DEKALB
PUBLIC LIBRARY
DE KALB, IL 60115

WHAT IS SCIENTOLOGY?

WHAT IS SCIENTOLOGY?

The Comprehensive Reference on the World's Fastest Growing Religion

PUBLICATIONS, INC.

Compiled by staff of the Church of Scientology International

Published by **Bridge Publications, Inc.** 4751 Fountain Avenue, Los Angeles, California 90029

ISBN 0-88404-633-8

Published in other countries by **NEW ERA Publications International ApS** Store Kongensgade 55, 1264 Copenhagen K, Denmark

ISBN 87-7336-909-8

Grateful acknowledgment is made to L. Ron Hubbard Library for permission to reproduce selections from the copyrighted works of L. Ron Hubbard.

Based on the religious literature and works of L. Ron Hubbard, who developed *Scientology*® applied religious philosophy and *Dianetics*® spiritual healing technology, this book is presented to the reader as part of his personal research into life, and the application of same by others, and should be construed only as a written report of such research and not as a statement of claims made by the Church or the Founder. The attainment of the benefits and goals of Scientology philosophy requires each individual's dedicated participation, as only through his own efforts can he achieve these.

The *Hubbard*® Electrometer is a religious artifact used in the Church confessional. It in itself does nothing, and is used by ministers only, to assist parishioners in locating areas of spiritual distress or travail.

The *Purification* program cannot be construed as a recommendation of medical treatment or medication and it is not professed as a physical handling for bodies nor is any claim made to that effect.

Photography by Golden Era Productions except as listed (company and page number): Culver Pictures—65; ©1992 Sygma, Photographer: Bagglioni—77; The Bettman Archive—41, 75; ©1992 FPG International, Photographers: Peter Gridley—477, 479, Arthur Tilley—483, Michael Krasowitz—465, Dick Luria—469.

Printed in the United States of America

The full body of knowledge that comprises Scientology is contained in more than forty million spoken and written words on the subject—all by L. Ron Hubbard, the source and founder of Scientology. This volume was compiled to fill the need and demand for a concise reference on the subject. Contained herein is a complete description of Scientology: its religious philosophy, its organization, its activities and its influence on society.

Church of Scientology International

Table of Contents

Part Nine: A Scientology Catechism

Part Ten: References

Foreword

Despite this century's torrent of technological advances, our civilization is in dire need of help. Since the advent of an atomic age which spawned the distinct possibility that all life on Earth could be extinguished at the push of a button, two generations have grown up under that specter. Partially in consequence, life in our society has taken many strange twists: Children are forcibly administered tranquilizing drugs in schools in the name of control; workers are taxed one hour's wages for every three on the job; and our youth emerge from their schools unable to read or write. Whole populations are directed what to think, what to believe or what attitudes to hold through media manipulation. Such is the world that would be encountered by a time traveler from the start of this century; and surely he would find it strange.

It is not easy to live with purpose, dignity and happiness in a world so engrossed in materialism and so utterly blind to man's spiritual needs. Half an hour's walk through any urban landscape would convince virtually anyone that life could be a happier proposition.

Which brings up this relevant question: What is Scientology?

Scientology is an applied religious philosophy.

The fastest growing religious movement on Earth, Scientology has become a firmly established and active force for positive change in the world in less than half a century.

The Scientology religious philosophy contains a precise system of axioms, laws and techniques, exhaustively researched and documented as workable; as such, it provides the individual with the ability to dramatically improve conditions, not only in his own life but in the world around him.

In a word, Scientology works.

And this is why millions of people the world over use its principles in their daily lives, why a growing number of people find such relevance in Scientology for themselves, their families, their organizations, their nations and this entire civilization.

You will learn about Scientology in this book, about its basic principles, its history, its organizations, what it is doing to improve life in a troubled world and about the remarkable man who researched and developed Scientology—American philosopher and humanitarian L. Ron Hubbard.

Fundamentally, Scientology is about the individual man or woman. Its goal is to bring an individual to a sufficient understanding of himself and his life and free him to make improvements where he finds them necessary and in the ways he sees fit.

Scientology is a workable system. Evidence of this may be seen in the lives of millions of Scientologists and the positive effects they create. People improve their lives through Scientology. As Scientologists in all walks of life will attest, they have enjoyed greater success in their relationships, family life, jobs and professions. They take an active, vital role in life and leading roles in their communities. And participation in Scientology brings to many a broader social consciousness, manifested through meaningful contribution to charitable and social reform activities. Through hundreds of separate community outreach programs, Scientologists help the needy and disadvantaged on every continent.

Scientology contains effective answers to society's most crucial problems, among them drug abuse, crime, education and decay of moral values.

All Scientologists are drug free, and spearhead effective actions in countries around the world to get others off drugs. Scientologists have helped millions of underprivileged children to dramatically improve their reading level, vocabulary and comprehension, and the record of Scientology's fight for human rights is unparalleled.

Scientology is not authoritarian. There is no enforced belief. Rather, a maxim in Scientology is that only those things which one finds true for himself are true. In Scientology you learn to think for yourself—it is a voyage of self-discovery.

In the interests of making *What Is Scientology?* useful to as many as possible, it has been organized with the assumption that the reader has little or no familiarity with the subject. Consequently, the book is best read in sequence, since more advanced concepts build upon information in earlier chapters. The primary purpose was to produce a book that fully answers the question "What is Scientology?" Millions of words have been written on the subject of Scientology, and in this volume we present the fundamentals. Photographs, diagrams and graphs illustrate many points of importance.

Scientology is about the individual man or woman. Its goal is to bring an individual to a sufficient understanding of himself and his life and free him to improve conditions in the ways that he sees fit.

Thus, as a broad overview of Scientology, this book will be a useful reference text, both to those with specific questions about the subject and, through the selected writings of L. Ron Hubbard, to those who wish to generally know more about his philosophy and principles.

The Scientology religion consists of a growing worldwide network of churches, missions and groups. And like any great movement that has advocated change for

CHURCH OF
SCIENTOLOGY
THE L. RON HUBBARD LIFE EXHIBITION

the better, it has not been a stranger to controversy, attracting media attention in many countries. *What Is Scientology?* both examines and explains this phenomenon, chronicling the history of its battles against vested interests and correcting much of the misinformation that has been manufactured in an attempt to hinder its forward progress.

Scientology is a dynamic, expanding religion. Even as this book is going to press, it is expanding into more and more countries, cities, towns and hamlets of Earth. Soon, the chapters describing Scientology's influence in society will need augmentation. But the basic ideas of Scientology, the benefits it offers, will not change and so, if this volume succeeds in answering the question posed by its title, the intention for its publication will have been well served.

A civilization without insanity, without criminals and without war, where the able can prosper and honest beings can have rights, and where man is free to rise to greater heights, are the aims of Scientology.

In less than fifty years, Scientology has become an indelible part of this civilization's fabric. It is here to stay.

How has this happened in so short a time? The answers are contained within.

The headquarters of the Church of Scientology International in Los Angeles, California

This half-million square foot facility serves tens of thousands of Scientologists living in the greater Los Angeles area.

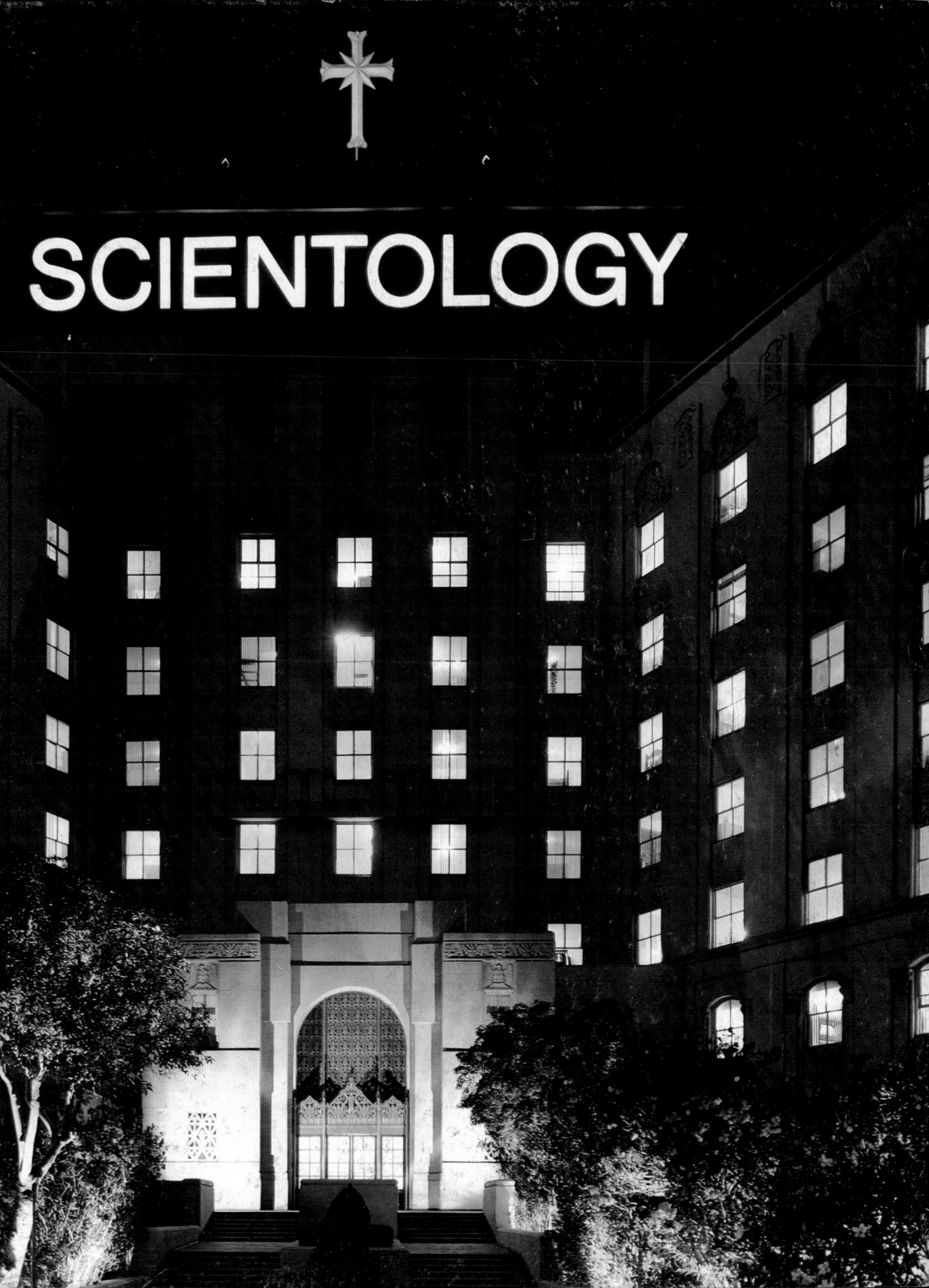

SCIENTOLOGY

Celebrity Centre International, located in Hollywood, California, heads a worldwide network of organizations which help the many Scientology artists, athletes and business professionals. Scientology Celebrity Centres can be found in many major cities including Paris, Vienna, Hamburg, Düsseldorf, Munich, London, New York, Las Vegas, Nashville and Washington, DC.

Tokyo, Japan

Zurich, Switzerland

Toronto, Canada

Scientology churches exist in most major cities around the world. Some of them are shown here.

Hamburg, Germany

Johannesburg, South Africa

Washington, DC, USA

Frankfurt, Germany

Los Angeles, USA

Sussex, England

The Saint Hill College for Scientologists is situated on fifty-five acres of rolling countryside in Sussex, England. Students from many countries come here to study the advanced graduate courses it offers. Church members also do these courses at similar advanced Scientology organizations in the United States, Denmark and Australia.

Sydney, Australia

Copenhagen, Denmark

Located in Clearwater, Florida, this is one of thirteen buildings comprising the Scientology religious retreat known as the Flag Land Base.

Students from around the world study advanced Scientology courses in this building at the Flag Land Base.

Freewinds

*The **Freewinds**, operating out of her home port in the Caribbean, offers Scientologists the highest levels of spiritual advancement, off the turbulent crossroads of the world.*

Part One

Scientology: Its Background and Origins

Scientology follows a long tradition of religious philosophy and practice. Its roots lie in the deepest beliefs and aspirations of all great religions, thus encompassing a religious heritage as old and as varied as man himself.

Though drawing upon the wisdom of some 50,000 years, it is factually a new religion, one which has isolated fundamental laws of life and, for the first time, developed a workable philosophy that can be applied to help one achieve a happier and richer existence. Scientology is therefore something one *does,* not merely something one believes in—an important point which will be greatly clarified as you read on.

That Scientology's development and rapid promulgation was made possible, in part, by advances in the physical sciences through the first half of the twentieth century is significant. For Scientology constitutes man's first real application of scientific methodology to spiritual questions.

Part one of this volume provides a firm grounding on the subject of Scientology. This covers three topics, with chapters devoted to each. The first provides a brief introduction to the Scientology religion and a basic explanation of its philosophy. The second traces the history of religious thought in order to place Scientology into its proper context and clarify the path it follows. The third chapter introduces the reader to the Founder of Scientology, L. Ron Hubbard.

Chapter 1

Introduction to the Scientology Religion

Thanks to scientific and technical advances over the last hundred years, most people are today materially wealthier than their forebears. Yet, by their own accounts, the quality of their lives has not kept step. In fact, it may be argued that people were once happier and more fulfilled. For some, material affluence breeds anxiety, a gnawing fear that if someone doesn't take away their hard-earned acquisitions, the end of their days will prematurely arrive to finish the job. Others find death easier to face than a lifetime of assembly-line slavery, while most, in a less dramatic fashion, simply buckle down to lives of quiet desperation.

As the twenty-first century dawns, most have no real grasp of those factors governing their existence. And yet, simply stated, had they a greater understanding of themselves and their fellows they would be able to improve conditions and thus live happier lives. This, then, is the function of Scientology: to enable man to improve his lot through understanding.

Before Scientology, the tremendous scientific advances of this era were not matched by similar advances in the humanities. Man's knowledge of the physical universe had far outdistanced his knowledge of himself. The resulting pressures from such an imbalance account for much that has unsettled society and threatens the future. In part, therefore, what Scientology represented to many when it appeared in the early 1950s, was a restoration of the balance.

Despite its many successes, science has not provided answers to questions man has been asking himself since time immemorial: Who are we? What do we consist of? Where do we come from? Where are we going? What are we doing? Indeed, these questions have always been the province of philosophy and religion, but traditional answers seemed immensely inadequate in the face of the H-bomb. Scientology, however, drawing on the same advances in knowledge that led to nuclear physics, supplied modern answers to these questions. And it supplied *workable* methods of application which made it possible for man to reach the ancient goal he has been striving toward for thousands of years: to know himself and, in knowing himself, to know and understand other people and, ultimately, all life.

Scientology is an *applied* religious philosophy. It holds in common many of the beliefs of other religions and philosophies, and considers man to be a spiritual being, with more to him than flesh and blood. This, of course, is a very different view to that espoused by prevailing scientific thought which views man as but a material object, a complex combination of chemical compounds and stimulus-response mechanisms.

Scientology believes man to be basically good, not evil. It is his experiences that have led him to commit evil deeds, not his nature. Often, he mistakenly solves his problems by considering only his own interests, which then causes trouble for both himself and others. Scientology believes that man advances to the degree he preserves his spiritual integrity and values, and remains honest and decent. Indeed, he deteriorates to the degree he abandons these qualities.

But because man is basically good he is capable of spiritual betterment, and it is the goal of Scientology to bring him to a point where he is capable of sorting out the factors in his own life and solving his own problems. Other efforts to help man often try to solve his problems *for* him and in this respect Scientology is different. Scientology believes that an individual placed in a position where he has higher intelligence, where he can confront life better, where he can identify the factors in his life more easily, is also in a position to solve his own problems and so better his own life.

Life has tended to force the individual into certain values. The stresses of existence have tended to fixate his attention to a point where his awareness of himself and his environment has been greatly diminished. Attendant to this lowered awareness are problems, difficulties with others, illness and unhappiness. The goal of Scientology is to reverse this diminishing awareness and, in that sense, wake the individual up. As one becomes more and more alert, his intelligence rises and he is capable of greater understanding and thus better able to handle his life. Scientology, then, contains solutions to the problems of living. Its end result is increased awareness and freedom for the individual and rehabilitation of his basic decency, power and ability. It can and does accomplish these ends routinely, daily, all over the world.

The word *Scientology* is taken from the Latin *scio,* which means "knowing in the fullest sense of the word," and the Greek word *logos,* meaning "study of." Scientology means literally "knowing how to know."

The source and founder of the Scientology religion is L. Ron Hubbard, who devoted his life to finding answers to questions that have troubled mankind for millennia. Mr. Hubbard's curiosity and boundless spirit of adventure inspired his search, even as a boy. However, the first fruits of his researches did not result in Scientology, but another subject, "Dianetics." The word *Dianetics* comes from the Greek words *dia,* meaning "through" and *nous,* meaning "soul."

Dianetics constituted L. Ron Hubbard's first breakthrough, and it was these initial discoveries which led to further researches and the exact isolation of the source of life itself. Man does not *have* a spirit. He *is* a spirit. Dianetics addresses and handles the effects of the spirit on the body and thus helps provide relief from unwanted sensations and emotions, accidents, injuries and psychosomatic illnesses (ailments caused or aggravated by mental stress). Scientology, on the other hand, addresses man directly, as a spirit, with the goal of increased awareness and ability as a spiritual being and the full realization of his immortal nature.

In over half a century of investigation, Mr. Hubbard isolated many, many fundamental truths about life, leading to his development of the Scientology philosophy and the subsequent growth of the Scientology religion.

A testament to the truths contained in Scientology lies in the fact that in less than two generations, the movement now flourishes on every continent with thousands of churches, missions and groups touching millions of lives daily. Part of every facet of society, Scientologists are businessmen, housewives, students, artists, celebrities, working people, scholars, soldiers, doctors, policemen and on and on.

Ever involved in the world around them, Scientologists naturally share with others that which they have learned in Scientology. Seeing that it could have relevance in their lives too, these people also become interested in what Scientology can offer *them.* And so Scientology grows, much the same as every great religion in history has grown, from individual to individual, bringing knowledge, wisdom and hope for a better life.

With Scientology, millions know life can be a worthwhile proposition, that men can live fulfilling lives in harmony with others and that the world can be a happier place. Scientologists work to create such a world every day, constantly joined by others who share this dream. The undeniable relevance of Scientology to the lives of these millions assures its permanence in our society. And that millions upon millions more will follow in this quest to create a better world.

Chapter 2

The Religious Heritage of Scientology

The dream of making the world a better place has long been embraced by every religious movement in history. Indeed, religion has served as the primary civilizing influence on the planet.

The knowledge that man is a spirit is as old as man himself. Only recently, with the advent of Western psychology, have notions cropped up that man is merely another animal, a stimulus-response mechanism. Such espousals stand at odds to every religious tradition, which variously speak of the "soul," the "spirit" or the "life force"—to encompass a belief held by all civilized men.

The Scientology religion follows just this tradition of man's search for his spiritual identity. In Scientology, the individual himself is considered to be the spiritual being—a thetan (pronounced "thay′-tn"). The term is taken from the Greek symbol or letter *theta* which has long served as a symbol for thought or spirit. Thus, although a new movement, Scientology is heir to the understanding of thinking men since the beginning of human history that man is a spiritual being who aspires to understand and improve life. The search was long, but it has been successful and answers now exist in Scientology for anyone who wishes to reach for them.

In Lascaux, France, 15,000 years before Christ, early man painted bulls and other images deep inside the walls of caves. His underlying belief held that such representations would bring the living animal within their grasp, and so guarantee a successful hunt.

Like this ancient man with his primitive spear, in his attempt to conquer the raging bull, human beings have been trying to understand themselves and their relationship to other living things and the physical universe for countless eons. That which has been recorded in cave paintings, on stone tablets and in ancient myths stands as a testament to this search.

For all the mystery surrounding himself, one of the first things man has innately known was that he was more than merely another beast of the forest, more than mere muscle and bone, but that he was somehow endowed with a spark of the divine, a spiritual being.

Such wisdom formed the basis of the first great civilization—the Egyptian, whose culture endured for twenty-seven centuries. As the earliest people to conquer man's deep-rooted fear of ancestral spirits, they were also among the first to propose that each man must provide for his own happy afterlife.

Despite considerable advances in the physical sciences, their gift of organization and their monumental art and architecture, the Egyptians still lacked the means to reverse the internal decay of their society. Beset with immorality and decadence, they were soon too enfeebled to resist the onslaught of Rome.

At approximately the same time as the Egyptians began erecting their "houses of eternity," further east in India, the early Hindu philosophers were also wrestling with life's most basic questions. Their revelations were first recorded in poems and hymns in the Veda some 10,000 years ago.

The doctrine of transmigration (the ancient concept of reincarnation)—that life is a continuous stream which flows ceaselessly, without beginning and without end—initially seemed to explain much of what plagued India. With the prospect of many lives, it was reasoned, a man had just as many opportunities to achieve self-knowledge. But such a belief offered little succor to the multitudes of impoverished. And so, as that misery continued to spread, concerned religious leaders began to challenge traditional doctrine.

Siddhartha Gautama, son of a wealthy Hindu rajah, spent years in search of fundamental truths, and declared that man could live a "Middle Path" between the extremes of sensual indulgence and drastic asceticism. Man, he proclaimed, is a spiritual being who can achieve an entirely new state of awareness which he termed ***bodhi.*** *For this reason, he is remembered today as the Buddha, revered for civilizing most of Asia. Unfortunately, however, he left no real means for others to actually attain those states of which he spoke.*

In Persia and much of the ancient world, philosophers and religious men continued their quest to divine the true nature of man, even studying the movements of the sun and stars in hopes of unlocking the mysteries of life.

In the seventh century B.C., *Zoroaster, born into a priestly family, came to believe himself a prophet. Forced to flee his native land for what he taught, he found asylum with King Vishtaspa in eastern Iran. There, the Persian religion of Zoroastrianism was born around the belief that only by defining "good" and "evil" could one hope to free himself of ignorance and achieve true happiness in the afterlife.*

A century later, the Chinese philosopher Lao-tse believed the world moved according to a divine pattern, one reflected in the rhythmic and orderly movements of nature. Saddened by the corruption of politicians and general social decay, he saw man ***striving*** *to be good, rather than let his inherent goodness come naturally from within. Eventually, so great was his disillusionment, he called for a return to a simpler golden age, and set out for the secluded countryside. Yet upon reaching the city's edge, Lao-tse was beseeched by the gatekeeper not to leave before recording his ideas for posterity.*

His manuscript, the ***Tao Te Ching,*** *became the basis of Taoism and held out yet another hope of higher states to which man could aspire.*

Tao *means simply "way" or "way to go." It is the way the universe moves—a universe to which man is inextricably linked. When men are most natural, they move according to the laws of interdependence and interaction of all universal laws, and so maintain a perfect harmony and balance. According to the* ***Tao,*** *it is* ***the*** *way—there is no other.*

Unfortunately, Taoism too did not provide a ***workable*** *means to reach that perfect harmony. Nor was any attempt made to provide such a means. For intrinsic in the Way, was the conviction that its basic truths were beyond words and could only be experienced. Hence the principles remained in the realm of esoteric knowledge.*

When the Delphic Oracle proclaimed the Greek philosopher, Socrates (470?–399 B.C.) to be the "wisest man in the world," Socrates countered that he was wise only in that he knew that he did not know. He believed man had a right to search for his own truth and that through increased understanding would become happier and more tolerant.

Socrates believed himself charged with a mission from God to make his fellow men aware not only of their own ignorance but also that knowledge could redeem them.

Socrates held that neither he nor anyone else had the right to force opinions on others. Rather, through systematic questioning, he sought to lead others to cast aside preconceptions and reach their own conclusions. He challenged falsehoods and pomposity, but his ironic criticisms and intellectual honesty were misunderstood by the authoritarians of his time.

Like many philosophers before him, Socrates' methods challenged established beliefs. As a result, in 399 B.C. he was convicted of both "denying the gods" and corrupting youth. Sentenced to drink a cup of hemlock, a bitter poison, he chose to die rather than compromise his stand against tyranny and suppression of the truth.

Prejudice and a general deviation from the road to philosophic truth about man sent even the highly learned Greek civilization to an inevitable and untimely end. First conquered by the Roman Empire, its cities were then mercilessly sacked by barbarians.

Like the philosophers of Greece, India and China, the Hebrews, too, sought to define the meaning of life. According to Jewish tradition, it was Abraham who first gained a special understanding of what lay at the heart of the universe and from that revelation came a belief in a personal god. He further believed that beneath the seemingly endless variety of life lay a single purpose, a single reality.

Judaism is the mother religion of both Christianity and Islam—the three dominant faiths in the Western world.

Two thousand years ago, Jesus of Nazareth brought new hope to man by preaching that this life was not all men might hope for, that man was more than only flesh and would continue to live, even after death. Implicit in his message was the promise of salvation from suffering and a promise of eternal peace.

At odds with the teachings of Jesus was traditional rabbinical belief that salvation would not come until the advent of a distant Messiah. Hence, the special appeal of Christ's message that the Kingdom of God was not only at hand, but lay within all those with faith.

Long fearing popular revolt, the Romans equated Christ's words with political insurrection. Rome had decreed that nothing should be held above imperial order and thus viewed Christ's wholly spiritual message as dangerously revolutionary, particularly his talk of the coming Kingdom.

Though crucified, the hope that Christ brought to man did not die. Instead, his death became symbolic of the triumph of the spirit over the material body and so brought a new awareness of man's true nature.

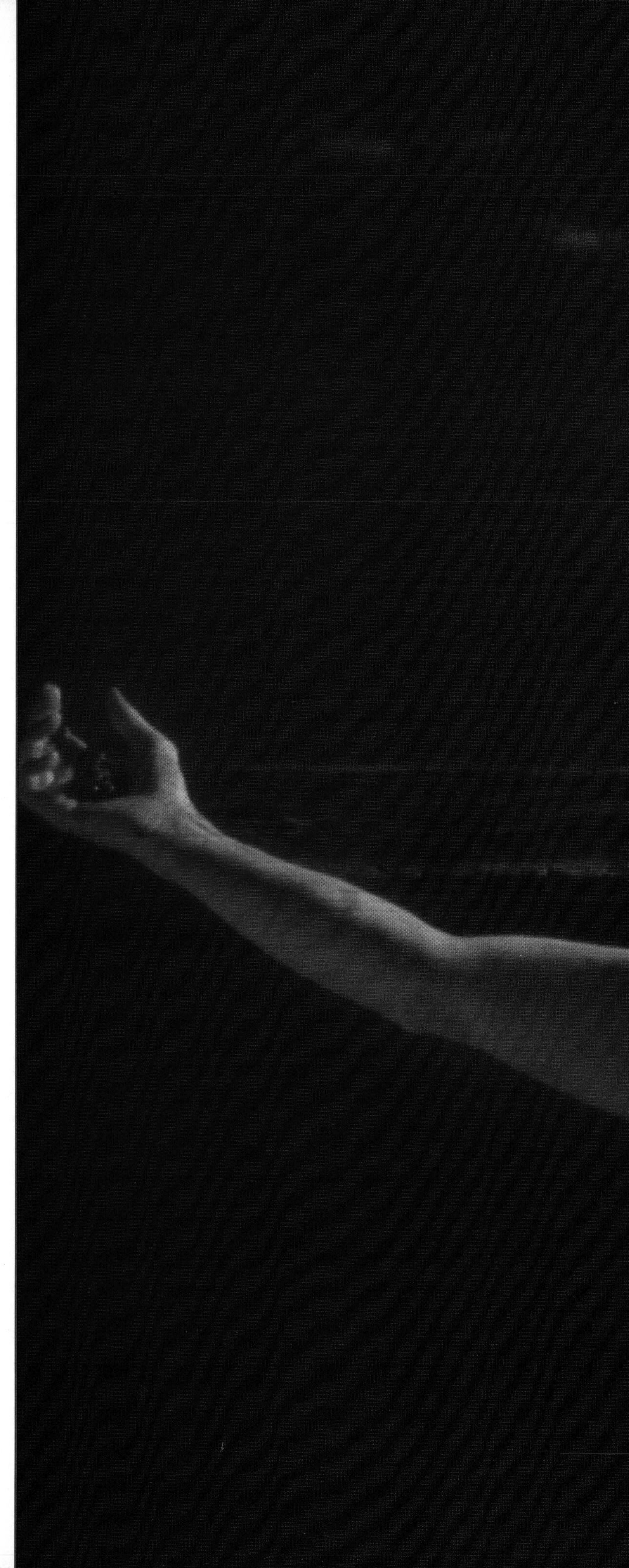

INRI

The Romans, however, continued to insist that man was just a material object. The psyche (a word meaning "spirit" or "breath of life") was thought to be given up when the man "himself," his body, had perished.

For all their military strength, the Romans never acknowledged or found ways to develop man's true potential and so, as did so many empires before them, they too perished.

About the same time Christ was teaching in the Middle East, the first Buddhist monks arrived in China. The Buddhism that first became popular in China during the Han dynasty (206 B.C.–A.D. 220) taught the indestructibility of the soul, the theory of karma and the values of charity and compassion. Buddhism spread through China, incorporating some of the practical and this-worldly philosophy of ancient China. It taught man a way to spiritual enlightenment despite resistance from the Taoists and later suppression by the state, when hundreds of monasteries were destroyed, and hundreds of thousands of monks and nuns were forced to return to lay life.

Despite such suppression, belief in the spiritual nature of man received even more impetus in the sixth century when the prophet Mohammed preached that there was only **one** *God and attempted to civilize an entire nation. He taught about the supremacy of the spiritual over the material, and beseeched man to seek his own salvation. His message was seen as a threat to the revenues of Mecca, and eventually led to his banishment.*

Within eight years, however, he returned triumphant and began his "Holy War" against infidels. He built the great Mohammedan Empire, which eventually reached from Spain to the borders of China.

The Crusades, the subsequent wars "in the name of religion" which swept Europe for hundreds of years, involved tens of thousands of people in continuous bloodshed. Nonetheless, with the Crusades came a vital cultural exchange. Men who had never traveled beyond the immediate vicinity of their manor, village or fiefdom were suddenly exposed to an entirely new world across the Mediterranean.

Toward the end of this period, in 1215, English barons forced King John to sign the famous Magna Carta. This historic document, a formal recognition of the rights of others, was built on the belief that the basic nature of man was good, not evil, and that he was capable of determining his own destiny.

The provisions included the guaranteed freedom of the church, respect for the customs of towns, protection of the rights of subjects and communities, and what would later be interpreted as a guarantee of the right of trial by jury. These represented the triumph of law over king, and thus reason over force.

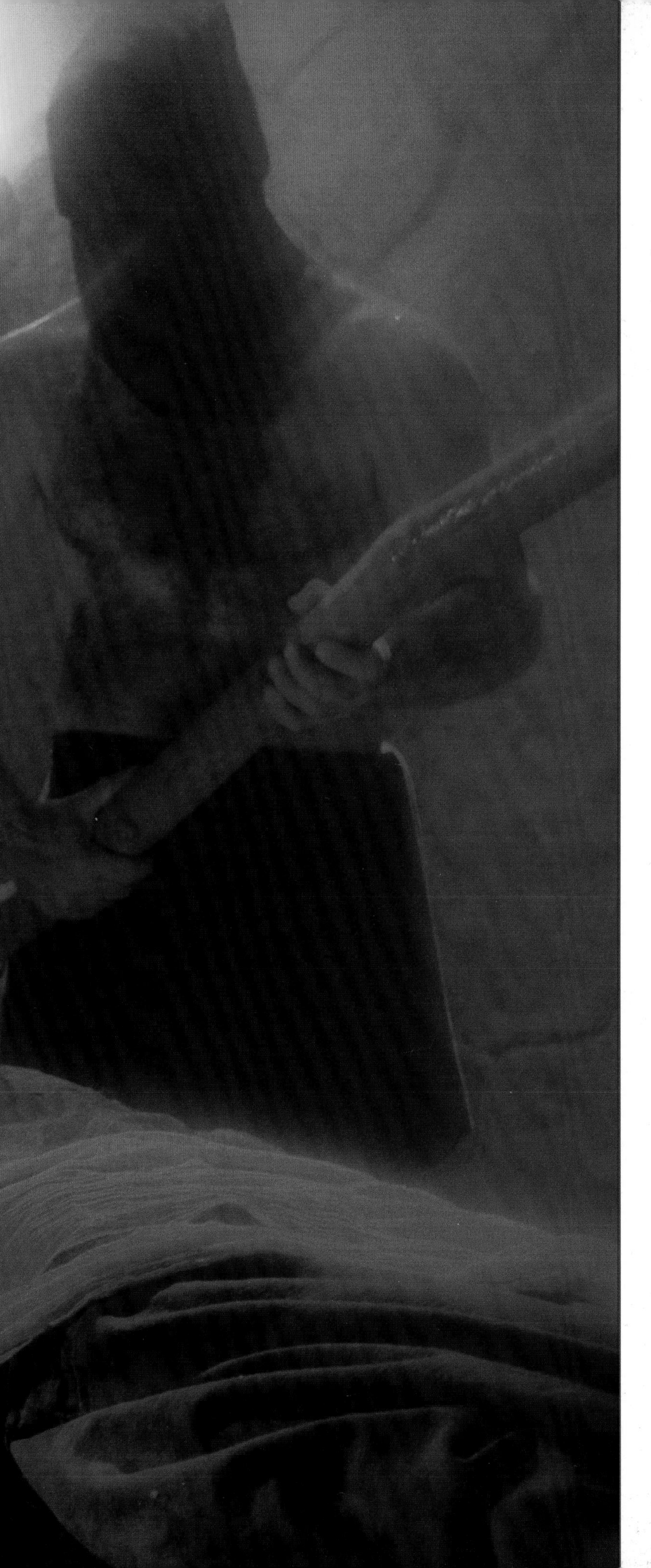

But the late fifteenth century ushered in the Inquisition, which again sought to quell man's sense of reason and his reach for spiritual enlightenment. Those subscribing to beliefs unacceptable to the Catholic church were tried and tortured until they renounced their "heretical views."

Anyone thought to have "strange" or "different" ideas could be labeled a blasphemer or even a witch, then burned at the stake if they refused to accept the established beliefs.

But man's desire to understand himself and the world around him could not be stopped and men like Leonardo da Vinci pursued their studies in the hope of finding the answers. A brilliant painter, engineer, astronomer and botanist, Leonardo helped launch the Renaissance and a new age of scientific discovery in the face of ridicule from the ignorant and bigoted. Even the most seemingly innocuous studies had to be undertaken with discretion, as the watchful eye of the Inquisition was ever present. In fact, many of his notes were written out so they could only be read in a mirror.

In the sixteenth century, Galileo dared to challenge long-held beliefs by publicly endorsing the Copernican theory that the Earth revolved around the sun and not the reverse. This was considered heresy by the still-active Inquisition.

Galileo was sentenced to an indefinite prison term by the Catholic church for his "crime." Only when he subsequently renounced Copernican theory was he allowed to return to his villa where he lived out the remainder of his life under house arrest by authority of the Inquisition, a broken man.

Fleeing suppression and intolerance in Europe, pilgrims of several faiths set sail for the New World where their aspirations of freedom were probably best summed up by Thomas Jefferson's Declaration of Independence. He wrote, ". . . that all men are created equal, that they are endowed by their Creator with certain inalienable Rights, that among these are Life, Liberty and the pursuit of Happiness." The light of spiritual freedom was once again burning bright.

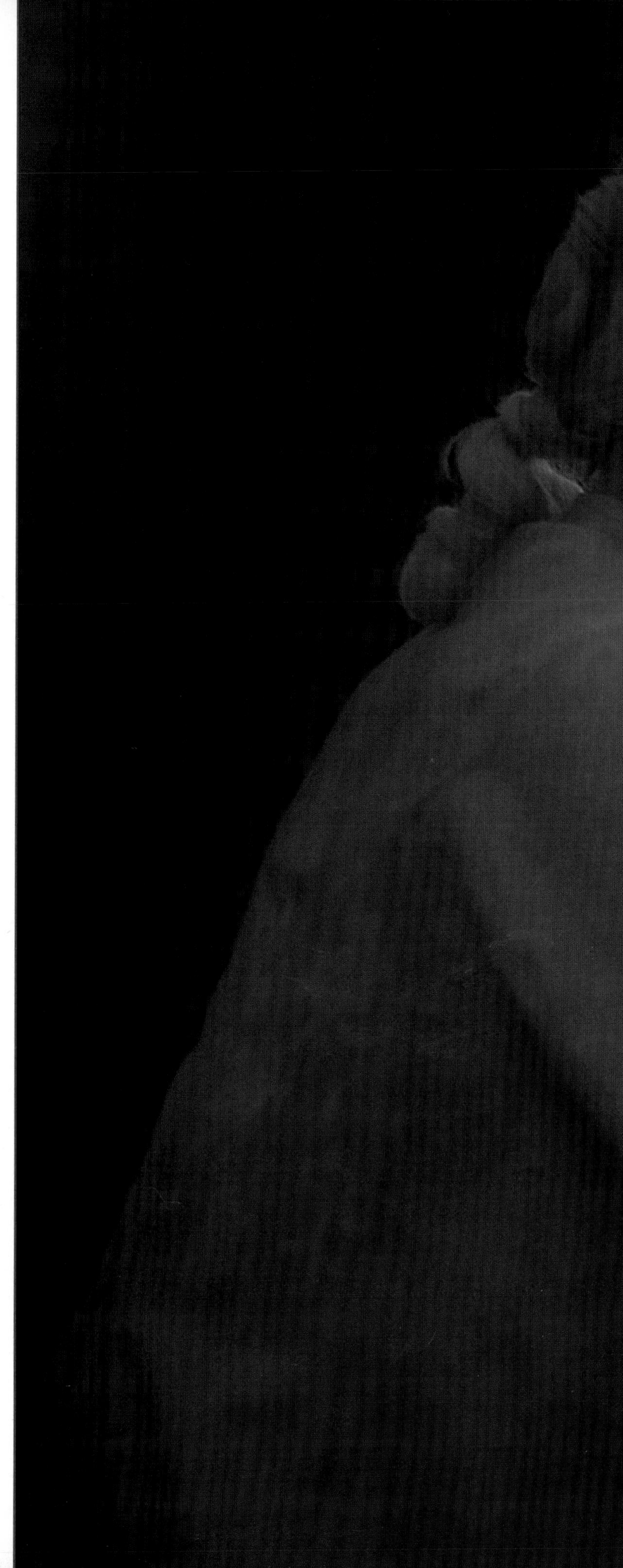

There were some however, like Charles Darwin, who had a very different message: Man was but another rung on the evolutionary ladder, and could never hope to raise himself to greater levels of awareness. Darwin's man-from-mud theory, the idea that life was a chance happenstance resulting from a chain reaction in a sea of ammonia, soon took hold in the scientific community. Ironically, however, that very same theory may be traced to an ancient Egyptian myth wherein man was seen as emerging from a primordial ocean.

MAN
APE

Professor Wilhelm Wundt, a German psychologist and Marxist at the University of Leipzig, proclaimed that man's soul—if indeed he had one—was irrelevant, as man could only be understood in terms of physically observable phenomena. A search for the spiritual nature of man, he reasoned, was a waste of time as there was no psyche. Thus psychology became the study of the spirit which denied the spirit. The subject of psychology thereafter became prevalent in universities.

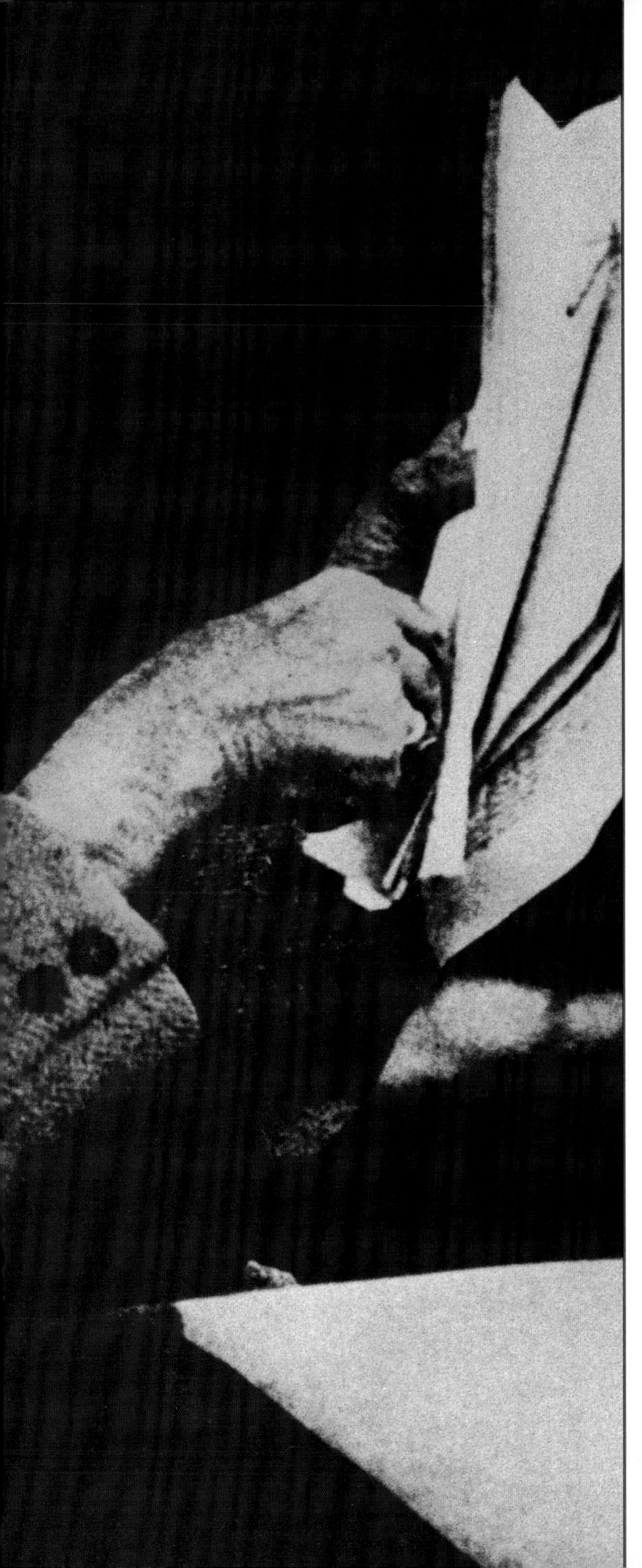

Sigmund Freud further reinforced this "modern" concept of man, arguing that all impulses stemmed from his repressed and uncontrollable sexual desires. Such impulses were then "analyzed" as primitive and instinctive, not that different from those which drive an animal.

Although Freud himself broke new ground with his recognition that man could overcome physical ills through addressing the mind, the real value of his work was soon buried in a hodgepodge of theories from others.

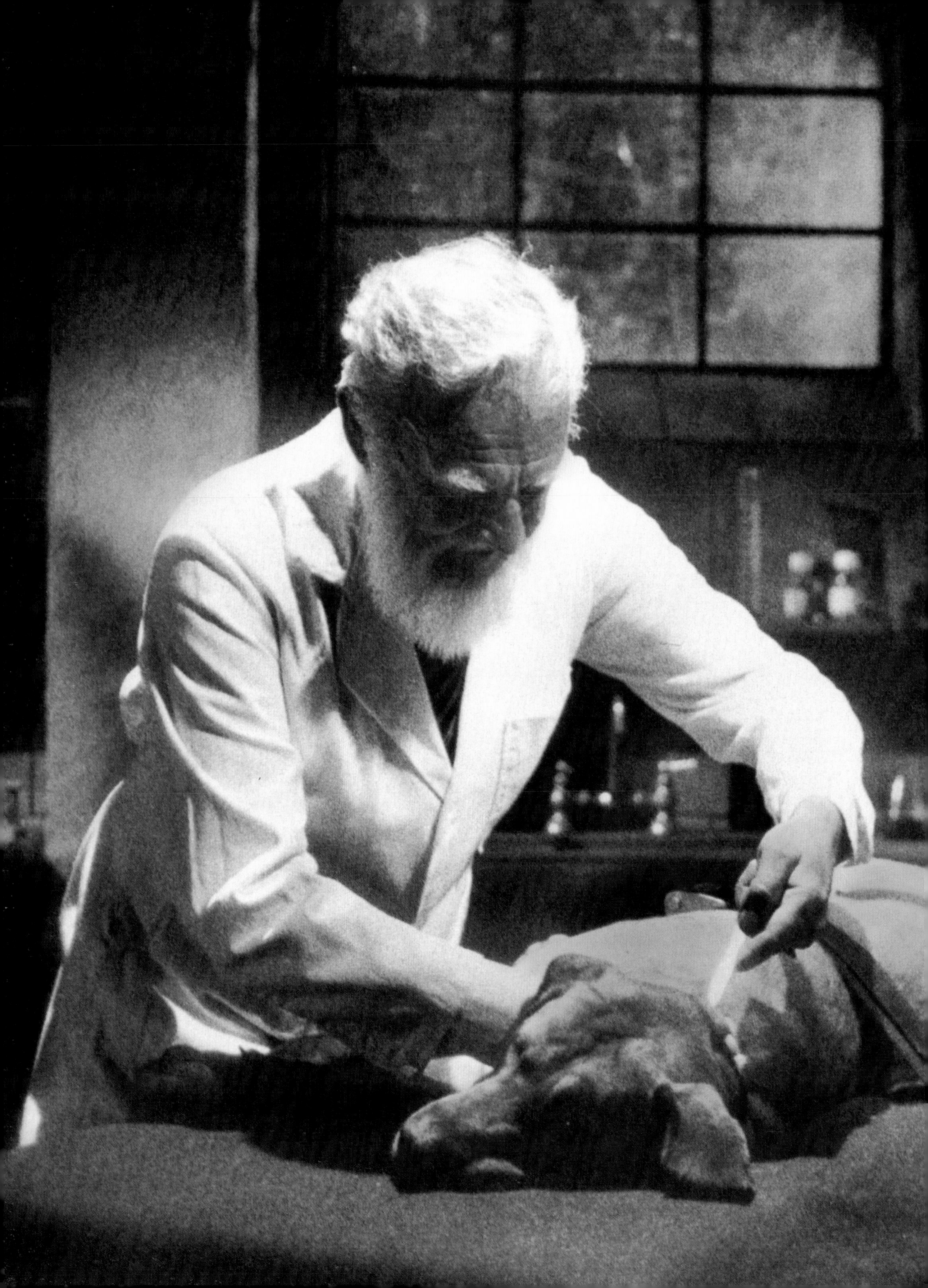

In Russia, former veterinarian Ivan Petrovich Pavlov served the dictator Stalin with experiments to discover how man could be controlled to better serve the state. He reasoned that if dogs could be made to slaver on command, so could human beings. Man had now been reduced to the level of a mindless animal—and thus psychiatry was born, as a tool for tyrannical governments.

Convinced that man is only a body, psychology and psychiatry have forwarded the idea that there is no soul, merely a physical brain, an aggregation of tissue and nerve cells.

And since man no longer has a soul, he can be degraded still further through all manner of barbaric "treatments." In fact, the array of primitive methods dreamed up by "modern" psychiatrists includes hypnotic drugs, lobotomies, electric shock and bolts to the brain while a person is drugged and comatose—each of which leaves a person little more than a vegetable.

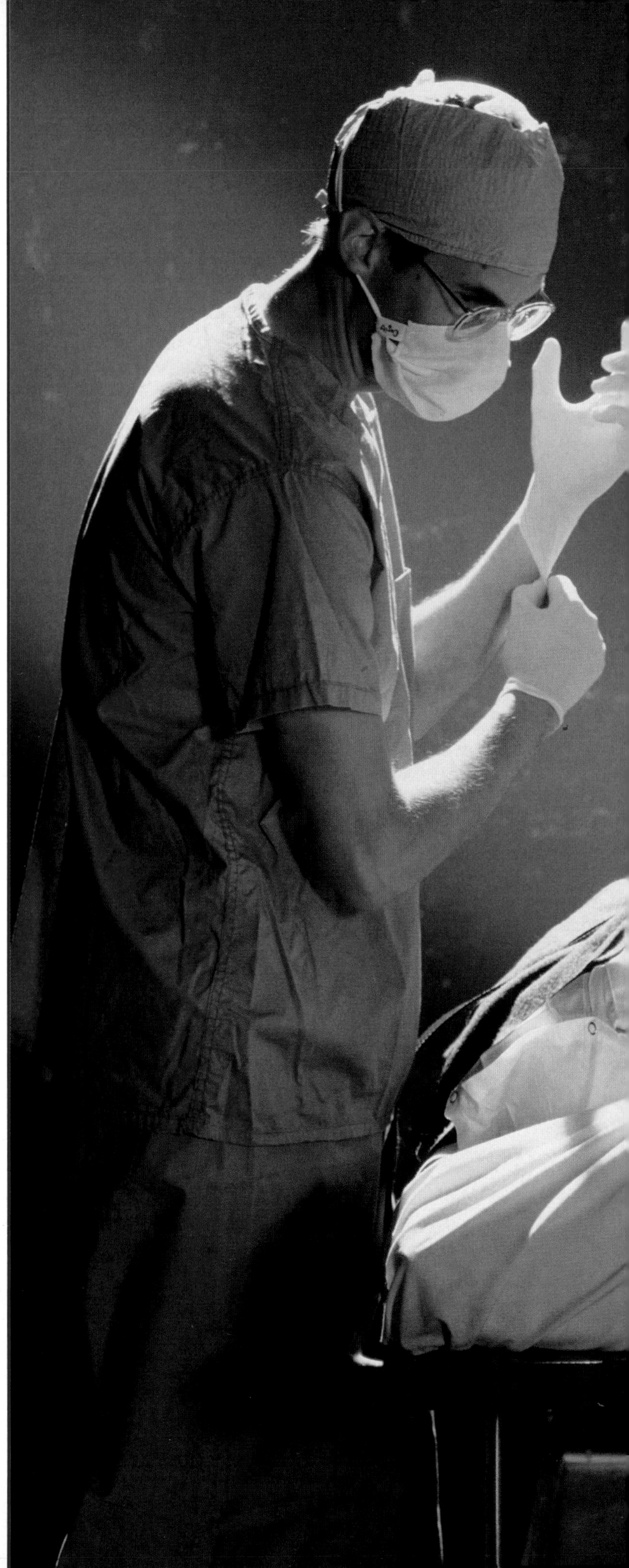

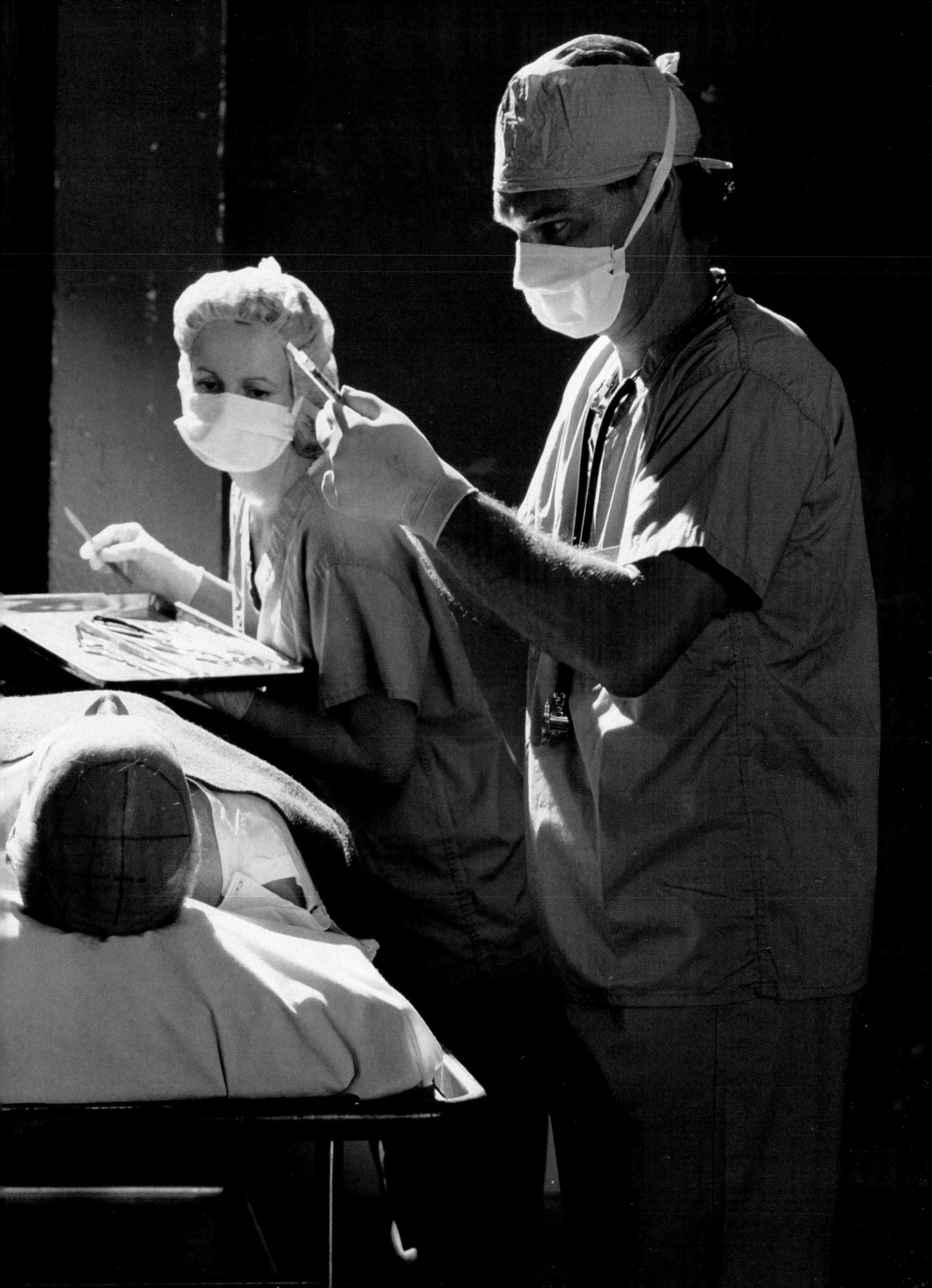

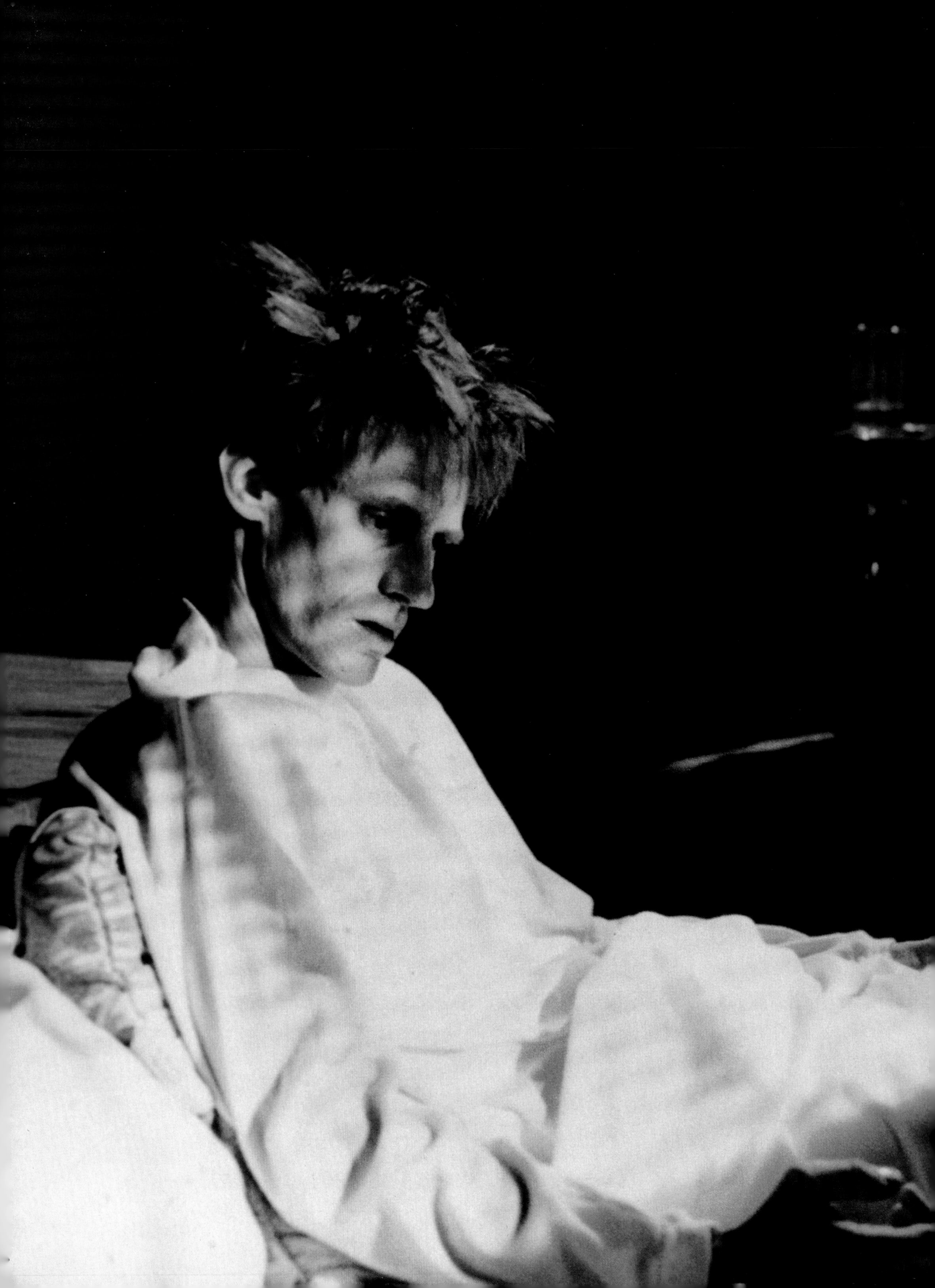

The psychologist believes in materialism. This is the principle that all is purely matter—hopes, dreams, love, inspiration—all just chemical reactions in the brain. Following from this theory, he has attempted to create a society where the body is glorified over the spirit, and where material possessions are more important than one's spiritual well-being.

In such a society, where spiritual values are no longer given credence, man soon loses touch with both his past and his future. Religion, then, becomes an "opiate," while the new high priests of psychiatry, handsomely supported by taxpayers, conduct worthless government studies that provide no solutions.

Even today, new ideas are fought by totalitarian states, and learning is restricted to the privileged few, in an attempt to keep the majority ignorant. Book burnings are another phenomenon of our own time, reminiscent of the Inquisition.

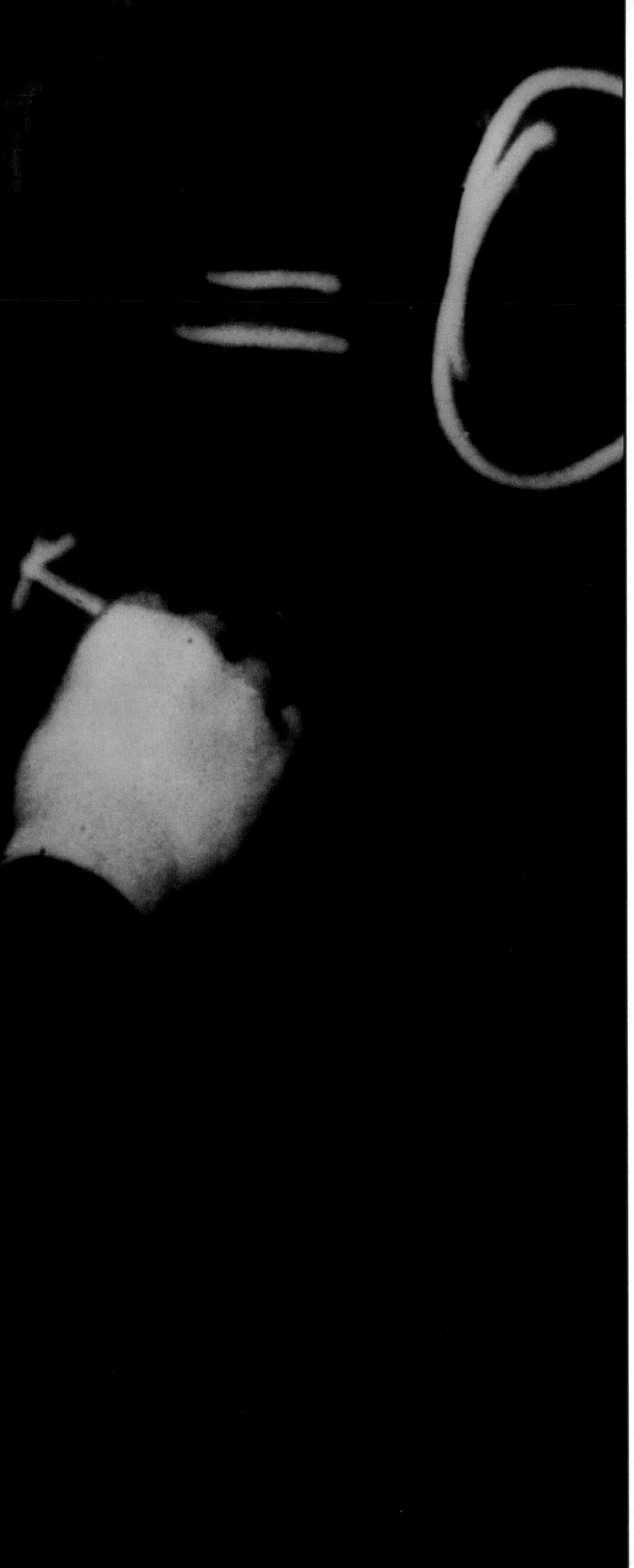

But wisdom and spiritual values cannot be suppressed. All men at all times have sought spiritual release. All individual quests and all philosophies and religions have one goal and one goal only: to discern the true essence of man and his relationship to the universe.

Unfortunately, the humanities have failed to keep pace with scientific developments. A preoccupation with all things physical has left the humanities far behind.

Science advanced to where it could send rockets into space. But, until now, the greatest challenge of all was ignored, the improvement of man himself.

At this point in the history of our civilization we have, frighteningly enough, developed the capabilities to destroy all life on the Earth.

One madman in a position of power could wreak the ultimate destruction for all living things. Lacking a real understanding of man or a workable technology to improve man, governments are unable to forge their own destinies and the potential for chaos is very real.

Perhaps it has taken the potential for ultimate destruction to bring about the ultimate in hope for mankind: a twentieth-century religion, utilizing a truly workable technology to bring man to an understanding of himself and his fellows. Both the atom bomb and this technology were born at the same time—in the crucible of the last world war. Fortunately, we can now end not only war, but crime and insanity on Earth, once and for all. We can reverse the dwindling spiral of life on this planet.

Man can find answers to his timeless questions and gain true spiritual freedom—with Scientology.

Chapter 3

L. Ron Hubbard: The Founder of Scientology

L. Ron Hubbard is the Founder of Scientology. He has described his philosophy in more than 5,000 writings, including dozens of books, and in 3,000 tape-recorded lectures. Those who regularly employ his teachings to improve themselves and help their fellows come from all walks of life, while Scientology missions and churches have been established on six continents.

The universal acclaim for the man—including thousands of awards and recognitions from individuals and groups and the unprecedented popularity of his works among people from all walks of life—is but one indicator of the effectiveness of his technologies. More importantly, there are millions of people around the world who consider they have no greater friend.

Although long celebrated as a writer, novelist and explorer, it was the 1950 publication of *Dianetics: The Modern Science of Mental Health* that initially focused world attention on L. Ron Hubbard. That book, which marked a turning point in history, provided the first workable approach to solving the problems of the mind, the first hope that something could be done about the causes of irrational behavior—war, crime and insanity. Dianetics is something that anyone can use to help improve himself and his fellows. Hence, when the book was released, Amherst College Political Science Professor, Dr. Frederick L. Schuman's declaration in the *New York Times*: "History has become a race between Dianetics and catastrophe. Dianetics will win, if enough people are challenged in time to understand it."

Although most men might have been satisfied with such an accomplishment, L. Ron Hubbard did not stop at Dianetics. Yes, he had solved the riddle of the human mind, but there still remained unsolved questions regarding the nature of the human being himself, outstanding puzzles concerning that long-sought-after "something" we call *life*. And from his methodical and wholly scientific research into this problem came the applied religious philosophy of Scientology, offering not only greater happiness and ability but also solutions to such seemingly hopeless social problems as drug abuse, the decline of moral standards and illiteracy—always providing effective and workable solutions as he found them.

The story of Dianetics and Scientology began long before the publication of Mr. Hubbard's first book on the subject. Indeed, even in his early youth he exemplified a rare sense of purpose and dedication which, combined with his adventurous spirit, made him a living legend. His life-long search for answers to the human condition was equally adventurous; for unlike other philosophers content to view events from an ivory tower, he knew that to really understand one's fellow man, one had to be part of life. One had to rub elbows with all kinds and types of people. And, one had to explore the nooks and crannies of all existence.

This chapter will cover the key incidents that shaped L. Ron Hubbard's life, and the important milestones on the road to his discoveries. By any measure, it was an immensely full and interesting life, but the true value of it lies in the legacy that he left mankind.

Son of naval commander Harry Ross Hubbard and Ledora May Hubbard, L. Ron Hubbard was born on March 13, 1911 in Tilden, Nebraska. At the age of two, he and his family took up residence on a ranch outside Kalispell, Montana, and from there moved to the state's capital, Helena.

As a young boy he learned much about survival in the rugged Far West—with what he called "its do-and-dare attitudes, its wry humor, cowboy pranks, and make-nothing of the worst and most dangerous." Not only could he ride horses at the age of three and a half, but was soon able to rope and break broncos with the best of them.

L. Ron Hubbard's mother was a rarity in her time. A thoroughly educated woman, who had attended teacher's college prior to her marriage to Ron's father, she was aptly suited to tutor her young son. Under her guidance, Ron was reading and writing at an early age, and soon satisfying his insatiable curiosity about life with the works of Shakespeare, the Greek philosophers, and other classics.

When his father's naval career necessitated that the family leave Montana for a series of cross-country journeys, Ron's mother was also on hand to help him make up what he missed in school.

It was also through these early years that Ron first encountered another culture, that of the Blackfoot Indians, then still living in isolated settlements on the outskirts of Helena. His particular friend was an elderly medicine man, commonly known as "Old Tom."

Establishing a unique friendship with the normally taciturn Indian, Ron was soon initiated into the various secrets of the tribe, their legends, customs and methods of survival in a harsh environment. At the age of six, he became a blood brother of the Blackfeet, an honor bestowed on few white men.

In early 1923, when Ron was twelve, he and his family moved to Seattle, Washington, where his father was stationed at the local naval base. He joined the Boy Scouts and that year proudly achieved the rank of Boy Scout First Class. The next year he became the youngest Eagle Scout ever, an early indication that he did not plan to live an ordinary life.

At the end of that year, young Ron traveled to the nation's capital via the Panama Canal, meeting Commander Joseph C. Thompson of the US Navy Medical Corps. Commander Thompson was the first officer sent by the US Navy to study under Sigmund Freud, and took it upon himself to pass on the essentials of Freudian theory to his young friend. Although keenly interested in the Commander's lessons, Ron was also left with many unanswered questions.

THEORY
DREAMS
EGO
SUB

In 1927, at the age of sixteen, Ron took the first of his several voyages across the Pacific to Asia. There, both on his own and in the company of an officer attached to the British legation, he took advantage of this unique opportunity to study Far Eastern culture. Among others he befriended and learned from was a thoroughly insightful Beijing magician who represented the last of the line of Chinese magicians from the court of Kublai Khan.

Although primarily renowned as an entertainer, Old Mayo was also well versed in China's ancient wisdom that had been handed down from generation to generation. Ron passed many evenings in the company of such wise men, eagerly absorbing their words.

It was also through the course of these travels that Ron gained access to the much talked-about but rarely seen Buddhist lamaseries in the Western Hills of China—temples usually off-limits to both local peasants and visiting foreigners.

Among other wonders, Ron told of watching monks meditate for weeks on end, contemplating higher truths. Once again then, he spent much of his time investigating and questioning, seeking answers to the human dilemma.

Beyond the lamasery walls, he closely examined the surrounding culture. In addition to the local Tartar tribes, he spent time with nomadic bandits originally from Mongolia. He further traveled up and down the Chinese coast exploring villages and cities, delving into the fabric of the nation. And everywhere he went, one question was uppermost in his mind: "Why?" Why so much human suffering and misery? Why was man, with all his ancient wisdom and knowledge accumulated in learned texts and temples, unable to solve such basic problems as war, insanity and unhappiness?

By the age of nineteen, long before the advent of commercial airplane or jet transportation, he had traveled more than a quarter of a million miles, including voyages not only to China but also Japan, Guam, the Philippines and other points in the Orient. In a very real sense, the world itself was his classroom, and he studied in it voraciously, recording what he saw and learned in his ever-present diaries, which he carefully preserved for future reference.

Everywhere he went, he also took the time to help and teach others. On a remote Pacific island, for example, he proved to the terrified natives that the groans of a ghost in a supposedly haunted cave were nothing more than the rushing of underground water.

In the South Pacific islands, Ron continued his search by venturing deep into the jungles of Guam where he located an ancient Polynesian burial ground, a place steeped in the tradition of heroic warriors and kings. Though his native friends were fearful for him, he explored the sacred area—his initiative drawn from the ever-present desire to know more.

These sojourns in Asia and the Pacific islands had a profound effect, giving Ron a subjective understanding of an Eastern philosophy that had predated even the Greeks.

Yet for all the wonders of these lands and all his respect for those whom he encountered, he still saw much that concerned him: Chinese beggars willing themselves to die above open graves in Beijing, children who were less than rags, widespread ignorance and despair. And in the end, he came to the inescapable conclusion that despite the wisdom of its ancient texts, the East did not have the answers to the miseries of the human condition. It remained evident in the degradation and sorrow of its people.

Returning to the United States in 1929, Ron resumed his formal education. After attending Swavely Prep School in Manassas, Virginia, he was graduated from the Woodward School for Boys in Washington, DC.

FRIDAY OCT 4 1929
ENGLISH: POETRY
FOOT
METER
RHYME
5
ambic pentameter
went | to meet | the bark king dog ||

He enrolled at George Washington University. His university subject should probably have been ethnology, since he was already an expert in many different cultures—from the Philippine pygmies to the Kayan shamans of Borneo to the Chamorros of Guam. But fate and his father placed him, fortunately, in mathematics and engineering instead. With his knowledge of many cultures and his growing awareness of the human condition, his background in engineering and mathematics would serve him well in undertaking a scientific approach to solving the riddles of existence and man's spiritual potential.

Theorizing that the world of subatomic particles might possibly provide a clue to the human thought process, he enrolled in one of the first nuclear physics courses taught in the United States. Moreover, he was concerned for the safety of the world, recognizing that if man were to handle the atom sanely for the greatest benefit, he would first have to learn to handle himself. His aim, then, was to synthesize and test all knowledge for what was observable, workable and could truly help solve man's problems. And to that end, he set out to determine precisely how the mind functioned.

124
1821
MOLECULAR
HUBBARD

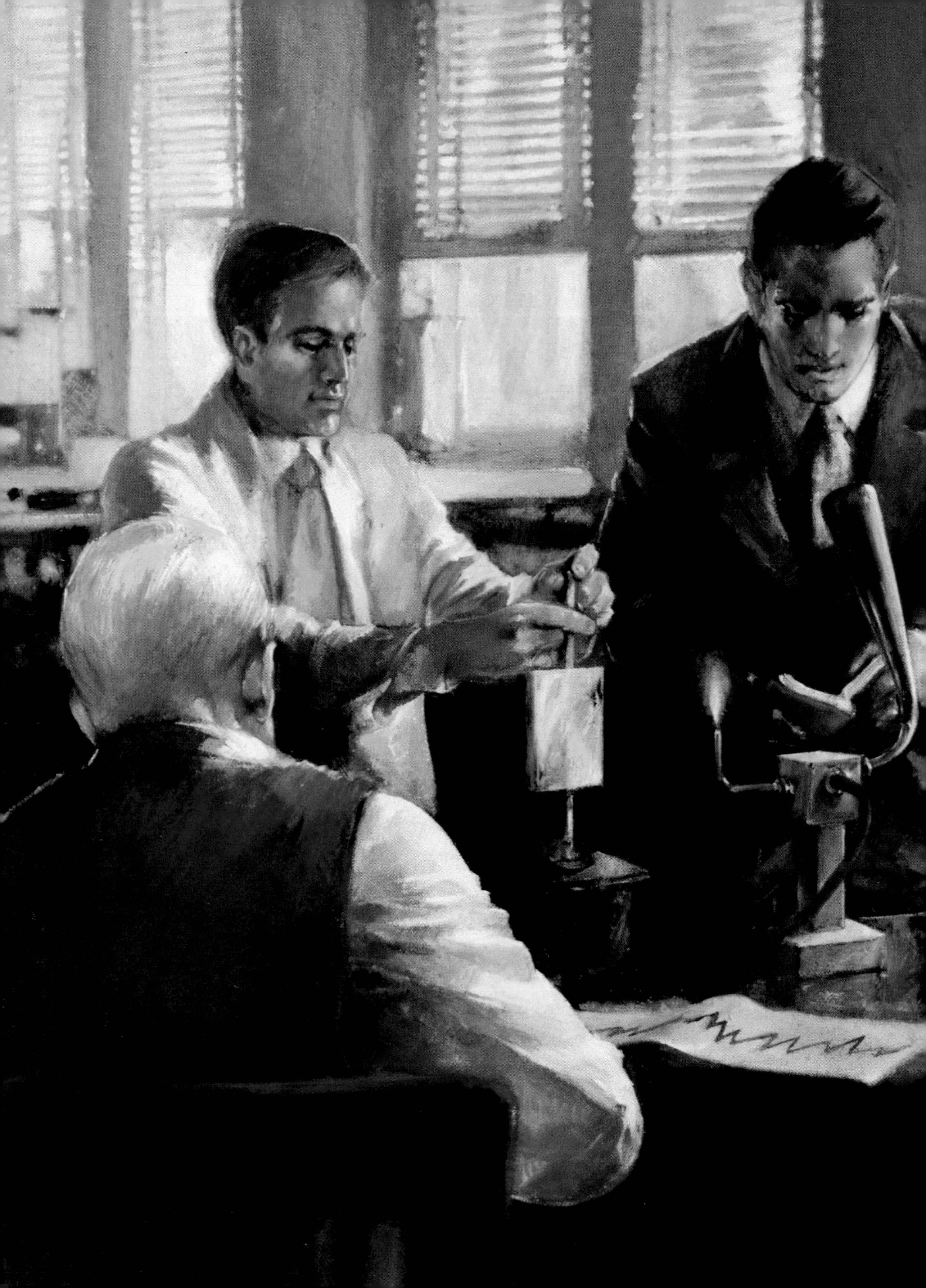

In one of his first pioneering experiments on the subject, he employed a sound wave measuring device called a Koenig photometer. Two students read poetry from extremely different languages—Japanese and English—into the device. He found that the device identified the speech as poetry regardless of language. When haiku was read in the original Japanese, the wavelengths produced by the Koenig photometer were the same as those produced when English verse was read.

Here, then, he concluded, was scientific evidence that people were not so different as he had been led to believe, that there was indeed a meeting ground, and all minds did in fact respond identically to the same stimuli.

EASTERN SPIRITUALISM

Reasoning that questions arising from his experiments would best be answered by those who were paid to know about the mind, Ron took these discoveries to the psychology department. Rather than answers, however, he found that the George Washington University psychologists had no comprehension or understanding of the results—but more importantly—they weren't even interested in such things.

Stunned, he soon came to the realization that no one knew how the mind worked. And furthermore, no one in the fields of psychology or psychiatry was about to find out.

Not only were there no answers in the East, there were none to be found in any Western center of culture.

"To be very blunt," he put it, "it was very obvious that I was dealing with and living in a culture which knew less about the mind than the lowest primitive tribe I had ever come in contact with. Knowing also that people in the East were not able to reach as deeply and predictably into the riddles of the mind as I had been led to expect, I knew I would have to do a lot of research."

Deciding that formal study had nothing more to offer, L. Ron Hubbard left college in the depths of the Depression, again taking his quest to learn about life out into the world. He said of this period, ". . . my writing financed research and this included expeditions which were conducted in order to investigate primitive peoples to see if I could find a common denominator of existence which would be workable."

He directed two expeditions, the Caribbean Motion Picture Expedition, a two-and-a-half month, 5,000-mile voyage aboard the four-masted schooner, **Doris Hamlin**, and the West Indies Mineralogical Expedition, which completed the first mineralogical survey of the island of Puerto Rico under US rule. Upon his return to the United States, and with scientific grants few and far between, he began to write his way to fame and fortune, supporting his research by becoming one of the most popular writers of the 1930s.

As the editor of **Thrilling Adventures** magazine, one of the more than 30 magazines he headlined, wrote in October 1934, "L. Ron Hubbard needs no introduction. From the letters you send in, his yarns are among the most popular we have published. Several of you have wondered, too, how he gets the splendid color which always characterizes his stories of the faraway places. The answer is: He's been there, brothers. He's been and seen and done. And plenty of all three."

While continuing to write for his New York editors as well as screenplays for Hollywood such as **Secret of Treasure Island**, he never stopped his vital researches into man.

Five Novels
L Ron Hubbard
ARGOSY
L RON HUBBARD

L. Ron Hubbard was searching for a principle which would lead to the unification of knowledge and explain the meaning of existence—something other philosophers had set out to find in the past with varying degrees of success. In fact, many Western philosophers had given up on the idea that different peoples held anything in common and were no longer even asking questions about the life force or the essence of life. Man had become just another animal, mere flesh and bones.

Yet Mr. Hubbard saw man in a very different light. Although he had no name for it yet, he felt certain that life was more than a random series of chemical reactions, and that some sort of intelligent urge underlay our actions. Organizing the tremendous body of data he had acquired—from his travels, research and experiments—he embarked upon a new experimental path, this time to determine how cells functioned. And following an elaborate series of experiments in early 1938, he made a breakthrough of magnitude: he isolated the common denominator of existence. SURVIVE.

That man was surviving was not a new idea. That this was the single basic common denominator of existence was.

The predominant theory of the time held that life was simply a chance chain reaction in a sea of ammonia. Disproving this materialistic belief and forming the basis for all his later work, his findings were compiled into a philosophic manuscript, "Excalibur," written during the first weeks of 1938.

He wrote: "I suddenly realized that survival was the pin on which you could hang the rest of this with adequate and ample proof. It's a very simple problem. Idiotically simple! That's why it never got solved. Nobody has ever looked at anything being that simple to do that much. So what do we find as the simplicities of solution? The simplicities of solution lie in this: that life, all life, is trying to survive. And life is composed of two things: the material universe and an X-factor. And this X-factor is something that can evidently organize, and mobilize the material universe."

Recalling the writing of "Excalibur," the first of his many manuscripts on the subject of life, he noted, "I began to hammer out that secret and when I had written ten thousand words, then I knew even more clearly. I destroyed the ten thousand and began to write again."

The response of those who read this manuscript was dramatic, and more than a few publishers eagerly sought to publish it. He declined. " 'Excalibur' did not contain a therapy of any kind but was simply a discussion of the composition of life. I decided to go further," he added.

Ron continued to fund his research by his ever more popular fiction writing. His stories and novels spanned every genre from adventure and travel to mystery, western, romance, science fiction and fantasy. Writing not of machines and robots but of real men and real adventures, he pioneered a whole new era of science fiction writing as one of the creators of what came to be known as the "Golden Age of Science Fiction."

His expeditions continued as well. Elected a member of the prestigious Explorers Club in New York City, he was bestowed custody of their flag, a high honor in the field of exploration, for the Alaskan Radio Experimental Expedition in May, 1940. This expedition greatly assisted in the codification of the coastal charts of British Columbia and Alaska, while augmenting his knowledge of more cultures—the Tlingit, the Haida and the Aleut Indians of Alaska.

In December 1940, L. Ron Hubbard earned his "License to Master of Steam and Motor Vessels" from the US Department of Commerce. Three months later, he obtained a second certificate attesting to his marine skill: "License to Master of Sail Vessels, Any Ocean."

Throughout all of this, however, Ron was continuing in his quest to answer the riddles of man. His writings and explorations had the purpose of financing his researches and expanding his knowledge of the world and life.

Then came the war.

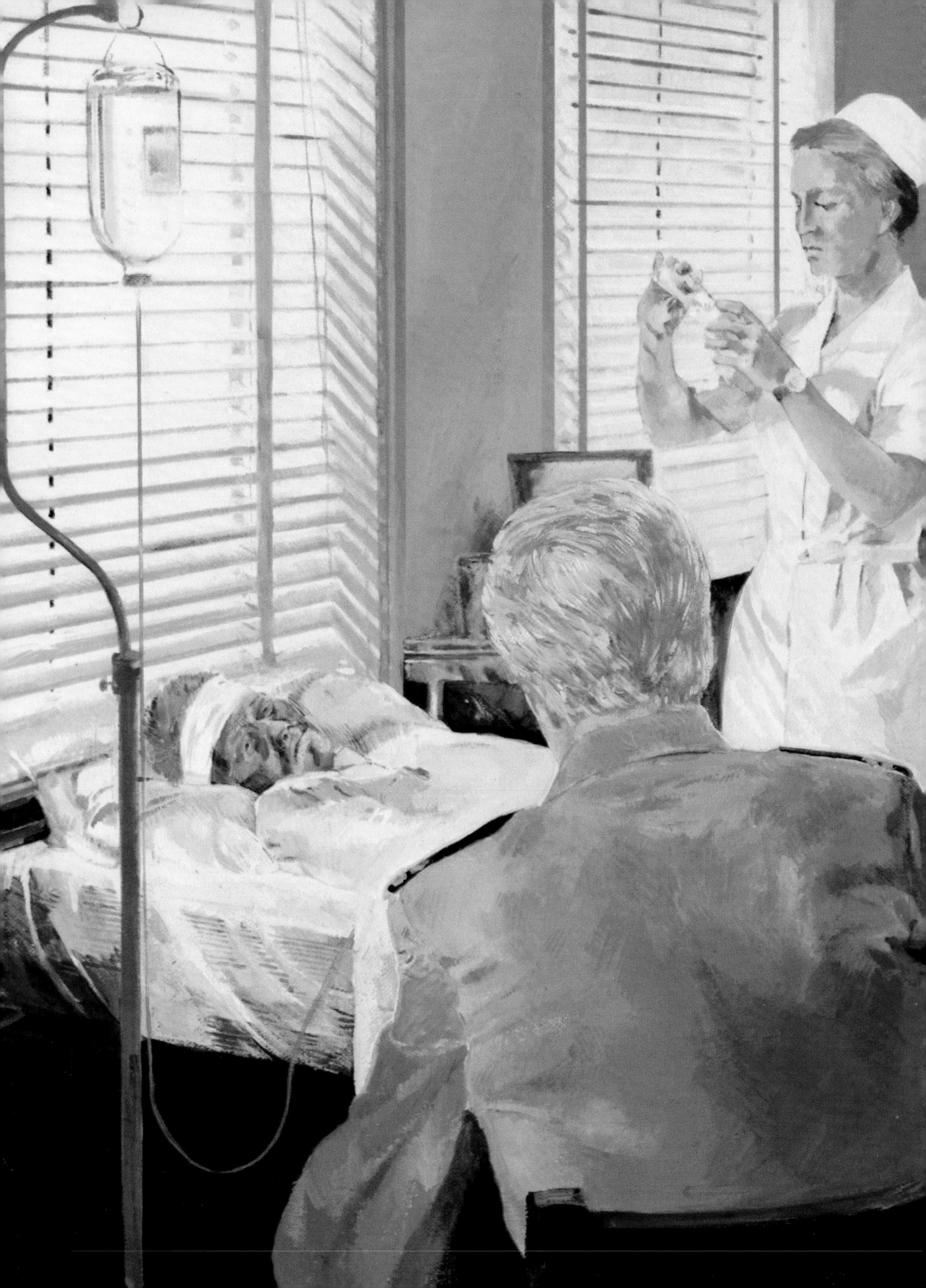

At the outbreak of World War II, Mr. Hubbard was commissioned as a lieutenant (junior grade) in the US Navy and served as a commander of corvettes. He saw action in both the Atlantic and Pacific, and thoroughly distinguished himself in the eyes of those who served beneath him. Yet he was not a man who enjoyed war, and having seen enough killing to last him a lifetime—and the effects of that bloodshed on men's sanity—he vowed to redouble his efforts to create a saner world. With this same sense of compassion, he also did all he could to safeguard his crews, prompting one of his men to write:

"I feel I owe you a tremendous debt of gratitude. First for your acquaintance. Secondly because you have portrayed to me all the attributes of a 'story book' naval officer. I can see for myself that you were an officer and a gentleman long before Congress decided so."

In 1945, left partially blind with injured optic nerves and lame from hip and back injuries, Mr. Hubbard was hospitalized at Oak Knoll Naval Hospital in Oakland, California. Among the 5,000 naval and Marine Corps patients at Oak Knoll were hundreds of former American prisoners liberated from Japanese camps on South Pacific islands. Many were in terrible condition from starvation and other causes, unable to assimilate protein.

In an attempt to resolve this problem, Navy physicians were administering testosterone, a male hormone. This medical treatment, however, was not getting effective results on all patients, and Mr. Hubbard utilized the opportunity to not only help his fellow servicemen, but to test a theory he had developed in application.

"All I was trying to establish," he wrote, "was whether or not the mind regulated the body or the body regulated the mind. Therefore, if on some of these patients hormones did not work and on some of them they did, there might be a mental reason. If those patients on whom it did not work had a severe mental block, then it was obvious that regardless of the amount of hormone or medical treatment the person received, he would not get well. If the mind were capable of putting this much restraint upon the physical body then obviously the fact that was commonly held to be true, that structure monitors function, would be false. I set out to prove this. . . . I was not interested in endocrinology but in resolving whether or not function monitored structure or structure monitored function."

In case after case, he found that by utilizing techniques he had developed, previously unresponsive patients immediately improved with medical treatment once the mental blocks were removed.

In fact, function did monitor structure. As Ron noted at the time, "Thought is boss."

This was a revolutionary concept, cutting across misconceptions which had plagued Eastern philosophy and science for centuries.

With peace restored at war's end, Mr. Hubbard immediately set out to further test the workability of his breakthroughs. This was intensive research. For subjects he selected people from all walks of life—in Hollywood, where he worked with actors and writers; in Savannah, Georgia, where he helped deeply disturbed inmates in a mental hospital; and in Washington, DC, New York City, New Jersey, Pasadena, Los Angeles and Seattle. In all, he personally helped over four hundred individuals before 1950, with spectacular results. And he used the same procedures to cure injuries and wounds he himself had received, fully recovering his health by 1949.

So complete was his recovery, that officers from the Naval Retiring Board reviewing Lt. Hubbard's case were actually upset. After all, they reasoned, how could a man physically shot to pieces at the end of the war pass his full physical examination? The only answer, they concluded, was that L. Ron Hubbard must be somebody else. And when they found that all was in order, they designated him fit for active duty.

DIANETICS
THE
ORIGINAL
THESIS
by
L. Ron Hubbard

Returning to Washington, DC, Ron compiled his sixteen years of investigation into the human condition, writing the manuscript "The Original Thesis" (today published under the title **The Dynamics of Life***), a paper outlining the principles he was using. He did not offer it for publication. He gave a copy or two to some friends, and they promptly duplicated it and sent it to* ***their*** *friends who, in turn, made copies and sent it to others. In this way, passed hand to hand, Dianetics on its own became known the world over. Word spread that he had made a revolutionary breakthrough. L. Ron Hubbard had found the source of human aberration and had developed a technique of the mind that worked. Dianetics was born.*

The first published article on Dianetics, entitled "Terra Incognita: The Mind," appeared in the Winter/Spring 1949–1950 issue of the **Explorers Club Journal.** *Shortly thereafter, Ron found himself literally deluged with letters requesting more information on the application of his breakthroughs. Hoping to make his discoveries available to the broad public, and at the insistence of those working with him at the time, he offered his findings to the American Medical Association and the American Psychiatric Association. The response was most enlightening. Not only did the health care establishment claim no interest in his work, they declined to even examine his results.*

Thereupon a new lesson was learned.

A workable technology of the mind, that anyone could use to help himself and others, was totally at odds with the entrenched medical and psychiatric establishment. They preached that the mind was so complex it could only be understood by "experts" (themselves). They depended upon government appropriations and research grants and perceived Dianetics as a threat to these vested interests (ignoring the fact that Mr. Hubbard had always funded his own research). A technology that anyone could use posed a threat to their monopoly and their billions of dollars. They not only refused to accept Dianetics, they tried to suppress its use. If helping others was their sole purpose, certainly they would have embraced a new, completely proven technological breakthrough and assisted its release for the benefit of society. But they did not, and thus one can only conclude that their true motives were more sordid—the control of others toward their own interests, or, in one word, greed.

L. Ron Hubbard's friends and associates were aghast at the responses from the bastions of healing. On the one hand were hundreds of case histories with rave testimonials from those who had studied and used Dianetics and thousands of letters from people wanting to know more. On the other hand were the few "experts," who had resorted to 220 volts of electricity to cure problems of the mind, who had never studied the subject of Dianetics but nonetheless, didn't want it.

And so the decision was made. L. Ron Hubbard would go directly to the public with a handbook, detailing his discoveries and the techniques he had developed. Never before had there been such a text on the mind, a work expressly written for the man on the street.

The announcement was made, and all across the nation people eagerly anticipated its release.

"There is something new coming up in April called Dianetics," *wrote national columnist Walter Winchell on January 31, 1950.* ***"A new science which works with the invariability of physical science in the field of the human mind. From all indications, it will prove to be as revolutionary for humanity as the first caveman's discovery and utilization of fire."***

Winchell's prediction proved correct.

Dianetics: The Modern Science of Mental Health *was published on May 9, 1950. The response was instantaneous and overwhelming. Almost overnight the book became a nationwide bestseller, with 25,000 letters and telegrams of congratulation pouring in to the publisher. The book hit the* ***New York Times*** *bestseller list where it remained week after week, month after month, forever changing L. Ron Hubbard's life and, as we shall see, the lives of millions.*

A New Era For Mankind

The publication of *Dianetics* ushered in a new era of hope for mankind, and with it a new phase of L. Ron Hubbard's life. Although from this point forward, his life would prove just as adventurous as the previous 39 years, it is not the details that are most important, but the accomplishments which form the subject matter of this book.

The first indication that he was to be a public figure came immediately after the release of *Dianetics*. Although Ron had originally planned yet another expedition following the completion of *Dianetics*, so great was the popular response to his work that he had to change those plans. Thus, instead of exploring islands off Greece, he soon found himself lecturing on Dianetics to packed halls across the nation. It was also at this time that the first Hubbard Dianetics Research Foundation was formed in Elizabeth, New Jersey, and people began arriving in droves to study the new techniques and find out more about Dianetics.

By late fall of 1950, there were 750 groups across the country applying Dianetics techniques, while newspaper headlines proclaimed, "Dianetics Taking US by Storm," and "Fastest Growing Movement in America."

Ron's research continued, and in March 1951 he completed his next book, *Science of Survival*. In this 500-page work, he further explored the nature of thought and life, offering readers an understanding of, and a new means to predict human behavior. The book is oriented around a chart, the Hubbard Chart of Human Evaluation, which explains the various emotional tones of individuals, exactly delineated, and with the precise procedures to bring anyone to the highest level and thus ultimate survival.

In 1951 he wrote a total of six books, continuing to research and perfect the technologies of Dianetics with which he had resolved the problems of the human mind. But this still left many unanswered questions, questions which man had been pondering since the beginning of recorded history. "The further one investigated," he wrote, "the more one came to understand that here, in this creature *Homo sapiens*, were entirely too many unknowns."

And so, within a year and a half of the release of *Dianetics: The Modern Science of Mental Health*, L. Ron Hubbard had embarked upon another journey of discovery—entering the realm of the human spirit. This track of research, begun so many years earlier as a young man traveling the globe in search of answers to life itself, was to span the next three decades. And as breakthrough after breakthrough was codified, the philosophy of Scientology was born, giving man, for the first time, a route to higher levels of awareness, understanding and ability that anyone could travel.

Given the inherently religious nature of Mr. Hubbard's work through these years, it was only natural that those surrounding him would come to see themselves, not only as students of a new philosophy but also as students of a new religion. And so, in 1954, Scientologists in Los Angeles established the first Church of Scientology. L. Ron Hubbard founded the subject—early Scientologists began the Church.

As more and more people discovered Ron's breakthroughs, Scientology churches sprang up rapidly around the world. Meanwhile, through his writings and lectures, he continued to make his discoveries available to all those seeking answers.

In 1959, Mr. Hubbard and his family moved to England, where he purchased the Saint Hill Manor in East Grinstead, Sussex. This was to be his home for the next seven years, and the worldwide headquarters of the Church of Scientology.

There, in addition to his constant writing and lecturing, he began intensively training Scientologists from around the world so that they, in turn, might return to their homelands and teach others. The mid-1960s saw him develop a step by step route for anyone to reach states of higher awareness. He also codified administrative principles for the operation of Scientology organizations—work which brought about the expansion of Scientology into a global network.

On September 1, 1966, with Scientology established as a worldwide religion, Mr. Hubbard resigned his position as Executive Director of the Church and stepped down from the boards of all Church corporations in order to fully devote himself to researches into the highest levels of spiritual awareness and ability. On the threshold of breakthroughs that had never before been envisaged, he returned to the sea, in part to continue his work in an undistracted environment.

On board ship for the next seven years, he again traveled extensively, while devoting his attention to ever-worsening problems facing society through the late 1960s and early 1970s. Of special note from this period is the drug rehabilitation program he developed, recognized today by government studies around the world as the most effective in existence. It was also during this period that he developed the highest levels of Scientology, refinements of application, new administrative principles, and advances in the field of logic—all of which are explained later in this book.

Returning to shore in 1975, Ron continued his travels—first from Florida to Washington, DC and Los Angeles before finally settling in the southern California desert community of La Quinta near Palm Springs, his home until 1979. There, searching for new ways to make Dianetics and Scientology more easily accessible, he wrote dozens of training films on the subjects to visually demonstrate proper application of technical principles. He directed many of these films himself.

Long concerned with accelerating social decay, Mr. Hubbard wrote a nonreligious moral code based on common sense in 1980. Published in booklet form, it is entitled *The Way to Happiness.* In explanation of this work, L. Ron Hubbard said, "Reading the papers and wandering around in the society, it was pretty obvious that honesty and truth were not being held up to the standards they once had. People and even little kids in schools have gotten the idea that high moral standards are a thing of the past. Man has in his hands today a lot of violent weapons. He doesn't have the moral standards to go with them."

Loudly applauded by community and civic groups around the world, *The Way to Happiness* spread across the planet. An entire grass-roots movement formed to disseminate and use the booklet to uplift the decency and integrity of man. To date, 35 million copies have been distributed with millions more being demanded each year.

In 1980, he celebrated his 50th anniversary as a professional writer by again turning his prodigious energy to the field of fiction. He wrote *Battlefield Earth: A Saga of the Year 3,000,* an epic science fiction novel, followed by the ten-volume *Mission Earth* opus, a satirical romp through the foibles of our civilization. All eleven books went on to become *New York Times* and international bestsellers, a consecutive bestseller record unmatched by any writer in history.

Returning to his more serious work with continued research into man's spiritual potentials, Mr. Hubbard traveled extensively through California in the early 1980s. In 1983, he finally resided in the town of Creston, near San Luis Obispo. Here he completed his research and finalized the Scientology technical materials he had spent most of his life developing.

Dianetics' popularity spans four decades, remaining on bestseller lists around the world today.

Today, those materials are recorded in the tens of millions of words on the subject of the human spirit which comprise Dianetics and Scientology philosophy. The over 25 million words of his lectures—just those that are on tape—are enough to fill over 100 volumes of text.

In fact, it may well be that L. Ron Hubbard's works include more literature, recorded research and materials than any other single subject of philosophy, the spirit or religion. All of these materials are available to anyone who desires an improvement in his life. Well over 100 million of his books are in circulation today.

Having fully completed his research and seen its broad application expand to six continents and over 60 countries around the world, improving the lives of millions of people, L. Ron Hubbard departed this life on January 24, 1986. Instead of an end, however, it marked the beginning of an unprecedented expansion of Scientology around the world, as more and more people continue to benefit from his technologies.

As just one indication of Mr. Hubbard's continued popularity, fully 38 years after its initial publication, *Dianetics: The Modern Science of Mental Health* achieved the unheard of, returning to the top of the *New York Times* bestseller list in 1988. It still rides on bestseller lists around the world to this day and has thus far sold 15 million copies.

No less dramatic was the popular acceptance of Mr. Hubbard's other discoveries. To date, for example, more than 100,000 people have been freed from drugs, utilizing his rehabilitation methods, in centers across the globe, including the world's largest drug rehabilitation and training facility in Oklahoma.

For many more throughout the world—two million in South Africa alone—the name L. Ron Hubbard means literacy and an ability to learn any subject, thanks to his developments in the field of study.

Thousands of people each year discover Dianetics and Scientology in L. Ron Hubbard's books. They are available in over 30 languages and in bookstores around the world. Each individual book in this photograph is a separate work of Mr. Hubbard's, including 3 encyclopedic series: 18 volumes of his technical writings, 100 volumes of transcripts of his public lectures, and a 12-volume set of his administrative works.

KNOWINGNESS
L. RON HUBBARD
TECHNICAL BULLETINS
The Hope of Man
THE HUBBARD KEY TO LIFE COURSE
THE HUBBARD LIFE ORIENTATION COURSE
L. RON HUBBARD
FOUNDER
The International #1 Self-Help Bestseller
DIANETICS
The Modern Science of Mental Health
L. RON HUBBARD
Tens of Millions of Copies Sold Internationally
L. RON HUBBARD
The Way to Happiness
A COMMON SENSE GUIDE TO BETTER LIVING
#1 Bestselling Self Help Author
L. RON HUBBARD
CLEAR BODY
CLEAR MIND
EFFECTIVE PURIFICATION PROGRAM
14. BE WORTHY OF TRUST
Unless one can have confidence in the reliability of those about one, he, himself, is at risk. When those he counts upon let him down, his own life can become disordered and even his own survival can be put at risk.
Book One
Chapter Three
The Goal of Man

Mr. Hubbard's breakthroughs in administration have enabled thousands of professionals in industry, business and community affairs to bring sanity and stability to their workplaces and their groups.

Every day, Mr. Hubbard's discoveries on the subject of ethics help bring new order into people's lives, into their families, their communities and their environment. A long-confused subject, it has been endowed with new clarity and workability.

The accolades for his work would alone fill a volume, awards recognizing his literary works, his humanitarian contributions, his discoveries including Dianetics. In 1988, *Publisher's Weekly,* the prestigious journal of the book and publishing industry, bestowed on Mr. Hubbard their Century Award in recognition of *Dianetics* being on its bestseller list for over 100 weeks. No wonder *Magazine and Bookseller,* a leading publication of the US book trade wrote, "*Dianetics* by L. Ron Hubbard seems to go on and on."

But the greatest reward, particularly in Mr. Hubbard's mind, were the lives he was able to touch through Dianetics and Scientology. Today, millions of people are using his principles and are finding they work. And through this application, L. Ron Hubbard's dream, a dream that perhaps summarizes the hopes of thinking men throughout the ages—"a civilization without insanity, without criminals and without war, where the able can prosper and honest beings can have rights, and where man is free to rise to greater heights"—is not only possible but attainable.

What you are about to read in this book will provide a firm appreciation of L. Ron Hubbard's contributions to mankind, and everything contained in these pages derives from his work. Although one can enjoy the benefits of Scientology without fully knowing Mr. Hubbard, one cannot understand the man without understanding Scientology—for it is his work and his work alone.

Every few hundred or a thousand years, some genius rises and man takes a new step toward a better life, a better culture. Such a man is L. Ron Hubbard, the Founder of Scientology.

L. Ron Hubbard's many accomplishments have earned him thousands of acknowledgments and recognitions from around the world, a few of which are pictured here.

Personal Integrity By L. Ron Hubbard

WHAT IS TRUE FOR YOU is what you have observed yourself
And when you lose that you have lost everything.

What is personal integrity?
Personal integrity is knowing what you know—
What you know is what you know—
And to have the courage to know and say what you have observed.
And that is integrity
And there is no other integrity.

Of course we can talk about honor, truth, all these things,
These esoteric terms.
But I think they'd all be covered very well
If what we really observed was what we observed,
That we took care to observe what we were observing,
That we always observed to observe.

And not necessarily maintaining a skeptical attitude,
A critical attitude, or an open mind.
But certainly maintaining sufficient personal integrity
And sufficient personal belief and confidence in self
And courage that we can observe what we observe
And say what we have observed.

Nothing in Dianetics and Scientology is true for you
Unless you have observed it
And it is true according to your observation.
That is all.

Part Two

Scientology Principles and Application

The full story of the development and codification of Scientology can be found in scores of books, more than 15,000 pages of technical writing and more than 3,000 taped lectures. All told, these works represent a lifetime of research by L. Ron Hubbard to discover a workable means to set men spiritually free—to replace ignorance with knowledge, doubts with certainty and misery with happiness.

Today, the fruits of L. Ron Hubbard's work are available to anyone who wishes to reach for them. And no matter how different Scientologists may be—whether teachers and businessmen, housewives and athletes, artists and secretaries—they hold one vital factor in common: having significantly bettered their lives, they know that Scientology works.

Nothing in Scientology, however, need be taken on faith. Its truths are self-evident, its principles are easily demonstrable and its technology can be seen at work in any church of Scientology. One need only open the door and step through.

CHAPTER 4

A DESCRIPTION OF SCIENTOLOGY

Scientology: *Scio* (Latin), know, *logos* (Greek), the word or outward form by which the inward thought is expressed and made known. Thus, Scientology means knowing about knowing.

Scientology is a twentieth-century religion. It comprises a vast body of knowledge extending from certain fundamental truths, and prime among those truths: Man is a spiritual being endowed with abilities well beyond those which he normally envisages. He is not only able to solve his own problems, accomplish his goals and gain lasting happiness, but also to achieve new states of awareness he may never have dreamed possible.

In one form or another, all great religions have held the hope of spiritual freedom—a condition free of material limitations and misery. The question has always been, however, how does one reach such a state, particularly while still living amidst a frantic and often overwhelming society?

Although modern life seems to pose an infinitely complex array of problems, Scientology maintains that the solutions to those problems are basically simple and within every man's reach. Difficulties with communication and interpersonal relationships, nagging insecurities, self-doubt and despair—each man innately possesses the potential to be free of these and many other concerns.

Scientology offers a pathway to greater freedom. While the *hope* for such freedom is ancient, what Scientology is *doing* is new. The way it is organized is *new.* The technologies with which it can bring about a new state of being in man are likewise *new.*

Because Scientology addresses man as a spiritual being, it stands completely apart from other philosophies which see man as a product of his environment or his genes—fixed in the limitations under which he was born.

Rather, Scientology is the *study and handling of the spirit in relationship to itself, universes and other life.* Based upon the tradition of fifty thousand years of thinking men, it is built upon the fundamental truths of life. From these principles, exact methods by which one can improve conditions were derived; and unlike other efforts of improvement, which offered only rules by which men should live, Scientology offers real tools for use in everyday life. Thus, it does not depend upon a system of beliefs or faith. The emphasis is squarely on an exact *application* of its principles toward the improvement of one's life and the world in which we live.

To understand exactly how Scientology is utilized, something should be known of the track of research L. Ron Hubbard traveled and the antecedent of Scientology—Dianetics.

DIANETICS: UNDERSTANDING THE MIND

Dianetics: *Dia* (Greek) through, *nous* (Greek) soul.

*The Dianetics symbol uses the Greek letter **delta** as its basic form. The stripes are green for growth, and yellow for life. The four green stripes represent the four subdivisions of man's urge to survive which are delineated in Dianetics.*

Prior to 1950, prevailing scientific thought had concluded man's mind to be his brain, i.e., a collection of cells and neurons, and nothing more. Not only was man's IQ considered to be unimprovable, but with the formation of his cerebral cortex, his personality was likewise established. These theories were, however, inaccurate and consequently science has never evolved a workable theory of the mind nor a means to resolve problems of the mind.

L. Ron Hubbard changed all that with *Dianetics: The Modern Science of Mental Health*. Its publication in 1950 marks a watershed in the history of man's quest for a true understanding of himself.

Dianetics is a methodology which can help alleviate such ailments as unwanted sensations and emotions, irrational fears and psychosomatic illnesses (illnesses caused or aggravated by mental stress). It is most accurately described as *what the soul is doing to the body through the mind.*

Like Scientology, Dianetics rests on basic principles, easily learned, clearly demonstrated as true, and every bit as valid today as when first released in 1950.

THE GOAL OF LIFE

The concise statement of the goal of life itself was one of the most fundamental breakthroughs of Dianetics. This, the dynamic principle of man's existence, was discovered by L. Ron Hubbard and from this many hitherto unanswered questions were resolved.

The goal of life can be considered to be *infinite survival.* That man seeks to survive has long been known, but that it is his primary motivation is new. Man, as a life form, can be demonstrated to obey in all his actions and purposes the one command: "SURVIVE!"

This is the common denominator of all life, and from it came the critical resolution of man's ills and aberrations.

Once "Survive!" was isolated as the primary urge which explained all of a life form's activities, it was necessary to study further the action of survival. And from that research it was discovered that when one considered pain and pleasure as part of the equation, he had at hand the necessary ingredients with which to understand all of life's actions.

Survival is not only the difference between life and death. There are various levels of survival.

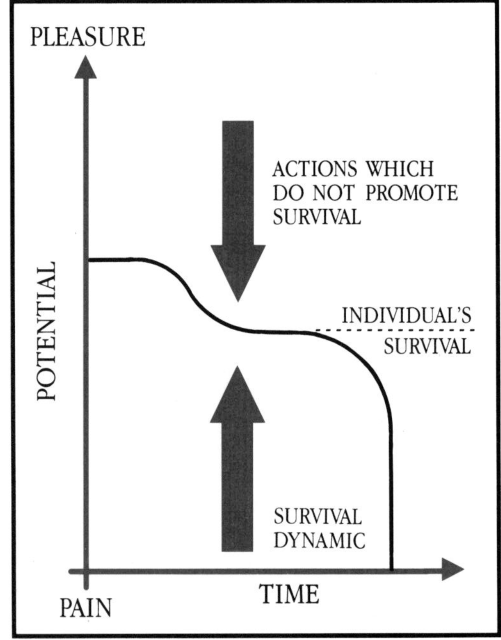

The better one is able to manage his life and increase his level of survival, the more he will have pleasure, abundance and satisfaction.

Pain, disappointment and failure are the result of actions which do not promote survival.

SURVIVAL AND THE MIND

Dianetics states that the purpose of the mind is to solve problems relating to survival.

The mind directs the individual in the effort of survival and bases its operations upon the information that it receives or records. The mind records data using what are called *mental image pictures.*

Such pictures are actually three-dimensional, containing color, sound and smell, as well as other perceptions. They also include the conclusions or speculations of the individual. Mental image pictures are continuously made by the mind, moment by moment. You can, for instance, examine the picture of what you had for breakfast this morning by recalling breakfast; and similarly recover a picture of an event which occurred last week by recalling it; or even recall something which happened a much longer time ago.

Mental image pictures are actually composed of energy. They have mass, they exist in space, and they follow some very, very definite routines of behavior, the most interesting of which is the fact that they appear when somebody thinks of something. If you think of a certain dog, you get a picture of that dog.

The consecutive record of mental image pictures which accumulates through a person's life is called the *time track.* The time track is a very accurate record of a person's past. As a rough analogy, the time track could be likened to a motion-picture film—if that film were three-dimensional, had fifty-two perceptions and could fully react upon the observer.

The mind uses these pictures to make decisions that promote survival. The mind's basic motivation, even though a person might fail in an undertaking or make a mistake, is *always* survival.

That being the case, why don't all of the actions dictated by the mind result in enhanced survival? Why do people sometimes experience irrational fears, doubt their own abilities or entertain negative emotions which seem uncalled for by circumstances?

As a rough analogy, the time track could be likened to a motion-picture film, if that film were three-dimensional, had fifty-two perceptions and could fully react upon the observer.

Mental image pictures are recorded in the analytical mind.

Mental image pictures containing physical pain and painful emotion are recorded in the reactive mind.

THE PARTS OF THE MIND

L. Ron Hubbard discovered that the mind has two very distinct parts. One of these—that part which one consciously uses and is aware of—is called the *analytical mind.* This is the portion of the mind which thinks, observes data, remembers it and resolves problems. It has standard memory banks which contain mental image pictures, and uses the data in these banks to make decisions that promote survival.

However, two things appear to be—but are not—recorded in the standard banks: painful emotion and physical pain. In moments of intense pain, the action of the analytical mind is suspended and the second part of the mind, the *reactive mind,* takes over.

When a person is fully conscious, his analytical mind is fully in command. When the individual is "unconscious" in full or in part, the reactive mind cuts in, in full or in part. "Unconsciousness" could be caused by the shock of an accident, anesthetic used for an operation, the pain of an injury or the deliriums of illness.

When a person is "unconscious," the reactive mind exactly records all the perceptions of that incident, including what happens or is said around the person. It also records all pain and stores this mental image picture in its *own* banks, unavailable to the individual's conscious recall and not under his direct control. Though it may appear that a person knocked out in an accident is unconscious and unaware of happenings around him, his reactive mind is actually industriously recording everything for future use.

The reactive mind does not store memories as we know them. It stores particular types of mental image pictures called *engrams.* These engrams are a complete recording, down to the last accurate detail, of every perception present in a moment of partial or full "unconsciousness."

This is an example of an engram: A woman is knocked down by a blow to the face. She is rendered "unconscious." She is kicked in the side and told she is a faker, that she is no good, that she is always changing her mind. A chair is overturned in the process. A faucet is running in the kitchen. A car is passing in the street outside.

The engram contains a running record of all these perceptions.

The problem with the reactive mind is that it "thinks" in *identities,* one thing *identical* to another. The equation is A=A=A=A=A. A reactive mind computation about this engram would be: the pain of the kick *equals* the pain of the blow *equals* the overturning chair *equals* the passing car *equals* the faucet *equals* the fact that she is a faker *equals* the fact that she is no good *equals* the fact that she changes her mind *equals* the voice tones of the man who hit her *equals* the emotion *equals* a faker *equals* a faucet running *equals* the pain of the kick *equals* organic sensation in the area of the kick *equals* the overturning chair *equals* changing one's mind *equals* . . . But why continue? Every single perception in this engram *equals* every other perception in this engram.

In the future, when this woman's present environment contains enough similarities to the elements found in the engram, she will experience a reactivation of the engram. For example, if one evening the faucet were running and she heard the sound of a car passing outside and, at the same time her husband (the man in her engram) was scolding her about something in a similar tone of voice as used in the original engram, she could experience a pain in the side (where she was kicked earlier). And the words spoken in the engram could also become *commands* in the present: She might feel that she was no good, or get the idea that she was always changing her mind. The reactive mind is telling the woman that she is in dangerous quarters. If she stays, the pain in the areas where she was abused could become a predisposition to illness or a chronic illness in themselves. This phenomenon of "awakening" the old engram is called *restimulation.*

The reactive mind is not an aid to a person's survival for the excellent reason that though it is sturdy enough to hold up during pain and "unconsciousness," it is not very intelligent. Its attempts to "prevent a person from getting himself into danger," by enforcing its engram content, can cause unevaluated, unknowing and unwanted fears, emotions, pains and psychosomatic illnesses that one would be much better off without.

The Solution to the Reactive Mind

Having discovered the existence of the reactive mind and its engrams, L. Ron Hubbard developed very precise techniques to address it. These techniques can effectively "erase" the contents of the reactive mind and eliminate the ability of such recordings to affect the person without his conscious knowledge. Furthermore, it makes these formerly hidden memories available to the individual as memory in the analytical mind. The effectiveness of these techniques, astonishing in many cases, has been documented in a multitude of case histories over nearly a half-century of application.

The Clear

The goal of Dianetics is a new state for the individual, sought throughout history but never attainable before Dianetics. This state is called "Clear." A Clear is a person who no longer has his own reactive mind and therefore suffers none of the ill effects that the reactive mind can cause.

The Clear has no engrams which, when restimulated, throw out the correctness of his computations by entering hidden and false data.

Becoming Clear strengthens a person's native individuality and creativity and does not in any way diminish these attributes. A Clear is free with his emotions. He can think for himself. He can experience life unencumbered by inhibitions reactively dictated by past engrams. Artistry, personal force and individual character are all residual in the basic personality of the person, not the reactive mind.

Clears are self-confident, happy and generally successful—in both careers and interpersonal relationships. It is a highly desirable state for any individual and is attainable by virtually anyone. In fact, thousands upon thousands of people have achieved the state of Clear, a living tribute to the workability of L. Ron Hubbard's discoveries and the technology he developed.

A Clear is a person who no longer has his own reactive mind.

The Attributes of Clear

Clear is a state that has never before been attainable in man's history. A Clear possesses attributes, fundamental and inherent but not always available in an uncleared state, which have not been suspected of man and are not included in past discussions of his abilities and behavior. The Clear is:

- *Freed from active or potential psychosomatic illness or aberration*
- *Self-determined*
- *Vigorous and persistent*
- *Unrepressed*
- *Able to perceive, recall, imagine, create and compute at a level high above the norm*
- *Stable mentally*
- *Free with his emotion*
- *Able to enjoy life*
- *Freer from accidents*
- *Healthier*
- *Able to reason swiftly*
- *Able to react quickly*

Happiness is important. The ability to arrange life and the environment so that living can be better enjoyed, the ability to tolerate the foibles of one's fellow humans, the ability to see the true factors in a situation and resolve problems of living with accuracy, the ability to accept and execute responsibility, these things are important. Life is not much worth living if it cannot be enjoyed. The Clear enjoys living to a very full extent. He can stand up to situations which, before he was cleared, would have reduced him to a shambles. The ability to live well and fully and enjoy that living is the gift of Clear.

Scientology: A Knowledge of Life

For all that Dianetics resolved in the field of human behavior and the mind, there still remained one outstanding question. When someone was looking at a mental image picture, *who* was looking at that picture?

The breakthrough came in the autumn of 1951, after Mr. Hubbard observed many, many people using Dianetics and found a commonality of experience and phenomena. After carefully reviewing all relevant research data, Mr. Hubbard isolated the answer: Man was neither his body nor his mind, but a spiritual being. This was the source of all that is good, decent and creative in the world: the individual being himself. With this discovery, L. Ron Hubbard founded the religion of Scientology, for he had moved firmly into the field traditionally belonging to religion—the realm of the human soul.

The term *soul,* however, had developed so many other meanings from use in other religions and practices that a new term was needed to connote precisely what had been discovered. The term Mr. Hubbard chose was *thetan,* from the Greek letter *theta,* θ, the traditional symbol for thought or life.

A thetan is the person himself, not his body or his name or the physical universe, his mind or anything else. It is that which is aware of being aware; the identity which IS the individual. One does not *have* a thetan, something one keeps somewhere apart from oneself; he *is* a thetan.

Very pertinent to Mr. Hubbard's research at this juncture was his examination into the phenomena known as exteriorization. Although various religious texts make mention of it, no one had ever considered the matter with such careful scrutiny. From this research, Mr. Hubbard concluded that the thetan is able to leave the body and exist independent of the flesh. Exteriorized, the person can see without the body's eyes, hear without the body's ears and feel without the body's hands. Man previously had very little understanding of this detachment from his mind and body. With the act of exteriorization attainable in Scientology a person gains the certainty he is himself and not his body.

The Parts of Man

From this discovery, Mr. Hubbard went on to precisely delineate the parts of man.

First there is the body itself. The body is the organized physical composition or substance of man, whether living or dead. It is not the being himself.

Next, there is the mind, which consists essentially of pictures.

Finally, and most important, there is the thetan. The thetan is not a thing. It is *the creator of things.*

The seniormost of the three parts of man, obviously, is the thetan, for without the thetan there would be no mind or animation of the body, while without a body or a mind there is still animation and life in the thetan.

The thetan utilizes his mind as a control system between himself and the physical universe. The mind is not the brain. The brain is part of the body and does not determine intelligence. It can be likened to a switchboard. If one said that a telephone switchboard was the intelligence of the corporation it served, this would be like saying the brain was the intelligence of the person. It is just not true. The brain is simply a conduit that, like a telephone wire, carries messages. The mind accumulates recordings of thoughts, conclusions, decisions, observations and perceptions of a thetan throughout his existence. The thetan uses his mind in the handling of life and the physical universe. The body (including the brain) is the thetan's communication center. It is a physical object, not the being himself.

The thetan is the source of all creation and *is* life itself. It becomes fully apparent

The Scientology symbol is an S imposed over two triangles. The S stands for Scientology. The two triangles represent important concepts in the Scientology religion. The lower triangle is made up of affinity, reality and communication, which together equate to understanding. The top triangle consists of another set of closely interrelated factors—knowledge, responsibility and control.

for the first time in man's experience that the spirit is immortal and possessed of capabilities well in excess of those hitherto predicted. The exteriorization of the thetan from his body accomplishes the realization of goals envisioned—but questionably, if ever, obtained—in spiritualism, mysticism and such fields.

Recognition of the thetan makes possible gains in ability and awareness—improvements which are not attainable in any practice holding man to be only a body and thus entirely subject to physical universe limitations. Psychology, for instance, had worked itself into a dead end. Having no concept of the existence of an animating factor to life, it had degenerated into a practice devoted solely to the creation of an effect on living forms.

In Scientology, however, the thetan himself is directly addressed. Such an approach to improvement accomplishes increased spiritual freedom, intelligence and ability for the individual, and clarifies any part of life.

THE EIGHT DYNAMICS

Because the fundamentals upon which Scientology rests embrace all aspects of life, certain key principles can be broadly employed to better any condition. Scientologists use these principles in their daily lives, and their use alone can often make the difference between success and failure. Moreover, the principles greatly clarify what is so often confusing and bewildering.

Suppose, for example, life could be correctly compartmentalized so that its many activities, often confused and blurred, could suddenly assume a new clarity? Suppose, for instance, that all the activities in one's varied life could not only be understood for what they really are, but harmonized with all others?

This is possible in Scientology through delineation of the eight dynamics.

The basic command "Survive!" obeyed by all of life is subdivided into eight compartments so that each aspect of life can be more easily inspected and understood. These eight compartments are called the eight *dynamics* (*dynamic* meaning urge, drive or impulse). L. Ron Hubbard had observed and delineated the first four of these dynamics in Dianetics. When his research led him into the realm of Scientology, he was able to amplify these first four and delineate the remaining four dynamics.

Through Scientology, a person realizes that his life and influence extend far beyond himself. He becomes aware also of the necessity to participate in a much broader spectrum. By understanding each of these dynamics and their relationship, one to the other, he is able to do so: and thus increase survival on all these dynamics.

The *first dynamic* is SELF. This is the effort to survive as an individual, to be an individual. It includes one's own body and one's own mind. It is the effort to attain the highest level of survival for the longest possible time for self. This dynamic includes the individual plus his immediate possessions. It does not include other people. It is the urge to survive as one's self. Here we have individuality expressed fully.

The *second dynamic* is CREATIVITY. Creativity is making things for the future and the second dynamic includes any creativity. The second dynamic contains the family unit and the rearing of children as well as anything that can be categorized as a family activity. It also incidentally includes sex as a mechanism to compel future survival.

The *third dynamic* is GROUP SURVIVAL. This is the urge to survive through a group of individuals or as a group. It is group survival, the group tending to take on a life and existence of its own. A group can be a community, friends, a company, a social lodge, a state, a nation, a race or in short, any group. It doesn't matter what size this group is, it is seeking to survive as a group.

The *fourth dynamic* is SPECIES. Man's fourth dynamic is the species of mankind. This is the urge toward survival through all mankind and as all mankind. Whereas the American nationality would be considered a third dynamic for Americans, all the nationalities of the world together would be considered the fourth dynamic. All men and women because they are men and women seek to survive as men and women and for men and women.

The *fifth dynamic* is LIFE FORMS. This is the urge to survive as life forms and with the help of life forms such as animals, birds, insects, fish and vegetation. This includes all living things whether animal or vegetable, anything directly and intimately motivated by life. It is the effort to survive for any and every form of life. It is the interest in life as such.

The *sixth dynamic* is the PHYSICAL UNIVERSE. The physical universe has four components. These are matter, energy, space and time. The sixth dynamic is the urge to survive of the physical universe, by the physical universe itself and with the help of the physical universe and each one of its component parts.

The *seventh dynamic* is the SPIRITUAL DYNAMIC, the urge to survive as spiritual beings or the urge for life itself to survive. Anything spiritual, with or without identity, would come under the heading of the seventh dynamic. It includes one's beingness, the ability to create, the ability to cause survival or to survive, the ability to destroy or pretend to be destroyed. A subheading of this dynamic is ideas and concepts and the desire to survive through these. The seventh dynamic is life source. This is separate from the physical universe and is the source of life itself. Thus there is an effort for the survival of life source.

The *eighth dynamic* is the urge toward existence as INFINITY. The eighth dynamic is commonly supposed to be a Supreme Being or Creator. It is correctly defined as infinity. It actually embraces the allness of all.

Simply delineating these dynamics clarifies and brings order into existence. One can observe these dynamics in one's own life, note which one or ones need improvement and, through Scientology, bring these factors into greater harmony.

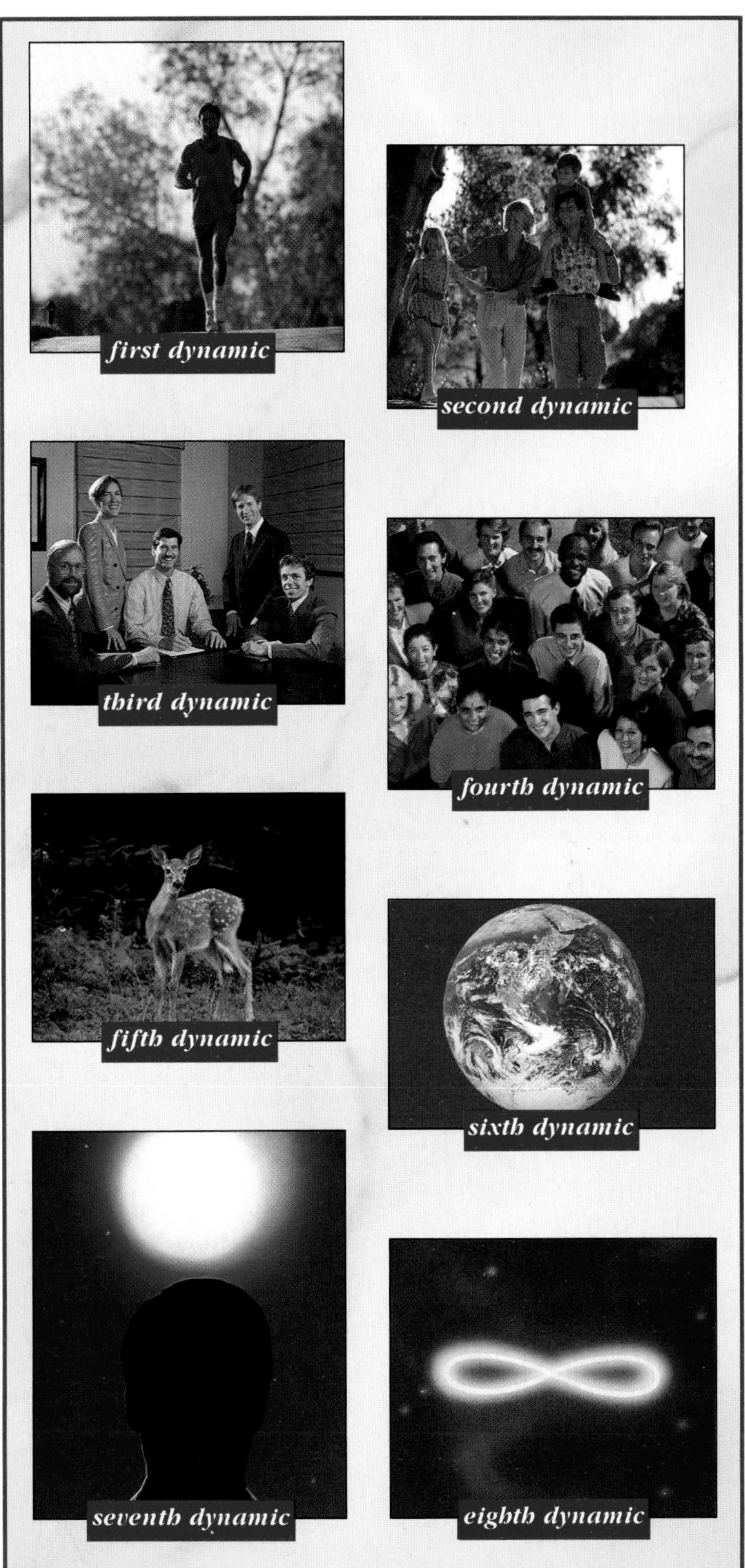

The basic command "Survive!" obeyed by all of life can be compartmented into the eight **dynamics (dynamic** *meaning urge, drive or impulse). A knowledge of the dynamics allows one to more easily inspect and understand any aspect of life.*

THE TONE SCALE

Another tool drawn from the body of Scientology and commonly used in everyday life is the Tone Scale. Codified from many, many hours of exhaustive testing and observation, the Tone Scale plots emotions in an exact ascending or descending sequence. Until Mr. Hubbard's examination of this matter, emotions were something we all suffered or enjoyed, but never fully understood.

Have you ever attempted to raise the spirits of someone mourning a recent loss with a cheerful word? The response is usually a fresh outpouring of tears.

Or someone whose outlook and response to life is a chronic apathy, no matter what is happening around him? The person seems to be in good health, has a loving family and an enviable job, but nothing makes any difference. The person just isn't interested.

The Tone Scale precisely illuminates what is occurring with individuals such as these, how best to communicate with them and how to help them.

One can find himself or any individual on this Tone Scale and thus know how, using Scientology, he may best be moved up to the higher tones where increased beingness, competence, self-esteem, honesty, well-being, happiness and other desirable attributes are manifested.

These emotional levels are thoroughly detailed in Scientology, but this simplified version will serve to show different emotions and their relative positions on the scale:

40.0 Serenity of Beingness
30.0 Postulates
22.0 Games
20.0 Action
8.0 Exhilaration
6.0 Aesthetic
4.0 Enthusiasm
3.5 Cheerfulness
3.3 Strong Interest
3.0 Conservatism
2.9 Mild Interest
2.8 Contented
2.6 Disinterested
2.5 Boredom
2.4 Monotony
2.0 Antagonism
1.9 Hostility
1.8 Pain
1.5 Anger
1.4 Hate
1.3 Resentment
1.2 No Sympathy
1.15 Unexpressed Resentment
1.1 Covert Hostility
1.02 Anxiety
1.0 Fear
0.98 Despair
0.96 Terror
0.94 Numb
0.9 Sympathy
0.8 Propitiation
0.5 Grief
0.375 Making Amends
0.3 Undeserving
0.2 Self-Abasement
0.1 Victim
0.07 Hopeless
0.05 Apathy
0.03 Useless
0.01 Dying
0.0 Body Death

From knowledge of a man's level on the scale, much can be determined about his attitudes, behavior and survival potential.

When a man is nearly dead, he can be said to be in chronic *apathy.* And he behaves in certain specific ways. This is 0.05 on the Tone Scale chart.

When a man is chronically sad about his losses, he is in grief. And, once again, behaves in a predictable manner. This is 0.5 on the chart.

When a person is not yet so low as grief but realizes losses are impending, or is fixed chronically at this level by past losses, he is in *fear,* around 1.0 on the chart.

Just above fear, past or impending losses generate hatred in the person. However, he dare not express this as such, so the hatred comes forth covertly. This is 1.1, *covert hostility.*

An individual fighting against threatened losses is in *anger* and manifests predictable aspects of behavior. This is 1.5.

The person who is merely suspicious that loss may take place, or who has become fixed at this level, is resentful. He is in *antagonism,* which is 2.0 on the chart.

Above antagonism, the situation of a person is not good enough for him to be enthusiastic, not bad enough for him to be resentful. He has lost some goals and cannot immediately locate others. He is said to be in *boredom,* or at 2.5 on the Tone Scale chart.

At 3.0 on the chart, a person has a *conservative,* cautious aspect toward life, but is reaching his goals.

At 4.0 the individual is *enthusiastic,* happy and vital.

Very few people are naturally at 4.0 on the Tone Scale. A charitable average is probably around 2.8.

This scale has a chronic or an acute aspect. A person can be brought down the Tone Scale to a low level for ten minutes and then go back up, or he can be brought down for ten years and not go back up.

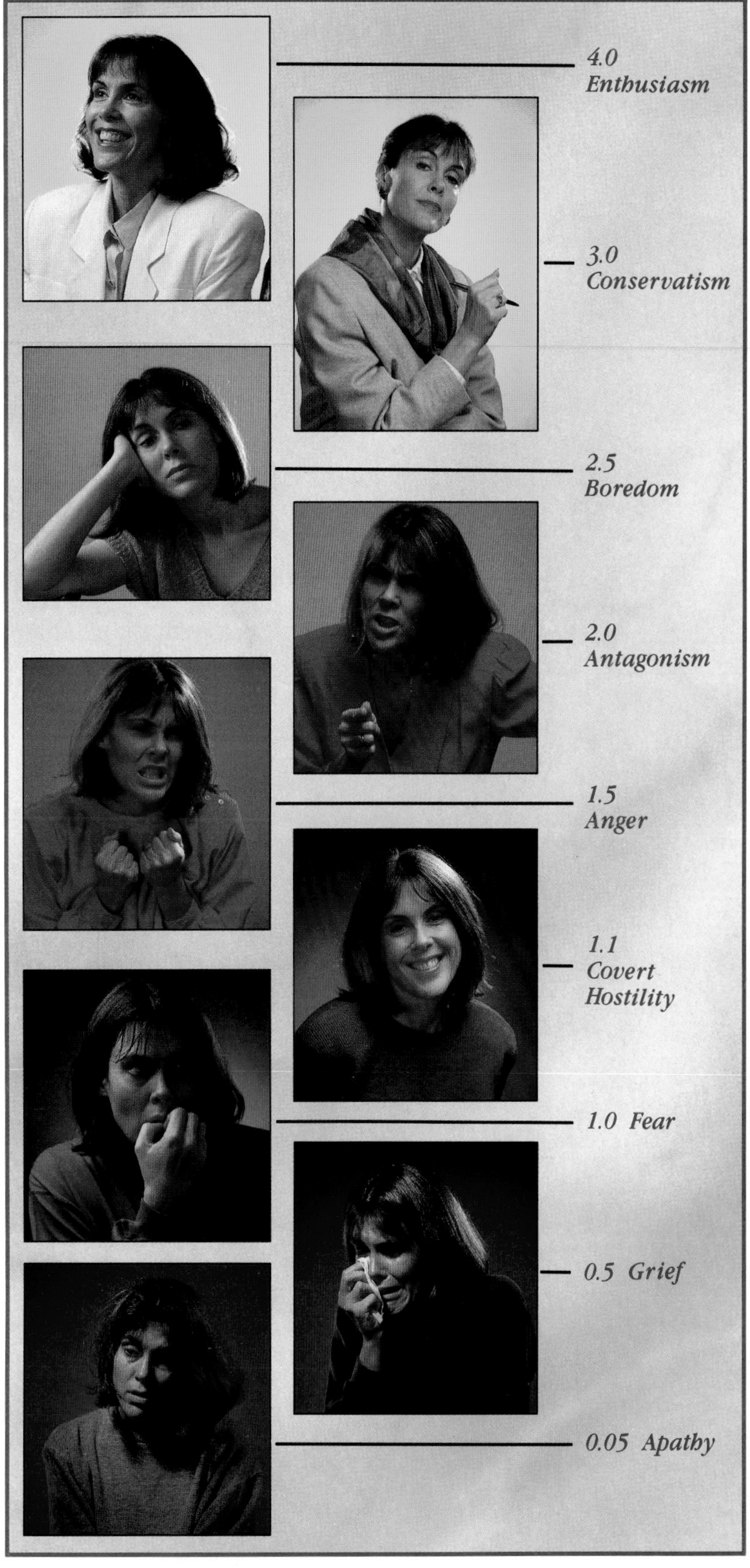

An abbreviated version of the Tone Scale, which plots emotions in an exact sequence. Through knowledge of the scale, one can understand and predict the actions of others.

A man who has suffered too many losses, too much pain, tends to become fixed at some lower level of the scale and, with only slight fluctuations, stays there. Then his general and common behavior will be at that level of the Tone Scale.

The simplest thing to know about this scale is that people find it difficult to respond to communication which is too far above where they are stuck. If you try to help someone in *apathy* by talking to them in *enthusiasm,* you will probably not have much success. The gap between such extremes is not easily bridged unless you understand the Tone Scale.

Using knowledge of the Tone Scale, however, you would recognize the emotion one-half to one full tone above the person, communicate in that tone and thus bring him up to higher tones. By moving up the scale gradiently it is possible to help someone overcome fixed conditions and regain a more happy and vital outlook.

The Tone Scale is of enormous value in life and its relationships. Mr. Hubbard thoroughly researched human behavior and the full body of his work in this area furnishes an accurate description of the attitudes and behavior of others. By knowing where a person falls on the scale, one can precisely predict his actions. Knowledge of the Tone Scale gives one a greater understanding of his fellows than ever before available.

Affinity, Reality and Communication

Another tool of considerable importance in Scientology, and one that greatly assists interpersonal relationships, is the principle of affinity, reality and communication. These three interdependent factors may be expressed in a triangle. The first corner of the triangle is *affinity,* which is the degree of liking

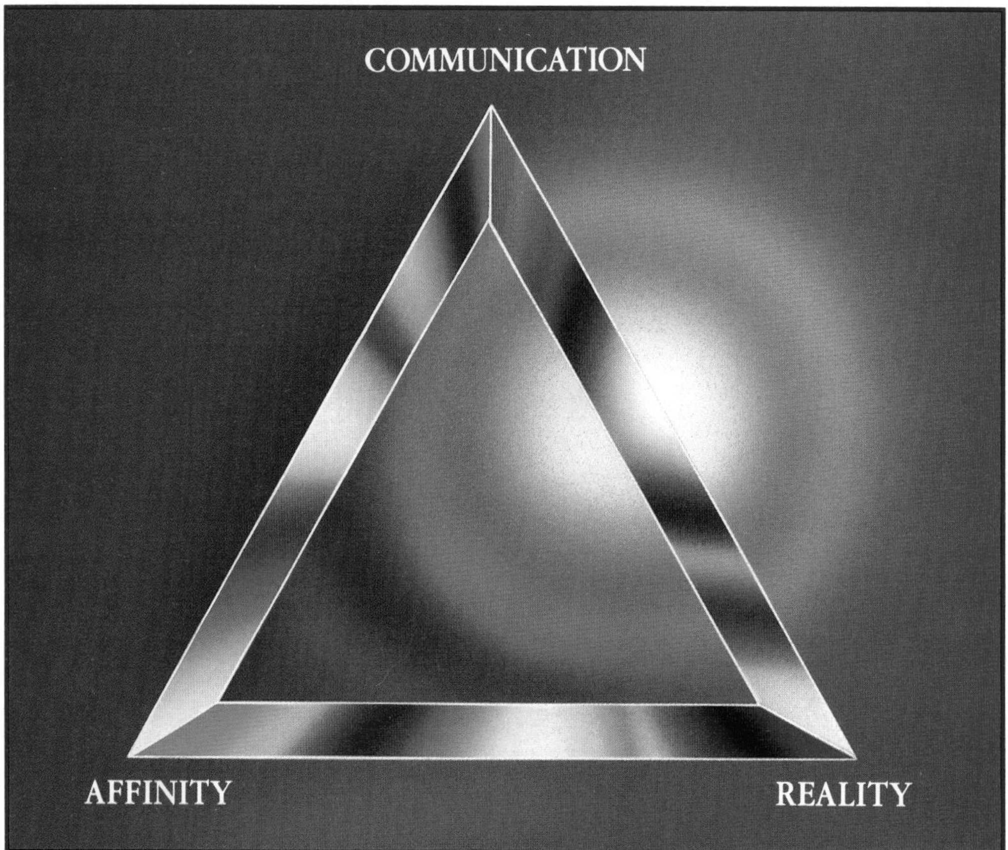

The component parts of understanding.

or affection or lack of it. It is the feeling of love or liking for something or someone.

The second corner of the ARC triangle is called *reality,* which could be defined as "that which appears to be." Reality is fundamentally agreement. What we agree to be real is real.

The third corner of the triangle is *communication,* defined as the interchange of ideas or objects between two people. In human relationships this is more important than the other two corners of the triangle.

The interrelationship of the triangle becomes apparent at once when one asks, "Have you ever tried to talk to an angry man?" Without a high degree of liking and without some basis of agreement there is no communication. Without communication and some basis of emotional response there can be no reality. Without some basis for agreement and communication there can be no affinity. Thus these three things form a triangle. Unless there are two corners of a triangle, there cannot be a third corner. Desiring any corner of the triangle, one must include the other two.

The ARC triangle is not equilateral. Affinity and reality are much less important than communication. It might be said that the triangle begins with communication, which brings into existence affinity and reality.

Great importance is placed in Scientology on the factor of communication, as Scientologists know that communication is the bridge to higher states of awareness and happiness.

These three terms—affinity, reality and communication—add up to understanding. They are interdependent one upon the other, and when one drops the other two drop also. When one point of the ARC triangle rises, the other two rise also.

The ARC triangle has many uses in life. It answers the question of how to talk to someone—if one uses the triangle and chooses a subject on which the person being talked to can agree, affinity will rise and communication will be better. Using the principle that raising any corner of this triangle raises the other two, one can improve his relationship with anyone.

THE SCOPE OF SCIENTOLOGY

Although there are substantially many more ways in which these principles and others may be used to better conditions, one need not spend months studying Scientology before it can be used. People have been led to believe that life is complex and man unknowable, but Scientology holds the opposite view: It is possible for anyone not only to know himself in the fullest sense of the word, but also to gain control over life. Moreover, Scientology is organized so that one may easily employ just a single principle to work remarkable changes.

But quite apart from the immediate bettering of relationships, or sorting out the confusion in one's life, these principles are actually part of the practice of Scientology, and that practice is dedicated to—and has the technology to—consistently raise individuals on the Tone Scale, increase their ARC, and broadly improve their dynamics.

To fully appreciate the depth and scope of the religion, and the actual practice of these principles and others, it is necessary to gain some understanding of the most important applications of Scientology—auditing and training—the subject of the next chapter.

CHAPTER 5

THE PRACTICE OF SCIENTOLOGY

Within the vast amount of data which is the religious *philosophy* of Scientology there are many principles which, when learned, give one a new and broader view of life. Scientology as a philosophical system contains many data one can use to *think with.* Knowing the Tone Scale, for instance, a person can see how best to deal with a grumpy child, mollify an upset friend or get an idea across to a staid employer. These principles amount to a huge area of observation in the humanities. The data exists for a person to think with, to work with, to wonder with, to accept or reject as he wishes. It is a body of knowledge there for the learning. There is nothing authoritarian in it. It is valuable purely as a body of knowledge.

From this body of wisdom the second division of Scientology—the applied philosophy—is derived. And the extraordinary achievement of Dianetics and Scientology has been the development of exact, precise methods to increase man's awareness and capabilities. Other efforts along this line achieved only sporadic or temporary results—if any. Using Scientology, invariable improvements can be obtained when exactly applied.

The importance of application in Scientology comes from the fact that L. Ron Hubbard developed as part of his philosophy an actual *technology* with which his discoveries could be used to effect improvement in people. *Technology* means the *methods of application* of the principles of something, as opposed to mere knowledge of the thing itself. And, using L. Ron Hubbard's technology, applying the methods, one can heighten his perceptions and awareness, increase his abilities and lead a better, more fulfilling life. In short, one can be unhindered by others' ideas that man cannot change and that one can be no better than he was born to be.

Throughout the remainder of this book the term *technology* is used with regard to the application of Scientology principles. Many technologies are extant today, technologies to build bridges and technologies to fire rockets into space. But with the work of L. Ron Hubbard, for the first time there exists a provenly workable technology to improve the functions of the mind and rehabilitate the potentials of the spirit. This is auditing.

A DESCRIPTION OF AUDITING

Although the purely philosophical aspects of L. Ron Hubbard's work are sufficient in themselves to elevate this civilization, only auditing provides a precise path by which any individual may walk an exact route to higher states of awareness.

The goal of auditing is to restore beingness and ability. This is accomplished by (1) helping the individual rid himself of any disabilities and (2) increasing individual abilities. Obviously, both are necessary for an individual to achieve full potential.

Auditing, then, deletes those things which have been added to the person's reactive mind through life's painful experiences and, as well, addresses and improves the person's ability to confront and handle the factors in his life.

Scientology auditing could be described as a very unique form of personal counseling which helps an individual look at his own existence and improves his ability to confront what he is and where he is. There are vast differences between the technology of auditing and other forms of counseling. There is no use of hypnosis, trance techniques or drugs during auditing. The person being audited is completely aware of everything that happens. Auditing is a precise, thoroughly codified activity with exact procedures.

A person trained and qualified in applying auditing to individuals for their betterment is called an *auditor. Auditor* is defined as *one who listens,* from the Latin *audire* meaning to *hear* or *listen.* An auditor is a minister or minister-in-training of the Church of Scientology.

A person *receiving* auditing is called a *preclear*—from pre-Clear, a person not yet Clear. A preclear is a person who, through auditing, is finding out more about himself and life.

The period of time during which an auditor audits a preclear is called an *auditing session.* A session is conducted at an agreed-upon time established by the auditor and preclear.

Auditing uses *processes—exact* sets of questions asked or directions given by an auditor to help a person find out things about himself and improve his condition. There are many, many different auditing processes, and each one improves the individual's ability to confront and handle part of his existence. When the specific objective of any one process is attained, the process is ended and another can then be run to address a different part of the person's life.

An unlimited number of questions *could,* of course, be asked—which might or might not help a person. The accomplishment in Dianetics and Scientology is that L. Ron Hubbard isolated the *exact* questions and directions to invariably bring about improvement.

The questions or directions of the process guide the person to inspect a certain part of his existence and what is found will naturally vary from person to person, since everyone's experiences are different. Regardless of experience or background, however, the individual is assisted in locating not only areas of upset or difficulty in his life, but in locating the source of the upset. By doing this, any person is able to free himself of unwanted barriers that inhibit, stop or blunt his natural abilities and increase these abilities so that he becomes brighter and more able.

There are no variables in the technology of auditing. No random results or haphazard applications. Auditing is not a period of vague free association. Each process is exact in its design and in its application, and attains a definite result when correctly administered.

Scientology auditing can bring any person from a condition of spiritual blindness to the brilliant joy of spiritual existence.

The Importance of Communication

Mr. Hubbard knew from his researches that only by enabling a person to find his own answers to the problems of his life could improvements be attained. As this cannot be forced on a person, auditing relies for its workability upon good communication between the auditor and preclear. The preclear is fully alert during a session and becomes even more alert and brighter as auditing progresses. The auditor and preclear work *together* to help the preclear defeat the preclear's reactive mind. It is not something *done to* the person, but involves his active participation to increase his self-determinism.

Auditing depends utterly on a full knowledge and understanding of the basics of communication. These are thoroughly analyzed in Scientology in many lectures, books and other writings. Several courses of study exist which deal exclusively with the laws and fundamentals of communication and their application.

Communication is vital in auditing and *is* what makes it possible for the process to work.

The Auditor's Code

The auditor maintains and practices a code of conduct toward his preclear known as the "Auditor's Code." This is a doctrine of strictly followed rules to ensure a preclear gets the greatest possible gain from auditing, and was evolved over many years of observation. It is the code of ethics which governs an auditor's actions.

Auditing is most successful when the auditor acts toward the preclear according to the Code. The auditor, for example, never tells the preclear what he should think about himself, nor offers his opinion about what is being audited. A goal of auditing is to restore the preclear's certainty in his own viewpoint; evaluation for the preclear only inhibits attainment of this goal. Hence, its prohibition by the Code.

The qualities instilled by the Auditor's Code are essentially those held to be the best in people. An auditor shows his preclear kindness, affinity, patience and other such virtues, to assist the preclear in confronting areas of upset or difficulty.

The E-Meter

Auditing is assisted by use of a specially designed meter which helps the auditor and preclear locate areas of spiritual distress or travail. This instrument is called an *Electropsychometer*, or *E-Meter*. The E-Meter measures the mental state or change of state of a person and thus is of enormous benefit to the auditor in helping the preclear locate areas to be handled. The reactive mind's hidden nature requires utilization of a device capable of registering its effects—a function the E-Meter does accurately.

When the E-Meter is operating and a person holds the meter's electrodes, a very tiny flow of electrical energy (about 1.5 volts—less than a flashlight battery) passes down the wires of the E-Meter leads, through the person's body and back into the E-Meter. The electrical flow is so small, there is no physical sensation when holding the electrodes.

The pictures in the mind contain energy and mass. The energy and force in pictures of experiences painful or upsetting to the person can have a harmful effect upon him. This harmful energy or force is called *charge*.

When the person holding the E-Meter electrodes thinks a thought, looks at a picture, reexperiences an incident or shifts some part of the reactive mind, he is moving and changing actual mental mass and energy. These changes in the mind influence the tiny flow of electrical energy generated by the E-Meter, causing the needle on its dial to move. The needle reactions on the E-Meter tell the auditor where the charge lies, and that it should be addressed by a process.

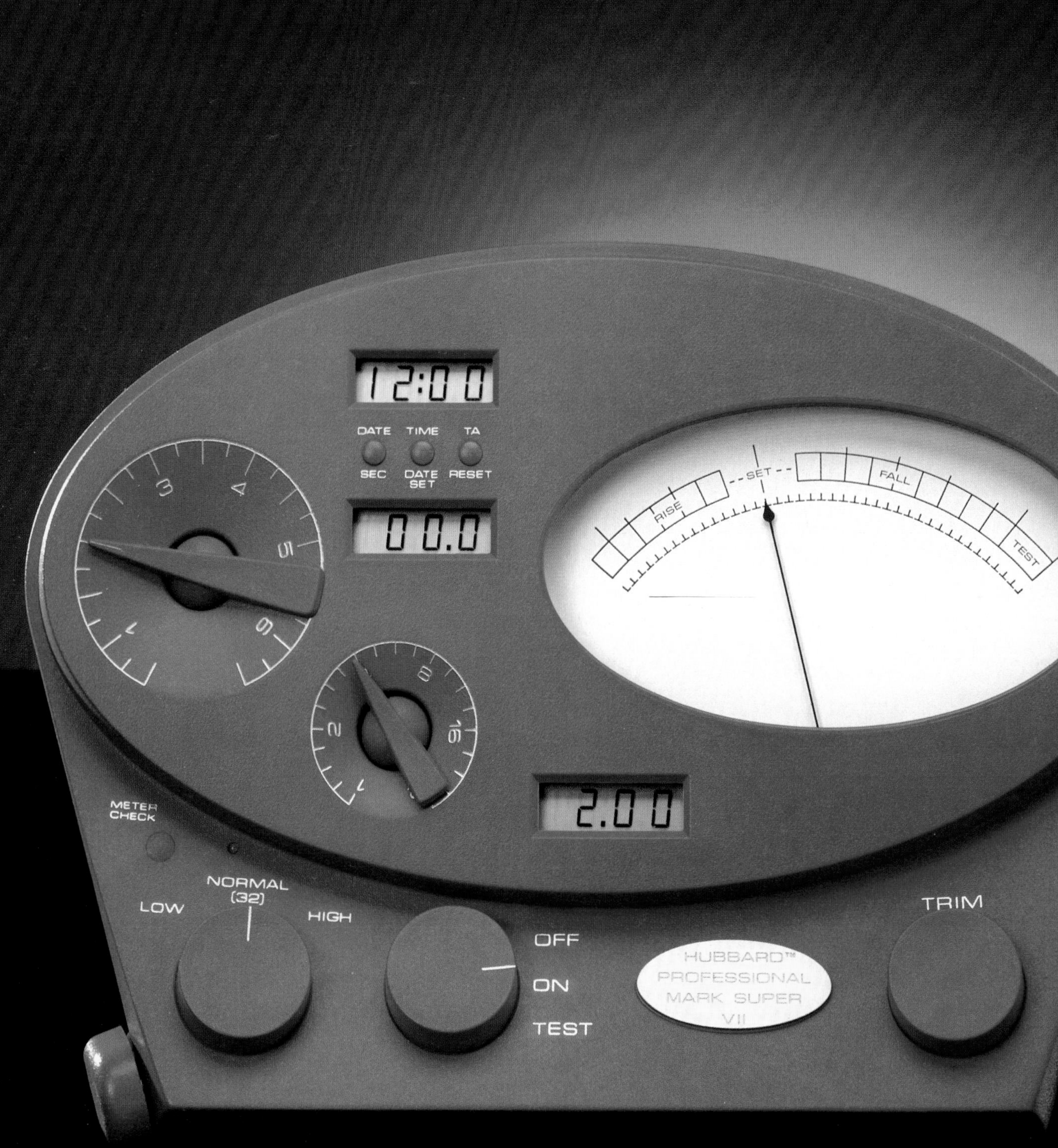

12:00
DATE
TIME
TA
SEC
DATE SET
RESET
00.0
RISE
SET
FALL
TEST
2.00
METER CHECK
LOW
NORMAL (32)
HIGH
OFF
ON
TEST
HUBBARD™
PROFESSIONAL
MARK SUPER
VII
TRIM

Different needle movements have exact meanings and the skill of an auditor includes a complete understanding of all meter reactions. Using the meter, the auditor ensures the process covers the correct area in order to discharge the harmful energy connected with that portion of the preclear's reactive mind. When charge lessens, the person heightens his ability to think clearly in the area being addressed and his survival potential increases proportionately. As a result, the preclear discovers things about himself and his life—new realizations about existence, the milestones that mark his gains.

These realizations result in a higher degree of awareness and consequently a greater ability to succeed.

HOW AN AUDITING SESSION IS CONDUCTED

Auditing then consists of certain elements: the preclear, the auditor, the auditing process, communication, the Auditor's Code and the E-Meter. In combination, they address the reactive mind and effect its resolution.

The auditing session takes place in a quiet, comfortable place where it will not be disturbed. Usually the auditor and preclear are seated across a table or desk from one another with an E-Meter set up for the auditor's use.

Before a program of auditing begins, the preclear is familiarized with the elements of auditing during a period of orientation so he knows what to expect in a session. The auditor also ensures the preclear has no distractions or upsets to prevent him from devoting his full attention to the process used in the session.

Different types of auditing are used for the preclear, depending upon his concerns during the session and his earlier auditing. Though auditing addresses the individual, and each

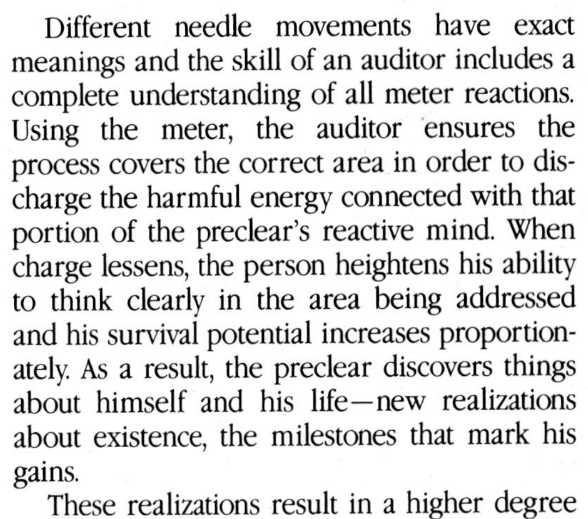

The Electropsychometer, or E-Meter, measures the mental state or change of state of a person, helping the auditor and preclear locate areas of spiritual distress or travail so they can be addressed and handled.

individual is different, a precisely delineated gradient of processing steps is used to achieve personal freedom for everyone.

By use of exact questions and the E-Meter, the auditor first locates an area of charge in the preclear's reactive mind to address with the process. When the auditor finds something in the reactive mind, the meter needle surges, indicating that the subject of his questioning contains charge.

Once an area of charge or upset has been located, the auditor then asks the process question or gives the directions needed to assist the preclear in examining it, because he is now inspecting his reactive mind.

The auditor guides the preclear to look at the area more thoroughly. He continues the process and makes notes of the meter reactions and data recovered by the preclear to help chart progress. He maintains the Auditor's Code, never evaluating the data being recovered by the preclear. As the process continues, more and more data from that area of the reactive mind, heretofore hidden from the person's conscious awareness, becomes available in the analytical mind of the preclear.

The process questions and directions help the preclear discharge the harmful energy or force connected with incidents or situations in his past. As the charge lessens, the preclear's awareness of the area increases.

The auditor continues to guide the preclear's attention to the area. Reactions on the E-Meter aid him to direct the preclear to pull more and more data, previously unknown to the preclear, out of the reactive mind and return it to his analytical awareness. Ultimately, the preclear becomes completely aware of the content and is able to view it as it is, without his awareness clouded by reactivity.

This is an auditing session. The auditor is on the left; the preclear is on the right.

During auditing, a preclear has many realizations about life. Such discoveries are called, in Scientology, *cognitions*. A cognition is something a person has come to realize. It is a "What do you know, I just realized why I always felt that way about . . ." kind of statement. Cognitions result in a higher degree of awareness and consequently greater abilities to succeed in life. When such a realization occurs, that portion of the reactive mind ceases to register on the E-Meter and the needle freely sweeps the dial rhythmically back and forth, a phenomenon plainly visible to the auditor.

The preclear will have gained a higher degree of awareness and rid himself of, perhaps, an irrational fear, psychosomatic illness or disability. The source of what had been bothering him was previously unknown, but, once discovered, its power is nullified. That particular process employed in the auditing session has served its purpose and can be ended. The auditor now proceeds onto additional processes in further auditing the preclear.

As more and more areas of the reactive mind are addressed and alleviated through auditing, its adverse effects continue to lessen and the individual becomes happier and more in control of his life.

With auditing, a person can be more self-confident, effective and successful in his endeavors.

WHY AUDITING WORKS

In a session, the analytical mind of the preclear is assisted by the analytical mind of the auditor in order to vanquish the preclear's reactive mind.

The preclear is victimized by his reactive mind. When this is restimulated, a person is affected by the harmful energy it contains. Since the reactive mind is hidden, the preclear cannot handle it by himself—witness the thousands of years man has philosophized, "soul searched" and tried to understand himself and his motives with no lasting result. In the absence of an auditor, the strength of the preclear's dynamic thrust is *less* than the force capable of being exerted by the reactive mind.

One of the primary reasons auditing works is because the strength of the auditor's dynamic thrust is added to the preclear's dynamic thrust and these two combined are *greater* than the single force of the preclear's reactive mind. Working together and applying L. Ron Hubbard's precise technology, the preclear's reactive mind can be erased.

Each time an area of charge is released from the reactive mind, the preclear's awareness increases. This increase of awareness builds from auditing session to auditing session and the preclear gradually becomes more and more aware of who he is, what has happened to him and what his true potentials and abilities are.

VALIDATION OF RESULTS

Routine testing by Scientology organizations of every preclear has made Dianetics and Scientology the most validated practices in the field of the mind and spirit.

Auditing gains which a person feels subjectively can be shown objectively through testing during the course of an auditing program. Numerous tests are used by technical staff to help gauge a preclear's progress. There are IQ, personality, aptitude, coordination and other tests a preclear takes prior to starting an auditing program. These provide a prediction of how much auditing it may take to achieve a certain result with the preclear. When the preclear is retested afterwards, the improvements he is experiencing personally can be plotted on a graph which validates his gains. The results are used by the auditor to help determine further processes to audit.

Though testing is primarily meant to assist technical staff to deliver a preclear the greatest benefits in his auditing, the consistent results observed have changed man's viewpoint of himself in many regards. Prior to Dianetics, psychiatry and psychology were adamant in their assertion that a person's IQ could not be changed. Their pronouncements were disproven in the face of study after study wherein persons showed dramatic increases in IQ after auditing.

Another routine test is the Oxford Capacity Analysis (OCA). This test accurately measures the preclear's estimation of ten different personality traits. These rise markedly in auditing, reflecting the preclear's gains. Preclears report being calmer, more stable, more energetic and more outgoing as a direct result of auditing and scores on the OCA furnish corroborative data.

Aptitude tests are also a reliable indicator of auditing results. Improvements in aptitude test scores correlate with a decrease in accident-proneness. Many other tests are available which test coordination and different perceptions such as vision, hearing, colorblindness, balance and so on, and these, too, improve as a result of auditing.

Naturally, individual progress is variable since it is largely influenced by the preclear's dedication and the frequency of sessions. Therefore, clearly defined rates of improvement are impossible to establish. The Church makes no claims or guarantees of the gains someone will make in auditing. Church staff, however, have seen so many remarkable improvements in test scores that they expect such as a matter of course.

COMPARISON TO EARLIER THERAPIES

Auditing is quite different, both in terms of approach and result, from other efforts which purport to be therapeutic.

In psychoanalysis, for instance, the analyst does not accept what the person says but interprets it, evaluates his condition for him, reads sexual significance into the person's statements and tells him why he is worried, all of which merely confuse a person further and have no therapeutic effect. In auditing, what the preclear says is never evaluated and his data is never refuted. To do so would totally violate the Auditor's Code. Nor in auditing is the preclear encouraged to ramble on without guidance, ransacking the millions of incidents in his reactive mind and restimulating many, in the hope he might stumble across the right one.

In more brutal practices such as psychiatry, force (physical, chemical or surgical) is used to overwhelm the person's ideas and behavior and render the patient quiet. There is no thought of gain or therapy here but only of making patients more manageable. Auditing bears no resemblance to any part of this field.

Likewise, auditing bears no resemblance to psychology, which is primarily the study of observing responses to stimuli and provides no means of producing actual improvement.

Other practices such as hypnotism consider that a person has to be put into a state of lessened awareness (i.e., a trance) before anything can be done. Auditing is quite the opposite and seeks to wake people up, not put them to sleep.

Some past efforts to help man tried to do so by enforcing moral codes or standards of behavior and conduct but, having no knowledge of the reactive mind or means to relieve its irrational dictates, they effected no lasting improvements.

Auditing is quite different from these past therapies, many of which were impositive and some, like psychiatry, which were actually harmful. In auditing one follows a precisely mapped route which leads to specific gains and it is only the individual being audited who says whether these have been achieved or not. The preclear determines when he has regained an ability or rid himself of a barrier to living, not anyone else. The auditor keeps working with the preclear until the preclear knows of his own volition that he has made it. It is not the auditor or anyone else in Scientology who says the preclear has made a gain. The preclear himself knows.

Given that the goal of auditing is rehabilitation of one's own potentials, the gains can really be determined in no other way.

Auditing is made up of common denominators which apply to all life. There are no variables in auditing; the same procedures apply to all cases. This is a considerable achievement, and is the one which makes auditing Scientology's most important use.

Only auditing restores to the individual his native potentials, enabling him to be the person he knows he really is. Only auditing frees a person from the traps of the reactive mind.

A DESCRIPTION OF SCIENTOLOGY TRAINING

A fundamental idea of Scientology is that increased awareness is the only factor which offers any road to increased survival and happiness.

Through auditing one becomes free. This freedom *must be* augmented by knowledge of how to *stay* free. Scientology contains the anatomy of the reactive mind in its axioms and the discipline and know-how necessary to handle and control the laws of life. The practice of Scientology, then, is composed in equal parts of auditing and training in Scientology principles which includes the technology of their application. Knowing the mechanisms by which spiritual freedom can be lost is itself a freedom and places one outside their influence.

Auditing lets one see *how* something happened, training teaches one *why.*

Therefore, because of the importance of training, one will find Scientologists studying the works of L. Ron Hubbard in any church of Scientology. If one were to look in on them, anywhere in the world, the scene would be the same:

Students seated at tables study the written works of L. Ron Hubbard, dictionaries at hand. Some, wearing headphones, listen to his lectures, while others drill the principles of application—all in the precise sequence as laid out by their materials.

There are no teachers present. Instead, an ambulatory Course Supervisor moves from student to student, monitoring their progress, while a Course Administrator provides any needed materials. Here one sees enthusiastic students, not only assimilating data, but actually learning how to apply it.

This is Scientology training and it is unique in the field of learning.

Training is the way to learn the technology of Scientology. Technology implies *use.* There is a gap between knowledge and the application of that knowledge. By becoming trained, a person becomes able to use the truths found in Scientology to accomplish the purpose of improving conditions in life.

Because Scientology is an applied religious philosophy, the study of Scientology emphasizes application. What exactly does one do to reunite a father and a son, to ease the suffering of a widow or repair a failing marriage? Other practices espouse how one must maintain faith, work out differences or endure with dignity. But does such advice, however well meaning, actually make a difference?

When a student enrolls on a Scientology course aimed at providing him the means to better any relationship, he will actually acquire an understanding of the subject, and equally important, the skill to apply it.

By way of an example, let us suppose that a Scientologist is faced with the prospect of a friend's impending divorce. A trained Scientologist has learned *why* a marriage—any marriage—fails. He understands why good communication ceases between partners and how affinity becomes lowered. Knowing this, he can do something effective to salvage a marriage. He knows methods of reestablishing communication between estranged husbands and bitter wives, and how to rekindle love all but extinguished by marital transgressions. Training in Scientology gives him what nothing else can: a truly workable means of dealing with real-life situations. Someone who has only been audited as a preclear might understand part of a problem in his own marriage but he will not have a complete understanding of it, much less the skills necessary to help others understand theirs.

Any person's involvement with Scientology therefore invariably includes gaining knowledge through education in Scientology principles. By learning the subject, one comes to *own* the knowledge of Scientology for himself and so is able to improve his own life and the lives of others.

How Are Scientologists Trained?

During his research, L. Ron Hubbard made many advances in how best to educate people and these are applied in courses delivered by the Church. He isolated the fundamentals of learning and codified these into a technology of study. Study technology is a separate field in itself, with application to any subject of learning. It is used in all Scientology training but is equally useful in the study of *any* subject.

Among elements unique to Scientology course rooms is the Course Supervisor, an expert in the technology of study, adept at locating and handling any barriers or obstacles to understanding which a student might encounter. The Supervisor does not lecture, nor in any way add his own rendition of the subject. This point is important because the results obtained in Scientology come only from closely following the technology exactly as written by Mr. Hubbard. The subject has already been researched, tested and well proven as workable in application. Verbal renditions passed on from teacher to student would inevitably contain alterations from the original, however unintentional, until Scientology's efficacy would be lost. This is why considerable attention is paid to ensuring a student receives only the pure rendition as written or spoken by Mr. Hubbard himself.

Instead, the Supervisor helps the student grasp the materials, always stressing understanding and application. This method of education has been found to graduate students who understand more and are far better able to use what they have learned than traditional methods of instruction.

Scientology training allows students to learn at their own pace. Each course is organized around what is called a *checksheet.* This is another innovation in the technology of study developed by Mr. Hubbard. A checksheet is a means of arranging and presenting the materials of a subject in a step-by-step manner to facilitate learning. Checksheets lay out the sequence of study and the practical application drills to be followed.

The materials of a Scientology course consist of books, other publications, films and recorded lectures by L. Ron Hubbard. These are laid out in the checksheet and the student studies them in the order listed. The student progresses from one step to the next only when he is ready. There is no "getting left behind," no expecting the student to blindly accept the data, or other such humiliations all too prevalent in the society's educational system. A Scientology course is solely for the benefit of the student; his own advancement in knowledge is the determining factor of progress.

Since the emphasis is on doing, not study for the sake of study, the student soon finds himself working with other students on the practical aspects of his course. Students study together to become proficient in what they have learned, and an atmosphere of mutual assistance pervades the course rooms.

In addition to studying his materials, each Scientology course requires direct application by the student of the data learned. As one progresses through the checksheet, he is required to demonstrate concepts, apply the information to situations in his own life and practice the procedures or techniques being studied until proficient in their use. A balance is struck between study of Scientology principles and practical application of these principles. The product of a Scientology course is someone who not only understands what he has studied but who can demonstrate this understanding through application.

There are course rooms for reading assignments and listening to taped lectures, while other course rooms are reserved for students drilling the application of their materials.

Another feature of Scientology training is the use of films as a tool to teach correct technical application. These films cover specific aspects of Scientology, showing exactly how they are applied in auditing. The films were written by L. Ron Hubbard and many of them were also produced, directed and narrated by him.

When someone completes a course they are awarded a certificate of accomplishment to signify attainment of a particular level of knowledge or skill.

SCOPE OF TRAINING IN SCIENTOLOGY

The broad scope of Scientology is divided into numerous courses, ranging from introductory courses that teach basic principles, to more extensive ones that train professional auditors, to courses which contain knowledge about the ultimate capabilities of the thetan, to those that cover the full philosophic and technical materials of Dianetics and Scientology. There is much to know but all of it is knowable and as one learns more, his view of life becomes clearer and more understandable.

At the heart of all instruction in Scientology are the auditor training courses offered in the Academy of Scientology in any church.

Scientology Academy training gives one an understanding of man, his potentials and the difficulties that confront him, far in excess of anything taught in the humanities or social sciences. Here, one becomes aware of how Scientology principles apply to situations anywhere in life. With this knowledge a person understands why some people are successful while others fail. He understands why one man is happy while another is not. He knows why some relationships are stable and why others fall apart. Life is not a mystery to someone who has studied Scientology. In this respect, training offers every bit as much personal insight as does auditing.

All lives are occasionally beset with trouble. A child falls and gets a scrape, the drinking problem of a neighbor's wife is discovered, a friend's business is failing, a parent becomes ill. The trained Scientologist can bring to bear what he has learned in the Academy to any situation in life and *he can do something about it.*

In a Scientology course room, people study Dianetics and Scientology materials at their own pace with the help of trained Course Supervisors. In addition to reading L. Ron Hubbard's writings and listening to his recorded lectures, students practice the application of those materials to improve their own lives and help others.

The skills acquired in training are a discipline in living and a know-how of the parts of life. Training in Scientology is the bridge between one's own learning and experience and livingness, and the truths offered to him in Scientology. It is a bridge from every human being to an understanding of life.

The Academy courses teach different aspects of this understanding as well as methods of their application, a combination which brings about certainty that one does, in fact, *know.* Since life is an *activity,* the emphasis is on *application.* The student, then, learns the actions which constitute their most important application, auditing. This encompasses an understanding of the communication which takes place between auditor and preclear and how to foster good communication.

Once one has learned to do this within the discipline of auditing it becomes simple to do it in life. The student thoroughly studies the theory and mechanics of the E-Meter and then drills with it until he is proficient in its handling and operation. He learns the basic rules of auditing and how to administer a session standardly to a preclear. Each step is studied and then drilled to competence. He watches training films in the Academy film room in order to learn the correct way to perform a particular aspect of auditing. He learns the various codes, laws and axioms that pertain to auditing so that he has a thorough grasp of these basics.

Later steps of his training build upon earlier steps and the student is gradually brought up to actual handling of specific laws by which life operates. The student next learns exact auditing processes and drills them with other students to the point of proficiency.

After two weeks of intensive training the student can complete enough study and drilling to be ready to begin auditing another on elementary processes. His preclear can be a friend, a fellow student, church staff member or anyone. His sessions are carefully supervised by highly trained auditors in the church who help him correctly apply his materials. The student audits his preclear daily and fulfills specific auditing requirements listed on his checksheet. *Application,* whether in life or in auditing, is the prime purpose of his training.

By bringing improvement to another person the student gains the certainty that he in fact does understand his materials. He confirms his competence in handling the elements of life and his certainty in his own abilities rises. This is a factor equally as important to one's spiritual advancement as the personal gains one receives from being audited.

L. Ron Hubbard stressed that half the gains in Scientology come from training in its principles. The truth of this becomes obvious when one considers how much a knowledge of Scientology clarifies a person's view of life. This naturally includes a greater understanding of what goes on in his own auditing sessions and so makes his own progress as a preclear more rapid and certain. Such understanding is gained by training.

In addition, there is considerable pride and personal satisfaction seeing another become more able and happier as a result of one's help. But regardless of whether one chooses to audit professionally, one is alive, and, trained in Scientology, he has new understandings he can use.

After completing the auditing requirements on the checksheet, the student is graduated from his course. An auditor does six major courses in sequence as part of his Academy training. The completion of each signifies a level of skill attained by the auditor and is denoted by a classification, Class 0 through Class V. More advanced classifications, numbering up through Class XII, can be obtained on higher-level training courses available at specific churches around the world. Each course follows the efficient and thorough pattern of instruction described earlier, but adds more advanced theory and procedures. The result is an auditor who becomes more and more knowledgeable in the subject. In this way the different levels of training parallel the levels through which a preclear advances in auditing.

Upon completion of specific training courses, the graduate gains further know-how in applying what he has learned under highly qualified supervision on an internship. Interning turns an auditor into an expert by *doing*. The auditor audits many different preclears on actions in which he has been trained. Such experience imparts the unshakable certainty that comes only from experience of doing something over and over.

Auditing techniques work 100 percent of the time if they are applied correctly. Though the basic principles of auditing are simple in themselves, skill in the application of auditing techniques must be gained by an auditor before he will be able to produce invariable results.

Precision is a requisite for accomplishing many things in life but when one is dealing with life itself, which *is* the preclear, slight variations in application of a procedure can considerably lessen the result obtained. It has long been established that greater gain accrues when the procedure is delivered precisely in all its aspects. The miracles of auditing are the culmination of dozens, even hundreds, of precisely learned, drilled and applied points concerning the wording of procedures, operation of the E-Meter, communication with the preclear and so on. The many steps of an auditing session, correctly taken, result in giant strides of improvement for the preclear.

A highly trained auditor spends thousands of course room hours learning his skills and perfecting them in practice. It is usual for an auditor-in-training to put in forty or more course hours per week. He invests far more time in a study of the mind than does a practitioner in any similar field. At the highest levels of classification, an auditor will have studied a number of course hours comparable to twelve years of classes at a college or university.

Training in Scientology enables one to face and handle existence. The skills of effective communication, of how to really help another, and how to face whatever life may present—all of these attributes have as many applications as there are situations in life requiring a handling.

The need for auditors is great since it is plain that individuals can be salvaged only one at a time. Unlike congregational religions, this salvation ultimately occurs in Scientology in the one-on-one relationship between auditor and preclear. Many Scientologists train to become auditors, and anyone who wishes to help his fellow man can do the same. But of no less importance, one can gain greater skill in handling life than he ever thought possible. There is no more worthwhile purpose than helping one's fellows and no better way to accomplish this purpose than by becoming an auditor. Auditors apply what they have learned to help others with auditing and to change conditions wherever they find that conditions need improving.

This is the mission of the trained Scientologist, and it is in his understanding, his compassion and his skill that the dreams of a better world reside.

THE VALUE OF SCIENTOLOGY

Through auditing and training, Scientologists have come to understand that much in our modern world is transitory and impermanent and based on things not surviving or on things that are in fact being destroyed. They know the practice of Scientology can rehabilitate the individual to his full potentials and that these gains last forever, bringing him to a realization of his own immortality.

Caught on an economic treadmill, hit at every side with the materialism of our age, it is hard for many to grasp that higher states could even exist.

But they do exist.

One sees this for himself when he reaches for them.

Once one starts moving up, there is no wish to stop. The scent of freedom is too strong.

The practice of Scientology is concerned with a better state for man and opens the way with a certain and sure bridge into a future. The way has been dreamed of in ages past. For man it never existed until now.

It exists in Scientology.

CHAPTER 6

THE BRIDGE TO A BETTER LIFE

That man could improve and better himself is a traditionally held belief. This idea tended to become obscured by the nineteenth-century theories of psychology which claimed otherwise—that we remain as we were born. More than that, psychology offered the novel—but utterly false—idea that man was only an animal and therefore could not improve his ability, could not improve his behavior and could not improve his intelligence.

Because of this, man in general now finds it rather hard to grasp the older and truer idea that man is a spirit and that he can reach for and attain higher states.

Yet betterment *is* a reality. Many higher states of existence are available to man, and these are attainable through Scientology. L. Ron Hubbard provided a precise delineation of these states, and then clarified how they could be attained by arranging them on a chart which graphically showed each step of the route upward.

Life is improved on a gradient. It is improved a little and then it is improved a little more and then a little more. It does not happen all at once. One cannot expect to be handed a totality of improvement in an instant, like being injected with a syringe that magically cures everything—unless of course one subscribes to the nonsensical idea that a living being has nothing to do with life. What is improved in Scientology is the individual and his awareness. It is not his body, his credit cards, his automobiles or other attendant and appendant machinery surrounding him. The individual himself is improved.

If one had a person with a very serious illness, his mind would be so thoroughly occupied with that condition that he could envision little more than recovery. If in this state someone were to propose the idea he might return to his job and play for the company football team within a week, it is doubtful he would even listen. When the pain subsided and he began to contemplate sitting up, this would be a substantial gain; after which he might even entertain the idea of going downstairs. But if at any point of improvement he were asked to consider the rigors of his job or the company team, it would constitute too big an improvement in too short a time.

Similarly, spiritual advance occurs a bit at a time and one cannot expect someone to immediately leap to the highest levels. The chart Mr. Hubbard devised indicates not only attainable improvements, but also the proper progression, thus avoiding the inevitable setback when attempting to attain too much too soon. An orderly progression, one improvement at a time, as Mr. Hubbard laid out, enables one to ascend at a satisfactory pace to a very high state indeed.

The chart which shows these gradations to betterment is called the *Classification, Gradation and Awareness Chart of Levels and Certificates.* It is divided into two sides—the left-hand side showing training steps one takes in Scientology, and the right-hand side showing the auditing steps.

Classification refers to training in Scientology and the fact that certain actions are required, or skills attained, before an individual is *classified* as an auditor at any particular level and allowed on to the next class.

Gradation refers to the gradual improvement that occurs in Scientology auditing. There are grades to a road and there are grades to steps. There can be shallow or steep steps, or even a vertical ascent, which is not a gradient. The desirable road is a gradual grade upward.

One's *awareness* improves as one progresses in Scientology. By receiving both training and auditing, each equally necessary, one's awareness increases. The levels of awareness are listed in the center of the chart and correspond precisely to one's progress in training and progress in auditing.

Man, in his religious heritage, has long imagined a bridge across the chasm between where one is now and a higher plateau of existence. Unfortunately, many of those attempting to cross that chasm fell into the abyss.

Employing this metaphor, the Classification, Gradation and Awareness Chart represents, in fact, the bridge which spans the chasm and brings one to the higher plateau. This is the vision man has cherished for at least ten thousand years, and it is now attainable by following the steps as laid out on the chart. It is an exact route with standard procedures providing uniformly predictable gains when correctly applied. The bridge is complete and can be walked with certainty.

The reader will find a copy of the chart inside the back cover showing the Bridge as developed by L. Ron Hubbard. This chart is intended to serve the reader as a helpful guide to Scientology services described in chapters to follow. (Instructions for its use are provided on the chart itself and any unfamiliar term is explained in the glossary at the back of the book.) Running up the center of the chart is a series of awareness levels, numbered from −34 at the bottom to +21 at the top. These levels represent what the individual person is aware of in his or her life.

Everyone is *somewhere* on these levels of awareness. The goal of Scientology is to assist the individual to raise his awareness higher and higher. Each rise in awareness is accompanied by increased ability, intelligence and survival potential.

As one improves, one naturally becomes aware of the next step. A person in "unexistence" (−34 on the scale), for example, when he improves becomes aware of "disconnection." In other words, disconnection (−33 on the scale) is an improvement over no existence at all. In realizing that one is truly disconnected from life, he is at least now in a position to rectify that condition. And so it goes for each level of awareness. A person who has recognized that he is introverted (−11) can then and only then recognize that he is numb (−10 on the scale), and thus gets no reaction from life. As a person progresses up the scale, he becomes aware in turn of the next higher stage.

The chart, then, is a map of what one individual can become aware of. It is, however, important to note that the chart stresses one's personal awareness, not what others may have observed about his behavior. Thus, again, we find that what matters is the individual, for that is what is addressed and improved.

At the level of "need of change" (−4) one is aware that he needs change in his life, and has actually reached quite a high state of awareness. Many people are not up to this level, and are therefore stuck in the unfortunate condition of wondering how they can endure that which they believe cannot be changed. Scientology is for the person who sincerely wants change, wants to become better and more able. Scientology thus helps the able to become more able.

As one moves up this bridge, he becomes a trained auditor and learns to help another as well as receive his own auditing. He achieves the state of Clear, advances to the highest levels of auditor training and the highest states of awareness as a spiritual being. The awareness levels are paralleled by the various techniques and activities which approximate them and bring about further improvements as one progresses.

As is evident from the chart, one must move up both sides, training and auditing, if one is to make it all the way. One must learn the axioms of existence by training in Scientology if one is to attain a higher awareness of life. One must experience how these axioms relate to himself through auditing if he is to fully understand himself and his relationship to life. Attempting to walk only one side of the Bridge is like trying to climb a hill by hopping on one leg. But an individual moving up *both* sides of this chart, one step after another, will arrive at the top.

The chart is a guide for the individual from his first awareness of Scientology to each higher state. *Man has never before had such a map.* It is the Bridge to Total Freedom. It *is* the route. It is exact and has a standard progression. One walks it and one becomes free.

THE GOAL OF SCIENTOLOGY

The goal of Scientology is making the individual capable of living a better life in his own estimation and with his fellows.

Although such a statement may seem simple and modest, the ramifications are immense and embody the dream of every religion: the attainment of complete and total rehabilitation of man's native, but long-obscured abilities—abilities that place him at knowing cause over matter, energy, space, time, form, thought and life.

Yet even well before one reaches this state, the changes Scientology can bring are profound. Personal relationships can be repaired or revitalized. Personal goals can be realized and happiness restored. Where once there were doubts and inhibitions, there can be certainty and self-confidence. Where once there had been unhappiness and confusion, there can be joy and clarity.

Those who have seen Scientology at work today cannot easily close their eyes to the results or fail to acknowledge that it truly does work. For Scientology has taught that a man *is* his own immortal soul. In Scientology, the riddle has been solved and the answer found simple.

Note: The next several chapters cover the auditing and training services found on the chart, providing descriptions of the primary ones listed. One can turn to the appropriate chapter in Part 3 for information about any particular service.

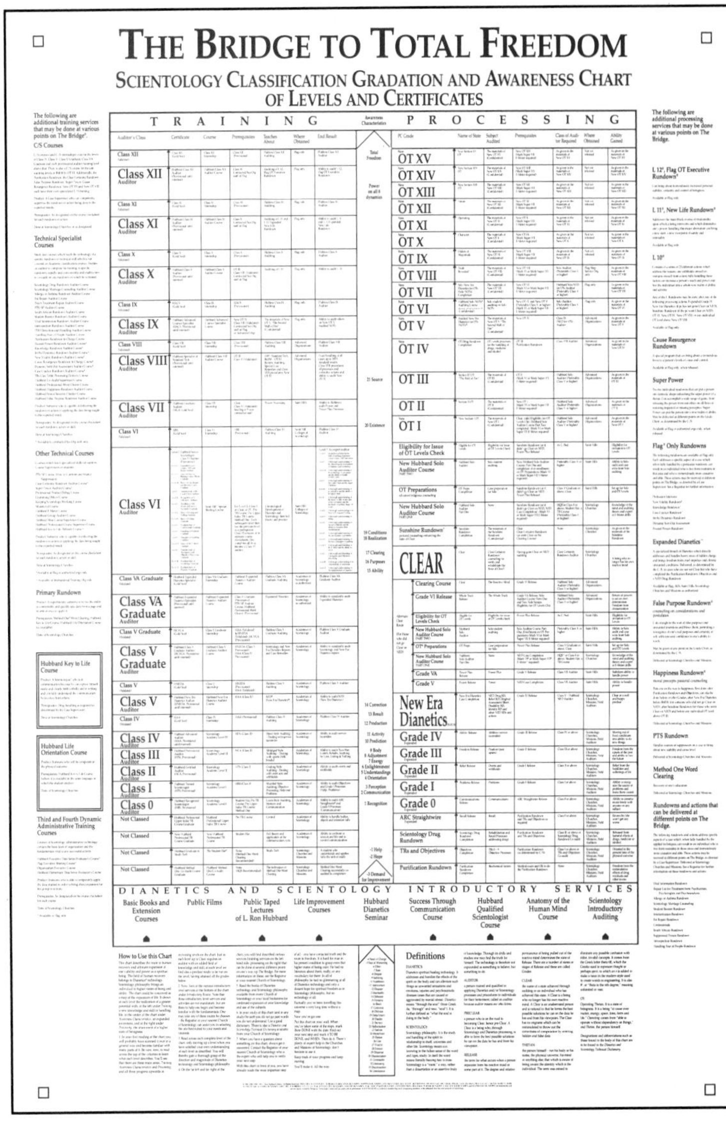

THE BRIDGE TO TOTAL FREEDOM

SCIENTOLOGY CLASSIFICATION GRADATION AND AWARENESS CHART OF LEVELS AND CERTIFICATES

A full-size copy of this chart has been included at the back of the book.

PART THREE

THE SERVICES OF SCIENTOLOGY

People benefit from Scientology through specific services which translate its philosophic concepts into practical methods of application. These divide roughly into courses of training and levels of auditing. Each service has an end result, enabling a person to rise higher in awareness and ability. His problems resolve, his relationships improve and his outlook brightens. He understands himself better and becomes more able.

Scientology can be addressed to *any* area. An arrangement of clearly defined services makes it possible for someone to learn and apply different aspects of the subject. In this way people progress up the Bridge.

The chapters in this part describe the services of Scientology. These follow the pattern of the Classification, Gradation and Awareness Chart, starting with introductory books and services and progressing up to different auditing levels and courses of training. All categories of service offered in churches and missions are covered, including a system of ethics which helps people apply Scientology for the greatest gains.

Each chapter describes a category of service and may be read independently of the rest. If the reader is especially interested in one in particular, he can find it listed in the table of contents and read that chapter first. All should be read though, in order to gain a full appreciation and understanding of the Scientology services that make up the Bridge to Freedom.

CHAPTER 7

BASIC BOOKS, EXTENSION COURSES AND LECTURES

Any fundamental of Dianetics and Scientology can be found in L. Ron Hubbard's books and lectures. And any one of his books offers more insight into Dianetics and Scientology than could be gleaned from a thousand magazine articles or interpretations of his work. The best way to find out about something is to go directly to its original materials. In Dianetics and Scientology, these are Mr. Hubbard's books and lectures.

L. Ron Hubbard's books have been read by millions and he is recognized as the most popular author of self-betterment books of all time. His first book on the subject, *Dianetics: The Modern Science of Mental Health,* remains a bestseller more than forty years after its initial publication, a feat unparalleled in publishing history.

All his works are straightforward, exact and written to be understood by anyone. They contain practical knowledge that lends itself to immediate application.

There are many books one can read to find out about Dianetics and Scientology, and so decide for oneself whether the observations and phenomena Mr. Hubbard describes are true. Several of those which contain explanations of the most fundamental principles are described here:

BOOKS ON DIANETICS

The Dynamics of Life

In his introduction to the book, L. Ron Hubbard wrote:

"Dianetics offers the first anatomy of the human mind and techniques for handling the hitherto unknown reactive mind, which causes irrational and psychosomatic behavior. It has successfully removed any compulsions, repressions, neuroses and psychoses to which it has been applied."

The Dynamics of Life

This is the first formal record of L. Ron Hubbard's researches on the function of the human mind. It is the original thesis on his work and explains those ideas which formed the basis of his research.

The Dynamics of Life contains the first description of many basic concepts which were later expounded in *Dianetics:* the nature of engrams and their relation to aberration, the earliest description of auditing principles, including the code of conduct followed by the auditor. The book further contains the original discussion of the axioms by which auditing actually works.

Dianetics: The Modern Science of Mental Health

Dianetics: The Modern Science of Mental Health

This book marks a turning point in man's knowledge and understanding of himself. In *Dianetics,* L. Ron Hubbard details the dynamic principle of existence (Survive!) and provides the first accurate description of the human mind, what it consists of and how it operates. He describes in great detail the source of all human aberration: the reactive mind and its engrams.

Having discovered this barrier to rationality and survival, L. Ron Hubbard developed a technology to eradicate its harmful effects, resulting in a new state of existence for man, the state of Clear. The auditing techniques for erasing engrams covered in *Dianetics* are more widely used today than in 1950.

Dianetics: The Evolution of a Science

Science of Survival

Self Analysis

Dianetics 55!

As an organized approach to life, *Dianetics: The Modern Science of Mental Health* has brought about great changes predicted by a university professor writing in the *New York Times:*

"As with all great books, the impact of *Dianetics* means the world will never be the same again."

Dianetics: The Evolution of a Science

L. Ron Hubbard traces the exact sequence of events leading to his discoveries about the human mind and his detection of that part of the mind responsible for man's nonsurvival behavior.

The book describes the full potential of the mind and details how Mr. Hubbard was able to isolate an individual's basic personality. He discloses how painful or traumatic events exterior to the individual can become fused with his innermost self, thereby causing fears, insecurities and psychosomatic ills. At a young age, L. Ron Hubbard became greatly intrigued by the mystery of man and his mind. *Dianetics: The Evolution of a Science* is the story of how he came to make the breakthroughs which solve this mystery.

Science of Survival

"While all men are created with equal rights under the law, an examination of the individuals in the society rapidly demonstrates that all men are not created with equal potential value to their fellows," wrote L. Ron Hubbard in *Science of Survival.*

Following a year after *Dianetics: The Modern Science of Mental Health, Science of Survival* is the authoritative work on the subject of human behavior. It is a detailed account of L. Ron Hubbard's observations of man and his discoveries of how man thinks and acts. In the boom following the release of *Dianetics,* much data accumulated on the application of auditing and great advances were made in furthering man's understanding of himself. These advances are contained in *Science of Survival.*

The book is organized around the Hubbard Chart of Human Evaluation which clarifies the seeming confusion of human conduct into definite categories which Mr. Hubbard observed through his research. A chapter of *Science of Survival* is devoted to each column of the chart and explains that column in detail.

One can use *Science of Survival* to accurately predict what another will do in any situation in life, even those with whom one has not had extensive prior experience. By noting the state of another's possessions, for instance, one could predict with keen accuracy his attitude toward children or the state of his health. *Science of Survival* can be used to help one choose employees, friends, those one should avoid and those one can trust and support.

Self Analysis

As L. Ron Hubbard wrote in this book, "Your potentialities are a great deal better than anyone ever permitted you to believe." *Self Analysis* is the first book ever written which provides definite techniques to improve memory, speed reaction time, handle psychosomatic illness and reduce stress.

Self Analysis offers the means to self-discovery through a series of processes designed to give an individual the clearest look he has ever had into his past.

A battery of tests at the beginning of the processing section enables the reader to assess his condition before starting, and provides a gauge of improvements achieved as he continues. The reader then launches into an analysis of his past, guided by specific and easily followed directions. Through the use of a special disk provided with the book, the reader's perception of his past quickly opens. Through the processing contained in *Self Analysis,* a person can discover that he is a much better friend to himself than he ever thought possible.

Dianetics 55!

The quality of one's life is dependent upon his ability to communicate. L. Ron Hubbard's researches into the subject of communication and how to communicate effectively are covered fully in this book.

L. Ron Hubbard carefully analyzes the subject of communication, dissecting it into components and describing the complete cycle of communication between any two people. A thorough understanding of this book alone could assure success in any endeavor.

Communication is central to the workability of Dianetics and Scientology and this book is Mr. Hubbard's most complete exposition on the subject. In fact, it is *the* manual on communication and thus vital to both living and auditing.

Child Dianetics

Here is a new approach to rearing children utilizing the principles of Dianetics. With the technology provided in this book, one can help a child become calm, happy and self-confident.

There is much practical data in the book, detailing how one can establish a trusting relationship with a child, how much control to exert and how to educate without breaking or discouraging a child. The book also clarifies the reason for childhood revolts, and how best to handle such upsets. A child can be taught honesty and integrity without overwhelming his self-determinism, and this is clearly explained.

A child is a man or woman who has not attained full growth. With this view of children and the practical measures in Mr. Hubbard's book, one can engender a child's love and respect, and help him grow to lead a happy and successful adult life.

Books on Scientology

Scientology: The Fundamentals of Thought

Mr. Hubbard declared this work to be the first Scientology book. In it, he introduces and explains many of the basic principles of the Scientology religion. This work is a broad summation of his research and contains a complete description of Scientology's most fundamental ideas: the cycle of action, the conditions of existence, the ARC triangle and the parts of man.

The materials described in this book *are* how life works. These data are exact and provide a clear, succinct understanding of the Scientology fundamentals.

A New Slant on Life

This collection of thirty essays by L. Ron Hubbard covers a variety of subjects—including the true story of Scientology, two rules for happy living, the anatomy of failure, professionalism, how to live with children, justice, knowledge and the first usable description of what constitutes true individual greatness.

A New Slant on Life contains both philosophical writings elucidating the Scientology religion, and practical data any reader can use to enhance his life.

The Problems of Work

Work is a large and important part of life for nearly everyone. It is also a major source of many upsets, anxieties and frustrations. L. Ron Hubbard analyzes the subject of work itself in this book and provides pragmatic data to help one succeed at his job and make his working hours calmer, less confusing and more enjoyable.

In *The Problems of Work,* Mr. Hubbard clearly isolates the problems encountered on the job—whether on the assembly line as a shop foreman or even as the CEO. He offers solutions to frayed tempers, exhaustion and the common feeling that one can't possibly accomplish all there is to do. There

Child Dianetics

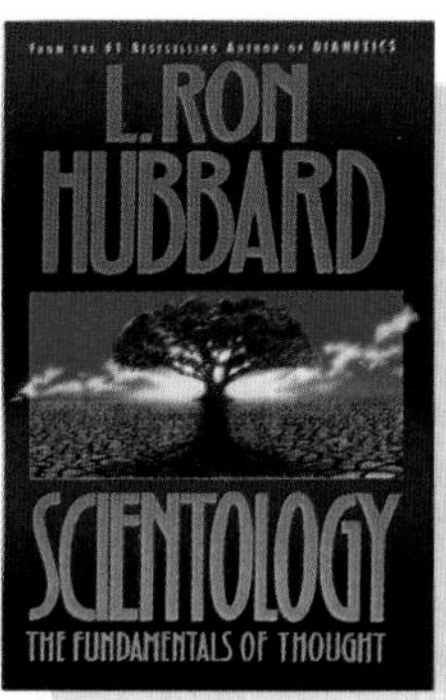

The Fundamentals of Thought

A New Slant on Life

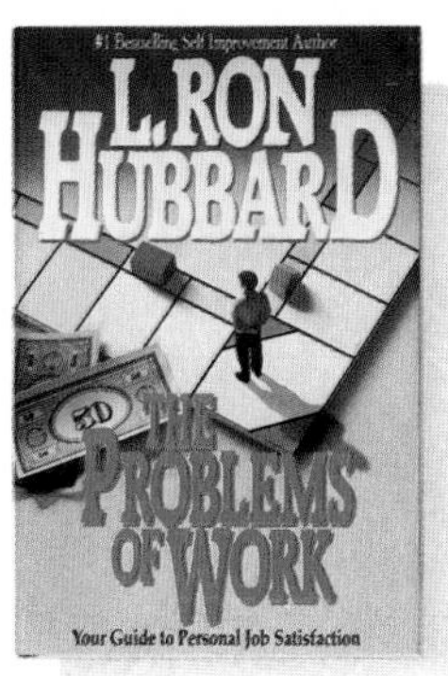

The Problems of Work

are ways to handle the confusions that surround any job or activity. There are secrets to efficiency. There are even ways to speed recovery from the burns, bruises or sprains that occur on the job or around the home. Mr. Hubbard covers all this in *The Problems of Work*.

Scientology 0-8

Scientology 0-8: The Book of Basics

Gathered here are the fundamental philosophic and technical data of Scientology. It is essentially a distillation of the entire materials of Scientology. In fact, the title of the book means, "Scientology, zero to infinity," the numeral 8 being the symbol for infinity stood upright.

Some of the data included are the Axioms of Dianetics and Axioms of Scientology. These are the self-evident agreements upon which the subjects were developed. Included too, are Mr. Hubbard's discoveries of the fundamentals underlying all forms of thought, known as the Logics.

Mr. Hubbard was able to plot many of his observations onto scales of attributes or characteristics of life. The many scales he discovered are included. Use of these scales enables one to understand the extremes and intervening gradients of such things as responsibility, motion, emotion, affinity, time sense, awareness and knowingness itself.

Scientology 0-8 contains the central, senior data of life, concisely stated.

Understanding: The Universal Solvent

Understanding: The Universal Solvent

Quotations from the works of
L. Ron Hubbard

"The only richness there is is understanding," wrote L. Ron Hubbard. This and hundreds of other quotations have been compiled into a volume of inspirational passages extracted from his millions of published words.

First and foremost, Mr. Hubbard was a writer, and while his enduring legacy stems from his researches, mastery of the language allowed him to convey his discoveries in terms that are often strikingly beautiful. The real strength of his writing however, comes from the truths he conveyed, and this book is filled with his wisdom on such subjects as understanding, communication, survival, goals, happiness, leadership, civilization, freedom, art, human relationships, morals and ethics and many more.

Understanding: The Universal Solvent conveys the essence of the Scientology philosophy and at the same time speaks volumes about its author. One could read this work and know at once what L. Ron Hubbard believed and what he strived to achieve.

EXTENSION COURSES

In order to help people better learn the data in Mr. Hubbard's books, the Church provides extension courses which can be done at home. Each extension course covers the entirety of one of Mr. Hubbard's books and is designed to give the reader a full understanding of the subject matter.

One receives an extension course lesson book, which he completes as he reads the book. After reading each section of the book and filling in the corresponding lesson, he then mails it to his local Scientology organization. There, a church staff member grades the lesson, sends a reply and helps with any difficulties. Extension courses can deepen one's understanding of Dianetics and Scientology books, and are an excellent way to acquire the material.

PERSONAL ACHIEVEMENT SERIES LECTURES

To relate his discoveries firsthand, L. Ron Hubbard delivered thousands of lectures to eager audiences all over the world. He lectured extensively throughout the United States, then moved on to London, Melbourne and Johannesburg, to name but a few cities that received him. He lectured to both those only recently acquainted with his works, and to seasoned practitioners.

The selected lectures listed below are particularly apt as introductions to the Scientology philosophy, roughly an hour in length. Each lecture imparts some of the fundamental wisdom of Dianetics and Scientology as well as providing an insight into L. Ron Hubbard himself. Listening to Mr. Hubbard lecture reveals his vitality, humor and enthusiasm as no written work can.

The lectures deal with a wide variety of topics but all communicate something of the flavor of the Scientology religion and its positive view of man's potentials. One can gain real insight into Scientology from hearing L. Ron Hubbard explain the subject. A listing of the titles in the series gives some idea of this:

The Hope of Man

Scientology and Ability

Money

The Story of Dianetics and Scientology

Health and Certainty

Man's Relentless Search

The Machinery of the Mind

Operation Manual for the Mind

The Dynamic Principles of Existence

Miracles

The Dynamics

Scientology and Effective Knowledge

The Road to Truth

Formulas for Success—The Five Conditions

Power of Choice and Self-determinism

The Deterioration of Liberty

Differences Between Scientology and Other Studies

Man: Good or Evil?

The Affinity-Reality-Communication Triangle

Increasing Efficiency

The Road to Perfection—The Goodness of Man

These and other books and lectures by L. Ron Hubbard are available in bookstores, libraries and through Scientology churches, missions and groups.

CHAPTER 8

INTRODUCTORY SERVICES

Though Scientology is immense in scope, one need not familiarize oneself with everything before applying its tenets to life.

The Church offers various introductory services for those who either want help with current problems or simply wish to explore the subject.

Introductory courses and activities provide much insight into the basics of Scientology and furnish data one can immediately apply to improve one's life. Such services are usually short in length and can be done in a few evenings at a church or mission. Their value lies in the instant benefit one gains from practical answers to the problems of life. Several, but by no means all, of these are described in this chapter.

LIFE IMPROVEMENT COURSES

Scientology Life Improvement Courses contain simple basics of Scientology technology which bring immediate improvement in a specific aspect of an individual's life.

The confusions of modern living require solutions. A problem in a relationship, a business or family situation can consume far too much attention. Each Life Improvement Course contains basic Scientology data one can use to rectify problems and improve conditions. There are courses on marriage, interpersonal relations, overcoming the ups and downs in life, personal values and integrity, working more efficiently, raising children, understanding others, and many more.

In every sense of the word, then, these are "how to" courses. Each is illustrated to facilitate understanding, with an emphasis on practical application. One learns the theory of basic Scientology principles, then applies these in course room exercises until one can do so in his life.

Consider, for example, an employee with an unresolving problem with a superior at a job which he otherwise enjoys. Any prospects for advancement are blocked but his current position is better than he would have at another company.

People have solved such situations by quitting, hardening themselves to the disappointment, growing increasingly bitter about management and so on, none of which actually *handle* the problem with the boss.

Rather than such losing propositions, one could take the Life Improvement Course which deals with improving relationships. He would soon discover definite ways, based on Scientology fundamentals, to improve his relationship with others. He would learn the true basis of interpersonal relations and then practice the precise steps needed to improve or repair any relationship. He would learn principles of communication and their application. He would learn the Third Party Law, the discovery made by L. Ron Hubbard concerning the underlying cause of *any* conflict, and how to employ this discovery to resolve strife. Given these and other tools, he could actually *change and improve* the situation with his boss. He would have found things he

A person can make rapid improvement in a specific area of his life with a Life Improvement Course. These provide Scientology fundamentals directly related to the area for which a person wants immediate help.

could actually *do*—not only for his own benefit, but *also* for the benefit of others.

Life Improvement Courses are unique to Scientology. Unlike other movements, with belief systems, Scientology provides practical knowledge. A technology about man leading to higher levels of awareness and ability is something that should be applicable to the everyday concerns of people. These applications exist in Scientology on Life Improvement Courses.

HUBBARD DIANETICS SEMINAR

Over four decades of results demonstrate beyond doubt that Dianetics works. Any person can experience the workability of Dianetics technology for *himself* by attending a Dianetics Seminar and getting Dianetics auditing.

Here, a person is audited on Dianetics and begins to rid himself of the barriers to his confidence, well-being and success.

The seminar begins with the viewing of a video explaining basic Dianetics principles and what happens in an auditing session. The person reads selected portions of *Dianetics: The Modern Science of Mental Health* and is then paired up with another student to practice the auditing procedure. After only a few hours the student is familiar enough with Dianetics technology to begin auditing another person or to receive auditing himself. Students audit each other under the guidance of experienced seminar supervisors, highly trained in Dianetics auditing. Those enrolling on the seminar receive as much Dianetics auditing as they wish, and gain a firsthand understanding of its power.

On the Dianetics Seminar, students pair up and audit each other as much as they want, giving them the firsthand experience of the results of Dianetics and the mutual gain of helping another person.

Through Hubbard Dianetics Seminars, thousands and thousands of people have received Dianetics auditing and started on the road to Clear.

The Success Through Communication Course

Many, many people experience difficulties in communicating. Some have trouble expressing themselves, while others feel uncomfortable in certain social situations. Still others find it difficult to initiate a conversation, while some do not know how to end one. A man cannot get a better job because he does not make an effective sales presentation. A girl cannot keep a boyfriend because she is too shy. An executive does not know how to talk to his employees and so lacks support. Communication difficulties are among the biggest problems people have in everyday living.

One of the greatest discoveries of Scientology is the delineation of the components of communication. All the gains experienced in Scientology stem in one way or another from a knowledge and application of communication. Scientologists have become known around the world as *the* experts on the subject of communication.

The exact technology of how to communicate effectively is taught on the Success Through Communication Course. L. Ron Hubbard developed eighteen separate communication drills to teach a student the basic elements of good communication. The student is paired up with another student and the two work together. Students read a drill and then practice it. Experienced Course Supervisors are always on hand to help with difficulties and ensure smooth progress. Each drill builds on the preceding drill, and as the student moves through these drills he makes the happy discovery that he truly has gained new communication skills. The drills teach one such social and business necessities as how to start talking to anyone, how to get one's point across, how to listen effectively and how to end a conversation.

An ability to communicate well is highly rewarded in life as evidenced by the esteem accorded artists, entertainers, television personalities and the like. But on a more personal scale, one who can truly communicate gets the more desirable job, has the better friends, the deeper relationships and a smoother life than one who cannot communicate.

Hubbard Qualified Scientologist Course

A person is part of life whether he is happy about it or not. There are basic laws to the way life operates and a knowledge of these laws can make life easier to understand and provide tools with which he can improve conditions. This is the subject of the Hubbard Qualified Scientologist Course.

This course offers a broad survey of key Scientology principles. The student studies six of L. Ron Hubbard's basic books and receives a thorough introduction to Scientology. He watches a filmed interview with L. Ron Hubbard in which he discusses how he developed Dianetics and Scientology and explains his philosophy.

There are many practical assignments providing the student with an opportunity to apply what he has studied to real life situations. From such application, he sees for himself how these principles work and so makes them his own, not merely an intellectual pursuit.

The student learns to audit basic Scientology processes and gains experience applying these to others. He drills communication fundamentals and learns how to properly deliver an auditing session. He drills different auditing techniques, then both audits another and receives auditing himself. These techniques include methods to assist those suffering from illness or an accident, how to make an intoxicated person sober, and processes which greatly raise one's awareness of his past—processes, incidentally, that are so powerful they have been known to entirely alleviate neuroses.

On the Hubbard Qualified Scientologist Course a person gets an excellent subjective understanding of what Scientology is all about, sees it working in others and experiences it working in himself.

These are the course materials and books studied by students on the Hubbard Qualified Scientologist Course. They give one a firm grounding in basic Scientology principles which he can apply to his life, making him a qualified Scientologist.

THE ANATOMY OF THE HUMAN MIND COURSE

The human mind has an exact anatomy. Before Dianetics, however, this anatomy was entirely unknown because those seeking to understand the mind did so from a wholly materialistic standpoint.

The Anatomy of the Human Mind Course contains the precise description of the mind, its components, its workings and its relationship to an individual.

The course consists of twenty lectures, detailing every aspect of the mind. The first period of each course consists of a talk on one portion of the mind. In the second period, students gain actual experience with what was discussed. Demonstrations are performed, examples are found and the students are helped to gain an understanding of such basics as the reactive mind, mental image pictures, engrams, the analytical mind, the body, its nervous system, and aberration.

The Anatomy of the Human Mind Course imparts a real understanding of Dianetics principles and their value to one's life.

SCIENTOLOGY INTRODUCTORY AUDITING

The best way to find out what Scientology auditing can accomplish is to get some.

In mapping the route to higher states, L. Ron Hubbard developed processes which take a person from wherever he is to the next higher level of awareness. There are many processes which do exactly that for the person just beginning auditing. Introductory processes address immediate concerns of an individual and can produce remarkable changes in conditions and his attitudes toward them. That they are introductory in no way lessens their precision or their potential for giving someone insight into a part of his life. Mr. Hubbard designated these processes as particularly applicable for someone with no previous auditing. They give a person his initial auditing gains, which, because they are his first, can be among the most memorable he will ever experience.

Another type of introductory auditing is called "assist auditing." This includes techniques which help a person recover more rapidly from bruises, burns, illnesses, upsets or other mishaps. Assists can actually be done on anyone, no matter how little or how far he has progressed in Scientology. The noticeable improvement that can occur from doing an assist on a burn or bruise makes it a very appropriate introduction to auditing. Someone whose headache has been alleviated by an assist obtains an excellent reality on the workability of auditing.

After a person has received some individual auditing there is another way to continue to receive auditing gains. This is through Group Processing. Mr. Hubbard developed certain auditing processes that are delivered to large numbers of people simultaneously. These techniques are administered by a single auditor to groups gathered in rooms or halls, and provide gains to many in one session. Even Scientologists who are not currently receiving individual auditing attend Group Processing sessions. Group Processing is for everyone, from those who have only experienced a little auditing to those who have had a lot. Though simple, Group Processes sometimes produce startling results and are always enjoyable.

Life does not have to be an unhappy plight. But one would be hard pressed to find a person who has not had his share of knocks or who cannot name an aspect of life he would wish to improve. Like a man dying in a desert for want of water, the world is full of people who lead an unhappy existence for want of answers to vital questions.

Millions have found these answers on introductory services at a Scientology church or mission.

CHAPTER 9

THE PURIFICATION PROGRAM: REHABILITATING A DRUGGED AND POISONED WORLD

Our planet has hit a barrier which prevents any widespread social progress—drugs and other biochemical substances.

The culture was severely harmed by the massive proliferation of drugs which began in the 1960s and today continues unabated. For many years prior to that turbulent decade, psychiatrists had busily endorsed the use of drugs as a solution to a multitude of mental and emotional conditions. LSD, for example (and L. Ron Hubbard warned of its danger to society as early as 1951) was heavily promoted and used by psychiatry during the 1950s and 1960s as a treatment for mental conditions. Subsequently, it was pushed out into the society and billed as a means of attaining enlightenment. In such a wise, the illegal street drug market boomed. Narcotics, stimulants and other substances found wider and wider acceptance in the society. Abuse of such drugs, once confined to a small segment of the population, grew to epidemic proportions in the 1960s among college students and spread from there.

Abetted by giant pharmaceutical firms and much media attention, psychiatry made drug taking an acceptable, mainstream activity for many. In addition to LSD, drug companies unleashed a torrent of drugs into the society—heroin, methadone and countless tranquilizers among others—that have proven to be nightmares for mankind. Added to an increasing use of marijuana, mescaline and other psychedelics, the availability and acceptability of drugs increased enormously.

A common tactic to gain acceptance for a pharmaceutical drug is to release it amid massive public relations campaigns professing the drug's efficacy and safety. But often, cases discrediting the claims of safety and revealing instead harmful side effects soon begin to accumulate. In the mid-1800s, opium addiction begat morphine which was touted by the medical establishment as nonaddictive treatment for opium addiction. But by 1870, morphine was recognized as more addictive than opium. This led to the development of heroin, extolled as a nonaddictive substitute for morphine. Within fifteen years this claim had clearly been shown to be otherwise. Following World War II, psychiatrists began pushing a new drug, methadone, as a cure for heroin addiction, thus foisting a century-old con game on a growing number of victims—all while reaping huge appropriations of public funding for its implementation.

Other prescription drugs such as Valium, Librium, Xanax, Oraflex, Halcion and Prozac were all claimed to be safe, but each has been found to have harmful side effects. Psychiatrists have earned hundreds of millions of dollars prescribing these drugs—and then treating the problems created by their own prescriptions.

The pharmaceutical drug companies reap huge profits, literally tens of billions of dollars a year, from the widespread use of drugs to treat an ever-increasing list of symptoms for new illnesses "discovered" each year by the psychiatric profession. Drugs have, for example, even become

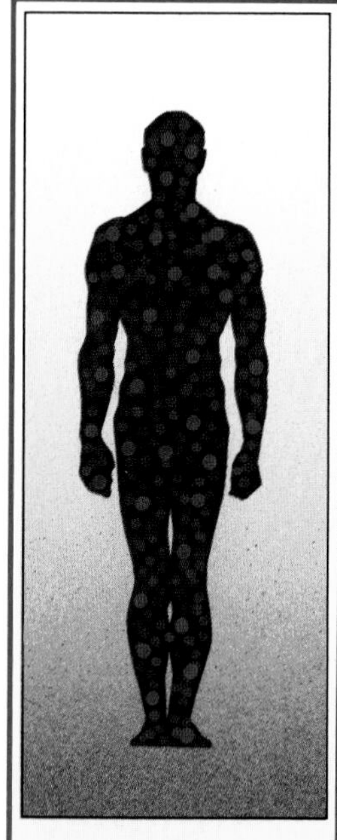

We live in a chemical-oriented society. The Environmental Protection Agency reports that the average American consumes 4 pounds of pesticides each year and has residues from over 400 toxic substances in his body. More than 3,000 chemical additives are found in the food we eat.

entrenched in the educational system. Today, a child labeled "hyperactive" can be given the psychiatric drug Ritalin in the classroom. And hundreds of psychiatric drugs are consumed by millions to "solve" a multitude of modern problems such as sleeplessness, nervousness, stress or just plain boredom.

These illnesses, all of which are given credence with sophisticated names, become official during the American Psychiatric Association's annual convention. Psychiatrists proffer a newly discovered illness and a vote is taken, with a majority consensus creating an official new disease. Why "official"? Official diseases can be treated and paid for by insurance companies, and in that way the psychiatric–drug manufacturer coalition ensures an ever-increasing source of income. Without question this is the greatest fraud of the twentieth century. It remains suppressed through the billions of dollars vested interests have at their disposal for high-tech PR campaigns and expensive marketing strategies, which in turn create the advertising revenues for a media which would be financially crippled if it exposed the scam.

All this is quite in addition to the widespread consumption of illegal drugs (many of which were originally prescription drugs), which are figured to be a 500 billion dollar a year industry in themselves. By some estimates, marijuana is now the biggest cash crop in America. Cocaine and its derivatives became very fashionable in the 1970s and are now widely abused, due in part to false data from psychiatrists who claimed as recently as 1980 in their own texts that cocaine usage was not addictive. They could not have been more wrong. Many medical and psychiatric drugs—heroin, LSD, methadone, Methedrine and tranquilizers, to name a few—were poorly controlled by those professions and allowed to proliferate on the illegal market, further exacerbating the problem. Right now, the most widely prescribed antidepressant, Prozac, is also the hottest kid on the block in the illegal street drug market.

Drug taking seems to be part of being alive in our modern world.

Additionally, technological advances this century have produced many unfavorable byproducts harmful to an individual's well-being. Smog, for instance, was unknown before the rise of manufacturing centers in Britain. Every major city on Earth now advises its inhabitants daily about the quality of air they are breathing. A hundred years ago, the main food preservatives were salt or ice. Today, nearly any packaged food has a list of the artificial ingredients it contains that is longer than the list of natural ingredients. Environmental disasters such as Chernobyl, to say nothing of radiation exposure from widespread nuclear bomb testing, did not exist fifty years ago.

We live in a chemical-oriented society. The Environmental Protection Agency reports that the average American consumes four pounds of pesticides each year and has residues from over 400 toxic substances in his body. More than 3,000 chemical additives are found in the food we eat.

There is no escaping our contaminated civilization and, furthermore, it has been found that these substances can put individuals in a condition which prevents personal improvement.

The drug problem was not of major concern in 1950 when L. Ron Hubbard released *Dianetics*. By the 1960s, however, the frightful specter of drugs had arrived and Mr. Hubbard's research showed that this was a major barrier to a person's spiritual betterment. Drugs, he discovered, affect the mind adversely and block any progress in auditing.

The way a being perceives much of existence is via the sensory channels of the body. The body is a communications center for the being, with the brain acting as a switchboard for translating thought into action. The biochemical actions of drugs alter the normal operations of this pattern, often with harmful or even disastrous consequences.

L. Ron Hubbard researched this barrier to spiritual freedom long before it was recognized by others as the huge social concern it is today. His work yielded a truly effective handling for the adverse biochemical effects of drugs and other toxins.

He made the discovery that residues from drugs and other toxins lodge in the fatty tissues of the body and stay there, even years after they have been ingested. And that these residues can continue to affect the individual adversely long after the effect of the drug has apparently worn off. Such deposits have been known to cause lessened perception, tiredness, confused thinking and a host of other symptoms in people—all of which are counter to what is being achieved through auditing. Cases have been documented where a person reexperienced the effects of LSD years after having taken the drug.

Realizing that this biochemical factor had to be handled before any lasting spiritual gain could be made through auditing, L. Ron Hubbard devised what independent researchers acknowledge as the most effective detoxification program in existence, the Purification program.

Developed solely as a handling for this barrier to spiritual gain caused by drugs, the Purification program is a carefully designed combination of exercise, vitamins, nutrition and sauna use which dislodges drug residues and other toxins from the fatty tissues so that these substances can then be eliminated from the body. A person undergoing the program is closely monitored by specially trained personnel in liaison with medical doctors to ensure that each aspect of the program is administered correctly and the desired benefits are attained.

Once the person has been freed from the harmful effects of these drug residues and other toxins, he is in a far better position to improve as a spiritual being, something many thousands of people have attested to.

After the release of the program in 1980, news of L. Ron Hubbard's breakthrough reached medical circles and the scientific community. Since then, numerous studies of his method of detoxification have been undertaken—studies which validate the tremendous workability of the program.

In 1973, a disaster occurred in the state

On the Purification Rundown, running is done to get the blood circulating deeper into the tissues where toxic residuals are lodged and thus act to loosen and release the accumulated harmful deposits and get them moving.

Very important, then, is that the running is immediately followed by sweating in the sauna to flush out the accumulations which have now been dislodged.

Regular nutrition and supplemental nutrition in the form of megavitamin and mineral dosages and extra quantities of oil are a vital factor in helping the body to flush out toxins and to repair and rebuild the areas that have been affected by drugs and other toxic residuals.

A proper schedule with enough rest is mandatory, as the body will be undergoing change and repair throughout the program.

of Michigan. Cattle feed had mistakenly been contaminated with a toxic fire retardant. The subsequent contamination of milk, meat and other products was widespread, and five years later, 97 percent of the residents of the state had detectable amounts of the fire retardant in their fatty tissues. A group of Michigan residents had been monitored since the initial contamination and the concentration of the toxin had not reduced. The doctors monitoring the study concluded that the toxins were there to stay.

In 1982, a group of these subjects was put through the Purification program. Biopsies of fatty tissue before and after showed a decrease of the fire retardant and other toxins of over 20 percent. A follow-up examination four months later proved even more significant: Levels of toxins continued to decrease after the program had been completed and showed an average decrease of over 40 percent of the toxins.

The deadly chemical dioxin—Agent Orange—was used to defoliate trees during the Vietnam War. Exposure to the chemical resulted in dioxin poisoning of American servicemen. Years later no effective handling had been developed. Then a Florida cardiologist conducting tests on a person who had been exposed to the chemical but who had done the Purification program, found that his patient's level of the chemical had reduced by 29 percent immediately after the program and an astounding 97 percent eight months later—and that all symptoms of dioxin poisoning had disappeared. These and other similarly impressive studies validate the workability of the Purification program.

L. Ron Hubbard's Purification program is the solution to the blight of drugs. Hundreds of thousands of people have been freed from the harmful effects of drugs and other toxins through its use. Many who have completed the program report that, along with eradicating any craving for drugs, they can see or hear better than before, that they are able to learn new subjects much more easily, that they get along better with people, and that they generally feel healthier and happier.

The entire program is explained in detail in the book *Clear Body, Clear Mind: The Effective Purification Program,* including the discoveries which led to its development and an exact description of how and why it works. One can read this book and then, by following the procedures detailed in the text, administer the Purification program to himself to detoxify his own body.

Despite their glorification by drug companies, psychiatrists, the media and the pusher in the streets, one is much better off without drugs.

Until such time as drug companies reform and science can give us advances that are not double-edged swords, the individual will have to contend with these factors.

In the eyes of many legislators, social scientists, educators and others, the drug problem is the most serious threat to our society. Drug companies, psychiatrists and criminal elements make billions in profits while shoving these deleterious and even lethal substances at the peoples of Earth. L. Ron Hubbard's Purification program has proven itself to be the most effective action one can take to free himself from the biochemical devastation caused by drugs.

After more than a decade of successful application and validation by independent researchers, that fact is indisputable.

Over 100,000 people have been freed from the effects of drugs using this technology and thousands more join the roster each month.

Mental and Spiritual Factors

The Purification program addresses the biochemical aspect of drugs and toxins. From a personal standpoint however, there are other factors to consider, mental and spiritual ones.

L. Ron Hubbard solved the mental and spiritual harm that drugs do with a series of actions comprising what is called the "Drug Rundown." A rundown designates a series of

These books cover in detail the technology and exact procedures of the Purification program, including a full textbook, an illustrated booklet and a manual to guide one's progress step by step through the program.

related actions in Scientology which culminate in a specific end result. In this case, the Drug Rundown consists of the auditing processes and actions necessary to free an individual from the damaging mental and spiritual effects of drugs. The Drug Rundown is delivered in churches and missions by highly trained auditors.

A person who has been on drugs often becomes disassociated from the world around him or even his physical self, as evidenced by the neglect many drug takers show for their hygiene, dress, health, job, friends and family, etc.

The reason is that, among other things, drugs dull a person's communication. This is most directly observed in the action of painkillers which shut off the person's feeling of pain, but it occurs with the use of other drugs as well. Emotions are suppressed with drug use, and perceptions become altered or shut off. A person often becomes less aware of things and people around him and so becomes less considerate and responsible, less active, less capable and less bright. The person factually becomes less conscious of what is happening in the present. One does not have to have been a heavy narcotics addict to experience a lessening of alertness, fogginess or other effects as a result of drug use.

Drugs do something else too: They stick a person's attention at points in his past. Mental image pictures restimulated from the reactive mind appear in the visions of hallucinations a person sees while on certain drugs. Attention often becomes stuck in these pictures after the drug has worn off, with the cumulative effect of the person not feeling "with it" or not feeling in present time.

This can be dangerous to the person himself and to others, as seen in the number of drug-related automobile accidents that occur, to say nothing of less serious accidents or goofs that happen because a person is unaware of what is going on around him. Drug use makes a person less alert mentally, can harm memory and has a host of other effects on attitudes and behavior—all residual consequences of the drugs, which persist indefinitely unless audited.

The spiritual effects of drug use can also be devastating. In the late 1960s, L. Ron Hubbard discovered that a person who had been heavily on drugs was not able to make spiritual gains from auditing. This condition had not been encountered earlier in his researches, as drugs had not yet encroached so deeply into society. But it became more and more prevalent and required a solution, as drugs now represented an increasingly serious block to self-betterment efforts.

The reason drugs are so harmful spiritually is because they can badly scramble the energy contained in the mind, disorienting and confusing the person. His awareness often diminishes and his capabilities of dealing with the energies and masses of reality become less. A person affected by drugs is less able to control the things in his environment and, despite whatever subjective feelings he may have to the contrary, he becomes less powerful and less able.

While on drugs, the pictures in the reactive mind can violently turn on, overwhelming the being and making him afraid to confront anything in the reactive mind thereafter. As a result, the person is stopped dead from any mental or spiritual gain.

Through the different auditing processes and drills of the Drug Rundown, a person is first brought to new awarenesses of his environment and the world around him. This has the effect of unsticking him from points in his past and brings him more into present time.

This is a very important factor in mental and spiritual ability. The more a person can exist in the present without his attention stuck in past incidents, the better able he is to deal with his life. He feels brighter, has increased perception, is better able to control himself and the things in his environment, and becomes more able to deal with others.

Getting the person into present time is not the total answer, however. The actual incidents from his reactive mind associated with drugs must also be addressed in auditing. Drugs scramble the mind to such a degree that freeing the person from these effects requires a precise and thorough approach.

First, experiences the person had while taking drugs are addressed using exact auditing procedures, and the charge in the reactive mind which has accumulated around these incidents is released. Attention that had been fixated by drugs, medicines and alcohol is freed, and the mental masses brought about by drugs are erased.

Drug taking invariably has numerous unwanted physical sensations, emotions, attitudes and other feelings connected with it. So the next stage of a Drug Rundown entails auditing on unwanted feelings connected with specific drugs taken by the person. These are addressed one by one and fully handled, freeing the person from their effects.

L. Ron Hubbard found, though, that people begin taking drugs for a reason: To ease the agony of a physical condition, to numb themselves against certain situations in their lives, to relieve boredom, to feel better; the number of possible reasons is as great as the number of people taking drugs. By taking drugs the person was trying to handle or cure something. At the bottom, then, the drug problem is essentially spiritual. The being in some way hurt and was led into the false solution that drugs could cure this. The solution, as many learned the hard way, turned out to be a trap from which there was no true escape until the drug-handling technology of L. Ron Hubbard.

A vital part of the Drug Rundown, then, includes finding the pains, emotions, sensations, feelings, etc., the person was suffering from—for which drugs became the cure. When these are found, each is addressed in auditing. Unless the reasons a person went on to drugs in the first place are resolved, the person is forever left with the original condition for which drugs were a "solution."

When the original problem has been addressed, the person himself is at last free from any effects of drugs and free from the need to take them. The full solution to the drug problem thus consists of handling all aspects of drug taking.

On Earth today, drugs are very, very big business. We live in a society where human values are routinely shunted aside for the economic concerns connected with drugs, both legal and illegal. The cost in crime, the cost in trying to control the problem, the cost in inefficiency, the cost simply in lives lived under the numbing influence of drugs cannot be calculated. For to do that, one would have to put a price on life itself.

So, what price the headache remedies, the soporifics, the pain relievers, the antidepressants that fill our medicine cabinets? What price the amphetamines given our schoolchildren, turning them into drug-dependent people? What price the narcotics that are used to negate a painful existence? What price the recreational drugs that provide escape from the boredom of affluence? What price these shackles that keep from us the sensations and joys of living itself?

A drug war rages on this planet. L. Ron Hubbard recognized the drug problem long before it became an international concern. And he developed a technology people can use to free themselves from this trap and remain free of it.

His technology is the weapon that can win this war.

Chapter 10

Study Technology: Effective Learning and Education

The future of our planet will one day rest in the hands of our children. How well equipped will they be to carry society forward? Perhaps the surest gauge is the success with which we are educating them for that role. Sadly, from all indications, this responsibility has not been met. At a time when quality education is more important than during any period in history, our schools are failing at an alarming rate.

Typical of the educational problems faced by most Western countries is the tragedy of the United States student. America once had one of the finest educational systems in the world, yet for nearly three decades that system continues to face a formidable crisis.

Over 25 percent of all students leaving or graduating high school lack the reading and writing skills required by the minimum demands of daily living.

The American high-school dropout rate hovers at around 30 percent to 50 percent in inner-city areas.

According to the president of one teachers' association, up to 50 percent of all new teachers quit the profession within the first five years.

SAT (Scholastic Aptitude Test) scores of American students have sunk to levels considerably lower than those achieved by students in the mid-1960s.

The news media regularly report on the continuing decline of standardized test scores, on overcrowding in classrooms, on public disenchantment about pouring more tax dollars into what they perceive to be an increasingly poor investment, and growing teacher disillusionment.

It is indeed a grim picture but is no better in most other parts of the world.

A British survey sponsored by *The Sunday Times* of London, for instance, found 42 percent of those surveyed were unable to add the menu prices of a hamburger, French fries, apple pie and coffee. One out of six British inhabitants could not correctly locate Great Britain on a world map.

From both official and media reports, the pattern of educational decline is evident in almost every Western country—places where excellence in public education was once taken for granted.

These dismal figures translate into an equally depressing economic scene. Internationally, the cost to business in lowered or wasted productivity, unemployment and crime is estimated at $300 billion annually. Businesses are forced to develop their own remedial programs to teach employees the basic reading, writing and computational skills necessary to function on the job.

There seems to be no shortage of ideas and theories on how to accomplish educational reforms. But these programs tend to create as many problems as they solve.

For example, after the crisis in education became headline news, America instituted "get tough" retention policies and added graduation requirements, on the assumption that a greater challenge for students would improve performance. The opposite occurred. The policies raised rather than lowered the dropout rate in some cities. The president of the American Federation of Teachers argued, "It's ridiculous to raise the hurdle for kids who are unable to jump in the first place."

A WORKABLE ANSWER: STUDY TECHNOLOGY

Failed attempts to improve education in recent decades raise one important question: With so much attention on improving the quality of education, with billions spent each year to remedy the situation, why has there been so little improvement?

There is an answer. Quite simply, these efforts have been directed at solving the wrong problems.

At the root of educational failures lies a fundamental situation that has been almost universally overlooked: *Students have never been taught how to learn.*

Students are thrown into their school years and basic subjects without ever first being taught how to go about learning those subjects. As they grow older they are confronted by more and more complex areas of study, still without ever having learned *how* to learn.

Learning how to learn has been the vital missing ingredient that has hampered all fields of study. It handicaps both children in school and people in life.

Without knowing how to learn what they are studying, a majority of students find education a trying and difficult process. They never master the ability to rapidly learn something with certainty and ease. Others, who apparently have less difficulty studying, find they are unable to apply what they have read.

It is a reality of the modern world that anyone in the work force, whether on the factory floor or in the executive suite, must have an ability to assimilate important information, retain it and then be able to apply it. This process, whether formal or informal, is what is meant by "study."

L. Ron Hubbard recognized the failings of modern education and training in 1950, many years before educational horror stories began to make headlines.

His extensive investigation into the problems of teaching others led to a breakthrough—the first comprehensive understanding of the real barriers to effective learning. From this, Mr. Hubbard developed a precise technology

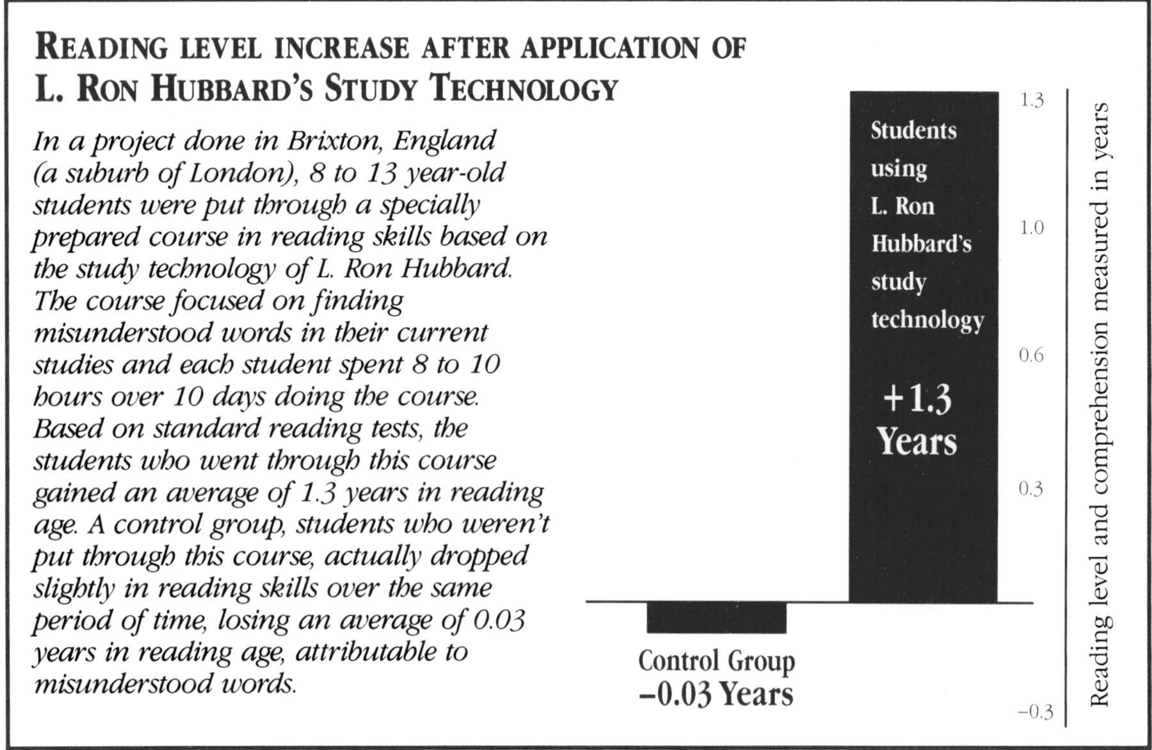

READING LEVEL INCREASE AFTER APPLICATION OF L. RON HUBBARD'S STUDY TECHNOLOGY

In a project done in Brixton, England (a suburb of London), 8 to 13 year-old students were put through a specially prepared course in reading skills based on the study technology of L. Ron Hubbard. The course focused on finding misunderstood words in their current studies and each student spent 8 to 10 hours over 10 days doing the course. Based on standard reading tests, the students who went through this course gained an average of 1.3 years in reading age. A control group, students who weren't put through this course, actually dropped slightly in reading skills over the same period of time, losing an average of 0.03 years in reading age, attributable to misunderstood words.

on how to learn *any* subject—a technology that ensures a person will not only fully grasp what he is studying, but proficiently apply what he has studied in work or in life.

These breakthroughs came to be known as "study technology," and provide the first fully workable approach to teaching people exactly *how to learn*. Study technology helps anyone learn anything. Used throughout Scientology in all churches, missions and groups, it is also widely used outside the Church in schools and businesses. Study technology opens the door to effective training and makes it possible to raise the general quality of education to new heights.

Study technology is based on laws that underlie all learning. It delineates the barriers which block a person's ability to grasp information and provides precise methodologies to overcome those barriers.

Study technology has been extensively tested and proven to achieve uniform, consistent results wherever it has been applied. Because it is based on fundamentals common to everyone, it cuts across any economic, cultural or racial lines and can be used by all, regardless of age. It is as effective in the executive suites of multinational corporations as it is in elementary school classrooms.

Outstanding improvements have been made by students of all ages in reading level, comprehension, vocabulary and mathematics when they have been instructed in study technology. A Los Angeles study showed an average gain of 1.8 years in vocabulary and comprehension after only 10 hours of tutoring in study technology. One student gained an almost unbelievable 5 years and 9 months in his test scores after 20 hours of instruction. All teachers involved in this study also reported an overall improvement in their students' ability to learn, ability to read and, an unexpected gain, in the general behavior of students as a direct result of study technology.

An Arizona study tested students after the beginning of a school year and then six months later. Teachers ran the classroom using study technology throughout the duration of the study. Standard reading tests were administered and showed an average gain of two years in comprehension and vocabulary. This is four times the expected gain, a remarkable achievement considering individual tutoring was not part of the study.

In South Africa one class of underprivileged high-school students was trained in study technology, and at the end of the school year achieved a 91 percent pass rate on the country's Department of Education examination. A control group, not so trained, had a 27 percent pass rate on the same test.

The numbers collected from these and many similar studies translate, really, into effective education for young people and an assurance they will grow to a confident, self-reliant adulthood with learning skills they will use every day of their lives.

Many principles and procedures make up study technology, but it only takes a brief discussion of a few of the most basic to provide an insight into what it is and what it can accomplish.

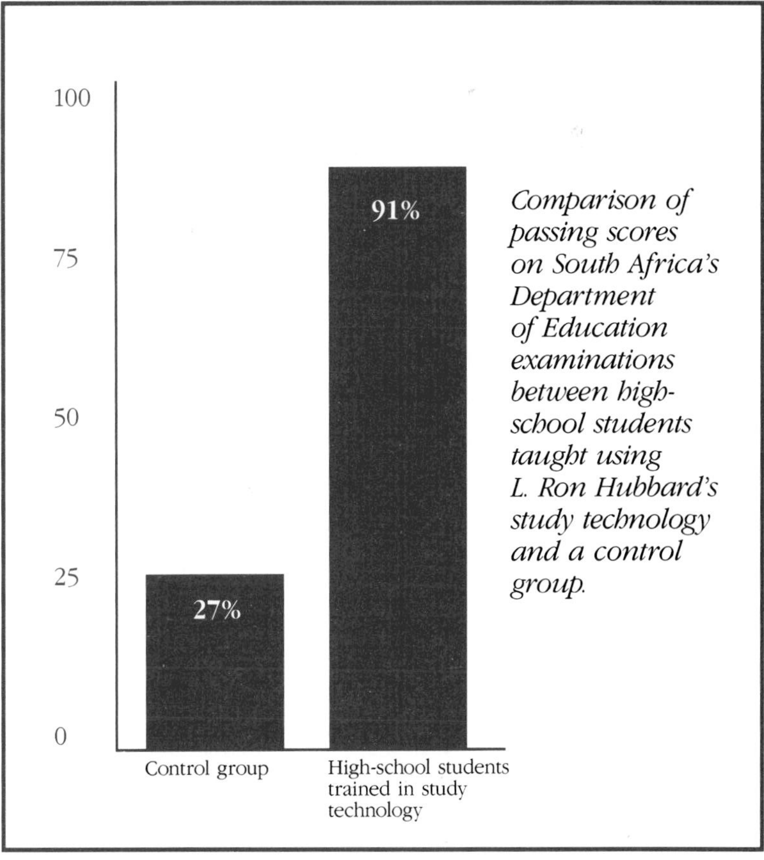

Comparison of passing scores on South Africa's Department of Education examinations between high-school students taught using L. Ron Hubbard's study technology and a control group.

THE BARRIERS TO STUDY

L. Ron Hubbard discovered three primary barriers which keep one from successfully studying a subject. Despite all that has been written on the subject, these three barriers, simple as they are, were never isolated as paramount to effective education. For want of this data, the toll in poorly educated students, unfulfilled potential and frustration is incalculable.

The First Barrier—Lack of Mass

Attempting to educate someone without the mass (or object) that he is going to be involved with can make study exceedingly difficult. This is the first barrier to study.

For example, if one is studying tractors, the printed page and the spoken word are no substitute for an actual tractor. Lacking a tractor to associate with the written word, or at least pictures of a tractor, can close off a person's understanding of the subject.

Definite physiological reactions occur when trying to educate a person in a subject without the thing actually present or available. A student who encounters this barrier will tend to feel squashed, bent, sort of spinny, sort of dead, bored and exasperated. He can wind up with his face feeling squashed, with headaches, and with his stomach feeling funny. He can feel dizzy from time to time and very often his eyes can hurt. These reactions are quite common but wrongly attributed to poor lighting, or studying too late at night, or any number of other incorrect reasons. The real cause is a lack of mass on the subject one is studying.

The remedy to this barrier is to supply the thing itself—in the example above, the tractor, or a reasonable substitute for one. Some educators have instinctively known this, but usually it was applied only to younger students and it certainly was never given the importance it warrants at any level of education.

The Second Barrier—Too Steep a Gradient

The next barrier is too steep a study gradient. That is, if a student is forced into undertaking a new action without having understood the previous action, confusion results.

There is a different set of physiological reactions which occur as a result of this barrier. When one hits too steep a gradient, a sort of confusion or reelingness is experienced.

Commonly, the difficulty is ascribed to the new action, when in fact it really stems from the previous action. The person did not fully understand some part earlier and then went into confusion on the new one. This barrier to study is very pronounced in subjects involved with activity.

Take the example of a person learning to drive. He cannot properly coordinate his feet and hands to manually shift the car into another gear while keeping to one lane. The difficulty will be found to lie in some earlier action about shifting gears. Possibly he was not yet comfortable shifting through the gears with the engine off and the car at rest. If this is recognized, the gradient can be cut back, and the person brought up to a point where he can easily shift the gears on a motionless car before performing the same action while in motion.

The Third Barrier—the Misunderstood Word

The third barrier to study is the most important of the three. It is the prime factor involved with stupidity and many other unwanted conditions.

This third barrier is the misunderstood word. A misunderstood definition or a not-comprehended definition or an undefined word can thoroughly block one's understanding of a subject and can even cause one to abandon the subject entirely.

This milestone in the field of education has great application, but it was overlooked by every educator in history.

Going past a word or symbol for which one does not have a proper definition gives one a distinctly blank or washed-out feeling. The person will get a "not there" feeling and will begin to feel a nervous hysteria. These are manifestations distinct from either of the other two barriers.

The barrier of the misunderstood word is far more important than the other two, however. It has much to do with human relations, the mind and different subjects. It establishes aptitude or lack of aptitude and is the key to what psychologists were attempting to test for years without recognizing what it was.

A person might or might not have *brilliance* as a computer programer, but his ability to *do* the motions of computer programing is dependent exclusively and only upon definitions. There is some word in the field of computer programing that the person who is inept did not define or understand and that was followed by an inability to act in the field of computer programing.

This is extremely important because it tells one what happens to doingness and that the restoration of doingness depends only on the location and understanding of any word which has been misunderstood in a subject.

Have you ever come to the bottom of a page only to realize you didn't remember what you had just read? That is the phenomenon of a misunderstood word, and one will always be found just before the material became blank in your mind.

This sweeping discovery is applicable to any sphere of endeavor, and opens wide the gates to education.

These barriers to study and their resolution are contained on a Scientology training course called the Student Hat. "Hat" is a Scientology slang term for a particular job, taken from the fact that in many professions, such as railroading, the type of hat worn is the badge of the job.

The Student Hat course covers the complete technology of how to study *any* subject effectively, providing the student with every needed tool. Much of the study technology is contained in a dozen lectures Mr. Hubbard gave on learning and education, and these are all included, along with many of his pertinent writings.

The materials comprising the Student Hat course contain all of L. Ron Hubbard's study technology, as contained in his written works and recorded lectures.

A full understanding of the barriers to study and how to recognize and fully handle them is gained on the course. The student learns how to clear up a misunderstood word so that he fully understands it and can use it in his speech and writing. One also becomes practiced in a precise method Mr. Hubbard developed to ensure comprehension in what one has studied.

In a technological society, someone who cannot easily assimilate data is in serious danger of being left behind. The Student Hat alone could invigorate the culture.

Study technology is universally applicable and has found wide utilization outside the Church: in schools, universities, businesses and other institutions. To make this technology available to all, the Church offers the following works in addition to the Student Hat materials:

Basic Study Manual

The major breakthroughs of study technology are described for any age or academic level from teenagers on up. All fundamentals are covered, giving a firm grounding to successful learning in any pursuit.

Learning How to Learn

Recommended as the first study book for children, this illustrated work teaches children how to study. Basic to all children's education, it teaches exact skills they need in order to begin learning.

Study Skills for Life

Written specifically for young teenagers, this book enables a person to learn the most basic aspects of study technology in an easy-to-understand format.

Two additional books exist to aid children in study:

How to Use a Dictionary Picture Book for Children

Many children have not been taught to use a dictionary. Thus, when a parent or teacher uses a word beyond their level of comprehension, they have no way to define it. *How to Use a Dictionary Picture Book for Children* teaches children how to find and understand words.

Grammar and Communication for Children

This simple English grammar book was written and illustrated to hold the interest of children. Its purpose is to show the young student the basics of grammar so he can understand and communicate well and does not develop a fear or distaste for the subject.

A Technology to Increase Comprehension

In the years following L. Ron Hubbard's breakthrough on the importance of the misunderstood word, he developed a considerable body of technology which enables one to deal with the misunderstood words or symbols he encounters.

The relay of ideas from one mind to another mind or minds depends upon words, symbols, sounds, pictures, emotions and past associations.

Primary among these, in any developed culture, are words. These can be written or spoken.

While whole subjects exist concerning the development and meaning of words, many of them very learned and worthwhile, practically no work was ever done on the effect of words or the consequences of their misuse or noncomprehension.

What was not studied or known before L. Ron Hubbard's development of study technology is that the flow of ideas in any message or field of learning can be blocked in such a way as to suppress further understanding or comprehension from that point forward. Further, the misunderstood word can even act in such a way as to bring about ignorance, apathy and revolt in the classroom and in the workplace depress productivity.

Not only did these factors remain undiscovered before Scientology, but also, of course, no technology existed to remedy the problem.

To enable a person to handle the effect of misunderstood words, L. Ron Hubbard developed the subject called Word Clearing. Word Clearing is part of the broader field of study technology, but in itself Word Clearing has many uses and applications. Word Clearing can be defined as "the subject and action of clearing away the ignorance, misunderstoods and false definitions of words and barriers to their use."

In his observations of society, Mr. Hubbard had noticed a deterioration in literacy during this century. This conclusion is inescapable if one compares the political speeches and literature of a hundred or even fifty years ago to those of today. He noticed that the public was more and more dependent upon radio, motion pictures and television, all of which contain the spoken word, and he considered the possibility that these messages were not being fully received or understood. His observations were confirmed when an advertising association undertook a survey which showed that television audiences misunderstood between one-quarter and one-third of all the material they watched—findings with alarming implications. Not only are there serious economic consequences, as the study pointed out, wherein up to one-third of advertising expenditures are wasted owing to the fact that the public does not understand the ads; but more importantly, such a gross level of noncomprehension can generate antipathy and even aggression among viewers.

When one speaks or writes, one has the responsibility to others of being understood. Further, one has a responsibility to oneself of ensuring that he understands what he sees and hears.

L. Ron Hubbard developed nine separate methods of Word Clearing and several related technologies for handling the effects of misunderstoods and false data in a person. Each method provides a different way of locating areas of noncomprehension, tracing this back to the misunderstood words underlying the problem and then getting these words fully understood so the person can use them in his own vocabulary.

Thousands of hours of research and hundreds of thousands of cases went into the development of these nine methods.

In the twelve or sixteen years or more that a student spends in school, the unknowing accumulation of undefined words and symbols can present a serious barrier to knowledge and productivity in life. Also, a person contacts words or symbols in everyday activities outside of the classroom which he does not understand and these, too, dull his capabilities.

With the techniques of Word Clearing, whole subjects and educations which were not understood at the time and could not subsequently be applied can be recovered and used. Such is the power of clearing misunderstood words.

Wherever communication is being engaged in, given or received, the technology of Word Clearing will find beneficial use.

Study technology is a complete subject in itself and used by millions of people all over the world, in schools, universities and businesses.

Mr. Hubbard once remarked, "The future is the only frontier without limit and the frontier that we all enter and cross no matter what we do."

Reading news headlines is enough to tell anyone that social problems are escalating in virtually every community and that these portend a bleak future. Drugs, crime, unemployment, poverty and violence are all indicators of how extensive educational failures have become. A great many of those enmeshed in such problems could have been happier, more productive individuals if they had simply learned how to learn. If used, study technology will salvage both our current and future generations.

CHAPTER 11

THE KEY TO LIFE: HANDLING A WORLD OUT OF COMMUNICATION

Communication is one of the key elements of living, a fact that becomes even more apparent as one progresses in Scientology. It is thus not unreasonable to say that a person is as alive as he or she can communicate.

Three cultural changes during the last half-century have combined to lessen this ability in a great majority of people.

After World War II, general education standards were lowered. New systems of education ignored such fundamentals as reading, writing and grammar. School systems adopted a permissive attitude toward education with the inevitable consequence that students learned less and less. The decline was progressive and hastened after 1950 when television became dominant in child care. Mothers plunked their children in front of the TV and let them fixate their attention, the continuous inflow of images serving as both leash and babysitter. The onset of the drug scourge in the 1960s further served to dull the minds of the TV generation.

These three factors have produced generations of people who are bombarded with a large amount of information which they do not comprehend and who have been placed in the role of mere spectators. They are, as a result, out of communication with life.

This has led to lawlessness, inflation, lowered production and many other societal problems, not to mention the individual frustration and unhappiness of wasted potential and wasted years. People ill-equipped for living in a highly technological society get trampled by those who are better equipped; and even the very bright are eventually impeded by those underfoot. Educators in the better private universities routinely find students who cannot read with comprehension, regardless of how well they scored on standardized admission tests.

L. Ron Hubbard recognized these phenomena in the 1950s, as we have seen in the last chapter, and by 1964 he developed the technology of how to study. However, in the late 1970s he saw that even this technology now required a more fundamental handling owing to the general cultural decline. He found that many people, even college educated, were unable to easily assimilate data, including his study technology.

"Functional illiteracy" describes the circumstance wherein an individual appears able to make his way in life, yet is actually so deficient in reading and writing that, for all but menial purposes, he is illiterate. A growing number of students have been little more than baby-sat in the school system for twelve years, then turned loose with almost no chance of contributing to society and with every chance that society will have to support them. The term, *functional illiteracy,* really means simply, "illiteracy" and is a condemnation of an educational system which, entrusted with educating our young people, fails them miserably and fails the rest of us as well.

Over 25 million Americans are illiterate, according to government figures. Another 45 million, at least, are only marginally capable of leading productive lives. These two categories amount to nearly 49 percent of all adult Americans and underscore the general decline in literacy.

Key to Life is a major breakthrough in the field of communication. Step by step, it strips away the reasons why a person cannot clearly comprehend what he reads, writes and hears and why others cannot comprehend him.

Tests made by Mr. Hubbard in the late 1970s revealed that college graduates, when examined on the common materials they would read for pleasure, were found to not understand much of what they read. They could pronounce words but could not define many of the words they pronounced! With respect to these people's ability to comprehend written materials, an *apparency* of understanding masked the actual state of affairs: that these people did not really comprehend what they were reading. Their ability to learn had been stymied.

The Hubbard Key to Life Course breaks through the barriers to comprehension and assimilation of data, utilizing thousands of pictures to communicate the fundamental factors of language.

HOW TO USE A DICTIONARY
PICTURE BOOK
SMALL COMMON
WORDS DEFINED
RON HUBBARD

THE HUBBARD
KEY TO LIFE
COURSE
LIFE

MAN
noun

SALLY
noun

CITY
noun

LOVE
noun

Not everyone suffers from this condition. But it does exist in varying degrees in nearly everyone. For example, in the sentence, "It's as good as gold," most people cannot define the word "as." Yet, "as" is a word used every day. This doesn't classify one as illiterate but it does serve to show that anyone's comprehension could be increased.

If one truly comprehended what he read and heard and if he were able to make himself comprehended by others, all of life would open to him. But to the degree he cannot express himself and make others understand him, and to the degree he cannot understand what others are communicating, life is closed off to him.

In solving the problem of a world out of communication, L. Ron Hubbard developed a thorough handling that not only brings an illiterate up to literacy but increases the ability of *anyone* to comprehend and to be comprehended.

The handling he devised is called the Hubbard Key to Life Course.

Key to Life is a major breakthrough in the field of communication. Step by step, it strips away the reasons why a person cannot clearly comprehend what he reads, writes and hears and why others cannot comprehend him.

In developing the Key to Life, there was a particular problem that cried out for a solution. On a wider sphere, this is a conundrum that has been faced, but not resolved, by every educator in history: How does one teach someone to understand and use the language without assuming that the person under instruction already knows at least some of what one is trying to teach him? How, for example, does one teach the meaning of a word without assuming the person already knows how to read the words being used to teach him? How does one teach the language without assuming the person already knows some of it?

For example, if one opens a dictionary to look up the definition of a word, one can encounter other words that are not understood. If one opens up a book on grammar, one is immediately hit with terminology that is not explained until later. Yet, when one encounters a misunderstood word, he ceases to understand and does not fully grasp or become aware of what follows. Understanding ceases on going past a misunderstood word. This datum is the single most important factor in the whole field of education. How, then, can one teach the language, its construction, its words and its use without laying the person open to misunderstood words?

In cutting this Gordian knot, L. Ron Hubbard solved the problem of literacy itself and of difficulties in comprehension, and so opened the door to a vastly increased understanding of life.

Needed was a way to bypass the possibility of misunderstood words in the student no matter how poor his level of comprehension. Words are used to communicate concepts from one person to another. But other means too can be used. A concept can be communicated by a sign, by a physical gesture, by a noise or by a picture, etc. By drawing a picture of a cat next to the words *felis domesticus,* one can communicate the concept of a house cat, which is what *felis domesticus* means.

The Key to Life Course utilizes thousands of pictures, drawn by top illustrators from Hollywood film studios, to communicate the concepts needed to teach the student the materials on the course. Concepts are defined using pictures as well as words to ensure that comprehension occurs.

In one of the books on the course, each concept in the entire book is illustrated as well as defined and assures comprehension without having to use complex definitions. This is a unique dictionary that fully defines each of the sixty most commonly used words in the language. With the use of pictures, the factor of misunderstood words is circumvented and a student can really learn the words he uses and reads most often, without getting hopelessly tangled up in the complexities of grammar. In this way, a person improves his understanding of what he hears or reads and improves his ability to make himself understood.

The importance of this approach becomes apparent when one realizes that it opens the door to fully learning the most commonly used words in the language, how the language is put together and how to use it. With such knowledge, a person is able to communicate and receive communication with a much higher level of comprehension.

Another breakthrough on Key to Life is a completely innovative approach to the subject of grammar. Mr. Hubbard simplified the language into its basic building blocks and showed people how to use those building blocks to better express their thoughts and understand what they read and hear.

In his book, *The New Grammar,* Mr. Hubbard resolves many of the confusions entered into the language by grammarians and turns grammar into something that one can *use* rather than something one merely *studies.*

Many people have a distaste for grammar because it has been stultified by grammarians into a maze of complex rules understandable not even to grammarians themselves. Mr. Hubbard showed instead that grammar is really something one *uses* in order to facilitate and enhance meaningful communication, and that grammar really has no other useful purpose. He has put together *the* book that at last clarifies the construction of the language. *The New Grammar* has drastically altered the concept of grammar for the thousands who have completed the Key to Life Course.

The Hubbard Key to Life Course produces a person who is literate and who can express himself easily and clearly, both verbally and in writing, and who can fully understand the communication he receives from others.

In our technological society, which regularly requires a high order of comprehension, the declining level of literacy is disastrous. There are many consequences if one does not understand things in life, and none are good.

The Hubbard Key to Life Course enables an individual to avoid these consequences in himself and opens up to him all of life.

"English is now the language of international communication. It is the language used by heads of state. It is the language of international business negotiation. It is the language of the majority of the rapidly growing masses of computerized information.

"Unfortunately, most persons educated by the public education systems in the United States are not competent in understanding and using English. As a teacher in one of the better private universities in the United States I am well aware that many of our students, even though they are among those ranking very high on standardized tests, are unable to read with comprehension. Failing to master the full resources of the English language, students become functionally illiterate.

"This inability to fully understand and use language causes problems in schools and businesses, and these problems affect wider areas of society. In this time of widespread illiteracy L. Ron Hubbard introduces a book that makes grammar understandable and useful to all.

"This book takes grammar and makes it easy. It helps individuals to understand the basic building blocks of the English language and how to use those building blocks to better communicate, express their thoughts and understand what they read.

"L. Ron Hubbard first gained fame as a writer at a time when even the popular magazines of the day expected their readers to appreciate breadth of vocabulary and variety of style.

"Only a professional writer with a writer's sensitivity to language could have written such an innovative approach to grammar. Only such a writer would see grammar not as full of constricting rules, but full of possibilities for rich expressions of thought and action.

"Teaching writers how to write in the 1940s, L. Ron Hubbard has now come full circle with this grammar book and returned to the field of teaching language.

"This is a brilliant book by a brilliant mind. In fact, it is a revolution in thought."

David Rodier, Ph.D.
Associate Professor of Philosophy
American University, Washington, DC

CHAPTER 12

THE LIFE ORIENTATION COURSE: ATTAINING COMPETENCE IN LIFE

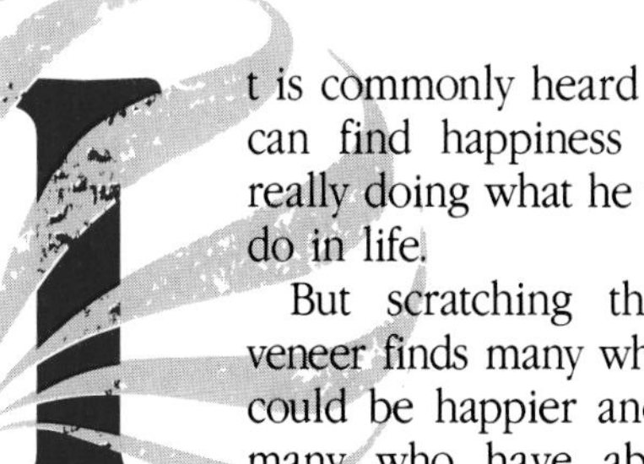

It is commonly heard that one can find happiness if he is really doing what he wants to do in life.

But scratching the social veneer finds many whose lives could be happier and just as many who have abandoned earlier dreams. One wanted to be a concert musician, but father fell ill and there was no one to run the store. One dreamed of medical school, but settled for teaching high school when a baby came due and a family had to be supported. One wanted to own a beauty shop, but problems in the marriage prevented it. One was going to be a jet pilot until faced with the seemingly impossible rigors of prerequisite studies.

What fulfillment has faded in the tides and fortunes of living? How many people have settled for a life in which they could get along, rather than the one in which they could flourish? Too many.

If one could conceive of doing what one truly loved, it is not hard to imagine the happiness that would follow. But, to the extent one does not follow his true interests, the factors in his life can be badly misaligned, breeding disharmony and unhappiness.

If all dynamics that constitute a person's life were aligned toward the attainment of a clear and worthwhile purpose, one would be well along a road to success, regardless of any personal advancements he was making spiritually through Scientology auditing or training.

One is often defined, and remembered, by what he does in life. Fundamentally, a thetan is the creator of things. On a day-to-day basis this is represented by his job, what he produces, how he supports himself and so on. Many individuals are not fulfilled in this part of their lives. Their activities are not aligned for optimum productivity, which causes innumerable complications. The man who is unproductive at his job brings his disgruntlement home, making his home life less pleasant. He finds less enjoyment in his leisure time. He may feel anxious about losing his job because the company will not be able to carry him forever if he is not contributing to it. His life would be more worthwhile if he were more productive at work. He certainly would be happier about himself if he could demonstrate a higher level of competence in his activities.

A person's competence can be directly addressed using the technology L. Ron Hubbard developed and made available on the Hubbard Life Orientation Course.

There are many parts to anyone's life—ambitions, friends and associates, a job and social involvements. There are obligations to fulfill, assets to protect, people to look after, a future to make. Just how many factors are there to a life? And what happens if one factor is missing or life is overbalanced in favor of another factor to the neglect of still others?

The Life Orientation Course sorts out every single area of a person's life, utilizing a specific series of steps. Mr. Hubbard observed that the totality of anyone's activities in life can be compartmented into twenty-one separate areas. The first step of the course involves the person's close inspection of each of these twenty-one areas

If one could conceive of doing what one truly loved, it is not hard to imagine the happiness that would follow. But, to the extent one does not follow his true interests, the factors in his life can be badly misaligned, breeding disharmony and unhappiness.

to gain a clear picture of where he stands. He then undertakes a searching study of the eight dynamics, with emphasis on his personal involvement on each dynamic. A special auditing process enables him to closely inspect his dynamics, providing him a clearer view of all life.

Now with a much better vantage point, he can view his life, dynamics, his influence over these dynamics, his decisions along these lines and how these have contributed to where he finds himself. Study alone could not bring about this awareness; the auditing is necessary. This is a more distinct view than ever available before. The individual's existence is being straightened out using the fundamentals on which life operates.

With this sufficiently broad view, he can begin to isolate the actions that promote increased survival from those actions which are nonsurvival. This entails more auditing, developed by Mr. Hubbard especially for the Life Orientation Course. This results in a firm subjective understanding of what happens in life if the dynamics go out of alignment.

The student next learns technology about the consequences of actions harmful to his dynamics and undertakes to locate and view all his transgressions against any part of his life. This tremendous unburdening of past misdeeds and mishaps truly means, for many people, the beginning of a new existence.

With attention unpinned from points in his past, he is ready to learn exact ways to improve his future. He learns the natural laws that govern existence and the tools necessary to arrest the decline that traps so many.

The student now learns how the different activities of his life must each result in something of real use and value. A person who has no real purpose in life or what he does or who produces nothing of value will be miserable. A specific product should result from activity in each part of his life.

His profession, for instance, results in a product which furthers his survival. A person produces something or provides

some service for which he is given money on which to live. The establishment and maintenance of his living quarters results in a completely different product, but one which also helps promote a different aspect of his survival. A comfortable, clean home is a pleasant place in which to live, certainly a valuable product in itself. Likewise, each activity in a person's life has a product, and these either aid or inhibit his success and survival depending on how good they are.

On the Life Orientation Course, the person arrives at a clear understanding of where he is heading in life, and what his true purpose really is. Such an awareness makes it possible to straighten out his life because he now sees where he is going. Once this is clear in his mind, he can align all the elements of his life to this purpose

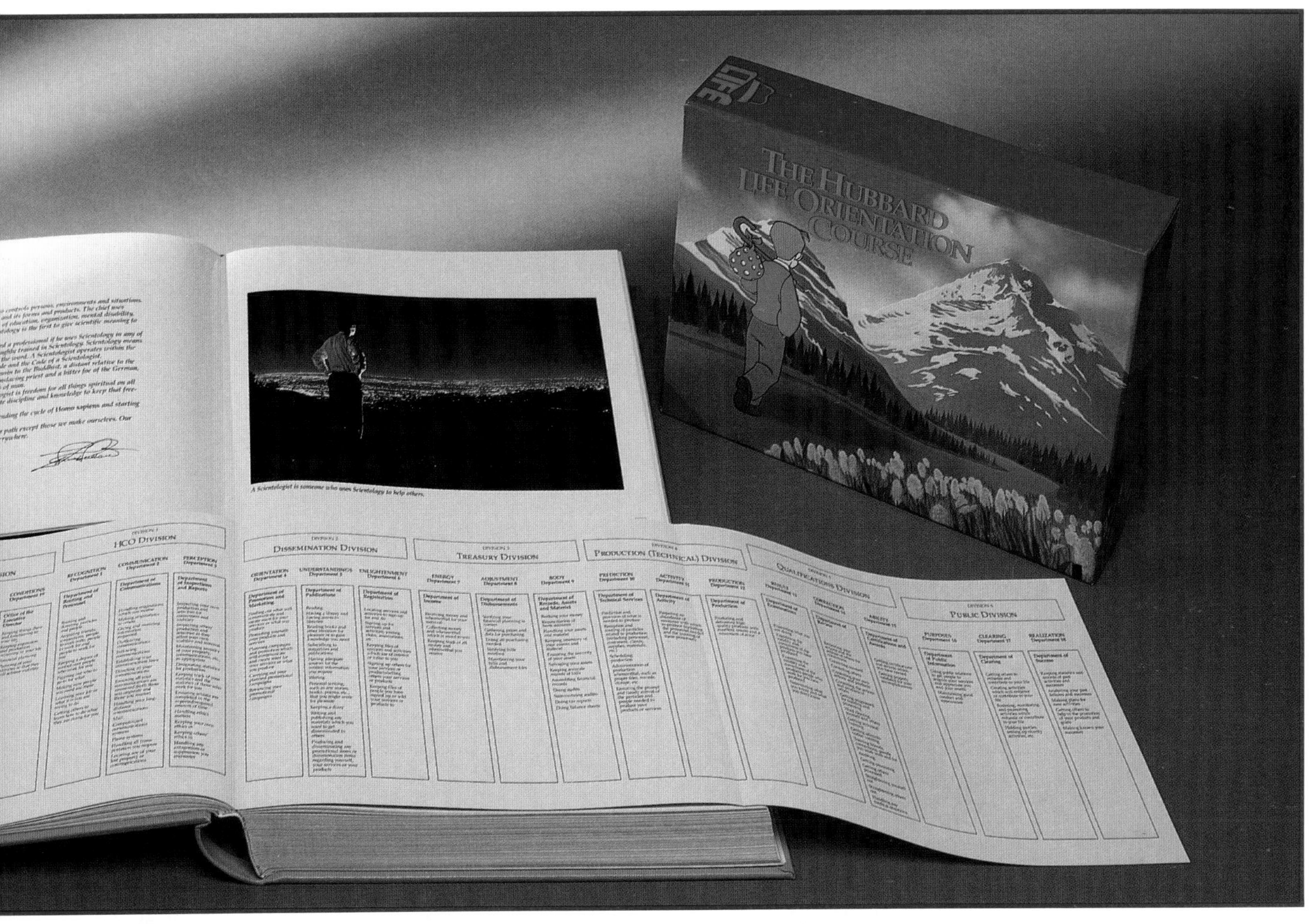

and get somewhere—the somewhere he always wanted to be.

The final step of the course gets the person totally oriented to his main product in life, how this fits in with the rest of his dynamics, and brings him to clearly view what he needs to do to viably produce it. This is a major advance because it results in someone who is causative, competent and productive in life.

With this ability gained, the individual's life is truly straightened out and he sees clearly where he is headed, now armed with the tools to make sure he arrives.

It is a great feeling to be oriented in life. Many forces are at work, thrusting one this way and that. People get caught up in them and are carried along, snowed under or left out.

The new alternative, attained on the Hubbard Life Orientation Course, is to get one's life in clear perspective and under control, with a certainty on the laws of life, knowing what one is doing to forward one's *own* purposes.

On the Life Orientation Course purpose, morale, fulfillment and happiness are in the offing.

A frank assessment of the lives of other people usually reveals that many are not leading the lives they would like, but in the manner life "has to be" for one reason or another. L. Ron Hubbard developed the Life Orientation Course to help people better understand where they are going in life and to help them make their lives more fulfilling.

The Life Orientation Course is a route *into* the activity of living. Spiritual gains from the rest of Scientology can be augmented greatly from the knowledge contained on this course.

CHAPTER 13

AUDITING SERVICES

Millions, attesting to the results of auditing, prove beyond doubt that auditing accomplishes far more to better man than any other means ever devised.

Through auditing, a person can rid himself of his reactive mind and the limitations it imposes upon him—limitations which were once thought "natural." Man's full potential, so often speculated about, can be realized. This potential is far, far higher than earlier practices and religions ever thought possible.

Millions of Scientologists have found out more about themselves through auditing and improved their lives as a direct result.

The different processes which comprise auditing technology can be likened to a road—an exact road, with exact steps that anyone can walk. L. Ron Hubbard developed many different auditing processes during his research. He arranged these in a sequence that enables an individual to achieve greater awareness and with this, higher states of existence leading to, ultimately, a recognition of his own immortal nature.

If one thinks about it for a moment, one will recognize that there are many states of existence in life. A man is rich or poor, well or sick, old or young, married or single.

Moreover, in Scientology it is known that there are many states of existence beyond that of so-called normal man. This has been touched on by earlier philosophies but what is new about Scientology is that one can predictably attain these higher states of existence.

Although some savants in the Himalayas have worked in this direction, Gautama Siddhartha (Buddha) spoke of it at length, at least fifteen or twenty years of hard work were required for what was, at best, an uncertain outcome.

With Scientology, there are no such uncertainties. Higher states of existence are attainable through auditing, and these states and how they can be attained are described here.

SCIENTOLOGY EXPANDED GRADES

When they begin auditing, people are usually too beset by problems to immediately face and handle the core of the reactive mind. A person is worried about his mortgage payments. He suffers from job stress. His child needs dental work. His marriage is shaky. His paycheck is shrinking in the face of escalating taxes and inflation, and on and on. The day-to-day pressures of life are simply too consuming; and so one needs increased abilities just to stay abreast of these pressures, much less to surmount and be free of them.

The Scientology Expanded Grades are a series of auditing processes which address and increase specific abilities in order to place the individual in a far better position to survive.

L. Ron Hubbard discovered that there are certain definite barriers to living successfully. If a person is able in these areas he can survive. If he is unable in these areas, he does not survive well and flounders.

The Expanded Grades consist of six separate grades (which are described below) and nearly 150 different processes on which a person is audited. Each grade was designed by Mr. Hubbard to enable the individual to rehabilitate or strengthen specific abilities needed to succeed in life.

When a particular process has been run to its desired result, the person's awareness increases in that area and he becomes more able in that regard. Running more processes on a similar subject returns more ability in the area. When all the processes of a grade have been run the person has become rehabilitated on the whole subject of that grade, at which point the next grade, and another area of ability, can be addressed.

In this way, the Expanded Grades improve the person's abilities gradiently—abilities which were so buried that one has come to believe that his failings were simply a "natural" consequence of life. In fact, however, such failings are not natural at all. Through Scientology Expanded Grades auditing a person's native potentials and characteristics become evident, and flourish.

The six Expanded Grades are:

Expanded ARC Straightwire: "ARC" refers to the components of understanding. "Straightwire" is another term for "straight memory," so called because in the auditing processes on this grade the auditor directs the memory of the preclear and in doing so is stringing wire, much on the order of a telephone line, between the preclear and the standard memory bank in the preclear's mind.

The concept of ARC is one of the most important factors in all of life. If a person can establish ARC for something he can truly understand it. As noted, the subject of Scientology is the person himself, and so it follows that the first grade would involve restoring a preclear's direct and immediate understanding of himself. This is accomplished through the processes of ARC Straightwire.

ARC Straightwire explores the capabilities of one's memory and mind. If a person could increase his ARC for himself, he would realize that he is possibly his own best friend. A person who truly likes himself is an important first milestone to reach on the road to freedom.

Expanded Grade 0: The ability to communicate is one of the most fundamental abilities of a being. This ability too often fades through the course of living. As a consequence, some people grow shy and retiring. Others suffer from knots in their stomachs at the prospect of addressing a crowd. Still others are unable to discuss certain subjects or grow uncomfortable in the presence of the opposite sex or with people not of their age bracket. The number of ways a diminished ability to communicate can manifest itself are really incalculable.

The processes of this grade address a person's ability to communicate and free him, in his *own* estimation, from any blocks in the area, thus restoring the ability to communicate to anyone about any subject. Although some may view such a state as an impossibility, factually thousands and thousands of people have received just such gains with Expanded Grade 0. And with the ability to communicate comes the joy of associating freely with others.

We instinctively revere the great artist, painter or musician and society as a whole looks upon them as not quite ordinary beings.

And they are not. They are a cut above man. He who can truly communicate to others is a higher being who builds new worlds.

Auditing can help an individual achieve this higher state of being—one who can communicate.

Expanded Grade I: This grade deals with the problems a person has in his life. One can be so enmeshed with unwanted situations that any chance for happiness seems remote indeed. The problems of relationships, finances, job, family, one's ambitions, etc., can absorb a tremendous amount of energy.

What distinguishes civilized man as MAN is that he is mired in problems which just get worse the more he tries to "solve" them.

L. Ron Hubbard discovered a precise mechanism common to all problems. Any problem, regardless of how complex or how big, has at its source one intention in opposition to another intention. The conflicts in a person's life all stem from opposing intentions. This mechanism makes a person indecisive, causes his worries and causes situations in his life to "hang up" and not resolve.

The processes on Expanded Grade I bring the preclear up to an ability to recognize the actual source of problems at which point they "vanish"—cease to be problems anymore. A person who can do this is too rare to be easily comprehended. Man *solves* problems. But a being in a higher state looks at them and they vanish.

The mechanisms and phenomena surrounding problems are things which man has never, before Scientology, examined or understood.

Someone with this ability—to make problems vanish with a glance—is certainly in a far better condition in life.

Expanded Grade II: People try as best they can to deal with the hostilities and sufferings of life. Hit with "the slings and arrows of outrageous fortune," one responds in kind, and finds himself in a trap from which there has never been an escape.

The trap is composed of a person's transgressions against the mores of his family, the society and the race. Throughout his life a person has agreed to certain codes of conduct. These are the mores by which he survives in harmony with others. When a person unthinkingly transgresses against the mores to which he has agreed or, with "good cause" knowingly offends them, his misery begins. Having transgressed, the person now feels he must hold back his deed from others, and he begins to withdraw or feel different from the person or group he has harmed. This is the mechanism by which people create misery, bitterness and hatred around themselves. This is the source of the guilty conscience, feelings of vengeance and, actually, all the sufferings and hostilities of life.

Expanded Grade II processes enable a person to take apart this mechanism for himself. It is a tremendous relief to fully view this aspect of one's past in the calm, analytical environment of an auditing session.

The processes of Grade II eradicate these hostilities and sufferings from a person's life and provide relief from the actions that have pinned one to his past.

Expanded Grade III: Man is chained to his prior upsets. He has never understood why he felt so upset about his family or people or situations.

Most people dwell perpetually on troubles they have had. They lead sad lives.

Freedom from upsets of the past, with the resultant ability to openly face the future, is almost an unknown condition to man. But this too can be achieved in auditing.

Times of upheaval can unknowingly pin a person's attention years after the episodes. On Grade III processes one locates specific incidents where upsetting change occurred in life and addresses these. The end result of Expanded Grade III is the freedom to face the future with an enhanced ability to confront, experience and find advantage in the inevitable changes of life.

Expanded Grade IV: The next barrier to ability is addressed on Grade IV. Habit patterns can be nearly impossible to break, yet these fixed conditions hold a person down and rivet his ideas and activities in ways that cloud his potential.

The mechanism by which one falls into such a trap revolves around the concepts of right and wrong. Inborn in everyone is the impulse to be right. A person tries to be right and fights being wrong, no matter how he views these ideas. In the upsets, troubles and failures of life, this impulse to be right and not be wrong can become confused. This results in patterns of conduct that are demonstrably not in the best interests of survival, for they are fixed and repeated over and over in a misguided effort to be right.

The processes of Grade IV enable the preclear to view himself in relation to all life and free himself from any patterns of thought and action which, while seeming to promote one's survival, in reality do everything but. When one makes such a discovery it can dramatically change one's life, and leads to a huge resurgence in the ability to choose, partake in and enjoy new activities.

Countless events over years and years of a lifetime diminish a person's abilities. Many of these events, too insignificant to even notice at the time, yet have telling effects. With auditing, it does not take but a small fraction of one's lifetime to restore abilities and even enhance them beyond what one thought possible. In two or three months of regular auditing a person can make tremendous strides towards a rehabilitation of his native abilities, and experience how good life can be with such barriers out of the way. The gain available from the Scientology Expanded Grades is considerable. It can literally bring one to new states of existence.

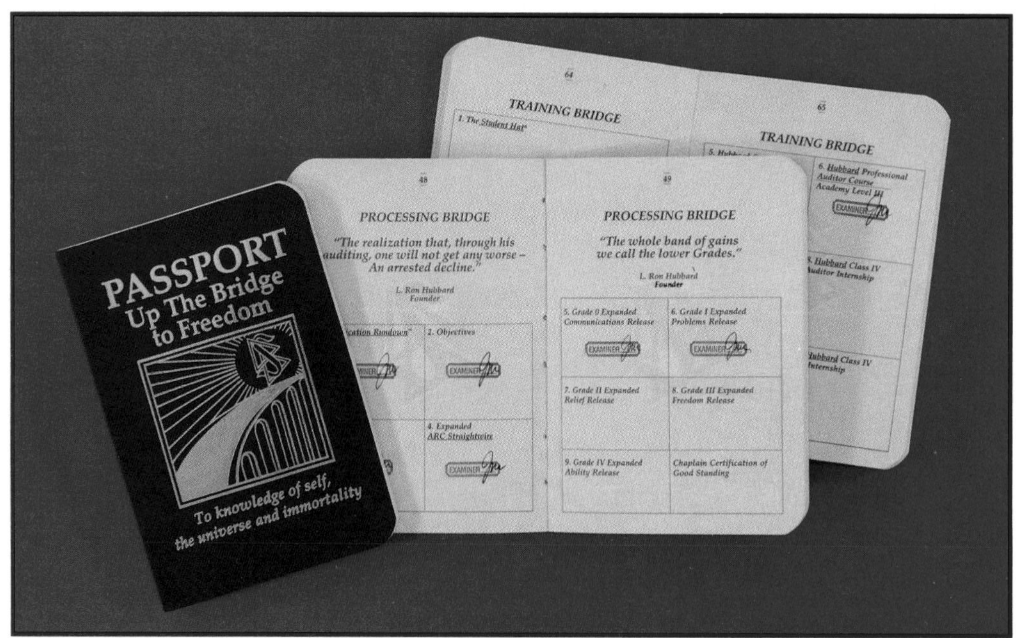

The Scientology Passport to Freedom, used by Scientologists to assist in tracking their orderly progress up the Bridge. As one finishes a grade, the passport is stamped to show completion.

NEW ERA DIANETICS AUDITING

A person able in an area can produce, perform, function and control activity in that area. An able acrobat, for example, performs stunts adroitly. An able chef prepares delicious food. But a person who has attained the abilities from the Scientology Expanded Grades is now able in *living* itself. As such he is more in control, brighter, and enjoys more personal power.

He is also now in a position to rid himself of his reactive mind and its contents. This accomplishment is not possible if a person is too distracted by his environment or cannot overcome the barriers to living the Expanded Grades handle.

Initially, by using the techniques contained in *Dianetics: The Modern Science of Mental Health,* engrams could be contacted and erased, resulting in more gains than were ever before available. The techniques invariably worked, but L. Ron Hubbard continued to research, seeking technology that offered faster and easier-to-attain results.

Refinements, such as the development of the E-Meter, made auditing swifter and more precise, as did development of the Scientology Expanded Grades. Building on the basic principles of Dianetics, Mr. Hubbard undertook further researches and developed more advanced Dianetics techniques. That these later refinements were built on the original axioms and procedures of Dianetics as initially released by him, is a great testimony to the accuracy of his original theories.

To give one an idea of just how effective Mr. Hubbard's new techniques were, consider this: Preclears who might have needed over 2,000 hours of auditing to achieve the highest results obtainable from 1950 technology might now achieve comparable gains in a tenth of that time with modern Dianetics and Scientology.

New Era Dianetics (NED) is the technology which contains L. Ron Hubbard's ultimate refinements of Dianetics auditing. He developed it following discoveries he made in 1978. Using New Era Dianetics technology, preclears can achieve the goals of Dianetics much, much faster than any early Dianeticist might have believed possible.

The reactive mind plagues a person with the unthinking, irrational dictates of its contents and imposes anxieties, fears, unwanted sensations and feelings, strange pains and a host of other undesirable effects. Freeing him from the command value such ills exert over his volition, provides new levels of self-determinism.

A person may have suffered the emotional upheaval of losing a loved one. NED auditing addresses these losses and, while it won't replace the affections held for the departed, it can free one from the spiritual trauma of the loss.

Many people are held back by what they consider their flaws or disabilities. NED techniques can erase the sources of these feelings and brighten a person's outlook and feelings about himself remarkably.

New Era Dianetics auditing consists of at least eleven specific rundowns (a series of auditing steps designed to handle a specific aspect of a case) and actions which address the engrams contained in the reactive mind. The different psychosomatic pains, sensations, emotions, feelings and so forth are used to trace back engrams in the reactive mind. Utilizing Dianetics auditing procedure, the preclear erases his engrams and nullifies their harmful energy.

The procedures of New Era Dianetics are precise. Completion of New Era Dianetics can make a well and happy human being with renewed health and his innate sanity recovered.

EXPANDED DIANETICS

This is a branch of Dianetics which uses New Era Dianetics in special ways for specific purposes. Some persons require Dianetics technology specially adapted to their individual requirements and this is delivered on Expanded Dianetics. While New Era Dianetics is very general in application, Expanded Dianetics is specifically tailored to the preclear's needs. It is not the same as New Era Dianetics and requires special training and advanced skills.

Some preclears have particularly heavy histories of drug taking. Others have been victimized by injurious psychiatric treatments or have unresolving psychosomatic complaints. People such as these benefit from the specially adapted technology contained in Expanded Dianetics, which consists of more than a dozen different auditing rundowns designed to address and handle such things as:

- Difficulties the preclear has in his environment
- Experiences of severe emotional stress
- Points of his past from which he cannot free his attention
- Areas of severe personal difficulty stemming from cruel impulses

Expanded Dianetics technology resolves the more difficult aberrations found in the reactive mind. Not every preclear requires Expanded Dianetics but it often brings a spectacular improvement in those receiving it.

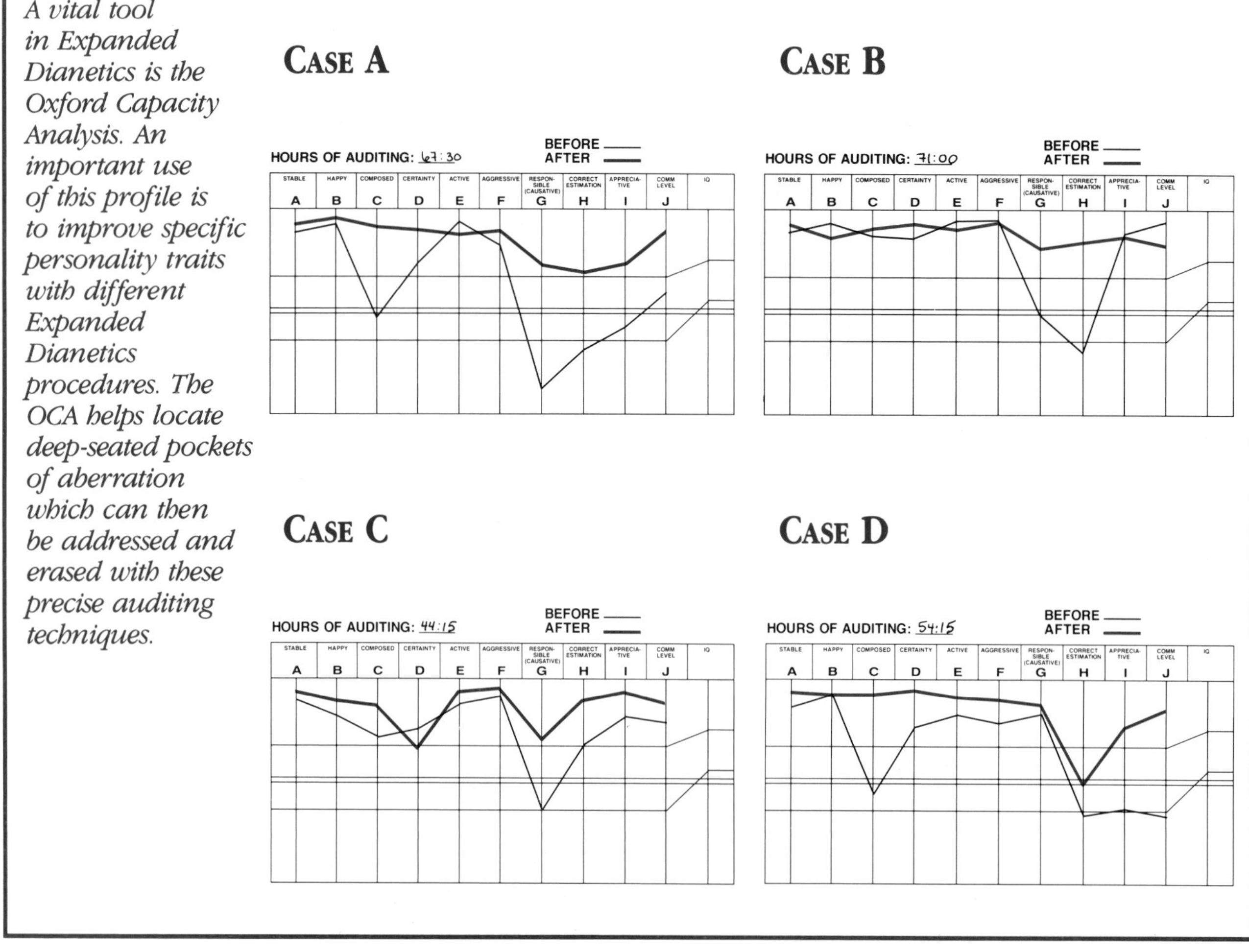

A vital tool in Expanded Dianetics is the Oxford Capacity Analysis. An important use of this profile is to improve specific personality traits with different Expanded Dianetics procedures. The OCA helps locate deep-seated pockets of aberration which can then be addressed and erased with these precise auditing techniques.

THE STATE OF CLEAR

The goals of Scientology predate all current ideas of "therapy" and are first found in religion and philosophy as long as 10,000 years ago. A Scientologist is trying to make people better and that is a new idea in the field of the human mind.

Clearing someone is erasing his reactive mind. All the misery man experiences is contained in the reactive mind.

There is a definite road out from reactivity, from aberration, from identifying everything with everything else. It leads to increased abilities, increased general performance and other exceptional gains that can be precisely measured and experienced. This road out has certain milestones which must be passed, and these are represented in the Expanded Grades and New Era Dianetics auditing.

The product of traveling the road that runs past these milestones is the erasure of reactivity. When this occurs the person achieves the state of Clear. It is not possible to attain this upper state by ignoring the lower grades.

A Clear is a person who no longer has his own reactive mind. He has vanquished it forever. Without the stimulus-response mechanisms of the reactive mind which can cause a person pain, unwanted sensations and negative emotions, a Clear can act rather than *react.* A Clear has a very high degree of personal integrity and honesty, and is living proof that man is basically good. His own basic beingness returns and his own basic personality flourishes. A person loses all the fears, anxieties and irrational thoughts that were held down by pain in the reactive mind and, in short, regains himself when he goes Clear. A person is much, much more himself without a reactive mind.

Until a person is cleared, no matter how able he becomes by virtue of earlier auditing, it is inevitable, just by the nature of the universe, that he will sooner or later sink back into the reactive mind. That is why clearing is vital. Clear is total erasure of the reactive mind and thus is a stable state, not subject to relapse.

When a person attains the state of Clear he is entitled to wear the Clear bracelet.

Each preclear is different and the type and amount of auditing necessary to erase the reactive mind is unique to each person. The state is therefore reached at either of two different places in a person's auditing. The first place is on New Era Dianetics. If a person does not achieve Clear on NED, he continues with further actions and attains it on the Clearing Course, a later service with a special auditing procedure. Other grades or auditing services do not result in Clear.

The state of Clear has never existed before. No matter how able a being may have been, no matter what powers he possessed, no matter his strengths, the reactive mind was still there, hidden, and eventually dragged him down again.

The full glory of the state of Clear has no comparable description in any literature existing in the culture, religious or otherwise. The state has been long sought but was impossible to achieve until the researches and breakthroughs of L. Ron Hubbard.

But the state does exist and it is attainable and many thousands of Scientologists all over the world are Clear, joined by more each day.

To acknowledge one's attainment of New OT VIII, a Scientologist may wear the OT bracelet.

THE STATE OF OPERATING THETAN

For thousands of years men have sought the state of complete spiritual freedom from the endless cycle of birth and death, a state of full awareness, memory and ability as a spirit independent of the flesh.

By eradicating the reactive mind in clearing we not only achieve an erasure of the seeming evil in man, we also overcome the barriers which made it so difficult to attain total spiritual independence and serenity. Thus, once a person achieves Clear he is now able to become refamiliarized with his native capabilities. As man is basically good, a being who is Clear becomes willing to trust himself with greater and greater abilities.

In Scientology, a state of complete spiritual freedom is attainable. It has been achieved not on a temporary basis but on a stable plane of full awareness and ability, unqualified by accident or deterioration. And it is not limited to a few.

It is called, in Scientology, "Operating Thetan." The definition of the state of Operating Thetan is "knowing and willing cause over life, thought, matter, energy, space and time."

The amount of spiritual gain available to a person is something rarely conceived. In an aberrated state where one's energy is primarily absorbed attempting to straighten out personal problems, a person is unlikely to lift his gaze to the glories that could be his as a fully rehabilitated and able being, not just as *Homo sapiens.*

On the auditing services above the state of Clear, called the "OT levels," one is no longer dealing with a person in relationship to his job, his house payments or his aches and pains. These will have been addressed at lower levels since it is necessary to free a person's attention from these matters in order to address higher aspects of existence. Having been freed of his own reactive mind, the person is able to undertake further steps in auditing by himself, becoming at the same time the auditor and the person being audited. This is "Solo auditing," learned on the Solo Auditor's Course. The Solo auditor uses communication drills, adapted to this level of skill, an E-Meter and exact processes, enabling him to rise into the realm of OT.

At the level of Operating Thetan one deals with the individual's own *immortality* as a spiritual being. One deals with the thetan himself in relationship to eternity; not to the eternity that lies *behind* him, but to the eternity which lies *ahead.*

On the OT levels one is rising to *eternity.* The vastness of time which has existed in the past is matched by at least as much time which lies ahead. *That* is eternity and a being will be in that eternity, and he will be in a good state or a bad state. One can step out of a job or a relationship or a worn-out suit of clothes, but one is not going to step out of life.

Contrary to those who teach that man cannot improve and that some seventy years in a body are all one can expect, there are states higher than that of mortal man. The state of OT does exist and people do attain it. Like any other gain in Scientology it is attained gradiently. Just as it would not be as beneficial to give someone New Era Dianetics auditing before improving his abilities with the Scientology Expanded Grades, so it is fruitless to try and move someone onto the OT levels before he is ready for them. One might as well pull a baby out of its bassinet and demand that he run. He won't make it until he has first learned to crawl and then walk. The reactive mind thoroughly blocks the thetan from regaining and exercising his native powers. But once this block is removed, the person can learn to operate as himself, a spiritual being.

The OT levels contain the very advanced materials of L. Ron Hubbard's researches and it is here the person achieves the ultimate realization of his own nature and his relationship to life and all the dynamics. Abilities return as he advances up through the OT levels and he recovers the entirety of his beingness.

Some of the miracles of life have been exposed to full view for the first time ever on the OT levels. Not the least of these miracles is knowing immortality and freedom from the cycle of birth and death.

The way is true and plainly marked. All one needs to do is to place his feet upon the first rung of the ladder and ascend to Clear and then walk upward to the level of Operating Thetan.

Auditing enables the individual to span the distance from *Homo sapiens,* with his drugs, his pains, his problems, upsets and fears, to higher states and freedom as a spiritual being. Such states are obtainable only through auditing. But they do exist and they are attainable and they fully restore a being to his native potential.

Throughout history man has had many solutions to the problems of existence and has sought far and wide for the answers to himself. Auditing *is* the solution and does provide the answers. Even a small amount of auditing can make this truth abundantly plain.

CHAPTER 14

AUDITOR TRAINING SERVICES

The influence of the reactive mind and its mechanisms present obstacles which destroy man's self-confidence, ruin his ambitions and cause his psychosomatic ills. Real and lasting happiness is difficult to attain if these obstacles remain unseen and unknown.

Training in Scientology principles enables one to unveil the reactive mind, understand its machinations and render them no longer mysterious. By understanding the factors of life and developing skills to handle them, happiness can be achieved.

There is factually no higher ability than the ability to restore life to its native potentials. Thus the value of Scientology technology is found in its actual application to oneself, a preclear or the situations one encounters in life. This chapter describes the primary training services offered in Scientology by which people learn this technology.

THE FUNDAMENTAL SKILLS OF AUDITING

Hubbard Professional TR Course

"TR" stands for *T*raining *R*outine and on this course a person gains expertise in that very vital ingredient for both successful living and auditing: communication.

As the most important part of the ARC triangle, communication is more important in auditing than the auditing technique used. Communication is what enables the auditor to help the preclear rid himself of his aberrations and regain his abilities. In life, communication is what enables one to perceive and deal with the world around him.

Before L. Ron Hubbard's researches into the subject, no one had isolated what the cycle of communication was, or its relationship to efforts to help man. But it is the essential element in *any* such effort, and so it is little wonder that earlier practices obtained no real or lasting results.

Hubbard Professional TR Course

The Hubbard Professional TR Course contains L. Ron Hubbard's discoveries about communication and teaches the skills needed to apply it effectively in life and in auditing. While the Success Through Communication Course gives one skills for handling communication in business or social situations, the Professional TR Course enables one to audit and to handle any situation in life with communication alone. This is a higher-level skill.

On the course, one studies the individual elements of communication and dissects the cycle of communication into each of its components, learning the principles of what communication is and how it is used. Technical training films written, directed and narrated by L. Ron Hubbard facilitate further understanding. The course even contains a set of very special auditing processes that students receive which gives them insight into some of the most basic laws in Scientology and lets them see how these apply to their lives and activities.

Once the student has completed his theory studies and auditing, he begins drilling the Training Routines (TRs), each of which develops skill in a basic part of communication. The drills begin with teaching the student how to face another person comfortably, even with distractions, since one cannot communicate well if one is shy, nervous or unwilling to simply be there to communicate. On subsequent drills, one learns how to deliver a communication so it arrives exactly where one desires, to let another person know that he has been heard and understood, to get one's questions answered (an important skill in living and a vital one in auditing) and to effectively handle what others say in order to maintain good communication with them. Each of these drills builds on the ones before it.

Students pair up and progress through each of the drills, mastering one before going on to the next. In doing the drills, the students become aware of poor communication habits or patterns they may have previously developed and they learn to communicate effectively.

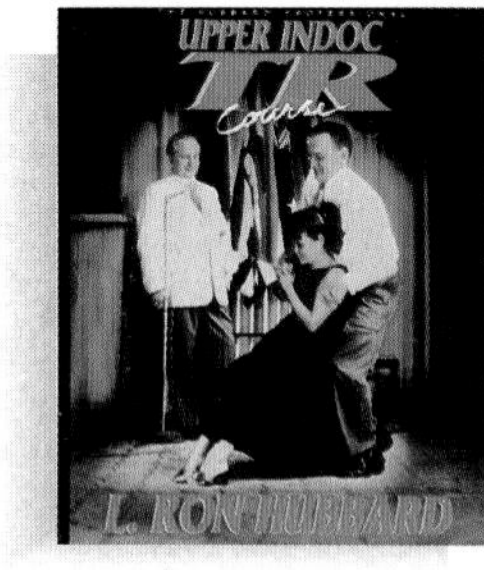

Hubbard Professional Upper Indoc TR Course

Hubbard Professional Upper Indoc TR Course

The next basic skill needed by an auditor or, for that matter, any successful person, is the ability to control things and to direct people and situations. Control is defined as the ability to start, change and stop something. One is successful in his life to the degree that he can start or change or stop the things and people within his environment.

This skill is learned on the Hubbard Professional Upper Indoc TR Course. "Indoc" is short for "indoctrination" (meaning "to teach") and Upper Indoc TRs, as they are called, are the series of TRs that follow Professional TRs in auditor training. This course teaches adroitness in starting, changing and stopping communication and directing other people. One's abilities in this area are thoroughly drilled until proficiency is attained.

To some, control may have a bad connotation but that is only due to past failures at controlling things or upsets stemming from times when one was poorly controlled.

But if one looks squarely at the subject, one can see that it is not possible to do much of anything in life if one cannot exert control. How, for example, can one drive a car one cannot start, change and stop? Control is a know-how vital to any endeavor, including auditing. Skillful control makes for more positive application of auditing techniques and greater gain for the preclear.

Control is a subject all auditors must master and, factually, is something everyone needs to know. The Professional Upper Indoc TR Course is where such expertise is learned.

ACADEMY AUDITOR TRAINING

The Academy Levels

The Academy Levels are a series of five auditor classification courses where the principles of Scientology and what it achieves become manifest.

Each Academy Level is an intensive two-week course which runs on a schedule of forty hours of course time per week. Students study either on a day schedule of eight hours of course periods five days a week, or on an evening and weekend schedule of three hours per evening and eight hours per day on the weekends. Each course consists of theory study and practical application of a specific aspect of Scientology technology. Each Academy Level corresponds to one of the Scientology Expanded Grades discussed in the last chapter and teaches the underlying principles of that Grade, as well as the auditing techniques.

Because each level deals with a specific aspect of life and the way to improve that aspect, by acquiring the data from these levels one becomes more causative overall. In short, the Academy Levels contain answers to the barriers that hold people back from success in their lives.

Level 0—Class 0 Auditor

(Hubbard Recognized Scientologist)

On Level 0, a person learns the basic actions of auditing, such as proper auditing session form and how to operate an E-Meter. He learns techniques which address communication and how to free another's abilities in this area.

The student reads five of L. Ron Hubbard's basic books and listens to seven selected lectures covering the subjects of communication and auditing fundamentals. He then learns the processes audited on ARC Straightwire and Expanded Grade 0.

Level I—Class I Auditor

(Hubbard Trained Scientologist)

This level teaches a person the anatomy of problems—why people get problems in the first place and the mechanics of eliminating problems.

The student reads two more basic L. Ron Hubbard books, hears eleven lectures on problems and their successful resolution through auditing and learns the auditing skills and processes of Expanded Grade I.

Level II—Class II Auditor

(Hubbard Certified Auditor)

Here, a person learns about the ramifications of harmful acts and how these affect survival. This course contains the technology of bringing relief from such hostilities and returning trust and honesty to life.

The student studies another book, hears fourteen lectures, then learns further techniques and the processes of Expanded Grade II.

Level III—Class III Auditor

(Hubbard Professional Auditor)

Level III covers the technology to free anyone from past upsets. One learns the mechanisms behind personal upheavals and how to alleviate the harmful aftereffects. The student learns more advanced E-Meter drills and more skilled auditing techniques which are used in the processes of Expanded Grade III.

Another book of Mr. Hubbard's and seven more lectures are part of the materials studied on this course.

Level IV—Class IV Auditor

(Hubbard Advanced Auditor)

The final Academy Level teaches the student how to handle fixed conditions in life. The technology of Level IV gives one the ability to change, to accept new ideas and to achieve his goals. Two more books are studied, seven lectures are heard and the Expanded Grade IV processes are taught.

The Academy Levels 0–IV constitute the basic Scientology auditor training. The student not only learns to help preclears in auditing, but also how to better handle his own life and help others deal with theirs.

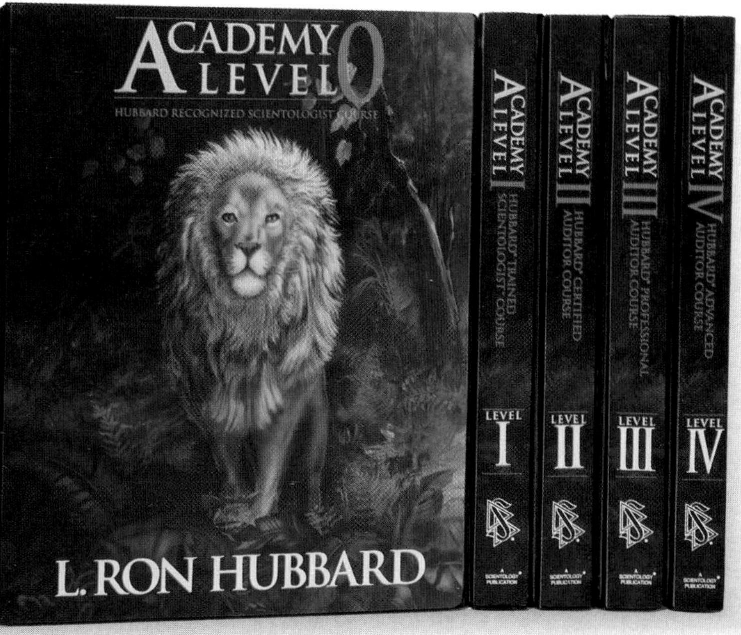

The Academy Levels – auditor training levels 0 – IV

Class V—Hubbard New Era Dianetics Auditor Course

The next training step upon completing Class IV Auditor training is the Hubbard New Era Dianetics Auditor Course which contains a summary and refinement of Dianetics, based on the decades of experience gained in the subject after its release. New Era Dianetics does not change any of the theories or principles of Dianetics as Mr. Hubbard originally developed them, but later breakthroughs resulted in this ultimate Dianetics technology, New Era Dianetics.

All Dianetics technology is included on this course including three basic books and five lectures on Dianetics and its use. With the procedures and techniques of NED auditing, an auditor can obtain results many times faster than earlier technology.

The student learns auditing procedures that effectively address any psychosomatic complaint a preclear may have. Over ten specific NED rundowns allow the auditor and preclear to erase engrams and often bring him to the state of Clear.

Clearing is within reach of millions and New Era Dianetics technology delivered well by NED Auditors is the primary means by which this will occur.

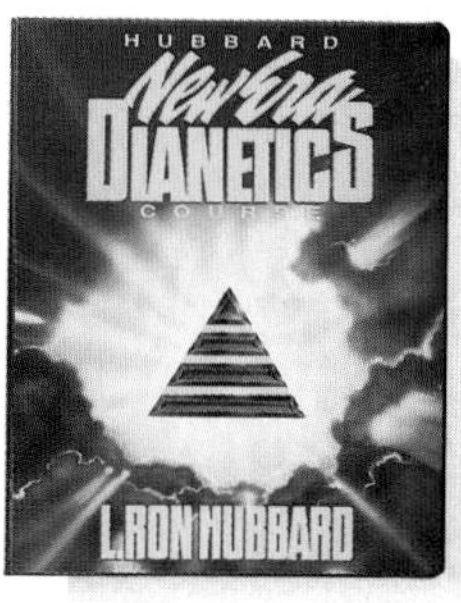

Hubbard New Era Dianetics Auditor Course

COMPREHENSIVE TRAINING: CLASS VI THE SAINT HILL SPECIAL BRIEFING COURSE

Auditor training courses in Academies of Scientology teach a person precise theory and techniques to handle the primary factors that complicate life and aberrate a being. In the interests of imparting data to a student that he can apply and get results with rapidly, Academy training courses are, by design, not comprehensive. Application is stressed in the Academy because in this way one can immediately get *results* that are obtainable with auditing and can at once start causing conditions in life to change for the better.

But a full understanding of Scientology and, therefore, of life could only be arrived at in one way: by following the path that L. Ron Hubbard himself took in order to find the way out of the trap. Walking the same road he walked, seeing the same things he saw would give one a total understanding of life, its mysteries and the technology for solving them. The course that traces every step of this path is the Saint Hill Special Briefing Course.

The Saint Hill Special Briefing Course is the largest single course in Scientology. It consists of a comprehensive and chronological study of the entire development of Dianetics and Scientology and contains the largest, broadest body of information on the subject of human behavior, the mind and life that has ever been available.

The course is named after Saint Hill Manor in England, Mr. Hubbard's residence during much of the 1960s, and where he taught the course from March 1961 to December 1966. This covers an intense period of his research, leading to many important discoveries. Auditors came from all over the world to Saint Hill

Saint Hill Special Briefing Course students study all materials shown here, including books, films, 12,000 pages of technical volumes and more than 450 recorded lectures.

and were present when Mr. Hubbard developed the Bridge to Total Freedom and many of the procedures that today form a large part of any preclear's auditing. The course was hugely popular and auditors who returned to their areas from Saint Hill were regarded with enormous respect. Demand for the training only available on the Briefing Course resulted in it being established in other areas of the world in organizations called "Saint Hills" as a tribute to the original home of the course.

Students study all of L. Ron Hubbard's books and technical bulletins and listen to recordings of more than four hundred of his lectures on the Saint Hill Special Briefing Course.

Due to the scope of the course and the setup necessary to deliver it, only selected Scientology organizations offer the Saint Hill Special Briefing Course. The course consists of sixteen individual checksheets, each requiring an average of three to four weeks of study. Each checksheet covers a specific period of Dianetics and Scientology technology and gives the student a full understanding of the theory and application of the materials of that period.

On the final two checksheets, the student audits extensively and becomes expert in the application of Dianetics and Scientology technology. Special training aids helping the student apply his materials are found only on the Saint Hill Special Briefing Course. All of L. Ron Hubbard's Technical Training Films are seen on the course.

The vast panorama of understanding the human mind and the secrets of life is only attained by an in-sequence study of all the developments one by one as they occurred, a consecutive chain of breakthroughs, each one a milestone in man's understanding of man. Such is available on the Saint Hill Special Briefing Course.

The Class VIII Course, one of the highest levels of auditor classification, stresses precision application of Scientology technology.

ADVANCED AUDITOR TRAINING

Several more classes of auditor training exist above the Saint Hill Special Briefing Course. These are Classes VII through XII. Each of these auditor classifications teaches advanced auditing techniques and requires that the auditor be very well trained on the lower classifications in order to apply them.

As Mr. Hubbard's research brought to view higher realms of awareness and ability, he codified auditing actions which would allow others to attain these. Of special distinction among the resulting courses is the Class VIII Auditor Course. This stresses an exact, unvarying standard of auditing technology application to all preclears.

Below Class VIII, an auditor learns different styles of auditing, processes, techniques and theory. One has to know all this data before taking the next step; one can then totally align all this knowledge into a simple but wholly effective ability to achieve stellar auditing results on *any* preclear. That is what a Class VIII Auditor can do, and there are no shortcuts to its attainment.

He is trained to administer auditing technology with flawless and invariable precision, a necessity for the advanced techniques and rundowns he learns here. He studies the materials of the course, including nineteen lectures, three times to reach the understanding which underlies a Class VIII Auditor's effortless competence. At Class VIII the highest standards of application are reinforced again and again until the student applies *them* and nothing else. He gains an absolute certainty in the precision of auditing and knows he can get results on any preclear with it. The power in the vast technical data of Scientology becomes concentrated into a relatively few essentials. In the hands of a Class VIII Auditor these essentials produce the high-velocity gains which result from perfect application.

Technical Specialist Courses

Factors can arise in a preclear's life which threaten to halt his progress on the Bridge. Different case problems can exist that are best handled by special processes and rundowns not contained in the normal course of auditing actions on the Bridge. So, in addition to the numbered auditor classifications, other training courses teach specialized techniques to help people resolve an array of conditions.

These are classified as Technical Specialist Courses. They comprise a body of postgraduate studies which train an auditor in the technology of a specific rundown or technical skill not covered in Academy classification courses. Each course is only a few days' duration and requires no interning. The procedure learned will resolve an exact condition in the preclear, enabling him to continue to progress up the Bridge.

Technical Specialist Courses are the most direct way for an auditor to learn all the procedures necessary to handle any preclear. (These techniques in addition to the full philosophical theory underlying them are included within the more extensive Saint Hill Special Briefing Course.) On Technical Specialist Courses an auditor learns how, for example, to repair victims of psychiatric abuse, to aid students in resolving study difficulties, to assist people in overcoming specific fears and to help others rid themselves of false purposes. These are all conditions that can slow a preclear's progress, but an auditor trained on Technical Specialist Courses is fully capable of helping any person resolve such barriers so that he may move on up the Bridge to Total Freedom.

The Technical Specialist Courses train an auditor on the specialized techniques to resolve a broad spectrum of mental and spiritual maladies. There are 19 separate courses, each covering a different subject.

PERFECTING SKILLS OF APPLICATION

Auditor Internships

After training, an auditor's skills are developed by experience in auditing others. This is done on internships which come after selected courses.

An internship is a period of serving as an intern under the supervision of technical experts. As in other fields such as medicine where medical school graduates intern under experienced doctors to learn the profession, the recently graduated auditor gets "on-the-job" practical experience working under veteran auditors in the organization. In this way, his skills are honed and polished to a very high level of proficiency.

An intern's auditing skills are carefully reviewed by technical experts. Practical application of actually auditing a preclear brings to light any weakness in the auditor's ability to apply all of his materials. Particular emphasis is then given to these areas until the auditor becomes competent in them. The pattern of auditing, combined with inspection and any needed correction of errors, soon brings about a high level of expertise. Interns audit daily, and work up to an ability to do as much as ten hours of flawless auditing in a single day.

When interns have audited in volume and polished any rough edges so they can think with their materials without hesitation on what to do in an auditing session, they are an internship graduate.

An auditor who completes an internship invariably becomes more accomplished by virtue of the intensive supervision and assistance given by more highly trained and experienced personnel. Internships are rigorous and make a course graduate into a top-flight professional auditor while also raising his general competence in life.

AUDITOR SUPERVISION

Successful auditing is a team activity requiring the work of additional people besides the auditor and preclear.

In order to ensure technology is applied correctly in all cases, auditing is overseen by another technically trained person called the Case Supervisor (C/S). The Case Supervisor directs auditing actions for each individual preclear under his care. *Case* is a general term for a person being treated or helped. The Case Supervisor's purpose is to see that the technology is standardly applied for the greatest possible benefit for the preclear. Ultimately, it is the Case Supervisor who is responsible for the technical quality in his area.

The Case Supervisor is a highly trained and interned auditor who does additional training in the technology of supervising auditing. Not every auditor becomes a C/S, but every Case Supervisor is a highly skilled auditor.

The Case Supervisor reviews all auditing sessions done by auditors under his charge. He verifies the auditor's application was standardly done. He directs the auditor on what process to run next on his preclear, based on an overall program of auditing drawn up especially for each individual to ensure his maximum progress. He helps the auditor apply the technology correctly and, if some error in procedure is made, he sees that the auditor is corrected. The C/S, not being directly involved in the session, studies the technical report made by the auditor; this distance often furnishes a clear and valuable view of the preclear's overall progress.

Case Supervisor training consists of courses, followed by internships of their own where the student learns the technology of case supervision and then gains practical experience supervising the auditing of others. There are C/S courses following Class IV, Class V, Class VI, Class VIII, Class IX and Class XII.

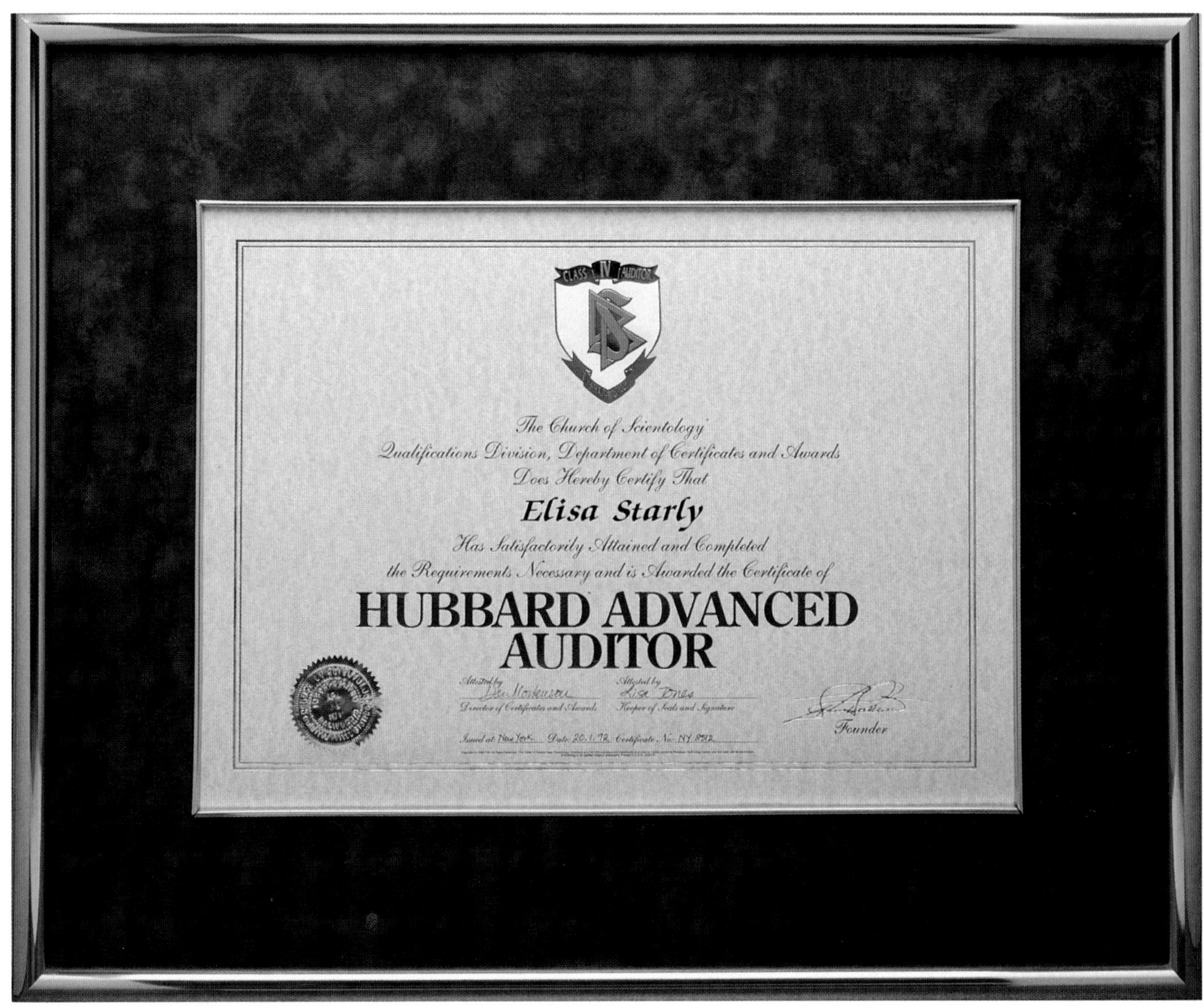

AN AUDITOR'S VALUE

Auditor training services gradiently make one more capable in life. Each course and internship builds on the preceding and makes an individual more and more confident and able.

Skills gained by training in the discipline of auditing are the superior skills of handling life. With them one can undo the pain, misery and failures of others and this has never been possible in history. The proficient auditor is valuable beyond compare to his fellows, to the world and to himself. An impulse to help resides in nearly everyone. Auditor training gives one the know-how to provide help of a higher order. An auditor is the only person in the world capable of actually *undoing* unhappiness in another. He is the only one who can help others restore their native powers. No better way to help exists, and no activity is more rewarding.

The successful completion of a Scientology training course is validated with certification. When one has passed a thorough period of internship, he earns a gold seal signifying that his certificate is permanent.

Chapter 15

Other Ministerial Services

It has long been the function of a church to provide guidance and succor to parishioners in times of need. In fact, beyond strictly spiritual concerns, the church has traditionally seen its mission as easing temporal suffering, helping where help is required and instilling dignity to the pivotal turning points of our lives.

The loss of a loved one, the illness of a relative, marital difficulties, family disputes, and the like—all constitute times when individuals seek guidance, support or solace in their church. Parishioners also turn to their church for weddings, christenings and funeral services. The Scientology Chaplain performs all of the above, but his primary function is to help solve the day-to-day problems that can occasionally keep a Scientologist from moving up the Bridge. Each church has a Chaplain who is well equipped with a variety of means to help resolve such troublesome situations. Whether dealing with someone who experienced the loss of a loved one, the disillusioned husband or wife, or helping Scientologists overcome barriers encountered along their route to freedom, his door is always open.

Helping to Keep People on the Bridge

So great are the pressures of modern life that every once in a while a Scientology student or preclear may find himself drawn off the Bridge by demands from his home, his workplace or neighborhood. While the many services offered by the Church relate to the totality of all life, the person has to be there to take advantage of them. Hence, one of the Scientology Chaplain's duties is to help parishioners stay on the Bridge. Although the particular reasons why someone might have difficulty can vary enormously, the Chaplain is superbly equipped to handle almost anything. He is well trained in Scientology communication principles, and so can help resolve disagreements between preclears, students or members of the staff. He understands the principles of Scientology counseling and can arrange auditing sessions for those who have slipped off the Bridge owing to an upset. He knows how to apply Scientology personality testing to pinpoint difficulties one might encounter in the home or office, or resolve disputes between individuals or marital partners.

Nor are the Chaplain's functions limited to resolving difficulties among the Scientology public. Utilizing the same skills with which he helps the parishioner in the community, he also does much to maintain the high morale of Scientology staff members. He knows that by caring for the morale of each individual, one can raise the morale of all.

In short, the Scientology Chaplain performs those duties that chaplains have always performed: He helps sort out problems, extends a hand to those who have fallen and works to instill a general well-being, buoyancy and confidence within all members of his group. There are also other ways Scientologists help their fellows through difficult periods.

ASSISTS

L. Ron Hubbard developed many, many techniques to help those suffering from illness or injury—techniques well known to a Scientologist when he enters the hospital or sickroom. These techniques constitute a body of technology classified as "assists," and are undertaken to help the spirit confront physical difficulties. These assists include the *Contact Assist,* designed to help an individual alleviate the mental or spiritual reaction to injuries and so greatly speed the healing process, and the *Touch Assist,* designed to reestablish communication with injured body parts. Both of these assists operate on the principle that if injured, one tends to mentally or spiritually withdraw from the injured area. Although a perfectly understandable reaction to pain, only by restoring communication with the injured area can one bring the spiritual element into the healing process—an element that physicians have long innately recognized but never before had a means to utilize.

HELPING THE FAMILY

The family is the building block of a culture, and when a society loses sight of that fact, it loses its foundations. With that in mind, L. Ron Hubbard did much to isolate the sources of familial problems and provide a means to bring family members back together again.

In the first bloom of love, it seems easy to commit oneself "till death do us part." As the years pass, however, those first sacred vows can too often lose their meaning, and thus marriages can end in divorce. In that the traditional core of the family unit is the relationship between a husband and a wife, Mr. Hubbard set out to discover the *real* reason behind marital failures and how to reignite that first spark of love.

Like the techniques employed to help the ill or injured, Scientology marriage counseling is an assist. It is intended to alleviate marital problems by addressing the root of all such difficulties: transgressions against the previously agreed-upon moral code that now inhibit communication and, in turn, hinder survival. Although forthrightness, honesty and open communication have long been known to form the basis of a healthy marriage, never before has there been a real method to help couples achieve that state.

Scientology marriage counseling helps create an atmosphere of honesty and open communication between marital partners.

In the interests of reestablishing open communication, the Scientology Chaplain conducts a marriage counseling session with both partners present—first the Chaplain addresses one spouse while the other looks on, and then their places are reversed.

By way of example, consider the adulterous husband. Quite apart from the health hazards of infidelity, the adulterer carries with him a deep and dark secret. He has broken his marriage vows. To hide his transgression, he lies; and with each new lie he grows more consumed with guilt and further out of communication with his wife. Although adultery may be one failing of a marriage, there are a thousand and more transgressions one might make against the moral code—and with each untold transgression and each new lie to cover it up, the marriage dies a little more.

With these principles firmly understood by both partners, the Chaplain proceeds to help the couple morally cleanse themselves. He very carefully maintains strict impartiality so that by no mannerism, tone of voice or word, does he give the impression that he favors one spouse over the other.

When the husband, for instance, has completed his session, he then looks on while the Chaplain addresses the wife. If the counseling sessions are standardly conducted with strict adherence to the Auditor's Code and other rules of auditing, both partners soon unburden themselves of barriers to marital harmony—the guilt, shame and lies are a thing of the past and communication is restored. Utilizing these procedures Scientology Chaplains have successfully salvaged thousands of marriages from the brink of dissolution.

Children

In addition to salvaging marriages, and as part of his larger effort to restore family unity, the Scientologist is often called upon to help the child. Children today are not only beset with the problems that have always troubled young people—nightmares, squabbles with friends, difficulties with their studies—but face a whole new host of ills as a consequence of our ailing society. Drugs and sexual abuse steal the happiness of children at an increasingly young age, while gang violence and rampant criminality endanger their lives; and one need only glance at an inner-city school to appreciate just how badly our society has served their welfare.

"Save the child," Mr. Hubbard wrote, "and you save the nation." Yet not only has today's society sadly neglected children, but even where efforts are made to help, too often they come to nothing for lack of any real know-how.

Long concerned with the well-being of man's future, L. Ron Hubbard developed dozens of techniques to enhance the welfare of a child. As a basic orientation, Mr. Hubbard points out that the child is not an *enfant terrible* who must be forcefully molded or broken if he is ever to behave as a responsible adult. Rather, the child must be seen for what he is: a fully aware individual in a body that has not attained full growth. And recognizing that what applies to an adult's behavior also applies to the child, the Scientologist may utilize the same means to help children that he employs to help adults.

The ill or injured child, and even infants, may be given Touch Assists. The young student suffering through his studies will find relief through the application of L. Ron Hubbard's study technology. The student who cannot get along with his friends can quickly resolve the matter with communication skills learned on a course specifically designed for him. And even very young children may receive auditing.

Possessing all these tools and more, the Scientologist is well equipped to counsel parents and help their children grow up happy, confident and able. He recognizes that the child is often wonderfully sane, that his values and sense of reality are acutely sharp, and if only adults around him would refrain from attempts to manage and fashion him into their image, he will become a fine, successful human being.

SCIENTOLOGY SERVICES

There are moments in everyone's life when a ceremony lends an appropriate dignity. When getting married, mourning a death or naming our children, most feel that a ceremony is appropriate. Scientology congregations celebrate weddings and christenings with their own formal ceremonies, hold Sunday services and mark the passing of their fellows with funeral rites. The Chaplain or minister conducts these functions with dignity and order, but they are not necessarily solemn. Church services are open to those of any denomination.

Sunday sermons generally revolve around primary points of the Scientology philosophy, including the idea that a person is not a body or mind, but a spiritual being. Other sermons might address any of the eight dynamics, the Axioms or the codes of Scientology. Although such sermons covering the basic truths of Mr. Hubbard's philosophy do much to refresh and revitalize Scientologists, the Chaplain is keenly aware that his sermons will also offer hope to the stranger burdened by life and the workaday world.

That so much of the Scientology minister's work is aimed at helping the infirm, the estranged, the saddened is traditional. What is not traditional, however, is that he can do more than offer sympathy and compassion that is based upon common sense and faith. With the tools provided by L. Ron Hubbard he can actually better conditions.

A traditional Scientology wedding ceremony

Chapter 16

Scientology Ethics and Judicial Matters

Because it has long been acknowledged that spiritual progress and proper conduct are inextricably linked, all great religious philosophies contain some form of ethical, moral and/or judicial system. Most obviously, one finds the Ten Commandments aimed at outlawing those transgressions deemed most offensive to God and most injurious to the Jewish people. Similarly, the Buddhists developed the concept of Right Livelihood, while Christian notions of sin fill a thousand pages or more. But merely setting down rules has never appreciably led to improvement, and it was not until L. Ron Hubbard defined and codified the subject, that there was any workable technology of ethics and justice for increased happiness, prosperity and survival.

Ethics

The Scientology system of ethics is based wholly on reason. Whereas morals, Mr. Hubbard pointed out, are essentially laws of conduct laid down from accumulated experience out of ages past and thus may no longer be entirely relevant to survival, ethics consists wholly of rationality toward the highest level of survival for all dynamics. True, in the absence of anything else, a moral code can provide a general yardstick for optimum conduct, and ethical conduct always includes an adherence to society's moral codes. But over time, morals can become outmoded, burdensome, and so invite revolt. Thus, although moral codes are respected, it is the adherence to ethical standards that holds the channels of the Bridge firmly open, enabling Scientologists to progress smoothly and without distraction.

Ethics may be defined as the actions an individual takes on himself to ensure his continued survival across the dynamics. It is a personal thing. When one is ethical, it is something he does himself by his own choice.

The logic of Scientology ethics is inarguable and based upon two key concepts: *good* and *evil.* Like ethics and justice, *good* and *evil* have long been subject to opinion, confusion and obfuscation. But to appreciate what Scientology ethics is all about, it must be understood that *good* can be considered to be a constructive survival action. It is something that, to put it simply, is more beneficial than destructive across the dynamics. True, nothing is completely good, and to build anew often requires a degree of destruction. But if the *constructive* outweighs the *destructive,* i.e., if a greater number of dynamics are helped than harmed, then an action can be considered good. Thus, for example, a new cure which saves a hundred lives but kills only one, is an acceptable cure.

Having thus defined what is good, evil then becomes the opposite of good, and constitutes anything which is destructive more than it is constructive along the dynamics. A thing which does more destruction than construction is evil from the viewpoint of the individual, the future race, group, species, life or physical universe matter that it destroys.

In summation, then, an act or conclusion

is as *right* as it promotes survival across the dynamics and to be entirely right would be to survive to infinity. Conversely, an act or conclusion is *wrong* to the degree that it is nonsurvival across the dynamics, injuring more than it aids.

With a firm understanding of these definitions, the Scientologist is well equipped to rationally determine the course of his actions.

The logic behind maintaining high ethical standards is simple. Although modern conceptions of ethics have become hopelessly convoluted with common conflict of interest and gray areas of choice, it cannot be forgotten that greater survival for both individuals and groups comes through abiding by these agreements. Hence, the Scientologist is lawful with regards to his country, fair in his dealings with others and faithful in his relationships. He knows that because every individual is essentially good, he has an innately acute sense of what is ethical and what is not. Thus, when one violates one's personal sense of ethics, he soon loses self-respect and begins to deteriorate from that point forward.

CONDITIONS OF EXISTENCE

With the basic definitions of *ethics, good* and *evil* in place, and the basic *necessity* for ethical conduct established, Mr. Hubbard proceeded to develop a means of allowing one to gradiently raise his ethics level and so increase survival in any area of his life. It is a system of betterment unlike any other, and contains nothing of the "Go-and-sin-no-more" approach that many find so difficult to follow. Rather, it is predicated on the idea that there are degrees of ethical conduct, that things may be surviving more or less well, but can still be greatly improved. Hence, Mr. Hubbard set out to delineate the various ethical states or *conditions* which constitute the degree of success or survival of something, and precisely how to better that condition of survival.

These conditions are not static states, but either improve or worsen, depending upon one's actions. Indeed, it is a fact that nothing remains exactly the same forever, for such a condition is foreign to life and the universe. Things grow or they lessen. They cannot apparently maintain the same equilibrium or stability.

Everything in existence is in one condition or another. A person is in some condition personally, his job is in a condition, his marriage is in a condition and so on. Mr. Hubbard isolated and described these states, then determined what it would actually take to move from any given condition to a higher one. In all, Mr. Hubbard delineates twelve separate conditions. They range from a state of complete confusion where an individual is in no position to produce any product to a condition of stable power wherein very little if anything can imperil his position. Along the way to power, he will pass through such other conditions as normal operation wherein he is gradually taking on more control, producing more and more, but has still not achieved permanent stability. As he continues to properly apply himself, he will eventually move into a condition of affluence—or, failing to take proper steps, may sink into a state of emergency.

Like every fundamental truth in Scientology, the conditions encompass the whole of life. They represent descriptions of actual laws that apply to everything from the growth of trees to the running of an automobile to the raising of a child. Yet discovering these conditions of existence was not all Mr. Hubbard accomplished; he also discovered the exact actions or steps anyone under any circumstances can take to better any condition of existence.

Those steps to improving conditions are aptly called formulas. They are precisely laid out for each condition, and only by following the specific formula for the condition in which one finds oneself can an individual move on to the next higher condition.

To take a very common example, consider the subject of personal relationships between a man and a woman. Obviously, when a couple first begins dating, however strong the attraction, they are not in the same condition as a married couple. Likewise, the marriage beset with strife owing to adultery is not surviving well—and is thus in a lower condition than the entirely harmonious marriage. Yet regardless of how poorly a marriage may be surviving, how bitter the arguments, how seemingly unresolvable the strife, there are *always* steps one can do to better the condition of that marriage. And by continuing to apply those steps, ascending through successively better conditions, one can, with remarkable certainty, always improve that marriage.

The same conditions and their specific formulas can be used to better anything, from personal happiness to the performance of a high-school athletic team to the performance of a multinational corporation. If, to take another example, an employee suddenly finds himself demoted to a lower position in his company, there are specific ways and means by which he can climb back up the corporate ladder. Similarly, if the employee suddenly finds himself promoted to a higher position with a substantial pay increase, a precise application of the Scientology ethics conditions will keep him from falling into the trap of suddenly spending more than he makes or assuming that he is now forever blessed in his boss's eyes.

The important point to recognize here, is that the Scientology conditions formulas are not arbitrary. Yes, they serve to raise a Scientologist's ethics level and so speed his progress on the Bridge. But they also can raise the ethics level, and thus the survival of anyone in any circumstance; for the conditions describe what governs all existence, and if followed, they *do* lead to improvement. Conversely, if these conditions are not followed, the individual, his career, his relationships or even his possessions will deteriorate to the next lower condition.

Scientologists use these conditions formulas to handle personal situations, family activities, successes and failures on the job and relationships with other people. The conditions formulas can be applied to *any* situation on *any* dynamic. They *are* the tools by which one makes changes in his life and the world around him.

Spotting one's condition in an area of his life and applying the formula to raise it is the primary activity of ethics. Churches have a staff member, the Ethics Officer, who helps parishioners determine which condition applies to a part of their lives and how, in turn, to apply the right formula. A person may have trouble applying the formulas, as life's complexities can sometimes make it difficult to sort out which formula needs to be applied or how best to proceed with the steps. The Ethics Officer is there to help Scientologists at such times. This is valuable because problems can arise in life that threaten to hinder one's progress up the Bridge. Properly applied, ethics will get one moving again.

Because the conditions formulas follow natural laws that embrace all life's endeavors, they naturally open the door to increased survival on any dynamic and in any course of action. Moreover, the conditions formulas are quickly learned, easily applied and can immediately set one on the road to happiness, success and well-being.

STATISTICS: THE MEASUREMENT OF SURVIVAL

As a further word on the Scientology ethics conditions, mention should be made of how Scientologists use statistical measurement to eliminate the guesswork of applying conditions formulas. Simply put, a statistic is a basic tool for the measurement of survival potential. A statistic is a number or amount compared to an earlier number or amount of the same thing. Statistics refer to the quantity of work done or the value of it and are the only sound measure of any production or any activity. Although one normally thinks of statistics in terms of, say, items sold or payment received, anything can be analyzed in terms of statistics—from gardening to golf. Moreover, only by monitoring statistics can one be certain that he is pinpointing the proper condition, whether bettering or worsening, and not relying on rumor or hearsay. Thus, with an understanding of how to compile, graph and compare statistics, the Scientologist is amply equipped to determine exactly *what* condition an activity is in, and thus exactly what steps he must take in order to better that condition.

THE ANTISOCIAL PERSONALITY

Another key aspect of the Scientology ethics system is the recognition of the antisocial personality. Reflective in man's earliest ethical codes is an innate sense that there are those among us—about 2½ percent of the population—who possess characteristics and mental attitudes that cause them to violently oppose any betterment activity or group. Within this category, one finds the Adolf Hitlers and the Genghis Khans, the unrepentant murderers and the drug lords. Although most blatantly antisocial types may be easy to spot, if only from the bodies they leave in their wake, others are less obviously seen. Enterprises may seem to crumble for no apparent reason, marriages may mysteriously disintegrate and a thousand more ills may affect those associated with the antisocial personality. In fact, all told, 20 percent of the entire population suffers, in one form or another, from a connection with the antisocial personality. For that reason Mr. Hubbard offers very specific guidelines for their detection.

To ensure that these guidelines never perpetuate a witch hunt or an unjust condemnation, he also provides a precise description of the social personality—the category that embraces the great majority of mankind. Moreover, Mr. Hubbard continually stresses that, regardless of apparent traits, all men are basically good—even the most seemingly unrepentant.

The importance of detecting the antisocial personality becomes eminently clear when one considers his effect on the lives of those around him. It has been found that a person connected to an antisocial personality will suffer greatly decreased survival, impeding not only his progress in Dianetics and Scientology but all aspects of his life. Then, too, as his conditions worsen, his ensuing troubles tend to spill over into the lives of others. Hence such a person is designated a "potential trouble source." With the standard application of materials found in Mr. Hubbard's *Introduction to Scientology Ethics,* however, the potential trouble sources can be swiftly helped. Factually, Scientologists use these materials every day to repair marriages, bring parents and children closer together and trade misery for health and happiness.

THE THIRD PARTY LAW

Another key tool that Scientologists regularly use to better their lives, remove barriers that may slow their progress on the Bridge and generally improve conditions is the Third Party Law. This law, defined for the first time by Mr. Hubbard, illuminates the underlying cause of all human conflict—whether in the home, the community or the nation. Precisely stated, the law is this:

> "A THIRD PARTY MUST BE PRESENT AND UNKNOWN IN EVERY QUARREL FOR A CONFLICT TO EXIST.
>
> "or
>
> "FOR A QUARREL TO OCCUR, AN UNKNOWN THIRD PARTY MUST BE ACTIVE IN PRODUCING IT BETWEEN TWO POTENTIAL OPPONENTS.
>
> "or
>
> "WHILE IT IS COMMONLY BELIEVED TO TAKE TWO TO MAKE A FIGHT, A THIRD PARTY MUST EXIST AND MUST DEVELOP IT FOR ACTUAL CONFLICT TO OCCUR."

The jealous business associate who continually slanders one to a boss, the spiteful neighbor who slyly belittles a wife to a husband, the disgruntled ex-employee who bad-mouths a company to customers—all may constitute the hidden third parties in a conflict that is severely injurious to survival. And unless those third parties are detected, that hidden but very real third party can wreak considerable havoc in terms of worsening conditions on any number of dynamics. Thus, it is not uncommon to find the Third Party Law used in conjunction with the conditions formula steps to, say, salvage a marriage or friendship. As with the detection of the antisocial personality, however, Mr. Hubbard was careful to precisely delineate the application of this tool so that it is not used unjustly.

SCIENTOLOGY JUSTICE

For all the tools that a Scientologist possesses to better his conditions and raise his ethics level, it is occasionally necessary, for the protection of the many, that the group step in and take proper action when the individual fails to take such action himself—hence the Scientology justice system. The basic idea behind Scientology justice is as simple and rational as the underlying theory of Scientology ethics. Justice exists to protect decent people. It is necessary in any successful society. Without it the brute attacks the weak, the good and the productive. The concept and practice of justice as it exists in society today, however, is increasingly ineffective.

That justice system is bogged down in a morass of Latinized grammatical complexities and has become, sadly, a matter of which attorney can present the better argument. Right and wrong, guilt and innocence are relegated to bit players in the show. A lawyer defending a criminal on trial for armed robbery, for instance, is not interested in establishing guilt or innocence; he is looking for a loophole or technicality on which the case can be dismissed and his client set free—whether guilty or not. Few have the wealth necessary to even try to pursue justice through the courts and even if one prevails, attorney costs often make it a Pyrrhic victory. The due process of the court system is in a virtual gridlock of motions, countermotions, depositions, injunctions, appeals, claims and counterclaims.

Scientology has another system, one unlike any other. Jurisprudence exists within Scientology which is both rapid and fair, and Scientologists utilize this to protect the decent and the productive.

Scientology justice is administered in accordance with a precise set of easily understandable ecclesiastical codes clearly delineated, broadly published and well known by Scientologists. Justice actions are conducted entirely in accordance with these codes, and whether they have been violated or not; suspicion, opinion or caprice play no part. The codes protect the rights of any Scientologist in good standing with the Church.

The sole purpose of justice in Scientology is to establish the truth of a matter and determine guilt or innocence. With this established, proper restitution of wrongs can be made. Scientologists with disputes can use Scientology justice to settle matters amicably. Any Scientologist can avail himself of the justice system to resolve civil disputes, be they with another Scientologist or even a non-Scientologist. And because Scientology justice is fair, economical and occurs without delay, Scientologists find it of great value.

Any justice action in Scientology is completed within a week of being convened, saving the parties involved the unnecessary stress of lengthy delays. Situations are resolved rapidly, with assurance that the outcome will result in the greatest good for the greatest number.

Church justice codes delineate four general classes of crimes and offenses: errors, misdemeanors, crimes and high crimes. These range from minor unintentional errors or omissions in applying Church policy or Scientology technology, to felonies and serious ecclesiastical offenses.

Justice proceedings are effected by bodies formally convened by duly authorized members of the church with the sole purpose of carrying out one particular justice action. These temporary bodies consist of church staff members or other Scientologists who otherwise carry on with their normal duties and activities, but who are given the responsibility of acting on behalf of the group in the matter before them. No attorneys are used and the entire business of a justice action in Scientology is to determine with accuracy the truth of the situation and to see that any wrong is rectified accordingly. There are no legal maneuverings or technicalities which obscure establishing rightness or wrongness, innocence or guilt. One is expected to present the truth, and knowing that the procedures are fair, this is what happens. An accused has access to any reports against him and has the right to face and question his accusers.

Four main types of bodies constitute the Scientology system of justice.

A Court of Ethics is convened when known evidence exists of an offense committed against the justice codes by a person. A staff member is appointed as Hearing Officer and adjudicates the facts of the matter and makes a recommendation based on these. The convening authority may direct amends based on the findings commensurate with the offense.

A Board of Investigation has the duty to discover the cause of conflicts amongst Scientologists or poor performance in an area in the Church. A three- to five-member board is appointed to conduct an investigation. The board reports on its findings but recommends no disciplinary actions. It may recommend a Committee of Evidence be convened should it uncover serious offenses.

A Chaplain's Court exists where grievances may be heard and disputes brought to speedy and equitable resolution. The Chaplain hears all matters, or when requested and allowed by the Chaplain, a body of three people is selected mutually agreeable to both parties. Scientologists use this means of civil justice because it is faster and fairer than what they would receive from any court system. If two Scientologists cannot resolve, say, a personal financial matter, they can bring this before the Chaplain's Court and get it handled rapidly and fairly. The alternative would be to bring costly and time-consuming suit in the legal system.

A Committee of Evidence is convened to try more serious matters. This is a fact-finding body composed of between four and seven members. Its duty is to conduct an inquiry into known offenses, hear evidence from witnesses it calls, arrive at a finding and make a full report and recommendation to its convening authority for his action.

Punishment is not a factor in Scientology justice, since it has long been proven in society that punishment more often than not simply hardens the punished person into patterns of destructive behavior. Instead, those guilty of ecclesiastical offenses are instructed to make amends for any damage done by their actions, perform what amounts to community service on behalf of those wronged, and other such actions. In this wise, Scientology justice helps an individual apply ethics to himself and his activities and move up the conditions.

Scientology justice protects the group from the destructive actions of individuals as well. A person who refuses to act ethically and who commits crimes against the group in general may be brought before a justice action in an effort to straighten him out. Depending on the severity of his offenses, a Committee of Evidence may recommend suitable restitution and penalties, taking into consideration any mitigating circumstances. The most extreme penalty that can be leveled at a person is expulsion from the Church. This can occur when blatant actions intended to destroy Scientology or Scientologists are committed, or when the person has clearly proven that he is no longer in agreement with and is actively opposing the Church's goals. Such a person has demonstrated that he opposes what Scientology stands for. By publicly announcing the person's expulsion, Scientologists in good standing are alerted and can avoid being harmed by him until such time as his actions are more in accord with the group.

No further action is taken by the Church or its members as justice has been done by expelling the individual from the group. The exclusion from Scientology is the harshest judgment faced by any Scientologist for it effectively bars any further progress on the Bridge. Once expelled, the person must go his own way and sort out his life without further communication, assistance or guidance from the Church, which is extremely busy giving its help to those who honestly desire it. The expelled individual is no longer a part of Scientology and its benefits are not his to enjoy, including access to Scientology justice procedures, no matter what difficulties he encounters.

With any justice action, even expulsion from the Church, if the individual concerned does not feel justice has been done, he has avenues of recourse to determine the facts and correct matters, if needed. Because Scientology justice is predicated solely on establishing truth, the honest individual is secure in the knowledge that he will receive fair treatment.

The Scientology justice codes align with the mores and legal codes of the society. Acts considered criminal by society are considered criminal by the Church and Scientologists. Scientologists do not tolerate illegal activities of any sort. Experience has taught that those who seriously violate the laws of the land are incapable of maintaining the ethical standards required to accomplish spiritual advancement.

Scientology justice is a new system, one which serves the individual and the group equally well. Its procedures are valuable to Scientologists as they offer a system where disputes can be resolved, truth is made known and increased survival occurs.

The book *Introduction to Scientology Ethics* contains the full scope of Scientology ethics technology and the Scientology justice system in clearly laid-out terms.

ETHICS, JUSTICE AND MANKIND

Scientology ethics, explained L. Ron Hubbard, are reason. They provide the means by which men conduct themselves toward their long-term survival, the survival of their families, their groups, their planet and more. Implicit within the subject is the recognition that all things are, to one degree or another, interdependent upon all else and that only by constantly considering the survival of the many can the individual ensure his own survival.

With this thinking firmly in mind the Scientologist obeys the law, remains faithful to his spouse, truthful in his business dealings and otherwise conducts himself in accordance with honesty, integrity and decency.

Scientologists understand that rules and laws form the agreements by which a group, society or nation survives, and that high ethical standards, far from inhibiting the enjoyment of life, foster it.

Yet what of the rest of the world?

For want of a workable system of ethics and justice, whole civilizations have gone to ruin, whole forests have been laid to waste and whole sections of our cities have been reduced to racial battlegrounds. Simultaneously, we have witnessed the steady disintegration of the family, a general decay of sexual values, escalating drug abuse, theft, assault and on and on until it seems there is no hope at all—except this: The Scientologist must also live in this society, and he truly does possess the tools to make a difference.

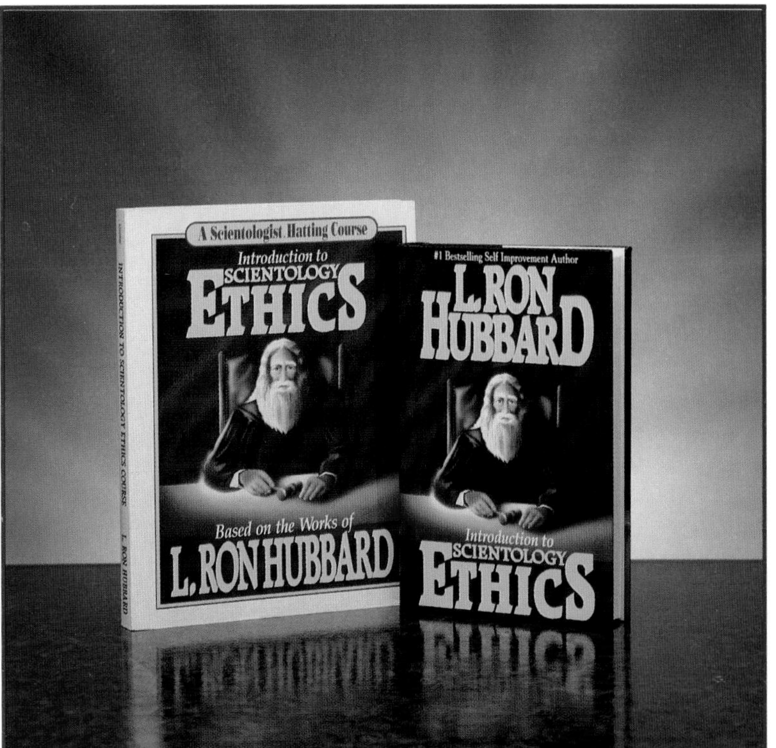

*The **Introduction to Scientology Ethics** book and course provide one with a full understanding of Scientology ethics and justice technology.*

Part Four

The Effectiveness of Scientology

Millions of applications over the course of several decades show Dianetics and Scientology to be workable beyond any methods man ever had before. The point cannot be stressed enough: Answers have been found to the problems of life. They exist in Scientology and people discover this fact for themselves every day.

At a time where many unworkable "solutions" are offered, disappointment can blind people to something which really does work. The effective results of Dianetics and Scientology, then, warrant some comment. The next chapter has been written by individual Scientologists, for their statements are the best testament to its workability.

There is a pathway to full spiritual awareness and an understanding of life. It is clearly mapped and has been traveled with great success by many. The recommended course of progress up this bridge to freedom is described in this part.

Even when progress in Scientology seems balked or when difficulties arise, there are solutions which enable advancement to continue. L. Ron Hubbard isolated reasons for *any* apparent failures in application and thoroughly codified technologies to resolve these, making Scientology, as is covered in Chapter 19, a subject capable of correcting itself. Scientology is an activity where, ultimately, everyone wins.

CHAPTER 17

SUCCESSES OF SCIENTOLOGY

If one honestly avails himself of the technology and sincerely applies himself to gain the benefits offered, there are apparently no limits to what can be achieved.

This chapter is devoted to the stories of individual Scientologists and tells of the gains and results they have experienced. It is in these that the worth of Scientology finds its truest expression.

The opinions of experts or the pronouncements of authorities bear little importance. It is by each individual's reckoning whether or not he arrives at a better place.

People who have benefited come from all over the globe and from all walks of life. L. Ron Hubbard's technology knows no economic, ethnic, racial, political or religious barriers. Wisdom is for any man who chooses to reach for it.

Literally millions of stories are on file in churches and missions in all parts of the world. These are not the stories of the privileged or select. They are the successes of everyday people who were looking for answers and who were bright enough to know when the answers had been found.

The following should not be construed as claims made by the Church concerning personal benefits any individual will experience. The Church provides the services. The results speak for themselves.

The main thing that has really impressed me about Scientology is that there is the most brilliant tech for anything and everything in your life. I've become a more powerful individual with increased abilities. I never even conceived that I could experience these kinds of gains prior to Scientology.

There is a way to handle every part of life with Scientology, and a way to exist that is far beyond any dream that you could ever dream. All of my dreams keep becoming realities and that's very exciting!

Through Scientology, things happen a lot quicker. What used to take weeks or months sometimes happens in days or even minutes!

Life is at my fingertips and with Scientology I've found I can have or be whatever I want.

Kelly Preston
Actress

In January of 1975 I was working on my first film in Durango, Mexico. There I met an actress who gave me the book ***Dianetics.*** *During the five weeks we were filming she gave me some auditing sessions and applied some basic principles. That was when I became involved in Dianetics—because it worked. When I returned to the United States I began Scientology training and auditing. My career immediately took off and I landed a lead role on the TV show "Welcome Back Kotter" and had a string of successful films. I have been a successful actor for 17 years and Scientology has played a major role in that success.*

I have a wonderful child and a great marriage because I apply L. Ron Hubbard's technology to this area of my life.

As a Scientologist I have the technology to handle life's problems and I have used this to help others in life as well.

I would say that Scientology put me into the big time.

John Travolta
Actor

The single greatest thing that studying Scientology has done for me is that it's helped me become freer. Freer to create life as I want to, without being thrown off from my objectives. One of the first simple successes was that I learned to handle and remove my own self-imposed barriers and restraints. Through further study, my ability to handle life around me also increased. This freedom has been hard won, but the rewards are great.

My study of Scientology has also enabled me to write more music. I have become quicker and am able to use all of the musical abilities that I already have. I gained a new understanding of what the proper importances are in the process of creating music.

Scientology has helped me to live better. Using the basic principles of Scientology has become a natural way of life for me. From Scientology I've gotten a freedom to learn whatever I want to learn in life and I'm gaining new abilities all the time.

Chick Corea
Eight-Time Grammy Award Winning Jazz Musician & Composer

I sought out other solutions, I tried other philosophies and never found one that really indicated the truth to me.

Scientology presented precepts to me that really made me feel like I had found, at last, the guidelines that I had been searching for.

Before Scientology I had one dream of making a living, doing voice-overs for animation. After I became a Scientologist my abilities have expanded so far and above what I originally dreamed for myself that I've amazed even myself at my enormous increase of abilities.

I've gotten an Emmy, a platinum and a gold album. I've written and starred in a one-woman show and I have a bright future as a producer.

*I've got two beautiful children, an incredibly supportive husband, a staff working with me for the same products, future dreams and goals and **all** of this is because I became a Scientologist.*

Nancy Cartwright
Actress/Writer/Producer & Voice of Bart Simpson

Scientology makes people free, sane and able. It makes it possible to be more oneself, with the ability to create and change anything being a natural and expected phenomenon. It puts you at cause over your life and makes it easy for you to take responsibility not only for your own life, but for the world.

Scientology is sanity and if people who aren't in Scientology knew just how sane their lives could be, they would run to find out about it.

Anne Archer
Actress

Scientology has enabled me to see clearly what my goals in life are. Before I became a Scientologist I was a professional race car driver but quit. I got involved with Dianetics and Scientology and through my studies and auditing I was able to rekindle my purpose in life and return to my profession. My capabilities increased and I became more certain. As a result, I won the 24 hours of Le Mans. Without Scientology I would never have accomplished this nor found the happiness I now have in life.

Philippe de Henning
Champion Racer & Winner
of the 1987 Le Mans

I have been in Scientology for over 21 years. In those years I have worked hard to make my dreams a reality. Very few dreams have escaped me and I am extremely thankful now for my successes both professionally and personally. The role Scientology has played in my life has been vital. Without it I simply cannot imagine where I would be right now. It has been the source of answers and resolution for every conceivable problem, upset, fear and obstacle life has thrown at me. I have found amazingly that the answers were simple yet totally effective, the resolutions easy and completely workable. Life is not easy. Sometimes life is cruel—even vicious—I've been there, I've felt it. But I've also felt hatred, anger, upset and pain lift off of me and go away forever with Scientology auditing. I've seen the worst possible dilemmas evaporate with the application of Scientology technology—just like magic. But it's not magic—it's Scientology. Easy to understand and apply by anybody, anywhere, anytime. Scientology works.

Billy Sheehan
Internationally Renowned
Rock Bassist

Scientology not only revitalized me as an artist, it revitalized me as a person. I had given up on singing and on life before Scientology—and this was after a long, successful singing career of 23 years. You have to realize how far gone I was. I didn't think there was any hope and all my dreams were gone.
The difference in the quality of my life before and after Scientology is quite simply day and night. So many friends tell me that I look ten years younger than I am! Perhaps even more important is that I feel the way I used to in my early 20s. Every person deserves the chance to feel the renewal of life, energy, power and hope.

Maxine Nightingale
Vocalist

Scientology changed my life because it gave me a direction, it gave me something that I believe in and it gave me truth.
As an artist I have been knocked down I don't know how many times and each time by applying basic principles of Scientology I have been able to bounce back stronger than before.
In a world where nuclear war threatens annihilation and where the Earth's natural resources are being destroyed to a point where no one can live on it, I am proud to be a Scientologist and learn the data about happiness, about life and about responsibility.
I thank L. Ron Hubbard for everything he has done for me and for mankind.

Julia Migenes
Opera Star

After Vietnam I was floundering. The technology of Dianetics and Scientology revitalized my life. I was searching for answers to life and found them. The tools I got from Scientology ethics and administrative technology boosted me to the top of my profession. All of these tools have expanded my awareness and abilities to the point where I can make a difference.

Bill Moon
Research Analyst

I started in Scientology in 1977 and soon realized the data contained in Scientology would make a huge difference in my life. All the courses and auditing have been extraordinarily enlightening and valuable. My wife and I use Scientology to create a wonderful marriage. In fact, I'm sure there's not a day that I don't apply what I've learned in Scientology dozens (and probably hundreds) of times in a variety of ways.

Scientology is such a key part of my life today that it really constitutes an approach to living that is optimum for me as an individual, as a member of a family, as a member of the groups I belong to, and as a citizen of the world.

Scientology founder L. Ron Hubbard was a great man. We should all be thankful for the insights and knowledge he made available for all people.

Terry Jastrow
Seven-time Emmy Award–winning Producer/Director
ABC Sports

I came to America 9 years ago when I was 23 years old. I barely spoke English and couldn't write or read English at all. But I had a dream to make it in this free land. I had no idea how I was going to do that. I was alone here, no friends, my life was just crazy.

Five years ago, I started my first Scientology service. From that point on, my life has improved.

I have become a lady full of confidence. I am now engaged to a wonderful man and I own my own company which is expanding and doing very well. I have learned to read and write English. All of these wins and gains I attribute to Scientology.

Hellen Chen
Business Executive

When I was first introduced to Scientology, I was doing well in life but I knew there was more. I wanted to know what made people tick and how one could improve his own condition. Now I have the answers to those questions and more. They are contained in the vast wealth of knowledge of Scientology.

Billy Evans
Publisher

As a child I had everything—wonderful parents, a beautiful home, a terrific life. Then my parents moved when I was a teenager and I snapped. We quit communicating and I spent years rebelling against them. We were so out of touch by 1969 it was unbelievable. I was on a quest to find out why I felt the way I did. In 1969 I read the book ***Dianetics*** *by L. Ron Hubbard and that day my life changed. I started the Communications Course and immediately understood how to solve the problem with my parents. I went from a rebellious individual trying to hurt my parents to a very happy person. I am now in* ***terrific*** *communication with my parents. I have handled the problems that held me down so I don't have to pass them on to my son. I am successful at whatever I do and I find life just gets better and better.*

Tory Bezazian
Mother

Scientology has greatly increased my abilities to understand myself and others. The auditing procedures have far exceeded any of my expectations. The difference it has made in my life is so remarkable that I could say life was like trying to walk in a pool of quicksand before Scientology.

I think so much more clearly. Problems are easily solved now after the training and auditing I have had.

I've been in Scientology since 1986. I just wish I had found it sooner because it would have made my life so much easier.

Ward Cole
Dentist

As a kid growing up I was very shy, withdrawn, afraid of people and generally unhappy. All these uncomfortable feelings were still there during high school and later in college. The most I could hope for was to make each day as bearable as I could, yet I felt life should be happier.

These ill feelings weren't going to go away all by themselves. I was going to have to DO something about them and what I did was Scientology.

I enrolled on a Scientology communication course and to my surprise and delight my shyness started to disappear and my fear was less and one by one all these uncomfortable feelings started to go away. It was like shedding a skin. And what I found underneath all of this was ME! The more I used what I learned in Scientology the more ME I became. Scientology really works! I became more outgoing, more confident, honest and ethical. I found my integrity. I liked people a lot more, and life became FUN, just like I always thought it should be.

Michael Manoogian
Logo Designer

I found out about Scientology through a newspaper in Tokyo. I was a very unstable person before Scientology. For example, when I set out to do something, the opinions or influence of others used to have an effect of swaying me off what I was aiming for. I eventually felt I could not trust others, and lost my self-confidence.

However, through Scientology I've now found out why and learning this new knowledge gave me back my confidence. I'm working as a translator now, and feel able to do anything I set out to do.

Yoko Suzuki
Japanese Translator

Scientology has had a major impact upon both my personal life and my artistic life. It has contributed tremendously to the survival and expansion of both.

As an artist I have had difficulties that were very hard to confront—phenomena such as "stage fright" or "the blank page when writing that first line." The "solutions" to these and other problems, in the form of drugs and alcohol, had plagued me for a long time.

Scientology supplies a technology that assisted me in confronting and handling such situations **very** *effectively. My ability to create impact as an artist has increased tremendously due to Scientology auditing and training.*

Marital and familial relationships had long been an unstable area for me. Scientology handled this area of my life and has given me the ability to create a very sane and healthy family and the best possible environment in which to bring up my children.

Applying Scientology technology, for me, has been the smartest decision I could have possibly made toward the betterment of my life and the lives of those around me.

Mark Isham
Grammy Award–winning Musician/Composer

Before Scientology I was extremely shy. I had a big problem even beginning a conversation with someone. I had a lot of trouble making new friends and I was generally an introverted person.

Scientology completely handled this. I have lost my fear of communicating and I found I could talk to people and make friends easily.

I am able to work out problems until all parties are happy. Scientology has made parenting really fun. My daughter grew up in Scientology, she is able to communicate, stays away from drugs and other teen insanities and she and I have a great relationship.

Scientology has given a sense of purpose to my life.

Barbara Pease Stewart
Businesswoman

By the time I was 17 years old, I was doing a lot of drugs and was going downhill fast. I had dropped out of high school and left my chances of a good education and successful life behind. I had no real hope or desire to succeed in life. I did L. Ron Hubbard's Purification program and my life was literally saved. I continued in my trade and did volunteer work helping others get off drugs. At the age of 21 I went into business on my own. I now had a strong need for skills at handling life. I turned to Scientology and again found my answers. If not for Scientology technology I am certain I would not be alive today. It truly is a miracle that now, at the age of 31, I own real estate and a million-dollar-a-year business. I am a successful businessman, I have a great marriage and I am happier than ever. I am really winning in life.

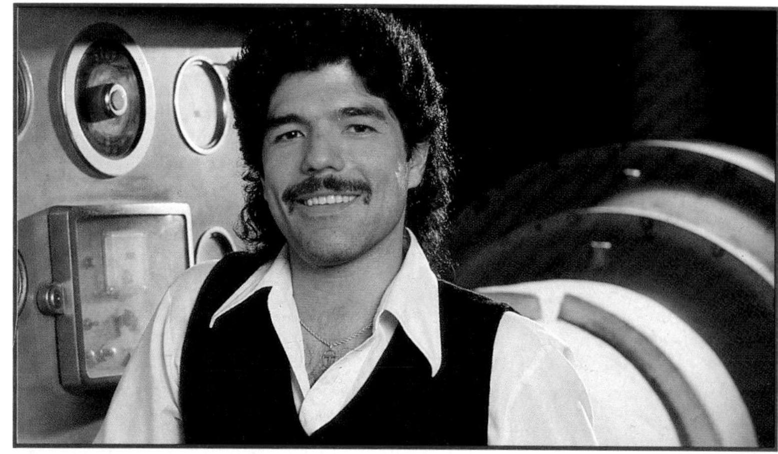

Robert Hernandez
Air Conditioning Business Owner

Before Scientology I never felt confident in my abilities at work, I was introverted and my drive to succeed was getting weaker by the day. With Scientology I've been able to turn this all around. Scientology has increased my ability to handle all areas of my life. I now have a great husband who I love more and more each day and I also have a fantastic career. It is actually hard to think what life would be like without Scientology.

Stephanie Rose
Radio Broadcaster

Scientology counseling has expanded my reach for my family, my friends and mankind. I really want to help them survive. I find I have very little attention on myself personally as I have personal fulfillment, leaving time for involvement in my children's schooling and community activities. I now have a high personal esteem for my friends and family.

Barbara Levine
Housewife

I was a fire fighter in the LA City Fire Service for 26 years. I felt I was failing because I was losing ground in the course of life. In 1977 I read in L. Ron Hubbard's ***Dianetics*** *about how the reactive mind robs one of his self-determinism, and about the state of Clear. I had to find out for myself. Later, after my Scientology studies, my life turned around. It improved my performance as a fireman and vastly lessened the fear of a job filled with fear.*

Pete Andreasen
Fireman

I have studied, for some 20 years now, the various technologies that exist in Scientology. I have firsthand knowledge and experience of the workability of this subject in assisting an individual to dramatically enhance the quality of his life. I can honestly say that I know who I am and that I am much more capable of controlling life (as opposed to life washing me downriver and into the ocean). I am happy. I am successful.

Bill Johonnesson
Management Specialist

Before Scientology I had no real purpose. I didn't know what I was going to do next week, let alone with my life. I was very unhappy. My sister started telling me about all these amazing and wonderful things that were happening in her life and I wanted to experience these things myself. I went to the Church of Scientology and started the Success Through Communication Course and it was unbelievable. But it didn't end there. I did the Basic Study Manual course. I couldn't believe someone could actually learn how to study. Since then I have done many courses and read several books and apply the things I've learned in life. I thank L. Ron Hubbard for his technology for now I am truly happy.

Paul Girard
Printer

I found that embarking on a career in art had its drawbacks. Drugs seem to be everywhere in the art world. The myth that "artists need to be crazy to be creative" is rampant. It is no wonder that many artists have failed, given up their hopes and are no longer creating. When I discovered Scientology, I learned that you can overcome the critics and the drugs. And the myth? Well, that's all it is—a myth. A sane artist has a much better chance at succeeding and surviving as an artist. Scientology has given me the knowledge, ability and strength to maintain my sanity even when the world gets crazy.

Bobbie Kitchens
Artist

Scientology helped me as a former Vietnam combat pilot and later as an experimental test pilot, to conquer alcohol abuse which came from my involvement with the Vietnam conflict. I have given numerous interviews around the country on the subject of the Gulf War and its relationship to the Vietnam conflict. Before Scientology I was afraid of talking in front of groups of people. Now I no longer fear getting up and speaking to others. I am much happier now.

Glen Barton
Pilot

At thirty-five years old, I was not happy and wasn't getting what I wanted from life. I felt if I waited it out or tried harder, things would change. As each failure came my way, whether it be in relationships or career, my world just seemed to get a little smaller. I wondered why the fearlessness and enthusiasm I once had was gone. I did not have the ability to change things so passed time waiting for fleeting moments of happiness. I got interested in Scientology and found that something could be done. I found there is hope and made successes out of my failed purposes and goals. Due to Scientology I have a great marriage, my life is better and I'm able to win again.

Janice Sturgiss
Mother

Scientology has made it possible for me to change my life and the lives of others. It provided me with tools that I could apply to realize my potential. Not long after I became a Scientologist I got my role as Mary Ellen on the TV show "The Waltons." Through what I have learned in Scientology I am able to confront and handle difficult situations without relying on other people for solutions. I apply what I've learned to other people and have had a positive effect on their lives as well. Scientology has made me much happier.

Judy Norton
Actress/Singer

I got into Scientology when I was fifteen and at that point I was going downhill pretty fast—with school and family and just about everything. I received Scientology auditing and my life has forever changed. The drowning, "there's-no-hope" feeling has disappeared. I have become cause over more of life and I don't go the effect of others' ideas, opinions or suppression. This has allowed me to expand. I thank L. Ron Hubbard and Scientology for this new life.

David Flate
Office Manager

Four years ago I was combating depression. Now people ask me if I have always been so cheerful. It makes me think of the times that I didn't want to go on. Scientology has given me the key to knowledge and a way to solve problems so that the answers fall right into place.

With what I learned from Scientology I was able to help my mother who was taking the drug Prozac after surgery. She felt no reason to go on living although she has always been very full of life. I worked with her, using a special Scientology assist to soothe her nerves, and she responded remarkably well. Without Scientology, I would have had to just sit back and do nothing for my mother in her time of need.

Bonnie Jean Damico
Hairdresser

We really don't know how we would've kept our marriage together if it wasn't for Scientology. There is so much stress that is placed upon a marriage that it's sometimes difficult to know that you are making the correct decisions. Through Scientology we look forward to each and every day as an adventure, instead of just "getting by." L. Ron Hubbard developed a great deal of technology that has enabled us to face the challenges brought on by day-to-day living. It's really helping our marriage ***work.***

Mr. and Mrs. Sutton
Writers, Illustrators & Publishers of Children's Books

My life is infinitely better since my first introduction to Scientology. Before Scientology, I was on an emotional "roller coaster." Anytime I'd win at something or gain a moment of happiness, if it was on a Tuesday, you could predict that by Wednesday I'd be down in the dumps again. This "up and down and up and down" was such a point of upset and hopelessness for me that I finally resigned myself to the fact that this was something I was going to have to live with for the rest of my life.

In 1988, as a result of Scientology auditing, this phenomenon ceased for all time. I was shocked. I couldn't believe it. I was no longer on the "helpless" receiving end of life. I am resilient, strong, more self-assured and, most importantly, more able to handle what I encounter.

Physical aches and pains I'd associated with writing my songs have vanished. On stage, I feel much more creative and I am enjoying myself more up there.

My awareness of, interest in and love for other people has risen markedly and the more I study Scientology, the more I feel like I'm coming out of a long, deep sleep. What a relief!

Thank you, L. Ron Hubbard, for this chance to live the full-blown "Technicolor" life I've always dreamed of.

David Pomeranz
Songwriter/Recording Artist

Scientology gave me and my family a new life. It enabled my kids to survive "teenage madness." Scientology has helped me do a good job of making my marriage survive—I have a really strong relationship with my wife. It has enabled me to understand people so I can cooperate with others. I have increased my ability to help others just by talking and listening to them.

Joe Duncanson
Electrician

The first thing that struck me about Scientology is that it made sense. I could think with the data. The second was that it actually WORKED and that is why I became a Scientologist. I've been a Scientologist for over 20 years and I'm still awed daily by the things I've learned through Scientology. Not only did my dreams come true but along the way the quality of my life became rich, filled with decency and integrity. Scientology is simply the finest thing I have encountered in my entire existence. Today I have a magnificent wife, four incredible children and I wake up each morning knowing that I am contributing to the betterment of my family, society and the world around me. Scientology has made it possible for me to lead a full and productive life.

Jeff Pomerantz
Actor and Founder of Hollywood Says No to Drugs

By the time I got into my late thirties, my life was a mess. Not only did I have a serious problem with alcohol and drugs but I also had been divorced twice. Although I wanted to change things in my life, no matter how hard I tried, nothing worked. Then I found out about Scientology. My life changed. Now I have a wonderful wife and marriage of 14 years, I have great kids and they are doing well. I am happy.

John Taufer
Building Contractor

I have been involved in Scientology for 12½ years. Earlier as a student I had felt inadequate in my studies. In Scientology I found out that I had missed basic steps in my education and I was able to resolve my study problems and go on to fulfill my goals to work with children. Now I am a teacher and I use that same technology with my students. Once they learn how to study and apply what they have learned, they have been able to come up 2–3 grades in 8 months. The students are bright, confident and proud of their achievements. It has been a great joy and privilege to share L. Ron Hubbard's study technology with my students.

Carol Loweree
Teacher

Man, I was a mess after getting out of college. Drugs, fear, alienation, stagnation; these were the makeup of my existence. By applying Scientology to myself and my environment I was able to pull myself up by the bootstraps. Today I'm married to a wonderful lady who recently gave birth to our first child, Molly, and she is the greatest. I have a new life and love it. I look forward to living it each and every day. Scientology is all about improving and living life with enthusiasm.

Bob Sullivan
Fisherman

I think the most essential thing for an artist, in order to develop and mature, is to get information that he or she can use in terms of communication skills and in terms of affinity and reality with people. The Tone Scale is invaluable wisdom for any artist. I think Scientology is essential. It's been the most practical tool for me to have. I love being a Scientologist. I'm proud to have parents and grandparents who are Scientologists. I love being an individual and expressing myself and Scientology has enabled me to do that.

Kate Ceberano
Australia's Top Female Vocalist

Before I found Scientology I was a stressed-out executive who was running on tranquilizers and martinis to get through the day. I had ulcers and back problems, and I felt I would burn out before I was forty. I was out of communication with my family and my business associates. Scientology helped me to discover who I really am, which enabled me to pursue my goals in life. I no longer require drugs or alcohol to remain stress free and my body problems have ceased. As the result of Scientology training and counseling I now have a happy marriage, my own successful interior design firm and I have become an accomplished public speaker. Scientology works because it has the technology to change the conditions in life.

Lee Cambigue
Business Executive

Scientology training has changed my life and made me able to function more at cause because I am now able to know that what I am doing is right.

Linda Tucker
Office Manager

With Scientology, I've gained an enormous understanding and love for life and my perceptions have increased. As an artist, that's priceless. My business has skyrocketed and the demand for my work keeps increasing. Scientology gave me the realization of my unlimited potential and the ability to achieve any goal I set for myself. For this I am forever grateful.

James T. Sorensen
Photographer

I have been a Scientologist since 1970, and I have not been the same since the first day I entered the Detroit organization.
I knew at once that Scientology was what I had been looking for all of my life.
It is difficult for me to imagine what I was like before I became a Scientologist as it was akin to being totally blind. I am no longer entangled in the confusion of what most people consider daily life.
Using Scientology has definitely enhanced my well-being and creates a safer environment for those I come into contact with.
My ability to confront life, handle situations and to take responsibility for myself and others has markedly improved. I can honestly say without the merest shadow of a doubt that had it not been for L. Ron Hubbard and Scientology I would not be as happy nor as successful as I am today.

John W. Frencher
Businessman

If anyone had told me years ago that I would be where I am today I would not have believed them, but here I am! I have an absolutely wonderful marriage. My husband and I have a growing and happy relationship. We can talk to our children about anything and they know they can talk to us. This fact alone is the most valuable thing about Scientology—it helps people get into real communication. Even my parents who are not Scientologists tell me the world would be a wonderful place if all children were as active, helpful and honest as ours are.

Dorda McDaniel
Store Owner

*I went with a friend to the church of Scientology. I didn't believe them, I didn't trust them. I knew nobody could do what they had told me. But I made a deal with the person I saw. "I will read your book [**Dianetics**]. If I like it, I will be back." That was spring, 1975. Over the years Scientology and Dianetics has not failed to work when applied. I see it work every day!*

Roy Brock
Roofer

I began taking drugs when I was 14 years old. By the time I was 17 years old I had become an addict. I tried several programs to handle my addiction and none of them worked.
In 1973 I went to Narconon LA. There, using L. Ron Hubbard's drug rehabilitation technology I was able to successfully come off of drugs. After graduating the Narconon program, I read ***Dianetics****, became a trained auditor and received auditing myself. My insecurities, fears and losses in life were handled with Scientology auditing. I can honestly say Scientology saved my life. Today I run a very successful Narconon drug rehabilitation center. I have 3 teenagers that I have raised successfully and most of all I have my life back. I would strongly suggest that anyone out there who is looking for a better life pick up a* ***Dianetics*** *book and read it. It will change your life forever!*

Jeannie Trahant
Program Director,
Narconon Los Angeles

Before I became a Scientologist, I was hopeless. I came to realize that my life had no real meaning even though I was "doing well." Then I found Scientology. I discovered why I felt so hopeless. I found that I actually had a purpose for life! I met my wife then and we were married. My career boomed. My income shot up 300 percent in less than two years! Now it's been 15 years and I'm doing really well. I enjoy my two wonderful children, and I enjoy my work immensely. Things have come a long way since those hopeless years—thanks to Scientology.

Ed Beckman
Computer Consultant

Twelve years ago, I was successful in the business world but my life was really a mess. I was married to a banker hooked on drugs and had no strength to face the future.
With Scientology, I now live a wonderful life and I truly enjoy what life has to offer. I am in control of my own life now and, best of all, I can help others live better and happier lives, thanks to Scientology.

Lily Guerrero
Sales Manager

Being a professional driver dealing with the public and their need to be across town NOW used to be stressful for me. Before Scientology I had no idea about being in control of my vehicle and therefore had my fair share of accidents. After each shift I would be wiped out. Now, I handle my car with certainty and do the impossible as far as my clients are concerned. I'm rarely stressed and when my shift is over I still have plenty of energy to play with my 9-month-old son. Not bad for an old coot of 50, eh?

Henry Baumgard
Taxi Driver

A friend of mine had a copy of ***Dianetics*** *on her bookshelf and I had seen it advertised on TV. So I bought the book and started to read it. I came to a part that really made sense to me so I wanted to get some auditing. I called the 1-800 number in the back of the book and was referred to a church of Scientology. My life hasn't been the same since. After a short time I had gotten rid of the need for alcohol and drugs and to this day I haven't felt the need to go back to them.*

Peter Finnegan
Technician

In my career Scientology is the thing that has made it possible to be in show biz for 21 years. I love the people and I love the work. Scientology has helped me to handle the everyday problems of life, handle confusions and keep my goals focused. It has made my life fulfilling as an actor, father and American citizen and has made it possible for me to fulfill my own American Dream. Being a Scientologist has clarified knowing what freedom really is.

Michael D. Roberts
Actor

Before Scientology, I was using street drugs. It was destroying my life. With Scientology, I have not taken drugs for twenty years. Through the Scientology courses that I have taken, I lead a happy and successful life with a great marriage and two incredible kids. I don't honestly think that I would be alive today had it not been for Scientology and the technology that it has for handling people with drug problems. My life is on the right road now—thanks to Scientology.

Art Stein
Real Estate Manager

I came to the United States from Mauritius in 1978. I found out about Scientology and it assisted me in making an easier and more comfortable transition to a new, different country. I learned how to really communicate to others and with L. Ron Hubbard's study technology my command of the English language increased 100 percent.

Françoise Hooks
Legal Secretary

Scientology has been a tremendous asset for my brothers and I as individuals, as a family and in our highly successful firm. The breadth of knowledge available from the subject is hard to conceive. Most notable is the ability to communicate on any subject. That, coupled with L. Ron Hubbard's enormous insights into the mind of man, and the study and administrative technology he has developed, gives one a huge leg up on any endeavor. Being happy with oneself, one's family, one's business activities and life generally is a fantastic accomplishment and the knowledge that one can improve from there still, is incredible; yet we have found it truly achievable with Scientology.

Matt Feshbach
Feshbach Brothers
Investment Managers

Since becoming a Scientologist I feel very stable and a lot happier than I did before. My understanding of this world was almost nonexistent before Scientology. Now life isn't a mystery to me anymore. I'm not afraid or worried about my past, present or future. I'm now able to handle difficult situations with Scientology technology. I continue to maintain a happy marriage and good relationships with my friends and family. I can't imagine life without Scientology.

Gigi Boratgis
Piano Teacher

One of the principles of Scientology is "if one knows the technology of something he cannot be the adverse effect of it." In Scientology there is a wealth of know-how on life. I have achieved many goals using the technologies of L. Ron Hubbard. One of the things I have gained through Scientology is to set a target for goals that I want to achieve and then push them through to attainment.

Craig Hooks
Carpet Salesman

From 1972 through 1980, my business merely plodded along. In 1981, I was introduced to L. Ron Hubbard's technology which I quickly applied to my business. In a short period of time, I became the nationally recognized leader of the upscale car detailing industry. I was featured in a number of national news media including ABC, NBC and CBS national news. Scientology works for me—not only in business but in my marriage as well.

Steve Marchese
Automotive Detailer

Before I was a Scientologist, I was unsure of myself and nervous and shy dealing with men. I got confused and annoyed easily if things did not go my way. Now, after 18 years of being a Scientologist, I cannot believe that I am the same person. I feel so calm. I am self-assured. It's a great feeling.

Carmen Suarez
Manager

I didn't know how bad my life was until I did my very first course, a communications course. Since that time I've been able to apply Scientology to every part of my life. I'm co-founder and executive director of The School of the Natural Voice here in Los Angeles. I have hundreds of singers come to me for voice lessons. Most of my time is spent applying the simplest Scientology technology to their lives, just to help them gain confidence in themselves and their ability. My own singing career has flourished through the use of Scientology. I apply the administrative technology to my business and it's helped me build a business I never knew I had the potential to do. It's one thing for me to sit here and spout off about how great Scientology is and have someone else read what I'm saying and say, "Oh yeah, well you're just saying those things because someone asked you to." All I can say is take ONE PIECE OF DATA and apply it to a part of your life standardly and see what happens. I'm amazed at how it works exactly the way it's supposed to work every time.

Gloria Rusch-Novello
Singer/Writer/Actress

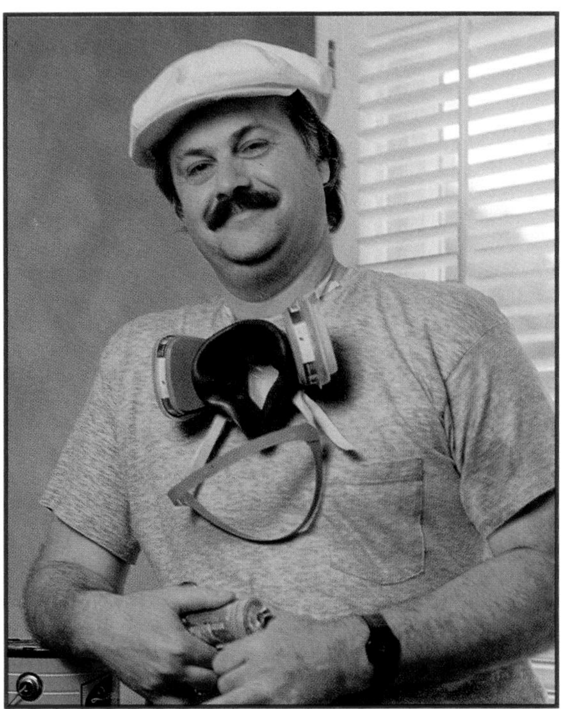

*Scientology has helped me bring up a teenage boy in a troubled world. We are the best of friends. With Scientology and the precepts of **The Way to Happiness** by L. Ron Hubbard, I have gotten through the rough years.*

Bob Cook
Painter

Before Scientology I knew that I wanted to have a good marriage, happy family and to be successful in life, but it seemed that I kept running into closed doors which I could not open. I got into Scientology in 1972 and knew that I had found a way to achieve my childhood goals and dreams.
Scientology gave me the tools I needed and the understanding which I so lacked, and what was even more important: a way to apply this knowledge to better my life. As I improved and became more capable, it had a definite effect on others as well.
Scientology literally saved my life. I look back on the course of destruction I was on, and had it not been for Mr. Hubbard's technology, I would not have been able to achieve what I have today, a happy family and marriage and success in what I do helping others make their lives more worthwhile.

Jane Allen
National Spokesperson
Citizens Commission on Human Rights

I was 37 years old when I first learned about Scientology. I figured I was doing about average for my peer group: My second marriage was in trouble; my business was heading out of control; I was drinking heavily and taking cocaine two to three nights a week on a gradually increasing basis. Now, nine years later, my marriage is happily intact, my business is stably expanding, I take no drugs, have only an occasional beer or glass of wine and I've never been happier, healthier or more prosperous in my life. I can see now what I only dimly suspected back then—that my life was headed down a long, dark chute to nowhere. Only one thing altered that course for me: the truth and wisdom contained in the teachings of L. Ron Hubbard.

Terry Johnston
Farmer

One of the best things that I have gotten from Scientology is a future—a real future. I had what I considered was a good job, but I wasn't going anywhere that interested me. I knew there was something missing in my life. Now I have no doubt about who I am or about the direction I am going. Without Scientology this just would not have happened. My activities are directed now and the goals I made much, much earlier in my life are now defined and real. I recommend Scientology to anyone who wants to put direction into their life and set their goals straight.

Gary Nordfors
Carpenter

I have had the most wonderful experiences using L. Ron Hubbard's writings on education and art to help others develop musical skills and talents. The information I learned in Scientology about art has allowed me to pursue my own expressions amid the confusion of "authorities" and conflicting data one often finds in art.

Carole Blum
Music Teacher

Scientology auditing gives you the ability to be as great as you can be. And it takes the stops off the things that prevent you from succeeding.

Floyd Mutrux
Writer/Director/Producer

Life is much simpler and fun as a Scientologist. Before, I was reeling from a marriage which ended sadly in divorce. I didn't understand the opposite sex. My personal life was practically nonexistent. Constant headaches were handled by taking 8–12 aspirin daily. Employees were often hard to understand and difficult to manage.

When I learned about Scientology and started applying it in my life, here's what happened: I started having fun in life again.

Today I have a lovely wife and five great children.

I successfully made a career change from retail consumer electronics to commercial printing and successfully brought it about. Today, I'm President, CEO and sole shareholder of a multi-million-dollar printing plant in southern California.

Employees are easy to understand and a joy to work with.

Oh, and the headaches? Haven't had one in years, nor even a cold for that matter! Aspirin and drugs are a thing of the past. Scientology has had a tremendous effect on my life, my family, friends and associates. I recommend it to anyone that wants to have a happy and successful life.

Geoffrey Pick
Printing Company Owner

Before I found out about Scientology I had no purpose. I worked as a parole officer and because I had very few successes the vast majority of the parolees failed and were reincarcerated. I tended to consider myself a failure.

Since entering Scientology my life has been turned around. My energy level is much better and my outlook on life is very positive.

Rod Randall
Retired Parole Officer

Before I was introduced to Scientology, I was moving about in life uncertain of how to create stable success for myself as an artist, in my marriage and for others around me. I just left it to hard work and luck. I now have confidence that I can tackle any venture in life and be able to make it work for the benefit of myself and others around me. This confidence comes from the clarity and workability of a lifetime of research and hard work by L. Ron Hubbard. I am deeply indebted to him.

Pat Frey
Florist

Well, I didn't have an occupation. At the time, my idea toward life was to see how little I could do and basically how much and how many kinds of drugs I could take. I wasn't doing anything with my life. When I got into Scientology a lot changed right away. For the first time ever, I saw that there was hope and that was very encouraging. When I received Scientology counseling to handle my drug problem, my life started going up and up and up and hasn't stopped since.

Keith Code
Top Motorcycle Instructor

I had set high goals in life but was not achieving them, and was backsliding in life. Then I found Scientology and my life turned around. I now have a lot of self-confidence. If it was not for my experiences in Scientology, I would never have had the courage to start my own business.

Jeff Evans
Automotive Machinist

Scientology has had the most profound effect on the raising of our children. By knowing that each of our children are total individuals we have developed an incredible relationship. When I communicate with our children I use everything I learned in Scientology. My husband, Dr. David Singer, and I have a wonderful marriage because we have used Scientology philosophy to create it from the start. Our children, as a result, have grown up in a very safe environment because we have such a happy marriage.

Diana Venegas
Fashion Designer

Being an actress in Los Angeles, with all the stress and insecurities that the film business can put on an artist, it is very easy to get screwed up. And believe me—I was before I got into Scientology. My life was a total mess. A friend of mine told me about Scientology. I was hesitant at first, then I started reading books by L. Ron Hubbard. They were so right on, the principles so simple and true. I started learning more and more and my life started to change. My career as an actress is in the best place it's ever been. Through Scientology I truly have gained a certainty and confidence that I thought only other people could have. I would never have believed my life would be this good.

Kimberly Kates
Actress

Before Scientology, I found it difficult to communicate with others and make progress towards my goals in life. I was moody and difficult with friends, family and acquaintances. Now, by applying what I have learned through Scientology, I know how to make things go right in my life, I have a wide circle of friends and I am happy beyond any earlier expectations. L. Ron Hubbard was a man of brilliance, and more, he used the brilliance to help better the lives of others.

Doug Walker
Writer

Before Scientology I had my own company that was doing okay, but I didn't have the faintest idea how to get along with people on a professional level. I didn't know how to lead without building up animosity or how to be liked and still have control. It seemed that as a leader one had to continually assert oneself, much like a bull in the field running over a herd of cows. Very macho!
Needless to say, this approach didn't work very well.
Then I found Scientology.
I learned how to handle people effectively while still managing to keep my sense of humor. I learned how to understand people (including myself) and how to get the most out of people and also how to give. I learned how to help other people get along with others. All this has led me to a good, healthy, sane life.

Robert McFarlane
Businessman

I owe my life to Scientology—both literally and figuratively. Prior to getting involved in Scientology I was heavily dependent on drugs. I was killing myself. One day a friend told me about Scientology. It contains so much simple data that is immediately applicable in life. I gained the ability to face life and learned the power of real communication. Scientology technology helped me free myself from drugs and create a new life.

Ron Penner
Caterer

About 5½ years ago I was miserable. When things didn't go well I blamed someone else. I was always broke and relied heavily on my parents to bail me out. I was at a point where I knew I needed to change. I had read other self-help books, and I would get fired up for about a day, but that was it. Then I read ***Dianetics****. Wow! Something clicked when I was reading it and I knew that this was it. It made sense and was something that I could* ***do*** *and* ***see*** *the results of, and they stayed with me. From that moment on, my life has been getting better.*

Michael Klaumann
Photographer

Our overall success with Scientology includes terrifically increased stability and significantly fewer upsets in life. In fact, it's even hard for us to get a good fight going now. Using Scientology we make life exciting and worthwhile. It's that simple.

David and Sue Minkoff
Physicians

Before Scientology I had no real direction in life and was definitely the effect of it. I had a profession that I was pursuing (being a pilot) but I didn't have the data necessary to learn to do it.

Through studying Scientology I have learned how to communicate and to confront life head-on. I can honestly say that I am no longer the effect of my environment or my future and I'm doing exactly what I want to do in life.

Randy Hepner
Jet Pilot

The technology I learned from L. Ron Hubbard's study course has helped me so much that I wish I had it while I was in college and in professional school.

Dr. Steven Lund
Management Consultant

I used to have a fear of crowded places. Every time I'd go to the grocery store or to a movie or almost any place where there were a lot of people, I'd go into a panic; my heart would race, my hands would sweat and I would feel as though I was about to pass out. This problem was completely handled in one hour of Scientology auditing and it has never recurred. If I had gone to a psychiatrist, I am sure it would have cost tens of thousands of dollars and years of therapy and probably still would not be handled.

Dianne Cook
Bookkeeper

Scientology has changed my whole life for the better. It has given me a better understanding of myself, of others and of life. This makes life much more livable. I would never have the terrific marriage I now have without Scientology. The gains I have had in Scientology enable me to experience events without getting overwhelmed by them, making me a better problem solver and more stable. My ethical and moral standards have risen incredibly, which is a real asset. With Scientology, life is easier, simpler and more fun.

Bill Greenwald
Commercial Real Estate Broker

Four years ago I had a beat-up old pickup, my wife had left me and I had no job. It was then that I discovered Scientology and got a renewed attitude toward life. Where things were not possible for me they were now possible. My life has expanded incredibly. I now have my own contracting business, and my wife and I got back together through Scientology Marriage Counseling. We are now very happily married.

Tim Van Pelt
Plumbing Contractor

One day I realized that I was not going anywhere. I was broke and unhappy. I lost my driver's license, couldn't work and left Colorado. I moved to LA and then turned to Scientology. The results were instant. Scientology enabled me to completely turn my life around. I am now doing all the things I have ever wanted to do. I can communicate with people, something I could never do before. I can achieve anything I want. I attribute this directly to Scientology.

Jim Blythe
Window Cleaner

As a medical professional I am concerned with matters which deal with life. The knowledge about life which I have obtained from Scientology has been an incredible help to me. I have seen so many young doctors become hardened, disillusioned and lose compassion because of the suffering to which they are exposed.
Being a Scientologist and knowing Scientology has allowed me to grow in compassion and understanding and has made me more effective in helping my patients, my children and others.

Megan Shields
Physician

SUCCESSES FROM SPECIFIC SERVICES

Millions of successes are on file in churches of Scientology around the world relating benefits received from Scientology training and auditing services. Here is a representative sampling of gains Scientologists report having experienced from individual services spanning the Bridge to Total Freedom.

Introductory Books and Services

Twenty years ago, although I had a good job and had recently gotten married, I was dissatisfied with life and was seldom really happy. My day-to-day existence seemed futile and had little direction or purpose.

I suspected that there must be more to life than what I was experiencing, but it was all a mystery to me.

I picked up a book one day, entitled ***A New Slant on Life****. In this book by L. Ron Hubbard I found answers to my problems. I went to the Church of Scientology and got onto a course on communication and suddenly had some tools to change unwanted conditions.*

My life started to turn around.

Today, I own my own successful business, the expansion of which I directly attribute to the use of L. Ron Hubbard's principles. I have been happily married for over 23 years and have a teenage daughter who is also happy and doing well in life. Not only am I happier and more successful than I thought possible, but I am now involved in the Church of Scientology's community affairs programs, helping other people to get off drugs and helping to make known the harmful effects of drugs.

I am enjoying life and have never looked back!

R.T.

After reading some of L. Ron Hubbard's books in 1976 and taking a course, I found my teaching profession was more enjoyable and productive because now I could understand and therefore handle "problems" that came up.

My children in class were happier, too!

My life changed dramatically.

Old body aches and pains from an international track and field career vanished with the application of Mr. Hubbard's spiritual technology. With my new awareness and confidence, I stepped into the business world and started my own business. My life is a happy one, filled with new discoveries at every turn. I find it amazing that we are

born into this life and are not given an instruction manual on how to live it! I now have one!
I highly recommend the use of L. Ron Hubbard's technology to anyone who wishes he had a "manual" that would better life. You will find, as millions have, that true joy and happiness can be achieved.

I.P.

I wish I had found Scientology 20 years ago when I was first looking for answers to my life. I went to a lot of meetings and read a lot of books and tried a lot of different things but then I just sort of got on with my life. I happened upon ***Fundamentals of Thought*** *one day in a bookstore, stayed up all night reading it and my life has not been the same since. I immediately saw how I had a problem relating to others in many cases, and with the materials L. Ron Hubbard presented in the book I was able to improve the way I deal with other people which has made them and me a lot happier.*

M.T.

Sometimes in life achieving a goal large or small can seem very complex and possibly there are barriers to accomplishment. After having studied the entire book ***Fundamentals of Thought*** *I found I was able to simply play the game of life, knowing with certainty that things would turn out right—and that's exactly what happened! I became more able to make a clear, precise decision about something I wanted to do. And this certainly made the greatest difference in getting it done.*
I was able to improve my relationship with my husband, my parents and my son through understanding them better. My work became not just easier, but more enjoyable. I was able to enjoy being with people so much more and better deal with even difficult circumstances. Best of all, I am in a much better position to help others. So many times I've had a friend or acquaintance who I could have helped. Before, I would have been sad for them because there was nothing I could have done. But now I have solutions that work.

T.L.

Before the Success Through Communication Course I was having a rough time talking to people. I wouldn't be able to start a conversation or if I had to leave, I couldn't end one either. But then I did this course and I am now able to talk to people and get my communications across. I can also answer questions easily without being embarrassed and can make friends much more easily and just lead a happier life.

C.E.
Success Through Communication Course

I was dancing ballet and teaching in a university. I had broken a bone in my left foot and was unable really to perform anymore. I'd opted to teach instead of dance. I had had an operation to remove the bone and in fact ended up standing up through my last four months of lectures at the university due to hip pain that started just after the foot operation.

One of my university colleagues told me I should get and read a book called **Dianetics: The Modern Science of Mental Health.** *I read the book over three days practically night and day. It made so much sense to me I KNEW it must work.*

I went with a friend to the Dianetics center and received some Dianetics auditing as mentioned in the book. After the second session I was entirely well. The pain in my hip disappeared and to this day has never returned. I resumed dancing and even started performing again.

D.A.
Introductory Auditing

The course has meant regained knowledge, regained awareness, abilities, freedom to speak my mind, listen better, hear more, speak more precisely and clearly and it goes on and on. A miracle has occurred to me!

M.A.
Success Through Communication Course

I was withdrawn, extremely shy and afraid to communicate. Then I did the Success Through Communication Course. As a result, the world became brighter and people were less of a threat to me. I became happier and willing to hold a conversation with anyone. There was a feeling of control in my environment and the sensation of being very big as a spirit. It was the best feeling I had ever experienced.

N.D.
Success Through Communication Course

My son died in an accident and in the weeks that followed I was constantly thinking about the moment when my father told me about his death. During all my daily activities I appeared to be functioning properly, but that moment was constantly replaying in my thoughts. I doubt I would have been able to continue to function much longer without it really driving me crazy. After one session of introductory Dianetics auditing, six weeks after his death, that "tape" stopped playing constantly and I was able to proceed with my daily routine and obligations much more easily.

I do not believe I would have been okay without this auditing. My life would probably have completely fallen apart.

S.R.
Introductory Auditing

My success ranks with biblical references to the blind seeing, the lame walking and people being raised from the dead! What the top medical authorities in the fields of internal medicine, orthopedics, radiology and neurology could not handle in 3 years, my auditor with LRH tech handled in one afternoon! I can move my previously debilitated left arm with ease and comfort now. This morning I could not raise it from my side without terrible pain!

The spiritual cause of the problem is resolved and the problem no longer exists.

P.W.
Introductory Auditing

Purification Program

I did the Purification program shortly after getting started in Scientology. I was amazed at the changes it produced in me.

It enhanced my perceptions and as a fine artist this is invaluable. It also helped increase my speed in completing my artwork. I was far less moody and much more stable mentally than ever before. These factors allowed me to be more successful in my business relationships and with people in general. It was a great experience.

W.D.
Purification Program

As a Bachelor of Medicine, I found it very interesting to study the Purification program. I found it so interesting that I began the program at the church of Scientology.

After completing the program, I noticed a tremendous upsurge in physical and mental well-being.

Mentally I feel relaxed, my memory has improved a great deal and I feel much less dispersed and freer emotionally. The changes are so vast that I must say that this program has changed my life and my only wish is that these discoveries by L. Ron Hubbard will be broadly implemented to handle our "drug society" which is in so much need of them.

J.M.B.
Purification Program

I did the Purification program and the results were amazing. During the early part I felt for days like I was "stoned." I would get up in the morning in a mental fog. It was definitely reminiscent of the old times when it was miserable to go to work and the future seemed unimportant. My reaction to pressure situations was just to say, "To hell with it" and ignore it. After some time on this program this went away and by the time I was done I felt more bright and awake than I have ever felt. It has been a couple of years since I did the program, and this feeling has persisted. My life has changed.

S.G.
Purification Program

Prior to taking drugs I was full of life, energy and dreams. Life was simple and uncomplicated. I had a very good family life—one in which I loved and trusted my parents. I had good friends that I enjoyed honest relationships with. More than anything I wanted to be happy and have a game to play in which I would win.

But something happened along the way. I got involved with drugs. I was not trying to destroy myself—drugs were the "in" thing—to many people in my generation they were considered part of the "answer." It was too late by the time I realized that drugs were destroying my life. I had become "spaced out" from drugs, and detached from life. Those things that I had held precious in my youth—family, morality and honest friendships—were a thing of the past. Really caring about life and other people were beyond my grasp. What relationships I did have became superficial.

I remember wondering if I could ever really care about someone again. I was scared, as I realized that I was not the same person I had been before drugs. I was not as sharp, my mind was a fog. I was bitter and untrusting. If there was one part of my life that I wanted to change it was the fact that I had done drugs. There was not a day that went by that I did not worry about this. This only heightened my despair as I knew that I couldn't turn back time. Even after quitting drugs entirely I remained aware of the fact that I was not the same person that I had been before. The guilt, bitterness and sorrow were staggering. Then I did L. Ron Hubbard's Purification program. It handled the effects of the drugs that I had taken. I got my energy back and I am no longer walking around in a fog. I can think clearly and my mind is quick and decisive again. I have my drive back and I'm a part of life. I feel real emotions again that have been shut off for years. I can confront having real and honest relationships with others and I'm restoring those which I lost.

I only hope that everyone else who has been involved with drugs, be they street drugs, medicinal drugs, etc., has the same opportunity as I have had and that they do this program. It will change their lives for the better, and there is an awful lot of good that can be done with one's life to have that ruined by drugs. L. Ron Hubbard's Purification program performed a miracle for me. It gave me back my life and I am living proof of that.

B.D.
Purification Program

Study Technology

I have been a teacher for nearly twenty years and a student for nearly fifty years. In that time I have seen and experienced much that has been described as "education." Some of it has been good, but an overwhelming amount of it had little or no lasting value.

As a student I found it very difficult to exercise anything other than my memorization skills. I just memorized things without really understanding why I was doing it. The purpose was really just "to get the grade."

My first course in the study technology developed by L. Ron Hubbard completely revitalized me as a student and provided me with the tools to approach study with a purpose and to really learn something for application. It was this technology that gave me my first real interest in teaching. I realized that with the basic tools provided by this exceptional technology, not only was I able to learn anything I set my mind to, but I could help someone else to learn successfully as well.

For nearly 20 years I have been working with students of all ages from around the world, and have found that they all suffer from the same study-related problems and that once in possession of Mr. Hubbard's breakthrough technology they have the tools necessary for successfully learning anything.

I can think of no greater gift than to give a child (or adult) these easily mastered study tools. They last for a lifetime; they open wide the doors of the future and they unlock potential that was always there.

B.W.
Student Hat

This is the most powerful course I have ever done. The wins, gains and changes have been phenomenal. I have changed so much as a student it is hard to believe. I can actually study comfortably now. This material hit into very basic inabilities and has totally changed them around. I have so much more power to operate and I have regained a marvelous sense of who I am and my own ability to communicate.

S.R.
Student Hat

The technology of L. Ron Hubbard is really incredible—specifically his study technology. I studied for nineteen years. I was in a university and I noticed that I started to feel kind of "stupid." I couldn't grasp the information in my courses as fast as I could before. I started having trouble with my studies. With the study technology of L. Ron Hubbard, everything changed. All my troubles went away and my brightness came back. I was better than ever. Just to give an example: I'm French and I tried to learn English in French schools for eight years. At the end of that time, I knew only ten to twenty words. I started to learn English with L. Ron Hubbard's study technology. Three months later I was able to have a conversation with any English-speaking person. Today, my ability to speak English is impressive. This technology is priceless.

P.M.
Student Hat

I just finished my Student Hat course and I feel great about it. My trouble in school was that I never knew how to study. I was always a kid with cheat sheets in the desk and instead of writing a report by myself, I'd copy the data verbatim from the source.

I now know how to study—and if someone can learn to study then they can learn anything they want to and do it. I never knew before how important proper study technology is, but now I love it. I apply the study technology constantly as it is invaluable. I'd never be without it.

E.B.M.
Student Hat

Key to Life

I have gained **myself** *on this course; a certainty of my true beingness and an ability to duplicate others and to be duplicated by others. My confront of life and my willingness and ability to communicate has soared.*

I feel like a new being who has shed tons of confusions and fears and who has tools that will enable me to live life.

T.P.
Key to Life Course

The Key to Life has been the most rewarding course I have done in my life.

"A man is as alive as he can communicate," L. Ron Hubbard wrote. I am ten times more alive than I was when I began this course and have the potential to become many times more so! So much of life's agony is just a failure to understand what was communicated.

R.F.
Key to Life Course

Thoroughly confused and stultified by the educational system, I somehow stumbled through life this far. How, I don't know.

It took this course to undo years of incorrect training and education and then put a foundation there that will stand for the rest of my life. I now feel that I have a chance in life and that I have the ability to go forward and succeed. The course has indeed been aptly named—The Key to Life.

F.A.
Key to Life Course

I have just finished the Key to Life Course. It is indescribable in terms of personal wins and abilities regained or polished up.

If someone had told me that I would experience this much gain, this much revitalization and resurgence from doing the Key to Life, I don't think I would have believed them. The wins are incomparable, that's just how basic and powerful this course is.

S.S.
Key to Life Course

Auditor Training

The Academy Levels were the first courses I did where I learned how to audit and really help another person by handling any difficulties to do with communication. I finished studying the course and then took my first preclear into session. He was a very shy young man who talked with a slight stutter and walked through a room looking at the floor to avoid having to look at and talk to other people. I took him into session and audited him for a few hours.

As we walked out of the room after session, he gave me a big grin and said, "Well, let's give this a test." He then walked right up to the first person we met and started chatting, laughing and really enjoying himself, and continued getting into communication in a totally relaxed manner with the people in the room. There were no signs of his stutter. It was like watching a totally different person from the shy person of a few hours earlier, and it left me feeling very, very happy that I had been able to apply what I had learned to produce this incredible result.

H.N.
Academy Level Training

This was possibly the most demanding training I've ever done—and the most rewarding. In learning to audit, I've seen sick people jump out of bed and dance after a session. I've watched psychosis melt away before my eyes. I've seen preclears who felt they had no recall of the past suddenly remember. I've seen major life ruins vanish in one short session, after years of the preclear trying to handle them with other means.

D.M.
Academy Level Training

I just completed training on the Academy Levels and the knowledge contained in them has changed my life in numerous ways. I am now much more at cause and know how things are going to go in my life.

The most rewarding part of the Academy Levels is to sit down in the auditing room with another person and administer the processes and experience the elation when my preclear gets rid of some aberrated pattern he's had all his life.

One has to do it to experience it. The preclear's complexion gets bright, his eyes very bright and clear and a big smile comes across his face and he looks at you with a "what do you know, I thought I would have to live with that for the rest of my life!" expression that tells you what's occurred to him and you know you have made life and livingness a brighter activity for that person. I cannot thank L. Ron Hubbard enough for all the love and caring he put into this work, to ensure that each person who wants to help others change will understand and be able to apply his discoveries.

P.C.
Academy Level Training

I was educated for four years at one of the finest universities in the world but I honestly have to say that there were any number of lectures I heard while doing the Saint Hill Special Briefing Course which taught me more about myself, others and life than any ten courses I took in college. L. Ron Hubbard's depth of understanding of life and the mind was so far beyond anything my professors could teach me that doing the Briefing Course was like a university education several times over.

By the time I did the course I was already a trained and experienced auditor but studying all the materials of Dianetics and Scientology in the order that L. Ron Hubbard discovered them gave me a total understanding of his technology and I was able to make it my own because I followed and understood exactly how he did it.

As an auditor I have all the technology under my belt now and I know I can help any person improve. Helping someone else discover more about himself is the most satisfying activity I know and the Briefing Course is the course that teaches you all the technology of how to do this. I have learned in Scientology that there is a technology to life and that once you've learned it, you know it forever. The Saint Hill Special Briefing Course is the most thorough education in life that exists anywhere.

D.K.
Saint Hill Special
Briefing Course

What I got out of the Saint Hill Special Briefing Course was an unshakable certainty and an understanding of a tremendous body of truths which left me with the true beingness of a Scientologist and an auditor.

I solved aspects of my own life just by mere knowledge of this data but above and beyond this I gained the know-how of clearing another being of the barriers to his freedom. That is the bottom line and is something that can never be taken away from me—the knowledge of how to free a being.

P.A.
Saint Hill Special
Briefing Course

Listening to the Saint Hill Special Briefing Course lectures was the most rewarding training I have ever done as an auditor. Every detail of research that L. Ron Hubbard did at Saint Hill during the 1960s is covered in these tapes and listening to them is really like sitting right next to him and learning how he developed the Bridge to Total Freedom, step by step.

These lectures not only cover all the basic underlying theory of the Bridge but also address just about every facet of life. Mr. Hubbard gives incredible facts about man's past, politics, religion, study, different cultures, music, art and a myriad of other subjects. Once you have heard all these lectures you have a comprehensive understanding of life.

What I gained as an auditor from these

tapes and this course was a complete certainty on auditing basics.

Auditing became the simplest thing in the world to do because any and all seeming complexities got swiftly eradicated and I just knew that I was able to get any preclear through anything in auditing with ease and with 100 percent results every time.

G.M.
Saint Hill Special
Briefing Course

My life changed radically from the knowledge gained on the Saint Hill Special Briefing Course, and I will continue to put every part of what I have learned into application.

Without doubt, the Saint Hill Special Briefing Course was the most spectacular adventure of my life. I gained a wealth of knowledge and understanding broad enough and technically perfected to the point where I know with absolute certainty how to set any individual free.

I was put in awe many times over at the simplicities and truths presented on the course and I felt myself changing as I have never felt before.

While the course taught me the technology of auditing, what I really learned was the technology of LIFE. I stepped into a new realm of capability and stability and really assumed the beingness of an auditor the way L. Ron Hubbard intended.

I am forever grateful to L. Ron Hubbard for this legacy of technology, for it is a truly amazing body of truths expansive enough to fill the universe, yet maintaining a total simplicity. With it we can free and are freeing beings.

P.A.
Saint Hill Special
Briefing Course

The Class VIII Course has resulted in a quantum leap in my auditing skills. Whereas earlier I felt that I had a mountain of information that I had to remember and use while auditing, now I am just there, relaxed and in communication with the preclear and naturally doing the next correct thing without having to think about it.

Auditing has been reduced to a simplicity where the tech is simply part of me—I own it and can use it with no effort, worry or thought. I can only liken it to an athletic skill. A great athlete is so highly trained that he doesn't think about his next action as that would be much too slow—he simply does it.

I feel honored and privileged to be among the elite of Scientology auditors and being able to help others so effectively in ways that have never before been possible. Auditing is now easy and pure pleasure with every session ending in an excellent result. Thank you, Ron, for this priceless gift—you have made my life truly worthwhile.

L.D.S.
Advanced Auditor
Training

Dianetics and Scientology Auditing

Scientology Expanded Grades have noticeably increased my ability to learn. In my business, I must do extensive reading and research, and I am now able to absorb and understand a much higher volume of material. This ability has been invaluable to me.
Due to Expanded Grades auditing I have become much happier and find my respect for others has increased. My energy level has risen to the point where I've started my own business and have become revitalized as a writer and financial lecturer.
Probably the most amazing thing which has happened to me was the fact of a 20 percent increase in my IQ.

K.G.
Scientology Auditing

The end result of my Drug Rundown restored me to my teenage years—when I was honest, didn't take drugs or alcohol; when I was so full of life and enthusiasm; when everything was new and wonderful and I could do anything. All I had to do was decide I wanted something or to do something and it happened. That state has been restored to me now. I'm 53.

S.L.D.
Dianetics Auditing

After completing Grade II I feel terrific. I feel energetic, enthusiastic and yet at peace with myself. I also sense a new awareness. I can also look back at past hurts, anxieties and frustrations and feel that they will not have any impact on future decisions.

P.N.
Scientology Auditing

I was looking for a way to handle the emotional pain left over from being abused as a child. I went to a psychologist and she said, "I don't know how to help you." Another one said, "All we can do is 'reprogram' you." The third one told me maybe she could do something but that it would take thirty years. Then a friend told me Scientology could handle my problem, like that! It's true. Since I have had Scientology auditing I no longer have to live in the past—I can live in the present and create my future. And it all happened faster than I would have imagined possible!

M.S.
Scientology Auditing

Prior to coming into Scientology I had received a major operation on my nasal passages which were blocked, causing extreme sinusitis. The medical specialist told me that although he could help by removing the blockage, in his experience it would not fully resolve the problems I was having which he felt may be psychosomatic. He was right. Although I experienced relief, I was still crippled by blinding headaches and sinusitis and would literally have to go to bed as it hurt so much. Then came Scientology auditing. One day in my auditing I contacted something which had to do with the extreme pain I was suffering. Suddenly I felt a crunch—I could physically sense the bones in the left part of my face changing. Right afterwards my face felt as if it had woken up after being asleep. It began tingling. The huge pressure build-up from my sinuses had completely disappeared—gone.

I knew that it was over. I no longer felt any sinus pain—I could breathe—I felt alive again.

To this day, twenty years later, it's never returned. What happened to me during that auditing was a miracle.

C.M.
Scientology Auditing

My wife was seven months pregnant when she became very ill and had surgery performed in her abdomen. After the operation the doctor told me she would need to remain in intensive care for several days. He explained that, being pregnant, the pain from the surgery would be very intense and would last for many days. He estimated it would take five days before she could walk.

While she was in intensive care, I audited her and in less than 24 hours she was walking up and down the hall, and in 48 hours she was released from the hospital. The head doctor examined her and told me her recovery was miraculous!

E.E.
Scientology Auditing

I was wearing glasses when I went for my first Dianetics session. I had been wearing them for six years and my vision was steadily deteriorating. During the session I discovered why I had started wearing glasses. All of a sudden I felt a tremendous surge of inner strength and certainty. I took my glasses off and I felt terrific. Things looked really clear. That was over twenty years ago and I haven't worn glasses since. Today my vision is almost perfect. Dianetics really works.

R.B.
Dianetics Auditing

After getting Grade 0 I honestly feel like a new person. It's a wonderful feeling knowing that I can communicate and that I want to communicate. Through this auditing I realized that I have an absolute love for being in communication with people and things. This was a life-changing experience.

A.T.
Scientology Auditing

I have had many personal successes with Scientology auditing. My ability to let others be, without the need to interfere and unnecessarily interrupt or control them came way up. This was a big win, in the work environment particularly. Also, I found changes in life, often disconcerting in the past, became something I just took in stride. All in all, my ability to confront and handle the pressures and stresses of day-to-day interrelationships increased dramatically and I find myself calmer and enjoying life much, much more.

K.R.
Scientology Auditing

In 1977 I had a serious problem with drugs. I was drinking morning, afternoon and night, as well as using cocaine five to six times a week. Life was gray. I felt hopeless, and there seemed to be no way out. Then I was introduced to the technology of L. Ron Hubbard and believe me, life has not been the same. My drug problem was history after three months. I began to take courses at the church of Scientology on communication, auditing and life. Today, over ten years later, I still have no more urges or cravings for drugs and alcohol.

D.H.
Scientology Auditing

One of my biggest wins in Scientology came at the end of Grade I, which deals with problems. I went from being a problem to being a problem solver. If you can confront, you can break a problem into pieces. I gained the ability to make problems undo.
Before this auditing, any problem would give me a headache. I would come to a screeching halt, be really upset and would not be able to sleep. Through Scientology auditing on the Grades, I understood how problems are structured, and how all problems are put together. There is no problem I cannot handle.

S.S.
Scientology Auditing

There is so much for me to say about this fantastic auditing. It handled areas of myself and my life that I've wanted handled for so long. I'm incredibly happy. I don't know when I've really ever attained this before.
One of the biggest things that occurred was that I gained self-respect—something I've been without for a very long time.
I now have the ability to inspect situations with myself and others and handle accordingly without shame, blame, regret or worry about the future.
It's a great life I have and will continue to have. I have a fresh start now!

K.S.
Scientology Auditing

I was very ill for months in the hospital. I was under intensive care for weeks with a bleeding ulcer infection and kidney failure. My heart stopped three times. I was unconscious for over a week, and I did not want to live. The doctors were going to give up on me and stop the treatment. The nurses did not expect me to survive. My wife had a very hard time with it and she couldn't even call to see how I was doing; she had to have someone else call for her. She then received some Dianetics auditing and came to grips with it, at which point she was able to come into my room in the hospital and give me some auditing. She came in every day. I soon started becoming more aware of my environment and had a determinism to survive. It made life bright enough to live. I am now recovered and would not have lived if it weren't for the technology of L. Ron Hubbard that helped us get through it.

B.G.
Dianetics Auditing

Three years ago I had an automobile accident. One of the results was a partial paralysis of my left arm. This was devastating because I'm a guitarist. After a single Dianetics auditing session I regained some use of my left hand that three years of hard work had not accomplished. I am awaiting further sessions with open arms! It's a miracle!

C.T.
Dianetics Auditing

My life was chaos and headed on a downward spiral before Scientology. From my early teens I had a history of violence. By the time I was 25, I had personally been involved in 200 fights and domestic altercations. I had suffered multiple fractures and broken bones. I only lost one of the fights, such was my anger and desire to destroy that which offended me.
I could see no way of stopping, even though I knew that the end for me was either death or jail for killing someone else.
My parents and close friends were very concerned as they could see the writing on the wall—it was just a matter of time. Fortunately I discovered Scientology at age 25 and through auditing I was able to find the true source of my anger and over a period of months of auditing, it disappeared. I didn't become "adjusted" or nonemotional. On the contrary, for the first time I was able to experience the correct emotion based on what was happening around me and I was in control rather than blindly reacting to every bad situation in the same emotional band—ANGER!
I now live a happy and productive life with my wonderful wife and daughter. This auditing has given me the chance to live the kind of life that I have always wanted to live—that of a productive and contributing member of our society. Because of Scientology I am proud of who I am and what I am doing.

R.M.C.
Scientology Auditing

I used to have epilepsy. Through Dianetics auditing, I discovered that the convulsions which traumatized my life for more than 16 years stemmed from a series of electric shocks that my mother underwent when she was pregnant with me.

During the 16 years I suffered attacks of excruciating blinding and stabbing pains through my eyes and head. My body would go rigid and my throat, mouth and arms would go numb. Then I would throw up every twenty minutes for eight hours before the pain would subside. These attacks occurred from the ages of 11 to 27 years—until I had Dianetics auditing.

These attacks vanished after Dianetics auditing at the age of 27. Today, ten years later, I have helped hundreds of people achieve similar results with Dianetics auditing.

J.B.
Dianetics Auditing

Over 2 years ago I had a severe accident where I smashed both ankles. The bones were in 15 pieces and the surgeon was not positive he could even put them all back together. He said I would never run and may not ever walk. It took all sorts of screws, pins, wire and steel plates just to hold all the pieces together while they healed.

I got daily auditing starting the day after the accident, which not only greatly eased excruciating pain both mentally and physically but also produced miracles. My doctors were amazed as they could not believe my speedy recovery. I was walking within months and now I dance, run and play sports which my doctors doubted would ever be possible. There is absolutely no way this would have occurred without L. Ron Hubbard's technology.

G.C.
Dianetics Auditing

Several years ago I got a spasm back pain that kept me immobile and in agony constantly. I'd had these before and the only solution from the doctor was to prescribe muscle relaxers and painkillers. Although these ended the pain, they dulled my judgment and I would make poor decisions even though I "felt good" or at least "felt no pain." Some of my judgments gravely affected my life. The doctor prescribed more pills but I decided to ride it out. I'd rather have pain and some wits about me than to feel nothing and be stupid. After three days and nights of screaming pain and convulsions I was ready to crawl to the store for my drugs. I even threatened someone with harm if they didn't get my drugs right now while I was flat on my back and couldn't move. But my husband brought me to an auditor instead. The pain of crawling into the chair was the last I had to suffer. Three hours later I walked out, felt wonderful and was anxious to get on with life and work.

T.K.
Dianetics Auditing

In the fall of 1990 I developed a physical condition which I had never encountered before. Over three months I visited several doctors to try to determine what it was and to find out how to cure it. Finally after seeing a specialist it was diagnosed as a chronic vascular disease that there was no cure for. I was told by this specialist that I would probably have it for the rest of my life. This news was very upsetting to me. I was 28 years old at the time. Then I got some auditing. After less than one hour I felt much better. Not only that, the physical condition stopped spreading. Within a week of daily auditing, all physical evidence of the condition was gone. It is 1½ years later and the disease has not returned.

J.M.
Dianetics Auditing

In this session, a series of incidents from my childhood that were causing me a tremendous amount of guilt and heartache was completely relieved. This was unconfrontable before. In fact, I'd never been able to talk about it, not in 27 years. My auditor had me return to the moment it happened and go over the incident several times. I was wide awake and fully alert throughout.
As we began, I felt again the same fear and frustration I felt in the incident, but as we continued, the bad feeling was completely discharged and I began to feel much better. By the end of my Dianetics session I was totally free of any effects from this nightmare that had been ruining my life. It's a real miracle—I feel like a 200-pound weight is off my shoulders!
As a Doctor of Dentistry, I'd wholeheartedly recommend Dianetics auditing to anyone. I see now that when you get rid of the upsets, guilt, anger, etc., your whole life changes for the better.

S.C.
Dianetics Auditing

Nearly one year ago my father was struck down by a massive heart attack which left him completely disabled.
We were told by the doctor that he probably would not survive as he was 78 years old and the damage was too great. He was discharged to a convalescent center renowned for its success in stroke rehabilitation.
Two days after he arrived we were told by the director that my father would not benefit from the program as he was too far gone, that it was hopeless and she would not be able to help him.
I gave my father Scientology auditing every day. Day by day he improved until finally six weeks later he walked out of that facility!!!
The same physical therapist who had told us that there was no hope confessed to my sister that in her twenty years' experience with stroke patients she had never seen anyone come back the way my father had.

A.A.
Scientology Auditing

New Era Dianetics auditing is absolutely incredible. I never realized really what an engram could do and how solidly fixed they were in one's mind or how insidiously they aberrate you. Then I had a session of New Era Dianetics and I was utterly amazed at what happened. This particular engram was quite severe and I was a little more than nervous to go through it, but with the help of my auditor, I made it through. We ran it several times, each time picking up more of the engram that was hidden beneath unconsciousness and pain. After we had run all the emotional pain out of this engram, I had an incredible realization about my life and why I had been unconsciously behaving in certain ways. That unwanted aspect of myself is gone now, never to return. I couldn't stop smiling for days after that! It was incredible, I felt as if I were floating when I walked. I had never felt so good, and this was just **one** *engram.*

J.J.
Dianetics Auditing

New Era Dianetics auditing has completely changed my life. Things that seemed unresolvable resolved in the first 4–5 hours. Until I experienced it for myself, the reactive mind was not really tangible to me; but let me tell you, when you get in session with an auditor trained on New Era Dianetics and an E-Meter you instantly find and resolve those things that have been haunting you for years. I would never have believed it if someone had told me what had been underlying all my fears and anxieties. Each session ended with me finding out something about myself that I didn't know before and with a new feeling of freedom. I can't say enough about New Era Dianetics auditing—there is no aberration that can hide from its incredible ability to dig out of the reactive mind that which keeps you pinned down in life.

L.D.
Dianetics Auditing

Before I got Expanded Dianetics auditing, I had problems and conflicts with those I worked with and was in trouble all the time. Expanded Dianetics is very powerful and thorough. I found the very source of my problems with other people and blew this away! It became a pleasure to work with others. I discovered why there were certain locations—cities and even whole countries—I hated or feared. This was fully resolved (prior to my auditing I disliked the city I was in so much that I stayed inside all the time and would only venture out when forced to). Turmoil and strife disappeared and it was possible for other people to live happily with me for the first time!

A.A.
Dianetics Auditing

Every two weeks I used to get a migraine headache which literally did not allow me to get up from bed. This was ruining everything I wanted to do in life.
Then I received New Era Dianetics auditing and in the three-hour session I eradicated the source of the migraines. Today, a year and a half later, I've not had another headache. I'm living a new life.

A.P.
Dianetics Auditing

Years ago I was burglarized at home. Two guys entered and I was beaten severely and raped. I had 27 fractures in my face and jaw. The doctors said I'd lose my eyes. I was an emotional wreck, unable to face my friends or any part of life. I was terrified by this experience and unable to confront it.
I turned to Scientology auditing. The improvement was so miraculous that one friend who had come with me dropped to her knees and cried. Within two days the emotional trauma was gone. I completely regained my self-confidence and self-respect. This made it possible for my body to heal much faster. Scientology auditing got me over a tragic experience and has enabled me to lead a better life than I ever thought possible.

V.F.
Scientology Auditing

State of Clear

Achieving the state of Clear is the most important thing that has happened in my life. Not only because I was relieved of my past unwanted emotions that were affecting my life and making it difficult to be happy, but also because I opened a new door of happiness. I'm now able to help others a great deal more as I can understand them in a way that was not possible before. Abilities that I did not know I had became evident and as a result I could experience and give greater happiness to others.
My dreams and goals are alive and I have certainty that they will happen. My strength and persistence as an individual have been unblocked.

T.L.
State of Clear

Do I feel wonderful! Having recently achieved the state of Clear, everything around me is so calm and my awareness of the environment and life itself has expanded tremendously. I am now able to view life's problems analytically and come up with sound, rational decisions for each and every one of them. My energy level has increased tenfold and I tackle life with an enthusiasm I never had before. Being Clear has enabled me to begin accomplishing all of those things I wanted in life.

J.L.
State of Clear

I have just achieved the state of Clear! It is nothing short of miraculous to be rid of one's reactive mind and to have the accompanying freedom, happiness and new-found abilities that I know are lasting. When I first read the Dianetics book and learned for the first time the truth about the mechanics of the mind and how it all works, I wanted to go Clear.

It is an incredible relief to finally understand myself and to know with certainty the cause of man's aberrations, his downfalls, his sorrows and that these can be eradicated to make way for a new life of competence and happiness. The day-to-day problems and obstacles in life no longer pin me down in unwanted conditions. I am able to set and reach any goals that I create and positively affect my relationships with others and family.

Since achieving the state of Clear, I notice that my family and friends are doing far better as well, and I am much more capable of helping them. The doors to my future have blown wide open with potential and possibilities.

G.A.
State of Clear

It is nearly beyond my power of expression to describe the state of Clear—this crystal, shining, effortless state. It is the most basic and the most noble part of ***me.*** *It is all that I knew I ever was, absolutely unadulterated by past failure, social machinery or false identity. I have the complete freedom of basic personality. Man has perhaps glimpsed this state when witnessing individual acts of mercy, kindness, creativity, courage, truth or any other attribute we commonly personify through art. It isn't a temporary condition or something that will pass, like the happiness we feel during some great moment in our lives. It is lasting and permanent. This is the beginning of something new and great for me and a brand-new vista for mankind as well.*

N.K.N.
State of Clear

The big question for me was why was I not succeeding in life—why was living so difficult, painful and full of heavy effort?
I read the book **Dianetics** *and adopted the goal of becoming Clear. I worked toward this goal and experienced my first big lesson—life was really worth living and change was possible.*
Through auditing, my goal was achieved and I went Clear. I couldn't adequately describe the enormous change that occurred.
I am no longer in the chaos of confusion that prevails around me but I stand now in the center of the whirlwind of living. I am calm, confident and understand myself for the first time—it is the greatest experience in my life—I am free. Life is wonderful as a Clear.

N.N.
State of Clear

Before going Clear I was dissatisfied with life, I felt trapped in some way. I was on a treadmill, and there didn't seem to be any way to get off of it. Going Clear really opened the door to my life and my abilities.

I now see a strong, vibrant future and a way to achieve my goals. It's hard to imagine how I lived at all before I went Clear. My whole concept of what living means has changed and I wouldn't trade it for anything!

C.J.
State of Clear

It's been many years since I went Clear but the feeling of vitality has never faded.

Being Clear, I am able to see things as they are, rather than viewing them through my own reactivity. I notice that though other people might get very upset or frustrated about problems and troubles, I can just view the actual situation and decide on the best solution to handle it rather than automatically REACTING or losing my temper and saying something I would later regret.

With my marriage, being Clear has had a tremendous effect. I feel that communication is the basis of a good marriage. Because I am Clear my ability to communicate is very good and I have a very happy marriage. I have been able to enter a newly chosen career full speed ahead, without veering off onto any side roads or worrying if it was all going to work. It's very easy to do things because I'm definite in my decisions. I know what I can achieve.

Achieving the state of Clear released me from the barriers of life and left me with a definite sense of freedom.

D.F.
State of Clear

OT Levels

It seems I've been searching for eons for what I know now. I feel at peace. I am calm and certain. Things that never made sense now make sense. It's so hard sometimes to say enough to really acknowledge the magnitude of what processing is and does. OT levels are the most precious thing in the universe.

R.M.
OT Levels

On OT II I have gained competence, respect for myself and others, a deeper understanding of life, an amazement with the simplicity of things, and a sense of well-being.

M.P.
OT Levels

The OT levels create such a feeling of freedom you become able to set your own future and go where you want to go. The OT levels take you to an incredible new realm of self-awareness—but the result is the ability to get more done in life!! I am more part of life and I have the ability to join in and make life happen the way I want it.

C.M.
OT Levels

Moving through the OT levels is like nothing I've ever experienced before. Through them you find the answers to things you never imagined existed. These answers unlock the very truths of life for you. The OT levels are like removing shackles from yourself as a spiritual being—ones you weren't aware you carried with you. I found that I'd been so used to dealing with life in a certain way that I surprised myself when I no longer became upset or acted negatively on my job or in my relationships. My life became calm, it became sane and I became truly cause over each of my dynamics. The OT levels gave me the freedom and understanding of life that has enabled me to accomplish goals I never dreamed were possible.

S.M.
OT Levels

On the OT levels I learned the ultimate truths of man and myself. And the truth does make you free. And with that freedom has come a joy I have never known before. It is a happiness that spills over into the lives of everyone I touch. As if I am so rich in happiness I have plenty left over to give.

I have seen with clarity beyond the cycle of life and death, and risen to an immense vista of freedom where such things as friendships, affections and my personal identity can last beyond one life.

To say my future looks exceedingly bright is an understatement. I am a ***free being!***

S.H.
OT Levels

This was truly the most amazing action I've ever done in Scientology. The power and simplicity of this OT level frequently left me at a loss of words for what had occurred in my universe—the changes were that fast and big. I am now looking forward to an eternal future of new abilities and a new-found insouciance to play the game of life.

M.H.
OT Levels

I can't describe how wonderful I actually feel. Calm, serene—that's it. Also a very deep knowingness. There are things now that I know about why we are like we are (or were, in my case!), about our true nature—and I can testify, MAN IS GOOD. There's no doubt about that. As for myself, I now know that I can be anything I want. It's that easy! I can choose my own path. Many, many additives are gone, leaving more and more and more of just myself. Life is truly beautiful and bright.

The amount of very deep-rooted basic stuff handled is almost unbelievable. The amount of gain is like nothing I've ever experienced in Scientology before. It's a quantum leap.

B.M.
OT Levels

The greatest change for me on this OT level is really finding myself more and more as I always wished to be. I have completely lost all self-invalidation. Things I previously thought as "too hard" or "impossible" or "too exhausting" are now reachable. This level goes deep into the salvation of man. I know I'll never make the same mistakes again.

M.B.
OT Levels

On this OT level I was able to resolve situations that had worried me for an eternity in a matter of minutes. I have become cause over any situation in my life. I can handle, resolve and accomplish what I decide to. Life can be handled totally and solely on a spiritual level. My ability to spot the exact source of a situation and then handle it immediately is unstoppable.

B.R.
OT Levels

I have regained the power of boundless and limitless persistence. I have regained myself and have no questions as to who I am or why I am. I have regained the spirit of play and the ability to permeate that I had lost and forgotten long ago. This was truly magnificent!

N.B.
OT Levels

My understanding of the human condition has vastly expanded. My care for other people has risen enormously. My life is much calmer now. I am much, much less likely to become upset. The gains I have achieved are greater than anything I have ever experienced. Peace of mind and spirit is priceless.

P.J.B.
OT Levels

Chapter 18

Recommended Course of Progress

The amount of research L. Ron Hubbard conducted on man, the mind and life is towering. He wrote millions of words and delivered many millions more in lectures. By his own creed, wisdom is only worthwhile if it can be shared, and Mr. Hubbard spent years making his materials readily available for anyone with a desire to improve his life. Today, the Church carries on that intention.

Why is there so much information? Dianetics and Scientology contain answers to the broadest field of all, the field of life. And the materials of Dianetics and Scientology are a precisely laid route to higher states of ability and awareness.

However, of greater importance than the sheer quantity and exactitude of material is the fact that one can begin to apply the technology as soon as he has learned any of it. It is not required to sequester oneself away for twenty years on a mountaintop or in a university to see improvement. One is alive now. With L. Ron Hubbard's technology, one can improve now.

With the multitude of services available, the question naturally arises, "Which is the best way to travel up the Bridge?"

There are three general avenues of progress. Each has its advantages. They are: (1) training as an auditor, (2) individual professional auditing as a preclear and (3) a combination of the first two that includes individual professional auditing and auditor training, done concurrently. Below is a discussion of each avenue with recommendations on how to make the most certain progress.

Training as an Auditor

Decades of people moving up the Bridge to Total Freedom have shown that training as an auditor is the most optimum way to progress in Scientology. The value of Scientology training cannot be overstated, since training provides the understanding of life necessary to live successfully.

Before one can succeed in any game he must learn its rules and develop the necessary skills. Without the rules, one upsets the other players; and without the skill, one can hardly play, much less win. Training in Scientology teaches one the rules and develops the needed skills, but here the game is life itself. And with Scientology it is a game where everyone wins.

It is proven that a person who is technically trained in Scientology is much more able to handle work and personnel than an untrained individual. How can people handle life if they have no expert knowledge of how to go about it?

It is not expected for someone who becomes trained as an auditor to then only audit. That is a limited view of Scientology and its applications to life. While the skill of a trained auditor in auditing someone is the most valuable skill of all, a trained Scientologist is more effective in the factories, the offices, the homes and the neighborhoods than someone who is not trained.

Training as a professional auditor has the further advantage of being the most economical course of action to take. As a trained auditor one can receive his own auditing by exchanging with another auditor, and in this fashion get himself up the processing side of the Bridge. He is thus able to move up both sides of the Classification, Gradation and Awareness Chart at the same time and gain both an objective and subjective understanding of the technology.

The Hubbard Method One Co-audit Course trains a student so he can help another recover his education.

Students on the Scientology Drug Rundown Co-audit Course learn and then co-audit techniques to free one another from the mental and spiritual damage of drugs.

As an auditor, one can *do* far more to improve people and conditions in life. Foremost amongst things an auditor can do is free another spiritually and no activity is more valuable than that.

Through auditing a person becomes free and only an auditor can make that happen.

By looking at the training side of the Classification, Gradation and Awareness Chart one can see the progression of courses necessary to become an auditor. This sequence usually begins with one or more introductory services, as described earlier, which lead up onto the training side of the Bridge.

After a person has done one or more introductory services, the Student Hat course is a vital first major service. It has been found that the single biggest pitfall in training has been the lack of knowledge of study technology or its proper application. While this is easily remedied once discovered, the student who knows and applies study technology throughout his studies invariably speeds through his courses and becomes an accomplished auditor.

Another indispensable service is the Method One Word Clearing Co-audit Course. Method One is one of the nine methods of Word Clearing. A person can learn to audit this procedure and then co-audit it with another student. Method One Word Clearing is an auditing procedure in which the auditor and preclear search for and clear out of the way any basic word and meaning errors in the preclear's past. The value of doing this can be appreciated when one realizes that with Method One Word Clearing, whole subjects and even entire educations that were not understood at the time can be recovered for the preclear. A person can get hung up at points where he accumulated misunderstoods. Method One frees the person from these points and makes it possible for him to *use* his education.

Either the Student Hat or Method One

Word Clearing may be done first, but both are necessary for successful and rapid study.

A student with a long history of drug use may find the effects of drugs severely inhibit his studies. In some cases it is necessary that a student do the Purification program and the Drug Rundown before he can adequately progress. This imposes no economic difficulties on the student, since the needed processes and actions can be done co-audited at any church or mission.

The next key elements to be learned are the communication skills as taught on the Hubbard Professional TR Course and the Hubbard Professional Upper Indoc TR Course. Here, the student masters the communication cycle, which is vitally important in auditing, and the subject of control, which is also indispensable. Many difficulties in the application of auditing can be traced to a faulty understanding of TRs and how to use them.

Once a student has mastered study technology and the TRs, he is ready to learn the theory and techniques of Scientology Expanded Grades auditing. This material is covered in Academy Levels 0–IV, as described in previous chapters. The importance of applying the materials on any training course cannot be overstressed. One does drills to learn how to operate the E-Meter, drills to learn how to properly do each action associated with an auditing session and drills on the techniques used in auditing. All this drilling leads up to an ability to *apply* the technology. It is vital then that students spend adequate time on their drills and learn each one well.

Since definite skills are attained with any training course, it behooves the student to put in as much course time as possible and study outside of course hours as well. In this way course progress is rapid.

After finishing the Academy Levels 0–IV, the auditor should now intern as a Class IV Auditor. An internship gives needed experience as an auditor, polishes the skills learned in the Academy and develops certainty in oneself and one's abilities. Each higher classification attained should be followed by an internship for that class, so experience is gained at each level as one moves up.

Training in Scientology most definitely should include the Saint Hill Special Briefing Course. This course contains all the materials of Dianetics and Scientology necessary for a full understanding of life. By doing the Saint Hill Special Briefing Course, one can also co-audit with another student on any process or action taught on the course, and the student is thus able to receive as much auditing as he desires.

Complete mastery of auditing technology comes with training on the Class VIII Course. The Class VIII Course trains an auditor in the precise standard of application for any case.

By training as an auditor one moves up the entire Bridge in the most economical way possible, gets all the data and all the gains there are to be had. Many Scientologists have advanced far in Scientology by training as auditors. It is the most highly recommended way to progress.

Individual Professional Auditing

An alternate way to move up the Bridge is to receive individual processing in the Hubbard Guidance Center of a church or mission. This is much faster than training as an auditor in terms of one's own personal progress up the auditing side of the Bridge. It is, however, not as economical because it requires special attention from several staff members to provide the individual service.

Receiving professional auditing in the HGC enables one to receive service in intensive numbers of hours which makes for very rapid progress. The interruptions and upsets of day-to-day living intrude minimally when auditing is done every day for some hours, and a person soon rises above situations which would have dragged him down earlier. More gain is achieved per unit of time when auditing is done this way.

Before beginning auditing, it is wise to become fully familiar with a set of guidelines which, if followed, help ensure that the greatest gains are made in one's sessions. These are supplied by the person in the church who oversees the administration of all auditing, called the Director of Processing. (*Processing* is another word for *auditing*.) These guidelines cover such points as getting sufficient sleep the night before a session, eating properly and refraining from the use of drugs or alcohol for the duration of the auditing, except for medications administered under the care of a physician. Too, the person should keep his personal life as ethical as possible, since problems in one's relationships with others can take up an inordinate amount of auditing time, time that could otherwise be spent on progress up the Bridge.

Any training the person receives before embarking on auditing will be to his advantage. Even a person who has read books on Dianetics and Scientology will be more conversant with what is taking place in his sessions. At some point, in order to make it all the way up the Bridge, one will require auditor training, so the more one knows about the technology early on, the better off he is.

It is important that enough auditing be obtained at the outset to ensure that adequate progress can be attained. An estimate of how many hours will be required to reach a specified point on the Bridge can be ascertained by church technical staff based upon tests and other evaluations made before a preclear starts his auditing. Arrangements to have enough auditing time reserved in advance help ensure that one will reach the level he seeks.

The specific processes that a person receives are determined by the Case Supervisor. Since everyone is different it is impossible to state beforehand exactly how each preclear should progress. The basic route for all persons, however, is laid out on the Classification, Gradation and Awareness Chart and includes, for any case, the Expanded Lower Grades; New Era Dianetics; clearing, either on New Era Dianetics or on the Clearing Course, and each OT level.

Many people who have experienced skilled auditing say it is the most valuable activity there is. Those who move up the Bridge through professional auditing can do so rapidly.

PROFESSIONAL AUDITING AND TRAINING

A third main avenue Scientologists use to progress up the Bridge is by combining professional auditing in the Hubbard Guidance Center with auditor training in the Academy. When the person is not in session as a preclear, he is a student in a course room studying to be an auditor.

This has the advantages of rapidity of progress up both sides of the Grade Chart. One's gains in auditing are augmented by the gains of training, making it an excellent way to progress for those who have the time to do both concurrently.

It should be noted that TRs are not done simultaneously with auditing and so those who wish to study Academy Level training material while receiving auditing in the HGC should do their Professional TR Course and Professional Upper Indoc TR Course beforehand. Experience has taught that apart from teaching auditing skills, the TRs result in vast personal changes and gain as the student's ability to confront and handle communication improves. For this reason, TR training should not be intermixed with auditing.

The above are the three main ways Scientologists progress up the Bridge to Total Freedom. Different people usually find that one way suits them better than the others, but regardless of which route one takes, the adventure of Scientology is a journey of awakening and self-discovery unlike anything else in life.

RECOMMENDED COURSE OF PROGRESS

1

TRAINING AS AN AUDITOR

- Teaches the most valuable skill of all—auditing
- Increases ability to handle life
- Most economical
- Enables one to co-audit up the Bridge

2

INDIVIDUAL PROFESSIONAL AUDITING

- Fastest route up the Bridge
- Intensive auditing makes further progress per hour of auditing
- Full services of the Hubbard Guidance Center to ensure maximum gains

3

PROFESSIONAL AUDITING AND TRAINING

- Enables progress up both sides of the Bridge
- Person can study on course when not in session
- Auditing gains are augmented by gains in training

CHAPTER 19

ANY REASONS FOR DIFFICULTIES AND THEIR CORRECTION

According to the personal accounts of Scientologists in Chapter 17, the gains to be had in Scientology are considerable, even miraculous. By far the largest percentage of people who take part in Scientology training or auditing achieve gains comparable to those. Occasional failures have, however, been reported in Scientology. But, when Scientology appears to go wrong, there is invariably a specific error that has been made in the application of technology which, when remedied, enables it to then work and achieve the expected results. It is a fact that *Scientology works 100 percent of the time when it is properly applied to a person who sincerely desires improvement in his life.*

Such a statement is all the more remarkable when one considers that the general attitude of man toward help or improvement has considerably worsened under the relatively recent influences of psychiatry and psychology. For concurrent with the rise of these two fields came soaring violent crime rates, the creation and rapid proliferation of drug abuse, plummeting educational standards, a weakening of moral standards and a legion of social, economic and other ills. Such a correlation is not coincidental.

These problems of modern living are directly consequential to the massive injection of false psychiatric and psychological solutions into the culture. The steady decay of social institutions in this century followed the ill-considered adoption of psychiatric dogma in the management of our schools, family affairs, child rearing, interpersonal relationships, the arts, criminal justice, politics and other areas.

Furthermore, psychiatric propagandizing against traditional moral values has clouded the concepts of right and wrong and produced generations of people who are confused about themselves, their marriages, their families, their communities and where they are going in life.

Dianetics and Scientology entered a world battered by half a century of this false mental technology and two paramount facts became clear. The abilities of many people to actually perceive, think and reach rational conclusions had noticeably lessened; and many had grown chronically cynical, disabused of the notion that improvement or real help was possible. Dianetics and Scientology, however, *do* produce positive results, spectacular even, if one honestly studies, understands and applies the data. There are methods to produce results even among those who have been victims of this general societal malaise. In fact, the technology of Dianetics and Scientology has proven to be invariably correct. It is therefore of some value to examine why there have been occasional failures and to see exactly how this has been due to incorrect application and not flaws in the existing technology. The fact is, various types of errors can be made, both in training and processing, which could prevent the technology from being exactly applied. The following is a description of these, and how they are easily corrected.

ERRORS IN TRAINING

Wrong Purpose for Studying

Before even starting to study a subject, a person can make a fundamental mistake—trying to study it for some other reason than to really learn, understand and apply it.

Some of the wrong reasons for study include: to earn a certificate or degree, to gain status, to pass an examination, to impress someone or to obey the wishes of a parent or family member.

These reasons might result in a degree, but are no guarantee that a person will be able to *apply* the material he has studied.

If a person studies a Dianetics or Scientology course for the wrong reason, he will only hinder his chances for real improvement.

This could result in a failure to really understand the course and get the full gains possible.

A student should study with the purpose of application in mind. Scientology courses are arranged so that they are easy to get through, step by step. Upon graduation from the course, the student knows the materials he has studied and can apply the data to handle his job, his environment and his life.

The Barriers to Study

In his extensive study of education and learning, L. Ron Hubbard discovered the actual barriers to study which can prevent a person from understanding a subject or from even *wanting* to study. These barriers can get in the way of one's study in a Scientology course room or in life.

The barriers to study have been fully researched and described by Mr. Hubbard; courses exist at churches and missions of Scientology where people can learn what these barriers are and how to easily overcome them.

Past Study Failures

After failures as a student prior to Scientology, a person can become so convinced that he cannot study that he won't even try to study again, or when attempting to study, runs into past failures and doesn't progress. There are various remedies available to students in Scientology to help them overcome such problems and regain the ability to learn quickly and competently.

Past Bad Study Experiences

Past approaches to education have not known the precise causes of study difficulties and, due to this, the methods for handling have not always been effective.

Some of the past handlings for poor study included:

■ Dunce caps on the students while they sat in the corner. This activity has never made any student brighter, but only succeeded in humiliating students, leaving them with less desire to learn.

■ Trick methods of studying and memory systems whereby the student is taught to parrot off facts as a substitute for actual understanding. While a student employing such techniques might look like he has learned something, these methods impart no real knowledge a person can *use*.

■ The use of drugs to quiet a student and make him less active—purportedly to enable him to concentrate and to lengthen attention span. In actual fact, this method makes a student dull and less able to learn for he is less in communication with his physical surroundings. Such drugs also have extremely damaging side effects, which have included instances of suicide.

■ Pain and duress to force a person into obedient study. Examples of this are rapping knuckles with a ruler, spankings and other threats of punishment if a student did not learn as the teacher demanded. Students "taught" in this method often dislike study and have great difficulty with it in future attempts. Pain and duress also stand as a confession from the teacher that he has failed in his job.

It has never been successful to override a person's own determinism to "make" them do something. Consulting someone's understanding and encouraging their sincere willingness and desire to learn has always succeeded. Teaching someone with the idea they are stupid and must be forced to learn destroys the individual's initiative.

In Scientology the actual causes for study difficulties have been isolated. L. Ron Hubbard's study technology can handle reasons why a student would have trouble in study and even more importantly, once a student is taught the technology of study, he can actually prevent difficulties from occurring.

Problems with Earlier Similar Subjects

When a student has developed misconceptions or misunderstandings in subjects studied earlier, it can hinder him in current studies. The later subject can seem complicated or incomprehensible due to confusions stirred up by unwitting association with the earlier subject.

A housewife who has trouble baking may not realize that her botched recipes stem from earlier confusions in her study of arithmetic in school.

An advertising agency copywriter whose clients are unhappy with his ads does not see that his confusions on grammar from high school are ruining his professional life.

A photographer who cannot take a good picture might not connect his difficulties with earlier studies and misconceptions of color harmony in a painting class.

This inability to grasp a current subject is the result of confusions from earlier subjects. The housewife could make better cakes if she understood that half a pint was eight ounces, not four ounces. The ad copywriter could be more successful if he saw that behind his stilted prose lay confusions in grammar. The photographer might take award-winning photos if he knew how to use colors for more pleasing arrangements.

There is a specific handling for such examples as the above—to find the *earlier* subject and clear up the misconceptions and misunderstandings in *it.* The student will then be able to learn the current subject.

This procedure is followed in a Scientology course room, and study failures due to confusion with earlier studies are handled or prevented.

False Ideas or Information

In day-to-day living people often accept ideas without question if they appear to make sense. False ideas and information can come from newspapers, radio, TV or textbooks. They can even come from parents or friends. If a person has been given a lot of false information or concepts in an area, it is difficult to study and apply the subject as it just doesn't make sense.

The subject of religion, for instance, has been seriously muddied up by the mechanistic philosophies of the last century with their false ideas that man is an animal.

Fortunately, there is a very simple procedure developed by L. Ron Hubbard for handling this problem. It helps the person locate the false data he has acquired on a subject, and assists him in stripping it away, thereby freeing up his ability to think in the area where he was formerly confused.

Studying While Tired, Hungry or on Drugs

Trying to study and learn without being well rested and well fed is a student error. It is very hard to understand the information being studied when one's attention is fixed on one's body. It is also a mistake to drink alcohol or to take any kind of drugs while attempting to study.

Taking drugs while studying would defeat the purpose of training, which is to increase a person's awareness and ability. Drugs, whether medical or street drugs or even alcohol, have the opposite effect and impair the senses, the intelligence and the ability to view things clearly. Many medical drugs cause serious side effects, such as hallucinations or mental disturbances. For this reason, taking drugs while on a Scientology course is forbidden.

Even if a person is no longer taking drugs, if he has taken many drugs in the past, he may have trouble studying until the effects of the drugs have been eradicated.

Persons who have taken drugs do the Purification program and receive processing on Objectives and the Drug Rundown. These actions handle the damage caused by drugs and enable one to think clearly and study once again.

Receiving Training While Connected to Someone Who Is Against Spiritual Betterment

A student connected to a person who does not want to see him become better and more self-determined will not be able to get and keep his gains from Scientology training. There is a great amount of information available in Scientology which fully describes this phenomenon and explains how to deal with it.

Suppose a wife is unhappy being a housewife and wants a career of her own where she can use her abilities yet she is too timid to resolve the matter with her husband, who is violently opposed to the idea and believes a wife's place is in the home.

She does a course in Scientology and starts to become stronger and more self-confident. The husband, viewing her progress as a threat to his own plans and comfort, tells his wife that he will divorce her and leave her with no support if she does not stop attending Scientology courses. Or perhaps she comes home after going to course, tells her husband how much she is learning and how great she feels, and he sourly states that he does not see any difference in her. This situation will cause a phenomenon whereby the person feels much better at first and is steadily improving but then loses her gains.

Training must not be continued over such an unhandled situation, as study under this kind of duress will not produce the intended results.

Fortunately, the exact technology to resolve this exists in Scientology and it can be handled quite rapidly. The wife would sit down with a trained Scientologist who would assist her in communicating with her husband. The situation would be resolved in such a way that her own spiritual betterment was not slowed, but also so that her husband's wishes were also respected and accommodated.

In some cases, the cause of this "up-and-down" phenomenon in a person's life cannot be immediately located in the person's environment. If this is the case, there is also special auditing available to help a person discover the real causes and thus become stable in life.

The technology to help people communicate with and deal with others in their environment who are antagonistic to their plans or desires for personal and spiritual betterment is available at Scientology churches and missions.

Schedules

Just as in any well-run organization, Scientology courses are run according to an agreed-upon schedule adhered to by all students. Course periods start and end at an exact time. Each student has the responsibility to arrive on time for course and to follow his course schedule. Students shuffling in at odd hours distract those already studying and contribute to a failure to really understand the material. The remedy is simple: by sticking to the schedule, a minimum of time is wasted and the student can get on with his course.

If a student is having difficulty following the course schedule, he should see his Course Supervisor for assistance.

Illness

It is an error for a person to continue studying in a Scientology course room if he is physically ill. If one is not feeling well while studying on a Scientology course or is unable to attend the course because of illness, he should let the Course Supervisor know right away. The Supervisor can arrange auditing to help handle the emergency if needed, relieve any spiritual or mental trauma and help speed recovery.

Materials

All Scientology courses have course packs and other materials that the student needs to have on hand to study the course.

A lack of needed materials obviously would prevent the student from getting on with his studies. Fortunately, the Church makes these easily available and, if the student does not speak English, most materials have been translated into the student's language.

Ask the Supervisor, Not a Student

Students in a Scientology course room agree to follow a guide for students which includes simple, common-sense rules that experience has shown make study much easier.

Included in these guidelines is the basic rule that if the student doesn't know something or is confused about course data, he should ask a Supervisor and get his confusion cleared up before continuing. He should not ask another student as this can create progressively worsening misconceptions, since other students don't necessarily know the answers. If the student asks the Supervisor he will be referred to the correct answer contained in his course materials.

Materials are made available in many languages so parishioners around the world can advance in their study of Scientology.

Distractions While Studying

If a student has heavy problems in his life these can weigh on him during his time on course and distract his attention from what he is trying to learn. The Course Supervisor can often be of assistance in such matters and should be consulted, though sometimes auditing is necessary to resolve the situation.

Some students have been in course rooms where the indiscreet "extracurricular" activities of the students and even the teacher or professor have gotten in the way of actual learning. In a Scientology course room it is the right of all students to learn undistracted by unethical interpersonal relationships. The basic rule is, "Do not engage in any sexual activities (or involvements) that could impede or interrupt the processing or training of another Scientologist." When this is violated, one's own self-improvement actions are actually impeded. The correct action is not to engage in such activities.

Dishonesty

Occasionally a student gets through his course dishonestly by falsely signing off items on his checksheet he hasn't done or pretending to have completed a course with full understanding of the material when he *hasn't* fully understood it.

Such a student is only cheating himself. This is easily handled by applying the study technology and owning up to any prior failures to do so. The student will then be able to study honestly and succeed.

Training in Scientology is done on a gradient with more basic courses coming before more advanced materials. If prerequisites to a course are falsified, the student will not grasp the materials or skills taught on the course. Any inclination not to honestly walk each step of the Bridge resolves with the application of auditing and other procedures. In this way the full gains can be attained.

Not Following the Auditor's Code

Even for "student auditors," the Auditor's Code, the code of conduct that must be followed by all auditors, still applies. Not following the Code can lead to not getting results on one's preclears. If one feels he can't apply the Code, he should get help from the Supervisor.

Supervisor's Permission

A student should not receive processing from or give processing to anyone under any circumstances without the direct permission of the Director of Training and the Case Supervisor. The exception is if an emergency assist is needed due to injury or illness.

Scientology was not designed to be mixed with other practices; therefore, engaging in any rite, ceremony, practice, mental exercise, meditation, food therapy or any similar occult, mystical or other similar practice while on course without the express permission of the Director of Training is an error.

If a person is involved with any of the above, he should simply inform the Director of Training who will either give him authorization to go ahead with the handling he wishes to do, or otherwise help him remedy the situation he is trying to handle.

It is also an error to give processing to anyone who:

1. Expects to be cured of any terminal illness.

2. Has an extensive institutional or psychiatric history which includes heavy drugs, shocks of various kinds and/or so-called psychiatric brain operations. By "institutional history" is meant having been knowingly or unknowingly given such treatment in a public or private institution for the insane, a psychiatric ward in a hospital, a psychiatrist's, psychologist's or other mental practitioner's clinic or office or a mental health center. It is not that such individuals cannot, in many instances, be helped. But they require many more hours of auditing than someone who has not been so harmed and often, too, due to the damage received in such "treatment" are so unstable as to require

more attention and facilities than the church could possibly provide. Therefore, in order to do the greatest good for the greatest number, it is more survival to use Scientology to bring about improved conditions in the individuals in society who are already capable and who would progress fastest. These people, made even more capable, will increase their spheres of influence. The society will then support constructive reform measures such as eliminating the unworkable and even debilitating practices of psychiatry and psychology. And the Church spearheads and supports such efforts so as to prevent further harm by these professions.

Moreover, in that their condition was not brought about by the Church, but rather by psychiatrists, they fall outside the zone of responsibility of Scientology.

3. It is also an error to process a third category of individual, which includes members of organizations who by their conduct show themselves to be hostile to the best interests of mankind. This includes members of police spy organizations, government spy organizations such as the CIA or FBI, or other such federal agencies in any country. This category would include also those who have publicly attacked Scientology in the media or who have attacked or harmed other self-betterment groups.

   It has been found that all such attacks on Scientology were instigated by those who either knew full well that their allegations were false or had no information on the subject in the first place. Such persons constitute a minor percentage of the population and work against any self-betterment group or activity, for they perceive the improvement of others as a threat to their power.

ERRORS IN AUDITING

Just as there are guidelines for a student on training, there are also guidelines which the preclear should follow to get the most out of his auditing. Some of the errors that a student can make in a course room are also applicable to preclears. The most common errors made by preclears and how these can be easily remedied are as follows:

Not Getting Sufficient Food or Sleep

Just as being well fed and well rested are requirements for a student, so they are for a preclear.

Not getting enough sleep while getting audited can slow one's progress and keep one's attention on the body. The preclear should get seven or eight hours of sleep a night (or more if he needs it) to ensure he is well rested.

Snacking on soft drinks and chips instead of nutritious meals with plenty of vegetables and protein is also a mistake. If the preclear feels run-down or has attention on his body, he will have less attention to give to the processes in session. To get the most gains, one's concentration has to be on the process.

If one's diet is not providing adequate nutrients, many preclears have found vitamin and mineral supplements helpful. Vitamins B_1 and E taken during auditing have been found especially beneficial. L. Ron Hubbard discovered in his research that preclears require a certain amount of mental energy to carry through with processing. Vitamins B_1 and E can be helpful in generating that energy.

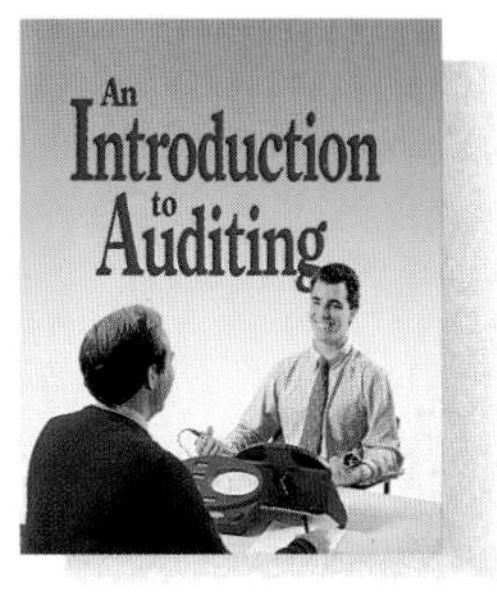

This booklet is provided to all persons newly beginning auditing. It lays out guidelines to follow in order to get maximum gain from one's auditing.

Misunderstood Words

As mentioned in a previous chapter, one of the barriers to study is a phenomenon that occurs when words one reads or hears are not fully understood. This applies in processing as well. If a person who is being audited does not really understand what the auditor is saying or asking, he might well be trying to do something totally different from what the auditor and the process intend. He might experience a lack of gains, become puzzled, and possibly would not want to receive any further auditing.

To prevent this situation from occurring, a person about to receive auditing is given a thorough understanding of the basic terms and concepts used in processing. The exact procedures to be followed are reviewed until the person feels confident that he understands them.

If later during processing a question or uncertainty comes up, the person should tell the auditor immediately. The auditor will assist him in clearing up any misunderstood words and getting any questions answered.

Having Attention on Something Else

Sometimes a person tries to receive auditing while having his attention on something else. Perhaps he knows that the money he put in the parking meter will run out in half an hour, or he knows that if he has not completed his session at a certain time, no one is going to pick up his children from the babysitter.

Situations like this must be handled *before* processing takes place. The preclear simply works to find a solution, such as parking in another spot or getting someone else to pick up the children.

Not Following Instructions

An auditor knows what he is doing and in working with people his goal is to *free* the individual, not suppress him. No matter if it seems difficult at times to do as he says, it will be to the preclear's advantage to do so. Following instructions to the best of one's ability is the keystone of fast progress. The auditor will be the most understanding person the preclear knows; cooperation with him will save many hours.

Not Staying in Communication with the Auditor

The preclear should remain in communication with his auditor. If he feels an unusual or new sensation, he should inform the auditor; he can help to the degree that communication with him is maintained. If the auditor does something that the preclear doesn't like, the preclear should inform the auditor immediately. The communication should not be kept to oneself or saved for the neighbors. Failure to maintain good communication can stop auditing progress entirely. If the preclear feels something is wrong, he should say so. Auditors are usually perceptive but few are psychic.

To receive help as a preclear, a person has to be honest with his auditor. If he doesn't tell his auditor what is really going on—even things he's done that he is ashamed of or for which he thinks he'll be thought less of—he will simply block his own progress up the Bridge. A preclear should also take responsibility for his own case. As he consciously works toward his own improvement he will enhance his progress. He should follow instructions, but help the auditor by remaining in communication with him and by telling him whenever he feels there is something he would like to talk about or work on.

Not Understanding the Auditor's Code

The Auditor's Code (see Chapter 33) is the governing set of rules for the general activity of auditing. The preclear should understand that the auditor is guided in his conduct as an auditor by the Auditor's Code. One point of the Code states that he is not allowed to sympathize with the preclear, but instead must be effective in helping the preclear. He also is trained not to evaluate for a preclear or to tell him what to think about his case in session.

Confusions about the E-Meter

The E-Meter is a very accurate instrument and the full gains in auditing are impossible without its use. Confusions about what the E-Meter does or how it works can get in the way of auditing.

The meter does not diagnose or cure anything. Its value is in helping the auditor locate areas of spiritual travail and charge in the preclear's reactive mind, and in this capacity it is invaluable.

At the beginning of auditing the preclear is shown how to hold the meter electrodes, and has the meter's use in auditing explained to him. The meter electrodes and other conditions need to be adjusted to fit the preclear for comfort or else false readings can be obtained which can mislead the auditor in session. For instance, if the preclear's hands are excessively dry and calloused, a hand cream may need to be applied in order to ensure proper skin contact. Such things as an uncomfortably cool auditing room or wearing shoes that are too tight can also affect the operation of the meter. The auditor is trained to check for and handle this kind of thing before session.

Self-Auditing

Sometimes a person engages in what is called "self-auditing." This consists of going around running concepts or processes on oneself. It is out-of-session wondering and chewing on one's reactive mind.

This is an error, as the person himself does *not* know how to resolve the problem. Most people have been trying to figure out what is wrong with themselves all their lives without success, so the self-auditing approach does not work.

Auditing is a team activity, with the auditor and the preclear working together. The auditor gives the auditing command, the preclear looks to his reactive mind, gets the answer to the question, tells the auditor, and then the auditor acknowledges the answer. In this way the preclear and auditor work together to handle the preclear's reactive mind.

(Self-auditing is not to be confused with *Self Analysis* auditing. *Self Analysis* auditing is done using the exact commands in the book *Self Analysis* by L. Ron Hubbard and actually amounts to being processed by the author. Neither is it the same thing as Solo auditing which is a precise technology developed by Mr. Hubbard to enable one to attain various of the OT levels.)

Discussing One's Case

Case has an exact technical definition in Scientology. It means the entire accumulation of upsets, pain, failures, etc., residing in the preclear's reactive mind. This is what is handled with auditing.

Discussing one's case with anyone else besides an auditor in session is forbidden as this can cause problems in session. If a preclear has done this he should let his auditor or Case Supervisor know. The Case Supervisor is the staff member who directs the auditor and guides him in what auditing actions are done for each individual preclear under his care.

If one does wish to say something about his case before going into session or in between sessions, there is a staff member one can visit, called the Examiner. The preclear can tell the Examiner anything he wishes the Case Supervisor to know, and it is part of the Examiner's duty to make sure the Case Supervisor receives the communication.

Actions Unknown to Case Supervisor

Sometimes people get into situations where they are being audited by an auditor, and at the same time are given other Scientology actions by someone else, such as another auditor or staff member or maybe a friend or family member. This should be avoided, as such other actions, unknown to the Case Supervisor, could foul up the person's case. If this situation arises, it should be immediately communicated, so the auditor can ensure that any needed handling is done.

Fooling Around with Processes

Another error consists of fooling around with nonstandard processes outside of session, without a meter; it is sometimes done by students, stirring up cases. Such activity is forbidden. Standard auditing occurs in session with a trained auditor using proper procedures developed by L. Ron Hubbard.

Taking Drugs or Medicine

Taking drugs while receiving processing is an error just as it is while receiving training, and for the same reasons. Drugs, whether medical or street drugs or even alcohol, should not be consumed while a person is receiving processing.

Illness

It is important if a person becomes ill or has an injury while receiving auditing, even if it is just a cold, to let his auditor know. It is a mistake to not mention an illness or injury, as this will only slow progress.

By informing his auditor right away, the auditor can work out the correct auditing steps and suggest medical attention if needed.

If one needs to get an assist on an emergency basis, this is fine, but make sure that the person who gives the assist writes down what occurred in the session and gets it into the auditing folder (the folder which holds all the records of auditing sessions and other vital data on a preclear's case). In this way the Case Supervisor will be fully informed of all actions taken.

Receiving Processing While Connected to Someone Who Is Against Spiritual Betterment

Just as with training, it occasionally happens that a person receiving auditing is associated with someone who does not care for the fact the person is trying to improve himself. For reasons of their own, a friend or family member sometimes feels threatened if anyone in their vicinity seeks to become brighter or more able. In such instances the person being audited sometimes has to suffer another person's displeasure at his becoming better. Those being audited while connected to people antagonistic to their hopes for improvement may have trouble keeping their gains from auditing. The stress they are subjected to between sessions from the antagonistic person can pose too much of a distraction to the auditing. If the preclear feels this is occurring he should make the situation known. He can then receive assistance from staff in the organization to resolve the source of the antagonism and restore enough harmony so that auditing may progress as expected.

Breaking Auditing Appointments

An auditor's time is very valuable. If an auditing appointment is made, it is a mistake not to keep it. No matter what "emergencies" or other factors arise. If the preclear doesn't show up for session one too many times, he shouldn't be surprised to find that his auditor has been assigned to somebody else! There is a great demand for auditing and people who can keep their auditing appointments naturally get first preference.

If a session absolutely has to be missed or one has to go out of town, he should be sure to let his auditor know with plenty of advance warning.

Not Getting Enough Auditing

Auditing should be given and received intensively, and in sufficient quantity to ensure a stable improvement can be achieved.

Life tends to knock a person about somewhat, and can prevent one from making steady gains if too much time passes between individual sessions. Additionally, it can be predicted based on a person's current case state that it will take a certain amount of hours of auditing to achieve a specific result. The preclear should ensure he has secured enough hours of processing to attain the end result.

Denying One's Integrity

One of the most basic truths of Scientology is that something is not true if it is not true for the individual himself. No one but the individual himself can determine that he has benefited from auditing. If one claims to have benefited for specious reasons such as to be better thought of by one's friends or to have the status of having attained a higher level on the Bridge, this inevitably causes problems sooner or later. Each level of auditing builds on the earlier levels below it and if one skips through lower levels in a desire to get to a higher level, this eventually shows up and needs to be corrected. What happens is that the gains from the higher levels are unobtainable when the lower levels have not been honestly achieved. This is corrected by going back and honestly doing the missed levels, which then enables the full gains to be reached.

Getting Discouraged Easily

Do *not* be discouraged easily. Give the processes a fair chance to work. A preclear will often experience different emotions or attitudes during the course of processing, and discouragement can be one of them.

The only way out is the way through. Sometimes a preclear has to have the courage to persist through a difficult spot in auditing to emerge with the full gains that can be had.

But *do* persist. If the auditor and the preclear work together as a team, results will occur every time. Man has spent countless years sinking into his present state. Processing will not handle every problem a person might have in a day or a week. But the technology is available to greatly increase a person's ability and to restore his health, self-confidence and happiness. Man *can* pull himself up.

Scientology does not claim to be a perfect system. It is a *workable* system, and *does* produce definite, predictable and positive results, far in excess of any other practice.

It is the responsibility of the individual student and preclear to apply Scientology exactly, just as it is the auditor's and Course Supervisor's. When applied exactly, it gives 100 percent success.

Remedying Case Difficulties

Scientology's workability is enhanced by the unique aspect of being able to correct itself. Problems that arise or errors made in its application can be rectified and L. Ron Hubbard developed a corrective technology to accomplish this.

He devised auditing techniques to remedy any error that can occur during the course of an auditing session. These locate the error and get it out of the way. He developed these over the course of more than twenty years' research into the application of auditing techniques and thorough study of auditing done by other auditors. The result is a standard corrective technology that keeps the bumps on the road as incidental as can be expected when one is handling something as tumultuous as life.

Everybody is different. In moving up the Classification, Gradation and Awareness Chart, aspects of a person's life may need to be addressed that are not a part of the general run of processing delivered on the chart. Case conditions can exist which, while not requiring attention in the majority of persons being audited, nevertheless could stall the progress of some people.

L. Ron Hubbard's intention was to provide a technology that brought freedom to *all,* not just to many or to most. To this end, he was constantly alert to phenomena showing up in people's progress in auditing which indicated conditions that might require special procedures in order to completely resolve them.

As a result, a large amount of auxiliary auditing actions were developed so a person's progress up the Bridge could be made smoother. These help a person sort out a specific problem he may be having in his life, such as problems with his marriage. Other actions can address past therapies the person has been engaged in which had adverse effects. One may have trouble with his profession which could be resolved more rapidly by a concentrated address to that specific situation rather than in the general course of auditing. Difficulties one has as a student might be the subject for another auditing action that concentrates on that area.

Life can present different situations that stall a person's progress. Sometimes these can knock the person off the Bridge entirely, but L. Ron Hubbard devised handlings even for that. People who have stumbled on the Bridge have gotten patched up and gotten going again, often at an improved rate of advance.

The idea of a corrective technology to repair any errors in application is, in the field of the humanities, unique to Dianetics and Scientology. L. Ron Hubbard developed this technology in order that failures would be minimized and that any error would be remediable. This is routinely accomplished whenever misapplications of Dianetics and Scientology occur. This is the reason why one finds so many successes in Scientology. L. Ron Hubbard did his researches with an eye toward anyone being able to improve and indeed has made Scientology the game where everyone wins.

Part Five

Churches of Scientology and Their Activities

Parishioners study Scientology technology and receive auditing in Scientology churches around the world. Yet whether in London, Sydney, San Francisco or any of hundreds of other locations on every continent, a church of Scientology has the same basic organizational structure and pattern of operation and performs the same functions. Each church has a common purpose to make the technology of L. Ron Hubbard available and to ensure it is properly learned and applied to the improvement of its parishioners and those in its local community. For these reasons, a church of Scientology is unique among churches—busy, bustling and geared to efficiency.

In order to minister to the spiritual needs of expanding congregations and to ensure uniform application of Dianetics and Scientology, the worldwide churches of Scientology are organized in a hierarchical structure which includes the many public and special service organizations. This section provides an explanation of that hierarchy and how it functions to keep Scientology expanding. The Church has done much to improve society with its betterment and reform efforts and these programs too, are covered, demonstrating that spiritual gains achieved in Scientology translate into effective action to change our troubled world.

Chapter 20

What Occurs in a Church of Scientology

A church of Scientology is a special place, quite different from the popular conception of a church. The church is not only open on Sundays. The Scientology community around a church come and go at different times during the week, and it is an integral part of their lives. It is where they come to study Scientology technology, receive auditing, coordinate community activities or simply to meet friends. Through its doors, they walk a road that can be walked nowhere else, a road to personal discovery, awareness and truth.

The atmosphere in a church of Scientology is what one would expect to find in a place where people are doing well, where they are learning about things, where they are actively pursuing their goals and succeeding. It is *alive,* cheerful and the hope of a better world seems to imbue every activity. The church is a friendly place and anyone is welcome.

Churches are staffed by dedicated Scientologists who leave their homes each morning knowing that when they return in the evening they will have spent the day helping their fellows become happier and freer. In a thoroughly materialistic and often cold world, there are not many who can say the same.

The church is open seven days a week. Delivery of service to church members usually begins at 9:00 A.M. and continues throughout the day. Many churches have two sets of staff, one for weekdays and another to service parishioners on evenings and on the weekends. The Day staff work from 9:00 to 6:00. The second staff (called the Foundation staff) take over from the Day staff at dinner time and keep the church open until 10:30 at night during the week and from 9:00 to 6:00 on weekends. When not working, both Day and Foundation staff tend to the rest of their lives which includes their families, other obligations and, of course, their own progress in Scientology.

The church is always there, literally as well as figuratively, and Scientologists count on it as a stable reference point in their lives. Scientologists tend to be very active in life and are, of course, not always at the church, but they know when they need something, someone will be there to help them.

The Preclear

Most parishioners come to the church for two primary services: to receive auditing or to study on a training course. The church is organized around the administration of these activities and all staff, in one way or another, help ensure that these services are standardly delivered. To understand how the church operates, consider the progress of a typical parishioner arriving there for auditing services. He has, for instance, progressed part of the way to Clear and is returning after an absence to continue further auditing. The church Registrar helps enroll him for his next services. Processing is best done in closely spaced blocks of auditing, at least 2½ hours per day for five consecutive days in a week. This 12½-hour block is called an "intensive." Auditing progress is faster and smoother when delivered on an intensive basis, for life's distractions intrude less. The preclear might enroll for 75 hours of auditing, planning to complete this over the next six weeks.

Auditing is delivered in that part of the organization called the Hubbard Guidance Center (HGC). The HGC is staffed with professional auditors and numerous other personnel necessary for efficient delivery of auditing. After enrolling with the Registrar, the parishioner meets with the Director of Technical Services in the HGC, who sets the schedule for his auditing. Some parishioners find it more conducive to receive their auditing in the mornings, some in the afternoons, some in the evenings. These preferences are taken into account. What matters is that the parishioner receives his auditing predictably and regularly.

When the schedule has been arranged, the person next sees the Director of Processing, the administrator over all auditing delivered to church members. The Director of Processing selects an auditor for the parishioner, and arranges for a battery of tests to be taken. These tests serve to monitor the preclear's progress as he continues up the Bridge. The test results and records from his previous auditing are passed to the Case Supervisor, who then writes a program of auditing actions to ensure the greatest and swiftest gain.

The next day the person returns to the church to commence his auditing. His first stop is the HGC lounge, which exists so auditors can locate their preclears readily. He arrives a little early, and while waiting, meets fellow Scientologists also receiving service, giving him the opportunity to rekindle old friendships or make new ones.

At the appointed hour, the preclear's auditor meets him in the lounge and takes him to the auditing room where the next 2½ hours will be spent making further progress up the Bridge to Clear. Other auditors and preclears come and go throughout the day as the HGC conducts its activities.

When the session is over the auditor takes the preclear to a staff member called the Examiner. The preclear says anything he wishes about the auditing he has just received or anything he would like his Case Supervisor to know. The Examiner's purpose is to ensure that auditing technology has been applied standardly. The information from the Examiner assists the Case Supervisor to ensure all auditing progresses smoothly for the benefit of the preclear. After seeing the Examiner, the preclear is complete until the next day, when the same basic routine occurs again. Rapid gains in awareness and ability happen when auditing is delivered in this way. At the end of the day, all the auditors turn in reports of their sessions and administrative staff route these to the Case Supervisor, who further checks that the auditing was standardly delivered and directs the next day's auditing.

The Student

Students arriving at the church for training also see the Registrar to enroll. Following this, the student visits the church bookstore and obtains the materials needed for his studies. Depending on the course, he will require Scientology books, taped lectures, a pack of technical materials (called bulletins), an E-Meter and accessories, or a combination of these. The bookstore is fully stocked and supplies all Scientologists and the public at large with these items.

The student then goes to the Academy, where all auditor training courses are delivered. Like any course room, Academy courses run on set schedules. Course starts at 9:00, runs until lunch and resumes in the afternoon until dinner, with a midafternoon break. A full-time student can put in 40 hours of course time per week on such a schedule and make very rapid progress through his training. On the Foundation schedule, courses run from 7:00 to 10:30 so Scientologists with day jobs can train. On weekends, course runs from 9:00 to 6:00, similar to the weekday schedule.

The Director of Training is in charge of all training activities and is assisted by the Director of Technical Services, who, as in the case of preclears, also works out student schedules. The Church recognizes the vital necessity for anyone to train in Scientology regardless of other activities in their life. For example, a working mother whose job and family demands do not permit the standard five-night-a-week and weekend schedule, may have allowances made and special schedules arranged. So as not to disrupt those on standard schedules, these part-time students have their own course room. Full-time students study a minimum of 40 hours per week and in practice it is expected that part-time students study at least 12½ hours a week. Less than this has been found to disproportionately extend the amount of time it takes a student to graduate.

Once a course schedule is set, the Course Administrator is seen. He is in charge of all materiel in the course room—its tables and chairs, tape playback machines, films, dictionaries and reference books, etc. After giving the student his course checksheet, he logs him in the course roll book. The Course Supervisor then greets the student and orients him to the Academy, its layout, schedule and rules. He works closely with the student throughout his training, answers questions, helps him with any problems and ensures he understands his materials.

The Course Supervisor ensures students understand and can apply what they are studying.

The Course Supervisor begins each course period with a roll call and then study begins. He personally sees each student and together they work out how much progress the student can make that day. This is the student's goal for the day and the Supervisor and his other personnel assist the student as needed to reach the target he has set for himself.

The course room has a staff member who is expert in locating and clearing student misunderstoods. He is called the "Word Clearer" and is someone the student can go to if difficulties arise in study. The Word Clearer uses study technology and Word Clearing to resolve any inability to understand or apply what is being learned so the student may continue smoothly. The course period ends at its scheduled time, students put away their materials and leave for the day. The next day, course begins again with roll call and the routine is repeated.

When a student completes his course requirements he sees the Examiner who verifies the student's checksheet is complete and that he knows and can apply his materials. In some cases a written examination is administered.

Once a week, usually on Friday, students, preclears and other Scientologists gather for graduation. This is a time for parishioners to acknowledge those students and preclears who have completed a course or level of auditing during the week. Completions have a chance to share their gains with the assembly, which encourages everyone's progress up the Bridge. Graduation also provides an informal setting in which Scientologists may socialize.

While most people recognize the need for a stronger emphasis on religion in their lives, as a general rule, none are as actively committed to the practice of their religion as Scientologists. Whereas many members of congregational religions meet only on Sundays, Scientologists in addition to their career and family commitments, may spend several hours each day, five days a week for a period of several weeks at their church while receiving auditing or training. Many are also highly committed to church-sponsored community betterment programs. Such dedication to moving up the Bridge and forwarding the aims of the Church, is indicative of the fact that Scientologists have experienced, firsthand, the benefits of Mr. Hubbard's technology. They know they have become brighter, more aware and more able—all to the benefit of their careers, their families and their lives in general—and know, too, that such gains can be had by others. As they see it, practice of the religion itself—auditing and training—is truly bettering the world, and this world very much needs improving.

To assist those not currently enrolled on training or auditing, the church offers "home-study" extension courses based on L. Ron Hubbard's books. Many Scientologists also find it helpful and enjoyable to read L. Ron Hubbard's books or listen to his taped lectures on their own, as these works in themselves provide valuable insight into the everyday events of life.

Other Church Activities

When parishioners are not currently on a service at the church, they still want to remain in touch and the church is organized to encourage this. Each church publishes its own magazine which keeps parishioners abreast of news, recent course and auditing completions, upcoming events such as seminars or celebrations and the like. Church staff maintain contact with parishioners by mail and help arrange their return for further service.

Scientologists celebrate several meaningful occasions throughout the year, among them L. Ron Hubbard's birthday, the New Year, the anniversary of Dianetics and Auditor's Day. Parishioners are briefed on important church affairs and activities and updated on the overall expansion of Scientology. In addition to the thousands attending at the central location (which varies from event to event in cities around the world), events are also telecast to all

Scientology churches across the globe, such as Los Angeles, New York, Toronto, London, Paris, Berlin, Barcelona, Sydney, Milan, Johannesburg, Copenhagen, Clearwater and scores of other cities in numerous countries. These events draw parishioners by the thousands to their local churches or public auditoriums to enjoy the event telecast. As well as being informative briefings, these occasions instill a sense of unity among Scientologists everywhere.

Individual churches also regularly host smaller events for local parishioners, including tape plays of L. Ron Hubbard's lectures, Sunday church services, briefings from top auditors and open houses for those new to Scientology and members of the local community.

The church makes every effort to let a person find out for himself what Scientology has to offer in accordance with Mr. Hubbard's principle that, in Scientology, it is only what you find true for yourself that is true. Regular introductory lectures are conducted on basic Dianetics and Scientology principles. Free personality testing is offered to help people isolate the exact areas in their lives they can improve upon and gives them direction as to how this might be accomplished. Films are shown which explain different Dianetics and Scientology concepts. Church staff are always more than happy to answer questions. In particular, the church Registrar is an expert regarding church services and assists individuals in selecting those services which best help them to advance on the Bridge.

Churches offer an array of services designed for a new person. These are delivered in a part of the organization separate from the HGC and the Academy, catering mostly to beginning students. Here, a person just finding out about Dianetics and Scientology can receive services at an introductory level.

Although many Scientologists live some distance from their churches, the church continues to remain a focal point in their lives even when they are not actively involved in an auditing or training service. A Scientologist who has completed professional auditor training and established a practice in the field, for instance, can receive case supervision services and materials from the church.

If a parishioner has difficulty moving up the Bridge or hindrances in any part of his life, the church Ethics Officer helps him apply ethics technology to improve his condition. And when traumatic or personally upsetting situations arise—perhaps a marital quarrel or a dispute with another Scientologist—the Chaplain is always available.

Each Sunday, the Chaplain conducts services open to anyone of any denomination who shares the hope of a better and happier future for man. For the person new to Scientology, this is an opportunity to gain a better understanding of the religion. For the Scientologist, it provides the chance to gain further insight into familiar concepts.

The Chaplain also performs Scientology weddings, christenings and funerals for parishioners and their family members.

Scientologists form numerous groups to aid local programs, particularly in the areas of social reform, education, drug abuse and neighborhood betterment. The church also lends its support to many community-sponsored organizations, and often provides facilities to those who work toward similar goals.

All Scientology activities in the local area fall under the Executive Director and his Executive Council. He is in charge of the church and sees to the well-being of church members, his staff and the expansion of Dianetics and Scientology in his city or area.

But there is even more to a church than what goes on inside. As a central point from which dedicated Scientologists come and go, applying what they have learned to help those around them, the church, in turn, becomes a central point of betterment for the whole community. Thus as the church itself flourishes, so too do those around it.

Scientology events, celebrations and briefings are held several times a year and are attended by thousands of parishioners. Events held at a central location, such as this New Year's gathering, are telecast to churches around the globe. Here, Church leaders have an opportunity to talk to other Scientologists and brief them on Church activities and expansion news from different parts of the world.

SYSTEM OF DONATIONS

Some churches have a system of tithes, others require their members to pay for pew rentals, religious ceremonies and services. In the Church of Scientology, parishioners make donations for auditing or training they wish to take. These contributions by Scientologists are the primary source of financial support for the church and fund all the community programs and social betterment activities of Scientology. Scientologists are not required to tithe or make other donations.

The church also has a "Free Scientology Center" where parishioners may receive auditing without donation, from ministers-in-training. Auditor training is encouraged by making it very economical and by also offering scholarships to deserving Scientologists. This has a dual benefit, creating valuable auditors who can help their fellows, and who can also co-audit their way up the Bridge with another student without charge.

Ideally, Dianetics and Scientology services would be free, and all Scientologists wish they were. But those are not the realities of life. When one considers the cost of delivering even one hour of auditing, requiring extensively trained specialists, and the overhead costs of maintaining church premises, the necessity of donations becomes clear.

The donation system in Scientology is the most equitable as those who use the facilities of the church are the ones who most directly contribute to its upkeep and continued existence. Naturally, no donation is expected from those not receiving auditing or training. And church doors are always open to those who wish to learn more about the philosophy of Scientology, be they parishioners or not. There are tape plays of L. Ron Hubbard's lectures, introductory lectures, books available, people to discuss questions with, and of course the more traditional church activities—Sunday services, sermons, weddings, christenings, funerals—all of which are provided without any donation necessary.

Scientology does not have hundreds of years of accumulated wealth and property like other religions—it must make its way in the world according to the economics of today's society.

Scientologists' donations keep the church alive and functioning, fund its widespread social reform programs, make Scientology known to people who may otherwise never have the opportunity to avail themselves of it and help create a safe and pleasant environment for everyone.

SCIENTOLOGY ADMINISTRATIVE TECHNOLOGY

Scientology is an entirely new activity, and cannot be organized along general religious or secular lines. Unlike other churches, it provides services for parishioners seven days a week, not merely on Saturdays or Sundays. Its primary services, however, are not congregational, where one minister serves the needs of hundreds or a thousand parishioners at once. Nor is it a social or commercial activity, for its province is strictly spiritual, providing freedom to man through the exact application of a precise technology administered like no other.

Recognizing this, L. Ron Hubbard spent many years developing a wholly new system of organization designed specifically for the purpose of making auditing and training broadly available and accessible. This system contains all functions an organization must perform in order to efficiently provide for its parishioners and is based upon what is called an "organizing board."

The Scientology organizing board has been used in all Dianetics and Scientology organizations since it was developed in 1965. It is an arrangement of functions necessary to obtain a product. The church's product is not a manufactured item, it is totally freed beings.

This pattern contains seven divisions which describe all the actions encompassed by the organization. Each division is subdivided into three departments. In these seven divisions and their twenty-one departments one finds all the functions, duties, positions, sequences of action and command channels of the organization.

The Divisions 1 through 7 of the organizing board are laid out in a sequence known as the *cycle of production.* L. Ron Hubbard discovered that for any cycle of action to complete successfully, it must go through these seven main stages. That is, to produce something of value, an organization must have all seven divisions operating.

The organizing board works as follows: The first division of the organization is the Hubbard Communications Office—so named because its main functions were originally part of L. Ron Hubbard's office in the early days of Scientology. This division establishes and keeps the church running. The functions include hiring personnel, answering the phones, handling the mail, delivering internal communications, filing reports on the church's operations and administering its ethics and justice system.

The next division, Division 2, is the Dissemination Division. *Dissemination* means to spread or scatter broadly. In a Scientology church, this division makes Scientology services and materials widely known. It produces mailings and publications, such as the church's magazine, which are sent to all parishioners, and operates the church bookstore. The staff in this division inform individuals about Scientology. Church members often write to request information or to arrange for services. Those letters are answered within this division.

Division 3 is the Treasury Division. All corporations, even religious ones, are required to keep proper financial records. Donations from parishioners provide the wherewithal for the church to disseminate Scientology, carry on its work in the community and continue to make auditing and training available. Division 3 invoices donations, pays the bills, disburses other monies and keeps financial records. It also provides for the upkeep and ensures the continued value of the organization's premises and equipment.

The Technical or Production Division of the organization, Division 4, provides the major training and auditing services of the Bridge. It gives excellent and fast service, schedules people for auditing, and provides high-volume, high-quality Scientology training and processing. The Technical Division is the central activity of the organization. It produces the product by which the organization expands and survives. The Technical Division contains more staff than other divisions, as these are needed to assist parishioners with arrangements for service, provide course supervision and other course room services, and deliver auditing. The other divisions in the organization factually exist to facilitate the Technical Division's production of its product.

The next division, Division 5, is the Qualifications Division. The functions of this division are unique to Scientology churches. Whereas many organizations maintain quality control over products, this division does much more: It sees to the enhancement, correction and care of those who actually *produce* the product. If a staff member in any way has difficulties performing his duties, he receives immediate attention and help from Division 5. Without such concern for its members, an organization may eventually fail. In addition to its routine correction duties, Division 5 trains and audits the staff. It also corrects students and auditors on any inability to apply what they have learned and runs the internship to make auditor training course graduates into top-flight professionals. And it verifies that the full gains of all auditing have been received by church parishioners.

Division 6 is called the Public Division. In a Scientology church, Division 6 introduces new people to Scientology through lectures and films, open houses, Sunday church services and tape plays. It also offers introductory courses. This division reaches into the community to provide needed assistance and contribution to local social programs. Through the Public Division, the church performs many goodwill actions which benefit the community. Additionally, Scientologists often form "field groups" which offer basic Dianetics and Scientology services to the public. Division 6 assists setup of field groups and missions in new areas so more people can benefit from Dianetics and Scientology.

The last division is the Executive Division, Division 7, which keeps the overall activity viable and expanding through careful planning and supervision. The Executive Director is located here. Division 7 is responsible for legal affairs and government relations. Another important executive in each church is the L. Ron Hubbard (LRH) Communicator—a position established when Mr. Hubbard served as Executive Director of the Church and maintained a local representative in each church to facilitate his communication channels. Today, the LRH Communicator sees that the church adheres to Mr. Hubbard's writings. The LRH Communicator also preserves the L. Ron Hubbard office maintained in all churches as a mark of respect for the Founder of the religion. The LRH Communicator's duties are especially key because it is the standard application of L. Ron Hubbard's technology which makes the gains and accomplishments of Dianetics and Scientology possible.

This pattern of organization also serves as a "philosophical system" by which any organization or even one's own life can be analyzed. Each division contains three smaller departments, making twenty-one departments in all. The departments correspond to levels of awareness as found on the Classification, Gradation and Awareness Chart. The design of the organization, then, follows the progression of a person up the Bridge itself. A person comes into the church through Reception in Division 1, is routed to Division 2 where he enrolls on his service, makes his donation in Division 3, receives his service in Division 4, is verified as having achieved the full result in Division 5 and stays connected up with the organization through its field activities in Division 6, all of which is coordinated and directed by Division 7.

The organizational pattern, then, is actually an upward spiral with Division 7 adjacent to but higher than Division 1. When parishioners reenter the organization for further services, they are on a higher plane. Through this pattern and system people receive the knowledge and abilities of Scientology.

Each division produces a specific product which contributes to the overall cycle of production of the organization. Each department within a division produces its own product, which in turn contributes to the product of the division.

The organization corrects itself through the Qualifications Division, under the authority of the Executive Division.

These principles of organization apply to an individual's own life as thoroughly as they do to a large corporation composed of many thousands. The functions and activities contained in the divisions and departments exist in a person's life. For instance, a person produces a product on his job; that is his Division 4, Technical. He handles his finances; that is his Division 3, Treasury, and so on. A person can look over the divisions and departments and see what is missing in his own life.

An organization, or a life, fails because it is lacking one or another of these divisions. But, by knowing and applying this pattern and its principles, organizations and individuals can expand and prosper.

All Scientology churches or groups are covered by the organizing board. The divisions are manned in such a way that the maximum amount of service can be delivered to parishioners. A ratio exists between number of staff needed to deliver training and auditing services to number of staff needed to administer and support delivery. The Technical and Qualifications Divisions (Divisions 4 and 5) are the primary portions of the organization which deliver auditing and training services to public and staff. These require many staff to supervise students, audit preclears, train staff, run an internship and so on. The organization is manned in a ratio of one staff member in

Technical or Qualifications Divisions to one staff member in all the other divisions. This has been found to satisfy demand for auditing and training and administrative support services.

The staff in Division 4 (Technical Division), for instance, need to be supplied with a building, furniture, utilities and so forth. They need somebody to sign up new preclears for service, somebody to pay the electric bill, somebody to keep the premises clean and other actions which can be efficiently done by others, leaving the technical staff free to deliver services.

Man has a tendency to fill all the boxes on an organization chart. This is extremely inefficient and hinders expansion. Allotting personnel to every post regardless of need leaves some posts overloaded and others underworked. The formula of one administrative staff member for every technical staff member handles this. Thus, the Technical and Qualifications Divisions are heavy with personnel, containing five times as many as each of the other divisions.

In expanding the organization, each department acquires five subsections, every subsection acquires five units.

Such a pattern of organization is remarkable in its effectiveness. Application of it in churches of Scientology has provided a stable, constantly expanding structure which has contributed greatly to the Church flourishing around the world. It was designed not to make money or to make Scientologists. Its whole purpose is to forward the "Ability to Better Conditions," which is the mission of Scientology. A simplified version of the organizing board is contained at the end of this chapter.

The Technology of Administration

Having described the basic organizational form, one can now begin to understand the specific policies upon which that framework functions. These precise and workable administrative policies were also developed by Mr. Hubbard through years of research and experience, and constitute a tremendous body of material relating to the survival of a group.

As with everything Mr. Hubbard accomplished, his discoveries came from hard-won experience. He isolated administrative fundamentals for every level of organization from top to bottom. When Executive Director of Scientology organizations internationally, he worked in virtually every position and function, ironing out difficulties and forming the policy for smooth and efficient operation. He wrote policies covering the theory and particulars of every working facet in a Scientology organization. In total, these spell out the basic laws of the third dynamic (group survival) and constitute a body of knowledge as important to administration of groups as his writings on Dianetics and Scientology are to rehabilitation of the spirit.

Staff members therefore study this administrative technology avidly. In applying auditing technology they have learned that an exact procedure results in the improvement of a specific condition in the preclear. Likewise, it is apparent that by following and maintaining exact administrative procedures, one can remedy, handle or reinforce situations relating to the group.

All of this administrative technology has been arranged into a twelve-volume set of reference texts. Volume 0, the *Basic Staff Hat,* contains all policies pertinent to any church staff member and provides a thorough orientation to the organization for new staff members. Seven of the remaining volumes, numbered one through seven, correspond to the same numbered divisions of the organizing board. Volume One, for example, covers Division 1; Volume Two, Division 2; and so on. Each divisional volume contains all the policies pertaining to the purpose and functions of that division. Organized in this way, any person in the organization can easily find the policies which describe his own functions within the group. Or he can refer to other volumes and gain an understanding of any duty in the organization and thus work more efficiently and harmoniously as a group member.

The remaining volumes encompass Mr. Hubbard's writings on the subject of management and executive know-how.

These books contain a codification of all the ingredients required to successfully operate Dianetics and Scientology organizations. When any necessary functions are found to be missing, the organization is, to that degree, unsuccessful. And to the degree that each function is present and operating, the organization thrives.

Mr. Hubbard also devised the means to monitor the production of any post in the organization, using statistics to ensure that no individual is lost in the group. By staticizing activities, church executives can direct the activities of the organization more efficiently. This single principle allows for the exact isolation of areas or functions which require attention, and its application alone has dramatically enhanced the success of many organizations. The entire body of technology concerning statistics is intimately related to application of the principles of the conditions of existence—statistics are a guide to the application of the correct condition. As each staff position contributes to the overall well-being of the group, it follows that one can use these principles to enhance the survival of the entire organization.

In his policies, L. Ron Hubbard further delineated the purposes, functions and products of every post and, in turn, every department, so organization members could work as a team and achieve their overall product. In so doing, he codified a workplace technology applied all over the world today by Scientology churches, missions and groups.

Church executives train on courses which cover the totality of these volumes and learn to apply them in their day-to-day running of the organization.

Although Mr. Hubbard developed this technology to help administer Dianetics and Scientology, parishioners who worked outside the organization began to apply these principles to other groups as well. L. Ron Hubbard discovered and delineated the basics on which *any* group operated and, as such, these breakthroughs are broadly applicable. Since then his administrative principles have been used by many other organizations around the world with extraordinary success.

These volumes contain the codification of the administrative technology required to successfully operate Scientology organizations.

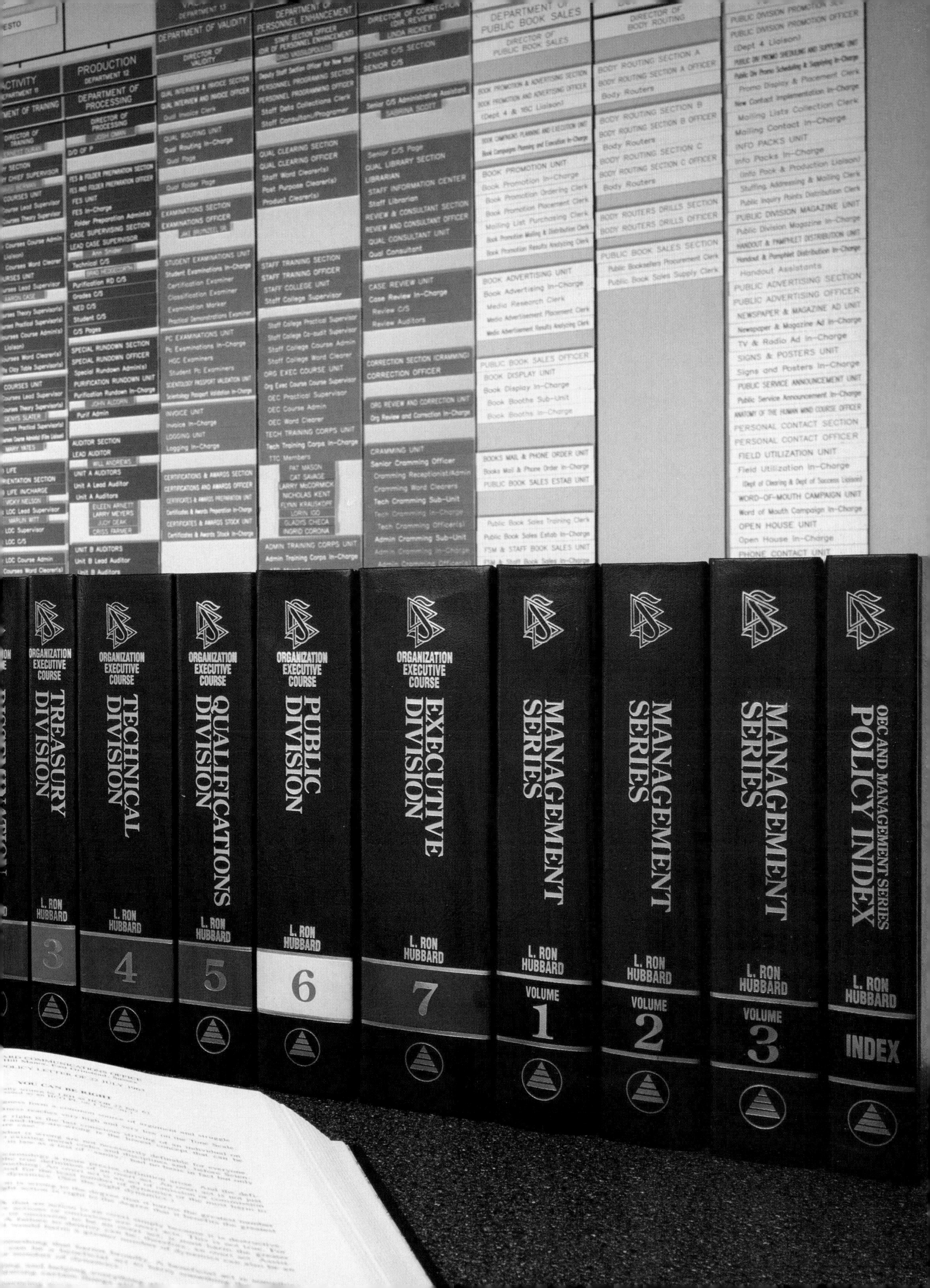
ORGANIZATION EXECUTIVE COURSE
TREASURY DIVISION
L. RON HUBBARD
3
ORGANIZATION EXECUTIVE COURSE
TECHNICAL DIVISION
L. RON HUBBARD
4
ORGANIZATION EXECUTIVE COURSE
QUALIFICATIONS DIVISION
L. RON HUBBARD
5
ORGANIZATION EXECUTIVE COURSE
PUBLIC DIVISION
L. RON HUBBARD
6
ORGANIZATION EXECUTIVE COURSE
EXECUTIVE DIVISION
L. RON HUBBARD
7
MANAGEMENT SERIES
L. RON HUBBARD
VOLUME 1
MANAGEMENT SERIES
L. RON HUBBARD
VOLUME 2
MANAGEMENT SERIES
L. RON HUBBARD
VOLUME 3
OEC AND MANAGEMENT SERIES
POLICY INDEX
L. RON HUBBARD
INDEX
PRODUCTION
DEPARTMENT OF PROCESSING
DEPARTMENT OF VALIDITY
DEPARTMENT OF PERSONNEL ENHANCEMENT
DEPARTMENT OF PUBLIC BOOK SALES

ORGANIZING BOARD

(Simplified version, showing the organizational pattern used in all churches of Scientology)

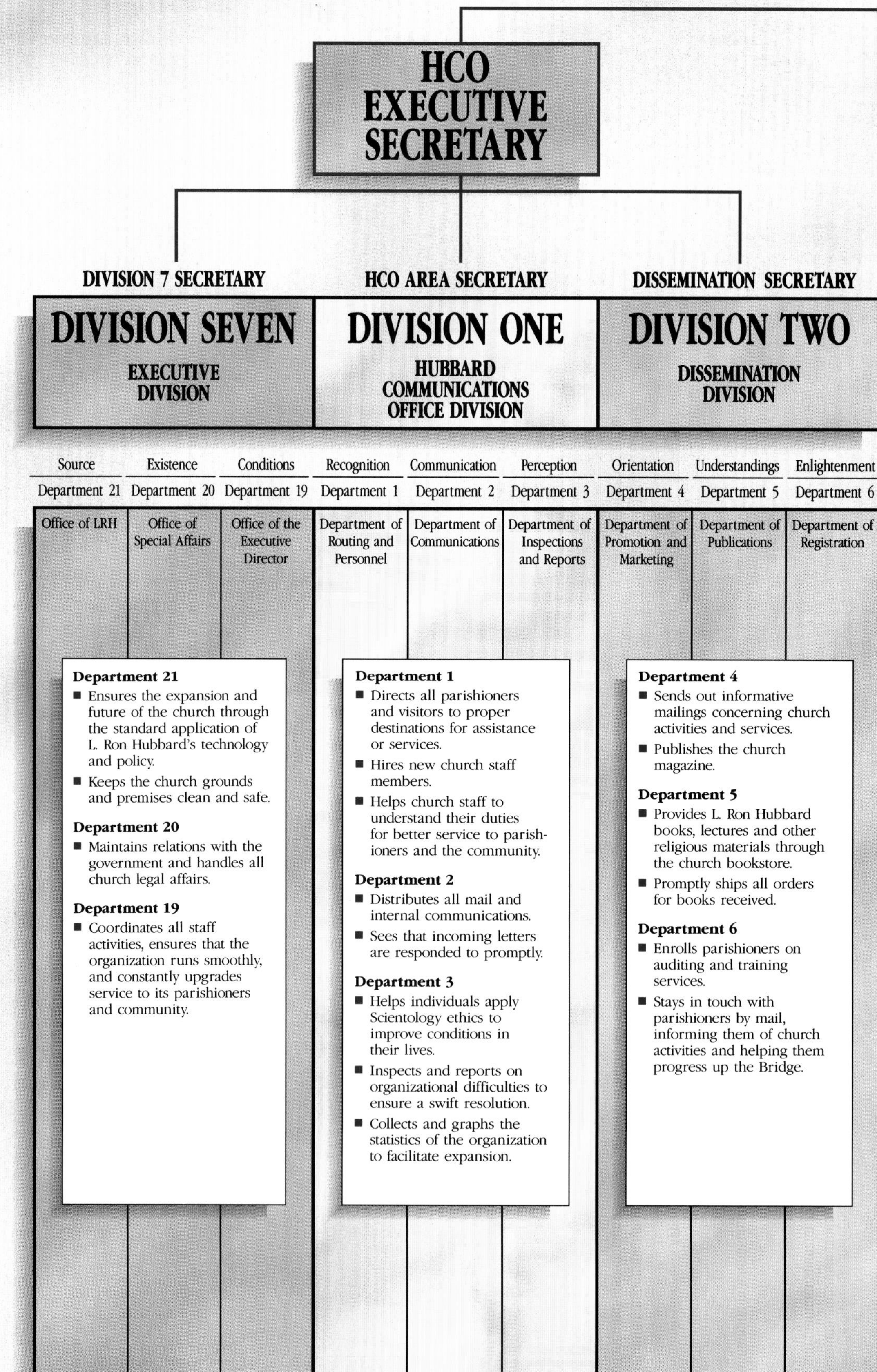

EXECUTIVE DIRECTOR

ORGANIZATION EXECUTIVE SECRETARY

TREASURY SECRETARY	TECHNICAL SECRETARY	QUALIFICATIONS SECRETARY	DISTRIBUTION SECRETARY
DIVISION THREE TREASURY DIVISION	**DIVISION FOUR** TECHNICAL DIVISION	**DIVISION FIVE** QUALIFICATIONS DIVISION	**DIVISION SIX** PUBLIC DIVISION

Energy	Adjustment	Body	Prediction	Activity	Production	Result	Correction	Ability	Purposes	Clearing	Realization
Department 7	Department 8	Department 9	Department 10	Department 11	Department 12	Department 13	Department 14	Department 15	Department 16	Department 17	Department 18
Department of Income	Department of Disbursements	Department of Records, Assets and Materiel	Department of Technical Services	Department of Activity	Department of Production	Department of Examinations	Department of Review	Department of Certifications and Awards	Department of Public Information	Department of Clearing	Department of Success

Department 7
- Invoices parishioner donations and maintains records of donations received.

Department 8
- Sees to the material needs of the church and its staff by purchasing all items required to keep the church functioning.
- Pays any bills incurred by the church.

Department 9
- Cares for all church furniture, equipment and the like, ensuring such property is well maintained and properly functioning.
- Keeps records of church accounts.

Department 10
- Sees that parishioners are well cared for and receive rapid service.
- Helps arrange housing for out-of-town parishioners.
- Provides technical staff with needed supplies and materials to deliver auditing and training.

Department 11
- Standardly delivers Scientology training services to all parishioners.
- Graduates auditors who can help others move up the Bridge.

Department 12
- Standardly delivers auditing to church parishioners with excellent results.

Department 13
- Verifies that students and preclears have received the full results of their services.

Department 14
- Locates and corrects failures to standardly apply the technology.
- Cares for church staff by providing them with auditing and training.

Department 15
- Issues certificates to those who complete church services.

Department 16
- Makes Dianetics and Scientology more broadly known and delivers introductory lectures to inform people about the subjects.

Department 17
- Provides introductory training, auditing and seminars.
- Delivers chaplain services including marriage counseling.
- Performs ministerial services including weddings, naming ceremonies and Sunday services.

Department 18
- Appoints and assists volunteer ministers to perform their functions in the community.
- Helps open new Dianetics and Scientology groups in the area.
- Assists the local community with church goodwill programs.

Chapter 21

Scientology Around the World

The rapid expansion of Scientology has been due, in large part, to the scores of churches of Scientology. These now exist in most major cities throughout the world and provide auditing and training services to individuals who want to advance up the Bridge.

Although each church is usually incorporated separately, with its own board of directors and executives responsible for its activities, these churches together form the stable building blocks of an international network which spans the globe.

To clarify this further, however, it should also be understood that these churches are part of a hierarchical structure arranged in a pattern which matches the Classification, Gradation and Awareness Chart of Scientology. In other words, at the lower level of this hierarchy individuals and organizations provide beginning-level auditing and training; and, at the upper level, church organizations deliver the highest levels of auditing and training. It is a logical sequence of organization, one that reflects the progress of Scientology parishioners up the Bridge.

Below the local churches are individual Scientologists and various groups that support them; above them are higher-level churches which deliver more advanced levels of auditing and training. Generally, the higher-level organizations deliver all services of the organizations beneath them. Spanning everything is an ecclesiastical management structure that supports, coordinates and assists the activities of each and every organization, in order for Scientology as a whole to achieve its aims.

This ecclesiastical hierarchy is paralleled by a corporate structure, as is the case in many religions. Religious nonprofit corporations provide the Church with a legal identity that allows it to interact with society; open bank accounts; purchase goods and services; and enter into contractual relationships with other corporations and individuals. These separate corporations are each fully independent and responsible for their own activities and well-being, though they receive ecclesiastical guidance and assistance from others and form part of the larger picture which is the religion of Scientology.

From top to bottom, in this ecclesiastical hierarchy, Scientologists are united in action by common purposes.

FIELD AUDITORS AND DIANETICS COUNSELING GROUPS

At the lowest level of the Scientology hierarchy are field auditors and Dianetics Counseling Groups. Any properly qualified individual Scientologist may become a "field auditor" and deliver auditing and introductory services. People often find that when they become trained in Scientology they want to help others with what they have learned, and this is frequently how field auditors get started—auditing friends and family.

Field auditors operate either alone or as part of a Dianetics Counseling Group with other auditors who work together to contact new people, get them started on the Bridge and then refer them to a church of Scientology where they continue their auditing and training. In either case, they offer auditing services up to the classification training levels of the auditors involved. This is an outreach activity that is an important aspect of the religion's expansion.

Field auditors and Dianetics Counseling Groups are assisted by the International Hubbard Ecclesiastical League of Pastors (I HELP). I HELP, located in Los Angeles, California, was created to provide auditors who deliver services outside organized churches and missions with the guidance they need to operate successfully. It aids auditors in the field to minister to the public by providing them with materials, publications and consultation services. It also offers assistance with any administrative or technical difficulties they may encounter. I HELP ensures field auditors maintain high standards of application and discipline.

Field auditors and Dianetics Counseling Groups provide the following religious services:

I HELP

- INTRODUCTORY LECTURES
- TAPE PLAYS OF L. RON HUBBARD'S LECTURES
- HUBBARD DIANETICS SEMINAR
- SUCCESS THROUGH COMMUNICATION COURSE
- OTHER INTRODUCTORY SERVICES FOR PEOPLE NEW TO SCIENTOLOGY
- PURIFICATION PROGRAM
- DIANETICS AND SCIENTOLOGY AUDITING THROUGH NEW ERA DIANETICS AND EXPANDED DIANETICS

Scientology Missions

Scientology missions comprise the next level of the ecclesiastical hierarchy. A mission is a religious nonprofit corporation granted the right to provide elementary Dianetics and Scientology services. Missions are a front-line dissemination activity of Scientology that reach out to those who have not previously come in contact with the religion. Missions do not have full church status, nor do they have the authority to train or ordain Scientology ministers. They are often started in areas of the world not previously introduced to Scientology. There are hundreds of missions located on every continent on Earth.

Missions offer all the introductory and beginning services of Dianetics and Scientology, including extension courses, Life Improvement Courses, Dianetics Seminars, the Success Through Communication Course, the Student Hat course, Hubbard Qualified Scientologist Course and certain co-auditing courses where students learn to audit each other on specific actions. Missions may also deliver all auditing actions up through New Era Dianetics, including introductory auditing, Expanded Lower Grades and Expanded Dianetics.

Scientology Missions International (SMI) is the mother church for all missions. SMI provides guidance and help for existing missions, keeps the far-flung network of missions in communication with each other, and assists Scientologists to open new missions, encouraging them particularly in countries and cities where no missions already exist. Any qualified Scientologist may open a mission and contribute to the advancement of Scientology into society.

After a mission or group expands, it can eventually become a Scientology church. There are many more missions than there are Scientology churches, each reaching out into the society and bringing Dianetics and Scientology to mankind through beginning services.

There are hundreds of missions located in scores of countries around the world.

They deliver the following religious services:

- Introductory lectures, films and tapes
- Extension courses
- Life Improvement Courses
- Hubbard Dianetics Seminar
- Success Through Communication Course
- Other introductory services for people new to Scientology
- Scientologist hatting courses
- The Student Hat
- Purification program
- Auditing through New Era Dianetics and Expanded Dianetics

Class V Organizations

Above missions in the Scientology hierarchy come the churches of Scientology. The first echelon of churches provide beginning and intermediate Dianetics and Scientology training and auditing. This includes all religious services that missions may deliver, and they additionally train auditors to the level of Class V Graduate Auditor. For this reason they are known within Scientology as Class V organizations.

Class V organizations can also provide other services such as training on Technical Specialist Courses, the Hubbard Key to Life Course and Hubbard Life Orientation Course. Only churches have the authority to train and ordain Scientology ministers.

Many Class V organizations establish smaller offices in nearby areas and towns to provide introductory services, after which public then go to the central church for further training and auditing.

Each church in each city is the center of Scientology activity in that area and functions as the source and dissemination point of the technology. It is the core of Scientology in its district, playing a major role in helping individuals and groups provide Dianetics and Scientology services to the public.

Class V organizations make Dianetics and Scientology broadly known to people in their area, and also assist Scientologists to set up groups and missions which in turn contact and service their local public and in this way expansion continues to keep up with the increased demand for L. Ron Hubbard's technology.

Class V organizations are concerned with the quality of technical delivery in local missions and groups and among field auditors, ensuring that the technologies of Dianetics and Scientology are standardly applied so parishioners receive the expected gains.

The church is the central point for numerous community activities. Blood drives, antidrug rallies, toy drives, entertaining the elderly, cleaning up local parks, crime watches and the like are often spearheaded by the church.

Scientology Class V organizations provide a safe and stable point for all the Scientology activities in an area to help parishioners move up the Bridge to Total Freedom.

Scientology Class V churches are located around the world with more opening all the time.

They deliver the following religious services:

- All introductory services provided by missions
- All auditing through New Era Dianetics and Expanded Dianetics
- Auditor training to the level of Class V Graduate
- The Minister's Course and ordaining ministers
- Technical Specialist Courses
- The Hubbard Key to Life Course
- The Hubbard Life Orientation Course
- Solo Auditor Course Part One
- Clear
- Sunshine Rundown

Celebrity Centres

L. Ron Hubbard once wrote, "A culture is only as great as its dreams, and its dreams are dreamed by artists." Artists supply the spark of creativity and the vision of what could be leading us into tomorrow.

Artists wield enormous influence over society, setting cultural trends and forwarding new ideas, both good and bad. In the sixties, musicians promoted drugs, and helped lead an entire generation into the drug culture. On the other hand, many artists work to raise public awareness of environmental concerns. By example, and through their art, they influence millions. By improving the lives of artists, great progress can be achieved to better the condition of society—for any artist with an increased ability to communicate, who is drug free and has high moral standards imparts a positive influence to many others.

To forward their dreams and help artists elevate the culture, L. Ron Hubbard established Celebrity Centres. They are located in cities around the world and assist artists to achieve their goals through the application of Dianetics and Scientology. They offer services to artists and professionals in such fields as the performing arts, fine arts, sports and business. Church of Scientology Celebrity Centres deliver the same services as Class V organizations and missions but additionally provide special services which help artists apply Scientology principles to their chosen fields. A training service exists, for instance, which covers L. Ron Hubbard's codification of the field of art.

The availability and types of services offered accommodate the unique needs and aspirations of these individuals. Apart from providing a location where Scientology artists are able to meet each other, Celebrity Centres also offer a distraction-free environment where they can concentrate on their auditing and training.

There are thirteen Church of Scientology Celebrity Centres which provide the following religious services:

- All services provided by Class V churches
- Specialized Scientology courses for artists

Saint Hill Organizations

The original Saint Hill church organization was located at Mr. Hubbard's home, Saint Hill Manor, in East Grinstead, Sussex, England. It was there that Mr. Hubbard delivered the Saint Hill Special Briefing Course (SHSBC), the most extensive auditor course in all of Scientology.

When other organizations were formed in Copenhagen and Los Angeles to meet the demand for SHSBC training, they were named "Saint Hill" organizations, as they specialize in delivering the Saint Hill Special Briefing Course.

Saint Hill Organizations are centralized church colleges for advanced auditor training. They provide extensive training facilities to parishioners from both local areas and remote locations. Most Saint Hill students arrange their schedules so they can devote themselves to an intensive period of training—several months to a year—on the Briefing Course. Thus, Saint Hills have a high concentration of full-time students, who study in an environment uniquely suited to auditor training.

Saint Hills play an important role in the religion of Scientology as they train expert auditors who gain a comprehensive understanding of life. A chronological study of the development of the Scientology philosophy from its beginning to the present gives graduates of the Briefing Course a wide-ranging ability to benefit society and their fellow man.

In 1983, the newest Church of Scientology Saint Hill Organization opened in Sydney, Australia.

There are Church of Scientology Saint Hill Organizations located in four cities around the world.

They deliver the following religious services:

- All auditing and training services provided by Scientology Class V churches
- Power Processing
- The Saint Hill Special Briefing Course
- Class VII Auditor training
- Auditing services on the Grade Chart through Eligibility for OT levels auditing
- Solo Auditor Course Part Two

Advanced Organizations

Advanced Organizations (AOs) are located in Los Angeles, East Grinstead in England, Copenhagen and Sydney. They offer advanced auditing and training, with an emphasis on auditing. This is where a person progresses through the OT levels, to the completion of OT Section V. Advanced Organizations also train auditors on the Class VIII Auditor and C/S Courses.

The Advanced Org churches service parishioners from a wide area who move up the Bridge from missions and Class V orgs. In the case of the Advanced Organization Los Angeles for instance, parishioners from all over the United States, Canada, Mexico and South America travel to Los Angeles to progress up the OT levels or do Class VIII Auditor training.

The staff at these higher-level churches require a higher level of training in Scientology in order to administer these advanced levels of the Bridge.

There are four Church of Scientology Advanced Organizations.

They deliver the following religious services:

- All auditing and training services provided by Class V churches
- All processing services from Grade VI Release through New OT V New Era Dianetics for OTs
- Doctorate Series Course for OTs
- Class VIII Auditor and C/S training

FLAG SERVICE ORGANIZATION

The Flag Service Organization (FSO) is a religious retreat for Scientologists of every nationality. It provides the highest levels of religious services. (The term *Flag* denotes that this organization was first established on a ship, the *Apollo.* Beginning in 1967, Mr. Hubbard conducted his research into the upper levels of Scientology with a group of dedicated Scientologists aboard three ships. These advanced services were then delivered aboard the *Apollo,* flagship of the flotilla, until land-based organizations were established for greater accessibility. This is more fully described later in this chapter.)

The FSO, in Clearwater, Florida, is the largest single Scientology church in the world, with well over 750 staff members. As people travel there from all over the world to receive auditing and training, staying for several weeks or even months at a time before returning home, the FSO also provides accommodations for its parishioners in a distraction-free environment so they can make the most progress on the Bridge during their stay, without the turbulence of the day-to-day world.

Here, auditors train to the level of Class XII, which is the highest auditor classification in Scientology. The FSO also delivers Dianetics and Scientology services from the bottom of the Bridge through to New OT VII, plus certain specialized auditing services only available there.

Auditor training above Class VIII is exclusive to the FSO. Included among its staff are the most experienced and highly trained auditors, case supervisors, course supervisors and other training specialists on the planet. The FSO sets the technical standard in Scientology and enjoys a reputation for the highest standards of technical perfection. Churches and missions from around the world send their technical staff to be trained to Flag standards.

The Flag Service Organization is unique. It delivers all religious services available in all lower organizations. Additionally, it delivers:

- NEW OT VI AND NEW OT VII (SOLO NEW ERA DIANETICS FOR OTS)
- AUDITOR TRAINING THROUGH CLASS XII
- SPECIALIZED AUDITING AVAILABLE ONLY AT THE FSO INCLUDING:

  L10 Rundown

  L11 New Life Rundown

  L12 Flag OT Executive Rundown

  New Vitality Rundown

  Profession Intensive

  Knowledge Rundown

  Case Cracker Rundown

  Interiorization by Dynamics Rundown

  Dynamic Sort-out Assessment

  Fixated Person Rundown

FLAG SHIP SERVICE ORGANIZATION

Whereas the FSO offers the highest level of auditor training and auditing from the bottom of the Bridge up through OT VII, the delivery of OT VIII, the most advanced OT level available, is entrusted to the Flag Ship Service Organization (FSSO). This church is located aboard a ship, the 450-foot motor vessel *Freewinds*. This ship forms an ideal religious retreat off the crossroads of society where full attention can be devoted to spiritual advancement. Parishioners normally stay for several weeks to receive OT VIII and also to take special training courses which help a person enhance his abilities as an OT. This setting makes an ideal environment, far from everyday distractions, for the delivery of these advanced spiritual services.

The Church of Scientology Flag Ship Service Organization only delivers specialized religious services to advanced Scientologists.

- NEW OT VIII, THE HIGHEST AUDITING LEVEL AVAILABLE IN SCIENTOLOGY
- THE HUBBARD KEY TO LIFE COURSE
- THE HUBBARD LIFE ORIENTATION COURSE
- THE NEW HUBBARD PROFESSIONAL TR COURSE
- SPECIAL TRAINING COURSES TO ENHANCE ABILITIES AS AN OT

THE CHURCH OF SCIENTOLOGY INTERNATIONAL

The system of ecclesiastical management used in the Church was developed to individually care for the large number of Scientology churches, missions and groups which exist, while at the same time providing the broad planning and direction needed to advance the propagation of Scientology in the world.

Individual churches of Scientology are governed by their own council of executives from that local church. The executive council is fully responsible for the application of Scientology policy and technology to ensure the expansion of Dianetics and Scientology in that area.

However, to assist individual churches, and ensure the overall expansion of Scientology, there is a mother church for all Scientology—the Church of Scientology International (CSI), located in Los Angeles.

Through CSI's ecclesiastical management activities, individual Scientology churches receive guidance in applying the scriptures both technically and administratively.

CSI broadly plans and coordinates Scientology expansion overall; providing programs to be carried out by the individual organizations and groups, and then helping with their implementation toward expansion.

CSI provides specialized training programs for church executives on the entirety of Scientology administrative technology which allows them to better serve their parishioners. This training is conducted at CSI's headquarters in the Hollywood Guaranty Building in Los Angeles.

In addition to coordinating the overall expansion of Scientology, CSI sees to the distribution of Scientology scriptures, both in written and audiovisual form. Golden Era Productions produces all the E-Meters, religious training films, slide shows and videos of Scientology and the recorded lectures of Mr. Hubbard.

Translations of L. Ron Hubbard's books, courses, lectures and films into many languages is also a function of Golden Era.

Church management provides ecclesiastical guidance to each of the Scientology organizations, coordinates the activities and expansion of Scientology internationally and in doing so makes it possible for Dianetics and Scientology to meet the demand for its services from people around the world.

Religious Technology Center

Utmost importance is given to the precise application of Dianetics and Scientology, because, when standardly applied, with the honest cooperation of one who is seeking spiritual betterment, it works 100 percent of the time. Such a technology has never before existed. Millions of people around the world regard this technology as valuable beyond comparison, and it is of great interest to Scientologists everywhere that it be maintained in a pure state, exactly as L. Ron Hubbard developed it.

In the past—in fact, since the beginning of Dianetics in 1950—some unscrupulous individuals have attempted to misuse the technology of Dianetics and Scientology for their own personal profit. Mr. Hubbard's intention from the beginning was that the benefits of Dianetics and Scientology be available to all, and Scientologists work hard to keep it so. Scientology was developed to rehabilitate the spirit—not to make money.

Within the Church itself, numerous staff see to proper application and protection of the technology and these responsibilities permeate the ecclesiastical hierarchy.

To help maintain the purity of the technology both inside and outside the Church, many of the words and symbols of the Scientology religion have been registered as trademarks with appropriate government agencies in countries all over the world.

This ensures nobody can deliver some offbeat version of Dianetics and Scientology and represent it as real Scientology.

The enforcement of the trademarks of the Scientology religion guarantees its integrity and prevents corruption or perversion.

Until 1982, all the trademarks and service marks were owned by L. Ron Hubbard. In May of that year he gave the marks of the Scientology religion to a newly formed church, Religious Technology Center (RTC).

RTC possesses ultimate ecclesiastical authority over the international hierarchy concerning the maintenance and standard application of L. Ron Hubbard's technology. RTC owns all the Scientology trademarks and service marks and controls their licensing and use. RTC is not part of the management structure of the Church. Its purpose is to safeguard the proper use of trademarks, to protect the public, and to make sure that the technologies of Dianetics and Scientology remain in good hands. It sees to the pure and ethical ministration of Scientology religious services.

This provides protection for the parishioner. It means that a person knows when he goes to a Scientology organization to receive a specific service, he will get exactly that service. It protects unsuspecting persons, should unscrupulous individuals outside the Church try to pervert and use L. Ron Hubbard's technology to further their own ends. Thus, the technology is kept pure. This is the intention of all Scientologists and RTC receives their wholehearted support in maintaining it.

Scientology Staff Members

Scientology missions and Class V churches are administered by staff members who contract to work for the Church for either two-and-a-half or five years at a time, in order to make Scientology and Dianetics available to all who reach for it.

Some staff positions are technical, requiring auditor or other specialized training; others are administrative and help keep the church functioning and provide the support so auditing and training can be delivered. In order to accomplish these duties, staff members work at the organization from morning to evening, with a period set aside for Scientology training and auditing. As with any other job, they return to their homes and families at the end of the day.

Every position in a church is different, but there are exact duties for each and staff members study policies which delineate these specific functions. Each job or position is called a hat, taken from the fact that in many professions such as railroading, the type of hat worn is the badge of the job. Staff engage in 2½ hours of study or auditing each day and, when they have completed the hatting courses and know how to do their jobs, many proceed on to other training, perhaps as an auditor, or use this time to move up the Bridge as a preclear.

Those staff who have signed a five-year contract may be sent for full-time training at a higher organization—either technical training at Saint Hill or the FSO, or administrative training at the mother church. This training can last up to a year, but in any event results in a highly trained church administrator, auditor or case supervisor.

There is also an entirely different category of staff in Scientology: members of the Sea Organization.

Entrusted with delivery of the most advanced levels of Scientology, the Sea Organization had its beginnings in 1967 when, after resigning all corporate and administrative responsibilities, L. Ron Hubbard set to sea with a handful of veteran Scientologists to research and develop the OT levels. For many years, the Sea Org operated from a fleet of ships, headed by its flagship, the *Apollo*. Sea Org members, in keeping with the tradition of these beginnings still wear maritime uniforms and have ratings and ranks, though the majority of Sea Org members are located on land today.

This group is a religious order within the hierarchical structure of Scientology and spans various churches and corporations. Sea Org members are responsible to the board of the church corporation they work in. Today there are almost 5,000 Sea Org members, the dedicated core of the religion, each of whom has signed a pledge of eternal service to Scientology and its goals.

All Church organizations above the level of Class V are manned by Sea Org members. This includes the Saint Hills, Advanced Orgs, FSO, FSSO and all of CSI and RTC.

Sea Org members continue the tradition of competent and professional teamwork that was the hallmark of the years at sea. New Sea Org members undergo rigorous basic training designed to raise their ability to confront and deal with their environment, their competence and their ethics level.

Sea Org members, having devoted their lives to their religion, work long hours for little pay and live a communal existence with housing, meals, uniforms, medical and dental care provided by the Church. They receive training and auditing during a portion of each day, but otherwise dedicate themselves to whatever their assigned task may be in the furtherance of the objectives of Scientology. Sea Org members achieve a great deal and have a high esprit de corps and sense of accomplishment.

The Sea Organization is dedicated to achieving the objective of a cleared planet through the standard application of the technologies of Dianetics and Scientology. It is a challenge met with determination and dedication.

COOPERATION AND EXPANSION

Each echelon in the Scientology hierarchy has a distinctly different responsibility. Together, they form a global network that has contributed to the rapid growth of the Church over nearly four decades.

Over the past thirty years, the growth factor of the Church has dramatically increased. In the past decade, Scientology has opened new organizations in more than fifty countries. In one recent six-month period alone, more than two hundred new Scientology groups became active. In less than four decades, Scientology has grown from a handful of organizations to a worldwide network.

Every duty in every organization—from the highest levels of Church management, down to the churches, missions, groups and auditors which offer services directly to those new to the subject—exists to help get the technology of Dianetics and Scientology known and used. Scientology continues to expand because it gets results: bringing people happiness, self-confidence, freedom from drugs, freedom from psychosomatic pain and fear, the ability to learn, stable relationships and a host of other priceless gains achieved every day in churches around the world. There is no more valuable activity on Earth, and thus the horizons for Scientology are bright and unbounded.

Whether a person wishes to attend a lecture on basic principles of Scientology, or receive auditing and training at the highest levels of the Bridge, there is a Scientology organization to provide him the services he needs. The object of any of these organizations is totally freed beings, a goal they help achieve daily.

Chapter 22

The International Association of Scientologists

The International Association of Scientologists (IAS) was formed at a convention held at Saint Hill Manor in East Grinstead, Sussex, England, in 1984. Delegates from around the world representing the Scientologists in their areas gathered in recognition of the need to unite all Scientologists as one international body. Its purpose is to assure the survival of the religion and guarantee that Scientology will be practiced for all time through a strong group that is composed of those who believe in the rights of man and freedom of religion.

The IAS is today a membership organization open to all Scientologists from all nations. It unifies the members and provides a forum to keep them informed of important developments and sharing the successes of the religion around the world. It is the strength of the individual members of the team, briefed and coordinated one with another that gives strength to the group. All great movements have succeeded based on the personal conviction and dedication of their members to overcoming any barriers to achieving their objectives.

Regrettably, history has seen many attempts to suppress religious freedom and human rights. From the persecution of early Christians in Rome, to the nineteenth-century assault on Mormons in the United States, to the slaughter of Jews in Nazi concentration camps, many faiths have suffered dearly. The International Association of Scientologists also serves the purpose of protecting Scientology from similar attempted persecution.

For this reason, in the 1984 convention at Saint Hill Manor, in addition to forming the IAS and adopting a constitution and electing a board, the delegates also formulated and signed the Pledge to Mankind to rededicate themselves to the aims of Scientology. A copy of the Pledge to Mankind is included in the reference section of this book.

The IAS was enthusiastically embraced by Scientologists all over the world and, through their financial support and membership activities, rapidly became a major force, both protecting the religion and supporting the Church and individual Scientologists in their actions for social reform.

Each year, delegates representing Association members from all areas of the world gather at an Annual Convention of Delegates to review the accomplishments of the previous year, plan for the next and elect the board members of the Association as necessary. The Annual Convention of Delegates is held in different locations around the world, together with a large anniversary celebration. Significant accomplishments and progress toward the aims of Scientology are acknowledged and the event is broadcast to members in many countries.

Membership in the Association

Members of the International Association are entitled to certain rights and privileges. Churches of Scientology have adopted membership in the International Association of Scientologists as their membership system

The logo for the International Association of Scientologists

and grant special privileges and benefits to Association members designed to help them move more quickly up the Bridge.

Membership in the Association is open to any Scientologist. There are three categories of membership in the Association:

1. Introductory Membership

An introductory free membership is offered to new Scientologists. It is valid for a period of six months and is not renewable. Beginning members receive magazines and promotional materials from the IAS.

2. Annual Membership

Annual membership is valid for one year. It entitles the holder to benefits of the Association including a membership card and copies of *IMPACT*, the Association's magazine.

Also included are written briefings to keep members abreast of events and occurrences in Scientology, invitations to Association briefings and events, and the right to participate in IAS award programs and projects.

3. Lifetime Membership

Lifetime membership is valid for the lifetime of the holder and entitles him to all benefits and privileges of the Association.

In addition to the three categories of membership, there are special honor statuses awarded for extraordinary contributions toward achieving the goals of the Association. These honor statuses are valid for the duration of the membership of the holder. There are several categories awarded according to the level of support: "Sponsor of the Association," "Member of the Honor Roll," "Patron of the Association," "Patron with Honors," "Patron Meritorious," "Gold Meritorious" and "Member of the Senior Honor Roll." These statuses are acknowledged through publication to all members of the names of the individuals so awarded, presentation of special pins and plaques and award dinners held to honor the recipients.

Also, anyone who is in agreement with the Pledge to Mankind and the Aims of Scientology, even if he does not attend a church of Scientology or participate in its religious services may, upon contribution to the Association, be accorded the status of Associate. Associate status does not entitle the holder to the benefits and privileges of membership.

IMPACT Magazine

All members receive *IMPACT* magazine which contains news and information relating to every Scientologist, including official news of the Association, major actions undertaken by the Association and its members, and announcements of services for its members.

IMPACT reports particularly on notable activities of Association members around the world who forward the aims of Scientology. IAS members contribute in many ways: They make Scientology more widely known, get it more widely used and help make the truth about the practices and value of the Scientology religion broadly understood.

ASSOCIATION SUPPORT

The Association provides support to members engaged in activities which greatly assist the expansion of Scientology or directly contribute to the eradication of threats to the well-being of mankind. The Association makes monetary grants and calls upon its members to support such worthy projects, which results in many Scientologists volunteering their time and effort. In this way, the Association helps individual members gain valuable support from their fellow Scientologists to carry out worthwhile projects.

FREEDOM MEDAL WINNERS

Each year the Association recognizes individuals who have defended the cause of religious and personal freedom. They are awarded the Freedom Medal by the Association at its anniversary celebration in October. There are no higher honors accorded the contributions of a Scientology parishioner than an IAS Freedom Medal.

The International Association of Scientologists works ceaselessly to forward the aims of Scientology and welcomes the membership of all who would aid in bringing hope to mankind.

The International Association of Scientologists Freedom Medal awarded annually to Scientologists in recognition of outstanding achievements

Chapter 23

A Vital Force in the Community

That a church would involve itself in charitable works and community betterment is both natural and traditional. For if it can be said that all great religions sprang from what is decent and beneficent in man, then it follows that charity and social responsibility are logical extensions of spiritual values. Prior to government welfare programs, for example, only the church could be counted upon to provide for the needy and the destitute, and through much of the world it is still only the church that provides.

Recognizing this tradition, and inspired by the many works of Mr. Hubbard, the Church of Scientology has become a notably vital force in the community.

Social betterment programs are fully supported by Church management, and every local church has a department devoted to carrying out these activities. It is from here that local Scientologists are coordinated and directed in programs which address the specific needs of their communities. Local Scientologists volunteer their services for these programs and, consequently, many individual Scientologists are leaders in community improvements.

In particular, the Church of Scientology has focused on four areas of concern: drug abuse, community betterment, criminal reform and charitable contribution. The Church and its members' motives are simple: Keenly conscious of his place in the world, the Scientologist knows that the only optimum solution is that which brings the greatest benefit to the greatest number of dynamics. To that end, his guidelines are rationality and an acute awareness that all dynamics are inextricably linked so that one man's well-being cannot be divorced from the well-being of all.

It is with this broad view in mind, then, that the Church and Scientologists are committed to social betterment—in the local neighborhood, the nation or in the world as a whole. The tools employed are those acquired from study of L. Ron Hubbard's works, including Mr. Hubbard's drug rehabilitation technology, his literacy programs, his essays on safeguarding the environment and, perhaps most important, the immense compassion for others that pervades everything he wrote.

The Church's areas of concern tend to center on those that each community regards as most pressing. Church environmental projects, for example, were prompted by a recognition that whole cities have quietly and sadly given up hope for a better future in the face of urban disintegration. That entire sectors of the population have emerged from schools without basic skills to survive has prompted Church educational programs. And the fact that even fundamental concepts of human decency are now under assault, has motivated Scientology's community cleanup campaigns world over. Then too, Scientologists tend to help where they themselves feel help is most needed, which is why their efforts are so diverse.

Utilizing L. Ron Hubbard's technology, Scientology churches are often catalysts for constructive change and provide rallying points for those who seek to improve conditions in their communities.

Antidrug Projects

Drug abuse is arguably the greatest problem society faces, directly and indirectly pushing crime to previously unimagined proportions. Quite apart from the individual tragedies involved, drug abuse has turned inner cities into battlegrounds and led to dwindling moral values and a general disregard for even the most basic ethical conduct. Moreover, and this is of special concern to Scientologists, drug abuse of all kinds lessens individual awareness, which when spread across whole sectors of society, does much to undermine the culture. With the world's most effective and statistically successful drug rehabilitation program, Scientologists have helped thousands of hard-core users free themselves from addiction and the lasting effects of substance abuse. But treating the victim of drug abuse on an individual basis is only one way Scientology meets the problem.

Uniting concerned community groups, staging public awareness forums, antidrug rallies and educational conferences, the Church of Scientology is at the forefront of the international grass-roots fight against drugs.

Scientologists are at the forefront of the fight against drugs, spearheading programs in cities around the world to provide effective solutions to reducing drug abuse.

Using programs developed and supervised by their local churches as a focal point, Scientologists then reach out effectively into society.

In the United States, for instance, the Church-sponsored "Lead the Way to a Drug-Free USA" national campaign has helped millions of people by fighting further drug proliferation.

It has done this by raising funds for youth groups such as "Teen Canteen," an organization that helps runaway teens solve their problems; by enlisting the aid of celebrities for concerts with antidrug themes; and by hosting conferences of community leaders and antidrug activities, such as the one in Washington, DC which led city commissioner Bob King to present the Church's local "Lead the Way" program with a proclamation lauding its efforts in the war against drugs.

Nor was he by any means the only one to recognize the Church's efforts. Not long after the establishment of "Lead the Way" in the District of Columbia (DC), the director of the Office for Substance Abuse Prevention of the US Department of Health commended the Church for its drug-fighting initiative, writing, "It is because of the participation of dedicated groups like yours that we are making progress in the reduction of alcohol and other drug problems."

In 1991, "Lead the Way" began to broaden its influence with the inception of its first national conference in Washington, DC in the Sam Rayburn Congressional Office Building. More than 100 leaders in the antidrug field from around the country attended, including members of drug rehabilitation and social betterment groups, congressional aides, government official and media representatives. By bringing community leaders together, the conference helped expand antidrug programs to a truly concerted national level.

The Church has also enlisted the direct support of government officials. In Philadelphia, for example, it received a special recognition from the city's drug czar, who heads the Mayor's Office on Drug Control. But then, he went a step further and, in order to assist the Church's "active and cooperative participation in the war on drugs," as he put it, he became a national advisor to the "Lead the Way to a Drug-Free USA" campaign.

Dr. Hans Janitschek, author and consultant to the United Nations, neatly summed up the activities of "Lead the Way":

"In a world where serious problems such as drug abuse receive much attention, much talk and little in the way of effective action, 'Lead the Way to a Drug-Free USA' is a breath of fresh air.

"It has pooled together action-oriented individuals and groups from throughout the world in a shoulder-to-shoulder effort to bring to our communities REAL help for drug addicts, REAL preventative actions that keep our kids off drugs, and a REAL network of like-minded leaders who seek a drug-free USA."

Drug abuse knows no international boundaries, however, and Scientologists are active in many other nations. A glimpse of these activities reveals how pervasive and effective this work is.

In Canada, members of the Church of Scientology founded the national "Say No to Drugs, Say Yes to Life" campaign, which serves as a key force in turning youth away from drugs before they start.

Aimed at gaining the support of entertainment and sports figures because of their appeal to youth, the "Say No to Drugs, Say Yes to Life" campaign enlisted the Toronto Maple Leafs hockey team, the Toronto Blue Jays baseball team, the Toronto Argonauts and the Saskatchewan Roughriders football teams, all of whom have signed the "Say No to Drugs, Say Yes to Life" Honor Roll.

Members of the Church additionally gained the support of Canadian city officials to endorse the campaign. In eleven cities in the province of Ontario, for instance, mayors have proclaimed March 13—L. Ron Hubbard's birthday—"Say No to Drugs, Say Yes to Life" Day in their cities. Each proclamation has credited the Church, and one of them, from the mayor of Brampton, Ontario, specifically commended the Church for "helping educate communities toward an understanding that to achieve their goals, they must be drug free."

Canadian law enforcement officials, who regularly deal with drug-destroyed lives, also support the Church. Police welcome the enthusiasm that Scientologists bring to activities against this tragic scourge. In fact, to encourage others, the police force of Mercier, near Quebec, celebrated its 21st anniversary by publishing a booklet which included a long description of the Church's antidrug work.

AROUND THE WORLD

European members of the Church feel the desire to help no less than their fellow Scientologists in North America. Consequently they have joined in the fight against the truly pandemic drug problem.

Scientologists in Germany, France, Switzerland, Denmark, Belgium, Holland, Austria, Sweden, Norway, Italy and the United Kingdom lead successful and popular "Say No to Drugs, Say Yes to Life" campaigns.

The Italians, who also have a "Say No to Drugs" Honor Roll, enlisted the support of Philips, Italy's most famous volleyball team. While touring Italy, members of the legendary Spanish football team, Real Madrid, each signed the honor roll. And, further maintaining a high profile in the field of sports, the Church antidrug campaign sponsors major sporting events to heighten public awareness of the problem and its solution.

Other avenues are also utilized. In particular, the Church conducts regular drug-free musical concerts throughout Italy, enlisting the support of popular musicians.

But arguably no other program has such a direct practical impact as the Church's response to the widely acknowledged health menace of used hypodermic syringes discarded in public parks by addicts.

Groups of church volunteers and celebrities lead regular citywide drives to round up and safely dispose of these potentially lethal hazards. Rome, Verona, Padova, Torino, Brescia, Pordenone, Novara, Monza, Florence and Milan have all benefited from such cleanup drives.

The achievements of Scientology's Italian volunteers have earned recognition from not only those local Italian mayors and city officials who witness the goodwill firsthand, but from members of the Italian Parliament as well.

Scientologists in Scandinavia are no less active. In Sweden, parishioners of all ages, carrying banners and placards, regularly conduct "Say No to Drugs, Say Yes to Life" marches down major thoroughfares to raise public awareness of the issue.

In Denmark, the "Say No to Drugs, Say Yes to Life" association has taken a more adversarial position. There, they have been educating members of Parliament, city officials, police chiefs and other community leaders on the dangers of drug use—particularly the liabilities of methadone. Originally billed as a solution to heroin addicts, methadone ultimately proved to be just as addictive. Acutely aware that substituting one drug for another is no solution at all, Danish Scientologists have loudly decried this psychiatric "quick fix," with thousands of signatures on the "Say No to Drugs, Say Yes to Life" Honor Roll. Danish Scientologists also run a radio station which broadcasts effective life improvement tips—including advice on saying no to drugs.

Germany also faces a methadone problem of frightening proportions, and Scientologists in Hamburg published a brochure describing the destructiveness of methadone "therapy," and distributed more than 50,000 copies of it throughout the city. This led to a long-overdue national exposé of the abuses occurring in Hamburg's "Needle Park."

As elsewhere, concerts and rallies effectively mobilized public concern for Germany's drug crisis and helped many among Germany's youth understand that one does not have to take drugs to be happy and successful in life.

In Switzerland, where antidrug events are regularly held in Lucerne, Basel, Bern, Lausanne and other cities, Scientologists also take an activist role. Working with other local organizations, the church in Zurich launched a petition drive that closed an infamous park to drug addicts and pushers, amid widespread media coverage.

Support for the Church's antidrug activities has come from both federal and state members of Parliament. In Geneva, the mayor signed the "Say No to Drugs, Say Yes to Life" Honor Roll and became an honorary member of the association.

Here too, Swiss Scientologist sports celebrities give many antidrug lectures to schoolchildren and raise public awareness of the drug problem by answering questions about drugs at "Say No to Drugs" public information stands.

French Scientologists, including well-known and popular celebrities have organized marches, concerts and street events promoting the Church's antidrug message, reaching hundreds of thousands of Parisians. Contacting still more through the media, celebrities regularly discuss the workability of L. Ron Hubbard's drug rehabilitation technology. A set of radio cassettes produced on the Church's "Say No to Drugs, Say Yes to Life" campaign is played on radio stations throughout France.

In Spain, where drug trafficking has earned the nation the title "drug crossroads of Europe," local Scientologists formed a "Freedom Without Drugs" association and conducted a series of antidrug events in Madrid.

Utilizing public events with just as much efficiency, Mexican Scientologists run a "Say No to Drugs" campaign, with well-known entertainers in cities such as Torreón, Guadalajara and Mexico City.

Similarly, South African Scientologists inaugurated a "Say No to Drugs, Say Yes to Life" Honor Roll, with events at schools, clubs and other organizations. To date, tens of thousands of South Africans have signed the honor roll, including the mayors from Port Elizabeth, Cape Town and Soweto.

In both Australia and New Zealand, Scientologists campaign against drug abuse with a "Say No to Drugs, Say Yes to Life" Honor Roll, receiving support from a wide range of sports celebrities, including the legendary New Zealand All Blacks rugby team, and many famous automobile and motorcycle racing stars.

The work of Scientologists on the antidrug front has been widely recognized. Scores of cities throughout the world have issued commendations to the Church for its antidrug work. From Perth to Adelaide in Australia, from Madrid to Stockholm to Milan in Europe, from Cape Town to Pretoria in South Africa, from more than forty cities in the United States and fifty in Canada, city governments have recognized the value of the efforts of Scientologists in this area. In fact, whenever one finds a church of Scientology, one will find a coordinated and concerted effort to turn youth away from drugs and rehabilitate the addict.

Throughout the world, members of the Church are spreading the word that a drug-free life is a better, more productive and happier one. Literally hundreds of hours of public service announcements and radio or television programs provided by the Church are broadcast every week. These programs often contain readings from the works of L. Ron Hubbard on such subjects as helping others overcome difficulties, how to improve home and community conditions and—as an underlying message—that no problem, not even epidemic drug use, is too large to surmount so long as people care enough and are determined enough to persevere.

REDUCING CRIMINALITY

Inexorably linked with both drug abuse and urban decay is crime. To the degree that a man perceives his environment as a threat, Mr. Hubbard wrote, he will not thrive. With that in mind, Scientologists have dedicated themselves to the reduction of criminality in an effort to further safeguard their environment. Of course, they believe the ultimate solution to crime is the eradication in individuals of criminal impulses, made possible with Scientology auditing technology. Witness the case of a Melbourne, Australia resident who, after receiving Scientology auditing, turned himself in to local authorities and confessed to having stolen eight hundred dollars years earlier. His reason: He decided that he could not achieve spiritual gain until he had taken full responsibility for past transgressions and repaid the money, which he did. The judge said this action was unheard of and reduced the penalty to a suspended sentence, describing the man's behavior as exceptional and stating that it clearly showed he had been rehabilitated.

At the same time, Scientologists have also joined law enforcement officers around the world in their fight to reduce senseless criminal violence.

In San Francisco, California, for example, Scientologists spearheaded the creation of a Neighborhood Crime Watch program designed to protect those who live in the community near the church.

In Montreal, Canada, the church of Scientology sponsors a contest inviting the public to write essays regarding crime reduction as a means of raising public awareness of, and appreciation for, the daily task of law enforcement officials.

In an effort to ease police–public tensions in Mexico City, Scientologists conducted seminars to teach police officers better human relations techniques. Members of the Mexican Federation of Dianetics delivered seminars to 250 policewomen from the central police headquarters in Mexico City.

When the 1992 Los Angeles riots shook the city, *The Times* of London reported, "Further east, at the fabled intersection of Hollywood and Vine, 300 members of the Church of Scientology ignored the citywide curfew and surrounded an entire block to protect their building. By midnight it was one of the very few blocks on Hollywood Boulevard where no business had been torched or looted."

With an all too obvious need to rebuild their city in the wake of the Los Angeles riots, community leaders gathered in a spirit of cooperative endeavor to heal the city's wounds, among them the president of the Church of Scientology International. Invited to serve on the board of a newly formed group called Los Angeles Model Plan, he soon took an active part in the "healing" process. The group, which also includes Los Angeles City Council members, a California state senator, the president of the Los Angeles United Way and other leaders, was specially formed to address the problems of education, a matter of great concern to Scientologists.

Scientologists also spearheaded the formation of East Hollywood People Against Crime, which brought that community together in an effective campaign to reduce local crime. Under the Church's leadership, events were held to wipe out graffiti covering twenty-eight gang-ridden city blocks, and funds were raised to purchase equipment for neighborhood foot patrols.

Acknowledging the difficult task performed by law enforcement officials, Scientologists encourage citizen support for their work. Churches regularly present special awards to police officers in recognition of the value of police work in their local communities. The Church supports the efforts of police forces to help create an environment where citizens can safely walk the streets and raise their children.

While crime has become an increasing factor in the lives of people throughout the world, in these and many other ways Scientologists are contributing to the creation of a safe environment.

ENVIRONMENTAL REVITALIZATION PROJECTS

Because individual churches and their parishioners are involved in their communities, environmental efforts naturally tend to reflect community needs. Thus in one city, Scientologists can be found heading recycling projects, public park cleanups and the removal of graffiti; while in another they can be found planting trees or protecting wildlife.

In Los Angeles, for instance, a murals project sponsored by the Church's Community

Outreach Group and the Church's Visual Artists Association beautifies the environment. Through the years, scores of large murals have been provided to Dependency Courts and related facilities for children throughout Los Angeles County. The Community Outreach Group has received city, county and state recognition as a result, in fact, being named the community group of the year in Los Angeles.

Equally energetic is the Tustin, California "Scientologists for a Better Community" who enhance their city's image with graffiti cleanups and by painting murals. While in Orlando, Florida, Scientology received the city's 1990 "Church Volunteer of the Year" award for its contributions to the cleanup and restoration of the local historic train station and surrounding streets.

In Santa Barbara, California, the church is a participant in California's "Adopt a Highway" program, taking responsibility for maintaining the cleanliness of a portion of a major highway.

Ecologically minded South African Scientologists celebrate Earth Day each year with educational campaigns to stress the importance of safeguarding and improving their environment. They have also helped with clean-up events at local parks and beaches. A church-organized antilitter campaign in Durban, South Africa, involving hundreds of volunteers from both the church and the community, received special recognition and a warm letter of thanks from the Durban City Council.

In Australia, the "Clean Up Australia Day" organization recognized the Church of Scientology's community clean-up events with a proclamation acknowledging the Church's "outstanding contribution." Scientologists run a constant educational campaign in Melbourne and other Australian cities to reduce pollution in the environment.

Scientologists are constantly engaged in smaller, unreported projects—discouraging neighborhood youth from defouling property with spray cans, or encouraging those around them to use litter baskets. These activities are all part of Scientology's larger world view that no dynamic can thrive unless all thrive, and that each man is not only vitally linked to all other men but also to the world in which he lives.

Ethnic Affairs and Civil Rights

By the Creed of the Church, "All men of whatever race, color or creed were created with equal rights." In its efforts to secure freedom and human rights for all individuals, the Church of Scientology has provided effective assistance for members of minority groups who have suffered hardship because of race or belief.

In the United States, the Church of Scientology maintains an Office of Ethnic and Cultural Affairs, to coordinate Church efforts on behalf of all minorities.

Churches have continuously affirmed the truth that although one man's skin may be white and another's black, red or yellow, the spirit has no color.

One of the services of the Church's Office of Ethnic and Cultural Affairs for many years has been to publish a popular column, syndicated in newspapers around the country, providing positive guidelines on educational reform, self-esteem and other applications of L. Ron Hubbard's technology. The column has exposed government abuses against minorities and championed the cause of equal rights and equal opportunity for all.

In fact, the Church provided the first national exposure of widespread racial discrimination against IRS employees by IRS officials. In 1990 Scientologists investigated and exposed voluminous reports received on the IRS's discriminatory policies and practices in Chicago; New York; Los Angeles; Indianapolis; Kansas City; Jackson, Mississippi and Norfolk, Virginia.

Scientologists have also investigated and challenged racially motivated police brutality on the streets of Los Angeles. The Church helped initiate reforms of the Los Angeles Police Department.

In Washington, DC, Scientologists established an award-winning program which has assisted hundreds of African-American inner-city children to raise their scholastic competence and self-esteem. Many Scientologists volunteer their time every weekend to help these underprivileged children and, as a result, have received community awards for their hard work, dedication and results.

To increase understanding and tolerance between diverse groups, to ensure justice for all regardless of color or creed—these are not merely words to the Scientologist, but deeply felt convictions, seen as a true cornerstone for survival.

Supporting Goodwill and Community Organizations

In cities on every continent, members of the Church donate thousands of hours in community work and provide assistance to a wide range of other goodwill and community groups.

The Church supports and contributes to other established community programs such as the Red Cross, the Cystic Fibrosis Foundation and local community groups in cities around the world. Church members' support of and contribution to these programs range from broad participation in drug-free blood drives, to citywide collection of holiday toys for needy children, to donations of food and clothing for underprivileged families.

For years, the church of Scientology in Portland has provided assistance to the Northeast Emergency Food Program, sponsored by Ecumenical Ministries of Oregon. The Portland church displays the award certificate received for "outstanding contribution" to the program's fund-raising efforts.

In Orange County, California, Scientologists helped form a local chapter of the "Food for All" program with Lutheran Social Services and Presbyterian and Catholic groups in the area which provides food for the homeless.

The Church of Scientology of St. Louis raises funds for the US Marine Corps "Toys for Tots" program, while also carrying out a successful education program aimed at safeguarding children from crime. Both the Marine Corps and *The Police News* of Missouri have recognized the church for its community service activities.

In Dallas, Scientologists raised thousands of dollars on behalf of Bryan's House, a facility that helps children suffering from AIDS.

Church members in Sacramento head a project called "Operation Caring"—a community outreach program providing support and companionship for the elderly.

In Arizona, church volunteers participated in a pledge drive to support public television, raising $25,000—more than double the target set by the local public television station.

In Australia, the Church of Scientology of Sydney works hand in hand with the Salvation Army, running the local drive for food, clothes and toys. Church volunteers in Australia also conduct clothing drives for underprivileged families and provide musical entertainment for the elderly.

In Germany, church volunteers also provide musical entertainment for the elderly at old-age homes, while in nearby Belgium, local Scientologists supported an annual 24-hour bicycle race, raising funds for cancer research.

Honoring a long tradition of helping the needy, and particularly children, over the Christmas holidays, Scientologists help spread Christmas goodwill in cities around the world. From California to New York, Scientologists in the United States collect food and gifts to cheer the holidays of those in need.

For many years the church in Los Angeles has worked with the Department of Children's Services of Los Angeles County to provide toys and holiday entertainment for foster children under the department's care. These children are, most commonly, from broken families or victims of abuse. Over the years, the various contributions made by Scientologists have resulted in many commendations from the department.

In 1991 the department asked the church to provide gifts and entertainment for more children than ever before. Responding to the call, church staff and volunteers organized a massive toy drive that resulted in more than 5,500 gifts for these children, who otherwise would have gone without.

Scientologists also provided entertainment at nine separate parties throughout Los Angeles County, some of them attended by several hundred children. These holiday events culminated in an enormous party for more than 3,000 children.

In addition to these activities in the Los Angeles area, for years the church has sponsored the popular "Winter Wonderland" in Hollywood, complete with the film capital's largest Christmas tree and many tons of snow. Santa lights the tree during the annual Christmas parade and the setting plays host to thousands of children and their parents. Winter Wonderland is a tradition begun by L. Ron Hubbard's gift of a Christmas tree donated to the city each year, and carried on by the church as a goodwill activity in the Hollywood area.

Clearwater, Florida Scientologists are active in the Women's Auxiliary, providing hundreds of Christmas presents to underprivileged children via the local Marine Corps Reserve. Also through the Women's Auxiliary, gifts were provided to the Future Homemakers of America for children of Florida migrant workers. A choir comprised of children of church staff makes numerous holiday season appearances each year at retirement homes and other care facilities in the Clearwater area. Scientologists also participate in such community events as the annual Clearwater Christmas Parade. Each year, Scientologists organize a toy drive and party for Clearwater's foster children.

Also in Florida, the Miami church annually supports the Salvation Army's toy drive for tens of thousands of local children; across the country in Seattle, the church donates a large Christmas tree to the community every year. Scientologists there help organize events in celebration of the tree's arrival and to foster holiday spirit. Seattle Scientologists also collect toys for the Seattle Police drive for underprivileged children.

The Children's Choir of the Church of Scientology of St. Louis specializes in bringing holiday season joy to the elderly. As the manager of a local home for seniors wrote, "In today's world of so busy lives, the seniors are too often forgotten. Your visit put a smile on their faces as well as in their hearts."

In the United Kingdom, as elsewhere around the world, Scientology performers visit homes for disadvantaged children and the elderly, providing music and other entertainment.

In Australia, Scientologists also collect food, clothing and toys each year and distribute them to the needy, and Christmas carolers visit local nursing homes.

In Vancouver, the church's participation in the city's toy drive has received widespread appreciation from community officials and press coverage. The church has, as well, been instrumental in the success of the Vancouver Christmas Cruise, enlisting the participation of yacht owners who offer children free excursions and toys.

The Toronto church is the site of a Christmas street festival, where toys are passed out by Santa to hundreds of area children. Toronto Scientologists also sponsor a special Christmas distribution of gifts to underprivileged children.

Canadian Scientologists team up with local law enforcement officers and firefighters in Ottawa and Montreal for annual toy drives and caroling for underprivileged youth and residents of care centers.

Nor does Scientology charity in Canada stop with Christmas. Year around Canadian church members greet and care for arriving immigrants and refugees and their families—and round-the-clock as necessary. The Church of Scientology of British Columbia was acknowledged with a certificate of appreciation for "generous contribution" from the Immigrant Services Society of British Columbia for helping newly arrived refugee families.

In Montreal, the church is an active fund-raiser, joining forces with the Canadian National Hockey Team for various charities. Scientologists in Montreal support the Cerebral Palsy Association, led by a Scientologist who serves as vice-president of the association's fund-raising committee.

In addition to these charitable activities and programs, the Church supports one other community effort—the Volunteer Minister program.

The good works of the Church are covered in the media around the world, with hundreds of articles every week.

SOUTHERN MAIL

Non à la drogue

Fenelon Falls And Area Gazette

SUPPORTS 'No to Drugs Campaign'

Schools, clubs sign petition against drugs

Los Angeles TODAY

Bakersfield News

Daily News

SERVING THE SAN FERNANDO AND NEIGHBORING VALLEYS

THURSDAY, SEPTEMBER 6, 1990

Churches fight drug abuse

BOSTON HERALD

Pollution claim disputed

The Anchorage Times

THE TORONTO STAR

The Portland Observer

July 4th Celebration To Include Food Drive

Spring

Neighbor

Parties brighten holidays for

Children get gifts from volunteers

HOTLINE

Deutsche Presse

The Vancouver Sun

BRITISH COLUMBIA'S NEWSPAPER

Inter-faith task force launches strategy against drug abuse

July 19, 1990

SOUTH WEST DE... HERALD

THE FOOTHILL LEADER

State budget crisis reminder of New York

Wednesday, Aug. 5, 1992

TAMPA ...ARA

THE Sunday NEWS

Scientologists Say no

Daily Camera

July 29, 1990 Boulder, Colorado 25 Cents

Dianetics Foundation recognizing drug-free businesses

MATTERS OF FAITH

Giving thanks

New Haven Register

Francisco

Today in The C...

Bay briefs

Church of Scientology gives books to library

SAN FRANCISCO POST

THE POST, Sunday, December 29, 1991 Page 1

Church Supports Toy Drive

CONTRAST January 17, 1986, Page 11

Church launches an anti-drug campaign

stampa SERA CRONACA

...eguaci di L. Ron Hubbard raccolgono siringhe sui viali

La Gazzetta di Ravenna

«Scientology» Raccolta di siringhe nei parchi e giardini

Questa ma...

Rac... in p...

Quella di...

...youth

...e Canada Times

Friday, August 11, 1989

291 Dundas St., West, Toronto, Ontario M5T 1G1

Pirates At Caribana Say No To Drugs

STAR-NEWS

...DAY, FEBRUARY 12, 1990

...roubled kids ... in county facility

People

HAROLD N. HUBBARD

Hollywood Independent

Scientologists form crime watch group

FREE COPY

CALIFORNIA EXAMINER

The First Independent and Largest Filipino Weekly Newspaper in California

The Bakersfield News Observer

WEDNESDAY, JULY 11, 1990

Church Of Scientology And Neighborhood Watch Hold Fundraiser To Fight Crime

Free

"An independent newspaper se...

Church of Scientology blood drive May 12

...s Tree

THE ORANGE COUNTY Register

THURSDAY, DECEMBER 19, 1991

Scientology aids homeless vets

Religion

Scientologists crusade for rights

...resentatives of the Church of ...ology were in St. Catharines

...form people of their basic rights under the charter," Miss Crellin told The Standard in an interview.

The Church of Scientology is concerned with the rights issue, she said, because it was the victim of a raid by Ontario government authorities last March at its main headquarters in Toronto that involved the seizure of a quarter million documents, many of them personal files of church members. So far,

public generally has been receptive to the Scientology campaign. Copies of the Rights, obtained from the government and suitably ..., were snapped up ... they were offered during ... Miss Crellin said the ... Scientology has the support ... faiths in its quest for religious freedom.

...rive

...is Spokes...

November 15, 1990

...of Scientology ...use & food drive

food contributions is Nov. 21st at which time the food will be given to the Emergency Foodshelf Network Inc. The food drive will end with an Open House on Nov. 21st from 10:00am until 4:00pm. There will be continuous showings of

Los Angeles Times

JUNE 24, 1990

Scientologists Lead Way in Crime Fight

Gangs: Neighbors have joined members of the Church of Scientology in an East Hollywood

mally like to keep a low profile. But members began passing out 5,000 flyers to area residents asking them to meet and plan for the defense of their community—a mix of noisy commercial boulevards and quiet residential streets—and they began lobbying for a greater police presence in the area.

As many as 200 church members and neighborhood residents showed up at the first meeting, held three weeks ago

dents block by block, and has begun graffiti eradication measures. The first "paint-out" in early June drew more than 150 people, who covered up graffiti over a 28-block area, and more than 100 area residents attended a cookout and organizational meeting last Sunday, according to a Scientology spokeswoman.

Officer Richard Ledesma of LAPD's Northeast Division said the crime watch group is already making its

TAMPA TR...

Thursday, September 17, 1992

CLEARWATER

- Scientologists collecting for Andrew victims

The Church of Scientology is

VOLUNTEER MINISTERS

In the mid-1970s, L. Ron Hubbard concluded that criminal activities were rising in proportion to the decline in religious influence. He further noted that many had no place to turn when they needed solutions to life's problems. Yet Scientology contains data that anyone can use in any part of their lives, data people can use to help each other. When Scientology is used, conditions do improve. The way to a better society is to make it available as broadly as possible. One of the key ways the Church fosters this idea is through the Volunteer Minister program.

The program makes help broadly available by providing fundamental aspects of Scientology technology to *anyone,* Scientologist and non-Scientologist alike. To supply this technology *The Volunteer Minister's Handbook,* by L. Ron Hubbard, was published in 1976. Since then, thousands of individuals have performed a vital role as Volunteer Ministers in their communities.

The Church takes an active role to help them by distributing the handbook, offering training and certification on its materials, putting Volunteer Ministers in contact with each other and assisting them to start in their ministry. The Volunteer Minister program is nonsectarian and, in addition to training lay people, also trains ministers of other denominations to render more effective assistance to those around them.

There are no restrictions on who may become a Volunteer Minister or what he may do to assist others. Anything a minister would do, a Volunteer Minister does. And any area of life can benefit from his help.

The Volunteer Minister's Handbook is the result of hundreds of thousands of hours of research and application. It teaches many of the helpful fundamentals of Scientology in a series of simple and swiftly learned lessons. After studying these lessons, one can immediately begin ministering to the needs of the community in a volunteer capacity. Volunteer Ministers need not belong to any association or congregation. All one requires is knowledge of the handbook and the desire to help.

Those following any faith may become a Volunteer Minister. But he *is* a minister and he helps his fellow man. He does not shut his eyes to the pain, evil and injustice in the world. Rather, he is trained to handle such misery and help others achieve the relief that comes from the application of Scientology technology to conditions in life. People in all areas can do something for their fellow man through the Volunteer Minister program.

A Volunteer Minister eases the tribulations of people. He saves troubled marriages, helps failing students, resolves conflicts between individuals and groups, rescues drug addicts from the agony of withdrawal convulsions, eases physical discomfort and assists the injured. Such are just some of the miracles Volunteer Ministers accomplish every day. He supplies services which are lacking in the society, and there is a tremendous amount he can do.

Each section of *The Volunteer Minister's Handbook* teaches a body of basic Scientology technology on a different subject. With each lesson learned, the Volunteer Minister becomes more able to effectively deal with situations he sees in life:

A person smashes his hand in a car door. The Volunteer Minister is taught assist technology and so can help alleviate the pain and help the injury heal more rapidly. He applies similar techniques to ease illnesses as well. A married couple has constant arguments. The Volunteer Minister knows the mechanisms which underlie marital conflicts and can counsel them, restore harmony and save the marriage. Two shop owners in the neighborhood are in conflict. With what he is taught, the Volunteer Minister can locate the real source of the conflict and resolve it. A friend has fallen on hard times and is using drugs. The Volunteer Minister has studied how to get him off drugs and can help him straighten out his life. A restaurant owner's business has taken a downturn. The Volunteer Minister can isolate the reason for this and help the owner right his business. These are not unusual

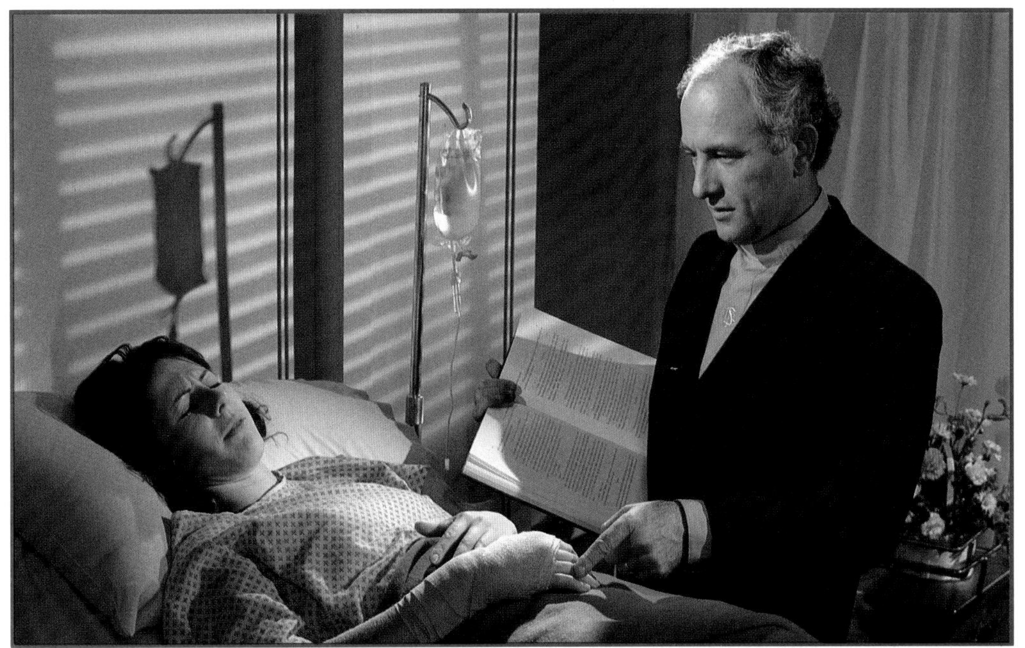

The ***Volunteer Minister's Handbook*** *provides Scientologists and non-Scientologists alike with fundamental Scientology technology to aid the injured, handle troubled marriages and rescue drug addicts from their addiction.*

circumstances; they happen all the time. Ordinarily, people are helpless in such situations, even if they want to help; a Volunteer Minister, on the other hand, has been trained to render effective assistance. And so he does something about it.

If the person desires to do it, an optional course is offered at his church or mission. Such training at the church, by virtue of assistance from experienced personnel, can better equip a Volunteer Minister to perform his duties.

Volunteer Ministers frequently form groups with each other which enable them to better serve the community. Such groups allow newer ministers to gain experience by working with more practiced ones. Some even have congregations, holding Sunday services or seminars with topics relevant to their communities and individual interests.

Volunteer Ministers also work with and assist ministers of other denominations. All churches are involved in helping their fellow man and can work together to accomplish these goals. Upon invitation, Volunteer Ministers deliver sermons at other churches.

By mutual cooperation and assistance, ministers of all denominations strengthen the force of religion in the world. In so doing they help reverse the cultural decay stemming from the rampant materialism plaguing modern society.

The good works of Volunteer Ministers are noticed by the society at large. A perfect example came from a South African Volunteer Minister, the Reverend William Mesilane. This sixty-nine-year-old minister of the Christ Assembly Church utilized Scientology technology to help people in his community.

"He eased someone's pain using the Touch Assist on the train from Maclear to Sterkstroom," the newspaper reported. "He saw a woman crying, who jumped with terror if anyone spoke to her. He asked her what was wrong and she did not know. He offered to do a Touch Assist, which took twenty minutes. During that time, the train conductor came and watched him at work, as well as curious passengers. At the end of the Touch Assist the woman was laughing and calm."

"William claims he took on a new lease in life when he began to study the handbook. He eagerly plans to use all he learns to help his people further."

As more and more people see the value of bringing true help to another, the Volunteer Minister program spreads further throughout the society. By freely offering his assistance to those who need it, the effective contributions of the Volunteer Minister are making the world a better place.

LONG-RANGE GOAL

Although it may be reiterated that the Church has received thousands of awards and commendations for its work within communities, these are incidental to both the intention and the deed. Scientologists help because help is part of the fabric of their religion, and L. Ron Hubbard has always stressed the importance of taking responsibility for one's fellows.

It should also be pointed out that, in addition to these listed activities, a legion of unheralded Scientologists in countries all over the world engage in a host of unreported activities. Whether they are organized by the Church, or simply the actions of individual Scientologists who willingly accept responsibility for their fellows and their neighborhoods, it is part and parcel of the broader view that there is no finer satisfaction than that which comes from helping. Thus, wherever one finds a church of Scientology, one also finds a steady, if unpublicized, effort to help where help is needed.

Reducing criminality and drug abuse, community cleanup and charitable contributions—when one considers the larger purpose of Scientology, it is no accident that members of the Church have chosen to focus their social betterment programs on these areas. For although the primary emphasis of Scientology remains on bettering the individual, on bringing him to greater heights of spiritual awareness, the long-range aim has always been the same—a civilization without insanity, without criminals and without war, where the able can prosper and honest beings can have rights, and where man is free to rise to greater heights. And so, as the numbers of Scientologists continue to grow, so, too, is their presence increasingly felt as a vital force in the community.

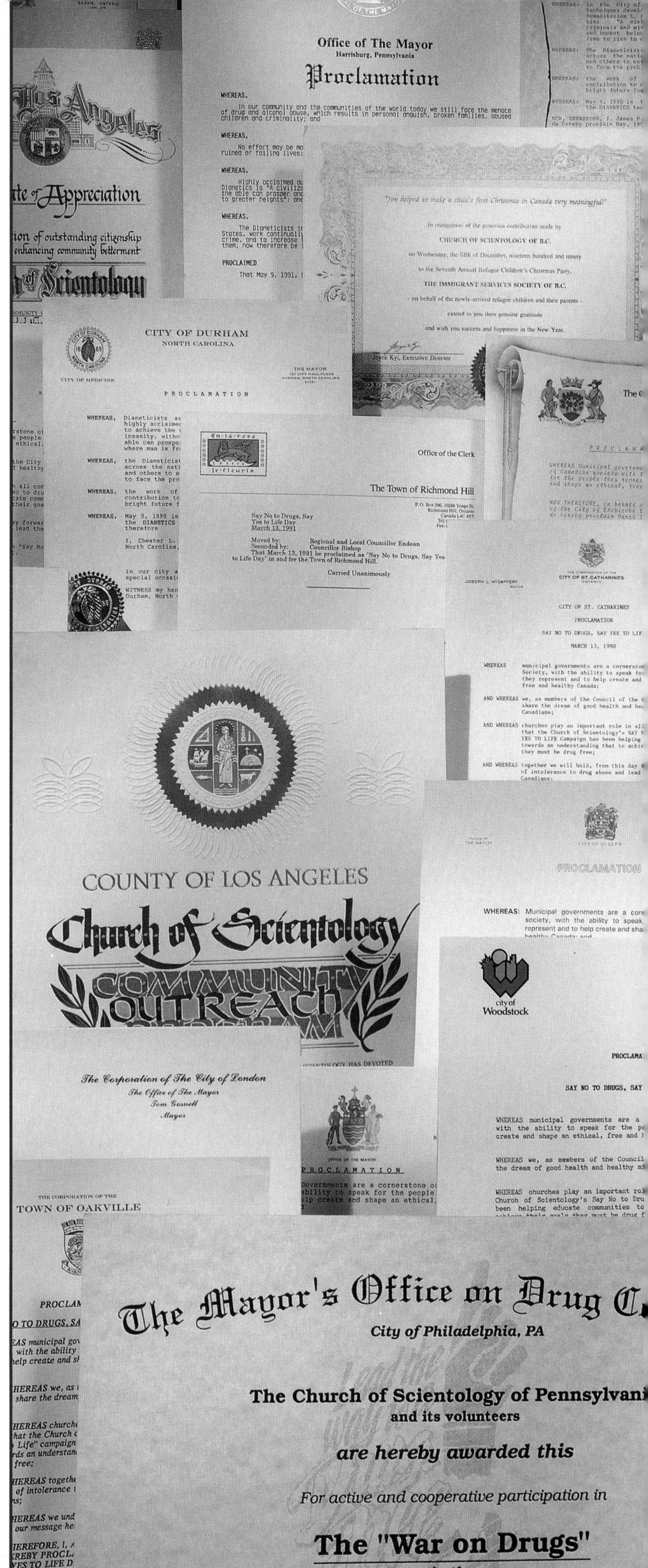

Some of the numerous recognitions the Church has received for its community activities

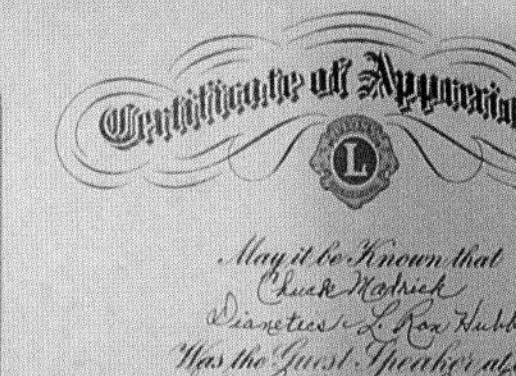

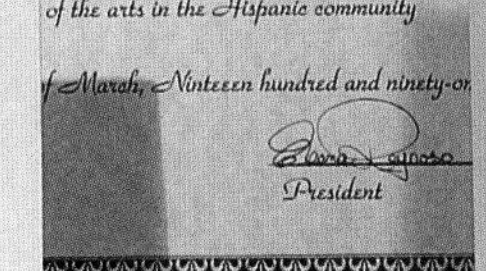
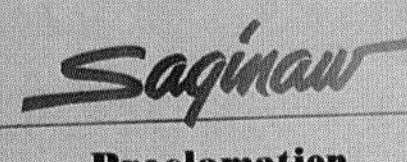
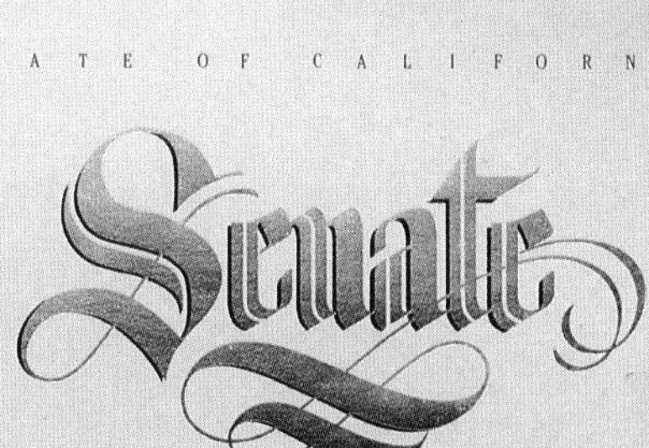

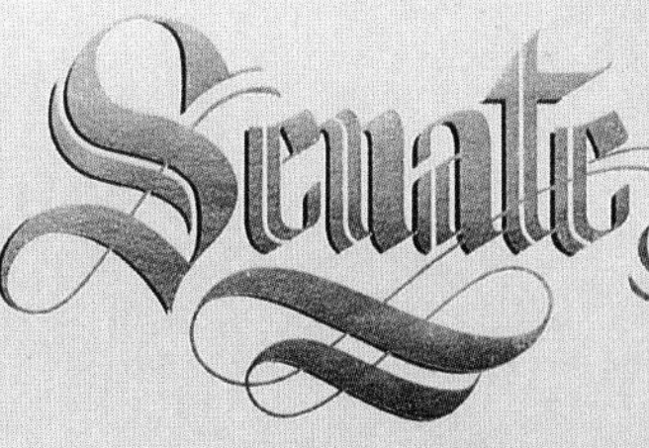

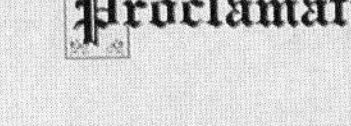

The Corporation of the Town of Whitby
PROCLAMATION
California Legislature Assembly
County of Los Angeles
The Community Outreach Group of the Church of Scientology
Office of the Mayor
The Corporation of the Township of Richmond
Proclamation
Centro Literario Anacaona Hispanoamerica
presents this
Certificate of Appreciation
Certificate of Appreciation
Saginaw
Proclamation
State of California
Senate
Rules Committee
Resolution
PROCLAMATION
WHEREAS: Municipal governments are a cornerstone of Canadian society with the ability to speak for the people they represent and to help create and shape an ethical, free and healthy Canada; and
City of Waterloo
Brian Turnbull, Mayor
Town of Ajax
Proclamation
City of Oshawa
City of Los Angeles
State of California
RESOLUTION
WHEREAS, THE Outreach Group of the Church of Scientology
HAS DEVOTED THOUSANDS OF HOURS TO ASSIST THE DEPARTMENT OF CHILDREN'S SERVICES PROVIDE BETTER CARE FOR AND RESPOND TO THE NEEDS OF CHILDREN AND THEIR FAMILIES; AND
WHEREAS, MEMBERS OF THE GROUP DESIGNED AND PAINTED THE ENTIRE FAMILY VISITATION ROOM AND PAINTED A LARGE MURAL IN THE CHILDREN'S WAITING AREA OF THE WEST LOS ANGELES OFFICE AND HAS PAINTED ANOTHER 10 MURALS FOR THE PRIVATE AND PUBLIC WAITING AREAS OF THE VAN NUYS DEPENDENCY COURT HOUSE; AND
WHEREAS, FIFTEEN MEMBERS OF THE GROUP HAVE DONATED THEIR WEEKEND TIME FOR ONE AND A HALF YEARS TO COMPLETE THE PROJECT:
PROCLAMATION
Senate
California Legislature
JULY 13, 1989
The Great Seal of the State of California

Chapter 24

Spearheading Social Reform

While religious leaders have long recognized that man's spiritual well-being cannot be entirely divorced from temporal concerns, few churches have dedicated themselves so thoroughly to the cause of social reform as the Church of Scientology. Through its diligent and aggressive activities, it is recognized by many as a leading champion of human rights, one that involves itself in arenas wherever injustice has been perceived.

For a church to actively involve itself—as the Church of Scientology has done—in the exposure of psychiatric abuses around the world, Internal Revenue Service (IRS) illegalities in the United States, international law enforcement corruption and a host of other ills that plague society, may seem unusual, but the fact is Scientologists care as much about the here and now as the hereafter. The Creed of the Church specifically addresses the inalienable rights of all men, regardless of race, color or creed, and the actions of Scientologists everywhere have given these words true substance.

These endeavors by Scientologists who care enough to investigate, to overcome the resistance of powerful vested interests, and even to place themselves at risk, have also resulted in remarkable achievements. Laws have been passed, lives saved, victims rescued, restitution paid, criminals arrested and life-threatening activities halted. In a word, they have resulted in justice, a sometimes rare commodity in today's world.

Scientologists have, in a very real sense, drawn the line. They have raised their voices in the collective cry: "Enough!" Enough butchery of innocents, enough enslavement of the weak, enough intolerance, enough abuse of power by those who hold it. Enough. While such statements may sound inflammatory, verging on drama and exaggeration, they are not—except to those too timid to see, those who huddle in the security of their homes and jobs, or those who, when they witness evil on the evening news or upon the streets of their cities say, "This has nothing to do with us."

That the presence of evil is as real as the shadows that dog our footsteps will be shown in this chapter. It is man's burden and will continue to be so for as long as it has nothing to do with us. No matter how technologically advanced our age, no matter how "enlightened" the opinions on talk shows or the advice so liberally handed out in magazines, it is not enough. As repugnant as the thought may be, there are those among us on a mission of destruction, and it will take more than talk to abort such missions.

Scientologists are acutely aware of this. And thus they have taken the task of man's freedom upon themselves. For as has been implied and discussed and stated in this book, the mission of Scientology involves spiritual freedom. But just as there can be no soaring flight while anchored to the ground, so there can be no true and lasting spiritual freedom while tyranny and injustice govern any man among us.

The Code of Honor of a Scientologist states quite plainly: "Your integrity to yourself is more important than your body." And while no ethical code can be enforced, it is a beacon that stands as an ideal. To many Scientologists it is even more—it is a reality to live by. Which is why they are willing to draw that line, to persist against unfriendly fire, and to show by deeds that enough is indeed enough.

To carry these battles forward, the Church and concerned Scientologists have founded a number of nonprofit organizations such as the Citizens Commission on Human Rights (CCHR) and the National Commission on Law Enforcement and Social Justice (NCLE) which seek social reform in the areas of psychiatric excess and corruption in law enforcement, respectively. And, to quickly and broadly bring the results of its research in these areas and others into the light of day, the Church publishes an international journal.

FREEDOM MAGAZINE

With its main editorial offices in Los Angeles, *Freedom* magazine is published in nine countries and five languages. In addition to breaking stories on the enforced drugging of school children, psychiatric brutalities and more, *Freedom* has, since founded in 1968, become widely recognized as one of the foremost voices for taxpayer rights and tax agency reform.

A forum for hard-hitting, investigative journalism, *Freedom* has taken on stories that other media have been reluctant to investigate or publish. And as its readership has grown, so has public awareness of areas in need of social reform.

CITIZENS COMMISSION ON HUMAN RIGHTS

From the United States to Australia, South Africa to Germany, the Church has relentlessly exposed psychiatric criminality and oppression—all in pursuit of a civilization "where man is free to rise to greater heights," as Scientology states in its aims.

In 1969, the Church established the Citizens Commission on Human Rights. Since then it has expanded around the world. Today, CCHR International, located in Los Angeles, supervises offices in most major cities in more than two dozen countries including the United States, United Kingdom, France, Germany, Norway, Switzerland, Denmark, Sweden, South Africa, Canada, Italy, Spain, Mexico, Netherlands, Israel, Australia, New Zealand and others.

Psychiatry Unmasked

During investigations into basic human rights abuses, one of the more fertile fields trod by the Church of Scientology, interestingly enough, has been the practice of psychiatry—interesting because it is a field which claims both humanitarian motive and leadership in the treatment of "mental health." It is a positioning that for many years has filled its trough with lucrative government appropriations and given it no small measure of societal power.

Based upon the realities, however, a more apt analogy might be that it has been looting the coffers for many years, for if, as is true for most of us in society, payment is received in return for a valuable service or product, psychiatry has been pulling the wool over government eyes for a very long time. Having taken the high ground much earlier this century simply due to the fact that nothing much had been done as far as studies of the mind were concerned, psychiatry stepped into the void and declared its leadership position. There were no competitors to speak of, for medicine had its hands full with advances in physical treatment and virtually no interest in the mind. And so, initially at least, in a society newly infatuated with the claims of science, there was little opposition to these new theories that claimed for themselves the same scientific status. Funded by governments interested in the control of populations, psychiatrists donned white cloaks in their laboratories, ran their tests on mice and monkeys and dogs and issued scholarly papers, written in a rapidly developed lexicon virtually incomprehensible to the layman—or the politician.

In truth, and as time finally proved, it was simply another case of an emperor with no clothes. The problem was not minor, however; it lay in the basic premise. Any researcher faces many choices in virtually limitless directions. And more than a century ago, psychiatry and its cousin, psychology, chose a certain path which has since, with minor exceptions, been slavishly followed. The premise was that man was an animal (thus the experiments on animals), that all mental activity originated in the brain (thus physical treatment of this physical organ was a primary solution), and that he responded to environmental stimuli (thus his behavior could be manipulated by such stimuli). Psychiatry has done little to diverge from this premise.

Unfortunately, the path has led only to a dead end. The fact of the matter is that these self-appointed experts have never discovered and do not know to this day that the mind is composed of mental image pictures, that the brain is simply a conduit, and that man is a spiritual being. Such oversights would be ludicrous and even amusing if the consequences were not so disastrous.

For today, as psychiatry still stumbles in circles around that cul-de-sac into which they were led, they have had to step over the bodies of the victims lying in their wake. Even a car mechanic learns about engines—what they are, what motivates them, how they work—before diving in with a wrench. Psychiatry has not only missed this basic premise, but its tools are dangerous. In lieu of understanding, their only instruments are a vast cornucopia of mind-altering pharmaceuticals, electroshock machines and surgeons' knives. And as the basic premise is inaccurate, and they actually have no idea *what* they are treating (other than easily observed symptoms), the results are naturally dismal.

The obvious question that arises is what does one do in such circumstances? They have claimed a leadership position by virtue of the fact there were no other candidates, and now they are expected to deliver. Unfortunately, they have virtually no idea what they are doing. It is a difficult position to be in. And so we have the undeniably applicable maxim: Desperate men do desperate things.

L. Ron Hubbard was one of the first to notice the nakedness of this emperor—and the desperation of his acts. From his earliest contact with the field in the late 1940s, he saw that something was very wrong: an arrogance, a venality, a disconcern for the individual and a serious incompetence. He noted with due outrage that for all the talk of enlightened psychiatric care, unmanageable patients were still routinely warehoused in dreadful conditions, drugged into vegetative states that left them permanently impaired, and punitively electroshocked. He also noted that, beyond food, clothing and a padded cell, psychiatry possessed no tools at all for dealing with the mentally ill.

To sum up, Mr. Hubbard wrote, psychiatry stood for ineffectiveness, lies and inhuman brutality. Its basic assumption revolved around the idea that with enough punishment, anyone could be restored to sanity; and if all else failed, one could always sever the patient's prefrontal lobes. With this and more in mind, Mr. Hubbard declared it to be the Scientologist's duty "to expose and help abolish any and all physically damaging practices in the field of mental health." Thus came about the formation of CCHR—the Citizens Commission on Human Rights.

Chelmsford—The Endless Sleep

Chelmsford is a name that Australian members of CCHR will probably never forget. For many, it was their first contact with unmitigated evil. And for all of them, it tested both their courage and their ability to persist in the face of derision, disbelief and an uncaring bureaucracy.

The Sydney Morning Herald
Wednesday, August 10, 1988
Royal commission into mental health will investigate Chelmsford
Govt picks inquiry judge

The Gazette
Aussies hear bizarre tale of drugs, death at hosp

The Newcastle Herald
WEDNESDAY, AUGUST 17, 1988
Commission to 'lift lid' on Chelmsford

The Courier-Mail
BRISBANE, Tuesday, December 27, 1988
Call for nationwide 'deep sleep' probe

The Adv
Horror hospital

The Sydney Morning Herald
Wednesday, March 15, 1989
Nurse feared for life, hearing told

The Sydney Morning Herald
Wednesday, August 17, 1988
Deep sleep inquiry granted

THE DAILY Telegra

THE AGE
Friday 4 January 1991
Chelmsford: the story of a medical nightmare

THE GLOBE AND MAIL
Dark episode of death revealed in Australia
1,160 killed or damaged by therapy

The Church's exposure of the atrocities at Chelmsford resulted in an international scandal and much-needed psychiatric reform.

For Australians as a whole, the name of Chelmsford is today synonymous with madness, barbarism and horror; of psychiatry run amok, of bizarre experiments that, one magazine claimed, "rival those performed by Dr. Josef Mengele in Nazi Germany." New South Wales Health Minister, Peter Collins, called it "the darkest episode of the history of psychiatry in this country." And in mute witness, at least forty-nine crematoriums and cemeteries around Sydney hold Chelmsford's victims.

The Chelmsford Private Hospital in Sydney's northwest Pennant Hills was headed up by Dr. Harry Bailey who by 1963 had started to administer what is called deep sedation therapy, or more commonly, deep sleep therapy. As a later story by the *Sydney Morning Herald* described it, the title was a misnomer.

"First of all it isn't a therapy," having shown no therapeutic benefits. "Nor is it sleep. It is a coma induced by large doses of barbiturates."

Bailey's technique for handling mentally disturbed Chelmsford patients who were sent to him for help and care was essentially simple, if heavy-handed. He would place them in a coma for up to two weeks, during which period he would administer daily doses of electroshock therapy and/or psychosurgery, often without the consent or knowledge of the "sleeping" patient.

From mid-1963 to 1979, during his autocratic reign at Chelmsford, the deaths from this "treatment" mounted. Then there were the suicides by patients who were able to make it out of the facility alive, although the number of these was difficult to verify.

In the mid-1970s, CCHR began to receive reports of what was happening at Chelmsford. And by 1978, after investigating, it had collected hard evidence of six deaths related to deep sedation therapy. At that point, CCHR went public.

What followed was a significant demonstration of the unwillingness of authorities to view emperors in their nakedness—and failure of the psychiatric establishment to police itself. It was, in fact, a tedious merry-go-round of letter writing and lobbying. The Royal Australian and New Zealand College of Psychiatrists was given the evidence, and did nothing. The state of New South Wales Attorney General Department was given the evidence, and did nothing. The Minister of Health was given the evidence, and did nothing. The Health Commission and the Medical Board were given the evidence, but they each referred CCHR to the other. Meanwhile, public relations attacks were mounted against CCHR.

It took CCHR ten years of persistent investigation and bulldog-like determination before the New South Wales government appointed a Royal Commission in 1988 to look into deep sleep therapy in Chelmsford and throughout the state. Finally, after the two-year inquiry was completed and the full litany of horrors was uncovered—which included the possibility of 183 patient deaths, either at Chelmsford or within a year of discharge—a thorough shake-up of mental health care in New South Wales was recommended, along with a mental health patient bill of rights.

And what of psychiatry's stance after CCHR first uncovered what was happening at Chelmsford? It was ignored for as long as possible. However, this comment by a leading international figure provides an apt summation of psychiatric concerns. On January 6, 1981, Sir Martin Roth, Professor of Psychiatry at Cambridge University, wrote to another psychiatrist, who was calling for an inquiry, that the "Scientologists and other organizations will have obtained ammunition for years or decades to come. There is, therefore, a pressing need for maintaining strict confidentiality at this stage until one can set these barbarities in the context of contemporary practice in psychiatry in a carefully prepared statement that comes from colleges and other bodies concerned."

Scientology's remorseless work to uncover the truth was not without compensation. Deep sleep therapy was banned in New South Wales. Chelmsford was closed. And, of even more significance, many of the surviving victims who received electroshock therapy took their cases to the Crime Victims Compensation Board. So far, the board's tribunal has recognized in more than thirty of these cases that the patients were indeed subjected to acts of violence, and has accordingly awarded them compensation. Two of the psychiatrists who worked at Chelmsford finally faced criminal charges in 1992. And CCHR continued its work, exposing psychiatric abuses at Townsville Hospital in the northern state of Queensland. In practices frighteningly similar to Bailey's deep sleep treatments, sixty-five deaths were attributed to "unlawful and negligent treatment" after CCHR triggered a government investigation.

Finally, what of Bailey himself? He was never prosecuted. In September, 1985 he killed himself with the same drugs he had been feeding to his own patients. In his suicide note he blamed Scientologists, saying, "They have finally won."

Psychiatric Slave Camps

In the 1970s, a traveling windowpane salesman lost his way in the semirural countryside outside of Johannesburg, South Africa. Stopping to ask directions at what seemed to be a desolate mining compound, he happened upon a troubling sight: a naked and obviously terrified native woman was attempting to flee a uniformed guard.

The salesman happened to be a Scientologist and mentioned what he had seen to the Church. As the South African edition of *Freedom* began to investigate, what emerged was a story that would long stand as a dark symbol of psychiatric greed and inhumanity.

That apparently abandoned mining compound was one of thirteen psychiatric facilities owned and operated by the Smith-Mitchell Holding Company, a group that by the mid-70s was absorbing about one-third of the South African mental health budget. Nine of these facilities were for black patients; four for whites.

What CCHR uncovered was shocking. In 1976, more than 70 percent of all black certified mental patients in South Africa were in the hands of this group. The Smith-Mitchell hospitals had a patient population of more than 10,000. And the blacks were treated little better than animals, providing 12-hour-a-day forced labor to line the pockets of their keepers. Nutrition was minimal, patients slept on mats on bare concrete floors, and in some institutions there was only one nurse on duty for anywhere from 300 to 1,000 patients. Nor were there equipped medical facilities, and at least one patient died a day. Accurately described by media as "hidden slave camps" and "human warehouses," most of these Draconian camps were hidden from view, and surrounded by spiked fences.

Troublesome patients were made tractable with a trip to the nearest state hospital where electroshock therapy was administered—without anesthetic.

The exposure of these grim revelations in Church publications brought an understandable wave of public outrage, both in South Africa and overseas. The World Health Organization and the United Nations Commission on Human Rights investigated and confirmed the atrocities uncovered by CCHR. Of even greater significance, and as a direct result of CCHR's work, in 1991 the United Nations unanimously issued for the first time a body of principles to protect persons with mental illness and improve mental health care—a mental health bill of rights.

CCHR and US Psychiatric Institutions

Since the late 1960s CCHR has investigated a virtually endless array of psychiatric abuses in the United States. In 1976, for instance, it provided California lawmakers with evidence and witnesses documenting the unexplained deaths of more than 100 people at the Camarillo and Metropolitan State psychiatric institutions. These exposés led to an investigation by the California state legislature and resulted in substantial administrative changes in both institutions.

In 1990 a similar pattern of abuse was discovered at the Patton state psychiatric institution in San Bernardino, California. CCHR discovered that the death rate at Patton had increased five times since the head of the institution had assumed office. Again, the California legislature investigated and the executive director was forced to resign.

CCHR was also instrumental in 1976 for laws passed in California to restrict the use of electric shock and lobotomies. The measures prohibited the use of these brutal practices on children and required that psychiatrists fully inform adult patients of the damaging effects and helpful alternatives before either procedure could be consented to.

Psychiatrists and Sexual Abuse

Although the Chelmsford atrocities and the disgraceful South African mental health camps are broad and telling examples of psychiatric desperation, there is a less dramatic yet extremely pervasive form of abuse which, mainly through the efforts of CCHR, has made headlines throughout the United States: psychiatric sexual abuse.

A growing problem among psychiatrists and psychologists, the sexual exploitation of patients—men, women and children—had long gone unreported owing to the unique and powerful control mental health professionals hold over their patients. Less than 5 percent of patients sexually assaulted by their therapists ever take action against them. And there are even cases on record wherein psychiatrists have actually used their instruments of trade—electroshock and heavy sedation—to silence patients they have sexually abused.

While there have been widespread reports of these abuses in institutions, CCHR investigations and the appearance of more and more newspaper accounts show the problem is not limited to those who have been committed to psychiatric care. It ranges from one-man practitioners in small towns and cities, to high officials. Early in 1992, for instance, John Hamilton, deputy medical director of the American Psychiatric Association, stepped down from office and had his license suspended for a year—after having sexual relations with a patient who was courageous enough to file a complaint. Ironically, Hamilton wrote and edited the APA peer review manual.

However, this type of rap on the knuckles is all too common—and, more unfortunately, all too rare. In the last ten years, the APA has suspended or expelled only 113 psychiatrists for exploiting patients. These are mild actions when one considers findings of the California task force that about 66 percent of those who are sexually exploited by mental health practitioners experience serious emotional repercussions, and 1 percent even commit suicide.

The intrinsic problem here, of course, is that like doctors and lawyers, psychiatrists righteously and loudly claim that a peer review system is firmly in place to handle member malfeasance. Outsiders, particularly those involved in enforcement of laws, are not needed, thank you. However, the reality demonstrated in all these professions shows serious flaws. Two factors come into play: A peer is after all an equal and a member of the same group and, unless one is motivated by deeply rooted ideals, it is, to say the least, uncomfortable to reprimand one's equals; and, perhaps of more pertinence, if judgments are too harsh they are invariably publicized, thus airing the profession's dirty linen. Bad publicity is anathema to a profession already standing on shaky ground. And faced with this disturbing threat, ranks tend to close rather quickly.

Therefore, knowing full well that the psychiatric community has consistently demonstrated an inability to police its own actions, CCHR has long felt it only just that the perpetrators of actions that break the law of the land should face criminal prosecution. And so, it has taken it upon itself to see that they do. Victims of psychiatric abuse have little other recourse. Virtually nobody else is willing to stand up for their rights, perhaps because of the societal stigma attached to mental difficulties. More and more, however, they turn to CCHR as the word goes out that Scientologists care.

Thus, in 1991 and 1992, CCHR has been responsible for the prosecution of scores of criminal psychiatrists, psychologists, psychiatric workers and psychiatric facilities. In the first nine months of 1992 thirty-six of these people were put behind bars, a clear sign of increasing activity since the twenty-one who were sentenced in 1991.

While exploitation of women patients is common, CCHR's investigations have revealed that the majority of these cases involve even more distasteful acts against children.

- One of the first cases CCHR investigated was that of Orange County psychiatrist, James Harrison White, who had sexually assaulted a 15-year-old boy. White was sentenced in 1990 to six years and eight months in prison. The Senior Deputy District Attorney, Dennis D. Bauer wrote to CCHR:

"I commend you and your staff for the tireless energy and unselfish commitment to solving one of society's neglected and secret problems . . . 'experimental psychiatry.' "

- That same year, another case involved the Children's Farm Home, a residential center for children with behavioral and emotional problems, in Oregon. Three men, William Henry Dufort, psychiatrist and director, another psychiatrist and a case worker, were all charged with sexual assault and/or sodomy of young boys under their care. Dufort was charged with forty-three counts and sentenced to forty-eight years in prison.

- On July 27, 1992, Alan J. Horowitz of Schenectady, New York was sentenced to ten to twenty years in prison for sodomizing a nine-year-old psychiatric patient the previous year. Allegedly, he has assaulted a string of children from California to Israel to New York in the past twenty years.

The problem is widespread. Each year, CCHR investigates scores of crimes such as these and ceaselessly lobbies for stronger laws against psychiatric rapists, in particular to make sexual relations with patients by psychotherapists and/or other mental health practitioners illegal. After many years of CCHR efforts, such a law was passed in California in 1989. By 1992 ten states had these laws and the Church was actively working with other states to enact similar legislation.

Psychiatric Drugs

When LSD was accidentally discovered, it was not put on the shelf, but actively developed by its maker and subsequently heavily promoted by noted psychiatrists and psychologists from the 1950s on. By the mid-60s it started to become a campus fad.

Around the same time, however, as *Freedom* exposed, it was also being given to unknowing US soldiers by their government. The results of these experiments included death, birth defects in offspring and lifelong psychotic reactions for some of the victims.

Due to the work of the Church, which located a number of these unfortunate veterans, the Army conducted a program to locate and notify all who had been tricked into participating in these covert psychiatric mind-control programs.

Psychiatric drugs have long been a CCHR target. Mind-altering, with immensely powerful and dangerous side effects, they have been used extensively by psychiatrists who lack real answers to problems they don't understand. From Valium, which was the psychiatric "wonder drug" of the 60s—until it was found to cause violent rages and to be highly addictive—to today's destructive drugging of more than a million US schoolchildren with Ritalin, psychiatric drugs have done nothing but further destabilize individuals in our society.

Ritalin, a powerful amphetamine-like drug prescribed by psychiatrists for so-called hyperactive children of all ages, has turned essentially normal, healthy children into depressed, listless, and sometimes violent or suicidal addicts. In fact, Ritalin is bought on the street by heroin addicts. Through an educational program directed at parents, to information campaigns aimed at banning the drug, CCHR is enlightening society to its dangers.

*Some of the many issues of **Freedom** magazine published and distributed by the Church to educate the public on important social issues*

Score Two for Religious Freedom
IRS Stopped by Wall of Separation; Agency Ordered to Pay Legal Costs
Retaliation...Or Just Plain Harassment?
Le magazine d'investigation de l'Eglise de Scientologie.
Dans les écoles primaires : quand les psychiatres s'en
LA NUOVA INTOL
FREEDOM
INVESTIGATIVE REPORTING IN THE PUBLIC INTEREST
PUBLISHED BY THE CHURCH OF SCIENTOLOGY SINCE 1968
Psychiatry Creates Violence
FREEDOM CANADIAN EDITION
THE WAR — See Page 3 —
SPECIAL REPORT
Health Minister Asked to Probe Cover-Up of Crimes
Queen Street Mental Health Centre
Psychiatric Victim
The Making of a Killer
PSYCHIATRIC DRUG RUINS
HUMAN RIGHTS ADVOCATE OF THE MONTH:
Jim Garrison: The Killing of John Kennedy
IRS Targets Small Businesses
Whatever Happened to The American Dream?
Designer Drugs
IN THE FOOTSTEPS OF THE GREATEST
Readin', 'Ritin' and Ritalin
How Psychiatric Drugs Are Turning Our Children Into Robots
Ritalin in the Streets
Illegal Use of Psychiatric Drugs Escalating in U.S. Cities
PSYCHIATRIC TERROR
ERNEST HEMINGWAY LAST STAND
Taxpayers' Bill of Rights
Help for the Beleaguered Citizen
Destructive Effects Ignored by Air Force
Exposing a Criminal Clique
Indiscretions of "CAN" Revealed
IRS: Playing God
Xanax: A Psychiatric Chemical Nightmare
"It's A Little Pill Waiting To Take Your Life Away From You"
TAXPAYERS' RIGHTS
YES
NO
Leaked Document Shows
IRS Sabotaging Congress' Intent
Speaking Out Against IRS ABUSES
More and more people are calling for an end to IRS criminality. This issue highlights some of the individuals who are doing something about exposing IRS abuses and protecting individual rights.
Senator Harry Reid
Charles T. Pherigo
Holier Than Thou
IRS Hypocrisy Revealed in Survey
Racism Rampant
Rescuing the U.S. Economy
A National Sales Tax
PROZAC CRASH!
Investors Abandon Killer Drug

The latest wonder drug, Prozac, which is linked with violence, permanent mental instability and death, has been consistently exposed by CCHR. The Food and Drug Administration has received more adverse reaction reports on this drug since it was introduced in 1987 than any drug in history. Yet it is still being prescribed to millions of people around the world. CCHR has conducted a massive public awareness campaign to make the facts known, demanding its removal from the market.

No battle is one-sided, however, and Scientology has been subjected to predictably intense and unrelenting attacks by the enormously wealthy psychiatric drug companies. Small wonder, when one considers that Prozac is the single largest worldwide moneymaker in Eli Lilly & Co.'s arsenal of drugs. Utilizing a malleable media, they have strafed Scientology from every possible angle. Still, as noted, these assaults were predictable and the Church has refused to be intimidated. Principle is a far more substantive and defensible stance than greed.

Psychiatric Fraud

Greed is, of course, what motivates the fraudulent—a category of criminal that has been no stranger to the ranks of psychiatry. According to investigations by CCHR, the mental health system is riddled with them.

In 1992 a hearing before the US House of Representatives Select Committee on Children, Youth and Families heard numerous cases of such abuse provided to the committee by CCHR and others. These incidents ranged from adolescents and children subjected to psychiatric practices they never needed in the first place, to institutions that hired "bounty hunters" to kidnap patients they could hold against their will—all for the insurance money.

Insurance has, in fact, been a major area of psychiatric fraud, particularly among private hospitals. The giant psychiatric hospital chain National Medical Enterprises (NME), and its subsidiary organization, Psychiatric Institutes of America, has, for example, been under investigation in Texas, Florida and New Jersey by officials ranging from attorneys general to state insurance commissioners—investigations helped by information from CCHR. In 1992 ten insurance companies filed suit against NME for defrauding them and trampling on the rights of mental health patients.

But NME is no lone offender. Other organizations, including Community Psychiatric Centers, Charter Medical Corp., and Hospital Corp. of America have also been investigated.

The widespread industry abuses discovered by CCHR and other investigators include: sending patients back into the street as soon as insurance ran out after the thirty days most companies were willing to pay for inpatient care; paying social workers, school counselors, crisis hot-line workers and even ministers to refer patients; abusing children with violent therapy; diagnosing without sufficient detail; and, multiple unnecessary treatments. Preying on the young and/or helpless is a common theme.

Fraud, however, wears as many faces as its participants can dream up schemes. In 1989 CCHR uncovered and exposed documents to show that two psychiatric facilities in Los Angeles that had been paid hundreds of thousands of dollars in government funding, did not even exist—except on paper.

Whether involving fraud, physical and mental abuse, unethical behavior or the poisoning of our children with drugs, CCHR's tireless work against psychiatric wrongdoing has been lauded by law enforcement, politicians, human rights groups and those victims who had been unable to stand alone against these brutal practices.

In 1986 the United Nations recognized CCHR's work in a report stating, "The main task of CCHR has been to achieve reform in the field of mental health and the preservation of the rights of individuals under the Universal Declaration of Human Rights.

"CCHR has been responsible for many great reforms. At least thirty bills throughout the world, which would otherwise have inhibited even more the rights of mental patients, or would have given psychiatry the power to commit minority groups and individuals against their will, have been defeated by CCHR actions."

Psychiatry too has recognized CCHR's work, although not necessarily with such admiration. In fact, with CCHR's revelations in South Africa, Australia, the United States, Germany, Canada, Italy, France, Switzerland and other countries, psychiatry had no choice but to realize that in Scientology it faced its worst enemy.

How to Start a CCHR

Forming a CCHR does not demand prior expertise or research. The primary prerequisite is a willingness and desire to do something to eliminate psychiatric abuse and restore human rights. Anyone wishing to start a CCHR chapter should merely contact their nearest CCHR office.

CCHR members have already compiled the successful actions needed to set up a local chapter, how to document abuses, what to look for when touring a psychiatric institution and numerous other helpful pointers. These are included in the information packets needed to start a CCHR chapter.

National Commission on Law Enforcement and Social Justice

Information is one of the most valuable commodities in this technological age. From the exchange of demographics to the sale of names for mailing lists, there are a thousand seemingly innocuous business activities that deal in information. But there is a more sinister aspect to consider. For instance, false and inaccurate reports in computer data banks have been known to ruin innocent lives. The man who has an incorrect credit report entered and can suddenly no longer get credit; the law-abiding citizen who has the same name as a criminal and unexpectedly finds himself under arrest; these situations are not that uncommon. And even more dangerous are files that have the authority of national governments behind them.

The problem of false reports in government agency files has, for many years, been of primary concern to the Church of Scientology, and in 1974 it formed the National Commission on Law Enforcement and Social Justice (NCLE) to reform the entire system of secret government dossiers.

The Church found that the basic rights and freedoms of citizens in all countries could be seriously jeopardized by uncorrected information, particularly in government files. And the potential for harm and abuse was compounded by the fact that many agencies shared their information data bases—an act that knows no international boundaries.

In today's computer age, false information can spread more quickly than germs—and become just as destructive. Data, accurate or not, filed by an authorized agency in one country, can spread throughout the world in the form of secret government dossiers that are simply assumed to be accurate. The potential for abuse is obvious. Government files can, and have, been deliberately poisoned by interested sources.

NCLE's early investigations of the origins of false information in government files—particularly those in foreign countries—led to a murky source about whom little was then known: the International Criminal Police Organization (Interpol). Originally formed to track international criminals, Interpol is a private organization—a fact unknown to the public before NCLE exposed it—and not subject to the direction, review or authority of any government.

Documents obtained by NCLE proved conclusively that Interpol was feeding false reports from law enforcement groups to government agencies in countries around the world. Numerous cases were documented of individuals jailed, harassed and even physically abused by police officials because of these reports.

And investigation into the history and activities of Interpol exposed for the first time that it had a long and close relationship with Nazi Germany. In fact, NCLE revealed in 1974 that the relationship had not completely ended with the Second World War: The president of this private organization between 1968 and 1972 had actually been a Nazi SS officer during the war.

Not surprisingly with such a background, evidence was also uncovered and widely exposed connecting Interpol with drug trafficking and other criminal activities on an international scale.

Government Investigations Confirm Church Findings

In 1976 NCLE researchers testified before the US Senate hearings on Interpol and presented information they had thus far gathered on the agency.

Following on the heels of this report, NCLE helped formulate questions for a US General Accounting Office (GAO) investigation into Interpol's activities. The GAO's report contained the following conclusions which confirmed NCLE's exposés:

▪ No government or state body monitors the activities of Interpol and there is no control over the distribution of information disseminated through Interpol.

▪ There were no guidelines from Interpol's headquarters governing exchange of unverified accusations, raw intelligence or other data, potentially regarding innocent citizens.

▪ Although a private organization, Interpol could carry out police, diplomatic, intelligence, law enforcement and other functions without effective oversight by any US government agency.

▪ None of the cases inspected by GAO investigators showed that Interpol was engaged in the combating of crime syndicates or major criminals.

A further GAO investigation into Interpol in 1986 recommended that the organization be required to verify the accuracy of reports it receives and disseminates. This and two subsequent investigations in 1990 were initiated by the GAO as a result of new information uncovered by NCLE and the Church's *Freedom* magazine and turned over to congressional offices.

Interpol: Promoting Drugs?

Although Interpol has publicly claimed since 1972 that the "war on drugs" has been its "number one priority" and that it has had the major drug trafficking routes "under investigation," researchers for NCLE and *Freedom* magazine found and exposed evidence that Interpol officials have in fact been involved in drug trafficking themselves:

▪ In April 1970, two members of the US State Department's Agency for International Development (AID) investigated drug law enforcement in Bolivia and reported that two former Interpol chiefs had been dismissed for corruption and suspected involvement in drug dealing.

▪ During the 1970s and into the 1980s, Interpol chiefs from the following countries were arrested, charged and convicted of drug trafficking: Mexico, Panama, Peru, Ecuador, Bolivia and Colombia.

▪ Incredibly, in a 1987 ceremony, Interpol Secretary General Raymond Kendall awarded the organization's highest honor, a bronze medal for "international effectiveness in combating drug trafficking," to former Panamanian dictator Manuel Noriega who, at the time, was under investigation in the United States for drug trafficking and money laundering. Furthermore, information from former high-ranking Panamanian officials had just been made public which implicated Noriega in a multibillion-dollar drug smuggling ring. Noriega was subsequently tried and found guilty in the United States on drug trafficking charges and sentenced to forty years in prison.

Over the years, investigations of Interpol by NCLE and *Freedom* have disclosed more and more criminal activities involving violations of the basic rights of individuals. The results of these investigations have been presented to government officials across the world, and have led to long-needed curtailment of Interpol corruption. These have included the Council of Europe, the European

Freedom** magazine and the Church-sponsored National Commission on Law Enforcement and Social Justice investigated and exposed widespread criminal activities on the part of Interpol, including drug trafficking and money laundering. The Church uncovered and released the photograph above showing the Interpol Secretary General presenting then Panamanian dictator, Manuel Noriega, an award for his "anti-drug activities" in 1987, just before Noriega was indicted as a major international drug trafficker. The results of the Church's research are summarized in the widely distributed publication, **Private Group, Public Menace—Interpol: A Police Organization Involved in Criminal Activities.

Parliament, the US Congress and federal parliaments and congresses of many other countries.

Material relating to Interpol corruption and its violations of individual rights was so extensive, the Church published a handbook, *Interpol: Private Group, Public Menace,* which clearly exposed the public danger inherent in Interpol.

When the executive director of the US National Association of Chiefs of Police received a copy of *Interpol: Private Group, Public Menace,* he felt the information was so important that he contacted the Church to arrange a mailing to over 15,000 chiefs of police across the country.

In the United States, state governments, now aware of the liability, enacted laws to keep their files out of Interpol hands. Various national police agencies in Europe also no longer trust or use Interpol, and an organization of five European countries (Germany, France, Belgium, the Netherlands and Luxembourg) signed a treaty which prohibits Interpol from accessing their police data bases.

Throughout the world, NCLE is alerting government and law enforcement officials to the abuses and dangers of Interpol. And the reform measures enacted continue to spread, little by little, ensuring greater protection of individual rights for all.

How to Start an NCLE Chapter

If you care about individual rights, privacy and freedom, you can start an NCLE chapter by contacting NCLE's main office in Los Angeles, California.

Freedom of Information

In 1822 James Madison, fourth president of the United States and a primary creator of the democratic principles which form the American system of government, wrote a letter putting forward a basic proposition concerning democracy:

"A popular government, without popular information, or the means of acquiring it, is but a Prologue to a farce or a Tragedy; or, perhaps, both. Knowledge will forever govern ignorance; and a people who mean to be their own Governors must arm themselves with the power which knowledge gives."

Passed into law in 1966 and greatly strengthened in 1974, the US Freedom of Information Act is a worthy effort by Congress to breathe life into Madison's words.

Under this act, a citizen can request access to any records of the executive branch of the federal government. The act provides that those records *must* be released to the requester unless they are shielded from disclosure by some provision of the Freedom of Information Act itself, or by some other federal law.

As Madison implied, a knowledgeable and informed citizenry is able to make intelligent decisions regarding its own future. And the Freedom of Information Act is one of the most valuable tools allowing people to learn exactly what their government is doing—and if government agencies have files about them. When one considers that Martin Luther King, Jr., was the subject of tens of thousands of government documents peppered throughout FBI and IRS files, one can see why this is sometimes worth knowing. However, King had no access to a workable Freedom of Information Act at that time.

The concept of freedom of information has not been without opposition. More than a few government agencies have waged pitched court battles to preserve their secrecy.

To help counter these and other attempts to circumvent the law, the Church of Scientology submitted an open letter to Congress on July 4, 1981, signed by 146 organizations opposing an effort at that time to limit the effectiveness of the act.

Widely recognized among public interest groups as a leading expert on freedom of information legislation, the Church of Scientology has also earned a substantial reputation for its role in informing US citizens of their rights under the Freedom of Information Act. Nor have Scientologists limited their energies in these matters to the United States. When freedom of information legislation was passed in France (1978), Canada (1982), Australia (1982), New Zealand (1983), Italy (1991) and Belgium (1991), members of the Church played a decisive role to bring these laws about.

In 1991 Scientologists also assisted passage of a new law in France providing individuals greater access to the files of *Renseignements Généraux* (General Information), the French intelligence police, known as the "RG."

In 1992 an international conference on freedom of information, organized by a Scientologist, was held in Hungary with speakers from the United States, Canada, Sweden, Portugal, Scotland and Germany, and delegates from Czechoslovakia, Yugoslavia, Romania, Albania, Bulgaria, the Ukraine, Latvia and Poland. This three-day international meeting, attended by 120 people and cosponsored by the Hungarian Ministry of the Interior and Ministry of Justice, under the auspices of the Council of Europe, brought a vital message on the subject for all those emerging from former political repression.

Broad public education concerning freedom of information is essential if people are to understand their rights. In the mid-1970s the Church of Scientology published the first of its informative booklets on freedom of information—a layman's guide for filing requests and overcoming arbitrary refusals to provide valid information.

A revised and updated edition was published in 1989 and distributed as a public service to more than 60,000 individuals and groups. Entitled *How to Use the Freedom of Information Act: Holding the Government Accountable for Its Actions,* the revised handbook received countless accolades by letter and in the media.

This handbook, printed and distributed by the Church to hundreds of thousands of citizens, has made individual rights known and has provided individuals with simple directions for using the Freedom of Information Act and informed them of their rights under this law.

Fighting for Freedom of Information

Ever willing to fight unwarranted government secrecy in the courts, the Church of Scientology's litigation with various US government agencies has established legal precedents further empowering the citizen with his right to monitor his government.

In May 1991, for example, a federal court in the United States credited the Church, in a case it brought against the Internal Revenue Service, for helping bring about significant reform. "Furthermore," the court stated, "communications between the IRS and the Church indicate that this litigation contributed to the IRS' decision to review its procedures and that resulting improvements in these procedures will enable better handling of over 1,000 cases involving identical legal issues."

In another precedent-setting case that will be of value to everyone, because it sets a standard to be obeyed by government in the future, the US Court of Appeals for the District of Columbia ruled that the National Security Agency could not simply assert that it was unable to locate records in response to a Church FOIA request. The court ordered the agency to conduct new searches, stating, in part, "If the agency can lightly avoid its responsibilities by laxity in identification or retrieval of desired materials, the majestic goals of the act will soon pass beyond reach."

In yet another case, a federal judge in Los Angeles granted *Freedom* magazine's motion to require the IRS to produce a detailed and specific index of records being withheld by the agency, rather than merely listing them out by general category.

And with each success through and for the Freedom of Information Act comes not just another victory for Scientology, but a victory for all those who might one day suffer from government secrecy.

It was in acknowledgment of such unprecedented efforts that noted author and expert on US intelligence matters, Victor Marchetti, declared:

"I would like to commend the Church of Scientology for its faith in itself and its determination to work within the constitutional democratic system of our nation. It has fought the good fight against great odds openly and legally . . . and it has survived . . . which is more of a tribute to its membership than it is to our own government. By its tenacity and determination, the Church of Scientology has forced that government to adhere to the Constitution . . . something that will benefit all Americans in the long run."

Religious Freedom

According to the Creed of the Church of Scientology, Scientologists believe that all men have inalienable rights to their own religious practices and their performance, and that no agency less than God has the power to suspend or set aside these rights.

However, like all of man's treasured freedoms, freedom of religion is maintained only through vigilance and refusal to succumb to those who seek to enslave and suppress.

Over the years, the Church of Scientology has been a leader in championing the cause of religious freedom for all. It strongly believes that as the United States was founded on this principle, separation of church and state forms an essential base for all other freedoms. And that continuous attempts by government to encroach upon this right must be strenuously fought, for this is the sign of an oppressive government.

During the 1970s one of the methods used by vested interests to undermine religious freedom in the United States was a broad-scale propaganda and lobbying campaign directed at both state and federal legislatures. Efforts were made to introduce bills which would have legalized the activities of anti-religious hate groups, restricted the legitimate dissemination activities of churches and given state agencies the green light to take control of day-to-day church operations.

Through the dedicated work of Scientologists and friends in other religious groups, antireligious legislation of this type met defeat in Alabama, California, Connecticut, Delaware, Florida, Illinois, Kansas, Massachusetts, Michigan, Minnesota, New Jersey, New York, Nevada, North Carolina, Ohio, Oregon, Pennsylvania and Texas.

Milestone Victories

A landmark California case, which began in 1979 as an attempt to subjugate religion under a psychiatric yoke, ended with passage of a law that protects churches from punitive damage claims by antireligious interests.

The case, involving a frivolous lawsuit filed against a Christian church over the suicide of a parishioner, progressed through a series of rulings and appeals in California state courts over a period of ten years. The Church of Scientology worked with more than 1,500 religious organizations in opposing the suit and making its ramifications known to other religions and the public.

In the eventual 1989 decision, the US Supreme Court endorsed a California Supreme Court decision which held that the state's laws forbid the filing of such cases against churches. The right to free practice of religion was upheld, and this attempt to position psychiatrists as overseers of religion was dismissed.

In another milestone victory, the Church of Scientology mustered interfaith support for a bill prohibiting claims for punitive or exemplary damages against religions, with strictly defined exceptions.

Many religious groups joined the Church in support of the bill, including the California Catholic Conference, the California Council of Churches, the Church of Jesus Christ of Latter-day Saints and the National Congress for Religious Liberty.

Two years of concerted efforts culminated on September 27, 1988, when California Senate Bill No. 1 was signed into law by the California governor.

Establishing an Important Precedent

Churches have traditionally been guardians of freedom, protecting citizens against government attempts to dilute or eradicate their rights, and therefore they have often come under attack. To help protect churches from unwarranted government intrusion the 1984 Church Audits Procedures Act was passed by Congress "to give churches a special audit procedure to require the IRS to take greater care in the examination of churches."

This law is a step intended to help close the door on IRS intimidation and attempts to silence religions and subvert their role in society.

The Church of Scientology has blocked efforts by the Internal Revenue Service (IRS) to undermine this act, and in the course of doing so has preserved the rights of all religions in the United States.

The Church of Scientology has long been a vocal critic of government abuses, and some IRS officials saw the law as an obstacle to their habitual circumvention of constitutional safeguards. The IRS commissioner from 1981 to 1986 called the law's regulations "little more than a series of mechanistic tests and hoops for the Service to jump through."

The Church of Scientology established the first major court precedent strengthening the Church Audit Procedures Act in 1990 when the US District Court in Boston ruled against the IRS' request to rummage through 200,000 pages of church documents.

This Church of Scientology case was observed widely by many religious leaders as the first major test of the law—with an outcome that would be significant for all churches in the United States.

After the Church's courtroom triumph, the *Legal Times* reported, "Other church groups are hailing the decision as a victory for religious freedom, and warn that the IRS had better think twice before sticking its nose in religious organizations' business again."

Establishing Religious Freedom Week

With the groundswell of public support for religious freedom generated by Church of Scientology initiatives, leaders of other mainstream religions joined in petitioning the US Congress to enact an annual national Religious Freedom Week.

The original Religious Freedom Week resolution was signed into law by the president of the United States on September 20, 1988 and has now become an annual national tradition.

Another publication provided by the Church as a public service to all citizens

The Religious Freedom Week celebrations, in which churches of nearly every faith participate, have brought about a renewed awareness throughout the country of the importance of defending the right for all citizens to practice their faith according to their own conscience.

Crusades for Religious Freedom

Throughout Europe, Religious Freedom Crusades organized by the Church of Scientology have been conducted in response to threats from antireligious influences.

In France, 2,500 Scientologists assembled in Strasbourg to proclaim a "Declaration of Religious Freedom" which was subsequently accepted by the Council of Europe.

In Germany, the Church of Scientology played a key role in establishing the ecumenical "European Council of Religious Movements" whose members represent their respective churches and religions in dealing with issues of religious freedom.

In its battles against attempts to violate or negate religious freedom, the Church of Scientology and its members have maintained a firm stance that religious freedom must be preserved for all faiths.

RELIGIOUS FREEDOM
CRUSADE
UPHOLD
THE
FIRST
AMENDMENT
THE SUN
NEVER
SETS ON
SCIEN-
TOLOGY
RELIGIOUS FREEDOM
CRUSADE
DAY 13

Tens of thousands of Scientologists gathered in Los Angeles, California in a Crusade for Religious Freedom.

The work of Scientologists on behalf of religious freedom is nondenominational; it is carried out with the view that liberty of religious belief and practice is the cornerstone of freedom itself, and that when one religion is infringed upon, the rights of all men are endangered.

An Ongoing Crusade Against Injustice

These are just some of the highlights of the Church of Scientology's ongoing work to eradicate injustice, abuse of the weak and betrayals of public trust. It is no easy task; social reform requires constant vigilance and a willingness to confront those ugly facts most of us would like to ignore.

A just and enlightened civilization does not tolerate brutalities toward the helpless among its citizens. Nor does a true civilization allow monolithic governments to subvert the rights of its most honest and productive people. It is often said that power corrupts. And so it has been in many civilizations that have come and gone in ages past. When citizens feel they can no longer do something about injustice, they have taken a giant step toward abdicating their rights to freedom.

Scientologists have the courage and determination to do something about it. They have, indeed, drawn the line, not just for themselves, but for all men of goodwill. While some of the dreadful things that happen in this world may seem far distant from the life you live, you should know this: that what Scientologists are doing, they are doing for you. And in doing so, they are bringing all mankind closer to a higher and better civilization.

Part Six

The Association for Better Living and Education (ABLE)

It is impossible to ignore the signs of decay in modern society—drug abuse, criminality, failing education and moral decline. They are issues discussed at every political convention, in every civic group and nearly every home. They are also issues of pressing concern to Scientologists, for they, too, must live in this world—thus, the formation of ABLE, the Association for Better Living and Education.

Coordinating the efforts of Scientologists to eradicate these problems through the use of L. Ron Hubbard's technology, ABLE has proven itself to be the most successful organization of its kind in the world. This chapter describes the various activities of ABLE and how it is making a difference.

CHAPTER 25

ABLE: SOLUTIONS TO A TROUBLED SOCIETY

Since its earliest days, the Church of Scientology has been concerned about the decline in society at large, well knowing that Mr. Hubbard's technology had wide applications that would be of inestimable benefit beyond the religious arena. Beginning in the 1960s, Scientologists became involved in a number of social betterment activities to reverse this decline.

As the aims of Scientology seek evolution to higher states of being for both the individual and society, these activities have grown increasingly important to the Church and, in 1988, it formed the Association for Better Living and Education (ABLE) to support, promote and expand the social betterment organizations that use Mr. Hubbard's technologies in society.

Today, under the umbrella of ABLE, thousands of Scientologists and non-Scientologists alike are extensively involved in many community groups and programs which apply the discoveries and technology of L. Ron Hubbard toward the resolution of society's most devastating problems: rampant drug and alcohol abuse, widespread illiteracy, escalating crime and the dramatic decline in personal integrity, ethics and moral values.

Located in Los Angeles in the Hollywood Guaranty Building, ABLE's activities are supported at the Church's highest ecclesiastical levels. There is also substantial direct financial sponsorship by the Church and donations by its members, all of which amount to many millions of dollars a year to help these programs carry out their activities.

The function of ABLE is to assist social betterment groups to accomplish their purposes through advisory and fund-raising services, as well as to carry out promotional and public relations campaigns. These campaigns address individuals and groups (such as corporations, clubs, institutions, departments of local and national governments, etc.) to inform them that the solutions to the problems of today's society can be found in ABLE's social betterment groups.

To assist these groups, ABLE has offices around the world covering all continents, and regional offices where they are needed. In addition to providing books and materials, ABLE also sends administrative and technical experts to outer areas to help resolve any difficulties they might be having and ensure that Mr. Hubbard's technology is being correctly applied so that the full results are attained.

ABLE supports groups which apply the technology of L. Ron Hubbard to handle four of the most severe blights in society:

Drug and alcohol abuse: Narconon International, which oversees a global network of drug rehabilitation and drug education centers, is dedicated to restoring drug-free lives to drug-dependent people, and also delivers educational programs to help people avoid the trap of drugs.

Crime: Criminon International is aimed at restoring a sense of responsibility to criminals so they can become productive members of society and at bringing about reform so that prisons actually rehabilitate.

Education: Applied Scholastics International assists students, parents, teachers, educational organizations and businesses

The offices of Association for Better Living and Education in Los Angeles

around the world to eradicate illiteracy with Mr. Hubbard's study technology.

Morals: The Way to Happiness Foundation is creating a groundswell of international support for moral reform utilizing Mr. Hubbard's nonreligious moral code, *The Way to Happiness.*

These organizations have succeeded in salvaging many lives through the application of L. Ron Hubbard's technology. Each has made vital contributions to improving life in a troubled world.

ABLE exists to bring about genuine betterment of conditions on a planetwide scale, a goal shared by all Scientologists. ABLE and its programs are supported by thousands of Scientologists around the world, volunteering their time and providing donations. Neither the Church nor its parishioners receive monetary remuneration for this charitable activity. Those involved, however, are rewarded with a great deal of personal satisfaction.

The staff of ABLE and the groups they support are applying L. Ron Hubbard's technology to bring sanity to a troubled and dying society. They are on the front lines, creating a new civilization here on Earth, one in which drugs, illiteracy and crime are things of the past. And, fortunately for the future well-being of mankind, their activities continue to grow.

NARCONON:
DRUG REHABILITATION

Narconon (meaning *no drugs*) began in 1966 through the efforts of Arizona State Prison inmate William Benitez. A hard-core addict from the age of thirteen, then serving his fourth prison term, Benitez had unsuccessfully tried numerous ways to kick his drug habit.

In Mr. Benitez's words:

"My failure to come off drugs wasn't due to not wanting to. Believe me, I really tried. I read and read . . . Freud, Jung, Menninger—and studied one philosophy after another, everything I could get my hands on to find out about myself. I underwent psychiatric aid and participated in all sorts of programs and as time went on, I knew less about myself instead of more. The only thing that kept me from putting a gun to my head was that I knew someday I would make it. I felt so sorry for my friends who were constantly trying to get off drugs. I wanted to help them and yet I couldn't even help myself. . . . I was so tired of the life of addiction, thieving, prostitution and all that goes with it. On my fourth and last trip to Arizona State Penitentiary, I was tried as a habitual criminal which sentence carried a mandatory fifteen years to life, of which I received fifteen to sixteen years. It was at this point that I began to go into agreement with the idea that once you were an addict, you remained an addict."

His search for solutions led him to L. Ron Hubbard's *Scientology: The Fundamentals of Thought,* and with the principles in this book, he was at last able to kick his addiction.

As Mr. Benitez continued his studies, he soon realized that L. Ron Hubbard's mental and spiritual discoveries offered the first real hope for addicts, and began applying that material to help other inmates.

"When first applied to a pilot group at Arizona State Penitentiary in 1966," Mr. Benitez reported, "it consisted only of the basic communication exercises. Yet, seven out of ten of the first group in their own words, 'made it.' Their success spread at grass-roots level to other prisons, and drawing on further research by L. Ron Hubbard, the program was expanded."

An initial group of ten grew to one hundred inmates within the first year. And, although originally organized to help heroin addicts, Narconon's usefulness and workability led to enormous interest from the general prison population. In 1967 prison officials granted permission for any inmate to join the group, and thereafter Narconon was opened to all who wished to improve their lives.

Mr. Benitez wrote to L. Ron Hubbard, who encouraged him to expand the program. The church of Scientology in Phoenix also assisted by donating materials, and the most effective drug rehabilitation program in the world had been born.

By 1970, Mr. Benitez had been released from prison and traveled to Los Angeles to assist in opening the national office of Narconon. This bureau became known as Narconon US, and commenced a program of expansion throughout the United States.

Initial Narconon programs in California institutions such as California's Rehabilitation Center in Norco, the California Men's Colony in San Luis Obispo and the Youth

Training School in Ontario were well received and highly successful.

An official evaluation of the ten-month program at the Youth Training School showed that disciplinary offenses among the control group increased 10 percent during the second five-month period, while those of the Narconon group decreased by 81 percent. The grade average of the control group increased from C to C+, while that of the Narconon group increased from C– to B–.

Narconon successes continued to mount. In May 1972, a program was started at the Ventura School for Boys and Girls in Ventura, California. After considerable expansion it later received funding from the California Youth Authority.

That same year, Narconon opened its first residential programs, making it possible to take an addict through the Narconon withdrawal program and other Narconon courses. This expansion was an important step for Narconon as it brought all stages of rehabilitation into the safety of a residential environment.

The Narconon Program: Producing New Lives Without Drugs

The need for effective drug rehabilitation technology is today greater than ever before, for the scope of the problem is vast. Internationally, the illegal narcotics industry has estimated annual revenues of between $500 billion and $1 trillion.

This astonishing statistic is only one indicator of the many social repercussions of drug abuse. Criminals on drugs, for example, are responsible for the vast majority of all crimes committed. According to US Justice Department studies, three out of four suspects arrested for crimes of violence test positive for illegal drugs.

To meet this crucial need for effective drug rehabilitation, Narconon has expanded greatly in the years since its founding. As the program moved into other countries, Narconon International was formed to direct the drug education and rehabilitation activities of Narconon and provide assistance and support to Narconon centers and their staffs throughout the world. Narconon International has a goal to achieve a drug-free Earth. It provides effective and complete drug rehabilitation for those enslaved by drugs and works to prevent our future generations from ever becoming addicted. Located in Los Angeles, Narconon International today supervises worldwide drug education and drug rehabilitation programs.

Narconon centers are located throughout the world, with more opening every year. Currently, Narconons operate in Canada, Denmark, France, Germany, Italy, the Netherlands, Spain, Sweden, Switzerland, the United Kingdom and the United States. Today there are 34 Narconon organizations in 11 countries, and more than 25,000 people had availed themselves of Narconon services by 1992.

Narconon also operates the largest training and rehabilitation facility of its kind in the world, the Narconon Chilocco New Life Center near Newkirk, Oklahoma. Set on 167 acres of lush Great Plains landscape, it was formerly the site of the Chilocco Indian Agricultural School, and was developed with the agreement of leaders from five Native American tribes.

This peaceful campus brings a new life to many in need of rehabilitation with the highest quality and most effective drug rehabilitation program available in the world. It is also here that Narconon personnel come from many countries for training to administer this Narconon program to others. Narconon Chilocco is the international training center, turning out highly qualified and competent staff trained in L. Ron Hubbard's technology so that it can be delivered in all nations. These dedicated Narconon staff return to their cities and countries to bring a new life to drug and alcohol abusers there.

Narconon's efficacy comes entirely from the technology developed by L. Ron Hubbard who, years before the drug crisis became headline news internationally, had extensively researched the antisocial side effects of drugs.

He discovered the insidious effects not only of illegal or "street" drugs but also of alcohol and psychiatric drugs—the latter often far more devastating and injurious than the original condition they were intended to "cure."

Narconon utilizes a completely *drug-free* rehabilitation program to restore life to drug and alcohol abusers and give them back control of their lives.

Compared to other programs in the drug rehabilitation field Narconon's results are exceptional. While most programs have a 15 percent success rate, two independent studies of Narconon showed that 84.6 percent of graduates from a 1981 Swedish program no longer used drugs, and in Spain, a 1985 study found 78.37 percent were still drug free a year later.

In a field loaded with drug programs that substitute addictions with yet more drugs, L. Ron Hubbard developed exact techniques to deal with the physical *and* mental damage brought about by substance abuse. None of these techniques involve the use of methadone or any other substitute drug.

The Narconon program today consists of a series of exercises, drills and study steps done in a precise sequence. The techniques and learning programs help the individual withdraw from current drug use; get into communication with others and the environment; remove the residual drugs from his body; gain control of himself and his environment and reach the point where he can take responsibility, not only for himself, but also for others. The Narconon program consists of the following:

1. Drug-Free Withdrawal—The first step of the Narconon program helps the individual cease current drug use rapidly and with minimal discomfort through proper nutrition, vitamins and care from experienced Narconon staff. Various assists help the person come off the drugs with minimal discomfort.

2. Therapeutic TR Course—Once withdrawal is complete, a series of communication drills (called training routines, or "TRs") are used to extrovert the person and get him in touch with others and with the environment. Each TR increases the person's ability to face life and communicate with others.

3. The Narconon New Life Detoxification Procedure—Next, the person cleanses his body of drug residues and other toxic substances through a regimen of exercise, sauna and nutritional supplements as described in the book *Clear Body, Clear Mind: The Effective Purification Program* by L. Ron Hubbard. Drug residues remain locked in the fatty tissues of the body and can be released into the bloodstream years after the person has stopped taking drugs, thus rekindling old cravings for drugs. This step purges the body of these residues and other toxins.

4. The Learning Improvement Course—Here, the student gains the ability to study and retain knowledge, along with the ability to recognize and overcome the barriers to study. He can now proceed with further educational steps to prepare him to lead a productive and ethical life.

5. The Communication and Perception Course—On this step, the student repeats the TRs, plus additional exercises which get him into full communication with others and his environment. The exercises pull the person's attention off himself, where it has been fixed by drugs, and out to the world around him. The student also helps another student do the exercises, which not only gives him increased responsibility, but a tremendous sense of pride and satisfaction because of this newly gained ability to help others.

6. The Ups and Downs in Life Course—Now the student gains the knowledge to spot and handle those influences in his environment that would cause him to lose any gains he has made. He learns the characteristics of the antisocial personality and the social personality so he can recognize the two, spot the differences between them and better choose his friends and associates. Completing this course makes a person less susceptible to those who would influence a reversion to drugs.

The Narconon program consists of a series of exercises, drills and study steps done in a precise sequence. The study materials and workbooks shown here guide the individual through the program.

7. The Personal Values and Integrity Course—The student gains the data he needs to improve his survival potential. The course teaches the student about the eight dynamics, ethics, honesty and integrity, showing him how to correct contrasurvival behavior by ridding himself of the effects of past harmful deeds.

8. The Narconon Changing Conditions in Life Course—This course covers the ethics technology of L. Ron Hubbard and shows the student exactly how to apply it to improve conditions in his life, something the student needs if he is to reassert his self-determinism.

9. The Narconon "The Way to Happiness" Course—Based on a nonsectarian moral code called *The Way to Happiness,* this course gives the student a guide to living a life where real happiness is attainable.

This comprehensive program addresses and handles the reason why the individual started using drugs in the first place and arms him with the knowledge and certainty he needs to lead a happy, drug-free life. Vocational training programs are also available to develop needed job skills so graduates can better support themselves.

Narconon programs are delivered by dedicated individuals who choose to work with Narconon because it has proven itself in the drug rehabilitation field. In some cases these staff are Scientologists. In many other cases, they are those who have progressed themselves from addict to ex-addict to contributing Narconon staff member.

Effective Drug Education Lectures

Prevention is also an important part of the Narconon program.

The international spokesperson for Narconon is actress Kirstie Alley. She tirelessly promotes the benefits of a drug-free life attainable through Narconon, with numerous radio and television interviews and public appearances at fund-raising events.

Other Narconon spokespersons delivered nearly ten thousand lectures on drug abuse to approximately three-quarters of a million students in the 1980s and early 1990s.

These "Truth About Drugs" lectures result in a dramatic change in attitude toward drugs. A 1989 study by the Foundation for Advancements in Science and Education measured the attitude change of students from the second grade to twelfth grade in high school and concluded:

"Narconon's drug education program is effective in teaching students about the adverse consequences of drug abuse and has a very positive influence on the attitudes of students toward drugs. The most dramatic effect on attitude [was] observed in the borderline group of students—those indicating that they might use drugs in the future."

Of the students in this category, 86 percent indicated that they were less likely to use drugs following the presentation.

Film and television actress, Kirstie Alley, is Narconon's international spokesperson.

Scientologists Support Narconon

While talk of drug and alcohol abuse is endless, solutions do not come as easily. Nearly 80 percent of the American public, for instance, believe that drug abuse is a concern that the US government must deal with immediately, yet 70 percent feel their government's "war on drugs" is ineffective.

Scientologists strongly believe that both drug education and real rehabilitation are vital. Based on results, Mr. Hubbard's technology provides the most effective solutions to drug and alcohol abuse.

In nearly three decades of service in the war against drugs, Narconon has shown itself to be the most effective rehabilitation program there is. It is something that the peoples of Earth urgently need.

Thus, Scientologists support Narconon. Many contribute time and energy to help Narconon staff, serving as part-time volunteers in Narconon's community and prison programs.

Administrative staff in Narconon's worldwide network help acquire donations for new premises or materials, and assist to recruit staff for these programs. Scientology churches, through ABLE, have donated millions of dollars, as well as materials, furniture and supplies to Narconon programs. And individual Scientologists have also enthusiastically contributed financially to support Narconon.

This combination of dedicated staff and L. Ron Hubbard's technology has served Narconon for over twenty-five years as the acknowledged pacesetter in the field of drug and alcohol prevention, education and rehabilitation.

Expansion Because of One Reason: Results

From the simple beginnings and single L. Ron Hubbard book, to the full lineup of today's Narconon program, the fact of workability lies at the core of Narconon's success. Professionals in the field of drug rehabilitation from many countries have attested to Narconon's results.

For instance, one leading researcher in the field of public health, well known for his work with professional football players in America, Dr. Forest Tennant, remarked on the excellence of the Narconon program:

"Narconon has emerged during the past decade as one of the premier residential treatment centers for persons who have severe drug dependence. I have referred patients to Narconon centers in recent years and I have seen the tremendous results."

He further stated, "Of particular note is that, although the use of vitamins, minerals and amino acids is now standard treatment, I thought it was false in 1974 when I first heard of Narconon's belief in the use of megavitamins. Further, Narconon was also one of the first to reveal that drugs are retained in the body, a belief which I also believed false in 1974 when I first heard it. There is now unquestionable scientific evidence that, when drugs such as marijuana, cocaine, PCP or methamphetamines are taken, the drugs do go into body fat and remain for weeks or months. Accordingly, it is entirely possible that Narconon was simply twenty years ahead of its time. . . ."

Kent McGregor, a nationally respected American drug abuse consultant whose career in drug prevention began with then-president Richard Nixon's "war on drugs," said this about Narconon:

"I have been to some of the high-powered programs in the nation and I can say, unequivocally, that what you are doing here is better than anything I have seen anywhere else. Even to the point that if [my sons] . . . had a drug problem, I would bring them here. And that's over the other programs I talked about."

Narconon is accredited by the prestigious Commission for Accreditation of Rehabilitation Facilities (CARF), widely recognized as the foremost authority on drug rehabilitation programs in the United States. CARF's standards are the highest in the nation and have been adopted by many states and federal agencies as the benchmark for all rehabilitation programs to measure up to.

Narconon is also recognized by numerous governments as a safe and highly effective program.

In Sweden, Denmark, Italy, the Netherlands and Switzerland, governments provide funding for Narconon's drug education efforts and support delivery of the drug rehabilitation program.

The Parliamentary Assembly of the Council of Europe recognized the success of L. Ron Hubbard's drug rehabilitation technology and Narconon in a resolution passed in January 1988.

More and more, judges and government agencies today refer drug addicts to Narconon for rehabilitation, rather than to jail or prison. Such an option is given by courts in Denmark, Germany, Italy, the Netherlands, Spain, Sweden and the United States.

Two decades of success prove that the Narconon program gets *real* results, far better than any other drug rehabilitation program in the world. Narconon has documented many, many cases of successful release from drugs and resultant drug-free lives.

A parole agent from the California Department of Youth Authority commented on the effectiveness of Narconon:

"I am very impressed by some of the gains I have seen in wards placed in Narconon. One of the most dramatic changes I ever noted was produced in a ward who had failed to show improvement in other local drug treatment programs. At Narconon he made rapid and outstanding improvement. The improvement was due to the Narconon program alone since all other factors remained constant."

Another California Youth Authority representative had this to say about Narconon's approach to drug abuse prevention and rehabilitation:

"As one of our more congenial community resources, Narconon has produced results with some of our wards, where other programs have failed. It is reassuring to have an organization such as Narconon that meets the needs of our parolees and goes a little beyond—they care."

Like many others, a New London, Connecticut attorney who studied the results of Narconon's residential program responded to the Narconon program with great admiration:

"Without equivocation, of all the social agencies with which I have had contact over the past two years, Narconon is the one to which I turn when all other possibilities have vanished. It is staffed with youthful, outgoing, knowledgeable and dedicated men and women who can communicate properly with their 'clients.' Let me offer my highest possible commendation: that this is the number one social agency serving the community in the reduction of crime and drug abuse."

An official with the Canadian Penitentiary Service wrote:

"The Narconon program is the only program I have observed to produce quick and stable results in assisting addicts to give up their dependency on drugs. I have been employed in Corrections since 1964 and have had the opportunity to participate in and observe varied treatment programs for addicts, but this is the first program that I have observed to achieve what it claims to achieve."

A former Los Angeles public health official who witnessed results in the early years of Narconon's residential program said this:

"It is one of the few programs which has enabled drug/alcohol abusers to evolve a rational, humanistic approach to social and personal tensions. Narconon has proven its success inside institutions and on the streets. It is well staffed and well organized; people associated with its programs are dedicated and cooperative. I therefore highly recommend Narconon."

The head of a Russian delegation from the Ministry of the Interior, which seeks solutions to the drug problem in Russia, concluded after his study of several Narconon facilities:

"The only place in the world where I have seen with my own eyes drug addicts fully cured from heroin and cocaine is Narconon. This technology is not only taking the person off the addiction, it also . . . keeps them cured and ethical and in a high moral state.

". . . I see these methods as the future hope for all those unfortunate addicts in Russia and the other republics."

How a Narconon Program Is Started

Anyone interested in pioneering a Narconon program should contact the nearest Narconon center or Narconon International or an ABLE representative who will provide the needed assistance. (See the list of centers and offices in the back of this book.)

The first step to opening a Narconon is recruiting others interested in working in the field of drug rehabilitation. A willing and able staff is the nucleus of any successful Narconon. These individuals are then trained to deliver the program. Staff training facilities exist to make this as easy as possible.

Narconon International helps obtain suitable premises and ensures that all local regulations and requirements are met.

Manuals and other materials are available from Narconon offices to set up and operate one's own Narconon center and to contact and help those in need of Narconon's services.

Representatives from Narconon International and Narconon's regional offices assist in all aspects of getting the new center set up and running successfully. They place one in contact with referral agencies that lead to people in need of the program, help locate local sources of funding and provide organizational advice and direction.

Donations may be needed for beginning expenses and course materials. In many cases the local community has assisted in donating furnishings, bedding, food and sometimes money to new Narconon programs. The Narconon consultant advises how to go about obtaining donations for these important prerequisites.

The drug problem ranks high among the vital concerns of society. Untold numbers of lives have been ruined. But there is a viable solution, one that restores self-respect and a willingness to be a part of life once more. L. Ron Hubbard's technology, applied throughout the world by Narconon, is the road back. Each time a person is rehabilitated through Narconon, the scourge of drugs disappears a little more from the world. Narconon offers hope that drug abuse will one day be a thing of the past.

Germany

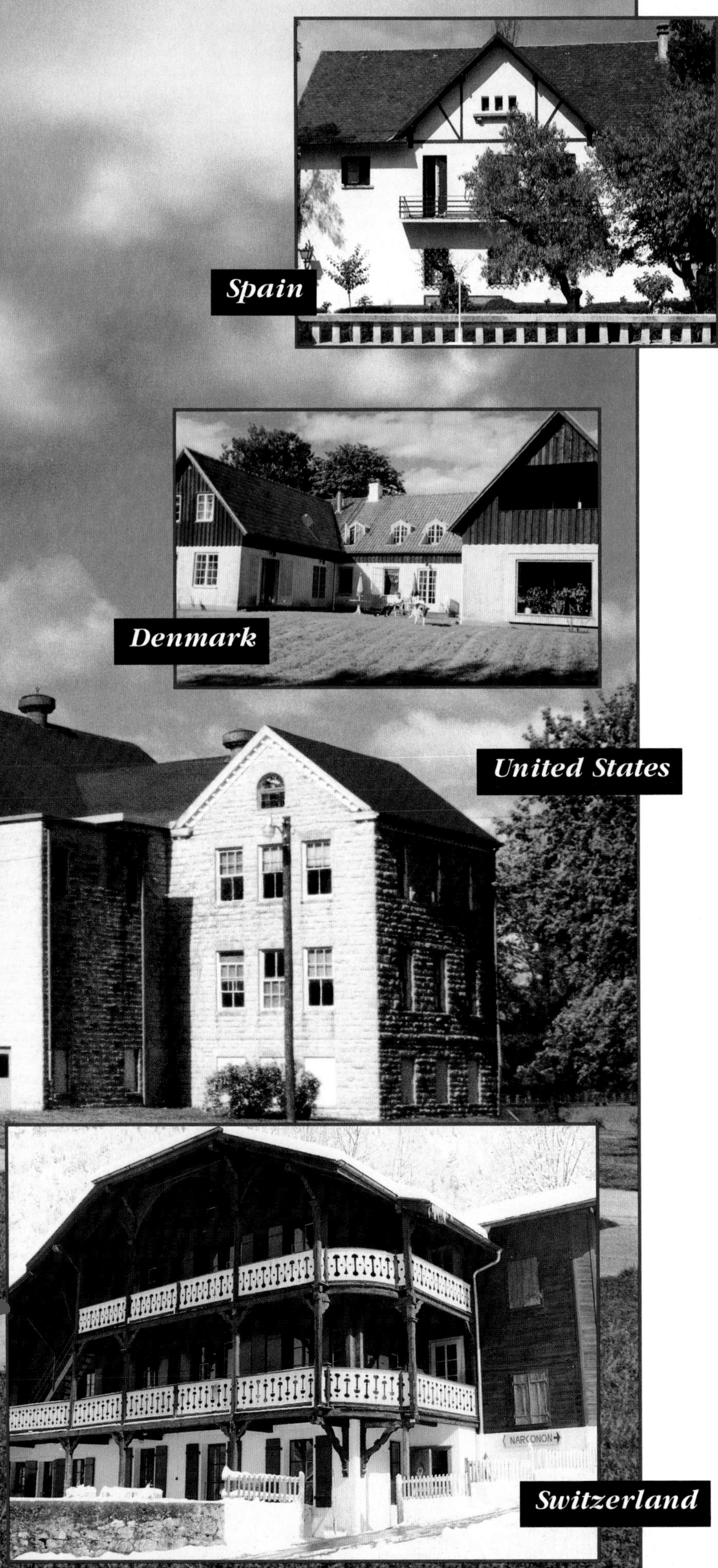

Narconon centers are located in eleven countries around the world, several of which are pictured here. Narconon's international training facility (center) is in Chilocco, Oklahoma.

SUCCESSES OF NARCONON GRADUATES

The drug problem ranks high among the vital concerns of society. Untold numbers of lives have been ruined. But there is a viable solution, one that restores self-respect and a willingness to be a part of life once more. L. Ron Hubbard's technology, applied throughout the world by Narconon, is the road back. Each time a person is rehabilitated through Narconon, the scourge of drugs disappears a little more from the world. Narconon offers hope that drug abuse will one day be a thing of the past.

I came here already destroyed. I had lost about twenty kilos in the streets. I was gaunt, pale and could not physically move as a result of daily drug abuse. This was occurring physically, but it was not all [of it], as morally I arrived with no hope of anything and full of doubts as to whether or not I would ever want to make it in life. Nothing mattered in life.

I had been in two [other rehabilitation] centers, but I got nothing from being in these centers. I started the [Narconon] program and bit by bit I became freer of drugs. I started to regain my lost hopes and desire to live again. But not only that, I am now happy without having to live with drugs—to wake up in the morning with a desire to smile and with the thought that I start a new beautiful day and that the road for better days will continue.

M.B.

I was a drug addict for four years. During this time I used every drug there is. For two years I was very, very heavily addicted to heroin. I almost died from this. Since joining Narconon my whole life has changed. I am now able to communicate much easier with anybody. I have learned to control myself and my environment much better. I now have responsibility (which I couldn't face up to before). I don't need drugs anymore because I am now higher than I have ever been on drugs. I thank you L. Ron Hubbard and everyone helping people with Narconon.

D.K.

The first time I walked in the Narconon office I was desperate. My son had not spent more than a few months out of jail at any given time period for over five years and all of his incarcerations had been directly related to drug and alcohol offenses. Counseling, and even hospitalization, had not helped. You were my last hope.

As I read the letters on the wall in the waiting room I remember my eyes stinging with tears. I wondered if I would ever be able to write a letter thanking Narconon for the successful treatment of my son.

There were a lot of rocky moments for all of us during the instruction stage; phone calls, home visits, even a few disappointments. When he finished the program I don't think any of us knew for sure what the final outcome would be. That was almost two years ago and with a happy, grateful heart I am writing you and your dedicated, wonderful, committed staff to let you know that the program proved successful. The nightmare of drug and alcohol abuse is finally in the past. My son has become a happy and confident individual, with your assistance. The program established itself to be the best investment we could have ever made. Would I recommend Narconon to anyone? In a heartbeat! May God bless each and every one of you. Keep up the great work.

N.N.

For a while, I thought drugs were fun. But then they almost killed me the way they have so many other musicians. I did the Narconon program and it literally saved my life. I have lived drug free for a number of years now and continue to reach new levels of creativity and satisfaction with life. Now it's life that's fun. I would have hated to have missed it!

N.H.

From this day on I will be all I can be in this world thanks to Narconon. The staff are very brave people here at Narconon. They are good people and without them and their kindness I would never have made it. I feel great today, and I will feel great tomorrow too, because I am a drug-free person.

S.B.

I came here beaten up by the use of drugs. I was at the point where I wanted to die, my attitude and perception of life was all screwed up. I am now a new person. This program has saved my life. I have had so many wins and realizations. I do know that I have the ability, the technology and the courage to lead a drug-free life. I would really encourage others to do this program and get the gains I have got.

D.K.

Narconon saved my life. For years, seventeen to be exact, I battled with drugs and alcohol. This program was the only one that showed me how to stay off drugs and how to live my life honestly, and work toward happiness.

L.V.

Having now completed this program I can say without any reservation whatsoever, I feel I am living proof that there is certainly more to life than three bottles of wine or the equivalent consumption each evening.
Without the Narconon program and the compassion of the staff who deliver it, I would not be as alive as I am today and I would certainly not be looking forward to life as I am. So a big, big thank you and my eternal affinity and love for saving my life.

M.B.

I am a fully recovered drug addict. My life was in total ruin before I entered the Narconon program in 1989. Today I have a happy and productive life. After I completed my program at Narconon, I wanted to give others what was given me. Narconon gave me my life back and I have seen and helped countless others to achieve what I have. Drugs only bring about insanity and health problems that put us all at risk. L. Ron Hubbard has given us the technology so that we all can be free. I am more than happy to help make this happen.

K.D.

I am a staff member here at Narconon Los Angeles. Working here is the best thing I have ever done. I am a former drug user who was addicted to drugs for twenty years.
It wasn't until I came to Narconon that I came to a total understanding of why I did drugs. I not only learned why I did drugs, but I also learned how to confront difficult situations, how to communicate with people and how to control my life. I now can handle situations logically and analytically rather than running for a syringe or a pill.
Working at Narconon I have seen people walk in the door messed up on drugs and alcohol. They're in bad shape mentally and physically.
To see these people turn their lives around and become happy, confident and productive is the most rewarding feeling a person can ever feel. To really help people and see the results of the Narconon program is nothing short of a miracle.

P.J.

CRIMINON:

CRIMINAL REFORM

Each day in the United States, more than 31,000 petty and hard-core criminals are released back into their communities. Within one year, up to 80 percent, or more than 25,000 of these men and women a day, will have committed ten or twenty more crimes before being arrested again and sent back to prison.

The figures speak for themselves. The 80 percent recidivism rate makes a mockery of current psychiatric-oriented rehabilitation methods, demonstrating that, for all intents and purposes, there is in fact no such thing as criminal rehabilitation. A report published recently by the National Council on Crime and Delinquency in America concurred, stating that there was "little evidence that either institutional programs or noninstitutional efforts to rehabilitate offenders make any appreciable difference."

And so go the revolving doors of the US penal system.

L. Ron Hubbard once quite accurately pointed out that although the percentage of criminals is relatively small, the amount of grief and turmoil they create in the world is out of all proportion to their numbers. "Thus," he concluded, "the criminal mind is a subject one cannot avoid in research as it is a major factor in the distortion of a culture."

From the need to remedy this glaringly destructive societal flaw—and through the fruits of L. Ron Hubbard's research—Criminon (which means "without crime") was born in New Zealand in 1970. A branch of Narconon, it is an organization that operates within the penal system to rehabilitate criminals and restore their sense of worth so that they can become productive members of society.

Criminon actually grew out of the very successful Narconon prison programs. By the 1980s, with increased drug usage in all sectors of society, the Narconon program shifted its emphasis to community-based activities. At that point, Criminon expanded into the correctional facilities to fill a need.

Criminon program results have been astoundingly successful. A Butler County, Alabama study among juvenile offenders who were exposed to a part of the program, for instance, showed that only 2 percent of the pilot group were recidivist; of a comparable control group not on the program, the usual 80 percent were recidivist. These figures, too, speak for themselves.

Rehabilitating a Sense of Responsibility

Headquartered in Los Angeles, Criminon today runs programs in 203 prisons and penal institutions in 39 states. So far, in the last five years, more than 3,200 inmates have successfully participated in the programs. This success naturally raises basic questions: What makes Criminon different? What does it do? Perhaps the best place to start is with what Criminon does not do:

Criminon does not drug inmates. It does not use punitive restraints. It does not use aimless conversation for lack of a better tool. It is not psychiatry or psychology.

From psychiatry's ineptitude within the penal system—in spite of the immense funding and power bestowed upon it—the uncharitable conclusion could be drawn that rehabilitation is not necessarily what it intends to accomplish. However, the more obvious and arguable point is that it is unable to rehabilitate criminals because it has no knowledge of what makes a criminal. Unproven theories are easy to come by, and psychiatry/psychology has no lack of them. Criminality is blamed on everything from poor environmental conditions, inherited drives, biological imbalances in the brain, to "sluggish nervous systems."

Criminon's success, on the other hand, is due to the fact that in order to devise *workable* rehabilitation methods, Mr. Hubbard extensively researched criminality until he found the actual source of what makes a criminal. And from this point of truth, he was able to develop workable methods.

"Do you know that there is not a criminal anywhere in any prison who is not a criminal because he was degraded and lost his personal pride?" Mr. Hubbard asked in one of his lectures. "I have done a very thorough cross-check of this—what they call 'bad women,' 'criminal men.' Their badness and criminality is immediately traceable to a loss of their powers and personal pride, and after that they were 'bad'; they were 'dangerous.'

"If you want to rehabilitate a criminal, just go back and find out when he did lose his personal pride. Rehabilitate that one point and you don't have a criminal anymore."

By addressing this point of rehabilitation, Scientologists through their support of Criminon are taking effective action to end this repeating cycle of criminality and reform the prison system.

The Program

L. Ron Hubbard made an important discovery more than three decades ago—he conclusively proved that man was basically good. Ironically, this is nowhere more evident than in our prison population, as proven by the fact of their incarceration. Men who commit wrongful deeds against their fellows *want* to be caught, which explains why criminals invariably leave clues and make the job of the police that much easier.

What they do not necessarily want, however, is punishment. As all men are basically good, those who err seek to be rendered less harmful to society and can be rehabilitated.

The key element of the Criminon program is The Way to Happiness Extension Course, based on a booklet of the same name. As the first step toward rehabilitation, this correspondence course is designed to give students knowledge of right and wrong conduct. A nonreligious moral code, *The Way to Happiness* is practical and incisive, and provides fundamental guides to behavior—a vital step, often overlooked in the family life and education of the criminal. Critical values ranging from love and kindness, to basics such as hygiene and common courtesy are covered.

Students do practical exercises on this course and mail them in to Criminon staff and volunteer groups of Scientologists around the country who grade the exercises. They maintain communication with the inmate and encourage him. When the course is completed, Criminon issues a certificate.

Other elements in the Criminon course, some of which are delivered in prisons by staff and volunteers to the inmates, are similar to those used in Narconon drug rehabilitation programs. They include the following:

- The Learning Improvement Course. As many inmates suffer literacy problems, this course in study skills is invaluable as a tool both during incarceration and upon release. As it provides the ability to learn any subject, it is a fundamental that will help in vocational and other training.
- The Communication and Perception Course. These communication exercises increase the inmate's ability to face life and not withdraw from it—the very act that exacerbated the criminal condition.
- The Ups and Downs in Life Course. As recidivism is often due to the return of an inmate to his previous environment, this invaluable course helps him learn the social and antisocial characteristics of his friends and associates. The person is thus less susceptible to bad influences.
- The Personal Values and Integrity Course. This study of the eight dynamics, ethics and integrity, helps the inmate take responsibility for, and rid himself of, his past misdeeds.

And as with the Narconon program, other courses address subjects such as how to change conditions in life, how to contribute effectively and other basics vital to successful living.

All in all, the Criminon program totally replaces the unworkable rehabilitation methods that only exacerbate crime. It directly and effectively rehabilitates individuals so that criminal behavior becomes a thing of the past and remains that way.

Because of its workability, word of Criminon is spreading rapidly from prison to prison. And of the thousands of prisoners released every day, more and more will be truly rehabilitated. In time, the revolving door will be closed.

PRISONERS SPEAK OF RESULTS

Thousands of letters and testimonials from prisoners describe how Criminon helped them cope with prison life, increased their self-worth and happiness, and began to change their outlook and behavior for the better.

This course has taught me the many changes that life can take and it has polished my ability to deal with those changes. It has taught me the importance of trust and the importance of fulfilling my obligations. I have to be an industrious individual in society. I have a four-year-old son and I am a single parent and it is very important to remember that setting good examples enhances your child's chances of becoming a more successful and industrious member in this society. It has also taught me a little of what my religion teaches me and that is knowledge of self and discipline, which are the main ingredients that 75 percent of this nation lacks.

Q.W.B.
Detroit

I am so thankful to you for The Way to Happiness Course. I had lost all my self-respect and personal pride. I didn't care for myself or anyone else. However, through this course I have gotten all my pride back and my self-respect as well. I didn't think I could ever face my family or the world again. But thanks to The Way to Happiness Course I can hold my head up again. I also know for sure that I will never again commit another crime or come back to prison.

C.P.
Western United States

The Way to Happiness Course has been a large part of my getting back my self-respect. The time I spent working the lessons, and then putting the lessons to work, were a big part of my feeling human again. I believe so strongly in this program that I have told many others about the course and will continue to do so in the future. Thank you Criminon for making these programs available to me and others in my position.

J.C.
El Reno
Correctional Facility
Oklahoma

Before entering this program [Criminon] I didn't know what success was. I didn't even know the tremendous feeling of self-assurance you adopt from this program. I can now honestly say that the works of L. Ron Hubbard are very inspiring. They have taught me the value of hard work and self-awareness. Others around me have noticed the change in my whole being. My attitude, my patience, my ability to deal with hostile situations with calm assurances, this is something I never had or was able to do. But with what I have learned on this program I have attained those characteristics and more.
I feel in control of my life, and although I am presently a guest of the state (prisoner) in a correction facility, I never felt more free in my life!!
I know when I am released I can truly be happy and prosper in society because I no longer have a destructive nature. Rather I have come to learn of a productive and positive way to go about life thus making my survival and those around me safe with room to grow.

T.W.
Delaware State Prison

We are very grateful and appreciative of the books and tapes that you [Library Donation Service] donated. Your books were very beautiful and from the moment we received them they became very much in demand because they relate to us as people in a way we never have seen before. There is great truth in this philosophy you gave us, and we are very much in your debt.

The tape lectures of Mr. Hubbard's have changed the lives of a lot of people here. We started a night class and over fifty inmates have attended. Some of the men said that if they heard this tape before they got in trouble with the law, they would have never wound up in jail.

How can we make it available to more people? This stuff really can prevent crime.

S.P.
Federal Correctional Institution
Florida, USA

For many years I seemed to be living in a very dark room. When I completed the [Criminon] course it was like someone had switched the light on in this dark room and I beheld some pretty good things in there. I saw kindness, love, respect, self-control, honesty and many, many more beautiful things. What's amazing in all of this, it was myself that I saw. I realized for the first time in my life I had sincerely and truly found myself. The other amazing thing is, I didn't hate myself anymore because I understood.

R.P.
Kingston Penitentiary
Ontario, Canada

Since I've been doing this course, I have gone seven months major ticket free [without major disciplinary action], which I have never done and I'm involved in a trade called food tech and I'm steadily bettering myself. I would like everyone to know that this course has done a great deal for me and I'm very thankful for it. 'Cause now I feel ready for the real world and ready for the people around me. Thank you!

J.W.
Lakeland Correctional Facility
Michigan, USA

After thirty-eight years trying to understand life, I became very confused and wound up serving three years in a penitentiary and at the end of my rope.

Mentally battered and exhausted, I came across a book called ***Dianetics: The Modern Science of Mental Health.*** *At this point a change had occurred within. I started to think clearly, my life suddenly had meaning. I understand myself and others better, I feel freedom within and I have become a very happy individual because of these books and courses by L. Ron Hubbard.*

I'm afraid to think what could have happened to me, had I not come across this data. However, I have come across this data, I have used it and studied it and I am truly free and happy because of it.

Now, you have also come across this same data. What are you going to do with it? Do you want happiness and freedom in your life? Do you want to be a winner? Well! It's your move!

R.V.P.
Canada

While taking The Way to Happiness Course I felt a renewed sense of pride in who I really am and my capabilities to do good. I have regained certainty that I am not a bad person. I made a mistake and I have paid my debt to society. Now this course has re-lighted in me to be good and do good, because only that will ensure my happiness and the happiness of others.

T.A.C.
Indiana Reformatory USA

APPLIED SCHOLASTICS:

SOLUTIONS IN EDUCATION

As early as 1950, L. Ron Hubbard expressed his deep concern over the poor quality of so-called "modern" education.

"Today's children will become tomorrow's civilization," he wrote. "The end and goal of any society as it addresses the problem of education is to raise the ability, the initiative and the cultural level, and with all these the survival level of that society. And when a society forgets any one of these things it is destroying itself by its own educational mediums."

Decades later, Mr. Hubbard's observation has proven accurate and the continued disintegration of many of our institutions can be predicted unless the deterioration of society's educational systems is arrested.

There is hope, however, because Mr. Hubbard developed breakthrough educational technology capable of turning schools into institutions of unprecedented learning excellence.

Improving Education with L. Ron Hubbard's Study Technology

The ability to understand and retain data, the ability to actually learn, is vital for virtually everyone in today's world, be they adult or child. New technologies, the constant avalanche of information, even something as simple as reading the directions of household electronic equipment requires comprehension.

L. Ron Hubbard's study technology is thus an advance of gigantic significance in a world where educational standards have steadily declined, where education has abdicated its responsibility to the extent that it does not even teach our students to learn how to learn.

Study technology is a vast body of knowledge that not only consistently teaches people to learn how to learn, but delineates the three major barriers to effective study. Armed with these and the other tools provided, anyone can successfully study. It amounts to nothing less than a revolution in the field of education.

It is the job of Applied Scholastics to get this technology into the hands of a world that sorely needs it and revitalize our abilities to study.

Applied Scholastics International is a nonprofit, public benefit corporation whose purpose is to improve education worldwide. Located in Los Angeles, it has affiliated offices in Canada, Mexico, the United Kingdom, South Africa, Denmark, Sweden, Germany, Austria, France, Italy, Australia, Malaysia, China, Russia and Venezuela. Its materials are translated into many different languages.

In the 1960s, public school teachers who knew of L. Ron Hubbard's study technology used it in their public school classes and reported great improvement in learning abilities among their students.

In 1971, the first educational organization specializing in the use of study technology was started in California by a Scientologist teacher.

Then, in 1972, Applied Scholastics was founded to advance the application of Mr. Hubbard's study technology outside the churches of Scientology and thus broadly remedy learning difficulties for people of all ages and intellects.

Formed by a team of educators and teachers from a number of American schools and universities, Applied Scholastics today coordinates the many programs throughout the world which utilize study technology. Through ABLE, the Church and its members support and sponsor Applied Scholastics because it has a proven solution to the debacle in education today.

More than 3 million people have participated in Applied Scholastics programs throughout the world. L. Ron Hubbard's study technology is delivered by 156 groups in 29 countries in all 6 continents.

Working at the grass-roots level and with educational authorities, Applied Scholastics addresses six main areas of education: teacher training; schools; English as a second language; tutoring individuals; training business staff to apply the study technology; and, training human resource professionals so that they, in turn, can train their staff. This involves, of course, both adults and children.

Among the Applied Scholastics International affiliates throughout most of Europe, there is the Association for Effective Basic Education in Denmark; Centers of Individual and Effective Learning in Switzerland; Modern Instruction Centers in Italy; Studema in Sweden; the Effective Education Association and Basic Education and Supplementary Teaching Association in the United Kingdom; and the list goes on, with new organizations and affiliates opening each year.

In the growing number of schools and colleges affiliated with Applied Scholastics, students who are taught study technology from an early age are routinely eager, bright and interested in life around them.

Among the many schools in the United States which use study technology are:

Oregon's Delphian School, which occupies an 800-acre campus near Portland, enrolling students from around the world in a full-time academic program. It also operates training and apprenticeship programs for teachers, educators, school administrators and parents.

Ability Plus School, located in southern California, teaches students of all ages from toddlers through high school. The school also offers apprenticeships for teacher trainees in their state-licensed preschool and supplementary teacher training based on the study technology.

Florida's True School, where students are also enrolled on a full curriculum, is noted for its community outreach program called "Operation: Educate America." The school provides speakers to other community

Learning How to Learn
A first study book for children.

How to Use a Dictionary
Teaches children how to find and understand words using a dictionary.

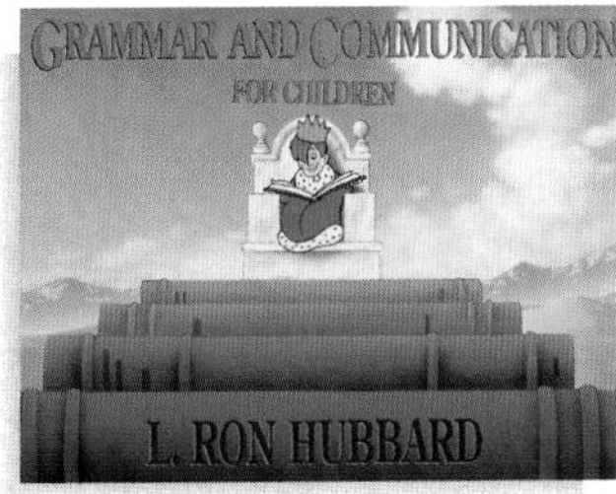

Grammar and Communication
A simple, illustrated English grammar book written to show the young student the basics of grammar.

Study Skills for Life
The basic aspects of study technology written for teenagers.

Basic Study Manual
The major breakthroughs of study technology are described and illustrated for any age or academic level.

The following are some of the many organizations that have used L. Ron Hubbard's study technology:

ALLSTATE INSURANCE
EXECUTIVE SOFTWARE
GENERAL MOTORS
LANCÔME
REALWORLD CORPORATION
STERLING MANAGEMENT SYSTEMS
SURVIVAL INSURANCE
TIGRE LIS ENTERPRISES
U-MAN INTERNATIONAL
EPSON AMERICA
BUICK
OHIO INSTITUTE OF TECHNOLOGY
TRANSWESTERN INSTITUTE
INTERFACE COMPUTERS
VOLKSWAGEN/AUDI
PERRIER
ELIZABETH ARDEN
NATIONAL CASH REGISTER
CITROËN
CYANAMID
MOBIL OIL
TRUST BANK OF SOUTH AFRICA

groups to publicize the urgency of improving American education.

These and other schools throughout the world routinely graduate eager, literate students who can make their way in life.

Increasing Productivity in the Workplace

One of the major concerns of business, particularly in the United States, lies in the dismal statistic that 27 million, or 20 percent of America's adults, are functionally illiterate, with basic skills below a fifth-grade level. Another 45 million adults are marginally literate.

This failure of our educational system costs American business and industry billions of dollars a year. Companies have thus found it necessary to introduce extensive, and expensive, training programs. In fact, US business spends about $45 billion annually to train from the top of the corporate ladder to the bottom. This does not include the staggering amount the government spends to train workers—with little result.

L. Ron Hubbard's study technology, furnished by Applied Scholastics, provides vitally necessary educational programs to a wide variety of businesses to increase employee efficiency, initiative and performance. It is currently used by thousands of businesses around the world.

Businesses that utilize study technology range from General Motors and Mobil Oil to Electronic Data Systems and Perrier, phone companies, computer software and hardware manufacturers, retail chains, clothing manufacturers, beverage companies, restaurants and more.

General Motors, for instance, spent millions of dollars on a computer system that nobody could use. For years they tried to train new operators, and failed. Their intensive lecture seminars resulted only in sleeping students, or those who begged for a break. They were almost ready to scrap the system.

Consultants trained in the application of the study technology, came into the company and rewrote a 1,000-page manual with graphics, a checksheet and a full glossary. They also put students through a study course prior to the computer course. The result was a meteoric reduction in ramp-up time—the time it takes graduates to apply what they have learned on the job. Normally six to twelve months, it was cut down to an unheard-of three weeks.

Programs tailored for executives raise the ability to assimilate, evaluate and retain large amounts of information—skills important for any executive.

Employees unable to read company manuals or follow written instructions are also put through Applied Scholastics courses, resulting not only in greater efficiency, but in enhancement of their entire lives.

Applied Scholastics has trained thousands of company executives and employees on L. Ron Hubbard's study technology. These innovative study materials, provided by ABLE and used internationally by Applied Scholastics groups, teach students of all ages.

Teacher Training Programs

Applied Scholastics also trains teachers to apply study technology and runs successful programs in many countries which accomplish this. These programs supply needed teaching skills based on L. Ron Hubbard's methods and rekindle the infectious enthusiasm for learning that every good teacher brings to his classroom.

Teachers throughout the world are today giving new meaning to what they do. Education Alive, for instance, the Applied Scholastics affiliate which delivers L. Ron Hubbard's study technology in South Africa and other parts of the continent, was established in 1975 and since then has trained more than 2 million students. Greatly helping to improve the deplorable educational standards for Blacks in that troubled land, Education Alive has also trained literally tens of thousands of teachers since its inception. In one teachers' college, for instance, the dropout rate for teacher trainees fell dramatically to only 2 percent after Education Alive services.

In South Africa, L. Ron Hubbard's study technology has been taught to 2 million underprivileged children.

When Mr. Hubbard visited South Africa in the early 1960s, he predicted a series of massive social upheavals and a severe rift between Black and White communities there. To avert disaster, he advised measures and provided the technology that would enable the country's large Black population to become literate.

The appreciation and increased hope and human dignity resulting from Education Alive's programs is clear from this teacher's remarks:

"I stand like a warrior to conquer all difficulties I have come across with much ease. The entire world has become a phenomenon that needs restudy and to be observed with a different perspective. . . ."

Encouraged by Education Alive's results, major corporations have provided financial support for its vital work.

As one teacher wrote, "Education Alive has rescued me, and saved the lives of many pupils, students and teachers, as well as employees. I honor L. Ron Hubbard and his successors for the work they have done for the African child. Everybody who has heard these lectures is thirsty for further lessons and, at the same time, in a hurry to go out and experiment with these wonderful methods of teaching."

In the People's Republic of China, a country with many millions of illiterate people, Applied Scholastics International has been active since 1984. Since then, more than 5,000 teachers and industrial managers have been trained in study technology.

In the Yunnan provincial capital city of Kunming, junior high school English teachers are now required by the City Education Bureau to use the Chinese translation of Mr. Hubbard's study materials for their teacher training.

The Shandong Education Commission cosponsored a correspondence course for teachers to allow L. Ron Hubbard's study technology to reach the population more quickly. And the major textbook publisher in China, in preparation for more extensive use of the study technology throughout the country, trained its editorial staff in Applied Scholastics courses.

In Costa Rica, extensive teacher training on study technology has resulted in a more rapid and thorough application of English as a second language for teachers. In recognition of the role Mr. Hubbard's study technology has played in raising the standard of education there, a representative of the Costa Rican Ministry of Education presented a plaque to Applied Scholastics at its twentieth anniversary celebration in Los Angeles in 1992.

"On behalf of Costa Rica, we are pleased to present this token of our appreciation to Applied Scholastics for its support in the teaching of English to Costa Rica's teachers," said Dr. Humberto Perez.

"We congratulate Applied Scholastics on this anniversary and hope that its relationship with Costa Rican education will grow and strengthen in the future."

A long-term professor of English at a California university had this to say about the results of study technology:

"I have never felt so good about my work nor achieved such consistent academic successes as I have since I incorporated the study technology of L. Ron Hubbard into my classes. No teacher should enter a classroom without this knowledge. No student should exit a school without this knowledge. This is what we all should have known long ago and didn't. Thank you, L. Ron Hubbard, for your gift to humanity."

These are only some of the many thousand testimonials from teachers around the world.

Spectacular Results of Study Technology

Even among gang members in the riot-torn Los Angeles city of Compton, California, L. Ron Hubbard's study technology has been winning endorsements. Introduced to community leaders and educators, in a grass-roots program coordinated by the Church, L. Ron Hubbard study technology has been described by youth counselors as "heaven sent." For not only have younger children markedly increased their reading and communication skills with the application of Mr. Hubbard's study materials, but even gang members, normally disdainful of any remedial education program, are willingly attending study classes. "These study materials," commented a community minister who is helping institute the program, "will set people free."

Additionally, working with African-American churches, Applied Scholastics initiated a program to train parents to be tutors so that they can pass the study technology on to families and other members of the community. Since then, the program expanded to south central Los Angeles, another area plagued by illiteracy.

Because of its enormous value and wide application, this study technology has been widely used with spectacular results.

- In New Zealand, students in a girls' school showed an increase of twelve IQ points on the Otis Lennon Mental Ability Test after completing a course based on Mr. Hubbard's learning methods.
- College students at the East Los Angeles College in California received twenty hours of instruction in the study technology. Tested before and after the course in vocabulary, reading comprehension, arithmetic reasoning, arithmetic fundamentals, language mechanics and spelling, the students improved an equivalent of approximately one grade level in each area tested.
- Another study conducted in England showed that students shot ahead 1.29 years in their reading levels after just ten hours of study using Mr. Hubbard's study technology. Comparatively, no gain in reading levels was found in a control group of students not instructed in study technology.
- In a separate project in Los Angeles, high-school students tested after a forty-hour period of classroom instruction

in study technology showed a remarkable average gain of over two years per student. In a similar project in South Africa, the average gain in reading age was two years and three months.

■ In Mexico City, the study technology was introduced into a private school. High-school students in one class had failed 95 percent of their materials. After application of L. Ron Hubbard's study technology, the class passed 90 percent of the materials the following year.

Applied Scholastics International and its associated groups are bringing the study technology of L. Ron Hubbard to people from all walks of life—technology that is not only successful beyond any other approach to education, but fully capable of generating a renaissance in learning.

Every day, in businesses, schools and learning centers all over the world, more and more individuals are having the door of opportunity opened to them through the study technology of L. Ron Hubbard.

Delphi, Oregon, USA

Ability School, Virginia, USA

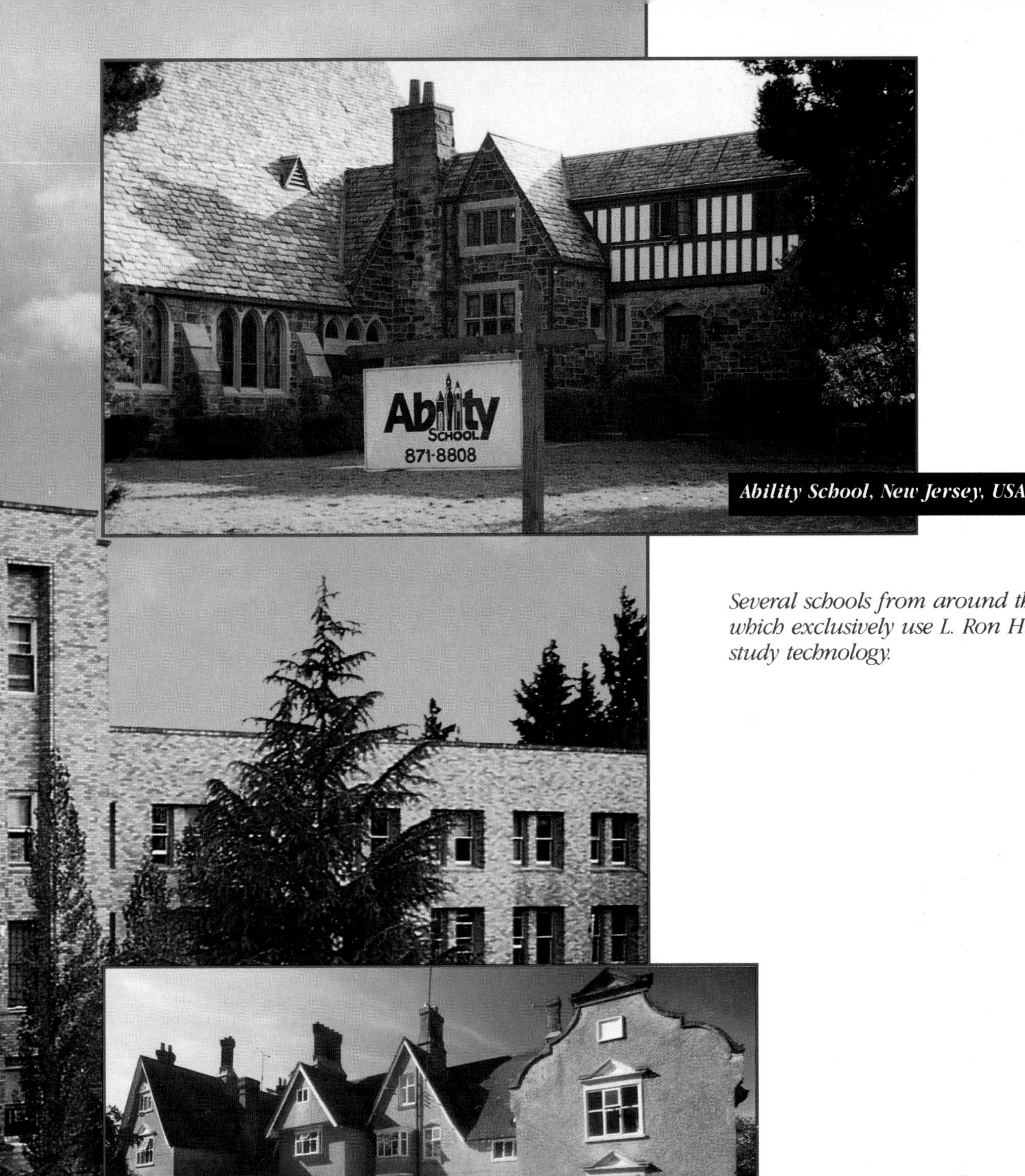

Ability School, New Jersey, USA

Greenfields School, Sussex, England

Several schools from around the world which exclusively use L. Ron Hubbard's study technology.

SUCCESSES IN APPLICATION

Every day, in businesses, schools and learning centers all over the world, more and more individuals are having the door of opportunity opened to them through the study technology of L. Ron Hubbard.

I am a teacher by profession. I have taught boys and girls who are now teachers, graduates, clergymen, doctors, etc. But after I took up studies of L. Ron Hubbard's study technology . . . I felt ashamed of myself when I started to look back at all the long period of my teaching career. I thought the dropouts who left school were permanently stupid and dull. I am now able to carry on even with retarded children. Hats off to those who have sown this seed until it reached me!

E.G.

As a teacher of English as a second language in a large inner-city high school in Manhattan, I have successfully used the study technology to help my students become more able people and acquire a greater understanding of the lessons they were taught.

Other teachers and administrators in my school have noticed the change and improvements in my students' test scores and speaking ability, as well as the atmosphere in my classroom.

Their praise has validated my application of Mr. Hubbard's study technology and its goals: that being a good teacher produces students who can apply what they have learned.

L.K.

I had to send my daughter to a state school in Holland. After one year at school she had to wear glasses, started to stutter and had a lot of trouble with her math. Even though I was helping her at home, the problems became worse and she became very unhappy.

My son also went to the same school and he became very introverted and quiet. His teacher told me he was deaf (reason for being quiet) and he had an underlying psychological problem. Well, he had been a very lively child up until then and not deaf—I can assure you of that!

We decided to move and bring our children to Greenfields School which uses L. Ron Hubbard's study technology in all its classes. Even though there was a language barrier they both felt much happier at their new school.

Within no time my son was a happy, very lively boy again and all the signs of his "problems" were gone, and he could still hear very well.

My daughter's problem with math came down to not knowing the three barriers to study and how to handle them. She actually loves math now and her stuttering completely disappeared. The use of study technology has saved my children's school life without a doubt!

I.M.H.

I've finally gotten the data that's been denied to me for so long! I've wanted to know how to study so earnestly throughout my so-called education. It is safe to say that I've learned more on this course than the entirety of my previous schooling.

J.D.

I have been in a school without the study technology and I know that L. Ron Hubbard's study technology that I use is much better. When I study I learn much faster and I love what I learn about. When I use this, I stay at a nice steady pace. I also know now what I am learning, I can use, because I really understand what I am learning.

C.B.

I am a teacher at the Ohio Institute of Technology. This is an electronics technical school and we have students from all social backgrounds and educational levels. I used the methodology as laid out in the ***Basic Study Manual*** *for two quarters at the Institute and met with tremendous success. The school administration was so impressed with my results that they have given me three months' leave of absence to get more training in the technology developed by Mr. Hubbard.*

C.K.

Using L. Ron Hubbard's basic study techniques, we found profound jumps in productivity among staff. Employees stopped making costly mistakes.

R.H.

At the time I was first introduced to Mr. Hubbard's theories and methods, I was very discouraged about what was happening to student literacy and motivation. I was even considering tendering my resignation. However, after learning about the basic barriers to study and what could be done about them, I began using more and more of the data with students. Eventually, I created an entire study skills course and also taught my grammar and writing course fully utilizing the study technology. The result has been one rehabilitated English teacher and hundreds of enthusiastic, rejuvenated students.

B.E.P.

I can think of no more valuable and necessary element of any course of study, practical or theoretic, than study technology courses.

R.V.D.

Some people try to say common things with uncommon words instead of saying uncommon things with common words. But this course taught me to understand simple words which turn out to be the ones we often don't understand. I have changed a great deal in just two days of this course. Yesterday I spent my day practicing what I learned and it became great fun. I no longer worry about how I am going to study. L. Ron Hubbard's study technology is amazing.

P.R.N.

Our company is one of the leading software manufacturers for micro and personal computers. This is a highly competitive, high-technology business and demands top standards of excellence in communication and education.

All of our executives and staff apply the study technology developed by L. Ron Hubbard and this fact has been very instrumental in our success. This technology is fundamental not only to our high-technology business but any activity where individuals must learn skills in order to survive; in other words, all of life.

D.Y.

It helped me on my report card. It helped me in math, social studies, science, health, listening and following directions, finishing work on time, keeping materials in order and it helped me be more dependable. It helped me so I wouldn't be held back. I improved in eight different subjects.

C.A.

THE WAY TO HAPPINESS FOUNDATION:

IMPROVING MORALS IN TODAY'S WORLD

Every culture in every age has relied upon a moral code to provide broad guidelines for conduct that is conducive to survival. Although much in these past moral codes may not seem particularly relevant to the late twentieth century, when those codes were written they were entirely relevant. They helped ensure the perpetuation of the family, the group and nation. They provided the means by which people upheld the basic tenets of honesty and mutual trust. In short, the moral code supplied the overriding principles by which men could live peaceably, prosperously and in harmony with one another.

Today's declining moral standards have long been a point of grave concern. If art and entertainment are any reflection of our culture, then we live in genuinely frightening times. It is an era of gratuitous violence wherein we have the potential for immense destruction, but no corresponding moral standards to check that destruction. It is an age of senseless killing, unrestrained greed and such profoundly deep cynicism that even the concept of morals often brings sneers.

But just as all ancient cultures required a moral code for their survival, so too does our own culture desperately need such a code by which we may live. Judging by modern crime rates, divorce rates, substance abuse and falling confidence in government, one could predict that the seeds have been sown for a serious social upheaval unless countered by a commensurate effort to restore traditional values.

L. Ron Hubbard was keenly aware of this situation in 1980 when he observed that our modern world lacked a code of morals befitting our faster, high-tech and highly pragmatic society. Old values had been broken but not replaced by new ones, and many were left to flounder on rapidly shifting sands of societal change. Moreover, the moral codes of ages past were religiously based and demanded a faith that many could not muster in this era of waning church attendance. Thus, Mr. Hubbard set out to write a new moral code, one that was based not on faith, but on common sense; one that appealed purely to man's reason and his natural inclination to better survival.

That moral code is *The Way to Happiness.* It is the first moral code based wholly on common sense, and the only one that is entirely nonreligious in nature. It carries no other appeal than to the good sense of the individual man or woman, boy or girl who reads it. Beneath the many differences of national, political, racial, religious or other hue, each of us as individuals must make our way through life. Such a way, *The Way to Happiness* teaches, can be made better if the precepts it presents are known and followed, and if one gets others to know and follow them as well.

Life in an immoral society can be much worse than simply difficult. One's own survival is constantly under threat as even the most basic human values are held up to ridicule. To counter such declining moral trends, *The Way to Happiness* contains twenty-one separate precepts—each constituting a rule for living and has relevance for anyone in our global village. "Safeguard and Improve Your Environment" it advises. "Be Worthy of Trust." "Fulfill Your Obligations." These and the other precepts are fully explained with examples of how each should be applied in one's life and how one can make it known by others. Regardless of the course of any person's life, the precepts can be likened to the edges of the road: Violating them, one is like the motorist who plunges onto the verge—the result can be wreckage of the moment, the relationship, the life. Abiding by the precepts gives one a chance to attain true and lasting happiness.

Mr. Hubbard offered *The Way to Happiness* to others as something they would find useful in their efforts to live more successfully. People read it. They understood its sensible argument for adopting values which foster greater survival for all. Realizing the code's intrinsic value, Scientologists were among the first to use it in their daily lives. The code began to spread through the society from hand to hand, city to city, country to country. To date, many tens of millions of copies of the booklet have been passed out in more than forty countries and translated into seventeen languages.

A Better Life for Millions

The Way to Happiness Foundation, based in Los Angeles, was organized to meet the grass-roots demand for *The Way to Happiness* and to provide copies to the many millions of interested people.

By promoting the booklet's distribution and use, The Way to Happiness Foundation is changing the lives of the many people reached with it—and thereby improving conditions in communities around the world.

The booklet enjoys widespread popularity because it is effective in reestablishing moral values wherever its message is heard. It has received four US Congressional recognitions and has been enthusiastically endorsed by police, civic leaders, businessmen, educators and other groups who have distributed it broadly. Hundreds of groups and officials have used the booklet to bring about greater harmony in their communities.

Distribution occurs through sponsorships; any individual or group may donate copies to youth groups, schools, clubs, social service agencies, military organizations or any of a multitude of other groups. These then distribute the booklets to their members or people with whom they are in contact.

Thousands of schools and millions of students participate in the broad promotion of *The Way to Happiness* precepts. With the help of sponsoring groups, local schools and youth organizations initiate projects that range from cleaning up the environment to

MORAL PRECEPTS FROM THE WAY TO HAPPINESS

1. *Take Care of Yourself*
2. *Be Temperate*
3. *Don't Be Promiscuous*
4. *Love and Help Children*
5. *Honor and Help Your Parents*
6. *Set a Good Example*
7. *Seek to Live with the Truth*
8. *Do Not Murder*
9. *Don't Do Anything Illegal*
10. *Support a Government Designed and Run for All the People*
11. *Do Not Harm a Person of Good Will*
12. *Safeguard and Improve Your Environment*
13. *Do Not Steal*
14. *Be Worthy of Trust*
15. *Fulfill Your Obligations*
16. *Be Industrious*
17. *Be Competent*
18. *Respect the Religious Beliefs of Others*
19. *Try Not to Do Things to Others that You Would Not Like Them to Do to You*
20. *Try to Treat Others As You Would Want Them to Treat You*
21. *Flourish and Prosper*

setting good examples for peers and helping rid schools of drugs.

One of the many sponsoring groups is the Concerned Businessmen's Association of America (CBAA), a nonprofit, charitable educational organization founded in 1981. Through its efforts, many young people are no longer involved in drug abuse, crime and gang violence. Since CBAA began, more than six million copies of *The Way to Happiness* booklet have been distributed throughout the school system, with over five million students participating in its programs—involving more than seven thousand elementary, junior high and high schools.

CBAA has conducted two very successful nationwide campaigns based on *The Way to Happiness*: "Set a Good Example" and "Get Drugs off School Grounds."

These consist of two contests, one for individual students who demonstrate how they use the precept "Set a Good Example" in their lives, and one for schools, promoting their efforts to keep drugs off their campuses. More than thirty state governors, along with directors of state alcohol and drug-abuse programs and departments of education in hundreds of communities, have endorsed the "Set a Good Example" contest using *The Way to Happiness.*

One Ohio school, prior to becoming involved with one of these contests, had routine violence, crime and drug abuse among its students and tested well below the average national reading level. After participating in the program for two years, the school was declared drug-free and reading levels had risen well above the national level.

The Way to Happiness is reaching into the hearts of our cities, where gang violence and street warfare have become a way of life. The simple reading of this book to hundreds of gang members has actually brought reform. In Los Angeles, for example, after hard-core gang members read (or were read to, in some cases) *The Way to Happiness,* they voluntarily removed graffiti from 130 buildings in their neighborhood, while passing out hundreds of copies of the booklets to neighbors.

Many concerned citizens use *The Way to Happiness* to bring their communities together. Such was the case during and after the 1992 Los Angeles riots. The Way to Happiness Foundation volunteers passed out hundreds of thousands of copies throughout the city while assisting on food drives and cleanup actions.

Said one south central Los Angeles community leader who heads an organization called Parents of Watts: "We've been giving out this book now for about two or three months. Nothing different has come into the community except this particular book—and we do see a change and we have to relate it to *The Way to Happiness.*"

Many other campaigns have been sponsored around the world. In the South African township of Soweto, a campaign based on the precept "Safeguard and Improve Your Environment" was supported by the largest food chain in the country and two major labor unions. Still another campaign in the South African city of Pietermaritzburg was highly successful in easing racial tensions.

Also in South Africa, in 1992, the South African police requested 114,000 copies of *The Way to Happiness* booklet—one for every policeman in the country.

Children and teenagers all over the world regularly participate in community cleanups based on the precept, "Safeguard and Improve Your Environment."

The Youth Service Bureau, a national organization founded to prevent delinquency and divert youth from the criminal justice system, is one of many groups that distributes *The Way to Happiness.* Its executive director, who uses the book with the bureau's youth counselors, reported: "Our youthful clients lack a set of principles by which they can live a successful, happy life. *The Way to Happiness* certainly focuses on 21 positive principles which, if applied, would lead to a happy and successful life, rather than a life of drugs, crime and welfare."

On a similar note, a Girl Scout official wrote, "Thank you for sending the booklets and thank Mr. Hubbard for writing it. I only wish it could be distributed to every family in the country. The positive impact it could have (if ideally everyone *used* it) is mind-boggling. You can be sure that the people we distribute it to will put it to wise and frequent use!"

Throughout the United States, tens of thousands of corporate executives, professionals and travelers read copies of *The Way to Happiness,* compliments of hotels that provide the booklet in their guest rooms.

Upon ordering a stock of books for his guests, one Hilton Hotel manager remarked, "It is obvious that the morals and integrity of a large portion of our population are lacking today. Your book says it simply, as it should be, and hopefully will play on the conscience of many people to realize the need to adjust their lifestyles for a more healthy and vital environment, not only for themselves but for everyone around them."

Worldwide Recognition

In one year alone, 324 major recognitions were received by the Foundation, 131 of them from government officials worldwide acknowledging *The Way to Happiness* for its role in fostering greater social responsibility and tolerance.

One former Toledo, Ohio police officer remarked, "After having read *The Way to Happiness,* I've never felt so uplifted. In a world so wrought with destruction these days, it's a blessing to have such a publication available to help instill strong moral values in our youth today."

In Moscow, the chief of the city's police force—one of the largest in the world—ordered 5,000 copies of the Russian edition of the book for his officers noting: "This book is recommended to you by the Moscow City Police Department in hopes that it will help you lead a better and happier life."

Even the drug-torn nation of Colombia has felt the impact. The country's largest and most influential newspaper, *El Tiempo,* distributed copies of the booklet to all subscribers and printed a series of quotes from the booklet in its editions. Referring to the violence that had shaken the nation, the newspaper president stated, "The root of this illness is not in politics but in the soul of our people. When I read *The Way to Happiness,* I realized that this is our solution for social and personal illness."

One Colombian army general was so taken with the work that he had 30,000 copies distributed to soldiers fighting the drug war. Yet another general urged judges in Colombia's demoralized justice system to follow *The Way to Happiness* to restore justice in the country.

Colombia's Minister of Education endorsed the booklet, announced a "Set a Good Example" contest, and suggested all teachers, alumni, directors of education and parents organize classrooms where *The Way to Happiness* would be available to help people discuss and handle their problems.

The president of Olympian International (and a world-renowned trainer and sports physician) helped get copies of *The Way to Happiness* to many Olympic athletes, explaining: "It's a wonderful way to educate the people on the harmful effects of drugs and to build their self-esteem for better understanding right and wrong by using their common sense."

And the Minister of Foreign Affairs in Austria said: "After reading about your international campaign based on tolerance, trust and understanding I must say that the values expressed in your activities should be the basis of human life on this Earth."

In *The Way to Happiness,* L. Ron Hubbard has given everyone a guide by which they can chart a course to a world where violence is not a solution to the bumps in the road and where mutual respect and trust make the way smoother for all. Like gentle oil spread upon the raging sea, the calm generated by *The Way to Happiness* will flow outward and outward. The Way to Happiness Foundation helps the revitalization of moral values in our world by assisting in every way possible the spreading of this common-sense guide to better living.

WINNING WITH *THE WAY TO HAPPINESS*

Moral values have been heavily assaulted in this century. Many people have recognized the decline within their own lifetimes and avidly support the concepts expressed in **The Way to Happiness.** *It has been used by tens of millions around the world, helping spread a common-sense approach to living in our turbulent world.*

I am writing this letter in reference to one of the greatest self-esteem/self-help books I have come across in quite a while, The Way to Happiness. *As a police officer, many situations that I see along with other officers, are often sad ones. So many people seem to be unable to pull within themselves to find good.*

The Way to Happiness *book encourages people to search for the goodness within themselves and spread that goodness to others.*

Officer F.P.
Hartford Police Department

We think that the publication of the book in Lithuanian would be useful and beneficial. Our community, having experienced a long and severe period of communist oppression, is in great demand of spiritual values such as honesty, conscientiousness, sincerity and tolerance. These qualities will help us to overcome the severe inheritance and to advance on the road of freedom and independence to the European community of nations.

Professor L.A.
Ministry of Energy, Lithuania

We like The Way to Happiness *booklet because the way we work with children around here is to recognize that they seem to be in the dark about how to handle life. They need real direction, so we try to provide the lantern that lights up the road for them.*

The Way to Happiness *booklet has the true ingredients for this. It provides moral support, common sense, the real basic things these children need to know to avoid trouble and it is not so lengthy that they can't get through it.*

The mother I gave the booklet to told me it helped her to phrase what she had always wanted to tell her children but couldn't find the words for. She said this booklet refreshes the things I have always known. Things I felt I myself or someone ought to write a book on so our children could know them. That won't be necessary now that we have The Way to Happiness *booklets.*

Everyone we give booklets to expresses their appreciation. Teachers, parents, clergy, and the citizens here have all wanted extra copies for their friends so they have joined us in efforts to get the booklet into the hands of every parent in the area. We already have requests for over 25,000 copies.

A.H.
Director, Parents of Watts

Participating with The Way to Happiness *has been most rewarding to me. I have thoroughly enjoyed hearing my patients' favorable responses. Many have personally thanked me for* The Way to Happiness *booklet and were pleased to get another to pass it on to friends.*

I encourage anyone considering participating in The Way to Happiness *program to do so. The more people who have access to this booklet, the better our society will be.*

M.S.
D.D.S.

Thank you so much for the beautiful book, The Way to Happiness. *It is beautifully bound and has a beautiful message. It is a wonderful and insightful guide to living a more peaceful life on a personal and world-wide basis.*

T.L.
United States Senate
Washington, DC

Reading the book was very interesting and helpful. I have no doubt that reading and using this guide can help people think and behave in a more positive way. Allow me to express to you my sincere appreciation of the blessed activity of The Way to Happiness Foundation and my best wishes to your success in disseminating the message of peace and harmony.

R.A.
Knesset Member
Jerusalem, Israel

We love your Way to Happiness *booklet. The* values, *moral and ethical, are exactly what we believe schools should emphasize. Maybe, if we start them young, they will have the foundation for happiness. Our students find it easy to understand and direct and to the point.*

L.H.
Principal
Board of Education
City of New York

After having read The Way to Happiness, *I've never felt so uplifted. We here at ADD LOVE Productions, have provided our children's performing group, The Positive Force Performers, each with their own copy to study. To date, we've distributed over 1,500 copies throughout Toledo, Ohio and Detroit, Michigan during our special presentations. Everyone who has received a copy only had the highest praise for its positive message. In a world so wrought with destruction these days, it's a blessing to have such a publication available to help instill strong moral values in our youth today.*

D.A.
Executive Producer
ADD LOVE Productions

Thanks for sending copies of The Way to Happiness! *We love the whole concept, and it goes hand-in-hand with our mission—which is to inspire girls in the highest ideals of character, conduct and patriotism in order to help them reach their full potential. The book will be invaluable for use in troop meetings, service unit gatherings, and as inspiration to many of our volunteers.*

M.C.
West Texas Girl Scout Council, Inc.

Please accept my thanks for the wonderful book, The Way to Happiness. *It is filled with gems, and it certainly gives some interesting pointers on happiness.*

G.P.
US Congressman
Washington, DC

City of Phoenix
Office of the Mayor
A Proclamation
City of Burbank
Proclamation
Narconon Day
City of Santa Monica
Proclamation
City of Philadelphia
Proclamation
County of Los Angeles
With sincere congratulations and best wishes, the Board of Supervisors of the County of Los Angeles does hereby join in the celebration of the
Benefit Event
Narconon
Chilocco
Office of the Mayor
City of Columbus
Ohio
PROCLAMATION
Proclamation
For the City of Pawtucket by His Honor
Mayor Brian J. Sarault
CITY OF KANSAS CITY, MISSOURI
EMANUEL CLEAVER II, MAYOR
PROCLAMATION
Proclamation
Office of the Governor
PROCLAMATION
* APPLIED SCHOLASTICS DAY IN ARIZONA *
State of Tennessee
THE SENATE
SENATE JOINT RESOLUTION NO. 301
By Senator Rusty Crowe
&
Representatives Charles Allen & Ruth Robinson
A RESOLUTION
Honoring students from SCIENCE HILL HIGH SCHOOL for their exemplary contributions to their school and community.
Resolution
By the Honorable Rebecca Q. Morgan, 11th Senatorial District;
Relative to Commending
The Delphi Academy
A PROCLAMATION
DESIGNATING
JUNE
AS
"SET A GOOD EXAMPLE"
MONTH
City of Hawthorne
State of California
The City of Inglewood
Proclamation
California Legislature
Resolution
CONCERNED BUSINESSMEN'S ASSOCIATION
"LOVE AND HELP CHILDREN"
MARCH 1990
City of PORTLAND, OREGON
Proclamation
WHEREAS, the future of succeeding generations and therefore the progress of the United States, and communities therein, depends upon the education of our children and workforce; and
Commonwealth of Massachusetts
State Senate
Official Citation
Flint
The Mayor
Proclamation
State of Rhode Island and Providence Plantations
OFFICE of the GOVERNOR
The Governor of the State of Rhode Island
PROCLAMATION
WHEREAS, founded on the inspiration of William Benitez inside the walls of Arizona State Prison twenty-five years ago, the Narconon Program treats thousands of individuals throughout the world who suffer from drug and alcohol addiction; and
WHEREAS, aiming to make our society drug-free, Narconon is fighting the war through prevention and education in our schools, juvenile facilities, and community organizations, as well as offers rehabilitation to those already addicted; and
Resolution of Commendation
WHEREAS, today's youth are tomorrow's civilization and the youth of Santa Clara County California and America are the hope of the future; and
WHEREAS, drugs are a serious threat to the future of today's youth which undercuts the objectives of our schools, whose purpose is to prepare youth for life in our society; and
WHEREAS, the Concerned Businessmen's Association of America out of a concern for our youth and their future, created the American Set A Good Example Contest and Campaign To Get Drugs Off School Grounds and out of our communities; and
WHEREAS, Students of Delphi Academy in Palo Alto, California achieved first place national honors in the 1989-1990 junior high school competition from among more than 5000 schools enrolled in the nationwide Set A Good Example Contest; and
WHEREAS, the students and faculty of Delphi Academy deserve to be honored and highly commended as a drug-free school setting an outstanding example;

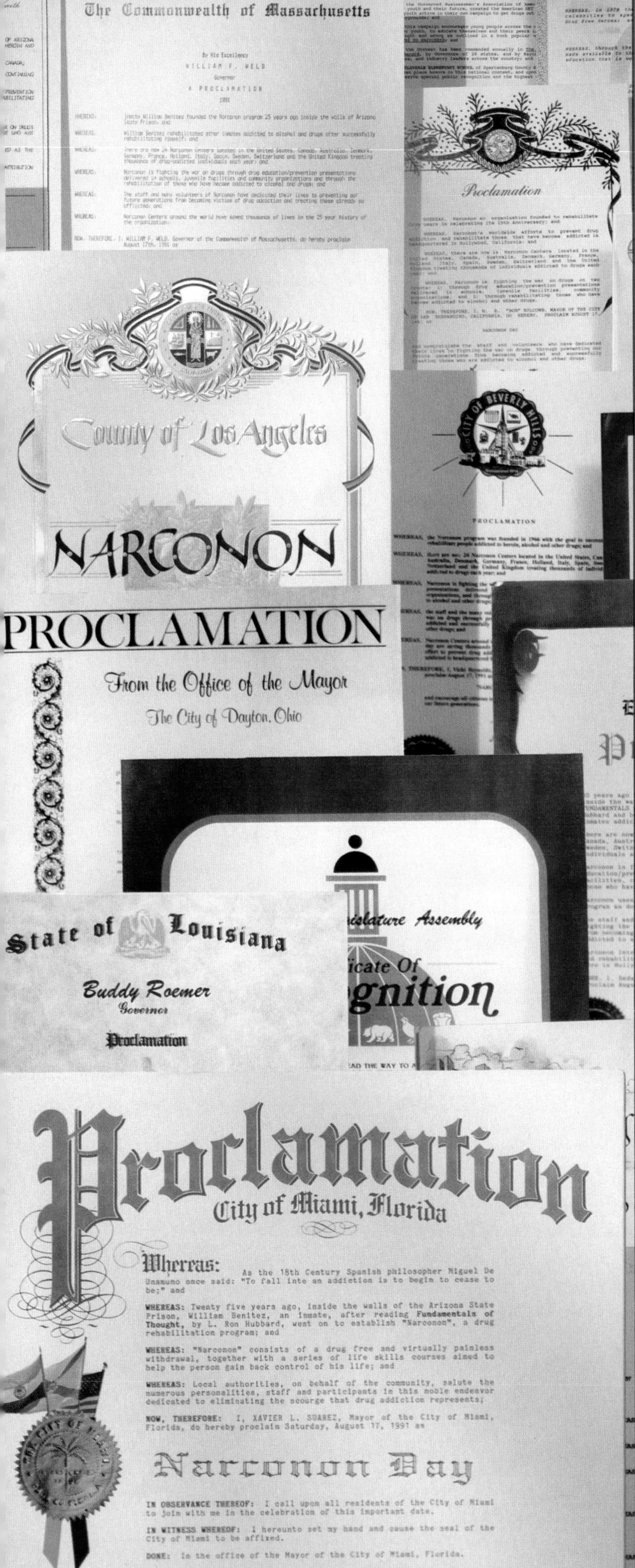

A Better World Through ABLE

ABLE's support and promotion of invaluable social betterment programs today offers new hope for millions of individuals on six continents. From the addicted who find new meaning in drug-free lives, to the illiterate who learn to read and suddenly find a future, from criminals who once again find pride in who they are and their potentials, to children who discover the value of morals, ABLE is helping and changing lives.

And to understand why the Church of Scientology supports all the programs of ABLE, one need only look again at some of the many success stories presented in this chapter.

While ABLE's mission is to reverse the decline of our civilization—to once again make learning a joy, our streets safe, our people able to face life sanely and rationally—the satisfaction gained by the staff of ABLE and its Scientology supporters and volunteers comes from helping individuals, those basic building blocks of our society so often ignored and overlooked. There is no greater fulfillment in any act than there is in safeguarding life, in restoring to an individual hope and pride and competence.

The successes of ABLE are successes for all. And the Church of Scientology and its members will continue to do all they can to bring about a better world through the application of the technology of L. Ron Hubbard.

These are some of the thousands of recognitions and proclamations saluting community betterment programs that are supported by ABLE.

Part Seven

World Institute of Scientology Enterprises (WISE)

If Scientologists are to survive in this world, L. Ron Hubbard explained, they must see to the survival of all men. They must dedicate themselves to the eradication of injustice, constantly work to raise levels of ethics and restore sanity in all sectors of society.

Although members of the World Institute of Scientology Enterprises represent a diverse group—from presidents of advertising companies to owners of repair shops—each has discovered a vital fact: that the same administrative policies used to expand Scientology organizations may also be used to expand any organization. And, as this chapter details, because expansion goes hand-in-hand with ethics, they are making the entire business community a better place in which to work.

Chapter 26

Wise: Enabling Groups to Flourish and Prosper

Until Dianetics and Scientology, no one knew the principles of a successful group any more than they knew the principles of the human mind.

Recognizing that what all too often passes for life in the modern workplace is endless drudgery, inefficiency, insecurity and bureaucratic entanglements, individuals began to utilize the same administrative principles L. Ron Hubbard developed for use in Scientology churches to improve their own businesses, organizations, groups and even their personal lives.

Their reasoning was simple: If Mr. Hubbard's administrative policies could bring sanity, stability and expansion to a Scientology organization, surely the application of those policies could do the same outside the Church. Why, for example, must a businessman suffer sleepless nights through uncertain economic times when Mr. Hubbard's policies so plainly outlined the means of survival in any economic climate? Why, too, must one suffer from continual infighting, backbiting and day-to-day duress when Mr. Hubbard so precisely laid out rules for group harmony? Moreover, many had long been utilizing principles from such Scientology books as *Problems of Work* to help resolve problems in group situations. Some even compiled their own manuals using some of Mr. Hubbard's material for use in training their employees, while others used what they knew to assist colleagues.

Thus it was that the World Institute of Scientology Enterprises (WISE) was born in 1979. A religious fellowship organization, WISE is made up of businessmen and professionals in numerous fields, who share a common certainty that only through the application of Mr. Hubbard's administrative technology can one do for the third (group) dynamic what Scientology does for the individual: eliminate confusions, replace hardship with happiness, and generally better survival.

Their tools, available in any church bookstore and many public libraries, are the twelve encyclopedia-sized volumes comprising the *Organization Executive Course* (OEC) and *Management Series* volumes. These works are a result of Mr. Hubbard's research and codification of the Scientology religion and were written for church administration. They address the subject of life in a group with the same thoroughness and attention to fundamental truths as Mr. Hubbard's writings on Scientology address the life of an individual. Thus, just as Dianetics and Scientology opened the way to an understanding of the mind and the spirit, the volumes of the OEC lead to an understanding of just what comprises a successful group. Be it a local Boy Scout troop or the largest government agency, with the principles contained in the OEC, one can turn any group into a productive, smooth-running and expanding concern.

These volumes contain practical knowledge in all areas of administration and organization. With their principles, one can solve problems ranging from the hiring of a secretary to the implementation of

The offices of WISE International, located in Los Angeles

multinational corporate plans. Similarly, by employing the principles contained in the Scientology organizing board, one can remarkably streamline all aspects of operation. And because the fundamentals of the organizing board apply equally well to one or one thousand, even the individual can greatly improve his life by simply aligning his activities according to the Scientology organizing board. In fact, with the application of the data in even a single volume, any group or personal activity can be immediately bettered.

Because every group, from a softball team to a steel mill work force, seeks to achieve some goal, the OEC material on the use of statistics to monitor progress toward that goal is particularly valuable. Utilizing Mr. Hubbard's principles, one can even better define goals and employ a precise system for laying out the steps to achieve them. The entire subject of logic is described—how to think and how to make logical decisions about any aspect of living. Ethics technology, including the correct application of the conditions of existence, is covered in detail, and there is a series of policies on the subject of establishing any organization and the personnel within it. In fact, there is no sphere of organizational knowledge not contained in the OEC.

Simply put, this technology encompasses the basic laws needed to succeed in any endeavor in any zone of application. No wonder then that individuals regularly use this technology in not only their careers but *also* their personal lives. With such knowledge so readily available, it was only natural that businessmen and professionals would begin implementing these discoveries to better relationships within their fields of practice and with their friends and families. Today, this technology is utilized with excellent results by thousands of individuals, groups and organizations. Its use results in increased survival and well-being, allowing any group to flourish and prosper.

The WISE membership is administered by WISE International, a religious nonprofit corporation located in Los Angeles. WISE members forward a basic principle of honesty and fairness to create a sane and productive working environment where everyone can flourish and prosper. If a WISE member violates these agreements, WISE International does everything possible to correct the member through proper training in ethics and justice codes before revoking his membership.

THE BENEFITS OF MEMBERSHIP

WISE members share a commonality of interest. They conduct business with one another, provide referrals and gain access to other like-minded individuals which may not otherwise be available.

The administrative functions of WISE also include supplying different members' benefits. These include issue authority (for use of copyrighted L. Ron Hubbard materials in publications), newsletters, membership directories, seminars, conventions and arbitrations for business disputes.

Some members employ the administrative principles solely within the framework of their own business or profession. Others study Mr. Hubbard's administrative breakthroughs and become consultants. A WISE consultant is a skilled expert in administration, who is trained on the technology contained in the OEC volumes and has learned how to help others apply it. WISE itself does no consulting. But the WISE members who are professional consultants routinely produce spectacular results when called in to help. WISE consultants have rightly earned the reputation of resolving situations that others, lacking their know-how, have been unable to crack. For the technology they have at their fingertips undercuts and corrects even the most difficult organizational problems.

In order to ensure proper and standard use of copyrighted materials, consultants are licensed by WISE. This acts as a safeguard against offbeat activities or the publication of altered versions held out to be the technology of L. Ron Hubbard. Being a WISE member in good standing is an assurance to others that one is maintaining the high level of ethical standards and conduct contemplated in Mr. Hubbard's writings.

WISE also furnishes arbitration services to its members. These are conducted in accordance with the ethics and justice codes of Scientology. As such they are swift, fair and determine, based on facts, restitution for any wrongs that may have been committed. This is an extremely valuable service, saving WISE members a great deal of the time, money and uncertainty that is part and parcel of the legal system.

A membership card for WISE International

For these reasons, WISE membership has grown since its inception in 1979, to more than 2,700 individuals, groups and companies (many with hundreds of employees). WISE members are found in more than 30 countries and many sectors of society. They are sought after for their high ethical standards and knowledge of administration and management principles and procedures. Recently, WISE members have been called upon to assist in the organization and management of newly privatized businesses and industries in Russia and other countries formerly under communist rule.

THE WISE CHARTER COMMITTEE

To ensure that high ethical standards are maintained by its members, WISE has established local Charter Committees, composed of the most ethical and trusted WISE members (called Charter members). The purpose of the Charter Committee is to use the Scientology system of ethics and justice to create a more ethical business environment.

Charter Committees are self-governing entities that regulate their own territories and members in achieving WISE's objective: the productive and standard use of L. Ron Hubbard's administrative technology to improve third dynamic conditions.

Through the administration of standard Scientology ethics and justice procedures to their members, Charter Committees arbitrate and rapidly and fairly resolve business disputes.

THE HUBBARD COLLEGE OF ADMINISTRATION

Because so many businesses and industries now use Mr. Hubbard's technology, WISE has established the Hubbard College of Administration to expand the business professional's ability to tackle the challenges of administering and running a group, company or organization. The Hubbard College provides training in L. Ron Hubbard's management technology.

Whether one is learning specific tools to apply to his or her own business or studying to become a consultant to help others, the Hubbard College provides the highest caliber of L. Ron Hubbard's administrative technology.

The curriculum is laid out in such a way that even the novice can rapidly grasp the basics and move on to more advanced training within a very short period of time. Hubbard College courses are available on either a full- or part-time basis.

A businessman or woman who studies at the Hubbard College first spends some time with an adviser to clarify the purpose of their study. Then an individualized program is developed with the focus on applying the technology to their area. Some of the aspects in which graduates have directly and positively affected the well-being of their companies are: increased production, reduced stress, streamlined organization, improved management/staff relations and heightened ethical levels amongst employees.

One of the most comprehensive courses for resolving undesirable third dynamic situations teaches the student to apply Mr. Hubbard's discoveries in the field of logic. Through this course, the business professional or consultant becomes expert in perceiving *through* the "apparent" reasons for a problem and zeroing in on the true underlying source of the decline or difficulty.

The Hubbard College also delivers specialist courses covering such subjects as:

- the application of ethics to business
- executive essentials and leadership
- management by statistics
- communication lines
- public relations
- the use of surveys
- how to increase personnel and company efficiency
- developing effective company policy
- how to put planning into implementation
- hiring of personnel
- the use of testing in personnel hiring and placement
- troubleshooting, and
- computers

The WISE Hubbard College of Administration where students learn the administrative technology developed by L. Ron Hubbard

SUCCESSFUL APPLICATIONS

By the early nineties, 35,000 of these courses had been delivered. Successes reach far more broadly than business and professional application, however. Many of the College's course graduates report that, as a result of the organizational know-how they have gained, other areas of life improve as well—a better overall outlook, marriages salvaged, happier family life, achievement of personal goals, etc.

Evidence from one chiropractor who had received assistance from a WISE member applying the administrative technology:

"My practice had a lot of disorder and inefficiencies before you came in. Thanks to the Hubbard data and your help, I am now achieving the success I have worked so hard for.

"But more important for me, I also have the quality of life and am enjoying my success thanks to your program. Even though production and income [are] higher, I actually am able to spend more time with my family. My personal life has improved along with the practice."

And from another: "Seven weeks ago I was unsure as to whether or not I would continue practicing chiropractic. I had lost my sense of purpose and felt overwhelmed with confusion and sadness at the condition of the world, where I found myself and in life. Not a pretty picture. As a last resort I attended [a WISE] introductory seminar.

"On December 30, 1991, I took myself to the introductory seminar. On December 31st I decided to sign up for a complete management package. I immediately noticed a dramatic change in one of my chiropractic assistants, and for myself the decision to begin the management program signified a clear commitment to my belief in myself. All was not lost after all.

"Now only seven weeks later, my original failing practice has almost doubled and . . . I know my purpose and willingly accept the responsibility that goes along with it. I am filled with energy and find true happiness in my work. I feel like this is my first year in practice instead of my seventh."

An Allstate insurance industry executive wrote this testimonial concerning the implementation of Mr. Hubbard's administrative procedures in his office by another WISE member:

"I'm convinced that the training provided by you and your firm had a good deal to do with the positive results we experienced during the last year.

"Our production results were above goal; we have a better partnership atmosphere in the region; our managers feel they are in better control of their destiny rather than letting the environment control them."

The manager of a famous Hollywood restaurant reported: "Using the organizational technology of L. Ron Hubbard has done more in the last 11 months than the 20 years before to make the restaurant an efficient, effective and profitable organization. In my opinion, no other investment could have come close to that performance."

A technology consultant who worked as a staff scientist at Massachusetts Institute of Technology, wrote: "I highly recommend that any serious student in the business would observe for himself the practical method that Mr. Hubbard has developed."

A marketing executive reported: "L. Ron Hubbard has developed extremely workable procedures for predicting and handling the problems that accompany periods of rapid growth. As a result of knowing and applying these procedures we now find ourselves well organized to deal with our current high level of production, and we are prepared to expand further without undue strain on our resources.

"We consider Hubbard administrative technology to be a fundamental key to our continued success."

A major corporation executive said: "As president of my company, it has been my good fortune to be connected with the WISE organization, receiving business consultation. I have tried many other business technologies, especially in the areas of marketing and management leadership, and was very discouraged at the results. In a very short time working with a WISE consultant, using the administrative technology

Robert Goldscheider, a management technology consultant for thirty-three years, has been special counsel to multinational corporations, the UN Industrial Development and the World Intellectual Property Organizations. He observed the application of Mr. Hubbard's administrative technology in the business world.

"Having had a firsthand opportunity to delve rather deeply into the administrative writings of L. Ron Hubbard, I am impressed. The technology is infused with common sense and practicality.

"Particular aspects, proven to be successful at all levels of the corporations I visited and analyzed, include:

"AVAILABILITY—The entire body of his administrative technology is carefully recorded in bound volumes, indexed and cross-referenced by title, subject and date. This affords a stability at all levels where corporate executives and staff alike can become acquainted with policy and cooperate as a group.

"THE ORG BOARD—The organizing board pattern is an innovative discovery which can be adapted to accommodate a large multipurpose corporation or customized to the needs, purposes and strategies of a particular organization.

"MANAGEMENT BY STATISTICS—A carefully organized reporting system, broken down to quantify and qualify virtually every aspect of operations relevant for sensitive management control. The ability to react very promptly to developments is one of the attributes of LRH administrative technologies, and is perhaps the key reason they have been successfully applied so consistently.

"INDIVIDUALITY—The techniques and systems developed to choose the correct personnel for a job, and how to train and stabilize them to perform their functions, has never before been so well described or completely delineated.

"In my opinion, the management technologies of L. Ron Hubbard superbly take into account long-run policies and daily needs of modern business and administrative operations. If the MBA products of our most eminent business schools had measured up to these standards in the past decade, I doubt that the American and world economies would be in their current disarray.

"I know of no other body of administrative laws and methods which is as complete, as workable and as broadly applicable as Mr. Hubbard's. His philosophy of organizational know-how and his lucid explanations for its application deserve wide use in industry, commercial enterprises, and government."

Robert Goldscheider, Chairman
The International Licensing Network, Ltd., Technology Management Consultants

of Mr. Hubbard, I found I could easily apply the information and raise the production level of my company. I have also noticed a marked increase in the morale of my staff due to the material they learned through WISE courses."

A chartered accountant stated: "With the direction from the WISE membership I was able to find the exact L. Ron Hubbard administrative technology which I needed to handle a major problem with my company. By training my staff on courses at the Hubbard College, I have easily doubled my production. Without WISE membership assistance and L. Ron Hubbard's administrative technology made available, I would not have been able to locate or handle this problem at all."

According to a highly successful investment counselor: "L. Ron Hubbard's management technology is world-class. It is an innovative and remarkably workable method of improving conditions. Being a WISE member and using this technology has allowed me to improve my business and to face head-on the challenges of work and life with a smile and with enthusiasm.

"This is priceless data. It's also simple and basic. Results are immediate. If you are having any business difficulties this stuff can turn your entire career or business around in a matter of days. It's that powerful."

And, from an insurance adjustment company senior executive: "L. Ron Hubbard administrative technology has been the management technology that I have followed since I started our insurance adjusting company in 1979. This technology has taken my company from a one-man operation out of a rented house to the fastest growing insurance adjusting company in southern California with over 140 employees.

"Prior to studying and applying this technology, I studied business administration throughout my more than six years in college. I had been attempting to get answers in the areas of personnel, client relationships, finance, production, quality of work product and marketing. Somehow the answers I got were vague and not data that could be readily applied.

"I came upon Hubbard Management Technology in the early 70s and decided it was worth looking into. And that it was. I have taken courses in this technology and apply it to my company on a daily basis. Almost all of our employees have graduated from the more advanced programs.

"Through WISE membership this technology has been made available. I urge all businessmen to become WISE members and take advantage of its services and benefits."

And one member reports the outcome of a WISE arbitration: "The thought of an arbitration used to cause me to sweat cold bullets . . .

"Then I got an arbitration from WISE. The results were amazing. And yes, I felt much better afterwards. But the real bonus was the end result—fairness. Both parties had to confront their own responsibility in the matter and the ethics of the situation was taken into account, not just the technicalities of some obscure law . . . I thoroughly recommend it. Really for the first time, it is possible to resolve disputes sanely, without paying exorbitant sums on legal fees."

Why Is WISE Important?

Inflation, recession, lowered productivity, imbalance of trade, bankruptcy, soaring national debts, strikes, unemployment, poverty and want—these well-known symptoms of economic decline and instability on this planet are actually indicators of a much deeper problem—a crippling lack of administrative know-how. If today's businesses and governments could grasp and competently apply the basic principles of organization and administration, they would be able to enact workable solutions to end economic chaos rather than perpetuate it. Increased survival on the third dynamic would ensue.

WISE offers the hope of improvement in this sphere of society. WISE members bring sanity and order into their environment. Every WISE member is a point of stability that reduces confusion in this uncertain world. Businesses can prosper, governments can rule wisely and populations can live without economic duress. With L. Ron Hubbard's administrative technology, the goals that have evaded society for so long are within reach.

Part Eight

The Statistics and Growth of Scientology

No religion in history has spread as fast or as far in as short a time as Scientology. Today it is practiced in more than 30 languages in 74 countries on every continent.

This part details the expansion of Scientology from its birth in the United States in the early 1950s to its scope today. The next five chapters cover a wide variety of data on Scientology and Scientologists, the "firsts" which have spurred its ascendancy, the history of its expansion, documentation of the sources who have opposed it and the predictions about Scientology by sociologists, religionists and others.

Here is a look at the phenomenon of a new religion emerging and flourishing in a time of generally declining religious influence.

Chapter 27

Demographic and Statistical Facts About Scientology

This chapter presents facts and figures about Scientology which detail its rapid dissemination and growth around the world. These include results of an extensive demographic survey of Scientologists from every continent which provide a picture of who they are, what they are like, their attitudes, lifestyles and more.

Scientologists represent a tremendously varied cross section of society, and include Kenyan farmers, Norwegian fishermen, Brazilian soccer players, Japanese businessmen, Italian educators and on and on. To typify a Scientologist, one must disregard age, race, occupation, nationality or political allegiance, for Scientologists cover the entire spectrum.

Scientologists are healthy (over half do not miss a single day of work in any given year), active (a majority are involved in some form of church, human rights, environmental or charitable activity) and successful in their work (¾ in the US earn more than the national average wage). Scientologists are also drug free (none at all use illegal street drugs).

Such figures run counter to many current trends in society and underscore the fact that Scientology helps people lead better lives. More people are discovering and embracing Scientology every day. Its expansion increases because it continues to offer meaningful solutions to universal problems.

WORLD EXPANSION OF DIANETICS AND SCIENTOLOGY

1955

1975

1992

Countries in Which Dianetics and Scientology Services Are Delivered

1. Algeria
2. Argentina
3. Australia
4. Austria
5. Belgium
6. Brazil
7. Bulgaria
8. Canada
9. Chile
10. China
11. Colombia
12. Costa Rica
13. Croatia
14. Cuba
15. Czechoslovakia
16. Denmark (including Greenland)
17. Dominican Republic
18. Ecuador
19. El Salvador
20. Estonia
21. Ethiopia
22. Finland
23. France
24. Germany
25. Ghana
26. Greece
27. Guatemala
28. Honduras
29. Hungary
30. India
31. Indonesia
32. Ireland
33. Israel
34. Italy
35. Ivory Coast
36. Japan
37. Kenya
38. Luxembourg
39. Malta
40. Malaysia
41. Mexico
42. Nepal
43. Netherlands
44. Netherlands Antilles
45. Nicaragua
46. Nigeria
47. Norway
48. New Zealand
49. Pakistan
50. Peru
51. Philippines
52. Poland
53. Portugal
54. Puerto Rico
55. Romania
56. Russia
57. Saudi Arabia
58. Sierra Leone
59. Singapore
60. Slovenia
61. South Africa
62. South Korea
63. Spain
64. Sweden
65. Switzerland
66. Taiwan
67. Tanzania
68. Turkey
69. Uruguay
70. United Kingdom
71. United States
72. Venezuela
73. Zaire
74. Zimbabwe

CHURCHES, MISSIONS AND ORGANIZATIONS:
OVER 40 YEARS OF GROWTH

L. Ron Hubbard's technology is made available to individuals through a growing number of organizations around the world that provide a broad range of services from education and drug rehabilitation to Scientology auditing and training.

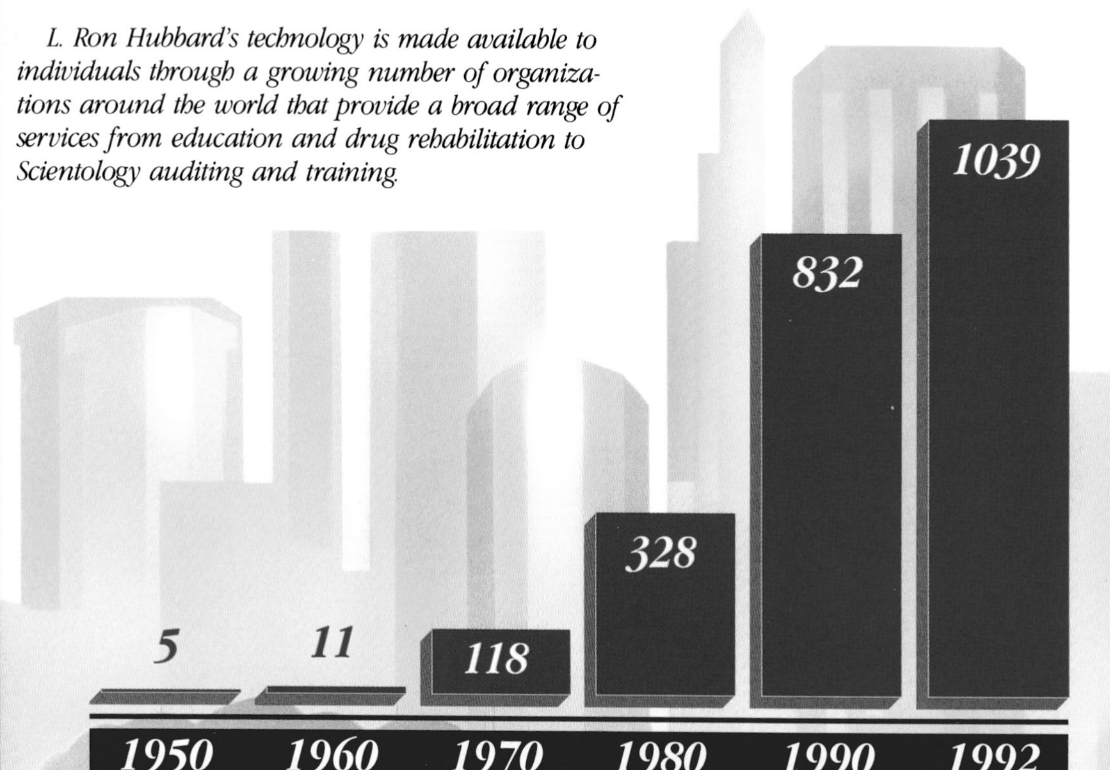

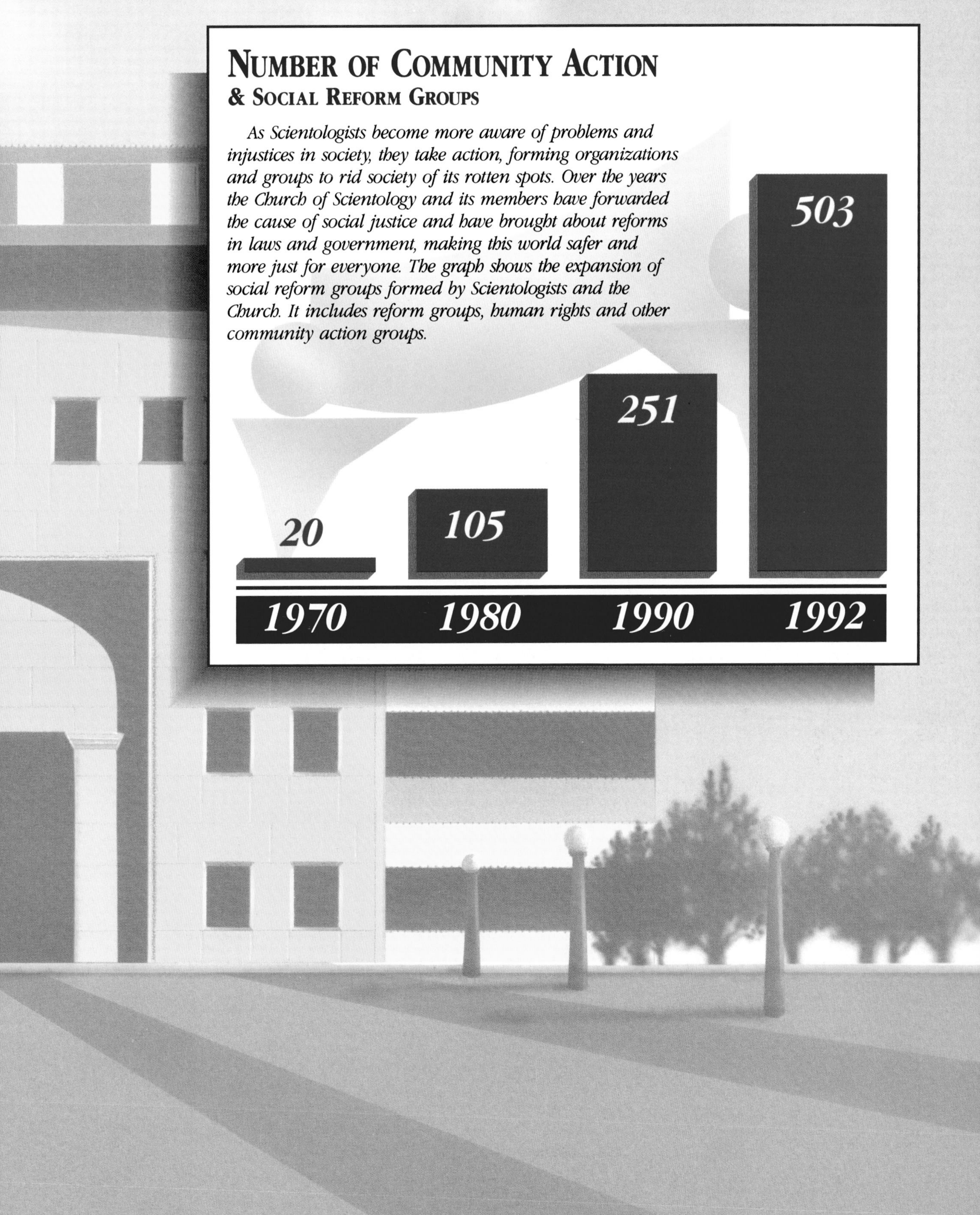

NUMBER OF COMMUNITY ACTION
& SOCIAL REFORM GROUPS
As Scientologists become more aware of problems and injustices in society, they take action, forming organizations and groups to rid society of its rotten spots. Over the years the Church of Scientology and its members have forwarded the cause of social justice and have brought about reforms in laws and government, making this world safer and more just for everyone. The graph shows the expansion of social reform groups formed by Scientologists and the Church. It includes reform groups, human rights and other community action groups.
20
105
251
503
1970
1980
1990
1992

Church of Scientology Staff

Contracted Scientology Staff in Churches and Missions Internationally

With the expansion of Dianetics and Scientology, the need for staff to train and audit members of the Church has increased commensurately. In the last two decades the number of contracted Scientology staff in churches and missions around the world has grown by more than 4 times. This reflects more organizations and the growth of existing ones.

(1970 is the first year that accurate records for contracted staff internationally are available.)

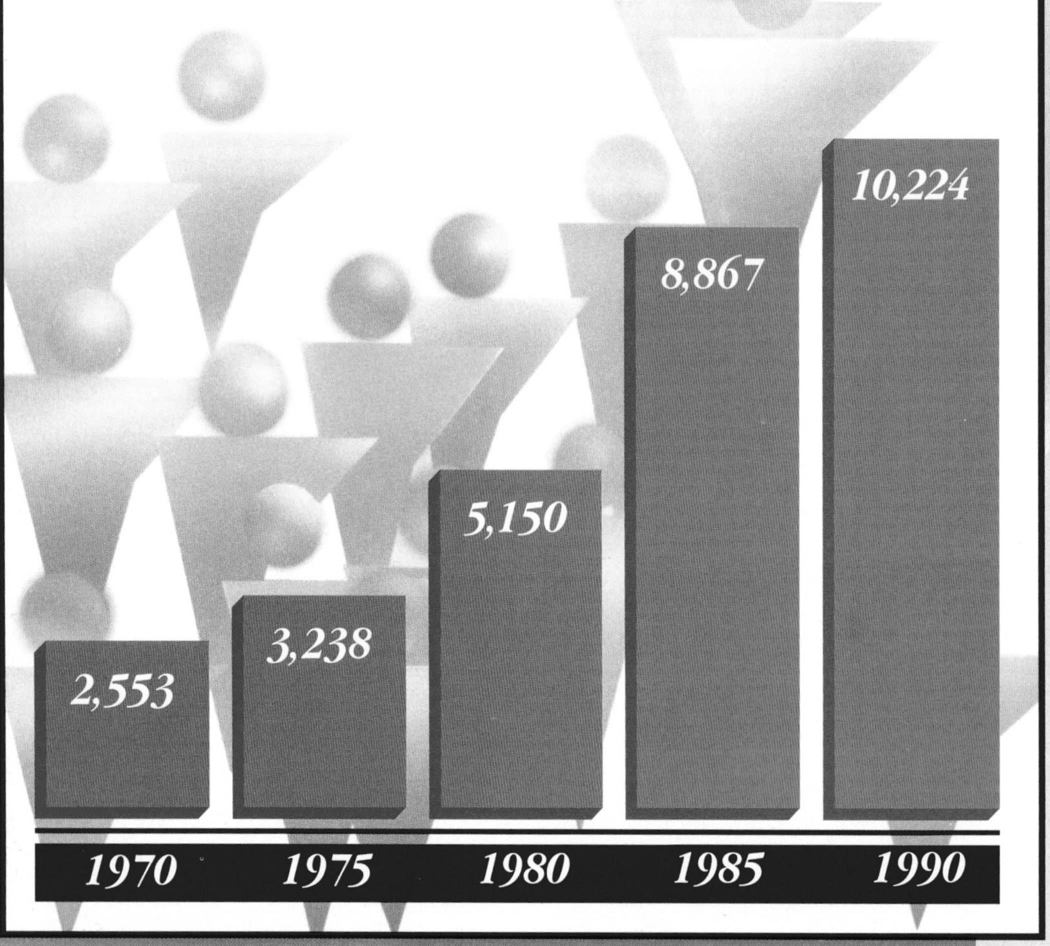

Percentage Distribution of Church and Mission Staff

The graphic below shows the global distribution of Scientology staff.

SERVICES OF THE CHURCH OF SCIENTOLOGY

NUMBER OF PEOPLE
PARTICIPATING IN SCIENTOLOGY FOR THE FIRST TIME (PER YEAR)

A fair gauge of just how many people are interested in Scientology can be seen in the following graph, which reflects the annual number of individuals entering a church or mission for the first time, obtaining a service, book or lecture. The volume each year has increased by over 5½ times since 1970—to almost half a million new people a year in 1990.

Number of Auditing Hours

Delivered Yearly in Churches and Missions (Not Cumulative)

The number of yearly auditing hours delivered in church organizations is seen in the graph below. In just the last decade, auditing hours have almost doubled and the 10-year total is over 10 million hours. There are countless hours of auditing delivered outside churches and missions around the world every day which are not included in the figures below.

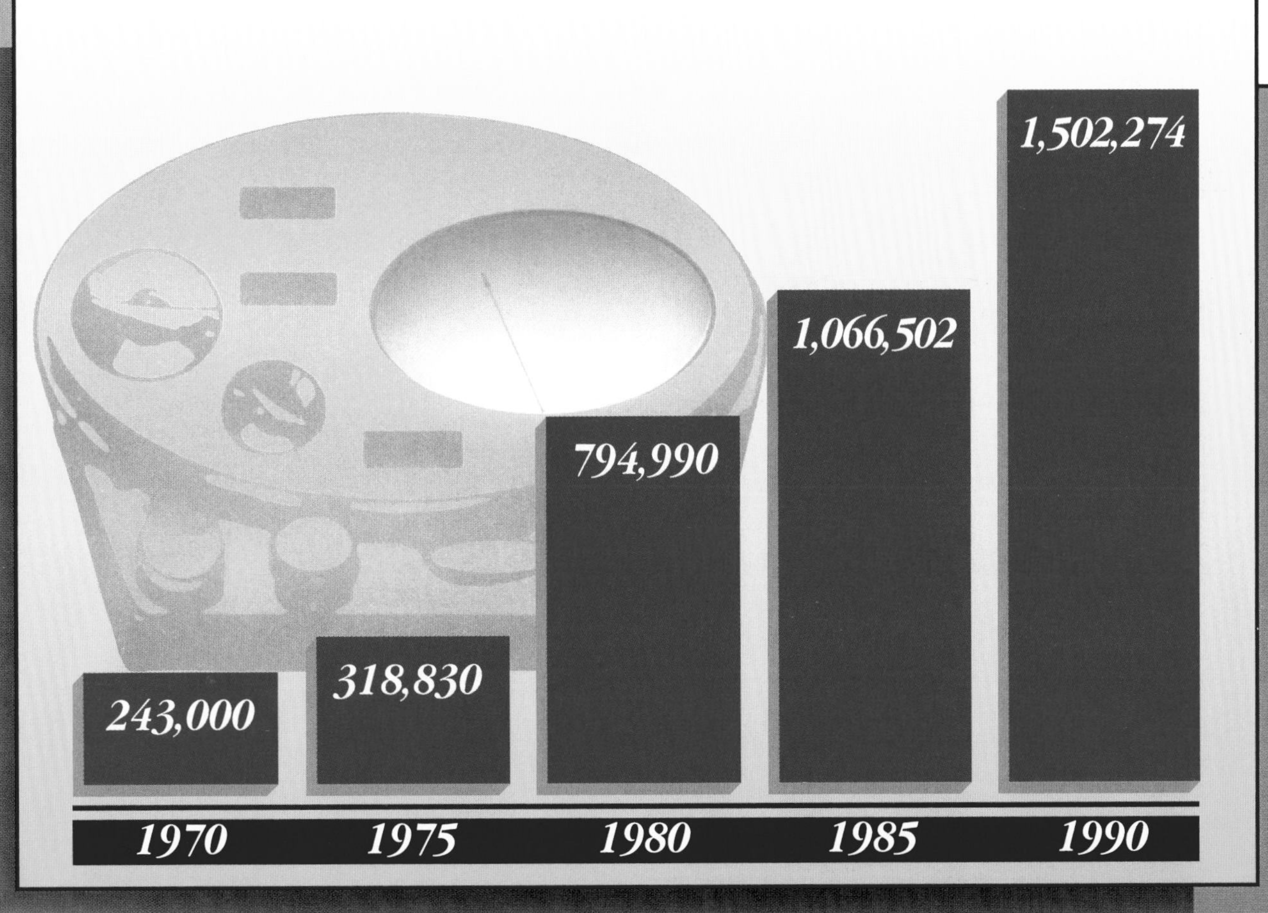

Scientology Magazine Distribution

Growing in Circulation

Churches and missions produce their own periodicals which are regularly mailed to their members.

Three of the Church's more important publications are ***The Auditor****, the magazine of all Saint Hill Organizations,* ***Source*** *magazine, the publication of the Flag Service Organization and* ***Advance!*** *which is the magazine of the Advanced Organizations. Their increasing circulation reflects the constant growth of these organizations.*

SOURCE CIRCULATION

1975	1980	1990	1992
38,000	73,000	133,000	144,000

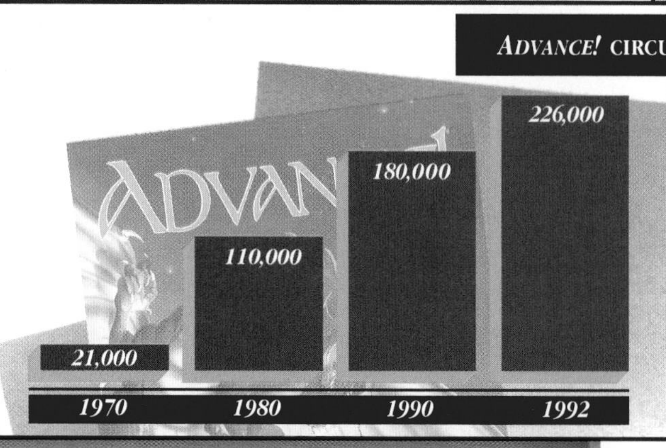

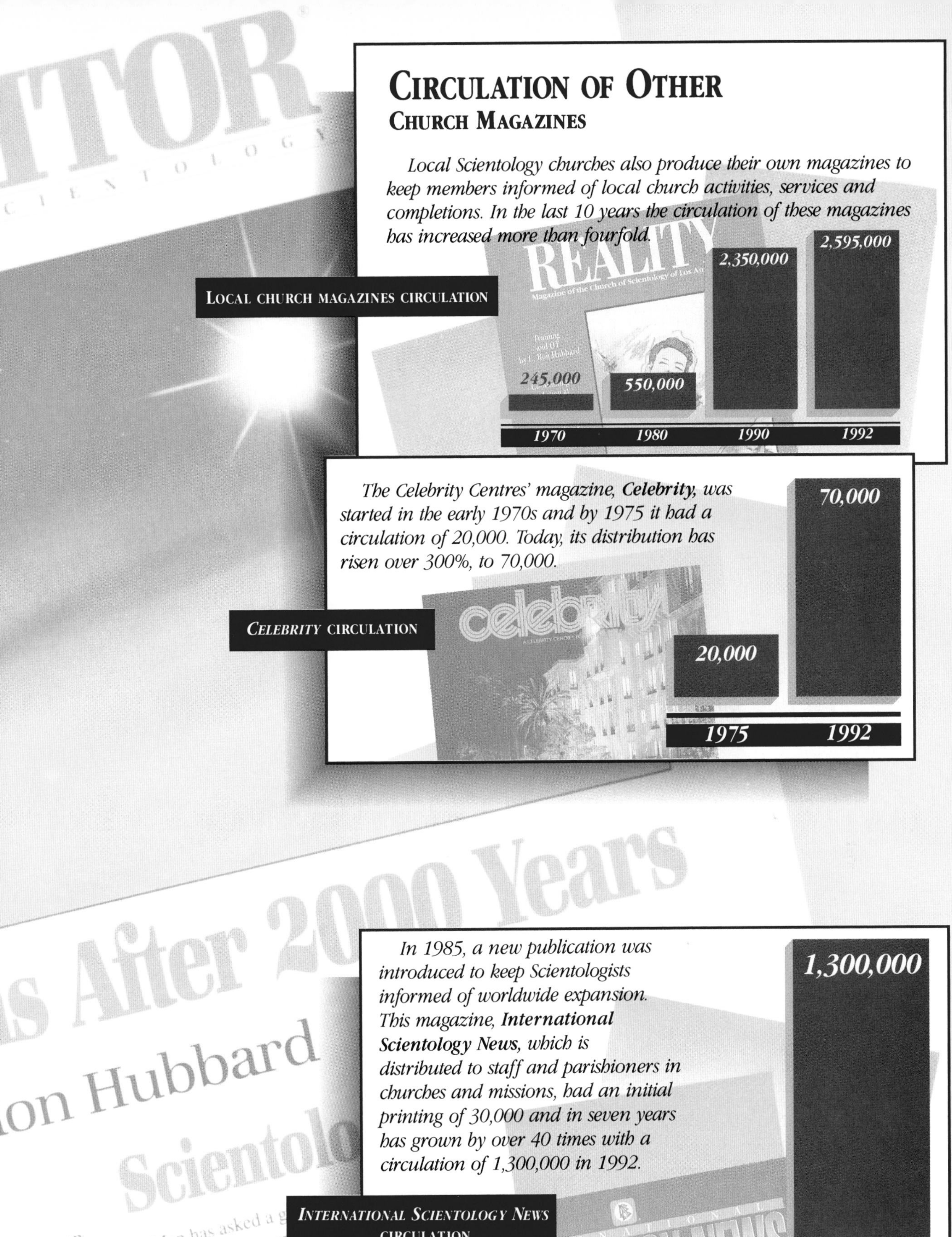

Circulation of Other Church Magazines

Local Scientology churches also produce their own magazines to keep members informed of local church activities, services and completions. In the last 10 years the circulation of these magazines has increased more than fourfold.

Local church magazines circulation

1970	1980	1990	1992
245,000	550,000	2,350,000	2,595,000

The Celebrity Centres' magazine, ***Celebrity****, was started in the early 1970s and by 1975 it had a circulation of 20,000. Today, its distribution has risen over 300%, to 70,000.*

Celebrity **circulation**

1975	1992
20,000	70,000

In 1985, a new publication was introduced to keep Scientologists informed of worldwide expansion. This magazine, ***International Scientology News****, which is distributed to staff and parishioners in churches and missions, had an initial printing of 30,000 and in seven years has grown by over 40 times with a circulation of 1,300,000 in 1992.*

International Scientology News **circulation**

1985	1992
30,000	1,300,000

Positive Response to Dianetics and Scientology

In 1988, the Church of Scientology hired an independent national research company to conduct two public opinion surveys: one among those who had purchased copies of ***Dianetics: The Modern Science of Mental Health*** *and the other among members of the Church.*

An extraordinarily high consensus of opinion was revealed. In fact, the research company admitted that it had never seen responses so uniformly favorable.

Dianetics Improves Lives

When ***Dianetics*** *bookbuyers were asked, "Would you say that applying the techniques in* ***Dianetics*** *has changed your life?" 79% responded affirmatively. 90% felt that* ***Dianetics*** *was successful in "helping man to improve his potential," while 84% felt that the book "helped people become more successful" and "taught people how to be happier."*

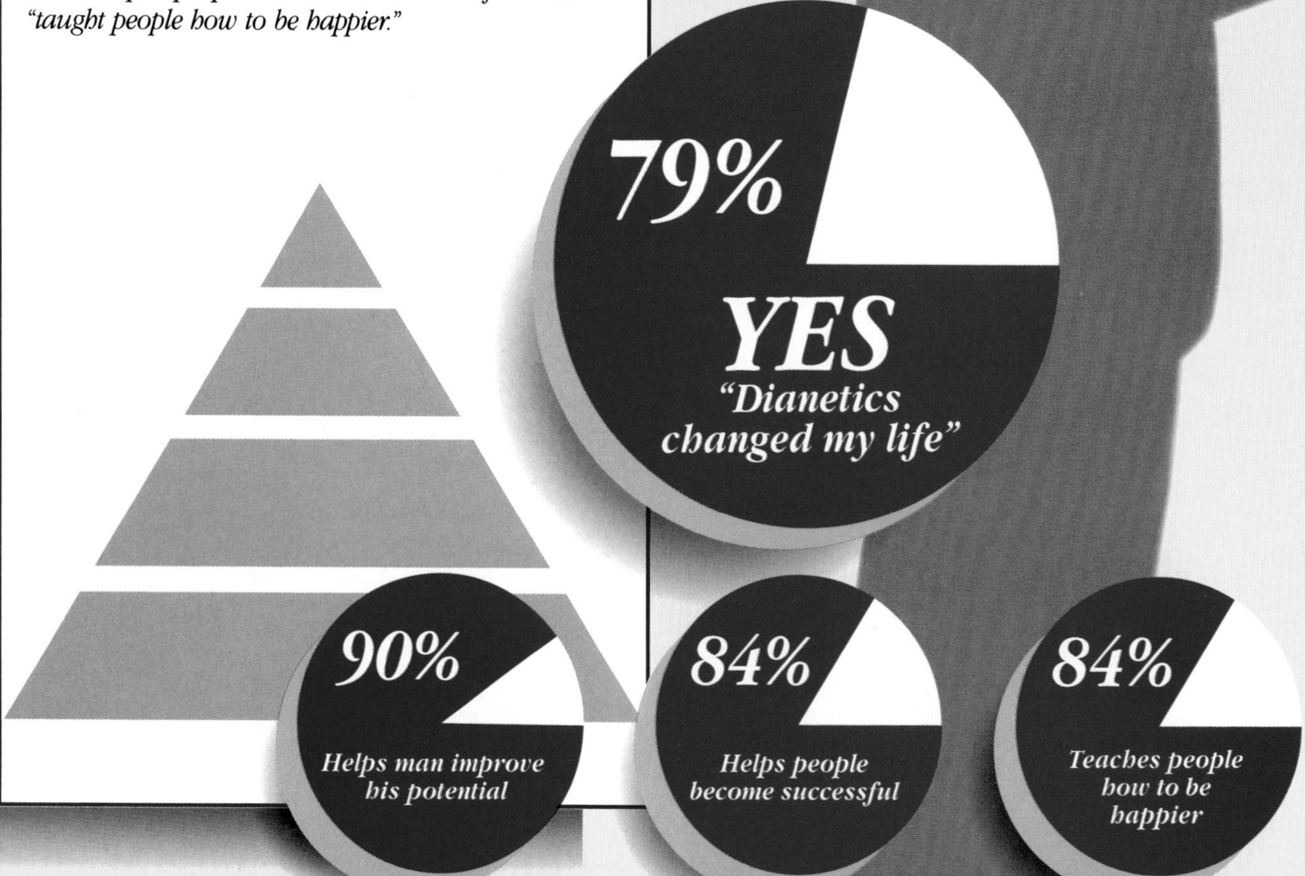

Scientology Makes a Difference

In a survey among Church of Scientology members, 97% responded that Scientology has made "a great deal" of difference in their lives, with the remaining 3% responding that it had made some difference. 91% stated that Scientology had either "exceeded" or "met" their expectations.

97%
"Scientology made a great deal of difference"

91%
"Scientology exceeded/met my expectations"

Ninety-six percent of Church members reported that they had received auditing, with 97% of those who had been audited saying it was helpful and 95% stating they wanted more.

97%
"Auditing was helpful"

95%
Wants more auditing

Eighty-eight percent of the Scientologists said that the idea of becoming an auditor themselves was appealing. 100% of those surveyed agreed that Scientology successfully "teaches people to think more clearly."

These responses are testimony to the workability of Dianetics and Scientology.

100%
"Scientology teaches people to think more clearly"

88%
"Becoming an auditor is appealing"

L. Ron Hubbard's Books

Public Popularity

The popularity of Scientology can be measured by the number of Dianetics and Scientology books in public hands. The total number of L. Ron Hubbard's nonfiction titles sold since 1950 is 58,222,612. The rate of increase in public demand is possibly best seen in the number of ***Dianetics: The Modern Science of Mental Health*** *books sold since its release in 1950. The graph below shows the cumulative* ***Dianetics*** *sales over the last 22 years.*

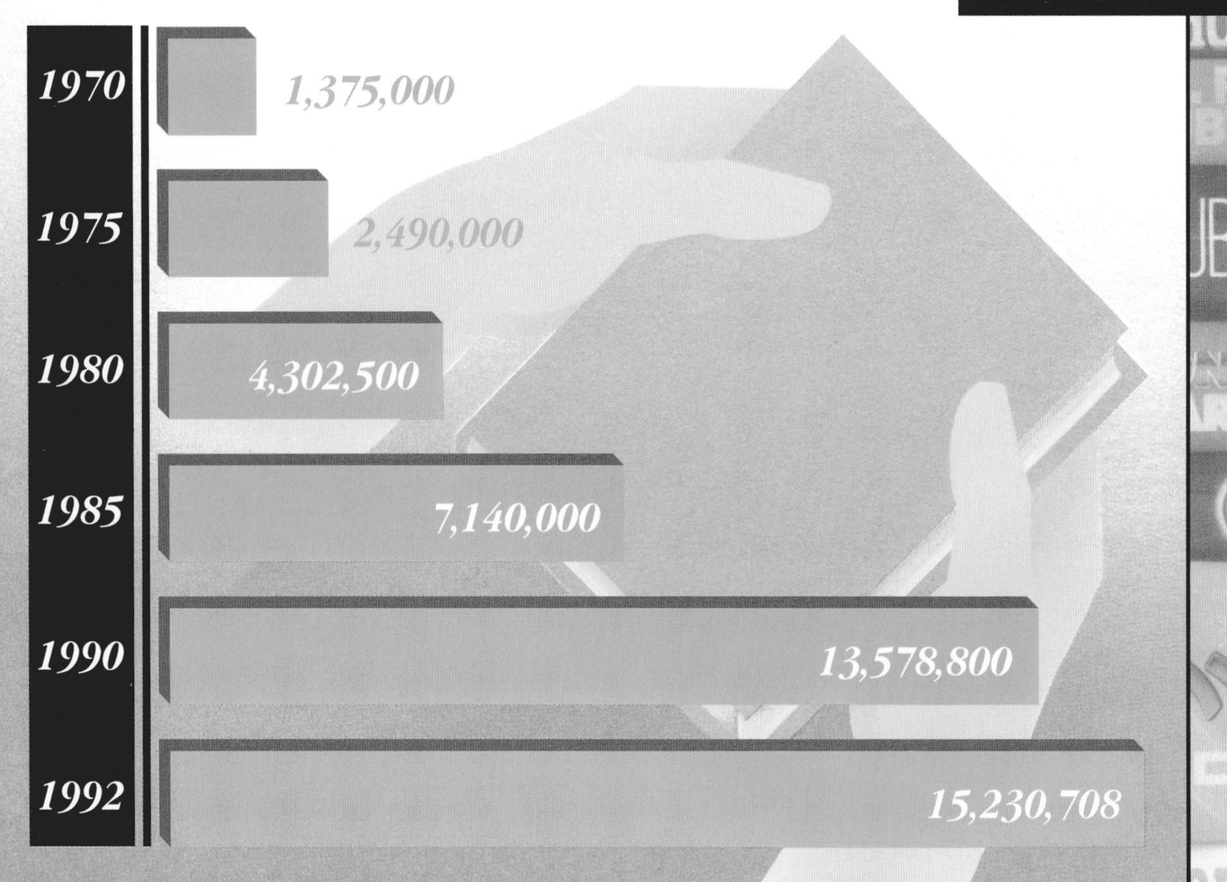

L. Ron Hubbard's works are in such huge demand around the world that they are distributed in the 103 countries shown below.

1. Algeria
2. Argentina
3. Australia
4. Austria
5. Bahamas
6. Belgium
7. Belorussia
8. Bolivia
9. Brazil
10. Bulgaria
11. Cameroon
12. Canada
13. Chile
14. China
15. Colombia
16. Congo
17. Costa Rica
18. Croatia
19. Cuba
20. Cyprus
21. Czechoslovakia
22. Denmark (includes Greenland)
23. Dominican Republic
24. Ecuador
25. Egypt
26. El Salvador
27. Estonia
28. Ethiopia
29. Finland
30. France (includes Reunion Island, Polynesian Islands—Tahiti, St. Pierre & Miquelon)
31. French Guiana
32. French Polynesia
33. Germany
34. Ghana
35. Greece
36. Guadeloupe
37. Guatemala
38. Guyana
39. Haiti
40. Honduras
41. Hungary
42. Iceland
43. India
44. Indonesia
45. Ireland
46. Israel
47. Italy
48. Ivory Coast
49. Jamaica
50. Japan
51. Jordan
52. Kenya
53. Korea
54. Kuwait
55. Latvia
56. Lebanon
57. Lithuania
58. Luxembourg
59. Madagascar
60. Mali
61. Malta
62. Malaysia
63. Mauritius
64. Mexico
65. Monaco
66. Morocco
67. Netherlands
68. Netherlands Antilles
69. Nepal
70. New Zealand
71. Nicaragua
72. Nigeria
73. Norway
74. Pakistan
75. Peru
76. Philippines
77. Poland
78. Portugal
79. Romania
80. Russia
81. Senegal
82. Singapore
83. Slovenia
84. South Africa
85. Spain
86. Sri Lanka
87. Sudan
88. Sweden
89. Switzerland
90. Taiwan (Formosa)
91. Tanzania
92. Thailand
93. Trinidad
94. Tunisia
95. Turkey
96. Ukraine
97. United Arab Emirates
98. United Kingdom (includes Bermuda, Gibraltar, Hong Kong & Montserrat)
99. United States (includes Puerto Rico)
100. Uruguay
101. Venezuela
102. Zaire
103. Zimbabwe

To meet the worldwide demand for L. Ron Hubbard's works, his books have been published in the 31 languages listed below.

1. Afrikaans
2. Arabic
3. Bahasa Indonesia
4. Chinese
5. Czechoslovakian
6. Danish
7. Dutch
8. English
9. Finnish
10. French
11. German
12. Greek
13. Hebrew
14. Hungarian
15. Italian
16. Japanese
17. Korean
18. Norwegian
19. Polish
20. Portuguese
21. Punjabi
22. Russian
23. Serbo-Croatian
24. Sotho
25. Spanish
26. Swahili
27. Swedish
28. Taiwanese
29. Urdu
30. Xhosa
31. Zulu

Social Betterment and Reform Activities

Number of Social Betterment Groups

The Church of Scientology and its members actively participate in bettering society by establishing nonchurch groups and organizations around the world. Using L. Ron Hubbard's technology, Scientologists help children with school and study problems; work to rehabilitate drug addicts and criminals and bring about a safer environment through programs to increase moral values. The graph below shows the number of officially established and recognized groups using L. Ron Hubbard's technology to better social problems. There are many thousands of others less formally organized, but no less dedicated or effective—however, there are no accurate records of them available.

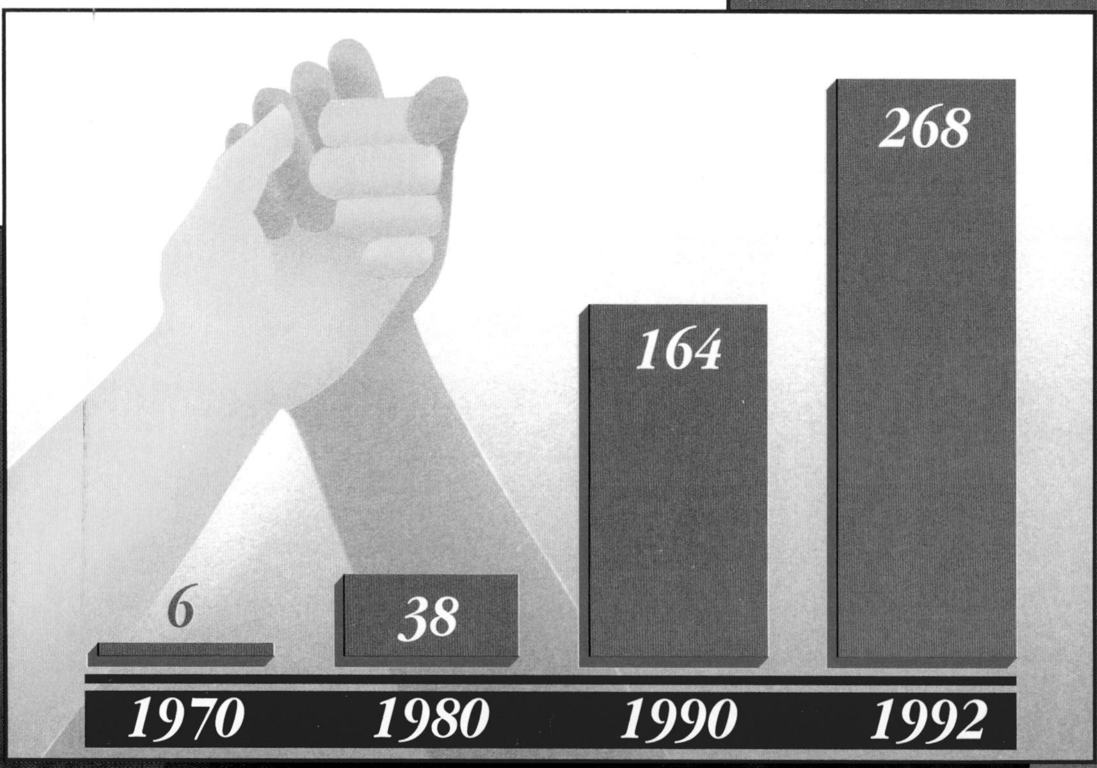

NARCONON
DRUG EDUCATION

Narconon (the drug rehabilitation program that uses L. Ron Hubbard's technology in this field) not only gets people off drugs, but also delivers drug education lectures and seminars to schools and community groups.

Starting their educational program in the early 1980s, in response to the onslaught of cocaine and crack addiction among Western youth, Narconon has delivered an average of more than 2 lectures per day reaching over 66,000 people a year.

Through its actions, Narconon has helped hundreds of thousands of students and adults avoid the horrors of drug use. The figures below are cumulative for each area.

NARCONON CENTER	NUMBER OF LECTURES	NUMBER OF ATTENDEES
Greater Los Angeles	5,327	203,576
Boston	1,704	168,143
Italy	1,500	300,000
Chilocco	534	24,750
Malmö	90	5,348
Huddinge	400	12,000
Spain	31	2,280
Switzerland	2	80
Denmark	137	4,176
Canada	98	7,806
Cumulative Total:	9,823	728,159

Effectiveness of Narconon
Demonstrated by Government Study

In 1987, a study was completed and released by an independent sociological research group in Spain on the success of Narconon. The research group, often used by the Spanish government, confirmed the remarkable results of Narconon.

Of the students surveyed, 69.2% were still off drugs two years later. Over two-thirds of those who had received other types of rehabilitation treatment stated that the effects from these treatments had been negative and unsuccessful, while 86.5% rated Narconon as very positive and 89.2% stated that the Narconon staff were very qualified.

69.2%

Still off drugs after 2 years

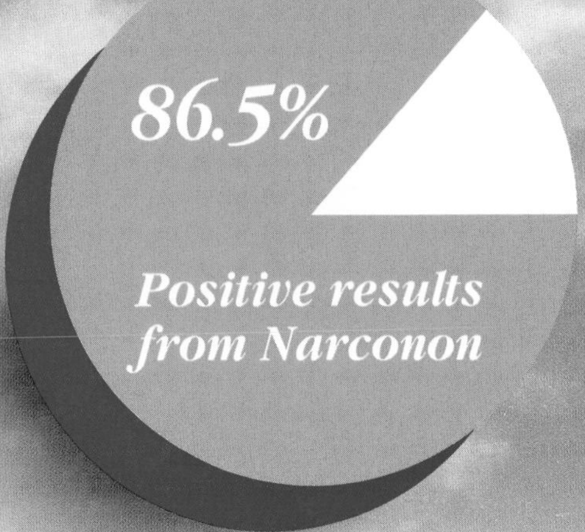

86.5%

Positive results from Narconon

89.2%

Narconon staff are very qualified

POSSIBLY THE MOST REVEALING STATISTIC WAS *the fact that **all** the students who had completed the program had subsequently not been involved in any criminal activities, yet those who had completed other programs before Narconon had not only not been cured of their drug addiction, but were also continuing to sell drugs and commit other criminal acts.*

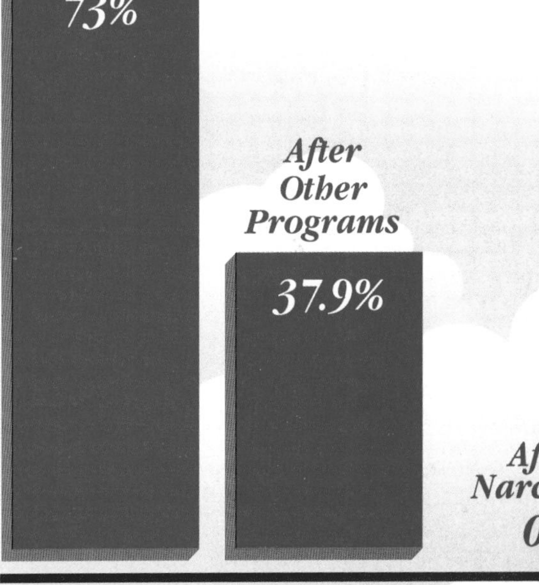

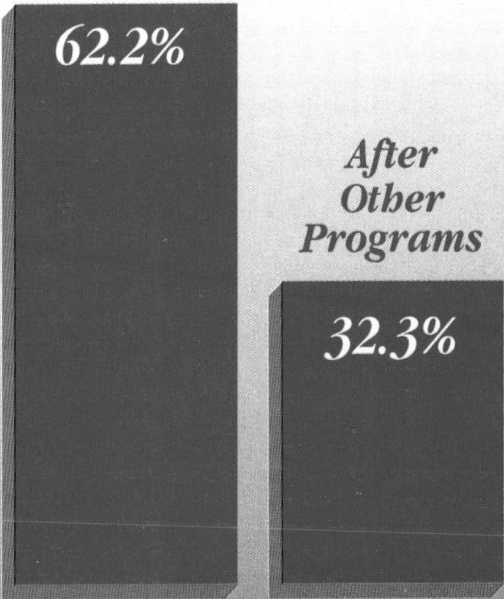

Vital Statistics of Scientologists Across the World

What Are Scientologists Like?

What are their backgrounds and how do they live? What is important to them and what are their habits and interests? To answer these questions, surveys were mailed to Scientologists around the world. The statistics and graphs on the following pages reflect the results—showing attitudes, lifestyles and backgrounds of Scientologists. (A margin of ±3% is allowed to cover both statistical and sampling errors.)

How Were You Introduced to Scientology?

Scientologists want their friends to know about what they find helpful. It is no surprise then that well over half of today's Church members were first introduced to Scientology through a friend or relative.

Through Reading a Dianetics or Scientology Book 20.6%
Through a Personality Test 18.0%
Through an Advertisement 4.8%
Lecture 3.1%
Other 0.9%
Through a Friend or Relative 52.6%

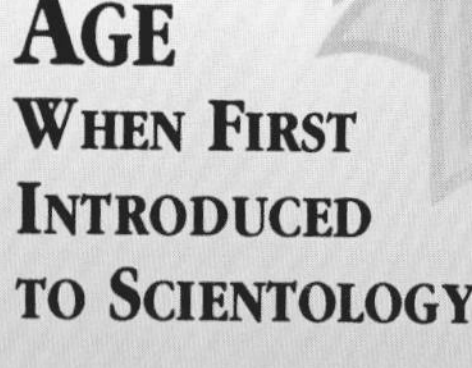

Age When First Introduced to Scientology

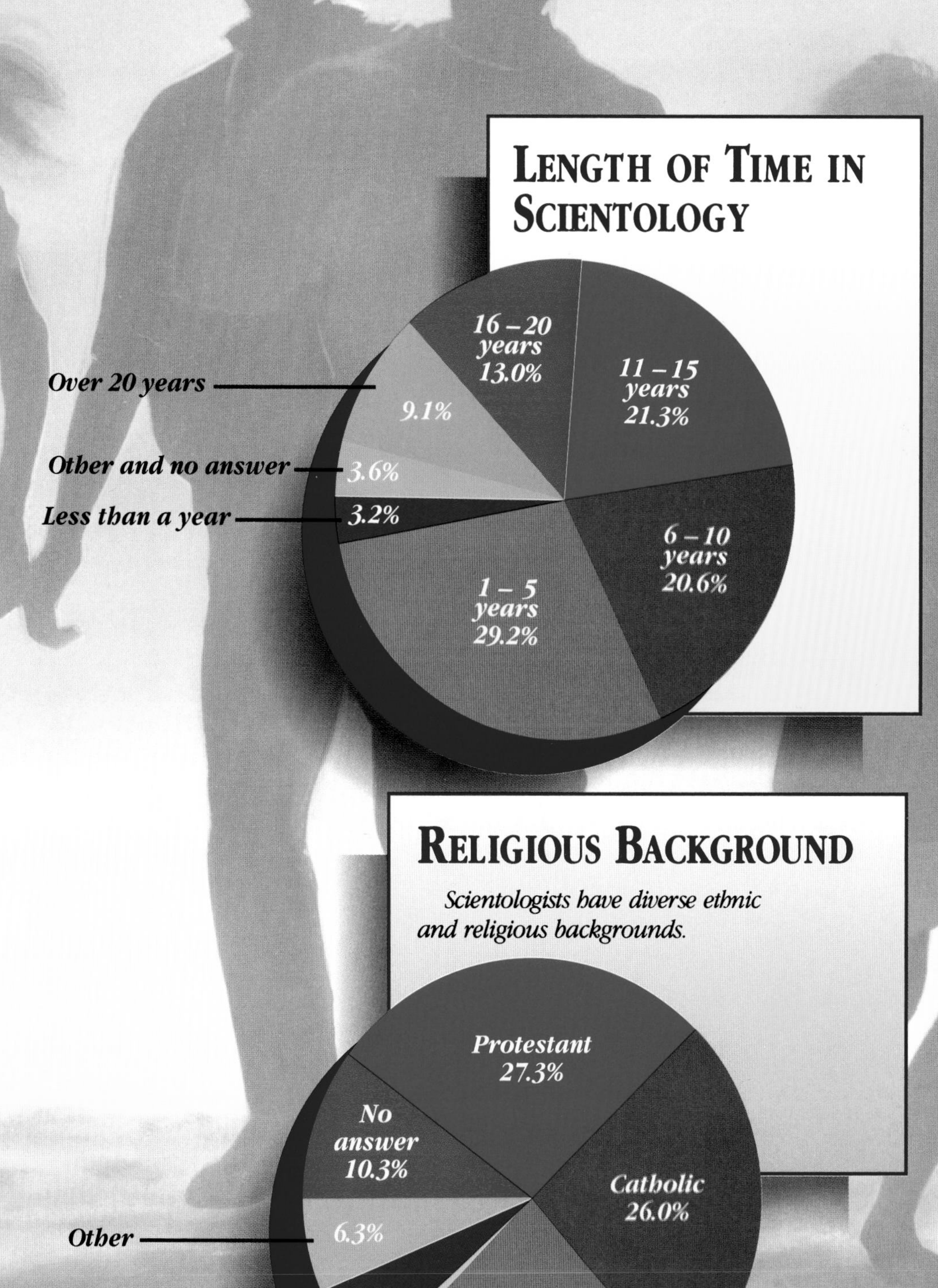

LENGTH OF TIME IN SCIENTOLOGY
16 – 20 years 13.0%
11 – 15 years 21.3%
Over 20 years
9.1%
Other and no answer
3.6%
Less than a year
3.2%
6 – 10 years 20.6%
1 – 5 years 29.2%
RELIGIOUS BACKGROUND
Scientologists have diverse ethnic and religious backgrounds.
Protestant 27.3%
No answer 10.3%
Catholic 26.0%
Other
6.3%
5.3%
Judaism
None 23.8%
Eastern 1.0%
(Hindu, Buddhist, Eastern Philosophy)

Marital Status

Statistics show that the marriage rate more than doubles after involvement in Scientology. Marriage is seen as vital to three times as many after Scientology as before. More than just recognizing the value of creating and maintaining successful relationships, Scientologists have the technology to bring these about and consequently they have close, happy families and long-lasting marriages.

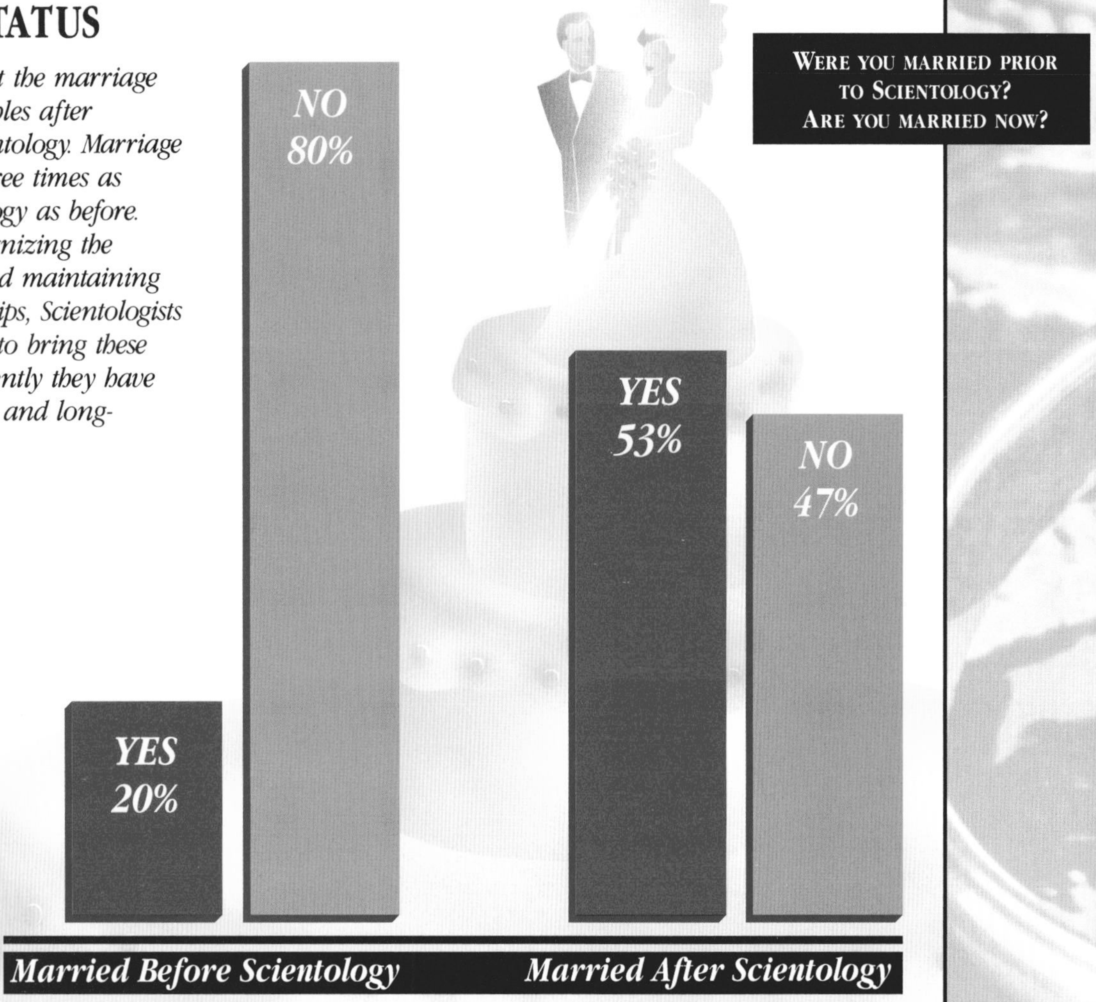

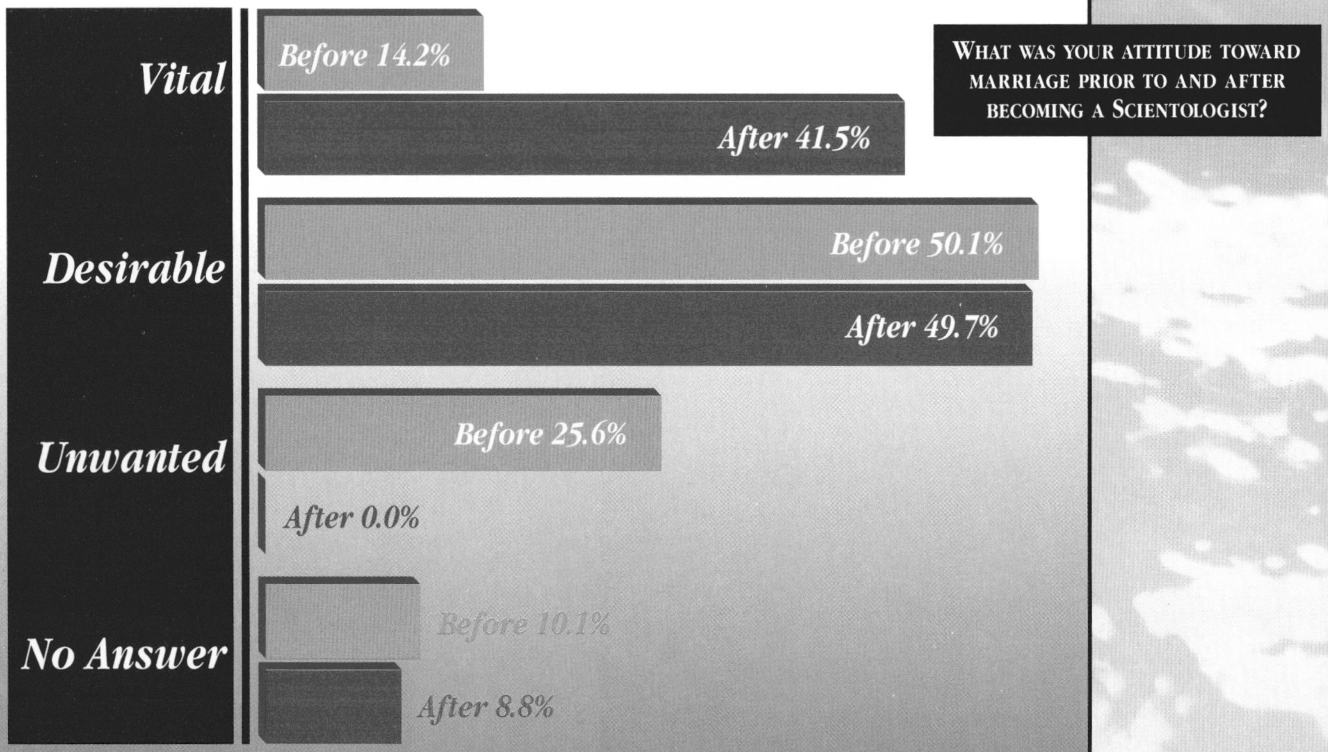

Were you married prior to Scientology? Are you married now?

	YES	NO
Married Before Scientology	20%	80%
Married After Scientology	53%	47%

What was your attitude toward marriage prior to and after becoming a Scientologist?

	Before	After
Vital	14.2%	41.5%
Desirable	50.1%	49.7%
Unwanted	25.6%	0.0%
No Answer	10.1%	8.8%

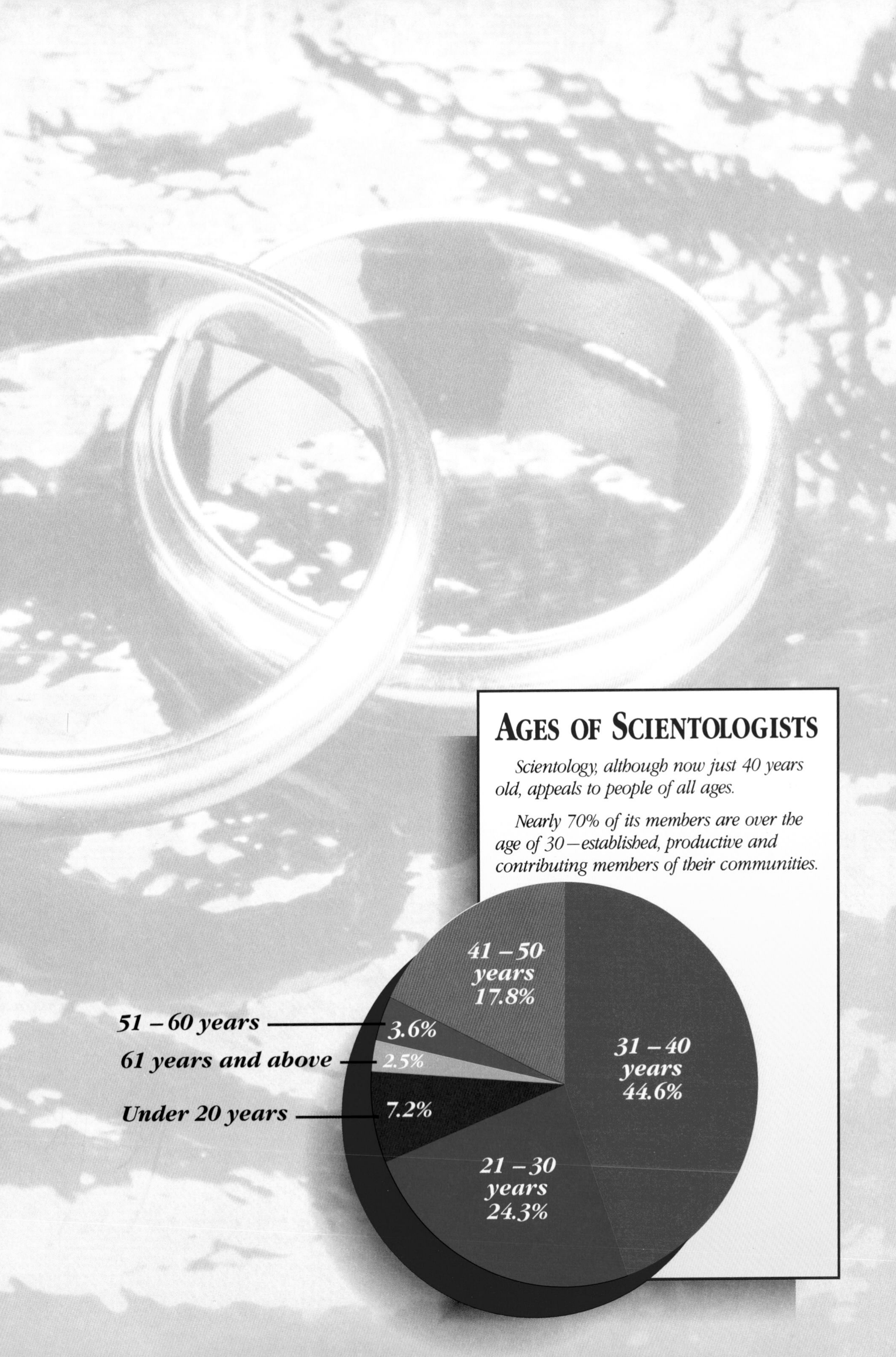
AGES OF SCIENTOLOGISTS
Scientology, although now just 40 years old, appeals to people of all ages.
Nearly 70% of its members are over the age of 30—established, productive and contributing members of their communities.
41 – 50 years 17.8%
51 – 60 years
3.6%
61 years and above
2.5%
Under 20 years
7.2%
31 – 40 years 44.6%
21 – 30 years 24.3%

Scientologists
and Their Families

Over 97% of Scientology's married couples have children. They enjoy raising children, as do many other parents, and ensure that their children are involved in community and school projects, sports and other activities to give them a well-rounded upbringing.

(As a comparative, US census statistics show that 51% of America's married couples do not have children.)

How many children do you have?

2 Children 37.8%
3 Children 15.2%
4 Children 7.3%
5 or more Children 3.6%
No Children 2.8%
1 Child 33.3%

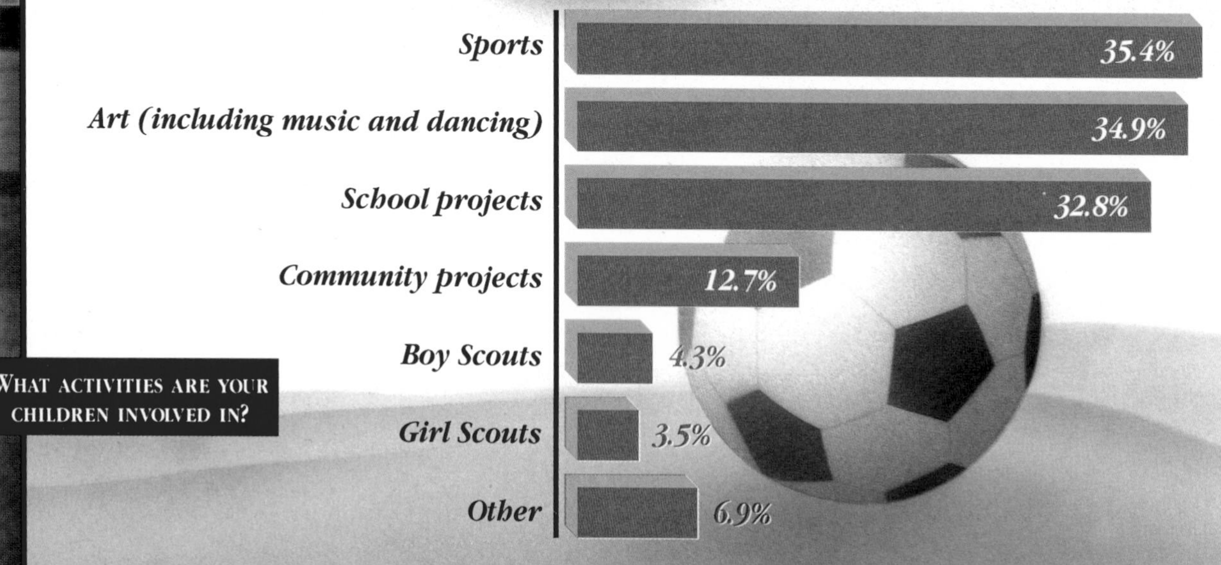

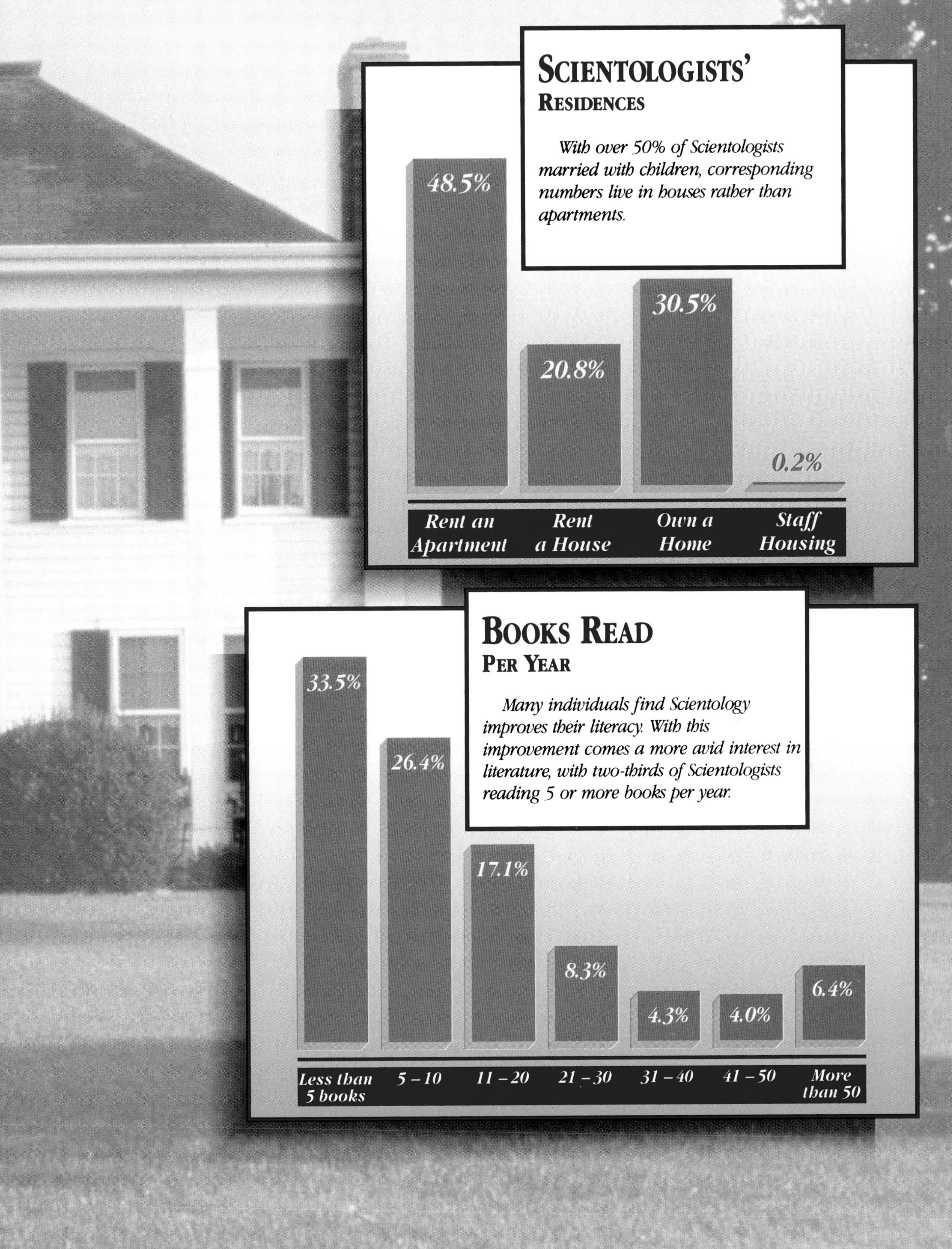

SCIENTOLOGISTS' RESIDENCES
With over 50% of Scientologists married with children, corresponding numbers live in houses rather than apartments.
48.5%
20.8%
30.5%
0.2%
Rent an Apartment
Rent a House
Own a Home
Staff Housing
BOOKS READ PER YEAR
Many individuals find Scientology improves their literacy. With this improvement comes a more avid interest in literature, with two-thirds of Scientologists reading 5 or more books per year.
33.5%
26.4%
17.1%
8.3%
4.3%
4.0%
6.4%
Less than 5 books
5 – 10
11 – 20
21 – 30
31 – 40
41 – 50
More than 50

SCIENTOLOGISTS
& THEIR EDUCATION

Scientologists are well educated, with over 80% graduating high school and 23% graduating college including postgraduate work. Compared to the average educational levels found in the United States, the percentage of Scientologists graduating high school is more than 8% higher and those graduating college is more than 30% higher than the norm.

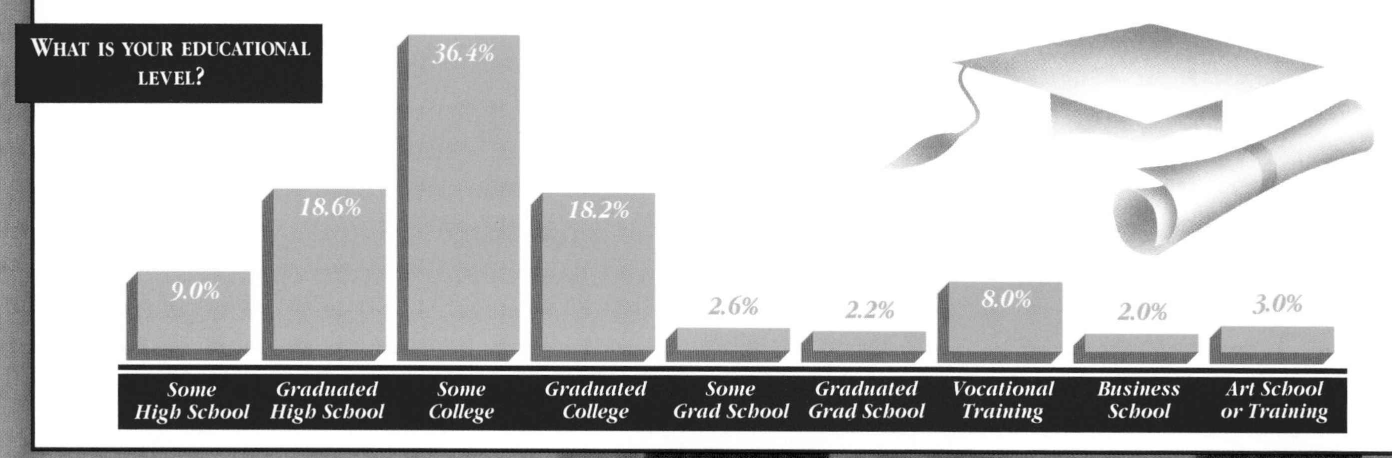

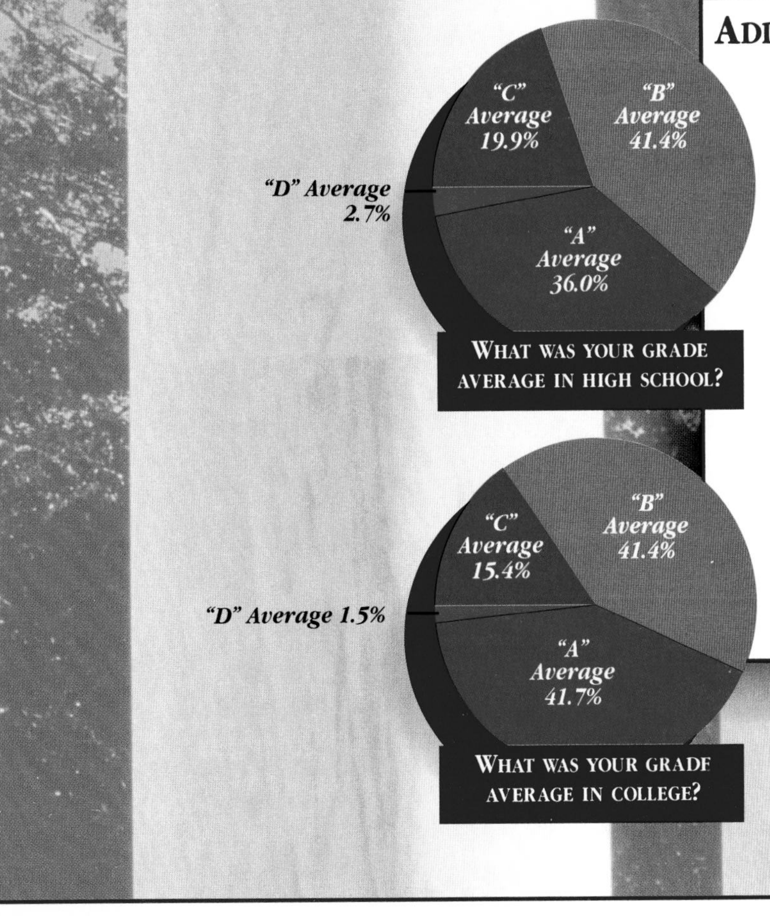

ADDITIONAL QUESTIONS *were asked to find out what kind of grade average students who were Scientologists attained while attending high school and college. Over three-quarters reported that they maintained a "B" average or above and found that Scientology helped them not only study better, but also better apply what they learned.*

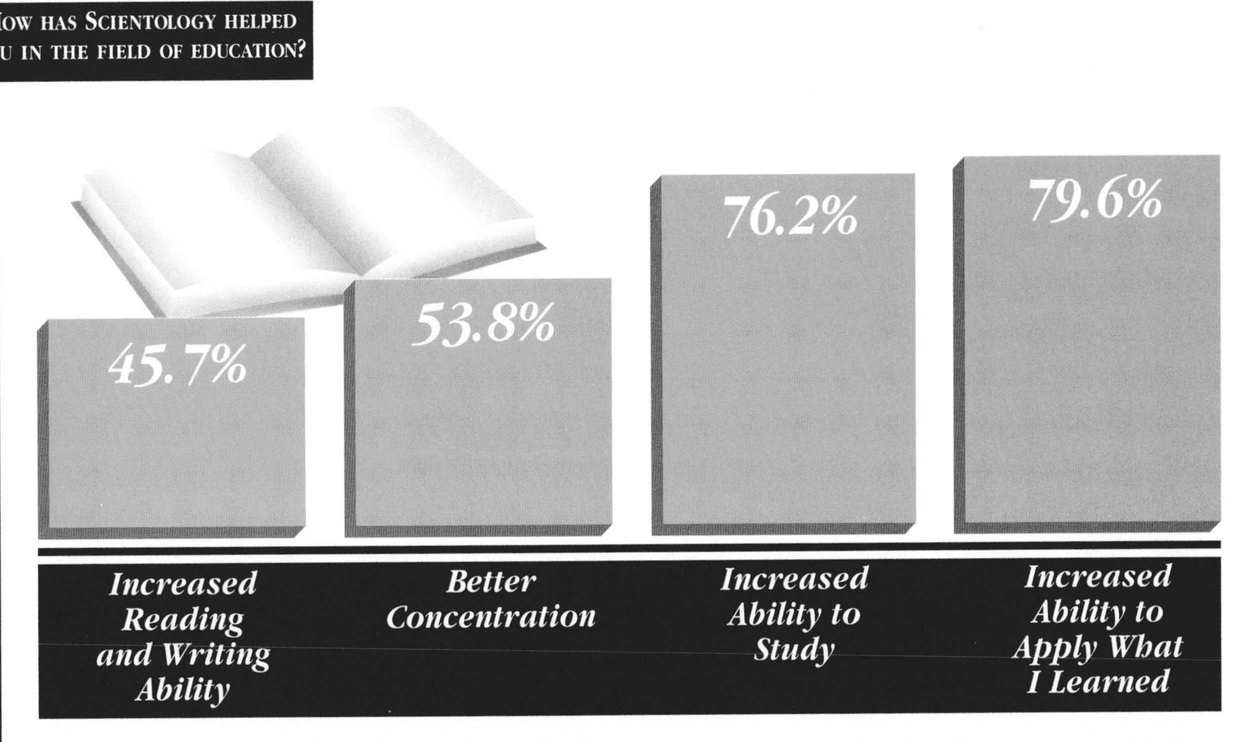

Scientologists & Work

Scientologists find that no matter what their occupation, Scientology helps them improve their competence. As a result they are more productive and valuable to their profession.

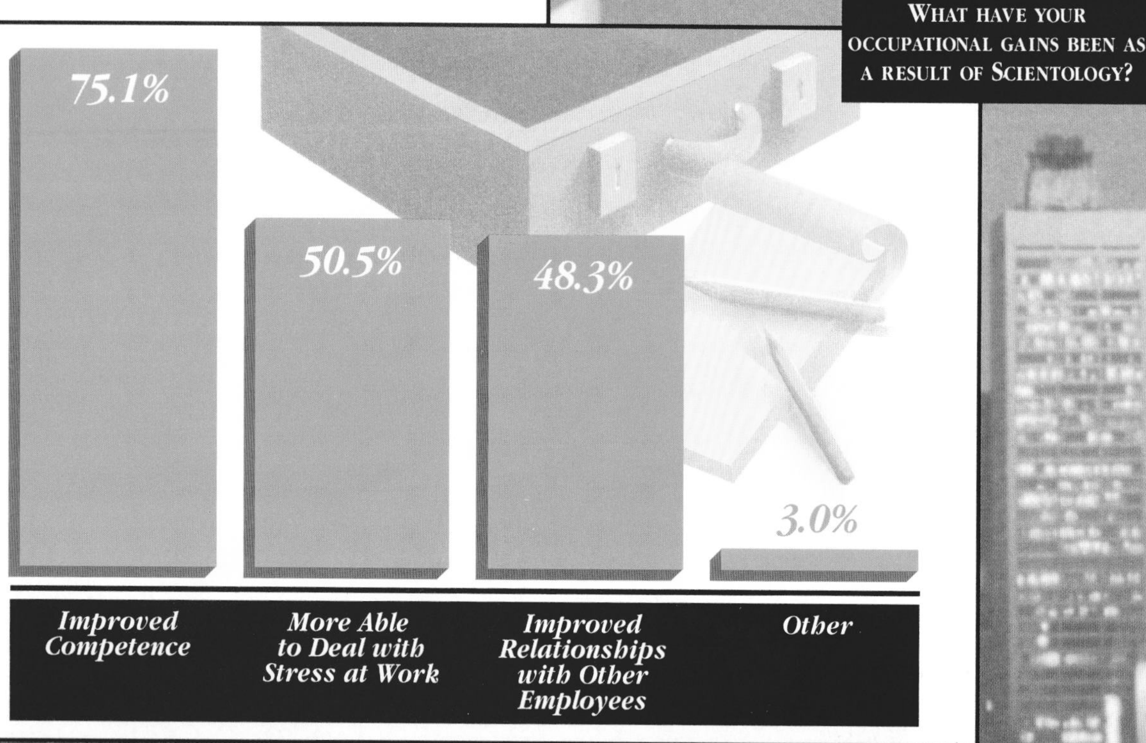

What is your current occupation?

Managerial Position	16.5%
Arts, Technical & Engineering	15.6%
Owner or Part-owner of Company	14.0%
Sales	10.2%
Computers	8.1%
Teaching	6.2%
Medical (including Nursing, Dental, etc.)	5.8%
Construction	5.5%
Student	4.8%
Marketing & Advertising	4.6%
Clerical	4.5%
Secretarial	4.0%
Communications	2.7%
Law	1.3%
Sports	0.9%
Civil Service	0.8%
Armed Forces	0.5%

Income Information

Per an independent national research group study of individuals who have purchased and read the book **Dianetics**, 84% of **Dianetics** book readers felt that Dianetics helped people become more successful. One measurement of success is the amount of income one makes.

Today's average annual wage in the United States is $22,563: Of Scientologists surveyed 60% make in excess of $30,000 annually, and almost 80% exceed $20,000. Clearly the overwhelming majority of Scientologists have achieved greater success.

Scientologists do not look toward others to help them survive. They work hard to support themselves and their families. The percentage of Scientologists on welfare (which includes Scientologists in such countries as Sweden, Denmark and the United Kingdom where public assistance is even more prevalent than in the United States) is less than half of the average in the United States, which today is estimated at 4%.

Do you receive welfare?

NO

98.1%

What is your average yearly income bracket since Scientology?

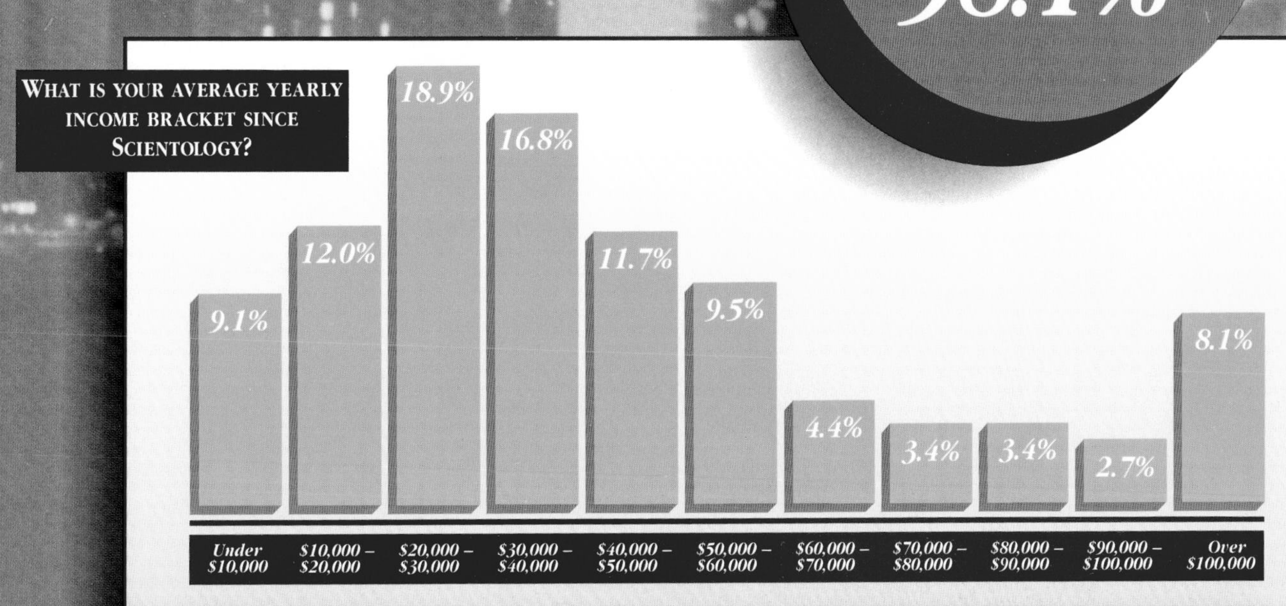

SCIENTOLOGISTS' HEALTH

Scientologists make productive employees. Almost 75% report they are ill less often than they were before Scientology. More than half report that, in the last year, they did not miss any days of work due to illness, and over 85% fall under the United States absenteeism average of almost 5 days missed a year due to illness.

A health-and-employee-benefits insurance expert reviewed the medical expenses for the 1,200 staff of the Church of Scientology International. He stated that its per capita medical costs ran between 10% and 20% of the national average.

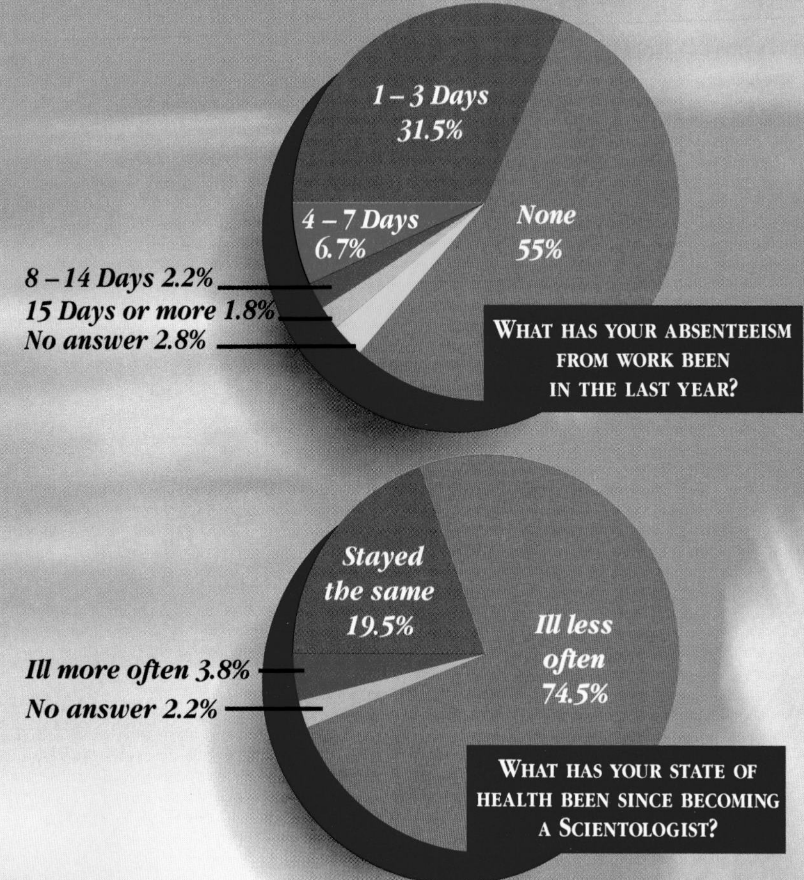

SCIENTOLOGISTS ARE LESS ACCIDENT-PRONE

Scientologists find that auditing and training greatly improve awareness of surroundings. In being more aware of one's environment, Scientologists tend to be less accident-prone than others. The following statistic shows that after Scientology the number of individuals involved in accidents is dramatically decreased.

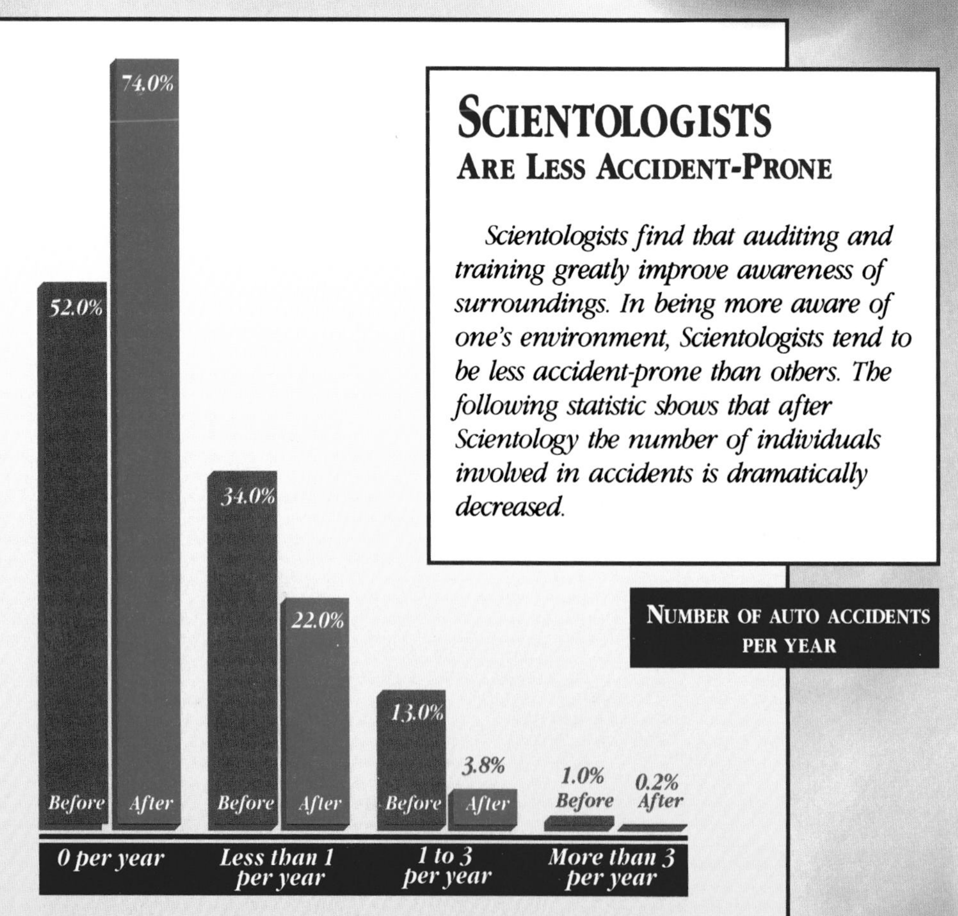

Exercise Habits of Scientologists

Scientologists are active and extroverted—over 75% exercise at least once a week.

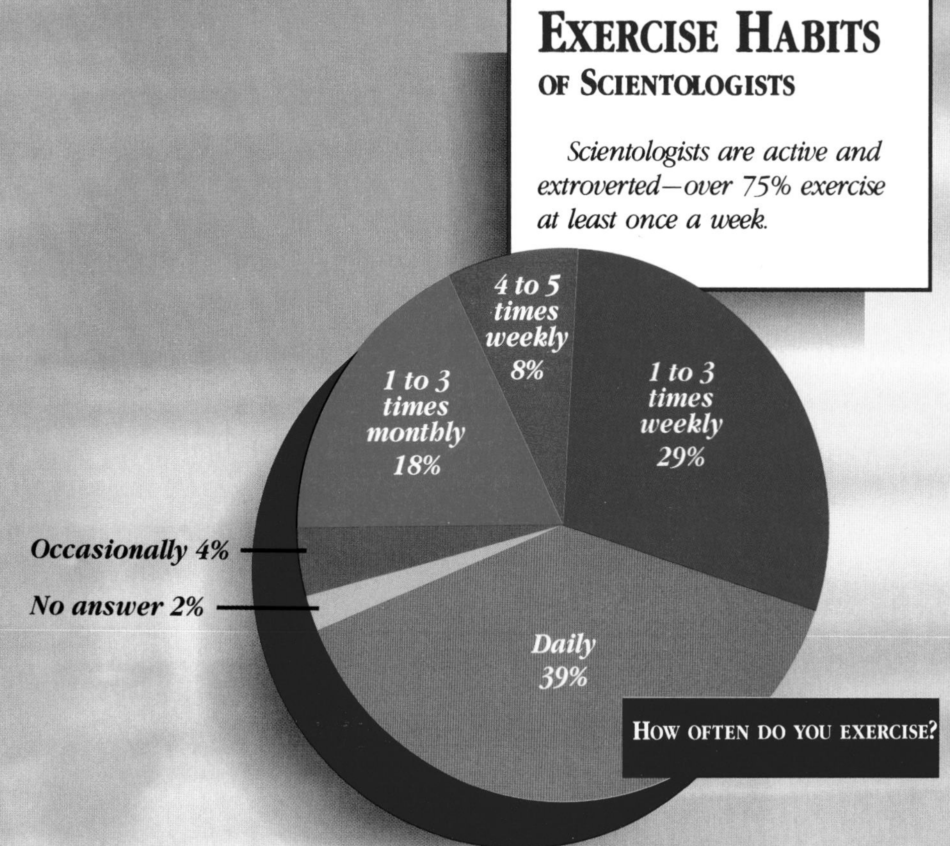

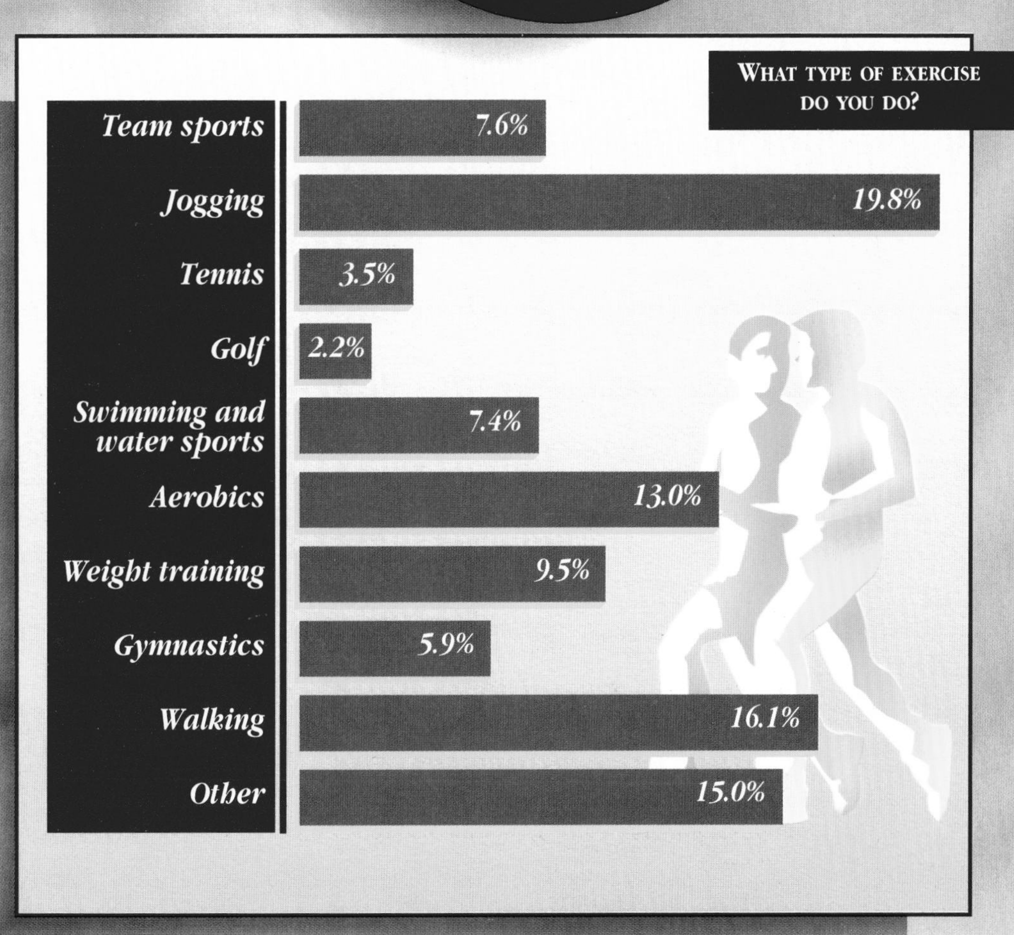

Drug Intake
of Scientologists

In a drug-ridden culture, it is a fact that all Scientologists are drug free. 100% say they take no street drugs at all. This statistic is even more dramatic when compared to the 1990 US government figures showing that over 50% of those between the ages of 18 to 25 use drugs.

Had you taken street drugs prior to being in Scientology?

YES 61.5%
NO 38.5%

Do you currently take street drugs?

NO 100%

Have you used medical drugs during the last year?

NO 81.6%
One time 11.1%
More than one time 5.0%
Currently taking medical drugs as prescribed 2.3%

ALCOHOL USE
BY SCIENTOLOGISTS
Recent alcohol-use surveys done in the United States revealed that 7% drank alcohol daily, 56% sometimes and 37% never. In comparison, Scientologists' use of alcohol is lower than averages for the US and no Scientologist surveyed drinks on a daily basis.
HOW OFTEN DO YOU USE ALCOHOL?
Never
50.8%
No answer 1.9%
1 – 5 times per year 11.0%
6 – 12 times per year 9.3%
Rarely/Special Occasions only 27.0%

Scientology Training

The training level of Scientologists reflects the constantly increasing number of new people coming into the Church and starting on the training Bridge. There are more people on Academy Level training than ever, and as their numbers grow, the volume of new people moving onto the beginning of the Bridge grows even faster.

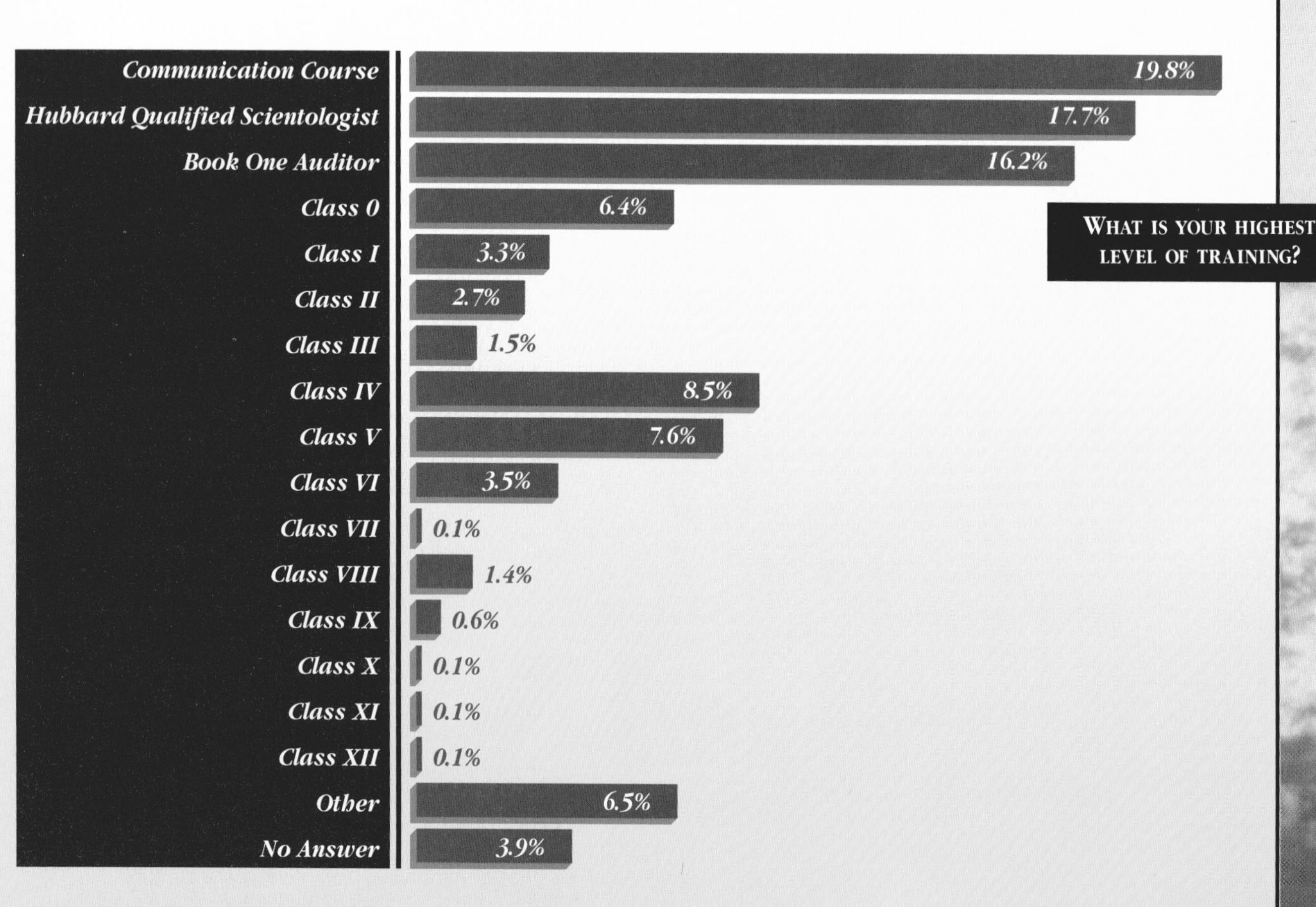

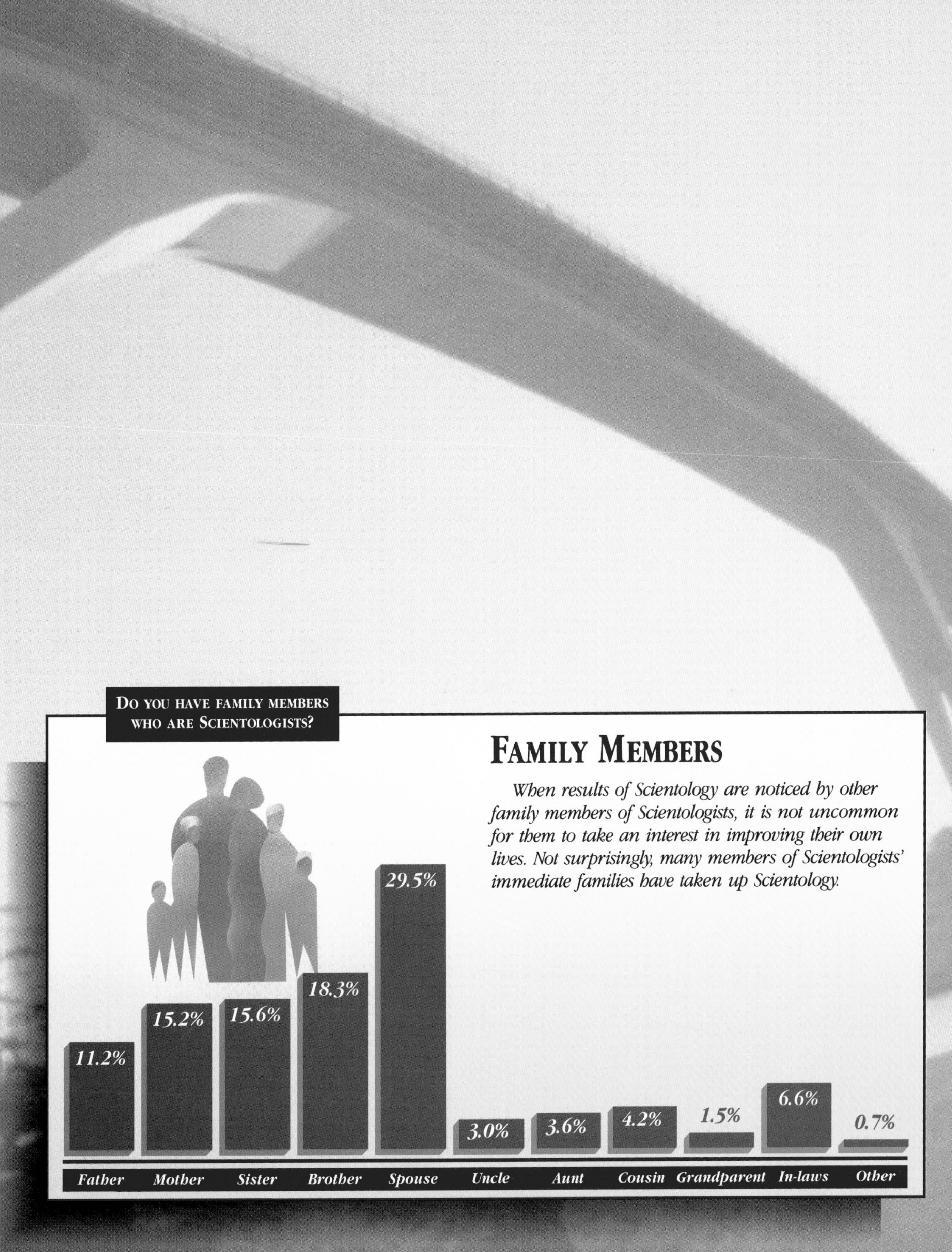

Do you have family members who are Scientologists?
FAMILY MEMBERS
When results of Scientology are noticed by other family members of Scientologists, it is not uncommon for them to take an interest in improving their own lives. Not surprisingly, many members of Scientologists' immediate families have taken up Scientology.
11.2%
15.2%
15.6%
18.3%
29.5%
3.0%
3.6%
4.2%
1.5%
6.6%
0.7%
Father
Mother
Sister
Brother
Spouse
Uncle
Aunt
Cousin
Grandparent
In-laws
Other

SCIENTOLOGISTS' ATTITUDES TOWARD LIFE

Scientologists live honest and ethical lives. They are interested in the well-being of others while achieving their own potentials. They have a positive outlook on life.

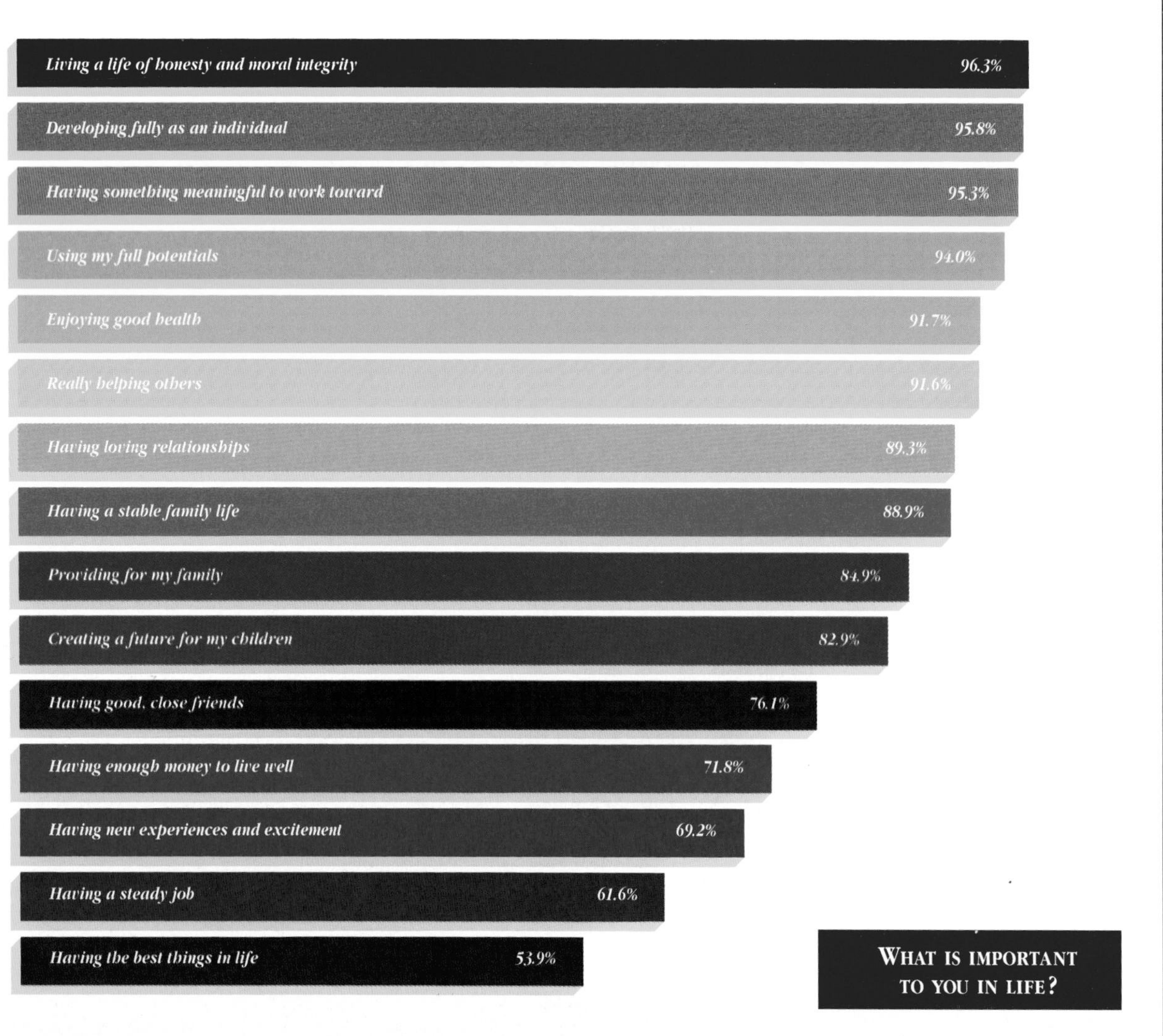

SCIENTOLOGISTS' INVOLVEMENT IN COMMUNITY ACTIVITIES

As seen in the preceding pages, Scientology helps improve and better one's own life. But for Scientologists it is just as important to become involved in activities to better the quality of life around them. As seen in this graph, Scientologists are involved in diverse activities to better the community and society.

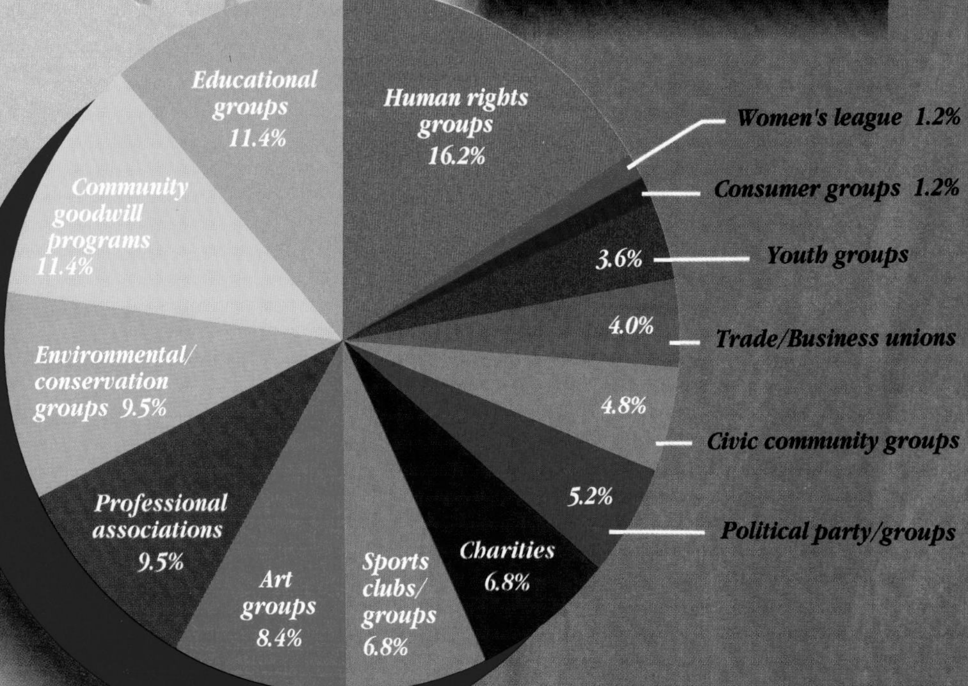

Scientology Works

As you read these words, the statistics of Scientology will have changed. A week, a month, a year from now they will have changed again as this vital religion reaches further into a troubled world. Its presence will be felt in more countries; its materials will be translated into more languages; it will continue to be the fastest growing religion in the world.

*The only possible reason for this phenomenon is that Scientology **works**. And once people read a book, hear a lecture or take a course they find for themselves that it works and pass the news on to others. Scientology offers man his greatest hope for a new world, free of the misery, pain and conflict that has plagued us for so long.*

CHAPTER 28

THE FIRSTS OF DIANETICS AND SCIENTOLOGY

Once upon a time, L. Ron Hubbard wrote, some remote ancestor discovered the secrets of controlling fire, and from that unsung first came a whole host of firsts upon which every succeeding culture was founded. Previously inedible foodstuffs could be made palatable. Inclement weather could be borne, metals could be forged. Civilization began. And although that mythical pyrotechnician has long been forgotten, the fruits of his invention still form the backbone of our culture today.

Similarly, with L. Ron Hubbard's discovery of Dianetics and Scientology came a whole host of firsts that will continue to reshape our culture. For when one has made a truly basic and fundamental discovery in any field, many lesser discoveries proceed thereafter and many "firsts" occur. This has been the case with Dianetics and Scientology.

To begin with, Dianetics and Scientology offer the first axiomatic construction of the basic laws of thought and behavior in man. These axioms predict and explain all questions relating to human behavior and so constitute an achievement that many had previously attempted to no avail. It was also through the course of his initial research that Mr. Hubbard discovered the dynamic principle of all existence: Survive.

With Dianetics and Scientology came the first description and classification of all parts of the human mind, thus correcting decades-old fallacies found in Freudian theory and the work of Pavlov, including the false notion that man cannot remember before the age of three.

And with this delineation of the mind, comes the first workable description of the so-called unconscious mind—which, in fact, was shown not to be unconscious, but merely hidden. Following this discovery, Mr. Hubbard provided the man in the street with the first means whereby anyone could apply simple techniques to better themselves and their fellows—Dianetics.

Of no less importance, particularly when considering future generations, is Mr. Hubbard's discovery that regardless of all earlier claims to the contrary, the human fetus is acutely aware of his environment—what is said in the mother's presence, what she ingests and any injuries she may suffer. So, too, is the child acutely aware of his environment at birth. And only by safeguarding these very formative periods, can one safeguard his future.

From the utilization of Scientology and Dianetics principles comes the first effective guidelines for the raising of children, the resolution of marital difficulties and maintaining the well-being of the family. Previously, theories on family life were derived primarily from psychology, and proved not only useless but, in many instances, destructive.

Although psychology and psychiatry have long held that one's IQ is inherent and fixed, the application of Dianetics and

Scientology auditing has proved this not to be true. Intelligence can be raised, as thousands of case histories show.

Dianetics and Scientology are the first technologies of the mind and spirit subjected to validation tests, which confirm Mr. Hubbard's projections. And, in consequence, Scientology and Dianetics became the first to offer man truly new states of existence far in excess of anything previously imagined possible.

Scientology was the first to isolate the basic life unit, i.e., that which perceives and generates energy, but is distinct from either the mind or body. This discovery resolves long-outstanding questions and has enormous impact on the lives of millions around the world.

From the revelations of Scientology came the first complete understanding of the phenomenon of death, the first real definition of man's spiritual potential and a truly eternal view of his destiny.

Moreover, Scientology offered man the first means of determining for himself what it means to be a spirit, delineating his potentials, the ways in which he operates and his relationship to the universe.

Dianetics was the first subject to determine the *exact* cause of psychosomatic illness, offering a provenly workable resolution to such. Correlative to this, Dianetics proved to be the earliest field to establish that function monitors structure, despite widespread medical beliefs to the contrary. Thus it was determined that the mind could indeed change the body and, that by addressing mental problems, one could radically enhance the body's ability to heal itself. Similarly, the tenets of Scientology defined, for the first time, the mechanistic limits of medicine.

Dianetics was the first to not only define the sources of psychosomatic illness but also the *extent* of the mind's impingement on the body. Freud and Breuer had vaguely known that psychic trauma led to hysterical paralysis, digestive dysfunctions and other ailments. Before Dianetics the severity and scope of psychosomatic illness was not known.

The Scientology E-Meter is the first device to accurately measure thought.

As Mr. Hubbard continued his research into mental phenomena, he soon made another revolutionary discovery: the Emotional Tone Scale, whereby human emotions are plotted in exact ascending sequence to enable the prediction and analysis of human behavior.

Mr. Hubbard's emergency assists provide the first delineation of how an injury affects the communication channels of the body—how a knowledge of nerve and energy flows can lead to truly lifesaving results through a restoration of communication to injured body parts.

Mr. Hubbard was also the first to determine the effects of aspirin and other pain depressants and soporifics on the mind and nervous system, and how to eliminate those effects.

Equally dramatic are Mr. Hubbard's discoveries relating to psychosis, or the obsessive desire to destroy. In 1970, the true cause of psychosis was isolated, and subsequently, Mr. Hubbard offered the first and only remedy for the condition. This, quite naturally, eliminates the need for earlier barbaric treatments and makes possible an alleviation of insanity throughout the society.

Scientology offers man the first system of bettering individuals through the improvement of their communication skills, with techniques that greatly increase one's ability to relate to his fellows. Mr. Hubbard's discoveries on the subject, which included defining the component parts of communication and led to the communication formula, represent an entirely new approach to communication.

Part and parcel of the above, Scientology is the first to precisely isolate barriers to study and provide the means to remove those barriers. From this discovery came a technology whereby anyone could successfully study any subject and, just as importantly, could successfully *apply* the fruits of his study. With this breakthrough came also solutions to the mutinous and rebellious conduct which had become the order of the day in modern schools. In short, then, Scientology provided the first effective resolution of all problems relating to learning.

Also in the field of learning, Mr. Hubbard was the first to develop a speedy and permanent handling for both illiteracy and "hidden illiteracy," thus stripping away the reasons why one cannot clearly comprehend what he reads, writes and hears and why others cannot comprehend his communication. Inclusive in these discoveries, Mr. Hubbard offers a revolutionary approach to English grammar, which constitutes the last word on this long-misunderstood subject.

Scientology is also the first to make whole classes of backward children averagely bright using drills which the teacher can do for a few minutes a day. Never before had something like this been accomplished.

Because one cannot address the problems of modern society without also addressing the problems of substance abuse, Mr. Hubbard also became the first to develop an entirely workable means of handling drug and alcohol addiction. Contained within his revolutionary solution to substance abuse is a technology for not only eradicating the craving for drugs and alcohol, but also the reason why one began taking such substances in the first place.

Mr. Hubbard was also the first to discover that, even long after one has ceased taking drugs, residual amounts of those drugs still remain in the body's fatty tissues. Mr. Hubbard's *Purification program* is the first means of ridding the body of environmental toxins picked up through the normal course of living in a highly polluted world.

Mr. Hubbard examined the questions of management—a subject that, like the mind, man previously had no real conception of and certainly no means of resolving. From this examination came the first precise tools of management, including the first effective methods of monitoring production by statistics, and of reversing the downward trend of any organization. In a related study, Mr. Hubbard further determined the first means of resolving all difficulties in the workplace, while offering principles to handle exhaustion, reduce injuries and vastly increase efficiency.

Mr. Hubbard addressed the question of ethics, and from that investigation came the world's first wholly rational ethics system whereby anyone can better his condition in any area of his existence. Also as part of this research, he determined the root cause of criminality, the precise mechanism whereby transgressions lead to increasing disability and unhappiness, and exactly how to restore one's happiness.

Mr. Hubbard may be further credited with the first breakthrough in centuries on the subject of logic, which had previously lacked any applicable use. Mr. Hubbard's discoveries on the subject offer man a truly workable breakdown of the subject, define its terms and offer methods to facilitate the perception, isolation and resolution of any problem.

Scientology offers the first real answer to that age-old question, "What causes war?" For although it was commonly held that "It takes two to make a fight," Mr. Hubbard found that behind every conflict is a hidden third party. With the application of this principle, any conflict may be resolved.

Just as questions of ethics and logic had baffled men for centuries, so, too, had the subject of aesthetics. Addressing the subject as a matter of "pure research," he devised the first workable definition of *art* and the first codification of the subject—which has led to a full revitalization of talents for many of the world's most respected figures of literature, music, drama and other arts. Mr. Hubbard was first to answer the question, "How good does a work of art have to be?"

These, then, are some of the firsts of Dianetics and Scientology. More important, however, are what can be accomplished with them. If one honestly avails himself of the technology and if one sincerely applies himself to gaining the benefits offered, there are apparently no limits to what can be achieved in Scientology.

Many, many people, millions in fact, have partaken of the services of Dianetics and Scientology over the last four decades. Their experiences point to the indisputable fact that Scientology, when properly applied to a person who is honestly seeking to improve and who is willing to communicate, produces results which match or exceed anyone's expectations.

A wide, wide range of benefits have been reported by Scientologists from their participation in Scientology. The conditions that can be improved by wholehearted application of the technology have been thoroughly documented since the 1940s. Following is a long and varied enumeration of what individuals have reported that Scientology achieves and the conditions it handles. None of these benefits are claims made by the Church; they are simply statements made by individuals about what they have achieved.

Although we shall never forget the name of L. Ron Hubbard, as we have forgotten that first bold experimenter with fire, the end results are quite similar: With fire came the means to establish civilization; with Dianetics and Scientology come the means to make a civilization of which we can be proud.

WHAT INDIVIDUALS SAY THEY HAVE ACHIEVED FROM SCIENTOLOGY

- Increased efficiency
- Increased energy and vitality
- Increased self-confidence
- Increased intelligence quotient
- Alleviation of neuroses
- Alleviation of psychoses
- Relief from mental trauma of injury or illness
- Faster recovery from broken bones, bruises, burns and injuries
- Alleviation of illness symptoms, colds, fevers, coughs and the like
- Salvaged marriages
- Happier relationships
- Ability to study any subject and be able to understand and apply it
- Improved school grades
- Better work habits
- Recovery from bereavement over loss
- Alleviation of psychosomatic illness
- Alleviation of painful memories
- Alleviation of postpartum depression
- Better communication skills
- Certainty of oneself as a spiritual being able to exist separate from the body
- Better performance in athletics

- Increased ability in artistic endeavors
- Increased literacy and ability to express oneself easily and clearly, both verbally and in writing
- Increased ability to understand others
- Ability to communicate freely with anyone on any subject
- Ability to recognize the source of problems and make them vanish
- Greater affinity for others
- Better relations at work
- Fewer problems in life
- Fewer colds and illnesses
- Fewer days absent from work
- Relief from the hostilities and sufferings of life
- Freedom from the upsets of the past and ability to face the future
- Freedom from fixed conditions and increased ability to do new things
- Increased well-being
- Ability to handle sources of personal suppression
- Certainty of one's immortality
- Increased self-determinism
- Freedom from the restimulative effects of drug residuals and other toxins
- More enjoyment from work
- Relief from the harmful effects of drugs, medicine or alcohol
- Better organization in one's life
- More and better friendships
- Increased competence
- Alleviation of cruel impulses and chronic unwanted conditions
- Increased personal stability
- Improved memory
- Raised ethical standards
- Ability to think clearly and rationally
- Improved relationships with others
- Improved family relations
- Rehabilitation of criminals
- Better rearing of children
- Improved reaction time
- Improved perceptions (sight, hearing, taste, etc.)
- Fewer physical ailments
- Improved concentration
- Rehabilitation of drug addicts and habitual drug users
- Restoration of sense of self-worth
- Alleviation of guilt feelings
- Increased creativity
- Increased productivity at work
- Increased happiness

Chapter 29

The History of Scientology's Expansion

The story of Dianetics and Scientology expansion is a simple one. Having developed the world's first workable technology of the mind and an applied religious philosophy that struck a vital chord in so many people, L. Ron Hubbard found that word of his discoveries began to spread. And as he continued researching, his further milestone discoveries created greater and greater interest.

In order to make these discoveries available, training centers, missions and churches were founded; and as more and more people discovered that Dianetics and Scientology worked, the cycle perpetuated itself.

This is the broad view. For a real sense of the story, however, one must return to early January 1950, when word of the forthcoming *Dianetics: The Modern Science of Mental Health* generated so many advanced orders that the publisher literally had to force his way past a mound of envelopes that had been dropped through the mail slot of his office door.

Dianetics Bursts on the Scene

Published on May 9, 1950, *Dianetics: The Modern Science of Mental Health* quickly led to a national movement. Bookstores, unable to keep copies on the shelves, slipped them beneath the counters for favored customers. Campus discussion groups and Dianetics clubs sprang up from coast to coast. Having grasped the essentials of Dianetics from their reading, thousands were either auditing or receiving auditing, while a number of hospitals adopted Mr. Hubbard's technology as the *only* effective means of helping those suffering from psychosomatic ills. As for the author, by late summer 1950, readers were actually camping on his lawn in the hopes that he might consent to offer personal instruction.

To meet this demand, the Hubbard Dianetic Research Foundation opened in Elizabeth, New Jersey in June 1950. There, Mr. Hubbard delivered the first Professional Auditors Course to students arriving from across the nation. With sales of the book approaching the 100,000 mark, five more branch offices soon opened in Chicago; New York; Washington, DC; Los Angeles and Hawaii.

Concurrent with the establishment of the Dianetics offices, those first hectic months after publication saw Mr. Hubbard on the lecture circuit—first to Los Angeles where, with little promotion, more than 6,000 people welcomed him to the Shrine Auditorium; then on to the San Francisco Bay area for a series of lectures in Oakland. Returning to Los Angeles, Mr. Hubbard continued lecturing and instructing students. When these students returned to their home towns to audit friends, family members and associates—the word continued to spread.

Having spent the spring of 1951 in pre-communist Havana, Cuba, where relative anonymity afforded him the opportunity to complete his second major work on Dianetics, *Science of Survival,* Mr. Hubbard accepted an offer to pursue his research and instruction at a newly opened Dianetics Foundation in Wichita, Kansas.

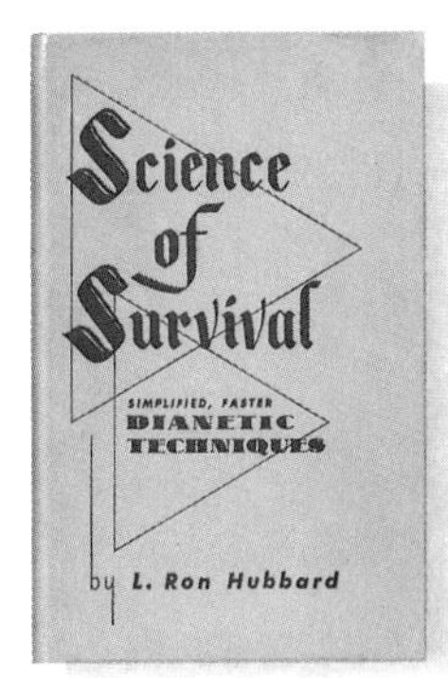

*The first editions of **Dianetics: The Modern Science of Mental Health** and **Science of Survival**, released in 1950/51*

Here Mr. Hubbard formed the first organization that he himself actually administered, the Hubbard College. This organization trained auditors under his personal supervision, and only when those auditors could competently demonstrate auditing skills and results were they certified.

As news of Mr. Hubbard's return to the United States circulated, scores of students appeared, so that by June 1951 the First Annual Conference of Hubbard Dianetic Auditors brought 114 leading auditors to Wichita. Thereafter, Mr. Hubbard continued to lecture and oversee auditor training, while delivering a series of evening talks to the Wichita Chamber of Commerce on how his discoveries might be employed to expand their community.

Scientology Is Announced

With the continuation of his research through the autumn and early winter of 1951, Dianetics auditors were invited to study a new subject, one which would place them squarely in the spiritual realm—Scientology. By early spring 1952, some 15,000 persons were utilizing Scientology principles toward the betterment of their lives.

In order to train and audit these founding Scientologists, a Scientology center was established at 1407 North Central Avenue, Phoenix, Arizona. There, the recently formed Hubbard Association of Scientologists International (HASI) offered two classes of membership, one technical and one general. To keep HASI members informed of technical breakthroughs and Association news, the first *Journal of Scientology* was published in August 1952—a typewritten mimeograph, partially funded with paid notices from HASI members offering instruction and auditing in such cities as Boston; Detroit; Philadelphia; Chicago; Honolulu; and Little Rock, Arkansas.

As news of Scientology moved east across the Atlantic and interest took root in England, Mr. Hubbard was asked to lecture in London. Arriving in September 1952, he found a surprisingly substantial Scientology community. Under his supervision, England soon had nine certified Scientology auditors and many more students in training at the London center. And to help ensure the growth rate continued, introductory lectures were given in London's Hyde Park.

Back in the United States, Scientologists were equally enthusiastic, touring the length and breadth of California to offer free auditing demonstrations and Group Processing—all, as the *Journal* reported, "in a very spirited fashion."

The Philadelphia Doctorate Course

After delivering a series of lectures to the newly formed Hubbard Association of Scientologists in London and completing his landmark work, *Scientology 8-8008,* Mr. Hubbard returned to the United States for a celebrated series of December 1952 lectures in Philadelphia. Known as the *Philadelphia Doctorate Course,* these lectures described the full range of man's spiritual potential as well as a wide analysis of human behavior. As recordings of these lectures began to circulate throughout the Scientology field, and a third printing of *Scientology 8-8008* rolled off the press, the ranks of Scientology kept increasing on both sides of the Atlantic.

By early 1953, Mr. Hubbard resumed his instruction of auditors at the Hubbard Association of Scientologists International center in Marlborough Place, London. The organization now boasted many more auditors in training and a burgeoning field of preclears. Concurrently, American Scientologists opened new centers in Houston, Texas; Hollywood and El Cerrito, California. In order to apprise them of the latest technical breakthroughs, the Hubbard Communications Office in London opened and the first *Professional Auditor's Bulletins* were published.

The Church Is Born

"After a very careful examination of a poll," declared Scientologists in a 1954 *Journal of Scientology,* "one would say very bluntly: Scientology fills the need for a religion." Consequently, and independently of

Mr. Hubbard, the first Church of Scientology was founded by parishioners in Los Angeles.

At about the same time in Phoenix, a major Scientology and Dianetics congress was soon underway. Featuring L. Ron Hubbard's lectures, seminars and auditing demonstrations, the congress attracted 450 Scientologists from across the United States.

Also indicative of expansion through this period: news that Scientology had taken root in Australia; word from South Africa where 35 Scientologists had enrolled on a course taught in Durban; a notice from New Zealand (which now had a church in Auckland) that a Phoenix-trained auditor opened a course for 24 new Scientologists, and letters from Tel Aviv and Cairo where Scientologists were desperately hungry for more books. All told, by the summer of 1955 there were eight buildings in Mr. Hubbard's Phoenix center, and 22 full-time staff members.

Although still lagging in comparison, Great Britain now boasted nearly 500 auditors offering services in such towns as Farnham, West Croydon and Liverpool. As the worldwide Scientology network grew, Mr. Hubbard moved to more centrally located Washington, DC where, in July 1955, the Founding Church of Scientology and the first Academy of Scientology were formed. Here also, the first Scientology distribution center was established to oversee the printing and dissemination of material around the world. To ease the administration of this now sizable organization, Mr. Hubbard drafted the first of what would ultimately be volumes of administrative policies laying out the functions, actions and duties of the organization.

Books Create Worldwide Growth

Dissemination, L. Ron Hubbard advised in January of 1957, was a matter of getting Scientology books into the hands of the public. The prolific Mr. Hubbard had by now written *The Fundamentals of Thought, The Problems of Work, Scientology: A History of Man, Self Analysis in Scientology* and *How to Live Though an Executive.* Inspired by his words, Scientologists distributed books at an unprecedented rate. As a result of the growth that followed, the Hubbard Association of Scientologists International gathered in Washington, DC to appoint a new secretary for Great Britain to help oversee the broadening activities throughout the British Isles. Also resolved at that Washington conference: the establishment of offices in the then Union of South Africa, where the Church of Scientology of Johannesburg had also been founded. Nor was South Africa the only far-flung land where Scientology was taking root, for as of June 1958 *Scientology: The Fundamentals of Thought* had been translated into Greek.

Returning to London in the fall of 1958, after lectures in Washington, Mr. Hubbard found plans in place for a new London educational center. The center was to utilize Scientology techniques for the advancement of British schoolchildren. The project sparked so much interest among Londoners that a number of those who turned up for the first public lecture had to be turned away for want of available seating.

The hall was also crowded in New Delhi when a sister project initiated a course to train ranking members of the Indian government (including the Minister of Labor) on how Scientology principles might be utilized in the educational realm.

A few thousand miles to the southeast, excitement continued to build in Auckland, New Zealand where the book campaign was in full swing and demand was so high that the local Scientology bookstore regularly sold out its stock. Keeping books in stock also proved a problem in Australia, South Africa, France and outlying areas of England and the United States—continents now dotted with Scientology churches and missions. The largest concentration, however, still remained in the United States, where some 500 turned up at Washington, DC's Shoreham Hotel in July 1959 for 9 hours of lectures by L. Ron Hubbard on new clearing procedures. Eight weeks later another 400 met at London's Royal Empire Society Hall in Trafalgar Square, while dozens of advanced students attended the First Melbourne Advanced Clinical Course.

Saint Hill Manor near East Grinstead in Sussex, England. The Saint Hill Castle, home of the Advanced Organization church, is in the background.

The Move to Saint Hill

To establish a central training, management and dissemination point, Mr. Hubbard and his family moved to Saint Hill Manor in East Grinstead, Sussex, England. Here, in July 1959, the Hubbard Communications Office Worldwide was established. In keeping with his advice from two years earlier, one of the first departments to be established was a shipping office for books—and orders poured in so quickly that they could not be filled fast enough. To help staff members cope with the demand for books and services, 1959 saw such administrative policy letters as "How to Handle Work" and "How to Get Approval of Actions and Projects."

"Hubbard Communications Office is now safely and securely established at Saint Hill Manor, East Grinstead, Sussex," Mr. Hubbard had written in the closing days of 1959, and by early 1960 the half-hundred acres at Saint Hill were the scene of much activity. Cables and telegrams arrived at all hours of the day and night with requests for more books, advice and reports of expansion in 11 different countries.

To ensure orderly growth, Mr. Hubbard continued his study of administrative procedure, codifying the basic principles and drafting appropriate policy letters. Meanwhile, the call went out for staff to help with everything from delivering messages and typing, to training and auditing, to executive functions.

With the firm establishment of these worldwide organizational basics at Saint Hill the previous summer, Scientology entered into an accelerated period of expansion through 1960. After yet more lectures at his home, Mr. Hubbard set off to South Africa in September. There, he standardized the administration of a steadily building organization before moving on to Washington for another series of lectures. Returning to Saint Hill in early January 1961, he found letters from such frontiers as Cuba, where a resident doctor was attempting to organize a correspondence course; Thailand, where pioneer Scientologists offered an introductory Scientology course to the monks of a Bangkok monastery; and Israel, where a number of teachers were reading *Dianetics*. There were also letters from Bombay where educators were utilizing Scientology principles, and more orders for books from Peoria, Illinois to Auckland, New Zealand.

The Saint Hill Special Briefing Course

Following another trip to South Africa in late January of 1961, when another church was founded in Cape Town, Mr. Hubbard returned to Saint Hill and initiated the famed Saint Hill Special Briefing Course. In a matter of months, study space was at such a premium that students were regularly found auditing on the tennis court and lawns—prompting Mr. Hubbard to initiate plans for the conversion of buildings. And as those Briefing Course graduates returned to their home towns telling of their successes, new pioneer groups were soon established.

Armed with the fruits of new technical breakthroughs, Scientologists continued to reach into society—into Mexico where a Spanish translation of *Scientology: The Fundamentals of Thought* had sparked a small movement in Mexico City; and into France where a pair of Scientologists had recently founded a Parisian church of Scientology and now needed French translations of Scientology materials.

Once again, to guarantee a steady but orderly rate of expansion, Mr. Hubbard drafted further administrative policy letters in 1963 to outline such organizational fundamentals as the delineation of duties for a staff member and the importance of administration. Through the implementation of these and other policy letters, as well as steady dissemination in the field, the mid-60s saw 4 newly founded Scientology churches around the world, including Port Elizabeth and Durban, South Africa; Detroit, Michigan; and Honolulu, Hawaii. With these churches in place, the total number of Scientology churches had reached 13 by the end of 1964.

Meanwhile, as Scientologists had continued to arrive at Saint Hill for training and auditing, the organizational staff likewise increased. Mr. Hubbard, continuing his technical research and breakthroughs, presented 7 lectures on the field of education in 1964, which formed the basis of study technology.

By 1965, more than 200 staff provided services to Scientologists and, all told, some 1,000 hours of auditing were delivered every week. To impress upon them just how vital it was to maintain standard application of Dianetics and Scientology through each and every one of those hours, and, in fact, for all time, Mr. Hubbard issued 2 more administrative policy letters: the very critical issues "Keeping Scientology Working" and "Safeguarding Technology." Additionally, the first Foundation (at Saint Hill) was founded in June to meet the increasing demand of the local population for services during evenings and weekends.

The Bridge to Freedom

With the release of the Classification and Gradation Chart in September 1965, delineating the exact steps of auditing and training on the Bridge to Total Freedom, Scientologists now had an exact route to follow to achieve the state of Clear. This included the release of the Scientology Grades 0–IV to establish a firm foundation at the beginning of the Bridge.

Concurrent with his technical research, Mr. Hubbard had been examining the very basics of organization as part of his continuing efforts to make his technology readily available and standardly delivered. As a result, in November Mr. Hubbard announced the Seven-Division Organizing Board—immediately implemented at Saint Hill, sent out to organizations around the world, and becoming the standard pattern of operation still in use today.

In consequence, Scientology continued to reach new areas in Australia where more Scientology lectures and demonstrations were organized; in South Africa where a Cape Town Scientologist launched a course for businessmen; and in New Zealand where Scientologists wrote in their thanks for the new international *Auditor* magazine telling of technical advances and success. And with every issue of *The Auditor* came news from other corners of the world, instilling a sense of unity among Scientologists, be they in Alberta, Canada; Port Elizabeth, South Africa; Puerto Rico; or Glenrock, Illinois.

The State of Clear and Beyond

Continuing his technical research through the early months of 1966, L. Ron Hubbard announced a breakthrough of supreme importance: The state of Clear was now attained with certainty by any well-trained auditor. A few months later, Mr. Hubbard released the first two OT levels beyond the state of Clear, and with these new levels now available Scientologists flocked to Saint Hill from around the world.

By mid-May 1966, the first Clears were attesting at Saint Hill, and the routine attainment of this long-dreamed-of state was particularly meaningful to Scientologists. Clears were often featured on the cover of *The Auditor,* and returning to their homelands, were regularly called upon to speak. Their success, in turn, inspired others to move out into the world—auditing, setting up introductory courses and generally spreading the word. To that end, two enterprising Scientologists began translating Scientology materials into Danish, while others were either opening or expanding Scientology centers in Austin, Texas; Buffalo, New York; Manchester, England; Guadalajara, Mexico and The Hague, Netherlands.

With the pattern of organizations now in place and the field continuing to expand at a healthy rate, Mr. Hubbard took another critical step for the future. He resigned Scientology directorship to devote himself fully to further research. In September 1966, all his administrative duties were turned over to Executive Council Worldwide and 100 staff charged with the responsibility of administering the existing Scientology network and ensuring its further expansion.

The Sea Organization Begins

To support L. Ron Hubbard's ensuing research and the delivery of soon-to-be-released OT Levels III, IV, V and VI, the Sea Organization was formed on August 12, 1967. Its first operational vessels were the *Enchanter* (later rechristened the *Diana*) and the *Avon River* (rechristened the *Athena*). Within a few months the *Royal Scotman* (rechristened the *Apollo*), became the third vessel. With these research vessels operating and a dedicated team for support, Mr. Hubbard continued to provide Scientology with technical breakthrough after technical breakthrough.

OT III Released

On September 9, 1967, in a particularly important recorded message, Mr. Hubbard announced that he had discovered the means to eradicate those mental factors which stand in the way of peace and tolerance for mankind. This new level of the Scientology Bridge was OT III.

Further growth followed, with 104 organizations, missions and field groups in twelve countries around the world. All told, Scientologists were now delivering some 50,000 auditing hours per year. By the end of 1967 there were also over 500 Clears.

To provide Scientologists with the fruits of Mr. Hubbard's upper-level research, 1968 saw Sea Organization teams establish Advanced Organizations in Edinburgh, Scotland and Los Angeles, as well as an American Saint Hill Organization in Los Angeles.

The ***Apollo****, flagship of the Sea Organization from 1968 to 1975*

The year 1968 additionally signaled a significant boom in churches around the world. For instance, hundreds of students could be found in the Academy during any given course period. Likewise, San Francisco's newly formed church of Scientology, with 23 staff members, reported large numbers of students on course, as did Detroit, Toronto and London. More than 400 Scientologists convened at a Saint Hill graduation to hear those who had recently completed the OT levels and the one-thousandth Clear attested in March. A broader look at statistics revealed 15,000 professional auditors, and by this time, some 3,000,000 people had purchased Scientology books or services from 37 official Scientology churches worldwide.

As Scientologists continued to reach deeper and deeper into society, however, they increasingly came face to face with society's problems—in particular, drug abuse which had risen to epidemic proportions by 1968. To help reverse the trend, Mr. Hubbard began a comprehensive research program to search out a means to alleviate not only the effects of drug abuse but also the causes. This work led to the first Drug Rundown in 1968, allowing still more to ascend the Bridge.

The First Class VIII Auditors

To ensure that each and every organization standardly delivered auditing services, Mr. Hubbard launched a new advanced training course in August 1968 to emphasize standard technical application. This was the Class VIII Auditor Course conducted aboard the *Apollo* and attended by top auditors from churches around the world.

With the release in 1969 of the Hubbard Standard Dianetics Course to simplify and standardize Dianetics procedures, and the earlier arrival of the first Class VIII graduates to ensure standardized application of all auditing, Scientology course rooms were soon packed, from New York to New South Wales. As more and more students continued up the Bridge, a third Advanced Organization and Saint Hill was opened in Denmark.

"By rehabilitating the artist," Mr. Hubbard had said, "one does much for rehabilitating the culture." With this incentive, the first Scientology Celebrity Centre was established in 1969. Aimed at assisting the now numerous artists and celebrities who had found Scientology technology indispensable to their creative well-being, the course rooms of the Los Angeles Celebrity Centre were soon also filled with students. In addition to regular Scientology services, Celebrity Centre provided a forum for poets, playwrights, actors, painters and musicians—all part of the effort to help revitalize the arts.

Meanwhile, by August 1970, as demand for advanced levels continued to increase, the Edinburgh Advanced Organization was forced to move to larger quarters at Saint Hill.

Flag Management Is Formed

In the interest of further expansion, L. Ron Hubbard developed a completely new system of management and established the Flag Bureaux aboard the *Apollo* in 1970 to carry out this function for all of Scientology. To relay and implement the Flag Bureaux's orders, liaison offices were opened in Los Angeles for the United States, Saint Hill for the United Kingdom and Copenhagen for Europe.

In April 1970, Mr. Hubbard invited executives from all churches to attend his Flag Executive Briefing Course on the flagship *Apollo.* The end result placed true administrative experts in all local churches. And with the later publication of the *Organization Executive Course* and *Management Series* volumes, all policy was now readily available to the 2,553 staff of the 118 churches and missions in 20 nations.

As of early 1971, 250 professional auditors had joined the Los Angeles Auditors Association to deliver the newly expanded Scientology Lower Grades. Later this same year, Mr. Hubbard released three new auditing rundowns: L10, L11 (the New Life Rundown) and L12 (the Flag OT Executive Rundown). These rundowns were delivered only by the first, specially trained Class XII Auditors aboard the *Apollo.* At the same time, fellow auditors were busy at newly formed churches in Las Vegas, Nevada; Pretoria, South Africa; Göteborg and Stockholm, Sweden; Copenhagen, Denmark; Munich, Germany; Plymouth, England; Buffalo, New York and Boston, Massachusetts.

Employing new technical releases containing refinements of study techniques to greatly speed students through their courses, 1972 saw Scientology increase in size under Sea Organization guidance. All told, these breakthroughs helped push the number of Clears to the 4,000 mark by early 1974; while future Clears stepped onto the Bridge at newly opened Scientology churches in Sacramento, California; Ottawa, Ontario; Manchester, England; Malmö, Sweden; Vancouver, British Columbia; Portland, Oregon and Vienna, Austria.

After months of research and compilation, the *Dianetics and Scientology Technical Dictionary* was completed in early 1975. This long-awaited work defined all Dianetics and Scientology words and abbreviations used in connection with auditing and training, and thus greatly aided study.

The Flag Land Base Established

Another milestone for 1975 was the landing of the Sea Organization, and the establishment of the Flag Land Base in Clearwater, Florida. Located in the 11-story Fort Harrison Hotel and the nearby Clearwater Bank Building, the Flag Land Base constituted the largest single Scientology organization in history. As the spiritual headquarters of the Church and the only place where preclears could receive the special L Rundowns, it was soon drawing Scientologists from all over the world.

Nineteen seventy-five also saw the opening of Chicago's church of Scientology, another church in Philadelphia and the first Canadian pocket book edition of *Dianetics.*

A new Spanish translation of *Dianetics* was released in Mexico in 1976, and some 12 million television viewers watched as Hispanic celebrities told of its benefits.

In August, 10,000 Scientologists convened for a convention in Anaheim, California. And all the while, Scientology and Dianetics continued to repair lives around the world: in the Philippines where business leaders discovered L. Ron Hubbard's technology, and in the slums of London where his study technology was put to good use helping impoverished children.

Approximately one hundred miles east of Los Angeles, at the desert community of La Quinta, Mr. Hubbard established a Scientology training film studio (Source Productions) in 1977. Under his personal direction, in an 8-month period, Source Productions produced a public Scientology information film and 7 technical instruction films to preserve the standard training and application of Scientology long into the future.

The same year, to accommodate the flood of Scientologists arriving for services, the 520,000 square foot Cedars of Lebanon complex in Hollywood was purchased—soon to be the new home of the Church of Scientology Los Angeles, the American Saint Hill Organization, the Advanced Organization and various administrative offices. This was also a big year for the Flag Land Base with the release of two L. Ron Hubbard written and directed public information films, *The Secret of Flag Results* and *The Case He Couldn't Crack.* And to help keep all running smoothly, L. Ron Hubbard's dictionary of Scientology management terms was released.

The Year of Technical Breakthroughs

Christened "The Year of Technical Breakthroughs," 1978 was another landmark with the release of New Era Dianetics, providing lightning-fast gains for those who were not yet Clear. In cities across the world—now including Oslo, Norway; Bern, Switzerland; and Milano, Italy—students entered course rooms to learn the techniques of NED.

Later that year, New Era Dianetics for OTs (New OT V) was introduced. As word of the truly extraordinary gains this level offered circulated, Scientologists began pouring into the Flag Land Base.

Still more technical releases were celebrated in 1979, most notably the Purification program to rid the body of harmful residuals of drugs and environmental pollutants.

In order to handle the subsequent flood of Scientologists arriving at Flag, the 100-room Sandcastle Hotel, half a mile from the Fort Harrison Hotel, was purchased and renovated.

By the end of June 1980, more than twenty new churches had been founded in locations as diverse as Brussels, Belgium and Bogotá, Colombia.

New OT VI and VII Released

The most significant achievement of 1980 was the release in September of another two OT levels, New OT VI and VII. Expanding the scope of gains available for the individual beyond any commonly envisioned state, these levels were soon bringing still more Scientologists to the Flag Land Base.

Mr. Hubbard issued several new bulletins on how best to make Scientology known in the early 1980s; and cities where demand was so great that new Scientology churches were opened included: Phoenix, Arizona; Edmonton, Canada; Albuquerque, New Mexico; Berlin, Germany; Geneva, Switzerland; Tel Aviv, Israel; Canberra, Australia; Cincinnati, Ohio; Quebec, Canada and four in Mexico City.

A part of Golden Era Productions' facilities where Scientology religious training films and audio properties are produced and technical compilations occur

The first L. Ron Hubbard lecture series on cassette was released in 1980 by Golden Era Productions—formerly Source Productions at La Quinta and now relocated to a nearby 500-acre property to facilitate not only film production, but also audio and technical compilations for speeding Scientologists up the Bridge. And for an indication of just how big Scientology had grown by 1980: Dianetics and Scientology were now available in 52 countries at 328 organizations, missions and auditor groups, serviced by 5,150 staff who helped deliver 794,990 auditing hours that year.

With liaison offices now established for Canada and Latin America, a total of 8 such offices were ensuring steady expansion under Sea Organization direction. As of 1981, twelve of Mr. Hubbard's technical training films were completed and released to help standardize Scientology training. Mr. Hubbard also released the Sunshine Rundown to heighten one's awareness of new abilities as a Clear.

New Directions in Management

Nineteen eighty-one additionally saw several key administrative changes, initiated in response to a problem that many organizations suffer through rapid expansionary periods. In 1981, after a series of Sea Organization inspections of the Guardian's Office (GO), it was found that the GO—a small unit of the Church established in 1966 to protect the Church from external threats—had become entirely autonomous, operating without regard to Mr. Hubbard's policies and was, in fact, attempting to usurp control of the Church.

Further investigation by Sea Org executives revealed that the GO's corruption was so extensive it had been hindering Church expansion internationally—inhibiting both public and staff from advancing up the Bridge. As a result of these investigations, Sea Org officials disbanded the Guardian's Office entirely.

To safeguard these administrative changes, the corporate structure of the Church was updated and the Church of Scientology International was formed as the international mother church.

With all Church organizations now fully aligned with Mr. Hubbard's policies, preclears began moving far more speedily and confidently to Clear and beyond. As a result, there was a surge in the total number of Clears and OTs produced at the Flag Land Base and Advanced Organizations.

Nineteen eighty-two brought the formation of the Religious Technology Center, a corporation to which L. Ron Hubbard donated all trademarks of Dianetics and Scientology. Its purpose: To safeguard the proper use of trademarks, to protect the public and to make sure that the powerful technology of Dianetics and Scientology remains in good hands and is properly used.

To cope with the new administrative load, July of 1982 saw the establishment of the International Network of Computer Organized Management (INCOMM). Utilizing computer systems, based upon Mr. Hubbard's developments in the field, INCOMM fully computerized international church management to facilitate efficiency of operations and the huge rate of Scientology expansion.

As just one more indication of how quickly Scientology was now expanding through the early 1980s, a new Advanced Organization opened in Sydney, Australia.

Dianetics: *Perennial Bestseller*

To spread word of technical breakthroughs and generally inform the world of just what Scientology has to offer, the Planetary Dissemination Organization was founded in 1983. One of the organization's first tasks: to make *Dianetics* even more widely available. And the result a few months later: *Dianetics* once again reached the bestseller lists with the 7 millionth copy sold.

Concurrently, new churches were founded in Hamburg, Bern, Zurich and Verona, soon followed in the US with churches in Long Island, New York and Orange County, California. And to serve the artistic community in New York, a Celebrity Centre organization was opened there.

Two more German churches opened in 1984 and, by then, scores of Scientology churches and missions spanned the globe. It seemed only appropriate then, that on October 7, 1984 the International Association of Scientologists was formed at Saint Hill in England, to unite Scientologists from all nations.

Man has long suffered from inability to consistently pursue his true purposes, and in 1984 Mr. Hubbard released the solution to such problems: the False Purpose Rundown. As with all earlier technical releases, Scientology course rooms from Sydney to St. Louis were soon filled with auditors learning how to remove those factors which obscure a being's real purposes. So great were the numbers of students and preclears at the Flag Land Base that the Flag Bureaux, previously located in Clearwater, was moved to Los Angeles in order to make more room for more delivery to parishioners and consolidate management. As an added bonus, Scientologists were soon to be listening to the first of Mr. Hubbard's lectures in Clearsound—a revolutionary development in tape restoration making possible the release of all of Mr. Hubbard's lectures from 1950 forward.

Nineteen eighty-five saw the 150th church open in Monza, Italy. To fill the demand around the world for taped lectures (over 90,000 students and preclears completed services in 1985) a full production and recording studio was established at Golden Era Productions. And, looking to the future, for a glimpse of what was to come: Sea Organization teams began scouting for a new motor vessel for the delivery of Scientology's most advanced auditing level.

While the Sea Organization was ensuring the availability of the OT levels, other Scientologists were making L. Ron Hubbard's work better known to those who had not yet stepped onto the Bridge. As a result of these efforts: copies of *Dianetics* selling

*The Sea Org Motor Vessel **Freewinds** sailed on her maiden voyage out of Curaçao on June 6, 1988.*

in Gdańsk, Poland for the first time; a Peruvian mission established in Lima; a team of three Scientologists distributing Scientology materials in Hong Kong; and, a Celebrity Centre in Nashville, Tennessee opening its doors in 1987. New Scientology missions also opened in Puerto Rico, North Carolina, Palm Springs and Zaire and—fulfilling the long-laid seeds—Ambala, India.

And lest one had any doubts as to just how many were now reaching for L. Ron Hubbard's works; *Dianetics* reached the number one position on the *New York Times* bestseller list. Concurrently, *Dianetics* was released, and became instantly popular in a new quarter—mainland China—with the first printing selling out in less than 2 weeks.

Painstakingly researched, the new fully up-to-date Scientology Academy Levels were released in the first days of 1988. Also in 1988, the greatly improved Mark Super VII E-Meter was released. Further plans to make L. Ron Hubbard technology available to larger numbers led to the formation of the Association for Better Living and Education (ABLE). Among other projects ABLE would soon help initiate—bringing L. Ron Hubbard study technology to classrooms in China where 190,000 copies of *Dianetics* had sold by this point. In order to handle equally impressive North American sales of L. Ron Hubbard books, Bridge Publications (formerly the Publications Organization, United States) moved into new and larger quarters in Los Angeles.

New OT VIII—Truth Revealed

After four years of intensive work locating, purchasing and refitting, the Sea Organization motor vessel was christened the *Freewinds*. Setting sail on June 6, 1988, she was not only the first Sea Organization vessel to see service in 13 years, but she is the only place where Scientologists can take the highest available step on the Bridge: New OT VIII, Truth Revealed.

The unveiling of two new facilities was cause for celebration among Scientologists in 1989. The first was the 12-story, 110,000-square-foot Hollywood Guaranty Building, which was to serve as the home of international church management. The second was the Saint Hill Castle, a building modeled after a medieval English castle, that Mr. Hubbard originally conceived and designed in 1965. It now offered advanced Scientology services and the Saint Hill Special Briefing Course. Three more new churches opened in 1989: one in Atlanta, Georgia; another in Hanover, Germany and the third in Stuttgart.

These three churches brought the total number of Scientology organizations, missions and field groups up to 830, with some 10,000 staff members delivering services to over 200,000 students and preclears for a grand total of 1.4 million auditing hours per year. That same year also saw Scientologists moving into society with 251 social reform groups and 164 social betterment groups.

While the demand for Dianetics and Scientology in China was growing, another Asian nation was responding in a significant way to Mr. Hubbard's technology: Japan. In a matter of months, the first Scientology church in Tokyo was delivering courses and auditing to scores of Japanese citizens.

RON
HUBBARD

Into the Nineties

With the full implementation of L. Ron Hubbard's policies, advices, directives and technical material, the early 1990s presaged a new era of unprecedented expansion.

Among the highlights: Thousands of Scientologists poured into their churches to enroll on the Hubbard Key to Life Course, first made available on May 9, 1990; the March 13, 1991 release of the complete *Organization Executive Course* and *Management Series* volumes containing all of L. Ron Hubbard's organizational policies; soon followed by the 18-volume collection of Mr. Hubbard's technical writings.

More than 700 invited guests—including leaders of the business community, the arts and political dignitaries—were on hand for the 1991 opening of the L. Ron Hubbard Life Exhibition in Hollywood.

Auditor's Day, 1991, celebrated the completion of a 5-year program to compile, verify as totally accurate, and make available all of L. Ron Hubbard's auditing and training technology on the Bridge to Total Freedom. And with this, the final Classification, Gradation and Awareness Chart was released at an event at Saint Hill in England.

In July 1992, the newly restored Celebrity Centre International was officially opened to service the many artists in Scientology.

And with the iron curtain down, such formerly inaccessible nations as Russia, Hungary and what had been East Germany, were soon reaching for L. Ron Hubbard's technology. To meet their needs, a Sea Org liaison office opened in Russia, while teams flew in to deliver Mr. Hubbard's educational and administrative technologies. And with those formerly Eastern-bloc nations now enjoying Mr. Hubbard's materials—bringing the total number of countries offering Scientology up to 74—new translations of his work followed. In all, there were now 422 translated titles available in 31 languages.

Finally, and for another view of just how broad Scientology had become—now that there were 1,039 Scientology organizations, missions and groups around the world—the yearly number of Scientology book sales of 1967 were currently exceeded every day. There were also over 1.5 million auditing hours delivered in 1991—or more auditing in just 12 days than in the whole of 1967, and a 1991 survey revealed that Dianetics and Scientology had become so widely known they were household words.

But however great the numbers become—the new preclears and auditors sitting down for their first session, the new readers picking up their first copies of *Dianetics*—the story of Scientology expansion is still a simple one: Having discovered that L. Ron Hubbard's technology works, people make it known to others.

The 1991 grand opening of the L. Ron Hubbard Life Exhibition, which contains 30 audiovisual displays depicting the life and accomplishments of Mr. Hubbard

CHAPTER 30

FUTURE PREDICTION OF SCIENTOLOGY

If a founding Scientologist had been asked in 1952 to predict the impact of Scientology on the world forty years later, would he have been able to imagine the extent to which it has grown today? Would he have been able to envision from a stucco building in Phoenix, Arizona, the more than one thousand churches, missions and groups that exist today? Would he have been able to envision the hundreds of thousands who have been helped to rid themselves of the curse of drugs, or the millions who have been placed on the road to literacy through the use of L. Ron Hubbard's technologies?

Surely, these pioneer Scientologists had some idea of what potential L. Ron Hubbard's discoveries held for mankind, just as today Scientologists envision even greater expansion in the future.

Today, Scientology is the fastest growing religion on the planet—and so long as Mr. Hubbard's technologies are available to all who wish to reach for them, and so long as they are applied standardly, Scientology will continue to grow.

To understand what this growth might mean to a troubled world, religious leaders, professionals, educators and others have offered the following predictions on the future of the Scientology religion.

"The movement founded by L. Ron Hubbard will engage itself increasingly in the design of a new world following the collapse of the Soviet Union and Communism. A new awakening of spiritual powers is taking place and his vision will help shape events."

Hans Janitschek
President
Society of Writers
United Nations

"Scientology has come a long way, and has grown in numbers.

"There are so many people of different types—and into different activities—art, human rights, rehabilitation and more.

"Obviously, it will last. It can be geared to individual interests, and even if the interests change, people can use the basic technology to adapt to new ones."

Loretta Needle, B.A.
University of Toronto

"Scientology is a practical religious theology which embodies the technology of helping people discover themselves and at the same time to become aware of the evils that plague our society, such as the prevalent use of dangerous psychiatric drugs.

"The pastoral counseling program of Scientology puts man in touch with reality and enhances and strengthens his relationship with God and his fellow man.

"The beauty of Scientology is you don't have to give up your religious upbringing to become a Scientologist. You can still remain in your original church.

"Scientology has a great future because it helps those who are in frustration and despair to shift their position to a helpful and useful one."

Rev. Dr. Leo Champion
Pastor
Fellowship Missionary
Baptist Church
Milwaukee, Wisconsin

"In looking at the future of Scientology, as a sociologist I am cautious about predicting long-range futures. But I may say this, if it is a futile undertaking it will not last, but if it has a providential function this will manifest itself in time. So it would be wise for us to let it be lest we be opposing providence in the age of religious freedom. This was Gamaliel's advice on the Christians to his fellow Jews. If it had continued to be taken (as it was by his immediate listeners) thousands of years of conflict between the great religions of the Book might have been saved. (Acts 5:34–39)"

Noel Ryan
Sociologist
Australia

"Like so many relatively new religions, the Church of Scientology has been forced to spend much of its time and resources fighting religious prejudice and prosecution. Despite those pressures, the Church has been a real force for good in the lives of many of its adherents and a champion of religious freedom."

Robin Johansen
Attorney and Religious
Freedom Fighter

"Your Church's noble principles of high ideals and ethical living along with the beliefs of accepting so many aspects of knowledge meets very close to the ideals of the American Institute of Islamic Studies. I find it a pleasure and privilege to reach out for common thoughts. The future looks so optimistic that we shall convey our common principles to the world side by side."

Amir Gillani
President
American Institute
of Islamic Studies
Toronto, Canada

"There are many Bible-believing Evangelicals and others in the established Christian community who have not yet accepted the Church of Scientology. Nevertheless, they should thank the Lord for them, because the Scientologists have fought a lot of battles that have helped protect and safeguard freedom for us all.

"Because of these efforts, Scientology is continuing to gain more and more acceptability among leaders in the religious community, and the Church has won most of its battles. However, while they are enjoying a breathing period, be assured there are a lot more battles to be fought, and won, down the road."

Rev. Jim Nicholls
Producer of "Voice of America"
Radio and TV Show

"I have traveled far and wide throughout my professional life and see the peoples of Earth as incredibly diverse in character as well as needs. Oftentimes our efforts to understand and help them have been too narrow. In the many years I have worked with the Church of Scientology the one thing which has impressed me the most and which will characterize the Church far into future centuries is its ability to deal with humankind as a whole.

"At the heart of Scientology's activities is the betterment of all people no matter what creed, what race, what socioeconomic status to develop themselves spiritually and mentally so that each individual can improve his own life. Scientology's far-reaching goals are designed to tend to each individual uniquely with compassionate concern and commitment. These rare attributes are essential in these times of trouble and uncertainty and most assuredly provide the Church with a platform for growth and strength in the years to come."

L. Fletcher Prouty
Col. US Air Force (Ret.)

"As American society becomes more diverse in the years ahead, we will be looking for leadership from those organizations that represent the moral tenets which united us as a country: personal responsibility, compassion, tolerance, respect and a commitment to community. The Church of Scientology is one of those organizations—as its commitment to the Hollywood community so clearly demonstrates."

Mark A. Robbins
1992 Republican Candidate
for Congress 29th
District of California

"The Church of Scientology is an important force in our society seeking to enhance the people's ability to know what our government is doing, is not doing and why, and otherwise striving to enable citizens to make the government more accountable for its actions. I believe that in the future, when the need for such efforts will be more necessary, the Church's role will be even stronger and more effective."

Quinlan J. Shea, Jr.
Former Senior Justice
Department Official
Director Center for Citizen
Access to Government
Information

"For many years an international organization has been masquerading as a legitimate defender of the citizens of the world. This agency, INTERPOL, while claiming to work against criminals has protected terrorists like George Habash, drug dealers such as Manuel Noriega, crooked banks like BCCI and others. For many years Nazis and former Nazis led INTERPOL.

"It has been the Church of Scientology that has taken the leadership to unmask this canard. By doing so, it is helping get rid of drug dealers, crooks and terrorists from the planet. This is the type of social action that all religious organizations should emulate."

Steve Frank
Public Affairs
Consultant

"It is notable that while the major denominations in Canada are careless about religious rights (and, therefore, careless about the ultimate welfare of our people), Scientologists have courageously and at great cost struggled against state abuses of these and other rights. If they hold out and succeed, all of us will one day have to bring our proper thanks that through their endurance we enjoy our freedom."

The Right Reverend
Juris Calitis, D.D.
Evangelical Lutheran
Church in Canada

"Drugs are the scourge of mankind, and they are the problem we must solve as we exit the twentieth century. The twenty-first century promises hope because Scientology is here and has the solutions to drugs."

Bob King
Advisory Neighborhood
Commissioner,
Washington, DC

"Scientology has a background of benefiting its members as well as the general public through a number of social betterment programs in areas like drug rehabilitation, education and government reform. This broad spectrum of beneficial activities is a tribute to the Church as well as its members and is something I believe guarantees the Church of Scientology a bright future."

Dr. Isaac N. Brooks, Jr. Ph.D.
Executive Chairman
National Task Force
on Religious Freedom
Legislation and Litigation
Washington, DC

"The mind is a magnificent thing, and Scientologists rightfully are against mind-altering drugs. We cannot continue to destroy the minds of people with drugs. This goes against nature. Scientology is on the right track, giving the mind a chance to work on its own."

Lillian Ray
Assistant Deputy Mayor
for Drug Control Policy
Philadelphia, Pennsylvania

"Scientology provides technology for improving a person's ability to study and educate himself. They also are accomplishing much in fighting crime and keeping people from returning to drugs. Provided they can make this more known in the society, it can be very helpful in changing the direction of the society. Scientology will be very helpful in improving everyday life."

William Orozco
Former Representative for
California State Senator
Diane Watson

"It's the largest growing religious movement in the entire world. I see the future for Scientology just being bigger and bigger."

Richard Allatorre
Former State Assemblyman
California

"It's a new religion, and it will meet many difficulties. But Scientology stands on fine ground, and all resistance will be broken down."

Harry Widemyr
Social Inspector
Sweden

"I think the Church's involvement in such issues as religious freedom and ending psychiatric abuses within the field of mental health demonstrate the Church is interested in more than just spirituality, but in enabling all people to enjoy their human rights. The support for these efforts can only grow."

Cedric Hendricks
Congressional Aide
Washington, DC

"There is and will be a more positive view of Scientology through the actions of community work and the various community outreach programs that the Church presents.

"It has been a fulfilling experience working with Community Outreach staff for over ten years.

"I look forward to a long relationship utilizing the talent, the time, and dedication to helping young people which has been our source of contact over the years."

Carole J. Simpson
County of Los Angeles
Department of Children Services

"On the threshold of the twenty-first century Scientology will continue to grow and be very strong and effective in its impact around the world. They will continue to be admired for putting hands and feet to their beliefs. Their example in fighting for religious freedom will continue to inspire all other faith groups in the ongoing struggles for religious freedom. Keep on keeping on."

Rev. Wm. Solomon
Executive Minister
Metro Toronto Black Clergy Association

"Scientology relies on the energy of each and every one of its members. As a result, as the energy and enthusiasm of its members grow so will Scientology and its many programs designed to help society."

Carlos A. Rodriguez
Political Consultant

"It is inevitable that Scientology will expand because from my experience, the types of people I have met are walking advertisements for it. I think more and more people are looking for a practical philosophy."

The Hon. Herbert Graham
Former Member of West Australian Parliament

"As the Church of Scientology is a well-arranged organization, I see very good survival chances for its future. This is because the survival of a religion depends very much on its organization."

Dr. Rainer Flasche
Philipps University
Marburg, Germany

"Observers of the Church [of Scientology] seem to be predominantly of the opinion that as a phenomenon it will develop and become larger due to the symptoms shown by unsolved problems and conflicts in our technical-scientific world."

Rudolf Grimm
Reporter
Berlin, Germany

"Special attention belongs to Scientology however . . . It is the forerunner of coming religions and philosophical movements with absolutely separate ethics, no longer bound to Western ethical ideas."

Pfarrer Haack
Evangelical Expert
Germany

"Scientology is likely to be engaged more and more in public affairs. The main problem will be abuse and false information peddled by its opponents and those in public affairs who wish the public to be kept in ignorance. It is my view that the public generally who have little knowledge of the Church of Scientology will learn more—particularly through the media, who I believe will be paying more positive attention to its activities."

Arthur Lewis, MP
United Kingdom

"It's far better known than it was a few years ago. People are more aware now. As society becomes more complex, people will want to associate with something to get a handle on life. I see this as a religious movement with all churches."

Michael Franchetti
Former Deputy Attorney General
California

"I feel [Scientology's] future is good, given the conditions in society today—and the need for people to find themselves. It's a good future, but a rough one, as long as organizations with strong religious prejudices exist and want to create problems for others. It's unfortunate, but inevitable."

Professor J. Stillson Judah
The Graduate Theological Union
San Francisco

"It is axiomatic in the history of religion that when a new religious movement publishes, it is here to stay. Scientology surely has *published,* a lot, in its quest to help man help himself. The eight million adherents of the Church are here to stay—with increasing benefit of the human family.

"The Scientologists we are privileged to know are sincere, dedicated human beings who are striving hard for the betterment of all."

Marvin Bordelon
President
American Conference
on Religious Movements

"I expect the Church of Scientology increasingly to contribute positively to interfaith understanding in a true spirit of dialogue. This will be a valuable and welcome development. Such cooperation and dialogue will, in itself, help to break down barriers and increase trust, and will produce a broad stream of people of faith and ethics seeking and working for world peace."

Rev. Brian Cooper
Chairman
Christian Peace Conference
England

"I am confident that the Church of Scientology will continue to be on the cutting edge of government reform simply because the Church has been doing it for years and doing it well. Scientology does this type of work better than any other organization in the country."

Wayne C. Bentson
FOIA Specialist
Western Information Network

"The Church is expanding more and more rapidly from what I see on the TV and on the radio. The Church will move into the mainstream of society. Scientology will be the focus point in the 1990s and will set the direction in which this country will go.

"Scientology will be known as the place to go where people really care."

Bill Hoston
Political Activist
Los Angeles

"Scientology offers a true bridge between the East and the West and Scientologists can effectively help solve the great problems that plague both cultures.

"Scientology will become a major religion in the Western world before the end of the century."

Loek Hopstaken
Postal Manager
Amsterdam, Netherlands

"As an attorney, concerned resident of Hollywood and former Chairman of the Board of Directors of the Hollywood Chamber of Commerce I wanted you to know that we are proud of Scientology's accomplishments here in 'Tinsel Town.' Please, continue to let your 'light shine' and share your success with others.

"The Church has been active in the Hollywood area for over a decade and continue to be 'excellent' citizens, good neighbors and a positive influence in the community."

John O. Adams, Esq.
Honorary Director
Hollywood Chamber of Commerce

"I see the Church of Scientology becoming a very strong community structure. What I see happening is [a] continued reach out to assist those who are not members and the formation of a working unit with the Church made up of people of all religions."

Lester Smith, Jr.
Founder and President
of The Natural High
Entertainment Group, California

"I would see the Church of Scientology being a part of all the other churches who recognize that there must be a new direction and a coming together of all churches for the betterment of mankind.

"Each Church has its unique role. Basically I see the role of the Church of Scientology as cleaning man's thinking, redirecting man's thinking, because obviously the old thought process has gotten us in the mess that we have. We must look at old values, old ways of doing things and not be afraid to question. And if we find that these values are incorrect in view of new enlightenment, then be willing to change—not feel threatened by new ideas, but embrace them and give them a chance to be proved or disproved."

Rev. E.L. Woods
Pastor of Ebony Missionary
Baptist Church
Los Angeles, California

"The laws of our land are often administered in an unfair and unequal manner. In the future, however, I see the technology of the Church of Scientology assisting those in the judicial system in equitably administering these laws. In this manner, the judicial system can effectively contribute to bringing about the aims of Scientology as outlined by L. Ron Hubbard."

Reginia Rogers Jackson
Attorney
Washington, DC

"Scientology's Citizens Commission on Human Rights is fighting a cause, the abuses of psychiatry and the devastation of their drugs to which the general public is beginning to awaken. They are creating a safer world for us all."

Ann Tracy
Prozac Survivors
Support Group Director
Utah Branch

"It is obvious that the Church of Scientology feels a moral responsibility to attack serious social problems and improve conditions. I see the Church building on this background and expanding its activities into the practical hard-nosed field of education where it can play a major role in resolving some of the bitter conflicts which are preventing the proper education of our children. We need our children to be literate to have real-world skills. I see the Church of Scientology playing a major role in making this happen."

Patrick Groff, Ed.D.
Professor Emeritus
San Diego State University

"Based on the time I've been in Hollywood and seen what the Church of Scientology has accomplished, all indications appear that the Church in the next five years will continue to make progress in the community, specifically as it relates to handling gang violence, graffiti, etc.

"The outreach achieved is significant and I think it is very positive. The Church continues to have faith and continues to help those in need of direction, upgrade their properties, and contribute to community development."

Frank L. Buckley
Board Member
Hollywood Chamber of Commerce

"We, at the Bible Holiness Movement, have—over the years—been gratefully aware that the Church of Scientology has actively endeavored to express its committal to the God-given rights and liberties, including religious freedom, that are essential to society, and this with them has not been an abstract ideal but an essential practical effort along with other religious and concerned bodies of people.

"It is also good to have known personally of many instances when these Scientologists have acted on behalf of others who would differ with them, simply on the basis of principle and human compassion. Two instances come to mind, one where an

Evangelical youth was under illegal effort to force a denial of faith in Christ, and the other of compassionate and effective effort in improving the lot of South African Black mental patients who were suffering vicious abuse in a form of virtual slavery.

"What of the future? It would be our hope and expectation that the Scientologists will continue in their social conscience and concern for human liberty."

Wesley H. Wakefield
Bishop General of the
Bible Holiness Movement

"The trend today is for people to go back to conservatism.

"As long as the Church of Scientology provides a visible alternative it's going to grow and expand.

"We are through the permissive age and people are questioning values. You will get larger if you continue to provide an active social side to the Church.

"If you continue to reassure people that it isn't all hopeless and the world isn't coming to an end you'll continue to do well."

Robert Carr
Journalist
Ontario Parliament
Press Gallery

"Scientology will endure. It will be accepted more and more into normality as with other religious associations."

Svante Nycander
Writer
Sweden

"The delightfully informative L. Ron Hubbard Life Exhibition, combined with Celebrity Centre's magnificently restored Manor Hotel, have created for the citizenry of Hollywood two brilliant examples of the Church's commitment to improve not only the cultural scene, but also to add vision and financial resources to the increasingly important community revitalization program. Add to that the Herculean 'neighbor safety' efforts of staff and membership during the recent civil unrest in Los Angeles, and you have created a blueprint for a successful future throughout the community."

Michael Teilmann
Teilmann International
Productions
Hollywood, California

"I feel that the Church has been a great help to many people. It has brought enlightenment—I hope you continue in your strides."

Lilyann Mitchell
***Argus** Newspaper*
England

"Scientology has shown its valuable place in society not only in its stand against religious suppression but by providing education and study technology for people of all races. This ensures the most fundamental of all human rights, the right to literacy. The Church of Scientology will be here as a guiding light for future generations."

Ron Segal
Education Committee
United Nations Association
of Australia

"Because the Church of Scientology has a legitimate philosophy on the human situation, it will endure. I see it outliving and speeding the demise of its main antagonist, the state-sponsored religion of psychiatry. Despite the current financial power of psychiatry and its ability to spread its dark message that man is but an animal, I believe the day will come when the Church of Scientology will be joined by other churches dancing on psychiatry's coffin."

Seth Farber, Ph.D.
Executive Director
Network Against Coercive
Psychiatry

Although these views greatly vary, all have common denominators; that Scientology has workability, has produced results and is a growing authority in the humanities and spiritual nature of man.

The future, L. Ron Hubbard said some twenty years ago, would tell more than he ever could about the value of his work.

Thus far it has told an extraordinary story—a story of millions who have found a way to better themselves and their fellows through the use of this technology, of new rights for the mentally ill, of new lives for drug abusers and of new hope for the illiterate.

But what does the future hold from this point forward? Many of those who have attempted to halt Scientology in the past are still with us, and it is not unreasonable to assume that there may be future battles to fight. But in the final analysis, authority belongs to those who can DO the task in any given field. Authority sustained by pompousness, the laws passed and "we who know" cannot endure.

Scientology has the answers. Authority belongs to those who can do the job. And Scientology will inherit tomorrow as surely as the sun will rise.

CHAPTER 31

THOSE WHO OPPOSE SCIENTOLOGY

Dianetics did not come quietly into the world. Even before publication of L. Ron Hubbard's *Dianetics: The Modern Science of Mental Health,* excitement had been created on a relatively small scale—small, in hindsight of what was to come later. It had begun with a mimeographed copy of his earlier work *Dianetics: The Original Thesis,* which was passed hand to hand around the country, and soon followed by an article in the *Explorers Club Journal.*

Then, on May 9, 1950 *The Modern Science of Mental Health* reached the bookstores. Almost immediately, a groundswell of public enthusiasm vaulted the book onto national bestseller lists. Stores simply could not keep copies in stock as hundreds of thousands across the nation formed themselves into auditing groups, and Mr. Hubbard's discoveries even began to take root on distant shores. To meet the astonishing response from all sectors of society—the fashionable, the academic and, most importantly, the man on the street—the publisher instantly ordered further printings. Yet still supply could barely keep pace with demand. By the end of six weeks, Dianetics was not merely a phenomena; it was the beginning of the global movement that continues to grow today.

There were, however, a scant few among society's ranks who were not quite so enthusiastic, i.e., certain key members of the American medical/psychiatric establishment. That their numbers were pitifully small—literally measured in the dozens—did not necessarily concern them. They were well entrenched and well connected; and when they decided that Dianetics must be stopped to preserve their kingdom, they were fully prepared to make use of every one of those connections.

Thus it was that two diametrically opposed forces were unleashed on May 9, 1950. On the one hand stood the hundred thousand and more everyday men and women who eagerly read and applied *Dianetics* with extraordinary success. On the other stood a small clique of medical and psychiatric practitioners, who knew nothing of the human mind, and had not even read *Dianetics.* Nonetheless, they were certain that a handbook, which made self-improvement possible to anyone, would constitute a severe financial loss to the healthcare establishment. After all, they reasoned, how can psychiatrists expect to command large salaries if the man on the street knew more about the mind than they did? Seen within this context then, May 9, 1950 not only saw the birth of Dianetics, but also psychiatry's first shot that began a war.

THE REAL ISSUES

To understand the forces ranged against L. Ron Hubbard, in this war he never started, it is necessary to gain a cursory glimpse of the old and venerable science of psychiatry—which was actually none of the aforementioned. As an institution, it dates back to shortly before the turn of the century; it is certainly not worthy of respect by reason of age or dignity; and it does not meet any known definition of a science, what with its hodgepodge of unproven theories that have never produced any result—except an ability to make the unmanageable and mutinous more docile and quiet, and turn the troubled into apathetic souls beyond the point of caring.

That it promotes itself as a healing profession is a misrepresentation, to say the least. Its mission is to control.

Psychiatry as we know it today is more priesthood than science. Its conglomeration of half-baked theories is handed down by an arbitrary elite—authorities who have attained such status through who they know and who can sweet-talk the government into parting with yet more grant money.

While as for what they actually *do*, there are only three primary methods of "treatment"—electroshock, psychosurgery and psychotropic drugs.

To illustrate the unscientific basis of this "science," in Fascist Italy in the 1930s, Professor Ugo Cerletti noted that back in A.D. 43 or so, Roman citizens would sometimes try to rid themselves of headaches by putting a torpedo fish on their heads. A torpedo fish generates about 25 volts of electricity. Perhaps it was just coincidence that the Empire fell soon after that, but be that as it may, Cerletti was undeterred by this observation and set off on a new path. He began his experiments by killing dogs with huge jolts of electricity. However, before he could significantly reduce Rome's canine population, inspiration came in the form of a visit to a pig slaughterhouse. There, much to his delight, he found that pigs were not killed by the electricity administered, but only sent into epileptic convulsions, whereupon their throats could conveniently be cut by the butchers. After experimenting further—and losing a great many pigs—to discover how much electricity it would take to kill one of the porcine creatures, he was ready for man. The unfortunate vagrant he chose (generously supplied by the police) received 70 volts to the head, fell, then shouted, "Not a second [one]. It will kill!" Later, it was discovered that human beings could withstand between 140 and 150 volts to the brain. Thus electroconvulsive shock therapy (ECT) was born.

Psychosurgery had equally shabby beginnings, according to the medical historians. In 1848, Phineas Gage of Vermont was peering into a blasting hole when a charge detonated and blew a metal tamping rod through his brain—an unfortunate accident that he managed to survive. But, his astute physician noted with amazement, Gage had changed! A most noticeable change—from efficient and capable, to self-indulgent and profane. Thus Gage made his place in history as the first person to survive a lobotomy. The man who actually established himself as the father of the lobotomy (a procedure conducted on intractable patients to make them more manageable) was Dr. Egas Moniz. He operated on about one hundred patients. However, in at least one case, the operation might have been a success but the doctor died: he was shot by one of his lobotomized patients. That in 1949 he was given the Nobel prize for this questionable advancement is one of the saddest ironies of medical history. Nonetheless, it assured that many followed his path.

As for drugs, witch doctors have used the natural variety for centuries. Today's pharmaceutical psychotropic drugs began their development with attempts to brainwash recalcitrant citizens and political prisoners. Virtually all of the original research—in Russia, Germany and the United States—was funded by intelligence agencies. Once again, the aim was to make individuals more tractable and malleable. And, in the United States, at least, most of it was illegal, conducted on unknowing servicemen and citizens. Except, of course, in the oft-cited instance of CIA psychiatrist, Dr. Louis Jolyon West, who was the only man known to have killed an elephant with LSD.

That all of this experimentation—drugs, psychosurgery, ECT—has never cured anyone of anything but, on the contrary, has either made people more manageable or damaged them beyond recognition, has never stopped the psychiatric community from continuing these practices. After all, these are the only tools they have. Without them, they would have nothing to sell.

Which brings up a crucial point: to whom do they sell their services? Not to the broad public (and only sometimes even to their own patients), for the majority have no faith in this parody of science and would never even entertain the idea of actually visiting a psychiatrist. Then, of course, there is also the shame and embarrassment associated with going to a psychiatrist—which is largely due to the way psychiatrists themselves have characterized mental illness in a sales campaign that backfired. The only customers they have, the only ones willing to pay for their services (and very generously) are governments, particularly the clandestine arms of the government, or those that desire to control people, be they prisoners, children or society's unwanted.

These, then, constitute the force that tried to stop Dianetics and Scientology.

And this is the world Dianetics entered. A world where psychiatry was entrenched among the US intelligence services, living off the fat of government grants, and experimenting—with the help of ex-Nazi scientists—on an oblivious public. A world where their critics were simply labeled insane and "in need of psychiatric help."

Thus the battle lines were drawn. Dianetics offered a means to happiness, stability and success. It provided a solution to psychosomatic illnesses. It created an interest in the workings of the mind among people of all classes and ages. And it gave the man in the street a method that, for the first time, he himself could utilize to improve his own condition. Additionally, it should be kept in mind that L. Ron Hubbard achieved something that psychiatrists have long been attempting to achieve: to write a book about the mind that was genuinely popular, that people actually wanted to read, that was both understandable and applicable.

But Dianetics did more. It labeled the latest and greatest psychiatric drugs as dangerous. And it directly exposed the inhuman crimes of psychiatrists and the harm they caused with ECT and lobotomies, clearly substantiating the irreparable damage these treatments caused to healthy brain tissue.

That mental health professionals were incensed by Mr. Hubbard's not-so-gentle upbraiding is understandable, particularly as he was not a member of their elitist clique. But when all was said and done, the issue was clearly financial: How long could one continue to convince the American taxpayer to foot the bill for multimillion-dollar psychiatric appropriations in the face of what Dianetics could accomplish for the price of a book?

THE MARSHALING OF FORCES

Among the many, many positive reviews and articles on *Dianetics* were a few strategically placed "hits" specifically designed to dampen public enthusiasm.

These first negative "reviews" on *Dianetics* came through the American Medical Association—a group instinctively opposed to any unregulated or nonmember means to better health and living. But it was not as it appeared; more the result of a ventriloquism act. The actual link to the AMA was made by the American Psychiatric Association (APA) medical director, Dr. Daniel Blain, who well knew that psychiatry enjoyed nothing close to the credibility of its medical colleagues, and none of the clout. The voice of the AMA was essentially that of he and his colleagues.

But using the AMA to take potshots was only the first round. The full APA plan was far more elaborate. First, false propaganda was to be published in "authoritative" journals; then, once the "experts" had passed judgment, these opinions would be given to mainstream media sources. Dossiers would be created to contain all this unflattering "information" and passed still further afield including, of course, to appropriate government agencies.

Although simple in both design and execution, the consequences would be far reaching. Indeed, to one degree or another, the subsequent attacks on Dianetics and Scientology were but a result of this original scheme to fabricate dossiers and then spread them far and wide.

MIND CONTROL EXPOSED

During the continual process of Dianetics research, both as an auditor and as an observer of other auditors, Mr. Hubbard naturally came into contact with a wide variety of cases. And, it was inevitable that these would include those who had been in the hands of psychiatrists closely allied to the intelligence community.

Thus it came about, fully twenty-five years before the facts were made public by Congress, that Mr. Hubbard was the first to announce and decry government mind manipulation programs. Eventually, of course, these and other revelations of Central Intelligence Agency criminality would entirely reshape public perception of this group of spies from a patriotic and somewhat glamorous image to that of a rogue agency of dirty tricksters, with its own citizens as victims.

The vehicle was his 1951 book *Science of Survival,* and in it he described in no uncertain terms the combined use of pain, drugs and hypnosis as a behavioral modification technique of the worst kind. It was, he said, so extensively used in espionage work, it was long past the time people should have become alarmed about it. It had taken Dianetic auditing to discover the widespread existence of these brainwashing techniques, and, he added, the only saving grace was that Dianetics could undo their effects.

With such covert government activity so openly addressed by Mr. Hubbard and Dianeticists, he had compounded his "crime": In his first book, he offended psychiatrists; in his second, the intelligence community. That the two, already closely connected, should now draw even closer in the common effort to stop him, was not surprising. What was surprising was the velocity and frequency of subsequent attacks. By the mid-1950s, as we shall see, at least half a dozen Federal agencies were brought into the effort to suppress Dianetics and its assault on the mental health field, including the Federal Bureau of Investigation (FBI), the Internal Revenue Service (IRS) and the Food and Drug Administration (FDA).

"You would have thought that at the very least I was inciting whole populations to revolt and governments to fall," a slightly bemused Mr. Hubbard later wrote of these events. "All I really was doing was trying to tell man he could be happy, that there was a road out of suffering and that he could attain his goals."

THE BATTLE MOUNTS

Yet even while Mr. Hubbard successfully told man he could be happy and the numbers of Scientologists mounted, psychiatry was attempting to strengthen its grasp on society.

The plan involved what came to be known as the Siberia Bill, actually named the Alaska Mental Health Bill. The more popular title came from the fact that the proposed outcome of this cherished psychiatric plan was likened to a Siberia-type camp for mental health patients in the frozen wastelands of Alaska. Presumably, this was far enough away from the well-traveled roads of the world to allow psychiatrists to conduct their mind control and other experiments on a captive population, unhindered by the glare of publicity. To ensure a captive population, the measure incorporated a "simplified commitment procedure," so simple, in fact, that it eradicated such wasteful and costly activities as jury trials and legal defenses and allowed any peace officer, friend, medical doctor and, of course, psychiatrist, to institute commitment proceedings.

But just after January 1956, and the bill's unanimous, yet barely noticeable, passage through Congress, a coalition of members of the Church of Scientology and civil rights groups launched a campaign to inform the American public just what this bill held in store for them. Under the rallying cry, "Siberia, USA!" a massive letter-writing campaign inspired political opposition.

When it was over, the commitment section of the bill was deservedly dead, leaving merely an act to authorize mental health funding to the territory of Alaska.

A wounded psychiatry struck back, this time utilizing the FDA as its main battering ram. Thanks to the Freedom of Information Act, Scientologists later uncovered a mountain of documents which well demonstrated the activities of the participants—egged on by members of both the AMA and APA. A veritable beehive of activity took place, with letters and meetings between interested psychiatric parties, the Department of Justice, the Washington, DC police department, the United States Post Office, the AMA, of course, and even the US Army's Criminal Investigation Command—all continuously linked and regularly prodded by a now extremely nervous psychiatry.

The upshot of all these schemes? The first action was a ludicrous failure; the second a waste of time, the third an embarrassment.

The first, based on a psychiatrist's "tip" that the Church was using illegal drugs, led to a "raid" on the Washington, DC church by a US deputy marshal who seized a few bottles of said drug. When it turned out to be a compound of the commonly available vitamin B_1, vitamin C, niacinamide and calcium, that case obviously went nowhere.

Drug dealing proving an unworkable premise, the FDA and other interested agencies decided that Scientology practicing medicine without a license would prove fertile ground for exploration. On March 19, 1959 FDA agent Taylor Quinn infiltrated the church, taped a religious service, and passed the information on to the US Attorney's Office. Unfortunately, as he reported to the FDA, the church had required him to sign a contract that he was not to learn to cure anyone. Nor was there any evidence of fraud.

With both drugs and illegal healing dead-ended, the only avenue remaining to the FDA was the E-Meter. Perhaps, they theorized, it was used to "diagnose" or "cure illness." So, on January 4, 1963, US marshals, deputized longshoremen, and armed police barged their way into the Founding Church of Scientology in Washington, threatened the staff, and left with two vans of not only E-Meters, but books, scriptures and other materials.

Still, as outrageous as it was, it didn't match the sheer audacity of what happened in Seattle where the FDA's fingerprints were figuratively all over the handgun that was used to murder the head of the church there.

A local resident, Russell Johnson, who had heard about the FDA's actions in Washington, DC, thought they would provide a sympathetic ear to his current problem. He called them to complain about "the practices of a Dr. William Fisk who operates as the Church of Scientology" and claimed Fisk was attempting to seduce his wife.

The enterprising FDA official he spoke to immediately suggested that Johnson join forces with the FDA as an "undercover agent" and infiltrate the church. Johnson dutifully did this, reported in, and was instructed to return and get further information.

Johnson carried his duties as an intelligence agent into tragic and bloody extremes. On September 10, 1963, he walked into the Seattle church and shot and killed the Executive Director before a roomful of horrified congregation members.

The FDA then carried the concept of expediency to new and distasteful heights. Instead of confessing that one of its "agents" had just committed murder, it contacted the Seattle police department and arranged to send its own people illegally into church premises with the homicide team, to further gather information for its "investigation." As usual, however, the FDA discovered nothing illegal in the church.

Altogether, for more than a decade the FDA would remain obsessed with the

E-Meter. With other government agencies, it would repeatedly infiltrate the Church with agents and informants, employ bugging devices, place a "cover" on Church mail, and obtain confidential Church bank account information.

It would get nowhere. In 1969, the Washington, DC Federal Appeals Court ruled the Church a bona fide religion protected by the US Constitution, and that the E-Meter had not been improperly labeled or used.

Still, it was not until 1973 that a reluctant FDA finally returned those stolen church materials: 5,000 books, 2,900 booklets, and the E-Meters.

MEDIA–GOVERNMENT COLLUSION

There remains one illuminating point to the FDA fiasco. It involves the enlistment by the FDA of *The Saturday Evening Post* and their star feature writer, James Phelan.

After being approached by the AMA to do a story on Scientology, the *Post* assigned the piece to Phelan, who traveled to England to interview Mr. Hubbard. He was warmly welcomed and assisted in every manner possible, as befits a seemingly interested and unbiased journalist, which is how he represented himself.

That Phelan was anything but that was borne out by two facts: Immediately upon his return to Washington and *before* the story was published, he gave his story to the FDA for coordination purposes; and, the resulting story was a hatchet job of the first order—an unrestrained attempt to smear both Mr. Hubbard and Scientology, obviously a flanking action to the FDA's attempted case against use of the E-Meter.

Phelan was followed by many others—a long string of stories through the years, concocted to create a climate conducive to governmental harassment. It was a similar pattern to that which occurred in Germany in the 1930s—the very successful media actions to create public "indignation" that would legitimize not only the most blatant violations of civil rights, but, indeed, the Holocaust.

THE IRS CAMPAIGN

The FDA had conclusively proven its incompetence, not only by botching its mandate to destroy Scientology, but by taking so long to do it—thus allowing Scientology to grow meteorically, both in the United States and around the world. Thus, the FDA was dismissed to do what it does best: harass vitamin salesmen, and give carte blanche to powerful drug companies well before completion of the product safety tests.

The weight of the mission now fell on IRS shoulders. Actually, the IRS had been part of the same program, harassing the Church since the early 1950s, denying tax-exempt status to various Scientology churches, and issuing Federal tax liens against others. It also provided information to the post office to "support a charge of misrepresentation," and informed the Department of Labor that "LSD and perhaps other drugs are widely used by the members while assembled" and that the Church used "electric shock" on its parishioners—well aware that these were gross and ludicrous falsehoods.

IRS illegalities were the subject of 1976 Congressional hearings that found the IRS had been engaged in "intelligence gathering" and had been used as a political weapon disrelated to tax concerns. Thus among the materials turned up through the Freedom of Information Act was a St. Louis IRS file labeling the Church as politically subversive to justify further harassment. This charge, it should be mentioned, is particularly outrageous in view of the fact that Scientology is one of the most politically nonpartisan religions on Earth—fighting discrimination and injustice on the left, the right and all points in between.

The whole tedious history of IRS attacks would fill a book. In fact, it fills scores of filing cabinets of documents obtained under the Freedom of Information Act, revealing not merely a genuinely shocking parade of IRS dirty tricks, but also a mad agency scramble to fabricate a case—any kind of case—against the Church of Scientology.

Specifically, these documents tell of IRS attempts to redefine the term *church,* expressly to disqualify Scientology from tax-exempt status. And when that didn't work, an even more unbelievable story unfolded: In an attempt to circumvent the fact that the Church committed no crimes, the IRS engaged in a truly Machiavellian scheme which they pursued for several years.

The plan called for nothing short of complete destruction of the Church. As part of the agenda: infiltration of the Church with a network of undercover agents and the manufacture of evidence. Forged documents were to be seeded into Church files where, through the course of a planned IRS raid, they would be conveniently found and used as evidence for prosecution. The infiltrators were not only to be rewarded financially when Church assets were looted, but they were also to be installed as IRS puppets running a fully tax-exempt church that would use the name but bear no resemblance to Scientology.

Yet, even as the IRS were implementing their plans—attempting to infiltrate church premises, working out how to forge and plant documents—Church attorneys exposed all. In addition to concerns over ensuing public outrage at this exposure, the IRS now had to contend with another problem; one doesn't spend several years investigating a church at enormous cost to the taxpayer only to report that no crimes were found.

In a last-ditch effort to save face, not to mention careers, the IRS tried to persuade the Department of Justice to bring some kind, any kind, of prosecution as a justification for what they had done. Justice may be blind, but it's not stupid, and Justice Department attorneys rebuked the IRS and refused to entertain any prosecution or even further investigation. After all, anyone could see that no crimes had been committed beyond those of the IRS themselves.

The Church, on the other hand, with an abundance of evidence filed a $120 million damages suit in Federal Court in August 1991. That suit named seventeen Washington, DC and Los Angeles-based Internal Revenue Service officials. It charged agency officials with waging a thirty-three-year campaign of illegal acts, violating the constitutional rights of the Church and large numbers of its parishioners.

BEHIND THE WORLDWIDE CAMPAIGN

The previous pages might lead one to believe that the forty-year assault against Scientology has assumed large proportions, but the source must be remembered—that small but influential circle of psychiatrists. Nor have the means changed over the years: false allegations selectively planted in the media, then seeded into federal files as background "fact."

It is a method, with small adjustments, that has also served to cause trouble overseas. The international pipeline leaves the US, primarily through FBI and CIA links, and discharges among the voluminous dossiers of Interpol, a private organization which worked closely with the Nazis during World War II, and had as its president an ex-SS officer as late as 1972—as the Church was the first to expose.

Interpol (originally designed to coordinate criminal apprehension between countries) is convenient on three counts: First, because it is a private organization, it is above the laws of any country, free to amass secret dossiers and spread them far and wide; second, files bearing the authoritative Interpol stamp are assumed to be true; and, third, it has a decades-old relationship with the FBI, one of the main repositories of false reports on Scientology in the US. In fact, FBI files contain virtually every rumor ever disseminated about Scientology, further substantiating Congressional findings that the FBI was often used to launch politically motivated attacks against targets that had committed no crimes at all.

And Interpol was well used, beginning in the 1960s. What happened over the next two decades was fairly predictable: attacks against Scientology by government agencies in England, France, Germany, Italy, Spain and Australia—all with fervent media support involving the most outrageous allegations. Still, as usual, in every instance, Scientology has prevailed.

So it goes. Key psychiatric figures, their US government allies and psychiatric colleagues overseas—together they have spent untold millions of dollars around the world to stop Scientology.

And they never have.

THE END OF THE FIGHT

While psychiatry had US government agencies infiltrating, raiding and investigating the Church in the early and mid-1960s, and inquiries in Australia and Great Britain underway during the same decade, the technologies of Scientology and Dianetics were widely available in five countries. Despite unabated attacks, these technologies became available in five more countries by the mid-1970s, in fifty-six countries in the late 1980s, and in seventy-four countries by the turn of the 1990s. All of which demonstrates that psychiatry has been about as effective in stopping Scientology as it has been in treating mental illness.

It has, in fact, become increasingly evident that psychiatry offers no valuable contribution to society whatsoever. Electric shock, brain operations, and indiscriminate drugging of patients in nineteenth-century-like horror chambers passed off as mental hospitals, have killed and maimed people on a daily basis. And during the period psychiatry has held its position of authority, the most dramatic era of social unrest, civil disobedience, drug proliferation and criminality in the history of the Western world has gained momentum.

Today, there are 500 Dianeticists and Scientologists to every psychiatrist, and while Scientology expands, enrollment in psychiatric university curriculums has slid to a drastic low since a peak in the 1960s. Without government appropriations, even these few psychiatrists would not be able to economically survive, for they have nothing to offer worth a cent of the public's money. Hence, while Scientology is more visible than ever, with churches dotting every continent on Earth and millions of parishioners around the world, one is hard pressed to find even a single psychiatrist with a shingle on his door. True, one can still find them in scuffed-linoleum offices of state and county hospitals, and lodged in the federal bureaucracy. But when was the last time anyone saw a sign advertising: lobotomies, electric shock and seriously incapacitating drugs?

In short, then, while psychiatry, which lives off government handouts, is shrinking; Scientology, which receives only public donations from people who know it works, is growing faster than any religion in the world. And if Scientology had anything to hide, it would not have survived the relentless attacks detailed in this chapter.

Thus the story of the attacks against Scientology is basically very simple. Dianetics and Scientology cut across vested interests which then ruthlessly attempted to destroy it. The issue was never any wrongdoing by the Church, merely encroachment on turf claimed by a mental health industry who would stop at nothing to preserve their stake.

Still, while psychiatry's offensive against Scientology has been all but defeated, the battle is not over. Their traditional allies and symbiotic partners have been the drug companies. Psychiatry invents the "disease"—the pharmaceutical companies invent the "cure." The side effects of the drugs ensure that the patient stays with the psychiatrist and, based upon these symptoms, a new disease is created. Which is the tail and which the dog in this vicious circle is debatable, but in any event, the drug companies jumped on the bandwagon. They stand to lose literally billions of dollars *a year* when people fully discover that ills and addictions can be resolved without mind-bending and mood-altering chemicals.

It would be well to remember, then, that when alarming reports are heard about Dianetics and Scientology, they stem from those who would prefer to manhandle problems with mind-altering drugs or enough electricity to throw a pig into convulsions—and as any fool knows, sticking one's finger in a light socket or clamping electrodes to one's skull cures nothing. (Even psychiatrists are not that stupid. When widely offered $10,000 to undergo their own "treatment," not one has ever agreed to subject himself to electroconvulsive therapy.)

The lessons of history provide the best context within which to consider such attacks. Every great movement which has opened new vistas and shaken the strongholds of archaic thought has been attacked by those who profit from the persistence of outmoded ideas. Thus, as Scientologists continue their work toward a new civilization without insanity, criminality or war, those with billion-dollar vested interests in just those ills will continue to lash out.

Yet it is ironic to view these attacks in the context of time. Scientology did not choose to fight this battle with psychiatry and, indeed, was not the one to fire the opening salvos. Mr. Hubbard was simply the one to come up with real answers to problems of the mind. Perhaps sensing that implicit in a solution to the mind lay their own demise, psychiatrists decided to destroy him and his technology. And just as they feared, Scientology has become their nemesis, exposing their brutality and their crimes.

But even as their tirades drone on, there is another point they should consider: The world which they helped create, a world where the wasted insane wander aimlessly through our inner cities, where senseless criminality claims a new life every few minutes, and entire generations sag under the double onslaught of drug dependency and illiteracy, this is a world in which they too must live.

And so, in the end, even those who attempted to stop Scientology will ultimately benefit from its victory.

THE TRUE STORY OF SCIENTOLOGY BY L. RON HUBBARD

The true story of Scientology is simple, concise and direct. It is quickly told:

1. A philosopher develops a philosophy about life and death.

2. People find it interesting.

3. People find it works.

4. People pass it along to others.

5. It grows.

When we examine this extremely accurate and very brief account, we see that there must be in our civilization some very disturbing elements for anything else to be believed about Scientology.

These disturbing elements are the Merchants of Chaos. They deal in confusion and upset. Their daily bread is made by creating chaos. If chaos were to lessen, so would their incomes.

The politician, the reporter, the medico, the drug manufacturer, the militarist and arms manufacturer, the police and the undertaker, to name the leaders of the list, fatten only upon "the dangerous environment." Even individuals and family members can be Merchants of Chaos.

It is to their interest to make the environment seem as threatening as possible, for only then can they profit. Their incomes, force and power rise in direct ratio to the amount of threat they can inject into the surroundings of the people. With that threat they can extort revenue, appropriations, heightened circulations and recompense without question. These are the Merchants of Chaos. If they did not generate it and buy and sell it, they would, they suppose, be poor.

For instance, we speak loosely of "good press." Is there any such thing today? Look over a newspaper. Is there anything **good** *on the front page? Rather, there is murder and sudden death, disagreement and catastrophe. And even that, bad as it is, is sensationalized to make it seem worse.*

This is the coldblooded manufacture of "a dangerous environment." People do not need this news; and if they did, they need the facts, not the upset. But if you hit a person hard enough, he can be made to give up money. That's the basic formula of extortion. That's the way papers are sold. The impact makes them stick.

A paper has to have chaos and confusion. A "news story" has to have "conflict," they say. So there is no good press. There is only ***bad*** *press about everything. To yearn for "good press" is foolhardy in a society where the Merchants of Chaos reign.*

Look what has to be done to the true story of Scientology in order to "make it a news story" by modern press standards. Conflict must be injected where there is none. Therefore the press has to dream up upset and conflict.

Let us take the first line. How does one make conflict out of it? No. 1, ***A philosopher develops a philosophy about life and death.***

The Chaos Merchant ***has*** *to inject one of several possible conflicts here: He is not a doctor of philosophy, they have to assert. They are never quite bold enough to say it is not a philosophy. But they can and do go on endlessly, as their purpose compels them, in an effort to invalidate the identity of the person developing it.*

In actual fact, the developer of the philosophy was very well grounded in academic subjects and the humanities, probably better grounded in formal philosophy alone than teachers of philosophy in universities.

The one-man effort is incredible in terms of study and research hours and is a record never approached in living memory, but this would not be considered newsworthy. To write the simple fact that a philosopher had developed a philosophy is not newspaper-type news and it would not disturb the environment. Hence, the elaborate news fictions about No. 1 above.

Then take the second part of the true story: ***People find it interesting.*** *It would be very odd if they didn't, as everyone asks these questions of himself and looks for the answers to his own beingness, and the basic truth of the answers is observable in the conclusions of Scientology.*

However, to make this "news" it has to be made disturbing. People are painted as kidnapped or hypnotized and dragged as unwilling victims up to read the books or listen.

The Chaos Merchant leaves No. 3 very thoroughly alone. It is dangerous ground for him. ***People find it works.*** *No hint of workability would ever be attached to Scientology by the press, although there is no doubt in the press mind that* ***it*** *does work. That's why it's dangerous. It calms the environment. So any time spent trying to convince press that Scientology works is time spent upsetting a reporter.*

On No. 4, ***People pass it along to others,*** *the press feels betrayed. "Nobody should believe anything they don't read in the papers. How dare word of mouth exist!" So, to try to stop people from listening, the Chaos Merchant has to use words like* ***cult.*** *That's "a closed group," whereas Scientology is the most open group on Earth to* *anyone. And they have to attack organizations and their people to try to keep people out of Scientology.*

Now, as for No. 5, ***It grows,*** *we have the true objection.*

As truth goes forward, lies die. The slaughter of lies is an act that takes bread from the mouth of a Chaos Merchant. Unless he can lie with wild abandon about how bad it all is, he thinks he will starve.

The world simply must ***not*** *be a better place according to the Chaos Merchant. If people were less disturbed, less beaten down by their environments, there would be no new appropriations for police and armies and big rockets and there'd be not even pennies for a screaming sensational press.*

So long as politicians move upward on scandal, police get more pay for more crime, medicos get fatter on more sickness, there will be Merchants of Chaos. They're paid for it.

And their threat is the simple story of Scientology. For that is the true story. And behind its progress there is a calmer environment in which a man can live and feel better. If you don't believe it, just stop reading newspapers for two weeks, and see if you feel better. Suppose you had all such disturbances handled?

The pity of it is, of course, that even the Merchant of Chaos needs us, not to get fatter, but just to live himself as a being.

So the true story of Scientology is a simple story.

And too true to be turned aside.

Part Nine

A Scientology Catechism

Throughout history, religions have traditionally published summaries of their basic principles in catechism form. The following chapter will answer some of the most commonly asked questions people have about the fundamentals of Dianetics and Scientology.

When individuals first hear about the subject, their questions are usually quite diverse. They range from "Why is Scientology called a religion?" and "What is the difference between Dianetics and Scientology?" to "Who was L. Ron Hubbard?" to "What is the E-Meter and how does it work?"

These questions, and many others, are answered in the following pages.

Chapter 32

Answers to Common Questions

What does the word Scientology mean?

The word *Scientology* means "the study of knowledge" or "knowing about knowing" from the Latin word *scio* which means "know" or "distinguish," and from the Greek word *logos* which means "reason itself" or "inward thought." So it means the study of wisdom or knowledge, or "knowing how to know." *Scientology* is further defined as the study and handling of the spirit in relationship to itself, universes and other life. The word was coined by L. Ron Hubbard.

What is Scientology about?

Developed by L. Ron Hubbard, Scientology provides *exact* principles and practical technology for improving self-confidence, intelligence and ability. Scientology does not require faith or belief—one can apply the principles and see for oneself if they work and are true.

Scientology addresses the spirit—not simply the body or mind—and is therefore completely apart from materialistic philosophies which hold that man is a product of his environment—or his genes.

Scientology is a religion by its basic tenets, practice, historical background and by the definition of the word *religion* itself. It is recognized as such by courts in country after country around the world, including the highest courts in the United States, Australia, Germany, Sweden, Italy, Denmark and many others.

All denominations are welcome in Scientology.

Scientology is a *route,* a way, rather than a dissertation or an assertive body of knowledge.

Through its drills and studies one may find the truth for oneself. It is the only thing that can show you who *you* really are.

The technology is therefore not expounded as something to believe but something to *do.*

How did Scientology start?

L. Ron Hubbard began his studies of the mind in 1923. In 1947 he wrote a manuscript detailing some of his discoveries. It was not published at that time, but circulated among friends, who copied it and passed it on to others. (This manuscript was formally published in 1951 as *Dianetics: The Original Thesis* and later republished as *The Dynamics of Life.*)

As copies of the manuscript circulated, Mr. Hubbard began to receive an increasing flow of letters requesting further information and more applications of his new subject. He soon found himself spending all his time answering letters and decided to write a comprehensive text on the subject.

His first published article on the subject, "Terra Incognita: The Mind," appeared in the Winter/Spring 1950 issue of the *Explorers Club Journal,* followed by the book *Dianetics: The Modern Science of Mental Health,* which was published in May 1950.

It became a nationwide bestseller almost overnight. By late summer, people across the country were not only reading the book, but were also organizing their own groups for the purpose of applying Dianetics techniques. The book has remained a bestseller ever since, again becoming number one on the *New York Times* bestseller list, almost four decades after its initial publication. It continues to appear on bestseller lists around the world.

During the course of thousands of hours of Dianetics counseling on thousands of individuals all over the country, incontrovertible evidence was amassed about the fundamentally spiritual nature of man. L. Ron Hubbard himself had discovered early in his research that man was a spiritual being, inhabiting a body and using a mind. These discoveries led him to realize that he had entered the realm of religion.

In 1954, the first Church of Scientology was formed in Los Angeles by a group of Scientologists. Within a few years churches had been formed across the country and around the world.

In the years that followed, L. Ron Hubbard completed his research into the spiritual nature of man. Today, all his writings on the subject are available to anyone who wishes to study Scientology. Although Mr. Hubbard departed his body in 1986, he is still with us in spirit and the legacy of his work continues to help people around the world.

How come it's all based on one man's work?

In the early 1950s, L. Ron Hubbard wrote: "Acknowledgment is made to fifty thousand years of thinking men without whose speculations and observations the creation and construction of Dianetics would not have been possible. Credit in particular is due to:

Anaxagoras, Thomas Paine, Aristotle, Thomas Jefferson, Socrates, René Descartes, Plato, James Clerk Maxwell, Euclid, Charcôt, Lucretius, Herbert Spencer, Roger Bacon, William James, Francis Bacon, Sigmund Freud, Isaac Newton, van Leeuwenhoek, Cmdr. Joseph Thompson (MC) USN, William A. White, Voltaire, Will Durant, Count Alfred Korzybski, and my instructors in atomic and molecular phenomena, mathematics and the humanities at George Washington University and at Princeton."

Why is Scientology called a religion?

Religion is defined as "Any specific system of belief and worship, often involving a code of ethics and a philosophy. . . ." *(Webster's New World Dictionary, Third College Edition)*

Religious philosophy implies study of spiritual manifestations, research on the nature of the spirit and study of the relationship of the spirit to the body; exercises devoted to the rehabilitation of abilities in a spirit.

Scientology is a religion in the most traditional sense. It deals with man as a spirit and is distinguishable from material and nonreligious philosophies which hold man to be a product of material circumstances. Scientology does not demand blind faith, but endeavors to help the individual discover past experiences and shed the trauma and guilt (sin) which encumber him.

The Church of Scientology also conducts basic services such as sermons at church meetings, christenings, weddings and funerals.

Why is Scientology a church?

The word *church* comes from the Greek word *kurios* meaning "lord" and the Indo-European base *kewe,* "to be strong." Current meanings of the word include "a congregation," "ecclesiastical power as distinguished from the secular" and "the clerical profession; clergy."

The word *church* is not only used by Christian organizations. There were churches ten thousand years before there were Christians, and Christianity itself was a revolt against the established church. In modern usage, people speak of the

Buddhist or Moslem church, referring in general to the whole body of believers in a particular religious teaching.

A church is simply a congregation of people who participate in common religious activities; *church* is also used to refer to the building where members of a religious group gather to practice their religion and attain greater spiritual awareness and well-being.

Scientology helps man become more aware of God, more aware of his own spiritual nature and that of those around him. Scientology scriptures recognize that there is an entire dynamic (urge or motivation in life) devoted to the Supreme Being (the eighth dynamic), and another dynamic that deals solely with one's urge toward existence as a spirit (the seventh dynamic). Acknowledgment of these aspects of life is a typical characteristic of religions. Thus, Scientology is a religion and the use of the word *church* when referring to Scientology is correct.

In the 1950s, Scientologists recognized that L. Ron Hubbard's technology and its results dealt directly with the freeing of the human spirit, and that greater spiritual awareness was routinely being achieved. There was no question in their minds that what they were dealing with was a religious practice; thus, in the early 1950s, they voted that a church be formed to better serve the needs of Scientologists. The first church of Scientology was incorporated in 1954. Since that time, dozens of court rulings in many different countries have upheld the fact that Scientology is a religion.

What Scientology Does for the Individual

How does Scientology work?

Scientology philosophy provides answers to many questions about life and death; it encompasses an exact, precisely mapped-out path. Through application of Scientology technology in an auditing session, a person is able to remove barriers and unwanted conditions and so become more himself. As a person progresses, he often reaches out to help others in the ways he has been helped.

In developing Scientology, L. Ron Hubbard found the means to develop a technology to free the human spirit and thereby allow man to really know himself. He thoroughly tested all of his procedures and recorded for future use those that proved most workable in bringing about uniformly predictable results. These comprise standard Scientology technology.

That which is real to the person himself is all one is asked to accept of Scientology. No beliefs are forced upon him. By training and processing, he finds out for himself the answers he is looking for in life.

What does Scientology accomplish?

Since Scientology is an *applied religious philosophy,* the stress is on application and workability. It addresses the individual and brings about self-improvement by increasing a person's awareness and ability to handle life. It differs from other religious philosophies in that it supplies the means through which a person can increase his ability to effectively handle the problems and situations he and others face in life.

What claims are made for Scientology?

Scientology can increase a person's awareness and its application can help one to achieve greater happiness, self-confidence and ability.

Man has often been attracted to philosophies that sound plausible but which have no technology that can be applied to bring about desirable changes in one's life. Scientology and Dianetics, on the other hand, supply the tools with which an individual can improve his own life and the lives of those around him.

Scientology philosophy is based on the premise that man is basically good and that man can improve conditions in his life. However, Scientology cannot promise to do anything by itself. Only the individual can bring about his own improvement by applying Scientology tenets to himself, his life and others in his environment.

How do people get into Scientology?

Usually by word of mouth, often by reading a book or seeing promotional materials or taking a personality test at a church of Scientology. Sometimes by meeting a Scientologist and seeing that he has "something"—a positive attitude toward life, certainty, self-confidence and happiness—which they too would like. Fundamentally, people get into Scientology because they want to improve something in their lives or because they wish to help others improve themselves and thus make a better civilization.

Scientology and Other Practices

Is Scientology like hypnotism, meditation, psychotherapy or other mental therapies?

There is no resemblance. In fact, it was as a result of L. Ron Hubbard's investigation of hypnotism and many other mental practices that he saw the need for practical answers to man's problems. In his book, *Dianetics: The Modern Science of Mental Health,* he wrote that he had found hypnotism and psychotherapy to be dangerous and impractical. Nearly all other methods of alleged mental science are based on principles that are quite the opposite of those used in Scientology. They treat man as a "thing" to be conditioned, not as a spiritual being who can find answers to life's problems and who can improve enormously.

Is Scientology a secret society?

Not at all. Scientology churches are open—you can go in at any time. Scientology literature is freely available to anyone. There is no demand for the individual to withdraw from society; on the contrary, Scientologists become *more* involved in life around them, as they want to take responsibility for improving conditions.

In what way does Scientology differ from other religions and religious philosophies?

Nearly all religious philosophies share a belief in helping man live a better life. In Scientology, this concept is expressed as one of the aims of the Church, which is to achieve a world without insanity, war and crime.

While Scientology religious philosophy has much in common with other religions in this regard and in terms of its basic religious concepts and its outreach into the community with social reform programs, the most valuable asset that Scientology has to offer is a wealth of technology which brings about greater spiritual awareness.

In Scientology there is no attempt to change a person's beliefs or to persuade him away from any religion to which he already belongs. Scientology helps people to achieve their goals: (1) through reading the materials contained in the books and publications; (2) through the unique counseling technology called auditing; (3) through training courses which utilize L. Ron Hubbard's discoveries in the field of education. Scientology makes it possible for *any* religion to attain its goals and is therefore a religion of religions.

Does Scientology interfere with other religions?

Scientology is all-denominational in that it opens its membership to people of all faiths. Part of the Church's Creed states that "all men have inalienable rights to their own religious practices and their performance."

Membership in Scientology does not mean that there is any necessity to leave your current church, synagogue, temple or mosque.

What does Scientology think of other religions?

Scientology respects all religions.

Scientology does not conflict with other religions or other religious practices. Quite often Scientology church members rekindle a greater interest than ever in the subject of religions—including the one of their birth.

What does Scientology have to say about Christianity?

Scientologists hold the Bible as a holy work and have no argument with the Christian belief that Jesus Christ was the Savior of Mankind and the Son of God. We share Christ's goals for man's achievement of wisdom, good health and immortality. Christianity is among the faiths studied by Scientology ministerial students.

There are probably many types of redemption. That of Christ was to heaven.

SCIENTOLOGY BELIEFS

Is man a spirit?

Yes. Here's a short exercise you can do to find out for yourself.

Close your eyes and get a picture of a cat.

Done?

That which is looking at that cat is you, a spirit.

How does one know man is a spirit?

It is a matter that each individual must examine for himself. Scientologists believe man is more than a mind and body and that it is he, himself, the spirit, who can control his mind and body.

Do you think your body would *do* anything by itself if it were not guided by you, the being?

What is the Scientology concept of God?

The Church has no dogma concerning God, and each person's concept is probably different. As a person becomes more aware of himself, others, the environment and God, each person attains his own certainty as to who God is and exactly what God means to him. The author of the universe exists. How God is symbolized or manifested is up to each individual to find for himself.

In his book *Science of Survival,* L. Ron Hubbard writes: "No culture in the history of the world, save the thoroughly depraved and expiring ones, has failed to affirm the existence of a Supreme Being. It is an empirical observation that men without a strong and lasting faith in a Supreme Being are less capable, less ethical and less valuable to themselves and society. . . . A man without an abiding faith is, by observation alone, more of a thing than a man."

Can't God be the only one to help man?

Scientologists take the maxim quite to heart that God helps those who help themselves. They believe that each person has the answers to the mysteries of life; all he requires is awareness of these answers, and this is what Scientology helps a person achieve. Man is accustomed to asking for pat answers. Scientology requires that the person think for himself and thus help himself become more intelligent, happy and healthy.

Does Scientology believe in brotherly love?

Yes, and perhaps goes a step further. L. Ron Hubbard wrote that "To love is the road to strength. To love in spite of all is the secret of greatness. And may very well be the greatest secret in this universe."

Why do Scientologists want to help people?

For several reasons. First, because Scientologists themselves have been helped enormously—and they want others to share the same successes. Second, Scientologists understand that life is not lived alone. An individual has more than just one dynamic (the urge to survive as self). He wants to help his family, his groups, mankind itself and living things survive better.

Does Scientology recognize good and evil?

Yes, in Scientology, a very clear distinction is made between good and evil. Those actions which enhance survival on the majority of the eight aspects or dynamics of life are good, and those which destroy or deny these aspects of life are evil. Decisions are then based on enhancing the majority of these dynamics of life.

Good may be defined as constructive. *Evil* may be defined as destructive.

Does Scientology believe man is sinful?

It is a basic tenet of Scientology that man is basically good, but that he is aberrated (capable of erring or departing from rational thought or behavior) and therefore commits harmful acts or sins, thus reducing his awareness and potential power.

Through Scientology he can confront his actions, erase the ignorance and aberration which surrounds them and know and experience truth again.

All religions seek truth. Freedom of the spirit is only to be found on the road to truth.

Sin is composed, according to Scientology, of lies and hidden actions and is therefore untruth.

Will Scientology put one in control of his mind?

Yes. As you are a spiritual being, quite separate from your mind and your body, Scientology will help *you* achieve a far better command over your mind, just as it helps you to intelligently control all aspects of your life.

Is Scientology about the mind?

No. Scientology is about the individual himself as separate and distinct from the mind. Dianetics concerns the mind and contains the most advanced technology of the mind man has.

Does Scientology believe in mind over matter?

Scientology addresses you—not your mind, not your body, but you.

Scientologists have found that the spirit is *potentially* superior to material things, and that the spirit, i.e., you, if cleansed of past traumas, transgressions and aberrations, can make miraculous changes in the physical universe that would not otherwise be possible.

Does Scientology believe one can exist outside of the body?

Before entering Scientology many people experience the feeling of looking down on one's body, and by achieving greater spiritual awareness through Scientology, this experience becomes nothing out of the ordinary. Scientology believes that man is not his body, his mind or his brain. He, a spiritual force, energizes the physical body and his life.

Scientology proved, for the first time, that man was a spiritual being, not an animal.

Does Scientology believe in reincarnation or past lives?

Reincarnation is a definite system and is not part of Scientology. It is a fact that unless one begins to handle aberrations built up in past lives, he doesn't progress.

The definition of the term *reincarnation* has been altered from its original meaning. The word has come to mean "to be born again in different life forms," whereas its actual definition is "to be born again into the flesh or into another body."

Today in Scientology, many people have certainty that they have lived lives prior to their current one. These are referred to as past lives, not as reincarnation.

Individuals are free to believe this or not; past lives are not a dogma in Scientology, but generally Scientologists, during their auditing, experience a past life and then *know* for themselves that they have lived before.

To believe one had a physical or other existence prior to the identity of the current body is not a new concept—but it is an exciting one.

In Scientology, you are given the tools to handle upsets and aberrations from past lives that adversely affect you in present time, thus freeing you to live a much happier life.

Does Scientology believe in charity and welfare?

It does. However, Scientologists also believe in the principle that exchange is necessary. If a person only receives and never gives, he will not be a happy person and will lose his own self-respect. Therefore, any Scientology-sponsored charity programs also encourage those receiving the charity to make some form of contribution by helping others so that self-respect can be maintained.

Does Scientology hold any political views?

Scientology is nonpolitical. By its Creed, "All men have inalienable rights to conceive, choose, assist or support their own organizations, churches and governments." Scientologists are free to hold their own political views, vote for the candidates of their choice, etc., and are not given direction from the Church as to what position to take on political issues or candidates. The Church believes there should be separation of church and state.

Can children participate in Scientology? How?

Yes, there are many children who participate in Scientology. There are no age restrictions as to who can take Scientology courses or receive auditing. Some churches also deliver special courses and study programs specifically designed for young people. If the person is below the legal age, he must first get written consent from his parents or guardian to take Scientology services. Scientologists generally want their children to have Scientology available to them so are quite agreeable to have their children take Scientology services.

What does Scientology say about the raising of children?

L. Ron Hubbard has written a great deal about raising children. In Scientology, children are recognized as people who should be given all the respect and love granted adults.

Scientologists believe children should be encouraged to contribute to family life, not just be "seen and not heard" as the old saying goes. Children are spiritual beings, and as such they need to exchange with those around them in order to thrive and live productive, happy lives. For more information on handling children, the book *Child Dianetics* and the course "How to Be a Successful Parent" are recommended.

Most children raised in good Scientology homes are above average in ability and quickly begin to understand how and why people act as they do. Life thus becomes a lot safer and happier for them.

Can one make up his own mind about Scientology?

One can and indeed one should. Scientology enables you to think for yourself. There is no purpose served in studying Scientology because someone else wants you to. But if you've taken a good look at your life and have decided that you want to make it better, the best thing is to start and find out for yourself what Scientology can do for you. One should read one of the basic books by L. Ron Hubbard, such as *Dianetics: The Modern Science of Mental*

Health or *Scientology: The Fundamentals of Thought.*

What is real in Scientology for you is what you find in it that is real for you.

What is the Scientology cross?

It is an eight-pointed cross representing the eight parts or dynamics of life through which each individual is striving to survive. These parts are: the urge toward existence as self, as an individual; the urge to survive through creativity, including the family unit and the rearing of children; the urge to survive through a group of individuals or as a group; the urge toward survival through all mankind and as all mankind; the urge to survive as life forms and with the help of life forms such as animals, birds, insects, fish and vegetation; the urge to survive of the physical universe, by the physical universe itself and with the help of the physical universe and each one of its component parts; the urge to survive as spiritual beings or the urge for life itself to survive; the urge toward existence as infinity. To be able to live happily with respect to each of these spheres of existence is symbolized by the Scientology cross.

As a matter of interest, the cross as a symbol predates Christianity.

What religious holidays do Scientologists celebrate?

Scientologists celebrate several major holidays annually. These include the birthday of L. Ron Hubbard (March 13); the date marking the initial publication of *Dianetics* (May 9); Auditor's Day, in honor of all auditors (second Sunday in September); and the International Association of Scientologists Anniversary, to mark the founding of this organization which unites, supports and protects the Scientology religion and Scientologists in all parts of the world (October 7).

Additionally, each local country or area may observe its own significant dates, such as the founding of the church in its area or the opening of the first Dianetics or Scientology organization in that country. Members of the Church also observe traditional religious holidays such as Christmas.

SCIENTOLOGY'S FOUNDER

Is L. Ron Hubbard still alive?

No. L. Ron Hubbard passed away on January 24, 1986, but he remains with us in spirit and through the legacy of his technology and its continual application around the globe.

Who was L. Ron Hubbard?

L. Ron Hubbard is the Founder of Dianetics and Scientology and the author of its scriptures. His research on the mind and life is recorded in the tens of millions of words on the subject of the human spirit which comprise Dianetics and Scientology philosophy. His works cover subjects as diverse as drug rehabilitation, education, marriage and family, success at work, administration, art and many other aspects of life.

His best-selling self-help book *Dianetics: The Modern Science of Mental Health* alone has sold millions and millions of copies and has continued to appear on the *New York Times* and other bestseller lists around the world over four decades after its original publication.

Testimony to the applicability and workability of his discoveries are the millions of happy and successful people and the hundreds of Dianetics and Scientology churches, missions and groups internationally.

L. Ron Hubbard dedicated his life to helping others. He saw that times needed to change, and he created a workable technology so that needed changes could occur for millions of people. He departed his body on January 24, 1986 leaving with us his life's work which is continued today through the application of his discoveries which help millions around the world.

What was L. Ron Hubbard's role in the Church?

L. Ron Hubbard founded the Scientology philosophy. A group of Scientologists then formed the first Church of Scientology in Los Angeles in 1954.

Mr. Hubbard ran the early Dianetics and Scientology organizations until 1966, when he retired from running them on a day-to-day basis and turned this function over to Scientology Church executives. He continued to take an interest in the Church's expansion and advised on administrative matters when specifically asked for advice, but he mainly spent his time researching the upper levels of Scientology and codifying the technology.

Has L. Ron Hubbard's death affected the Church?

L. Ron Hubbard recorded the results of all his research in writing, on film or in taped lectures so that the technology would be preserved. As a result, Scientology has continued to expand, and its future survival is assured.

All great religious leaders of the past have died. Their work flourishes. Men die. Wisdom and ideas do not.

How did L. Ron Hubbard rise above the reactive mind when others didn't?

He applied to himself the principles he had found.

Did L. Ron Hubbard make a lot of money out of Scientology?

No. He received no royalties from the fees paid to Scientology organizations for training and processing. In fact, L. Ron Hubbard forgave Scientology churches a thirteen-million-dollar debt in 1966 when he retired as Executive Director.

He made his money from the royalties on his books. One book alone, *Dianetics,* has sold *millions* of copies, and his total book sales of both fiction and nonfiction are in excess of one hundred million copies around the world, including more than twenty national bestsellers in the 1980s.

In fact, Mr. Hubbard's books still sell by the millions each year and the royalties from the sale of these books and his life's fortune were willed to the Church to help ensure the future application of his technology to the betterment of mankind.

Was L. Ron Hubbard a millionaire?

L. Ron Hubbard was one of those fortunate people who never made problems over money. He inherited some wealth at an early age, but in the early 1930s became one of the highest paid writers in America long before *Dianetics.*

He was a millionaire several times over from his book royalties. His public book sales continue to be astronomical.

How is it that one man could discover so much information?

He simply cared enough to want it and had the intelligence and persistence to research and find it.

Few men have been trained in all the Eastern philosophies and in the highest levels of Western science as well.

Knowing that his research was only as valuable as it provided workable solutions to man's problems, he tested all of his discoveries and found the most effective methods for applying the results of his research. His workable methods enabled him to continue research into higher and higher realms of spiritual awareness.

Do Scientologists believe that L. Ron Hubbard was Jesus Christ?

No. L. Ron Hubbard personally stated he was a man as others are men. He was a much-loved friend and teacher and continues to be respected and loved.

Did L. Ron Hubbard go Clear?

Yes. In order to map the route for others he had to make it himself.

Scientology Attitudes and Practices

How do Scientologists view life?

As a game—a game in which everyone can win. Scientologists are optimistic about life and believe there is hope for a saner world and better civilization and are actively doing all they can to achieve this.

What moral codes do Scientologists live by?

There are four main codes that Scientologists apply in life. One is the Auditor's Code which gives the basic rules an auditor must abide by to ensure excellent auditing results.

Another is the Code of a Scientologist, guidelines which Scientologists agree to follow in order to achieve the aims of Scientology.

There is an ethical code, called the Code of Honor, that Scientologists use in dealing with their fellow men.

L. Ron Hubbard has also written a nonreligious moral code called "The Way to Happiness" which gives basic precepts for a happy life. This moral code is used by Scientologists and non-Scientologists alike, with tens of millions of copies distributed in communities all around the world.

What is Scientology's view on drugs?

Scientologists consider that drugs cause damaging effects on a person—physically, mentally and spiritually. They decrease awareness and hinder abilities. They are a "solution" to some other problem, which themselves become a problem.

Scientologists do not take street drugs or mind-altering psychiatric drugs.

Scientologists do use prescribed drugs as part of medical programs from competent physicians, but have found that as a result of auditing, they need to take medical drugs much less frequently and also that medications such as antibiotics seem to work more rapidly when being audited.

For more information about drugs and what can be done about them, the book *Clear Body, Clear Mind: The Effective Purification Program* is recommended.

Why are there so many young people on staff in Scientology?

Many Scientologists are under thirty-five. We find that young Scientologists enjoy the lifestyle working in the Church. It may be that due to the expansion of Scientology they find that there are many opportunities to achieve responsible positions quite rapidly. Many families have three generations working in Scientology. There are also a great many older people in Scientology.

Do you have any special dietary laws or rules against smoking or drinking in Scientology?

No. There are no dietary laws whatsoever and no general prohibitions against smoking or drinking. The only guidelines in Scientology are that no alcohol is allowed twenty-four hours prior to or during auditing sessions, and that no drinking is allowed twenty-four hours prior to or during study. The effects of the alcohol would make it impossible to get the gains one can get from auditing and training.

Smoking is forbidden in course rooms or during auditing sessions, as such would distract oneself and others. Rules for student behavior are laid out in a Church policy called the "Students' Guide to Acceptable Behavior."

Do Scientologists use medical doctors?

Yes. The Church of Scientology has always had the firm policy of sending sick parishioners to medical doctors to handle the physical aspect of any illness or injury. A Scientologist with a physical condition is instructed to get the needed medical examination and treatment. He then resumes his auditing so as to handle any spiritual trauma connected with the physical condition. There are also many medical doctors who are Scientologists.

In Scientology does one have to sacrifice one's individuality?

No. People are unique, even though they have in common certain problems and aberrations. As they become disentangled from the stimulus-response part of their mind, they become more themselves, more unique, more individual and learn to believe in themselves. In fact, becoming more aware of and able to express one's own unique beingness is encouraged in Scientology. Scientology teaches one to maintain his personal integrity and to develop fully as an individual.

What benefits can one get from Scientology?

In reviewing success stories written by Scientologists, there are a few common themes that stand out. One is that many people have attained the ability to communicate in relationships, whether with family members and spouses, friends, or even mere acquaintances; another is that they are freed from stress at work and in other areas of their lives; another common one is that they can expand their potential and do things they never thought possible.

What is Scientology's system of ethics?

L. Ron Hubbard has defined *ethics* as "reason and the contemplation of optimum survival."

In Scientology, ethics is a rational system based on a number of codes of practice.

L. Ron Hubbard has pointed out: "Dishonest conduct is nonsurvival. Anything is unreasonable or evil which brings about the destruction of individuals, groups, or inhibits the future of the race."

Man has long postulated a means by which he could put himself on the right path. As long ago as 500 B.C., religions recognized that confession frees a person spiritually from the burden of sin.

In Scientology, it has been found that a Confessional (a type of auditing) assists the person who has transgressed against his own and his group's moral code to unburden himself and again feel good about himself and be a contributing member of the group.

L. Ron Hubbard has written: "No man who is not himself honest can be free—he is his own trap. When his own deeds cannot be disclosed, then he is a prisoner; he must withhold himself from his fellows and is a slave to his own conscience."

In addition to the Confessional, Scientology's ethics system includes a body of technology called conditions formulas. Mr. Hubbard discovered that there are various states of existence in which an individual operates (called "conditions") and that there are exact formulas connected with these operating states. Each formula has a number of exact steps.

A person can determine what condition or operating state any area of his life is in and apply the conditions formulas to move it into a higher condition.

While very simple, such actions are quite powerful and have enabled millions of individuals to improve conditions in their lives in ways they never thought possible.

These are just two of the tools from the wealth of ethics technology that exists in Scientology. Complete information on this subject is contained in the book *Introduction to Scientology Ethics* by L. Ron Hubbard.

What does "clear the planet" mean?

It means that Scientologists want to clear the planet of insanity, war and crime, and in its place create a civilization in which sanity and peace exist. In order to do this, they must help individuals become clear of their own individual insanities and regain awareness that they are basically good.

What does "suppressive person" mean?

According to L. Ron Hubbard, a suppressive person is "a person who seeks to *suppress,* or squash, any betterment activity or group. A suppressive person suppresses other people in his vicinity. This is the person whose behavior is calculated to be disastrous." Well-known examples of such a personality are Napoleon and Hitler.

Mr. Hubbard found that a suppressive person, also called an antisocial personality, has definite antisocial attributes.

The basic reason the antisocial personality behaves as he or she does lies in a hidden terror of others.

To such a person every other being is an enemy, an enemy to be covertly or overtly destroyed.

The fixation is that survival itself depends on "keeping others down" or "keeping people ignorant."

If anyone were to promise to make others stronger or brighter, the antisocial personality suffers the utmost agony of personal danger.

Because of this, the suppressive person seeks to upset, continuously undermine, spread bad news about and denigrate Scientology and Scientologists. The antisocial personality is against what Scientology is about—helping people become more able and improving conditions in society.

For the good of the Church and the individuals in it, such a person is officially labeled a suppressive person so that others will know not to associate with him.

For more understanding of suppressive persons and how to handle them, the book *Introduction to Scientology Ethics* is recommended.

What is disconnection?

A Scientologist can have trouble making spiritual progress in his auditing or training if he is connected to someone who is suppressive or who is antagonistic to Scientology or its tenets. He will get better from Scientology, but then may lose his gains because he is being invalidated by the antagonistic person. In order to resolve this, he either handles the other person's antagonism with true data about the Church, or as a last resort when all attempts to handle have failed, he disconnects from the person.

In 1983, L. Ron Hubbard clearly defined the two terms, "disconnect" and "handle," as related to this subject:

"The term *handle* most commonly means to smooth out a situation with another person by applying the technology of communication.

"The term *disconnection* is defined as a self-determined decision made by an individual that he is not going to be connected to another. It is a severing of a communication line.

"The basic principle of handle or disconnect exists in any group and ours is no different.

"It is much like trying to deal with a criminal. If he will not handle, the society resorts to the only other solution: It 'disconnects' the criminal from the society. In other words, they remove the guy from society and put him in a prison because he won't *handle* his problem or otherwise cease to commit criminal acts against others."

A person who disconnects is simply exercising his right to communicate or not to communicate with a particular person. This is one of the most fundamental rights of man. "Communication, however, is a two-way flow," Mr. Hubbard pointed out. "If one has the right to communicate, then one must also have the right to not receive communication from another. It is this latter corollary of the right to communicate that gives us our right to privacy."

Another example is marriage. In a monogamous society, the agreement is that one will be married to only one person at a time. If one partner, say the husband, starts to have second dynamic relations with a person other than his partner, the wife has the right to insist either that this communication cease or that the marriage itself ends.

In this example, the optimum solution would be for the wife to resolve the situation through communication so that her husband, who is violating the agreements, is handled. But if this is not possible, then the wife has no choice other than to disconnect (sever the marriage communication lines if only by separation). To do otherwise will only bring disaster, as the wife is connected to someone antagonistic to the original agreements on which the marriage is based.

With the technology of handle or disconnect, Scientologists are, in actual fact, doing nothing different than any society, group or marriage down through thousands of years.

Is Scientology a cult?

Assuming that modern usage of the word *cult* implies an elite secrecy and unthinking zealotry, then consider this: Scientology is the fastest growing religion in the world today. The materials that comprise Scientology scriptures are fully codified, broadly published and available to anyone. Churches and missions are open to the public seven days a week. Anyone can come in for a tour and see for himself what the Church is all about.

Scientology is unique in that it contains no dogma and its adherents are not told or forced to "believe" anything. In Scientology, what is true for the individual is only what he has observed and knows is true for him. Scientology is a technology one can use and through its use discover its workability for oneself.

Scientologists come from all walks of life, ranging from teachers to businessmen, physicians, housewives, artists, engineers, nurses, construction workers, celebrities, marketing and administrative personnel, secretaries, athletes, civil servants and many others.

The Church and its actions are far from secretive; there is nothing mystical about Scientology or its members or practices. The Church's leaders are in close touch with the membership; they hold a number of briefing events each year which are attended by tens of thousands.

Scientologists actively improve their communities; they are out there, involved, visible and effective.

The fact of the matter is there isn't a religion today that hasn't been called a cult at some point in its history by antagonistic interests. Nazis thought Jews and Eastern European religious sects to be cults. In the sixteenth century Catholics considered reform churches cults. Earlier than that Roman rulers considered the Christian community a cult. History has taught us to beware of those who would label *any* religious group a cult. It is traditionally the first step before wholesale persecution, and is always the statement of an unenlightened and uninformed individual, usually with ill motives as the Nazi history makes so clear.

Does Scientology engage in brainwashing or mind control?

No. In fact, what we do is exactly the opposite. We free people and enable them to think for themselves.

Millions of Church members from literally all walks of life have attested to the positive benefits received from Scientology. A common theme to their personal success stories is that they are now more in control of their lives than they ever have been.

In fact, Mr. Hubbard was one of the first to discover and expose *actual* mind control and brainwashing experimentation conducted by United States military and intelligence agencies during and after World War II.

He called these techniques "pain-drug-hypnosis" or PDH.

In his 1951 book, *Science of Survival,* Mr. Hubbard wrote:

"There is another form of hypnotism . . . This form of hypnotism has been a carefully guarded secret of certain military and intelligence organizations. It is a vicious war weapon and may be of considerably more use in conquering a society than the atomic bomb. This is no exaggeration. The extensiveness of the use of this form of hypnotism in espionage work is so wide today that it is long past the time when people should have become alarmed about it. It required Dianetic processing to uncover pain-drug-hypnosis. Otherwise, pain-drug-hypnosis was out of sight, unsuspected and unknown."

Not only did he uncover such blatantly destructive experimentation, but the technology he developed, Dianetics, could *undo* the effects of PDH and free a person from the grip of mind control.

Years after Mr. Hubbard learned about these government-sponsored psychiatric mind control experiments, documents released under the Freedom of Information Act detailed the extent to which these techniques were being used.

Over the years, the Church of Scientology has exposed numerous instances of brainwashing or mind control practices, such as those involved in so-called "deprograming." In this case, individuals are taken captive and forced to renounce their chosen religious or political group, generally using some form of coercion, food or sleep deprivation and sometimes drugs.

Such practices are diametrically opposed to the aims of Scientology, which are to free man and return to him his ability to control his own life.

Does Scientology actively promote for new members?

Yes. Scientologists make the technology broadly available to others because they want others to receive the same gains they have experienced. The Church wants more people to know and apply the works of L. Ron Hubbard and actively and vigorously promotes this.

Does one really need Scientology to do well in life?

That is a question you will have to answer for yourself. A Scientologist's viewpoint is that while some people might be surviving quite well without Scientology, they can always do better and expand their potentials even further. In fact, Scientology was developed to help the able become more able and one usually finds the people doing best in life are the first ones to embrace Scientology.

If you are interested in self-improvement, Scientology provides a tested route by which you can obtain tremendous benefits and learn to use your mind, talents and abilities to the fullest.

If you know people who are doing well but have never heard of Scientology, the question is: "Could they be doing better?"

Does one have to believe in Scientology?

No. One is not expected to believe in Scientology. One is only expected to study and apply the data and see for himself if it works for him. To quote L. Ron Hubbard, "Anything that isn't true for you when you study it carefully isn't true."

Why do Scientologists sometimes seem so intent on what they are doing?

If you had a chance to change yourself and civilization so greatly, you would be interested as well.

What do the terms preclear, student *and* auditor *mean?*

A *preclear* is someone who is receiving Scientology or Dianetics auditing on his way to becoming Clear. Through auditing he is finding out more about himself and life.

A *student* is one who reads in detail in order to learn and then apply the materials he has studied. One studies Scientology for itself and uses it exactly as stated, then forms his own conclusions as to whether or not the tenets he has assimilated are correct and workable.

An *auditor* is a Dianetics or Scientology practitioner trained in the technology of auditing. *Auditor* means "one who listens" (from the Latin word *audire*). An auditor listens and computes, applying standard technology to preclears to help them achieve the abilities as stated on the Classification, Gradation and Awareness Chart. An auditor's job is to ask the preclear to look, and get him to do so.

What is the E-Meter and how does it work?

E-Meter is a shortened term for *electropsychometer*. It is a religious artifact used as a spiritual guide in auditing. It is for use only by a Scientology minister or a Scientology minister-in-training to help the preclear locate and confront areas of spiritual upset.

In itself, the E-Meter does nothing. It is an electronic instrument that measures mental state and change of state in individuals and assists the precision and speed of auditing. The E-Meter is not intended or effective for the diagnosis, treatment or prevention of any disease.

The book *Understanding the E-Meter* offers a simple explanation of how the E-Meter works and what it actually measures. In order to understand what the E-Meter does, it is necessary to understand some basic Scientology concepts.

There are three basic parts of man—mind, body and thetan. The thetan is an immortal spiritual being—the individual himself. He (the thetan) inhabits a body, which is a carbon-oxygen machine. He has a mind, which is a collection of mental image pictures he has created.

These pictures have weight and mass and can impinge on the person when he is emotionally upset.

This is what makes the E-Meter read—the impingement of such pictures against the body.

The E-Meter puts a very small electrical current (approximately one and a half volts) through the body. This is about the same amount of current as in the average battery-powered wristwatch.

When a person thinks a thought, looks at a picture, reexperiences an incident or when he shifts some part of the pictures in his mind, he is moving and changing actual mental mass and energy. These changes in the person's mind affect the tiny flow of electrical energy generated by the E-Meter, which causes the needle on its dial to move.

The E-Meter thus measures changes that are caused by the spiritual being in his own mind (i.e., the movement of mental masses around him) and in this capacity, it is a religious artifact.

The E-Meter is used to help the individual who is being audited uncover truth. By locating areas of mental or spiritual trauma, the E-Meter helps both the auditor and the preclear locate exactly what to address in auditing.

THE ORGANIZATIONS OF SCIENTOLOGY

Scientology is a philosophy. Why does it need to be organized?

Scientology is an *applied* religious philosophy. Therefore organization is needed to make the technology available and teach people to apply it.

How many people work in a Scientology church?

The number of staff varies from church to church. Small churches may have 20 and large ones over 500.

How is Scientology organized?

There is a "mother church" which is the Church of Scientology International. It is headquartered in Los Angeles. It is responsible for the ecclesiastical supervision of the rest of the Scientology churches around the world, which are organized in a hierarchical structure not dissimilar to that of the Catholic Church. (For more information about the structure of the Church, see Part 5.)

Where are Scientology churches located?

Scientology churches and missions exist all over the world. There are a great many churches and far more missions in various countries.

What does a Scientology church or mission actually do?

The main activities of Scientology churches and missions are training Scientology ministers and providing auditing. The church also conducts Sunday services, weddings, funerals and christenings and delivers other chaplain services. The church helps the individual become more able to help himself and to help others. This is done by training and auditing.

What is the Office of Special Affairs?

The Office of Special Affairs (OSA) deals with legal affairs for the Church. It also publishes the facts about the social betterment works of Scientology, informing the government, the media, other religions and other groups with interests similar to those of the Church. OSA also oversees the social reform programs of the Church, among which are those that expose and effectively handle violations of individual and human rights.

What is the Flag Service Organization?

The Flag Service Organization (FSO), often referred to as "Flag," is located in Clearwater, Florida. It delivers advanced spiritual training and auditing. It retains its name from the days when it used to operate from the flagship *Apollo.* ("Flag" in nautical terms means "the flagship" or the vessel which gives orders to others.)

What is the Flag Ship Service Organization?

The Flag Ship Service Organization is located aboard the 450-foot ship called the *Freewinds,* and is an advanced religious retreat that delivers the level of auditing called New OT VIII and specialized training to Scientologists.

What is the Sea Organization?

The Sea Organization (commonly referred to as the Sea Org) is a confraternal organization existing within the formalized structure of the Church. It is composed of the most dedicated Scientology staff who have decided to devote their lives to the delivery and expansion of Scientology.

The Sea Organization has no separate corporate structure or identity and its members work for various different churches of Scientology and are subject, as are all other employees of that church, to the orders and directions of the board of directors.

The Sea Org was established in 1967 and once operated from a number of ships. It was set up to help L. Ron Hubbard with research of earlier civilizations and to carry out supervision of Church organizations around the world to keep Scientology expanding. It is also entrusted to deliver the advanced services of Scientology.

The Sea Organization retains its name in celebration of the fact that the Founder's life was majorly connected with the sea. It exists to help keep Scientology working.

Is it true that people in the Sea Org sign a billion-year contract?

Yes, they do. It is a symbolic document which, similar to vows of dedication in other faiths and orders, serves to signify an individual's eternal commitment to the goals, purposes and principles of the Scientology religion. Sea Org members have dedicated their lives to working toward these ends and toward a world without war, drugs, crime and illiteracy.

Why does Scientology have ministers? Are all Scientologists ministers?

The Church of Scientology has ministers to deliver Scientology religious services to church parishioners. Only those who specifically enroll in and graduate from the Scientology Minister's Course and its prerequisites, and fulfill the requirements for ordination are Scientology ministers. All Scientology auditors are required to become ordained ministers; however, they are allowed to audit as ministerial students while fulfilling their ordination requirements.

What are field staff members?

Field staff members are individual Scientologists who disseminate Scientology, provide books to interested friends, family members and associates and introduce (or select) people to the Church. They are appointed by their nearest Scientology organization. Because they have had gains from Dianetics and Scientology themselves, they naturally want to share it with others.

Why is everything copyrighted and trademarked in Scientology?

Scientology and Dianetics are technologies that work if applied exactly. If they are altered, the results will not be uniform.

For this reason, the technology is copyrighted and the words and symbols which represent the technology are trademarked. This way, nobody can misrepresent something as standard Scientology or Dianetics that really isn't.

In fact many persons have tried to rip off and profit from the technologies of Dianetics and Scientology. The subjects were developed for spiritual salvation, not for anyone's personal enrichment. Through ownership of the trademarks and copyrights, such ill-intentioned actions are prevented by the Church.

CHURCH FUNDING

Why do Scientologists make donations?

Some churches have a system of tithes, others require their members to pay for pew rentals, religious ceremonies and services. In the Church of Scientology, parishioners make donations for auditing or training they wish to take. These contributions by Scientologists are the primary source of financial support for the Church and fund all the community programs and social betterment activities of Scientology. Scientologists are not required to tithe or make other donations.

Ideally, Dianetics and Scientology services would be free, and all Scientologists wish they were. But those are not the realities of life. When one considers the cost of delivering even one hour of auditing, requiring extensively trained specialists, and the overhead costs of maintaining church premises, the necessity of donations becomes clear.

The donation system in Scientology is the most equitable as those who use the facilities of the Church are the ones who most directly contribute to its upkeep and continued existence. Naturally, no donation is expected from those not receiving auditing or training. And church doors are always open to those who wish to learn more about the philosophy of Scientology, be they parishioners or not. There are tape plays of L. Ron Hubbard's lectures, introductory lectures, books available, people to discuss questions with, and of course the more traditional church activities—Sunday service, sermons, weddings, christenings, funerals—all of which are provided without any donation necessary.

Scientology does not have hundreds of years of accumulated wealth and property like other religions—it must make its way in the world according to the economics of today's society.

Scientologists' donations keep the Church alive and functioning, fund its widespread social reform programs, make Scientology known to people who may otherwise never have the opportunity to avail themselves of it, and help create a safe and pleasant environment for everyone.

Why does one have to make donations to separate organizations for their services?

Scientology churches and missions are separate corporations and have separate financial records. The donations that go to each church for services delivered by that church must be separately banked and accurate records kept in alignment with the accounting procedures and laws in each country.

What about those who cannot afford to make donations for services?

There is a Free Scientology Center in churches of Scientology where those who cannot afford the donations can receive free auditing from ministerial students.

Many Scientology services are free and the knowledge is free to all men. There are also books, books, books and free public lectures, Sunday services and other religious services for which there is no cost. Books can be obtained in the local area either by going to a church of Scientology, a public bookstore or local library.

But it's interesting that once a person becomes more causative through the application of Scientology technology in his life, he does not usually need or want free services for very long. He becomes capable of holding a good job and thereby able to exchange for the services he wants.

Ministers-in-training can receive free auditing from other students while they are doing their training.

Is the Church profit-making?

No. Scientology churches are nonprofit organizations, as the donations all go back into the support and expansion of the Church.

How much does it cost to go Clear?

The cost varies from individual to individual depending on which route to Clear one takes.

One route is to pay for professional auditing and get audited all the way up to Clear. The preferred route, however, is to get trained as an auditor and co-audit with another Scientology student. The co-auditing route to Clear requires far less donations than professional auditing plus one helps another to progress. As professional auditing is much more expensive for the organization to deliver (requiring several staff to service one parishioner) the donations are necessarily higher. Training donation rates are much more economical and an incentive for persons to train while they co-audit without cost to the state of Clear.

No matter which route one chooses to achieve the state of Clear, all who have attained it express the pricelessness of the increased spiritual freedom they have achieved.

How well paid are Scientology staff?

The pay varies from church to church and from time to time. Staff are paid in proportion to the amount of donations received by their individual organizations. Thus, staff members are in control of how much they make by virtue of how well they perform individually on their own jobs.

In any event, Scientology staff aren't motivated by money and in no instance anywhere in the church structure is pay exorbitant. Scientology staff are motivated by a desire to help, not get rich.

SCIENTOLOGY BOOKS

What is the best book for a beginning Scientologist to read?

Dianetics: The Modern Science of Mental Health, which is the best-selling self-help book of all time, is the book recommended for beginners who are interested in the mind and how it works. This book has been a bestseller for over forty years.

In 1977, *Publishers Weekly* called *Dianetics: The Modern Science of Mental Health* "perhaps the best-selling non-Christian book of all time in the West." In 1988, *Publishers Weekly* awarded *Dianetics* its prestigious "Century Award" for more than 100 weeks on its bestseller list, officially designating it the No. 1 best-selling self-help book of all time.

If a person is more interested in starting with a broad summary of L. Ron Hubbard's research and findings about man as a spiritual being and basic principles of life, the first recommended book is *Scientology: The Fundamentals of Thought.* (Chapter 41 gives a more detailed explanation of the books available and suggested course of reading.)

Are the books difficult to understand?

Not at all. The books are quite easy to understand. Depending on what aspect of Scientology and Dianetics you are most interested in, any church Bookstore Officer can recommend the best sequence in which the books should be read.

Where can L. Ron Hubbard's books be purchased?

All of his books are available at missions and churches of Scientology. Many of his books are also available in popular bookstores and in libraries in cities all over the world.

What books should one read to get information about:

1. Dianetics:
   The Basic Dianetics Picture Book
   Dianetics: The Modern Science of Mental Health
   The Dynamics of Life
   Dianetics: The Evolution of a Science
   Child Dianetics
2. Basic Scientology principles:
   The Basic Scientology Picture Book
   Scientology: The Fundamentals of Thought
   A New Slant on Life
   Scientology 0-8: The Book of Basics
3. Self-help, tests and processes:
   Self Analysis
4. Handling the residual effects of drugs and toxins:
   Purification: An Illustrated Answer to Drugs
   Clear Body, Clear Mind: The Effective Purification Program
5. Basic principles of communication:
   Dianetics 55!
6. Predicting human behavior and understanding people:
   Science of Survival
7. How to increase success on the job:
   The Problems of Work
   How to Live Though An Executive
8. Basic principles of organization:
   The Organization Executive Course volumes 0–7
9. Basic principles of management:
   Management Series volumes 1, 2 and 3
10. The principles of ethics and how to use them to live a more productive life:
    Introduction to Scientology Ethics

11. Study methods:
    Basic Study Manual
    Learning How to Learn
    Study Skills for Life
    How to Use a Dictionary Picture Book for Children
12. Procedures to increase one's spiritual awareness and abilities:
    The Creation of Human Ability
    Advanced Procedure and Axioms
    Scientology 8-8008
    Scientology 8-80
13. Past lives and how they relate to this life:
    Have You Lived Before This Life?
    A History of Man
14. The application of basic Scientology technology to help others improve their lives:
    The Volunteer Minister's Handbook

These books were all written by L. Ron Hubbard or compiled from his works, and are just a few of the dozens and dozens of Scientology and Dianetics books available at churches of Scientology.

How can one get happiness out of a book?

The key to happiness is knowledge. Scientology and Dianetics books contain knowledge one can actually apply in life.

Being able to accomplish these improvements definitely makes people happier.

Dianetics

What is Dianetics?

L. Ron Hubbard discovered the single source of stress, worry, self-doubt and psychosomatic illness—the reactive mind. In his book *Dianetics: The Modern Science of Mental Health* he described the reactive mind in detail and laid out a simple, practical, easily taught technology to overcome it and reach the state of Clear. Dianetics (which means "through soul") is that technology.

What is the mind? Where is the mind?

The mind is basically a communication and control system between the thetan—the spiritual being that is the person himself—and his environment. It is composed of mental image pictures which are recordings of past experiences.

The individual uses his mind to pose and resolve problems related to survival and to direct his efforts according to these solutions.

What is the difference between the analytical mind and the reactive mind?

The analytical mind is the conscious, aware mind which thinks, observes data, remembers it and resolves problems. The reactive mind is the portion of a person's mind which works on a totally stimulus-response basis, which is not under his volitional control, and which exerts force and the power of command over his awareness, purposes, thoughts, body and actions.

What is the difference between Scientology and Dianetics?

Dianetics is a technology which uncovers the source of unwanted sensations and emotions, accidents, injuries and psychosomatic illnesses, and which sets forth effective handlings for these conditions.

Dianetics comes from the Greek *dia* meaning "through" and *nous,* "soul." It is further defined as "what the soul is doing to the body."

Scientology is the study and handling of the spirit in relationship to itself, universes and other life. It is used to increase spiritual freedom, intelligence and ability and to enable a person to realize his own immortality.

Dianetics and Scientology are *separate* subjects, but the delivery of each has in common certain tools like the E-Meter and the basic rules of auditing.

SCIENTOLOGY AND DIANETICS COURSES

What training should a person take first?

The first action a person should take in his Scientology training is to read a book, such as *Dianetics: The Modern Science of Mental Health* or *Scientology: The Fundamentals of Thought.* He can study these on an extension course which is designed to help people understand the basic fundamentals of L. Ron Hubbard's books and find out about Scientology for themselves. The lessons in the course are completed and mailed in to the Extension Course Supervisor who grades them and informs the student by return mail what his grade is and any parts of the book he may have misunderstood.

After completing a book or extension course, he should go into a church and see one of the Public Division Registrars who can help him decide which course he should do next. There are many different services available. For instance, many Life Improvement Courses exist, on such subjects as marriage, children, work, relationships with others and personal integrity. These help a person move from effect to cause in a specific area of life. Or there is the Hubbard Dianetics Seminar which utilizes Dianetics auditing techniques based on *Dianetics: The Modern Science of Mental Health,* providing as much Dianetics auditing to a person as he wants and giving him experience applying Dianetics to another. There is also the Success Through Communication Course which teaches the basic communication skills one needs to succeed in social or other situations.

Factually, it is best to talk to someone to find out which of the many courses available is addressed most directly to what one wants to handle or improve in life.

What does one get out of Scientology and Dianetics courses?

Training gives a person the knowledge and tools to handle life. A basic datum in Scientology is that what one learns is only as valuable as it can be applied, and as it helps one do better in life. This is why Scientology is correctly called an *applied* religious philosophy. The information and technology a person learns is not just to increase his understanding (although it will definitely do that as well), but it is for USE.

Although many Scientologists become practicing Scientology ministers, many others simply use the data in their everyday lives, on the job, and with their friends and family members. They report that life becomes more confrontable, their abilities increase and they are happier because they are winning in the game of life.

How are Scientology and Dianetics training different from studying philosophy or other religions?

The major difference is that Scientology and Dianetics training give one *tools* to use in life. Whereas studying other philosophies or religions may provide information that is interesting, only in Scientology does the individual get the exact tools he needs to change and improve conditions in his life.

Should I get my auditing before I get trained?

L. Ron Hubbard has written many times about the fact that 50 percent of one's gains are from training and 50 percent are from auditing. It is actually impossible to successfully make it through the upper processing levels of Scientology without also being trained. Therefore, to get the most from Scientology, one progresses in his training simultaneously with or at a comparable rate to his progress in auditing.

When can I take Scientology courses?

Most churches of Scientology are open from 9:00 in the morning until 10:30 at night weekdays and 9:00 a.m. to 6:00 p.m. on weekends. Several different course schedules are offered within these hours.

How are Scientology courses run?

Scientology training is unique. Each course is done by following a checksheet. A checksheet is a list of materials, divided into sections, that lay out the theory and practical steps which, when completed, lead one to a study completion. The items contained on the checksheet, such as books, recorded lectures and other written materials, add up to the required knowledge of the subject. Each student moves through his checksheet at his own rate. This ensures nobody is ever held back by slower students, and no one is under pressure from faster students. A trained Course Supervisor is always available to help the student, to refer him to the exact materials, to answer his questions and to ensure he is applying standard study technology to gain the full benefits from his studies.

When do I actually gain experience in auditing others?

Every major training course in Scientology is followed by an internship. This is a period of auditing others under the supervision of technical experts. In this way, an auditor's skills are honed and polished to a very high level of proficiency.

When can I take the Minister's Course?

This course can be studied by any Scientologist who is training in Scientology or Dianetics. The course provides an appreciation of the world's great religions, the religious background and philosophy of Scientology, the ethical codes of Scientology and the ceremonies of the Church. One also learns to deliver services and carry out basic ministerial duties.

How long do courses take?

Each course takes as long as it takes—since the student goes through each course at his own pace, he regulates his own progress. How long it takes depends on how diligently he applies study technology and how honestly he completes each item on his checksheet before proceeding to the next. The length of each course will also depend on how many hours he studies per week. On the average, Scientology courses take anywhere from a few days (for most introductory courses) to several months (for more advanced training).

Introductory services are designed to take one week at 2½ hours a day. Academy training to become an auditor is generally two weeks, at forty hours a week, for each individual level.

The required time to complete the more advanced courses is quite extensive. The Saint Hill Special Briefing Course, which is a chronological study of Scientology and Dianetics from 1948 to the present, takes approximately one year, at forty hours a week. This course gives the Scientologist the entire philosophic and technical development of the subject, and is the most extensive training course in Scientology.

Church staff ensure that auditors are professionally and thoroughly trained so that they can achieve the best results with their preclears.

Are Scientology Course Supervisors university trained?

According to demographic studies, a high proportion of Scientologists have graduated from college or university studies. However, this is not a prerequisite for becoming a Scientology Course Supervisor.

In Scientology, there is a very precise technology of how to supervise and successfully help students through their courses. All

Scientology Course Supervisors are trained in this technology to ensure that students get the most from their training.

SCIENTOLOGY AND DIANETICS AUDITING

What is the difference between the auditing and training routes in Scientology?

The reference that best explains the difference between these two routes is the Classification, Gradation and Awareness Chart.

On the right side of the chart there are various steps a person moves through as he receives auditing. Each grade listed has a column for "Ability Gained" that describes the increasing levels of awareness and ability achieved at each stage. In auditing, one is working toward improving himself and regaining recognition of and rehabilitating his spiritual nature and abilities. This is done on a gradient (a gradual approach to something, taken step by step), so those states of being which are seemingly "too high above one" can be achieved with relative ease.

The left-hand side of the chart describes the gradient steps of training on which one gains the knowledge and abilities necessary to audit another on each level. Each course listed includes a description of the subject matter that is taught at that level. In training, one is learning about the various facets of life with a view to helping others.

These two different paths parallel each other. Optimally, a person follows both paths.

The chart is a guide for the individual from the point he first enters Scientology, and shows him the basic sequence in which he will receive his auditing and training.

Do all the people on staff in Scientology receive auditing as well as training?

Yes, auditing and training of staff members is part of the exchange for their work in Scientology organizations.

Why does one have to wait six weeks for auditing if one has been habitually using drugs?

Research has shown that it takes at least that long for the effect of drugs to wear off. Quite simply, auditing is not as effective while drugs are in the system because a person on drugs is less alert and may even be rendered stupid, blank, forgetful, delusive or irresponsible.

Will antibiotics prevent me from getting auditing?

No. Antibiotics work differently than drugs. If the preclear has a doctor's prescription for antibiotics and is taking these to handle an infection, he should be sure to let his Director of Processing know, but this will not prevent him from receiving auditing. Many people claim that antibiotics work more rapidly and effectively if one is receiving auditing at the same time.

Is it okay to take any sort of drugs when you are in Scientology?

Except for antibiotics or prescribed medical drugs by a medical doctor, no.

If one has a medical or dental condition requiring treatment and wishes to take some medical drug other than antibiotics, he should inform his Director of Processing. A medical or dental consultation will be advised and a handling worked out in liaison with the Director of Processing to best accommodate one's progress in Scientology.

Any other drug use, such as the use of street drugs or psychiatric mind-altering drugs, is forbidden.

Drugs are usually taken to escape from unwanted emotions, pains or sensations. In Scientology, the real reasons for these unwanted conditions get handled and people have no need or desire for drugs. Drugs dull people and make them less aware. Scientology's aim is to make people brighter and more aware.

Drugs are essentially poisons. Small amounts may act as a stimulant or as a sedative, but larger amounts act as poisons and can kill one.

Drugs dull one's senses and affect the reactive mind so that the person becomes less in control and more the effect of his reactive mind, a very undesirable state.

Despite the claims of psychiatrists that drugs are a "cure-all," at best they cover up what is really wrong, and at worst, actually harm one. The real answer is to handle the source of one's troubles—and that is done with Scientology.

How many hours of auditing a day do people receive?

This depends upon one's particular auditing program. Some receive longer or shorter hours of auditing than others, but an average would be 2½ hours a day. Auditing is best done intensively, at least 12½ hours a week. The more intensively one is audited, the more rapid progress he makes as he is not bogged down by current life upsets. Therefore it is best to arrange for many hours of consecutive auditing, i.e., 50 to 100 hours at 12½ hours a week minimum.

Of course, one is not always receiving auditing so when one is, his best chance of making rapid progress is intensively.

Has the technology of auditing changed since the early days of Scientology?

The basics of auditing have not changed, but there have been considerable advances and refinements in auditing processes over the years. L. Ron Hubbard continued his research and development of Scientology auditing technology throughout his life, and completed it before he passed away. All of his technology is now available and laid out in an exact sequence of gradient steps in which it should be used.

What will I get out of auditing?

Scientology auditing is delivered in a specific sequence which handles the major barriers people encounter when trying to achieve their goals. After receiving auditing, you will start to recognize for yourself that you are changing, that your outlook on life is improving and that you are becoming more able. In Scientology, you will not be told when you have completed an auditing level—you will know for yourself, as only you can know exactly what you are experiencing. This gives you the certainty that you have attained what you want to attain from each level.

There will also no doubt be some outwardly demonstrable or visible changes that occur: Your IQ may increase, you might look healthier and happier, and may well have people comment on how calm or cheerful you look or, for instance, how you are doing better on your job.

Results like these are the products of auditing. Each person knows when he has achieved them.

Does auditing really work in all cases?

Dianetics and Scientology technologies are very exact and well-tested procedures that work in 100 percent of the cases in which they are applied standardly.

The only proviso is that the preclear must be there on his own determinism and must abide by the rules for preclears during his auditing to ensure optimum results. The Church makes no guarantee of results as auditing is something which requires the active participation of the individual. Auditing is not something done *to* an individual—it is something done in which he is the active participant.

What auditing handles physical pains or discomfort?

Dianetics auditing is used to help handle physical pains or discomfort stemming from the reactive mind.

What can auditing cure?

Scientology is not in the business of curing things in the traditional sense of the

…me one spends each week on … Those who get intensive auditing … not stop along the way progress …

…goes Clear, will he lose his …ns?

…on the contrary, a Clear is able to use … experience any emotion. Only the …ful, reactive, uncontrolled emotions are …e from his life. Clears are very respon…e beings. When one is Clear, he is more …mself. The only loss is a negative—the …eactive mind—which was preventing the individual from being himself.

What can you do when you are Clear?

A Clear is able to deal causatively with life rather than react to it. A Clear is rational in that he forms the best possible solutions he can with the data he has and from his own viewpoint. A Clear gets things done and accomplishes more than he could before he became Clear.

Whatever your level of ability before you go Clear, it will be greatly increased after you go Clear.

Are Clears perfect?

No, they are not perfect.

Being a Clear does not mean a person who has had no education, for example, suddenly becomes educated. It does mean that all the abilities of the individual can be brought to bear on the problems he encounters and that all the data in his analytical memory banks is available for solution to those problems.

A Clear has become the basic individual through auditing. The basic individual is not a buried, unknown or a different person, but an intensity of all that is best and most able in the person.

Do Clears eat food and sleep?

Most definitely.

Do Clears get colds and get sick?

A Clear can still get sick, but this occurs much less often than before he became Clear. In other words, a Clear still has a body, and bodies are susceptible at times to various illnesses. However, no longer having his reactive mind, he is much more at cause and is not adversely affected by many of the things that would have caused psychosomatic illnesses before he went Clear.

To measure a Clear only by his health, however, would be a mistake because this state has to do with the individual himself, not his body.

If Clears no longer have a reactive mind, why do they still need to get auditing?

There are many more states of awareness and ability that can be achieved above the state of Clear as he is only Clear on the first dynamic. Once Clear, an individual wants to continue his auditing to achieve these higher states.

THE STATE OF OPERATING THETAN

What is meant by Operating Thetan (OT)?

Operating Thetan is a state of beingness above Clear. *Thetan* refers to the spiritual being, and *operating* means here "able to operate without dependency on things." An Operating Thetan (OT) is able to control matter, energy, space and time rather than being controlled by these things. As a result, an OT is able to be at cause over life.

There are numerous auditing steps on the Bridge called OT levels. People on these levels are progressing to the state of full OT and becoming more and more OT along the way.

How would you describe the state of Operating Thetan?

OT (Operating Thetan) is a state of spiritual awareness in which an individual is able to control hi[illegible] ment. An OT is some[illegible] knows and can creat[illegible] vival effects on all of [illegible] been fully refamiliari[illegible] ities as a thetan and ca[illegible] ingly be at cause over [illegible] energy, space and time.

As a being becomes [illegible] he becomes more po[illegible] responsible.

Why are the OT mater[illegible] confidential?

Because understanding [illegible] apply the OT materials are [illegible] having fully attained the e[illegible] awareness and abilities per[illegible] tion, Gradation and Awarene[illegible] these materials are released [illegible] only to those who have hones[illegible] earlier states.

A SCIENTOLOGY CAREE[illegible]

Can one audit as a career?

Yes. There are many Scientol[illegible] ters who audit full time as their [illegible] Auditing provides a rewarding car[illegible] one in which you are always helpi[illegible] and constantly seeing miraculous [illegible] your preclears. It is very satisfying [illegible] that you are making people's lives [illegible] and saner.

Auditors are very valuable and i[illegible] demand.

L. Ron Hubbard's opinion of audi[illegible] well known: "I think of an auditor as [illegible] son with enough guts to *do som[illegible] about it.* This quality is rare and this q[illegible] is courageous in the extreme. It i[illegible] opinion and knowledge that auditors [illegible] amongst the upper tenth of the upper t[illegible] tieth of intelligent human beings. Their [illegible] to do, their motives, their ability to gr[illegible] and to use are superior to that of any ot[illegible] profession."

Of what value would it be to have my child trained as an auditor?

First of all, it would provide a young person with certainty and knowledge in dealing with every possible type of human problem, be it interpersonal, familial, organizational, ethical, moral or religious. Secondly, it would provide a career of fulfillment in aiding people from all walks of life to gain greater awareness and respect for themselves and others.

Auditors are in demand in every church of Scientology and mission throughout the world. Therefore, your child would be fulfilling a great demand and contributing greatly to making this world a saner place by getting trained as an auditor.

Can one make Scientology a career in some other way than by being a minister?

Yes, there are thousands of professional Scientologists who work full time in churches and missions throughout the world as executives or administrative staff. There are also those who further the dissemination of Scientology on a one-to-one basis or through the dissemination of Scientology materials and books, those who hold jobs in the Church's social reform groups and those who work in the Office of Special Affairs involved in community betterment or legal work. All of these provide rewarding careers as each forwards the expansion of Scientology and thereby makes it possible for more and more people to benefit from its technology.

SCIENTOLOGY IN SOCIETY

I've heard that Scientologists are doing good things for society. What are some specific examples?

These activities would fill a book in themselves, and are covered in more detail in Part 5 of this book, but here are just a few examples that are typical of the things that Scientologists are doing around the world.

Scientologists regularly hold blood drives to get donations of blood for hospitals, the Red Cross and other similar organizations. As Scientologists do not use harmful drugs, these donations of drug-free blood are welcomed by those in charge of health care.

Scientologists regularly hold drives to get donations of toys, food and clothing to make life happier for those in need.

During the annual holiday season, Scientologists are particularly active in this sphere. In downtown Hollywood, California, for example, Scientologists build a "Winter Wonderland" scene each Christmas, complete with a large Christmas tree, Santa Claus and even "snow," creating a traditional Christmas setting for children who otherwise might never see one.

In Canada, a group of Scientologists spends many weeks each year raising funds to sponsor visits to summer camps by underprivileged children.

Church members utilize their artistic talents to bring new experiences and joy to children by performing puppet shows in orphanages, schools and shopping malls, and magic shows for children in foster homes.

Scientologists can also be found in many communities contributing to the care of the elderly. They visit old-age homes and provide entertainment, draw sketches or just drop by and talk with senior citizens.

You will find Scientologists helping with "community cleanup" campaigns and assistance to the injured at Veteran's Administration hospitals.

Scientologists have taken a leading role fighting drug abuse, actively educating community officials and groups on the dangers of drugs and solutions to the problems. There are many groups utilizing L. Ron Hubbard's technology and freeing people from the detrimental effects of drugs.

L. Ron Hubbard's technology on how to study has been used by Scientologists around the world to help students and teachers alike. One place where this technology has made major inroads combating illiteracy is in South Africa, where well over a million native Africans have improved their ability to study.

Another important area of activity for Scientologists is raising moral standards in society. Scientologists all around the world have distributed tens of millions of copies of the nonreligious moral code called "The Way to Happiness," now available in more than twenty different languages. Its use has led to a revitalization of purpose for people of all ages who apply its simple truths to their lives and to the environment around them.

The Church and many of its members are also engaged in interfaith activities, the main thrust of which has been to work with leaders of other faiths in the areas of interreligious dialogue, religious freedom, constitutional law and "religion in society" issues—all aimed toward protecting and forwarding the freedom of religion for everyone.

Another prevalent activity for Scientologists is to expose and eradicate the violations of human rights perpetrated by psychiatry. Many Scientologists do this as members of the Citizens Commission on Human Rights (CCHR), a reform group which was established by the Church in 1969.

They actively investigate psychiatric abuses and bring these to the attention of the media, legislators and other groups concerned with protecting people from brutal psychiatric techniques. Such practices as psychosurgery, electroshock treatment and the administration of dangerous psychiatric drugs have destroyed the minds and lives of millions of individuals. Through the efforts of Scientologists working for CCHR, public awareness of the disastrous results of psychiatric methods has been raised and major steps taken to outlaw such practices.

Is Scientology active in Black communities and countries?

Definitely. By the Creed of the Church, "All men of whatever race, color or creed were created with equal rights." Thus, there are no limitations placed on who can receive and benefit from Scientology services.

There are Scientologists of all races, colors and religious backgrounds.

For example, there are Dianetics and/or Scientology organizations in Ghana, Zaire, Zimbabwe, Ethiopia and Sierra Leone, among other countries, and Black Scientologists are applying Scientology technology in their communities wherever possible. The Church maintains a Department of Ethnic Affairs specifically to interact and work with minorities.

Do doctors, schools, social workers, businessmen and other professional people use Scientology?

Yes, they do. There are members of all of these professions who use Scientology technology to improve the results being obtained in their fields of endeavor.

Schools and universities in many countries apply L. Ron Hubbard's study methods to improve literacy and teaching success, drug rehabilitation groups use his drug rehabilitation technology to successfully get people off drugs, doctors observe basic Dianetics principles to speed up the recovery of their patients, businessmen apply L. Ron Hubbard's administrative procedures to create thriving businesses.

Scientology applies to all spheres of life and uniformly gets results when standardly used. Therefore, there is hardly an area of social or community concern where you will not find people using some aspect of L. Ron Hubbard's technology.

Why has Scientology sometimes been considered controversial?

Like all new ideas, Scientology has come under attack by the uninformed and those who feel their vested interests are threatened.

As Scientologists have openly and effectively advocated social reform causes, they have become the target of attacks.

For those vested interests who cling to a status quo that is decimating society, Scientology's technology of making the able more able poses a serious threat. Attacks follow as an attempt to stop application of Scientology technology.

When the Church steps in to handle the attack, the conflict grabs the attention of the press, which lives on controversy. Regardless of the unfounded nature of the attackers' claims, reporters freely promote the controversy. Those seeking to stop Scientology then join the media in regurgitating and regenerating the created controversy.

Scientology has always flourished and prospered in the face of attacks. In every case where public disputes have been manufactured, intentional and blatant false reports about Scientology and its founder have been discovered to be the common denominator. As the falsehoods are proven lies, the controversy quickly fades, and the truth about Scientology, what the Church really is and what its members do replaces it. The source of these attacks and the controversy they have generated is detailed in Chapter 31 of this book.

Why has Scientology been to court a lot of times?

The Church has gone to court in many countries to uphold the right to freedom of religion. In Australia, as one example, legal actions by the Church brought about a landmark victory which greatly expanded religious freedom throughout that country.

In the United States, the Church's use of the Freedom of Information Act, taking government agencies to court and holding them accountable to release vital documents to the public on a variety of subjects, has been heralded as a vital action to ensure honesty in government.

In certain cases, the Church has used the courts to protect its copyrighted materials, or to ensure its rights and the rights of its members are safeguarded.

During the history of the Church, a few unscrupulous individuals, lusting for money, have observed how Scientology is prospering and rapidly expanding, and have abused the legal system to try to line their own pockets. In the handful of cases where such attempts have occurred, they have uniformly failed.

Are there any laws against the practice of Scientology? Has it been banned?

Of course not.

In fact, the Church has received numerous recognitions, citations and validations from various governments for contributions to society in the fields of education, drug and alcohol rehabilitation, crime reduction, human rights, raising moral values and a host of other fields.

How does Scientology view deprogramers and groups that attempt to force people to denounce their chosen religion?

These so-called "deprogramers," better described as psychiatric depersonalizers, are money-motivated individuals who kidnap others for profit. Their methods include brainwashing, imprisonment, food and sleep deprivation and various forms of torture.

Such activities are clearly against the principles held by Scientologists—and have been proven to be against the law as well. Psychiatric depersonalizers in many countries have gone to jail for their violent and illegal practices.

Situations in which families have expressed concern over family members' involvement in various religions can generally be handled with communication. No one need resort to violence and mercenaries to resolve the upset.

The Church does not condone the use of violence and advocates that each person has an inalienable right to their own beliefs.

Why is Scientology opposed to psychiatry?

As the stepchildren of the German dictator Bismarck and later Hitler and the Nazis, psychiatry and psychology formed the philosophical basis for the wholesale slaughter of human beings in World Wars I and II. Psychiatry uses electric shock, brain-mutilating psychosurgery, and mind-damaging drugs to destroy a person and make him "docile and quiet" in the name of "treatment."

Psychiatric methods involving the butchering of human beings and their sanity are condemned by the Church. Scientologists are trying to create a world without war, insanity and criminality. Psychiatry is seeking to create a world where man is reduced to a robotized or drugged, vegetable-like state so that he can be controlled.

A primary difference between Scientology and psychiatry is that psychiatrists routinely tell their patients what they think is wrong with them. This interjects lies or ideas which are not true for the individual himself, and thus psychiatric "therapy" violates the basic integrity of the individual.

On the other hand, Scientology technology enables a person to find out for himself the source of his troubles and gives him the ability to improve conditions in his own life and environment.

The underlying difference is the fact that Scientology recognizes that man is a spiritual being, while psychiatrists view man as an animal. Scientology is a religion. Psychiatry is strongly opposed to all religions as it does not even recognize that man is a spiritual being.

Scientologists strongly disagree with the enforced and harmful psychiatric methods of involuntary commitment, forced and heavy drugging, electroconvulsive shock treatment, lobotomy and other psychosurgical operations.

By the Creed of the Church of Scientology, the healing of mentally caused ills should not be condoned in nonreligious fields. The reason for this is that violent psychiatric therapies cause spiritual traumas. At best, psychiatry suppresses life's problems; at worst, it causes severe damage, irreversible setbacks in a person's life and even death.

Why do some people oppose Scientology?

There are certain characteristics and mental attitudes that cause a percentage of the population to oppose violently any betterment activity or group. This small percentage of society (roughly 2½ percent) cannot stand the fact that Scientology is successful at improving conditions around the world. This same 2½ percent is opposed to any self-betterment activity. The reason they so rabidly oppose Scientology is because it is doing more to help society than any other group.

Those who are upset by seeing man get better are small in number compared to the millions who have embraced Scientology and its efforts to create a sane civilization and more freedom for the individual.

Is Scientology trying to rule the world?

No. Scientology's aim, as expressed by L. Ron Hubbard, is that of creating "a civilization without insanity, without criminals and without war, where the able can prosper and honest beings can have rights, and where man is free to rise to greater heights. . . ."

"We seek no revolution. We seek only evolution to higher states of being for the individual and for society."

Scientology does want to improve and reform societal ills, and Scientologists believe there can be a better world by doing so.

It is not Scientology's mission to save the world. It is Scientology's mission to free *you.*

Can Scientology do anything to improve the world situation?

Yes, and it does so every single day.

By making the able individual in society more able and more certain of his abilities, and by continuing the Church's expansion and social reform programs throughout the world, the world can become a better place.

It is possible to bring people to higher levels of communication with the environment and those around them. And as one raises the level of communication, one raises also the ability to observe and change conditions and thereby create a better world and a better civilization.

The Aims of Scientology By L. Ron Hubbard

A civilization without insanity, without criminals and without war, where the able can prosper and honest beings can have rights, and where man is free to rise to greater heights, are the aims of Scientology.

First announced to an enturbulated world in 1950, these aims are well within the grasp of our technology.

Nonpolitical in nature, Scientology welcomes any individual of any creed, race or nation.

We seek no revolution. We seek only evolution to higher states of being for the individual and for society.

We are achieving our aims.

After endless millennia of ignorance about himself, his mind and the universe, a breakthrough has been made for man.

Other efforts man has made have been surpassed.

The combined truths of fifty thousand years of thinking men, distilled and amplified by new discoveries about man, have made for this success.

We welcome you to Scientology. We only expect of you your help in achieving our aims and helping others. We expect you to be helped.

Scientology is the most vital movement on Earth today.

In a turbulent world, the job is not easy. But then, if it were, we wouldn't have to be doing it.

We respect man and believe he is worthy of help. We respect you and believe you, too, can help.

Scientology does not owe its help. We have done nothing to cause us to propitiate. Had we done so, we would not now be bright enough to do what we are doing.

Man suspects all offers of help. He has often been betrayed, his confidence shattered. Too frequently he has given his trust and been betrayed. We may err, for we build a world with broken straws. But we will never betray your faith in us so long as you are one of us.

The sun never sets on Scientology.

And may a new day dawn for you, for those you love and for man.

Our aims are simple, if great.

And we will succeed, and are succeeding at each new revolution of the Earth.

Your help is acceptable to us.

Our help is yours.

Part Ten

References

CHAPTER 33

THE CREEDS AND CODES OF SCIENTOLOGY

The parishioners of every religion are bound together by creeds and codes.

These serve to state their aspirations, their duties, their mores and their beliefs. They further align purposes and reinforce the basic tenets of the religion.

The codes and creeds of Scientology were written by L. Ron Hubbard in the 1950s during the formative years of the religion. These set the guidelines for conduct and expansion and still serve those ends today.

Included are codes for the auditor, the supervisor, the manager and additional codes by which all Scientologists strive to live. Like all Scientology, the usefulness of these principles determines their worth. Scientologists follow them in their application of Scientology technology, their dealings with others, the administration of their groups and the practice of their religion.

The Creed of the Church of Scientology

The Creed of the Church of Scientology was written by L. Ron Hubbard shortly after the Church was formed in Los Angeles on February 18, 1954. After he issued this creed from his office in Phoenix, Arizona, the Church of Scientology adopted it as official because it succinctly states what Scientologists believe.

We of the Church believe:

That all men of whatever race, color or creed were created with equal rights;

That all men have inalienable rights to their own religious practices and their performance;

That all men have inalienable rights to their own lives;

That all men have inalienable rights to their sanity;

That all men have inalienable rights to their own defense;

That all men have inalienable rights to conceive, choose, assist or support their own organizations, churches and governments;

That all men have inalienable rights to think freely, to talk freely, to write freely their own opinions and to counter or utter or write upon the opinions of others;

That all men have inalienable rights to the creation of their own kind;

That the souls of men have the rights of men;

That the study of the mind and the healing of mentally caused ills should not be alienated from religion or condoned in nonreligious fields;

And that no agency less than God has the power to suspend or set aside these rights, overtly or covertly.

And we of the Church believe:

That man is basically good;

That he is seeking to survive;

That his survival depends upon himself and upon his fellows and his attainment of brotherhood with the universe.

And we of the Church believe that the laws of God forbid man:

To destroy his own kind;

To destroy the sanity of another;

To destroy or enslave another's soul;

To destroy or reduce the survival of one's companions or one's group.

And we of the Church believe that the spirit can be saved and that the spirit alone may save or heal the body.

The Auditor's Code

This code first appeared as a chapter in the book *Dianetics: The Original Thesis* (later retitled *The Dynamics of Life*) written by L. Ron Hubbard in 1947 and eventually published in 1951.

The ensuing years saw a great deal of auditing done by auditors other than Mr. Hubbard and from these experiences he was able to refine the Code and thus improve the discipline of auditing.

The Auditor's Code was revised in 1954, appearing in Professional Auditor's Bulletins 38 and 39.

Over the next four years, several additions were made to the 1954 Code, one of which appeared in the book *Dianetics 55!* Another was released in Hubbard Communications Office Bulletin of 1 July 1957, ADDITION TO THE AUDITOR'S CODE, and two more items were added when the Auditor's Code of 1958 was published.

The Auditor's Code 1968, released in October of that year, was issued as a Hubbard Communications Office Policy Letter. It was released in celebration of the 100 percent gains attainable by standard tech.

Hubbard Communications Office Policy Letter 2 November 1968, AUDITOR'S CODE, added three more clauses to the Code.

The final version of the Code was published by Mr. Hubbard on 19 June 1980.

The Auditor's Code is a fundamental tool of not only auditing but of life. As L. Ron Hubbard wrote in *Dianetics,* "The Auditor's Code outlines the *survival conduct pattern* of man. The Clear operates more or less automatically on this code." Because the basic axioms of Dianetics and Scientology comprise the fundamentals of thought itself, what works in auditing also works in life.

I hereby promise as an auditor to follow the Auditor's Code.

1 I promise not to evaluate for the preclear or tell him what he should think about his case in session.

2 I promise not to invalidate the preclear's case or gains in or out of session.

3 I promise to administer only standard tech to a preclear in the standard way.

4 I promise to keep all auditing appointments once made.

5 I promise not to process a preclear who has not had sufficient rest and who is physically tired.

6 I promise not to process a preclear who is improperly fed or hungry.

7 I promise not to permit a frequent change of auditors.

8 I promise not to sympathize with a preclear but to be effective.

9 I promise not to let the preclear end session on his own determinism but to finish off those cycles I have begun.

10 I promise never to walk off from a preclear in session.

11 I promise never to get angry with a preclear in session.

12 I promise to run every major case action to a floating needle.

13 I promise never to run any one action beyond its floating needle.

14 I promise to grant beingness to the preclear in session.

15 I promise not to mix the processes of Scientology with other practices except when the preclear is physically ill and only medical means will serve.

16 I promise to maintain communication with the preclear and not to cut his communication or permit him to overrun in session.

17 I promise not to enter comments, expressions or enturbulence into a session that distract a preclear from his case.

18 I promise to continue to give the preclear the process or auditing command when needed in the session.

19 I promise not to let a preclear run a wrongly understood command.

20 I promise not to explain, justify or make excuses in session for any auditor mistakes whether real or imagined.

21 I promise to estimate the current case state of a preclear only by standard case supervision data and not to diverge because of some imagined difference in the case.

22 I promise never to use the secrets of a preclear divulged in session for punishment or personal gain.

23 I promise to never falsify worksheets of sessions.

24 I promise to see that any fee received for processing is refunded, following the policies of the Claims Verification Board, if the preclear is dissatisfied and demands it within three months after the processing, the only condition being that he may not again be processed or trained.

25 I promise not to advocate Dianetics or Scientology only to cure illness or only to treat the insane, knowing well they were intended for spiritual gain.

26 I promise to cooperate fully with the authorized organizations of Dianetics and Scientology in safeguarding the ethical use and practice of those subjects.

27 I promise to refuse to permit any being to be physically injured, violently damaged, operated on or killed in the name of "mental treatment."

28 I promise not to permit sexual liberties or violations of patients.

29 I promise to refuse to admit to the ranks of practitioners any being who is insane.

The Code of Honor

The Code of Honor first appeared in Professional Auditor's Bulletin 40 on 26 November 1954. As Mr. Hubbard himself explained:

"No one expects the Code of Honor to be closely and tightly followed.

"An ethical code cannot be enforced. Any effort to enforce the Code of Honor would bring it into the level of a moral code. It cannot be enforced simply because it is a way of life which can exist as a way of life only as long as it is not enforced. Any other use but self-determined use of the Code of Honor would, as any Scientologist could quickly see, produce a considerable deterioration in a person. Therefore its use is a luxury use, and which is done solely on self-determined action, providing one sees eye to eye with the Code of Honor.

"If you believed man was worthy enough to be granted by you sufficient stature so as to permit you to exercise gladly the Code of Honor, I can guarantee that you would be a happy person. And if you found an occasional miscreant falling away from the best standards you have developed, you yet did not turn away from the rest of man, and if you discovered yourself betrayed by those you were seeking to defend and yet did not then experience a complete reversal of opinion about all your fellow men, there would be no dwindling spiral for you."

"The only difference between paradise on Earth and hell on Earth is whether or not you believe your fellow man worthy of receiving from you the friendship and devotion called for in this Code of Honor."

1 Never desert a comrade in need, in danger or in trouble.

2 Never withdraw allegiance once granted.

3 Never desert a group to which you owe your support.

4 Never disparage yourself or minimize your strength or power.

5 Never need praise, approval or sympathy.

6 Never compromise with your own reality.

7 Never permit your affinity to be alloyed.

8 Do not give or receive communication unless you yourself desire it.

9 Your self-determinism and your honor are more important than your immediate life.

10 Your integrity to yourself is more important than your body.

11 Never regret yesterday. Life is in you today, and you make your tomorrow.

12 Never fear to hurt another in a just cause.

13 Don't desire to be liked or admired.

14 Be your own adviser, keep your own counsel and select your own decisions.

15 Be true to your own goals.

Code of a Scientologist

The Code of a Scientologist was first issued as Professional Auditor's Bulletin 41 in 1954. In it, L. Ron Hubbard provides a Scientologist with guidelines in dealing with the press and in fighting for human rights and justice through social reform. It is a vital code for any Scientologist active in the community. The code was reissued in 1956 in the book, *Creation of Human Ability.* Revised in 1969 and again in 1973, the code is given here in its final version.

As a Scientologist, I pledge myself to the Code of Scientology for the good of all.

1 To keep Scientologists, the public and the press accurately informed concerning Scientology, the world of mental health and society.

2 To use the best I know of Scientology to the best of my ability to help my family, friends, groups and the world.

3 To refuse to accept for processing and to refuse to accept money from any preclear or group I feel I cannot honestly help.

4 To decry and do all I can to abolish any and all abuses against life and mankind.

5 To expose and help abolish any and all physically damaging practices in the field of mental health.

6 To help clean up and keep clean the field of mental health.

7 To bring about an atmosphere of safety and security in the field of mental health by eradicating its abuses and brutality.

8 To support true humanitarian endeavors in the fields of human rights.

9 To embrace the policy of equal justice for all.

10 To work for freedom of speech in the world.

11 To actively decry the suppression of knowledge, wisdom, philosophy or data which would help mankind.

12 To support the freedom of religion.

13 To help Scientology orgs and groups ally themselves with public groups.

14 To teach Scientology at a level it can be understood and used by the recipients.

15 To stress the freedom to use Scientology as a philosophy in all its applications and variations in the humanities.

16 To insist upon standard and unvaried Scientology as an applied activity in ethics, processing and administration in Scientology organizations.

17 To take my share of responsibility for the impact of Scientology upon the world.

18 To increase the numbers and strength of Scientology over the world.

19 To set an example of the effectiveness and wisdom of Scientology.

20 To make this world a saner, better place.

The Supervisor's Code

Just as auditors must follow a code of conduct, so too does the Supervisor in a Scientology course room. Unlike teachers in many traditional classrooms, Course Supervisors do not set themselves up as "authorities" who tell their students what to think, or espouse their opinions on the subject. Instead, students are guided to find the answers for themselves in Dianetics and Scientology materials.

In the following code, Mr. Hubbard sets forth the key guidelines that ensure instruction in a Scientology course room is standard and professional, with maximum benefit to the students. This code is followed by Supervisors in churches of Scientology throughout the world, guaranteeing a high level of training in the technology. It was first published in 1957.

1 The Supervisor must never neglect an opportunity to direct a student to the actual source of Scientology data.

2 The Supervisor should invalidate a student's mistake ruthlessly and use good ARC while doing it.

3 The Supervisor should remain in good ARC with his students at all times while they are performing training activities.

4 The Supervisor at all times must have a high tolerance of stupidity in his students and must be willing to repeat any datum not understood as many times as necessary for the student to understand and acquire reality on the datum.

5 The Supervisor does not have a "case" in his relationship with his students, nor discuss or talk about his personal problems to the students.

6 The Supervisor will, at all times, be a source-point of good control and direction to his students.

7 The Supervisor will be able to correlate any part of Scientology to any other part and to livingness over the eight dynamics.

8 The Supervisor should be able to answer any questions concerning Scientology by directing the student to the actual source of the data. If a Supervisor cannot answer a particular question, he should always say so, and the Supervisor should always find the answer to the question from the source and tell the student where the answer is to be found.

9 The Supervisor should never lie to, deceive or misdirect a student concerning Scientology. He shall be honest at all times about it with a student.

10 The Supervisor must be an accomplished auditor.

11 The Supervisor should always set a good example to his students: such as giving good demonstrations, being on time and dressing neatly.

12 The Supervisor should at all times be perfectly willing and able to do anything he tells his students to do.

13 The Supervisor must not become emotionally involved with students of either sex while they are under his or her training.

14 When a Supervisor makes any mistake, he is to inform the student that he has made one and rectify it immediately. This datum embraces all phases in training, demonstrations, lectures and processing, etc. He is never to hide the fact that he made the mistake.

15 The Supervisor should never neglect to give praise to his students when due.

16 The Supervisor to some degree should be pan-determined about the Supervisor–student relationship.

17 When a Supervisor lets a student control, give orders to or handle the Supervisor in any way, for the purpose of demonstration or other training purposes, the Supervisor should always put the student back under his control.

18 The Supervisor will at all times observe the Auditor's Code during sessions and the Code of a Scientologist at all times.

19 The Supervisor will never give a student opinions about Scientology without labeling them thoroughly as such; otherwise, he is to direct only to tested and proven data concerning Scientology.

20 The Supervisor shall never use a student for his own personal gain.

21 The Supervisor will be a stable terminal, point the way to stable data, be certain, but not dogmatic or dictatorial, toward his students.

22 The Supervisor will keep himself at all times informed of the most recent Scientology data and procedures and communicate this information to his students.

The Credo of a True Group Member

In our bureaucratic age, members of a group are often left feeling hopeless and ineffective in the face of seemingly insurmountable difficulties. Some even come to feel they might be better off without allegiance to any group. But inevitably, no one can survive alone, and denying oneself membership in a group is denying oneself that certain pride and satisfaction which can only come through teamwork.

In his research into the technology of groups, L. Ron Hubbard codified the key principles which members of any group should follow to attain its goals. These are offered in the following code, written in January 1951.

With these guidelines, a person can greatly increase his contribution to a group, while at the same time maintaining his own self-determinism.

1 The successful participant of a group is that participant who closely approximates in his own activities the ideal, ethic and rationale of the overall group.

2 The responsibility of the individual for the group as a whole should not be less than the responsibility of the group for the individual.

3 The group member has, as part of his responsibility, the smooth operation of the entire group.

4 A group member must exert and insist upon his rights and prerogatives as a group member and insist upon the rights and prerogatives of the group as a group and let not these rights be diminished in any way or degree for any excuse or claimed expeditiousness.

5 The member of a true group must exert and practice his right to contribute to the group. And he must insist upon the right of the group to contribute to him. He should recognize that a myriad of group failures will result when either of these contributions is denied as a right. (A welfare state being that state in which the member is not permitted to contribute to the state but must take contribution from the state.)

6 Enturbulence of the affairs of the group by sudden shifts of plans unjustified by circumstances, breakdown of recognized channels or cessation of useful operations in a group must be refused and blocked by the member of a group. He should take care not to enturbulate a manager and thus lower ARC.

7 Failure in planning or failure to recognize goals must be corrected by the group member for the group by calling the matter to conference or acting upon his own initiative.

8 A group member must coordinate his initiative with the goals and rationale of the entire group and with other individual members, well publishing his activities and intentions so that all conflicts may be brought forth in advance.

9 A group member must insist upon his right to have initiative.

10 A group member must study and understand and work with the goals, rationale and executions of the group.

11 A group member must work toward becoming as expert as possible in his specialized technology and skill in the group and must assist other individuals of the group to an understanding of that technology and skill and its place in the organizational necessities of the group.

12 A group member should have a working knowledge of all technologies and skills in the group in order to understand them and their place in the organizational necessities of the group.

13 On the group member depends the height of the ARC of the group. He must insist upon high-level communication lines and clarity in affinity and reality and know the consequence of not having such conditions. *And he must work continually and actively to maintain high ARC in the organization.*

14 A group member has the right of pride in his tasks and a right of judgment and handling in those tasks.

15 A group member must recognize that he is himself a manager of some section of the group and/or its tasks and that he himself must have both the knowledge and right of management in that sphere for which he is responsible.

16 The group member should not permit laws to be passed which limit or proscribe the activities of all the members of the group because of the failure of some of the members of the group.

17 The group member should insist on flexible planning and unerring execution of plans.

18 The performance of duty at optimum by every member of the group should be understood by the group member to be the best safeguard of his own and the group survival. It is the pertinent business of any member of the group that optimum performance be achieved by any other member of the group whether chain of command or similarity of activity sphere warrants such supervision or not.

The Credo of a Good and Skilled Manager

Leadership is considered a rare commodity, a gift possessed by a few uncommon individuals. And after a few years in a high executive position, whether in the private or the public sector, many individuals wonder whether this gift is in fact illusory.

In his management technology, L. Ron Hubbard developed a large body of guidelines that enable executives and managers not only to apply their powers with intelligence but to exercise sane leadership that will enable their groups to flourish and prosper. Following this code can greatly increase one's success as a manager in any group, from a business to a commonwealth of nations. This code was also written by Mr. Hubbard in 1951.

To be effective and successful a manager must:

1 Understand as fully as possible the goals and aims of the group he manages. He must be able to see and embrace the *ideal* attainment of the goal as envisioned by a goal maker. He must be able to tolerate and better the *practical* attainments and advances of which his group and its members may be capable. He must strive to narrow, always, the ever-existing gulf between the *ideal* and the *practical.*

2 He must realize that a primary mission is the full and honest interpretation by himself of the ideal and ethic and their goals and aims to his subordinates and the group itself. He must lead creatively and persuasively toward these goals his subordinates, the group itself and the individuals of the group.

3 He must embrace the organization and act solely for the entire organization and never form or favor cliques. His judgment of individuals of the group should be solely in the light of their worth to the entire group.

4 He must never falter in sacrificing individuals to the good of the group both in planning and execution and in his justice.

5 He must protect all established communication lines and complement them where necessary.

6 He must protect all affinity in his charge and have himself an affinity for the group itself.

7 He must attain always to the highest creative reality.

8 His planning must accomplish, in the light of goals and aims, the activity of the entire group. He must never let organizations grow and sprawl but, learning by pilots, must keep organizational planning fresh and flexible.

9 He must recognize in himself the rationale of the group and receive and evaluate the data out of which he makes his solutions with the highest attention to the truth of that data.

10 He must constitute himself on the orders of service to the group.

11 He must permit himself to be served well as to his individual requirements, practicing an economy of his own efforts and enjoying certain comforts to the wealth of keeping high his rationale.

12 He should require of his subordinates that they relay into their own spheres of management the whole and entire of his true feelings and the reasons for his decisions as clearly as they can be relayed and expanded and interpreted only for the greater understanding of the individuals governed by those subordinates.

13 He must never permit himself to pervert or mask any portion of the ideal and ethic on which the group operates nor must he permit the ideal and ethic to grow old and outmoded and unworkable. He must never permit his planning to be perverted or censored by subordinates. He must never permit the ideal and ethic of the group's individual members to deteriorate, using always reason to interrupt such a deterioration.

14 He must have faith in the goals, faith in himself and faith in the group.

15 He must lead by demonstrating always creative and constructive subgoals. He must not drive by threat and fear.

16 He must realize that every individual in the group is engaged in some degree in the managing of other men, life and MEST and that a liberty of management within this code should be allowed to every such submanager.

Thus conducting himself, a manager can win empire for his group, whatever that empire may be.

Chapter 34

The Axioms of Dianetics and Scientology

Representing the basic truths of life, the Logics and Axioms form the foundation upon which the philosophy of Dianetics and Scientology was built. Mr. Hubbard spent more than fifty years distilling the accumulated sum of man's wisdom, probing ever deeper into life's mysteries in order to discover them.

These are the central considerations and natural laws which contain the answers to life and its interaction with the physical universe.

The entirety of the subjects of Dianetics and Scientology flow from these basic truths. No later discoveries fell outside the bounds of truth described in these Logics and Axioms.

The chapter ends with The Factors, which embody the general considerations by which the game of life is played.

The Logics

The Logics were written by L. Ron Hubbard from a summary of information which began in November of 1938 and were published in 1951. They have never varied since that time.

The Logics form a gradient scale of association of facts necessary to understand and resolve any problem. They can be used to predict behavior and clarify the entire field of thought. The Logics are a method of thinking and could be called "how to think." In fact, the basic common denominators of all education can be found in the Logics.

Logic 1 Knowledge is a whole group or subdivision of a group of data or speculations or conclusions on data or methods of gaining data.

Logic 2 A body of knowledge is a body of data, aligned or unaligned, or methods of gaining data.

Logic 3 Any knowledge which can be sensed, measured or experienced by any entity is capable of influencing that entity.

COROLLARY: That knowledge which cannot be sensed, measured or experienced by any entity or type of entity cannot influence that entity or type of entity.

Logic 4 A datum is a symbol of matter, energy, space or time, or any combination thereof, in any universe, or the matter, energy, space or time itself, or any combination thereof, in any universe.

Logic 5 A definition of terms is necessary to the alignment, statement and resolution of suppositions, observations, problems and solutions and their communication.

DEFINITION: Descriptive definition: one which classifies by characteristics, by describing existing states of being.

DEFINITION: Differentiative definition: one which compares unlikeness to existing states of being or not-being.

DEFINITION: Associative definition: one which declares likeness to existing states of being or not-being.

DEFINITION: Action definition: one which delineates cause and potential change of state of being by cause of existence, inexistence, action, inaction, purpose or lack of purpose.

Logic 6 Absolutes are unobtainable.

Logic 7 Gradient scales are necessary to the evaluation of problems and their data.

This is the tool of infinity-valued logic: Absolutes are unobtainable. Terms such as good and bad, alive and dead, right and wrong are used only in conjunction with gradient scales. On the scale of right and wrong, everything above zero or center would be more and more right, approaching an infinite rightness, and everything below center would be more and more wrong, approaching infinite wrongness. All things assisting the survival of the survivor are considered to be right for the survivor. All things inhibiting survival from the viewpoint of the survivor can be considered wrong for the survivor. The more a thing assists survival, the more it can be considered right for the survivor; the more a thing or action inhibits survival, the more it is wrong from the viewpoint of the intended survivor.

COROLLARY: Any datum has only relative truth.

COROLLARY: Truth is relative to environments, experience and truth.

Logic 8 A datum can be evaluated only by a datum of comparable magnitude.

Logic 9 A datum is as valuable as it has been evaluated.

Logic 10 The value of a datum is established by the amount of alignment (relationship) it imparts to other data.

Logic 11 The value of a datum or field of data can be established by its degree of assistance in survival or its inhibition to survival.

Logic 12 The value of a datum or a field of data is modified by the viewpoint of the observer.

Logic 13 Problems are resolved by compartmenting them into areas of similar magnitude and data, comparing them to data already known or partially known, and resolving each area. Data which cannot be known immediately may be resolved by addressing what is known and using its solution to resolve the remainder.

Logic 14 Factors introduced into a problem or solution which do not derive from natural law but only from authoritarian command aberrate that problem or solution.

Logic 15 The introduction of an arbitrary into a problem or solution invites the further introduction of arbitraries into problems and solutions.

Logic 16 An abstract postulate must be compared to the universe to which it applies and brought into the category of things which can be sensed, measured or experienced in that universe before such postulate can be considered workable.

Logic 17 Those fields which most depend upon authoritative opinion for their data least contain known natural law.

Logic 18 A postulate is as valuable as it is workable.

Logic 19 The workability of a postulate is established by the degree to which it explains existing phenomena already known, by the degree that it predicts new phenomena which when looked for will be found to exist, and by the degree that it does not require that phenomena which do not exist in fact be called into existence for its explanation.

Logic 20 A science may be considered to be a large body of aligned data which has similarity in application and which has been deduced or induced from basic postulates.

Logic 21 Mathematics are methods of postulating or resolving real or abstract data in any universe and integrating by symbolization of data, postulates and resolutions.

Logic 22 The human mind* is an observer, postulator, creator and storage place of knowledge.

**The human mind by definition includes the awareness unit of the living organism, the observer, the computer of data, the spirit, the memory storage, the life force and the individual motivator of the living organism. It is used as distinct from the brain which can be considered to be motivated by the mind.*

Logic 23 The human mind is a servomechanism to any mathematics evolved or employed by the human mind.

POSTULATE: The human mind and inventions of the human mind are capable of resolving any and all problems which can be sensed, measured or experienced directly or indirectly.

*COROLLARY: The human mind is capable of resolving the problem of the human mind. The borderline of solution of this science lies between **why** life is surviving and **how** life is surviving. It is possible to resolve **how** life is surviving without resolving **why** life is surviving.*

Logic 24 The resolution of the philosophical, scientific and human studies (such as economics, politics, sociology, medicine, criminology, etc.) depends primarily upon the resolution of the problems of the human mind.

Note: ***The primary step in resolving the broad activities of man could be considered to be the resolving of the activities of the mind itself. Hence, the Logics carry to this point and then proceed as axioms concerning the human mind, such axioms being substantiated as relative truths by much newly discovered phenomena. The ensuing axioms, from Logic 24, apply no less to the various "ologies" than they do to de-aberrating or improving the operation of the mind. It should not be thought that the following axioms are devoted to the construction of anything as limited as a therapy, which is only incidental to the resolution of human aberration and such things as psychosomatic illnesses. These axioms are capable of such solution, as has been demonstrated, but such a narrow application would indicate a very narrow scope of view.***

The Dianetic Axioms

L. Ron Hubbard found that man is obeying very, very definite laws and rules which could be set forward in axioms. The very first and most fundamental of these is: The dynamic principle of existence is survive. That is the basic axiom of Dianetics.

The Dianetic Axioms were put together in the fall of 1951 after careful examination over a long period of time.

These 194 Dianetic Axioms contain a codification of the factors underlying all mental aberration.

Axiom 1 The source of life is a static of peculiar and particular properties.

Axiom 2 At least a portion of the static called life is impinged upon the physical universe.

Axiom 3 That portion of the static of life which is impinged upon the physical universe has for its dynamic goal, survival and only survival.

Axiom 4 The physical universe is reducible to motion of energy operating in space through time.

Axiom 5 That portion of the static of life concerned with the life organisms of the physical universe is concerned wholly with motion.

Axiom 6 The life static has as one of its properties the ability to mobilize and animate matter into living organisms.

Axiom 7 The life static is engaged in a conquest of the physical universe.

Axiom 8 The life static conquers the material universe by learning and applying the physical laws of the physical universe.

SYMBOL: The symbol for the LIFE STATIC in use hereafter is the Greek letter THETA.

Axiom 9 A fundamental operation of THETA in surviving is bringing order into the chaos of the physical universe.

Axiom 10 THETA brings order into chaos by conquering whatever in MEST may be prosurvival and destroying whatever in MEST may be contrasurvival, at least through the medium of life organisms.

SYMBOL: The symbol for the PHYSICAL UNIVERSE in use hereafter is MEST, from the first letters of the words MATTER, ENERGY, SPACE and TIME, or the Greek letter PHI.

Axiom 11 A life organism is composed of matter and energy in space and time, animated by THETA.

SYMBOL: Living organism or organisms will hereafter be represented by the Greek letter LAMBDA.

Axiom 12 The MEST part of the organism follows the laws of the physical sciences. All LAMBDA is concerned with motion.

Axiom 13 THETA operating through LAMBDA converts the forces of the physical universe into forces to conquer the physical universe.

Axiom 14 THETA working upon physical universe motion must maintain a harmonious rate of motion.

The limits of LAMBDA are narrow, both as to thermal and mechanical motion.

Axiom 15 LAMBDA is the intermediate step in the conquest of the physical universe.

Axiom 16 The basic food of any organism consists of light and chemicals.

Organisms can exist only as higher levels of complexities because lower levels of converters exist.

THETA evolves organisms from lower to higher forms and supports them by the existence of lower converter forms.

Axiom 17 THETA, via LAMBDA, effects an evolution of MEST.

In this we have the waste products of organisms on the one hand as those very complex chemicals which bacteria make and, on the other hand, we have the physical face of the Earth being changed by animals and men, such changes as grass holding mountains from eroding or roots causing boulders to break, buildings being built and rivers being dammed. There is obviously an evolution in MEST in progress under the incursion of THETA.

Axiom 18 LAMBDA, even within a species, varies in its endowment of THETA.

Axiom 19 The effort of LAMBDA is toward survival.

The goal of LAMBDA is survival.

The penalty of failure to advance toward that goal is to succumb.

DEFINITION: Persistence is the ability to exert continuance of effort toward survival goals.

Axiom 20 LAMBDA creates, conserves, maintains, requires, destroys, changes, occupies, groups and disperses MEST.

LAMBDA survives by animating and mobilizing or destroying matter and energy in space and time.

Axiom 21 LAMBDA is dependent upon optimum motion. Motion which is too swift and motion which is too slow are equally contrasurvival.

Axiom 22 THETA and thought are similar orders of static.

Axiom 23 All thought is concerned with motion.

Axiom 24 The establishment of an optimum motion is a basic goal of reason.

DEFINITION: LAMBDA is a chemical heat engine existing in space and time motivated by the life static and directed by thought.

Axiom 25 The basic purpose of reason is the calculation or estimation of effort.

Axiom 26 Thought is accomplished by THETA FACSIMILES of physical universe, entities or actions.

Axiom 27 THETA is satisfied only with harmonious action or optimum motion and rejects or destroys action or motion above or below its tolerance band.

Axiom 28 The mind is concerned wholly with the estimation of effort.

DEFINITION: Mind is the THETA command post of any organism or organisms.

Axiom 29 The basic errors of reason are failure to differentiate amongst matter, energy, space and time.

Axiom 30 Rightness is proper calculation of effort.

Axiom 31 Wrongness is always miscalculation of effort.

Axiom 32 THETA can exert itself directly or extensionally.

THETA can direct physical application of the organism to the environment or, through the mind, can first calculate the action or extend, as in language, ideas.

Axiom 33 Conclusions are directed toward the inhibition, maintenance or accelerations of efforts.

Axiom 34 The common denominator of all life organisms is motion.

Axiom 35 Effort of an organism to survive or succumb is physical motion of a life organism at a given moment in time through space.

DEFINITION: Motion is any change in orientation in space.

DEFINITION: Force is random effort.

DEFINITION: Effort is directed force.

Axiom 36 An organism's effort can be to remain at rest or persist in a given motion.

Static state has position in time, but an organism which is remaining positionally in a static state, if alive, is still continuing a highly complex pattern of motion, such as the heartbeat, digestion, etc.

The efforts of organisms to survive or succumb are assisted, compelled or opposed by the efforts of other organisms, matter, energy, space and time.

DEFINITION: Attention is a motion which must remain at an optimum effort.

Attention is aberrated by becoming unfixed and sweeping at random or becoming too fixed without sweeping.

Unknown threats to survival when sensed cause attention to sweep without fixing.

Known threats to survival when sensed cause attention to fix.

Axiom 37 The ultimate goal of LAMBDA is infinite survival.

Axiom 38 Death is abandonment by THETA of a life organism or race or species where these can no longer serve THETA in its goals of infinite survival.

Axiom 39 The reward of an organism engaging upon survival activity is pleasure.

Axiom 40 The penalty of an organism failing to engage upon survival activity, or engaging in nonsurvival activity, is pain.

Axiom 41 The cell and virus are the primary building blocks of life organisms.

Axiom 42 The virus and cell are matter and energy animated and motivated in space and time by THETA.

Axiom 43 THETA mobilizes the virus and cell in colonial aggregations to increase potential motion and accomplish effort.

Axiom 44 The goal of viruses and cells is survival in space through time.

Axiom 45 The total mission of higher organisms, viruses and cells is the same as that of the virus and cell.

Axiom 46 Colonial aggregations of viruses and cells can be imbued with more THETA than they inherently contained.

Life energy joins any group, whether a group of organisms or group of cells composing an organism. Here we have personal entity, individuation, etc.

Axiom 47 Effort can be accomplished by LAMBDA only through the coordination of its parts toward goals.

Axiom 48 An organism is equipped to be governed and controlled by a mind.

Axiom 49 The purpose of the mind is to pose and resolve problems relating to survival and to direct the effort of the organism according to these solutions.

Axiom 50 All problems are posed and resolved through estimations of effort.

Axiom 51 The mind can confuse position in space with position in time. (Counter-efforts producing action phrases.)

Axiom 52 An organism proceeding toward survival is directed by the mind of that organism in the accomplishment of survival effort.

Axiom 53 An organism proceeding toward succumb is directed by the mind of that organism in the accomplishment of death.

Axiom 54 Survival of an organism is accomplished by the overcoming of efforts opposing its survival.

(Note: Corollary for other dynamics.)

DEFINITION: Dynamic is the ability to translate solutions into action.

Axiom 55 Survival effort for an organism includes the dynamic thrust by that organism for the survival of itself, its procreation, its group, its subspecies, its species, all life organisms, material universe, the life static and, possibly, a Supreme Being. (Note: List of dynamics.)

Axiom 56 The cycle of an organism, a group of organisms or a species is inception, growth, re-creation, decay and death.

Axiom 57 The effort of an organism is directed toward the control of the environment for all the dynamics.

Axiom 58 Control of an environment is accomplished by the support of prosurvival factors along any dynamic.

Axiom 59 Any type of higher organism is accomplished by the evolution of viruses and cells into forms capable of better efforts to control or live in an environment.

Axiom 60 The usefulness of an organism is determined by its ability to control the environment or to support organisms which control the environment.

Axiom 61 An organism is rejected by THETA to the degree that it fails in its goals.

Axiom 62 Higher organisms can exist only in the degree that they are supported by the lower organisms.

Axiom 63 The usefulness of an organism is determined by the alignment of its efforts toward survival.

Axiom 64 The mind perceives and stores all data of the environment and aligns or fails to align these according to the time they were perceived.

DEFINITION: A conclusion is the THETA FACSIMILES *of a group of combined data.*

DEFINITION: A datum is a THETA FACSIMILE *of physical action.*

Axiom 65 The process of thought is the perception of the present and the comparison of it to the perceptions and conclusions of the past in order to direct action in the immediate or distant future.

COROLLARY: The attempt of thought is to perceive realities of the past and present in order to predict or postulate realities of the future.

Axiom 66 The process by which life effects its conquest of the material universe consists in the conversion of the potential effort of matter and energy in space and through time to effect with it the conversion of further matter and energy in space and through time.

Axiom 67 THETA contains its own THETA UNIVERSE effort which translates into MEST effort.

Axiom 68 The single arbitrary in any organism is time.

Axiom 69 Physical universe perceptions and efforts are received by an organism as force waves, convert by facsimile into THETA and are thus stored.

DEFINITION: Randomity is the misalignment through the internal or external efforts by other forms of life or the material universe of the efforts of an organism, and is imposed on the physical organism by counter-efforts in the environment.

Axiom 70 Any cycle of any life organism is from static to motion to static.

Axiom 71 The cycle of randomity is from static, through optimum, through randomity sufficiently repetitious or similar to constitute another static.

Axiom 72 There are two subdivisions to randomity: data randomity and force randomity.

Axiom 73 The three degrees of randomity consist of minus randomity, optimum randomity and plus randomity.

DEFINITION: Randomity is a component factor and necessary part of motion, if motion is to continue.

Axiom 74 Optimum randomity is necessary to learning.

Axiom 75 The important factors in any area of randomity are effort and counter-effort. (Note: As distinguished from near perceptions of effort.)

Axiom 76 Randomity amongst organisms is vital to continuous survival of all organisms.

Axiom 77 THETA affects the organism, other organisms and the physical universe by translating THETA FACSIMILES into physical efforts or randomity of efforts.

DEFINITION: The degree of randomity is measured by the randomness of effort vectors within the organism, amongst organisms, amongst races or species of organisms or between organisms and the physical universe.

Axiom 78 Randomity becomes intense in indirect ratio to the time in which it takes place, modified by the total effort in the area.

Axiom 79 Initial randomity can be reinforced by randomities of greater or lesser magnitude.

Axiom 80 Areas of randomity exist in chains of similarity plotted against time. This can be true of words and actions contained in randomities. Each may have its own chain plotted against time.

Axiom 81 Sanity consists of optimum randomity.

Axiom 82 Aberration exists to the degree that plus or minus randomity exists in the environment or past data of an organism, group or species, modified by the endowed self-determinism of that organism, group or species.

Axiom 83 The self-determinism of an organism is determined by its THETA endowment, modified by minus or plus randomity in its environment or its existence.

Axiom 84 The self-determinism of an organism is increased by optimum randomity of counter-efforts.

Axiom 85 The self-determinism of an organism is reduced by plus or minus randomity of counter-efforts in the environment.

Axiom 86 Randomity contains both the randomness of efforts and the volume of efforts. (Note: An area of randomity can have a great deal of confusion, but without volume of energy, the confusion itself is negligible.)

Axiom 87 That counter-effort is most acceptable to an organism which most closely appears to assist its accomplishment of its goal.

Axiom 88 An area of severe plus or minus randomity can occlude data on any of the subjects of that plus or minus randomity which took place in a prior time. (Note: Shut-off mechanisms of earlier lives, perceptics, specific incidents, etc.)

Axiom 89 Restimulation of plus, minus or optimum randomity can produce increased plus, minus or optimum randomity respectively in the organism.

Axiom 90 An area of randomity can assume sufficient magnitude so as to appear to the organism as pain, according to its goals.

Axiom 91 Past randomity can impose itself upon the present organism as THETA FACSIMILES.

Axiom 92 The engram is a severe area of plus or minus randomity of sufficient volume to cause unconsciousness.

Axiom 93 Unconsciousness is an excess of randomity imposed by a counter-effort of sufficient force to cloud the awareness and direct function of the organism through the mind's control center.

Axiom 94 Any counter-effort which misaligns the organism's command of itself or its environment establishes plus or minus randomity or, if of sufficient magnitude, is an engram.

Axiom 95 Past engrams are restimulated by the control center's perception of circumstances similar to that engram in the present environment.

Axiom 96 An engram is a THETA FACSIMILE of atoms and molecules in misalignment.

Axiom 97 Engrams fix emotional response as that emotional response of the organism during the receipt of the counter-effort.

Axiom 98 Free emotional response depends on optimum randomity. It depends upon absence of or nonrestimulation of engrams.

Axiom 99 THETA FACSIMILES can recombine into new symbols.

Axiom 100 Language is the symbolization of effort.

Axiom 101 Language depends for its force upon the force which accompanied its definition. (Note: Counter-effort, not language, is aberrative.)

Axiom 102 The environment can occlude the central control of any organism and assume control of the motor controls of that organism. (Engram, restimulation, locks, hypnotism.)

Axiom 103 Intelligence depends on the ability to select aligned or misaligned data from an area of randomity and so discover a solution to reduce all randomity in that area.

Axiom 104 Persistence obtains in the ability of the mind to put solutions into physical action toward the realization of goals.

Axiom 105 An unknown datum can produce data of plus or minus randomity.

Axiom 106 The introduction of an arbitrary factor or force without recourse to natural laws of the body or the area into which the arbitrary is introduced brings about plus or minus randomity.

Axiom 107 Data of plus or minus randomity depends for its confusion on former plus or minus randomity or absent data.

Axiom 108 Efforts which are inhibited or compelled by exterior efforts effect a plus or minus randomity of efforts.

Axiom 109 Behavior is modified by counter-efforts which have impinged on the organism.

Axiom 110 The component parts of THETA are affinity, reality and communication.

Axiom 111 Self-determinism consists of maximal affinity, reality and communication.

Axiom 112 Affinity is the cohesion of THETA.

Affinity manifests itself as the recognition of similarity of efforts and goals amongst organisms by those organisms.

Axiom 113 Reality is the agreement upon perceptions and data in the physical universe.

All that we can be sure is real is that on which we have agreed is real. Agreement is the essence of reality.

Axiom 114 Communication is the interchange of perception through the material universe between organisms or the perception of the material universe by sense channels.

Axiom 115 Self-determinism is the THETA control of the organism.

Axiom 116 A self-determined effort is that counter-effort which has been received into the organism in the past and integrated into the organism for its conscious use.

Axiom 117 The components of self-determinism are affinity, communication and reality.

Self-determinism is manifested along each dynamic.

Axiom 118 An organism cannot become aberrated unless it has agreed upon that aberration, has been in communication with a source of aberration and has had affinity for the aberrator.

Axiom 119 Agreement with any source, contra- or prosurvival, postulates a new reality for the organism.

Axiom 120 Nonsurvival courses, thoughts and actions require nonoptimum effort.

Axiom 121 Every thought has been preceded by physical action.

Axiom 122 The mind does with thought as it has done with entities in the physical universe.

Axiom 123 All effort concerned with pain is concerned with loss.

Organisms hold pain and engrams to them as a latent effort to prevent loss of some portion of the organism.

All loss is a loss of motion.

Axiom 124 The amount of counter-effort the organism can overcome is proportional to the THETA endowment of the organism, modified by the physique of that organism.

Axiom 125 Excessive counter-effort to the effort of a life organism produces unconsciousness.

COROLLARY: Unconsciousness gives the suppression of an organism's control center by counter-effort.

DEFINITION: The control center of the organism can be defined as the contact point between THETA *and the physical universe and is that center which is aware of being aware and which has charge of and responsibility for the organism along all its dynamics.*

Axiom 126 Perceptions are always received in the control center of an organism whether the control center is in control of the organism at the time or not.

This is an explanation for the assumption of valences.

Axiom 127 All perceptions reaching the organism's sense channels are recorded and stored by THETA FACSIMILE.

DEFINITION: Perception is the process of recording data from the physical universe and storing it as a THETA FACSIMILE.

DEFINITION: Recall is the process of regaining perceptions.

Axiom 128 Any organism can recall everything which it has perceived.

Axiom 129 An organism displaced by plus or minus randomity is thereafter remote from the perception recording center.

Increased remoteness brings about occlusions of perceptions. One can perceive things in present time and then, because they are being recorded after they passed THETA *perception of the awareness unit, they are recorded but cannot be recalled.*

Axiom 130 THETA FACSIMILES of counter-effort are all that interpose between the control center and its recalls.

Axiom 131 Any counter-effort received into a control center is always accompanied by all perceptics.

Axiom 132 The random counter-efforts to an organism and the intermingled perceptions in the randomity can reexert that force upon an organism when restimulated.

DEFINITION: Restimulation is the reactivation of a past counter-effort by appearance in the organism's environment of a similarity toward the content of the past randomity area.

Axiom 133 Self-determinism alone brings about the mechanism of restimulation.

Axiom 134 A reactivated area of the past randomity impinges the effort and the perceptions upon the organism.

Axiom 135 Activation of a randomity area is accomplished first by the perceptions, then by the pain, finally by the effort.

Axiom 136 The mind is plastically capable of recording all efforts and counter-efforts.

Axiom 137 A counter-effort accompanied by sufficient (enrandomed) force impresses the facsimile of the counter-effort personality into the mind of an organism.

Axiom 138 Aberration is the degree of residual plus or minus randomity accumulated by compelling, inhibiting or unwarranted assisting of efforts on the part of other organisms or the physical (material) universe.

Aberration is caused by what is done to the individual, not what the individual does, plus his self-determinism about what has been done to him.

Axiom 139 Aberrated behavior consists of destructive effort toward prosurvival data or entities on any dynamic, or effort toward the survival of contrasurvival data or entities for any dynamic.

Axiom 140 A valence is a facsimile personality made capable of force by the counter-effort of the moment of receipt into the plus or minus randomity of unconsciousness.

Valences are assistive, compulsive or inhibitive to the organism.

A control center is not a valence.

Axiom 141 A control center effort is aligned toward a goal through definite space as a recognized incident in time.

Axiom 142 An organism is as healthy and sane as it is self-determined.

The environmental control of the organism motor controls inhibits the organism's ability to change with the changing environment, since the organism will attempt to carry forward with one set of responses when it needs by self-determinism to create another to survive in another environment.

Axiom 143 All learning is accomplished by random effort.

Axiom 144 A counter-effort producing sufficient plus or minus randomity to record is recorded with an index of space and time as hidden as the remainder of its content.

Axiom 145 A counter-effort producing sufficient plus or minus randomity when activated by restimulation exerts itself against the environment or the organism without regard to space and time, except reactivated perceptions.

Axiom 146 Counter-efforts are directed out from the organism until they are further enrandomed by the environ at which time they again activate against the control center.

Axiom 147 An organism's mind employs counter-efforts effectively only so long as insufficient plus or minus randomity exists to hide differentiation of the facsimiles created.

Axiom 148 Physical laws are learned by life energy only by impingement of the physical universe producing randomity, and a withdrawal from that impingement.

Axiom 149 Life depends upon an alignment of force vectors in the direction of survival and the nullification of force vectors in the direction of succumb in order to survive.

COROLLARY: Life depends upon an alignment of force vectors in the direction of succumb and the nullification of force vectors in the direction of survive in order to succumb.

Axiom 150 Any area of randomity gathers to it situations similar to it which do not contain actual efforts but only perceptions.

Axiom 151 Whether an organism has the goal of surviving or succumbing depends upon the amount of plus or minus randomity it has reactivated. (Not residual.)

Axiom 152 Survival is accomplished only by motion.

Axiom 153 In the physical universe the absence of motion is vanishment.

Axiom 154 Death is the equivalent to life of total lack of life-motivated motion.

Axiom 155 Acquisition of prosurvival matter and energy or organisms in space and time means increased motion.

Axiom 156 Loss of prosurvival matter and energy or organisms in space and time means decreased motion.

Axiom 157 Acquisition or proximity of matter, energy or organisms which assist the survival of an organism increase the survival potentials of an organism.

Axiom 158 Acquisition or proximity of matter, energy or organisms which inhibit the survival of an organism decrease its survival potential.

Axiom 159 Gain of survival energy, matter or organisms increases the freedom of an organism.

Axiom 160 Receipt or proximity of nonsurvival energy, matter or time decreases the freedom of motion of an organism.

Axiom 161 The control center attempts the halting or lengthening of time, the expansion or contraction of space and the decrease or increase of energy and matter.

This is a primary source of invalidation, and it is also a primary source of aberration.

Axiom 162 Pain is the balk of effort by counter-effort in great intensity, whether that effort is to remain at rest or in motion.

Axiom 163 Perception, including pain, can be exhausted from an area of plus or minus randomity, still leaving the effort and counter-effort of that plus or minus randomity.

Axiom 164 The rationality of the mind depends upon an optimum reaction toward time.

DEFINITION: Sanity, the computation of futures.

DEFINITION: Neurotic, the computation of present time only.

DEFINITION: Psychotic, computation only of past situations.

Axiom 165 Survival pertains only to the future.

COROLLARY: Succumb pertains only to the present and past.

Axiom 166 An individual is as happy as he can perceive survival potentials in the future.

Axiom 167 As the needs of any organism are met it rises higher and higher in its efforts along the dynamics.

An organism which achieves ARC with itself can better achieve ARC with sex in the future; having achieved this it can achieve ARC with groups; having achieved this, it can achieve ARC with mankind, etc.

Axiom 168 Affinity, reality and communication coexist in an inextricable relationship.

The coexistent relationship between affinity, reality and communication is such that none can be increased without increasing the other two and none can be decreased without decreasing the other two.

Axiom 169 Any aesthetic product is a symbolic facsimile or combination of facsimiles of theta or physical universes in varied randomities and volumes of randomities with the interplay of tones.

Axiom 170 An aesthetic product is an interpretation of the universes by an individual or group mind.

Axiom 171 Delusion is the postulation by the imagination of occurrences in areas of plus or minus randomity.

Axiom 172 Dreams are the imaginative reconstruction of areas of randomity or the resymbolization of the efforts of theta.

Axiom 173 A motion is created by the degree of optimum randomity introduced by the countereffort to an organism's effort.

Axiom 174 MEST which has been mobilized by life forms is in more affinity with life organisms than nonmobilized MEST.

Axiom 175 All past perception, conclusion and existence moments, including those of plus or minus randomity, are recoverable to the control center of the organism.

Axiom 176 The ability to produce survival effort on the part of an organism is affected by the degrees of randomity existing in its past. (This includes learning.)

Axiom 177 Areas of past plus or minus randomity can be readdressed by the control center of an organism and the plus or minus randomity exhausted.

Axiom 178 The exhaustion of past plus or minus randomities permits the control center of an organism to effect its own efforts toward survival goals.

Axiom 179 The exhaustion of self-determined effort from a past area of plus or minus randomity nullifies the effectiveness of that area.

Axiom 180 Pain is the randomity produced by sudden or strong counter-efforts.

Axiom 181 Pain is stored as plus or minus randomity.

Axiom 182 Pain, as an area of plus or minus randomity, can reinflict itself upon the organism.

Axiom 183 Past pain becomes ineffective upon the organism when the randomity of its area is addressed and aligned.

Axiom 184 The earlier the area of plus or minus randomity, the greater self-produced effort existed to repel it.

Axiom 185 Later areas of plus or minus randomity cannot be realigned easily until earlier areas are realigned.

Axiom 186 Areas of plus or minus randomity become increased in activity when perceptions of similarity are introduced into them.

Axiom 187 Past areas of plus or minus randomity can be reduced and aligned by address to them in present time.

Axiom 188 Absolute good and absolute evil do not exist in the MEST universe.

Axiom 189 That which is good for an organism may be defined as that which promotes the survival of that organism.

COROLLARY: Evil may be defined as that which inhibits or brings plus or minus randomity into the organism, which is contrary to the survival motives of the organism.

Axiom 190 Happiness consists in the act of bringing alignment into hitherto resisting plus or minus randomity. Neither the act or action of attaining survival, nor the accomplishment of this act itself, brings about happiness.

Axiom 191 Construction is an alignment of data.

COROLLARY: Destruction is a plus or minus randomity of data.

The effort of constructing is the alignment toward the survival of the aligning organism.

Destruction is the effort of bringing randomity into an area.

Axiom 192 Optimum survival behavior consists of effort in the maximum survival interest in everything concerned in the dynamics.

Axiom 193 The optimum survival solution of any problem would consist of the highest attainable survival for every dynamic concerned.

Axiom 194 The worth of any organism consists of its value to the survival of its own THETA along any dynamic.

The Prelogics

L. Ron Hubbard analyzed life in its relationship to matter, energy, space and time and as a result evolved the Prelogics. These were published in late 1951 as a result of many years of research into the nature of life and the spirituality of man.

All manifestations of thought and all difficulties of thought find as their basic the Prelogics.

Knowledge is a pyramid, and knowledge as a pyramid has a common denominator which evaluates all other data below it. At the top point of this pyramid, we have what could be called a Q, and it could also be called a common denominator. It is in common to every other datum in this pyramid full of data.

The Qs are the highest echelon from which all other things are derived.

Q came from *quod* in Q.E.D. (*quod erat demonstrandum,* meaning "which was to be shown or demonstrated," used especially in mathematical proofs).

Actually, Q can be defined this way: It is the level from which we are now viewing, which is a common denominator to all experience which we can now view. This is the level which acts as a common denominator to all this experience, and is the highest level from which we are operating. This data, then, would stand behind everything else that we do.

Q simply means the most common datum that sums all other data.

Q1 The common denominator of all life impulses is self-determinism.

Q2 Self-determinism may be defined as the location of matter and energy in space and time, as well as a creation of time and space in which to locate matter and energy.

Q3 The identification of the source of that which places matter and energy and originates space and time is not necessary to the resolution of this problem at this time.

Q4 Universes are created by the application of self-determinism on eight dynamics.

Q5 Self-determinism, applied, will create, conserve, alter and possibly destroy universes.

The Scientology Axioms

In the Scientology Axioms, written by L. Ron Hubbard in 1954, we have a condensation and a recapitulation of all the earlier Axioms and Logics, boiled down to a more practical, more fundamental and more forthright list. They compare best, perhaps, to the axioms of geometry; they are certainly as self-evident as that. But the axioms of geometry are really much cruder than the Scientology Axioms, since geometry proves itself by itself and the Axioms of Scientology prove themselves by all of life.

Axiom 1 Life is basically a static.

DEFINITION: a life static has no mass, no motion, no wavelength, no location in space or in time. It has the ability to postulate and to perceive.

Axiom 2 The static is capable of considerations, postulates and opinions.

Axiom 3 Space, energy, objects, form and time are the result of considerations made and/or agreed upon by the static and are perceived solely because the static considers that it can perceive them.

Axiom 4 Space is a viewpoint of dimension.

Axiom 5 Energy consists of postulated particles in space.

Axiom 6 Objects consist of grouped particles.

Axiom 7 Time is basically a postulate that space and particles will persist.

Axiom 8 The apparency of time is the change of position of particles in space.

Axiom 9 Change is the primary manifestation of time.

Axiom 10 The highest purpose in the universe is the creation of an effect.

Axiom 11 The considerations resulting in conditions of existence are fourfold:

a. *AS–ISNESS is the condition of immediate creation without persistence, and is the condition of existence which exists at the moment of creation and the moment of destruction, and is different from other considerations in that it does not contain survival.*

b. *ALTER–ISNESS is the consideration which introduces change, and therefore time and persistence, into an AS–ISNESS to obtain persistency.*

c. *ISNESS is an apparency of existence brought about by the continuous alteration of an AS–ISNESS. This is called, when agreed upon, reality.*

d. *NOT–ISNESS is the effort to handle ISNESS by reducing its condition through the use of force. It is an apparency and cannot entirely vanquish an ISNESS.*

Axiom 12 The primary condition of any universe is that two spaces, energies or objects must not occupy the same space. When this condition is violated (a perfect duplicate) the apparency of any universe or any part thereof is nulled.

Axiom 13 The cycle of action of the physical universe is create, survive (which is persist), destroy.

Axiom 14 Survival is accomplished by alter-isness and not-isness, by which is gained the persistency known as time.

Axiom 15 Creation is accomplished by the postulation of an as-isness.

Axiom 16 Complete destruction is accomplished by the postulation of the as-isness of any existence and the parts thereof.

Axiom 17 The static, having postulated as-isness, then practices alter-isness, and so achieves the apparency of isness and so obtains reality.

Axiom 18 The static, in practicing not-isness, brings about the persistence of unwanted existences, and so brings about unreality, which includes forgetfulness, unconsciousness and other undesirable states.

Axiom 19 Bringing the static to view as-is any condition devaluates that condition.

Axiom 20 Bringing the static to create a perfect duplicate causes the vanishment of any existence or part thereof.

A perfect duplicate is an additional creation of the object, its energy and space, in its own space, in its own time using its own energy. This violates the condition that two objects must not occupy the same space, and causes the vanishment of the object.

Axiom 21 Understanding is composed of affinity, reality and communication.

Axiom 22 The practice of not-isness reduces understanding.

Axiom 23 The static has the capability of total knowingness. Total knowingness would consist of total ARC.

Axiom 24 Total ARC would bring about the vanishment of all mechanical conditions of existence.

Axiom 25 Affinity is a scale of attitudes which falls away from the coexistence of static, through the interpositions of distance and energy, to create identity, down to close proximity but mystery.

By the practice of isness (beingness) and not-isness (refusal to be) individuation progresses from the knowingness of complete identification down through the introduction of more and more distance and less and less duplication, through lookingness, emotingness, effortingness, thinkingness, symbolizingness, eatingness, sexingness, and so through to not-knowingness (mystery). Until the point of mystery is reached, some communication is possible, but even at mystery an attempt to communicate continues. Here we have, in the case of an individual, a gradual falling away from the belief that one can assume a complete affinity down to the conviction that all is a complete mystery. Any individual is somewhere on this Know to Mystery Scale. The original Chart of Human Evaluation was the emotion section of this scale.

Axiom 26 Reality is the agreed-upon apparency of existence.

Axiom 27 An actuality can exist for one individually, but when it is agreed with by others it can be said to be a reality.

The anatomy of reality is contained in isness, which is composed of as-isness and alter-isness. An isness is an apparency, not an actuality. The actuality is as-isness altered so as to obtain a persistency.

Unreality is the consequence and apparency of the practice of not-isness.

Axiom 28 Communication is the consideration and action of impelling an impulse or particle from source-point across a distance to receipt-point, with the intention of bringing into being at the receipt-point a duplication and understanding of that which emanated from the source-point.

The formula of communication is: cause, distance, effect, with intention, attention and duplication with understanding.

The component parts of communication are consideration, intention, attention, cause, source-point, distance, effect, receipt-point, duplication, understanding, the velocity of the impulse or particle, nothingness or somethingness.

A noncommunication consists of barriers. Barriers consist of space, interpositions (such as walls and screens of fast-moving particles) and time. A communication, by definition, does not need to be two-way. When a communication is returned, the formula is repeated, with the receipt-point now becoming a source-point and the former source-point now becoming a receipt-point.

Axiom 29 In order to cause an as-isness to persist, one must assign other authorship to the creation than his own. Otherwise, his view of it would cause its vanishment.

Any space, energy, form, object, individual or physical universe condition can exist only when an alteration has occurred of the original as-isness so as to prevent a casual view from vanishing it. In other words, anything which is persisting must contain a "lie" so that the original consideration is not completely duplicated.

Axiom 30 The general rule of auditing is that anything which is unwanted and yet persists must be thoroughly viewed, at which time it will vanish.

If only partially viewed, its intensity, at least, will decrease.

Axiom 31 Goodness and badness, beautifulness and ugliness are alike considerations and have no other basis than opinion.

Axiom 32 Anything which is not directly observed tends to persist.

Axiom 33 Any as-isness which is altered by not-isness (by force) tends to persist.

Axiom 34 Any isness, when altered by force, tends to persist.

Axiom 35 The ultimate truth is a static.

A static has no mass, meaning, mobility, no wavelength, no time, no location in space, no space. This has the technical name of "basic truth."

Axiom 36 A lie is a second postulate, statement or condition designed to mask a primary postulate which is permitted to remain.

EXAMPLES:

Neither truth nor a lie is a motion or alteration of a particle from one position to another.

A lie is a statement that a particle having moved did not move, or a statement that a particle, not having moved, did move.

The basic lie is that a consideration which was made was not made or that it was different.

Axiom 37 When a primary consideration is altered but still exists, persistence is achieved for the altering consideration.

All persistence depends on the basic truth, but the persistence is of the altering consideration, for the basic truth has neither persistence nor impersistence.

Axiom 38 1. Stupidity is the unknownness of consideration.

2. Mechanical definition: Stupidity is the unknownness of time, place, form and event.

1. Truth is the exact consideration.

2. Truth is the exact time, place, form and event.

Thus we see that failure to discover truth brings about stupidity.

Thus we see that the discovery of truth would bring about an as-isness by actual experiment.

Thus we see that an ultimate truth would have no time, place, form or event.

Thus, then, we perceive that we can achieve a persistence only when we mask a truth.

Lying is an alteration of time, place, event or form.

Lying becomes alter-isness, becomes stupidity.

(The blackness of cases is an accumulation of the case's own or another's lies.)

Anything which persists must avoid as-isness. Thus, anything, to persist, must contain a lie.

Axiom 39 Life poses problems for its own solution.

Axiom 40 Any problem, to be a problem, must contain a lie. If it were truth, it would unmock.

An "unsolvable problem" would have the greatest persistence. It would also contain the greatest number of altered facts. To make a problem, one must introduce alter-isness.

Axiom 41 That into which alter-isness is introduced becomes a problem.

Axiom 42 Matter, energy, space and time persists because it is a problem.

It is a problem because it contains alter-isness.

Axiom 43 Time is the primary source of untruth.

Time states the untruth of consecutive considerations.

Axiom 44 Theta, the static, has no location in matter, energy, space or time, but is capable of consideration.

Axiom 45 Theta can consider itself to be placed, at which moment it becomes placed, and to that degree a problem.

Axiom 46 Theta can become a problem by its considerations, but then becomes MEST.

MEST is that form of theta which is a problem.

Axiom 47 Theta can resolve problems.

Axiom 48 Life is a game wherein theta as the static solves the problems of theta as MEST.

Axiom 49 To solve any problem it is only necessary to become theta, the solver, rather than theta, the problem.

Axiom 50 Theta as MEST must contain considerations which are lies.

Axiom 51 Postulates and live communication not being MEST and being senior to MEST can accomplish change in MEST without bringing about a persistence of MEST. Thus auditing can occur.

Axiom 52 MEST persists and solidifies to the degree that it is not granted life.

Axiom 53 A stable datum is necessary to the alignment of data.

Axiom 54 A tolerance of confusion and an agreed-upon stable datum on which to align the data in a confusion are at once necessary for a sane reaction on the eight dynamics. (This defines sanity.)

Axiom 55 The cycle of action is a consideration. Create, survive, destroy, the cycle of action accepted by the genetic entity, is only a consideration which can be changed by the thetan making a new consideration or different action cycles.

Axiom 56 Theta brings order to chaos.

COROLLARY: Chaos brings disorder to theta.

Axiom 57 Order manifests when communication, control and havingness are available to theta.

DEFINITIONS:
Communication: the interchange of ideas across space.
Control: positive postulating, which is intention, and the execution thereof.

Havingness: that which permits the experience of mass and pressure.

Axiom 58 Intelligence and judgment are measured by the ability to evaluate relative importances.

COROLLARY: The ability to evaluate importances and unimportances is the highest faculty of logic.

COROLLARY: Identification is a monotone assignment of importance.

COROLLARY: Identification is the inability to evaluate differences in time, location, form, composition or importance.

The above is a summary of states of being which can be used to create, cause to persist, or destroy.

Having agreed to the mechanics and retaining the agreements, the thetan can yet make innumerable postulates which by their contradiction and complexity, create, cause to persist, and destroy human behavior.

The Factors

(Summation of the considerations and examinations of the human spirit and the material universe completed between A.D. *1923 and 1953.)*

1 Before the beginning was a Cause and the entire purpose of the Cause was the creation of effect.

2 In the beginning and forever is the decision and the decision is TO BE.

3 The first action of beingness is to assume a viewpoint.

4 The second action of beingness is to extend from the viewpoint, points to view, which are dimension points.

5 Thus there is space created, for the definition of space is: viewpoint of dimension. And the purpose of a dimension point is space and a point of view.

6 The action of a dimension point is reaching and withdrawing.

7 And from the viewpoint to the dimension points there are connection and interchange. Thus new dimension points are made. Thus there is communication.

8 And thus there is light.

9 And thus there is energy.

10 And thus there is life.

11 But there are other viewpoints and these viewpoints outthrust points to view. And there comes about an interchange amongst viewpoints; but the interchange is never otherwise than in terms of exchanging dimension points.

12 The dimension point can be moved by the viewpoint, for the viewpoint, in addition to creative ability and consideration, possesses volition and potential independence of action; and the viewpoint, viewing dimension points, can change in relation to its own or other dimension points or viewpoints. Thus comes about all the fundamentals there are to motion.

13 The dimension points are each and every one, whether large or small, *solid.* And they are solid solely because the viewpoints say they are solid.

14 Many dimension points combine into larger gases, fluids or solids. Thus there is matter. But the most valued point is admiration, and admiration is so strong its absence alone permits persistence.

15 The dimension point can be different from other dimension points and thus can possess an individual quality. And many dimension points can possess a similar quality, and others can possess a similar quality unto themselves. Thus comes about the quality of classes of matter.

16 The viewpoint can combine dimension points into forms and the forms can be simple or complex and can be at different distances from the viewpoints and so there can be combinations of form. And the forms are capable of motion and the viewpoints are capable of motion and so there can be motion of forms.

17 And the opinion of the viewpoint regulates the consideration of the forms, their stillness or their motion, and these considerations consist of assignment of beauty or ugliness to the forms and these considerations alone are art.

18 It is the opinions of the viewpoints that some of these forms should endure. Thus there is survival.

19 And the viewpoint can never perish; but the form can perish.

20 And the many viewpoints, interacting, become dependent upon one another's forms and do not choose to distinguish completely the ownership of dimension points and so comes about a dependency upon the dimension points and upon the other viewpoints.

21 From this comes a consistency of viewpoint of the interaction of dimension points and this, regulated, is TIME.

22 And there are universes.

23 The universes, then, are three in number: the universe created by one viewpoint, the universe created by every other viewpoint, the universe created by the mutual action of viewpoints which is agreed to be upheld—the physical universe.

24 And the viewpoints are never seen. And the viewpoints consider more and more that the dimension points are valuable. And the viewpoints try to become the anchor points and forget that they can create more points and space and forms. Thus comes about scarcity. And the dimension points can perish and so the viewpoints assume that they, too, can perish.

25 Thus comes about death.

26 The manifestations of pleasure and pain, of thought, emotion and effort, of thinking, of sensation, of affinity, reality, communication, of behavior and being are thus derived and the riddles of our universe are apparently contained and answered herein.

27 There *is* beingness, but man believes there is only becomingness.

28 The resolution of any problem posed hereby is the establishment of viewpoints and dimension points, the betterment of condition and concourse amongst dimension points, and, thereby, viewpoints, and the remedy of abundance or scarcity in all things, pleasant or ugly, by the rehabilitation of the ability of the viewpoint to assume points of view and create and uncreate, neglect, start, change and stop dimension points of any kind at the determinism of the viewpoint. Certainty in all three universes must be regained, for certainty, not data, is knowledge.

29 In the opinion of the viewpoint, any beingness, any thing, is better than no thing, any effect is better than no effect, any universe better than no universe, any particle better than no particle, but the particle of admiration is best of all.

30 And above these things there might be speculation only. And below these things there is the playing of the game. But these things which are written here man can experience and know. And some may care to teach these things and some may care to use them to assist those in distress and some may desire to employ them to make individuals and organizations more able and so give to Earth a culture of which we can be proud.

Humbly tendered as a gift to man by L. Ron Hubbard, 23 April 1953

CHAPTER 35

L. RON HUBBARD A CHRONICLE

To appreciate the scope of L. Ron Hubbard's life, his varied experiences and the many lands he visited in pursuit of answers to the human dilemma, the following chronicle has been provided. It is designed to give readers some feel for his progress and the sequence of steps leading to the discoveries for which he is so respected today.

13 March 1911:

L. Ron Hubbard is born in Tilden, Nebraska. In September the Hubbard family—Ron, his father, Harry Ross Hubbard, an officer in the US Navy, and mother, Ledora May—move to Durant, Oklahoma.

1913–1917:

In 1913, settling in the city of Kalispell, Montana, Ron first encounters the Blackfoot Indians at a tribal dance on the outskirts of town. The Indians are much taken with young Ron's inquisitiveness and the beginnings of a bond are established.

From Kalispell, Ron moves to Montana's capital at Helena, where during the summer months he usually resides at the family ranch, affectionately known as the "Old Homestead." During the harsh winter months, a three-story red brick house on the corner of Helena's Fifth and Beatty Streets serves as Ron's home.

Among other colorful figures in this still pioneer setting, Ron meets Old Tom, a Blackfoot Indian medicine man. A unique and rare relationship is established as the elderly shaman passes on much of the tribal lore to his young friend.

Many a Saturday finds Ron and his friends panning for gold in the gullies for pocket money, while afternoons are spent riding broncos on the surrounding plains.

At the age of six, Ron is honored with the status of blood brother of the Blackfeet in a ceremony that is still recalled by tribal elders.

1918–1921:

In the spring of 1918 Ron and his grandfather embark on an "automotive adventure"—from Helena to Portland, Oregon, in a Model-T Ford.

After returning to Helena, Ron takes his first adventure by himself, traveling to Tacoma, Washington to meet up with his father. He then moves with his parents first to San Diego and then a year later to Oakland, California.

1922–1923:

Ron moves north to Puget Sound in Washington State. He joins the Boy Scouts of America in April 1923. As a member of Tacoma Troop 31, he becomes a Second Class Scout on 8 May and two months later, on 5 July, advances to First Class Scout.

In October, Harry Ross Hubbard receives orders to report to the nation's capital. Ron and his parents board the USS *Ulysses S. Grant* on 1 November 1923 and sail to New York from San Francisco through the recently opened Panama Canal. They then journey to Washington, DC. During this voyage, Ron meets Commander Joseph "Snake" Thompson, who has recently returned from Vienna and studies with Sigmund Freud. Through the course of their friendship, the commander spends many an afternoon in the Library of Congress teaching Ron what he knows of the human mind.

By 11 December 1923, Ron, now part of Washington's Boy Scout Troop 10, earns his Carpentry, First Aid and Fireman merit badges.

1924–1925:

In the month of January 1924 Ron earns his Electricity, Personal Health, Photography and Public Health merit badges.

In February, after earning his Safety First, Craftsmanship, Swimming, Physical Development and Pioneering merit badges, Ron obtains his Life Scout and Star Scout medals.

In March, Ron obtains his Handicraft, Automobiling and Pathfinding merit badges. On 20 March Ron represents Troop 10 while visiting President Calvin Coolidge and five days afterwards, on 25 March, becomes the nation's youngest Eagle Scout. The next day, Ron leaves Washington and returns to Montana by cross-country train.

While in Montana, Ron continues his scouting activities, organizes scouting events and acts as an Assistant Scoutmaster. In 1925 Ron moves to Seattle where he attends Queen Anne High School.

1926–1929:

After completing the school year in early June 1927, Ron travels to San Francisco, boarding a steamer to meet his father in Guam. By way of Hawaii, Japan, China, the Philippines and Hong Kong, Ron arrives at the island of Guam during the first week of July, 1927. There, he befriends the local Chamorros and teaches in the native schools. Throughout these travels, Ron's observations and adventures are carefully recorded in diaries. A few years later, Ron will draw upon these experiences for his adventure and action fiction.

By late September 1927, Ron returns to Helena where he joins the Montana National Guard's 163rd Infantry. While at Helena High School he becomes an editor of the school's newspaper.

For the annual Vigilante Day Parade on 4 May, Ron organizes and enters a group of classmates dressed as pirates of the Spanish Main and wins the prize for "Most Original" cast.

Finding classrooms and schools too confining, Ron ventures out alone again and travels aboard the USS *Henderson,* returning to the Orient.

Through the next fourteen months Ron journeys inland to the Western Hills of China, out again to Japan, then down to the Philippines and further south to Java. He plies the waters of the China coast as a helmsman and supercargo aboard the *Marina Maru*—a twin-masted coastal schooner.

In China, he becomes close friends with British intelligence officers, Buddhist priests, US Marines and the last remaining magician from the line of Kublai Khan's court.

By late September 1929, he returns to the United States, completing his high-school education in Washington, DC. Writing and delivering a speech on the United States Constitution and the guarantees of individual liberty, he wins a scholastic oratory contest.

1930–1933:

Graduating from Woodward School for Boys in 1930, Ron enrolls at George Washington University. Here he studies engineering and atomic and molecular physics and embarks upon a personal search for answers to the human dilemma. His first experiment concerning the structure and function of the mind is carried out while at the university.

Ron joins the 20th Regiment, Company G of the US Marines, becoming a drill sergeant and turning out a prize-winning company. He performs as the balladeer for the local radio station WOL and writes serial drama shows. He also becomes a surveyor as part of a team sent to verify the Canadian/US border in Maine.

Taking his thirst for adventure to the skies, he is introduced to glider flying and quickly becomes recognized as one of the country's most outstanding pilots. With virtually no training time, he takes up powered flight and barnstorms throughout the Midwest. Due to reports he files on airport conditions, twelve unsafe airports are closed.

A national aviation magazine reports that Ron set a national soaring record for sustained flight over the same field.

Writing for the nationwide *Sportsman Pilot* magazine, Ron details the latest aviation developments and advises fellow pilots on flight procedures in adverse conditions.

He helps run the university flying club and is secretary of the George Washington University chapter of the American Society of Civil Engineers. As an editor and writer with the college newspaper, *The University Hatchet,* he writes his first published fiction story, *Tah.* He also wins the Literary Award for the best one-act play, *The God Smiles.*

In the spring of 1932, Ron organizes and heads the Caribbean Motion Picture Expedition. The two-and-a-half-month, 5,000-mile voyage aboard the 200-foot, four-masted schooner, *Doris Hamlin,* proves a unique and rewarding experience for over fifty college students. The voyage collects numerous floral and reptile specimens for the University of Michigan, and photographs are sold to the *New York Times.*

Shortly after Ron's return to the US he embarks on another adventure, the West Indies Mineralogical Expedition. Through April of 1933, Ron not only completes the first mineralogical survey of Puerto Rico, but writes articles for *Sportsman Pilot* magazine on flying through the Caribbean islands. He additionally investigates and explores some of the area's diverse cultures and beliefs, including voodoo and Espiritismo.

Returning to the mainland in the spring of 1933, Ron begins his professional fiction-writing career. Ron writes a story a day and after a few short weeks of work nets his first sale to New York publishers. February 1934 sees the publication of Ron's first adventure fiction story, *The Green God.*

1934–1936:

Throughout this period, L. Ron Hubbard writes. Seated at his Remington manual typewriter, he easily produces 100,000 words of fiction a month.

Ron writes western, detective, adventure, action, and even romance stories. In 1935 he is elected president of the New York Chapter of the American Fiction Guild, offering leadership to such stellar names as Raymond Chandler, Dashiell Hammett and Edgar Rice Burroughs. In his capacity as president, he also pens articles for writer magazines. He appears on radio shows advising both novice and professional colleagues on how to improve the quality and salability of their stories.

Illustrating his prolific output as a writer, he completes 138 novels, novelettes and short stories in six years in just the genres of adventure, action, western, mystery and detective. This is an average of over one published story every two weeks, three times the output of most other writers.

So great is his production in so many varied styles and genres that he employs numerous pseudonyms so as not to dominate too many magazine covers. Among them:

Winchester Remington Colt
Lt. Jonathan Daly
Capt. Charles Gordon
Bernard Hubbel
Michael Keith
Legionnaire 148
Rene Lafayette
Ken Martin
B.A. Northrup
Scott Morgan
Kurt von Rachen
Barry Randolph
Lt. Scott Morgan
Morgan DeWolf
Legionnaire 14830
Capt. Humbert Reynolds

So intense is the demand for Ron's stories, that one complete issue of *Top-Notch* magazine is entirely written by him. In 1936 Ron writes his first book, *Buckskin Brigades.*

1937–1940:

Ron's popularity is now such that Hollywood seeks film rights to his stories and then enlists his services as a writer. After purchasing film rights to his novel, *Murder at Pirate Castle,* Columbia Pictures requests that he adapt this work for the screen under the title *Secret of Treasure Island.* Arriving in Hollywood in May 1937, Ron begins work on *Secret of Treasure Island* and goes to work on three other big screen serials for Columbia: *The Mysterious Pilot, The Great Adventures of Wild Bill Hickok* and *The Spider Returns.* Ron thus works on four of Columbia's big screen super serials. In his ten weeks in Hollywood, he not only writes over a quarter of a million words of scripts, but also continues producing for his New York editors.

Upon returning to New York, executives from Street and Smith, one of the world's largest publishing concerns, enlist Ron's expertise for their newly acquired magazine, *Astounding Science Fiction.* Ron is asked to help boost sagging sales with stories about *real* people—not robots, planets and spaceships. He accepts their proposal and the face of science fiction is changed forever.

His first science fiction work, *The Dangerous Dimension,* appears in the July 1938 issue of *Astounding Science Fiction.* Among other L. Ron Hubbard stories appearing in the pages of *Astounding* is the much acclaimed *Final Blackout* which is later released as a best-selling book.

In 1939 Street and Smith launch a second new magazine, *Unknown,* and it is soon filled with Ron's fantasy writings which could not be accommodated in *Astounding.* His first story in this genre is *Ultimate Adventure,* appearing in the April 1939 issue. Many more L. Ron Hubbard fiction works appear for the first time in *Unknown* including such legendary stories as *Fear, Death's Deputy, Typewriter in the Sky* and *Slaves of Sleep.* These stories are subsequently released as books in their own right.

On 19 February 1940 Ron is elected a member of the prestigious Explorers Club. Concurrently he plans an Alaskan expedition, and on 27 July 1940 his Alaskan Radio Experimental Expedition embarks from Seattle. His vessel is the 32-foot ketch, *Magician,* and she sails under Explorers Club flag number 105. Ron completes a voyage of some 700 miles, charting previously unrecorded hazards and coastlines for the US Navy Hydrographic Office. He also conducts experiments on radio directional finding, and examines local native cultures, including the Tlingit, the Haidas and the Aleutian Island natives. On 17 December 1940 the US Bureau of Marine Inspection and Navigation awards Ron his Master of Steam and Motor Vessels license.

In December he returns to Seattle, resuming his writing while presenting the US Navy with the hundreds of photographs and notations they had requested.

1941–1945:

On 29 March 1941 Ron receives his Master of Sail Vessel license for "Any Ocean."

On 2 July 1941 he is commissioned as Lieutenant (jg) of the United States Navy Reserve. With the outbreak of war in December 1941, Ron is ordered to Australia where he coordinates intelligence activities.

Returning to the United States in March, Ron takes command of a convoy escort vessel in the Atlantic, then a subchaser in the Pacific. He also serves as an instructor and chief navigation officer, and is selected to Princeton University's Military Government School.

In early 1945, while recovering from war injuries at Oak Knoll Naval Hospital, Ron conducts a series of tests and experiments dealing with the endocrine system. He discovers that, contrary to long-standing beliefs, function monitors structure. With this revolutionary advance, he begins to apply his theories to the field of the mind and thereby to improve the conditions of others.

1946:

After discharge from the US Navy in February 1946, Ron returns to writing, although his primary thrust continues to be the development of a means to better the condition of men. To help support this research, he writes thirty-one science fiction, fantasy, western, mystery and detective stories over the next three years. A few of the titles included in his work at this time are: *Blood on His Spurs, Ole Doc Methuselah, Killer's Law, Hoss Tamer* and *The Obsolete Weapon*.

1947:

Ron opens an office near the corner of La Brea and Sunset Boulevards in Los Angeles, where he tests the application of Dianetics among actors, directors, writers and others of the Hollywood community. These are the people who first receive the benefits of Ron's revolutionary breakthroughs in the field of the mind.

With test cases and research material in hand, Ron travels to Washington, DC where he compiles into manuscript form his sixteen-year investigation to determine the dynamic principle of existence. (The result of this work is published today as the book *The Dynamics of Life.*)

1948:

Ron accepts an appointment as a Special Police Officer with the Los Angeles Police Department and uses the position to study society's criminal elements.

Moving on to Savannah, Georgia, he volunteers his time in hospitals and mental wards, saving the lives of patients with his counseling techniques.

1949:

His as yet unpublished manuscript on Dianetics, which had been passed to a few friends for review, is copied and copied again until it circulates around the world. As a result of this enthusiastic response, Ron is urged by associates to write a popular book on the subject of Dianetics.

Late in the year, L. Ron Hubbard's "Terra Incognita: The Mind" the first published article on Dianetics, appears in the Winter/Spring issue of the *Explorers Club Journal.*

1950:

Ron is contracted by Hermitage House Publishing to write *Dianetics.*

In the first week of March he completes *Dianetics: The Modern Science of Mental Health.*

Ron writes *Dianetics: The Evolution of a Science* for magazine publication to promote and accompany the release of *Dianetics.*

On 9 May 1950, *Dianetics* is released and appears on the *New York Times* bestseller list, 18 June 1950. It remains on the bestseller list for 28 consecutive weeks and launches a national movement which will soon become the fastest growing such movement in America.

On 7 June Ron delivers his first recorded lectures on Dianetics in Elizabeth, New Jersey, where the Hubbard Dianetics Research Foundation is formed.

On 10 August, after moving to a new residence in Los Angeles, California, Ron delivers a lecture on Dianetics to a sell-out crowd of over 6,000 people at the Shrine Auditorium.

Through the remainder of the year, Ron continues to tour and speak in major cities and by the end of December he has delivered over 100 lectures and crisscrossed the country.

1951:

Ron writes six books which outline his discoveries in the field of the human mind and give practical technology to better human existence.

In addition to the printed word, he delivers 135 lectures on the subject of Dianetics.

After returning from Havana, Cuba, where he completes the book *Science of Survival,* he opens the first Hubbard College in Wichita, Kansas, delivering lectures and conducting courses.

In the fall of 1951, having discovered that man is most fundamentally a spiritual being, he begins a new line of research to determine what can be done to help an individual regain natural abilities. The philosophy which he forms from these discoveries is Scientology.

1952:

Ron moves to Phoenix, Arizona where he opens his office and establishes the Hubbard Association of Scientologists International.

In September, traveling to England, he establishes the Hubbard Association of Scientologists International in London.

In late November Ron returns to the United States, where in Philadelphia he delivers a Doctorate Course in Scientology with 63 lectures in 19 days providing a wide analysis of human behavior. The lectures are known as the Philadelphia Doctorate Course lectures. He then travels back to England where he begins plans for a research trip across Europe.

In addition to delivering 230 lectures on subjects such as emotional tones, communication and creativity, Ron writes of his further research on man's spiritual potential in four new books.

1953:

Motoring across Europe to Barcelona, he follows World War II invasion routes to study the effects of devastation on populations; he also researches European university systems.

Ron returns to Phoenix, where he releases new breakthroughs which enable the individual to explore his past and improve his reactions toward life. During this period, Ron also researches the basics of organization, developing principles that any group can use to survive and prosper. He delivers 274 lectures and writes two more books.

1954:

In recognition of the spiritual nature of Ron's philosophy, a number of Scientologists in Los Angeles, California form the first Church of Scientology in February.

Ron further researches and develops the philosophy of Scientology in Phoenix, continuing to lecture and write extensively.

1955:

In March, Ron moves from Phoenix to Washington, DC where the Founding Church of Washington, DC is formed with Ron as Executive Director. He drafts organizational policies and intensifies his work in developing an administrative technology to allow Scientology organizations to run smoothly and expand.

During October Ron returns to England to deliver lectures in London, while further establishing the London organization. Ron delivers over 235 lectures in this year, on subjects from counseling techniques to education and alcoholism. In December he travels to Ireland to initiate the formation of an Irish organization in Dublin and then returns to England.

1956:

Returning to Dublin, Ron researches and develops the exact steps and actions a person follows to establish a successful Scientology organization anywhere in the world.

He also writes a book containing simple but powerful precepts that allow anyone to immediately improve their life.

In Barcelona, Spain he conducts additional research, then returns to Washington, DC where he delivers a series of lectures which cover spiritual and material requirements of man. He then sails back to England aboard the *Queen Elizabeth,* during which time he writes a book providing solutions to day-to-day job stress. After delivering 18 lectures on human problems in London, he again returns to Washington.

While delivering more than 150 lectures, detailing solutions to such problems as environmental radiation and the failings of groups, Ron also runs both the Washington and London organizations during this year and finds the time to write two more books.

1957:

In February Ron travels to Puerto Rico where he continues researching and writing. In April he flies to London to deliver a series of lectures on auditing techniques and then travels to Washington. While still concentrating on further organizational and administrative developments and delivering over 135 public lectures, Ron also writes two books to better speed an individual's progress.

1958:

Ron delivers 122 lectures in 1958, including the Clearing Congress Lectures in Washington, DC, the first six of which are filmed. In October Ron sails to London aboard the RMS *Statedam.* In England, he delivers 32 lectures, while reorganizing local offices. With this accomplished, he sets sail back to Washington in early December aboard the *Saxonia.*

1959:

Ron defines the duties of the various echelons of Scientology organizations and delivers six lectures on auditing refinements in Washington, DC.

In March he begins negotiations to purchase Saint Hill Manor in Sussex, England which will be his home for the following seven years. By May, negotiations are completed and Ron moves his residence to the 55-acre estate. The worldwide headquarters of Scientology is moved to Saint Hill.

In yet another line of research, this one involving different orders of life, Ron conducts horticultural experiments in greenhouses at Saint Hill which bring about major increases in plant growth. His discoveries are written up in horticultural magazines internationally and receive wide coverage in daily newspapers.

The first E-Meter designed and built to Ron's exact specifications is produced.

On 16 October Ron begins an around-the-world trip, traveling to Greece, India, Melbourne, Hawaii, San Francisco and New York, arriving back at Saint Hill the first week of December.

In Melbourne alone, he delivers 38 lectures, and while in the United States he writes and issues an organizing board for American Scientology churches (a board which shows what functions are done, the order they are done in, and who is responsible for getting them done).

Upon his return to England, Ron appears on BBC television discussing his horticultural experiments. Shortly afterwards Ron travels to Washington, DC.

In all he gives 128 lectures this year and writes two books.

1960:

While in Washington, Ron delivers 18 lectures in one week outlining his discoveries on such subjects as the importance of honesty and individual responsibility. He then returns home to Saint Hill.

In March, after extensive research and investigation, Ron writes the book, *Have You Lived Before This Life?*

After delivering over 30 more lectures at Saint Hill and London, he travels to South Africa in September where he standardizes the operation and administration of South African organizations. At the end of the year, he once more returns to Washington, DC and finishes out the year by delivering three lectures.

1961:

After extending his stay in Washington for an additional 13 lectures he returns to Saint Hill for a week, then travels back to South Africa in late January. Here he not only delivers more than 20 lectures which further detail the means of realizing man's spiritual goals, but also develops a refined pattern of organization for Scientology churches.

Ron is awarded his second Explorers Club flag for his "Ocean Archaeological Expedition to study underwater sites of historical interest such as submerged cities."

In late March Ron returns to Saint Hill and begins to deliver the Saint Hill Special Briefing Course—a comprehensive training program for Scientology auditors in which the entire history of technical development is covered.

For the following five years, Ron dedicates his time to the full delivery of the Saint Hill Special Briefing Course to students from around the world. This is a period of intensive technical research on the route to Clear and advanced spiritual states. This time is also devoted to developing and standardizing administrative policy for the organizations.

1962–1963:

In the first week of September, Ron takes a short break from the Saint Hill Special Briefing Course and travels to Washington, DC to deliver a nine-lecture congress in three days.

In addition to running the Saint Hill organization and the Briefing Course, during 1963, Ron films a movie entitled *An Afternoon at Saint Hill.* The film provides a tour of Saint Hill and a view of activities there.

1964:

While continuing his work at Saint Hill, Ron conducts photographic shoots in the surrounding area and carries out a study of promotional actions at the request of a well-known local promoter of events.

In June Ron begins a series of lectures in which he unravels the complexities of study and education, giving a technology which anyone can use to improve the study of any subject. This becomes study technology, which is used around the world today in both Scientology organizations and in private and public education systems.

1965:

In January Ron travels to the Canary Islands to begin intensive research on the spiritual nature of man and his origins. He returns to Saint Hill later that month.

His activities during the remainder of the year bring major organizational and technical breakthroughs as a result of his years of work at Saint Hill.

The Classification and Gradation Chart is released, laying out the exact steps to follow in Scientology counseling and training to achieve higher states of awareness and ability.

In November Ron announces and implements the seven-division organizing board. This is a major breakthrough in the successful pattern of operation of any group. It has universal application and is in use today in all churches of Scientology and an increasing number of other organizations.

1966:

In February Ron returns to the Canary Islands to continue his advanced research of the spiritual nature of man. On 18 March he flies to Rhodesia where he investigates the ability of a single individual to single-handedly assist a small country to overcome its problems.

In July he returns to England and delivers the final lectures of the Saint Hill Special Briefing Course.

He releases the first advanced levels of Scientology counseling which take one beyond the state of Clear originally postulated in Dianetics. On 1 September 1966, L. Ron Hubbard resigns from all directorships and running of Scientology organizations.

He subsequently accepts his third Explorers Club flag for the Hubbard Geological Survey Expedition, which will find and examine ancient Mediterranean civilizations, amplifying man's knowledge of his history.

In December Ron purchases the sailing vessel, *Enchanter* (later renamed *Diana*).

1967:

On 2 January Ron arrives in Tangier, Morocco, and establishes a base for advanced philosophic studies. He travels to Las Palmas, Canary Islands, where he meets the *Enchanter* which arrives on 25 February.

With a group of dedicated Scientologists, most of whom had never been to sea, Ron forms the Sea Organization. He trains this inexperienced crew into a team of competent and professional mariners in a matter of months.

Joined by yet another vessel, the *Avon River* (later renamed the *Athena*), Ron and his crews conduct the Hubbard Geological Survey Expedition in the Mediterranean.

Ron's search for the truth results in one of his most significant breakthroughs in removing the barriers to man's ability to achieve full spiritual freedom. This research is fully codified and made available to advanced Scientologists.

In November Ron travels to England and accepts delivery of the 3,200-ton vessel *Royal Scotman* as a further expansion of the Sea Organization.

1968–1969:

Ron continues training the ships' crews while living aboard the *Royal Scotman* (which is renamed *Apollo*). Ron issues more than 300 instructional letters, covering all nautical duties from engine room maintenance to fire drills and from navigation to small boat handling.

In the fall of 1968, aboard the *Apollo,* he delivers 19 lectures and develops a new advanced course to train students to deliver Scientology counseling 100 percent standardly.

During 1969 he researches the effects and causes of drug addiction and drug use, developing procedures which address and solve the causes of, and remove the harmful mental effects brought about by such abuse. He issues these findings for broad use.

1970–1973:

Having developed a successful and standardized pattern of organizational form and function, Ron turns to resolving the problems of how to manage an international network of organizations.

Ron streamlines organizational management technology—laying out highly workable principles of personnel, organization and financial management and handling which are found today in the *Management Series* volumes.

His breakthroughs at this time include the first significant advances on the subject of logic since ancient Greece. Ron conducts a comprehensive study of all existing public relations theories and practices and also releases his discoveries in the field of PR, providing an entirely analytical and ethical approach to the subject.

In 1972 Ron carries out a sociological study in and around New York City. Through the remainder of the year and into 1973, he researches vitamins and nutrition—which will later become significant in his breakthroughs in the handling of the residual effects of drugs.

1974–1975:

In February 1974, while aboard the *Apollo,* Ron forms a music and dance troupe to provide entertainment and goodwill at Spanish and Portuguese ports of call. He personally instructs the musicians and dancers in artistic presentation, music, composition, sound, arranging and recording.

During October 1974 the *Apollo* sails across the Atlantic to Bermuda and then on to the Caribbean.

From February through June 1974, while in Curaçao, Ron takes a series of photographs for the island's tourist bureau and completes six photography projects for release in Scientology books and publications.

By mid-1975 the activities on the *Apollo* outgrow the vessel's capacity. Ron returns to the United States.

Ron settles in Dunedin, Florida, where he continues his research into music, examining choir music at local churches. He writes the scripts for the first Scientology educational films.

1976–1979:

Ron moves to a southern California desert ranch in La Quinta and establishes, trains and supervises a film production unit. Over the following three years he writes not only a feature-length screenplay, *Revolt in the Stars,* but also the scripts for 33 Scientology instructional films.

During this same three-year period he also shoots, directs and produces 7 films which are used in training Scientology counselors.

Ron discovers that drugs remain in the body even years after usage has ceased. Consequently, he develops the Purification Rundown to rid the body of harmful residual substances. Coupled with his 1969 discoveries, Ron's development of the drug rehabilitation program is complete. These techniques used by churches of Scientology and drug rehabilitation organizations around the world, allow anyone to free himself from the debilitating effects of drugs.

It is also in 1979 that Ron isolates and solves the problem of increasing illiteracy. His discoveries and solutions later become the published Key to Life Course—widely acclaimed for its miraculous results.

1980–1981:

During this period Ron devotes the majority of his time to writing.

He composes a nonreligious moral code, *The Way to Happiness,* as a solution to the eroding morals in society. The broad distribution and widespread acceptance of this code contributes to a grass-roots movement for improved moral values.

Ron also writes two feature-length screenplays and 50 film treatments for public films on Dianetics and Scientology.

To mark his 50th anniversary as a professional writer, Ron writes the international blockbuster, *Battlefield Earth: A Saga of the Year 3000,* the largest science fiction novel written to date.

As part of his 2 million word output during this period, he also writes his science fiction satire, 10-volume magnum opus, *Mission Earth.*

1982– 24 JANUARY 1986:

Ron establishes a California home on a ranch outside of San Luis Obispo. He researches and releases new Scientology technical materials which further expand the route to total freedom, all the way to the highest levels of Operating Thetan.

Battlefield Earth is released in 1982 and becomes an international bestseller. Ron composes music and lyrics for an accompanying album—the first-ever soundtrack for a book.

While the acclaim for *Battlefield Earth* continues to grow with its publication in new languages, the first volume of Ron's *Mission Earth* is published in 1985. As each volume of the dekalogy is released it becomes an immediate bestseller. The successive appearance of these volumes on the *New York Times* bestseller list constitutes a first in publishing history. Ron accompanies *Mission Earth* with another new music album.

In 1986 the music album *The Road to Freedom* is released. With music and lyrics written by LRH, it is Ron's statement of many basic principles of Scientology.

On 24 January 1986, having accomplished all he set out to do, Ron departs his body. With millions using his technology daily and crediting him with providing the sole means for their happiness and spiritual fulfillment, he has become one of the most beloved men in history. His many friends continue to express their thanks in acknowledgment of the fact that although his physical presence is gone, he is still very much with us in spirit and the legacy of his work lives on.

Chapter 36

Important Dates in Scientology

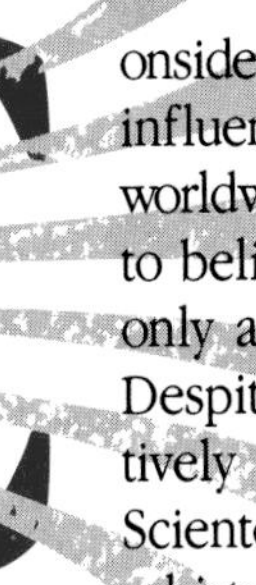

Considering the scope and influence of Scientology worldwide, it may be hard to believe the religion is only a few decades old. Despite its comparatively recent founding, Scientology has enjoyed a history that is remarkably rich in accomplishments. The most noteworthy are chronicled in the following pages, providing insight into Scientology's extraordinary vitality and growth.

APRIL 1950

Dianetics: Evolution of a Science published.

9 MAY 1950

Dianetics: The Modern Science of Mental Health published.

7 JUNE 1950

Hubbard Dianetic Research Foundation established. This was the first organization of Dianetics and headquartered, until 1951, in Elizabeth, New Jersey. Branch offices were located in New York, Chicago, Washington, DC, Los Angeles and Hawaii.

1951

First Dianetics group formed in Australia.

JANUARY 1951

Notes on the Lectures of L. Ron Hubbard published.

28 JUNE 1951

Science of Survival released at the 1st Annual Conference of Hubbard Dianetics Auditors in Wichita, Kansas as a limited edition manuscript.

AUGUST 1951

Hardcover edition of *Science of Survival* first published.

AUGUST 1951

Self Analysis published.

OCTOBER 1951

Child Dianetics published.

NOVEMBER 1951

Advanced Procedure and Axioms published in Wichita, Kansas.

DECEMBER 1951

Dianetics: The Original Thesis published.

1952

First Dianetics groups formed in Israel and New Zealand.

12 FEBRUARY 1952

The Hubbard College, the first organization established and controlled by L. Ron Hubbard, founded in Wichita, Kansas to train Dianetics auditors.

MAY 1952

The Wichita training center moved to Phoenix, Arizona. There, L. Ron Hubbard publicly announced the formal establishment of the philosophy of Scientology and the formation of the Hubbard Association of Scientologists International (HASI).

JULY 1952

Scientology: A History of Man published.

21 SEPTEMBER 1952

L. Ron Hubbard began delivery of the first training course for auditors in England. He also established the first British Scientology organization, and a London branch of the Hubbard Association of Scientologists International.

NOVEMBER 1952

Scientology 8-80 published.

DECEMBER 1952

Scientology 8-8008 published.

1 DECEMBER 1952

The first lecture of the Philadelphia Doctorate Course was delivered by L. Ron Hubbard in Philadelphia, Pennsylvania and he presented the first copies of *Scientology 8-8008.*

APRIL 1953

How to Live Though an Executive published.

30 September 1953

L. Ron Hubbard lectured at the First International Congress of Dianeticists and Scientologists in Philadelphia.

18 February 1954

The first church of Scientology founded in Los Angeles, California.

December 1954

Dianetics 55! published.

28 January 1955

The Church of Scientology of Auckland, New Zealand founded.

April 1955

The Creation of Human Ability published.

21 July 1955

Founding Church of Scientology of Washington, DC founded along with the first Academy of Scientology. To assist in the publishing and dissemination of Dianetics and Scientology books, a distribution center was also formed at this time.

15 November 1955

Church of Scientology of New York founded.

September 1956

Scientology: The Fundamentals of Thought published.

30 November 1956

Church of Scientology of Seattle, Washington was founded.

December 1956

The Problems of Work published.

11 March 1957

Church of Scientology of Miami, Florida founded.

May 1957

All About Radiation published.

11 November 1957

Church of Scientology of Johannesburg, South Africa founded.

December 1957

Control and the Mechanics of Start, Change, Stop published.

3 December 1957

Scientology: Clear Procedure, Issue One published.

1959

Release of the Hubbard Mark I E-Meter.

Spring 1959

Saint Hill Manor purchased by L. Ron Hubbard. Located in East Grinstead, Sussex, England, the manor served as Mr. Hubbard's residence, and as the communication center of Scientology.

26 June 1959

Hubbard Communications Office Worldwide was established at Saint Hill Manor.

26 October 1959

Church of Scientology of Paris, France founded.

23 November 1959

International Council for Dianetics and Scientology appointed.

1960

Release of the Hubbard Mark II E-Meter, soon followed by the Hubbard Mark III E-Meter.

March 1960

Have You Lived Before This Life? published.

20 JUNE 1960

Hubbard Association of Scientologists International established in Cape Town, South Africa.

30 DECEMBER 1960

Hubbard Communications Office, Ltd., incorporated in the United States.

3 JANUARY 1961

Release of the Hubbard Mark IV E-Meter.

28 JANUARY 1961

Church of Scientology of Cape Town, South Africa founded.

24 MARCH 1961

The Saint Hill Special Briefing Course began, drawing students from around the world. Mr. Hubbard personally delivered this course until 13 December 1966.

APRIL 1962

Church of Scientology of Port Elizabeth, South Africa founded.

SUMMER 1962

Release of the Hubbard Mark V E-Meter.

4 NOVEMBER 1963

Church of Scientology of Detroit, Michigan founded.

1 DECEMBER 1963

Church of Scientology of Durban, South Africa founded.

24 JANUARY 1964

Scientology Library and Research, Ltd., established to safeguard and preserve all Scientology materials.

MAY 1964

L. Ron Hubbard released the exact auditor training regimen, now known as the Academy Levels. These levels set exact standards and training requirements for certification.

JUNE–SEPTEMBER 1964

L. Ron Hubbard releases his breakthroughs in the field of education in seven lectures—the Student Hat tapes.

NOVEMBER 1964

The Book of Case Remedies published.

8 DECEMBER 1964

R6EW and Solo auditing released at Saint Hill Manor.

8 DECEMBER 1964

Church of Scientology of Hawaii founded.

MAY 1965

Power Processing, Grades V and VA on the Grade Chart, released at Saint Hill. L. Ron Hubbard personally trained the first auditors to deliver this new technology.

3 MAY 1965

The Classification, Gradation and Awareness Chart, listing the levels of training and grades of processing, laying out the Bridge to Total Freedom, was released by L. Ron Hubbard at Saint Hill. With the release of the "Grade Chart," lower-level auditing grades (Grades 0 through IV) were also released.

11 JUNE 1965

Hubbard College of Scientology Saint Hill Foundation founded. Subsequently, Foundations, which operate in the evenings and on weekends, were established in all Scientology organizations to facilitate the delivery of training and auditing services to the working public.

SEPTEMBER 1965

L. Ron Hubbard inaugurated the Clearing Course at Saint Hill Manor; the course is now available at the Advanced Organizations in Australia, United States, United Kingdom and Denmark, as well as the Flag Land Base.

20 NOVEMBER 1965

The seven-division organizing board issued by L. Ron Hubbard from Saint Hill.

DECEMBER 1965

Scientology: A New Slant on Life published.

30 DECEMBER 1965

Church of Scientology of Twin Cities, Minnesota founded.

19 FEBRUARY 1966

Narconon founded.

AUGUST 1966

Release of OT I.

SEPTEMBER 1966

Release of OT II.

1 SEPTEMBER 1966

L. Ron Hubbard resigned from the Board of Directors and post of Executive Director of Scientology organizations to continue his writing and research. He was given the title of Founder and his administrative duties were taken over by Executive Council Worldwide (WW).

27 JUNE 1967

Church of Scientology of Austin, Texas founded.

12 AUGUST 1967

The Sea Organization (or Sea Org) officially established.

8 SEPTEMBER 1967

Church of Scientology of Toronto, Canada founded.

18 SEPTEMBER 1967

Church of Scientology of Bulawayo, Zimbabwe founded.

20 SEPTEMBER 1967

In "Ron's Journal 67" (a recorded message to Scientologists) the major breakthrough level, OT III, the "Wall of Fire," is announced and released.

27 NOVEMBER 1967

The first Scientology Publications Organization (Pubs WW) established at Saint Hill Manor, England.

27 DECEMBER 1967

The first Advanced Organization, offering the advanced levels of Scientology to the public, was established aboard the *Royal Scotman,* the flagship of the Sea Organization. (This ship was later renamed the *Apollo.*)

JANUARY 1968

OT levels IV, V and VI released.

23 MAY 1968

Advanced Organization, Edinburgh, Scotland established.

JUNE 1968

Scientology Publications Organization moved from Saint Hill Manor to Edinburgh, Scotland.

5 JUNE 1968

Church of Scientology of Denmark, founded in Copenhagen.

12 JUNE 1968

Hubbard Academy of Personal Independence of Edinburgh, Scotland founded.

17 JUNE 1968

Church of Scientology of San Francisco, California founded.

AUGUST 1968

American Saint Hill Organization (ASHO) and Advanced Organization Los Angeles (AOLA) opened in Los Angeles, California. During this month L. Ron Hubbard released and personally supervised the Class VIII Course aboard the flagship *Apollo*. He also released the Drug Rundown—his breakthrough in handling the effects of drugs.

AUGUST 1968

The Phoenix Lectures published.

24 SEPTEMBER 1968

The Class VIII Auditor Course released.

31 OCTOBER 1968

Church of Scientology of Las Vegas, Nevada founded.

12 DECEMBER 1968

Church of Scientology of Pretoria, South Africa founded.

1969

First Dianetics groups in Germany, Greece and Mexico.

31 JANUARY 1969

The Church of the New Faith, founded in South Australia. This corporation consisted of Scientology churches in Adelaide, Melbourne, Perth and Sydney.

14 FEBRUARY 1969

Publications Organization moved from Edinburgh, Scotland to Copenhagen, Denmark.

APRIL 1969

Standard Dianetics released.

16 APRIL 1969

Church of Scientology of Göteborg, Sweden founded.

7 JULY 1969

Advanced Organization Denmark founded in Copenhagen to service European and African Scientologists.

7 JULY 1969

Church of Scientology of Saint Hill Europe founded.

22 JULY 1969

Church of Scientology of Copenhagen (a second church in Copenhagen, Denmark) founded.

9 OCTOBER 1969

Church of Scientology of Stockholm, Sweden founded.

1970

Criminon founded in New Zealand.

22 FEBRUARY 1970

Church of Scientology Celebrity Centre Los Angeles founded.

25 JUNE 1970

Expanded Lower Auditing Grades (Grades 0 through IV) released by L. Ron Hubbard.

17 AUGUST 1970

Advanced Organization United Kingdom moved from Edinburgh, Scotland to Saint Hill, Sussex, England.

20 SEPTEMBER 1970

L. Ron Hubbard released OT VII to Advanced Organizations around the world.

15 OCTOBER 1970

Church of Scientology of Munich, Germany founded.

NOVEMBER 1970

Scientology 0-8: The Book of Basics published.

NOVEMBER 1970

The Flag Executive Briefing Course begins with L. Ron Hubbard personally supervising and lecturing to the students aboard the flagship *Apollo*.

13 NOVEMBER 1970

The Flag Bureaux established by the Sea Organization aboard the *Apollo* to supervise Scientology expansion around the world.

19 NOVEMBER 1970

Continental Liaison Offices (CLOs) established to supervise church affairs in their respective continental areas: United States; United Kingdom; Europe; Australia, New Zealand and Oceania (ANZO); and Africa.

1971

Applied Scholastics founded.

1971

L. Ron Hubbard released three new rundowns: L10, L11 (the New Life Rundown) and L12 (the Flag OT Executive Rundown), only delivered by the most highly trained Sea Org auditors and C/Ses aboard the *Apollo*.

20 JANUARY 1971

Hubbard Scientology Organization of Plymouth, England founded.

11 FEBRUARY 1971

Church of Scientology Publications Organization United States established.

9 MARCH 1971

Church of Scientology of Buffalo, New York founded.

13 MARCH 1971

Church of Scientology of Boston, Massachusetts founded.

31 MARCH 1971

Church of Scientology of Vienna, Austria founded.

13 APRIL 1971

Church of Scientology of San Diego, California founded.

26 APRIL 1971

Church of Scientology of Portland, Oregon founded.

JUNE 1971

L. Ron Hubbard released Word Clearing Methods 1, 2 and 3.

1972

First Dianetics groups in Belgium and the Netherlands formed.

27 JANUARY 1972

Church of Scientology of St. Louis, Missouri founded.

FEBRUARY 1972

L. Ron Hubbard released Word Clearing Method 4.

13 MARCH 1972

Church of Scientology of Amsterdam, Holland founded.

4 APRIL 1972

Primary Rundown released.

15 APRIL 1972

Expanded Dianetics released.

22 MAY 1972

Church of Scientology of Melbourne, Australia reincorporated (formerly the Church of the New Faith).

June 1972

L. Ron Hubbard released Word Clearing Methods 5, 6, 7 and 8.

6 June 1972

Church of Scientology of Vancouver, Canada founded.

21 July 1972

Church of Scientology of Sydney, Australia founded (formerly the Church of the New Faith).

18 August 1972

Church of Scientology of Malmö, Sweden founded.

17 October 1972

Church of Scientology of Perth, Australia reincorporated (formerly the Church of the New Faith).

8 November 1972

Expansion of Scientology and Scientology churches in the United States resulted in the establishment of CLO Eastern United States in New York City and CLO Western United States in Los Angeles.

January 1973

Word Clearing Method 9 released.

24 January 1974

The Technical Breakthrough—The Introspection Rundown released.

12 March 1974

Church of Scientology of Manchester, England founded.

13 March 1974

Church of Scientology of Montreal, Canada founded.

13 March 1974

Church of Scientology of Ottawa, Canada founded.

22 March 1974

Church of Scientology of Sacramento, California founded.

15 June 1974

Church of Scientology of Denver, Colorado founded.

July 1974

The first *Organization Executive Course* volumes published making Mr. Hubbard's administrative policies broadly available around the world.

6 October 1974

The Vital Information Rundown released.

13 March 1975

Church of Scientology of Chicago, Illinois founded.

16 March 1975

Church of Scientology of Philadelphia, Pennsylvania founded.

June 1975

Dianetics and Scientology Technical Dictionary published.

October 1975

The Flag Service Organization moves ashore to temporary quarters in Daytona Beach, Florida retiring the flagship *Apollo.*

18 November 1975

Instituto de Filosofía Aplicada, A.C., Durango, Mexico City founded. (IFAD)

24 November 1975

Education Alive founded in South Africa.

6 DECEMBER 1975

Flag Land Base established when the Flag Bureaux and the Flag Service Organization moved from the flagship *Apollo* to the Fort Harrison Hotel and Clearwater Building in Clearwater, Florida. Here, the Flag Service Organization provides services to Scientologists from all over the world.

SPRING 1976

L. Ron Hubbard established Universal Media Productions in Clearwater, Florida, to produce Scientology films.

AUGUST 1976

The technical bulletins of Dianetics and Scientology released in published books for the first time.

24 AUGUST 1976

International Prayer Day, the Church's first International Conference for World Peace and Social Reform, was held in Anaheim, California, attended by 10,000 church members from around the world.

DECEMBER 1976

The Volunteer Minister's Handbook published.

DECEMBER 1976

Modern Management Technology Defined—Hubbard Dictionary of Administration and Management published.

FEBRUARY 1977

The former Cedars of Lebanon Medical Center in Hollywood purchased by the Church of Scientology as a major center for Scientology in the Los Angeles area.

27 SEPTEMBER 1977

The first of the Los Angeles service organizations, Church of Scientology of Los Angeles, moved into the former Cedars of Lebanon Medical Center building complex.

FALL 1977

Universal Media Productions was reorganized as Source Productions in La Quinta, California, to produce Scientology technical instructional films.

1978

First groups in Costa Rica, Pakistan, Saudi Arabia, Tahiti, Guatemala and Zambia formed.

9 MARCH 1978

Church of Scientology of Milano, Italy founded.

21 JUNE 1978

The first Hubbard Communications Office Bulletin on New Era Dianetics (NED) was written, introducing an effective refinement of Dianetics by L. Ron Hubbard, based upon thirty years of experience in the application of the subject.

20 JULY 1978

Church of Scientology of Bern, Switzerland founded.

24 SEPTEMBER 1978

Dianetic Clear Hubbard Communications Office Bulletin released.

SEPTEMBER 1978

Audited New Era Dianetics for OTs (New OT V) released.

1979

The first Dianetics group formed in Ecuador.

1 FEBRUARY 1979

The World Institute of Scientology Enterprises (WISE) founded to assist businessmen and women in improving efficiency, quality and ethical standards in their own businesses and in the business community at large.

13 MARCH 1979

The Hubbard Mark VI E-Meter was released.

JULY 1979

The Sandcastle, a hotel in Clearwater, Florida, purchased as part of the Flag Land Base, an advanced religious retreat for Scientologists.

20 SEPTEMBER 1979

Instituto de Filosofía Aplicada, A.C., Havre, in Mexico City founded.

DECEMBER 1979

The Purification Rundown released.

3 JANUARY 1980

Church of Scientology of Brescia, Italy founded.

29 JANUARY 1980

OT Drug Rundown (New OT IV) released.

31 JANUARY 1980

Church of Scientology of Cincinnati, Ohio founded.

7 FEBRUARY 1980

Asociación Cultural Dianética, A.C. (Asociación Civil), founded in Mexico City.

14 FEBRUARY 1980

Church of Scientology of Edmonton, Canada founded.

14 FEBRUARY 1980

Church of Scientology of Phoenix, Arizona founded. (In 1955, when L. Ron Hubbard moved Scientology organizations from Phoenix to Washington, DC, no formal church or mission remained, hence this date signifies the reopening of the Church of Scientology in Phoenix.)

13 MARCH 1980

Church of Scientology of Brussels, Belgium founded.

13 MARCH 1980

Church of Scientology of Novara, Italy founded.

1 MAY 1980

Instituto Tecnológico de Dianética, A.C., along with the Organizacion Desarrollo y Dianética, A.C., founded in Mexico City.

8 MAY 1980

Church of Scientology of Birmingham, England founded.

8 MAY 1980

Instituto de Filosofía Aplicada, A.C., Roma in Mexico City founded.

8 MAY 1980

Church of Scientology of Sunderland, England founded.

15 MAY 1980

Church of Scientology of Albuquerque, New Mexico founded.

15 MAY 1980

Church of Scientology of Columbus, Ohio founded.

15 MAY 1980

Centro Cultural de Dianética of Bogotá, Colombia founded.

22 MAY 1980

Church of Scientology of Basel, Switzerland founded.

22 May 1980

Church of Scientology of Angers, France founded.

27 May 1980

Church of Scientology of Berlin, Germany founded.

29 May 1980

Church of Scientology of Canberra, Australian Capital Territory founded.

June 1980

Research and Discovery Series Volume 1 published. Signifies the start of an extensive project to transcribe all of L. Ron Hubbard's lectures on the subjects of Dianetics and Scientology.

5 June 1980

Church of Scientology of Rome, Italy founded.

5 June 1980

Church of Scientology of Pasadena, California founded.

12 June 1980

Church of Scientology of Santa Barbara, California founded.

12 June 1980

Church of Scientology of San Fernando Valley, California founded.

12 June 1980

Church of Scientology of Kitchener, Canada founded.

19 June 1980

Church of Scientology of Padova, Italy founded.

26 June 1980

Church of Scientology of Oslo, Norway founded.

10 July 1980

Centro de Dianética Polanco, Mexico City founded.

10 July 1980

Church of Scientology of Geneva, Switzerland founded.

10 July 1980

Church of Scientology of Pordenone, Italy founded.

17 July 1980

Church of Scientology of Madrid, Spain founded.

August 1980

Source Productions becomes Golden Era Productions and is established as the international dissemination center for Scientology.

7 August 1980

Church of Scientology of Saint-Etienne, France founded.

September 1980

New OT VI and VII released—the Hubbard Solo New Era Dianetics for OTs (Solo NOTS) Course (New OT VI), utilizes technology developed by L. Ron Hubbard and enables a person to take the role of both auditor and preclear and actually audit himself on the level of OT VII, Solo New Era Dianetics for OTs, which has as its product Cause over Life.

25 September 1980

Scientology and Dianetics College Tel Aviv, Israel founded.

2 October 1980

Church of Scientology of Harare, Zimbabwe founded.

1981

CLO Canada established in Toronto and CLO Latin America (LATAM) established in Mexico City.

1 January 1981

Church of Scientology of Quebec, Canada founded.

19 February 1981

The Way to Happiness published.

19 March 1981

Church of Scientology of Johannesburg North, Johannesburg, South Africa founded.

19 March 1981

Asociación Cultural Dianética de Venezuela, A.C., founded.

May 1981

L. Ron Hubbard releases the Success Through Communication Course—teaching the fundamentals of communication and their application to life.

Spring 1981

Celebrity Centre moved into the famous Château Elysée, a French Normandie-style hotel in Hollywood, formerly the home of many prominent actors, actresses and other celebrities. In 1987, this building was registered as an historic landmark in the state of California.

October 1981

The first series of technical training films released.

1 October 1981

Church of Scientology Celebrity Centre Las Vegas founded.

1 November 1981

Church of Scientology International (CSI) founded as the mother church of Scientology. CSI is the corporation which houses international Church management.

3 December 1981

Church of Scientology of Winnipeg, Canada founded.

9 December 1981

Operation-Transport Liaison Office Iberia established in Madrid, Spain.

23 December 1981

Scientology Missions International (SMI) founded.

31 December 1981

Church of Scientology of Aarhus, Denmark founded.

31 December 1981

Church of Scientology of Barcelona, Spain founded.

7 January 1982

Church of Scientology, Celebrity Centre Paris founded.

2 February 1982

Church of Scientology of Torino, Italy founded.

10 February 1982

Church of Scientology of Verona, Italy founded.

4 March 1982

Church of Scientology of Clermont-Ferrand, France founded.

11 March 1982

Church of Scientology of Tampa, Florida founded.

11 March 1982

Church of Scientology of Lyon, France founded.

1 April 1982

Church of Scientology of Orlando, Florida founded.

16 May 1982

Religious Technology Center (RTC) incorporated. L. Ron Hubbard donated all trademarks of Dianetics and Scientology to RTC.

17 June 1982

Church of Scientology of Lisbon, Portugal founded.

17 June 1982

Church of Scientology of Kansas City, Missouri founded.

11 July 1982

The International Network of Computer Organized Management (INCOMM) was formed within the Church of Scientology International to establish and operate a major international management computer system which assists in the standard application of Scientology policy and technology and as a result facilitates rapid expansion.

29 July 1982

Church of Scientology New Haven, Connecticut founded.

5 August 1982

Church of Scientology of Brisbane, Australia founded.

5 August 1982

Church of Scientology of Brighton, England founded.

12 August 1982

Church of Scientology of Ann Arbor, Michigan founded.

1983

The Planetary Dissemination Organization formed to provide campaigns to make Dianetics and Scientology even more widely available.

6 January 1983

Organización Cultural Dianética de Guadalajara, A.C., founded in Guadalajara, Jalisco, Mexico.

5 May 1983

Church of Scientology of Hamburg, Germany founded.

16 June 1983

Church of Scientology of Zurich, Switzerland founded.

2 July 1983

Led by a team of Sea Organization members, the Advanced Organization Saint Hill Australia, New Zealand, Oceania (AOSH ANZO) opened its doors in Sydney, Australia to deliver advanced courses.

29 July 1983

Church of Scientology of Long Island, New York founded.

8 September 1983

Church of Scientology of Orange County, California founded.

10 November 1983

Church of Scientology Celebrity Centre of New York founded.

December 1983

Formation of the Office of Special Affairs International, a network within the Church of Scientology International which plans and supervises the legal affairs of the church, under the board of directors.

1 MARCH 1984

Church of Scientology Celebrity Centre Hamburg, Germany founded.

1 MARCH 1984

Church of Scientology of Düsseldorf, Germany founded.

JUNE 1984

First cassette lectures by L. Ron Hubbard on the subjects of Dianetics and Scientology released in a new sound-reproduction technology—Clearsound.

5 JUNE 1984

False Purpose Rundown released.

31 JULY 1984

The Way to Happiness Foundation incorporated in the state of California.

SEPTEMBER 1984

Purification: An Illustrated Answer to Drugs released.

SEPTEMBER 1984

Purification Rundown Delivery Manual published.

7 OCTOBER 1984

The International Association of Scientologists (IAS) formed and the Pledge to Mankind signed at Saint Hill in England, uniting Scientologists everywhere.

8 NOVEMBER 1984

Celebrity Centre International formed to give guidance to the network of Celebrity Centres throughout the world.

29 NOVEMBER 1984

Church of Scientology of Stevens Creek, San Jose, California founded.

DECEMBER 1984

The Flag Bureaux moved to Los Angeles to allow expansion of service delivery at the Flag Service Organization in Clearwater.

27 JUNE 1985

Church of Scientology Celebrity Centre Düsseldorf, Germany founded.

4 JULY 1985

Church of Scientology of Monza, Italy founded.

10 AUGUST 1985

Opening of the ninth Continental Liaison Office, CLO Italy, in Milano.

5 OCTOBER 1985

International Association of Scientologists Freedom Medal instituted by the International Association of Scientologists to acknowledge outstanding contributions toward the betterment of life and preservation of freedom on Earth. The first winners: Rev. Edgar Koons, Dr. Franklin Littell and Scientologists Jeff Pomerantz, Michel Raoust and Barbara Ayash.

17 DECEMBER 1985

Clear Certainty Rundown released.

1986

First groups in Chile and Kenya formed.

24 JANUARY 1986

L. Ron Hubbard departed this life at his ranch near San Luis Obispo, California, leaving a legacy of his life's work that lives on around the world.

13 MARCH 1986

The Road to Freedom music album, which set to music many basic principles of life, was released internationally. All songs and lyrics were written earlier by Mr. Hubbard.

19 June 1986

Church of Scientology Celebrity Centre of Portland, Oregon founded.

16 September 1986

The Sea Organization Motor Vessel *Freewinds* purchased.

7 October 1986

IAS Freedom Medals awarded to Rev. Jim Nicholls and Scientologists Dennis Dubin, Paul Rood and Don Moore at the annual convention in Toronto, Canada.

16 October 1986

Church of Scientology of Nuoro, Italy founded.

1987

First groups in Ghana and Dominican Republic formed.

12 March 1987

Church of Scientology Celebrity Centre of Dallas, Texas founded.

7 October 1987

IAS Freedom Medals awarded to Scientologists Peter Schless, Andrik Schapers, Philippe de Henning and Dennis Clarke at the annual convention in Paris, France.

1988

First group in Hungary formed.

7 January 1988

Church of Scientology of Lausanne, Switzerland founded.

13 March 1988

Advanced Organization Los Angeles and the Church of Scientology Orange County (California) were formally acknowledged for achieving the size of old Saint Hill. (The original Saint Hill organization, located at Saint Hill Manor, East Grinstead, Sussex, England, was very large when L. Ron Hubbard was its Executive Director. It is a purpose of all Scientology churches and organizations to minimally achieve the size that Saint Hill was when it was under Mr. Hubbard's direction. As each church or organization achieves this, they are acknowledged at the annual celebration of Mr. Hubbard's birthday.)

13 March 1988

Release of the Hubbard Professional Mark Super VII E-Meter developed according to L. Ron Hubbard's specifications and directions.

20 March 1988

Thirty-eight years after its initial publication, *Dianetics* reaches number one on the *New York Times* bestseller list, and remains on the list for a total of seventy weeks.

9 May 1988

Hubbard Dianetics Seminar released.

9 May 1988

Hubbard Dianetics Auditor Course released.

6 June 1988

Christening of the Sea Organization Motor Vessel *Freewinds* in Curaçao. Maiden voyage of the *Freewinds.*

6 June 1988

The Flag Ship Service Organization and the *Freewinds* Ship Organization began operation aboard the Sea Organization Motor Vessel *Freewinds.*

7 June 1988

At sea: The New OT VIII course room opened aboard the *Freewinds,* and with it, the delivery of New OT VIII, Truth Revealed, began.

7 October 1988

IAS Freedom Medal awarded to Scientologists Jan Eastgate, Rena Weinberg and Chick Corea at the annual IAS Convention held aboard the SMV *Freewinds.*

31 October 1988

Dianetics released in Chinese to the people of mainland China; became a number one bestseller overnight.

17 November 1988

Church of Scientology of Frankfurt, Germany founded.

31 December 1988

Ten new Life Improvement Courses released. Includes: Overcoming Ups and Downs in Life; How to Be a Successful Parent; How to Maintain a Successful Marriage; How to Improve Relationships with Others; The Dynamics of Money; Personal Values and Integrity Course; Starting a Successful Marriage; Financial Success Course; How to Live Though an Executive; and How to Make Work Easier.

31 December 1988

Church of Scientology of Tokyo, Japan founded.

1989

First groups formed in East Germany, Panama and South Korea.

13 March 1989

Advanced Organization Saint Hill United Kingdom and the Church of Scientology Hamburg (Germany) were formally acknowledged for achieving the size of old Saint Hill at the annual celebration of L. Ron Hubbard's birthday.

13 May 1989

The Flag Command Bureaux moved to the newly renovated Hollywood Guaranty Building, a twelve-story office building exclusively for international Scientology management and training of church executives from around the world.

October 1989

Church of Scientology of Hanover, Germany founded.

October 1989

Church of Scientology of Atlanta, Georgia founded.

October 1989

The Professional TR Course released with Clay Table Processing on communication.

6 October 1989

Completion and official opening of the Saint Hill Castle, a college for Scientology on the grounds of Saint Hill Manor, first envisioned and designed by L. Ron Hubbard in 1965. The first castle to be built in England for fifty-nine years, it was inspired by other historic castles, particularly an eleventh-century Norman castle at Tonbridge, Kent. It provides greatly expanded facilities for the Advanced Organization and Saint Hill UK and Saint Hill Foundation.

6 October 1989

IAS Freedom Medals awarded to Scientologists Judy Norton-Taylor, Nicky Hopkins and Boris Levitsky at the annual IAS Convention held at Saint Hill Castle in England.

December 1989

The Narconon Chilocco New Life Center, located on 167 acres on the Great Plains of Oklahoma, began delivery of the Narconon program. It is the largest drug rehabilitation center of any kind in the world.

28 December 1989

Church of Scientology of Stuttgart, Germany founded.

1990

First groups formed in Nigeria, Czechoslovakia, Taiwan, China, Romania, Algeria, Argentina, Yugoslavia and Russia.

13 March 1990

The Churches of Scientology Stevens Creek (California), Munich (Germany) and Zurich (Switzerland) were formally acknowledged for achieving the size of old Saint Hill at the annual celebration of L. Ron Hubbard's birthday.

9 May 1990

TRs and Objectives Co-audit Course released.

9 May 1990

Clear Body, Clear Mind: The Effective Purification Program released.

9 May 1990

The Hubbard Key to Life Course, *the* solution to a world out of communication, released to the public.

9 May 1990

The Churches of Scientology Milano (Italy) and Stuttgart (Germany) were formally acknowledged for achieving the size of old Saint Hill.

9 May 1990

Church of Scientology of Catania, Italy founded.

6 June 1990

The Hubbard Life Orientation Course released.

30 June 1990

The grand (official) opening of the Narconon Chilocco New Life Center at Chilocco, Oklahoma.

6 October 1990

IAS Freedom Medal awarded to Scientologists Jane Allen and Julia Migenes at the annual convention in Lausanne, Switzerland.

28 December 1990

Church of Scientology of Salt Lake City, Utah founded.

31 December 1990

Basic Study Manual published.

31 December 1990

Elementary and Executive Data Series Evaluator's Courses released.

1991

First groups formed in Poland, Bulgaria and Malaysia.

19 February 1991

Twenty-fifth anniversary of Narconon, which has grown from one program started by a prison inmate to a network of centers in twelve countries.

March 1991

The Church of Scientology of Mountain View, California founded.

13 March 1991

The new *Organization Executive Course* (OEC) and *Management Series* volumes were released, containing over 10,000 pages of L. Ron Hubbard's administrative technology, twice as many as in the OEC volumes issued in the 1970s. Along with the 44 tapes on the OEC, the Flag Executive Briefing Course tapes and the Establishment Officer tapes, also newly released, these materials comprise L. Ron Hubbard's complete technology of organization.

20 April 1991

Grand opening celebration of the L. Ron Hubbard Life Exhibition at the Hollywood Guaranty Building. The ribbon cutting was performed by the president pro tem of the California Senate and the president of the Hollywood Chamber of Commerce. The exhibition features more than thirty displays and audiovisual presentations on the life of L. Ron Hubbard.

6 May 1991

Opening of the newly built 25,000 square foot Sandcastle Technical Delivery Building in Clearwater, Florida, especially for the delivery of advanced levels.

9 May 1991

The *Technical Bulletins* volumes were released in a new edition of 18 volumes and over 11,000 pages. These contain all of L. Ron Hubbard's technical articles and bulletins on Dianetics and Scientology.

7 June 1991

Christening of the historic Sea Org vessel, *Diana,* a 62-foot ketch which played an important role in the early history of the Sea Org as the first Sea Org vessel. Completely restored, she returned to service to provide sea training for Sea Org members.

7 September 1991

Release of the new Saint Hill Special Briefing Course which includes 437 taped lectures reproduced and made available in Clearsound and with written transcripts.

7 September 1991

Release of the updated, finalized and totally complete Grade Chart including all new technical releases since its original issuance in 1965.

26 October 1991

IAS Freedom Medals awarded to Scientologists Keith Code, Kirstie Alley and Gabriele Segalla at the annual convention in Copenhagen, Denmark.

December 1991

Church of Scientology Puerto Rico founded.

1992

First groups formed in Philippines, Honduras, Brazil and Ivory Coast.

May 1992

The Children's Communication Course released.

May 1992

The release of twenty-three Technical Specialist Courses that train auditors to be able to handle a wide variety of conditions.

June 1992

How to Use Dianetics Video—A Visual Guidebook to the Human Mind released.

25 July 1992

Celebrity Centre International and the Manor Hotel (formerly the famous Château Elysée, a French Normandie-style hotel in Hollywood) restored and officially opened, now servicing celebrities and professionals from around the world.

August 1992

Sea Org members establish the first church offices in Moscow—OTL Russia.

September 1992

First group formed in Albania.

12 September 1992

Auditor's Day—Hubbard British Mark V E-Meter back in production and available for the first time since the late 70s. Manufactured by Golden Era Productions, it resembles the British Mark V exactly. While usable in all auditing up to the state of Clear, its re-release was intended to facilitate the need of student auditors co-auditing up the Bridge and to make such as economical as possible.

17 OCTOBER 1992

Presentation of IAS Freedom Medal to Scientologists John Travolta, Debbie Mace and Jerry Boswell at the annual IAS convention aboard the *Freewinds.*

17 OCTOBER 1992

The all-new *What Is Scientology?* (this book) is released at the annual IAS convention aboard the *Freewinds.*

CHAPTER 37

THE VICTORIES OF SCIENTOLOGY

For more than forty years, those who perceive Scientology as a threat to their vested interests have attempted to curb its expansion. Today, Scientology has expanded to the point where it cannot be stopped, and a summation of battles fought and won demonstrates the persistence of Scientologists and their active involvement to preserve religious freedom and the rights of man, not just for Scientology, but for everyone.

Witness Australia in 1965. In the state of Victoria, after a kangaroo court inquiry in which Scientologists were not even allowed to appear, the Church was banned. Naturally, such legislation was unenforceable, but it took eighteen years of sustained actions in the courts before Scientology not only won, but received full recognition in a landmark decision from the High Court of Australia that established the legal definition of religion in Australia.

So it has been in every country where Scientologists and their church have met with resistance from vested interests opposed to human betterment. For example, members of the British Parliament, urged on by psychiatric interests and the notorious yellow journalism of the British press, enacted a ban on foreign students entering the country to study Scientology. Exposure of the vested interests behind the ban, and a legal suit eventually forced a reversal of the decision twelve years later. Today, foreigners have free access to the many churches and missions that now dot the British Isles.

Many battles have been fought over the last three decades. And, as the following summary substantiates, all have been won. Scores of court decisions now affirm the religious bona fides of Scientology throughout the world. In every instance, those who would seek to destroy Scientology eventually disappear, while the Church continues to grow across the world.

Indeed, in every instance where Scientology has met resistance, the Church has emerged stronger, larger and with ever greater impact on society, testament to its validity and legitimacy. Any other movement subject to the magnitude of attacks sustained and overcome by Scientology would have long since ceased to exist.

LATE 1956

The so-called "Siberia Bill" was defeated by a coalition of citizen groups and Scientologists. If the measure, introduced in the US Congress in 1954, had passed, it would have allowed any peace officer or medical doctor to institute commitment proceedings against any US citizen. Legislation in Alaska would have made it possible for those dubbed "mentally ill" to be transferred to the territory of Alaska. After the serious human rights dangers of the bill were brought to public attention, it was killed.

JULY 16, 1957

The Church of Scientology of New York was recognized as tax exempt by the Internal Revenue Service as a religious organization.

JANUARY 4, 1963

The Founding Church of Scientology in Washington, DC was desecrated and looted by United States marshals and deputized longshoremen with drawn guns, acting for the US Food and Drug Administration (FDA). Five thousand volumes of Church scriptures, 20,000 booklets and 100 E-Meters were seized. It took 8 years of courtroom battle to finally obtain the return of the materials and victory for the Church. [See July 30, 1971 entry]

FEBRUARY 1, 1965

A Federal District Judge in Washington, DC ruled that Scientology ministers may refuse to violate confidences divulged to them by parishioners in pastoral counseling sessions.

FEBRUARY 5, 1969

In a landmark legal decision, the US Court of Appeals in Washington, DC ruled that Scientology was a bona fide religion and that auditing was an integral part of Scientology's religious doctrines and practices. The case had begun dramatically with the armed FDA raid on the Founding Church and seizure of E-Meters and Church literature. [See January 4, 1963 entry] Later all E-Meters and books were ordered returned to the church. [See July 30, 1971 entry]

JUNE 15, 1969

In a Scientology minister's draft exemption case, the US Court of Appeals ruled that the Church of Scientology was recognized as a church.

NOVEMBER 18, 1969

A court in Western Australia dismissed a case brought against the Hubbard Association of Scientologists International (HASI) for "practicing Scientology." (This case negated an unconstitutional law that had attempted to prohibit the practice of Scientology, following an "inquiry" held in the state of Victoria in 1965.) [See May 25, 1973 entry]

MAY 20, 1970

Narconon Los Angeles was recognized by the state of California as a nonprofit corporation.

OCTOBER 27, 1970

The Church of Scientology of Adelaide, Australia was granted exemption from payment of property tax on the basis that the property occupied by the church was used for religious purposes in the advancement of a religion.

DECEMBER 2, 1970

The Perth, Australia Court of Petty Sessions recognized Scientology as a religion and exempted a minister of the church from military service.

JULY 30, 1971

The US District Court for the District of Columbia ordered the Food and Drug Administration to return to the

Church the E-Meters and books that had been seized from the Founding Church 8 years earlier. In its decision, the court recognized the Church's constitutional right to protection from the government's excessive entanglement with religion. [See February 5, 1969 entry]

JUNE 19, 1972

In an immigration case concerning a foreign Scientology minister who sought permanent residence in St. Louis, Missouri, the court acknowledged the religious nature of the Church, recognized the applicant's status as a minister of the Scientology religion and granted her permanent residence in the United States on the basis of her status as a minister.

DECEMBER 22, 1972

Applied Scholastics Los Angeles was granted tax-exempt status by the Internal Revenue Service.

FEBRUARY 7, 1973

The attorney general of Australia wrote to the president of the Church announcing that the Church was now officially a recognized denomination. This letter provided federal recognition of the Church of Scientology in Australia.

MARCH 1, 1973

The IRS acknowledged the tax-exempt status of the Church of Scientology, Mission of Davis, California.

MAY 25, 1973

The Western Australia legislation aimed at restricting the activities of the Church of Scientology was formally repealed. [See November 18, 1969 entry]

JULY 27, 1973

The church in New South Wales, Australia was granted exemption from the payment of payroll tax.

NOVEMBER 2, 1973

The church of Scientology in Calgary, Alberta, Canada was exempted from paying business tax on the basis of being a nonprofit organization.

NOVEMBER 21, 1973

The Church of Scientology of Toronto was granted exemption from payment of business tax on the basis of being a religion.

NOVEMBER 22, 1973

The Church of Scientology was recognized as a bona fide religion by the Bavarian Ministry of Education and Culture.

MARCH 4, 1974

The Church of Scientology, Mission of Fort Lauderdale, Florida was recognized as a religious organization and granted exemption from sales and use tax by the Florida Department of Revenue.

MARCH 15, 1974

The Church of Scientology of Minnesota was granted exemption from paying income tax and employer's excise tax by the state Department of Revenue.

APRIL 11, 1974

The "Scientology Prohibition Act" of 1968, which had unsuccessfully attempted to prevent the practice of Scientology in South Australia, was repealed by the South Australian Parliament.

APRIL 18, 1974

A minister of the Church of Scientology of New Zealand was officially registered under the Marriage Act to perform marriage ceremonies.

APRIL 23, 1974

The minister for immigration in Australia lifted all previous restrictions on foreign Scientologists immigrating to Australia.

JULY 3, 1974

On March 11, 1970 the World Federation for Mental Health, Incorporated (WFMH), issued a Writ of Summons for defamation against the Church for statements made in *Freedom* magazine in the United Kingdom, characterizing the WFMH as a vast psychiatric conspiracy aiming to dominate and control governments by the use of degrading psychiatric treatment and misleading advice. On July 3, 1974, by order of Master Waldman, the action was dismissed with costs of £4,804.86 (approximately $10,000) and interest awarded against the WFMH. The WFMH subsequently retreated to Canada and reincorporated there to avoid payment.

OCTOBER 17, 1974

A decree was received from the Finance Management Department of the City of Zurich, Switzerland recognizing the Church of Scientology as a religious organization and exempting the Church from state and general municipal taxes.

DECEMBER 30, 1974

The US Department of State officially recognized the Church of Scientology as a religious denomination having a bona fide organization in the United States.

JANUARY 20, 1975

Narconon Los Angeles was officially recognized by the Internal Revenue Service as a nonprofit, tax-exempt organization.

APRIL 7, 1975

The church of Scientology in Las Vegas, Nevada was granted exemption from payment of city business-license tax based on its status as a nonprofit religious organization.

JUNE 4, 1975

The church of Scientology in Hawaii was granted tax-exempt status after the deposition testimony of an IRS agent revealed that the IRS' grounds for attempting to revoke the church's exemption had no basis in fact.

JUNE 16, 1975

The church of Scientology in Portland, Oregon was granted tax-exempt status by the Internal Revenue Service as a nonprofit religious organization.

JUNE 19, 1975

The church of Scientology in Seattle, Washington was granted tax-exempt status as a nonprofit religious organization by the Internal Revenue Service.

JULY 14, 1975

The Church of Scientology of Miami was granted tax-exempt status as a nonprofit religious organization by the Internal Revenue Service.

JULY 18, 1975

The churches of Scientology in Detroit and Buffalo were granted tax-exempt status by the Internal Revenue Service as nonprofit religious organizations.

JULY 22, 1975

The church of Scientology in Boston was granted tax-exempt status by the Internal Revenue Service as a nonprofit religious organization.

JULY 30, 1975

The church of Scientology in Nevada was granted tax-exempt status by the Internal Revenue Service as a nonprofit religious organization.

JULY 31, 1975

The church of Scientology in Minnesota was granted tax-exempt status by the Internal Revenue Service as a nonprofit religious organization.

AUGUST 4, 1975

The church of Scientology in Missouri was granted tax-exempt status by the Internal Revenue Service as a nonprofit religious organization.

AUGUST 28, 1975

The church of Scientology in Buffalo, New York was granted exemption from payment of property tax.

SEPTEMBER 5, 1975

The church of Scientology in Texas was granted tax-exempt status by the Internal Revenue Service as a nonprofit religious organization.

SEPTEMBER 18, 1975

The church of Scientology in Sacramento, California was granted tax-exempt status by the Internal Revenue Service as a nonprofit religious organization.

SEPTEMBER 26, 1975

The Church of Scientology of Florida was confirmed by the Department of Revenue as being exempt from Florida corporation income tax as a nonprofit organization.

AUGUST 1976

Mr. Herbert Graham, Deputy Premier of Western Australia, formally apologized for the passing of earlier legislation which had banned Scientology in his state, describing it as "the blackest day in the political history of Western Australia."

DECEMBER 8, 1976

In a decision in a case before the Stuttgart District Court, the Church of Scientology was recognized as a religious community.

MARCH 28, 1977

The Church of Scientology of New York's status as a tax-exempt, nonprofit religious organization, first recognized in 1957, was reconfirmed by the Internal Revenue Service.

JUNE 23, 1978

Based on its status as a religion, the Church of Scientology of Sydney, Australia was granted exemption from sales tax by the Australian Taxation Office.

DECEMBER 19, 1978

The Australian Taxation Office granted the Church of Scientology of Western Australia exemption from income tax based on its religious status.

FEBRUARY 9, 1979

In a judgment in a Church of Scientology tax case in Munich, Germany the court stated: "Scientology is not only a religion in the oldest sense of the word but also a religion in the common linguistic usage of the word."

MARCH 13, 1979

The church of Scientology in Melbourne, Australia was granted exemption from payment of income tax on the basis of being a religion.

FEBRUARY 12, 1980

In a tax case involving the Church of Scientology of California, the IRS stipulated that "Scientology is and at all relevant times was a religion within the purview of the First Amendment to the Constitution of the United States."

FEBRUARY 20, 1980

The Church of Scientology of St. Louis, Missouri was granted property tax exemption by the City of St. Louis on the basis that the church was a bona fide religion and used its property exclusively for religious purposes.

FEBRUARY 29, 1980

An appeals court acquitted a former executive of the church of Scientology in Paris of fraud charges, and at the same time recognized the Church as a religion. The appeals court decision overturned a lower court decision from 1978 when this executive had been investigated and tried in absentia. Two other former church executives who were similarly tried in 1978 were fully acquitted by the appeals court on December 21, 1981 and July 13, 1982.

JULY 16, 1980

A 1968 ban on the entry of foreign Church of Scientology students into the United Kingdom to study or work was lifted by the secretary of state for the Home Office.

AUGUST 29, 1980

The Church of Scientology of San Diego, California was granted tax-exempt status by the Internal Revenue Service as a nonprofit religious organization.

FEBRUARY 26, 1981

The Church of Scientology, Mission of Salt Lake City, Utah was acknowledged as tax exempt by the Internal Revenue Service as a nonprofit religious organization.

AUGUST 14, 1981

The Church of Scientology of San Francisco was granted exemption from California state taxes by the California Franchise Tax Board as a nonprofit religious organization.

OCTOBER 23, 1981

In a suit brought by a Scientologist, the DC Court of Appeals ruled for the first time that Interpol was not immune to suit in the United States for wrongs committed against US citizens.

NOVEMBER 1, 1981

The Church of Scientology International was founded, signaling a new era of Scientology management. A strong standardized corporate structure was required to facilitate the rapid expansion of Scientology and maintain high ethical standards in a widespread international network of churches. This followed a series of Sea Org inspections that discovered that the Guardian's Office (which had been established in 1966 to protect the Church from external attacks and care for its legal matters) had become entirely autonomous and corrupt. The Guardian's Office had been infiltrated by individuals antithetical to Scientology and had become an organization that operated completely apart from the day-to-day activities of the Church. Their secret actions in violation of Church policy had resulted in eleven members being jailed for obstruction of justice. Sea Organization executives overthrew the Guardian's Office and disbanded it. Part of the measures taken to ensure a similar situation could never recur was the formation of the Religious Technology Center on 1 January 1982. L. Ron Hubbard bestowed the trademarks of Scientology to RTC, whose purpose is to safeguard the proper use of the marks and ensure they remain in good hands and are properly used.

MAY 3, 1982

The Oregon State Court of Appeals threw out a 1979 verdict from an earlier trial against the church of Scientology in Portland and ordered a new trial for a woman who sued the church after being deprogramed and forced to renounce her religion. In its ruling, the Court of Appeals officially recognized Scientology as a bona fide religion. [See July 16, 1985 entry]

MAY 6, 1982

The church of Scientology in Montreal, Quebec, Canada obtained property tax exemption because it was recognized that the church building was owned by a religious institution.

JUNE 29, 1982

In a joint meeting of commonwealth and state attorneys general in Victoria, Australia, long-unenforced legislation against the practice of Scientology, which had been in place in Victoria since the 1960s, was repealed.

AUGUST 19, 1982

The Church of Scientology of Toronto, Ontario, Canada was granted unconditional exemption by the Customs and Excise Department from payment of federal sales tax on the sale of books written by L. Ron Hubbard.

JANUARY 7, 1983

The Regional Court in Munich, Germany validated the Church's policy on refunds, saying that the plaintiff had no valid claim to receive more money than the amount worked out as refundable in accordance with Church policy.

JANUARY 19, 1983

In a case brought by the Church to force the FBI and other US agencies to cease their unconstitutional conduct against the Church, the US District Court in Washington, DC found that the FBI had been improperly withholding documents concerning the Church and ordered the documents released. The court ruled the Church of Scientology was to be treated like all other mainstream denominations.

JUNE 18, 1983

A bogus probate case alleging, incredibly, that L. Ron Hubbard had passed away, filed in Riverside, California was dismissed. The judge found that L. Ron Hubbard was doing very well, that his personal affairs were in good order and that he was entitled to his privacy.

JUNE 28, 1983

A Massachusetts Superior Court judge ruled that the Church of Scientology "satisfies the criteria of a religion" as "the teachings involve a theory of the spiritual nature of man." The ruling also stated that the practice of auditing is central to the practice of Scientology, and that the organization of the Church has many resemblances to recognized hierarchical religious institutions.

OCTOBER 27, 1983

The Church of Scientology won a case against the high commissioner for payroll tax in Australia. In a 5–0 decision issued by the High Court of Australia, the judges stated: "The conclusion that it is a religious institution entitled to the tax exemption is irresistible." During this case, the Church established the legal definition of religion for the Australian Constitution for the first time in history.

JANUARY 23, 1984

The church of Scientology in Sydney, Australia was granted exemption from the payment of land tax, based on the fact that Scientology is a religion.

FEBRUARY 27, 1984

In four consolidated cases in Los Angeles, California, the US District Court of the Central District of California ruled: "This court finds that the Church of Scientology is a religion within the meaning of the First Amendment. The beliefs and ideas of

Scientology address ultimate concerns—the nature of the person and the individual's relationship to the universe."

MARCH 27, 1984

An appeals court upheld a November 1982 decision that found the Vancouver church of Scientology exempt from property tax as a religious organization.

MAY 11, 1984

A judge in Boston, Massachusetts ruled: "As far as I am concerned, Scientology is a religion. I don't think there should be any serious doubt about that. I will take judicial notice that it is a religion, period."

JANUARY 28, 1985

In a defamation case brought by a Scientologist against the International Criminal Police Organization (Interpol), Interpol was ordered to pay $55,681 in costs and attorney fees and also retracted the document containing false information on the Scientologist, which it had circulated to 125 countries.

JANUARY 30, 1985

The Stuttgart District Court reversed an earlier negative lower court ruling concerning church proselytizing because: "The conduct of the concerned served a direct religious purpose."

APRIL 30, 1985

The US Department of Justice was ordered to pay $17,097.72 to the Church of Scientology for improperly withholding documents which the Church had a right to receive, and for noncompliance with court orders.

MAY 15, 1985

The Social Security Agency of Angers, France ruled that a staff member of the Church of Scientology of Angers was not required to make Social Security payments because his commitment to the Church was of a purely spiritual nature and his work could not be compared to that of a normal wage earner.

MAY 20, 1985

A case was won in the District Court of Stuttgart acknowledging the Church's dissemination activities as part of the pursuit of its religion.

JUNE 5, 1985

In the case of the Church vs. the City of Munich, the appeals court announced that the court accepts (a) that auditing is an essential part of the teachings of Scientology according to the self-understanding of the Church; (b) that based on this, the term "commercial enterprise" cannot be applied to the Church.

JUNE 11, 1985

The Social Security Agency in Pau, France issued a decision granting exemption from making Social Security payments, due to the religious nature of the Scientologists' work.

JULY 16, 1985

A judge in Multnomah County, Oregon declared a mistrial in a second case involving a former parishioner of the church who had been kidnapped by deprogramers and then forced to renounce her religion. The judge's decision threw out a 39-million-dollar verdict against the church and declared that the court had not properly protected the rights of the church as a religion during the trial. This reversal came about after tens of thousands of Scientologists from around the world traveled to Portland for the first Religious Freedom Crusade and stood, shoulder to shoulder for 60 days, until justice was done. [See May 3, 1982 entry]

OCTOBER 28, 1985

The Church of Scientology of Melbourne, Australia was exempted from paying city taxes on the basis of being a religion.

NOVEMBER 20, 1985

A proceeding in the Padova Court in Italy for alleged labor law violations was dismissed because no violations were found; the church pursued religious aims; and church staff did not fall within the purview of the labor law.

1986

Education Alive South Africa was granted official tax-exempt status from the Commissioner of Inland Tax Revenue.

MARCH 26, 1986

In the United Kingdom, a permanent injunction was obtained against a group of individuals using copyrighted Church scriptures without permission. The group was also ordered to pay the costs of the case and £5,000 in damages.

MAY 5, 1986

The Bologna Court in Italy dismissed a baseless prosecution against Scientology staff on the basis that no crime was committed, also finding the Church to be a religion.

JUNE 5, 1986

A case involving the incorporation of the Scientology Mission of Ulm, Germany was decided in the Church's favor, validating the mission as a religious organization.

JUNE 23, 1986

In a court case involving an individual using copyrighted Church scriptures without permission, the United States Court of Appeals for the Second Circuit upheld the Religious Technology Center's ownership of the trademarks of Dianetics and Scientology and the right of the Church of Scientology International to enforce the proper use of the marks.

JULY 16, 1986

Five Seattle "deprogramers" pleaded guilty to charges that they had attempted to force a Scientologist to give up her chosen religious beliefs. The deprogramers were sentenced to one year's probation and fined $5,000.

AUGUST 11, 1986

A court in Denmark ordered three individuals to pay $175,000 in damages for theft of confidential Scientology scriptures from the Church of Scientology.

SEPTEMBER 4, 1986

All Scientology churches and missions in California were exempted from California State Unemployment Insurance Taxes, retroactive to January 1, 1984.

DECEMBER 8, 1986

The Immigration and Naturalization Service (INS) National Office issued an official ruling to regional and local INS offices, stating that the Church of Scientology is a bona fide religion and is to be treated as any other religion.

1987–1988

All Canadian churches of Scientology received official recognition from the Revenue Department of the federal government, validating staff members of those churches as religious workers and exempting the churches from unemployment insurance and pension plan payments for their staff.

JUNE 29, 1987

An injunction was granted by the Court of Appeal in Bern, Switzerland against the illegal duplication of copyrighted taped lectures on Scientology by L. Ron Hubbard.

NOVEMBER 19, 1987

Deprogramer Ted Patrick was ordered by a US District Court judge in Los Angeles to pay $184,900 in attorney fees and sanctions to a member of the Church of Scientology who had been kidnapped by Patrick in 1981 and held against her will for 38 days.

DECEMBER 29, 1987

Two deprogramers from England were convicted in Germany on charges of kidnapping a 32-year-old Scientologist. They spent six weeks in jail, were tried, sentenced and deported to England.

DECEMBER 31, 1987

The Tax Office in Pau, France issued a decision concerning the Pau mission, stating that donations for Scientology courses and auditing were tax exempt.

FEBRUARY 17, 1988

The Regional Court in Hamburg, Germany recognized Scientology as a bona fide religion and granted incorporation as a religious organization to the Church of Scientology's Hamburg Celebrity Centre.

MARCH 17, 1988

A German court cancelled proceedings against the Frankfurt mission, reaffirming the mission's incorporation as a charitable organization.

APRIL 7, 1988

The church of Scientology in Portugal was recognized and registered as a religious organization.

JUNE 10, 1988

The Inspector of Corporate Taxes in Amsterdam, Holland granted exemption from value added tax (VAT) and corporate tax to the Church of Scientology Amsterdam and cancelled assessments for corporate taxes for prior years.

JUNE 16, 1988

The Utah State Tax Commission found the Church of Scientology, Mission of Salt Lake City to be a religious institution and granted exemption from state sales and use tax.

JULY 11, 1988

Narconon in Germany was recognized as a nonprofit organization.

JULY 20, 1988

A Los Angeles Superior Court judge dismissed a billion-dollar lawsuit filed "on behalf of all disaffected Scientologists in the world." This was a total of 6 people—out of 8 million adherents around the world. Although the plaintiff's allegations were carried widely in the media, the judge dismissed the suit as entirely unsubstantiated. The judge ordered the plaintiffs on 7 separate occasions to provide evidence in support of their claims. They were unable to do so—he dismissed the suit as groundless. The dismissal was upheld on appeal in 1990 and costs of conducting this litigation were awarded to the Church.

SEPTEMBER 20, 1988

The week of 25 September was proclaimed by Congress and President Ronald Reagan as National Religious Freedom Week, due in large part to the work of members of the Church of Scientology in the US.

SEPTEMBER 28, 1988

The California governor signed into law a bill that protects churches and religious organizations from unfounded punitive damages claims. The law, first conceived by Scientologists, requires stringent proof of actual damages before such a claim is accepted for trial.

October 12, 1988

In a Berlin, Germany decision, the court recognized the Church as a religion.

December 30, 1988

The Tax Commission of the City of New York granted full property tax exemption to the church as a religious organization.

January 23, 1989

In Bolzano, Italy the court threw out charges against 11 Scientologists involved in the Bolzano church's delivery of the Purification Rundown. The charges, all based on false information supplied by a psychiatrist, were ruled as "unfounded" and the Scientologists were fully acquitted.

March 1989

The District of Schöneberg in Berlin, recognized the church as a religious organization.

June 7, 1989

The Frankfurt, Germany court ruled that auditing was the central religious practice of the Church and was covered under Freedom of Religion. The court further ruled that the religious services of the Church cannot be measured in monetary terms, and serve to forward the overall activity of the Church.

June 21, 1989

The Church of Scientology was victorious in a United States Supreme Court ruling that upheld the right of Federal courts to place legal restraints on the IRS when there is reason to suspect that the tax agency is likely to violate the law and abuse its powers.

July 19, 1989

The City of Munich, Germany dropped a case against the church and affirmed its religious status.

October 10, 1989

A Munich court ruled that the church should have no restrictions placed on its dissemination activities on city streets.

February 1990

The Federal Finance Office in Germany exempted Scientology Missions International, the mother church for Scientology missions, from paying tax on the tithes paid to them by German missions, and made the decision retroactive to 1982.

February 15, 1990

The Church of Scientology, Mission of Anchorage, Alaska was granted property tax exemption based on religious status.

February 15, 1990

Following 13 years of Trademark Office rejections of Church applications for trademark registration, the German Patent Court ruled that the term "Scientology" could be registered as a trademark.

March 27, 1990

The Monza Tax Commission in Italy ruled that the Church of Scientology was a tax-exempt organization and should not be subject to taxation because it is a religion.

April 4, 1990

The National Commission on Law Enforcement and Social Justice of San Francisco received tax-exempt status from the IRS.

May 23, 1990

The Citizens Commission on Human Rights was granted tax-exempt status by the IRS.

June 18, 1990

A judge ruled in favor of the Church of Scientology of Boston and denied the

IRS access to church records in the IRS's attempt to repeal the tax-exempt status of the Boston church, which was granted in 1975. The judge also reprimanded the IRS for intrusive and abusive practices. The IRS appealed the decision but lost again in the higher court. The church set a nationwide precedent that protects all religions from IRS meddling in church affairs.

SEPTEMBER 4, 1990

A Frankfurt, Germany court affirmed the religiosity of Scientology and its right to set up information stands and distribute information about Scientology throughout the city.

SEPTEMBER 18, 1990

A Valencia court ruled that Narconon is noncommercial and exempt from the payment of social security tax.

SEPTEMBER 20, 1990

A tax assessment against the church of Scientology in Torino, Italy was withdrawn because Scientology was a religion.

OCTOBER 31, 1990

In Hanover, Germany a court upheld the Church's constitutional right to disseminate its religion. The decision recognized the religiosity of the Church of Scientology.

JANUARY 16, 1991

In a lawsuit filed against two trademark infringers in Brisbane, Australia, a decision was obtained in favor of New Era Publications against all unauthorized use of the copyrighted materials of L. Ron Hubbard.

FEBRUARY 21, 1991

The local tax commission confirmed that the Scientology mission in Lecco, Italy did not have to pay value added tax because it is a church and delivering religious services.

MARCH 18, 1991

The United States Supreme Court issued a ruling that vacated an earlier $2.5 million judgment against the Church in a case involving a former member and sent the case to the California Court of Appeals with instructions to review its procedures against the US Constitution.

MAY 24, 1991

A US District Court judge in Los Angeles ruled that a Freedom of Information case brought by the Church against the Internal Revenue Service clearly served public benefit and caused the IRS to review its procedures which led to the resolution of nearly 1,000 similarly situated cases brought by other US citizens against the agency. The judge awarded monetary compensation to the Church of Scientology for the expenses it incurred in this suit against the IRS.

JUNE 3, 1991

A magistrate ordered the IRS to pay attorney fees for unnecessarily prolonging the litigation of a Freedom of Information Act suit filed by the Church of Scientology of Boston.

JUNE 21, 1991

A US District Court judge ordered monetary penalties against the IRS, who filed a motion solely to "harass, cause unnecessary delay, or needlessly increase the cost of litigation" in two Freedom of Information Act suits filed by the Church.

JULY 2, 1991

The Milan court in Italy after a two-year-long trial, acquitted all Scientologists charged with any crime; fully affirmed the religious nature of the Church; acknowledged the goal of Scientology as spiritual freedom; recognized the E-Meter as a religious artifact; and cited the technology of Scientology as effective in drug rehabilitation. This ended psychiatric-backed government attacks in Italy.

SEPTEMBER 1991

The Dresden mission in Germany became the first officially registered Scientology association in what had been East Germany, handing a defeat to the local antireligious movement who opposed the registration.

OCTOBER 18, 1991

The Federal Constitutional Court of Germany, the highest court in the land, overturned a decree by the City of Hamburg forbidding the Citizens Commission on Human Rights, a Church-supported group, to distribute fliers in the streets.

NOVEMBER 4, 1991

After three years of investigation by Spanish authorities, the national court in Spain dropped all charges that were an attempted direct attack against the religion of Scientology, and had earlier resulted in the unwarranted arrest of several members of the church based on false information.

DECEMBER 2, 1991

In Toronto, the court ruled that the Ontario Provincial Police 1983 raid of the church, the largest raid in Canadian history, was illegal and that all 2 million documents seized in the raid had to be returned. The church is suing the Ontario Provincial Police (OPP) and the Ministry of the Attorney General for $19 million. The complaint is based on the grave and unwarranted intrusion into church affairs and seeks to recover the costs of legal proceedings required to gain return of the materials.

JANUARY 23, 1992

The Hamburg Administrative Court recognized the local church's right to freely disseminate its religion and lifted all bans on promotion that had been placed by the city of Hamburg.

JUNE 17, 1992

The Superior Court in Germany accepted the religious and philosophical nature of the Church and concluded that the insinuations of a newspaper in Stuttgart were false facts and a violation of personal rights.

AUGUST 4, 1992

The Scientology Center of St. Petersburg became the first center in Russia to be incorporated.

AUGUST 14, 1992

The Oklahoma Board of Mental Health and Substance Abuse Services granted Narconon Chilocco an exemption from their certification process on the basis of Narconon's accreditation by the prestigious Commission on Accreditation of Rehabilitation Facilities.

AUGUST 17, 1992

In the first ruling of its kind, the US Ninth Circuit Court of Appeals ruled that the public have the right to sue the IRS to remove false information from their files. The case was brought to court by two Scientologists who had discovered a false and damaging report in their IRS files.

AUGUST 17, 1992

A United States District Court judge in Los Angeles ordered the IRS to pay $16,881.56 in attorney fees and costs to the Church of Scientology Western United States. The church prevailed in a Freedom of Information Act suit against the IRS and caused the IRS to release records that it had improperly withheld.

AUGUST 19, 1992

In cases involving the Church of Scientology International and the Church of Scientology Western United States, the US Court of Appeals for the Ninth Circuit held that the IRS must be held to a higher standard of proof when seeking records from churches.

CHAPTER 38

PLEDGE TO MANKIND

In 1984, the International Association of Scientologists drafted the following pledge as a statement of its position and aims. It was signed by representatives of Scientologists from around the world at Saint Hill Manor, in Sussex, England. It underscores the dedication and commitment of Scientologists everywhere.

PLEDGE to MANKIND

Time and again, throughout the troubled history of civilisation on this planet, new ideas, new religions and constructive thought have met with violent opposition. Such attacks come from those who would preserve the status quo and particularly from those who seek to preserve and enhance their position through the domination, subjugation and even destruction of others. For this reason new religions have been born in blood at the cost of great sacrifice and suffering by adherents. It is only through a unity of purpose and unswerving commitment by a dedicated group that new ideas and new religions survive and expand.

Scientology has been in existence now for some thirty-four years. During that time it has suffered all manner of attacks from the forces of oppression in various countries. Yet Scientology has survived and expanded because of the dedication of its members and because it is a force for goodness and freedo which is easily recognised by men of goodwill, despite the vicious lies which are spawned by those w would enslave mankind and which are carried by the media.

Scientology is experiencing the greatest expansion and prosperity in its history. Internatio scope, Scientology weekly frees more people from the debilitating effects of drugs, ignorance other sources of aberration and moves them on the path to greater awareness, self-respect and di all other groups combined.

Yet as we have learned in our thirty-four years, whenever we expand, we are attacked, com that expansion. And today is no exception.

In the United States, which was once thought to be a haven of religious liberty, we unprincipled attacks in the court system by those who would line their pocket coffers. Bigots in all branches of government, fearing the success of Scientology destruction through taxation and repressive legislation.

We have been subjected to illegal heresy trials in two countries before prejud who are not qualified or inclined to perceive the truth.

In Canada and Germany, our Churches have been subjected to vicious r genocide attacks on religions that took place in "less informed" ti

The news media chooses to ignore the good works and miraculous su to poison public opinion through vilification of the religion an

The detractors of Scientology know full well that it is a prov mankind from spiritual bondage. That is why they atta be threatened by a society which is more ethical, productive Scientology and Scientologists. Thus when we expand,

Up to this day, the responsibility for defending Scient few. And so it will continue in large measure.

Yet, in order to continue the quest for a new civili abound, the assistance and dedication of ea is essential. The road may be difficult and m and erosion of personal liberties at this ti prevail for the benefit of all mankind.

We, the undersigned, pledge ourselves, to achieving the aims of Scientolo the able can prosper and honest being

We invite Scientologists and

Witness our hand this Sev Sussex, England.

"Time and again, throughout the troubled history of civilization on this planet, new ideas, new religions and constructive thought have met with violent opposition. Such attacks come from those who would preserve the status quo and particularly from those who seek to preserve and enhance their position through the domination, subjugation and even destruction of others. For this reason new religions have been born in blood at the cost of great sacrifice and suffering by adherents. It is only through a unity of purpose and unswerving commitment by a dedicated group that new ideas and new religions survive and expand.

"Scientology has been in existence now for some thirty-four years. During that time it has suffered all manner of attacks from the forces of oppression in various countries. Yet Scientology has survived and expanded because of the dedication of its members and because it is a force for goodness and freedom which is easily recognized by men of goodwill; despite the vicious lies which are spawned by those who would enslave mankind and which are carried by the media.

"Scientology is experiencing the greatest expansion and prosperity in its history. International in scope, Scientology each week frees more people from the debilitating effects of drugs, ignorance and other sources of aberration and moves them on the path to greater awareness, self-respect and dignity than all other groups combined.

"Yet as we have learned in our thirty-four years, whenever we expand, we are attacked, commensurate with that expansion. And today is no exception.

"In the United States, which was once thought to be a haven of religious liberty, we are the targets of unprincipled attacks in the court system by those who would line their pockets from our hard won coffers. Bigots in all branches of government, fearing the success of Scientology, are bent on our destruction through taxation and repressive legislation.

"We have been subjected to illegal heresy trials in two countries before prejudiced and malinformed judges who are not qualified or inclined to perceive the truth.

"In Canada and Germany, our Churches have been subjected to vicious raids reminiscent of the historical genocide attacks on religions that took place in 'less informed' times and societies.

"The news media chooses to ignore the good works and miraculous successes of Scientology and instead seeks to poison public opinion through vilification of the religion and its Founder.

"The detractors of Scientology know full well that it is a proven, effective and workable system for freeing mankind from spiritual bondage. That is why they attack. They fear that they will somehow be threatened by a society which is more ethical, productive and humane through the influence of Scientology and Scientologists. Thus when we expand, to that degree we are attacked.

"Up to this day, the responsibility for defending Scientology has been on the shoulders of a desperate few. And so it will continue in large measure.

"Yet, in order to continue the quest for a new civilization where honest men have rights and freedoms abound, the assistance and dedication of each and every Scientologist and other men of goodwill is essential. The road may be difficult and may get worse due to the rapid decline of civilization and erosion of personal liberties at this time. But united in purpose and dedication, we shall prevail for the benefit of all mankind.

"We, the undersigned, pledge ourselves, without reservation or any thought of personal comfort or safety, to achieving the aims of Scientology: 'A civilization without insanity, without war, where the able can prosper and honest beings can have rights, and where Man is free to rise to greater heights.'

"We invite Scientologists and other well-intentioned people everywhere to join us in this pledge.

"Witness our hand this Seventh day of October, A.D. 34, Saint Hill Manor, East Grinstead, Sussex, England."

Chapter 39

The Holidays of Scientology

To commemorate memorable dates in its history, the Church of Scientology observes holidays in all parts of the world through the course of the year. The most significant are celebrated with internationally telecast events to link all Scientology churches. Regular church services are suspended for events, and in those cities where the local church simply cannot accommodate the thousands of parishioners attending the event, suitable auditoriums are rented. Major events are important to every Scientologist, be they in Africa, America, Asia, Australia or Europe as they provide a special sense of unity.

The major Scientology events feature briefings by senior church members on such subjects as the introduction of L. Ron Hubbard's works into new nations or sectors of society, the outstanding accomplishments of individual Scientologists and reviews of worldwide growth. Events further feature releases of new Scientology books, materials, courses and society betterment programs—all cause for celebration. Although highly dignified affairs, they are also joyous.

Other occasions, such as the founding of the church in a particular country or a city, may be locally observed. Traditional holidays, such as Christmas, Easter, the United States Independence Day and French Bastille Day are not listed, although Scientologists celebrate these occasions in their own countries according to custom. The following calendar lists major holidays around the world.

JANUARY

16 Recognition Day Africa, to celebrate recognition in 1975 of the church of Scientology in South Africa.

25 Criminon Day, to celebrate the 1970 founding of Criminon, the prison rehabilitation program.

28 National Founding Day New Zealand, to celebrate the founding of the first church in New Zealand, the Church of Scientology Auckland in 1955.

FEBRUARY

7 Recognition Day Australia, to celebrate the recognition in 1973 of the Church of Scientology across Australia, by the then Federal Attorney General, Senator Lionel Murphy. Scientology was recognized under Section 26 of the Commonwealth Marriage Act, 1961–1966.

18 National Founding Day United States, to celebrate the founding of the first church in the US, the Church of Scientology Los Angeles in 1954.

19 Narconon Day. On this day in 1966, an Arizona State Prison inmate initiated the Narconon drug rehabilitation program, which utilizes the technology of L. Ron Hubbard. Narconon has expanded to a network of more than thirty programs in countries throughout the world.

22 Celebrity Day, to celebrate the opening of the Celebrity Centre International in Los Angeles in 1970, dedicated to the rehabilitation of the culture through art.

MARCH

5 CCHR Day, to mark the formation in 1969 of the Citizens Commission on Human Rights. First formed in England, the commission is now a worldwide organization which has achieved major reforms internationally against psychiatric abuses.

13 MARCH

L. Ron Hubbard's Birthday

The birthday of the Founder of Dianetics and Scientology, March 13, 1911, is commemorated each year with a major celebration honoring L. Ron Hubbard's achievements and his continuing contributions to mankind. Outstanding churches and missions are recognized for service to their parishioners and communities during the previous year.

13 National Founding Day Belgium, to celebrate the founding of the first church in Belgium, the Church of Scientology Brussels in 1980.

13 National Founding Day Holland, to celebrate the founding of the first church in Holland, the Church of Scientology Amsterdam in 1972.

16 National Founding Day Italy, to celebrate the founding of the first church in Italy, the Church of Scientology Milano in 1978.

19 National Founding Day Venezuela, to celebrate the founding of the first Dianetics center in Venezuela, the Asociación Cultural Dianética de Venezuela, A.C., in 1981.

24 Student Day, to celebrate the commencement of the Saint Hill Special Briefing Course in 1961. The course was begun at Saint Hill Manor, East Grinstead, Sussex and in 1968 was expanded to the American Saint Hill Organization in Los Angeles. Today, the Saint Hill Special Briefing Course is also available in Copenhagen, Denmark; Sydney, Australia and at the Flag Land Base. This course, the largest in Scientology, covers the chronological development of Dianetics and Scientology.

31 National Founding Day Austria, to celebrate the founding of the first church in Austria, the Church of Scientology Vienna in 1971.

APRIL

4 Recognition Day Germany, to celebrate the recognition in 1974 of the church of Scientology in Munich.

16 National Founding Day Sweden, to celebrate the founding of the first church in Sweden, the Church of Scientology Göteborg in 1969.

20 L. Ron Hubbard Exhibition Day, to celebrate the opening in 1991 of the L. Ron Hubbard Life Exhibition in Hollywood, California. Featuring impressive audiovisual displays on the life and accomplishments of L. Ron Hubbard, the exhibition is visited by thousands of Scientologists and non-Scientologists annually.

25 Recognition Day New Zealand, to celebrate recognition of the Church in 1974 with Scientology ministers licensed to perform marriages.

MAY

9 MAY

Anniversary of Dianetics

The annual international celebration on this day salutes the publication of *Dianetics: The Modern Science of Mental Health* on May 9, 1950. It is the occasion when Scientologists and community leaders from around the world acknowledge the contributions Dianetics has made to the betterment of individuals and society at large and the daily miracles that occur through its widespread application.

15 National Founding Day Colombia, to celebrate the founding in 1980 of the first Dianetics center in Colombia, the Centro Cultural de Dianética in Bogotá.

22 National Founding Day Switzerland, to celebrate the founding of the first church in Switzerland, the Church of Scientology Basel in 1974.

25 Integrity Day, to mark the 1965 release by L. Ron Hubbard of his studies on ethics—the reason and contemplation of optimum survival.

JUNE

5 National Founding Day Denmark, to celebrate the founding of the first church in Denmark, the Church of Scientology Denmark in 1968.

6 JUNE

Maiden Voyage Anniversary

On this date in 1988, the Sea Org Motor Vessel *Freewinds* began her maiden voyage, during which

New OT VIII was released publicly. In memory of that day, OT VIII completions convene aboard the *Freewinds* for a week of special briefings and acknowledgments to new OT VIII completions for their work in disseminating and expanding Scientology.

12 National Founding Day Scotland, to celebrate the founding of the Hubbard Academy of Personal Independence in Edinburgh, Scotland in 1968.

17 National Founding Day Portugal, to celebrate the founding in 1982 of the first Dianetics institute in Portugal, the Instituto de Dianética in Lisbon.

18 Academy Day, in celebration of the 1964 release of L. Ron Hubbard's study technology.

26 National Founding Day Norway, to celebrate the founding of the first church in Norway, the Church of Scientology Oslo in 1980.

JULY

2 Advanced Organization Founding Day Australia-New Zealand-Oceania, to celebrate the opening in 1983 of the Advanced Organization and Saint Hill in Sydney.

7 Advanced Organization Founding Day Europe, to celebrate the opening of the Advanced Organization Denmark in 1969.

21 Founding Day Washington, DC, to celebrate the incorporation in 1955 of the Founding Church of Scientology and the opening of the first Academy of Scientology.

AUGUST

12 Sea Org Day, commemorating the establishment of the Sea Organization in 1967, is celebrated by all Sea Organization members throughout the world. Rank and rating promotion ceremonies are held, and speeches are delivered by leading Sea Organization members.

13 Advanced Organization Founding Day Los Angeles, to celebrate the opening of the American Saint Hill Organization and the Advanced Organization Los Angeles in 1968.

17 Advanced Organization Founding Day United Kingdom, to celebrate the opening of Advanced Organization United Kingdom at Saint Hill, Sussex, England in 1970.

SEPTEMBER

4 Clear Day, to mark the inauguration of the Clearing Course in 1965. First released at Saint Hill Manor, the course is now available to Scientologists at Advanced Organizations in the United Kingdom, the United States, Denmark and Australia as well as at the Flag Service Organization in Florida.

8 National Founding Day Canada, to celebrate the founding of the first church in Canada, the Church of Scientology Toronto in 1967.

SECOND SUNDAY IN SEPTEMBER

Auditor's Day

On this day auditors are acknowledged for their dedication in bringing man up the Bridge to Total Freedom. Top auditors from around the world are recognized for their efforts in helping their fellow man.

18 National Founding Day Zimbabwe, to celebrate the founding of the first church in Zimbabwe, the Church of Scientology Bulawayo in 1967.

20 National Founding Day Mexico, to celebrate the founding of the first Dianetics institute in Mexico, the Instituto de Filosofía Aplicada, A.C., in 1979.

21 National Founding Day England, to celebrate the beginning of Scientology in England, marking the opening of the London branch of the Hubbard Association of Scientologists International in 1952.

25 National Founding Day Israel, to celebrate the beginning of the first Scientology and Dianetics college in Tel Aviv, Israel in 1980.

October

7 October

International Association of Scientologists (IAS) Anniversary

Held at a different host city each year, members of the IAS gather to commemorate the founding of the IAS and to rededicate themselves to its aims. The annual IAS freedom awards are presented. This event coincides with the annual convention of IAS delegates.

15 National Founding Day Germany, to celebrate the founding of the first church in Germany, the Church of Scientology Munich in 1970.

26 National Founding Day France, to celebrate the founding of the first church in France, the Church of Scientology Paris in 1959.

November

11 National Founding Day South Africa, to celebrate the founding of the first church in South Africa, the Church of Scientology Johannesburg in 1957.

27 Publications Day, to celebrate the opening of the first publications organization, Publications Worldwide, at Saint Hill Manor in 1967.

December

6 Flag Land Base Day, to celebrate the opening of the Flag Land Base in Clearwater, Florida in 1975.

30 Freedom Day US, to celebrate the official recognition in 1974 of the Church of Scientology in the United States.

31 National Founding Day Spain, to celebrate the founding of the first church in Spain, the Church of Scientology Barcelona in 1981.

31 National Founding Day Japan, to celebrate the beginning of Scientology in Japan, which marks the opening of the Scientology Organization Tokyo in 1988.

31 December

New Year's Eve

This event welcomes in the new year with a review of accomplishments over the previous year and a look forward to the upcoming year and plans for further reach into new areas of society with L. Ron Hubbard's technology. Stellar accomplishments of Scientology parishioners helping new people to move up the Bridge to Total Freedom are acknowledged.

CHAPTER 40

THE COMPLETE SERVICES OF SCIENTOLOGY

Services are offered in Scientology which cover its full range of philosophic and technical data. Courses and auditing services exist which address any aspect of existence. No matter a person's condition in life, Scientology has services which can help improve it.

The listings in this chapter categorize and provide useful information about Dianetics and Scientology courses and auditing services. These are laid out in a sequence usually followed by Scientologists in obtaining them. The approximate length of time a particular service takes is noted, in addition to where one would normally obtain that service.

There are different levels of Scientology organizations, from those that primarily deliver the most basic services to those that provide increasingly advanced levels of training and auditing.

The vast majority of Scientology services are available in most cities around the world. They are delivered by field auditors, field groups, missions and Scientology Class V organizations.

The advanced training and auditing services are available only at higher-level organizations, due to the degree of skill and experience required of the delivery staff, yet are still very accessible. These services are delivered at Saint Hills, Advanced Organizations, the Flag Service Organization and the Flag Ship Service Organization.

Higher-level organizations have the capability to deliver all services including lower-level courses and auditing services, though they do not specialize in them.

For more information on any Dianetics or Scientology services, contact the Scientology church or mission nearest you. A list of Scientology organizations is included at the back of this book.

INTRODUCTORY SERVICES

There is an introductory service available for any person depending on his personal interest or immediate concerns. Introductory services provide information to a person who has had no or little prior contact with Scientology, answer his questions and help him begin to understand himself better.

There is no definite sequence in which the introductory services described below need be done, or how many must be done. Often a person will do one or a few before enrolling onto training in an Academy of Scientology or auditing in the Hubbard Guidance Center.

Introductory services are most frequently obtained from field auditors, field groups, missions and Class V organizations, which specialize in delivering such services.

■ ***Personality Testing and Evaluation***

Includes Oxford Capacity Analysis (personality profile which measures 10 different personality traits), IQ and aptitude tests. Trained staff evaluate the tests to help a person estimate his condition and make correct choices about his future.
1–2 hours

■ ***Introductory Lectures***

Lectures by church staff help a person gain an elementary understanding of Scientology and answer his questions.
1 hour

■ ***Introductory Tape Plays***

Selected lectures by L. Ron Hubbard convey basic principles of Dianetics and Scientology for people new to the subject.
1 hour

■ ***Introductory Films and Videos***

There are many films or videos which show how Scientology helps people improve their lives and what it offers to anyone. These cover a variety of different subjects and one even features an interview with Mr. Hubbard discussing Scientology principles. Running time for these is approximately 30 minutes each.

BOOKS AND EXTENSION COURSES

L. Ron Hubbard's books open the route to improvement and a better life. Extension courses are designed to accompany them and help the reader gain a deeper understanding through home study of the knowledge they contain. Each extension course consists of 20 lessons which take the reader through a particular book. Lessons help the student greatly increase his comprehension of what he is reading. The student answers lesson questions and mails them in to the organization, where staff grade and return them. At least one lesson per week is the minimum rate of progress, though most courses can be entirely completed in 2 or 3 weeks.

Extension courses exist for nearly all Mr. Hubbard's books. They are useful for the beginner in gaining an understanding of the subject and for the veteran Scientologist in filling out his knowledge of the subject while not on major church services. For this reason, extension courses are regularly delivered by all churches of Scientology including higher organizations.
For additional data see Chapter 7.

BASIC DIANETICS SERVICES

Those interested in Dianetics receive a thorough familiarity with the subject through the services listed here. Course lengths are figured on a part-time schedule of 3 hours per day, 5 days per week.
For additional data, see Chapter 8.

■ *Hubbard Dianetics Seminar*

Teaches basic auditing skills used in Dianetics and then gets students co-auditing with each other. Lets a person find out for himself that something can be done about the reactive mind. Students may co-audit as much as they want.
Seminars can be completed in 2 days full time (over a weekend) or during a week of evening classes, meeting each night for 3 hours. Naturally, this can take longer depending on how much co-auditing students want to do.

■ *Hubbard Dianetics Auditor Course*

The purpose of this course is to make a person into a Hubbard Dianetics Auditor and to see that the person receives Dianetics auditing himself. It contains further auditing techniques and a series of L. Ron Hubbard's lectures on Dianetics. Students co-audit as much as they want and make further progress toward Clear.
Course normally takes 3 weeks.

■ *Professional Dianetics Auditing*

This is auditing as taught on the Hubbard Dianetics Auditor Course but delivered by professionally trained staff in intensives of 12½ hours. A person receiving it does not train on Dianetics or audit another in return. Instead, professional Dianetics auditing is a rapid way to learn subjectively about Dianetics and experience its gains.

BASIC SCIENTOLOGY SERVICES

People interested in Scientology can do the following services. Each contains basic data and techniques of application. Course lengths are figured on a part-time schedule of 3 hours per day, 5 days per week.
For additional data, see Chapter 8.

■ *Life Improvement Courses*

These courses offer solutions to immediate concerns of the student. He learns specific things he can *do* about the condition he needs to change. Rapid improvement in a person's life is possible with these services in such areas as relationships, marriage, parenting, the workplace, personal values and others.
Most can be completed in 1 week.

■ *Success Through Communication Course*

Teaches communication skills for use in social or business situations. There are 18 separate drills learned, each one dealing with a different aspect of good communication.
1½ weeks

■ *Hubbard Qualified Scientologist Course*

Contains a broad survey of many Scientology basics and gives a student numerous techniques he can use to assist others. Students study from six of Mr. Hubbard's books, learn to audit and then give and receive as much co-auditing as they want. This course equips someone with a good working knowledge of fundamental Scientology data.
4 weeks

■ *Anatomy of the Human Mind Course*

Twenty lessons cover the makeup and mechanisms of the mind, man,

life and the universe. Each course period consists of a lecture on a different subject followed by demonstrations and practical application. Imparts a basic understanding of key principles of Dianetics and Scientology.
4 weeks—one lesson per evening for 20 evenings

- ***Basic Scientology Auditing Services***

One of the ways that people find out about Scientology is by receiving a session from an auditor.
For additional data, see Chapter 8.

- ***Introductory and Demonstration Auditing***

These auditing processes are ones designed for a person with no previous auditing experience and are delivered by professionally trained auditors. These processes result in a personal awareness that Scientology really works.
Individual sessions vary in length depending on the process being audited but may last an hour or more.

- ***Assist Auditing***

Scientology techniques can alleviate physical and mental trauma stemming from injuries or illnesses. These are used by Scientologists to help someone with burns, bruises, aches, pains, upsets and other such situations which occur in the course of living. Assists are rendered whenever the need for them arises, and are delivered by anyone qualified to do them.
Individual assist sessions vary in length depending on the assist process used.

- ***Group Processing***

Auditing procedures which can be delivered to a group of people simultaneously. Group Processing is delivered by any auditor who has been trained to audit groups. This type of auditing is not introductory as such; it is for persons who have previously received at least some individual auditing. Group Processing is regularly taken by Scientologists as it is an ideal service to receive when they are between major grades or levels of the Bridge. For this reason it is often also delivered in higher-level organizations.
Sessions last about 1 hour.

TRAINING SERVICES

Scientology organizations offer a wide range of training courses, for learning how to deliver auditing and gaining an understanding of the mechanics of life.

Most of the training services in Scientology are available at Class V organizations. More advanced training is available only at higher-level churches, which are Saint Hills, Advanced Organizations and the Flag Service Organization. Where delivery of a particular service is restricted to only certain organizations, this is designated below.

The average course lengths are estimated on the basis of a full-time study schedule of 8 hours per day, 5 days per week.
For additional data, see Chapter 14.

STUDY TECHNOLOGY SERVICES

■ ***Basic Study Manual Course***

Consists of the fundamentals of study technology, fully illustrated to facilitate comprehension. Designed for teenagers or older. Due to its broad application, this course is also delivered by field auditors, groups and missions.
1 week

■ ***Student Hat***

This is the course covering all aspects of study technology. It is a prerequisite course for all Academy training, enabling a student to fully understand his later studies or any subject in life. Also delivered by missions.
2 weeks

■ ***Hubbard Method One Co-audit Course***

Rapidly trains two people to co-audit Method One Word Clearing, a technique which locates and clears away misunderstood words and symbols from one's past. Completion of Method One greatly speeds progress on further courses, in addition to recovering a person's earlier education. Student learns enough basics to enable him to successfully co-audit with another. Also delivered by missions.
Course takes 4 days up to the auditing part of the course, which varies but ordinarily lasts another 2 or 3 weeks.

■ ***Primary Rundown***

A full course in study technology and augmented with thorough word clearing of all course materials. It results in the state of *superliteracy,* in which a person can comfortably and quickly take data from a page and be able at once to apply it.
4 weeks

KEY TO LIFE AND LIFE ORIENTATION COURSES

These are companion courses which boost any person to a much higher potential of ability and activity. Key to Life opens up all life to a person and puts him in communication. Directly following Key to Life, the Life Orientation Course enables him to use his new abilities to become competent in life.
For more information, see Chapters 11 and 12.
5 weeks for the Hubbard Key to Life Course; 4 weeks for the Hubbard Life Orientation Course

TR COURSES

TR courses contain drills in the cycle of communication, essential to auditing and any activity in life.
See Chapter 14 for more information.

- ***New Hubbard Professional TR Course***

A prerequisite to all auditor training, this course teaches the skills needed to be successful in auditing. Drills in communication (called "TRs" and numbered from 0–4) are studied and thoroughly drilled to mastery. The course also contains special auditing processes, available on this course only, to enhance the student's understanding of his materials.
3 weeks

- ***Hubbard Professional Upper Indoc TR Course***

Teaches further TRs needed to become wholly effective in all areas of auditing. These drills build on TRs 0–4 and bring a student to proficiency in handling people and communication while greatly increasing the student's ability to get his intention across. This is also a prerequisite to classed auditor training.
1½ weeks

- ***Therapeutic TR Course***

While TRs are the backbone of auditor training, they also result in remarkable case gains. This course is designed primarily for those taking the individual auditing route up the Bridge. Students do the TRs and experience the personal benefits these give, which also aids them in their further auditing. As this course is delivered as part of a person's case handling, it is also available at missions.
1½ weeks

AUDITOR TRAINING COURSES

- ***Auditor Classification Courses***

Auditor training teaches an understanding of life and know-how to handle it. Each auditor classification covers different aspects of Scientology principles and skills of application. It results in a certificate authorizing one to audit corresponding to the level on the processing side of the Bridge (i.e., Academy Level 0 teaches one to audit Grade 0 processes).
See Chapter 14 for further information.

Course		
Academy Level 0 *Hubbard Recognized Scientologist*	2	wks
Academy Level I *Hubbard Trained Scientologist*	2	wks
Academy Level II *Hubbard Certified Auditor*	2	wks
Academy Level III *Hubbard Professional Auditor*	2	wks
Academy Level IV *Hubbard Advanced Auditor*	2	wks
Class IV Internship	3	wks
Class V *Hubbard New Era Dianetics Auditor Course*	3	wks
Class V Internship	3	wks
Class V Graduate *Hubbard Class V Graduate Auditor Course*	3½	wks
Class V Graduate Internship	3	wks
Class VA Graduate *Hubbard Expanded Dianetics Auditor Course*	1½	wks
Class VA Graduate Internship	3	wks

■ *Technical Specialist Courses*

These teach a classed auditor skills to deliver a specific rundown or action. Technical Specialist Courses round out an auditor's training by giving him technology to handle a wide variety of conditions.

See Chapter 14 for more information.

Scientology Drug Rundown	2½	days
Scientology Marriage Counseling	3	days
Hubbard Happiness Rundown	2	wks
Allergy or Asthma Rundown	2	days
Est Repair	2	days
Psych Treatment Repair	2	days
PTS/SP	10	days
South African Rundown	10	days
Student Booster Rundown	2	days
Vital Information Rundown	2	days
Introspection Rundown	2	days
PDH Detection and Handling	5	days
Handling Fear of People	2	days
Hubbard Senior Security Checker	2	wks
Hubbard False Purpose Rundown	2	wks
Fixated Person Rundown	2	days
Knowledge Rundown	2	days
New Vitality Rundown	10	days
Dynamic Sort-out Assessment	2	days
Int by Dynamics Rundown	1	day
Profession Intensive	1	day
Case Cracker Rundown	2	days
Clear Certainty Rundown *Delivered at the Flag Service Organization or Advanced Organizations only*	1	wk

■ *Saint Hill Special Briefing Course (Hubbard Senior Scientologist, Class VI Auditor)*

This is the most comprehensive course in Scientology. The 16 separate checksheets listed below cover a complete chronological study of Dianetics and Scientology. The student acquires all auditing skills taught below this level in addition to a full command of the philosophical aspects of the subject.

See Chapter 14 for more information.

Delivered only at Saint Hill organizations and the Flag Service Organization.

Level A: *The Fundamentals of Dianetics*	3	wks
Level B: *The Fundamentals of Scientology*	3½	wks
Level C: *The Fundamentals of Havingness and Objectives Processing*	3½	wks
Level D: *The Basics of Metering*	3	wks
Level E: *The Principles of Auditing*	3	wks
Level F: *The Handling of Problems*	2	wks
Level G: *The Fundamentals of Confessionals*	4	wks
Level H: *The Basics of Listing*	3	wks
Level I: *The Basics of Listing and Nulling*	3½	wks
Level J: *The Handling of ARC Breaks and Service Facsimiles*	3½	wks
Level K: *The Recognition of Pc Indicators*	3	wks
Level L: *The Fundamentals of the Grade Chart*	3	wks
Level M: *The Basics of Case Repair and Resistive Cases*	3	wks
Level N: *The Developments and Techniques of Modern Auditing*	3½	wks
Level O: *Auditing the Expanded Lower Grades, New Era Dianetics and Repair Actions*	4	wks
Level P: *Auditing Expanded Dianetics and the Specialist Rundowns*	4	wks
Class VI Internship	4	wks

■ ***Advanced Auditor Training***

These classifications teach highly advanced auditing rundowns and skills. The level of Class VIII stresses complete mastery of all auditing fundamentals and makes an auditor who achieves spectacular gains on any preclear through totally standard delivery of the technology.

See Chapter 14 for more information.

With the exception of Class VIII, delivery of advanced auditor training is only to contracted staff members of Scientology organizations. These are delivered by Saint Hills (Class VII), Advanced Organizations (Class VIII) and the Flag Service Organization (Class VII to XII).

Course		
Hubbard Class VII Auditor Course *Hubbard Graduate Auditor*	1	wk
Hubbard Class VII Internship	3	wks
Hubbard Class VIII Auditor Course *Hubbard Specialist of Standard Tech*	6	wks
Class VIII Internship	3	wks
Hubbard Class IX Auditor Course *Hubbard Advanced Courses Specialist*	1	wk
Class IX Internship	3	wks
Hubbard Class X Auditor Course	1½	wks
Class X Internship	3	wks
Hubbard Class XI Auditor Course	1	wk
Class XI Internship	3	wks
Hubbard Class XII Auditor Course	1	wk
Class XII Internship	3	wks

MINISTERIAL COURSE

Required for ordination as a minister of the Church of Scientology and for permanent certification as an auditor. Provides a survey of religious studies throughout history and a study of the religious ceremonies and traditional religious services of Scientology.

OTHER SCIENTOLOGY COURSES

These provide data and teach a variety of technical skills of a non-auditor nature, such as supervising the Purification program or a course room.

Course		
Keeping Scientology Working Course	1	wk
PTS/SP Course How to Confront and Shatter Suppression	2	wks
Purification Rundown In-Charge Course	1	wk
Professional Product Debug Course	4	days
Cramming Officer Course	5	days
Cramming Officer Internship	3	wks
Hubbard Mini Course Supervisor Course	5	days
Hubbard Professional Course Supervisor Course	3	wks
Hubbard Professional Course Supervisor Internship	2	wks
Hubbard Co-audit Supervisor Course	4	days
Hubbard Professional Word Clearer Course	2	wks
Hubbard Professional Word Clearer Internship	2	wks
Hubbard Basic Art Course *Delivered only by Celebrity Centre organizations and higher-level churches*	4	days

CASE SUPERVISOR TRAINING

■ *C/S Classification Courses*

Beyond auditor training come skills needed to supervise auditing done by others. Each course teaches a different level of case supervision skills, building on what is learned on lower classifications. (See Chapter 14 for more information.) C/S courses are delivered by the same organizations that deliver the corresponding auditor classification levels.

Class IV C/S Course	2½	wks
Class IV C/S Internship	3	wks
Class V C/S Course	1	wk
Class V C/S Internship	3	wks
Class V Graduate C/S Course	1	wk
Class V Graduate C/S Internship	3	wks
Class VA Graduate C/S Course	1	wk
Class VA Graduate C/S Internship	3	wks
Class VI C/S Course	2	wks
Class VI C/S Internship	2	wks
Class VII C/S Course	3	days
Class VII C/S Internship	1	wk
Class VIII C/S Course	4	wks
Class VIII C/S Internship	3	wks
Class IX C/S Course	1	wk
Class IX C/S Internship	2½	wks
Class XII C/S Course	1	wk
Class XII C/S Internship	2	wks

■ *C/S Specialist Courses*

These teach skills to case supervise specialized auditing actions. Delivery of the Solo C/S, Clear Certainty Rundown C/S and Solo New Era Dianetics for OTs C/S Courses is restricted to higher-level organizations.

Purification Rundown C/S Course	4	days
Purification Rundown C/S Internship	1	wk
False Purpose Rundown C/S Course	4	days
False Purpose Rundown C/S Internship	1	wk
Solo C/S Course	3	wks
Solo C/S Internship	3	wks
Clear Certainty Rundown C/S Course	2	wks
Solo New Era Dianetics for OTs C/S Course	1	wk
Solo New Era Dianetics for OTs C/S Internship	3	wks

ADMINISTRATIVE TRAINING

These teach administrative technology necessary for group survival. These courses mainly exist to train Church staff members but Scientologists can train on this third dynamic technology as well.

Course		
Staff Status I	2	days
Staff Status II	5	days
Executive Status I	2	days
Hubbard Causative Leadership Course *Not including auditing actions that are part of course*	2	days
Hubbard Elementary Data Series Evaluator's Course	2	wks
Organization Executive Course *Includes study of OEC Volumes 0–7*	16	wks
Basic Staff Hat (Organization Executive Course Volume 0)	2	wks
Organization Executive Course, Volume 1	3	wks
Organization Executive Course, Volume 2	2	wks
Organization Executive Course, Volume 3	1	wk
Organization Executive Course, Volume 4	3	wks
Organization Executive Course, Volume 5	2	wks
Organization Executive Course, Volume 6	3	wks
Organization Executive Course, Volume 7	3½	wks
Flag Executive Briefing Course *Delivered at the Flag Service Organization only*	6	wks
Hubbard Executive Data Series Evaluator's Course *Delivered at the Flag Service Organization only*	4	wks

OT HATTING COURSES

These are special courses comprised of L. Ron Hubbard's lecture series that are particularly relevant to Scientologists on OT levels. Each course covers a different body of knowledge about the thetan's potentials and capabilities. These are delivered at the Flag Ship Service Organization for the purpose of providing Scientologists with training on the state of Operating Thetan.

Course		
The Time Track of Theta	3	days
The Route to Infinity	3	days
Secrets of the MEST Universe	5	days
The Perception of Truth	3	days
Universes and the War Between Theta and MEST	16	days
The Phoenix Lectures	9	days
The Creation of Human Ability	12	days
The Power of Simplicity	12	days
The Anatomy of Cause	9	days
The Whole Track	3	days
The Solution to Entrapment	10	days
The Ability Congress	5	days
State of Man Congress	4	days
The Doctorate Series Course for OTs *Also delivered by Celebrity Centres, Advanced Organizations and the Flag Service Organization*	4	wks

SCIENTOLOGIST HATTING COURSES

Designed for experienced Scientologists, Scientologist Hatting Courses provide extensive data on a single aspect of Dianetics and Scientology technology, such as ethics, the Tone Scale and dissemination, which greatly increase a Scientologist's knowledge of these areas. These services are also available from missions.

Course	Duration
Introduction to Scientology Ethics Course	5 days
Special Course in Human Evaluation	1 wk
Field Staff Member Specialist Course	2–3 days
Hubbard Dissemination Course	1½ wks

CHILDREN'S COURSES

Designed for children ages 8 through 12. Each is fully illustrated and teaches important skills for succeeding in school and with people. They cover a range of Scientology fundamentals but are presented at a level for young readers. Subjects dealt with include ARC, the eight dynamics, the parts of man, the Tone Scale and others. There are also children's courses which teach L. Ron Hubbard's study technology.

These courses are also delivered by field auditors, groups and missions.

They generally require 1 to 3 weeks of part-time study to complete.

AUDITING SERVICES

These are the main steps taken to advance a person all the way up to the highest states of awareness and ability. The services listed below are given in the basic sequence of progress, though individual progress may vary.
See Chapter 13 for more information.

Lower-level auditing services are most frequently delivered by field auditors, groups, missions and Class V organizations. Upper levels of auditing are delivered only in Saint Hills, Advanced Organizations, the Flag Service Organization or Flag Ship Service Organization, as designated below.

Note: When the length of time to complete a given series of actions or grades is given, these are only approximations and should be used as guidelines only. Each preclear varies in how long he takes to attain the designated result. An auditing process can take as little as minutes or as long as many, many hours over a number of sessions to achieve the end result.

■ ***Purification Rundown***

This rundown (also called Purification program) enables someone to attain freedom from the restimulative effects of drug residuals and other toxic substances.
See Chapter 9 for more information.
20 to 30 days at 5 hours per day

■ ***TRs and Objectives***

This service may be done on a co-audit basis on the TRs and Objectives Co-audit Course. Students learn auditing skills and then co-audit on processes which get the person into present time and oriented to his environment and the physical universe.
Co-audit course study is 4 days; length of auditing is two 12½-hour intensives.

■ ***Scientology Drug Rundown***

Students may co-audit this rundown by doing the Scientology Drug Rundown Co-audit Course, where they learn the technique of auditing out the harmful mental effects of drugs and then do so.
Co-audit course study is 3 days; length of auditing is one 12½-hour intensive.

■ ***Scientology Expanded Grades***

These are a series of six auditing levels which address and increase a preclear's abilities in a part of his life. The gains exceed by far anything man has had available to him previously. The amount of time it takes a preclear to move up through the Grades may vary depending on the case, but on the average is approximately a dozen 12½-hour intensives of auditing, delivered over a period of a few months. It is quite common for students training in the Academy to co-audit each other through all the Grades.

ARC Straightwire Expanded
Recall Release

Grade 0 Expanded
Communications Release

Grade I Expanded
Problems Release

Grade II Expanded
Relief Release

Grade III Expanded
Freedom Release

Grade IV Expanded
Ability Release

■ ***New Era Dianetics Auditing (NED)***

New Era Dianetics consists of over a dozen specific rundowns (a series of auditing steps designed to handle a specific aspect of a case) and actions which address the engrams contained in the reactive mind. Among these are actions which:

- Resolve any situation causing "ups and downs" in the preclear's life
- Increase the preclear's perception of and ability to control his environment
- Locate and handle any reasons the preclear began taking drugs
- Relieve trauma from losses suffered in life
- Audit out fixed computations which limit abilities and activity in life
- Resolve any difficulties with learning and education
- Alleviate a wide range of psychosomatic complaints
- Handle any disability the preclear considers he suffers from
- Enable the preclear to shed undesirable personality traits unknowingly adopted from others

These New Era Dianetics rundowns and actions are aimed at making a well and happy preclear. It can take approximately eight intensives of auditing to accomplish this, but the gains are tremendous—New Era Dianetics auditing can result in attainment of the state of Clear.
See Chapter 13 for more information.

■ ***Expanded Dianetics Auditing***

This is a specialized branch of Dianetics which directly addresses and handles heavy areas of hidden charge on a preclear's case and brings freedom from cruel impulses and chronic unwanted conditions. A person who did not attain Clear on New Era Dianetics would receive this auditing. An Expanded Dianetics program is tailored to each individual preclear's case and can take approximately six intensives of auditing.
See Chapter 13 for more information.

UPPER-LEVEL AUDITING

These are auditing levels which move a person into the highest levels of ability and freedom. Each has its own precise subject and techniques of delivery. Lengths of time to deliver any service can vary from person to person. Where any service is delivered is noted below.

■ ***Grade V***
Power Release

Grade VA
Power Plus Release

Grade VI
Whole Track Release

Clearing Course

These four services comprise an alternate route to Clear. A preclear who, upon completing New Era Dianetics and Expanded Dianetics, has not yet attained Clear, would receive auditing on Grades V and VA at a Saint Hill or higher-level organization. He would then train as a Solo auditor and do Grade VI and the Clearing Course at an Advanced Organization or the Flag Service Organization. The full alternate route to Clear takes, on an average, several months to travel.

■ ***Sunshine Rundown***

A short action done immediately after achieving the state of Clear, whether one goes Clear on New Era Dianetics or the Clearing Course. Delivered at Class V organizations or higher-level churches.

■ ***Solo Auditor Course***

This teaches full theory and practical skills of Solo auditing, necessary for anyone doing advanced auditing levels on the Bridge. This course consists of two parts: Part One, which covers all theory of Solo auditing, is delivered in Class V organizations. Part Two, which covers practical application of Solo auditing skills, is delivered only at Saint Hills, Advanced Organizations and the Flag Service Organization.

Hubbard Solo Auditor Course Part One	4	wks
Hubbard Solo Auditor Course Part Two	3	days

■ ***OT Preparations Auditing Eligibility for Issue of OT Levels Check***

Auditing actions which prepare a person to move smoothly onto the OT levels. Delivered at Saint Hills or higher-level organizations.

■ ***New OT I***
OT II
OT III—"The Wall of Fire"

After Clear, one arranges the time to Solo audit on New OT I through OT III without interruption. These services are available at an Advanced Organization or the Flag Service Organization. These three levels altogether can require several months' daily Solo auditing to complete.

■ ***New OT IV, OT Drug Rundown***

An audited level requiring 12½ to 25 hours to complete. Delivered at Advanced Organizations and the Flag Service Organization.

■ ***New OT V,***
Audited New Era Dianetics for OTs—"The Second Wall of Fire"

New OT VI,
Hubbard Solo New Era Dianetics for OTs Auditing Course

New OT VII,
Hubbard Solo New Era Dianetics for OTs Auditing

These three levels comprise the band of New Era Dianetics for OTs auditing. The first rundowns are done as an audited level, at an Advanced Organization or the Flag Service Organization. One then trains to audit New Era Dianetics for OTs Solo. New OT VII is a lengthy level, requiring a considerable amount of time to complete. One Solo audits at home daily, returning every 6 months to the Flag Service Organization for a check on one's progress. Though time in auditing stretches out quite a bit at these levels, the gains achieved are proportionately greater than those attained at lower levels.

■ ***New OT VIII, Truth Revealed***

This is the highest OT level now available. It is a Solo audited action, requiring about one month to complete. Delivered at the Flag Ship Service Organization only.

Further OT Levels to New OT XV to be released

OTHER AUDITING SERVICES

These are specialized auditing actions addressing specific aspects of the reactive mind or a person's spiritual abilities, received by preclears as directed by the Case Supervisor. Many of the actions below require about one 12½-hour intensive to complete. These services are delivered by auditors certified to deliver them.

Happiness Rundown
PTS Rundown
Method One Word Clearing
Vital Information Rundown
Repair List for Treatment from Psychiatrists, Psychologists and Psychoanalysts
Allergy or Asthma Rundown
Scientology Marriage Counseling
Student Booster Rundown
Interiorization Rundown
Est Repair Rundown
Confessionals
South African Rundown
Suppressed Person Rundown
Introspection Rundown
Handling Fear of People List
Hubbard Consultant Outpoint-Pluspoint Lists
False Purpose Rundown

FLAG SERVICE ORGANIZATION-ONLY AUDITING

These are advanced auditing rundowns requiring the most highly trained auditors. They address particular aspects of aberration or ability and people come from all over the world for the case benefits these actions bring.

The L Rundowns, as they are called, unlock some of a thetan's most powerful abilities, enabling him to operate much more effectively in any area of life. Each L Rundown requires approximately 25 hours to complete.

On the other rundowns listed below, the time estimate depends on the individual's case.

L10
L11, New Life Rundown
L12, Flag OT Executive Rundown
Cause Resurgence Rundown
Super Power
Profession Intensive
New Vitality Rundown
Knowledge Rundown
Case Cracker Rundown
Int by Dynamics Rundown
Dynamic Sort-out Assessment
Fixated Person Rundown

OTHER CHURCH SERVICES

Traditional functions delivered by churches are covered here, as well as non-audited services to help church members with specific needs. These services are delivered by all Scientology ministers.
See Chapter 15 for more information.

Sunday Church Services
Weddings
Funerals
Christenings
Chaplain's Assistance
Ethics Consultations
Word Clearing
Qual Consultation
Cramming

CHAPTER 41

SUGGESTED BOOKS, LECTURES AND VIDEOS

The best source of information on Dianetics and Scientology technology is the books and lectures of L. Ron Hubbard. This list of materials offers a path of discovery, from basic materials on the subjects to the more advanced or specialized. Some of the materials are available in public bookstores and libraries; the rest can be obtained at any of the Scientology organizations listed in Chapter 43. Many of these works have been translated into a number of different languages.

BOOKS

■ Basic information on Dianetics and its procedures

The Basic Dianetics Picture Book

Gives essential information to the new reader in abbreviated form with each principle clearly illustrated. Shows mechanisms of the reactive mind and how Dianetics auditing works.

Dianetics: The Modern Science of Mental Health

Basic text of Dianetics and the first accurate description of the human mind and Dianetics therapy. This handbook contains instructions one can apply, with no other training, and audit another on Dianetics.

The Dynamics of Life

L. Ron Hubbard's first book on his research into the mind and life. Contains several case histories of early auditing results.

Self Analysis

Over twenty auditing lists a person can use by himself to gain tremendous insight into his past. Contains a version of the Hubbard Chart of Human Evaluation and tests for reader to plot himself on the chart before and after auditing.

Dianetics: The Evolution of a Science

Traces the track of discovery which led to Dianetics breakthroughs. Details each milestone L. Ron Hubbard passed to chart the mind and develop technology to nullify engrams.

■ Books covering advanced Dianetics principles and procedures

Science of Survival

Most complete description of human behavior ever written. Built around the Hubbard Chart of Human Evaluation. Makes possible thorough prediction and understanding of human behavior.

Dianetics 55!

Full description of communication and its applications to life and auditing. L. Ron Hubbard's most complete exposition of the subject.

Notes on the Lectures of L. Ron Hubbard

Compiled from L. Ron Hubbard's lectures shortly after the publication of *Dianetics: The Modern Science of Mental Health*. Contains first descriptions of the Tone Scale and ARC triangle.

Advanced Procedure and Axioms

Advanced Dianetics principles and auditing techniques. Provides descriptions of mental phenomena discovered after publication of *Dianetics*. Appendix contains Tone Scale, Logics and Dianetics Axioms.

Handbook for Preclears

Written as an advanced personal workbook. A companion text to *Advanced Procedure and Axioms*. Contains auditing lists a person can do on his own or in conjunction with an auditor.

■ Dianetics principles and procedures to be applied to children

Child Dianetics

Explains a new approach to child rearing using Dianetics principles and technology. Contains many techniques for use with children of all ages.

■ Basic information on Scientology; the philosophy and practice of Scientology principles

The Basic Scientology Picture Book

An illustrated explanation of fundamental data of Scientology and their application to the individual in auditing. Includes the eight dynamics, the parts of man, ARC, the E-Meter, how auditing works and other basic principles.

Scientology: The Fundamentals of Thought

Basic text of Scientology. Describes many key philosophic principles and covers specific processes essential to increased ability.

A New Slant on Life

Collection of insightful writings on a wide variety of subjects including the two rules for happy living, justice, professionalism, marriage, what is greatness and over twenty others. Excellent as a broad survey of Scientology data.

Scientology 0-8: The Book of Basics

Compilation of the key knowledge of Scientology. Contains the Factors, Axioms, Logics, scales and codes of Dianetics and Scientology. Extremely useful reference work of fundamental data.

■ Advanced Scientology books, covering advanced information on Scientology principles and procedures

Scientology 8-80

Details Technique 8-80, a specialized form of Scientology, specifically, the electronics of human thought and beingness. Provides basic answers to goals of life in the physical universe.

Scientology 8-8008

Advanced explanation of techniques to rehabilitate abilities, ethics and goals. Was textbook for famous Philadelphia Doctorate Course lecture series given in late 1952. Book gives basic description of native potentials and abilities of the thetan.

The Creation of Human Ability

A manual containing over 100 auditing procedures aimed at restoring the thetan's determinism over his thoughts, decisions and actions.

■ Information on the subject of past lives

Scientology: A History of Man

Unique description of the principal events that have shaped man as he exists today. Describes common thetan experiences on the time track, explaining relationship between a thetan and his body and how electronics affect the thetan.

Have You Lived Before This Life?

First thorough account of the exploration of past lives. Dozens of case histories accurately reported which detail people's experiences with this phenomenon.

■ Books containing the full philosophic and technical data of Dianetics and Scientology

The Technical Bulletins of Dianetics and Scientology

Eighteen volumes containing all of L. Ron Hubbard's technical bulletins, articles and essays from 1950 to the present. Fully indexed. The broadest, most complete written record on the spirit, the mind and life in existence.

The Research and Discovery Series

A massive (over 100 volumes when complete) transcription and publication of all L. Ron Hubbard's recorded technical lectures and demonstrations. The only complete running record of all Mr. Hubbard's research into the mind and life. Supplemental material contained in each volume illuminates track of research and development.

■ Books covering the handling of drugs and toxins; how to rid one's body of unwanted toxins, drug residues and other harmful substances

Clear Body, Clear Mind: The Effective Purification Program

Comprehensive explanation of L. Ron Hubbard's breakthrough methodology for detoxifying the body of harmful drug residuals and other toxins. Contains all necessary data and technology to enable a person to do the entire program.

Purification: An Illustrated Answer to Drugs

Describes in picture form the harmful effects of drugs and other toxins on the body and how the Purification program eliminates these.

All About Radiation

Written in conjunction with a medical doctor, L. Ron Hubbard describes his research in the field of radiation. Explains the nature of radiation's effects on life. Provides means of preventing and counteracting these.

■ Books to improve job satisfaction and increase one's success in the workplace

The Problems of Work

Contains the fundamentals of workplace technology, such as how to handle confusions and be effective on the job. Applicable to any working environment or job.

How to Live Though an Executive

Advanced principles of administration such as how to efficiently run a company and how to handle employees, for executive use.

Organization Executive Course Volumes

Eight volumes plus an index volume which contain all L. Ron Hubbard's administrative policy. Contains the technology of groups and how to make them survive.

Management Series Volumes 1, 2 and 3

Full collection of third dynamic management technology. Contains all tools needed for successful management at any level: personnel, organizing, finance, data, targeting out group goals, management by computer, marketing, public relations and others.

■ Information on remedying difficulties with students and preclears

The Book of Case Remedies

Dozens of techniques applied to assist someone having difficulty as a student or preclear. The remedies resolve the problem and enable the person to progress again on the Bridge. Particularly valuable book for auditors, Case Supervisors or Course Supervisors.

■ Information on the subject of ethics, justice and morals

Introduction to Scientology Ethics

All fundamentals of Scientology ethics and justice systems. Includes all conditions formulas, ethics and justice codes of Scientology, application of ethics to others, and a fold-out copy of the organizing board; these are many tools to raise one's condition in life.

The Way to Happiness

A common-sense guide to better living. Written as a nonreligious moral code, it contains twenty-one precepts for successful living in a modern world. Over 40 million copies of the book have been distributed throughout the world.

■ Books of quotations from L. Ron Hubbard's writings

Understanding: The Universal Solvent

Hundreds of quotations on myriad subjects which convey the essence of Scientology.

Knowingness

A companion volume filled with hundreds of profound quotations from L. Ron Hubbard's writings.

■ E-Meter books, giving the full theory and use of the E-Meter

Understanding the E-Meter

Fully illustrated explanation of the principles and mechanics of the E-Meter. Includes photographs of every meter model ever developed.

Introducing the E-Meter

Basic book on E-Meter setup and operation. First book on E-Meter studied in Academy training.

E-Meter Essentials

Explains basics of recognition and interpretation of E-Meter reactions. Vital for correct use of the meter.

The Book of E-Meter Drills

The complete set of all drills developed by L. Ron Hubbard to train someone in proper use of the E-Meter. E-Meter training manual for auditors.

■ Books on study technology—for both children and adults

Basic Study Manual

Fundamentals of study technology for teenagers on up. Fully illustrated presentation of how to study to ensure comprehension and understanding and the ability to apply anything one studies.

Learning How to Learn
Introduction to learning for young students aged 8 to 12. Presents most basic data of study technology in fully illustrated format.

Study Skills for Life
Contains basics of study technology for young teenagers. Fully illustrated.

How to Use a Dictionary Picture Book for Children
Gives young students skills needed to use a dictionary, a vital necessity for learning. Fully illustrated.

Grammar and Communication for Children
Contains L. Ron Hubbard's breakthrough in the subject of grammar. Fully illustrated and presented for young students. Makes grammar understandable and something a person can *use* in his life.

■ Technology covering how to use basic techniques and procedures to enhance the survival of one's fellow man

The Volunteer Minister's Handbook
Full body of basic Scientology technology which anyone can read and apply to change conditions. Dozens of techniques and principles thoroughly explained to provide effective ways one can bring real help to others.

■ Ceremonial information

Ceremonies of the Church of Scientology
Contains the inspiring and beautiful church services, sermons and ceremonies.

■ Technology and know-how of art

Art
Contains all of L. Ron Hubbard's essays on art, used by artists to achieve their goals. Codifies for the first time artistic endeavors in any art form.

LECTURES

■ Lectures on personal achievement: The Personal Achievement Series

There are nearly 3,000 recorded lectures by L. Ron Hubbard on the subjects of Dianetics and Scientology. The following list presents a sampling of some of these lectures; each one is an excellent introduction to Dianetics and Scientology principles.

The Story of Dianetics and Scientology

L. Ron Hubbard shares his earliest insights into human nature and gives a compelling account of his experiences in developing Dianetics and Scientology.

The Road to Truth

Explains man's attempts to find truth and the traps and half-truths that he has fallen into on the way. Mr. Hubbard tells why this has occurred and how the road to truth can be traveled.

Scientology and Effective Knowledge

Describes why man has remained for so long at a loss for workable answers to life. Explains the relationship of observation to knowledge and reveals the key to truly knowing and understanding a subject.

The Deterioration of Liberty

Discusses three subjects—freedom, liberty, justice—important to man's survival. Analyzes how man loses his freedom and outlines the actions one can take to regain it, for himself and his fellows.

Power of Choice and Self-determinism

Man's ability to determine the course of his life depends on his ability to exercise power of choice. L. Ron Hubbard describes how one can increase the power of decision for himself and for others.

Scientology and Ability

Tells how a person becomes unable to cause things in his environment and explains workable methods which can be used to restore a person's ability and success in life.

The Hope of Man

Various men in history brought forth the idea that there was hope of improvement, but L. Ron Hubbard's discoveries in Dianetics and Scientology have made that hope a reality. Explains how Scientology has become man's one true hope for freedom.

The Dynamics

Data on the eight dynamics is covered here, including how man creates on them, what happens when a person gets stuck in just one dynamic, and how wars relate to the third dynamic.

Money

Explains what money really is and how a money system operates. Provides an understanding of how one can gain greater control over his own income and finances.

Formulas for Success—The Five Conditions

Natural laws govern the conditions of life, with exact steps to take in handling each of these conditions. Invaluable technology to help one succeed in *any* endeavor.

Health and Certainty

Explains how one's health is related to his certainty or lack of it, how false certainties can be forced on him. Shows the way to achieve certainty and improve one's condition in life.

Operation Manual for the Mind

Difficulties of trying to get along in life without knowing how the mind works are explored. Describes why man existed for thousands of years without any understanding of how his mind was supposed to operate, and how this problem has been solved in Scientology.

Miracles

Defines what a miracle is and sheds light on why they are so apparently lacking in the world today. Miracles are usually thought of as only having happened centuries ago in some distant place but this is not the case.

The Road to Perfection—The Goodness of Man

Unlike earlier practices that sought to "improve" man because he was "bad," Scientology assumes that man has good qualities that simply need to be increased. Shows how workable this assumption really is, and how one can begin to use his mind, talents and abilities to the fullest.

The Dynamic Principles of Existence

Some people seem more interested and involved in life than others, and generally have more fulfilling lives as a result. Discusses the importance of being a knowing part of and participant in any and all of the functions of life.

Man: Good or Evil?

Gives usable definitions of *good* and *evil,* and powerfully illustrates what man's basic nature really is. Man has struggled with the concepts of good and evil throughout his history. This lecture greatly illuminates them.

Differences Between Scientology and Other Studies

Oftentimes the important questions in life are the ones a person asks himself; and unlike other studies which try to force a person to accept beliefs, Scientology enables one to find his own answers. It points the way to true understanding of and belief in oneself.

The Machinery of the Mind

Gives an understanding of different mental phenomena, how these can cause a person to lose control and how one can regain power of decision and control of his life.

The Affinity-Reality-Communication Triangle

Explains how the ARC triangle works and how it can be used to resolve problems and improve personal relationships.

Increasing Efficiency

Inefficiency is a major barrier to success, but there are ways to increase one's efficiency. Provides data on how to increase one's effectiveness in life.

Man's Relentless Search

Describes what man is really searching for in life and how he can find it. His quest to find himself has repeatedly ended in failure and disappointment. With Scientology one's search no longer has to end this way.

VIDEOS

How to Use Dianetics

A succinct explanation of Dianetics principles and step-by-step instructions of how to do Dianetics auditing as taught in *Dianetics: The Modern Science of Mental Health*. The soundness of L. Ron Hubbard's theories and workability of his techniques are clearly demonstrated.

Introduction to Scientology

An hour-long interview with L. Ron Hubbard, who provides candid answers to many commonly asked questions about Scientology. The source of Scientology relates his researches into life and the development of Scientology, its fundamentals, procedures and organizations.

Chapter 42

Complete List of Books and Materials

The following pages contain a complete listing of Dianetics and Scientology books, technical and administrative issues, articles, films, recorded lectures, cassettes, E-Meters, insignia and special publications from 1948 to the present.

For ease of reference the categories of books, films and recorded lectures are noted in the listings by symbols.

BOOKS

One of the most acclaimed and widely read authors of all time, L. Ron Hubbard has sold in excess of 100 million published works throughout the world.

The books listed here include his non-fiction works on Dianetics and Scientology only.

Each entry lists title, publication date, original publisher and where first published. Where the book is a compilation of L. Ron Hubbard's works, this is also noted.

FILMS

Films are also included among Scientology materials. After doing extensive research on photography and film, Mr. Hubbard began producing films that would make it easier for students to learn the technology by actually *showing* them how to do it on film. As well as being valuable training tools, these films help to preserve the Scientology technology.

A number of films were made between 1958 and 1970. These are noted as they appeared.

In 1978, Golden Era Productions began producing a large number of new films, both technical training films for use on Scientology courses and films dealing with specific problems and concerns of society, intended for a general audience. Some of these films are still being produced—the list in this book covers only those released at the time of publication.

Each film is included by title and date of release.

RECORDED LECTURES

From 1948 on, L. Ron Hubbard delivered more than 3,000 public lectures on every aspect of the mind and life.

There are about 25,000,000 words on tape in archives which provide the consecutive path of discovery of Scientology technology. These lectures cover both Scientology philosophy and the technology of Scientology administration and auditing.

Since 1977, many of Mr. Hubbard's recorded lectures have been released to the public, as single cassettes or as cassette tape series. In order to ensure the highest quality sound on these cassettes, most have been produced using Clearsound state-of-the-art sound-reproduction technology. The project of reproducing these lectures on cassette is still in progress, and new cassettes and cassette series are being released on a regular basis to make the wealth of Dianetics and Scientology technology on tape easily accessible.

Issues and Articles

In addition to his books, Mr. Hubbard continuously released bulletins detailing technical breakthroughs as they occurred. Beginning with Dianetic Auditor's Bulletins (DABs) in 1950, and later in Professional Auditor's Bulletins (PABs), Hubbard Communications Office Bulletins (HCOBs) and other technical issues, he recorded and issued valuable advice and data on new discoveries.

Administrative breakthroughs were likewise issued immediately as policy letters for staff and public use. Various types of issues cover the administrative technology of Scientology organizations, the earliest of these being policy letters written for specific organizations such as the Hubbard Association of Scientologists International (HASI PLs) and the Founding Church of Washington, DC (FC PLs). Mr. Hubbard also recorded policy in several other forms, including LRH Executive Directives (LRH EDs), Secretarial Executive Directives (Sec EDs) and, most often, Hubbard Communications Office Policy Letters (HCO PLs).

Magazine articles provided another medium for the communication of Dianetics and Scientology technology. Magazines for Scientologists, such as the *Journal of Scientology* (JOS), *Certainty, Ability,* and *The Auditor,* often carried articles by Mr. Hubbard, as did the *Freedom* magazine put out by the Church.

Each of these individual writings has been included in the following list, along with the type of issue, the date of its original publication and date of any revision.

Insignia

Each of the insignia of Dianetics and Scientology is shown and described for the year it was adopted. The official insignia only are listed.

E-Meters

There have been a number of models of the E-Meter throughout the years of its development. Each meter is listed with its year of release.

Additional Materials

Several special categories of materials are covered, including charts and tools for auditors. Mr. Hubbard also composed music for several films, and their sound tracks are available on cassette.

Additionally, hundreds of course packs are available which accompany Dianetics and Scientology courses. These are not listed separately in this section, but each course has its own pack.

Translations

Translations of books, tapes, films and course packs are available in many languages. The translations listed are those available at time of publication. Many more translated materials and new languages are being added on a continuing basis.

1948

The first work describing the discoveries of Dianetics was written by L. Ron Hubbard in 1947, then distributed in manuscript form in 1948. This book marks the beginning of the materials of Dianetics and Scientology.

DIANETICS: THE ORIGINAL THESIS
by L. Ron Hubbard

The manuscript L. Ron Hubbard wrote detailing his Dianetics discoveries. Circulated amongst his friends, copied and passed on to others, it was first formally published in 1951 as Dianetics: The Original Thesis *and later republished as* The Dynamics of Life. TRANSLATIONS: Danish, Dutch, French, German, Italian, Norwegian, Portuguese, Spanish and Swedish.

1950

In early 1950, Mr. Hubbard published an article on Dianetics in the prestigious *Explorers Club Journal*, then went on to release *Dianetics: The Modern Science of Mental Health* in May of 1950. News of Dianetics soon spread nationwide, and he was deluged with demands for more data.

In August he lectured to a crowd of over 6,000 people at the Shrine Auditorium in Los Angeles, and within a few short months there were more than 700 groups practicing Dianetics in the US alone, led by the Hubbard Dianetic Research Foundation in Elizabeth, New Jersey and its offices in New York, Washington, DC, Chicago, Los Angeles and Hawaii.

Mr. Hubbard spent much of his time traveling across the US to lecture to the public, but he still found the time to write articles and technical bulletins describing new techniques, and to begin work on upcoming books covering his further advances in Dianetics.

ARTICLE Terra Incognita: The Mind

DIANETICS: THE EVOLUTION OF A SCIENCE
by L. Ron Hubbard

Written in early 1950, this manuscript was published first as a magazine article early in April 1950 and then as a book in September 1955 by the Hubbard Dianetics Research Foundation, Phoenix, Arizona. TRANSLATIONS: Danish, Dutch, French, German, Greek, Italian, Japanese, Spanish and Swedish.

DIANETICS: THE MODERN SCIENCE OF MENTAL HEALTH
by L. Ron Hubbard

Written in early 1950 in Bay Head, New Jersey and published by Hermitage House, New York, New York, May 9, 1950. TRANSLATIONS: Chinese, Danish, Dutch, Finnish, French, German, Greek, Italian, Japanese, Hebrew, Hungarian, Norwegian, Portuguese, Russian, Serbo-Croatian, Spanish, Swedish, Swahili and Taiwanese.

ARTICLE The Aims of the Hubbard Dianetic Research Foundation

SESSIONS AND DEMONSTRATIONS
ELIZABETH, NEW JERSEY

Following the publication of *Dianetics: The Modern Science of Mental Health*, the first Hubbard Dianetic Research Foundation was formed by a group of Dianeticists in Elizabeth, New Jersey. LRH lectured to staff and students at the Foundation, and recorded many of the auditing sessions he gave.

- 7 Jun Bringing Preclear to Present Time
- 7 Jun Auditing Toward Clear
- 7 Jun Repairing Past Auditing
- 8 Jun Auditing a Chronic Somatic
- 8 Jun LRH Auditing Demonstration
- 9 Jun LRH Auditing Demonstration

SATURDAY COURSE LECTURES
ELIZABETH, NEW JERSEY

- 10 Jun Dianetics: First Lecture of Saturday Course
- 10 Jun LRH Auditing Demonstration
- 17 Jun Recognizing Contact of Engram
- 17 Jun The Somatic Strip
- 24 Jun Running Out Birth
- 1 Jul Address of Auditor to Preclear
- 8 Jul How to Become an Auditor in One Easy Lesson
- 15 Jul Erasures
- 22 Jul Running Former Lives
- 22 Jul The Anatomy of the Demon Circuit
- 22 Jul Finding Dramatizations

MONDAY-WEDNESDAY-FRIDAY COURSE LECTURES
ELIZABETH, NEW JERSEY

- 12 Jun The Conduct of an Auditor
- 12 Jun Diagnosis
- 12 Jun LRH Auditing Demonstration
- 14 Jun Diagnostic Procedure
- 21 Jun A Talk with Two Co-auditing Teams
- 26 Jun Hypnosis
- 28 Jun Conception
- 5 Jul Application of Procedure
- 7 Jul Review of Material
- 7 Jul Operation of Valences and Demon Circuits
- 10 Jul A Summary of Standard Procedure
- 14 Jul Things an Auditor Must Not Do
- 14 Jul The Tone Scale in Action
- 17 Jul Derivation of Laws—Part I
- 17 Jul Derivation of Laws—Part II
- 19 Jul The Part Played by the Analytical Mind
- 21 Jul Manifestations Which Assist the Auditor
- 24 Jul Diagnosis Data
- 2 Aug The Importance of Getting Engrams
- 4 Aug Relation of Affinity, Communication and Reality

PROFESSIONAL COURSE LECTURES
ELIZABETH, NEW JERSEY

- 15 Jun Sound and Aberration
- 15 Jun Clears in This Society
- 15 Jun Case Factors
- 16 Jun LRH Auditing Demonstration
- 16 Jun Memory and Diagnosis
- 19 Jun Auditing an Illness Chain
- 19 Jun Handling of Cases
- 19 Jun The 15-Minute Assist
- 19 Jun LRH Auditing Demonstration
- 20 Jun Valences
- 20 Jun Analytical Mind
- 21 Jun Engrams
- 23 Jun Institutional Dianetics
- 26 Jun Demon Circuits
- 26 Jun Testing for the Right Engram
- 27 Jun Birth
- 27 Jun Sense of Reality
- 28 Jun Reduction of Engrams
- 29 Jun Research and Discovery
- 3 Jul Entering a Case
- 3 Jul Demonstration of Handling a Case
- 4 Jul Handling Somatics
- 4 Jul How to Do a Diagnosis
- 5 Jul Types of Cases
- 5 Jul The File Clerk and Valence Shifters
- 6 Jul Vicissitudes of the Preclear
- 8 Jul About Psychotics
- 10 Jul Getting a Case Rolling
- 11 Jul Standard Procedure and Accessibility
- 12 Jul Review of Standard Procedure
- 13 Jul Auditor's Skill—Part I
- 13 Jul Auditor's Skill—Part II
- 14 Jul Conception: The Sperm Sequence
- 14 Jul Circuitry
- 15 Jul Processing Children

In addition to giving lectures to students, Mr. Hubbard started writing bulletins which were distributed to auditors who were practicing Dianetics, to warn them of common errors and to impart new developments in the technology.

ISSUES

PRECAUTIONARY BULLETIN NO. 1	1 Jul	Auditor's Code—Breaking Of
PRECAUTIONARY BULLETIN NO. 2	1 Jul	Insanity "Caused by" Dianetics
RESEARCH BULLETIN NO. 2	1 Jul	Stuck on the Time Track
RESEARCH BULLETIN NO. 3	1 Jul	Sperm Sequence as Basic-Basic
DAB VOL. 1, NOS. 1–2	Jul–Aug	Standard Procedure

PUBLIC AND PROFESSIONAL COURSE LECTURES
LOS ANGELES, CALIFORNIA

Following an introductory lecture to over 6,000 people at Los Angeles' Shrine Auditorium, Mr. Hubbard gave a series of lectures and demonstrations at the Los Angeles department of the Hubbard Dianetic Research Foundation.

- 10 Aug Introducing Dianetics—Shrine Auditorium
- 15 Aug The Anatomy of the Engram
- 16 Aug Affinity, Reality, Communication
- 17 Aug Straightwire
- 18 Aug Denyers, Bouncers, Holders
- 18 Aug The Guk Formula
- 21 Aug Taking Inventory, SOP Step One
- 22 Aug Demonstration of Getting a Case Moving
- 22 Aug Opening the Case, SOP Step Two
- 23 Aug The Tools of the Trade
- 24 Aug Checking Perceptics
- 24 Aug Running Engrams, SOP Step Two
- 25 Aug Removing Demon Circuits and Valence Commands, SOP Step Three
- 25 Aug Paralleling the Mind
- 28 Aug Analytical Mind
- 28 Aug Spectrum from Psychosis to Clear
- 29 Aug Educational Dianetics
- 30 Aug Preventive Dianetics
- 30 Aug The Professional Auditor
- 31 Aug General Discussion of Auditing
- 31 Aug Medical Dianetics
- 31 Aug Demonstration of Running Down a Chain
- 1 Sep Child Dianetics
- 1 Sep Guk vs. Drugs: Effects in Auditing
- 1 Sep Auditing a Blind Preclear
- 4 Sep Advertising Dianetics—Propaganda—Push Buttons
- 5 Sep Political Dianetics
- 6 Sep Aesthetics
- 7 Sep Language Adjustment
- 7 Sep Valences and Valence Shifters
- 8 Sep The Complete Auditor

Issue

DAB VOL. 1, NO. 3 Sep How to Release a Chronic Somatic

Oakland Public Lecture Series
OAKLAND, CALIFORNIA

Traveling from Los Angeles to Oakland, Mr. Hubbard delivered the following series of lectures and demonstrations at the Oakland Municipal Auditorium. *(Four of these lectures are available on cassette in a series entitled, "Original Lectures and Demonstrations on Dianetics.")*

23 Sep Further Introduction to Dianetics
23 Sep What Dianetics Can Do
26 Sep Auditor's Code
26 Sep Demonstration of Procedure
26 Sep Standard Procedure Chart
27 Sep Demonstration
27 Sep Different Types of Cases
28 Sep How to Resolve Stalled Cases
28 Sep Running an Engram
29 Sep Guk and Freewheeling
29 Sep Running a Secondary

Article Oct The Analytical Mind

Issue

DAB VOL. 1, NO. 4 Oct Dianetics and Religion

Kansas City Lectures
KANSAS CITY, MISSOURI

From Oakland, Mr. Hubbard traveled to Kansas City, where he gave these public lectures.

21 Oct Introduction to Dianetics
25 Oct Clarification of Operation
25 Oct Demonstration
26 Oct Types of Cases and Methods of Resolving Them
26 Oct Demonstration
27 Oct Demonstration
27 Oct Restarting Stalled Cases
28 Oct Demonstration
28 Oct Improved Techniques

Issues

DESPATCH 1 Nov The Intensive Processing Procedure
DAB VOL. 1, NO. 5 Nov The Processing of Children

Professional Course Lectures
ELIZABETH, NEW JERSEY

Returning from Kansas City to his home in New Jersey, Mr. Hubbard brought the students and staff of the Foundation up to date on his latest discoveries and advancements in Dianetic techniques.

2 Nov Starting Off a New Preclear
4 Nov ARC and the Tone Scale
4 Nov Use of ARC in Auditing
7 Nov Practical Auditing
7 Nov The Art of Processing
8 Nov Child Dianetics—Part I
8 Nov Child Dianetics—Part II
9 Nov Group Dianetics
10 Nov Handling Psychotics
11 Nov Education and Dianetics
11 Nov Axioms and Fundamentals About Data
15 Nov Demonstration Research

Issue

ORGANIZATIONAL MEMORANDUM 16 Nov An Addition to Standard Procedure

Professional Course Lectures
LOS ANGELES, CALIFORNIA

After delivering the Professional Course in New Jersey at the beginning of November, Mr. Hubbard traversed the continent again to bring his newest developments to Los Angeles area Dianeticists.

20 Nov Thought, Life and the Material Universe
21 Nov Spectrums of Logic and Emotion
21 Nov Tone Scales of Affinity, Reality and Communication
22 Nov The Auditor's Code
22 Nov Accessibility
24 Nov The Accessibility Chart
24 Nov Opening the Case
25 Nov ARC and the Dynamics
25 Nov Running Standard Procedure
25 Nov The Anatomy of Circuitry
27 Nov Handling Chronic Somatics
27 Nov Handling the Stuck Case
27 Nov Straight Memory
27 Nov Tone Scales
28 Nov Valences and Demon Circuits—Part I
29 Nov Valences and Demon Circuits—Part II
29 Nov A New Straightwire Technique
30 Nov Questions and Answers
1 Dec Rudimentary Data on Groups
1 Dec Groups

Issues

HCO PL 24 Nov Instruction Protocol, Official
DAB VOL. 1, NO. 6 Dec Handling the Psychotic
DESPATCH 12 Dec Certification Board Duties and Responsibilities

Los Angeles Lectures
LOS ANGELES, CALIFORNIA

After delivering the Professional Course, Mr. Hubbard remained in Los Angeles to do further research, where he delivered these two lectures on Chain Scanning—a new technique which was still under development at the time.

19 Dec Chain Scanning
19 Dec Demonstration of Lock Scanning

1951

Early in 1951 Mr. Hubbard was in Palm Springs, California, compiling the Hubbard Chart of Human Evaluation. In the late spring, he traveled to pre-Communist Cuba, where he dictated the book *Science of Survival.*

By this time a Dianetics Foundation had formed in Wichita, Kansas, and in June Mr. Hubbard lectured there to over 100 auditors attending the First Annual Conference of Dianetics Auditors.

He spent much of the rest of the year giving lectures, doing research and writing up what he had found into books, issues and articles.

Notes on the Lectures of L. Ron Hubbard

Detailed notes and diagrams of Mr. Hubbard's November 1950 lectures in Los Angeles, made by staff of the Hubbard Dianetic Research Foundation; assembled and published at Mr. Hubbard's request so that they would be available for training purposes. Published by the Hubbard Dianetic Foundation, Inc., Wichita, Kansas, 1951.

Article Jan Dianometry, Your Ability and State of Mind

Issue

DAB VOL. 1, NO. 7 Jan Group Dianetics

The Dianetics Symbol

The Greek letter* delta *is the basic form. The dark stripes are green, which stands for growth. The light stripes are yellow, for life.

The four green stripes represent the four dynamics described in* Dianetics: *the urge to survive as self, family, group and mankind.

This symbol was designed in 1950 and has been in use ever since.

Mathison Model B Electropsychometer

Volney Mathison presented L. Ron Hubbard with the first electropsychometer (or E-Meter) in 1951, the Model B. It was used for research throughout 1951.

ELIZABETH LECTURES
ELIZABETH, NEW JERSEY

Taking a short break from his intensive work on the Chart of Human Evaluation, LRH traveled from Palm Springs, California to Elizabeth, New Jersey to brief auditors there on new techniques.

17 Jan The Third Dynamic
18 Jan Gradients of Accessibility
18 Jan Hurdy-Gurdy Straightwire and Haywire

ARTICLE Jan Diagnosis and Repair of Groups

ISSUES

CODE Jan The Credo of a True Group Member
CODE Jan The Credo of a Good and Skilled Manager
DAB VOL. 1, NO. 8 Feb The Theory of Affinity, Reality and Communication

RADIO BROADCAST LECTURES

The following series of fifteen-minute talks was recorded and broadcast over a network of 126 radio stations across the US.

7 Feb How to Straighten Out a Group
8 Feb Dianetics
9 Feb Valences and Straight Memory
12 Feb Grief and Valences
13 Feb Husbands and Wives Auditing Each Other
14 Feb Communication Breaks
15 Feb The Tone Scale of Groups and Nations

ISSUES

DAB VOL. 1, NO. 9 Mar The Problem of Sedation

DAB VOL. 1, NOS. 10–11 Apr–May Lock Scanning

RECORDED MESSAGE

This recorded address was sent by Mr. Hubbard from Wichita, Kansas to be played for those attending the New York Dianetic Association's First Anniversary of Dianetics celebration.

15 May Ron's May 15 Message

PROFESSIONAL COURSE LECTURES
WICHITA, KANSAS

After completing his latest book, *Science of Survival,* Mr. Hubbard lectured to Professional Course students at the Hubbard Dianetic Foundation in Wichita, Kansas, on the theory and procedures detailed in the book. *(To be released on cassette.)*

21 May Theta–MEST Theory
21 May The Tone Scale and Human Evaluation
4 Jun All Possible Aberrations
12 Jun Theory Behind Theta and MEST
12 Jun The Tone Scale in Life and Processing
12 Jun Demonstration: Validating Theta

ISSUE

DAB VOL. 1, NO. 12 Jun Preventive Dianetics

SCIENCE OF SURVIVAL: SIMPLIFIED, FASTER DIANETIC TECHNIQUES
by L. Ron Hubbard

This book was released as a limited manuscript edition on June 25–28, 1951 at the First Annual Conference of Hubbard Dianetic Auditors in Wichita, Kansas. The hardcover edition was published in August 1951 by the Hubbard Dianetic Foundation. The title was later changed to Science of Survival: Prediction of Human Behavior. *Included in each edition of* Science of Survival *is the Hubbard Chart of Human Evaluation.*
TRANSLATIONS: German and Italian.

FIRST ANNUAL CONFERENCE OF HUBBARD DIANETIC AUDITORS
WICHITA, KANSAS

L. Ron Hubbard gave attendees at the First Annual Conference of Hubbard Dianetic Auditors lectures centered on the latest advances in Dianetics, as covered in his book *Science of Survival. (To be released on cassette.)*

25 Jun New Techniques
25 Jun Human Evaluation
25 Jun Review of the Theta–MEST Theory
25 Jun Goals of Theta and MEST
25 Jun Aberration and the Dynamics
26 Jun Chart of Human Evaluation—Part I
26 Jun Chart of Human Evaluation—Part II
26 Jun New Viewpoint on Processing
27 Jun Civil Defense
27 Jun Validation Processing
27 Jun Demonstration Auditing
27 Jun Uses of Validation Processing
27 Jun Demonstration of Validation Processing
28 Jun The Complete Auditor—Part I
28 Jun The Complete Auditor—Part II
30 Jun MEST Straightwire

ISSUES

DAB VOL. 2, NO. 1 Jul Education and the Auditor
DAB VOL. 2, NO. 1 Jul Aberrations and Genius

ARTICLE Teaching

PROFESSIONAL COURSE LECTURES
WICHITA, KANSAS

For a period of five weeks Mr. Hubbard gave lectures each Monday afternoon to students at the Hubbard Dianetic Foundation in Wichita, covering auditing basics as well as his latest discoveries and refinements of procedure. *(To be released on cassette.)*

9 Jul Review of Validation Processing
9 Jul Extroversion
9 Jul MEST Processing
16 Jul Some Educational Data
16 Jul Being a Friend to the Preclear
16 Jul More on MEST Processing
23 Jul Basic Processing
30 Jul Basic Reason—Part I
30 Jul Basic Reason—Part II
30 Jul Perceptics
6 Aug Survival and the Human Mind
6 Aug Survival Processing

SELF ANALYSIS
by L. Ron Hubbard

Published by the International Library of Arts and Sciences, Wichita, Kansas, August 1951. Contains a simplified version of the Hubbard

MATHISON PROJECTION METER MODEL A

Also in 1951 the first projection meter was built, the Model A. This E-Meter was useful in the instruction of auditors because it was designed to project an image of the meter, allowing students to see needle reactions while LRH demonstrated auditing techniques.

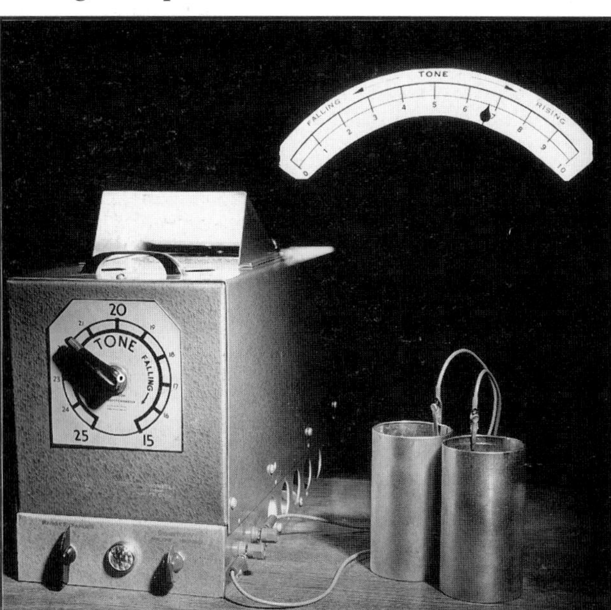

Chart of Human Evaluation.
TRANSLATIONS: Danish, Dutch, French, German, Italian, Japanese, Spanish and Swedish.

SPECIAL COURSE IN HUMAN EVALUATION
WICHITA, KANSAS

This series of lectures on human evaluation and its application in business, politics and domestic activities was given to a group of Wichita businessmen. *(Available on cassette.)*

13 Aug The Purpose of Human Evaluation
13 Aug The Dynamics of Existence
14 Aug Conquest of the Physical Universe
14 Aug Personality
15 Aug Self Analysis
15 Aug The Tone Scale
16 Aug Motion and Emotion
17 Aug Motion and the Tone Scale
17 Aug The ARC Triangle

ISSUES

LETTER 15 Aug "Dear HDA; . . ."
DAB VOL. 2, NO. 2 Aug An Essay on Management
DAB VOL. 2, NO. 2 Aug How to Pick Up Occluded Data
DAB VOL. 2, NO. 2 Aug The "26" Perceptics
DAB VOL. 2, NO. 3 Sep Basic Reason—Basic Principles
SUPPLEMENT NO. 1 TO *SCIENCE OF SURVIVAL* Sep All Possible Aberrations
SUPPLEMENT NO. 2 TO *SCIENCE OF SURVIVAL* Sep Validation Processing

PROFESSIONAL COURSE LECTURES
WICHITA, KANSAS

In lectures to students attending the Professional Course at Wichita, Mr. Hubbard discussed a variety of subjects including a new auditing technique known as Effort Processing. This powerful procedure addressed the effects of time, motion and directed effort on an individual. *(To be released on cassette.)*

20 Aug Motion and Effort—Part I
20 Aug Motion and Effort—Part II
27 Aug Motion and Emotion in Processing
27 Aug Line Charge
4 Sep Time and Motion
4 Sep Illusion
10 Sep Mimicry
10 Sep Arithmetic
10 Sep Theta Facsimiles
17 Sep Some Notes on Black Dianetics
17 Sep The Cellular Postulate
20 Sep Self-Determined Effort Processing
20 Sep Tactile Communication
20 Sep Randomity and Effort
20 Sep Auditing and Nutrition
24 Sep Effort Processing Fundamentals—Part I
24 Sep Effort Processing Fundamentals—Part II
1 Oct Self-Determined Effort Processing
1 Oct Progress of Dianetics Research
1 Oct Standard Procedure
1 Oct Group Processing Demonstration

THE OCTOBER CONFERENCE
WICHITA, KANSAS

This series of lectures was given to more than fifty auditors from all over the country gathered for a conference in Wichita. *(To be released on cassette.)*

8 Oct Axioms and Effort Processing
8 Oct The Logics
9 Oct Statics and Motions
9 Oct Axioms 1–14
9 Oct Effort Processing Summary
10 Oct Axioms 14–32
10 Oct Theory of Epicenters
11 Oct Axioms 33–49
11 Oct Epicenters and Self-Determinism
12 Oct Randomity and Emotion
12 Oct Effort in Engrams
12 Oct Conclusion Processing

THE DIANETICS AXIOMS
by L. Ron Hubbard

Published by Hubbard Dianetic Foundation, Wichita, Kansas, October 1951. This book was issued during the October Conference and was the first release of the Axioms of Dianetics. The Dianetics Axioms are now available in the books Advanced Procedure and Axioms, Handbook for Preclears *and* Scientology 0-8 *by L. Ron Hubbard.*

PROFESSIONAL COURSE LECTURES
WICHITA, KANSAS

While continuing his research and auditing through 1951, Mr. Hubbard also took time to lecture to students attending the Professional Auditor Course, staff auditors at the Wichita Foundation and conference attendees. *(To be released on cassette.)*

15 Oct ARC and Effort Processing
15 Oct Postulate Processing
22 Oct Clearing the Human Mind as an Electronic Computer

CHILD DIANETICS, DIANETIC PROCESSING FOR CHILDREN
by L. Ron Hubbard

Compiled from the research and lecture materials of L. Ron Hubbard by the staff of the Hubbard Dianetic Foundation of Los Angeles, California and published in Wichita, Kansas by the International Library of Arts and Sciences, October 1951. L. Ron Hubbard wrote the introduction in August 1951, about the same time as the book was actually typeset.
TRANSLATIONS: German, Italian and Spanish.

ISSUE

DAB VOL. 2, NO. 4 Oct Self-Determined Effort Processing

THE FOUNDATION AUDITOR'S COURSE
WICHITA, KANSAS

(To be released on cassette.)

23 Oct Methods of Processing
23 Oct Self-Determinism on the Dynamics
24 Oct Being Right
24 Oct Introduction to the Service Facsimile
25 Oct The Service Facsimile—Part I
25 Oct The Service Facsimile—Part II
26 Oct The Evolution of Man According to Theta Facsimiles
26 Oct How to Talk About Dianetics
29 Oct The Theta Facsimile—Part I
29 Oct The Theta Facsimile—Part II
29 Oct Learning

PROFESSIONAL COURSE LECTURES
WICHITA, KANSAS

(To be released on cassette.)

5 Nov Postulates and Emotion
5 Nov Love
12 Nov Basic Postulates
12 Nov Prime Thought
19 Nov Cause and Effect—Part I
19 Nov Cause and Effect—Part II
26 Nov An Analysis of Memory—Part I
26 Nov An Analysis of Memory—Part II
3 Dec Advanced Procedure
3 Dec Cause and Effect: Full Responsibility
10 Dec Dead Men's Goals—Part I
10 Dec Dead Men's Goals—Part II
17 Dec Seriousness and Approval
17 Dec Counter-Effort, Counter-Emotion and Counter-Thought

ADVANCED PROCEDURE AND AXIOMS
by L. Ron Hubbard

First published by the Hubbard Dianetic Foundation in Wichita, Kansas in November 1951. It was written as a companion book to Handbook for Preclears *which was published in December 1951.*

ISSUES

DAB VOL. 2, NO. 5 Nov An Essay on Authoritarianism
DAB VOL. 2, NO. 5 Nov A Brief History of Psychotherapy
SUPPLEMENT NO. 3 TO *SCIENCE OF SURVIVAL* MEST Processing
DAB VOL. 2, NO. 6 Dec Postulate Processing

HANDBOOK FOR PRECLEARS
by L. Ron Hubbard

This was the main theme of the Second Annual Conference of Hubbard Dianetic Auditors at which it was introduced. Published in December 1951 at Wichita, Kansas. It was later republished by Scientific Press in Phoenix, Arizona, under the title of Scientology Handbook for Preclears. *It contains the Hubbard Chart of Attitudes.*

ARTICLE Dec Suggested Method of Handling Handbook

SECOND ANNUAL CONFERENCE OF HUBBARD DIANETIC AUDITORS
WICHITA, KANSAS

The main theme of this conference was the new book *Handbook for Preclears,* which had recently been written and released, containing the Hubbard Chart of Attitudes. *(To be released on cassette.)*

27 Dec Miracles in Dianetics
27 Dec Counter-Emotion
28 Dec The Chart of Attitudes
28 Dec The Life-Continuum Theory
29 Dec The Emotional Curve
29 Dec The Goal of Processing: The Ideal State of Man
29 Dec Cause on All Dynamics
29 Dec Handbook for Preclears
30 Dec Effort Processing and the Life Continuum
30 Dec Yes, No and Maybe
31 Dec Forecast on New Techniques
31 Dec Auditing the Life Continuum
31 Dec Informal Discussion with Ron

1952

In 1952 LRH made spectacular new discoveries concerning man, his mind and his true spiritual nature. He had earlier discovered mental image pictures, and had been studying their characteristics and behavior: the reactive, stimulus-response mechanisms that

psychology itself had been familiar with, but never had analyzed.

Now he found out *what* was looking at the pictures. And described it. And found out that you could do things with it from a very practical standpoint that nobody had ever done before.

Exteriorization and exteriorization processes, the first E-Meter, formation of the Hubbard College and the Hubbard Association of Scientologists were only a few of Mr. Hubbard's activities in 1952.

ARTICLES

ARTICLE My Going Away Present
ARTICLE A Story

THE AUDITOR'S MANUAL

Staff written and edited. Published by the Hubbard Dianetic Foundation, Inc., Wichita, Kansas, 1952.

In addition to research, writing and administrative work, Mr. Hubbard responded to continuing demands with a full schedule of lectures and demonstrations to Professional Course students, Foundation staff and the general public.

PROFESSIONAL COURSE LECTURES
WICHITA, KANSAS

(To be released on cassette.)

7 Jan Survival
7 Jan Questions and Answers
11 Jan Service Facsimiles
11 Jan Past Life Auditing: Effort Processing
13 Jan Running Regret and the Emotional Curve
14 Jan The Impact of Dianetics on Society
14 Jan The Emotional Curve
16 Jan Running the Service Facsimile Chain
17 Jan Effort Processing: Intentions and Overt Acts
21 Jan The Anatomy of the Overt Act—Part I
21 Jan The Anatomy of the Overt Act—Part II
28 Jan The Anatomy of a Service Facsimile
2 Feb The Psychogalvanometer
2 Feb Mysticism

PUBLIC LECTURES
WICHITA, KANSAS

6 Feb Dianetics: The Modern Miracle
8 Feb Summary of the Service Facsimile Chain

HUBBARD COLLEGE LECTURES
WICHITA, KANSAS

(To be released on cassette.)

18 Feb Freedom
18 Feb The Code of Honor
18 Feb "Care of the Body"

SUMMARY COURSE LECTURES
WICHITA, KANSAS

(To be released on cassette.)

25 Feb Review of Progress of Dianetics and Dianetics Business
25 Feb Summary of Aberrative Incidents
3 Mar Scientology: Milestone One
3 Mar Outline of Therapy
3 Mar Demonstration of E-Meter
4 Mar Axioms and How They Apply to Auditing
4 Mar Thought, Emotion and Effort
4 Mar Discovery of Facsimile One
5 Mar Auditing Facsimile One
5 Mar Thought and Preclears
5 Mar Emotion
5 Mar Whole Track Facsimiles
6 Mar Effort and Counter-Effort
6 Mar Attack on the Preclear
7 Mar Facsimiles: How to Handle Recordings
7 Mar Indoctrination of the Preclear
8 Mar Effort and Counter-Effort: Overt Acts
8 Mar Indoctrination in the Use of the E-Meter
9 Mar Thought, Emotion, Effort and the Overt Act
9 Mar Training Auditors
9 Mar Demonstration: Metered Straightwire and Overt Act
10 Mar Organization of Data
10 Mar Theta Lines
10 Mar History of the Theta Line
10 Mar Principal Incidents on the Theta Line
10 Mar Running Effort and Counter-Effort

(The last four lectures of this course are available on cassette in a series entitled "The Time Track of Theta: More on the History of Man.")

ISSUES

DESPATCH 24 Jan "To the Students: . . ."
DAB VOL. 2, NO. 8 Feb Cause and Effect
SUPPLEMENT NO. 4 TO *SCIENCE OF SURVIVAL* Feb Effort Processing

ARTICLE Feb Processing of Auditors

SCIENTOLOGY AND DIANETICS ADVANCED PROCEDURES

Notes and transcripts on lectures by L. Ron Hubbard and others, Wichita, Kansas, January through March 1952. Compiled and published by the Central Pennsylvania Dianetics Group, Middletown, Pennsylvania.

PROLOGUE TO SURVIVAL, PART I, II AND III

Published by the Psychological Research Foundation, Inc., Phoenix, Arizona, March 1952. Based on the works of L. Ron Hubbard.

After moving his office from Wichita to Phoenix, Arizona, Mr. Hubbard resumed lecturing, covering his startling new discoveries and their application to improve people's awareness and abilities.

LECTURES
PHOENIX, ARIZONA

(To be released on cassette.)

15 Apr The Success of Dianetics
15 Apr Theta Bodies
16 Apr Anatomy of the Theta Body
16 Apr How to Audit a Theta Line
16 Apr How to Search for Incidents—Part I
16 Apr How to Search for Incidents—Part II
16 Apr Theta Body Demonstration

TECHNIQUE 80 LECTURES
PHOENIX, ARIZONA

(Available on cassette as a series entitled "The Route to Infinity.")

19 May Beingness
19 May Outline of Technique 80
19 May Wavelengths of ARC
20 May Decision
20 May Decision: Cause and Effect
21 May Therapy Section of Technique 80—Part I
21 May Therapy Section of Technique 80—Part II

ARTICLE 21 May Dianetics Jingles

SUMMER SESSION TECHNIQUE 88 LECTURES
PHOENIX, ARIZONA

(To be released on cassette.)

23 Jun Introduction
23 Jun Zero and Infinity
23 Jun Time
23 Jun Obsession
24 Jun Attention Unit Flows
24 Jun Attention Unit Running
24 Jun Concept Running
25 Jun Invalidation
25 Jun Overt Acts, Motivators and DEDS
26 Jun The Actions of Energy
26 Jun Technique 88 and the Whole Track—Part I
26 Jun Technique 88 and the Whole Track—Part II
27 Jun Confusions
27 Jun Acquisition of Bodies
27 Jun Theta and Genetic Lines
28 Jun Questions and Answers

MANUAL Jun Electropsychometric Auditing, Operator's Manual

INDIVIDUAL TRACK MAP
by L. Ron Hubbard

Published by the Office of L. Ron Hubbard, Phoenix, Arizona, June 1952. (The text of this book is printed in full in the Technical Bulletins *volumes.) New updated edition for use on New Era Dianetics was published in 1988.*

A KEY TO THE UNCONSCIOUS—SYMBOLOGICAL PROCESSING
by L. Ron Hubbard

Published by the Scientific Press, Phoenix, Arizona, June 1952. (The text of this book is printed in full in the Technical Bulletins *volumes.)*

TECHNIQUE 88 SUPPLEMENTARY LECTURES
PHOENIX, ARIZONA

(To be released on cassette.)

24 Jul Behavior of Energy as It Applies to Thought Flows
7 Aug Straightwire 88
7 Aug A Straightwire Process—Lecture I
7 Aug A Straightwire Process—Lecture II
28 Aug Ridge Running
28 Aug Talk to Associates about Fellowships, etc.

HEALTH AND HAPPINESS

Published by the Psychological Research Foundation, Inc., Phoenix, Arizona, 1952. Based on the works of L. Ron Hubbard.

WHAT TO AUDIT
by L. Ron Hubbard

Published in Phoenix, Arizona by the Scientific Press, July 1952. The same text was issued as History of Man *in London in July 1952.*

HISTORY OF MAN
by L. Ron Hubbard

Published by the Hubbard Association of Scientologists, London, July 1952. It contained the same text as in What to Audit. *A later edition was entitled* Scientology: A History of Man, *which is its current title. TRANSLATIONS:* French, German and Italian.

ARTICLE Jul A Step-by-Step Breakdown of 88

ISSUES

JOS Aug ISSUE 1-G	What Is Scientology?
JOS Aug ISSUE 1-G	Electronics Gives Life to Freud's Theory
JOS Aug ISSUE 1-G	The Handling of Arthritis
JOS Sep ISSUE 2-G	The Running of Concepts

THE PROFESSIONAL COURSE LECTURE SUMMARY
(also known as *Professional Course Booklets)*

Compiled and rewritten from transcripts of lectures given by L. Ron Hubbard during the spring and summer of 1952. This set comprised a list of 50 booklets. The first 27 booklets were originally entitled the Summary Course Booklets, *published by the Scientific Press, Phoenix, Arizona, March 1952. In May of 1952,* Professional Course Booklets *28 through 31 were published by the Scientific Press, Phoenix, Arizona. The balance of the* Professional Course Booklets *were issued throughout June, July and August 1952, published by the Hubbard Association of Scientologists, Inc., Phoenix, Arizona.*

SCIENTOLOGY: 88
by L. Ron Hubbard

A unique limited edition, handwritten by L. Ron Hubbard and printed on special lithographic plates. Distributed by the Hubbard Association of Scientologists, Phoenix, Arizona, September 1952. The technology from Scientology: 88 *can be found in* Scientology 8-80.

In September Mr. Hubbard flew to London, England, where he immediately began training auditors, writing a new book, establishing a new organization and launching several research projects. His agenda included several series of lectures to staff and students.

TECHNIQUE 88 SUPPLEMENTARY LECTURES
LONDON, ENGLAND

(To be released on cassette.)

21 Sep	Basis of Scientology—Stuck Flows
21 Sep	Lecture 101—London
22 Sep	Scientology—Flows, Tone Scale
23 Sep	The Resolution of the Second Dynamic Case Level V
23 Sep	Blanketing—Exteriorization
24 Sep	Scientology—The Three Types of Energy Flows

STANDARD OPERATING PROCEDURES FOR THETA CLEARING LECTURES
LONDON, ENGLAND

(To be released on cassette.)

Oct	Present Time Use of Energy Manifestations
Oct	Theory of Flows—Counter-Elasticity
Oct	Flows
Oct	Basic Summary on SOP of Technique 8-80
Oct	Phenomena of the Thetan
Oct	Service Facsimile Chain
30 Oct	The Role of Earth
30 Oct	Illusion Processing and Therapy

ARTICLES

JOS Sep ISSUE 3-G	Danger: Black Dianetics!
JOS Oct ISSUE 4-G	The Loophole in Guarded Rights
JOS Oct ISSUE 4-G	"Being Cause" Is Society's Major Aberration
JOS Oct ISSUE 5-G	Records of Mind Are Permanent

SELF ANALYSIS IN DIANETICS—A HANDBOOK OF DIANETIC THERAPY
by L. Ron Hubbard

Published in London, England by Derricke Ridgeway Ltd., October 1952. This was a revised edition of the original Self Analysis *and is now out of print—the original version was reinstated and is the book which is used today.*

ARTICLES

JOS Nov ISSUE 6-G	Procedures for Theta Clearing
JOS Nov ISSUE 6-G	E-Meter Is Precision Instrument When Used Skillfully by Auditor

SCIENTOLOGY 8-80
by L. Ron Hubbard

Published by the Hubbard Association of Scientologists, Phoenix, Arizona, November 1952. TRANSLATIONS: French.

LONDON LECTURES
LONDON, ENGLAND

(Available on cassette as a series entitled "Secrets of the MEST Universe.")

6 Nov	Methods of Research—The Thetan as an Energy Unit
7 Nov	Force as *Homo sapiens* and as Thetan—Responsibility
14 Nov	Be, Have and Do, Part I
14 Nov	Be, Have and Do, Part II
16 Nov	Self-Determinism and Creation of Universes

LOGICS AND AXIOMS LECTURES
LONDON, ENGLAND

(Available on cassette as a series entitled "The Perception of Truth.")

10 Nov	Introduction: The Q List and Beginning of Logics
10 Nov	Logics 1–7
12 Nov	Precision Knowledge: Necessity to Know Technology and Law
12 Nov	Logics 7–9 and 10–23

LONDON PROFESSIONAL COURSE LECTURES
LONDON, ENGLAND

(To be released on cassette.)

10 Nov	Introduction to the Course—Definitions of Dianetics and Scientology, Other Philosophies
12 Nov	8-8008 Continued, Time and Space
14 Nov	Time, Create, Destroy, Have
14 Nov	Standard Operating Procedure Issue 2, Steps 7, 6 and 5
14 Nov	SOP Issue 2, Step 5 (cont.) and Creative Processing Assessment
17 Nov	ARC, Motion, Emotion, Tone Scale, Flows, Ridges
17 Nov	Creative Processing
17 Nov	Ridges, Self-Determinism—Tone Scales
19 Nov	Attention, Part I
19 Nov	Attention, Part II
19 Nov	The Control of the Individual by an Unknown, Sound

THE SCIENTOLOGY SYMBOL

There are two triangles, over which is imposed the* S, *which stands for Scientology.

The lower triangle is the ARC triangle, whose points are* Affinity, Reality *and* Communication. *These are the three elements which combined give Understanding.

The upper triangle is the KRC triangle. The points are* K *for* Knowledge, R *for* Responsibility *and* C *for Control.

The KRC triangle acts like the ARC triangle. When one corner is increased the other two also rise.

The Scientology symbol first appeared in 1952.

It appears on auditors' blazer badges, Release pins and Clear bracelets. In addition it has been worn as lapel pins, tie tacks, rings of various designs, earrings, key rings, money clips, neckties, cigarette lighters, brooches and necklaces, and otherwise displayed in car badges, decals, flags, etc.

MATHISON MODEL H-52-1R

The model H-52-1R E-Meter became available in 1952 and was in use through 1954.

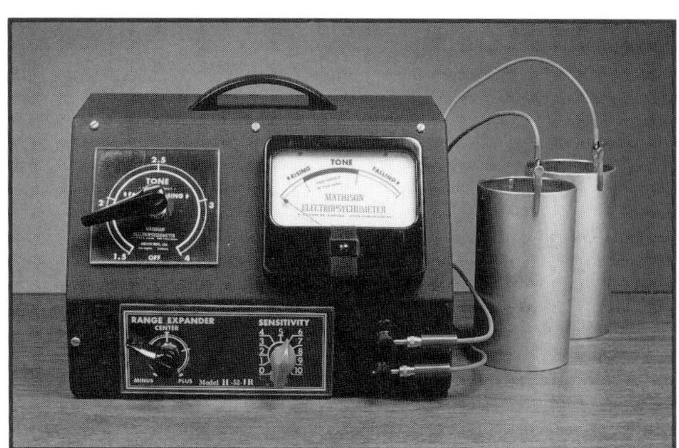

19 Nov Responsibility
20 Nov Creative Processing, Validation of MEST, Have and Agree
20 Nov Creative Processing Directed Toward Breaking Pc's Agreement with Natural Laws of the MEST Universe
20 Nov Assessment of Pc—The Dynamics: Be, Have, Do
21 Nov Creative Processing—How Different Levels of the Tone Scale React in Regard to Handling Illusions

ARTICLES

JOS ISSUE 7-G Nov Sanity Needs Creation–Destruction Balance
JOS ISSUE 7-G Nov The Components of Experience

SCIENTOLOGY 8-8008
by L. Ron Hubbard

Written by L. Ron Hubbard in England in October and November 1952. He had the first copy with him when he flew to the United States and presented it at the opening of the Philadelphia Doctorate Course on December 1st in Philadelphia, Pennsylvania. Published by the Hubbard Association of Scientologists, London, England, December 1952.

PHILADELPHIA DOCTORATE LECTURES
PHILADELPHIA, PENNSYLVANIA

This series of lectures was delivered to a class of thirty-eight auditors. Covering a wide analysis of human behavior, they gave a complete coverage of the latest auditing techniques and an expansion of the new professional course textbook, *Scientology 8-8008. (Available on cassette.)*

1 Dec Opening: What Is to Be Done in Course
1 Dec E-Meter: Demo
1 Dec Creative Processing, Demo of E-Meter Auditing
2 Dec Locks, Secondaries, Engrams, How to Handle Them
2 Dec The Gradient Scale of Handling Space, Energy and Objects
2 Dec The "Q": Highest Level of Knowledge
2 Dec A Thetan Creates by Postulates—Q2
3 Dec The Track of the Thetan/GE—Space/Time
3 Dec Anatomy of Processing—Energy, Phenomena/Sensation
3 Dec Specific Parts of Self-Determinism, Spacation
4 Dec Spacation: Energy Particles and Time
4 Dec Spacation: Locating, Space, Time
4 Dec Spacation: Anchor Points, Origin
4 Dec The Logics: Methods of Thinking
4 Dec The Logics: Infinity-Valued Logic
5 Dec Cycles of Action
5 Dec The Tone Scale: Moving the Pc up the Scale
5 Dec Conditions of Space/Time/Energy
6 Dec Axioms and Logics: Further Data
6 Dec Formative State of Scientology, Definition of Logic
8 Dec ARC/Cycles: Theory and Automaticity
8 Dec More on Automaticity
8 Dec ARC, Force, Be/Do/Have
9 Dec What's Wrong with This Universe: A Working Package for the Auditor
9 Dec Flows: Reverse Vector of Physical Universe
9 Dec Flows: Characteristics Of
9 Dec Flows: The Part Force Bears in Clearing
9 Dec Flows: The Part Space Bears in Clearing
10 Dec Flows: Patterns of Interaction
10 Dec Flows: Rate of Change, Relative Size, Anchor Points
10 Dec Flows: Basic Agreement and Prove It!
10 Dec Flows, Dispersals and Ridges
10 Dec Anatomy of the Genetic Entity
11 Dec 8-8008: Understanding the Phenomena
11 Dec The DEI Scale
11 Dec Structure/Function: Selective Variation Of
11 Dec Chart of Attitudes: Rising Scale Processing
11 Dec Rising Scale Processing
12 Dec Game Processing
12 Dec Games/Goals
12 Dec SOP Issue 3: Postulate, Creative Processing
13 Dec Standard Operating Procedure (SOP)
13 Dec On Auditing: How to Succeed/Fail, Assess
13 Dec SOP Assessment (cont.)
13 Dec Development of Scientology: Characteristics of a Living Science
13 Dec Goal: Rehabilitation of Thetan, Case Step I
15 Dec SOP: Issue 5
15 Dec SOP: Spacation
15 Dec SOP: Spacation (cont.)
16 Dec SOP: Spacation Step III, Flow Processing
16 Dec SOP: Issue 5
16 Dec Memory (Not Human Memory)
16 Dec Memory and Automaticity
17 Dec Summary to Date: Handling Step I and Demo
17 Dec Demonstration on Step I (cont.)
17 Dec Discussion of Demo: Above Agreement with Flows
17 Dec Continued Demonstration Step IV
18 Dec About the "Press" Tone Level: Psychometry
18 Dec Chart of Havingness
18 Dec How To Talk About Scientology
18 Dec How To Talk to Friends About Scientology
18 Dec Your Own Case: To You, the Student

ISSUE

MIMEOED HANDOUT Dec "The Aberration (above Time) . . ."

ARTICLES

JOS ISSUE 8-G Dec New Data Doesn't Invalidate Early, Proven Techniques
JOS ISSUE 9-G Dec Thetan, to Be "Sane," Must Learn How He's Been Caring for Body

1953

At the beginning of 1953, L. Ron Hubbard was operating from his office in London and delivering lectures. New lines for the issue of technical releases and updates were established with the Associate Newsletter and Professional Auditor's Bulletin.

In April, he released a book covering his breakthroughs on the technology of communication in management, entitled *How to Live Though an Executive.*

The Factors were also released in April. A masterpiece of simplicity and wisdom, these thirty statements comprise, as Mr. Hubbard put it, a "summation of the considerations and examinations of the human spirit and the material universe completed between 1923 and 1953 A.D."

During the summer months, he traveled across Europe continuing his research. Before the year was over he was again back in the US, delivering the first and second American Advanced Clinical Courses.

ARTICLE

JOS ISSUE 10-G Jan Preclears Must Be Audited According to Their Condition

Traveling between England and the United States, Mr. Hubbard lectured on such developments as the application of auditing to groups, and expanded on the material covered in his latest books.

LONDON GROUP AUDITOR'S COURSE LECTURES
LONDON, ENGLAND

Jan Educational System, How to Group Process
Jan History of the Organization, Self Analysis
Jan Mechanics of the Mind, Source of Data, Group Auditing and the Tone Scale
Jan Gradient Scales, Admiration Particle
13 Jan Creative Processing
15 Jan Mock-up, Certainty, Group Processing
Jan Raising Abilities

PHILADELPHIA DOCTORATE COURSE SUPPLEMENTARY LECTURES
LONDON, ENGLAND

(Available on cassette as part of the Philadelphia Doctorate Course Lectures.)

12 Jan Agree and Disagree: Have, Not Have
12 Jan Agree and Disagree: Have, Not Have (cont.)
12 Jan Anchor Points: Driving Them In and Out
14 Jan Group and Individual Processing
14 Jan SOP 5 Long Form Step I
16 Jan SOP 5 Long Form Step II
16 Jan SOP 5 Long Form Step II: Demonstration
19 Jan SOP 5 Long Form Step III: Differentiation on Theta Clearing
19 Jan SOP 5 Long Form Step III: Spacation
21 Jan SOP 5 Long Form Step IV: GITA
21 Jan SOP 5 Long Form Step IV: GITA (cont.)
23 Jan SOP 5 Long Form Step V: Additional Techniques
23 Jan SOP 5 Long Form Step VI
24 Jan Concluding Long Form of Step V: Admiration Processing

ISSUES

DESPATCH 30 Jan Processing Notes

BULLETIN DESPATCH late Jan Bulletin to Auditors Scientology 8-8008, Standard Operating Procedure 8

ARTICLES

JOS ISSUE 11-G Feb Preclears Should Be Processed; Education Isn't Auditor's Task
JOS ISSUE 12-G 15 Mar Auditor First Should Know Tools Before He Goes In for Artistic

LONDON SPRING LECTURES
LONDON, ENGLAND

Continuing his education of Scientologists in England, Mr. Hubbard gave these twenty hours of lectures covering his latest procedures and theory. *(To be released on cassette.)*

23 Mar Review of Dianetics, Scientology and Para-Dianetics/Scientology
23 Mar What's Wrong with the Pc and How You Can Do Something About It
24 Mar SOP Issue 5: Steps 1 to 7
24 Mar SOP Issue 5: (cont.)
25 Mar The Elements with Stress on How to Run Matched Terminals
26 Mar How and When to Audit
26 Mar Present Time
27 Mar SOP Utility
27 Mar Beingness, Agreement, Hidden Influence, Processes
27 Mar Data on Case Level 5, Step for Case 5
7 Apr Data on Case Level 5 (cont.)
7 Apr Exteriorization—Demonstration and Explanation
7 Apr Demonstration (cont.)
8 Apr Case Level 6 and 7
24 Apr The Factors
24 Apr SOP 8

ISSUES

LRH RESEARCH NOTES Spring "Anything to Which the Pc Agreed . . ."
DESPATCH Apr Advance Copy on Case Level V

HOW TO LIVE THOUGH AN EXECUTIVE: COMMUNICATION MANUAL
by L. Ron Hubbard

Published by the Hubbard Association of Scientologists, Phoenix, Arizona, April 1953.

SELF ANALYSIS IN SCIENTOLOGY
by L. Ron Hubbard

Published by the Hubbard Association of Scientologists, Philadelphia, Pennsylvania, April 1953. This was a modified version of the original Self Analysis *and is now out of print (although its text is contained in the* Technical Bulletins *volumes). The original 1951 edition of* Self Analysis *is in use.*

ARTICLES

JOS ISSUE 13-G Apr Marital Scientology
15 Apr Admiration Processing

ISSUES

ASSOCIATE NEWSLETTER 23 Apr "Several Items of Interest . . ."
ASSOCIATE NEWSLETTER 28 Apr "It Probably Has Not Occurred to the Field . . ."

ARTICLES

JOS ISSUE 14-G Apr Child Scientology
JOS ISSUE 15-G May "The Old Man's Casebook"

ISSUES

DESPATCH 1 May Scientology 8-8008, Unlimited Techniques
ASSOCIATE NEWSLETTER NO. 2 early May "Associate, Please Send Me . . ."

BIRMINGHAM LECTURES
BIRMINGHAM, ENGLAND

(To be released on cassette.)

21 May Three Universes
21 May Tone Scale—ARC, Present Time

ISSUES

DESPATCH May The Theta–MEST Theory Extended
ASSOCIATE NEWSLETTER NO. 3 mid-May "Enclosed Herewith, Prior to Release . . ."
PAB 1 10 May General Comments, Group Processing and a Summary of New Work: Certainties
PAB 2 end May General Comments, SOP 8 and a Summary of SOP 8-A, General Comment
ASSOCIATE NEWSLETTER NO. 4 end May "This Newsletter Concerns Itself . . ."
DESPATCH Give and Take Processing

THIS IS SCIENTOLOGY THE SCIENCE OF CERTAINTY
by L. Ron Hubbard

Published by the Hubbard Association of Scientologists, Philadelphia, Pennsylvania, June 1953. This book was later combined with the Scientology: Auditor's Handbook *and other material to make the book* The Creation of Human Ability. *Its text is contained in the* Technical Bulletins *volumes, as* Journal of Scientology *Issue 16-G.*

ARTICLE

JOS ISSUE 17-G Jun The Limitations of Homo Novis

ISSUES

PAB 3 mid-Jun Certainty Processing
ASSOCIATE NEWSLETTER NO. 5 18 Jun "After a Fast and Violent Passage . . ."
PAB 4 end Jun Beingness and Certainty Processing
ASSOCIATE NEWSLETTER NO. 6 Jul "This Is a Brief One About Organization . . ."
PAB 5 mid-Jul About PABs
ASSOCIATE NEWSLETTER NO. 7 late Jul "Strategy and Tactics . . ."

ARTICLE

JOS ISSUE 18-G Jul Off the Time Track

ISSUES

PAB 6 end Jul Case Opening
PAB 7 mid-Aug "Come On and Bear a Hand . . ."
ASSOCIATE NEWSLETTER NO. 8 late Aug "The Big News Is the International Congress . . ."
PAB 8 late Aug Viewpoint Processing
PAB 9 early Sep Formula H
ASSOCIATE NEWSLETTER NO. 9 4 Sep "Requested Report . . ."
PAB 10 late Sep Change Processing
ASSOCIATE NEWSLETTER NO. 10 late Sep Technique Bulletin

INTRODUCTION TO SCIENTOLOGY

Taken from the works of L. Ron Hubbard, published by the Hubbard Foundation, Philadelphia, Pennsylvania, late 1953. This notebook was awarded to all the students who successfully completed the course of the Foundation during the span of its existence: March 1952 through October 1953.

ON AUDITING

Taken from the works of L. Ron Hubbard, published in Ann Arbor, Michigan, late 1953.

FIRST INTERNATIONAL CONGRESS OF DIANETICISTS AND SCIENTOLOGISTS LECTURES
PHILADELPHIA, PENNSYLVANIA

This series of lectures was delivered to the nearly 300 delegates attending the

MATHISON H-53-DS

Since the range of earlier meters was insufficient to register all preclears, the Model H-53-DS (Double Scale) was designed with an expanded range. It was made available in 1953.

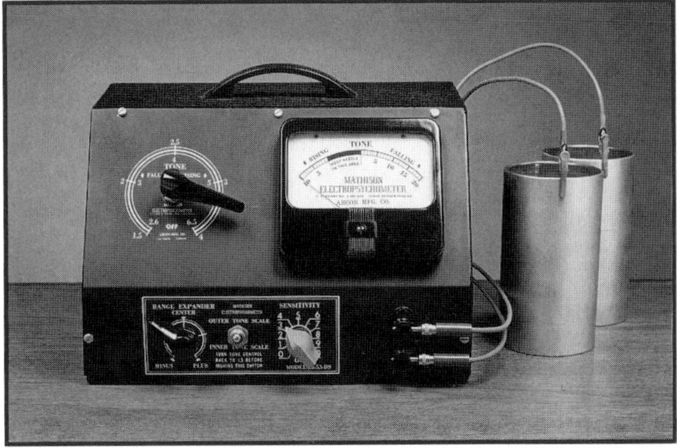

First International Congress of Dianeticists and Scientologists. *(To be released on cassette.)*

30 Sep History and Development of Dianetics
30 Sep The Problem to Be Solved
1 Oct Processing and Its Goals
1 Oct The Most Favorable Processes
1 Oct SOP 8, Step 5 and 4
1 Oct SOP 8, Step 6 and 7
1 Oct Demo—The Use of Q and A
2 Oct SOP 8, Step 1, 2, 3
2 Oct SOP 8, Short 8—Group Processing
3 Oct Six Steps to Better Beingness
3 Oct Uses and Future of Scientology
3 Oct Processes for Rough Cases
4 Oct Wasting
4 Oct Effort

LOOK DON'T THINK

L. Ron Hubbard lecture transcripts, Philadelphia Congress, September 30, 1953 through October 4, 1953. Published by Scientology Northern California, 1953.

FIRST AMERICAN ADVANCED INDOCTRINATION COURSE LECTURES

CAMDEN, NEW JERSEY

The lectures listed below, covering his latest and most advanced discoveries, were given by Mr. Hubbard to a hand-picked group of ten of the best auditors in the world. *(To be released on cassette as a series entitled "Exteriorization and the Phenomena of Space.")*

6 Oct Looking, Definition of Static
7 Oct Question and Answer, Step V
7 Oct Exteriorization
8 Oct Thetan Control, Part I—Handling Occlusion
8 Oct Thetan Control, Part II—Handling Occlusion

8 Oct Occlusion, Resolve Of
9 Oct Psychotics, Classification of Cases
9 Oct Occluded Case
12 Oct Exteriorization, Difficult Cases
12 Oct SOP: Step II
13 Oct Anesthesia in Bodies—Part I
13 Oct Anesthesia in Bodies—Part II
13 Oct Anesthesia in Bodies—Part III
14 Oct Randomity, Control and Prediction, Part I
14 Oct Randomity, Control and Prediction, Part II
14 Oct Inverted Dynamics
15 Oct Thinking Action, Machines
16 Oct Subjective Processes—Perimeter Processing
16 Oct Subjective Processes (cont.)
16 Oct Why a Thetan Is Stuck in a Body
17 Oct Thinking Processes
19 Oct Forget and Remember, Good and Evil
19 Oct Forget and Remember, Good and Evil (cont.)
19 Oct Change Processes, Action
19 Oct Change Processes (cont.)
20 Oct Certainty of Anchor Points Processing
20 Oct Certainty of Anchor Points Processing (cont.)
21 Oct Liabilities of Being Processed
26 Oct Restimulation of Engrams, Experiences
26 Oct An Assumption, Lines, Cords, Havingness
26 Oct Time, Assumption, Facsimiles, Overt Acts, DEDS
27 Oct Fixed Attention, Duplication, How to Audit Children
27 Oct Assessment, Memories, Ridges: Demo: Acceptance Level Processing
28 Oct Case Reports, SOP 8-C, SOP 8L
28 Oct Anchor Points, Space, Games, Indicated Drills of Processes
29 Oct Spacation, Anchor Points and Attention
29 Oct Study of the Particle
30 Oct The Particle with Regard to Time
30 Oct Consideration, Extent of Viewpoint, Step III Commands
30 Oct How to Run Change Processing
2 Nov Cause and Effect, Automaticity, Ridges Processing
2 Nov Occluded Case Reports—Black Spot Processing, Certainty
3 Nov The Logics—Their Relation to Aberration and Space
3 Nov Anchor Points and Space
3 Nov The Logics—Part II
4 Nov Randomity and Automaticity, Process to Resolve
5 Nov Certainty
5 Nov Communication—ARC—Demonstration
5 Nov Communication—ARC—Demo—Space
6 Nov Inverted Dynamics, Inflow-Outflow, Material, Time
6 Nov Space
6 Nov Demonstration: Havingness, Energy, Etc.
9 Nov Randomity, Anchor Points
9 Nov Exteriorization by Feeling
10 Nov Types of Processes, Space, Create-Destroy
10 Nov SOP 8-C Steps
11 Nov Group Processing
11 Nov Future Processing
11 Nov Questions: SOP 8-C, 3 Universes, SOP 8, Significances, Exteriorization
12 Nov Process to Use on Cases, Gradient Scales
12 Nov Self-determinism in Relation to a Thetan
12 Nov Gradient Scale Straightwire
12 Nov Gradient Scale Straightwire Demo (cont.)
13 Nov Final Talk on First Course
13 Nov Last Lecture of Advanced Course, Camden 1953 Reviewing Students' Ability to Process
13 Nov Group Processing After Afternoon Lecture

ARTICLE

JOS ISSUE 21-G	Oct	The Theory of Communication

ISSUES

PAB	11 Oct	What the Thetan Is Trying to Do
DESPATCH		This Is a List to Be Run by Change of Space Processing
PAB	12 late Oct	The Cycle of Action of an Explosion
DESPATCH	28 Oct	Step III Auditing Commands
PAB	13 mid-Nov	On Human Behavior

SECOND AMERICAN ADVANCED CLINICAL COURSE LECTURES

CAMDEN, NEW JERSEY

Due to the success of the First American Advanced Indoctrination Course and to meet demand for advanced training, a second, similar course followed almost immediately. *(To be released on cassette.)*

17 Nov Opening Lecture: Emotional Tone Scale
17 Nov SOP 8-C First Lecture
17 Nov Getting Up Speed—Part I
17 Nov Getting Up Speed—Part II
18 Nov Step 1 of 8-C, Beingness
18 Nov Black Mock-ups, Persistence, MEST
18 Nov Step II, Automaticities
18 Nov Waste a Machine
19 Nov Effects, Reaching End of Cycle

MATHISON HM-4

The Model HM-4 E-Meter was also introduced in 1953. HM-4 stands for Hubbard Meter #4—the first meter was the Model B in 1951, the second was the H-52-1R of 1952 and the third was the H-53-DS.

19 Nov More on Machines
20 Nov Resistance to Effect
20 Nov Plan of Auditing
23 Nov Formula "Phi," Creation of Mest
23 Nov Summary of Steps I, II, III of SOP 8-C
24 Nov Anchor Points, Knowingness of Location
24 Nov Steps 5, 6, 7; Duplication, Unconsciousness
24 Nov Additional Remarks
25 Nov Steps 5, 6, 7; Time
25 Nov SOP 8-C, Summary Of
26 Nov Electronic Theory, Anchor Points
26 Nov Exteriorization
26 Nov Additional Remarks
27 Nov Anchor Points, Justice
27 Nov Symbols
28 Nov Special Session—Experimental Process
28 Nov Demonstration: Group Processing
30 Nov Additional Remarks
30 Nov Mest, Universe, Agreements—Time, a Single Terminal
30 Nov Space, Perception, Knowingness
1 Dec Space, Lack of, Persistence
2 Dec Blackness
3 Dec Time a. a Barrier
3 Dec Time, Cause and Effect
4 Dec Plan of SOP 8-C
4 Dec LRH Questions the Class on Exteriorization
7 Dec Barriers, Occlusion
7 Dec Outline of SOP 8-C
8 Dec Essence of SOP 8-C
8 Dec Problems of Auditing
9 Dec Summary: The Dynamics
9 Dec Bodies
10 Dec Knowingness
10 Dec SOP 8-C: General Discussion
11 Dec SOP 8-C: Patter
13 Dec Force—Part I
13 Dec Force—Part II
14 Dec SOP 8-C: Step 8, Definitions
14 Dec Cause and Effect, Assignment of Cause, GE
15 Dec SOP 8-C: Step 5
15 Dec Energy Problems
16 Dec Techniques Which Do or Do Not Assign Cause/Technique to Assign Cause
16 Dec Comm Line: Overt Act–Motivator Sequence
17 Dec SOP 8-C: Formulas
17 Dec Space Opera
18 Dec The Only One
18 Dec Beingness
19 Dec SOP 8-C: General
19 Dec Mass
20 Dec Communication
20 Dec Auditing by SOP 8-C, Formula H
20 Dec Reach/Withdraw
21 Dec Ability to Accept Direction
21 Dec Knowingness and Certainty
21 Dec State of Man Today
21 Dec Group Processing
22 Dec Remedy of Havingness
22 Dec Postulates
22 Dec Group Processing

Issues

Associate Newsletter	19 Nov	"Dear Associates: Since Coming Back . . ."
PAB 14	Nov	On Human Character

Lecture
Camden, New Jersey

22 Dec Organization of Man

Lecture
Phoenix, Arizona

28 Dec Cycle of Action

Article

JOS Issue 22-G	Dec	What an Auditor Should Know

Issues

PAB 15	mid-Dec	Acceptance Level Processing
LRH Research Notes	Dec	"Motto of the Mest Universe"

International Congress of Dianeticists and Scientologists Lectures
Phoenix, Arizona

The latest Scientology techniques, which had been developed and perfected at the Advanced Clinical Courses, were presented to Scientologists from around the world at this congress. *(To be released on cassette.)*

28 Dec Goals of Scientology
28 Dec Mock-ups, Energy
28 Dec Basic Theory of Definitions
28 Dec Basic Theory of Definitions (cont.), Group Processing
28 Dec Group Processing—Part I
28 Dec Group Processing—Part II
28 Dec How to Be a Group Auditor
28 Dec Group Processing
29 Dec Create, Survive, Destroy Curve
29 Dec Use of SOP 8-C
29 Dec Role of the Auditor
29 Dec Group Processing—Short Lecture
29 Dec Design of SOP 8-C: Process for Groups, Percentages of Successes and Failures
29 Dec Group Process
30 Dec Talk on E-Meter
30 Dec Automaticity
30 Dec Group Processing
30 Dec Group Processing
31 Dec Step 5, SOP 8-C (Group Processing)
31 Dec Group Processing, Short Lecture
31 Dec Group Processing, Step 1, SOP 8-C
31 Dec Group Process for HAS Associate Groups
Dec Group Processing—Reach and Withdraw Across the Dynamics

Issue

PAB 16	late Dec	Acceptance Level Processing

1954

Mr. Hubbard spent 1954 in Phoenix, Arizona at the Hubbard College, where he lectured and delivered Group Processing on a nearly continuous basis. He delivered eight Advanced Clinical Courses (ACCs), each course six weeks in length. During this time period he delivered over 490 recorded lectures and Group Processing sessions to meet the demand for the technology.

He also originated two new publications to get the tech further disseminated: Operational Bulletins and *Ability* magazine.

Issue

PAB 17	mid-Jan	Future Processing

Article

Jan	An Invitation to Freedom, Man *Can* Save His Soul

Third American Advanced Clinical Course
Phoenix, Arizona

(To be released on cassette.)

4 Jan Introduction to the Third ACC
4 Jan Perception and Ownership
5 Jan Communication and Not Over-Instructing the Pc
5 Jan Boredom, Pace of Living, Truth

Mathison E-54

The Mathison E-54 meter was presented at the First International Congress of Dianeticists and Scientologists, September 1953, in Philadelphia, Pennsylvania, but it was overly complex and was never used much in auditing.

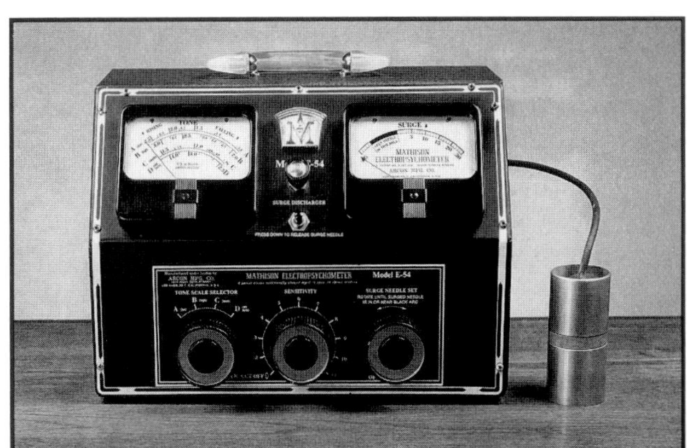

5 Jan Symbols and a Group Processing Demo
6 Jan Symbols and a Group Processing Demo (cont.)
6 Jan Symbols and a Group Processing Demo (cont.)
6 Jan Processing Demo: Randomity Plus Automaticity
7 Jan Communication
7 Jan Anchor Points, Flows
8 Jan Exteriorization from Masses
8 Jan How to Know What Pc Is Doing, Opening Procedures Plus Variations
11 Jan Exteriorization, Theory and Demo
11 Jan Exteriorization, Theory and Demo (cont.)
11 Jan Agreement, Motion and Perception
12 Jan Exteriorization, Acceptance and Rejection of Ideas
12 Jan Exteriorization, Lecture and Demo
12 Jan Exteriorization, Demo on Group
12 Jan Machines, Demonstration
12 Jan Special Message LRH to London Congress of Dianeticists and Scientologists
13 Jan Competence of Prediction, Demo
13 Jan Competence of Prediction, Demo (cont.)
13 Jan Exteriorization: Step I, Procedure
14 Jan Labels: In Society and Preclears
14 Jan Labels: Beingness and Justice
14 Jan Labels: Beingness and Justice (cont.)
15 Jan Present Time, Self Analysis
15 Jan Present Time (cont.)
15 Jan Present Time (cont.) and Demonstration
18 Jan Time: Barrier
18 Jan Time: Basic Process On
18 Jan Time: Sense, Particles, Survival Pace
18 Jan Processing Time on a Group
19 Jan Summary of Course to Date
19 Jan Exteriorization: Demonstration
19 Jan Communication by Emotion: Flows, Ridges
19 Jan Group Processing
20 Jan E-Meter, Use Of
20 Jan Audio (Beep) Meter Demonstration
20 Jan Exteriorization, Communication in Theta and MEST
21 Jan Livingness Processing Series
21 Jan Livingness Processing Series (Dyingness)
22 Jan Livingness Processing Series (Machinery)
22 Jan Livingness Processing Series (Demo)
25 Jan Goals of 8-0 (OT) Abilities
25 Jan Basic Data on 8-0 (OT)
26 Jan Exteriorization, Knowingness, Reality
26 Jan Instruction, Simplicity—Static and Zero, Science, Reason Why
27 Jan OT, Inversion: Courage and Mobility Parts I and II
28 Jan Exteriorization: Courage and Serenity Parts I and II
28 Jan Courage Processing
29 Jan Parked Personality: Exteriorization, Stuck Flows
29 Jan Simple Basis of Evaluating Cases
1 Feb Exteriorization, Taking Direction
1 Feb Processing Havingness Lecture
2 Feb Havingness Series (cont.), Acceptance and Rejection of Havingness
2 Feb Havingness Series (cont.), Comm Lines
3 Feb Havingness Series (cont.), Ownership
3 Feb Repairing a Case and Demo
4 Feb Review on Havingness and Demo
4 Feb Certainty: Maybes, Problems, Entrance
5 Feb Endowment of Livingness: Extroverting Attention
5 Feb Group Processing on Certainty, Eight Dynamics
8 Feb Summary of Course Data and Machinery
8 Feb Group Processing, Automaticities
9 Feb Auditing Groups
9 Feb Group Processing on Class: Barriers
9 Feb Short Discussion and Group Processing Demo
10 Feb Group Processing on Class: Being MEST
10 Feb Group Processing on Class: Black/White
10 Feb Group Processing on Class: Being MEST
11 Feb Group Processing on Class: Things to Be
11 Feb Group Processing on Class: Resist Effect
11 Feb Group Processing: Exterior
12 Feb Group Processing on Class: Sound
12 Feb Group Processing on Class: Balance
12 Feb Group Processing on Class: Time

ARTICLES

JOS ISSUE 23-G 15 Jan Man's Search for His Soul
JOS ISSUE 24-G Jan SOP 8-C: The Rehabilitation of the Human Spirit

ISSUES

PAB 18 late Jan Overt Acts
PAB 19 early Feb The Circuit Case
PAB 20 mid-Feb Two Answers to Correspondents: The Nonpersistence Case and Ridge Running

FOURTH AMERICAN ADVANCED CLINICAL COURSE LECTURES
PHOENIX, ARIZONA

(To be released on cassette.)

15 Feb Introduction to Fourth American ACC
16 Feb Group Processing: Ownership
17 Feb Group Processing: Not Suppressing Time
17 Feb Exteriorization Demonstration Process
17 Feb Demonstration Process
18 Feb Group Processing: Spotting Things
18 Feb Demonstration
18 Feb Group Processing: Things Telling Where Things Are
19 Feb Group Processing: Demonstration
19 Feb Group Processing: Second Dynamic
19 Feb Group Processing: Imagination
22 Feb Group Processing: Straightwire, Energy
22 Feb Group Processing: Consideration
23 Feb Group Processing: Certainty
23 Feb Group Processing: Ownership
24 Feb Group Processing: Time
24 Feb Group Processing: Stabilization Process
25 Feb Group Processing: Goals, Duplicating
25 Feb Group Processing: Being and Giving
26 Feb Group Processing: Havingness
26 Feb Group Processing: Changing Ideas
1 Mar Group Processing Series A: Be, Do, Have
1 Mar Group Processing Series A: Time
1 Mar Group Processing Series A: Certainties

BEEP METER

Though more a curiosity than an auditing tool, the "beep" meter was first available in 1954. It would give off a beep sound when a painful area of the body was located with a probe. LRH demonstrated and discussed this meter in his 20 January 1954 lecture entitled "Audio (Beep) Meter Demonstration."

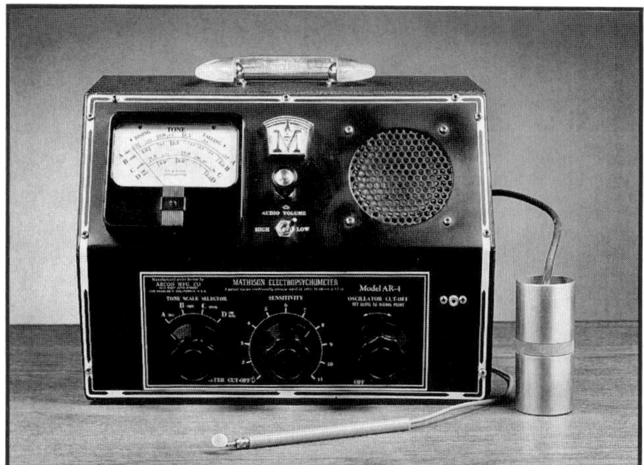

2 Mar Group Processing Series A: Exteriorization
2 Mar Group Processing Series A: Courage
2 Mar Group Processing Series A: Location
3 Mar Group Processing Series B: Sound
3 Mar Group Processing Series B: Light/Sound
3 Mar Group Processing Series B: Third Hour
4 Mar Group Processing Series B: Spaces
4 Mar Group Processing Series B: Attention
4 Mar Group Processing Series B: Work
5 Mar Group Processing Series C: Putting Things
5 Mar Group Processing Series C: Putting Things (cont.)
5 Mar Group Processing Series C: Putting Things (cont.)
8 Mar Group Processing Series C: Beingness
9 Mar Group Processing Series C: Basic Process
9 Mar Group Processing Series C: Beingness
12 Mar Group Processing Series C: SOP 8-C
12 Mar Group Processing Series C: Similarities and Definitions
15 Mar Group Processing Series D: First Hour
15 Mar Group Processing Series D: Talk/Beingness
15 Mar Group Processing Series D: Talk/Beingness and Basic Fundamentals of Existence
16 Mar Group Processing Series D: Second Hour
16 Mar Group Processing Series D: Talk/Beingness
16 Mar Group Processing Series D: Outline of Processes
17 Mar Group Processing Series D: Third Hour
17 Mar Group Processing Series D: Evaluation
17 Mar Group Processing Series D: Invalidation
18 Mar Group Processing Series D: Fourth Hour
18 Mar Group Processing Series D: Duplication and Comm
18 Mar Group Processing Series D: Following Orders
19 Mar Group Processing Series D: Fifth Hour
19 Mar Group Processing Series D: Senior Processes
19 Mar Group Processing Series D: Processes Talk
22 Mar Group Processing Series D: Sixth Hour
22 Mar Group Processing Series D Lecture: What Your Pc Is Trying to Do
22 Mar Group Processing Series D: Lecture/Pc
23 Mar Universe Series: All Cases
23 Mar Universe Series: Beingness
23 Mar Universe Series: Beingness (cont.)
24 Mar Universe Series: Group Processing
24 Mar Universe Series: Beingness and Protection
24 Mar Universe Series: Prediction
25 Mar Universe Series: Communication
25 Mar Universe Series: Outline of Processes
25 Mar Universe Series: More on Processes
26 Mar Universe Series: Group Processing
26 Mar Universe Series: Morals, Laws, Codes
26 Mar Universe Series: How Not to Get Results

PUBLIC LECTURE
PHOENIX, ARIZONA

Mar Background of Scientology

ISSUES

PAB 21 early Mar "The Following Is a Report..."
DESPATCH 10 Mar "Dear Associate, I Have Not Written You..."

ARTICLE

JOS ISSUE 26-G Mar The Road Up

FIFTH AMERICAN ADVANCED CLINICAL COURSE LECTURES
PHOENIX, ARIZONA

(Available on cassette as a series entitled "Universes and the War Between Theta and MEST.")

29 Mar Evolution and Use of Self Analysis
30 Mar Universes
31 Mar Simple Processes
1 Apr Basic Simple Procedures
2 Apr Presence of an Auditor
5 Apr Group Processing: Safe Place for Things
6 Apr Lecture: Universes
7 Apr Universe: Basic Definitions
8 Apr Universe: Processes, Experience
9 Apr Universe: Conditions of the Mind and Remedies
12 Apr Universe: Change and Rehabilitation
13 Apr Universe: Manifestation
14 Apr SOP 8-D
15 Apr Group Processing: Exteriorization and Stabilization
15 Apr Group Processing: Certainty Assessment
16 Apr SOP 8-D: Lecture
19 Apr Group Processing: Universe Assessment
19 Apr Group Processing: Area Assessment
20 Apr Group Processing: Remedying Havingness
21 Apr Elements of Auditing
21 Apr Group Processing: Reach for Present Time
22 Apr SOP 8-DA
23 Apr SOP 8-DB
26 Apr General Handling of Pc
27 Apr Anchor Points and Space
28 Apr Space and Havingness
29 Apr Space
30 Apr SOP 8-DA Through SOP 8-DH
3 May Viewpoint Straightwire
4 May Be, Do, Have Straightwire
5 May Efficacy of Processes
6 May Anatomy of Universes
7 May Energy—Exteriorization

ISSUES

PAB 23 2 Apr Havingness
DESPATCH 10 Apr Data Sheet, Advanced Course
DESPATCH 15 Apr SOP 8-D

ARTICLE

JOS ISSUE 28-G Apr Scientology: A New Science

ISSUES

PAB 24 16 Apr Certainty of Exteriorization
PAB 25 30 Apr Basic Procedures
DESPATCH 3 May Viewpoint Straightwire

PUBLIC LECTURE SERIES
PHOENIX, ARIZONA

While continuing his lectures to trained auditors, Mr. Hubbard also responded to the continuous public demand for Scientology technology by giving a series of public lectures on the fundamental tenets of Scientology.

MATHISON E-SERIES METER

More fancy and complex meters were also made available during 1954, called the E-Series meters; few were ever used in auditing as they were too complicated to be workable.

5 May Efficacy of Processes
5 May Remedying Reasons Why
5 May Rundown of Processes

ISSUES

DESPATCH 20 May I Training Department Organization
DESPATCH 20 May II Clinical Procedure

SIXTH AMERICAN ADVANCED CLINICAL COURSE LECTURES
PHOENIX, ARIZONA

(To be released on cassette.)

10 May Introduction, Materials and Publications
11 May Affinity, Reality, Communication
11 May Significance, Symbols, Orientation
11 May Goals of Scientology in Processing
12 May Goal of the Auditor
12 May Practical Applications of the Definitions of Scientology
12 May Basic Definitions
13 May Definitions: Cycle of Action and Time
13 May SOP 8-C by Definitions
14 May Randomity, Surprise and Prediction, Automaticity, Beingness
14 May Remedy of Havingness
14 May Command Postulates: Opening Procedure of 8-C
17 May Simple Processes, Specifics
17 May Simple Processes, Summary
18 May Barriers
18 May Barriers, Processing Of
18 May Present Time Straightwire
19 May Third Dynamics
19 May Communication and the Dynamics
19 May Imagination, Spots in Space
19 May Data Sheet, Viewpoint Processes
20 May How to Put Procedure Together
20 May Definitions ARC
20 May First Dynamic
21 May Consideration and Intention
21 May Practical Manifestations of Processing
21 May Seminar
24 May Conduct of the Auditor, Communication Lag
25 May Conduct of the Auditor, Older Therapies
25 May Connecting Point Between Older Therapies and Auditing
25 May Valences
25 May Beingness Processing
26 May Third Dynamic ARC
26 May Command Process
26 May Practical Aspects of Auditing
27 May How to Do Viewpoint Straightwire
27 May Demo Session by LRH
28 May Demo Session by LRH
28 May SOP 8-D with Wheel
31 May Know to Sex Scale
31 May Processing of Problems: Theta-MEST Theory
31 May Processing Attention, Beingness
31 May Procedure 30 Series: Granting Beingness
31 May Opening Procedure by Duplication—Part 1
1 Jun Opening Procedure by Duplication—Part 2
1 Jun Problems
1 Jun Granting Beingness
2 Jun When to Use Procedure 30
2 Jun Procedure 30 Series: How to Process a Case
2 Jun Procedure 30 Series: Granting Beingness
2 Jun Granting Beingness
3 Jun Study of Man: Demo of Procedure 30
3 Jun Consideration: Time, Beginning and End
4 Jun Know to Sex Scale: The Mind and the Tone Scale
4 Jun Imagination and Abilities
9 Jun Energy: Knocker-Offer Distraction of Attention
10 Jun Basic Elements of Scientology
11 Jun Procedure 30: Handling of Cases
11 Jun Processing Solutions: Procedure 30, Issue III
11 Jun Basic Impulses
11 Jun Basic Impulses (cont.)
12 Jun Lecture for HASI Standard Opening Procedure Issue V
14 Jun General Lecture
14 Jun Energy Machines, Survival
15 Jun Functional Processes
15 Jun Types and Forms of Commands
15 Jun Dependency
16 Jun Capabilities of Thetan
16 Jun Contact with the Public
16 Jun Make and Break Point of Cases, Dependency
17 Jun Betrayal, Ridicule, the Game Cycle
17 Jun Betrayal, Ridicule, the Game Cycle (cont.)
17 Jun Assists—Part I
17 Jun Assists—Part II
17 Jun Lecture on Group Processing
17 Jun Summary: Training Processing
18 Jun Summary: Processing Demos
18 Jun Certificates and Degrees

PHOENIX PUBLIC LECTURE
PHOENIX, ARIZONA

5 Jun Human Evaluation

UNIVERSE PROCESSES CONGRESS LECTURES
PHOENIX, ARIZONA

At the Universe Processes Congress (also called the Fourth International Congress of Dianeticists and Scientologists), delegates received fourteen hours of lectures and Group Processing from Mr. Hubbard. *(To be released on cassette.)*

5 Jun Opening Lecture—History of Dianetics and Scientology
5 Jun Procedure 30—Duplication
5 Jun Theta-MEST Theory—Tone Scale, Freedom, Space, Etc.
6 Jun Group Processes: Procedure 30, Step 1—Opening Procedure by Duplication
6 Jun Lecture and Processing
6 Jun Group Processing (Look at That Object)
7 Jun Scientology Workbook—*Journal of Scientology* 31-G
7 Jun Processing (Granting of Beingness) Session I
7 Jun Processing (Granting of Beingness) Session II
7 Jun Group Processing (What Do—Didn't Have)
7 Jun Theta-MEST Theory—Being a Problem Aspect
8 Jun Group Processing (Solution to Something)
8 Jun Processes of Exteriorization
8 Jun Group Processing (Straight Exteriorization Process)

GROUP AUDITOR'S HANDBOOK, VOLUME ONE
by L. Ron Hubbard

Published by Hubbard Association of Scientologists International, Phoenix, Arizona, June 1954. The Group Auditor's Handbook, Volume One, *was released at the Universe Processes Congress given in Phoenix, where it was made available to delegates and used by seminar leaders.*

THE MINISTER'S MEDALLION AND PIN

The minister's ceremonial medallion and ribbon was first introduced in 1954.

It is a gold cross on a white field, 2½ inches in diameter, ⅜ inch thick. The ribbon is black.

The minister's lapel pin is the same design as the minister's medallion but smaller.

These insignia are worn by ordained ministers of the Church of Scientology.

SCIENTOLOGY WORKBOOK

Taken from the works of L. Ron Hubbard, published by the Hubbard Association of Scientologists International, Phoenix, Arizona, June 1954.

ISSUE

PAB 28 11 Jun "My Dear Mr. Clouston: . . ."

SEVENTH AMERICAN ADVANCED CLINICAL COURSE LECTURES
PHOENIX, ARIZONA

(To be released on cassette.)

23 Jun Opening Procedure 8-C
23 Jun Further Uses of Opening Procedure 8-C
24 Jun Summary of Plan of Course
25 Jun Review of Procedure: PTP, ARC Straightwire, Two-way Comm
25 Jun Review of Procedure: Starting a Session, Two-way Comm
25 Jun Opening Procedure of 8-D: Demonstration
25 Jun Opening Procedure of 8-D: Demonstration (cont.)
28 Jun Exteriorization
28 Jun Exteriorization (cont.)
29 Jun General Lecture: Straightwire, Communication
30 Jun Rundown of Essentials
30 Jun Group Processing
30 Jun Group Processing and Lecture, Something, Nothing
30 Jun Lecture: Being Made Nothing and Having to Be Something
1 Jul Group Processing: Communication, Duplication, Spotting Spots
1 Jul Communication, Duplication and the Step V
1 Jul Exteriorization by Distance, Cause
1 Jul Exteriorization, Distance and Time
4 Jul Scientology and Living
5 Jul Things in Time and Space
5 Jul A Bright Resistive Case
5 Jul The Role of Laughter in Processing—Dangerousness
5 Jul Rundown of Cases
6 Jul Remedy of Havingness and Spotting Spots in Space
6 Jul ARC, Time, Life and Universe
7 Jul Intensive Procedure—Lecture 1
7 Jul Intensive Procedure—Lecture 2
7 Jul Intensive Procedure—Lecture 3
7 Jul Intensive Procedure—Lecture 4, Basic Processes, Patter
8 Jul Basic Individual Processes
9 Jul The Nature and Effect of Communication in Games
9 Jul Communication and Barriers in Society and the Pc
12 Jul Two Types of Cases
12 Jul Time: Havingness
12 Jul Intensive Procedure: Nothing–Something
13 Jul Auditor's Code in Practice
14 Jul Power of Life and Death
14 Jul Application of Theory to Cases, Life and Death, Only One
15 Jul The Difference Between a Good and a Bad Auditor
15 Jul SOP 8-D: Its Application
15 Jul SOP 8-D: Orientation Points
15 Jul Training of Auditors
16 Jul Teaching Formula: Duplication
19 Jul Scientology, Its General Background—Part I
19 Jul Scientology, Its General Background—Part II
19 Jul Scientology, Its General Background—Part III
20 Jul Bridge Between Scientology and Civilization
20 Jul Consideration, Mechanics and the Theory Behind Instruction
20 Jul Consideration and Isness
23 Jul Isness
23 Jul The Four Conditions of Existence—Part 1
23 Jul The Four Conditions of Existence—Part 2
23 Jul The Four Conditions of Existence—Part 3
23 Jul The Four Conditions of Existence—Part 4
23 Jul The Four Conditions of Existence—Part 5
26 Jul Two-way Communication and Present Time Problem
26 Jul Opening Procedure of 8-C
27 Jul Question and Answer Period
27 Jul Handling of Theta Bodies
27 Jul Things an Auditor Should Know
27 Jul Afternoon Lecture Remarks Especially on Telepathy and ESP
28 Jul Description Processing
28 Jul Group Processing
Jul Time
Jul Types of Processes
30 Jul Control

ISSUES

DESPATCH 15 Jul Training

DESPATCH 23 Jul Group Auditing Sessions

LECTURE
PHOENIX, ARIZONA

30 Jul Certificates of Dianetics and Scientology

SCIENTOLOGY: AUDITOR'S HANDBOOK—INCLUDING INTENSIVE PROCEDURE
by L. Ron Hubbard

Published by the Hubbard Association of Scientologists International, Phoenix, Arizona, August 1954. (This book, combined with other material, was published as The Creation of Human Ability, *1955.)*

ISSUE

PAB 32 7 Aug Why Doctor of Divinity?

AXIOMS LECTURES
PHOENIX, ARIZONA

These four half-hour talks were recorded by Mr. Hubbard in his Phoenix office with no audience present, for use on the Professional Course. *(Available on cassette as part of the series entitled "The Phoenix Lectures.")*

20 Aug Axioms: Part I
20 Aug Axioms: Part II
20 Aug Axioms: Part III
20 Aug Axioms: Part IV

GROUP AUDITOR'S HANDBOOK, VOLUME TWO
by L. Ron Hubbard

Published by the Hubbard Association of Scientologists International, Phoenix, Arizona, September 1954.

ISSUES

PAB 34 4 Sep Opening Procedure, SOP 8-C

DESPATCH 13 Sep Communication

CREED The Creed of the Church of Scientology

GROUP PROCESSING SESSION
PHOENIX, ARIZONA

14 Sep Dianetic Group Processing

ISSUE

PAB 35 18 Sep "What I Learned in Training"

LECTURE
PHOENIX, ARIZONA

28 Sep Church of Scientology Training Program and Lecture on Group Processing

ISSUES

BULLETIN Sep Fighting Process

PAB 36 1 Oct The Use of Scientology Materials

EIGHTH AMERICAN ADVANCED CLINICAL COURSE LECTURES
PHOENIX, ARIZONA

(Available on cassette as a series entitled "The Creation of Human Ability.")

4 Oct Introduction to the Eighth Unit
5 Oct Basic Elements of Processing
6 Oct Two-way Communication
7 Oct Elementary Straightwire
7 Oct Intensive Processing
8 Oct Opening Procedure of 8-C
11 Oct Opening Procedure by Duplication
12 Oct Remedy of Havingness
13 Oct Spotting Spots
19 Oct Axioms of Dianetics
20 Oct The Parts of Man: Overt Acts and Motivators
21 Oct R2-61: Good and Evil; R2-62: Overt Act–Motivator Sequence
22 Oct Second Lecture on Two-way Communication
25 Oct Communication and Straightwire
26 Oct Survive
27 Oct Hypnotism
28 Oct What Would You Do If . . . ?
29 Oct The Factors
1 Nov Third Lecture on Two-way Communication
2 Nov *Homo Sapiens*
3 Nov Shame, Blame and Regret
5 Nov Factors Present in Good and Bad Auditing
8 Nov Nonverbal Communication
9 Nov Application of Axioms to Auditing
10 Nov Definitions: Axioms
11 Nov The Scope of Dianetics and Scientology
12 Nov Question and Answer Period: Dissemination

ROUTE ONE LECTURES
PHOENIX, ARIZONA

These twelve fifteen-minute lectures give additional data on specific processing steps laid out in the *Scientology Auditor's Handbook* which was released in August 1954 (the original edition of the book now known as *The Creation of Human Ability*).

8 Oct Route 1, Step 4
8 Oct Route 1, Step 5
10 Oct Route 1, Step 6
10 Oct Route 1, Step 7
10 Oct Route 1, Step 8
10 Oct Route 1, Step 9
10 Oct Route 1, Step 10
10 Oct Route 1, Step 11
18 Oct Route 1, Step 12
18 Oct Route 1, Step 13
18 Oct Route 1, Step 14
18 Oct Route 1, Step 15

ISSUES

PAB 37 15 Oct The Communication Lines of Scientology

DESPATCH Oct Dianetics and Scientology, a Crusade

PUBLIC LECTURE AND GROUP PROCESSING SERIES
PHOENIX, ARIZONA

Throughout October, November and December of 1954, Mr. Hubbard gave Wednesday night public lectures and Group Processing sessions geared toward newer public interested in finding out more about Scientology. From mid-November through the beginning of December, he also lectured each morning to auditors on the Phoenix Certification Course.

20 Oct On Comprehending the Incomprehensible
20 Oct "Rising Scale" on the Tone Scale and "Find Something Incomprehensible"
20 Oct Group Processing
27 Oct Principal Difference Between Scientology and Dianetics
27 Oct "Electing Cause"—Something You Can't Control
27 Oct Life of Dynamics
3 Nov Organization of Scientology
17 Nov "Accept" and "Reject" (Group Processing)
17 Nov The Wrong Thing to Do Is Nothing
24 Nov Creation of Human Ability
24 Nov Group Process—"Find Shortest Communication Line"—"Create a Memory"
1 Dec Awareness of Awareness
1 Dec "Decide to Be Silent"—"Find Some Secrets"
8 Dec "Waiting," Something You Can Associate With
8 Dec Group Processing
15 Dec Acceptance Level

ISSUES

PAB 38 29 Oct The Auditor's Code 1954
PAB 39 12 Nov The Auditor's Code 1954 (Concluded)

PHOENIX CERTIFICATION COURSE LECTURES
PHOENIX, ARIZONA

(To be released on cassette.)

16 Nov Elementary Straightwire
17 Nov Background of Six Basic Steps
19 Nov Remedy of Havingness
22 Nov Levels of Case Ability
23 Nov Addressing Groups and Starting Sessions
24 Nov Following Orders
24 Nov Two-way Communication
30 Nov Solving Cases
1 Dec Opening Procedure of 8-C
3 Dec The Importance of Two-way Comm During Opening Procedure by Duplication
4 Dec Last Lecture

ARTICLE

JOS ISSUE 40-G Nov Validation of Scientology

ISSUES

PAB 40 26 Nov The Code of Honor
FOUNDATION BULLETIN VOL. 1, NO. 3 Dec Accent on Ability, New Trend Takes Form

ARTICLE

JOS ISSUE 41-G Dec Is It Possible to Be Happy?

NINTH ADVANCED CLINICAL COURSE LECTURES
PHOENIX, ARIZONA

(Available on cassette as a series entitled "The Solution to Entrapment.")

6 Dec Introduction to 9th ACC: Havingness
7 Dec The Essence of Auditing, Know to Mystery Scale
8 Dec Rundown on Six Basics
9 Dec Communication Formula
10 Dec The Practice of Dianetics and Scientology
13 Dec Conduct of the Auditor
14 Dec Mechanics of Communication
15 Dec Havingness
16 Dec Pan-determinism and One-way Flows
17 Dec History and Development of Processes: Games and the Limitations in Games
17 Dec History and Development of Processes: Question and Answer Period
20 Dec Games (Fighting)
21 Dec Anatomy of Games—Part I
21 Dec Anatomy of Games—Part II
22 Dec One-way Flows in Processing
22 Dec One-way Flows in Processing: Question and Answer Period
23 Dec Havingness and Communication Formulas
24 Dec Pan-determinism
24 Dec Pan-determinism: Question and Answer Period
27 Dec Training New People
27 Dec Curiosa from *Dianetics 55!*

The Ninth Advanced Clinical Course went through the end of 1954 and into the beginning of 1955, continuing with the following lectures:

3 Jan Auditing Requirements, Differences
4 Jan Time
4 Jan Question and Answer Period
5 Jan Exteriorization by Gradient Scale
5 Jan Auditing at Optimum
6 Jan Exteriorization
7 Jan Elementary Material: Know to Mystery Scale
10 Jan Education: Goals in Society—Adult Education
11 Jan Fundamentals of Auditing
11 Jan Auditors' Conference
12 Jan Definitions: Glossary of Terms—Part I
13 Jan Definitions: Glossary of Terms—Part II
14 Jan Definitions: Glossary of Terms—Part III
17 Jan Auditing Demonstration: Six Basics in Action
17 Jan Auditors' Conference
18 Jan Auditing Demonstration: Spotting Spots
18 Jan Auditors' Conference
19 Jan Auditing Demonstration: Exteriorization
20 Jan Background Music to Living
21 Jan Axioms: Laws of Consideration—What an Axiom Is

ISSUES

PAB 41 10 Dec The Code of a Scientologist
PAB 42 24 Dec Six Basic Processes

UNIFICATION CONGRESS OF DIANETICISTS AND SCIENTOLOGISTS LECTURES
PHOENIX, ARIZONA

This congress was marked by the release of a limited manuscript edition of Mr. Hubbard's newest book, *Dianetics 55!* The material in the book was expanded upon in the lectures to delegates. So successful was this congress that it was repeated in four additional places: New York City, London, Australia and New Zealand. *(To be released on cassette.)*

28 Dec Introduction
28 Dec Group Processing
28 Dec History of Dianetics
28 Dec Dianetics 1955
28 Dec Communication and ARC
29 Dec Games
29 Dec Group Processing
29 Dec Group Processing
29 Dec Terminals and Communication
29 Dec Errors in Communication: Aims and Goals of Dianetics and Scientology
30 Dec Communication and Problems
30 Dec Group Processing
30 Dec Problems and Games
30 Dec Group Processing
30 Dec Pan-determinism

DIANETICS 55!
by L. Ron Hubbard

A limited manuscript edition was available at the Unification Congress in Phoenix, Arizona, December 1954. Dianetics 55! *was published in April 1955 by the Hubbard Dianetics Research Foundation, Phoenix, Arizona.* TRANSLATIONS: Danish, French, German and Italian.

1955

Continuing his busy lecture schedule, Mr. Hubbard gave many talks at the Hubbard Professional College in Phoenix, Arizona through the end of May.

In June he traveled to Washington, DC, where he delivered two series of lectures and formed the Founding Church of Washington, DC. By October he had returned to London and begun delivery of the Fourth London Advanced Clinical Course (the first ACC that Mr. Hubbard himself conducted in England). He continued to research, write and lecture in England through the rest of the year.

NOTES ON LECTURES GIVEN BY L. RON HUBBARD AT PHOENIX, 1954

Taken from the lectures of L. Ron Hubbard, published by the Hubbard Association of Scientologists International, Johannesburg, South Africa, early 1955.

THE ELEMENTARY SCIENTOLOGY SERIES

Taken from the works of L. Ron Hubbard. Published by the Scientology Council, Los Angeles, California, early 1955.

L. RON HUBBARD'S PROFESSIONAL AUDITOR'S BULLETINS BOOK 1

(Professional Auditor's Bulletins 1–15)

Published by the Hubbard Communications Office, Washington, DC, 1955. (Note: The Professional Auditor's Bulletins written by L. Ron Hubbard also appear in the Technical Bulletins *volumes.)*

ARTICLE

JOS ISSUE 43-G Jan Phoenix Clinic

TENTH ADVANCED CLINICAL COURSE LECTURES
PHOENIX, ARIZONA

1955 opened with the Tenth Advanced Clinical Course, continuing the established pattern of personal instruction and auditing demonstrations from Mr. Hubbard. Though this was a separate course, it took place while the Ninth Advanced

Clinical Course was in progress. *(Available on cassette as part of the series "The Solution to Entrapment.")*

3 Jan Auditing Requirements, Differences
5 Jan Exteriorization by Gradient Scale
6 Jan Exteriorization
7 Jan Elementary Material: Know to Mystery Scale

Public Lectures and Group Processing Series
PHOENIX, ARIZONA

Despite a heavy schedule of teaching at Advanced Clinical Courses, Mr. Hubbard made time for a series of Wednesday evening lectures and Group Processing sessions for the general public.

5 Jan The Society at Large
5 Jan Group Processing
12 Jan Group Processing
12 Jan Games
19 Jan The Affinity-Reality-Communication Triangle
19 Jan Group Processing
26 Jan Goals of Dianetics and Scientology
26 Jan Group Processing
2 Feb Alcoholism
2 Feb Group Processing
2 Feb Variation on Six Basic Processes
9 Feb Miracles
9 Feb Session: Control of Body, Think a Thought
23 Feb Scientology and Ability
23 Feb Group Processing
23 Feb Session: Find a Mystery
2 Mar Increasing Efficiency
9 Mar Health and Certainty
9 Mar Session: Only One, Things Real and Unreal
9 Mar Group Processing
16 Mar Knowingness
23 Mar Scientology: A Technical Subject—Communication Lag, Principal Kinds Found in a Pc
30 Mar Conquered Territory
30 Mar Group Processing
6 Apr On the Second Dynamic
6 Apr Session: "What Could You Say To . . . ?"
13 Apr The Dynamic Principles of Existence—The Eight Dynamics
13 Apr Session: Find Present Time
20 Apr Para-Scientology—or Things That Go Boomp in the Night
20 Apr Session: Change and No-Change
27 Apr The Direction of Modern Scientology
27 Apr Gray Dianetics
27 Apr Session: "Something You Could Say to People" and Ownership
4 May Cause and Effect and Its Use in Processing
4 May Session: Cause and Effect
11 May Operation Manual for the Mind
11 May Session: "Enchantment" Processing

Issue

PAB 43 7 Jan Plotting the Preclear on the Tone Scale

Staff Auditors' Conferences
PHOENIX, ARIZONA

During January and February 1955, several conferences were held with staff auditors in Phoenix, briefing them on advances and refinements and discussing the results they were achieving.

10 Jan Staff Auditors' Conference Lecture: Exteriorization
11 Feb Staff Auditors' Conference
28 Feb Staff Auditors' Conference

Recorded Address

While delivering Advanced Clinical Courses in Phoenix, Arizona, Mr. Hubbard made a recording especially for delegates to the Third International Congress of Scientologists which was being held in London, England.

16 Jan Address to Congress Delegates

Issues

PAB 44 21 Jan Two-way Communication in Action
PAB 45 4 Feb Mimicry
PAB 46 18 Feb Straightwire
PAB 47 4 Mar Opening Procedure 8-C

Auditing Demonstrations
PHOENIX, ARIZONA

Presented on closed-circuit television to Advanced Clinical Course students, these sessions were also recorded on audio tape for future study and use.

8 Mar LRH Auditing Demonstration
14 Mar LRH Auditing Demonstration
14 Mar LRH Auditing Demonstration
15 Mar LRH Auditing Demonstration Parts I and II
16 Mar LRH Auditing Demonstration Parts I and II
17 Mar LRH Auditing Demonstration Parts I and II
18 Mar LRH Auditing Demonstration Parts I and II
21 Mar LRH Auditing Demonstration Parts I and II
22 Mar LRH Auditing Demonstration Parts I and II
23 Mar LRH Auditing Demonstration Parts I and II
24 Mar LRH Auditing Demonstration Parts I and II
25 Mar LRH Auditing Demonstration Parts I and II
28 Mar LRH Auditing Demonstration Parts I and II
29 Mar LRH Auditing Demonstration Parts I and II
1 Apr LRH Auditing Demonstration
1 Apr LRH Auditing Demonstration
4 Apr LRH Auditing Demonstration
7 Apr LRH Auditing Demonstration
19 Apr LRH Auditing Demonstration
20 Apr LRH Auditing Demonstration
21 Apr LRH Auditing Session—Demonstration Rud Session
25 Apr LRH Auditing Demonstration
26 Apr Discussion and Education of the Pc
26 Apr LRH Auditing Demonstration
27 Apr LRH Auditing Demonstration
27 Apr LRH Auditing and Discussion
28 Apr Demonstration Auditing—More Education on Ownership Process
29 Apr LRH Discussion and Auditing of Ownership and Control
7 May LRH Auditing Demonstration
8 May LRH Auditing Demonstration
9 May LRH Auditing Demonstration
10 May LRH Auditing Demonstration
13 May LRH Auditing Demonstration Parts I and II

Hubbard Professional College Lectures
PHOENIX, ARIZONA

(To be released on cassette.)

14 Mar "Death Wish" The Only One (The Mechanics and Solution of the Occluded Case)
26 Mar Axiom 51
2 Apr Axiom 51 in Action
9 Apr A New Understanding of the Six Basic Processes
16 Apr The Service Facsimile
23 Apr Thinkingness
30 Apr Ownership Processing
7 May Meaningness—Parts I and II
14 May The Tone Scale

Auditors' Conferences
PHOENIX, ARIZONA

(To be released on cassette.)

14 Mar Auditors' Conference
14 Mar How to Audit Paying Pcs
1 Apr First Hour Staff Auditors' Conference
4 Apr Scale of Awareness
8 Apr Staff Auditors' Conference
18 Apr Auditors' Conference
19 Apr Staff Auditors' Conference
21 Apr Auditors' Conference
29 Apr Sixth Hour of Staff Auditors' Conference
2 May Talk on "Think a Thought" in Connection with Ownership

The Scientology Cross

The Scientology sunburst cross, the basic design of which was found by L. Ron Hubbard in an ancient Spanish mission in Arizona, is the official insignia for Scientology ministers.

The cross is three inches high and two inches wide, made of sterling silver and hangs on a fine silver chain. It is worn by both men and women. Each of the eight points of the cross represents one of the eight dynamics.

Large Scientology crosses of wood and other materials are displayed in Scientology churches.

Very small versions are also worn as pins.

THE HUBBARD COMMUNICATIONS OFFICE INSIGNIA

This is a shield with the S and double triangle and the initials "HCO" placed vertically, to the right.

Below the shield on a banner is the motto of HCO, the Hubbard Communications Office, "Bring Order."

THE SCIENTOLOGIST, A MANUAL ON THE DISSEMINATION OF MATERIAL
by L. Ron Hubbard

Published by the Hubbard Association of Scientologists International, Phoenix, Arizona, March 1955. The text of this manual has been reprinted in full in the Technical Bulletins *and* Organization Executive Course *volumes.*

ISSUE

PAB 48 18 Mar Opening Procedure by Duplication

THE CREATION OF HUMAN ABILITY
by L. Ron Hubbard

Published by Scientology Publications in London, England in April 1955 and in the United States a few weeks later.

ISSUES

PAB 49 1 Apr The Remedy of Havingness
PAB 50 15 Apr Remedy of Havingness—The Process

LECTURE
PHOENIX, ARIZONA

18 Apr Dianetics and Scientology

ISSUE

PAB 51 29 Apr Spotting Spots

KEY TO TOMORROW
(also entitled *Scientology: Its Contribution to Knowledge*)

Taken from the works of L. Ron Hubbard, published by the Hubbard Communications Office, Phoenix, Arizona, May.

ARTICLE

ABILITY MINOR 4 early May The Scale of Awareness

ISSUES

PAB 52 13 May Auditing the "Whole Track"
PAB 53 27 May Ownership, Special PAB

ANATOMY OF THE SPIRIT OF MAN CONGRESS LECTURES
WASHINGTON, DC

One of the highlights of this congress was LRH's announcement of the new, expanded Tone Scale, showing how it complemented the Tone Scale already familiar to Dianeticists and Scientologists. *(To be released on cassette.)*

3 Jun The Hope of Man
3 Jun Practicalities of a Practical Religion
3 Jun History of Research and Investigation
4 Jun Direction of Truth in Processing
4 Jun The Tone Scale—Three Primary Buttons of Exteriorization
4 Jun Group Processing—Meaningness
4 Jun Composition of Beingness—Postulates, Exteriorization, Beingness
4 Jun Group Processing
5 Jun The Descent of Man
5 Jun How to Chart the Preclear—Knowingness and Unknowingness
6 Jun Six Basic Steps—Some Fundamentals of Auditing
6 Jun The Mechanisms of Ownership in Living
6 Jun Group Processing—Additional Processing on Meaningness
6 Jun The Game Called Man
6 Jun What Scientology Is Doing, Organizations, The Control and Direction of Man

ISSUES

CHART 4 Jun The Tone Plotting Scale
PAB 54 10 Jun Reality Level of Preclear

ARTICLE

ABILITY MINOR 5 mid-Jun The Hope of Man

STRAIGHTWIRE: A MANUAL OF OPERATION
by L. Ron Hubbard

Published by Hubbard Communications Office, Washington, DC, July. The text of this manual has been reprinted in its entirety in the Technical Bulletins *volumes.*

ISSUE

PAB 56 8 Jul Axiom 51 and Communication Processing

LECTURE
PHOENIX, ARIZONA

11 Jul Seven Basic Steps (Codification of the Hubbard Certified Auditor Course)

ARTICLES

ABILITY MINOR 6 mid-Jul The Adventure of Scientology
ABILITY MAJOR 5 early Aug With ARC
CERTAINTY VOL. 2, NO. 8 Aug An Idea Versus War

ISSUE

DESPATCH 5 Aug "The Secret Is . . ."

ACADEMY LECTURE SERIES
WASHINGTON, DC

Delivered at the Academy of Religious Arts and Sciences in Washington, DC, these lectures covered the latest techniques being taught on Scientology auditor training courses. *(Available on cassette as a series entitled "Conquest of Chaos.")*

23 Aug The Auditor's Public
23 Aug Axiom 53: The Axiom of the Stable Datum
30 Aug Rugged Individualism
30 Aug Union Station—R2-46
14 Sep The Unknown Datum—A MEST Shaking Lecture
21 Sep Postulates 1, 2, 3, 4 in Processing—New Understanding of Axiom 36

ARTICLE

ABILITY MAJOR 6 Basic Processes

ISSUE

PAB 60 2 Sep "Anything–Everything–Nothing"

ARTICLE

ABILITY 14 Start That Practice!

ISSUES

PAB 61 16 Sep Selling
PAB 62 30 Sep Psychiatrists

FOURTH LONDON ADVANCED CLINICAL COURSE LECTURES
LONDON, ENGLAND

Traveling to London in the autumn of 1955, Mr. Hubbard delivered an Advanced Clinical Course and a series of lectures to the general public. *(To be released on cassette.)*

3 Oct Fundamentals of Scientology and Rudiments of Auditing—Parts I and II
4 Oct 1st and 2nd Postulates in Living
4 Oct 1st to 4th Postulates in Living
5 Oct Smoothness of Auditing Parts I and II
6 Oct Communication and "I Don't Know" (Confusion)
6 Oct Stable Datum and Confusion
7 Oct Relations to Time Continuum
7 Oct Base Time and Time Continuum
10 Oct Establishing of the Auditor
10 Oct The Subject of Communication
11 Oct Data of Comparable Magnitude

11 Oct Communication Bridge, Confusion, Time Factor
12 Oct Communication and Intentions, Deterioration Of
13 Oct The Antiquity of Auditing
13 Oct Affinity, Reality and Communication
14 Oct Exteriorization and Interiorization
14 Oct Further Aspects of Exteriorization
17 Oct Tolerance of Havingness
17 Oct Establishing a Session
18 Oct Beginning and Continuing a Session
18 Oct Processing: Level One
19 Oct The Senior Desire of a Thetan
19 Oct Third Level of a Process
20 Oct The Pc's Present Time Problem—The Body
20 Oct An Understanding of Creative Processing
21 Oct Native State and Postulates 1, 2, 3, 4
21 Oct Native State and Communication
24 Oct Résumé of Creative Processes
24 Oct Lack of Terminals
25 Oct Engrams—Dissemination of Material
25 Oct The Handling of Confusion in Any Pc or on Any Dynamic
26 Oct Stable Datum and the Study of Science
26 Oct Solving Engrams with Stable Datum, Communication Terminals
27 Oct The Role of a Scientologist
28 Oct The Anatomy of Terminals
28 Oct Six Basic Levels of Processes
28 Oct Intolerance
31 Oct How to Audit
31 Oct Training of an Auditor
1 Nov The Preclear's Reality
1 Nov Improvement in Technology
2 Nov Trying and Communication
2 Nov Randomity and Automaticities
3 Nov A Review of the Fourth London ACC
3 Nov Attitude and Conduct of Scientology
16 Nov New Understanding of Universes
17 Nov End of Course Lecture

LONDON PUBLIC LECTURE SERIES
LONDON, ENGLAND

8 Oct Goals of Dianetics and Scientology
8 Oct Processing the Third Dynamic
15 Oct How Good Can You Get
15 Oct The Dynamics
22 Oct The Road to Perfection—The Goodness of Man
22 Oct Man: Good or Evil?
29 Oct The Machinery of the Mind
29 Oct Power of Choice and Self-Determinism

(The last five lectures of this series have been reproduced on cassette as part of the Personal Achievement Series.)

ISSUES

PAB 63 14 Oct Playing the Game
OPERATIONAL BULLETIN 1 20 Oct "The Following Auditing Commands . . ."
PAB 64 28 Oct First Postulate

ARTICLE

CERTAINTY VOL. 2, NO. 11 Nov The Six Levels of Processing

HUBBARD PROFESSIONAL COURSE LECTURES
LONDON, ENGLAND

(To be released on cassette.)

8 Nov Six Levels of Processing, Issue 5, Level One
8 Nov Six Levels of Processing, Issue 5, Level Two
9 Nov Six Levels of Processing, Issue 5, Level Three
9 Nov Six Levels of Processing, Issue 5, Level Four
10 Nov Six Levels of Processing, Issue 5, Level Five
10 Nov Six Levels of Processing, Issue 5, Level Six

ISSUES

OPERATIONAL BULLETIN 4 11 Nov Six Levels of Processing—Issue 5
PAB 65 11 Nov From a Lecture by L. Ron Hubbard on MEST Processing, 7 July 1951
OPERATIONAL BULLETIN 5 mid-Nov "Limited Company Proceeding . . ."

ARTICLES

ABILITY 16 What Are You Going to Do about It?
ABILITY 18 Letter to *Ability* Editor

ISSUES

PAB 66 25 Nov First, Second, Third and Fourth Postulates
OPERATIONAL BULLETIN 6 late Nov Processing Futures

LONDON AUDITORS' MEETING LECTURES
LONDON, ENGLAND

At these meetings with auditors in London, Mr. Hubbard delivered lectures on his latest developments. *(To be released on cassette.)*

1 Dec The Lowest Level Case
1 Dec The Fundamentals of Auditing Style
15 Dec Exteriorization by Separateness from Weakest Universe
22 Dec Matching Auditing to Tone

ISSUES

OPERATIONAL BULLETIN 7 6 Dec Intensive in Progress
OPERATIONAL BULLETIN 8 13 Dec Handling Press
OPERATIONAL BULLETIN 9 19 Dec The Turn of the Tide
PAB 68 23 Dec First and Second Postulate
OPERATIONAL BULLETIN 10 28 Dec "I Am Giving Here in Outline Form . . ."

RECORDED LECTURES

These lectures were recorded during 1955—their exact dates are unknown.

Elementary Straightwire
LRH Auditing—"What Wouldn't You Mind Fighting?"

1956

Early in 1956, Mr. Hubbard traveled from London, England to Dublin, Ireland, where he opened up a new Dianetics and Scientology organization.

Researching, writing and lecturing all the while, LRH then traveled from Dublin back to London, then to Barcelona, Spain, back to London, over to Washington, DC, back once more to London (sailing on the famous ocean liner *Queen Elizabeth* and writing *The Problems of Work* during the voyage), then again to Washington, DC, where he ended this very active and productive year with the Anti-Radiation Congress lectures.

LONDON AUDITORS' MEETING LECTURES
LONDON, ENGLAND

Continuing a series of technical lectures that he had started in December 1955, LRH gave the following talks at the London Auditors' Meetings in early 1956. *(To be released on cassette.)*

3 Jan Solution to Body Behavior—Part I
3 Jan Solution to Body Behavior—Part II
10 Jan Auditor Insight
12 Jan Anglo-Saxon Thought
16 Jan Repair and Remedy of Havingness
19 Jan Exteriorization
24 Jan The Role of Creation in Aberration
31 Jan Basic Lecture on Havingness
31 Jan GE Scientology
7 Feb The Game of Life (Exteriorization and Havingness)
9 Feb Sixth Dynamic Decisional Processing
14 Feb Aims and Goals of Scientology 1956
14 Feb Games Processing Applied to Auditing

ISSUES

OPERATIONAL BULLETIN 11 3 Jan "Now That the Happy Holidays Are Over . . ."
PAB 69 6 Jan Six Levels of Processing, Issue 7 (Revised)
OPERATIONAL BULLETIN 12 10 Jan An Experimental Arrangement of Level One
OPERATIONAL BULLETIN 13 17 Jan Operational Bulletins Growing Up
OPERATIONAL BULLETIN 13 APPENDIX 1 17 Jan Scientology Schools Curriculum
OPERATIONAL BULLETIN 14 24 Jan After the Flood
DESPATCH 25 Jan "The Recent Reports on Preclears Show . . ."
OPERATIONAL BULLETIN 15 31 Jan Long Continued Run

CREATIVE LEARNING—A SCIENTOLOGICAL EXPERIMENT IN SCHOOLS

Based on the works of L. Ron Hubbard. Published by the Hubbard Communications Office, London, England in early 1956.

HUBBARD PROFESSIONAL COURSE LECTURES
LONDON, ENGLAND

(To be released on cassette.)

6 Feb SLP 8, Level One, Theory
7 Feb SLP 8, Level One, Summation of Basic Theory
8 Feb Practical Application of Games to Processing
8 Feb SLP 8, Motives Of
10 Feb Application of Games to Processing (cont.)
10 Feb Use of Games Theory in Processing
14 Feb Application of Games to Processing—Comms and Vias
14 Feb The Various Ways of Processing a Preclear
14 Feb Games Applied to Processing Techniques

ISSUES

OPERATIONAL BULLETIN 16 7 Feb "Scientology US"
CEREMONY 7 Feb Founding Church of Scientology Funeral Service
OPERATIONAL BULLETIN 17 14 Feb Processing Results
PAB 72 21 Feb Changes for the PABs
PAB 74 6 Mar Office in Ireland

PAB 78 3 Apr Administration
PAB 79 10 Apr The Open Channel
PAB 80 17 Apr Scientology's Most Workable Process
PAB 81 24 Apr Purpose
PAB 82 1 May Scientology, The Fundamentals of Thought

LONDON PUBLIC LECTURE SERIES
LONDON, ENGLAND

5 May Latest Processes Today
31 Jul Games Processing

ISSUES

PAB 83 8 May The Conditions of Existence
DESPATCH 8 May Test Results
PAB 84 15 May The Reason Why
CEREMONY 15 May Scientology Wedding Ceremony
PAB 85 22 May The Parts of Man
PAB 86 29 May Causation and Knowledge
PAB 87 5 Jun Scientology Processing
PAB 88 12 Jun The Conditions of Auditing (concluded)
PAB 89 19 Jun Scientology, Revision of Translator's Edition
DESPATCH 26 Jun Current Processes
PAB 90 26 Jun The Organizations of Dianetics and Scientology
PAB 91 3 Jul The Anatomy of Failure
PAB 92 10 Jul A Critique of Psychoanalysis
DESPATCH 14 Jul Five Types of Valences
DESPATCH 20 Jul How to Really Split a Valence
DESPATCH 22 Jul Technical Bulletin
PAB 93 24 Jul A Critique of Psychoanalysis (cont.)

HUBBARD PROFESSIONAL COURSE LECTURES
LONDON, ENGLAND

(To be released on cassette.)

Aug The Auditor's Code
Aug The Code of a Scientologist
Aug Auditing Positions
3 Aug Axioms 1–5
Aug Axioms 6–10
Aug Facsimiles (Solids)
Aug Opening Procedure of 8-C
Aug Start, Change and Stop
Aug Games Theory
Aug Problems and Consequences
Aug Valences
Aug Knowingness
Aug Creative Processing, Motion Stops, Perception
Aug Exteriorization Procedures
Aug Scales, Motion
Aug Scales, Curiosity, Not-Know
17 Aug Confusion and Stable Datum
Aug Chronic Somatics
Aug The Auditing of Solids
Aug Not-Knowing
20 Aug Auditing as a Profession
27 Aug Auditors' Conference

ISSUES

HCOB 3 Aug Organizational Health Chart
HCO PL 3 Aug I Mail Line
HCO PL 3 Aug II Organizational Health Chart
BULLETIN 13 Aug Scientology Process Chart
PAB 94 15 Aug The Anatomy of Traps
HCOB 20 Aug HGC Procedure of Aug. 20
DESPATCH Aug The Goal of Auditors
DESPATCH 21 Aug Summary of Intensives Since June
BRIEFING BULLETIN Games Congress, Shoreham Hotel

ARTICLE

ABILITY 34 Havingness

GAMES CONGRESS LECTURES
WASHINGTON, DC

This congress included thirteen hours of Group Processing and lectures covering the subject of games and their importance in understanding man and improving his happiness and abilities. *(To be released on cassette as a series entitled "Games and the Spirit of Play.")*

31 Aug Spiritual and Material Requirements of Man
31 Aug Group Processing—Crave to Know
31 Aug The Anatomy of Human Problems
1 Sep Games Conditions vs. No-Games Conditions
1 Sep Third Dynamic Application of Games Principles
1 Sep Group Processing—"Keep It from Going Away"
1 Sep Auditing Procedure 1956
1 Sep Universe
2 Sep Havingness
2 Sep Group Processing: Hold It Still, Mama and Papa
2 Sep Group Processing: Hold It Still, Mama and Papa (cont.)
2 Sep Effectiveness of Brainwashing
2 Sep Demonstration of SCS

SCIENTOLOGY: THE FUNDAMENTALS OF THOUGHT
by L. Ron Hubbard

First published as a series of Professional Auditor's Bulletins starting in 1956. Scientology: The Fundamentals of Thought *was published in book form by the Hubbard Association of Scientologists International, Washington, DC in September 1956. TRANSLATIONS:* Danish, French, German, Finnish, Greek, Italian, Japanese, Dutch, Norwegian, Serbo-Croatian, Spanish and Swedish.

ISSUES

PAB 95 1 Sep Valences
HCO TECHNICAL BULLETIN 12 Sep The Summary of a Bulletin from the Academy in Washington, DC Concerning Training
PAB 96 15 Sep Justice

CONFERENCE AND LECTURE
LONDON, ENGLAND

20 Sep London Auditors' Conference
25 Sep Review of SLP 8

ISSUES

HCO PROCESSING SHEET 20 Sep "The Following Are Useful . . ."
HCOB 24 Sep Organizational Indoctrination
HCOB 26 Sep Registrar
ORG BULLETIN 26 Sep Procedure for Putting Auditors on Staff
HCO PL 26 Sep II Flow Line for Personnel
PAB 97 1 Oct Start-Change-Stop
HCOB 4 Oct High School Indoctrination

LONDON CONGRESS ON HUMAN PROBLEMS
LONDON, ENGLAND

This congress was held to discuss the major problems afflicting man at the time. *Certainty* magazine reported that in Mr. Hubbard's lectures to the more than 200 delegates, "He showed how salvation in our time lay in the application of the basic principles of modern knowledge as discovered, correlated and aligned in Scientology." *(To be released on cassette.)*

5 Oct Man's Relentless Search
5 Oct Portions of You
5 Oct Group Processing—Putting the MEST Universe There
6 Oct Youth—Today's Displaced Person
6 Oct Group Processing—"Keep It from Going Away" and "Granting Life"
6 Oct Uses of Scientology
7 Oct Salvation 1956
7 Oct Personal Efficiency
7 Oct Group Processing—Keeping Objects From Going Away
8 Oct Group Processing
8 Oct March of the Atom
8 Oct Today's Battle of Britain

ISSUES

LETTER 10 Oct "Dear Jean . . ."
PAB 98 15 Oct Creative Processes, Motions, Stops and Perceptions
HCOB 15 Oct Summary Research Project

ARTICLE

ABILITY 36 Randomity and Automaticity

FIFTEENTH AMERICAN ADVANCED CLINICAL COURSE LECTURES
WASHINGTON, DC

In addition to recent developments in auditing technology, this course included several important lectures on learning and education. *(Available on cassette as a series entitled "The Power of Simplicity.")*

15 Oct Opening Lecture
16 Oct Mimicry
17 Oct Complexity
18 Oct More on Mimicry
19 Oct Mechanics
22 Oct Scale of Reality
23 Oct "CRA" Triangle
24 Oct Cut Comm Lines (In and Out)
25 Oct Games vs. No-Games
26 Oct Learning Rates
29 Oct The Mind
30 Oct Education: Point of Agreement
31 Oct Rest Points and Confusion
1 Nov Coordination of Classes of Processes
2 Nov Wind-up on Stable Datum and Rest Points
5 Nov Radiation
6 Nov Time Track
7 Nov Creation
8 Nov Simplicity
9 Nov Skull Gazing
12 Nov Simplicity vs. Alter-Isness
13 Nov Aberration and the Sixth Dynamic
14 Nov Training Methods
15 Nov Diagnosis: How To
16 Nov Summary Lecture
23 Nov Farewell Lecture

ORGANIZATION SERIES LECTURES
WASHINGTON, DC

These lectures, given to organization staff and students, cover how to succeed and prosper and make progress professionally, in an auditing practice, in a Personnel Efficiency Course and other courses, and in group activities of any sort. *(Available on cassette as a series entitled "How to Present Scientology to the World.")*

18 Oct How to Create and Instruct a PE Course, Part I

18 Oct How to Create and Instruct a PE Course, Part II
25 Oct Education
25 Oct Methods of Education
1 Nov Tone Scale (Autumn 1956)
1 Nov How to Handle Audiences
8 Nov Research Report: Radiation, and Its Relationship to Processing
8 Nov Definition of Organization, Part I
15 Nov Definition of Organization, Part II
15 Nov Testing
22 Nov The Consequences of Organization
22 Nov The Deterioration of Liberty
29 Nov Hope
29 Nov The Scale of Havingness
6 Dec Money
6 Dec A Postulate Out of a Golden Age
13 Dec Confusion and the Stable Datum
13 Dec Randomity

Issues

HCO PL 26 Oct Gradient Scale of Personnel Procurement
HCOB 26 Oct HPA/HCA Training Processes
DESPATCH Oct/Nov Policy on Payment for Training and Processing
PAB 99 1 Nov Facsimiles and Solids
HCOB 9 Nov I Accounting Department, Washington
HCOB 9 Nov II Activities of Legal Department
HCOB 15 Nov HGC Preclear Complaints
PAB 100 15 Nov The Auditing of Solids
DESPATCH 19 Nov Staff Policy on Training and Indoctrination Courses
HCO TRAINING BULLETIN 30 Nov SLP 8
PAB 101 1 Dec Games Conditions Theory
HCOB 3 Dec BScn—HAA Techniques
HCO PL 11 Dec Tape Color Code
PAB 102 15 Dec A Case Report

The Problems of Work
by L. Ron Hubbard

First published by Scientology Consultants, Inc., Washington, DC, December 1956. *TRANSLATIONS:* Danish, Dutch, French, German, Indonesian, Italian, Japanese, Norwegian, Portuguese, Spanish and Swedish.

L. Ron Hubbard's Professional Auditor's Bulletins Book 2
(Professional Auditor's Bulletins 16–30)

Published by Hubbard Communications Office, Washington, DC, 1956.

L. Ron Hubbard's Professional Auditor's Bulletins Book 3
(Professional Auditor's Bulletins 31–46)

Published by Hubbard Communications Office, Washington, DC, 1956.

L. Ron Hubbard's Professional Auditor's Bulletins Book 4
(Professional Auditor's Bulletins 47–69)

Published by Hubbard Communications Office, Washington, DC, 1956.

(Note: The Professional Auditor's Bulletins written by L. Ron Hubbard also appear in the Technical Bulletins *volumes.)*

Anti-Radiation Congress Lectures
Washington, DC

The fourteen hours of lectures to this congress include discussion of the problem of nuclear radiation, its effects on society and on the individual, and how these can be dealt with. *(To be released on cassette.)*

29 Dec Opening Lecture
29 Dec Scientology View on Radiation
29 Dec Proofing Up a Body
29 Dec Group Processing—"Put It There"
29 Dec Group Processing—Confrontingness
30 Dec Solution to Psychosis
30 Dec Project Third Dynamic
30 Dec Insanity—Scarcity and Importances
30 Dec Group Processing—Mocking Up Bodies
30 Dec Group Processing—Making Problems and Confusions
31 Dec Background on Scale of Havingness
31 Dec Subzero Scales—Relation to Scale of Awareness
31 Dec Confrontingness
31 Dec Confrontingness (cont.)

1957

Mr. Hubbard taught three Advanced Clinical Courses in Washington, DC during 1957, and lectured at three congresses—one in London and two in Washington.

The lectures given to one of these congresses, the London Congress on Nuclear Radiation and Health, form the basis of the book *All About Radiation*, also first published during this year.

LRH's research into the field of education in 1957 resulted in vital technical issues on education in general and on the training of auditors—the foundations of modern Scientology study and training technology.

Issues

PAB 103 1 Jan The Code of a Scientologist
HCO PL 1 Jan FC Policy Letter

Scientology Training Course Manual: Field Validation and Hubbard Apprentice Scientologists
(also known as *HAS Training Manual*)

Taken from the works of L. Ron Hubbard, published by the Hubbard Association of Scientologists International, Washington, DC, 1957.

Sixteenth American Advanced Clinical Course Lectures
Washington, DC

Mr. Hubbard's lectures to students on this course included talks on the anatomy of traps, evil and how it affects man's abilities, and individual identity. *(Available on cassette as a series entitled "The Anatomy of Cause.")*

2 Jan Course Outline
3 Jan Reality Scale in Action
4 Jan Havingness in General and Bodies in Particular
7 Jan Learning Processes—No-Game Condition
8 Jan Agreements and Postulates of the Eight Dynamics
9 Jan Obnosis
10 Jan The Postulate of a Game
11 Jan Postulates of Action–Reaction
14 Jan Control
15 Jan Evil
16 Jan Havingness
17 Jan The Randomities of Communication
18 Jan Auditing Techniques: Self-Denial, Responsibility
18 Jan Question and Answer Period
22 Jan Auditing Techniques: Order of Processes
22 Jan Question and Answer Period
23 Jan Auditing Techniques: Scale of Processes
24 Jan Auditing Techniques: Altering Cases
24 Jan Question and Answer Period
25 Jan Auditing Techniques: Specifics
25 Jan Question and Answer Period
28 Jan Auditing Techniques: Stimulus-Response
28 Jan Question and Answer Period
29 Jan Auditing Techniques: Action and Reaction
29 Jan Question and Answer Period
30 Jan Auditing Techniques: Workable and Unworkable
30 Jan Question and Answer Period
31 Jan Auditing Techniques: Solids
31 Jan Question and Answer Period
1 Feb Auditing Techniques: Games Conditions
4 Feb Auditing Techniques: Procedure CCH
5 Feb Auditing Techniques: How Far South?
5 Feb Question and Answer Period
6 Feb Auditing Session on Processes of Intensive CCH
7 Feb Summation
7 Feb Question and Answer Period
8 Feb General Use of Procedure
8 Feb Question and Answer Period
11 Feb Question and Answer Period
12 Feb Final Lecture: Question and Answer

Issues

PAB 104 15 Jan Dissemination
HCO PL 25 Jan I Referrals to Field
HCO PL 25 Jan II Concerning the Separateness of Dianetics and Scientology
PAB 105 1 Feb The Story of a Static
HCO TRAINING BULLETIN 6 Feb Procedure CCH
POLICY 12 Feb "HCO Is Entitled . . ."
HCO PL 13 Feb "We Will No Longer . . ."
PAB 106 15 Feb Good Processes

Seventeenth American Advanced Clinical Course Lectures
Washington, DC

(To be released on cassette.)

25 Feb Opening Lecture: CCHs, The Future of Scientology
25 Feb Question and Answer Period
26 Feb ARC Triangle and Associated Scales
27 Feb Communication and Isness
27 Feb Question and Answer Period
28 Feb The Parts of Man
28 Feb Question and Answer Period
1 Mar Problems: Their Handling and Running
1 Mar Question and Answer Period About Problems and Responsibility
4 Mar Control
5 Mar The Scale of Techniques
6 Mar Control—The Lowest Possible Process
6 Mar Question and Answer Period
7 Mar "Ought to Be"
7 Mar Question and Answer Period
10 Mar Valences—Basic Personality
10 Mar Question and Answer Period
11 Mar Summary of Techniques

11 Mar Question and Answer Period
12 Mar Survival
12 Mar Question and Answer Period
13 Mar Techniques in Practice
14 Mar A Summary of an Intensive
15 Mar Exact Control
15 Mar Question and Answer Period
19 Mar Outline of Modern Intensive
19 Mar Question and Answer Period
20 Mar Game Conditions
21 Mar The Assist
22 Mar Effect: Axiom 10
25 Mar The Uses of Control
25 Mar Rest Points and Confusions
26 Mar Question and Answer Period
27 Mar Extroversion–Introversion, Its Relationship to Havingness and Communication
27 Mar Question and Answer Period
28 Mar Valences and Control
28 Mar Question and Answer Period
29 Mar The Professional Scientologist

ISSUES

HCO PL 28 Feb Hats
PAB 107 1 Mar Specific for Terror Stomach
HCOB 8 Mar Goals of Indoctrination Course
PAB 108 15 Mar Learning Rate (Part 1)
HCOB 20 Mar I Income Sources
HCOB 20 Mar II "I Wish to Thank the Staff..."
FC PL 20 Mar I Certificate Display
FC PL 20 Mar II Ministerial Ordination
FC PL 1 Apr I Always Register and Invoice
FC PL 1 Apr II Technical and Administrative Divisions
PAB 109 1 Apr Learning Rate (Part 2)
STAFF NOTICE 5 Apr Proportionate Pay Plan Proposal
HCOB 6 Apr Central Files and Procurement
HCO PL 8 Apr Advisory Committee
HCOB 8 Apr Group Auditing
HCOB 9 Apr List of "Purposes"
HASI PL 9 Apr I Employing and Discharging of Personnel
HASI PL 9 Apr II Dismissals and Post Changes
HCO PL 9 Apr I Communication Center
HCO PL 9 Apr II Bulletin Board
HASI PL 9 Apr III Grievances
HCOB 10 Apr "The HPA/HCA Full Course..."
HASI PL 10 Apr Student Intensives
NOTE 10 Apr Morale Note

LONDON CONGRESS ON NUCLEAR RADIATION AND HEALTH LECTURES
LONDON, ENGLAND

These lectures included data on nuclear radiation, its effect on health, and the latest advances in Scientology. *(Available on cassette as a series entitled "Radiation and Your Survival.")*

12 Apr Control, Communication and Havingness, Part I
12 Apr Control, Communication and Havingness, Part II
12 Apr Control Processes
13 Apr Radiation and the Scientologist
13 Apr Radiation and Scientology
13 Apr Radiation in War
13 Apr Group Processing: Emphasis on Control
13 Apr Group Processing: Emphasis on Control (cont.)
14 Apr The Reality Scale and the Effect Scale
14 Apr Scientology and Children
14 Apr The Organization and the Field
15 Apr The Control of Hysteria

ISSUE

PAB 110 15 Apr Education

ARTICLE

ABILITY 45 Today's Riches in Scientology

LECTURE
LONDON, ENGLAND

18 Apr Auditor's Training Evening, CCHs

ISSUES

HASI PL 19 Apr "Now that the Proportionate..."
HASI PL 21 Apr I Income
HASI PL 21 Apr III Information Boards
HCO PL 23 Apr "HCO Is Now Handling..."
HCO PL 28 Apr HCO Board of Review, Goal
HCOB 30 Apr Issue Authority for Mimeo
HCO PL 1 May Comm Center, Arrangement Of
PAB 111 1 May Eyesight and Glasses
HCO PL 2 May Dissemination
HCOB 3 May Training—What It Is Today, How We Tell People About It

ARTICLE

ABILITY 47 The Radiation Picture and Scientology

ISSUES

HASI PL 7 May Assignment of Auditors, Rooms, Students
HCO PL 9 May IV Mail
FC PL 9 May Bulletin Boards and Information Boards
FC PL 13 May Financial Enrollment Procedure
FC PL 14 May Hat Turnover
FC PL 15 May Central Files and Procurement
PAB 112 15 May The Rights of the Field Auditor

HUBBARD CERTIFIED AUDITOR COURSE LECTURES
WASHINGTON, DC

(To be released on cassette.)

15 May Comm Course, TRs 1, 2, 3, 4 and 5
16 May Procedure CCH: Background
16 May Procedure CCH: CCH Steps
30 May Outline of a Course and Its Purpose

ISSUES

FC PL 16 May Intensives for Staff
HCO PL 16 May Clarification of Invoicing Items
HCO TRAINING BULLETIN 17 May Definitions
HCO TRAINING BULLETIN 17 May Student Processing
HCO PL 18 May Policy on Signatures in Publications
FC PL 20 May Outside Auditing
HCO TRAINING BULLETIN 20 May Interim Process

ALL ABOUT RADIATION
by L. Ron Hubbard

Published by the Hubbard Communications Office, London, England, May 1957. *TRANSLATIONS:* Swedish, Danish, Dutch, French, German, Italian and Spanish.

ISSUES

FC PL 23 May Ordering People to Processing or Training
HCO PL 23 May I Responsibility for Issue
HCOB 24 May Stable Data for Instructors

ARTICLE

ABILITY 48 The Hubbard Certified Auditor Course

ISSUES

HCO INFO BULLETIN 1 Jun Rights of the Directors of Training and Processing, Staff Auditors and Instructors Regarding Preclears and Students
HCOB 3 Jun I Explanation of Aberrative Character of Radiation
HCOB 3 Jun II Auditing a Ten-Year-Old Child
FC PL 3 Jun Letter Writing, Amending CF and Procurement, Paper Of
FC PL 8 Jun Valuable Documents, Handling Of
HCOB 8 Jun The Teaching of the 18th ACC
HCO PROCESSING BULLETIN 10 Jun What to Tell New HGC Auditors to Process on Preclears
HCOB 11 Jun Training and CCH Processes
HCOB 13 Jun Student Intensives and Co-auditing Processes
HCOB 18 Jun People's Questions
HCO PL 24 Jun "When a New Post Is Created..."

STAFF AUDITOR CONFERENCE
WASHINGTON, DC

28 Jun Lecture
28 Jun Question and Answer Period

ARTICLE

ABILITY 49 What about Validation?

ADVANCED CLINICAL COURSE (ACC) PREPARATORY MANUAL FOR ADVANCED STUDENTS IN SCIENTOLOGY

Taken from the works of L. Ron Hubbard. Published by Hubbard Communications Office, London, England, summer of 1957.

ISSUES

PAB 115 1 Jul The Rehabilitation of Abilities
HCOB 1 Jul Addition to the Auditor's Code

ARTICLE

ABILITY 50 Levels of Skill

ISSUE

HCO PL 2 Jul Financial Reports, Washington, DC

FREEDOM CONGRESS LECTURES
WASHINGTON, DC

The Freedom Congress was so named because its subject was freedom from human confusion. In addition to lectures, Mr. Hubbard gave demonstrations of specific processes and training drills and delivered Group Processing to the congress delegates. *(Available on cassette.)*

4 Jul How We Have Addressed the Problem of the Mind
4 Jul Man's Search and Scientology's Answer
4 Jul Definition of Control
5 Jul Basic Theory of CCHs
5 Jul Group Processing: Acceptable Pressures
5 Jul Group Processing: Hold It on Earth

5 Jul Purpose and Need of Training Drills
5 Jul Training Drills Demonstrated
6 Jul Third Dynamic and Communication—High School Indoctrination Demonstration
6 Jul Demonstration of High School Indoctrination
6 Jul Tone 40 on an Object
6 Jul Levels of Skill
6 Jul Tone 40 on a Person
7 Jul Child Scientology
7 Jul CCH: Steps 1–4 Demonstration
7 Jul CCH: Steps 5–7 Demonstration

ISSUES

HCO PL 5 Jul Lonesome?
FC PL 10 Jul Hiring of Staff Auditors
PAB 116 15 Jul Solids and Chronic Somatics
HCO TRAINING BULLETIN 15 Jul "Our First Lesson in Training . . ."

EIGHTEENTH AMERICAN ADVANCED CLINICAL COURSE LECTURES
WASHINGTON, DC

(To be released on cassette.)

15 Jul Scientology and Effective Knowledge
15 Jul Question and Answer Period
16 Jul CCH Related to ARC
17 Jul Theory and Definition of Auditing
18 Jul What Scientology Is Addressed To
19 Jul The Five Categories
22 Jul Control
23 Jul The Stability of Scientology
24 Jul Auditing Styles
25 Jul Scales (Effect Scale)
25 Jul Question and Answer Period
26 Jul The Mind: Its Structure in Relation to Thetan and MEST
29 Jul Optimum 25-Hour Session
30 Jul Death
31 Jul Surprise—The Anatomy of Sleep
1 Aug Thinnies
2 Aug Ability—Laughter
2 Aug The Handling of IQ (Factors Behind)
6 Aug The Scale of Withhold
7 Aug CCH
8 Aug Confronting, Necessity Level
9 Aug Instructing a Course
16 Aug The Future of Scientology
23 Aug Axiom 53

ISSUES

HCO TRAINING BULLETIN 17 Jul Changes in Training Drills
HASI PL 26 Jul Funds or Favors Received

ARTICLE

ABILITY 51 The Adventure of Communication

ISSUES

HCOB 29 Jul Withholds and Communication
HCOB 31 Jul "More Workable Commands for Testing . . ."
PAB 117 1 Aug Confronting Present Time
FC PL 8 Aug Power of Veto
ACC BULLETIN 10 Aug CCH 18

ARTICLE

ABILITY 52 Confronting

ISSUES

HCO PL 15 Aug R Rev. 12 Jun 58 Ministerial Qualifications
PAB 118 15 Aug Validation Committee
HCO PL 19 Aug "Release All Certificates . . ."

ARTICLE

ABILITY 53 Communication

ISSUES

HCOB 29 Aug Government Project Stable Data
PAB 119 1 Sep The Big Auditing Problem
HCO PL 2 Sep Field Certificates
HCOB 2 Sep "When a Verbal Direction Is Given . . ."
HASI PL 2 Sep Executives
HCO PROCEDURE LETTER 3 Sep Method of Opening and Invoicing Mail
HCO TRAINING BULLETIN 3 Sep HPA/HCA Course Processes
HCO TRAINING BULLETIN 4 Sep Stable Data for Instructors
HASI PL 5 Sep I Validation of Staff
HASI PL 5 Sep II "All Preclears Are Expected To . . ."
HCO PL 5 Sep Testing

ARTICLE

ABILITY 54 More Confronting

ISSUES

HCOB 9 Sep Processes to Be Run on HGC Preclears from This Date
PAB 120 15 Sep Control Trio
HASI PL 16 Sep HGC Policy, Results or Else
HCO TRAINING BULLETIN 24 Sep Curriculum of CCH Class
HASI PL 26 Sep Filling Posts
HASI PL 27 Sep "It Has Come to My Attention . . ."

ARTICLES

ABILITY 55 The Saga of the 18th ACC
ABILITY 56 The Eighteenth ACC

ISSUES

PAB 121 1 Oct Rudiments and Goals
PAB 122 15 Oct The Five Levels of Indoctrination and Procedure CCH
HASI PL 24 Oct "Any Staff Member . . ."
HCO PL 29 Oct HCO Files
CHART 29 Oct A Basic Chart of Process Types

ARTICLES

ABILITY 57 Escape
ABILITY 58 We Are the Free People

ISSUES

PAB 123 1 Nov The Reality Scale
HCOB 2 Nov RA Rev. 22 Feb 75 An Objective Rundown
ORG INFO SHEET 6 Nov Duties of the Executive Director of the HASI (FC)
HCOB 13 Nov Project Clear Check Sheet
PAB 124 15 Nov Communication and Isness

ARTICLE

ABILITY 59 Why You Should Come to a Congress

HUBBARD CERTIFIED AUDITOR STUDENT MANUAL

Taken from the works of L. Ron Hubbard. Published by Hubbard Communications Office, London, England, November 1957.

ARTICLE

ABILITY 60 Scientology: The Philosophy of a New Age

SCIENTOLOGY: CLEAR PROCEDURE, ISSUE ONE
by L. Ron Hubbard

Published by Hubbard Communications Office, London, England, December 1957. Also printed in the Technical Bulletins *volumes.* TRANSLATIONS: Dutch, French, German, Spanish and Swedish.

ARTICLE

ABILITY 62 We Begin a Campaign

ISSUES

PAB 125 1 Dec The Parts of Man
HCOB 3 Dec Clear Procedure, Rewritten and Expanded from 30 Nov. 57 Definitions, Goals
HCOB 4 Dec Clear Procedure Continued, Step One: Participation in Session by the Pc
HCOB 7 Dec HGC Procedure
PAB 126 15 Dec Problems: Handling and Running
HCOB 16 Dec Present Time Problem
HCOB 18 Dec Psychosis, Neurosis and Psychiatrists
HCO PL 19 Dec Phone Bill
HCO PL 20 Dec Clarification of Public Relations Post
RESEARCH NOTE Dec *Ability* Book

ABILITY CONGRESS LECTURES
WASHINGTON, DC

The lectures of this congress centered on the return of ability to live—to understand oneself and others, to communicate, to have and achieve goals. *(Available on cassette.)*

29 Dec Experience—Randomity and Change of Pace
29 Dec The Clear Defined
29 Dec Clear Procedure
30 Dec Cause and Effect
30 Dec Creating a Third Dynamic
30 Dec Upper Route to Operating Thetan
31 Dec Responsibility—How to Create a Third Dynamic
31 Dec The National Academy of American Psychology
31 Dec Creative Processing Steps

CONTROL AND THE MECHANICS OF SCS

Taken from the works of L. Ron Hubbard. Published by Hubbard Association of Scientologists International, Washington, DC, December 1957.

1958

Mr. Hubbard spent much of his time in 1958 working and lecturing in London and in Washington, DC. He was involved in organizations on both sides of the Atlantic simultaneously, *while* keeping up a heavy schedule of research, writing and lecturing.

Among his major technical breakthroughs in 1958 were refinements of clearing technology, as detailed in the 19th American ACC lectures and Clearing Congress lectures, both given in Washington. Six of the Clearing Congress lectures were captured on color film and can still be heard and watched today.

Mr. Hubbard also made major developments in the technologies of auditing and auditor training, recorded in lectures, issues and articles.

HUBBARD AMERICAN BLUE E-METER

The new "American Blue" transistorized E-Meter was ready in time for the Nineteenth American Advanced Clinical Course in January, 1958. A meter was also developed around this time that projected and displayed the meter dial and the tone arm. It was used for classroom auditing demonstrations.

ACADEMY OF SCIENTOLOGY— INSTRUCTIONS AND INFORMATION FOR STUDENTS IN HCA, VALIDATION OR SPECIAL COMMUNICATION COURSES

Based on the works of L. Ron Hubbard. Published by the Hubbard Association of Scientologists International, Washington, DC, 1958.

ISSUES

PAB 127 1 Jan The Threat to Havingness
HCO PL 4 Jan R Field Offices
Rev. 30 Dec 58
ORG PL 10 Jan Inspection of Hat Folders
DESPATCH 11 Jan HGC Procedure
HCOB 13 Jan HGC Running of Pcs
PAB 128 15 Jan The Factors Behind the Handling of IQ
HCOB 15 Jan Field Office Communication
HCOB 18 Jan "The Reason the Auditor Is Having Trouble..."

NINETEENTH AMERICAN ADVANCED CLINICAL COURSE LECTURES
WASHINGTON, DC

(To be released on cassette.)

20 Jan The Four Universes
20 Jan The E-Meter
21 Jan Intensive Procedures
21 Jan Question and Answer Period
22 Jan The Bank Out of Control and Its Stabilization
22 Jan Question and Answer Period
23 Jan Clearing Fields
23 Jan Question and Answer Period
24 Jan E-Meter: Identification and Association
24 Jan Question and Answer Period
27 Jan Clear Procedure I: What It Is You Clear, Something and Nothing
27 Jan Question and Answer Period
28 Jan Clear Procedure II: Man the Animal and Man the God
28 Jan Question and Answer Period
29 Jan Clear Procedure III: One Clear Procedure
29 Jan Question and Answer Period
30 Jan Clear Procedure IV: Test for Clears
30 Jan Question and Answer Period
31 Jan Clear Procedure V: Importance of Theory Behind Clearing Procedure
31 Jan Question and Answer Period
3 Feb Clear Procedure VI
3 Feb Question and Answer Period
4 Feb Clear Procedure VII: How to Find a Preclear, Responsibility and Help
4 Feb Question and Answer Period
5 Feb Clear Procedure VIII: The Basic Approach to Clearing, Finding the Auditor
5 Feb Question and Answer Period
6 Feb CCH 0, SCS, Connectedness
6 Feb Question and Answer Period
7 Feb Help—How to Get Started
7 Feb Question and Answer Period and Group Processing
10 Feb Conduct of Clear
10 Feb Question and Answer Period
10 Feb The Key Processes of Clearing
11 Feb Question and Answer Period
12 Feb Havingness, Anaten, Flows—in Relation to Clearing
12 Feb Question and Answer Period
13 Feb Other Processes—The Help Button
13 Feb Question and Answer Period
14 Feb Responsibility for Mock-ups
14 Feb Question and Answer Period

ISSUES

HCOB 21 Jan I MEST Clear Procedure
HCOB 21 Jan II "An ACC Is a Special Activity..."
HCOB 24 Jan Outline of Activities
ORG PL 25 Jan Inept Students
HCOB 25 Jan II Reviewing Week's Profiles
HCOB 26 Jan Future Plans
HCO PL 27 Jan Duties of Personnel Post
HCOB 1 Feb Clearing of Fields
PAB 129 1 Feb Confronting
HCOB 3 Feb Free Clearing Project

ARTICLE

ABILITY 66 The Attainment of Clears

ISSUES

HCO PL 5 Feb "No New Charters or Contracts..."
HCOB 6 Feb CCH 0b—Help in Full, Starting Session
FC PL 8 Feb "Since People Will Begin to Expect..."
HCOB 13 Feb Rules Governing the Running of CCH 0b "Help"

ARTICLE

ABILITY 67 Man's Contest with the Machine Age

ISSUES

PAB 130 15 Feb "Death"
HCO PL 25 Feb Routing of Communication

ARTICLE

ABILITY 68 We Did It!

ISSUES

HCOB 1 Mar Processes
PAB 131 1 Mar The Scale of Withhold
PAB 132 15 Mar Report on Two Cases That Have Received Psychiatric and Euro-Russian Therapy from the Government
HCO PL 17 Mar Body Routing in Central Organizations
FC PL 19 Mar Transportation, Dir Admin Responsibility
HCOB 22 Mar Clearing Reality
FC PL 26 Mar Salary and Unit Pay

STAFF AUDITORS' CONFERENCES
WASHINGTON, DC

27 Mar Comments on Auditing
27 Jun Processing on Clearing

ARTICLE

ABILITY 70 Does Clearing Cancel the Need For Training?

ISSUES

HCOB 28 Mar Only Organization Offices Can Certify Clears
PAB 133 1 Apr Procedure CCH
HCOB 2 Apr ARC in Comm Course
HCO PL 7 Apr Routing of Org Board Changes
HCOB 8 Apr Auditing the Pc on Clear Procedure
HCOB 8 Apr II A Pair of Processes
HCOB 11 Apr CCH 88—Enforced Nothingness
PAB 134 15 Apr Procedure CCH Continued
HCOB 23 Apr Four Vital Training Data for Training Hats and Registrar

ARTICLE

ABILITY 72 How We Work on the Third Dynamic

ISSUES

HCOB 1 May Signs of Success
HCO PL 1 May I Employment Qualifications

HCO PL 1 May II Financial Management
PAB 135 1 May Procedure CCH Continued
HCOB 2 May Beingness Again

ARTICLE

ABILITY 73 Assists in Scientology

ISSUES

HCOB 9 May Who Should Take Which Class
PAB 136 15 May Procedure CCH Continued
HCOB 22 May "List the Enemies of Pc . . ."

ARTICLE

ABILITY 74 Scientology and the Reactive Mind

ISSUES

HCOB 24 May A Comment on Beingness Processing
FC PL 27 May Outside Auditing
HCO PL 28 May Incoming Calls for LRH
HCOB 29 May Standard Clear Procedure and an Experimental Road: Clearing by Valences
HCOB 29 May An Example of Clearing by Valences
PAB 137 1 Jun Some More CCH Processes
HCO PL 1 Jun Purchase Orders

ARTICLE

ABILITY 76 Offbeat Processing

ISSUES

HCOB 4 Jun Running Valences
FC PL 19 Jun Freeloaders

ARTICLE

ABILITY 77 Learning How to "Clear"

ISSUES

HASI PL 30 Jun Clear Bracelet Procedure
HCOB 30 Jun Procedure for Certifying Clears

CLEARING CONGRESS LECTURES
WASHINGTON, DC

The first six lectures of this congress were filmed in color and are available today in video cassette format. They contain a complete and simple presentation of the subject for the general public as well as the professional Scientologist—a spanning of interest and presentation of unusual accomplishment in itself.

4 Jul The Fact of Clearing
4 Jul The Factors of Clearing
4 Jul The Freedoms of Clear
5 Jul Prerequisites to Auditing
5 Jul Clear Procedure, CCH 0, Help
5 Jul Clear Procedure, Creativeness
6 Jul The Magic Button
6 Jul The Goal of Auditing
6 Jul Violence

ISSUES

HCOB 7 Jul Contents and Coverage of HCA/HPA Course
HCOB 9 Jul Staff Clearing
HCOB 12 Jul Standardization of Clear Processes for Guidance and Use of the HGCs

TWENTIETH AMERICAN ADVANCED CLINICAL COURSE LECTURES
WASHINGTON, DC

(To be released on cassette.)

14 Jul Opening Lecture
14 Jul Question and Answer Period
15 Jul ACC Procedure Outlined, E-Meter TRs
15 Jul Question and Answer Period
16 Jul Course Procedure Outlined
16 Jul Question and Answer Period
17 Jul Beginning and Ending Session—Gaining Pc's Contribution to the Session
17 Jul Question and Answer Period
18 Jul ACC Training Procedure
18 Jul Question and Answer Period
21 Jul The Key Words (Buttons) of Scientology Clearing
21 Jul Question and Answer Period
22 Jul The Rock
22 Jul Question and Answer Period
23 Jul Special Effect Cases—Anatomy Of
23 Jul Question and Answer Period
24 Jul Anatomy of Needles—Diagnostic Procedure
24 Jul Question and Answer Period
25 Jul The Rock: Putting Pc at Cause
25 Jul Question and Answer Period: Clearing the Command
28 Jul ACC Command Sheet; Goals of Auditing
29 Jul ACC Command Sheet (cont.)
30 Jul ACC Command Sheet (cont.)
31 Jul Running the Case and the Rock
1 Aug Case Analysis—Rock Hunting
1 Aug Case Analysis—Rock Hunting (cont.)
4 Aug Case Analysis—Rock Hunting (cont.)
4 Aug Question and Answer Period
5 Aug ARC
6 Aug The Rock, Its Anatomy
7 Aug The Most Basic Rock of All
7 Aug Question and Answer Period
8 Aug Auditor Interest
8 Aug Requisites and Fundamentals of a Session
15 Aug Summary of Twentieth ACC

ISSUES

HCOB 14 Jul 20th ACC Training Procedure
HCOB 15 Jul Carrying On
HCOB 28 Jul Clear Procedure
HCOB 29 Jul The Rock
HCOB 30 Jul The Handling of Hubbard Communications Offices
HCOB 5 Aug "The Basic Locating Question of the Rock . . ."
HCOB 10 Aug ACC Auxiliary Procedure
HCOB 20 Aug I Present Time Problem—Running Of
HCOB 20 Aug II Out of Sessionness

AXIOMS AND LOGICS
by L. Ron Hubbard

Published by Hubbard Communications Office, London, England, August 1958. This is a compilation of materials originally published between the years 1951 and 1955.

ISSUES

HCOB 25 Aug Administrative Stable Data
HCO PL 27 Aug I "The Washington, DC Central Organization . . ."
HCO PL 27 Aug II Executives of Scientology Organizations
HCOB 28 Aug Change Auditor's Code

HUBBARD "GREEN AND GOLD" UK METER

In Great Britain the "Green and Gold" meter was built. This E-Meter was used at the Fifth London Advanced Clinical Course.

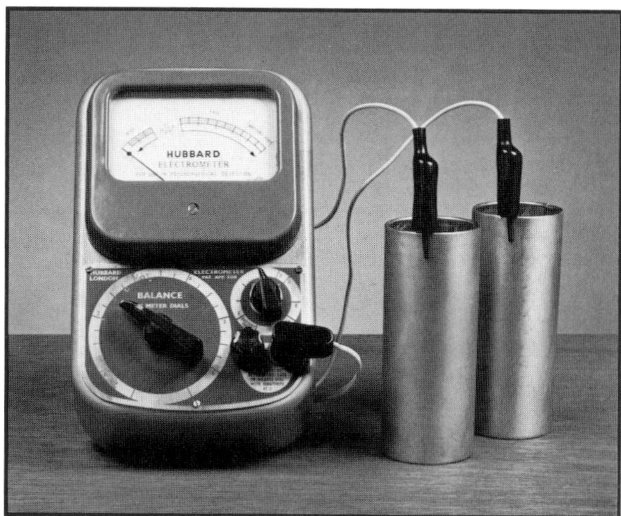

STAFF AUDITORS' CONFERENCES
WASHINGTON, DC

1 Sep How to Run Present Time Problems
27 Sep HGC Auditor Conference on Clear Procedure and Clearing People

ISSUES

HCOB 3 Sep "The Cost for an Individual..."
HCOB 12 Sep I Post Case Analysis Routine
HCOB 12 Sep II Havingness—New Commands
HCO PL 12 Sep Color Flash System Rewritten
HCOB 15 Sep More on Training Drill Two
HCO PL 17 Sep Who Can Order Printing
HCO PL 19 Sep A Model Hat for an Executive
HCOB 29 Sep Vital Training Data
HCO PL 1 Oct HCO Board of Review
HCO PL 2 Oct Sale and Conduct of Academy Courses
HCO PL 5 Oct How to Fill Jobs
FC PL 6 Oct Who Can Be Processed, Who Can Be Trained
FC PL 9 Oct Departments of FĆDC
HCOB 15 Oct ACC Clear Procedure

ACC CLEAR PROCEDURE (TWENTIETH AMERICAN ACC)
by L. Ron Hubbard

Published by Hubbard Communications Office, Washington, DC, October 1958. The text of this book appears in full in the Technical Bulletins ***volumes.***

ISSUE

PAB 146 15 Oct Procedure CCH

ARTICLE

ABILITY 83 New HCA Course You Can Begin at Home

LECTURE
LONDON, ENGLAND

Mr. Hubbard arrived in London on 17 October 1958 to give the London Clearing Congress, scheduled to start the following day. On arrival he gave a talk to the London staff on past ACCs, a new organization chart and organizational basics.

17 Oct Talk to Staff on Arrival in England

LONDON CLEARING CONGRESS LECTURES
LONDON, ENGLAND

In this congress Mr. Hubbard covered a broad range of subjects—from his experiences developing the technologies of Dianetics and Scientology, to the characteristics of Clears and the skills necessary to produce them, to the effects of Scientology's activities on the future of this civilization. *(To be released on cassette as a series entitled "The Origin of Aberration.")*

18 Oct The Story of Dianetics and Scientology
18 Oct The Skills of Clearing
18 Oct Confronting
20 Oct The Rock
20 Oct Confusion and Order
20 Oct The Future of Scientology and the Western Civilization

ISSUES

HCO PL 24 Oct I *Ability* Magazine
HCOB 25 Oct Abbreviations
DESPATCH Oct ACC Preclear Check Sheet, Fifth London ACC
HCOB 27 Oct How to Read Profiles on OCA: Comparing Current Week Profile with Week Before

FIFTH LONDON ADVANCED CLINICAL COURSE LECTURES
LONDON, ENGLAND

Auditing case histories from this month-long course, the most heavily attended ACC yet held, appear in the book *Have You Lived Before This Life? (To be released on cassette.)*

27 Oct Clearing and What It Generally Means to Man
28 Oct Compartmentation of Four Universes
28 Oct Question and Answer Period
29 Oct Types of Pictures
29 Oct Question and Answer Period
30 Oct Mental Image Pictures; Engrams
30 Oct Question and Answer Period
31 Oct Engrams
31 Oct Question and Answer Period
3 Nov The Detection of Engrams
3 Nov Question and Answer Period
4 Nov The Detection of Engrams with an E-Meter
5 Nov The Detection of Engrams Lecture 3
5 Nov Question and Answer Period
6 Nov Difficulties Encountered in Search for Engrams
7 Nov Detection of Circuits and Machinery
7 Nov Question and Answer Period
10 Nov Auditing: Its Skills
10 Nov Question and Answer Period
11 Nov The Skill of an Auditor—Part I
11 Nov Question and Answer Period
12 Nov The Skill of an Auditor—Part II
12 Nov Question and Answer Period
13 Nov The Attitude of an Auditor
13 Nov Question and Answer Period
14 Nov What an Auditor Is Supposed to Do with an Engram
14 Nov Question and Answer Period
17 Nov The Effect of the Environment on an Engram
17 Nov Question and Answer Period
17 Nov How to Audit an Engram; Use of an E-Meter
17 Nov Question and Answer Period
19 Nov How to Start and Run a Session
19 Nov Attitude and Approach to Auditing
28 Nov The Plan of Clearing
28 Nov Final Lecture

ISSUES

HASI PL 30 Oct Personnel Efficiency Foundation
HASI PL 31 Oct "Only 75 Copies..."
PAB 147 1 Nov Communication Course
HCOB 3 Nov American College of Personnel Efficiency, Dublin
HASI PL 6 Nov The Three-Basket System
HASI PL 7 Nov Registrar
HASI PL 7 Nov NO. 2 "The Output of Special Letters..."
HCOB 7 Nov HPA Courses for Staff
HCOB 11 Nov ACC Schedule
HCOB 13 Nov TR 9(b) and TR 9(c)
HASI PL 15 Nov I Informing Public of Test Results
HASI PL 15 Nov II How to Procure People
HCO PL 15 Nov I The Substance and First Duty of HCO
HCO PL 15 Nov II Legal Aid—HCO
HCO PL 15 Nov III Outstanding Copyrights and Marks
HASI PL 17 Nov Free Clear Estimates, Free Clear Tests
HCO PL 17 Nov I Project Engineering
HCO PL 17 Nov II Project Engineers, Three Types
HCO PL 17 Nov IV HCO Project Engineer: "Have You Lived Before?"
HCOB 17 Nov Clear Bracelets
OFFICE OF THE ED HASI 18 Nov Letter Policy
HCO PL 19 Nov Organization
HCO PL 22 Nov Owner of Materials, the Legal View
SEC ED 23 Nov Scientometric Testing
HCO PL 24 Nov R I Rev. 11 Feb 80 Magazine Policy
HCO PL 24 Nov II HASI Group Secretary
HCO PL 25 Nov HCO Board of Review, Function and Practice
HCOB 25 Nov Step 6
HCO TECHNICAL PL 25 Nov Techniques to Be Used on HGC Preclears
HCOB 26 Nov ACCs
HCO PL 27 Nov III Basic Financial Policy, HCO
MEMO 29 Nov Future Programs

ARTICLES

CERTAINTY VOL. 5, NO. 22 late Nov Violence
ABILITY 85 The Theory of Training in Scientology

ISSUES

PAB 149 1 Dec Dummy Auditing, Step Two: Acknowledgment
HCOB 1 Dec I "The Enrollees of the 5th London ACC..."
HCOB 1 Dec II Actions to Start an HCO
SEC ED 1 Dec Materiel Administrator Hat
HCOB 6 Dec How to Run an Engram, Brief Summary for HGC Use
HCOB 7 Dec Training Drill Change
HASI FINANCE PL 9 Dec Staff List, Notification to Payroll
HCO PL 13 Dec Important Information on Policy Letters
HCO PL 15 Dec R Corr. 6 Jan 59 Academy Training Curriculum and Examination
SEC ED 15 Dec Registrar Hat
PAB 150 15 Dec Dummy Auditing, Step Three: Duplication
HCOB 16 Dec Extension Course Curriculum
SEC ED 16 Dec Director of Administration—Hat
HCO SECRETARIAL PL 17 Dec Duties of Sec'l ED
HCOB 17 Dec I Basic Postulate of Overt Act–Motivator Sequence
HCOB 17 Dec II Auditing ARC Breaks on Registrar and Assistant Registrar
HCOB 20 Dec Processing a New Mother
SEC ED 20 Dec Certificates
HCO PL 20 Dec I HCO Communicator Basic Hat and Comm System, HCO Offices
HCO PL 20 Dec II Bad Clinical Results, Handling
HCOB 22 Dec New HGC Process, A New Straightwire
HCO PL 23 Dec I Quality of Presentations
HCO PL 23 Dec II Qualifications of HGC Staff Auditors
HCO SECRETARIAL LETTER 26 Dec Collection of Accounts
HCOB 26 Dec BScn/HCS Course
HCOB 27 Dec The First First Dynamic Process
HCOB 28 Dec Short-Sessioning

HCOB 31 Dec "Omit 'What Part . . .'"

HCO SECRETARIAL LETTER 31 Dec Routing of Profiles

ARTICLES

ABILITY 86M Something Has Happened!!!

CERTAINTY VOL. 5, NO. 23 Dec Healing and Clearing by Engram Running

L. RON HUBBARD'S PROFESSIONAL AUDITOR'S BULLETINS BOOK 5

(Professional Auditor's Bulletins 70–80)

Published by Hubbard Communications Office, Washington, DC, December 1958.

(Note: The Professional Auditor's Bulletins written by L. Ron Hubbard also appear in the Technical Bulletins *volumes.)*

1959

In 1959, Mr. Hubbard purchased Saint Hill Manor in Sussex, England, and moved his offices there.

Once established at Saint Hill he began a number of projects, including a series of experiments with plants and the nature of their life energy. His experiments and findings were widely publicized in the media. Many administrative policies were also formed here, because at that time LRH was directing the Scientology organizations and developing organizational technology to increase efficiency.

In addition to his projects at Saint Hill, LRH continued researching and writing; he also made time to travel, giving lectures and congresses in Washington, DC; London, England; and Melbourne, Australia.

ISSUES

DESPATCH Jan 21st Advanced Clinical Course Training Drills

HCOB 1 Jan Happy New Year

PAB 151 1 Jan Dummy Auditing, Step Four: Handling Originations

HCO PL 2 Jan I HCO Office Designations and Personnel

HCO PL 2 Jan II "Instructors or HCO Staff . . ."

SUCCESS CONGRESS
WASHINGTON, DC

Delegates to this congress were given lectures on new breakthroughs in the handling of engrams and the skills needed to apply them in making Clears. *(To be released on cassettes.)*

3 Jan The Future of Scientology
3 Jan Engrams and Clearing
3 Jan Preliminary to Engram Running
4 Jan Engram Running
4 Jan Overt Act–Motivator Sequence
4 Jan Leadership

LECTURE
WASHINGTON, DC

5 Jan Summary of Techniques and Processes in Use

TWENTY-FIRST AMERICAN ADVANCED CLINICAL COURSE
WASHINGTON, DC

(To be released on cassette.)

5 Jan The Basics of Scientology
6 Jan Compartmentation of Universes
7 Jan Types of Pictures
8 Jan Engrams
9 Jan Engrams; The Rock Engram
12 Jan The Detection of Engrams
13 Jan Detection of Engrams with an E-Meter
14 Jan Detection of Engrams: Finding Truth with an E-Meter
15 Jan More on Detection of Engrams
16 Jan Detection of Circuits and Machinery and the Observation of Special Types of Engrams
19 Jan Auditing Skills
20 Jan Skill of an Auditor
21 Jan Skills of an Auditor
22 Jan Attitude of an Auditor
23 Jan What an Auditor Is Supposed to Do with an Engram
26 Jan The Effect of the Environment on an Engram
26 Jan How a Process Works
27 Jan How to Audit an Engram
27 Jan What Doesn't Make an Auditor
28 Jan How to Start and Run the Session
28 Jan The Establishment of "R"
29 Jan Attitude and Approach of the Auditor
29 Jan Muzzled Auditing
30 Jan Plan of Clearing
30 Jan The Grouper
2 Feb Axiom 10
4 Feb Diagnosis of an Uncracked Case
6 Feb Processes Used in the Twenty-First ACC
6 Feb Setting Up Co-auditing Groups
13 Feb Summary of Data—Part I
13 Feb Summary of Data—Part II

ARTICLES

ABILITY 87 What Are Clears?

ABILITY 87 The 1959 HCA Course Becomes a Clearing Course

ISSUES

HCOB 5 Jan I Importance and Executives

HCOB 6 Jan I Field Activities

HCOB 6 Jan II Change of HCO PL of 15 December 1958

HCO PL 6 Jan HCO Personnel Training

SEC ED 8 Jan Reception Hat

HCOB 10 Jan HGC Allowed Processes

HCOB 11 Jan "An Amusingly Effective Process . . ."

HCOB 12 Jan Tone of Voice—Acknowledgment

HCO PL 13 Jan HCO Area Secretary Hat Material

PAB 152 15 Jan The Five Levels of Indoctrination

HCOB 19 Jan New HPA/HCA Course

HCOB 20 Jan ACC Preparatory Process Schedule for Running Engrams

HCO PL 20 Jan "When in Doubt about Copyrighting . . ."

SEC ED 22 Jan Letter Registrar Hat

SEC ED 22 Jan Mailing Lists and Field Auditors

HCOB 22 Jan Not-Is Straightwire

HUBBARD MARK I E-METER

In 1959, a company in England followed L. Ron Hubbard's instructions and produced the Hubbard Mark I E-Meter. The Mark I began a series of dependable and truly workable meters.

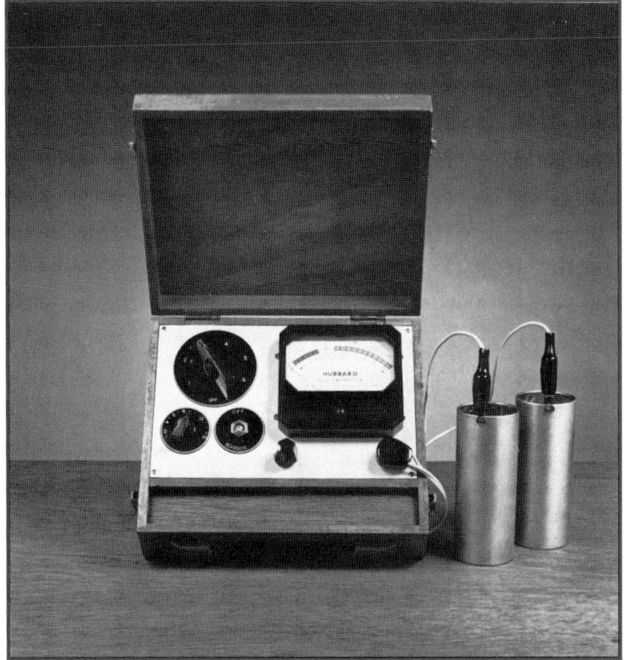

ARTICLE

ABILITY 88M A Campaign for Ethical Auditing

ISSUES

HCO PL 23 Jan Ethics
HCOB 24 Jan Scientology Axiom 58
HCO PL 26 Jan Scientology Magazines
SEC ED 29 Jan Secretarial to the Executive Director Hat
HCO PL 29 Jan HCO Communicator Hat
SEC ED 30 Jan Department of Promotion and Registration
SEC ED 31 Jan Promotional Letters
PAB 153 1 Feb CCH
HCOB 3 Feb I HGC Current Procedure
HCOB 3 Feb II Flattening a Process
HCOB 4 Feb Op Pro by Dup
SEC ED 4 Feb Policy—Certifying Clears
HCO PL 6 Feb HCO Accounts Worldwide
HASI PL 10 Feb Group Secretary
SEC ED 10 Feb The Advisory Council
SEC ED 10 Feb Central Files and the Addressograph (Use Of)
SEC ED 11 Feb The Dept of Promotion and Registration and CF Promotion Liaison
HCO PL 12 Feb Book Administrator
SEC ED 13 Feb Staff Processing and Training Policy
PAB 154 15 Feb CCH (Concluded)
HCOB 16 Feb HGC Processes for Those Trained in Engram Running or Trained in These Processes

STAFF AUDITORS' CONFERENCE
WASHINGTON, DC

16 Feb Staff Auditors' Conference

ISSUES

TRANSCRIPT Staff Auditors' Conference of February 16, 1959 Regarding HCOB 16 Feb. 59
SEC ED 17 Feb Extension Course Students, Letters
SEC ED 18 Feb Director of Materiel
SEC ED 18 Feb HGC Auditing Policies
SEC ED 18 Feb Thermostats in Buildings
SEC ED 19 Feb Use of Addresses in Letter Writing
HCOB 19 Feb Auditor's Code #19
SEC ED 23 Feb How to Interview People
SEC ED 24 Feb FC Communicator Basic Hat
SEC ED 24 Feb Secretary to Training Department Hat (Temporary Hat)
SEC ED 24 Feb Despatches to Advisory Council
SEC ED 24 Feb Shipping Department—Invoices
HCOB 24 Feb Selected Persons Overt-Withhold Straightwire
HCOB 26 Feb I Identification
HCOB 26 Feb II Engram Running on Old Dianetic Cases or Restarted Cases
SEC ED 26 Feb HCO Executive Secretary Continental
SEC ED 26 Feb Responsibilities of Assistant Org Sec
HCO PL 27 Feb Duty of Area Sec Re Personnel
HCOB 27 Feb How to Select Selected Persons
HCO PL 28 Feb HCO Board of Review Duties

ARTICLE

ABILITY 90M How to Study Scientology

ISSUES

HCOB 28 Feb I Analysis of Cases
HCOB 28 Feb II ARC Breaks with Auditors
HCOB 28 Feb III Clearing Commands
HCOB 1 Mar II Two Rules for Happy Living
PAB 155 1 Mar Processes Used in 21st ACC
HCO PL 1 Mar HCO Forbidden Activities
SEC ED 2 Mar Accounting System
HCO PL 2 Mar I HCO Cable and Despatch, Designation System
HCO PL 2 Mar II HCO Theory of Communication
SEC ED 3 Mar Book Section: Credits and Debits
SEC ED 3 Mar Staff Auditors
SEC ED 5 Mar Addressing Department—Hats
HCOB 6 Mar I Training Drills
HCOB 6 Mar II How to Do a Diagnosis on Dynamic Straightwire
SEC ED 7 Mar Materiel Administrator—Hat
SEC ED 7 Mar Processing Administrator—Hat
SEC ED 9 Mar The Purpose of the Lead Auditor
HASI PL 10 Mar "Permanent Staff Members . . ."
HCOB 10 Mar Supplemental Data Sheet to HCOB of 16 February 1959 and Staff Auditors' Conference of 16 February 1959
HCOB 13 Mar Muzzled Auditing
PAB 156 15 Mar Processes Used in 21st ACC
SEC ED 16 Mar HGC Psychotic Applicants
HCOB 17 Mar I An Insanity Questionnaire
HCOB 17 Mar II Do-It-Yourself Therapy
HCO PL 18 Mar "The Following Are . . ."
HCO PL 20 Mar Certificates Handling

ARTICLE

ABILITY 92M The Subject of Clearing

ISSUES

HCOB 24 Mar I HAS Co-audit
HCOB 24 Mar II Minimum Standards
HCOB 25 Mar HAS Co-audit and Comm Course
HCO PL 25 Mar Book Policy
PAB 157 1 Apr Processes Used in 21st ACC (Concluded)
HCOB 3 Apr HAS Co-audit and Comm Course

SPECIAL HUBBARD PROFESSIONAL AUDITOR'S COURSE LECTURES
LONDON, ENGLAND

The lectures given on this course were recorded and subsequently used in the training of Hubbard Professional Auditors the world over. *(To be released on cassette as a series entitled "The Skills of a Theta Being.")*

6 Apr Beingness and Communication
7 Apr Universes
7 Apr The Dynamics
8 Apr Scales
8 Apr States of Being
9 Apr Anatomy
9 Apr What Can Be Done with the Mind (Reality Scale)
14 Apr Mechanisms of the Mind
14 Apr Overt Act–Motivator Sequence
15 Apr Codes
15 Apr The Code of a Scientologist
16 Apr The Logics and Axioms of Dianetics and Scientology
16 Apr Axioms—Second Lecture
21 Apr Types of Auditing
21 Apr Modern Auditing Types
22 Apr Types of Cases
22 Apr Assessment
23 Apr Present Time
23 Apr Use of the E-Meter in Locating Engrams
28 Apr Theory of Processes
28 Apr Processes
29 Apr Specialized Auditing
29 Apr Processing of Children
29 Apr Mistakes in Auditing Style
30 Apr HAS Co-audit
30 Apr Electronic Phenomena of the Mind
30 Apr Confrontingness
1 May End of Course Lecture

ISSUES

HCO PL 6 Apr Clear Ads
SEC ED 6 Apr "The Organization Is As Apparent . . ."
SEC ED 8 Apr A Promotion Plan
SEC ED 8 Apr The Hats of the Department of Promotion and Registration
SEC ED 9 Apr Voluntary Help
SEC ED 9 Apr Addressograph Tabbing—Libraries
HCO PL 14 Apr New Book
HCOB 14 Apr Letter from Australia
HCOB 15 Apr Emotional Tone Scale Expanded
HCO PL 16 Apr Books, Cost Of
SEC ED 18 Apr "Bookbuyers Should Be Sold . . ."
SEC ED 18 Apr Addresses
HCOB 22 Apr Old and New Reality Scale
HCO PL 23 Apr I HCO Communicator Writes from South Africa
HCO PL 23 Apr II HAS Co-audit Courses
HCO PL 24 Apr I Final HPA Exam, HCO Board of Review
HCO PL 24 Apr III Organization Posts—Two Types
SEC ED 24 Apr Registrars—Materials Available To
HCO PL 29 Apr Defacing Books and Proper Addresses in Them
SEC ED 29 Apr Registrar—Dir of Processing, The Most Frequently Lost Line
HCO PL 30 Apr I Additional Staff Auditors
HCO PL 30 Apr II Long-Distance Program
HCO PL 1 May HAS Certificates
HCOB 3 May Solution to Solutions
HCOB 4 May I An Affinity Process
HCOB 4 May II How to Write a Curriculum
HCO PL 5 May Policy on Sec EDs and Hats
HCOB 7 May New Process
HCOB 8 May An Undoable Command

SIXTH LONDON ADVANCED CLINICAL COURSE LECTURES
LONDON, ENGLAND

(To be released on cassette.)

12 May Clearing
13 May Second Lecture on Clearing Methodology
14 May Clearing Technology
19 May The Theory of Clearing
20 May Clearing, Practice Of
21 May Clearing Process—Special Cases
26 May Clearing: Theta Clear Procedure
27 May Clearing: General Processes

28 May Clearing: General Cases—Communication Processes
2 Jun Clearing: Fixed Ideas
3 Jun Clearing: By Communication Processes, Specific
4 Jun Clearing: By Communication, Special Problems
9 Jun Clearing: Possibilities Of
10 Jun Clearing: Case Entrance Points
11 Jun Clearing: General Results

Issues

SEC ED 13 May HCO Book Administrator Hat
HCO PL 14 May III HCO Administrator
SEC ED 14 May A Staff Post
HCOB 20 May Know to Mystery Straightwire for Extreme Cases
HCOB 21 May HGC Allowed Processes and ACC Processes as of 21 May 1959
HCO PL 21 May I HCO Monies and Book Stocks
HCO PL 21 May II "The Symbol * on All Despatches..."
HCO PL 22 May I Advertisement for Field in *Certainty, Ability,* etc.—Minor Issues
HCO PL 22 May III Central Organization Efficiency
HCO PL 26 May I What an Executive Wants on His Lines
HCO PL 26 May II To Department Heads
HCOB 26 May Man Who Invented Scientology
HCO PL 28 May I New HCO WW Dept
HCO PL 28 May II Promotional Writing Fund
HCO PL 2 Jun I A Comment on Finance
HCO PL 2 Jun II Purchasing Liability of Staff Members
HCO PL 2 Jun III Correction of HCO PL 23 Dec 58, Qualification of HGC Staff Auditors
HCO PL 3 Jun Financial Management
HCO PL 4 Jun I Sale and Handout of *Certainty* Minors
HCO PL 4 Jun II Validity of Sec EDs
HCO PL 4 Jun III Definition of a Hot File
HCO PL 4 Jun IV Invoicing and Collection of Money
HCO PL 4 Jun V Instructions to Attorney or Solicitors, HCO Area Sec Enforce
SEC ED 4 Jun Definition of a Registration
HCO PL 5 Jun I Income Report Required
HCO PL 5 Jun II Handling of Bills
HCOB 5 Jun Formula 10
HCOB 6 Jun "When Cases Crack Well..."
HCOB 9 Jun Needed Material
HCOB 10 Jun Co-audit Formula
HCO PL 16 Jun Hat of PE HCO WW
HCO PL 18 Jun I US Mission Holders
HCO PL 18 Jun II Services Owing to Mission Holders
SEC ED 19 Jun Administrative Side of PE Foundation
HCO PL 21 Jun Signatures on Bulletins, Policy Letters and Sec EDs
HCOB 22 Jun How to "Sell Scientology"
HCOB 23 Jun I What Is Scientology?
HCO PL 26 Jun HCO WW Changes Quarters and Address
HCO PL 1 Jul I US Mission Queries
HCO PL 1 Jul II Responsibility for HCO Files
HCO PL 1 Jul III HCO Washington, DC
HCO PL 2 Jul II Developed Traffic, The Delirium Tremens of Central Orgs
HCO PL 2 Jul III Scientology Magazines
HCO PL 2 Jul IV Add Formula 10
HCOB 3 Jul General Information
HCO PL 4 Jul Actions for HCO Secretaries Faced with Illegal Usage

Theta Clear Congress Lectures
Washington, DC

Mr. Hubbard's lectures to congress delegates included the importance of co-auditing in accomplishing widespread clearing. *(To be released on cassette.)*

4 Jul HCO WW and Research
4 Jul Clearing
4 Jul HAS Co-audit
5 Jul Survive and Succumb
5 Jul Communication Processes
5 Jul How to Conduct a HAS Co-audit and Why

Issues

HCO PL 6 Jul II Outflow
HCO PL 7 Jul Staff Auditing Requirement
HCOB 9 Jul Definition of Scientology, Written by LRH for Legal When Setting Up HASI Ltd
HCOB 14 Jul Special Information for Mission Holders
HCO WW PL 17 Jul Duties at Saint Hill, HCO WW
HCOB 18 Jul I Technically Speaking
HCOB 18 Jul II Income Tax Reform
HCO PL 19 Jul I Accounts Inspection
HCO PL 19 Jul II New Corp—New Broom
HCOB 21 Jul HGC Allowed Processes
HCOB 22 Jul Actual Working Definition of Psychology
HCO PL 22 Jul Processing of Staff Members
HCO PL 25 Jul Membership Monies
HCOB 28 Jul Our Goals
HCO PL 28 Jul Organization of Corporations
HCOB 5 Aug HGC Processes
HCOB 7 Aug The Handling of Communication Processes, Some Rapid Data
HCO PL 10 Aug I Reception
HCO PL 10 Aug II Data Required as Reports from HCO Secretaries
HCO PL 12 Aug Cable, Don't Phone
HCOB 12 Aug A Second Type of HCO License
HCOB 13 Aug I Suggested HCA Course Schedule
HCOB 13 Aug II Mission Holders
HCOB 19 Aug I HAS Co-audit—Finding Terminals
HCOB 19 Aug II To a Roman Catholic
HCO PL 19 Aug I Writing of Letters by Staff Auditors
HCO PL 19 Aug III How to Handle Work
HCO PL 21 Aug Handling of Telex Machines
HCO WW PL 22 Aug HCO WW Projects
HCO PL 24 Aug I Tips to HCO Communicators
HCO PL 25 Aug Purchase Order System
HCO PL 26 Aug Promotional Functions of Various Depts
HCOB 27 Aug Growth with Competence
HCOB 31 Aug Some Observations on S22
HCOB 3 Sep Why "Victim" Works As a Process
HCO PL 4 Sep I Completed Staff Work (CSW)—How to Get Approval of Actions and Projects
HCO PL 4 Sep II Saint Hill Projects, Bonus and Quota System
HCOB 9 Sep A Short Story by Cable
HCO PL 12 Sep Programing
HCOB 14 Sep News Bulletin
HCOB 15 Sep Dissemination Tips
HCO PL 15 Sep I "No Changes of Positions..."
HCO PL 15 Sep II Hats and Other Folders
HCOB 23 Sep I Carrying Out Instructions
HCOB 23 Sep II The Perfect Dissemination Program
HCOB 23 Sep Correcting HCOB of 13 August 1959
HCO PL 25 Sep Accounting Records and Bills
HCOB 25 Sep HAS Co-audit
HCOB 26 Sep Data on Clearing a Staff Member after Specific Terminals Are Flat with Overt-Withhold Straightwire
HCOB 28 Sep Technical Notes on Child Processing
HCOB 29 Sep I Universe Processes
HCOB 29 Sep II The Organization of a PE Foundation
HCOB 5 Oct Universe Processes
HCO PL 5 Oct Tape and Record Production Hat
HCO PL 6 Oct Two Fine Magazines
HCO PL 9 Oct I Staff Auditors
HCO PL 9 Oct II Quota Revision
HCOB 13 Oct I A Useful Process
HCOB 13 Oct II DEI Expanded Scale
HCO PL 14 Oct I Comm Speed
HCO PL 14 Oct II Acting Executive Director
HCOB 15 Oct My Whereabouts in November
HCO PL 18 Oct Putting New Personnel on the Job and Taking Over When People Quit or Are Transferred
HCOB 20 Oct An Experimental Process
HCO PL 20 Oct HCO Order of Importance of Actions
HCO PL 21 Oct Routing of Bulletins and Policy Letters
HCO PL 23 Oct I Attention Registrars and Book Administrators
HCO PL 23 Oct II Academy Training
HCOB 25 Oct Psychoanalysis Goes Capitalistic
HCO PL 29 Oct I Processing of Academy Students
HCO PL 29 Oct II Service
HCO PL 29 Oct III Orders During Absence
HCOB 29 Oct III Communication Process Includes Havingness
HCOB 30 Oct To Retain Co-audit Pc's Interest in Case
HCOB 31 Oct Create Processes—Dangers and Advantages

Article

Ability 107 On Bringing Order

Melbourne Congress Lectures
Melbourne, Australia

This congress, given during one stop on a round-the-world tour, covered a wide range of subjects including current political systems, how to improve one's chances of surviving an atomic attack and the relation between complexity and unworkability. *(To be released on cassette.)*

7 Nov Welcome Address
7 Nov Recent Developments on OT
7 Nov The Route Through Step Six
8 Nov Importances
8 Nov Valences
8 Nov Final Lecture

FIRST MELBOURNE ADVANCED CLINICAL COURSE LECTURES
MELBOURNE, AUSTRALIA

(To be released on cassette.)

- 9 Nov The Know-How of Auditing
- 9 Nov Demonstration of an Assist
- 10 Nov Valence Splitting—Entering a Mind Process
- 10 Nov Demonstration of Knocking Down a Tone Arm
- 11 Nov Cycle of Action; Create, Destroy, Relative Importances
- 11 Nov Demonstration: Force Process—Discreditable Creation
- 12 Nov The Rule of the Weak Valence
- 12 Nov Demonstration: Dynamic Straightwire Assessment
- 12 Nov The Rehabilitation of Judgment
- 13 Nov How to Have a Game Instead of a Case
- 16 Nov The Collapsed Cycle of Action
- 16 Nov Getting the Pc into Session
- 17 Nov Case Assessment
- 17 Nov Demonstration: Case Assessment
- 18 Nov Alter-Isness—Keynote of All Destruction
- 18 Nov Demonstration: Minus Randomity Areas
- 19 Nov Minus Randomity—Clue to Case Assessment
- 19 Nov Intricacies of Create—Create Series
- 20 Nov Rationale of Create Series
- 20 Nov Responsibility of Creation
- 23 Nov Responsibility for Zones of Creation
- 23 Nov Demonstration: Responsibility for Destruction
- 24 Nov The Universe of a Thetan
- 24 Nov Demonstration: Turning on Pictures
- 25 Nov Counter-Create
- 25 Nov Individuation
- 26 Nov The Constancy of Fundamentals of Dianetics and Scientology
- 26 Nov The Handling of Cases—Greatest Overt
- 27 Nov Clearing Up the Whole Track
- 27 Nov Principal Incidents on the Track
- 30 Nov The Anatomy of Havingness
- 30 Nov Processes

ISSUES

HCOB 12 Nov	Acknowledgments in Auditing
HCOB 18 Nov	1st Melbourne ACC Material
HCO PL 20 Nov	Validation of Certificates
HCO PL 23 Nov	Employment of Criminals Forbidden
HCO PL 27 Nov	Key to the Organizational Chart of the Founding Church of Scientology of Washington, DC
HCOB 30 Nov	Allowed Processes 1st Melbourne ACC
HCO PL 7 Dec I	Former Saint Hill Staff
HCO PL 7 Dec II	Scientology Cleanup
HCOB 11 Dec	New Horizons in Scientology
HCOB 15 Dec	Urgent Change in All Co-audit Courses
HCOB 16 Dec	Responsibility for O/Ws

ARTICLE

ABILITY 110	Techniques of Child Processing

ISSUES

HCOB 23 Dec	Responsibility
HCO PL 28 Dec	Personnel Departure Requirement
HCOB 31 Dec R Rev. 9 Feb 89	Blow-Offs

ARTICLE

CERTAINTY SPECIAL ISSUE 3	Is It Possible to Be Clear?

CEREMONIES OF THE FOUNDING CHURCH OF SCIENTOLOGY
by L. Ron Hubbard

Published by Hubbard Communications Office, Washington, DC, 1959.

1960

Mr. Hubbard's schedule of lectures, congresses and Advanced Clinical Courses for 1960 took him to Washington, DC; London, England; Johannesburg, South Africa and to Saint Hill in England for the First Saint Hill Advanced Clinical Course.

His research led to major advances in auditing addressed to the subjects of help, responsibility and harmful acts. He also devoted time to finding new ways to apply Scientology broadly, to the betterment of large sectors of society.

ISSUE

HCO PL 1 Jan	Administrative Procedure for Reducing Overts

STATE OF MAN CONGRESS LECTURES
WASHINGTON, DC

In this congress, given at the Shoreham Hotel in Washington, DC, Mr. Hubbard covered the eight dynamics in detail, with particular attention to how the dynamics interrelate and how to improve conditions *across* the dynamics. *(Available on cassette.)*

- 1 Jan Opening Lecture
- 1 Jan Responsibility
- 1 Jan Overts and Withholds
- 2 Jan Why People Don't Like You
- 2 Jan Marriage
- 2 Jan Group Auditing Session
- 3 Jan Zones of Control and Responsibility of Governments
- 3 Jan Create and Confront
- 3 Jan Your Case

ISSUES

HCOB 2 Jan	HAS Certifications
HCOB 3 Jan	A Third Dynamic for Scientology

HUBBARD CLEARING SCIENTOLOGIST COURSE LECTURES
WASHINGTON, DC

Personally addressing the students of this course, Mr. Hubbard reiterated and expanded on auditing basics such as handling blocks to free communication and precise use of the E-Meter. *(To be released on cassette.)*

- 4 Jan E-Meter Phenomena
- 4 Jan E-Meter and Time Track Structure
- 5 Jan Processing Against an E-Meter
- 5 Jan Operating an E-Meter in Processing
- 6 Jan Case Procedure: Steps 1–6
- 6 Jan Identity
- 7 Jan Inability to Withhold
- 7 Jan Case Level and Needle State
- 7 Jan Specialized Problems
- 8 Jan Sessioning and Withholds

ISSUES

HCOB 7 Jan	The Unmoving Case
HCOB 8 Jan	OT Procedure for HCS/BScn Courses
HCOB 14 Jan	The Black Case
HCOB 18 Jan	Zones of Authority and Regulations of Saint Hill

HUBBARD MARK II E-METER

The Hubbard Mark II E-Meter was released in 1960.

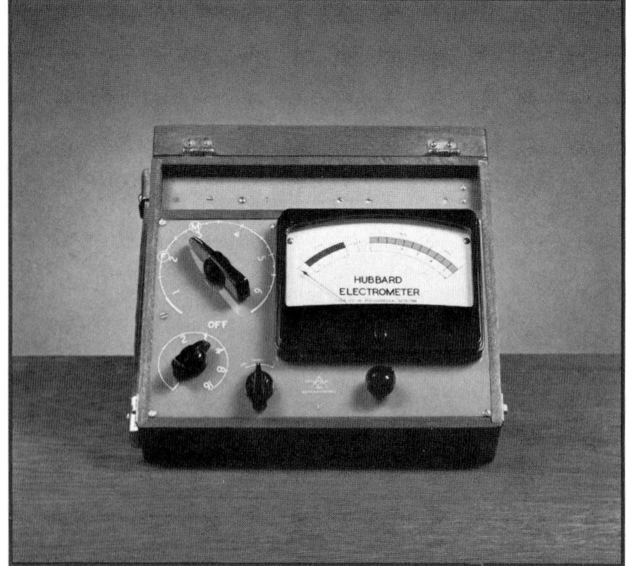

HCO PL 18 Jan	Qualifications of Permanent Staff Members
HCOB 19 Jan I	Tapes for Sale
HCOB 19 Jan II	Casualties
HCO PL 20 Jan	HCO WW Points of Concentration
HCOB 21 Jan I	Justification
HCOB 21 Jan II	Responsibility
HCOB 24 Jan	OT Procedure
HCO PL 27 Jan	Accounts Policies
HCOB 28 Jan	The Key to All Cases—Responsibility
HCOB 2 Feb	The Co-audit Team
HCOB 3 Feb	Security Check
HCOB 4 Feb I	Theory of Responsibility Processing
HCOB 4 Feb II	Overt Manifestations on a Low-Toned Case
HCOB 8 Feb I	Honest People Have Rights, Too
HCOB 8 Feb II	The Reputation of Saint Hill
HCOB 8 Feb III	Security Checks
HCOB 9 Feb I	Cancellation of Certificates
HCOB 9 Feb II	Research Advances
HCOB 10 Feb I	British E-Meter Operation
HCOB 10 Feb II	Restoration of Certificates
HCOB 11 Feb	Create and Confront

Article

Certainty Feb Vol. 7, No. 2	Why Some Fight Scientology

Issues

HCOB 18 Feb	How to Run O/W and Responsibility
HCOB 23 Feb	HPA Course Change Proposal to London
SEC ED 23 Feb	Outside Funds or Gifts—Staff Member Policy
HCOB 25 Feb	Scientology Can Have a Group Win
HCO PL 29 Feb	Organization Secretary Hat

Speech
London, England

End Feb — Opening Speech to Congress Delegates

Have You Lived Before This Life?
by L. Ron Hubbard

Published by Hubbard Communications Office, Saint Hill Manor, East Grinstead, Sussex, England, March 1960. Revised and expanded in 1977. *Translations:* Dutch, Danish, French, German, Italian and Spanish.

Issues

SEC ED 16 Mar	CF–Promotion Liaison Hat
HCOB 17 Mar	Standardized Sessions
HCO PL 18 Mar	*Have You Lived Before This Life?* Sales
HCO PL 21 Mar	Economy Wave
HCOB 21 Mar	Research Project
HCOB 24 Mar	Goals in the Rudiments

Article

Mar	How Do People Know They Have Lived Before?

Issues

HCO PL 29 Mar	HGC and Academy Prices for Minors
HCOB 30 Mar	Interrogation
HCOB 31 Mar	The Present Time Problem
HCO PL 31 Mar	Accounts Lines

Article

Ability 115	A Salute to the Central Organization Washington, DC and American Scientologists

Issues

HCOB 7 Apr I	A New Summary of Auditing
HCOB 7 Apr II	Check Sheet for HGC
HCO PL 9 Apr	Outflow
HCOB 11 Apr	The Purpose of HCO WW
HCOB 11 Apr	New Training Schedule
HCOB 14 Apr	New PE Data
HCOB 14 Apr	Flowers
SEC ED 21 Apr	Long Distance Phone Calls and Telegrams
HCOB 21 Apr I	Domestic Arrangements Changes
HCOB 21 Apr II	Presession Processes
HCOB 24 Apr	Concerning the Campaign for Presidency
HCOB 25 Apr	Send Your Clipping Files
HCO PL 25 Apr	Important Certification Change
HCOB 25 Apr	PrR Promotion
HCO PL 27 Apr	Security of Employment
HCOB 28 Apr	Books Are Dissemination
HCOB 29 Apr	The Scientific Treatment of the Insane
HCOB 30 Apr	ACC TRs
HCO PL 3 May	PE Literature
HCOB 4 May	Tapes
HCOB 5 May	Help
HCOB 7 May	Earmarks of a Hot Terminal
HCOB 10 May	Our Technical Program
HCOB 12 May	Help Processing
HCOB 19 May	How Help Became Betrayal
HCOB 22 May	Decertification, How You Should Support It
HCOB 23 May	Decertified Persons
HCO PL 23 May	Cancellation of Certificates
HCOB 26 May	Security Checks
HCOB 27 May II	"Dear Scientologist . . ."
HCOB 28 May	By Their Actions . . .
HCOB 30 May	Dynamic Assessment on Help
HCO PL 2 Jun	Requirements for Staff Posts
HCO PL 7 Jun I	Staff Auditing
HCO PL 9 Jun	HCO WW Internal Comm Schedule
HCOB 9 Jun	The Basic Assumptions of Scientology Versus Overts
HCOB 10 Jun I	What We Expect of a Scientologist *KSW Series 33*
HCOB 10 Jun II	HGC Preclear Assessment
HCOB 16 Jun	Hints on Running Cases with Help
HCO PL 20 Jun	Rush Magazine Note
HCOB 21 Jun	Religious Philosophy and Religious Practice
HCOB 23 Jun	The Special Zone Plan

London Open Evening Lectures
London, England

In addition to his schedule of research, writing and lectures and conferences with staff, Mr. Hubbard made time in June and July to give several lectures to newer public. *(To be released on cassette.)*

23 Jun	Difference Between Scientology and Other Studies
23 Jun	Confront
30 Jun	Some Aspects of Help
7 Jul	Help

Issues

HCOB 30 Jun	Create Again

Hubbard Mark III E-Meter

The Mark II was soon followed by the Hubbard Mark III E-Meter, also released in 1960.

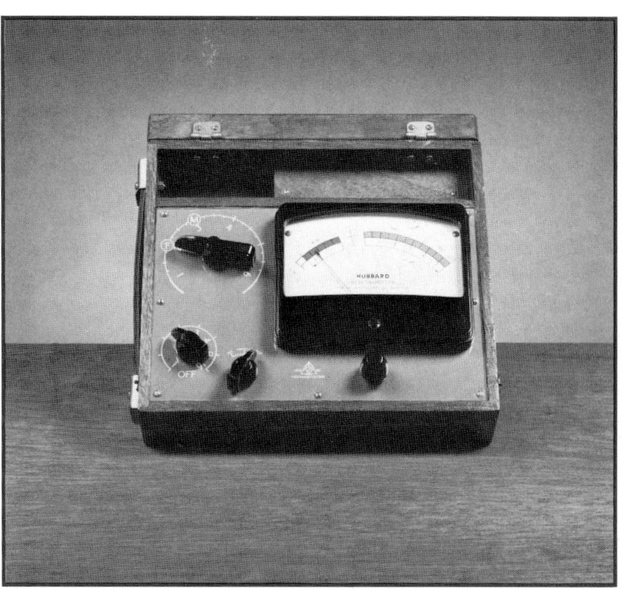

HCO PL	30 Jun	Administrative Traffic Trend
HCO PL	6 Jul	Working Hours, Office Staff
HCOB	6 Jul	Making Clears and Picking Up HGC Quality
HCOB	7 Jul	The Assessment of Help
HCOB	14 Jul	Current Rundown Concept Help
HCO PL	20 Jul	Director of Zoning Hat
HCOB	21 Jul	Some Help Terminals
HCOB	27 Jul	Double Action Cycles
HCO PL	28 Jul	Losses
HCO PL	3 Aug I	Magazine Advertisement Policy
HCO PL	3 Aug II	Security of Persons Leaving Staffs
HCO PL	4 Aug	ACC at Saint Hill
HCOB	4 Aug	Regimen 1

LONDON CONGRESS ON DISSEMINATION AND HELP
LONDON, ENGLAND

These lectures were given at a two-day congress with the theme of "dissemination and help," sponsored by the London Scientology organizations. *(To be released on cassette.)*

7 Aug	Clearing and Presessioning
7 Aug	Presessioning
7 Aug	Adjustment of the Cycle of Action in Presessioning

FIRST SAINT HILL ADVANCED CLINICAL COURSE LECTURES
SUSSEX, ENGLAND

The lectures given at the first ACC delivered at Saint Hill Manor included discussion of the sixth and seventh dynamics and the use of the E-Meter in clearing. *(To be released on cassette.)*

8 Aug	Introduction to Course
10 Aug	Regimen 1
12 Aug	Skill in Auditing
15 Aug	Auditor Requirements
16 Aug	Fundamentals with Regard to Cases
17 Aug	Elements of Presessioning
18 Aug	Organization Programs
19 Aug	Auditor Weakness
22 Aug	Why Auditing Works
23 Aug	Handling of Insanity
24 Aug	Basic Relationship of Auditing
25 Aug	Development of Scientology Data
26 Aug	Fundamentals and Cases
29 Aug	The Importance of an E-Meter
30 Aug	Circuits and Havingness
31 Aug	Theory on the 6th and 7th Dynamics
1 Sep	Common Denominator of Cases
2 Sep	Case Improvements
5 Sep	Successful Processes for Handling MEST
6 Sep	Correct Use of E-Meter
12 Sep	In-Sessionness
13 Sep	How Havingness Relates to Circuits
14 Sep	Formula of Havingness
15 Sep	In-Sessionness and Havingness
16 Sep	Final Lecture—6th and 7th Dynamics

AUDIBLE E-METER

This meter, on which reads were heard rather than seen, was developed for use by the blind. Several prototypes of this meter were made, the first in the early 1960s.

ISSUES

HCO PL	8 Aug	Persons Living In
HCO PL	11 Aug	Organization Information Center
HCOB	11 Aug	The Laws of Assessment
SEC ED	12 Aug	Department of Government Relations
HCO PL	15 Aug	Department of Government Affairs
HCOB	18 Aug	Vital Information
HCO PL	19 Aug	Registrar Lost Line
HCO PL	22 Aug	Department of Government Relations
HCO PL	25 Aug	Chicago Area
HCOB	25 Aug I	Powerful Presession Additions
HCOB	25 Aug II	New Definition of Psychosis
HCOB	26 Aug	Regimen Two
HCO PL	30 Aug I	Training Restrictions
HCO PL	30 Aug II	Special Zone Department
HCOB	1 Sep	Presession Two
HCOB	8 Sep	The Presessions of the 1st Saint Hill ACC
HCOB	15 Sep	The Tone Arm
HCO PL	17 Sep I	Giving the Pc Full Hours
HCOB	19 Sep I	Captive Brains
HCOB	19 Sep II	ACC Lecture Tapes
HCOB	22 Sep	Announcing New Technology
HCOB	23 Sep	Order of Test of Havingness and Confront Commands
HCO PL	28 Sep	HPA Grants
HCOB	28 Sep	Tips on How to Crack an HGC Case
HCOB	29 Sep	Havingness and Duplication
HCOB	6 Oct R Rev. 8 May 74	Thirty-six New Presessions
HCOB	10 Oct	Current News
HCOB	18 Oct	Terminal Stable Data
HCOB	20 Oct	Theory 67
HCO PL	22 Oct II	The Three Service Branches
HCOB	27 Oct	Revised Case Entrance
HCO PL	28 Oct I	New Testing Promotion Section
HCO PL	28 Oct II	HASI–HCO Relationship Discussed
HCO PL	31 Oct R I Rev. 24 Jan 91	Private Pcs
HCO PL	31 Oct II	US Appointment and Organizational Trend
HCOB	3 Nov	Failed Help
HCO PL	7 Nov	HCO Area Secretary Hat Addition
HCOB	10 Nov	Formula 13
HCOB	12 Nov	Clearing Routine
HCO PL	14 Nov	Urgent PrR
HCO PL	15 Nov R I Rev. 4 Feb 91	Modern Procurement Letters
HCO PL	15 Nov II	Staff Certificate Requirements
HCO PL	16 Nov	New Org Programs
HCOB	17 Nov	Starting Cases
HCO PL	18 Nov I	Staff Transfers and Dismissals
HCO PL	18 Nov II	Executive Time Salvage and Conferences Curtailed
HCO PL	19 Nov I	Pc Scheduling
HCOB	20 Nov	HAS Co-audit Ended
HCO PL	22 Nov	Warning on New PE
HCO PL	23 Nov I	Reports to OIC
HCO PL	24 Nov	Testing Promotion Revised
HCOB	24 Nov	The Unmoving Case
HCO PL	26 Nov	Permanent Staff Member Requirements
HCO PL	29 Nov	Testing Program Change
HCOB	1 Dec	New Formulas
HCO PL	2 Dec	Promotion on PE Foundation
HCOB	15 Dec	Presession 37
HCO PL	18 Dec	CF and Address Change
HCOB	19 Dec	PE Change
HCO PL	19 Dec	Spatial Reorganization
HCO PL	21 Dec I	Staff Clearing—New Policy
HCO PL	22 Dec	Important Change in Reports
HCOB	22 Dec I	HAS Co-audit Resumed
HCOB	22 Dec II	O/W, A Limited Theory
HCOB	29 Dec	The New PE and the New HAS Co-audit

ANATOMY OF THE HUMAN MIND CONGRESS LECTURES
WASHINGTON, DC

At the end of 1960, Mr. Hubbard traveled from South Africa to Washington, DC to deliver this congress on the 31st of December and the 1st of January 1961. *(Available on cassette.)*

31 Dec The Genus of Dianetics and Scientology
31 Dec The Things of Scientology
31 Dec A Talk on South Africa
1 Jan The Whole Answer to the Problems of the Mind
1 Jan The Field of Scientology
1 Jan Scientology Organizations

1961

1961 began with Mr. Hubbard in Washington, DC delivering the Twenty-second American Advanced Clinical Course and the Anatomy of the Human Mind Congress. Before the end of March he had traveled first to Saint Hill and from there to Johannesburg, South Africa, where he delivered more than twenty lectures and released a new organizational chart for use in Scientology organizations.

Certainly one of the most major events of 1961, though, was the opening of the most comprehensive, exhaustive auditor training course ever—the Saint Hill Special Briefing Course. Inaugurated on the 24th of March at Saint Hill Manor, this course rapidly became known the world over as *the* course where truly expert auditors were made.

TWENTY-SECOND AMERICAN ADVANCED CLINICAL COURSE LECTURES
WASHINGTON, DC

(To be released on cassette.)

2 Jan Present Time Problems—Why Cases Don't Move
2 Jan Present Time Problems and Withholds
3 Jan E-Meter
3 Jan Withholds
4 Jan The Mechanics of the Reactive Bank
4 Jan Clearing Procedure
5 Jan Dianetics and Present Time Problems
5 Jan Methods of Clearing Technology
6 Jan Dianetic Assist and Presession 38
6 Jan Clearing Routine

ISSUES

HCO PL 4 Jan I Urgent Mimeo Change
HCO PL 9 Jan Duties of HCO
HCO PL 10 Jan A Brief Outline of an HGC As Currently Done
HCOB 12 Jan New Help Data
HCO PL 16 Jan I Help Me Put in the New Lines
HCO PL 16 Jan II New Road
HCOB 19 Jan Additional HAS Processes

ANATOMY CONGRESS LECTURES
JOHANNESBURG, SOUTH AFRICA

The content and method of delivery of the Anatomy of the Human Mind Course was the key topic of the lectures at this congress. *(To be released on cassette.)*

21 Jan Opening Lecture
21 Jan The Parts of the Mind
21 Jan Aberration and the Handling Of
22 Jan Evolution of Early Research—Prehav Scale
22 Jan Things of Scientology: Cycle of Action, Time Track, Stable Datum
22 Jan Johannesburg Staff Intros, Lecture: Clearing Certs for Clears

THIRD SOUTH AFRICAN ADVANCED CLINICAL COURSE LECTURES
JOHANNESBURG, SOUTH AFRICA

(Reproduced on cassette for the South African Rundown Auditor Course.)

23 Jan HAS Co-audit Processes and E-Meter
24 Jan Presession 38
25 Jan Model Session Revised
26 Jan Difference Between Dianetics and Scientology—Presession 38
27 Jan Creative Ability
2 Feb Auditor Failures
3 Feb Regimen and Prehavingness—Advances
6 Feb Making Formulas Out of the Prehav Scale
7 Feb What Are You Auditing?
8 Feb Case Behavior Under Processing
9 Feb Mental Healing: Sanity and Insanity
10 Feb Organization Lines
13 Feb The Three Therapies of Earth
14 Feb Fundamentals of Auditing
15 Feb Havingness and Confront Scales
16 Feb Machines and Havingness
17 Feb Case Conditions

ISSUES

HCO PL 23 Jan PE Course Abolished
HCO PL 24 Jan A Test Policy on MD Referrals
HCOB 25 Jan Handling of Rudiments
HCOB 26 Jan The "Ultimate" Processes
HCOB 28 Jan New Assessment Scale
HCO PL 30 Jan II Case Files
HCO PL 31 Jan I Spheres of Influence
HCO PL 31 Jan II Message Placement
HCO PL 31 Jan III Academy Meters

ARTICLE

ABILITY 125 Personal Integrity

ISSUES

HCOB 2 Feb I Command Sheet, Prehavingness Scale
HCOB 2 Feb II UK Cases Different
HCO PL 4 Feb Types of Letters Established
HCO PL 7 Feb Proper Public Routing
HCOB 9 Feb New Presession Data and Script Change
HCO PL 10 Feb Professional Charges
HCO PL 12 Feb Certificates and Awards Revised List
HCO PL 13 Feb Permanent Staff Requirement Changes
HCO PL 14 Feb I Personnel Procurement
HCO PL 14 Feb II The Pattern of a Central Organization
HCOB 16 Feb Formula 19
HCO PL 17 Feb I HCO Continental
HCO PL 17 Feb II State of Emergency
HCO INFO LETTER 18 Feb Magazines
HCOB 18 Feb SOP Goals, Marvelous New Breakthrough, Be-Do-Have Coordinated
HCO PL 19 Feb II Accounts: How to Do a Payroll
HCOB 20 Feb Important Data on Goals SOP
HCO PL 21 Feb I Pattern for City Offices
HCO PL 21 Feb II Choosing PE and Registration Personnel
HCO PL 22 Feb I My Program to Raise Your Unit
HCO PL 22 Feb II Permanent Staff Exam

HUBBARD BRITISH MARK IV E-METER

The British Mark IV E-Meter was introduced in early 1961. As of June 1961, the only meter allowed in Academies of Scientology was the British Mark IV.

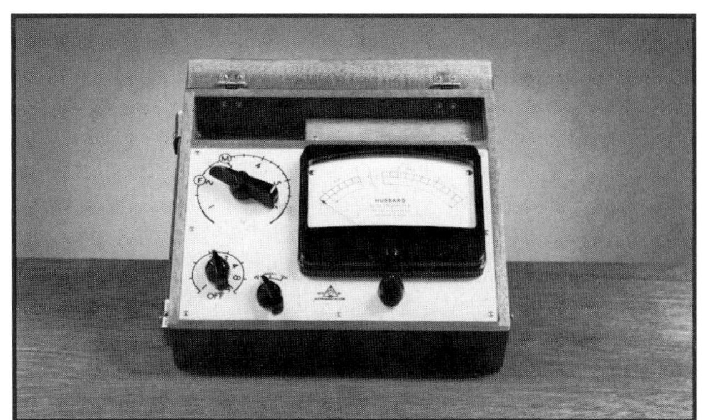

HCO PL 23 Feb Directives from a Board Member
HCOB 23 Feb PT Problem and Goals
HCO PL 26 Feb II Qualification of Executives
HCO PL 27 Feb Outside Pcs of Staff Members
HCO PL 2 Mar Automatic Evaluation Packet for PE Foundation
HCOB 2 Mar I New Prehav Command
HCOB 2 Mar II Use of SOP Goals Procedure
HCOB 2 Mar III Formula 20
HCO PL 12 Mar II Supplies of Central Organization Forms
HCO PL 12 Mar III Duties of the Assoc Sec's Sec in a Central Organization
HCO PL 13 Mar I Department of Official Affairs
HCO PL 13 Mar II Department of Official Affairs
HCO PL 13 Mar III Staff Auditor Training
HCO PL 13 Mar IV Free Courses
HCO PL 20 Mar I Mimeo and File Procedure
HCO PL 20 Mar II Basic Staff Auditor's Hat
HCO PL 22 Mar Staff Members Ordered to Processing
HCO PL 23 Mar Distribution of Bulletin Change
HCOB 23 Mar SOP Goals
HCO PL 24 Mar I Training Project Construction and Preparation
HCO PL 24 Mar II HGC Admin Partial Hat, Staff Auditor Assignment
HCO PL 24 Mar III Status of PE Courses
HCO PL 25 Mar Security Rules
HCO PL 26 Mar Animals Forbidden in House
HCO PL 28 Mar Personnel Policies, Staff Post Qualifications, Permanent Executives to Be Approved
HCOB 31 Mar SOP Goals Modified
HCO PL 31 Mar The Director of Processing's Case Checking Hat

ARTICLE

ABILITY 127 The 3rd South African ACC, Holding a Standard

ISSUES

HCO PL 2 Apr Staff Auditor Training, Sequence of Study
HCO PL 5 Apr I HCA/HPA or Practical Course Rundown for Academies
HCO PL 5 Apr II SOP Goals Goofs
HCOB 6 Apr I SOP Goals, Goals Assessment Problems Sorted Out
HCOB 6 Apr II SOP Goals, Repairing a Case
HCOB 7 Apr I Assessing for Goals and Terminals by Elimination
HCOB 7 Apr II SOP Goals, Modification I
HCO PL 7 Apr I Examinations of Academy Students to Be Done by Director of Processing
HCO PL 7 Apr RC II Johannesburg Confessional List
Rev. 15 Nov 87 *Confessional Form 1RA*
HCO PL 8 Apr OIC Board
HCO PL 9 Apr I Staff Intensives
HCO PL 9 Apr II City Offices, Successful Patterns
HCO PL 10 Apr HCO, Ltd., HPA/HCA Certificate Conditions
HCO PL 11 Apr How to Do a Staff Job
HCOB 11 Apr SOP Goals, Errors
HCOB 12 Apr Training Drills
HCO INFO LETTER 13 Apr Terror Stalks
HCO INFO LETTER 14 Apr I PE Handout
HCO INFO LETTER 14 Apr II New Book
HCO PL 17 Apr Training, Professional, New Policy
HCOB 23 Apr Change Processes
HCO PL 25 Apr I D of P Form
HCO PL 25 Apr II Association Secretary Duties
HCOB 27 Apr Change Processes
HCO PL 28 Apr II Central Organization Minimum Staff
HCOB 30 Apr R Change Brackets and
Rev. 25 Nov 73 Commands

E-METER ESSENTIALS
by L. Ron Hubbard

Published by Hubbard Communications Office, Saint Hill Manor, East Grinstead, Sussex, England, May 1961. *TRANSLATIONS:* Dutch, German, French, Italian and Spanish.

MAN FREE FROM MAN
Taken from the works of L. Ron Hubbard

Published by Hubbard Communications Office, Saint Hill Manor, East Grinstead, Sussex, England, May 1961.

ISSUES

HCO PL 2 May Procedure on Setting Up Central Orgs or City Offices
HCO PL 3 May Dining Room for Staff
HCOB 4 May Process Levels, Necessity for Training

The following lectures mark the beginning of the famous Saint Hill Special Briefing Course, delivered personally by L. Ron Hubbard at Saint Hill from 1961 through 1966.

During the next five and a half years, Mr. Hubbard lectured regularly to the students and personally oversaw their training so as to make them true *experts* who could be counted on to carry the latest technology and the highest standards of competence to the field. *(The full set of 437 Saint Hill Special Briefing Course Lectures, from 1961 through 1966, is available on cassette.)*

SAINT HILL SPECIAL BRIEFING COURSE LECTURES
SUSSEX, ENGLAND

7 May E-Meter Talk and Demo
12 May Assessment
19 May E-Meter
26 May On Auditing
1 Jun Flattening a Process and the E-Meter
2 Jun Flows, Prehav Scale, Primary Scale
5 Jun Routine 1, 2 and 3
6 Jun Security Checks
7 Jun Points in Assessing
8 Jun Question and Answer Period: Ending an Intensive
9 Jun Reading E-Meter Reactions
12 Jun E-Meter Actions, Errors in Auditing
13 Jun Seminar, Question and Answer Period
14 Jun Seminar: Withholds
15 Jun Not-Know
16 Jun Confront and Havingness—Routines 1, 2 and 3
19 Jun Question and Answer Period: Auditing Slowdowns
20 Jun Sec Check Questions, Mutual Rudiments
21 Jun Seminar: Auditing Speed
22 Jun Running CCHs
23 Jun Question and Answer Period: CCHs, Auditing
26 Jun Dealing with Attacks on Scientology
27 Jun CCHs—Circuits
28 Jun Raw Meat—Trouble-shooting Cases
29 Jun Wrong Target, Sec Check
30 Jun Training on TRs, Talk on Auditing
3 Jul Routine 1A—Problems
4 Jul Routine 1A—Problems and Solutions
5 Jul Question and Answer Period: Procedure in Auditing
6 Jul Routine 1A—Problems and Confront
11 Jul Routine 1A—Problems and Security Checks
12 Jul Question and Answer Period: Anatomy of Maybe, Solutions
14 Jul Checking Ruds and Withholds
18 Jul Can't-Have, Create, Fundamentals of All Problems
19 Jul Question and Answer Period: Auditor Effect on Meter
20 Jul Games Conditions
3 Aug Creation and Goals
4 Aug Methodology of Auditing—Not Doingness and Occlusion
8 Aug Forgettingness
9 Aug Question and Answer Period: Goals Search
10 Aug Question and Answer Period: Goals Assessment, Behavior of Pc
11 Aug Basics of Auditing, Matter-of-Factness
15 Aug Question and Answer Period: Anatomy and Assessment of Goals
16 Aug Unknown—Cyclic Aspect of Goals
17 Aug Rudiments, Valences
18 Aug Control of Attention
22 Aug PTPs, Unknownnesses
23 Aug Auditing Basics
24 Aug Rudiments
29 Aug Basics of Auditing
30 Aug Auditing Quality
31 Aug What is Auditing?
5 Sep Principles of Auditing
6 Sep Subjective Reality
7 Sep Reality in Auditing
12 Sep Clearing Breakthrough
13 Sep Sec Check and Withholds
14 Sep Goals and Terminals Assessment
19 Sep Question and Answer Period: Prehav, Sec Checks, ARC Break Process
20 Sep Seminar, Question and Answer Period: What Is Knowable to the Pc
21 Sep Smoothness of Auditing
26 Sep Teaching the Field Sec Checks
27 Sep Question and Answer Period: States of Beingness
28 Sep Grades of Auditors
3 Oct The Prior Confusion
4 Oct Moral Codes: What is a Withhold?
5 Oct Sec Checking: Types of Withholds
10 Oct Problems Intensive
11 Oct Problems Intensive Assessment
12 Oct Problems
17 Oct Problems Intensive Procedures
18 Oct Valences, Circuits
19 Oct Question and Answer Period: Flows
24 Oct Clearing
25 Oct Importance of Goals Terminals
26 Oct Security Checking: Auditing Errors
31 Oct Rudiments
1 Nov Formation of Commands
2 Nov How to Security Check
7 Nov Routine 3A
8 Nov Checking Case Reports
9 Nov Effective Auditing
14 Nov Routine 3D
15 Nov Routine 3D (cont.)
16 Nov Points in Assessing
21 Nov Running 3D

22 Nov Reading the E-Meter
23 Nov Auxiliary Prehav 3D Scale
28 Nov Havingness
29 Nov E-Meter Tips
30 Nov Parts of 3D
5 Dec Aspects of 3D
6 Dec Sec Checks Necessary
7 Dec Expectancy of 3D
12 Dec Sec Checks in Processing
13 Dec Assessing 3D
14 Dec Anatomy of Problems
19 Dec 3D Packages
20 Dec Upgrading Auditing
21 Dec Probabilities of 3D

Issues

HCO PL 10 May Staff Auditors
HCO PL 11 May I Student Training, Auditing Has Priority
HCOB 11 May I E-Meter Horror
HCOB 11 May II Assessment by Elimination, SOP Goals
HCOB 13 May Assessing for SOP Goals Improved
HCO PL 16 May HPA/HCA Requirement
HCOB 19 May Assessment Data
HCO PL 22 May The Only Valid Security Check
HCOB 23 May Prehav Scale Revised
SCALE May Secondary Scale
HCO INFO LETTER 23 May Telex From Ron to D of P London
HCO PL 24 May SOP Goals Assessments
SEC ED 24 May Responsibility for Results
HCOB 25 May Releasing and Preparing a Case for SOP Goals
HCO PL 26 May I Modification of HPA/HCA, BScn/HCS Schedule
HCO PL 26 May II Quality Counts *KSW Series 2*
HCO PL 26 May III Basic Staff Auditor's Hat
HCOB 29 May Clarification of "Change Processing"
HCO PL 29 May I Quality and Admin in Central Orgs *KSW Series 3*
HCO PL 29 May II Security of House
HCO PL 30 May I Current Office Work
HCO PL 30 May II How to Confess in HCO
HCOB 1 Jun Assessing
HCOB 5 Jun Processes Allowed
HCOB 7 Jun Academy Schedule, Clarification Of
HCO PL 7 Jun Orders
HCOB 8 Jun R Rev. 22 Feb 79 E-Meter Watching, Are You Waiting for the Meter to Play Dixie?

Article

ABILITY 129 The Sad Tail of PDH

Issues

HCO PL 9 Jun Technical Hat Checking, Vital Policy for HCO Area Sec *LRH Comm N/W Series 22*
HCOB 16 Jun CCHs and Routine 1
HCOB 17 Jun Primary Scale Amended
HCOB 19 Jun Sec Check Whole Track
HCOB 23 Jun Running CCHs
HCOB 27 Jun Routine One
HCO PL 29 Jun R Rev. 8 Nov 80 Student Confessional List *Confessional Form 5R*

Article

ABILITY 130 News News News

Issues

HCOB 6 Jul Routine 1A
HCO PL 7 Jul R II Rev. 5 Nov 80 Auditor Confessional List *Confessional Form 3R*
HCOB 10 Jul Metering Rudiments
HCO PL 22 Jul Executives' Pay

Article

ABILITY 131 Scientology's Future

Issues

HCO PL 4 Aug Private Mail and Telephone Calls
HCOB 10 Aug Information on Clears
HCO PL 14 Aug I City Offices
HCO PL 23 Aug HPA/HCA Policy
HCOB 23 Aug New Clearing Breakthrough!
HCOB 24 Aug Valences Key to Clearing
HCO PL 24 Aug HCO Organization, Future Plans
HCOB 31 Aug Advances in Technology
HCO PL 3 Sep HCO Vol Sec Policy Revised
HCOB 7 Sep New Facts of Life
HCO PL 12 Sep Curriculum for Clearing Courses
HCO PL 13 Sep I General Office Orders
HCO PL 13 Sep II HCO WW Security Form 7A
HCOB 14 Sep New Rudiments Commands
HCO PL 18 Sep R Rev. 16 Mar 89 HCO WW Security Form 7B
HCO PL 19 Sep Reality Test for Students
HCO PL 20 Sep Training Policy
HCO PL 21 Sep I Despatch Lines
HCO PL 21 Sep II Laundry
HCOB 21 Sep Security Check Children
HCOB 28 Sep HCO WW Security Forms 7A and 7B
HCO PL 29 Sep HGC Allowed Processes
HCO PL 2 Oct II Mission Policies
HCO PL 5 Oct Repairs and Cleaning of My Office
HCOB 5 Oct Clean Hands Make a Happy Life
HCO PL 6 Oct Staff Clearing
HCOB 6 Oct Training of Staff Auditors
HCO PL 7 Oct Friday Cables
HCO PL 9 Oct I Academy Training
HCOB 9 Oct Rudiments, Change In
HCO PL 9 Oct II HPA/HCA Rundown Change
HCO PL 10 Oct Problems Intensive for Staff Clearing
HCOB 12 Oct Student Practice Check
HCO PL 16 Oct Income Records
HCOB 17 Oct Problems Intensives
HCO PL 18 Oct Examinations
HCOB 19 Oct Security Questions Must Be Nulled
HCO PL 20 Oct RB Rev. 11 Jan 85 Non-Scientology Staff
HCO PL 23 Oct I E-Meters to Be Approved
HCO PL 23 Oct II HGC Preprocessing Security Check
HCO PL 23 Oct III Pay of Executives
HCO PL 25 Oct New Students Sec Check
HCOB 26 Oct Safe Auditing Table
HCO PL 27 Oct Professional Rates Restored
HCO PL 1 Nov HCO WW Security Form 5A
HCOB 2 Nov I The Prior Confusion
HCO PL 2 Nov II Training Quality *KSW Series 16*
HCOB 7 Nov Routine 3A
HCOB 9 Nov The Problems Intensive, Use of the Prior Confusion
HCO INFO LETTER 14 Nov Routine 3D
HCO PL 14 Nov Stabilization of Clears
HCO INFO LETTER 15 Nov Add Routine 3D
HCOB 16 Nov Sec Checking
HCOB 20 Nov Routine 3D Commands
HCO PL 21 Nov I Letter Writer's Code
HCO PL 21 Nov II HGC Processing Liability
HCO PL 23 Nov I Accounts
HCOB 23 Nov I Meter Reading
HCOB 23 Nov II Auxiliary Prehav 3D Scale
COMMAND SHEET 27 Nov Routine 3D Command Sheet
COMMAND SHEET 28 Nov Routine 3D Improved Commands of 28 November 1961
HCO PL 29 Nov Classes of Auditors
COMMAND SHEET 30 Nov Routine 3D Improved Commands of 30 November 1961
HCOB 30 Nov ARC Process 1961
HCOB 3 Dec Running 3D Levels
HCO PL 6 Dec Saint Hill Training Candidates from Organizations
HCOB 7 Dec Sec Checks Vital
COMMAND SHEET 7 Dec Command Sheet for Routine 3D
HCO PL 11 Dec RB Rev. 16 Mar 89 Organization Rudiments
HCO PL 12 Dec Training Activities
HCO PL 13 Dec Extension Course Completion
HCOB 13 Dec Varying Sec Check Questions
HCOB 14 Dec Rudiments, Modernized
HCO PL 15 Dec R Rev. 16 Mar 89 Rudiment Checklist for Orgs
HCO PL 19 Dec II Saint Hill Retreads
HCO PL 20 Dec Student E-Metering
COMMAND SHEET 26 Dec Command Sheet Routine 3D
HCO PL 27 Dec Sec Checks on Staff
HCOB 28 Dec I E-Meter Electrodes, a Dissertation on Soup Cans
HCOB 28 Dec II 3D Rules of Thumb

Clean Hands Congress Lectures
Washington, DC

Taking a short break from his heavy schedule of research, lectures and instruction at Saint Hill, Mr. Hubbard flew to Washington where he gave a nine-hour series of lectures on advanced auditing procedures and the technology of Scientology Confessionals. *(To be released on cassette as a series entitled "The Expansion of Havingness.")*

30 Dec Scientology, Where We Are Going
30 Dec Auditing Perfection and Classes of Auditors
30 Dec Parts of the 3D Package
31 Dec The Goals Problem Mass
31 Dec The E-Meter and Its Use
31 Dec Havingness, Quality of Reach
1 Jan The Valence, How It Works
1 Jan Goals Package Balance of Valences and Identification
1 Jan Effectiveness and Your Effectiveness Now

1962

Mr. Hubbard's most major activity in 1962, in the area of Scientology technology, was overseeing the Saint Hill Special Briefing Course. He delivered over 150 lectures to Briefing Course students, updating them on each research development and refinement as it was made, and inspecting and correcting their application of what they were learning.

In September, LRH took a short break from his intensive technical and administrative work at Saint Hill and flew to Washington, where he delivered 9 lectures in three days to delegates at the Clearing Success Congress.

ISSUES

HCO PL 6 Jan Laudatory Withholds, Know to Mystery Processing Check
HCO PL 7 Jan HCO Board of Review Class II Awards

SAINT HILL SPECIAL BRIEFING COURSE LECTURES
SUSSEX, ENGLAND

9 Jan Twenty-Ten, 3D Criss Cross
10 Jan Sec Checks, Withholds
11 Jan How to Audit
16 Jan Nature of Withholds
17 Jan 3D Criss Cross and GPM Anatomy
18 Jan How to Do 3D Criss Cross
23 Jan Basics of Auditing
24 Jan Training: Duplication
25 Jan Whole Track
30 Jan In-Sessionness
31 Jan Usages of 3D Criss Cross
1 Feb Flows
6 Feb Withholds
7 Feb Missed Withholds
8 Feb 3D Criss Cross Assessment
13 Feb Prepclearing
14 Feb Directing Attention
15 Feb Prepchecking
20 Feb What Is a Withhold?
21 Feb Use of Prepchecking
22 Feb Prepclearing and Rudiments
27 Feb Prepchecking and Basics
27 Feb Auditor's Code
1 Mar Model Session, Part I
1 Mar Model Session, Part II
19 Mar The Bad "Auditor"
19 Mar Mechanics of Suppression
20 Mar TV Demo: 3D Criss Cross Assessment, Part I
20 Mar TV Demo: 3D Criss Cross Assessment, Part II
21 Mar Object of Prepchecking
21 Mar Prepchecking, Zero Question
27 Mar Prepchecking Data
29 Mar CCHs
29 Mar Question and Answer Period: CCHs, 3D Criss Cross
3 Apr The Overt–Motivator Sequence
5 Apr Sacredness of Cases—Determinism
5 Apr As-isness: People Who Can and Can't As-is
17 Apr Auditing
17 Apr How and Why Auditing Works
19 Apr Gross Auditing Errors
19 Apr Determining What to Run
24 Apr Rundown on 3D Criss Cross, Part I
24 Apr Rundown on 3D Criss Cross, Part II
25 Apr TV Demo: Checking Line Plots
26 Apr Rundown on Prepchecking: Professional Attitude
26 Apr Rundown on Routine 3: Routine 3A Criss Cross
1 May ARC Breaks and Missed Withholds
1 May Routine 3G: Experimental Preview of a Clearing Process
2 May TV Demo: Prepchecking, Part I
2 May TV Demo: Prepchecking, Part II
3 May Craftsmanship: Fundamentals
3 May Prepchecking
15 May New Training Sections
15 May New TRs
16 May TV Demo: Patching Up 3D Criss Cross Cases
17 May Auditing Errors
17 May Prepchecking and Its Purposes
22 May Administration of Courses
22 May Missed Withholds
23 May TV Demo: Check on "What" Questions and Havingness Probe
23 May TV Demo: Fish & Fumble—Checking Dirty Needles
24 May E-Meter Data: Instant Reads, Part I
24 May E-Meter Data: Instant Reads, Part II
29 May Question and Answer Period: Goals Assessment, Havingness
29 May Security Check Prepchecking
30 May TV Demo: Getting Rudiments In, Part I
30 May TV Demo: Getting Rudiments In, Part II
31 May Value of Rudiments
31 May Middle Rudiments
12 Jun How to Do a Goals Assessment
12 Jun More on Middle Rudiments
13 Jun TV Demo: Checking Out a Goal, Part I
13 Jun TV Demo: Checking Out a Goal, Part II
14 Jun Future Technology
14 Jun Listing
19 Jun Do's and Don'ts of R3
19 Jun Question and Answer Period: GPMs, Release
20 Jun TV Demo: New Model Session
21 Jun Model Session Revised
21 Jun Question and Answer Period: TR 4, Model Session
26 Jun E-Meter Quality
26 Jun Prepchecking and the Time Track
28 Jun Rudiments
28 Jun Question and Answer Period: CCHs, Nulling Goals
10 Jul Repetitive Rudiments and Repetitive Prepchecking, Part I
10 Jul Repetitive Rudiments and Repetitive Prepchecking, Part II
12 Jul Meter Reading
12 Jul Meter Training
17 Jul E-Meter Reads and ARC Breaks
17 Jul Anatomy of ARC Breaks
19 Jul The E-Meter
19 Jul Question and Answer Period: Goals Lists, Field Auditors
24 Jul Routine 3GA, Part I
24 Jul Routine 3GA, Part II
26 Jul Routine 3GA Data
26 Jul Prepchecking with Mid Rud Buttons
7 Aug Routine 3GA Data on Goals, Part I
7 Aug Routine 3GA Data on Goals, Part II
8 Aug TV Demo: Routine 3GA, Nulling Goals
9 Aug Clearing
9 Aug Goals Listing
14 Aug Rock Slams and Dirty Needles
14 Aug World Clearing Program
15 Aug TV Demo: 3GA Dynamic Assessment
16 Aug 3GA Dynamic Assessment
21 Aug Finding Goals by Dynamic Assessment
21 Aug Basics of Auditing
22 Aug TV Demo: Dynamic and Item Assessment

ISSUES

HCO INFO LETTER 9 Jan 3D Criss Cross
HCO PL 10 Jan I HCO Standing Order No. 5, Students
HCOB 11 Jan Security Checking, Twenty-Ten Theory
HCO INFO LETTER 11 Jan Progress Report
HCO PL 17 Jan I Auditor Assignment
HCO PL 17 Jan II Responsibility Again
HCO PL 17 Jan III Org Rudiment Reports to Me
HCO INFO LETTER 22 Jan 3D Criss Cross, Method of Assessment
HCO PL 22 Jan Crash Program
HCO PL 23 Jan Permanent Executives
HCOB 25 Jan Flow Process
HCO PL 30 Jan Technical Director and Administrator
HCOB 1 Feb Flows, Basic
HCO INFO LETTER 1 Feb 3D Criss Cross Assessment Tips
HCO INFO LETTER 3 Feb 3DXX Flows Assessment
HCO PL 7 Feb Restriction on Saint Hill Area
HCOB 8 Feb Missed Withholds

HUBBARD BRITISH MARK V E-METER

The first British Mark V E-Meter became available in 1962. Its sensitivity range was greatly increased over all previous meters.

HCOB 12 Feb How to Clear Withholds and Missed Withholds
HCO PL 13 Feb 3D Criss Cross Items
HCOB 15 Feb Co-audit and Missed Withholds
HCO PL 18 Feb Fish and Game
HCOB 22 Feb Withholds, Missed and Partial
HCO PL 27 Feb Clean Hands Clearance Check
HCOB 1 Mar Prepchecking
HCOB 8 Mar The Bad "Auditor"
HCO PL 12 Mar I Staff Training
HCOB 15 Mar Suppressors
HCOB 21 Mar Prepchecking Data, When to Do a What
HCOB 29 Mar CCHs Again, When to Use the CCHs
HCO PL 4 Apr Training Course Regulations (Added)
HCOB 5 Apr CCHs, Auditing Attitude
HCO PL 6 Apr Technical Director Basic Hat
HCOB 11 Apr Determining What to Run
HCO INFO LETTER 11 Apr Dynamic Processing Checks
HCOB 12 Apr CCHs, Purpose
HCO PL 16 Apr I Comments on Letter Registrar Department
HCO PL 16 Apr II Regulations, Academies and Courses
HCO PL 18 Apr Furniture and Quarters
HCOB 26 Apr Recommended Processes HGC
HCO INFO LETTER 29 Apr Routine 3G (Experimental)
HCO PL 3 May Practical Auditing Skills
HCOB 3 May R Rev. 5 Sep 78 ARC Breaks, Missed Withholds
HCO INFO LETTER 8 May Only Saint Hill to Teach Special Briefing Course
HCOB 10 May Prepchecking and Sec Checking
HCO INFO LETTER 10 May Routine 3GA (Experimental)
HCOB 14 May Case Repair
HCO PL 14 May Training Sections
SEC ED 15 May CF/Addressograph, Handling of New Names
HCO PL 16 May HPA/HCA Training
HCO PL 21 May I Training, Classes of Auditors
HCO PL 21 May II Tape Examinations
HCOB 21 May Missed Withholds, Asking About
HCOB 22 May Model Session Change
HCOB 23 May E-Meter Reads, Prepchecking, How Meters Get Invalidated
HCO PL 24 May I Training, Session Cancellation, Auditing Section
HCOB 24 May Q and A
HCOB 25 May E-Meter Instant Reads
HCO PL 26 May Training Drills Must Be Correct
HCO PL 29 May Professional Rates
HCO PL 1 Jun Auditing, Rudiments Check Sheet
HCO PL 5 Jun I Permanent Staff Privilege
HCO PL 5 Jun II Class II Training Only by Academies and Saint Hill
HCO PL 7 Jun Professional Training to Be Done in Academy and Saint Hill Only
HCOB 8 Jun Rudiments Checking
HCOB 11 Jun Prepchecking the Middle Rudiments
HCOB 14 Jun Checking Needle in Rudiments Checks
HCO PL 14 Jun Professional Charges
HCO PL 21 Jun Staff Members Auditing Private Pcs
HCOB 24 Jun Prepchecking
HCOB 25 Jun E-Meter Standards
HCO PL 26 Jun Certification Requirements
HCOB 27 Jun Rundown on Routine 3GA
HCOB 28 Jun R Rev. 5 Sep 78 Dirty Needles, How to Smooth Out Needles
HCO PL 29 Jun Staff and Intern Auditors
HCOB 30 Jun ARC Process
HCOB 2 Jul Repetitive Rudiments
HCO PL 2 Jul Rudiments Policy
HCOB 3 Jul Repetitive Prepchecking
HCOB 4 Jul I Bulletin Changes
HCOB 4 Jul II Coachless Training, Use of a Doll
HCO PL 8 Jul Telephone Answering
HCO PL 9 Jul I Special Briefing Course
HCOB 12 Jul Motivatorish Cases
HCO PL 14 Jul Auditing Allowed
HCO PL 15 Jul Goals Prepcheck Form, Routine 3GA
HCO PL 17 Jul Routine 3GA, HCO WW R-3GA Form 1, Listing Prepcheck
HCO PL 19 Jul Clearing—Free Needles
HCOB 21 Jul Instant Reads
HCO PL 22 Jul Routine 3GA, Listing Wording
HCO PL 24 Jul Academy, Extra Weeks
HCO PL 30 Jul Certification and Validation Requirements
HCOB 30 Jul A Smooth HGC 25-Hour Intensive
HCO PL 31 Jul Oral Examination for HPA/HCA
HCOB 2 Aug CCH Answers
HCO PL 2 Aug I Accounts Information
HCO PL 2 Aug II New Work Arrangements, Outside Staff
HCO PL 2 Aug III Training Aids
HCOB 7 Aug Running CCHs
HCOB 10 Aug How It Feels to Go Clear
HCO PL 13 Aug Clearing
HCOB 21 Aug 3GA, Line Wording
HCOB 30 Aug Order of Prepcheck Buttons
HCO PL 30 Aug General Form of Release Contract
HCOB 31 Aug 3GA, Expanded Line Wording

CLEARING SUCCESS CONGRESS LECTURES
WASHINGTON, DC

This lecture series included data on Mr. Hubbard's most recent advances in clearing, the relationship between the various dynamics, exteriorization and the role Scientology organizations play in creating a new civilization. *(To be released on cassette.)*

1 Sep Presentation of the GPM
1 Sep The Point Where the Pc Begins to Get Clear
1 Sep Basic Purpose
2 Sep The Healing Effect of Preparatory Auditing (Suppress Button)
2 Sep Staff Introduction
2 Sep The Problems Intensive, Mechanics and Buttons
3 Sep World Clearing and You
3 Sep Your Scientology Orgs and What They Do for You

ISSUES

HCO PL 1 Sep Healing Promotion
HCOB 2 Sep Account of Congress Goal
HCOB 8 Sep 3GA, To Be Goals Line Listing
HCOB 12 Sep R Rev. 5 Sep 78 Security Checks Again
HCO PL 12 Sep II Saint Hill Graduates
HCO PL 12 Sep III Authorized Processes
HCO PL 13 Sep Comments about Letter Registrar
HCO PL 17 Sep R Rev. 24 Jan 91 An Arrangement of the Academy

SAINT HILL SPECIAL BRIEFING COURSE LECTURES
SUSSEX, ENGLAND

18 Sep Directing Pc's Attention
18 Sep 3GA Dynamic Assessment by Rock Slam
19 Sep TV Demo: Tiger Drill
20 Sep Listing Lines
20 Sep Geriatrics
25 Sep Current Trends
25 Sep 3GA Assessment
26 Sep TV Demo: Nulling Goals Session
27 Sep 3GA Listing, Part I
27 Sep 3GA Listing, Part II
2 Oct 3GA—Listing by Tiger Buttons, Part I
2 Oct 3GA—Listing by Tiger Buttons, Part II
3 Oct TV Demo: Prepchecking a Goal, Part I
3 Oct TV Demo: Prepchecking a Goal, Part II
4 Oct Modern Security Checking
4 Oct Making a Goal Fire
9 Oct Future Org Trends
9 Oct Instructors' Bugbear
11 Oct 3GA Goals Finding, Part I
11 Oct 3GA Goals Finding, Part II
23 Oct 3GA Criss Cross
23 Oct 3GA Criss Cross: Following the Rock Slam
25 Oct 3GA Criss Cross Data
25 Oct 3GA Criss Cross, Secondary Prehav Scale
30 Oct Prehav Scales and Lists
30 Oct Listing Goals
1 Nov The Missed Missed Withhold
1 Nov The Road to Truth
13 Nov The Difficult Case
13 Nov Entrance of Cases
15 Nov Terminals
15 Nov Clearing Technology
20 Nov Layout of the GPM
20 Nov Fundamentals of Auditing
22 Nov Question and Answer Period: Tiger Drilling, Clears
22 Nov Question and Answer Period: District Offices, Co-audits
27 Nov Routine 2-12, Part I
27 Nov Routine 2-12, Part II
29 Nov R2-12 Theory and Practice, Part I
29 Nov R2-12 Theory and Practice, Part II
11 Dec R2-12 Data
11 Dec Phantom R/S
13 Dec R2-12 Data: Needle Behavior
13 Dec Repair of R2-12

ISSUES

HCOB 19 Sep 3GA, Tips on Dynamic Assessment
HCOB 23 Sep A 40-Line List on a Doingness Goal
HCO PL 27 Sep I Valid Processes
HCO PL 27 Sep II Pay for Goals Finding
HCOB 27 Sep Problems Intensive Use
HCOB 1 Oct 3GA, Listing by Tiger Buttons, 114 New Lines for Listing
HCO PL 1 Oct The Plan for California
HCO PL 2 Oct I When You Need Reassurance
HCO PL 2 Oct II Termination and Classification
HCO PL 3 Oct Rooms, Emptying for Cleaning
HCOB 3 Oct Tiger Drilling
HCO PL 6 Oct I Accounts Irregularities
HCO PL 6 Oct II Car Washing
HCO PL 8 Oct I HGC Clearing
HCO PL 12 Oct II HPA/HCA Written Examination
HCOB 13 Oct Processes
HCOB 16 Oct Routine 3GA, Listing
HCO PL 16 Oct Auditing Hours Limited
HCOB 17 Oct Auditor Failure to Understand *Basic Auditing Series 6*

HUBBARD BRITISH MARK V E-METER

A new British Mark V E-Meter became available in 1963 with double the sensitivity of the first Mark V. The Mark IV and Mark V were both in use from 1963 through 1965. The Mark IV was discontinued in December 1965.

HCOB 18 Oct 3GA, Listing by Prehav
HCO PL 19 Oct II R3GA, HCO WW Form G3, Revised, Fast Goals Check
HCO PL 19 Oct I Preparation of HPA/HCA Certificates
HCO PL 21 Oct Auditing Supervisor and Auditing Instructors, Duties Of
HCO PL 24 Oct Emergency Headquarters
HCO PL 28 Oct I Z Unit, Case Review
HCO PL 29 Oct Religion
HCOB 29 Oct Preclearing Intensive
HCO PL 30 Oct I Security Risks Infiltration

ARTICLE The Place of the Scientist in Society

ISSUES

HCOB 7 Nov I Wrong Goals, Importance of Repair Of
HCOB 7 Nov II Routine 3-21, the Twenty-One Steps, Finding Goals
HCOB 7 Nov III "Roll Your Own" Prehav
HCO PL 8 Nov I Departure Form
HCO PL 8 Nov II Outside Staff Duties, Assignment Of
HCOB 8 Nov R Rev. 5 Sep 78 Somatics, How to Tell Terminals and Opposition Terminals
HCOB 11 Nov 3GAXX, Straightening Up 3GAXX Cases
HCOB 12 Nov 3GAXX, Dirty Needles and Incomplete Lists, How to Assess
HCO PL 12 Nov Purpose of the Saint Hill Special Briefing Course
HCO INFO LETTER 14 Nov Saint Hill Special Briefing Course
HCO PL 14 Nov Terminations from the Saint Hill Special Briefing Course
HCO PL 15 Nov Car Parking
HCOB 17 Nov Routine 3-21
HCO PL 18 Nov Address Machines
HCO PL 21 Nov Reissue of Materials
HCO PL 23 Nov Saint Hill Retread Fee
HCOB 23 Nov Routine Two-Twelve, Opening Procedure by Rock Slam, an HPA/HCA Skill
HCO PL 24 Nov Objective One
HCOB 24 Nov Routine 2-12, List One—Issue One, the Scientology List
HCOB 28 Nov R2-12, Practical Drills
HCOB 29 Nov I Routine 2-12, List One—Issue Two, the Scientology List
HCOB 29 Nov II Routines 2-12, 3-21 and 3GAXX, Tiger Drill (Small Tiger) for Nulling by Mid Ruds
HCO PL 1 Dec I V Unit, New Students, Saint Hill Special Briefing Course
HCO PL 1 Dec II Goals and Prepchecking
HCO PL 2 Dec Supervisor's Stable Data
HCOB 4 Dec Routine 2-12, List One—Issue Three, the Scientology List
HCO PL 4 Dec R2-12, Validation
HCO PL 5 Dec I Trips to Town
HCO PL 5 Dec II Administrator's Hat
HCO PL 6 Dec Saint Hill Special Briefing Course
HCOB 6 Dec R2-10, R2-12, 3GAXX Data, the Zero A Steps and Purpose of Processes
HCO PL 8 Dec Training, Saint Hill Special Briefing Course
HCOB 8 Dec Training, X Unit
HCOB 9 Dec Routine 2-12, List One, Add to List One, Issue Three
HCOB 10 Dec Routine 2-12, the Phantom Rock Slam, the Results of 2-12
HCOB 15 Dec R2-12, the Fatal Error
HCOB 30 Dec R Rev. 5 Sep 78 Routines 2-12 and 2-10, Case Errors

1963

While keeping the Saint Hill Special Briefing Course roaring ahead, LRH embarked on what he called "the most intense period of research I've yet done."

In addition to his work in the technical line, Mr. Hubbard made great strides in the field of administration—newly defining the activities of auditors and organizations across the world.

ISSUES

HCOB 1 Jan Academy Curriculum, How to Teach Auditing and Routine 2
HCOB 3 Jan Opposition Lists, Right and Wrong Oppose
HCO PL 4 Jan Pattern of District Office

SAINT HILL SPECIAL BRIEFING COURSE LECTURES
SUSSEX, ENGLAND

8 Jan R2-10 and R2-12
8 Jan Case Repair
10 Jan R2-12
10 Jan How to Audit
15 Jan R2-12 Dead Horses
15 Jan R2-12 Nevers
16 Jan TV Demo: TR 0 Demonstration
16 Jan TR 0 Lecture
6 Feb Instructors' Conference
7 Feb R3MX, Part I
7 Feb R3MX, Part II
12 Feb Routine 3M
13 Feb TV Demo: Ruds and Havingness
13 Feb Discussion of TV Demo Sessions
14 Feb Routine 3M Data
19 Feb Rundown on Processes
20 Feb TV Demo: Finding RRs
20 Feb Talk on TV Demo—Finding RRs
21 Feb R2 and R3: Current Auditing Rundown
26 Feb R3M: Current Rundown by Steps
27 Feb TV Demo: Case Repair
28 Feb Goals Problem Mass
5 Mar R2 and R3: Urgent Data
7 Mar When Faced with the Unusual Do the Usual
19 Mar R3M: How to Find Goals
20 Mar TV Demo: Rudiments and Havingness Session and Short Lecture
21 Mar R2G Series
26 Mar Case Repair
27 Mar TV Demo: Sec Checking—with Comments by LRH
28 Mar The GPM

ISSUES

HCO PL 15 Jan Routine 2-12
HCO INFO LETTER 16 Jan Our Role in the World
HCOB 27 Jan Routine 2—Simplified
HCOB 1 Feb Routine 3, Urgent—Urgent—Urgent, All Class III and IV Auditors
HCO PL 8 Feb Curriculum Change
HCO PL 9 Feb Saint Hill Course Goals
HCOB 11 Feb Current Auditing
HCO PL 11 Feb Auditing Regulations
HCO PL 13 Feb I V Unit
HCO PL 13 Feb II Academy Taught Processes
HCOB 15 Feb R2—R3, Listing Rules
HCO PL 21 Feb Goals Check
HCOB 22 Feb Routine 3M, Rundown by Steps

HCO PL 25 Feb R2—R3
HCOB 4 Mar Routine 2-10, 2-12, 2-12A
HCO PL 6 Mar Selling Techniques Forbidden
HCOB 6 Mar Correction to HCO Bulletin of February 22, 1963
HCO PL 6 Mar R3M, HCO WW Form G3, Revised, Fast Goals Check
HCOB 8 Mar Use of the Big Middle Rudiments
HCOB 9 Mar Routine 2 and 3M, Correction to 3M Steps 13, 14
HCOB 10 Mar Routine 2-10, 2-12, 2-12A (Also applies to Routine 3M), Vanished R/S or RR
HCO PL 12 Mar Staff Personnel Allowance, Saint Hill
HCO PL 13 Mar Amnesty
HCOB 13 Mar II The End of a GPM
HCOB 14 Mar Routine 2–Routine 3, ARC Breaks, Handling Of
HCO PL 15 Mar II Checksheet Rating System
HCOB 17 Mar R2–R3, Corrections, Typographicals and Added Notes
HCOB 18 Mar R2–R3, Important Data, Don't Force the Pc
HCO PL 20 Mar I HCO WW Electric Stencil-Cutting Machine
HCO PL 20 Mar II Self-determinism in Central Organizations
HCOB 23 Mar Clear and OT
HCO PL 23 Mar I Clear Test 1963, Issue II
HCO PL 23 Mar II Policies in Force, Org/Assoc Secs, HCO Secs
HCO PL 23 Mar III Classification of Auditors, Class II and Goals
HCO PL 29 Mar Clear Requirement
HCOB 30 Mar Routine 3M Simplified
HCO PL 2 Apr Construction Information
HCOB 2 Apr Diagrams Illustrating Tape of 28 March 1963
HCO PL 4 Apr II Director of Training Weekly Student Interviews
HCO PL 5 Apr Organization Students on Saint Hill Course
HCOB 6 Apr R3M2, What You Are Trying to Do in Clearing
HCOB 8 Apr I Routine 3M2, Listing and Nulling
HCOB 8 Apr II Routine 3M2, Corrected Line Plots
HCO PL 11 Apr II Emergency Library
HCO PL 13 Apr Policy of HGCs
HCOB 13 Apr Routine 2G, Original Routine 2, 3GA, 2-10, 2-12, 2-12A and Others Specially Adapted
HCOB 18 Apr Routine 3M2, Directive Listing

PROFESSIONAL AUDITOR'S CONGRESS
SUSSEX, ENGLAND

On a Saturday afternoon at Saint Hill, LRH gave these two lectures to professional Scientologists and students currently on course in the Academy of Scientology in London.

20 Apr What Clearing Is
20 Apr Basic Purpose

SAINT HILL SPECIAL BRIEFING COURSE LECTURES
SUSSEX, ENGLAND

2 Apr GPM Items
4 Apr Anatomy of the GPM
16 Apr Top of the GPM
18 Apr Directive Listing
23 Apr Goals
25 Apr Finding Goals
30 Apr Pattern of the GPM
2 May Running the GPM
14 May Implant GPMs
15 May TV Demo: Blocking Out and Dating Incidents
16 May The Time Track
21 May The Helatrobus Implants
22 May TV Demo: Engram Running—Helatrobus Implant Goal
23 May State of OT
28 May Handling ARC Breaks
29 May Programing Cases, Part I
30 May Programing Cases, Part II
11 Jun Engram Chain Running
12 Jun ARC Straightwire
13 Jun Levels of Case
18 Jun Beingness
19 Jun Summary of Modern Auditing
20 Jun History of Psychotherapy
25 Jun Modern Processes
26 Jun TV Demo: Listing Assessment for Engram Running, Part I
27 Jun TV Demo: Listing Assessment for Engram Running, Part II
9 Jul The Free Being
10 Jul Auditing Skills for R3R
10 Jul Auditing Session: Preliminary Steps of R3R, Part I
10 Jul Auditing Session: Preliminary Steps of R3R, Part II
11 Jul ARC Breaks
16 Jul Tips on Running R3R
17 Jul Dating
18 Jul Errors in Time
23 Jul Between Lives Implants
24 Jul ARC Breaks and the Comm Cycle
25 Jul Comm Cycles in Auditing
6 Aug Auditing Comm Cycles
7 Aug R2H Fundamentals
8 Aug R2H Assessment
14 Aug Auditing Tips
15 Aug The Tone Arm
20 Aug The Itsa Line
21 Aug The Itsa Line (cont.)
22 Aug Project 80
27 Aug Rightness and Wrongness
28 Aug The Tone Arm and the Service Facsimile
29 Aug The Service Facsimile
3 Sep R3SC
4 Sep How to Find a Service Facsimile
5 Sep Service Fac Assessment
10 Sep Destimulation of a Case
11 Sep Service Facs and GPMs
12 Sep Service Facsimiles
17 Sep What You Are Auditing
18 Sep Saint Hill Service Facsimile Handling
19 Sep Routine 4M TA
24 Sep Summary I
25 Sep Summary II: Scientology 0
26 Sep Summary III: About Level IV Auditing
15 Oct Essentials of Auditing
16 Oct The Itsa Maker Line
17 Oct Level IV Auditing
21 Oct Attack and GPMs
22 Oct The Integration of Auditing
23 Oct Auditing the GPM
29 Oct Routine 4
30 Oct R4 Case Assembly
31 Oct R4M2 Programing
5 Nov Three Zones of Auditing
7 Nov Relationship of Training to OT
26 Nov R4 Auditing
28 Nov TV Demo: Auditing Demo with Comments by LRH
28 Nov Seven Classifications
3 Dec Certifications and Classifications
4 Dec TV Demo: Basic Auditing—Lecture and Demo
5 Dec Basic Auditing
10 Dec Scientology Zero
12 Dec Summary of OT Processes
31 Dec Indicators

ISSUES

HCOB 23 Apr Routine 3M2, Handling the GPM
HCOB 24 Apr Routine 3M2, Tips, The Rocket Read of a Reliable Item
HCO PL 25 Apr R Rev. 29 Aug 90 Duties of a Staff Member
HCOB 25 Apr Meter Reading TRs
HCOB 28 Apr Routine 3, An Actual Line Plot
HCOB 29 Apr Routine 3, Directive Listing, Listing Liabilities
HCO PL 30 Apr The Saint Hill Staff Co-audit
HCOB 30 Apr Routine 3
HCOB 4 May Routine 3, An Actual Line Plot No. 2
HCOB 5 May Routine 3, R3 Stable Data
HCOB 8 May The Nature of Formation of the GPM
HCOB 12 May Routine 3, RI Form (GPM RI Form Corrected)
HCOB 13 May Routine 3, Routine 3N Directive Listing with New Routine 3 Model Session
HCO PL 15 May Instructor Hats
HCOB 15 May The Time Track and Engram Running by Chains, Bulletin 1
SEC ED 20 May Scientology Missionary Hat
HCOB 20 May Routine 3N, Proper Programing, Fast Blowing RIs
HCO PL 24 May Changes in Basement Student Facilities
HCOB 26 May Routine 3, Line Plot
HCOB 27 May Cause of ARC Breaks
HCOB 1 Jun Routine 2, New Processes
HCOB 4 Jun Routine 3, Handling GPMs
HCOB 8 Jun R Rev. 3 Oct 77 The Time Track and Engram Running by Chains, Bulletin 2
HCO PL 10 Jun Scientology Training, Technical Studies
HCO PL 17 Jun Staff Clearing Program
HCO PL 18 Jun Tape Release
HCO PL 24 Jun Review of Departments
HCOB 24 Jun Routine 3, Engram Running by Chains, Bulletin 3
HCOB 25 Jun Routine 2H, ARC Breaks by Assessment
HCOB 1 Jul Routine 3R, Bulletin 4, Preliminary Step
HCOB 5 Jul ARC Break Assessments
HCOB 9 Jul A Technical Summary, The Required Skills of Processing and Why
HCOB 14 Jul Routine 3N, Line Plots
HCOB 21 Jul Co-audit ARC Break Process
HCOB 22 Jul I You Can Be Right
HCOB 22 Jul III Org Technical, HGC Processes and Training
HCO PL 23 Jul Retreads on Saint Hill Special Briefing Course
HCOB 23 Jul Auditing Rundown, Missed Withholds, To Be Run in X1 Unit
HCOB 24 Jul R3N Corrections
HCOB 28 Jul Time and the Tone Arm
HCOB 29 Jul I Scientology Review
HCOB 29 Jul II R3R–R3N–R3T, Cautionary HCOB
HCO PL 30 Jul Current Planning
HCO PL 2 Aug I Public Project One
HCO PL 2 Aug II Saint Hill Course Changes
HCOB 4 Aug E-Meter Errors, Communication Cycle Error

HCOB	9 Aug	Definition of Release
HCO INFO LETTER	9 Aug	Public Meetings
HCOB	11 Aug	ARC Break Assessments
HCO PL	12 Aug	Certificates and Awards
HCOB	14 Aug	Lecture Graphs
HCO PL	14 Aug	Press Policies *PR Series 31*
HCOB	19 Aug	How to Do an ARC Break Assessment
HCOB	20 Aug	R3R—R3N, The Preclear's Postulates
HCO PL	21 Aug	Change of Organization Targets, Project 80, A Preview
HCOB	22 Aug	Tech Preparation for HCO PL 21 Aug. 1963, Project 80, The Itsa Line and Tone Arm
HCO PL	22 Aug	ARC Break Assessments on Staff
HCOB	24 Aug	Routine 3N, The Train GPMs, The Marcab Between Lives Implants
HCOB	1 Sep I	Routine Three SC
HCOB	1 Sep II	Scientology Two, Routine 1C
HCO INFO LETTER	1 Sep	Scientology One
HCO PL	3 Sep	Status of Auckland
HCOB	6 Sep	Instructing in Scientology Auditing, Instructor's Task, D of P's Case Handling
HCO PL	7 Sep	Committees of Evidence, Scientology Jurisprudence, Administration Of
HCOB	9 Sep	Repetitive Rudiments and Repetitive Prepchecking
HCO PL	22 Sep	Concerning Committees of Evidence
HCOB	23 Sep	Tape Coverage of New Technology
HCOB	25 Sep	Adequate Tone Arm Action
HCOB	28 Sep	Actual Goals
HCOB	1 Oct	How to Get Tone Arm Action
HCOB	2 Oct	GPMs, Experimental Process Withdrawn
HCO PL	4 Oct	Technical Council
HCO PL	7 Oct	Doors
HCO PL	8 Oct I	New Saint Hill Certificates and Course Changes
HCOB	8 Oct	How to Get TA, Analyzing Auditing
HCOB	16 Oct	R3SC Slow Assessment
HCOB	17 Oct I	R-2C Slow Assessment by Dynamics
HCOB	17 Oct II	R-2C Slow Assessment by Dynamics, Directions for Use of HCO Bulletin of October 17, AD 13, Issue I
HCO PL	23 Oct	Refund Policy
HCOB	31 Oct	R-2C Slow Assessment by Dynamics, Continued
HCO PL	4 Nov	Pay Card
HCO PL	11 Nov	Committees of Evidence
HCOB	25 Nov	Dirty Needles
HCO PL	26 Nov	Certificate and Classification Changes, Everyone Classified
HCOB	26 Nov	A New Triangle, Basic Auditing, Technique, Case Analysis
HCO PL	4 Dec	Org Staff W/H Checks
HCO PL	6 Dec	Org Programing
HCO INFO LETTER	10 Dec	The Dangerous Environment, The True Story of Scientology
HCO PL	11 Dec	Classification for Everyone
HCO PL	13 Dec	Co-audit
HCOB	14 Dec	Case Analysis, Health Research
HCO PL	27 Dec	The "Magic" of Good Management
HCOB	28 Dec	Routine 6, Indicators, Part One: Good Indicators
MESSAGE	late Dec	Ron's Journal

AZIMUTH ALIGNMENT METER

The Azimuth Alignment Meter became available in 1964. It was a "see-through" meter—the dial being glass both front and back. This enabled an auditor to look through the dial while writing to ensure that no movement of the needle was missed. It is a Mark V meter in function.

1964

In May, Mr. Hubbard created *The Auditor*, a new magazine sent out regularly from Saint Hill to swiftly carry information on his latest technical developments as well as news of Saint Hill and the wins of Saint Hill students and preclears.

Technical progress in 1964 included tremendous achievements in the field of education. Combining his own experiences as a student with observations made in training others, Mr. Hubbard developed Scientology study technology and recorded this revolutionary new tech in lectures to students on the Saint Hill Special Briefing Course.

In December of 1964, R6EW and Solo auditing were released at Saint Hill Manor.

SAINT HILL SPECIAL BRIEFING COURSE LECTURES
SUSSEX, ENGLAND

7 Jan	Good Indicators at Lower Levels
9 Jan	Bad Indicators
4 Feb	Auditor Self-criticism
6 Feb	The Communication Cycle in Auditing
25 Feb	What Auditing Is and What It Isn't
3 Mar	Auditing and Assessment
5 Mar	Case Analysis—Healing
10 Mar	Summary of Lower Levels—Clearing at Level IV
12 Mar	Track Analysis [filmed lecture]
12 Mar	Running GPMs [filmed lecture]
17 Mar	Lower Levels of Auditing
19 Mar	Flattening a Process
24 Mar	International City
10 Apr	How to Manage a Course
14 Apr	The Classification and Gradation Program
16 Apr	Auditing by Lists
21 Apr	Problems and Solutions
28 Apr	Wisdom as an Auditor
30 Apr	Effectiveness of Processing
19 May	The Preclear and Getting Auditing to Work
9 Jun	The Cycle of Action: Its Interpretation on the E-Meter
16 Jun	Communication, Overts and Responsibility
18 Jun	Studying: Introduction
30 Jun	Cause Level, OT and the Public
2 Jul	O/W Modernized and Reviewed
7 Jul	Dissemination
9 Jul	Studying: Data Assimilation
15 Jul	Organization Operation
28 Jul	Campaign to Handle Psychosomatic Ills
30 Jul	Psychosomatic: Its Meaning in Scientology
4 Aug	A Summary of Study
6 Aug	Study: Gradients and Nomenclature
11 Aug	Study: Evaluation of Information
13 Aug	Study and Education
1 Sep	The PE Course
3 Sep	Clearing, What It Is
15 Sep	Scientology and Tradition
22 Sep	A Review of Study
29 Sep	Gradients
13 Oct	Cycles of Action
20 Oct	Levels: The Reason for Them
27 Oct	The Failed Case
3 Nov	Programs
4 Nov	Comments on Clay Table TV Demo
10 Nov	PTPs, Overts and ARC Breaks
17 Nov	Styles of Auditing
15 Dec	Communication: A Gradient of Duplication

ISSUES

HCO PL 14 Jan I Continental and Area HCO Finance Policies
HCO PL 14 Jan II Future Continental Officer Status
HCOB 21 Jan Meter Level Warning
HCO PL 24 Jan I HCO (Sthil) Ltd., Course Staff Transfers
HCO PL 24 Jan II Scientology Library and Research, Ltd.
HCO PL 25 Jan Department of Enrollment
HCO PL 26 Jan HCO (WW) Ltd., Central Org Activities
HCO PL 29 Jan HCO (Sthil), Ltd., Charts, Routings and Publications, The Enrollment Department
HCO PL 31 Jan Corporation Coordinator
HCO PL 3 Feb HCO (Sthil), Ltd., Transport
HCO PL 5 Feb Founding Scientologist Certificate
HCO PL 9 Feb Comm Baskets
HCO PL 10 Feb Enrollment on Self-determinism
HCO PL 13 Feb Classification
HCO PL 15 Feb The Equipment of Organizations
HCO PL 20 Feb Regulations
HCO PL 21 Feb I Staff Regulations, Auditing versus Job
HCO PL 21 Feb III Issuing of Certificates
HCO PL 23 Feb Classification
HCO PL 24 Feb I SLR Ltd., Tape Copying
HCO PL 24 Feb II Org Programing
HCOB 1 Mar Meter Reads, Size Of
HCO PL 2 Mar Contracts and Services
HCO PL 7 Mar Director of Enrollment, The Letter Registrar, Administration
HCOB 10 Mar Basic Auditing, Nonreading Meters, Meter Flinch
HCO PL 11 Mar I Auditors Division, New HCO WW Organization
HCO PL 11 Mar II Departmental Changes, Auditors Division
HCO PL 11 Mar III Mission Program
HCOB 15 Mar I Overwhelming the Pc
HCOB 15 Mar II Meter, Everything Reading
HCO PL 18 Mar HGC Allowed Processes
HCO PL 19 Mar Staff Regulations
HCO INFO LETTER 20 Mar Postulates
HCO PL 1 Apr I New Mimeo Line, HCO Executive Letter
HCO PL 1 Apr II Saint Hill Personnel
HCO INFO LETTER 2 Apr Two Types of People
HCO PL 2 Apr I To the Saint Hill Student: Instruction Targets
HCO PL 2 Apr II Saint Hill Enrollment, Materials, Courses, and Use of Class VI Processes
HCO PL 2 Apr III Use of Recreation Facilities, 1964
HCOB 7 Apr Q and A
HCOB 10 Apr Auditing Skills
HCO PL 10 Apr I Balancing Income–Outgo, Paper, Postage and Printing
HCO PL 10 Apr II Scientology Courses
HCO PL 10 Apr III Domestic Staff
HCOB 13 Apr I Tone Arm Action
HCOB 13 Apr II Glossary of Terms

ARTICLE

THE AUDITOR 1 The Workability of Scientology

ISSUES

HCO PL 5 May Summary of Classification and Gradation and Certification
HCO PL 6 May I Accounts Policies
HCO PL 8 May Transport
HCO PL 12 May Theory Testing, Expiration Dates
HCO PL 13 May I Transport
HCO PL 25 May I Instructor's Conference Report Form
HCO PL 25 May II Press Relations
HCOB 27 May Auditing Assignments
HCO PL 28 May Reorganization
HCO PL 2 Jun Data for All Staff Members

ARTICLE

THE AUDITOR 2 The Gradation Program

ISSUES

HCO PL 9 Jun Reorganization
HCO PL 11 Jun I Central Organization and City Office Tape Service
HCO PL 11 Jun II New Students Data, Star-rated for New Students
HCO PL 16 Jun Personnel Records, Admin Certs
HCO PL 18 Jun New Posts
HCO PL 25 Jun Departmental Reports
HCO PL 26 Jun Staff Bonuses
HCOB 29 Jun Central Org and Field Auditor Targets
HCO PL 2 Jul Bulletin and Policy Letter Distribution
HCOB 7 Jul Justifications
HCOB 8 Jul I More Justifications
HCOB 8 Jul II Good Indicators
HCOB 10 Jul Overts—Order of Effectiveness in Processing

ARTICLE

THE AUDITOR 3 Ron's Journal No. 10

ISSUES

HCOB 12 Jul More on O/Ws
HCOB 24 Jul TA Counters, Use Of
HCOB 29 Jul Good Indicators at Lower Levels
HCO PL 30 Jul Gradation Program, Revised
HCO EXEC LETTER 6 Aug Accounts Unit
HCO PL 10 Aug Good Workers
HCO PL 12 Aug Policy on Technical Information
HCOB 14 Aug Prepcheck Buttons
HCOB 17 Aug Clay Table Work in Training and Processing
HCO PL 17 Aug Technical Info for Continental Mags
HCOB 18 Aug Clay Table Work, Covering Clay Table Clearing in Detail
HCO PL 21 Aug Staff Auditors
HCOB 23 Aug HQS Course
HCOB 24 Aug Session Must-Nots
HCO PL 26 Aug PE Course
HCO EXEC LETTER 1 Sep Technical Lectures by Other Personnel
HCO PL 5 Sep Examinations
HCOB 7 Sep I Clay Table Levels
HCOB 7 Sep II PTPs, Overts and ARC Breaks
HCOB 8 Sep Overts, What Lies Behind Them? *Word Clearing Series 11*
HCOB 9 Sep I Clay Table Healing
HCOB 9 Sep II Clay Table Clearing
HCO PL 9 Sep Purpose of Ad Comm
HCOB 12 Sep Clay Table, More Goofs
HCO PL 16 Sep I Understanding and Tape Lectures
HCO PL 16 Sep II Terminations
HCO PL 23 Sep Policies: Dissemination and Programs
HCOB 24 Sep Instruction and Examination: Raising the Standard Of *Word Clearing Series 33*
HCOB 27 Sep Clay Table Clearing
HCO PL 28 Sep Clay Table Use
HCO PL 30 Sep HCO Corporations

ARTICLE

THE AUDITOR 4 Ron's Journal No. 11

ISSUES

HCO PL 4 Oct Theory Checkout Data
HCO PL 8 Oct Artistic Presentation *Art Series 12*
HCO EXEC LETTER 12 Oct Congress Organization and Increasing Interest and Attendance
HCOB 17 Oct I Clay Table Data
HCOB 17 Oct II Getting the Pc Sessionable
HCOB 17 Oct III Clearing, Why It Works, How It Is Necessary
HCO PL 20 Oct Stickers for PABs Wanted
HCO PL 27 Oct R Rev. 15 Nov 87 Policies on Physical Healing, Insanity and Sources of Trouble
HCO PL 31 Oct Addressograph Equipment Warning

THE BOOK OF CASE REMEDIES—A MANUAL COVERING PRECLEAR DIFFICULTIES AND THEIR REMEDIES
by L. Ron Hubbard

Published by the Department of Publications, Worldwide, Saint Hill Manor, East Grinstead, Sussex, England, November 1964. Later revised in 1991. TRANSLATIONS: Dutch and Italian.

ARTICLE

THE AUDITOR 5 Gradation Program Reviewed

ISSUES

HCOB 1 Nov More Clay Table Clearing Goofs
HCOB 6 Nov Styles of Auditing
HCOB 12 Nov Definition Processes *Word Clearing Series 26*
HCO PL 13 Nov Provisional Class VI Classification
HCO PL 15 Nov I Transport Arrangements
HCO PL 15 Nov II Traffic Regulations Saint Hill
HCOB 16 Nov Clay Table Label Goofs

ARTICLE

CERTAINTY VOL. 11, NO. 11 Nov Socialism and Scientology

ISSUES

HCO PL 17 Nov I Off-Line and Off-Policy, Your Full In-Basket
HCO PL 17 Nov II Bonus
HCO PL 30 Nov RB Rev. 2 Feb 91 HCO Book Account
HCO PL 3 Dec R Rev. 7 Jul 83 Booming an Org Through Training

R6EW MATERIALS

The materials for this Solo-audited level were released 8 December 1964.

ISSUES

HCOB 10 Dec Listen-style Auditing
HCOB 11 Dec I Curriculum for Level 0–HAS
HCOB 11 Dec II Processes

THE SCIENTOLOGY PIN (OR MEMBERSHIP PIN)

Worn by members of the Hubbard Association of Scientologists International, a gold lapel-sized pin of the Scientology symbol.

Following the release of the Classification, Gradation and Awareness Chart of Levels and Certificates in 1965, a series of insignia became available that could be worn to show an individual's training level and grade of release.

AUDITOR BLAZER BADGE FOR CLASS IV AUDITOR

This is a shield with two horizontal stripes across the top.

The top stripe is yellow with the Roman numerals "0–IV" in red.

The second stripe is black with the word "auditor" in gold.

The bottom of the shield is green with a gold Scientology symbol.

Below the shield is a gold banner with the words "Standard Tech" in red.

HCO PL 11 Dec Full Table of Courses and Classification, Classification Correction
HCO PL 17 Dec Tape Prices
HCO PL 18 Dec I Saint Hill Org Board
HCO PL 18 Dec IV Re: OIC Data
HCO PL 21 Dec Address Lists to City Offices

The Mastery of GPMs Parts 1 and 2

A filmed lecture by L. Ron Hubbard given at Saint Hill Manor, East Grinstead, Sussex, England on December 22, 1964. This film is now part of Grade VI.

ISSUE

HCOB 26 Dec Routine 0A (Expanded)

The Pattern of the Bank, Parts 1 and 2

A filmed lecture by L. Ron Hubbard given at Saint Hill Manor, East Grinstead, Sussex, England on December 30, 1964. This film is now part of Grade VI.

The Bank and Its Pattern

A filmed lecture by L. Ron Hubbard given at Saint Hill Manor, East Grinstead, Sussex, England on December 30, 1964. This film is now part of the Clearing Course.

ISSUES

HCO PL 31 Dec I Certificates
HCO PL 31 Dec III Use of "Dianetics," "Scientology," "Applied Philosophy"

1965

Great advances were made in Scientology technical *and* administrative technology in 1965.

Mr. Hubbard codified the organizational technology he had developed in building Saint Hill into a big, rapidly expanding organization and released it in a flood of new HCO Policy Letters. In fact, 1965 was one of the richest years in Scientology history in terms of policy advances and releases.

1965 was also marked by spectacular progress in auditing and training technology. The route to total freedom was fully codified, and the first Classification, Gradation and Awareness Chart of Levels and Certificates was released in May. Power Processing was also begun in May, and in September, the Clearing Course was made available to students who had completed the prerequisite auditing steps.

ARTICLES

ARTICLE My Philosophy
THE AUDITOR 6 Healthy Babies

ISSUES

HCO PL 18 Jan Financial Management, Building Fund Account
HCO PL 21 Jan R I Vital Data on
Rev. 5 Apr 65 Promotion, The Fundamentals of Promotion
HCOB 25 Jan Definition of "Terminal"
HCO PL 28 Jan How to Maintain Credit Standing and Solvency
HCO PL 31 Jan Dev-t
HCO PL 7 Feb Keeping Scientology Working *KSW Series 1*
HCO PL 8 Feb Dev-t Analysis
HCO PL 10 Feb Ad and Book Policies
HCO PL 13 Feb I 1965 Saint Hill Objectives
HCO PL 13 Feb II Politics
HCO PL 14 Feb Safeguarding Technology *KSW Series 4*
HCO PL 20 Feb Appointments and Programs
HCO PL 22 Feb I Inspections
HCO PL 22 Feb II HCO Area Secretary Saint Hill
HCO PL 22 Feb III Executive Director Comm Lines
HCO PL 24 Feb Addendum to HCO PL of 7 Sept. 63, Committees of Evidence, Scientology Jurisprudence, Administration Of
HCO PL 27 Feb Course Pattern
HCO PL 28 Feb I Deliver
HCO PL 28 Feb II Course Checkouts, Twin Checking

THE BOOK OF E-METER DRILLS

by L. Ron Hubbard

Published by the Department of Publications, Worldwide, Saint Hill Manor, East Grinstead, Sussex, England, February 1965. Later revised in 1988. TRANSLATIONS: Danish, Dutch, French, German, Italian, Spanish and Swedish.

SAINT HILL SPECIAL BRIEFING COURSE LECTURES

SUSSEX, ENGLAND

2 Mar Technology and Hidden Standards
9 Mar The New Organizational Structure
16 Mar The Progress and Future of Scientology
30 Mar ARC Breaks and Generalities
6 Apr Org Board and Livingness
13 Apr The Lowest Levels
27 Apr Awareness Levels

ISSUES

HCO PL 1 Mar General Amnesty
HCO PL 2 Mar Purchase Order Filing
HCO EXEC LETTER 3 Mar II What's Coming Next
HCO PL 4 Mar I Reserved Payment Account
HCO PL 4 Mar RA II Technical and
Rev. 7 Jul 83 Policy Distribution
HCO PL 4 Mar III HCO Secretary WW
HCO PL 5 Mar I New Status of Honorary Awards
HCO PL 5 Mar II Policy: Source Of
HCOB 5 Mar II *Book of Case Remedies,* Application of Tech
HCO PL 6 Mar Amnesty Policy
HCO PL 7 Mar RA III Offenses and
Rev. 10 Jan 91 Penalties
HCO PL 7 Mar II Certificate Cancellation
HCO PL 8 Mar Board Decisions, Data Evaluation, Raw Data, Judging a Situation, Selection of Key Personnel
HCOB 10 Mar Words, Misunderstood Goofs *Word Clearing Series 14*
HCO PL 13 Mar I The Comm-Member System
HCO PL 13 Mar II The Comm-Member System, Routing Policies Section
HCO PL 13 Mar III The Structure of Organization, What Is Policy?
SEC ED 13 Mar Registrar Success
HCO PL 15 Mar I Registrars, CF and Address
HCO PL 17 Mar I Clearing and Training
HCO PL 17 Mar II Rights of a Staff Member, Students and Preclears to Justice
HCO PL 17 Mar III Administering Justice
HCO PL 17 Mar IV Organizational Suppressive Acts
HCO EXEC LETTER 18 Mar Justice
HCO EXEC LETTER 21 Mar PE Comes After They Have Read a Book
HCO PL 21 Mar Staff Members Auditing Outside Pcs
HCO PL 22 Mar Current Promotion and Org Program Summary, Membership Rundown
HCO PL 26 Mar RA II Field Staff
Rev. 8 Nov 84 Member I/C Hat, Field Staff Members *FSM Series 2*

HCO EXEC LETTER 27 Mar Confused Presentation Denies Service
HCO PL 27 Mar The Justice of Scientology, Its Use and Purpose, Being a Scientologist
HCO PL 28 Mar Emergencies and Accounts Personnel
HCO PL 29 Mar I Routing Despatches
HCO PL 29 Mar II Flows and Expansion, The Fast Flow System
HCO PL 29 Mar III Staff Regulations
HCOB 29 Mar ARC Breaks
HCO PL 31 Mar Justice Policy Letters Corrections
HCO PL 1 Apr HCO Communicator Has Program Checking Hat *LRH Comm N/W Series 21*
HCO PL 2 Apr I False Reports
HCO PL 2 Apr II Meter Checks
HCO PL 2 Apr III Heed Heavy Traffic Warnings
HCO PL 2 Apr IV Star-rate Checkouts for Process
HCO PL 2 Apr R V Rev. 14 Dec 80 Administration Outside Scientology
HCOB 2 Apr The Road to Clear
HCO PL 3 Apr Organization of a Scientology Org
HCOB 4 Apr ARC Breaks and Missed Withholds
HCOB 5 Apr A Conditions Test, Process I–X Registrars
HCO PL 5 Apr I Handling the Suppressive Person, The Basis of Insanity
HCO PL 5 Apr II The No-Gain-Case Student
HCO PL 5 Apr III Scientology Makes a Safe Environment
HCO PL 5 Apr IV Legal and Promotion
SEC ED 5 Apr Registrar, Your Orders
HCO PL 6 Apr Letter Reg Hat
HCO PL 7 Apr I Book Auditor
HCO PL 7 Apr II Healing Policy in Field
HCO PL 7 Apr III Amnesty, Cancelled Certs, Justice Comments
HCO PL 7 Apr RA IV Rev. 23 Sep 89 Book Income
HCOB 7 Apr Premature Acknowledgments
HCO PL 8 Apr I Justice Codes—HCO, Org Executive and Divisional Secretaries, Justice on, and Auditing Of
HCO PL 8 Apr R II Rev. 7 Jul 83 Cancellation of Mail Lists to Field Auditors
HCO PL 9 Apr Correction to Policy Letters on Certification and Awards
HCO PL 10 Apr Dismissals, Transfers and Demotions
HCO PL 12 Apr I Justice
HCO PL 12 Apr II Classification Pass Marks
HCO PL 14 Apr I Organization GPM Unit
HCO PL 14 Apr II Classification on GPMs
HCO PL 14 Apr III Field Auditor Rates
HCO PL 16 Apr I The "Hidden Data Line" *KSW Series 22*
HCO PL 16 Apr II Drills, Allowed
HCO PL 16 Apr III Handling the Public Individual
HCO PL 17 Apr Additional Mag Policy
HCO PL 18 Apr I Contests and Prizes
HCO PL 18 Apr II Prices Lowered Because of New Organization Streamline
HCOB 18 Apr How to Apply Level Processing
HCO PL 19 Apr Training and Processing Regulations, Tech Division, Qual Division, Technical Discipline, Students' Questions
HCO PL 21 Apr I Basic Certificates, Uncertified Personnel
HCO PL 21 Apr II Membership Attestations
HCO PL 22 Apr II Level 0 Comm Course
HCO PL 22 Apr III Booklets, Handouts, Mailing Pieces
HCO PL 23 Apr I Clarification, Auditing of Org Executives
HCO PL 23 Apr III Problems
HCO PL 24 Apr Review
HCO PL 26 Apr Sec ED Issue
HCOB 27 Apr Clay Table Healing Goof
HCO PL 27 Apr II Price Engram
HCO PL 27 Apr III Book Promotion Design
HCO PL 28 Apr I Color Flash System
HCO PL 28 Apr II Technical Personnel
HCO PL 28 Apr III Power Processes
HCO PL 29 Apr I Bonuses
HCO PL 29 Apr II Petition
HCO PL 29 Apr III Ethics, Review
HCO PL 30 Apr Emergency, State Of
HCO PL 1 May I Staff Member Reports
HCO PL 1 May II Order Board and Time Machine
HCO PL 1 May R III Rev. 29 Aug 90 Organization, the Design of the Organization
HCOB 5 May Application, More on the Application of Scientology to Children
HCO PL 5 May I Classification, Gradation and Awareness Chart
HCO PL 5 May II Supervisors
SEC ED 5 May "Free Memberships for Six Months . . ."
CHART Classification, Gradation and Awareness Chart of Levels and Certificates
HCO PL 7 May Cancellation, Mimeo Distribution Changes (Sec ED Distribution)
HCO PL 8 May I Cancellation of Assorted Directives
HCO PL 8 May II Results of HCO Technical Investigation
HCO PL 8 May III Flash Colors and Designations
HCO PL 9 May RA I Rev. 8 Nov 84 Field Auditors Become Staff *FSM Series 1*
HCO PL 9 May II Auditing Fees, Preferential Treatment of Preclears, Scale of Preference

Power Processing Materials

The issues covering this new level were released on 10 May 1965 to the auditors LRH was personally training to deliver it.

Issues

SEC ED 10 May Get Your Technical Division In, Fully Manned and Functioning!
HCO PL 10 May Releases, Vital Data

Saint Hill Special Briefing Course Lectures
SUSSEX, ENGLAND

11 May ARC Breaks and PTPs, the Differentiation
18 May Organization and Ethics
25 May The Five Conditions
8 Jun Handling the PTS
29 Jun The Well-Rounded Auditor
27 Jul Stages of Release
9 Sep Classification and Gradation [filmed lecture]

Issues

HCO PL 11 May I Ethics Officer Hat
HCO PL 11 May R II Rev. 7 Jul 83 HCO Book Account Policy, Receipt and Use of Membership Monies
HCO PL 13 May I Sale of Bulletins and Tapes Forbidden
HCO PL 13 May II SHSBC Unit Graduation
HCO PL 16 May I Important Explanation, Auditing Restrictions
HCO PL 16 May II Indicators of Orgs
HCO PL 16 May III Hubbard Recognized Scientologist
SEC ED 17 May Clarification of Sec ED 27
HCO PL 17 May I CCHs
HCO PL 17 May II Academy Processing
HCO PL 17 May III Free Scientology Center
HCO PL 20 May Power Processes
HCO PL 21 May Memorandum of Agreement
HCO PL 23 May II Rebates
SEC ED 24 May Examinations
SEC ED 26 May Re: Sec ED 29 (Tech Div)
HCO PL 26 May I Petitions

Auditor Blazer Badge for Class VI Auditor

This is a shield with two horizontal stripes across the top.

The top stripe is yellow with the Roman numeral "VI" in red.

The second stripe is black with the word "auditor" in gold.

The bottom of the shield is blue with a gold Scientology symbol.

Below the shield is a gold banner with the words "Standard Tech" in red.

THE POWER RELEASE PIN

For the preclear who has attained Grades V, VA or VI, a release pin with the S and double triangle (Scientology symbol) with the red R encircled by a gold wreath.

THE RELEASE PIN

A small lapel-sized pin. It is the Scientology symbol in gold with a red R (for Release) mounted on it. It signifies a release, Grades 0 through IV.

HCO PL 26 May II Communications, Registered Mail
HCO PL 26 May III Courts of Ethics
HCO PL 27 May Processing *KSW Series 31*
HCO PL 28 May I Some Allowed Ads, Book Ads
HCO PL 28 May II Mission Courses
HCO PL 31 May I Noise, Session Interruption
HCO PL 31 May II Mission Summary of Policy
HCO PL 2 Jun I Writing of an Ethics Order
HCO PL 2 Jun II Org Ethics and Tech
HCO PL 3 Jun R6EW
SEC ED 4 Jun "All Pcs Undergoing Power Processing . . ."
HCO PL 7 Jun I New Org Board Design
HCO PL 7 Jun II Entheta Letters and the Dead File, Handling Of
SEC ED 10 Jun PE and Lectures
HCO PL 11 Jun I The Foundation
HCO PL 11 Jun II Correction to HCO PL 26 May 65 II, Communications, Registered Mail
HCO PL 12 Jun The Foundation, Forming the Foundation
HCO PL 14 Jun I Folders, Marking Of
HCO PL 14 Jun II Six Power Processes
HCO PL 14 Jun III Politics, Freedom From
HCOB 14 Jun II Summary Report
HCO PL 17 Jun I Staff Auditor Advices
HCO PL 17 Jun II Scientology Pins
HCO PL 18 Jun I Grounds Regulations, Staff and Students
HCO PL 18 Jun II Areas of Operation
HCOB 18 Jun Clear and OT Behavior
HCO PL 21 Jun I Orgs Are Saint Hill FSMs
HCO PL 21 Jun II Distribution Division (Div 6)
HCO PL 26 Jun HGC Pc Review Auditing Form
HCOB 28 Jun Releases, Different Kinds
HCOB 30 Jun Release, Rehabilitation of Former Releases and Thetan Exteriors
HCO PL 30 Jun Ad

ARTICLE

THE AUDITOR 9 Org Staffs to Release

ISSUES

HCO PL 1 Jul I Ethics Chits
HCO PL 1 Jul II Comm Cycle Additives
HCO PL 1 Jul III Hats, the Reason For
HCO PL 1 Jul IV Letter Reg, Body Reg
HCO PL 3 Jul The Foundation Data
HCO PL 4 Jul Pc Routing, Review Code
HCO PL 6 Jul Releases
HCO PL 7 Jul Photos, News and Statistics for Mags and *Auditor*
HCO PL 9 Jul Qual Goofs
HCO PL 10 Jul Lines and Terminals Routing
HCO PL 11 Jul Assignment of Tech Personnel
HCO PL 12 Jul I Release Policies, Starting the Pc
HCOB 12 Jul States of Being Attained by Processing
HCO 13 Jul ADMIN LETTER Congresses
HCO PL 16 Jul Continental Magazines to Model After *Certainty*
HCO PL 19 Jul I Policy, How to Handle People Who Quote Policy to Show You They Can't Follow It
HCO PL 19 Jul II Separation Order
HCO PL 19 Jul III Release Checks, Procedure For
HCO PL 19 Jul RA IV Rev. 7 Jul 83 Discounts, Central Orgs, Books
HCOB 21 Jul Release Rehabilitation
HCO PL 22 Jul II Dissemination Materials to Saint Hill
HCO PL 23 Jul Priority of Power Processing
HCO PL 26 Jul Release Declaration Restrictions, Healing Amendments
HCO PL 28 Jul I Handling of Photographs
HCO PL 28 Jul II Case Supervisor, Special Attention
HCO PL 30 Jul Preclear Routing to Ethics
HCO PL 31 Jul Purposes of the Qualifications Division *KSW Series 12*
HCO PL 2 Aug I Executive Division
HCO PL 2 Aug II Chaplain
HCOB 2 Aug Release Goofs
HCOB 3 Aug Auditing Goofs, Blowdown Interruption
HCO PL 5 Aug Release Checkouts
HCOB 5 Aug Release Stages
HCOB 6 Aug Qualifications Technical Actions
HCO PL 6 Aug Technical Queries from R6 Graduates
HCO PL 7 Aug I Suppressive Persons, Main Characteristics Of
HCO PL 7 Aug II Floating Needle on Former Releases
HCO PL 9 Aug Release Checkouts
HCO PL 12 Aug Council and Ad Comms
HCO PL 13 Aug Foundation, Basic Course Organization
HCO PL 15 Aug Things That Shouldn't Be
HCO PL 16 Aug I Foundation, Basic Course Organization, Correction
HCO PL 16 Aug II Collection from SPs and PTSes
SEC ED 16 Aug Foundation
HCO PL 17 Aug I Return Address
HCO PL 17 Aug II Certification of Mission Students
HCO PL 20 Aug I General Amnesty
HCO PL 20 Aug II Continuing Pc to Third Stage Release
HCO PL 20 Aug III Appointment of Xerox Officer
HCO PL 20 Aug IV Scientology Org Uniforms, Saint Hill
HCOB 23 Aug Abbreviations and Symbols of Dianetics and Scientology
HCO PL 23 Aug I Classification at Upper Levels, Temporary Measure
HCO PL 23 Aug II Crediting of Auditor in Release Logbook
HCO PL 23 Aug III Deletion of TR 5
HCO PL 24 Aug I Pcs Released Routing
HCO PL 24 Aug II Cleanliness of Quarters and Staff, Improve Our Image
HCO PL 26 Aug RB Rev. 10 Jan 91 Ethics E-Meter Check
HCO PL 27 Aug Housing—Staff, Students, Preclears
HCOB 30 Aug R I Rev. 30 Dec 79 Art *Art Series 1*
HCOB 30 Aug II Release Stages
HCO PL 31 Aug Mail Opening

ARTICLE The Aims of Scientology

ISSUES

HCO PL 1 Sep II Publications
HCO PL 1 Sep R III Rev. 7 Jul 83 Mailing List Policies
HCO PL 1 Sep IV Some Tech Div Policies
HCO PL 1 Sep R V Rev. 27 Mar 78 Membership Policies
HCO PL 1 Sep VI Saint Hill Services and Prices
HCO PL 1 Sep VII Ethics Protection

The Materials of the R6 Bank

A filmed lecture by L. Ron Hubbard given at Saint Hill Manor, East Grinstead, Sussex, England on September 3, 1965. This film is now part of the Clearing Course.

ISSUES

HCO PL 4 Sep I Inspection Officer
HCO 6 Sep EXEC LETTER Upping Beginning Scientology Enrollments
HCO PL 8 Sep Supply Officer
SEC ED 8 Sep Distribution Division Info Packet
SEC ED 8 Sep Registration Packet
HCO PL 9 Sep Flowers, Care Of
HCO PL 12 Sep I Foundation Course Change

HCO PL 12 Sep R II E-Meters and Books
Rev. 4 Feb 91 for Academy Students
HCOB 13 Sep R I Out-Tech and How to
Rev. 16 Feb 81 Get It In
KSW Series 26
HCO PL 13 Sep II Issue Authority Required for Mimeo
HCO PL 13 Sep III Foundation Course Hours
HCO PL 14 Sep I Classification Is Required Before Moving to Next Level
HCO PL 14 Sep II Units and Bonuses for Org Exec Secs and HCO Exec Secs
HCO PL 14 Sep III New Car Park
HCO PL 16 Sep I Weekly Secretarial Personnel Report
HCO PL 16 Sep II Foundation
HCO PL 17 Sep Executive Letter Unit

SAINT HILL SPECIAL BRIEFING COURSE LECTURES
SUSSEX, ENGLAND

21 Sep Out-Tech
14 Oct Briefing of Review Auditors

ISSUES

HCO PL 21 Sep I Cleanliness and Tidiness of Premises
HCO PL 21 Sep II Auditor Estimation Test
HCO PL 21 Sep III Corporate Names, Group Names
HCO PL 21 Sep V E-Meter Drills
HCO PL 21 Sep VI Purposes of the Department of Registration
HCOB 21 Sep Out-Tech
HCOB 22 Sep Release Gradation, New Levels of Release
HCO PL 22 Sep Keys
HCO PL 23 Sep Keeping Stocks Up
HCO PL 24 Sep I Free Release Check
HCO PL 24 Sep III Ads and Info Packets
HCO PL 25 Sep Entheta Letters and the Dead File, Handling Of
HCOB 27 Sep Release Gradation, Additional Data

CLEARING COURSE MATERIALS

The written materials for the Clearing Course were first presented to students at its opening on 27 September 1965.

ISSUE

HCOB 29 Sep I Cyclical and Non-Cyclical Process Conclusions
HCOB 29 Sep II The Continuing Overt Act
HCO PL 30 Sep Statistics for Divisions

ARTICLES

THE AUDITOR 10 The States of Existence
THE AUDITOR 10 Preclears Should Demand Proper E-Meters Be Used

ISSUES

HCOB 1 Oct R Mutter TR
Rev. 24 Feb 75
HCO PL 5 Oct Routing, Ad Comm Reports and Minutes
HCO EXEC LETTER 10 Oct Government Conflicts
HCO PL 12 Oct Advisory Committees
HCO PL 13 Oct Dev-t Data, Executive Responsibility
HCO PL 14 Oct I Potential Trouble Source Routing
HCO PL 15 Oct R Field Staff Member
Rev. 8 Nov 84 Selection Papers and Commissions
FSM Series 3
HCO EXEC LETTER 15 Oct Field Staff Member Commissions
SEC ED 18 Oct Field Staff Member Program
HCO PL 19 Oct Release Declarations
HCO PL 21 Oct II Bills Payments
SEC ED 22 Oct FSM Selection Slips
HCO PL 23 Oct Dissemination Drill
HCO PL 25 Oct Saint Hill Solo Audit Course
HCO PL 26 Oct Low Statistics
HCO PL 27 Oct Grade Award Insignia
HCO PL 28 Oct Discounts
HCO PL 29 Oct I Student Auditing of Preclears
HCO PL 29 Oct II Ethics Authority Section, Office of LRH
LRH Comm N/W Series 18
SEC ED 2 Nov "In HCO Policy Letter . . ."
HCO EXEC LETTER 2 Nov Your Org—Reply Expected
HCO PL 2 Nov II Foundation Central Files Officer and Address In-Charge
HCO PL 2 Nov III Fast Line Sec EDs and Admin Orders
HCO PL 2 Nov IV Org Division, Income Dept
HCO PL 3 Nov I Equipment
HCO PL 3 Nov II Pc Scheduling
ADMIN DIRECTIVE 4 Nov Appearances Officer Hat Write-up
HCO EXEC LETTER 4 Nov "I Am Worried about Your Foundation . . ."
HCOB 5 Nov Five-Way Bracket on Help
HCOB 7 Nov Release Rehabilitation Error
HCO PL 7 Nov I Reception Log, In-the-Org List
HCO PL 7 Nov II Autographed Copies of Books by LRH
HCOB 8 Nov Suppressives and Hidden Standards
HCO PL 10 Nov The Cramming Section
HCO PL 12 Nov II Paint, Odorless
HCO PL 12 Nov III Transfers from SHSBC to Solo Audit Course
HCO PL 13 Nov Release Pins
HCOB 14 Nov Clearing Commands
HCO PL 15 Nov Reporting of Theft and Action to Be Taken
HCOB 16 Nov R I E-Meter Sensitivity
Rev. 22 Feb 79 Setting
HCOB 16 Nov II Commands for Upper Indoctrination TR 6, TR 7, TR 9
HCO PL 17 Nov The Basic Principles of Promotion
SEC ED 18 Nov Field Staff Member Courses
HCO PL 18 Nov I Appointment of Personnel
HCOB 19 Nov Problems Process
HCO PL 19 Nov Auditing Reports
HCO PL 20 Nov RA I The Promotional
Rev. 4 May 85 Actions of an Organization
HCO PL 20 Nov II Org Rudiments Section
HCO PL 21 Nov Check Signing
SEC ED 23 Nov Organization at Saint Hill
HCOB 24 Nov Search and Discovery
HCO PL 26 Nov R Financial Planning
Rev. 31 Oct 82 *Finance Series 40*
SEC ED 26 Nov Income Data
HCOB 26 Nov Information on Rehabilitation
HCOB 30 Nov Library Record of Levels
HCO PL 30 Nov Power Processing for the Public
HCOB 1 Dec CCHs
HCOB 6 Dec Low TA Cases
HCO PL 7 Dec Tape Color Flash Code
HCO PL 9 Dec R HCO Income,
Rev. 7 Jul 83 Memberships—Tape Plays
HCOB 10 Dec E-Meter Drill Coaching
HCO PL 13 Dec Numbering of Certificates
SEC ED 14 Dec Departmental Actions
HCO PL 15 Dec R I Student's Guide to
Rev. 25 Jul 87 Acceptable Behavior
HCO PL 15 Dec II Gifts
HCO PL 15 Dec III Ethics Chits
SEC ED 16 Dec Registration and Service
HCO PL 16 Dec I Copyright: USA
HCO PL 16 Dec II Organization of the Int Exec Division, Statistics of the International Executive Division
SEC ED 21 Dec Accounts Clearance
HCO PL 23 Dec RB Suppressive Acts,
Rev. 8 Jan 91 Suppression of Scientology and Scientologists
HCOB 27 Dec Vitamins
HCO PL 27 Dec RA LRH Communicator
Rev. 7 May 84 *LRH Comm N/W Series 2*

THE CLEAR AND OT BRACELETS

A Clear is signified by a silver identification bracelet with the S and double triangle on it. The bracelet is sterling silver. The underside bears the word "Clear," L. Ron Hubbard's initials, the engraved name of the person, the date they were declared Clear and their Clear number. An Operating Thetan is signified by a gold bracelet of the same design.

HCO PL 28 Dec RA E-Meters Allowed
Rev. 4 Feb 91

HCO PL 30 Dec PTS Auditing and Routing

SCIENTOLOGY: A NEW SLANT ON LIFE
by L. Ron Hubbard

A collection of the most popular magazine articles by L. Ron Hubbard. Published by Hubbard Communications Office, Worldwide, Saint Hill Manor, East Grinstead, Sussex, England, December 1965. TRANSLATIONS: Danish, Dutch, French, German, Italian, Spanish and Swedish.

1966

Early in 1966, Mr. Hubbard turned over his executive duties at Saint Hill and traveled to the Canary Islands to do advanced research. In March he flew on to the southern African country of Rhodesia (since renamed Zimbabwe), where he continued his research and investigated the relationship of the individual to a large group.

Returning to Saint Hill in July, he resumed lecturing to students on the Saint Hill Special Briefing Course, completing this monumental, six-year series of lectures and demonstrations in December.

Throughout this time, LRH continued researching new levels. In August, the first Operating Thetan level was released—OT I—followed by OT II in September.

On the first of September, LRH resigned from all directorships in Scientology organizations and devoted his time to lecturing and further research. Toward the end of the year, he was awarded his third Explorers Club flag, which he was to carry on a research expedition: the Hubbard Mediterranean Geological Survey Expedition, examining ancient Mediterranean civilizations and amplifying man's knowledge of his history.

WHAT ARE PEOPLE FOR?—AN INTRODUCTION TO SCIENTOLOGY
Taken from the works of L. Ron Hubbard

Published by the Hubbard College of Scientology, Saint Hill Manor, East Grinstead, Sussex, England, 1966. TRANSLATION: Danish.

ISSUES

HCO PL 4 Jan I Staff Meeting

HCO PL 4 Jan III Scientology Organizations Communications System: Despatches

HCO PL 4 Jan RA IV Sec EDs and HCO Exec Letters *LRH Comm N/W Series 3*
Rev. 7 May 85

HCO PL 4 Jan RA V Personnel, Staff Status
Rev. 25 Mar 89

HCO PL 4 Jan VI LRH Relationships to Orgs

HCO PL 6 Jan Credit and Discounts

HCO PL 7 Jan I Leaving Post, Writing Your Hat

HCO PL 7 Jan II Credit

HCO PL 9 Jan I OIC Section SH

HCO PL 9 Jan II International Changes or Area Changes of Address

HCO PL 9 Jan III Accounts, Invalidating

HCO PL 11 Jan Ad Council and Ad Comms, Orders, Issue Of

HCO PL 12 Jan Selectees Mailing, Selectee Advice Packets

HCO PL 13 Jan I Regulations for Auditing of Staff and Students

HCO PL 13 Jan II Records of Bank Deposits

SEC ED 13 Jan Intern Training

HCO PL 15 Jan I Hold the Form of the Org, Don't Bring About Danger Conditions

HCO PL 15 Jan II Office of the Treasurer

HCO PL 16 Jan R Danger Condition
Rev. 29 Nov 79

HCO PL 17 Jan I Unclassed Certificates—HAS, HBA, HQS

HCO PL 17 Jan II Organization Chart

SEC ED 17 Jan Distribution Action

HCOB 19 Jan Danger Conditions, Technical Data for Review Auditors

HCO PL 19 Jan I Danger Condition, Warning, The Junior Who Accepts Orders from Everyone

HCO PL 19 Jan RA II LRH Communicator Orders *LRH Comm N/W Series 4*
Rev. 7 May 84

HCO PL 19 Jan III Danger Condition, Responsibilities of Declaring

HCO PL 20 Jan II Division 7, International Executive Division, Offices of the HCO Exec Sec and Org Exec Sec Described

HCO PL 21 Jan Executive Division

SEC ED 21 Jan To Advisory Council Worldwide

HCOB 21 Jan S&D Errors

HCO PL 22 Jan Division Seven

HCO PL 23 Jan Accounting Policies of Scientology Companies

HCO PL 25 Jan II Communication Inspector Hat

HCO PL 26 Jan Int Exec Div Relation to Saint Hill Org

SEC ED 27 Jan Orders to HCOs

HCOB 28 Jan Search and Discovery Data, How a Suppressive Becomes One

HCO PL 30 Jan RA I Org LRH Communicator Reports to LRH Comm Int *LRH Comm N/W Series 5*
Rev. 7 May 84

HCO PL 30 Jan II Minimum Personnel of an Org

HCO PL 30 Jan III Accounts Procedures

HCO PL 30 Jan IV Check Signing Procedure

HCO PL 1 Feb I Staff Auditor and Supervisor Procurement

HCO PL 1 Feb II Danger Conditions, Inspections by Executive Secretaries, How to Do Them

HCO PL 1 Feb III HGC Cure, Intern Training and Staff Auditors

HCO PL 1 Feb IV Statistics, Actions to Take, Statistic Changes

ARTICLE

CERTAINTY 2 Feb Psychotics
VOL. 13, NO. 2

ISSUES

HCO PL 3 Feb I Legal, Tax, Accountant and Solicitor Mail and Legal Officer

HCO PL 3 Feb II Clearing Course, Submission of Folders

HCO PL 3 Feb IV Sec ED, Change in Issue and Use

HCO PL 3 Feb V Sec EDs, Definition and Purpose

HCOB 5 Feb I S and D Warning

HCOB 5 Feb II "Letting the Pc Itsa," The Properly Trained Auditor *Basic Auditing Series 8*

HCOB 9 Feb Release Grades

HCO PL 10 Feb I Checksheets, Course

HCO PL 10 Feb R II Tech Recovery
Rev. 22 Feb 79

HCO PL 10 Feb III Bonuses for Service Delivery

HCOB 11 Feb R Free Needles, How to Get Them on a Pc
Rev. 22 Feb 79

HCO PL 11 Feb Shipping Charges

HCOB 12 Feb The "Dangerous Auditor"

HCO PL 13 Feb I Personnel Control Officer

HCO PL 13 Feb II Sec EDs, Sec ED Okay (Continued), Policy Letter Changes and Origins

HCO PL 14 Feb Doctor Title Abolished

HCO PL 15 Feb I Attacks on Scientology

HCO PL 16 Feb Invoice Routing

HCO PL 18 Feb Attacks on Scientology (Continued)

HCO PL 23 Feb Appointments and Promotions

HCO PL 24 Feb Mail Statistic, Dir Comm's Function

HCO PL 25 Feb I Communications Functions

HCO PL 28 Feb Danger Condition Data, Why Organizations Stay Small

ARTICLE

CERTAINTY Mar What Is Greatness?
VOL. 13, NO. 3

ISSUES

HCO PL 1 Mar R II Executive Division Organization and Its Theory and Purpose
Rev. 14 Feb 91

HCO PL 3 Mar I Attacks on Scientology, Sex and Organizations

HCO PL 6 Mar I Rewards and Penalties, How to Handle Personnel and Ethics Matters

HCO PL 6 Mar II Statistic Graphs, How to Figure the Scale

HCO PL 7 Mar I HGC Cure (Continued)

HCO PL 7 Mar II Star-rates on Tech and Qual Staff

HCO PL 8 Mar High Crime *KSW Series 13*

HCO PL 12 Mar Board Minutes

HCO PL 13 Mar I Orders, Precedence of Personnel, Titles Of

HCO PL 15 Mar Corporate Address

SEC ED 17 Mar Expansion of Your Org

HCO PL 17 Mar Promotion of Saint Hill *Auditor* Issue Frequency

ARTICLES

ABILITY 179 Times Must Change

CERTAINTY Apr Economics
VOL. 13, NO. 4

An Introduction to Scientology

A one-hour filmed interview with L. Ron Hubbard answering questions commonly asked about Scientology. Filmed in April 1966. Available in a colorized version on video. TRANSLATIONS: Danish, Dutch, French, German, Italian, Spanish, Swedish, Finnish, Norwegian, Portuguese, Hungarian, Czechoslovakian, Polish, Urdu, Japanese, Korean, Taiwanese, Mandarin, Hebrew, Serbo-Croatian, Russian, Greek, Afrikaans and Arabic.

ISSUES

HCOB 3 Apr Dianetic Auditing Course
HCO PL 3 Apr Dianetic Auditor Course
HCO PL 19 Apr Congress Policies
HCO PL 29 Apr II Policy Checkouts and E-Meter
HCO PL 3 May R Reserve Fund
Rev. 2 Feb 91
HCO PL 7 May LRH Communicator, Issue Authority Of *LRH Comm N/W Series 20*
HCO PL 8 May RA LRH Communicator,
Rev. 7 May 84 No Other Hats *LRH Comm N/W Series 6*

Filmed Lectures

L. Ron Hubbard gave four filmed lectures at Saint Hill Manor in June 1966, which are now part of the Clearing Course. These films are entitled:

Composition of the Bank
The Technical Materials
General Information
Auditing Demonstration

ISSUES

HCO PL 4 Jun Board of Investigation
HCO PL 7 Jun OIC Publication and Distribution
HCOB 10 Jun I S&D Commands
HCOB 10 Jun II S&D—The Missed Item

SAINT HILL SPECIAL BRIEFING COURSE LECTURES
SUSSEX, ENGLAND

19 Jul About Rhodesia
21 Jul Dianetic Auditing
26 Jul The Classification Chart and Auditing
28 Jul Dianetic Auditing and the Mind
2 Aug Suppressives and GAEs
4 Aug Dianetics, Scientology and Society
16 Aug Releases and Clears
18 Aug Study and Intention
23 Aug Organization
25 Aug The Antisocial Personality
1 Sep Gradients and ARC
8 Sep States of Identity
1 Nov Government and Organization
29 Nov Scientology Definitions I: OT and Clear Defined
6 Dec Scientology Definitions II
13 Dec Scientology Definitions III

ISSUES

HCO PL 21 Jun Appointments, LRH Comm and Executive Secretary and Others
HCO PL 29 Jun Keep Academy Checksheets Up-to-Date
HCO PL 1 Jul Information Concerning the WW Time Machine
HCO PL 17 Jul I Despatches, Speed Up; Despatches, Staledate
HCO PL 17 Jul II Evidence, Admissibility of in Hearings, Boards or Committees
HCO PL 20 Jul RB Staff Status
Rev. 24 Nov 85
HCOB 20 Jul The Type Two PTS
HCO PL 21 Jul I Tech versus Qual
HCO PL 25 Jul Allocation of Quarters, Arrangement of Desks and Equipment
HCO PL 27 Jul Moving
HCO PL 31 Jul R Refund Notice
Rev. 28 Jan 91
HCO PL 1 Aug I Sign-ups and Discounts
HCO PL 1 Aug II Refund Addition
HCO PL 2 Aug I Graph Change, Ad Council Statistic
HCO PL 2 Aug II Dianetic Auditing
HCO PL 4 Aug Clears, Invalidation Of
HCO PL 5 Aug I Registered Mail
HCO PL 5 Aug RA II Chaplain's Court,
Rev. 7 Dec 88 Civil Hearings
SEC ED 5 Aug Successes of Scientology
HCO PL 8 Aug OT Color Flash, Color Flash Addition
HCOB 10 Aug Errors of Students
HCO PL 10 Aug Executive Director Sec EDs
HCO PL 11 Aug Lamps and Security

OT I MATERIALS

The materials for the first OT level, a Solo-audited action, were released to qualified Solo auditors on 14 August 1966.

ISSUES

HCO PL 15 Aug I Information Packets
HCO PL 15 Aug II Ethics Orders
HCO PL 16 Aug II Clearing Course Security
HCO PL 17 Aug Routing and Handling of SHSBC Students
HCO PL 22 Aug I Dead File: Restoration to Good Standing
HCOB 22 Aug Floating Needles, Listing Processes
HCOB 23 Aug Service Facsimile

INTRODUCING THE E-METER
by L. Ron Hubbard

Published by the Hubbard College of Scientology, Saint Hill Manor, East Grinstead, Sussex, England, September 1966. Later revised in 1988. TRANSLATIONS: Danish, Dutch, French, German, Italian, Spanish and Swedish.

OT II MATERIALS

The written materials for OT II were released in September 1966, to auditors who had successfully completed OT I.

ISSUES

HCO PL 1 Sep RA Founder
Rev. 8 May 73
HCO PL 6 Sep The Handling of Purchased or Rented Mailing Lists
HCO PL 9 Sep Security
HCO PL 13 Sep Requirement for Termination on the SHSBC and Enrollment on Solo Course
HCOB 20 Sep Minus Scale Releases: ARC Straightwire, Dianetic
HCOB 21 Sep ARC Break Needle
HCOB 27 Sep The Antisocial Personality, The Anti-Scientologist
HCO PL 30 Sep II OT Regulations

A NEW UNDERSTANDING OF LIFE

Published by the Hubbard College of Scientology, Saint Hill Manor, East Grinstead, Sussex, England, 1966.

ISSUES

HCO PL 5 Oct Students Terminating, Leave of Absence, Blown Students
HCO EXEC LETTER 5 Oct A New Pattern of Organization
HCO PL 6 Oct RC II Additions to HCO
Rev. 4 Feb 91 Div Account Policy
HCO PL 11 Oct Legal, Tax, Accountant and Solicitor Mail Incoming and Outgoing
HCO PL 12 Oct IV Examinations
HCO PL 12 Oct V Duration of SHSBC and Solo Course Requirements
HCO PL 13 Oct I Invoice Routing
HCO PL 13 Oct IV Advertisements Continental Magazines and *Auditor*
HCO PL 14 Oct Clearing Course Folders
HCO PL 17 Oct II Bonuses
HCO PL 18 Oct SH Staff Auditor's Purpose
HCO PL 20 Oct I Signatures of Policy Letters
HCO PL 20 Oct II Executives and Governing Body Errors and Answers *AKH Series 1*
HCO PL 21 Oct I Six-Department System
HCO PL 21 Oct II City Office System
HCO PL 21 Oct III City Office
HCO PL 21 Oct IV Evening Foundations
HCO PL 31 Oct I Actions, Executive, for Handling Disastrous Occurrences *AKH Series 2*
HCO PL 31 Oct R II Job Endangerment
Rev. 5 Mar 68 Chits *AKH Series 3R*
HCO PL 31 Oct III Boards of Investigation

ARTICLE

THE AUDITOR 18 What Every Auditor Should Know

ISSUES

HCO PL 1 Nov I Worldwide Organization
HCO PL 3 Nov Leadership *AKH Series 4*
HCO PL 6 Nov R I Statistic
Rev. 9 Nov 79 Interpretation, Statistic Analysis *AKH Series 5R*
HCO PL 6 Nov II Statistic Interpretation, Estate Statistic
HCO PL 7 Nov Clear Checkouts in Continental Orgs
HCO PL 10 Nov I Good versus Bad Management *AKH Series 6*
HCO PL 16 Nov Executive Facilities, Facility Differential *AKH Series 7*
HCO PL 17 Nov II Intervention *AKH Series 8*
HCOB 18 Nov Rehab on Self Analysis
HCO PL 21 Nov Ideas and Compilations Branch WW
HCOB 30 Nov Assessment for Service Facsimiles

ARTICLE

THE AUDITOR 19 Dianetics, Scientology and Beyond

ISSUES

HCO PL 4 Dec Expansion, Theory of Policy *AKH Series 9*
HCO PL 7 Dec RA Magazines Permitted
Rev. 5 Feb 91 All Orgs
HCO PL 12 Dec New Org Board Design (2)
HCO PL 15 Dec Financial Planning
HCO PL 16 Dec Clearing Course Regulation
LRH ED 20 Dec Tech and Qual Pre-examinations
HCO PL 21 Dec I Advisory Council
HCO PL 21 Dec II Executive Council
HCO PL 21 Dec III Office of LRH Supplies
HCO PL 23 Dec Saint Hill Income Peaks, Reinforcement of *Auditor* Promotion
HCO PL 24 Dec I How to Program an Org, Saint Hill Programs *AKH Series 10*

HCO PL 24 Dec II How to Program an Org, Corrections and Additions, Sequence of Programs Correction *AKH Series 11*
HCO PL 26 Dec PTS Sections, Personnel and Execs *AKH Series 12*
HCO PL 29 Dec Historical Precedence of Ethics

1967

In early January, LRH traveled from Saint Hill to the northern African city of Tangier, Morocco. There he set up a base where he could carry out advanced studies and research.

A short time later he traveled to Las Palmas in the Canary Islands, where he established the Sea Organization. In November, he returned to England where he accepted delivery of a 3,200 ton vessel, the *Royal Scotman.* Later renamed the *Apollo,* it became the flagship of the Sea Organization.

Amidst all of the tremendous organizational activity of 1967, Mr. Hubbard also made many spectacular technical advances, including the discovery and resolution of one of the most major barriers to man's attainment of full spiritual freedom: OT Section III, the Wall of Fire.

The Operating Thetan Symbol

The symbol used for OT activities is an oval O with a horizontal bar and a vertical bar down from its center to the bottom of the O. A person attaining Section V OT may have a wreath completely around the outside of the O. The OT symbol is worn on necklaces and rings.

Information for Releases
Taken from the works of L. Ron Hubbard

Published by the Hubbard College of Scientology, Saint Hill Manor, East Grinstead, Sussex, England, 1967.

Article

THE AUDITOR 25 Dianetics: Its Relationship to Scientology

Issues

HCOB 2 Jan I Sub-Zero Releases, Examiner's Safeguard
HCOB 2 Jan II Dating—Forbidden Words
HCO PL 17 Jan An Open Letter to All Clears
HCOB 19 Jan Manifestations of Engrams and Secondaries Further Defined
HCO PL 27 Jan Clearing and OT Course Reorganization
HCO PL 12 Feb The Responsibilities of Leaders *AKH Series 13*
HCO PL 22 Feb I Office of LRH
HCO PL 22 Feb II LRH Property, Building and Plans Branch
HCO PL 22 Mar I Personnel Requirement
HCOB 22 Mar II Alter-Is and Degraded Beings *AKH Series 14*
HCO PL 11 Apr Section III OT Prerequisite

Article

ABILITY 15 Jun Man from Mud

Issues

HCO PL 25 Jun Scientology Orgs Tax and Balance Sheets
HCOB 30 Jun Evidences of an Aberrated Area
HCO PL 24 Jul Fixed Public Consumption of Product

Article

THE AUDITOR 27 The Goal of Training

Issues

HCO PL 11 Aug I Second Dynamic Rules
HCO PL 11 Aug II Organization, Definition Of
HCO PL 11 Aug III OT Central Committee
HCO PL 15 Aug I Discipline, SPs and Admin, How Statistics Crash
HCO PL 15 Aug II Important Executive Action
HCOB 19 Aug The Supreme Test
LRH ED 1 Sep WW Emergency Condition
HCO PL 6 Sep II WW Division Reorganization
HCO PL 8 Sep I Statistics and Org Board Copies
HCO PL 8 Sep II Continental Liaison Officers at WW
HCO PL 10 Sep Statistic, GDS Div 6
HCO PL 12 Sep Post, Handling Of
HCOB 13 Sep Remedy B *Word Clearing Series 27*
HCO PL 15 Sep I Release and Clear Checkouts
HCO PL 15 Sep II Examiner Bonuses
HCO PL 15 Sep III The Supervisor's Code
LRH ED 15 Sep ARC Break Registrar
HCO PL 18 Sep Complexity and Confronting
HCOB 18 Sep Scales

Ron's Journal 67

In this recorded message, L. Ron Hubbard briefed Scientologists on a technical breakthrough of incredible magnitude: He had successfully mapped the route through the Wall of Fire—OT III—and made it possible for others to follow. *(Available on cassette.)*

20 Sep Ron's Journal 67

Affinity

A twenty-minute film based on the works of L. Ron Hubbard, produced at Saint Hill Manor, East Grinstead, Sussex, England in the autumn of 1967.

Issues

LRH ED 20 Sep "Failure to Apply . . ."
HCO PL 21 Sep I WW Income Outgo
HCO PL 21 Sep II Worldwide and Saint Hill Functions Redefined
HCO PL 21 Sep III International Officers at WW, Alert Council
HCO PL 23 Sep New Post Formula, The Conditions Formulas
HCOB 24 Sep "The Following Report . . ."
HCO PL 25 Sep Grades above Clear
HCO PL 1 Oct Uses of Orgs *AKH Series 15*
LRH ED 3 Oct Special Program, Fast Academies
HCO PL 4 Oct I Auditor and Org Individual Stats
HCO PL 6 Oct I HCO Exec Sec Condition
HCO PL 6 Oct R II Conditions of Liability and Doubt
Rev. 25 Sep 77
HCOB 8 Oct Clear Checks and Re-Clear Checks
HCOB 9 Oct RA Contact Assist
Rev. 13 Aug 87
HCOB 11 Oct Clay Table Training
HCO PL 12 Oct I Operational, Definition Of
HCO PL 12 Oct II Sea Org Resignations
HCO PL 12 Oct III Charges
HCO PL 15 Oct *Auditor* Magazine Success

Article

ABILITY 197 Politics

Issues

HCO PL 16 Oct Suppressives and the Administrator, How to Detect SPs as an Administrator *AKH Series 16*
HCO PL 18 Oct II WW—How to Comm to WW, Continental Liaison Officers
HCO PL 18 Oct III Policy and HCOB Alterations, High Crime
HCO PL 18 Oct V Conditions on Orgs or Divisions or Depts, Clarification

HCO PL 18 Oct VI Failure to Follow or Apply Condition

HCO PL 18 Oct VII Academy Checksheets, Supervisor Conditions

HCO PL 19 Oct I HCO Exec Sec Duties, Org Exec Sec Duties

HCO PL 19 Oct II WW Seven Divisions

HCO PL 20 Oct I Conditions, How to Assign *AKH Series 17*

HCO PL 20 Oct R II Conditions
Rev. 4 Mar 75 Penalties, New Employees and Persons Newly on Post

HCO PL 23 Oct Enemy Formula

HCO PL 26 Oct The Public Divisions

LRH ED 26 Oct Nine-Division Org

HCOB 5 Nov Critics of Scientology

HCOB 9 Nov Revision of Remedy A, Remedy B, and S and Ds *Word Clearing Series 28*

LRH ED 9 Nov Academy Checksheets

HCO PL 20 Nov Out-Tech

HCO PL 22 Nov RA Out-Tech
Rev. 12 Apr 83 *KSW Series 25*

HCO PL 23 Nov I Financial Lines and Legal Lines

HCO PL 23 Nov II Public Attacks, Legal Point

HCOB 28 Nov "The Key S&D Question . . ."

LRH ED 20 Dec Taxation

HCO PL 22 Dec Affluence Attainment

HCOB 27 Dec List Handling

HCO PL 28 Dec Qual Senior Datum

1968

Closely following the release of OT III, the next three OT levels—OT IV, V and VI—were released in January of 1968.

While carrying out his research on the upper levels of the Bridge, Mr. Hubbard was living aboard the flagship *Apollo,* where he was training Sea Org members in their duties as seamen and as highly effective organizational staff and executives.

He was also making major strides in nearly every other area of Scientology technology, including breakthroughs in handling the effects of drugs, study and effective education, repair of cases slowed or stalled in auditing, precise metering and fully standardized Grades auditing and case supervision.

In the fall of 1968, Mr. Hubbard called a select group of auditors from around the world to the flagship for a course that would make them true specialists of Standard Tech—the Class VIII Course.

A Test of Whole Track Recall
by L. Ron Hubbard

Limited first edition published by the Publications Organization, Worldwide, Saint Hill Manor, East Grinstead, Sussex, England, 1968. Later republished in Mission into Time, *1972.*

OT IV, V and VI Materials

The materials for all three levels were released simultaneously in January 1968. Scientologists came to the Advanced Organization aboard the *Apollo* from around the world to receive these OT levels.

Issues

HCO PL 3 Jan Speed of Service

HCO PL 5 Jan I Overfilled In-Basket, Bad News

HCO PL 5 Jan II Conditions Orders, Executive Ethics

HCOB 9 Jan Money Process

HCOB 13 Jan S&Ds

HCOB 16 Jan Starting of Preclears

HCOB 19 Jan S&Ds, S&Ds by Button

HCO PL 23 Jan Orders and Responsibility

HCO PL 28 Jan OT WW Liaison Unit, OT Central Committee

HCO PL 6 Feb Organization—The Flaw

HCO PL 7 Feb Fast Flow and Ethics

HCO PL 8 Feb I Statistic Rationalization *AKH Series 18*

HCO PL 8 Feb II Sea Org Zones of Planning

HCO PL 22 Feb Ethics and Admin, Slow Admin

Article

THE AUDITOR 34 Training and Life

Issues

HCO PL 2 Mar I Advanced Course Security Check

HCO PL 8 Mar Checksheets

HCO PL 11 Mar False Attestation

HCOB 12 Mar Mistakes, Anatomy Of

HCO PL 13 Mar Statistics

LRH ED 13 Mar New Qual Stat, GDS Qual Div

HCO PL 14 Mar Corrected Table of Conditions

HCO PL 16 Mar Post Changes

HCO PL 17 Mar "Boom Formula" Cancelled

Article

ABILITY 207 The Bridge from Chaos to Total Freedom

Issues

HCO PL 15 Apr "To Ensure Speed and Accuracy . . ."

HCOB 18 Apr Needle Reactions above Grade IV

LRH ED 28 Apr "When the Success Story Stat . . ."

HCO PL 28 Apr I Standard Executive Actions

Article

THE AUDITOR 36 What It Means to Be a Scientologist

Issues

HCO PL 4 May Handling Situations

HCOB 4 May Dianetic Courses, Stuck Pictures

HCO PL 7 May The Key Questions, Director of Success Duty

HCOB 7 May R Upper Indoc TRs
Rev. 2 Apr 90

HCO PL 9 May Sea Organization Personnel

HCO PL 10 May RA LRH Comms
Rev. 7 May 84 Functions *LRH Comm N/W Series 7*

HCOB 20 May Overt–Motivator Sequence

HCO PL 21 May Comm Procedure over Long Distances

HCO PL 22 May I Hiring Personnel, Line For

HCO PL 22 May III Translations

HCO PL 22 May IV OT Section Awards

HCO PL 23 May I WW and SH Recombined

HCOB 24 May Coaching

HCO PL 24 May Immigration Tip

HCO PL 26 May Boards of Investigation and Committees of Evidence, Termination Of

LRH ED 27 May Minimum Book Stocks

HCO PL 28 May I Books

HCO PL 30 May I Administration *AKH Series 20*

HCO PL 30 May II Communication

HCO PL 31 May I Scientology Technology *KSW Series 29*

HCO PL 31 May II Auditors

HCO PL 31 May III LRH Comm Log

Article

CERTAINTY Jun Scientology and the
VOL. 15, NO. 6 Group

Issues

HCO PL 5 Jun R III FSM Commissions
Rev. 8 Nov 84 *FSM Series 4*

HCO PL 5 Jun R II Weekly Book Stock
Rev. 28 Jan 80 Report Required

HCO PL 17 Jun HCO Book Account

HCO PL 18 Jun Ethics

HCO PL 20 Jun I Ethics Officers

The Sea Organization Symbol

The Sea Organization, founded 12 August 1967, is a fraternal organization existing within the formalized structure of the churches of Scientology.

The Sea Organization symbol is worn as cloth badges and rings. It is also worn on belt buckles, ties and other items of clothing and accessories.

The laurel wreath represents victory and has been used throughout history to crown poets, artists and champions. It not only represents the physical victory, but the series of inner victories achieved by the individual. It is associated with the head—traditional abode of the spirit.

The star is the symbol of the spirit. The five-pointed star signifies "rising up toward the point of origin."

The laurel wreath and star in combination signify the victory of the spirit. Its proper color is always gold. The star is not trapped in its victory, but is in the open field toward the top of the wreath, allowing free exit beyond its victory. The symbol is in a field of blue, symbolizing truth.

THE CLASS VIII BADGE

The Class VIII Badge is a shield with two horizontal stripes across the top with the word "auditor" and the Roman numeral VIII. The bottom of the shield contains the Scientology symbol and beneath that the banner with the words "Standard Tech."

The Class VIII Badge is all red with gold lettering and numbering. It is given to permanent Class VIII Auditors only.

THE DISTRIBUTION DIVISION 6 BADGE

The purpose of Division 6, the Distribution Divisions of the Church of Scientology, is to make Scientology grow. Its symbol and the symbol worn by its personnel is the affinity-reality-communication (ARC) triangle interwoven with the symbol for infinity.

HCO PL 20 Jun II Personnel
HCO PL 29 Jun Enrollment in Suppressive Groups

INTRODUCTION TO SCIENTOLOGY ETHICS
by L. Ron Hubbard

Published by the Publications Organization, Worldwide, Saint Hill Manor, East Grinstead, Sussex, England, July 1968. Revised and updated in 1989. TRANSLATIONS: Danish, Dutch, French, German, Italian, Spanish and Swedish.

ARTICLE

THE AUDITOR EXTRA — You as an Auditor

ISSUES

HCO PL 1 Jul Warning Signs
HCO PL 2 Jul I Org, Suppression Of
HCO PL 2 Jul II Office of LRH WW Reorganization
HCO PL 27 Jul A Tiger
HCO PL 30 Jul Gross Income Senior Datum

THE PHOENIX LECTURES
From lectures
by L. Ron Hubbard

Published by the Publications Organization, Worldwide, Saint Hill Manor, East Grinstead, Sussex, England, August 1968. (The lectures covered in this book are available on cassette.) TRANSLATIONS: Dutch, French, German and Swedish.

ISSUES

HCOB 1 Aug The Laws of Listing and Nulling
LRH ED 1 Aug Broad Public Questionnaire

ARTICLE

THE AUDITOR 39 The Cycle of Action

ISSUES

HCOB 5 Aug Change of Commands Overt-Motivator Sequence
HCOB 6 Aug R3H
HCO PL 10 Aug Legal and Dissemination
HCO PL 12 Aug I People Who Don't Do Their Jobs
HCO PL 12 Aug II Reasons Why Div 6s Don't Function
HCOB 14 Aug R Rev. 22 Jun 88 Remedy B Environment and "New Style" *Word Clearing Series 29*
HCOB 23 Aug I Arbitraries
HCOB 23 Aug II Workability of Tech
HCO PL 24 Aug Dissemination
HCOB 26 Aug I Rehab and Correction
HCOB 26 Aug II The Class VIII Course
HCOB 28 Aug I Out-Tech
HCOB 28 Aug II Drugs
HCOB 29 Aug Drug Data
HCOB 31 Aug Written C/S Instructions
HCOB 1 Sep Points on Case Supervision
HCO PL 2 Sep Chaplain
HCOB 4 Sep I "Don't Force a Pc Who Is Ill..."
HCOB 4 Sep II "When You Run a Valence Shifter..."
HCO PL 5 Sep Vital Org Activities
HCOB 6 Sep Checking for False Reads
HCO PL 7 Sep Review Complete, Pc Attestations
HCOB 10 Sep II Valence Shifter
HCOB 10 Sep III Standard Tech Data
HCOB 10 Sep IV Case Supervisor, Admin in Auditing
HCOB 10 Sep V Flunks
HCOB 11 Sep I False Reads
HCOB 11 Sep II Case Supervisor Data
HCOB 11 Sep III C/S Instructions
HCO PL 15 Sep Sea Org
HCOB 15 Sep I "The First Thing I Learned..."
HCOB 15 Sep R II Rev. 12 Jan 89 Tiredness
HCO PL 16 Sep Address Lists
HCOB 16 Sep I End Phenomena
HCOB 16 Sep II AOs—OT Sections
HCOB 17 Sep R I Rev. 31 Jan 75 Six Zones of Action
HCOB 17 Sep II Ethnics
HCOB 17 Sep III Gross Case Supervision Errors
HCOB 17 Sep IV Overrun Process
HCOB 19 Sep "Old Lists Are NOT TO BE COPIED..."
HCOB 20 Sep I Review, Ordering People To
HCOB 20 Sep II Glee *Word Clearing Series 12*
HCOB 22 Sep Rehabs
HCOB 23 Sep I Drugs and Trippers
HCOB 23 Sep II Violation of the Laws of Listing and Nulling
HCOB 23 Sep III New Rudiments

CLASS VIII COURSE LECTURES
SEA ORGANIZATION FLAGSHIP *APOLLO*

In September of 1968, a select group of auditors from Scientology organizations around the world were called to the Sea Organization's flagship *Apollo* for what was to be the toughest, most exacting technical course in Scientology history: The Class VIII Course. In a series of nineteen lectures, Mr. Hubbard delineated exactly what standard Scientology technology is, the spectacular results it invariably achieves, and precisely how, as Class VIIIs, course graduates would put it in and keep it in. The lectures are today an integral part of Class VIII Auditor training. *(Reproduced on cassette for the Class VIII Auditor Course.)*

24 Sep Welcome to the Class VIII Course, An Introduction to Standard Tech
25 Sep What Standard Tech Does
26 Sep The Laws of Case Supervision
27 Sep Standard Tech Defined
28 Sep Standard Green Form and Rudiments
29 Sep Mechanics of Techniques and Subject Matter
30 Sep C/S Do's and Don'ts, The Total Rationale and Background of Auditing
1 Oct Certainty of Standard Tech
2 Oct The Laws of Listing and Nulling
3 Oct Assists
7 Oct Assessment, Listing and Basics
8 Oct More on Basics
9 Oct Ethics and Case Supervision
10 Oct Auditor Attitude and the Bank
11 Oct Auditor Additives, Lists and Case Supervising
12 Oct Standard Tech
13 Oct Basics and Simplicities of Standard Tech
14 Oct New Auditor's Code
15 Oct Evaluation of Exam Answers and Data on Standard Tech

HUBBARD DIANETICS AUDITOR'S COURSE TEXTBOOK
Compiled from the works of L. Ron Hubbard

Published by the Publications Organization Worldwide, Edinburgh, Scotland, 1968.

ISSUES

HCOB 25 Sep Continuous PT Overts
HCOB 26 Sep "The Study of the 'Well Done' LRH C/S Folder..."
HCOB 27 Sep II ARC Straightwire
HCOB 28 Sep Dianetics
HCOB 29 Sep RA Rev. 18 Oct 86 List Correction—The Short L4
HCOB 30 Sep Lists

ARTICLE

THE AUDITOR 41 Scientology Technology

ISSUES

HCOB 4 Oct I Ruds
HCOB 4 Oct II "Pre-OTs Who Have Been Audited..."
HCOB 4 Oct III Advance Courses
HCO PL 4 Oct II Ethics Presence
HCOB 5 Oct ARC Break Needle
HCOB 7 Oct I Assessment
HCOB 7 Oct II ARC Break Needle
HCOB 8 Oct I Assessment: LX1
HCOB 8 Oct II Case Supervisor—Folder Handling

ARTICLE

THE AUDITOR 43 This Is the Auditor's Code of 1968

ISSUES

HCO PL 13 Oct RA Pc Examiner
Rev. 18 Oct 86

HCO PL 14 Oct RA The Auditor's Code
Rev. 19 Jun 80

HCOB 14 Oct I Meter Position

HCOB 14 Oct II Definition of Recall

HCOB 16 Oct Supervisor's Duty

HCO PL 16 Oct Treason Formula

HCO INFO LETTER 16 Oct E-Meters Replace Guns

HCOB 18 Oct Processing Sequence

HCO PL 19 Oct Course Completion, Student Indicators

HCOB 20 Oct The Purpose of Class VIII

HCOB 21 Oct R Floating Needle
Rev. 9 Jul 77

HCOB 22 Oct R Teaching the Class VIII
Rev. 31 Jan 75

HCO PL 24 Oct I Supervisor Know-How, Running the Class

HCO PL 24 Oct R II Supervisor Know-How, Handling the Student
Rev. 7 Jan 82

HCO PL 24 Oct III Supervisor Know-How, R-Factor to Students

HCO PL 24 Oct IV Supervisor Know-How, Tips in Handling Students

HCO PL 25 Oct Admin Know-How
AKH Series 21

HCO PL 26 Oct Executive Council

HCO PL 28 Oct I Press Releases

HCO PL 28 Oct II Classified Materials

HCO PL 29 Oct I Class VIII C/S Qual Stat

HCOB 1 Nov I High TA

HCOB 1 Nov II Overt–Motivator Definitions

HCOB 2 Nov R Case Supervisor, Class VIII, The Basic Processes
Rev. 31 Jan 75

HCO PL 5 Nov R Space Allocation
Rev. 8 Feb 89

HCOB 9 Nov Clearing Commands, All Levels

HCO PL 9 Nov Standard Admin

LRH ED 9 Nov Standard Admin

HCO PL 12 Nov R The Main Weakness
Rev. 11 Jan 89

LRH ED 16 Nov A Fable

HCO PL 21 Nov I Senior Policy

HCO PL 21 Nov II Photo Policy for Magazines

HCO PL 24 Nov II The Group Officer

HCO PL 26 Nov The Original *Auditor* Journal Policy

LRH ED 29 Nov The War

HCO PL 30 Nov OT Central Committee

HCO PL 2 Dec Gung-ho Groups

HCO PL 3 Dec Gung-ho Groups Policy Letter #2

HCOB 5 Dec Unresolving Cases

HCO PL 6 Dec Qualifications Check 7A

LRH ED 8 Dec Scarcity of Trained Auditors

HCO PL 9 Dec Qual Has No Backlog

HCOB 10 Dec Correction

LRH ED 11 Dec Services, Illegal Offering

LRH ED 13 Dec The Great "Charity" Swindle

HCOB 15 Dec RB L4BRB, For Assessment of All Listing Errors
Rev. 28 Apr 89

HCO PL 16 Dec Security Div 1

HCO PL 23 Dec Good Service

HCOB 26 Dec I The Third Party Law

HCO PL 26 Dec II Gung-ho Group Tech

HCO PL 30 Dec The Public Programs Officer

1969

While continuing to work closely with Sea Org officers and crew to expand Scientology across the world, Mr. Hubbard's work in the technical line remained at its usual rapid pace.

Major advances were made in the area of Dianetics auditing and case supervision, restoring this vital technology to full use and streamlining its application.

Drug use was also an area that received LRH's attention in 1969, with new procedures developed to solve the underlying *causes* of drug use and relieve its harmful effects.

ARTICLES

THE AUDITOR 44 Start a Scientology Group in Your Area

THE AUDITOR 44 The Value of Scientology

ISSUES

HCOB 5 Jan R Unresolving Cases, Additional Note
Rev. 13 Jan 89

HCOB 8 Jan Drugs and "Insanity" Noncompliance and Alter-Is

HCO PL 12 Jan High Ethics for High Conditions

HCO PL 13 Jan Unusual Favors

HCO PL 14 Jan I OT Orgs
Target Series 1

HCO PL 14 Jan II Spectatorism

HCO PL 16 Jan Targets, Types Of
Target Series 2

HCO PL 18 Jan II Planning and Targets
Target Series 3

LRH ED 20 Jan A Vital Target, Trained Auditor Program

HCO PL 24 Jan I Target Types
Target Series 4

HCO PL 24 Jan II Purpose and Targets
Target Series 5

HCO PL 25 Jan Targets and Computers
Computer Series 2
Target Series 6

HCO PL 26 Jan Compliance Reports

HCO PL 27 Jan Dev-t Summary List

HCO PL 30 Jan I Public Divisions Org Board

HCO PL 30 Jan R II Dev-t Summary List Additions
Rev. 21 Oct 80

HCO PL 31 Jan Humanitarian Objective and Gung-ho Groups

HCOB 3 Feb Triple Grades, Flows

HCO PL 3 Feb Public Image

HCO PL 5 Feb R I Code of a Scientologist
Rev. 15 May 73

HCO PL 5 Feb II PRO Actions
PR Series 35

HCO PL 5 Feb III Double Hats

HCOB 9 Feb Research Notes

LRH ED 9 Feb Organizational Intention

HCO PL 12 Feb Religion

HCO PL 13 Feb Ethics Protection, Conditions, Blue Star, Green Star, Gold Star

HCO PL 24 Feb Justice

ARTICLES

FREEDOM 27 Feb A Reason Psychiatric Front Groups Attack Scientology

FREEDOM 27 Feb Druidism and Psychiatry

ISSUE

HCOB 28 Feb Medical Doctors

ARTICLES

FREEDOM 1 Mar Fast Justice

FREEDOM 1 Mar Patriotism

FREEDOM 1 Mar Economics—War and Tax

FREEDOM 1 Mar Today's Terrorism

FREEDOM 3 Mar On Writing to Governments

ISSUES

HCOB 3 Mar Case Gain, Completing Levels
KSW Series 32

HCO PL 7 Mar Organization

ARTICLES

FREEDOM 11 Mar Brainwashing

FREEDOM 11 Mar British "Justice" and Evidence

ISSUES

HCOB 12 Mar II Physically Ill Pcs and Pre-OTs

HCO PL 15 Mar I Third Party, How to Find One

HCOB 17 Mar I Politics

HCOB 17 Mar R II Summary Report Form
Rev. 12 Nov 87
Auditor Admin Series 12RA

ARTICLES

FREEDOM 19 Mar Riots

FREEDOM Mar A Paper on the Difficulties of Researching in the Humanities, A Summary on Scientology for Scientists

ISSUES

HCOB 2 Apr RA Dianetic Assists
Rev. 28 Jul 78

HCO INFO LETTER 4 Apr Ron's Journal 1969 No. 3, Political Treatment

HCOB 5 Apr New Preclears, The Workability of Scientology

HCOB 6 Apr I Fundamental Auditing

HCOB 6 Apr II Dianetics Course Auditing Requirements

HCO PL 6 Apr Dianetics

HCO PL 7 Apr Org Reduction or Eradication

HCOB 17 Apr R I Dianetic Case Supervision
Rev. 25 Jul 78

HCOB 17 Apr II Dianetic Case Failures

HCO PL 20 Apr II Hats, Not Wearing

HCOB 22 Apr I Dianetics Versus Scientology

HCOB 22 Apr II Somatics and OTs

HCOB 23 Apr RA I Dianetics, Basic Definitions
Rev. 20 Sep 78

HCOB 23 Apr III Past Lives

HCOB 24 Apr RA I Dianetic Use
Rev. 20 Sep 78

HCOB 24 Apr R II Dianetic Results
Rev. 20 Jul 78

HCOB 26 Apr R Somatics
Rev. 11 Jul 78

HCOB 27 Apr II Dianetic Failures

HCO PL 27 Apr Death Wish

HCOB 28 Apr R High TA in Dianetics
Rev. 20 Sep 78

HCOB 29 Apr Assessment and Interest

HCOB 30 Apr Auditor Trust

ARTICLES

FREEDOM 1 May Justice

THE AUDITOR 49 The Value of Training

FREEDOM May Drug Addiction

ISSUES

HCOB 1 May Grinding Out Engrams

HCOB 7 May IV The Five GAEs

HCOB 7 May R V Floating Needle
Rev. 15 Jul 77

HCOB 7 May VI Summary of How to Write an Auditor's Report, Worksheets and Summary Report, with Some Additional Information

HCOB 8 May I Important Study Data

HCOB 8 May R II Teaching the Dianetics Course
Rev. 31 Mar 77

HCOB 9 May RA Case Supervising New
Rev. 21 Sep 78 Era Dianetics Folders
HCOB 11 May R I Meter Trim Check
Rev. 8 Jul 78
HCOB 11 May R II Forcing a Pc
Rev. 12 Oct 69

ARTICLE

FREEDOM 12 May Government and Revolt

ISSUES

HCOB 13 May Peculiarities
HCOB 14 May I Sickness
HCOB 14 May III Cultural Lag
HCOB 15 May Dirty Needle
HCO PL 16 May Course Administration
HCOB 17 May TRs and Dirty Needles
HCOB 18 May R Erasure
Rev. 3 Aug 78
HCOB 19 May RB Drug and Alcohol
Rev. 14 Nov 78 Cases, Prior Assessing
HCOB 20 May Keeping Dianetics Working in an Area
HCOB 21 May Assessment
HCOB 22 May Dianetics, Its Background
HCO PL 22 May Orders Versus Arbitraries
HCO PL 23 May Dianetic Contract
HCOB 23 May R Auditing Out Sessions,
Rev. 11 Jul 78 Narrative Versus Somatic Chains
HCOB 24 May I The Difficult Case
HCOB 24 May II Dianetic High Crimes
HCOB 27 May The VIII's Nightmare
HCOB 28 May RA I How Not to Erase
Rev. 21 Sep 78
HCOB 28 May II Dianetics and Results, Dianetic Counseling Groups
HCO PL 29 May Dianetic Certificates
HCOB 6 Jun Prediction and Consequences
HCOB 7 Jun R How to Make a Person
Rev. 13 Aug 87 Sober
HCOB 11 Jun Materials, Scarcity Of
HCO PL 12 Jun Dianetic Registration

ARTICLES

FREEDOM 15 Jun The Bland Personality
FREEDOM 15 Jun Control "Sciences"
FREEDOM 16 Jun How to Win an Argument
THE AUDITOR 48 Dianetics
FREEDOM 16 Jun Quackery and Fakery

ISSUE

HCO PL 17 Jun The Org Image
PR Series 36

ARTICLE

FREEDOM 23 Jun Crime & Psychiatry

ISSUES

HCOB 28 Jun RA C/S, How to Case
Rev. 21 Sep 78 Supervise Dianetics Folders

HCOB 16 Jul "I Have Made a Breakthrough . . ."
HCOB 17 Jul RB I New Era Dianetics
Rev. 4 Sep 78 Command Training Drills
HCOB 17 Jul II Flagrant Auditing Errors

ARTICLE

THE AUDITOR 50 Why Feel Guilty?

ISSUES

HCOB 19 Jul RA I Dianetics and Illness
Rev. 21 Sep 78
HCOB 21 Jul II One-Hand Electrodes
HCOB 22 Jul R I Auditing Speed
Rev. 20 Sep 78
HCOB 22 Jul II High TA Assessment
HCOB 23 Jul Auditor Assignment Policies
HCOB 24 Jul R Seriously Ill Pcs
Rev. 24 Jul 78
HCOB 27 Jul Antibiotics
HCOB 29 Jul The "Art" of Case Supervision
HCO PL 29 Jul II Course Administration, Roll Book
HCO PL 29 Jul III Completion of Cycles
HCOB 2 Aug R "LX" Lists
Rev. 4 Sep 78
HCOB 3 Aug R LX2, Emotional
Rev. 22 Aug 78 Assessment List
HCOB 9 Aug R I LX1 (Conditions)
Rev. 21 Aug 78
HCOB 9 Aug RA II Case Folder
Rev. 21 Sep 78 Analysis, New Era Dianetics
HCOB 15 Aug Flying Ruds
HCOB 16 Aug R Handling Illness in
Rev. 25 Sep 78 Scientology

ARTICLE

THE AUDITOR 23 Aug The New Dianetics

ISSUE

HCO PL 1 Sep R Counterespionage
Rev. 24 Sep 83

ARTICLE

THE AUDITOR 2 Sep Standard Dianetic Gains

ISSUES

HCO PL 2 Sep I Old ACC Students
HCO PL 2 Sep II Triple Grades
HCO PL 2 Sep IV Failed VIIIs
HCO PL 3 Sep I Former HDAs, HPAs
HCO PL 3 Sep II Successful Class VIIIs
HCO PL 8 Sep The Org Exec Course Introduction
HCO PL 9 Sep R How to Study This
Rev. 17 Jun 85 Course
LRH ED 11 Sep Org Affluences
HCO PL 14 Sep The Key Ingredients
AKH Series 22
HCOB 19 Sep Study Slowness

HCO PL 20 Sep Stability
HCO PL 21 Sep Staff Training Officer

ARTICLES

FREEDOM 24 Sep The Fight for Freedom
FREEDOM 24 Sep "Cult"
FREEDOM 25 Sep Drug Problems
FREEDOM 25 Sep Tangled Terms
FREEDOM 26 Sep Being Good
FREEDOM 26 Sep The Road Out
FREEDOM 29 Sep Student Victims

ISSUES

HCO PL 4 Oct Organizational Enturbulence
HCO PL 5 Oct R I Dianetic Courses,
Rev. 10 Dec 69 Wildcat
HCO PL 5 Oct II The Rehabilitation of Artists
HCOB 5 Oct I Triple Flows

ARTICLE

THE AUDITOR 11 Scientology, The Senior Science

ISSUES

HCO PL 7 Oct Fundamentals of Administration No. 2
HCO PL 9 Oct Publications Depts and Orgs, How to Straighten Out
HCO PL 10 Oct R Downstat Causes
Rev. 13 Feb 91
HCOB 12 Oct Dianetic Triples Plural Item
HCO PL 16 Oct Finance Course, Vital Action
HCOB 17 Oct RB Drugs, Aspirin and
Rev. 8 Apr 88 Tranquilizers
HCO PL 27 Oct I Dev-t
AKH Series 23

ARTICLE

FREEDOM 30 Oct Cultural Destruction

ISSUES

HCO PL 4 Nov Dev-t Graphed
HCOB 5 Nov R V LX3 (Attitudes)
Rev. 4 Sep 78
HCO PL 8 Nov Tech Services

ARTICLE

FREEDOM 9 Nov Too Many Enemies

ISSUES

HCO PL 10 Nov I FSM Awards
HCO PL 11 Nov I Accounts and PRO
PR Series 37
HCO PL 11 Nov II Promotion and Motivation
HCO PL 11 Nov III Mission Promotion Musts
HCO PL 12 Nov Appearance and PRO
PR Series 38
HCO PL 13 Nov I Internships and Case Supervisors
HCOB 14 Nov Medical Charts

HCOB 15 Nov R I Case Supervision,
Rev. 27 Jul 78 Auditing and Results
HCOB 15 Nov II Case Supervision, How It Goes Nonstandard

ARTICLES

FREEDOM 15 Nov Old-Fashioned Holdovers
FREEDOM 15 Nov A Champion

ISSUES

HCO PL 18 Nov I Central Files, Value Of, The Gross Income of the Org and Why
HCO PL 18 Nov II Dianetics, Right to Audit
HCO PL 18 Nov III Dianetics, Right to Teach
HCO PL 23 Nov I Individuals vs. Groups
PR Series 39
HCO PL 23 Nov II Allowed Technical Services
LRH ED 23 Nov Reform Mailing Result
LRH ED 23 Nov Ethics Program No. 1
HCOB 23 Nov RB III Student Rescue
Rev. 4 Sep 78 Intensive

ARTICLES

FREEDOM 25 Nov The Evolution of Totalitarianism
FREEDOM 25 Nov False Reports

ISSUES

LRH ED 25 Nov Registration
LRH ED 29 Nov Org Services
HCOB 2 Dec Rising TA
HCO PL 2 Dec R Freeloaders
Rev. 17 Jan 91
HCO PL 3 Dec II Issue Authority for Translations of Dianetics and Scientology Materials
HCO PL 7 Dec I Ethics, the Design Of
HCO PL 7 Dec II The Ethics Officer, His Character
HCO PL 7 Dec III More on Staff Member Reports
LRH ED 9 Dec RA Organization
Rev. 8 Jan 91 Program No. 1
HCO PL 9 Dec I How to Prevent an Ethics Officer from Doing His Job
HCO PL 9 Dec R II Purchasing from
Rev. 27 Mar 78 Pubs Org
HCO PL 10 Dec Superior Service Image
HCO PL 11 Dec R I Appearances in
Rev. 16 Sep 88 Public Divs
PR Series 40
HCO PL 11 Dec RB II Training of Clears
Rev. 25 Mar 89
HCO PL 13 Dec Post Transfers
LRH ED 14 Dec Magazines
HCO PL 15 Dec II Orders, Query Of
LRH ED 16 Dec Instant Service Project
LRH ED 16 Dec Org Image Program No. 1 US
LRH ED 20 Dec How to Raise Stats

A Summary on Scientology for Scientists
An article by
L. Ron Hubbard

Published by the Church of Scientology of California (Worldwide) Saint Hill Manor, East Grinstead, England, 1969.

How to Save Your Marriage
Taken from the works
of L. Ron Hubbard

Published by Scientology Publications Organization, Copenhagen, Denmark, 1969.

The Best of The Auditor

A collection of articles by L. Ron Hubbard from The Auditor *magazine, published by the American Saint Hill Organization, Los Angeles, California, 1969.*

Dianetics Case Histories Book

Staff compiled, published by the Sea Organization, Division 5 Flag, late 1969.

Reality

A film based on the works of L. Ron Hubbard produced in Copenhagen, Denmark in 1969.

1970

Working aboard the Sea Organization flagship *Apollo,* Mr. Hubbard continued to research intensively in the administrative and technical fields.

Having developed a successful and standard system of organization form and function, he turned to streamlining the technology of *management.* He released the highly workable principles and systems he evolved in series of policy letters covering the handling of data, personnel, organization and public relations—the first Management Series policy letters.

On the technical front, Mr. Hubbard resolved the mystery of the difficulties sometimes encountered by preclears after exteriorizing and released the technology to handle them—the new Interiorization Rundown. He also began writing series of technical bulletins covering the technologies of case supervision and Word Clearing. And in September 1970, OT VII was released.

Freedom

Based on the works of L. Ron Hubbard, this 20-minute film was produced in Los Angeles, California in 1970. The film includes a demonstration of Dianetics auditing.

Issues

HCOB 3 Jan — Triple Errors in Dianetics
LRH ED 14 Jan — Solvency
HCOB 15 Jan I — The Uses of Auditing
HCOB 15 Jan II — Handling with Auditing *KSW Series 17*
LRH ED 17 Jan — The Uses of Auditing, Handling with Auditing, Registrar Advice Form
HCO PL 18 Jan — "The Following Is a Letter..."
HCOB 19 Jan — Registrar's Advice Form
HCO PL 24 Jan — Tech/Admin Ratio
HCOB 29 Jan — Null Lists in Dianetics
HCOB 31 Jan — Withholds, Other People's

Articles

FREEDOM — Failures
THE AUDITOR 51 — What Your Donations Buy
THE AUDITOR 51 — Dianetics versus Scientology

Issues

HCO PL 4 Feb RA, Rev. 28 Jan 91 — Pc Application Form for Any Major Auditing Action
HCOB 4 Feb — Pc Application for Major Actions
HCO PL 5 Feb — Statistics, Management By
HCO PL 7 Feb II — HCO Makes the Org
HCO PL 9 Feb — Statistical Judgment
HCO PL 10 Feb RA I, Rev. 7 Jan 91 — Mission, Multiple Ownership
HCO PL 12 Feb RB I, Rev. 7 May 84 — LRH Comm and HCO ES Responsibility for Lines *LRH Comm N/W Series 8*
HCO PL 12 Feb II — EC WW, Primary Duties Of
HCOB 13 Feb — High TA, *Full* Handling Of
LRH ED 17 Feb — Stat Recovery, An Analysis of Broad Outnesses
HCOB 20 Feb — Floating Needles and End Phenomena

Article

FREEDOM 20 Feb — Professional Warfare

Issues

HCO PL 22 Feb — Celebrity Centre
HCO PL 23 Feb — Quality of Service
HCOB 26 Feb — Standard Tech and Invalidation

Article

FREEDOM 26 Feb — A Cause of Violence

Issues

HCO PL 28 Feb — Field Auditors
LRH ED 1 Mar — Recruit!
HCO PL 3 Mar — How to Write an ED or Order
HCO PL 12 Mar R, Rev. 20 Jan 89 — Source to Cause
HCOB 15 Mar — Double Folder Danger

Article

FREEDOM 18 Mar — Civil Rights

Issues

HCOB 20 Mar — Ally, Definition Of
HCO PL 24 Mar — A Matter of Orders
HCOB 27 Mar II — Green Form
HCO PL 28 Mar — R6EW and Clear
HCOB 29 Mar — Auditing and Ethics
HCOB 31 Mar — Dianetic TR Notes

Article

FREEDOM — The Enemies of Scientology

Issues

HCOB 1 Apr — Ethics Program No. 1 Case Actions
HCO PL 4 Apr — Power Change Violation Repair Formula
HCO PL 7 Apr RE, Rev. 27 Apr 89 — Green Form
LRH ED 8 Apr — Flag Executive Briefing Course
HCOB 8 Apr — GF 40 Handling—Clarification

American Mark V E-Meter

In 1970 the American Mark V E-Meter became available. This meter, along with the British Mark V and Azimuth Alignment Meter, became the standard meters.

HCO PL 9 Apr Conference Hats
HCO PL 10 Apr Conference Planning Officer
HCOB 11 Apr R Auditing Past Exterior
Rev. 23 Sep 78 *Int RD Series 6*
HCO PL 11 Apr I Third Dynamic Tech
HCO PL 11 Apr II Review Complete?
HCOB 16 Apr Arbitraries
HCO PL 16 Apr I Morale
HCO PL 17 Apr I Department 1
HCO PL 17 Apr II An Auditor and "The Mind's Protection"
HCO PL 18 Apr I Ethics and Missions
LRH ED 19 Apr Mimeo
HCO PL 21 Apr Field Ethics
HCOB 21 Apr Two-way Comm C/Ses
HCOB 22 Apr R Clay Table Demo
Rev. 2 Aug 89 Checkouts
HCO PL 23 Apr SH–UK ANZO–EU Relationships
HCO PL 25 Apr More on Lines and Hats
HCO PL 26 Apr R The Anatomy of
Rev. 15 Mar 75 Thought
Data Series 1R
HCOB 6 May R Blows, Auditing Past
Rev. 24 Sep 78 Exterior
Int RD Series 7
HCO PL 8 May Distraction and Noise
AKH Series 24
HCO PL 10 May Single Declare
KSW Series 14
LRH ED 10 May Lower Grades Upgraded
HCO PL 11 May Logic
Data Series 2
HCO PL 11 May-1 Further Illogics
Data Series 2-1
HCO PL 12 May Breakthroughs
Data Series 3
HCO PL 14 May Hat Checkout Sequence
HCO PL 15 May I Data and Situation Analyzing
Data Series 4
HCO PL 15 May II Information Collection
Data Series 5
HCO PL 16 May Institutional and Shock Cases, Petitions From
HCO PL 17 May R Data Systems
Rev. 16 Sep 78 *Data Series 6R*
HCO PL 18 May Familiarity
Data Series 7
HCO PL 19 May Sanity
Data Series 8
LRH ED 20 May The Ideal Org
LRH ED 21 May Fast Flow Grades Cancelled
HCO PL 23 May Errors
Data Series 9
HCOB 27 May R Unreading Questions
Rev. 3 Dec 78 and Items
HCOB 28 May Correction Lists, Use Of
HCOB 30 May R Interiorization
Rev. 23 Sep 78 Intensive, Two-way Comm
Int RD Series 3

HCO PL 30 May Cutatives
KSW Series 7
LRH ED 2 Jun Auditing Sales and Delivery Program #1
LRH ED 3 Jun What Was Wrong
LRH ED 3 Jun Orders to Divisions for Immediate Compliance
HCOB 5 Jun Triple Grades
LRH ED 6 Jun SH Pcs
HCO PL 8 Jun RC II Student Auditing
Rev. 11 Jan 85
HCOB 8 Jun Low TA Handling
HCO PL 10 Jun Public Divisions and Tech/Admin Ratio
LRH ED 11 Jun Auditing Mystery Solved
HCOB 12 Jun Programing of Cases
C/S Series 2
HCOB 13 Jun I Session Priorities, Repair Programs and Their Priority
C/S Series 3
HCOB 13 Jun II Hubbard Consultant, Study Stress Analysis
HCOB 14 Jun The Return Program
C/S Series 4
HCOB 15 Jun Repair Example
C/S Series 5
HCOB 16 Jun What the C/S Is Doing
C/S Series 6
KSW Series 20
HCOB 17 Jun RA Triple/Quad
Rev. 7 Apr 91 Rudiments and Overts
HCO PL 17 Jun RB I Technical Degrades
Rev. 25 Oct 83 *KSW Series 5R*
HCO PL 17 Jun II OIC Change, Cable Change
HCOB 19 Jun I C/S Q and A
C/S Series 7
HCOB 19 Jun II Chart of Human Evaluation
C/S Series 8
HCOB 21 Jun Superficial Actions
C/S Series 9
KSW Series 10

LRH Address
LOS ANGELES, CALIFORNIA

The Grand National Convention of Dianetics and Total Freedom was held in Los Angeles in July 1970. Shortly before the convention, Mr. Hubbard recorded a message to be played to the delegates. He discussed the early days of Dianetics and the tremendous improvements in auditing technology made through the years, including the development of Expanded Grades and standardized training.

21 Jun Expanded Grades and Training

Issues

HCO PL 23 Jun The Missing Scene
Data Series 10
HCOB 24 Jun Repairing a Repair
C/S Series 10
HCO PL 24 Jun I Management Cycle
HCO PL 24 Jun II Personnel Pools
HCOB 25 Jun I C/S Series 11
HCOB 25 Jun RC II Glossary of C/S
Rev. 16 Aug 89 Terms
C/S Series 12RC
KSW Series 9R
HCOB 30 Jun RA VIII Actions
Rev. 9 Apr 77 *C/S Series 13RA*
HCO PL 30 Jun The Situation
Data Series 11
HCOB 3 Jul C/Sing 2-way Comm
C/S Series 14
HCO PL 5 Jul How to Find and Establish an Ideal Scene
Data Series 12
HCO PL 6 Jul Irrationality
Data Series 13
HCO PL 7 Jul Working and Managing
Data Series 14
HCOB 14 Jul Solo Cans
HCO PL 14 Jul I Registrar Statistic
HCO PL 14 Jul II Hats, Basic and False
HCOB 15 Jul R Unresolved Pains
Rev. 17 Jul 78
HCOB 16 Jul The Psychiatrist at Work
HCO PL 20 Jul Cases and Morale of Staff
HCO PL 8 Aug Wrong Target
Data Series 15
HCO PL 13 Aug I Liabilities of PR
PR Series 1
HCO PL 13 Aug II The Missing Ingredient
PR Series 2
HCO PL 13 Aug III Wrong Publics
PR Series 3
HCOB 16 Aug R Getting the F/N to
Rev. 7 Jul 78 Examiner
C/S Series 15R
HCO PL 16 Aug Statistic Mismanagement
HCOB 20 Aug R Interiorization
Rev. 23 Sep 78 Rundown Musts
Int RD Series 8
HCOB 21 Aug Session Grading
C/S Series 16
HCOB 23 Aug R The Body
Rev. 7 Apr 91 Communication Process
HCOB 26 Aug R Incomplete Cases
Rev. 22 Sep 80 *C/S Series 17R*
KSW Series 15
LRH ED 26 Aug Case and Letter Reg Project #1
LRH ED 27 Aug Auditors Association Project in *Your* Area
LRH ED 27 Aug My Own Objectives
HCOB 28 Aug RB HC Outpoint–
Rev. 27 Jan 81 Pluspoint Lists RB
HCO PL 28 Aug I Control of Statistics
HCO PL 28 Aug R II Auditors
Rev. 16 Jan 75 Association
HCO PL 29 Aug I Personnel Transfers Can Destroy an Org
Personnel Series 1
HCO PL 29 Aug II Personnel Programing
Personnel Series 2
HCO PL 29 Aug III Recruit in Excess
Personnel Series 3
LRH ED 29 Aug Staff Training Pgm No. 2
HCO PL 30 Aug Recruiting Actions
Personnel Series 4
HCO PL 2 Sep II First Policy
LRH ED 4 Sep Gross Divisional Statistics
HCO PL 8 Sep RA Examiner's 24-Hour
Rev. 24 Oct 75 Rule

OT VII Materials

The written materials for OT VII were released on 9 September 1970.

Issues

HCO PL 10 Sep Transferitis
Personnel Series 5
HCOB 11 Sep R I Chronic Somatic,
Rev. 7 Jul 78 Dianetic Handling Of
C/S Series 18R
HCO PL 12 Sep Training
Personnel Series 6
HCO PL 13 Sep I Hats—Vital Data
Personnel Series 7
HCO PL 13 Sep II Basic Organization
Org Series 1
HCO PL 14 Sep I Cope and Organize
Org Series 2
HCO PL 14 Sep II How to Organize an Org
Org Series 3
HCO PL 15 Sep R Executive
Rev. 25 Apr 79 Responsibility for Training Staff
HCO PL 16 Sep Ethics and Personnel
Personnel Series 8
HCO PL 17 Sep Hats
HCO PL 19 Sep I Investigatory Procedure
Data Series 16
HCO PL 19 Sep II Narrowing the Target
Data Series 17
HCO PL 19 Sep III Summary of Outpoints
Data Series 18
HCOB 21 Sep R Study Definitions
Rev. 19 Mar 91 *Study Series 1R*
HCO PL 21 Sep Cope
HCO PL 22 Sep Hats
Org Series 4
Personnel Series 9
LRH ED 22 Sep Why Orgs Sag
HCO PL 23 Sep Quarters, Policy Regarding, Historical
HCO PL 24 Sep RA Issues—Types Of
Rev. 3 Jul 77
HCO PL 26 Sep III Org Board Cutatives
Org Series 5
HCO PL 27 Sep I Cutative Prices
Org Series 6
HCO PL 30 Sep I Checksheet Format
HCO PL 30 Sep II Credit Collections Defined

HCO PL 1 Oct Hats and Counter-Effort
Org Series 7

HCO PL 3 Oct RA Stat Interpretation
Rev. 27 Aug 82

HCOB 6 Oct Folder Error Summaries
C/S Series 19

HCO PL 6 Oct I Inspection of Low Stats

HCO PL 6 Oct II "Moonlighting"
Personnel Series 10

HCOB 8 Oct Persistent F/N
C/S Series 20
KSW Series 19

HCO PL 8 Oct Organizing and Product
Org Series 8

HCO PL 9 Oct The PR Personality
PR Series 4
Personnel Series 11

HCO PL 10 Oct Utilization

HCOB 13 Oct Course Supervisor Corrections

HCO PL 13 Oct II The Real Why
Data Series 19

HCO PL 14 Oct Division IV Org Board, Ideal Scenes and Stats

HCOB 18 Oct Auditor's Stats on F/N VGI
Auditor Admin Series 17

HCOB 22 Oct II "No Overts" Cases

HCOB 26 Oct III Obnosis and the Tone Scale

HCO PL 28 Oct Organizing and Hats
Org Series 9

HCO PL 29 Oct I The Analysis of Organization by Product
Org Series 10

HCO PL 29 Oct II An Org Board

SCIENTOLOGY 0-8: THE BOOK OF BASICS

by L. Ron Hubbard

Published by the Publications Organization, Copenhagen, Denmark, 1970. TRANSLATIONS: Danish, Dutch, French, German, Italian and Spanish.

ISSUES

HCO PL 1 Nov I Organization and Morale
Org Series 11

HCO PL 1 Nov II Use of I&R Form 1

HCO PL 2 Nov II The Theory of Scientology Organizations
Org Series 12

HCO PL 2 Nov III Responsibility

HCO PL 4 Nov R IV Estimated Purchase Orders
Rev. 7 Feb 91

HCO PL 7 Nov "Noise" and Organization

HCOB 10 Nov C/S Responsibility for Training
C/S Series 21

HCO PL 13 Nov Planning by Product
Org Series 13

HCO PL 14 Nov The Product as an Overt Act
Org Series 14

HCO PL 15 Nov Confessionals

HCO PL 18 Nov II PR Definition
PR Series 5

HCOB 20 Nov Organization Misunderstoods
Word Clearing Series 18
Personnel Series 12
Org Series 15

HCO PL 25 Nov Policy and Orders
Org Series 16

HCO PL 26 Nov More Outpoints
Data Series 20

HCOB 28 Nov Psychosis
C/S Series 22

HCO PL 1 Dec Reality of Products
Org Series 17

HCO PL 6 Dec Third Dynamic De-aberration
Personnel Series 13
Org Series 18

LRH ED 8 Dec Life Repair Block

HCOB 10 Dec RA I Clay Table Work in Training
Rev. 25 Jul 87

HCO PL 14 Dec Group Sanity
Org Series 19
Personnel Series 14

HCO PL 16 Dec R SH FSM Bonus Awards
Rev. 17 Apr 75

HCOB 23 Dec Fast Courses

HCO PL 23 Dec HCO Traffic

HCO PL 27 Dec Hats Program Pitfalls
Personnel Series 16

HCO PL 30 Dec Environmental Control
Org Series 20
Personnel Series 15

THE BACKGROUND AND CEREMONIES OF THE CHURCH OF SCIENTOLOGY WORLDWIDE

Based on the works of L. Ron Hubbard

Published by the Church of Scientology, Worldwide, Saint Hill Manor, East Grinstead, Sussex, England, 1970. TRANSLATIONS: Danish and German.

1971

In 1971 Mr. Hubbard carried on along similar lines to the work he had done in 1970, both technically and administratively.

Lecturing to top Scientology executives on the new Flag Executive Briefing Course—the Class VIII of administrative training—he revealed new management technology to be used in booming organizations across the planet.

Continuing to refine auditing and case supervision technology, LRH added nearly 50 new HCO Bulletins to the Case Supervisor Series and polished the technology of the Interiorization Rundown to make it even more precise and effective.

Great advances were also made in the areas of study and education, with many bulletins issued on the technology of Word Clearing. These HCO Bulletins and the study tech LRH had codified in the 1960s gave Course Supervisors and Word Clearers all the tools they needed to get students flying through their studies and effectively applying what they learned.

ISSUES

HCOB 2 Jan Illegal Auditing

HCO PL 4 Jan Competence

HCOB 4 Jan RA Exteriorization and High TA, The Interiorization Rundown Revised
Rev. 8 Apr 91
Int RD Series 2R

HCOB 13 Jan R Exteriorization
Rev. 24 Sep 78
Int RD Series 9

HCO PL 13 Jan Exam 24-Hour Rule (Additional Information)

FLAG EXECUTIVE BRIEFING COURSE LECTURES

SEA ORGANIZATION FLAGSHIP *APOLLO*

LRH established the Flag Executive Briefing Course in late 1970 to train Scientology executives up to full mastery of the technology of running an organization. These lectures to FEBC students form a vital part of the course, teaching the use of public relations technology, key principles of organizing any activity and the powerful Product–Organizing Officer System. Together with the course's written materials and practical drills, these tapes make a truly competent executive, capable of booming any organization. *(Reproduced on cassette for the Flag Executive Briefing Course.)*

17 Nov 70 Welcome to the FEBC

18 Jan PR Becomes a Subject

18 Jan The Product–Org Officer System, Part I

18 Jan The Product–Org Officer System, Part II

23 Jan How to Post an Org

23 Jan The Org Officer and His Resources, Part I

23 Jan The Org Officer and His Resources, Part II

ISSUES

HCO PL 19 Jan Duplicating Functions
Personnel Series 17
Org Series 21

HCO PL 25 Jan Squirrel Admin
Org Series 22

HCO PL 29 Jan RA Flag Banking Officers
Rev. 2 Feb 91
Finance Series 1RA

HCO PL 5 Feb VI CF and Address Presorting

HCO PL 6 Feb I Transferring Funds

HCOB 7 Feb R Administrative Training Drills, Admin TRs
Rev. 11 Aug 90

LRH ED 9 Feb Auditors Association

HCO PL 9 Feb Executive Misbehavior

HCO PL 10 Feb I Mimeo Files

HCO PL 10 Feb III "An I&R Form 1 . . ."
Personnel Series 18

HCOB 10 Feb Tech Volume and Two-way Comm

HCO PL 11 Feb RA Policy Knowledge Function
Rev. 7 May 84
LRH Comm N/W Series 9

HCO PL 12 Feb Hat Knock Off

HCO PL 13 Feb Financial Planning Tips
Finance Series 2

HCO PL 16 Feb II Lines and Terminals
Org Series 23

HCO PL 17 Feb RC Basic FBO Duties
Rev. 2 Feb 91
Finance Series 3RC

HCO PL 17 Feb -1RB Handling of Bounced Checks and Refunds
Rev. 2 Feb 91
Finance Series 3-1RB

HCO PL 21 Feb RA Supervisor Checkouts
Rev. 25 Jul 87

HCO PL 23 Feb The Magic Formula

HCO PL 24 Feb Operating at Risk

HCO PL 26 Feb I LRH Comm Troubles
LRH Comm N/W Series 10

HCO PL 26 Feb II Drills

HCO PL 27 Feb I Books

HCO PL 27 Feb II First Financial Policy

HCO PL 27 Feb RA III LRH Comm, New Basic Duties
Rev. 7 May 84
LRH Comm N/W Series 11

HCO PL 27 Feb RA IV LRH Comm Correction Form
Rev. 7 May 84
LRH Comm N/W Series 12

HCOB 28 Feb Metering Reading Items
C/S Series 24

HCO PL 1 Mar RB II Income Sources
Rev. 2 Feb 91
Finance Series 4RB

HCO PL 2 Mar Mimeo Section

HCO PL 4 Mar II How to Do Theory Checkouts and Examinations

HCOB 5 Mar The Fantastic New HGC Line
C/S Series 25
Auditor Admin Series 10

HCOB 6 Mar I New Uses for the Green Form
C/S Series 26

HCOB 6 Mar II Long C/Ses
C/S Series 27

HCO PL 6 Mar Line Design, HGC Lines, an Example
Org Series 24

HCOB 7 Mar RB Use of Quadruple Dianetics
Rev. 3 Feb 89
C/S Series 28RB

HCO PL 7 Mar Handling Overloaded Posts

HCOB 8 Mar R Case Actions, Off-Line
Rev. 25 Jul 78 *C/S Series 29R*

HCO PL 8 Mar R II Org Officer
Rev. 22 Apr 82 *Org Series 42*

HCO PL 8 Mar I Examiner's Form
Auditor Admin Series 11

HCO PL 9 Mar II Posting an Org Board—How to Put an HCO There, How to Put an Org There

HCO PL 10 Mar RA I FBO Hat
Rev. 2 Feb 91 *Finance Series 6RA*

HCO PL 10 Mar II Establishment and the HAS
Org Series 43

HCO PL 11 Mar Org Board and Production

HCO PL 12 Mar I Putting an HCO There, How to Establish a Division

HCO PL 12 Mar II Command Intention and Your Post

HCO PL 12 Mar III CO/ED Inspections

HCOB 14 Mar R F/N Everything
Rev. 25 Jul 73

HCO PL 14 Mar On Giving Checkouts

HCO PL 15 Mar RA II Data Series
Rev. 21 Sep 81 Auditing
Data Series 21RA

HCO PL 16 Mar R I What Is a Course?
Rev. 29 Jan 75 *KSW Series 27*

HCO PL 16 Mar II An Operating Standard Rule

HCO PL 16 Mar IV Lines and Hats
Personnel Series 19
Org Series 25

HCOB 19 Mar I C/Sing Auditor-C/Ses
C/S Series 30

HCOB 19 Mar II List 1C—L1C

HCO PL 19 Mar R I Personnel Prediction
Rev. 21 Jan 91 *Personnel Series 20R*

HCO PL 19 Mar RA II Bean Theory,
Rev. 27 Oct 82 Finance as a Commodity
Finance Series 7RA

HCO PL 25 Mar Valuable Final Products
Org Series 26

HCOB 27 Mar RA Dianetic Erasure
Rev. 21 Sep 78

FBDL 28 Mar Tech Delivery Situation

HCO PL 28 Mar I State of Orgs

HCO PL 28 Mar II Personnel Troubles

HCOB 31 Mar Programing and Misprograming
C/S Series 31

HCOB 4 Apr RB Use of Quad Dianetics
Rev. 3 Feb 89 *C/S Series 32RB*

HCOB 5 Apr RB I Triple and Quad
Rev. 3 Feb 89 Reruns
C/S Series 33RB

HCOB 5 Apr RA II Summary of How to
Rev. 2 Apr 90 Write an Auditor's Report and Worksheets for TRs and Objectives Co-audit

HCOB 6 Apr Non-F/N Cases
C/S Series 34

HCO PL 6 Apr Org Board Knowledge

HCOB 11 Apr RE L3RH, Dianetics and
Rev. 8 Apr 88 Int RD Repair List
NED Series 20

HCOB 19 Apr R Tech Quality
Rev. 18 Apr 91 *Cramming Series 1*

LRH ED 19 Apr Tech Delivery Quality

HCOB 21 Apr RD Quadruple Dianetics,
Rev. 3 Feb 89 Dangers Of
C/S Series 36RD

HCOB 26 Apr I TRs and Cognitions

HCO PL 26 Apr RC II FP Activation
Rev. 2 Feb 91 *Finance Series 5RC*

HCOB 27 Apr Education, Definition Of

HCOB 28 Apr Okays to Audit in HGCs

HCOB 30 Apr Auditing Comm Cycle

HCO PL 5 May I FEBC Graduate Policy

HCO PL 5 May RA II Reading Statistics
Rev. 27 Aug 82

HCO PL 5 May III FC Policy Letter

HCO PL 6 May Audience Alertness and Tape Players

HCO PL 11 May II Opinion Leaders
PR Series 6

HCO PL 11 May III Black PR
PR Series 7

HCOB 13 May Student Grasp of Materials
Word Clearing Series 57

HCO PL 17 May Justice—Correct Application

HCOB 23 May R I The Magic of the
Rev. 4 Dec 74 Communication Cycle
Basic Auditing Series 1R

HCOB 23 May R II The Two Parts of
Rev. 6 Dec 74 Auditing
Basic Auditing Series 2R

HCOB 23 May III The Three Important Communication Lines
Basic Auditing Series 3

HCOB 23 May R IV Communication
Rev. 4 Dec 74 Cycles within the Auditing Cycle
Basic Auditing Series 4R

HCOB 23 May R V The Communication
Rev. 29 Nov 74 Cycle in Auditing
Basic Auditing Series 5R

HCOB 23 May VI Auditor Failure to Understand
Basic Auditing Series 6

HCOB 23 May VII Premature Acknowledgments
Basic Auditing Series 7

HCOB 23 May R VIII Recognition of
Rev. 4 Dec 74 Rightness of the Being
Basic Auditing Series 10R

HCOB 23 May IX Metering
Basic Auditing Series 11

HCOB 23 May X Comm Cycle Additives
Basic Auditing Series 9

HCOB 26 May R TRs Course and
Rev. 23 Oct 83 Auditing, Mixing Major Actions
C/S Series 38R

HCO PL 27 May Service

HCO PL 28 May I Too Little Too Late
PR Series 8

HCO PL 28 May II Service and Workload

HCO PL 30 May Manners
PR Series 9

HCOB 31 May R Standard 12½-Hour
Rev. 21 Oct 71 Intensive Programs
C/S Series 39R

HCOB 2 Jun I Confronting
Study Series 2

HCOB 2 Jun II Overrun—Don't Use

HCO PL 2 Jun R II Breakthrough,
Rev. 28 Jul 83 PR and Production, Tone Scale Surveys
PR Series 10R

HCOB 3 Jun High and Low TA Breakthrough
C/S Series 37R

HCO PL 4 Jun Standard Admin

HCOB 7 Jun Low TAs
C/S Series 40

HCOB 9 Jun RA I C/S Tips
Rev. 28 Mar 77 *C/S Series 41RA*

HCOB 9 Jun II C/S Rules
C/S Series 42

HCOB 9 Jun III C/S Rules
C/S Series 43

HCOB 10 Jun I C/S Rules, Programing from Prepared Lists
C/S Series 44R

HCO PL 10 Jun Hatting Course Personnel

HCOB 15 Jun Hi-Lo TA Assessment Rules
C/S Series 37R, Addition

HCOB 16 Jun R IV Low TA Assessing
C/S Series 37R, Addition 2R

HCOB 19 Jun I C/S Rules
C/S Series 45

HCOB 19 Jun II Declares
C/S Series 46
KSW Series 18

HCOB 20 Jun The Supreme Test of a C/S
C/S Series 47

HCOB 23 Jun R The Secret of Fast
Rev. 25 Jul 87 Courses
Word Clearing Series 1R

HCOB 24 Jun Word Clearing
Word Clearing Series 2

HCO PL 24 Jun Trouble

HCOB 25 Jun R Barriers to Study
Rev. 25 Nov 74 *Word Clearing Series 3R*

HCOB 26 Jun I C/S Series 37R, Addition 3

HCOB 26 Jun RA II Supervisor Two-way
Rev. 11 Jan 89 Comm and the Misunderstood Word
Word Clearing Series 4RA

HCOB 27 Jun RA Supervisor Two-way
Rev. 20 Dec 88 Comm Explained
Word Clearing Series 5RA

HCOB 29 Jun RB Steps to Speed Student
Rev. 20 Dec 88 Product Flow
Word Clearing Series 7RB

HCO PL 29 Jun R I Policy on Psychiatric
Rev. 24 Jun 88 and Medical Failures

HCO PL 29 Jun II Public Warning on Psychiatry

HCOB 30 Jun RD I Expanded Green
Rev. 27 Jun 88 Form 40RF, GF 40XRF

HCOB 30 Jun RC II Standard C/S for
Rev. 3 Mar 89 Word Clearing in Session, Method One
Word Clearing Series 8RC

HCOB 1 Jul R I The Different Types of
Rev. 11 Jan 89 Word Clearing
Word Clearing Series 9R

HCOB 1 Jul RB II Speeding Up a Slow
Rev. 28 Dec 88 Course
Word Clearing Series 10RB

HCOB 2 Jul III Word Clearing Clarification
Word Clearing Series 13

HCOB 3 Jul R Auditing by Lists
Rev. 22 Feb 79

LRH ED 4 Jul Why Something New?

HCOB 5 Jul RB Assists
Rev. 20 Sep 78 *C/S Series 49RB*

HCO PL 6 Jul A Major Duty of the Hats Officer

HCO PL 7 Jul HCO Establishment Functions
Org Series 27

HCO PL 12 Jul Delivery Duties

HCOB 15 Jul II C/S Case Gain
C/S Series 50

HCOB 15 Jul RD III Drug Handling
Rev. 8 Apr 88 *C/S Series 48RE*
NED Series 9RC

HCO PL 16 Jul Violence

HCOB 17 Jul R Out of Valence
Rev. 6 Jul 78 *C/S Series 51R*

HCO PL 18 Jul I Stats and Progress Board

HCO PL 18 Jul II The Student Folder

HCOB 19 Jul Interns
C/S Series 52

LRH ED 20 Jul The Beginning and Maintaining of a Boom

HCO PL 21 Jul I HAS Standard Actions

HCO PL 21 Jul II HAS Apprenticing Actions

HCOB 22 Jul II Confronting, Addition
Study Series 3

HCO PL 22 Jul R CLOs, OTLs and Flag
Rev. 22 Jan 91 *AKH Series 25R*

HCOB 23 Jul R Assists
Rev. 16 Jul 78

HCO PL 23 Jul Telex Comm Clarity

HCO PL 25 Jul Hatting the Right Way

HCOB 28 Jul RB Dianetics, Beginning a
Rev. 8 Apr 88 Pc On
C/S Series 54RB
NED Series 8RA

HCO PL 28 Jul Admin Know-How No. 26

HCO PL 29 Jul I Why Hatting?
Org Series 28
Personnel Series 21

HCO PL 29 Jul III Penalties for the Hiring or Recruiting of Institutional or Insane Persons

HCO PL 30 Jul Mimeo Files Product

HCO PL 31 Jul The Usual

HCOB 2 Aug TRs, Solo Course and Advanced Courses

HCO PL 2 Aug Study Time

HCO PL 2 Aug RB II Public Executive
Rev. 10 Jan 91 Secretary Privilege

HCOB 4 Aug R Post Purpose Clearing
Rev. 26 Nov 74

HCOB 8 Aug The Ivory Tower
C/S Series 55

HCO PL 9 Aug I Writing Programs and Projects
Target Series 10
AKH Series 45

HCO PL 10 Aug HCO Cope Officer

HCO PL 11 Aug I Basic Hat Pack

HCO PL 11 Aug II Don't Unmock a Working Installation
Personnel Series 22

HCO PL 11 Aug III Infinite Expansion
Org Series 29

HCO PL 11 Aug V Security of Data

HCO PL 12 Aug I Hat Checksheet Requirements

HCO PL 12 Aug IV OT Courses

HCO PL 12 Aug V Ethics: Advanced Courses

HCO PL 14 Aug RC III Div 5 Mini Qual
Rev. 17 Feb 75 Org Board

HCOB 16 Aug R II Training Drills
Rev. 5 Jul 78 Remodernized

HCO PL 18 Aug On-Policy

HCOB 19 Aug RC II Quad Ruds, Long
Rev. 10 Apr 91 Duration

HCO PL 19 Aug Programs, Use of, How to Save Useless Work

HCO PL 20 Aug I HAS Troubles

HCO PL 20 Aug II Tech Establishment Officer

HCO PL 20 Aug III Musical Chairs

HCOB 23 Aug Auditor's Rights
C/S Series 1

HCOB 24 Aug II Assists Addition

HCO PL 24 Aug I Intern Checksheets, Okays to Audit

HCOB 25 Aug How to Get Results in an HGC
C/S Series 56
Auditor Admin Series 2

LRH ED 26 Aug On-Policy Registration

HCO PL 27 Aug Academy Certs Valid at SHs

HCOB 31 Aug R Confused Ideas
Word Clearing Series 16R

HCO PL 31 Aug I The Executive Council Network Disbanded

HCO PL 31 Aug Add Executive Council Network

HCO PL 31 Aug II Overload and Hatting

HCOB 1 Sep I A C/S as a Training Officer, A Program for Flubless Auditing
C/S Series 57

HCOB 2 Sep Words and Posts
Word Clearing Series 17

HCOB 4 Sep RA I How to Use a
Rev. 9 Feb 89 Dictionary
Word Clearing Series 22RA

HCOB 4 Sep II Alterations
Word Clearing Series 19

HCOB 4 Sep III Simple Words
Word Clearing Series 20

HCO PL 4 Sep RB FP and Necessities
Rev. 2 Feb 91 *Finance Series 37R*

HCO PL 5 Sep HCO Reception

HCOB 6 Sep Correct Sequence, Qualifications of Word Clearers
Word Clearing Series 21

HCOB 7 Sep Programing Cases Backwards
C/S Series 58

HCOB 8 Sep I Birth Control Pills

HCOB 8 Sep R II Case Supervisor
Rev. 20 May 75 Actions

HCO PL 8 Sep Instability

HCOB 13 Sep Troubleshooting
Word Clearing Series 23

HCOB 14 Sep R II Dianetic List Errors
Rev. 19 Jul 78 *C/S Series 59R*

HCOB 14 Sep III Word Clearing C/S No. 2

HCOB 15 Sep The Worst Tangle
C/S Series 60

HCOB 17 Sep Library
Word Clearing Series 24

HCOB 22 Sep The Three Golden Rules of the C/S, Handling Auditors
C/S Series 61

HCO PL 23 Sep Flag Banking Officer Purposes
Finance Series 9

HCOB 24 Sep RA Interiorization
Rev. 4 Feb 89 Rundown Correction Drill: Date to Blow/ Locate to Blow
Int RD Series 11R

HCO PL 24 Sep RC Assignment, Model
Rev. 26 Feb 89 to Be Used

HCOB 25 Sep RB Tone Scale in Full
Rev. 1 Apr 78

HCOB 28 Sep Know Before You Go
C/S Series 62

HCO PL 28 Sep Selling and Delivering Auditing

HCOB 30 Sep VI CCHs 5, 6 and 7

ARTICLE

FREEDOM Sep/Oct Psychology and Psychiatry, The Sciences of Saliva

ISSUES

HCOB 2 Oct C/Sing for New Auditors or Veterans
C/S Series 63

HCO PL 2 Oct HCO Puzzles

HCO PL 3 Oct How Ethics Gets Harsh

HCOB 5 Oct F/Ning Auditors
C/S Series 64

HCO PL 5 Oct Propaganda by Redefinition of Words
PR Series 12

LRH ED 7 Oct Tech Certainty and High Stats

HCOB 21 Oct Assists in Scientology

HCO PL 22 Oct RD Purchasing and
Rev. 2 Feb 91 Check-Signing Lines Modified
Finance Series 10RD

HCOB 24 Oct R I Op Pro by Dup—End
Rev. 2 Jan 75 Phenomena

HCOB 24 Oct II Vitamins

HCOB 24 Oct RA III False TA
Rev. 25 May 80

HCO PL 24 Oct Performance

HCOB 25 Oct Drug Drying Out

HCO PL 25 Oct I Comm Routing, How to Tie Up a Whole Org and Produce Nothing

HCO PL 26 Oct Tech Downgrades
KSW Series 6

HCOB 27 Oct Vitamin C

HCO PL 27 Oct Celebrity Centre Motto

HCOB 29 Oct RA Int Rundown
Rev. 24 Sep 78 Correction List Revised
Int RD Series 12

HCO PL 29 Oct II The Executive
Exec Series 1

HCO PL 29 Oct III Leadership
Exec Series 2

HCOB 31 Oct The Sequence of Programs
C/S Series 44R, Addition

HCO PL 31 Oct Full Hatting

THE BASIC DIANETICS PICTURE BOOK

Taken from the works of L. Ron Hubbard

Published by Publications Organization, U.S. Revised in 1972 and 1991. TRANSLATIONS: Chinese, Danish, Dutch, French, German, Greek, Hebrew, Italian, Japanese, Norwegian, Portuguese, Spanish, Russian and Swedish.

ISSUES

HCO PL 1 Nov RA II Prepayments Used
Rev. 19 Jul 79 for Books

HCO PL 1 Nov R IV CO and ED Penalty
Rev. 13 Feb 91 for False Completion Stats

HCOB 3 Nov Auditor's Worksheets
C/S Series 66
Auditor Admin Series 15

HCO PL 8 Nov RA I Internships,
Rev. 18 Aug 88 Electronic Attestation Form

HCO PL 8 Nov R II Complement
Rev. 23 Oct 75

HCOB 10 Nov R Tapes, How to Use
Rev. 21 Sep 74 *Word Clearing Series 25R*
Tape Course Series 6R

HCO PL 10 Nov Organization and Survival

HCOB 12 Nov RB False TA Addition
Rev. 25 May 80

HCO PL 12 Nov R II How to Raise
Rev. 6 Mar 73 Your Own Statistics and Pay

HCO PL 19 Nov R Director of
Rev. 24 Jan 91 Processing Hat

HCOB 20 Nov RA I HAS and
Rev. 10 Apr 91 Establishment Officer Specialist Auditing Program (Revised)

HCOB 20 Nov II Course Translation to Tape
Tape Course Series 1

HCOB 21 Nov I Dianetics and Scientology in Other Languages
Tape Course Series 2

HCOB 21 Nov R II Teaching a Tape
Rev. 23 Oct 74 Course
Tape Course Series 3R

HCO PL 21 Nov I Scientology Courses Examination Policy

HCOB 25 Nov II Resistive Cases, Former Therapy

HCO PL 25 Nov Inter-Org Exchange of Students and Fees

HCO PL 27 Nov I Money
Exec Series 3

HCO PL 27 Nov III Free Services = Free Fall

HCO PL 30 Nov Blind Registration

HCO PL 3 Dec Exchange
Exec Series 4

HCOB 5 Dec End Phenomenas

HCO PL 5 Dec R II How to Do Surveys
Rev. 10 Sep 88 *Marketing Series 20*
PR Series 13R

HCO PL 7 Dec I Advanced Course Violations

HCO PL 7 Dec IV Correction Division Purposes, Ideal Scenes, Products, Statistics

HCOB 8 Dec R The C/S and Cramming
Rev. 25 Aug 81 Cycles
Cramming Series 2
C/S Series 68R

HCOB 9 Dec RD PTS Rundown,
Rev. 28 Mar 89 Audited

HCO PL 9 Dec R What? No Auditors?
Rev. 22 Feb 75

HCO PL 11 Dec Earned Flag Certificates

HCOB 12 Dec How to Write Up a Cramming Order
Cramming Series 8
C/S Series 70

HCOB 16 Dec RB Interiorization Errors
Rev. 24 Sep 78 *C/S Series 35RB*
Int RD Series 10

HCO PL 16 Dec PRO Area Control
PR Series 10-1

HCOB 17 Dec RB Interiorization
Rev. 24 Sep 78 Summary
Int RD Series 15
C/S Series 23RB

HCOB 19 Dec D of P Operates by OCAs
C/S Series 71

HCOB 20 Dec Use of Correction Lists
C/S Series 72

HCOB 23 Dec RB The No-Interference
Rev. 2 Aug 90 Area Clarified and Re-Enforced
Solo C/S Series 10RB
C/S Series 73RB

HCO PL 29 Dec RB Flag Representative,
Rev. 4 Sep 90 Purpose Of

HCO PL 31 Dec Flag Rep Key Ingredients

THE BASIC SCIENTOLOGY PICTURE BOOK
Taken from the works of L. Ron Hubbard

Published by Publications Organization, US. Later revised in 1991. TRANSLATIONS: Danish, Dutch, French, German, Hebrew, Italian, Japanese, Norwegian, Portuguese, Spanish and Swedish.

1972

Early 1972 found L. Ron Hubbard aboard the flagship *Apollo,* researching, lecturing and overseeing the training of executives and auditors who had come from around the world for the highest levels of training available.

New achievements in the fields of study and education were made, with several new methods of Word Clearing released. These included the steps needed to bring about a brand-new state: *Super*literacy, the ability to comfortably and quickly take data from a page and be able at once to apply it.

BASIC STUDY MANUAL

Compiled from the works of L. Ron Hubbard by Applied Scholastics, Inc. Later revised in 1990. TRANSLATIONS: Italian, German and Spanish.

ISSUES

HCOB 2 Jan WC1 Comes First
Word Clearing Series 30

HCOB 3 Jan R Repairing a Case
Rev. 20 Jun 89 *C/S Series 69*

HCOB 7 Jan Training and Interning Staff Auditors

HCO PL 7 Jan R II Creating Survey
Rev. 10 Sep 88 Questions
Marketing Series 21
PR Series 14RA

HCO PL 15 Jan RC Riches or Poverty,
Rev. 10 Sep 90 the Quality of the Dissem Division, a Dissem Div Checklist for Quality

LRH ED 16 Jan Your Dissem Division

HCO PL 19 Jan Specialization

HCOB 20 Jan R PTS Rundown Addition
Rev. 8 Dec 78

HCO PL 21 Jan Hatting

HCO PL 22 Jan II Personnel Programing

HCO PL 26 Jan I Not-Dones, Half-Dones and Backlogs
Exec Series 5
AKH Series 29

HCOB 27 Jan Temperatures

HCO PL 31 Jan The Why Is God
Data Series 22

HCO PL 1 Feb II Accounts Policing

HCO PL 3 Feb Illegal Processing

HCOB 3 Feb R6EW–OT III, No-Interference Area

HCO PL 6 Feb Executive Intention
Exec Series 6

HCOB 7 Feb III Vitamin and Glandular Deficiency, Important Data All Levels

HCO PL 8 Feb R Targeting of Divisional
Rev. 21 Oct 80 Statistics and Quotas
Exec Series 7R

HCOB 15 Feb R False TA, Addition 2
Rev. 26 Jan 77

HCOB 16 Feb Talking the TA Down Modified
C/S Series 74

HCO PL 16 Feb The Purpose of the Department of Personnel Enhancement

HCO PL 17 Feb Proper Format and Correct Action
Data Series 23

HCO PL 18 Feb The Top Triangle
Exec Series 8

LRH ED 18 Feb Survey = Response

HCOB 18 Feb RA I False TA Addition 3
Rev. 25 May 80

HCO PL 21 Feb Qualities at the Top

HCOB 22 Feb RA Word Clearing
Rev. 8 Jul 74 Method 4
Word Clearing Series 32RA

HCOB 24 Feb Word Clearing OCAs
C/S Series 71A

HCO PL 24 Feb I Injustice

HCO PL 24 Feb II Estos
Esto Series 41

HCOB 26 Feb Word Clearing Series 15R

HCO PL 26 Feb R I Order or Chaos, the
Rev. 10 Sep 90 Quality of the HCO Division, an HCO Div Checklist for Quality

HCO PL 26 Feb R II Cause or Effect, the
Rev. 10 Sep 90 Quality of the Qual Division, a Qual Div Checklist for Quality

HCO PL 26 Feb R III Sanity or Psychosis,
Rev. 10 Sep 90 the Quality of the Tech Division, a Tech Division Checklist for Quality

HCO PL 26 Feb RA IV Viability or
Rev. 10 Sep 90 Liability, the Quality of the Treasury Division, a Treasury Div Checklist for Quality

HCO PL 26 Feb R V Coordination or
Rev. 10 Sep 90 Confusion, an Exec Div Checklist for Quality

HCO PL 27 Feb Routing
Exec Series 9

HCO PL 29 Feb I Correct Comm
Exec Series 10

HCO PL 29 Feb RA II Handling, Policy,
Rev. 3 Nov 90 Plans, Programs, Projects and Orders Defined
Data Series 24RA

ESTABLISHMENT OFFICER LECTURES
SEA ORGANIZATION FLAGSHIP *APOLLO*

Delivered to Flag Executive Briefing Course students aboard the *Apollo,* this series of lectures details the Establishment Officer system, how it relates to the Product–Organizing Officer system and how Establishment Officer technology can be utilized to create rapid and stable expansion in any organization. *(Reproduced on cassette for the Flag Executive Briefing Course.)*

1 Mar Estos Instant Hat, Part I
1 Mar Estos Instant Hat, Part II
2 Mar Evaluation and Handling of Personnel, Part I
2 Mar Evaluation and Handling of Personnel, Part II
3 Mar Handling Personnel, Part I
3 Mar Handling Personnel, Part II
4 Mar Hold the Form of the Org, Part I
4 Mar Hold the Form of the Org, Part II
5 Mar Revision of the Product–Org Officer System, Part I
5 Mar Revision of the Product–Org Officer System, Part II
6 Mar F/Ning Staff Members, Part I
6 Mar F/Ning Staff Members, Part II

ISSUES

HCOB 3 Mar Exercise

HCO PL 7 Mar R I The Establishment
Rev. 13 Apr 72 Officer
Esto Series 1R

HCO PL 7 Mar II Course Supervisors

HCO PL 9 Mar RA I Income Flows and
Rev. 2 Feb 91 Pools, Principles of Money Management
Finance Series 11RA

HCO PL 9 Mar II Hatting the Esto
Esto Series 2

HCO PL 9 Mar III Dev-t and Unhattedness
Esto Series 3

HCO PL 10 Mar Exec Esto Hatting Duties
Esto Series 4

HCO PL 13 Mar Production and Establishment, Orders and Products
Esto Series 5

HCO PL 14 Mar I Sequence of Hatting
Esto Series 6

HCO PL 14 Mar II Follow Policy and Lines
Esto Series 7

HCOB 15 Mar Cramming
Cramming Series 9

HCO PL 16 Mar I Look Don't Listen
Esto Series 8

HCO PL 16 Mar II Stuck In
Esto Series 9

HCO PL 16 Mar III Finance Directives Cancelled

HCO PL 16 Mar V What Is a Course, High Crime

HCO PL 18 Mar Files
Esto Series 10

HCO PL 19 Mar I C/Sing or Auditing Without Folder Study
Auditor Admin Series 5

HCO PL 19 Mar II Learning to Use Data Analysis
Data Series 25

HCO PL 20 Mar Auditors

HCOB 22 Mar RA Disagreement Check
Rev. 24 Mar 85

HCO PL 23 Mar Full Product Clearing Long Form
Esto Series 11

HCO PL 27 Mar Study

HCOB 27 Mar RD I Student Correction
Rev. 18 Oct 86 List—Revised

HCOB 27 Mar RA II Course Supervisor
Rev. 12 Jul 88 Correction List

HCOB 27 Mar RC III Auditor Correction
Rev. 12 Jul 88 List, Auditor Recovery

LRH ED 29 Mar Study and Tech Breakthrough

HCOB 30 Mar R The Primary
Rev. 30 May 72 Correction Rundown, Revised
Study Series 5R

EXPANDED DIANETICS LECTURES
SEA ORGANIZATION FLAGSHIP *APOLLO*

These lectures were given by L. Ron Hubbard to students he was personally training in the specialized data and advanced skills of his latest breakthrough in auditing technology, Expanded Dianetics. In addition to specifics on Expanded Dianetics procedures, he also covered vital data on misunderstood words and their handling, the anatomy of physical illness and the importance of standard auditor administration. *(Reproduced on cassette for the Expanded Dianetics Auditor Course.)*

30 Mar Expanded Dianetics
7 Apr Expanded Dianetics and Word Clearing
7 Apr Auditor Administration
7 Apr Illness Breakthrough

Issues

HCO PL 1 Apr Making an Executive *Esto Series 12* *Exec Series 11*
HCO PL 3 Apr Doing Work *Esto Series 13*
HCOB 3 Apr Primary Rundown Note *Study Series 6*
HCOB 4 Apr R I Primary Rundown (Revised) Rev. 30 May 72
HCO PL 4 Apr I Ethics *Esto Series 14*
HCO PL 4 Apr II Org Officers, Product Officers, Estos *Org Series 44* *Esto Series 42*
HCO PL 4 Apr R III Ethics and Study Tech Rev. 21 Jun 75 *Word Clearing Series 48*
HCO PL 6 Apr I Product Correction *Esto Series 15*
HCO PL 6 Apr R II How to Find a Why on a Person and Handle Rev. 21 Jan 91
HCOB 7 Apr RA Touch Assists, Correct Ones Rev. 25 Aug 87
HCO PL 9 Apr R Correct Danger Condition Handling Rev. 1 Dec 79
HCOB 10 Apr Pre-OTs Don't C/S *C/S Series 75* *Solo C/S Series 13*
HCO PL 12 Apr Handling Danger Conditions
HCOB 15 Apr RA Expanded Dianetics Series 1RA Rev. 24 Apr 91
HCOB 16 Apr R PTS RD Correction List Rev. 20 Dec 83
HCOB 17 Apr R C/Sing a PTS Rundown Rev. 20 Dec 83 *C/S Series 76R*
HCOB 19 Apr "Quickie" Defined *C/S Series 77* *KSW Series 8*
HCOB 20 Apr R I Suppressed Pcs and PTS Tech Rev. 23 Apr 91 *ExDn Series 4*
HCOB 20 Apr II Product Purpose and Why and W/C Error Correction *C/S Series 78*
HCOB 24 Apr I PTS Interviews *C/S Series 79* *ExDn Series 5*
HCO PL 24 Apr I Hatting the Product Officer of the Division *Esto Series 16*
HCO PL 24 Apr II Dones
LRH ED 24 Apr Auditor Recovery
HCOB 26 Apr The Glib Student *Study Series 8*
HCO PL 2 May RA Numbering of Mimeo Issues Rev. 29 Jun 77
HCO PL 3 May R Ethics and Executives Rev. 18 Dec 77 *Exec Series 12*
HCOB 3 May Havingness
HCOB 4 May Six Basic Processes
HCOB 5 May R The Remedy of Havingness Rev. 17 Jan 73
HCOB 6 May Remedy of Havingness—The Process
HCOB 7 May Expanded GITA
HCOB 8 May The Importance of Havingness
HCOB 10 May Robotism
HCO PL 12 May R PTS Personnel and Finance Rev. 27 Oct 82 *Exec Series 13R* *Finance Series 12R* *Personnel Series 25R*
HCO PL 13 May I Chinese School *Study Series 4* *Esto Series 17*
HCO PL 13 May II Handle
HCO PL 14 May Morale
HCO PL 28 May Boom Data, Publications Basic Function
HCO PL 3 Jun R Promotion Allocations Rev. 2 Feb 91 *Finance Series 13R*
HCOB 3 Jun RA PTS Rundown, Final Step Rev. 8 Dec 78
HCOB 9 Jun Grammar *Word Clearing Series 36*
HCOB 10 Jun I Bypassed Charge
HCOB 10 Jun RA VI The L3RH Rundown, Dianetic Track Repair Rev. 13 Jun 88 *NED Series 31*
HCO PL 11 Jun Product Officers
HCO PL 12 Jun R Length of Time to Evaluate Rev. 24 Jun 88 *Esto Series 18R* *Data Series 26R*
HCO PL 13 Jun Program Drill *Esto Series 19*
HCO PL 15 Jun R PR Area Control, Three Grades of PR Rev. 24 Jan 83 *PR Series 11R*
HCOB 15 Jun "Dog Pcs" *C/S Series 80*
HCOB 16 Jun RA Auditor's Rights Modified Rev. 7 Dec 76 *C/S Series 81RA*
HCOB 19 Jun Dinky Dictionaries *Word Clearing Series 37*
HCO PL 20 Jun Registrars and Notes
HCOB 21 Jun R I Method 5 Rev. 20 Feb 89 *Word Clearing Series 38R*
HCOB 21 Jun II Method 6 *Word Clearing Series 39*
HCOB 21 Jun III Method 7 *Word Clearing Series 40*
HCOB 21 Jun R IV Method 8 Rev. 8 Feb 89 *Word Clearing Series 41R*
HCO PL 24 Jun Posting *Esto Series 43*
HCO PL 25 Jun Recovering Students and Pcs
HCO PL 26 Jun Supervisor Tech *Esto Series 20*
HCO PL 28 Jun Files Accuracy *Esto Series 21*
HCO PL 14 Jul II Esto Failures *Esto Series 22* *Exec Series 14* *Org Series 30*
HCOB 20 Jul I Primary Correction Rundown Handling
HCOB 20 Jul II Distractive and Additive Questions and Orders
HCO PL 23 Jul RB The Vital Necessity of Hatting Rev. 11 Jan 91 *Esto Series 23RB* *Exec Series 15RB* *Org Series 31RB*
HCO PL 25 Jul The Form of the Org *Esto Series 24*
HCO PL 27 Jul Form of the Org and Schedules *Esto Series 25*
HCO PL 28 Jul Establishing, Holding the Form of the Org *Esto Series 26* *Exec Series 16* *Org Series 32*
HCO PL 7 Aug R PR and Causation Rev. 9 Aug 72 *PR Series 17R*
HCO PL 9 Aug Seniority of Orders
FBDL 10 Aug Magazines
HCOB 10 Aug Dianetic HCOB, Interest *C/S Series 82* *ExDn Series 6*
HCO PL 11 Aug I Films and Tapes Not Prohibited
HCO PL 11 Aug II Foundation and Day Orgs Separate
HCO PL 11 Aug R III Foundation Income Rev. 4 Sep 72
HCO PL 11 Aug IV Hatting Officer
HCOB 13 Aug RB Fast Flow Training Rev. 9 Aug 90
HCOB 16 Aug Flubless C/Sing *C/S Series 84*
HCOB 17 Aug RA Method 4 Notes Rev. 14 Jan 89 *Word Clearing Series 42RA* *Tape Course Series 10R*
HCOB 18 Aug Grammar Definition *Word Clearing Series 43*

Mission Into Time

Compiled by staff and published by the Publications Organization, Los Angeles, California, September 1972. Republication of A Test of Whole Track Recall, *1968.*

Issues

HCO PL 21 Aug Effective Hatting *Esto Series 27*
HCOB 2 Sep Cramming Motto *Cramming Series 10*
LRH ED 7 Sep Evaluation
HCO PL 8 Sep Efficiency and Flaps
HCO PL 9 Sep I LRH Income
HCOB 13 Sep Catastrophes from and Repair of "No Interest" Items *C/S Series 85* *ExDn Series 7*
HCOB 14 Sep Expanded Dianetics Case A *ExDn Series 8*
HCOB 15 Sep R Expanded Dianetics Case B Rev. 20 May 77 *ExDn Series 9R*
HCOB 18 Sep Expanded Dianetics Case C *ExDn Series 10*
HCOB 19 Oct Expanded Dianetics Case D *ExDn Series 11*
HCOB 20 Oct R Expanded Dianetics Case E Rev. 25 Jul 77 *ExDn Series 12R*
HCOB 21 Oct I Expanded Dianetics Case F *ExDn Series 13*
HCOB 22 Oct R Expanded Dianetics Case G Rev. 25 May 77 *ExDn Series 14R*
HCOB 24 Oct R Expanded Dianetics Case I Rev. 23 May 77 *ExDn Series 15R*
HCOB 25 Oct R Expanded Dianetics Case J Rev. 11 Jun 77 *ExDn Series 16R*
HCOB 29 Oct R Expanded Dianetics Case K Rev. 23 May 77 *ExDn Series 17R*
HCOB 30 Oct R Expanded Dianetics Case L Rev. 4 Jun 77 *ExDn Series 18R*
HCOB 1 Nov Expanded Dianetics Case M *ExDn Series 19*
HCOB 6 Nov Illiteracy and Work *Word Clearing Series 44*
HCOB 8 Nov RA The Dianetic Full Flow Table Rev. 27 Oct 85 *Auditor Admin Series 21RA*
HCOB 15 Nov II Students Who Succeed
HCO PL 21 Nov I How to Handle Black Propaganda *PR Series 18*

1973

Returning to the *Apollo* from several months spent in New York City doing sociological studies, Mr. Hubbard carried out research in the areas of vitamins and nutrition. His discoveries during this time formed the foundation for major advances he would make in later years in handling the effects of drugs and other toxic substances.

Issues

HCOB 4 Jan Confront *Study Series 9*

HCOB 20 Jan RE The Red Tag Line
Rev. 19 Apr 90 *C/S Series 86RE*

HCOB 30 Jan RE Method 9 Word
Rev. 16 May 84 Clearing the Right Way *Word Clearing Series 46RE*

HCO PL 7 Feb II Mimeo Supply Conservation

HCO PL 7 Feb III Mimeo File Folders and Files

HCO PL 7 Feb R IV Mimeo Files
Rev. 22 Mar 73

HCOB 5 Apr Axiom 28 Amended

HCO PL 12 May RC I Post Protection,
Rev. 7 May 84 LRH Communicators *LRH Comm N/W Series 15*

HCO PL 25 May Supplementary Evaluations *Data Series 27*

HCOB 11 Jul RB Assist Summary
Rev. 21 Sep 78

HCOB 29 Jul Art, More About *Art Series 2*

HCOB 30 Jul Scientology, Current State of the Subject and Materials

HCOB 2 Aug Pep

HCO PL 7 Aug R I Flag Representative,
Rev. 2 Jan 91 Purpose, Duties and Statistic

HCOB 10 Aug PTS Handling

HCO PL 15 Aug R Flag Representative,
Rev. 2 Jan 91 Orders To

HCO PL 24 Aug R Communication,
Rev. 2 Jan 91 Stopping Of

HCO PL 27 Aug Tech and LRH Comms *LRH Comm N/W Series 13*

HCO PL 28 Aug RA The Mission of the
Rev. 7 May 84 LRH Comm Network *LRH Comm N/W Series 14*

HCO PL 1 Sep Admin Know-How No. 30

HCO PL 11 Sep R Codes and Coding,
Rev. 21 Sep 81 Correct Practice Policy

HCO PL 19 Sep R I Checking Evals
Rev. 22 Jun 75 *Data Series 28R*

HCO PL 19 Sep-1 Checking Evaluations Addition *Data Series 28R-1*

HCO PL 19 Sep-2 Multiple Sit Eval Format *Data Series 28R-2*

HCO PL 20 Sep R Concerning
Rev. 12 Feb 91 Administration

HCO PL 24 Sep RA All Auditors—
Rev. 25 Jan 91 Ministers, Ministerial Board of Review

HCO PL 30 Sep I Outpoints, More *Data Series 29*

HCO PL 30 Sep II Situation Finding *Data Series 30*

HCO PL 15 Oct Administrative Skill *AKH Series 31*

HCOB 15 Oct RC Nulling and F/Ning
Rev. 26 Jul 86 Prepared Lists *C/S Series 87RC*

HCOB 19 Oct Mistakes and PTSness

HCO PL 21 Oct RA Case Supervisor
Rev. 9 Nov 83 Statistic

HCOB 21 Oct R The South African
Rev. 9 Apr 91 Rundown

HCO PL 26 Oct Staff Corrective Actions, Requiring Auditing Actions

HCO PL 28 Oct Celebrity Centre Purpose

HCO PL 4 Nov Publishing Policy, Books and Magazines

HCO PL 5 Nov Source Acknowledgment

HCOB 11 Nov Preclear Declare? Procedure

HCOB 15 Nov RA Fear of People List
Rev. 23 Apr 91

HCOB 16 Nov Study Tech and Post *Word Clearing Series 49*

HCO PL 19 Nov RA Organization
Rev. 21 Jan 91 Executive Course Checksheets

HCOB 20 Nov I Anti-Q and A Drill

HCOB 20 Nov II F/N What You Ask or Program *C/S Series 89*

HCOB 21 Nov The Cure of Q and A, Man's Deadliest Disease

HCO PL 21 Nov LRH Comm Drills

HCO PL 22 Nov Esto Series 30

HCOB 23 Nov RB Dry and Wet Hands
Rev. 25 May 80 Make False TA

HCOB 24 Nov RF I Hi-Lo TA
Rev. 26 Jul 86 Assessment C/S *C/S Series 53RM LF (Long Form)*

HCOB 24 Nov RE II Short Hi-Lo TA
Rev. 26 Jul 86 Assessment C/S *C/S Series 53RM SF (Short Form)*

HCO PL 25 Nov I Final Targets *Data Series 31*

HCO PL 25 Nov-1 Final Target Attachment *Data Series 31 Addition*

ORGANIZATION EXECUTIVE COURSE VOLUMES 0–7
by L. Ron Hubbard

Compiled by staff between 1969 and 1972 and published for Scientology staff use, these volumes of HCO Policy Letters were first made broadly available in 1973. Published by the American Saint Hill Organization, Los Angeles, California. Revised in 1991.

ISSUES

HCOB 5 Dec The Reason for Q and A

HCO PL 5 Dec R Q and A Checksheet,
Rev. 12 Dec 74 Checksheet of the Hubbard Causative Leadership Course *AKH Series 32R*

HCOB 6 Dec The Primary Failure *C/S Series 90*

HCO PL 14 Dec Target Troubles *Data Series 32*

HCOB 15 Dec The Continuous Missed W/H and Continuous Overt with Data on Degraded Beings and False PTS Conditions

L. RON HUBBARD'S PROFESSIONAL AUDITOR'S BULLETINS
(collections of bulletins issued as books)

L. Ron Hubbard's PABs—Volume 1 PABs 1–24, May 53—Apr 54

L. Ron Hubbard's PABs—Volume 2 PABs 25–49, Apr 54—Apr 55

L. Ron Hubbard's PABs—Volume 3 PABs 50–74, Apr 55—Mar 56

L. Ron Hubbard's PABs—Volume 4 PABs 75–99, Mar 56—Nov 56

L. Ron Hubbard's PABs—Volume 5 PABs 100–124, Nov 56—Nov 57

L. Ron Hubbard's PABs—Volume 6 PABs 125–160, Dec 57—May 59

(Note: The Professional Auditor's Bulletins written by L. Ron Hubbard are also available in the Technical Bulletins *volumes.)*

1974

Nineteen seventy-four opened with the announcement of an important technical breakthrough: the Introspection Rundown. Resulting from research and piloting done in the closing months of 1973, this powerful series of audited actions locates and corrects the causes of introversion; with these factors handled the person can again extrovert, *see* his environment and therefore handle and control it.

In February, Mr. Hubbard formed a music and dance troupe aboard the *Apollo* to provide entertainment and goodwill at the ship's Spanish and Portuguese ports of call. He personally instructed the musicians and dancers in artistic presentation, music, composition, sound, arranging and recording. Much of the technology he taught them is now found in the HCO Bulletins of the Art Series, contained in the *Technical Bulletins* volumes.

THE MANAGEMENT SERIES 1970–1974
by L. Ron Hubbard

Published by the American Saint Hill Organization, Los Angeles, California, 1974. Contains the Data Series, Public Relations Series, Personnel Series, Organizing Series, Finance Series, Executive Series and Establishment Officer Series.

Later revised and expanded into two volumes in 1983 and into three volumes in 1991.

HYMN OF ASIA: AN EASTERN POEM
by L. Ron Hubbard

Published by the Publications Organization, Los Angeles, California, December 1974.

ISSUES

HCOB 23 Jan RB The Technical
Rev. 25 Apr 91 Breakthrough of 1973! The Introspection RD

HCOB 27 Jan R3R Commands Have Background Data

HCO PL 9 Feb R Condition Below
Rev. 17 Feb 80 Treason, Confusion Formula and Expanded Confusion Formula

HCOB 15 Feb Service Facsimile Theory and Expanded Dianetics *ExDn Series 20*

HCOB 17 Feb Mutual Out-Ruds *C/S Series 91*

HCOB 20 Feb R Introspection RD,
Rev. 25 Apr 91 Additional Actions

HCO PL 26 Feb The Untrained PR *PR Series 20*

HCO PL 27 Feb Wasted Planning *PR Series 21*

HCOB 6 Mar Introspection RD, Second Addition, Information to C/Ses, Fixated Attention

HCOB 17 Mar Two-way Comm, Using Wrong Questions

HCO PL 17 Mar R Press Conferences,
Rev. 16 Sep 88 Preparation For *PR Series 22R*

HCOB 18 Mar R E-Meters, Sensitivity
Rev. 22 Feb 79 Errors

HCO PL 18 Mar The Press Book *PR Series 23*

HCOB 21 Mar End Phenomena

HCOB 10 Apr Stage Manners *Art Series 3*

HCOB 20 Apr R Introspection RD—
Rev. 25 Apr 91 Third Addition, Additional Introspection RD Steps

HCOB 23 Apr RB Expanded Dianetics
Rev. 24 Apr 91 Requisites *ExDn Series 21*

HCOB 25 Apr Rhythm *Art Series 4*

HCO PL 5 May Orders

HCO PL 9 May Prod–Org, Esto and Older Systems Reconciled

HCOB 31 May Unhandled Drugs and Ethics

HCO PL 11 Jun The "Economy"

HCO PL 22 Jun Tech

HCO PL 3 Jul RB Evaluation,
Rev. 29 Jan 79 Criticism Of *Data Series 33RB*

LRH ED 5 Jul Registration Pgm No. 2

LRH ED 6 Jul Additional Reges

HCOB 8 Jul R I Clear to F/N
Rev. 24 Jul 74 *Word Clearing Series 53R*

HCOB 8 Jul R II Word Clearing Errors
Rev. 24 Jul 74 *C/S Series 92R*
Word Clearing Series 51

HCO PL 13 Jul I Production Bugs
Org Series 33

HCO PL 13 Jul II Working Installations
Org Series 34

HCOB 17 Jul ExDn Case B
ExDn Series 9-1

HCO PL 18 Jul Situation Correction
Data Series 34

HCO PL 19 Jul Eval Correction
Data Series 35

LRH ED 25 Jul Books Make Booms

HCO PL 11 Aug Envisioning the Ideal Scene
Data Series 36

HCO PL 12 Aug Whys Open the Door
Data Series 37

HCO PL 13 Aug RA OEC "Policy" Clarified
Rev. 7 Feb 91

HCO PL 15 Aug Solo and Advance Course Checkouts

HCO PL 16 Aug RA Estates Restored to Dept 21
Rev. 13 Feb 91

LRH ED 22 Aug Registration

LRH ED 27 Aug RA Financial Planning Checklist for the Promotional Actions of an Organization
Rev. 5 May 85

HCO PL 27 Aug II Formulas

HCO PL 30 Aug R II Qual Stat Change, A New One
Rev. 31 Dec 75

HCO PL 31 Aug RA Keeper of Tech, Office of LRH
Rev. 27 Jul 86 *LRH Comm N/W Series 23*

HCOB 31 Aug RA New Grade Chart
Rev. 9 Apr 77 *C/S Series 93RA*

HCO PL 2 Sep RB Recruiting and Hiring
Rev. 23 Mar 89

HCO PL 5 Sep Book Sales to Individuals from Pubs

HCOB 7 Sep Superliteracy and the Cleared Word
Word Clearing Series 54

HCO PL 25 Sep Reduction of Refunds, C/Ses and Overload

HCOB 26 Sep Handling Flubbed Pcs

HCO PL 26 Sep RA New Case Supervisor Postings
Rev. 1 Mar 77

HCO PL 3 Oct Pluspoint List
Data Series 38

HCOB 6 Oct RA The Vital Information Rundown, The Technical Breakthrough of 1974
Rev. 23 Apr 91

HCOB 15 Oct Cramming over Out-Ruds
Cramming Series 11

HCO PL 19 Oct The Dramatization of Withholds on Vital Information Lines

HCO PL 27 Oct Safe Ground
PR Series 25

HCO PL 28 Oct Who-Where Finding
Data Series 39

HCOB 1 Nov RA Rock Slams and Rock Slammers
Rev. 5 Sep 78

HCOB 5 Nov Drugs, More About

HCO PL 9 Nov R Refunds and Repayments
Rev. 2 Oct 80

LRH ED 11 Nov Staff Pay

HCO PL 13 Nov HCO May Do Confessional Lists

LRH ED 14 Nov Phone Costs, or How to Get Wiped Out

HCO PL 15 Nov I Phone Tips

HCO PL 15 Nov II CFs, ARC Breaks In

HCOB 15 Nov R Student Rehabilitation List
Rev. 26 May 88

HCO PL 16 Nov RD Transfers and Removals and Permanent Postings Forbidden Locally
Rev. 30 Jun 89

HCO PL 19 Nov R Finance Stress in an Org
Rev. 31 Jan 91

HCO PL 28 Nov Building HCO

LRH ED 30 Nov Staff Pay

HCOB 1 Dec R Word Clearing Lists for Prepared Lists
Rev. 20 Jul 88

HCO PL 29 Dec Qualifications, Division Five Functions

1975

Mr. Hubbard's work in 1975 yielded new developments in Dianetics auditing, E-Metering, health, nutrition and dealing with the effects of drugs, management and finance.

Issues

HCO PL 8 Jan Compliance, How to Get One

HCOB 16 Jan R Past Life Remedies
Rev. 6 Jul 78

LRH ED 17 Jan How You Are Limiting the Size and Income of Your Org

HCOB 23 Jan The Purpose of Class VIII

HCOB 14 Feb R L10, L11 and L12 Prerequisites
Rev. 11 May 88

FREEDOM 23 Feb The Justice Department Versus Americans

Dianetics Today

Compiled by staff and published by the Publications Organization, Los Angeles, California, March 1975.

Issues

HCOB 7 Mar Ext and Ending Session

HCO PL 12 Mar I Grade Subsidy for Staff Forbidden in Other Orgs

HCO PL 12 Mar II The Ideal Org
Data Series 40

LRH ED 15 Mar How You Can Increase the Size and Income of Your Org

HCO PL 15 Mar Book Outlets of an Org

HCOB 18 Mar Meter Use in Qual
Cramming Series 12

HCOB 25 Mar Diet, Theory of a Natural Diet

HCO PL 26 Mar Cause

HCOB 29 Mar RA Antibiotics, Administering Of
Rev. 24 Mar 85

HCO PL 30 Mar PR and Information
PR Series 26

HCOB 19 Apr Out-Basics and How to Get Them In

HCOB 23 Apr RA Vanishing Cream and False TA
Rev. 25 May 80

HCO PL 9 Jun The Enemy Line
PR Series 27

HCO PL 23 Jun Ad Council Income Planning

Dianetics and Scientology Technical Dictionary

Based on the works of L. Ron Hubbard. Published by the Publications Organization, Los Angeles, California, June 1975. Later revised in 1987. *Translation:* Italian.

Issues

HCOB 23 Oct Technical Queries
Word Clearing Series 56

HCOB 26 Oct "Failed" Cases
C/S Series 95

HCO PL 26 Oct Gross Income/Corrected Gross Income Ratio, Failed Cases and Failed Students

New Vitality Rundown Lectures
Daytona, Florida

In late 1975 Mr. Hubbard gave twenty-two lectures to a specially picked team of auditors being trained on a new auditing rundown. Designed to handle cases that have not progressed well due to suppression or other factors, the New Vitality Rundown is delivered at the Flag Service Organization by auditors trained on the precise technology given in these lectures. *(Reproduced on cassette for the New Vitality Rundown Auditor Course.)*

29 Oct First Lecture—Special Rundown Pilot

30 Oct Second Lecture—Special Rundown Pilot

31 Oct Third Lecture—Special Rundown Pilot

1 Nov Fourth Lecture—Special Rundown Pilot

2 Nov Fifth Lecture—Special Rundown Pilot

3 Nov Sixth Lecture—Special Rundown Pilot

4 Nov Seventh Lecture—Special Rundown Pilot

5 Nov Eighth Lecture—Special Rundown Pilot

6 Nov Ninth Lecture—Special Rundown Pilot

7 Nov Tenth Lecture—Special Rundown Pilot

8 Nov Eleventh Lecture—Special Rundown Pilot

10 Nov Twelfth Lecture—Special Rundown Pilot

11 Nov Thirteenth Lecture—Special Rundown Pilot

12 Nov Fourteenth Lecture—Special Rundown Pilot

13 Nov Fifteenth Lecture—Special Rundown Pilot

14 Nov Sixteenth Lecture—Special Rundown Pilot

17 Nov Seventeenth Lecture—Special Rundown Pilot

18 Nov Eighteenth Lecture—Special Rundown Pilot

19 Nov Nineteenth Lecture—Special Rundown Pilot

20 Nov Twentieth Lecture—Special Rundown Pilot

21 Nov Twenty-first Lecture—Special Rundown Pilot

24 Nov Twenty-second Lecture—Special Rundown Pilot

Issues

HCO PL 8 Nov Non-Existence Formula Expanded

HCOB 20 Dec RC The Student Booster Rundown
Rev. 25 Apr 91

1976

At the end of 1975 and into 1976, Mr. Hubbard traveled from Florida to Washington, DC, across the United States to Los Angeles, California and finally to a ranch at La Quinta in the Southern California desert.

At his new home he continued researching and writing. In addition to numerous technical bulletins, several key HCO Policy Letters on training staff members and on how to improve an organization's productivity come from his work at this time.

Issues

HCO PL 1 Jan FSMs FOLOs Commissions
FSM Series 5

HCO PL 6 Jan RC Flag External Expenses
Rev. 2 Feb 91 *Finance Series 14RC*

HCO PL 6 Jan RC-1R Flag External
Rev. 2 Feb 91 Expenses Addition
Finance Series 14RC-1R

ARTICLE

FREEDOM 15 Jan The Vital Humanities

THE POLICY SUBJECT INDEX

Index to the Organization Executive Course *and the* Management Series *volumes, published by Publications Organization US, Los Angeles, California, March 1976. (Also known as the* Hubbard Communications Office Policy Letter Subject Index.*)*

ISSUES

HCO PL 21 May R HCO, the Elite Corps
Rev. 14 May 89

HCO PL 22 May Staff Section Officer Hat

HCO PL 23 May R Celebrities
Rev. 10 Jan 91

HCOB 27 Jul PTS Rundown and Vital Info RD Position Corrected

THE TECHNICAL BULLETINS OF DIANETICS AND SCIENTOLOGY
by L. Ron Hubbard

Compilation of L. Ron Hubbard's technical bulletins on Dianetics and Scientology. Published by Scientology Publications Organization, Copenhagen and Publications Organization US, Los Angeles, California, August 1976. Revised in 1991.

ISSUES

HCO PL 7 Aug I Product–Org Officer System, Name Your Product
AKH Series 33
Esto Series 31

HCO PL 7 Aug II Product–Org Officer System, Want Your Product
AKH Series 34
Esto Series 32

HCO PL 7 Aug III Product–Org Officer System, To Get You Have to Know How to Organize
AKH Series 35
Esto Series 33

HCOB 10 Aug R R/Ses, What They
Rev. 5 Sep 78 Mean

HCO PL 20 Sep The Stat Push
Org Series 35
Exec Series 17

HCO PL 20 Sep-1 Stat Push Clarified
Org Series 35-1
Exec Series 17-1

HCOB 20 Oct R I PTS Data
Rev. 25 Aug 87

HCOB 20 Oct II PTS Handling

HCOB 24 Oct RA Delivery Repair Lists
Rev. 12 Jul 88 *C/S Series 96RA*

HCO PL 24 Oct RF I Ex-Staff Free
Rev. 2 Aug 90 Service

HCO PL 24 Oct RA II Supervisors Can
Rev. 9 Aug 90 Become Professors

HCO PL 24 Oct R III Senior Case
Rev. 20 Jan 91 Supervisor Requirements

HCO PL 25 Oct Provisional Certificate Expiry

HCOB 26 Oct I Auditing Reports, Falsifying Of
C/S Series 97
Auditor Admin Series 25

HCOB 28 Oct Auditing Folders, Omissions in Completeness
C/S Series 98
Auditor Admin Series 26

HCO PL 4 Nov RB I Statistic Change,
Rev. 12 Feb 89 Gross Divisional Statistics, HCOs and Quals, OIC Cable Change

HCO PL 4 Nov-2 HCO Stat Penalty

HCO PL 10 Nov I Staff Courses Mandatory in Orgs

HCO PL 11 Nov RB I Statistic Change,
Rev. 20 Nov 84 HCOs and Qual, Definitions

HCO PL 12 Nov RC Statistic Change,
Rev. 25 Nov 85 Tech Sec Stat

HCO PL 13 Nov RA Professional Rates
Rev. 9 Nov 89

HCO PL 14 Nov Manning Up an Org
Exec Series 18
AKH Series 36
Org Series 36
Personnel Series 28

HCO PL 16 Nov Production Quotas
Exec Series 19
Org Series 37

HCO PL 27 Nov R Restoration of Local
Rev. 30 Jun 89 Control of Personnel Assignments and Comm Evs

HCO PL 30 Nov R Only SSO Can TIP
Rev. 25 Apr 79

MODERN MANAGEMENT TECHNOLOGY DEFINED—HUBBARD DICTIONARY OF ADMINISTRATION AND MANAGEMENT

Compiled from the works of L. Ron Hubbard, published by Publications Organization US, Los Angeles, California, December 1976.

THE VOLUNTEER MINISTER'S HANDBOOK
by L. Ron Hubbard

Published by Publications Organization US, Los Angeles, California, December 1976.
TRANSLATION: German.

ISSUES

HCO PL 6 Dec RB Illegal Pcs,
Rev. 8 Apr 88 Acceptance Of, High Crime PL

HCO PL 7 Dec Leaving and Leaves

HCOB 10 Dec RB Scientology F/N and
Rev. 25 May 80 TA Position
C/S Series 99RB

RON'S JOURNAL 28

L. Ron Hubbard recorded a special message for the staff of Scientology organizations in December, 1976.

1977

Living in southern California, Mr. Hubbard carried on with his work on films, writing scripts for eight new Scientology instruction films.

His technical and organizational research went ahead at full speed, making significant progress in such areas as E-Meter use, Word Clearing, study and training technology, case repair, handling the effects of drugs, the technology of Confessionals, Expanded Dianetics, marketing, data evaluation and ethics. Each new advance was released in HCO Bulletins and HCO Policy Letters.

CAN WE EVER BE FRIENDS?

A recorded lecture delivered by a minister of Scientology on the truth about Dianetics and Scientology, intended for those who have exhibited coolness or even antagonism toward the subject. *TRANSLATIONS:* Spanish, German, Dutch, Danish, French and Swedish.

CAN WE EVER BE FRIENDS?

Booklet published by the Church of Scientology of California, Worldwide, Saint Hill, England, 1977. Revised in 1989. TRANSLATIONS: French, German.

THE VOLUNTEER MINISTER BOOKLETS

Nine booklets published by Publications Organization, Los Angeles, California, 1977.

1. Communication
2. Understanding Others—Affinity, Reality, Communication
3. Do You Make Many Mistakes?
4. The Eight Dynamics
5. Assists
6. The Conditions of Existence
7. The Parts of Man
8. The Aims of Scientology
9. The Third Party Law

ISSUES

HCO PL 1 Jan RA Marketing Hat
Rev. 29 Aug 79 *Marketing Series 3*

HCOB 10 Jan I How to Win with Word Clearing
Word Clearing Series 55

HCOB 10 Jan II Ethics and Word Clearing
Word Clearing Series 50

HCOB 13 Jan RB Handling a False TA
Rev. 25 May 80

HCOB 21 Jan RB False TA Checklist
Rev. 25 May 80

HCOB 22 Jan In-Tech, The Only Way to Achieve It
Cramming Series 13
KSW Series 21

HCOB 24 Jan Tech Correction Roundup

HCOB 30 Jan R False TA Data
Rev. 25 May 80

HCOB 5 Feb Jokers and Degraders
C/S Series 100

HCOB 17 Feb R Course Necessities
Rev. 20 Feb 77

HCOB 24 Feb Expanded Dianetics Cases

HCOB 1 Mar II Confessional Forms

HCOB 1 Mar III Formulating Confessional Questions

HCOB 1 Mar IV A Valid Confessional

HCO PL 15 Mar RA Evaluation: The
Rev. 5 Nov 90 Situation
Data Series 41RA

HCOB 16 Mar The Gambler
ExDn Series 22

HCO PL 17 Mar RA Date Coincidence
Rev. 2 Nov 90 *Data Series 42RA*

HCO PL 18 Mar RA Evaluation and
Rev. 6 Nov 90 Programs
Data Series 43RA

HCO PL 18 Mar-1 R Evaluation Success
Rev. 14 Jun 77 *Data Series 43-1R*

HCO PL 20 Mar R Super Evaluation
Rev. 15 Jun 77 *Data Series 44R*

HCOB 27 Mar R Auditing the Pc at
Rev. 23 Apr 91 Cause
ExDn Series 23

HCOB 5 Apr Expanded Grades

HCO PL 10 Apr Dissemination Pieces, Stable Datum, Appearance, Layout and Design

HCOB 11 Apr List Errors, Correction Of

HCOB 17 Apr R Recurring Withholds
Rev. 16 Nov 89 and Overts

HCOB 7 May Long Duration Sec Checking

HCOB 9 May I Foreword of Expanded Dianetics Course

HCOB 9 May II Psychosis, More About
ExDn Series 24

HCOB 31 May LSD, Years After They Have "Come Off Of" LSD

HCOB 14 Jun RB Paid Completions
Rev. 11 Apr 91 Simplified

HCO PL 14 Jun RB I All Class IV Orgs,
Rev. 18 Jun 78 OIC Cable Change

HCO PL 14 Jun RA II All Sea Org Orgs,
Rev. 28 Jun 78 OIC Cable Change

HCOB 26 Sep R Art and
Rev. 30 Dec 79 Communication
Art Series 5

HCOB 4 Dec R Checklist for Setting
Rev. 19 Aug 87 Up Sessions and an E-Meter

The Secret of Flag Results

A film written by L. Ron Hubbard, produced by Universal Media Productions and released 9 December 1977.

1978

This was a landmark year for technical breakthroughs. In fact, in *Ron's Journal 30,* Mr. Hubbard called it The Year of Lightning Fast New Tech. Just a few of these spectacular new advances are listed below.

New Era Dianetics was released, a refinement of all previous Dianetics techniques combined with new developments to give much faster results and far higher gain per hour of auditing.

In September, a remarkable new OT level was released—an audited level called New Era Dianetics for OTs (New OT V).

The Sweat program, forerunner of the Purification program, gave new hope to those persistently troubled by the effects of drug residues in their bodies.

The advanced new Hubbard Professional Mark VI E-Meter was released in 1978, making possible much greater metering accuracy than ever before—and a resulting increase in pc wins and gains.

To give technical training a terrific boost in speed and accuracy, in 1978 LRH wrote scripts for three new technical training films and personally directed six such films. He also directed three new dissemination films to introduce people to Scientology and the Bridge to Total Freedom.

Issues

HCOB 6 Feb RD The Purification
Rev. 27 Mar 90 Rundown Replaces the Sweat Program
Purif RD Series 1R

HCO PL 23 Feb R Board of Review
Rev. 7 May 84 *LRH Comm N/W Series 19*

HCOB 26 Feb Internships Versus Courses

HCOB 19 Mar Quickie Objectives

HCOB 23 Mar RB Clearing Words
Rev. 16 Jan 89 *Word Clearing Series 59RB*

HCOB 27 Mar I Ethics Penalty for Word Clearers
Word Clearing Series 58

HCOB 3 Apr R TR Debug Assessment
Rev. 23 Dec 89

HCOB 26 May I Dianetics: Urgent Command Change

HCOB 2 Jun RC Cramming Repair
Rev. 18 Jun 88 Assessment List
Cramming Series 14

HCOB 2 Jun RC-1 Cramming Repair
Addition of 3 Jul 88 Assessment List Word List
Cramming Series 14-1

HCOB 15 Jun R "The Key to Expanded
Rev. 23 Apr 91 Dianetics . . ."
ExDn Series 25

HCOB 18 Jun R Assessment and How to
Rev. 20 Sep 78 Get the Item
NED Series 4R

HCOB 19 Jun Objective ARC
NED Series 3

HCOB 20 Jun Identity Rundown
NED Series 15

HCOB 21 Jun R New Era Dianetics
Rev. 8 Apr 88 *NED Series 1R*

HCOB 22 Jun RA New Era Dianetics
Rev. 8 Apr 88 Full Pc Program Outline
NED Series 2RA

HCOB 23 Jun RA Preclear Checklist
Rev. 8 Apr 88 *NED Series 16RA*

HCOB 24 Jun RA Original Assessment
Rev. 8 Apr 88 Sheet
NED Series 5RA

HCO PL 25 Jun Come-on Dissemination
Marketing Series 6

HCOB 26 Jun RA II Routine 3RA,
Rev. 15 Sep 78 Engram Running by Chains
NED Series 6RA

HCOB 28 Jun RA R3RA Commands
Rev. 15 Sep 78 *NED Series 7RA*

HCOB 29 Jun Disability Rundown
NED Series 14

HCOB 1 Jul The Dianetic Prepared Assessment Rundown Action Fifteen
NED Series 13

HCOB 2 Jul Dianetic Student Rescue Intensive
NED Series 11

HCOB 3 Jul R Relief Rundown
Rev. 22 Sep 78 *NED Series 10R*

HCOB 4 Jul R Second Original
Rev. 22 Sep 78 Assessment
NED Series 12R

HCOB 9 Jul RA Dianetic C/S-1
Rev. 8 Apr 88 *NED Series 21*

HCOB 11 Jul The Preassessment List
NED Series 4-1

HCOB 14 Jul R I Typical Dianetic Chain
Rev. 15 Sep 78 *NED Series 22*

HCOB 14 Jul R II A Typical Narrative
Rev. 15 Sep 78 Item
NED Series 23

HCOB 15 Jul RA Scientology Auditing
Rev. 10 Mar 84 C/S-1

HCOB 19 Jul Dianetic Persistent F/Ns
NED Series 17

HCOB 20 Jul After the Fact Items
NED Series 18

HCO PL 20 Jul Held From Above, Double-Hatting
Org Series 38

HCOB 21 Jul What Is a Floating Needle?

HCOB 22 Jul Assessment TRs

HCOB 23 Jul List of Perceptics
C/S Series 101

HCOB 24 Jul Dianetic Remedies
NED Series 24

HCO PL 24 Jul Subproducts, How to Compile a Subproduct List

HCOB 5 Aug Instant Reads

HCOB 7 Aug Havingness, Finding and Running the Pc's Havingness Process

HCOB 9 Aug I New Era Dianetics, A Requisite for Expanded Dianetics

HCOB 9 Aug II Clearing Commands
Word Clearing Series 52

HCOB 11 Aug I Rudiments, Definitions and Patter

HCOB 11 Aug II Model Session

HCO PL 15 Aug Chinese Schooling an Org Board

HCOB 21 Aug Running Flows That Won't Erase

HCOB 26 Aug R More on Drugs
Rev. 5 Oct 78

HCOB 3 Sep Definition of a Rock Slam

HCOB 5 Sep Anatomy of a Service Facsimile

HCOB 6 Sep I Following Up on Dirty Needles

HCOB 6 Sep II Service Facsimiles and Rock Slams

HCOB 6 Sep III Routine Three SC-A, Full Service Facsimile Handling Updated with New Era Dianetics

HCOB 7 Sep R Modern Repetitive
Rev. 21 Oct 78 Prepchecking

HCOB 8 Sep RB Mini List of Grade
Rev. 16 Nov 87 0–IV Processes

HCOB 10 Sep NED High Crime
NED Series 25

HCOB 12 Sep R I Dianetics Forbidden
Rev. 2 Dec 85 on Clears and OTs

HCOB 12 Sep II Overrun by Demanding Earlier Than There Is
NED Series 26

HCOB 13 Sep I R3RA Engram Running by Chains and Narrative R3RA—An Additional Difference
NED Series 27

HCOB 13 Sep II Clears, OTs and R/Ses

HCO PL 13 Sep "An Old Poem . . ."

HCO PL 15 Sep Confidentiality of Upper-Level Rundowns

HCOB 16 Sep Postulate Off Equals Erasure
NED Series 28

HCOB 19 Sep R I The End of Endless
Rev. 31 Jan 79 Drug RDs

HCOB 19 Sep R II The End of Endless
Rev. 31 Jan 79 Drug Rundowns Repair List

LRH ED 19 Sep AD 28, The Year of Technical Breakthroughs

New Era Dianetics for OTs (New OT V) Materials

This new, audited OT level was released 15 September 1978. The materials covering New OT V comprise over 60 HCOBs.

Issues

HCOB 20 Sep I An Instant F/N Is a Read

HCOB 20 Sep II LX List Handling

HCOB 20 Sep R III NED Auditor
Rev. 23 Apr 88 Analysis Checklist
NED Series 19R
C/S Series 103R

HCOB 24 Sep RB I The End of Endless
Rev. 4 Feb 89 Int Repair Rundown
Int RD Series 4RB

HCOB 24 Sep II Preassessment, AESPs and Int
Int RD Series 13

HCOB 24 Sep RC III Dianetic Clear
Rev. 18 Dec 88 *CCRD Series 1R*

HCOB 25 Sep R I Quad Commands for
Rev. 8 Apr 91 Int Buttons
Int RD Series 5R

HCOB 25 Sep R II Star-rate Checkouts
Rev. 4 Feb 89 for Interiorization Handling
Int RD Series 14R

HCO PL 27 Sep Examining Resources
Data Series 45

LRH ED 28 Sep The End of Endless Training

HCOB 3 Oct NED Rule
NED Series 29

HCOB 4 Oct Interiorization Handling Simplified
Int RD Series 1

HCOB 16 Oct I Repair Correction List

HCOB 16 Oct II C/S Checklist of Int Errors
Int RD Series 16
C/S Series 102

HCO PL 20 Oct Two-Bit FP
Finance Series 17

HCO PL 22 Oct Mistakes
Esto Series 44

HCOB 30 Oct R I Courses—Their Ideal
Rev. 3 Aug 83 Scene

HCOB 30 Oct R II C/S Series 53, Use Of
Rev. 26 Jul 86

HCO PL 8 Nov RB Senior HCOs Area
Rev. 5 Nov 79 and Continental

HCOB 10 Nov RA I Proclamation, Power
Rev. 26 Jul 86 to Forgive

HCO PL 10 Nov II "Power to Forgive" Certificate

HCOB 15 Nov Dating and Locating

HCOB 19 Nov L&N Lists—The Item "Me"

HCOB 27 Nov RB Word Clearing
Rev. 30 Apr 88 Correction List *Word Clearing Series 35RI*

HCOB 28 Nov Auditors Who Miss Withholds, Penalty

HCO PL 29 Nov How You Handle Demands for Personnel *Personnel Series 29* *AKH Series 37*

HCOB 30 Nov R Confessional Procedure
Rev. 10 Nov 87

HCOB 1 Dec RB Programing of
Rev. 18 Dec 88 Clears *C/S Series 113RA*

HCOB 3 Dec Unreading Flows

HCOB 4 Dec How to Read Through an F/N

HCOB 5 Dec RB Clear Data
Rev. 18 Dec 88 *C/S Series 105RB* *CCRD Series 4R*

HCOB 6 Dec Revivification

HCO PL 6 Dec Space Planning

HCOB 8 Dec R II Green Form and
Rev. 27 Jun 88 Expanded Green Form 40RF, Use Of

HCO PL 10 Dec RA Gross Book Sales—
Rev. 4 Feb 91 Definition

LRH ED 17 Dec Ron's Journal 30, 1978—The Year of Lightning Fast New Tech

HCO PL 28 Dec Use of *Big League Sales*

HCOB 29 Dec R The Suppressed Person
Rev. 20 Dec 83 Rundown, A Magical New Rundown

HCOB 30 Dec R Suppressed Person
Rev. 6 Jan 79 Rundown, Problems Processes

HCOB 31 Dec RA II Outline of PTS
Rev. 26 Jul 86 Handling

HCOB 31 Dec RA III Educating the
Rev. 21 Mar 89 Potential Trouble Source, The First Step Toward Handling: PTS C/S-1

1979

While supervising the training of a group of auditors selected to deliver a highly precise new auditing rundown, Mr. Hubbard found that many of them had difficulty with their TRs. In 1979 his search for the cause of this one outness and the means to terminatedly handle it led him to a series of discoveries that form the basis for the technology found today in the new Hubbard Professional TR Course, the Hubbard Key to Life Course and the Hubbard Life Orientation Course.

In December, LRH announced a new rundown designed to rid the body of harmful drug residuals and toxic substances. The successes from those who had participated in its piloting credited this new action with remarkable increases in their energy level, alertness, feeling of health and well-being and ability to think clearly. This new program, the Purification Rundown, is in use today throughout the world.

On the administrative front, 1979 saw the development of a powerful new technology for handling slowed or inadequate production: Debug Tech, consisting of a formidable battery of new technical tools including Crashing Misunderstood Word Finding, False Data Stripping, the Debug Tech Checklist and the Product Debug Repair List.

ISSUES

HCO PL 4 Jan The Ideal Ideal Scene *Data Series 46*

LRH ED 6 Jan Correction to Ron's Journal 30 Requirements for Super Power Auditors

HCO PL 6 Jan Financial Planning Regarding Property Renovations and Construction

HCOB 9 Jan BTB Cancellation

HCO PL 13 Jan Orders, Illegal and Cross

HCO PL 17 Jan A New Type of Crime

HCO PL 19 Jan RB I Scholarships, No
Rev. 30 May 89 Discounts

HCO PL 20 Jan Income Cutatives and Salary Sum

HCO PL 23 Jan Unevaluated Orders

HCOB 28 Jan C/S Qualifications

HCO PL 29 Jan Prices, Upper Org

HCO PL 30 Jan Positioning, Philosophic Theory *PR Series 30* *Marketing Series 5*

HCOB 31 Jan Mood Drills

HCOB 3 Feb R I Change the
Rev. 19 Dec 90 Civilization Eval

HCOB 3 Feb II Confront Tech Has to Be Part of the TR Checksheet

HCOB 7 Feb RA E-Meter Drill 5RB,
Rev. 10 Mar 88 Can Squeeze

HCO PL 7 Feb R The Basics of
Rev. 3 Sep 79 Marketing *Marketing Series 7*

HCOB 9 Feb R How to Defeat Verbal
Rev. 23 Aug 84 Tech Checklist *KSW Series 23R*

HCOB 15 Feb Verbal Tech: Penalties *KSW Series 24*

HCO PL 25 Feb R HCO Staff
Rev. 14 May 89 Qualification Requirements

HCOB 4 Mar R Art in Its Basics
Rev. 30 Dec 79 *Art Series 6*

HCOB 5 Mar RB Dianetic Clear False
Rev. 2 Dec 85 Declares

HCO PL 21 Mar R Sliding Scale of
Rev. 6 Dec 89 Pricing

HCO PL 25 Mar A New Hope for Justice

HCOB 26 Mar RB Misunderstood Words
Rev. 2 Sep 79 and Cycles of Action *Esto Series 35RB* *Word Clearing Series 60RB* *Product Debug Series 7R*

HCO PL 5 Apr I FSM Penalty for Refunds, Repayments and Bounced Checks

HCO PL 5 Apr RC II New FSM Account
Rev. 14 Feb 91 *FSM Series 6*

HCO PL 10 Apr RA Flag Rep Statistics
Rev. 12 Feb 91

HCOB 15 Apr Fine Arts Versus Illustrations *Art Series 7*

HCO PL 25 Apr Estates Production Statistics

HCO PL 1 May RB Clear Certainty
Rev. 18 Dec 88 Rundown: Administration *CCRD Series 3R*

HCO PL 27 May Book Sales Commission

HCO PL 7 Jun R I Data Series PLs,
Rev. 14 Jun 79 Use Of *Data Series 47*

HCOB 10 Jun A Professional *Art Series 8*

ARTICLE

FREEDOM Jun AMA . . . Up to Its Old Tricks

HUBBARD PROFESSIONAL MARK VI E-METER

The Mark VI E-Meter was released as the first OT meter. The Mark V proved not to be sensitive enough at upper levels—the Mark VI was more sensitive and it also had a newly designed meter movement.

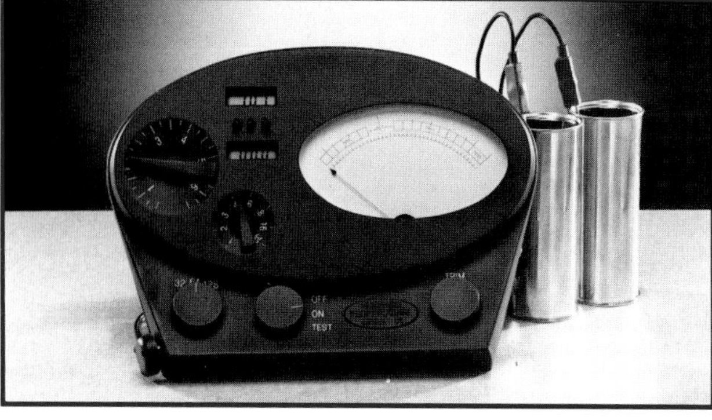

ISSUES

HCOB 17 Jun Crashing Mis-Us: The Key to Completed Cycles of Action and Products
Word Clearing Series 61
Product Debug Series 3

HCOB 18 Jun R The Crashing Mis-U
Rev. 27 Jun 88 Repair List—LC1R
Product Debug Series 4R
Word Clearing Series 62R

HCO PL 24 Jun Crime Additions

HCOB 7 Jul Crashing Mis-U Definition

HCO PL 10 Jul R I Publications
Rev. 26 Nov 79 Organizations Are Sales Organizations

HCO PL 16 Jul I Hubbard Key to Life Course High Crime

HCO PL 16 Jul II Delivering the Hubbard Key to Life Course, The Chicken and Egg Theory

HCOB 16 Jul The "Elusive" Mis-U or Crashing Mis-U
Word Clearing Series 63
Product Debug Series 5

HCOB 17 Jul RB I The Misunderstood
Rev. 26 Feb 89 Word Defined
Word Clearing Series 64RB

HCO PL 21 Jul Magazine Planning

HCO PL 25 Jul Magazine Motifs

THE TECHNICAL BULLETINS OF DIANETICS AND SCIENTOLOGY VOLUME XI, 1976–1978

Compilation of L. Ron Hubbard's technical bulletins on Dianetics and Scientology. Published by Publications Department Advanced Org/Saint Hill Denmark and Publications Organization US, Los Angeles, California, August 1979. Revised in 1991.

ISSUES

HCOB 7 Aug False Data Stripping
Product Debug Series 8
Esto Series 36

HCO PL 9 Aug I Call-in: The Key to Delivery and Future Income

HCO PL 9 Aug R II Service Product
Rev. 19 Nov 79 Officer
Org Series 39
Esto Series 39

HCO PL 9 Aug III Service Call-in Committee

HCOB 19 Aug RA High-Crime
Rev. 27 Aug 84 Checkouts and Word Clearing
Word Clearing Series 47

HCO PL 20 Aug Dianetics and Scientology Are New
Marketing Series 1
PR Series 34

HCOB 21 Aug Twinning

HCOB 23 Aug I Crashing Mis-Us, Blocks to Finding Them
Word Clearing Series 65
Product Debug Series 6

HCOB 23 Aug R II Product Debug
Rev. 14 Jun 88 Repair List
Product Debug Series 10R

HCOB 23 Aug R III Debug Tech
Rev. 23 Aug 84 *Product Debug Series 1R*
Esto Series 37R

HCO PL 23 Aug R II Debug Tech
Rev. 24 Jun 88 Checklist
Esto Series 38R
Product Debug Series 2R

HCO PL 23 Aug III Hubbard Key to Life Course Routing Forms

HCO PL 29 Aug R I Org Board for the
Rev. 14 Mar 80 Department of the Chaplain

HCO PL 29 Aug R II The Department of
Rev. 14 Mar 80 the Chaplain

HCO PL 1 Sep Marketing, Promotion and Dissemination, Defined
Marketing Series 2

HCO PL 2 Sep Surveys Are the Key to Stats
Marketing Series 4

HCO PL 4 Sep More on Marketing Basics
Marketing Series 8

HCO PL 5 Sep The Assembly Line for Produced Promo
Marketing Series 9

HCO PL 6 Sep The Relationship Between Design and Rough Layout
Marketing Series 10

HCO PL 19 Sep Promotion
Marketing Series 11

HCOB 24 Sep RA Flying Ruds in
Rev. 18 Oct 86 Cramming
Cramming Series 15

HCOB 25 Sep RB Method One Word
Rev. 1 Jul 85 Clearing
Word Clearing Series 34

HCO PL 26 Sep I FSM I/C Postings

HCO PL 26 Sep III Copywriting
Marketing Series 12

HCO PL 27 Sep Ads and Copywriting
Marketing Series 13

HCO PL 28 Sep RA XII Special Income
Rev. 2 Feb 91 *Finance Series 24RA*

HCOB 13 Oct Conceptual Understanding
Word Clearing Series 66

HCO PL 18 Oct R Viewpoint
Rev. 14 Sep 88 *Marketing Series 14R*

HCO PL 29 Oct SSO Responsibility for Standard Staff Courses

HCO PL 9 Nov R How to Correctly
Rev. 27 Aug 82 Determine a Stat Trend

HCO PL 13 Nov R I FSM Section,
Rev. 6 Feb 80 Department 18 Statistics

HCO PL 13 Nov R II Use of Airmail and
Rev. 7 Jul 83 Air Freight

LRH ED 1 Dec Ron's Journal 31, 1980—The Year of Expansion

HCO PL 1 Dec Survey Buttons Are Not the Message
Marketing Series 15

HCO PL 11 Dec I Department 17 Course Checksheets

HCO PL 11 Dec II Department 17 Course Checksheets, Addition

HCO PL 12 Dec R An Open Letter to
Rev. 8 Nov 84 All FSMs
FSM Series 7

HCO PL 13 Dec R Magazines, Dating
Rev. 16 Jan 80 Forbidden

HCO PL 15 Dec Surveying for Department 17 Services

HCO PL 18 Dec Enrollment on the Hubbard Key to Life Course

HCOB 21 Dec R Auditor Assignment
Rev. 30 Jul 90 Policies, Cramming Assignment Policies
C/S Series 107R
Cramming Series 16

HCO PL 23 Dec RB Tech/Admin Ratio
Rev. 25 Mar 89

HCOB 24 Dec R TRs Basics Resurrected
Rev. 19 Jun 86

HCO PL 26 Dec Execution of Evaluations
Data Series 48

HCO PL 30 Dec R Technical Training
Rev. 13 Feb 80 Corps

HCOB 30 Dec How to Build a Sauna
Purif RD Series 2

SCIENTOLOGY GROUP AUDITOR'S HANDBOOK VOLUMES I AND II

Compiled by staff and published by Publications Organization US, Los Angeles, California.

1980

Following on the release of the Purification Rundown in December of 1979, the new Scientology Drug Rundown was announced, using Scientology auditing techniques to relieve the mental and spiritual ravages of drugs. Another new OT level—the OT Drug Rundown (New OT IV)—was also released in January 1980.

The first of the *Research and Discovery Series* volumes was released in June. Containing transcriptions of Mr. Hubbard's thousands of technical lectures, arranged chronologically and projected to fill approximately 100 encyclopedia-sized books, this monumental set represents the complete running record of his research into the subject of the mind and life.

Two brand-new OT levels were released in September: the Hubbard Solo New Era Dianetics for OTs Course (New OT VI), which gives a person the technology he needs to audit himself on the next level, and new OT VII, Solo New Era Dianetics for OTs.

ISSUES

HCOB 3 Jan RA Purification Rundown
Rev. 8 Aug 83 and Atomic War
Purif RD Series 3

HCO PL 8 Jan Christmas Bonuses for Staff

HCO PL 9 Jan Departmental Mini Programs: The Key to Achievement
Exec Series 20

HCOB 12 Jan "To Do a Montage . . ."
Art Series 9

HCO PL 13 Jan Division 2/Division 6 Registrar Publics

HCO PL 25 Jan Executive Responsibility for Technical Excellence
KSW Series 11

HCO PL 27 Jan I Academies, Internships and Grade Auditing

HCO PL 27 Jan II Rudiments (ARC Break) Program

OT DRUG RUNDOWN (NEW OT IV) MATERIALS

The HCOBs describing how to run this new level were released on 29 January 1980 to auditors who had done all of the prerequisites.

ISSUES

HCOB 11 Feb R Illegal Pcs, Acceptance
Rev. 18 Oct 86 Of, Addition Regarding Purification Rundown
Purif RD Series 12

HCO PL 11 Feb II Org "Move" Mags

HCO PL 11 Feb III Org Magazines: Policy and Format

HCO PL 13 Feb Coordination Committees and Management Committees, Differences in Purpose and Function
AKH Series 40

HCO PL 14 Feb Order Versus Disorder
Org Series 40
Esto Series 40
Product Debug Series 9

HCOB 14 Feb R Research Data on
Rev. 13 Jul 85 Nutritional Vitamin Increases on the Purification Rundown
Purif RD Series 4

HCO PL 28 Feb Production and One's Standard of Living
Exec Series 21
Org Series 41
Finance Series 25

HCOB 29 Feb The Purification Rundown: Pregnancy and Breast-Feeding
Purif RD Series 6

HCOB 7 Mar Diets, Comments Upon

HCOB 13 Mar RA Conditional Step
Rev. 26 Jul 86 After the Purification Rundown
C/S Series 109RA
Purif RD Series 11

HCOB 5 Apr Q&A, the Real Definition

HCOB 10 Apr Auditor Beingness

HCO PL 18 Apr *The Auditor* Magazine: Policy and Format

HCOB 21 Apr R Pc Examiner
Rev. 18 Oct 86

HCOB 22 Apr R Assessment Drills
Rev. 26 Jul 86

HCOB 29 Apr R Prepared Lists, Their
Rev. 26 Jul 86 Value and Purpose

HCOB 3 May Pc Indicators

HCOB 12 May Drugs and Objective Processes

HCOB 18 May R Start-Change-Stop
Rev. 26 Jul 86 Commands

HCOB 21 May Purification Rundown Case Data
Purif RD Series 5

HCO PL 22 May R I Recruitment
Rev. 9 Feb 89 Breakthrough

HCOB 28 May RA Co-audit Defined
Rev. 20 Apr 90 *Co-audit Series 1RA*

HCOB 29 May RA Co-audits: How to
Rev. 20 Apr 90 Run Them
Co-audit Series 2RA

HCOB 30 May RA Supervising
Rev. 21 Apr 90 Co-audit TRs
Co-audit Series 3RA

HCOB 31 May RA Staff Co-audits
Rev. 21 Apr 90 *Co-audit Series 4RA*

Research and Discovery Series, Volume 1

Compiled from the taped lectures of L. Ron Hubbard from June of 1950. Published by Scientology Publications Organization, Copenhagen, and Publications Organization US, Los Angeles, California.

Issues

HCOB 19 Jun The Auditor's Code

HCOB 20 Jun L1C Word List

HCOB 22 Jun Int RD Correction List Words

HCOB 23 Jun RA I Checking Questions
Rev. 25 Oct 83 on Grades Processes

HCOB 23 Jun RA II Word Clearing
Rev. 26 Jul 86 Correction List Words

HCOB 28 Jun RA Student Correction
Rev. 18 Oct 86 List Words

HCOB 30 Jun RA Student Rehabilitation
Rev. 26 May 88 List Words

HCO PL 9 Jul R Ethics, Justice and the
Rev. 25 Mar 89 Dynamics

HCOB 12 Jul R The Basics of Ethics
Rev. 5 Nov 82

HCOB 23 Jul R Confessional Repair
Rev. 26 Jul 86 List—LCRE

HCOB 25 Jul RA Course Supervisor
Rev. 12 Jul 88 Correction List Word List

HCOB 29 Jul Criminals and Psychiatry

HCOB 30 Jul The Nature of a Being

The Technical Bulletins of Dianetics and Scientology Volume XII, 1978–1979

Compilation of L. Ron Hubbard's technical bulletins on Dianetics and Scientology. Published by Scientology Publications Organization, Copenhagen and Publications Organization US, Los Angeles, California, August 1980. Revised in 1991.

Issue

HCOB 2 Sep Repair Correction List Words

Hubbard Solo New Era Dianetics for OTs Auditor Course (New OT VI) and Solo New Era Dianetics for OTs (New OT VII)

These two new OT levels were released on 10 September 1980. Their written materials consist of 14 HCOBs.

Issues

HCOB 11 Sep L4BRB Word List

HCOB 16 Sep R PTS RD Correction List
Rev. 4 Jul 88 Word List

HCOB 17 Sep R I L3RH Word List
Rev. 8 Apr 88 *NED Series 20-1*

HCOB 17 Sep RA II Green Form Word
Rev. 28 Jun 90 List

HCOB 28 Sep R III Confessional Repair
Rev. 26 Jul 86 List—LCRE Words List

HCOB 6 Oct I General Staff Confessional List
Confessional Form 2R

HCOB 6 Oct II Supervisor Confessional List
Confessional Form 4R

HCO PL 15 Oct R Celebrity Centre
Rev. 4 Feb 91 Magazine, *Celebrity*

HCOB 23 Oct R Chart of Abilities
Rev. 16 Nov 87 Gained for Lower Levels and Expanded Lower Grades

HCOB 4 Nov I PRD Confessional List
Confessional Form 10RA

HCOB 5 Nov Returning Tours Confessional
Confessional Form 9RA

HCOB 8 Nov R C/S Series 53RM Long
Rev. 26 Jul 86 Form Word List

HCOB 12 Nov R I Case Supervisor
Rev. 12 Jul 88 Correction List

HCOB 12 Nov II Registrar and Sales Personnel Confessional List
Confessional Form 6RA

HCOB 18 Nov R I Auditor Correction
Rev. 12 Jul 88 List, Auditor Recovery Word List

HCOB 18 Nov R II Case Supervisor
Rev. 12 Jul 88 Correction List Word List

HCOB 23 Nov Case Supervisor Confessional
Confessional Form 8RA

HCOB 2 Dec Floating Needle and TA Position Modified

HCOB 19 Dec R Rehab Tech
Rev. 16 Nov 87

HCOB 21 Dec RA The Scientology Drug
Rev. 23 Apr 91 Rundown

HCOB 23 Dec R I Executive Correction
Rev. 12 Jul 88 List

HCOB 23 Dec R II Executive Correction
Rev. 12 Jul 88 List Word List

HCOB 25 Dec I LRH Communicator Confessional List
Confessional Form 12R

HCOB 25 Dec II Flag Rep Confessional List
Confessional Form 11R

The Learning Book

Compiled from the works of L. Ron Hubbard by the faculty of the Delphian School. Published by Heron Books. *Translations:* Chinese, Danish, Dutch, Finnish, French, German, Italian, Japanese, Portuguese, Russian, Spanish and Swedish.

"The Problem of Life" Music

Ten musical compositions from the music for the film, "The Problem of Life," composed by L. Ron Hubbard.

1981

Observing the decay of moral values in society, in 1981 Mr. Hubbard wrote *The Way to Happiness*—a common-sense guide to help people live happier lives. His intention was that the book be passed on from person to person in a grass-roots movement that would reverse the downward spiral of declining morality. Shortly after *The Way to Happiness* made its appearance, LRH also announced a new auditing rundown; called the Happiness Rundown, its purpose was to help remove barriers an individual might encounter in following the moral precepts *The Way to Happiness* book contains.

1981 was marked by dramatic changes in the Classification and Gradation Chart. First, the routes onto the Bridge were clarified and opened wide. The lower levels of auditing and training were also streamlined, making possible much smoother and faster progress upward. And a brand-new rundown was released for those who had just achieved the state of Clear: the Sunshine Rundown.

Issues

HCO PL 5 Jan RA Extension Courses
Rev. 13 Feb 91

HCO PL 8 Jan R Advanced Course
Rev. 3 Oct 88 Regulations and Security

HCO PL 22 Jan Orders of the Day

HCOB 29 Jan RA I FES Checklists and
Rev. 9 Apr 91 Summary
Auditor Admin Series 24RB

HCOB 29 Jan II HC Outpoint–Pluspoint Lists RB Words List

HCOB 13 Feb R Dictionaries
Rev. 25 Jul 87 *Word Clearing Series 67R*

HCOB 26 Mar R II Expanded Green
Rev. 4 Jul 88 Form 40RF Word List

HCOB 31 Mar R "Heavy Drug History"
Rev. 25 Apr 90 Defined

HCOB 1 Apr R II Interviews
Rev. 17 Jan 91

HCO PL 5 Apr RA Clear Certificates
Rev. 18 Dec 88 *CCRD Series 16R*

HCOB 10 Apr R Reach and Withdraw
Rev. 7 Aug 83

HCOB 4 May RA Study Green Form
Rev. 27 Jun 88 *Study Series 10RA*

HCOB 5 May R Study Green Form
Rev. 4 Jul 88 Word List

HCO PL 21 Jul R I What Is a Checksheet
Rev. 25 Jul 87

HCO PL 23 Jul R I The Use of
Rev. 10 Jan 84 Demonstration
Study Series 12

HCOB 23 Jul Pregnancy and Auditing

HCOB 29 Jul R Full Assist Checklists
Rev. 13 Apr 91 for Injuries and Illnesses

HCO PL 4 Aug R Pink Sheets
Rev. 30 Aug 83

HCO PL 9 Sep How to "Sell" Scientology to Your Friends
FSM Series 8

HCOB 15 Sep The Criminal Mind

HCO PL 20 Sep Dianetics and Scientology Redefined

HCOB 6 Oct Tech Films and Verbal Tech

HCOB 7 Oct R Method 3 Word Clearing
Rev. 30 Aug 83 *Word Clearing Series 31RD*

HCOB 8 Oct R III Word Clearing Method 2
Rev. 16 Jan 89 *Word Clearing Series 6RB*
Tape Course Series 9RA

HCO PL 20 Oct R PTS Type A Handling
Rev. 10 Sep 83

HCO PL 8 Nov RA Who May See Technical Training Films
Rev. 10 Nov 83

HCO PL 11 Nov R Policies on Film Usage
Rev. 30 Jan 91

HCOB 12 Nov RD Grade Chart Streamlined for Lower Grades
Rev. 20 Apr 90

HCOB 13 Nov What Tone 40 Is

HCOB 15 Nov R The Sunshine Rundown
Rev. 18 Dec 88

HCOB 29 Nov Dianetics and Scientology Compared to Nineteenth Century Practices

HCOB 5 Dec R Setting Up and Using a Reel-to-Reel Tape Player
Rev. 7 Oct 84 *Tape Course Series 7R*

HCOB 12 Dec The Theory of the New Grade Chart

HCOB 14 Dec The State of Clear

HCOB 15 Dec New Grade Chart Pc/Pre-OT Programing

HCOB 17 Dec Post Purpose Clearing Revived

HCOB 26 Dec Post Purpose Clearing for Management Teams and Executives

Holidays 81/82 Ron's Journal 33

THE WAY TO HAPPINESS
by L. Ron Hubbard

Paperback booklet; packets of 12 booklets each. Published by Regent House Publishers, Los Angeles, California. New paperback, hardback and leatherbound editions released in 1984 by Bridge Publications, Inc. *TRANSLATIONS:* Afrikaans, Arabic, Chinese, Danish, Dutch, Finnish, French, German, Greek, Hebrew, Italian, Japanese, Norwegian, Portuguese, Russian, Spanish and Swedish.

BASIC DICTIONARY OF DIANETICS AND SCIENTOLOGY
Based on the works of L. Ron Hubbard

Published by Scientology Publications Organization, Copenhagen, and Publications US, Los Angeles, California. *TRANSLATIONS:* Dutch, French, German, Italian, Japanese and Swedish.

RESEARCH AND DISCOVERY SERIES, VOLUME 2

Compiled from the taped lectures of L. Ron Hubbard, July–August 1950. Published by Scientology Publications Organization, Copenhagen, and Publications Organization US, Los Angeles, California.

1982

1982 saw the beginning of the computerization of Scientology management, using Mr. Hubbard's phenomenal breakthroughs in the application of computer technology. With new ideas for computer utilization far beyond the scope of the time, computers were being used to the utmost to help forward Scientology's efforts to improve conditions worldwide.

New advances were also made in the areas of Confessionals, E-Metering, study technology, auditing repair and case supervision, marketing, finance, management and ethics technology, with each new development made the subject of an HCO Bulletin or Policy Letter.

ISSUES

HCO PL 17 Jan What Is an Executive?
Exec Series 22

HCOB 19 Jan II High School Indoctrination

HCO PL 1 Feb Stature

HCO PL 5 Feb I Out-Ethics Symptoms

HCO PL 5 Feb II Books and Marketing
PR Series 44
Marketing Series 16

HCOB 15 Feb Freedom of Speech

HCOB 17 Feb Prejudice

HCO PL 18 Feb Changing Workable Finance Systems
Finance Series 27

HCOB 20 Feb Overts

HCO PL 24 Feb Economic Systems

HCO PL 28 Feb I News

HCO PL 28 Feb R III HCO Book Account Cash-Bills
Rev. 4 Feb 91

HCO PL 3 Mar The Qual Library

HCO PL 6 Mar R Confessional Tech Policies
Rev. 10 Dec 88

HCOB 8 Mar R Confessionals and the Non-Interference Zone
Rev. 24 Apr 83

HCO PL 9 Mar RB Eligibility for OT Levels
Rev. 6 Jan 85

HCOB 10 Mar Confessionals—Ethics Reports Required

HCO PL 11 Mar Proportionate Marketing
Finance Series 30
Marketing Series 17

RON'S JOURNAL 34 13 Mar The Future of Scientology

HCO PL 14 Mar Financial Irregularities

HCO PL 17 Mar FBO FP Adjudication
Finance Series 28

HCO PL 19 Mar Executive Success
Exec Series 23
Finance Series 31
Marketing Series 19

UNDERSTANDING THE E-METER

Compiled from the works of L. Ron Hubbard. Published by Bridge Publications, Los Angeles, California. Revised in 1988.

ISSUES

HCOB 20 Mar R Standards
Rev. 12 Apr 88

HCO PL 23 Mar R A Refined Definition of PR
Rev. 16 Sep 88 *PR Series 28RA*

HCOB 25 Mar R Objectives Not Biting
Rev. 16 Apr 90

HCO PL 29 Mar Personnel Policy
Personnel Series 30

HCOB 31 Mar R Basic Study Missed Withhold
Rev. 29 Dec 88 *Study Series 11R*
Word Clearing Series 68R

HCO PL 1 Apr The Safe Point
PR Series 19R

HCO PL 7 Apr Out-Ethics Indicators
LRH Comm N/W Series 16

HCOB 11 Apr Sec Checking Implants

HCOB 13 Apr Still Needle and Confessionals

HCO PL 15 Apr II The Counting of Gross Income
Finance Series 29

HCOB 16 Apr More on PTS Handling

HCOB 26 Apr The Criminal Mind and the Psychs

HCO PL 28 Apr The Rights of the Field Auditor

HCO PL 29 Apr II Field Auditor Fees

LRH ED 4 May Books Straight Talk

HCOB 6 May The Cause of Crime

HCO PL 9 May Books Are Assets
Finance Series 32

LRH ED 9 May Ron's Journal 35, From Clear to Eternity

HCOB 10 May OT Levels

HCO PL 10 May Bookstore Officer Hat

LRH ED 10 May R The Ridge on the Bridge
Rev. 21 Oct 82

HCO PL 25 May Kha-Khan

HCO PL 1 Jul Management Coordination
AKH Series 41

HCOB 11 Jul I Questionable Auditing Repair List

HCOB 11 Jul II Questionable Auditing

HCO PL 16 Jul R Fully Hatted Org Staff Members, HCO Gross Divisional Statistic
Rev. 30 May 89

HCO PL 19 Jul Failed PR
PR Series 45

HCO PL 22 Jul Knowledge Reports

HCO PL 27 Jul RA Deputy FBOs for Marketing of Org Resources for Exchange (D/FBO for MORE)
Rev. 2 Feb 91 *Finance Series 33RA*

HCOB 10 Aug OT Maxims

HCO PL 18 Aug R I Targets and Production
Rev. 28 Feb 84 *Target Series 8*
Computer Series 3
AKH Series 42R

HCO PL 18 Aug II Computers—Danger of Relying On
Computer Series 7

HCO PL 20 Aug Organizational Basics

HCO PL 22 Aug Battle Plans
Target Series 9
AKH Series 43

HCOB 25 Aug The Joy of Creating
Art Series 10

HCOB 26 Aug Pain and Sex

HCO PL 27 Aug Vital Data: Power and Affluence Conditions

HCO PL 2 Sep And That Is Banking
Finance Series 34

HCO PL 3 Sep Deputy FBO for Marketing of Org Resources for Exchange (D/FBO for MORE) Purpose
Finance Series 35

HCO PL 10 Sep Exchange, Org Income and Staff Pay
Finance Series 36

HCO PL 12 Sep PR Functions
PR Series 46

HCO PL 28 Sep The Basics of Statistics and Management

HCOB 28 Sep Mixing Rundowns and Repairs
C/S Series 115

HCO PL 29 Sep Misrepresentation of Dianetics and Scientology
KSW Series 30

HCO PL 12 Oct Corrupt Activities

HCOB 13 Oct Ethics and the C/S
C/S Series 116

HCO PL 14 Oct Why Things Are Evaluated
Data Series 49

HCO PL 27 Oct RA Cash-Bills Defined
Rev. 23 Sep 89 *Finance Series 38RA*

HCO PL 31 Oct Financial Planning—Responsibility For
Finance Series 39

HCO PL 1 Nov "Boom Formula" Cancelled

HCO PL 2 Nov Conditions Handlings

HCO PL 16 Nov Div 6A Stat Renamed and Redefined: Bodies in the Shop

BRONZE BUST OF L. RON HUBBARD

Large bust of L. Ron Hubbard for display on pedestal

CAR BADGE

Scientology symbol for use on cars

SOLO WINGS

Gold pin in the form of wings around a Scientology symbol for Solo auditors

HCO PL 30 Nov The Deputy CO or Deputy ED for Delivery and Exchange
HCO PL 18 Dec Ethics Conditions: Hang-up at Doubt
HCO PL 19 Dec I "Doing a Quicksilver" Forbidden *Org Series 45* *Personnel Series 31*
HCO PL 19 Dec R II Rev. 2 Jun 90 Repairing Past Ethics Conditions
HCO PL 22 Dec RB Rev. 15 Aug 90 Service Routes for New Public
HCO PL 24 Dec R Rev. 19 Feb 91 Service Routes into SO Orgs
HCOB 27 Dec Training and OT
HCO PL 29 Dec R I Rev. 21 Feb 91 Service Routes into the FSO
HCO PL 29 Dec RA II Rev. 21 Jan 91 The Tools of Management *Esto Series 45RA* *Org Series 46RA* *AKH Series 44RA* *Exec Series 24RA*

INTRODUCTORY AND DEMONSTRATION PROCESSES AND ASSISTS

Based on the works of L. Ron Hubbard. Published by Bridge Publications, Los Angeles, California.

RESEARCH AND DISCOVERY SERIES, VOLUME 3

Compiled from the taped lectures of L. Ron Hubbard, August–September 1950. Published by Bridge Publications, Los Angeles, California.

RESEARCH AND DISCOVERY SERIES, VOLUME 4

Compiled from the taped lectures of L. Ron Hubbard, September–November 1950. Published by Bridge Publications, Los Angeles, California.

RON'S JOURNAL 36: "YOUR NEW YEAR"

Powerful tape-recorded New Year's message from L. Ron Hubbard released on December 31, 1982, urging Scientologists to move up the Bridge.

1983

Among the new technical releases of 1983 was a vital new auditor training course, the Professional TR Course—featuring Mr. Hubbard's technical training film, "The Professional TR Course" and his latest TR training breakthroughs.

Mr. Hubbard also published new bulletins and policy letters on ethics technology, case supervision, Word Clearing, Confessionals, management, public relations and finance.

ISSUES

HCO PL 5 Jan Strategic Planning *AKH Series 46*
HCO PL 9 Jan R I Rev. 2 Feb 91 Viability, the Make-Break Point of an Org *Finance Series 41R*
HCO PL 9 Jan II Checklist for a Strategic Plan *AKH Series 47*
HCO PL 13 Jan The Business of Orgs
HCO PL 23 Jan Auditor Training Prerequisite
HCO PL 30 Jan Your Post and Life *Esto Series 46* *KSW Series 28*
HCO PL 31 Jan The Reason for Orgs
HCOB 8 Mar Handling PTS Situations
HCO PL 7 Apr Goodwill *Exec Series 25* *PR Series 47*
HCOB 12 Apr List of Keeping Scientology Working Series
HCOB 3 May Who or What Is a "C/S"? *C/S Series 117*
HCO PL 13 Jun R Rev. 17 Jan 91 Addition to HCO Gross Divisional Statistic, Fully Hatted Org Staff Members
HCO PL 31 Jul R I Rev. 21 Jan 91 Basic Management Tools *Esto Series 47R* *Org Series 47R* *Exec Series 26R* *AKH Series 48R*
HCO PL 31 Jul II Management Tools Breakthrough *Esto Series 48* *Org Series 48* *Exec Series 27* *AKH Series 49*
HCO PL 4 Aug R Rev. 2 Feb 91 Financial Planning Program No. 1 *Finance Series 42R*
HCO PL 6 Aug R Rev. 24 Dec 89 What a Professional TR Course Must Consist Of
HCOB 7 Aug Robotic TRs
HCOB 8 Aug Cycling Through TRs on a Professional TR Course
HCOB 19 Aug OT III Course Posh-Up
HCOB 27 Aug Words and Associations *Word Clearing Series 69*
HCO PL 28 Aug Spot Checks
HCOB 10 Sep PTSness and Disconnection

The Professional TR Course

Directed and narrated by L. Ron Hubbard, this film shows why TRs are vital in auditing and depicts all aspects of professional TR training. The TRs themselves are covered in detail, portraying exactly how each is done. TRANSLATIONS: German, Spanish, Italian, French, Norwegian, Portuguese, Danish, Dutch, Hebrew, Swedish and Japanese.

ISSUES

HCO PL 15 Sep LRH Comm and PRO *LRH Comm N/W Series 17*
HCO PL 2 Oct Solo Course Part One, Prerequisites
HCOB 23 Oct Sec Checking: Note
HCO PL 10 Nov TR and EM Films, Showing Of

MANAGEMENT SERIES VOLUMES 1 AND 2
by L. Ron Hubbard

Updated edition of the Management Series *volumes. Staff compiled and published by Bridge Publications, Los Angeles, California.*

RESEARCH AND DISCOVERY SERIES, VOLUME 5

Compiled from the taped lectures of L. Ron Hubbard, November 1950–May 1951. Published by Bridge Publications, Los Angeles, California.

THE ORIGINAL L. RON HUBBARD EXECUTIVE DIRECTIVES
by L. Ron Hubbard

Two-volume reprinting of all the LRH Executive Directives. Series 1—15 September 1966 to 28 April 1968, Series 2—10 May 1968 to 9 March 1969, Series 3—20 January 1969 to 13 March 1983. Published by Bridge Publications, Los Angeles, California.

THE PROFESSIONAL TR COURSE MOTION PICTURE SOUNDTRACK

Nineteen musical themes from the Professional TR Course film, composed by L. Ron Hubbard. Produced by Golden Era Productions.

RON'S JOURNAL 38, TODAY AND TOMORROW: THE PROOF

One-hour-long cassette from L. Ron Hubbard giving news of unprecedented expansion of the Church. Produced in Clearsound by Golden Era Productions.

1984

In addition to the many technical and administrative advances made in 1984, it was during this year that Mr. Hubbard's research in the field of sound culminated in the

development of Clearsound technology. This revolutionary tech made it possible to produce sound recordings and reproductions of unsurpassed clarity—a great step forward for musicians and cine professionals, invaluable in preserving and reproducing LRH's thousands of recorded lectures.

ISSUES

HCOB 3 Jan III Radiation and Liquids *Purif RD Series 7*

HCOB 10 Jan The Use of Demonstration *Study Series 12*

HCOB 16 Jan RA I The Happiness Rev. 27 Jun 89 Rundown *HRD Series 1RA*

HCOB 16 Jan II Repair of Past Cramming *Cramming Series 17*

HCOB 17 Jan Happiness Rundown Basics *HRD Series 2*

HCOB 18 Jan How to Audit the HRD *HRD Series 3*

HCOB 19 Jan Happiness Rundown Command Sheets *HRD Series 4*

HCOB 20 Jan HRD Precepts Assessment List *HRD Series 4-1*

HCOB 21 Jan R I Happiness Rundown Rev. 20 Jul 88 Repair List (HRL) *HRD Series 5R*

HCOB 21 Jan RA II C/Sing the Rev. 27 Jun 89 Happiness Rundown *HRD Series 6RA*

HCOB 21 Jan R III Delivery of the Rev. 20 Jul 88 Happiness Rundown to Clears and OTs *HRD Series 7R*

HCOB 23 Jan Drug Rundowns and Radiation

HCOB 27 Jan FSM Breakthrough, New FSM TRs—Controlling a Conversation

HCOB 1 Feb How to View Art *Art Series 11*

HCO PL 16 Feb What Is a Computer? *Computer Series 1*

HCOB 25 Feb Depth Perspective *Art Series 13*

HCOB 26 Feb I Color *Art Series 14*

HCOB 26 Feb II Art and Integration *Art Series 15*

HCOB 28 Feb Pretended PTS *C/S Series 118*

HCO PL 29 Feb Computer Ethics Points *Computer Series 6*

HCOB 2 Mar R O/W Write-Ups Rev. 24 Apr 90

HCOB 10 Mar I Message *Art Series 16*

HCOB 10 Mar II Oils Can Go Rancid *Purif RD Series 8*

HCO PL 20 Mar Targets, More About *Target Series 7*

HCO PL 27 Mar Three Classes of People *Esto Series 49*

HCOB 27 Mar Stalled Dianetic Clear: Solved *C/S Series 119*

HCO PL 28 Mar I The Stages of Analysis *Data Series 50*

HCO PL 28 Mar II Executive Posting Qualifications *Personnel Series 32* *Exec Series 28*

HCO PL 2 Apr "Upside Down" Graphs

HCO PL 6 May ARC Break Program, Additional Data

HCO PL 7 May The LRH Comm Network and Its Purpose *LRH Comm N/W Series 1*

HCOB 5 Jun R False Purpose Rundown Rev. 11 Jan 90 *FPRD Series 1R*

HCOB 6 Jun I Rock Slams, More About

HCOB 6 Jun II "Murder Routine"

HCOB 6 Jun III Missed Withhold Handling

HCOB 6 Jun R IV The "Lost Tech" of Rev. 12 Jan 90 Handling Overts and Evil Purposes *FPRD Series 2R*

HCOB 7 Jun The Prior Confusion: New Tech Breakthrough *FPRD Series 3*

HCOB 8 Jun Clearing Justifications *FPRD Series 4*

HCOB 9 Jun R Auditing the False Rev. 3 May 85 Purpose Rundown *FPRD Series 5R*

HCOB 10 Jun False Purpose Rundown Commands *FPRD Series 6*

HCOB 11 Jun C/Sing the False Purpose Rundown *FPRD Series 7*

HCOB 12 Jun False Purpose Rundown Auditor Errors *FPRD Series 8*

HCOB 13 Jun R False Purpose Rundown Rev. 1 Aug 90 Correction List *FPRD Series 9R*

HCOB 14 Jun False Purpose Rundown Basic Form *FPRD Series 10-A*

HCOB 15 Jun II False Purpose Rundown, Info for Orgs and Missions

HCOB 17 Jun Evil Purposes and False PR *C/S Series 118-1*

HCO PL 2 Jul Hatting and the Environment *Esto Series 50* *Exec Series 29*

HCO PL 8 Aug II Routing Forms, How to Write One

HCO PL 2 Oct R Scientology Rev. 18 Jan 91 Magistrate

PURIFICATION: AN ILLUSTRATED ANSWER TO DRUGS

A picture book compiled by staff and published by Bridge Publications, Los Angeles, California.

PURIFICATION RUNDOWN DELIVERY MANUAL

Compiled by staff and published by Bridge Publications, Los Angeles, California.

ISSUES

HCOB 8 Nov R Security Checker Rev. 18 Jun 89 Beingness

HCOB 22 Nov False Purpose Rundown Correction List Word List *FPRD Series 9-1*

RESEARCH AND DISCOVERY SERIES, VOLUME 6

Compiled from the taped lectures of L. Ron Hubbard, May–August 1951. Published by Bridge Publications, Los Angeles, California.

RESEARCH AND DISCOVERY SERIES, VOLUME 7

Compiled from the taped lectures of L. Ron Hubbard, August–September 1951. Published by Bridge Publications, Los Angeles, California.

1985

Living at his ranch near San Luis Obispo, California, Mr. Hubbard continued to develop new technology at the lower levels of the Bridge, while also pushing forward his research into the highest levels of OT.

In August he completed and released the Allergy or Asthma Rundown, a new series of auditing steps designed to help relieve mental and spiritual troubles associated with allergies and asthma.

The new Clear Certainty Rundown was completed in December, providing a complete and streamlined procedure for verifying and validating a person's achievement of the state of Clear.

For Clears, a completely new first step toward Operating Thetan was released: *New* OT I. This level, which replaced OT I, not only gives the Clear terrific case gains, but also builds his certainty and competence as a Solo auditor.

While advancing technical research, Mr. Hubbard also

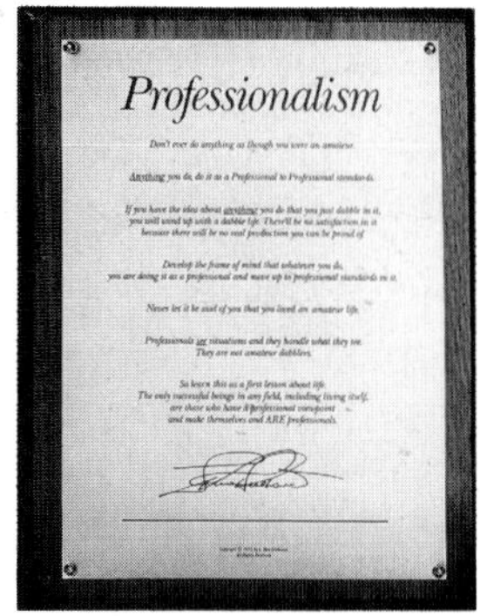

PLAQUE, "PROFESSIONALISM" BY L. RON HUBBARD

Article on professionalism by L. Ron Hubbard, suitable for wall-hanging.

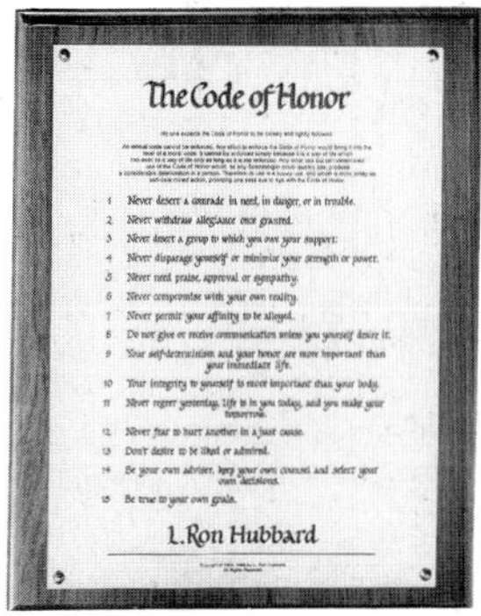

PLAQUE, "CODE OF HONOR" BY L. RON HUBBARD

The Code of Honor, suitable for wall-hanging.

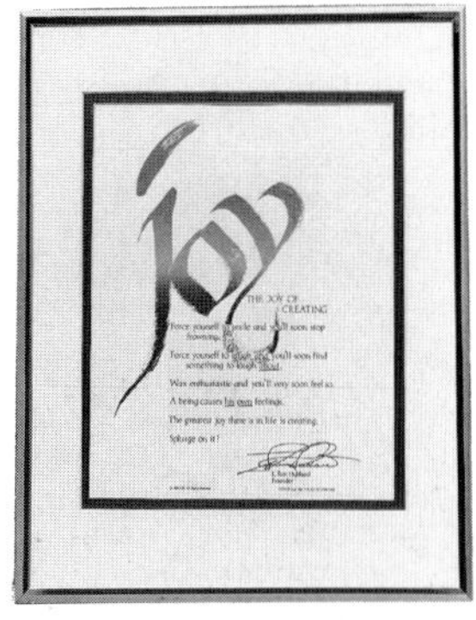

PLAQUE "JOY OF CREATING" BY L. RON HUBBARD

Calligraphic rendering of "Joy of Creating" in frame, suitable for wall-hanging.

CHURCH OF SCIENTOLOGY INTERNATIONAL RING

A gold ring with the Church of Scientology International symbol.

INTERNATIONAL ASSOCIATION OF SCIENTOLOGISTS PINS

Earned by persons who have contributed to the International Association of Scientologists: Membership Pin, Award Pin and Patron Pin.

found time to compose and write lyrics for a complete album of Scientology songs. Making musical statements of many of the basic principles of Scientology, the album was recorded and produced in 1986 by Golden Era Productions. The album provided an aesthetic way for Scientologists to introduce family and friends to the truths of Scientology.

The Tone Scale and The Tone Scale Drill Film

The first film, narrated by L. Ron Hubbard, goes through the different tone levels, giving a dramatic representation of each. The viewer is then instructed to watch the accompanying drill film to review the tone levels until he knows them fully. Available in English, German, Italian, French, Spanish, Danish, Swedish, Dutch, Portuguese and Hebrew. Produced by Golden Era Productions.

ISSUES

HCO PL	7 Jan	HCO Confessionals
HCO PL	22 Mar	Full Danger Condition Handling *Esto Series 51*
HCO PL	24 Mar	Responsibility, Control and Danger Conditions
HCO PL	1 May	Honesty and Case Gain *C/S Series 120*
HCOB	2 May	Responsibility, Definition Of
HCOB	12 May	Exec and Staff Member Form *FPRD Series 10-C*
HCOB	13 May	Second Dynamic Form *FPRD Series 10-D*
HCOB	14 May	Money and Finance Form *FPRD Series 10-E*
HCOB	15 May	Dissemination Form *FPRD Series 10-F*
HCOB	17 May	Auditor Form *FPRD Series 10-H*
HCOB	18 May	Student Form *FPRD Series 10-I*
HCO PL	21 May	Two Types of PTSes *C/S Series 121* *FPRD Series 11*
HCO PL	18 Jun	Product Orientation *Org Series 49* *Exec Series 30*
HCOB	2 Jul	Artist Form *FPRD Series 10-G*
HCO PL	3 Aug	Completing Conditions Formulas
HCOB	20 Aug	Sec Checker Form *FPRD Series 10-J*

NEW OT I MATERIALS

A brand-new OT level for the new Solo auditor, released 24 August 1985. Its materials consist of 7 HCOBs which replace the previous version of OT I.

ISSUE

HCOB	29 Aug	Allergy or Asthma Rundown

THE FUTURE OF SCIENTOLOGY AND WESTERN CIVILIZATION

by L. Ron Hubbard

Transcribed from a recorded lecture. International Association of Scientologists special gift edition. Published by New Era Publications, Copenhagen, Denmark.

ISSUES

HCOB Rev. 28 Mar 90	24 Oct R	Troubleshooting the Purification Rundown Pc *C/S Series 122R* *Purif RD Series 9R*
HCOB Rev. 28 Mar 90	25 Oct R	Purification Rundown Correction List *Purif RD Series 10R*

RESEARCH AND DISCOVERY SERIES, VOLUME 8

Compiled from the taped lectures of L. Ron Hubbard, given in October 1951. Published by Bridge Publications, Los Angeles, California.

ISSUES

HCOB Rev. 18 Dec 88	17 Nov R	Clear Certainty Rundown: Purpose *C/S Series 104RB* *CCRD Series 2R*
HCOB	21 Nov	First Dynamic Form *FPRD Series 10-K*
HCOB	22 Nov	Field Staff Member Repair and Revitalization List *FSM Series 9*
HCO PL	23 Nov	INCOMM *Computer Series 4*
HCO PL Rev. 18 Dec 88	2 Dec R	Clear Certainty Rundown, New Service *C/S Series 112RA*
HCOB	4 Dec	Case Evaluation and Children
HCOB Rev. 18 Dec 88	5 Dec R	Handling of Past-Life Auditing *C/S Series 123R*
HCOB Rev. 18 Dec 88	6 Dec R	C/S Study Requirement *C/S Series 106RB*

RESEARCH AND DISCOVERY SERIES, VOLUME 9

Compiled from the taped lectures of L. Ron Hubbard, November to December 1951. Published by Bridge Publications, Los Angeles, California.

THE ORGANIZATION EXECUTIVE COURSE VOLUME 0

by L. Ron Hubbard

New edition updated by staff with many new LRH policies added. Fully indexed and including insert of nine-division org board. Published by Bridge Publications, Los Angeles, California.

E-Meter Reads Drill Film

This film goes through all the various reactions of the needle on the E-Meter, enabling the audience to drill recognizing them many times. Produced by Golden Era Productions in English, Danish, Dutch, French, German, Italian, Spanish and Swedish.

1986

On 24 January 1986, having completed all he set out to do, Mr. Hubbard departed his body. However, he left a wealth of research material yet to be assembled and published, along with instructions as to *how* this work was to be done. Dedicated Sea Organization staff took up the task of making this legacy of as-yet-unpublished material available.

By the end of 1985, Mr. Hubbard had completed and codified new OT levels all the way through New OT XV. His New Year's message for 1986 included a very special gift for his friends—the first of these OT Levels, New OT VIII: Truth Revealed. The level was complete, but an ideal space for its delivery was needed—which was accomplished with the purchase of the ship *Freewinds.* New OT VIII was released on the *Freewinds* on 7 June 1988.

In addition to compiling and publishing materials not previously available, a continuing effort has been made to see that the entire legacy of Mr. Hubbard's work is made known—and easily accessible—to all the peoples of Earth. To this end a series of projects have been carried out to assemble and publish new editions of his works: books supplemented with glossaries and indexes to make data more easily located and understood; lectures produced using Clearsound technology so that every word can be clearly heard, then released with complete transcripts and glossaries; translated editions of books, films and recorded lectures; and new books and films to quickly communicate the truths of Dianetics and Scientology and how they can be used to improve life. This work has been going forward apace since 1986 and will continue for many years to come.

Ron's Journal 39: My New Year's Gift to You

In this special New Year's message for 1986, produced in Clearsound, L. Ron Hubbard announces the levels above New OT VII.

Road to Freedom

Songs composed by L. Ron Hubbard and performed by the Golden Era Musicians and numerous celebrities. "Thank You for Listening," the last song, is sung by L. Ron Hubbard himself. Produced in Clearsound on cassette and as a record album in English, French, German, Italian and Spanish. Released on 13 March, 1986 at L. Ron Hubbard's Birthday Event.

Hubbard Dissemination Course

Based on the works of L. Ron Hubbard, published by Bridge Publications, Los Angeles, California.

What Happened to These Civilizations?

A film that tells why numerous civilizations have failed and the answer to a new civilization that will bring hope to mankind. Produced in English, Portuguese, Danish, Dutch, Finnish, French, German, Italian, Norwegian, Brazilian, Hebrew, Greek, Spanish and Swedish. Released on May 9, 1986.

Issues

HCO PL 10 Jul I Keeping Admin Working *AKH Series 50*
HCO PL 10 Jul II Admin Degrades *AKH Series 51*
HCO PL 10 Jul III Admin High Crime *AKH Series 52* *Computer Series 5*

The Hope of Man

by L. Ron Hubbard

Transcribed from a recorded lecture. International Association of Scientologists special gift edition. Published by Bridge Publications, Los Angeles, California, 1986.

Books Make Booms Slide Show

L. Ron Hubbard directed the original photo story from which this slide show for staff on the importance of selling books was created. *TRANSLATION:* Italian.

My Philosophy

A cassette on which "My Philosophy," "A Description of Scientology" and "The Aims of Scientology," three of L. Ron Hubbard's powerful writings, are read by actor Jeff Pomerantz accompanied by music composed especially for the cassette. Produced in Clearsound. Released in September 1986.

1987

My Philosophy

A video presentation of L. Ron Hubbard's 1965 essay, "My Philosophy," narrated by actor Jeff Pomerantz, with never-before-seen photos of Mr. Hubbard's life. Produced by Golden Era Productions with transcript and glossary.

The Story of Book One

The story of the release of Dianetics: The Modern Science of Mental Health *in May 1950 and the grass-roots movement it sparked. Released by Golden Era Productions on 9 May 1987 in English. Rereleased in 1991 in English, Danish, Dutch, French, German, Hebrew, Italian, Spanish and Swedish.*

Issues

HCO PL 25 Jul Knowledge, Definition Of
HCOB 13 Aug Confessionals—Types of TRs
HCOB 15 Aug Unconscious Person Assist
HCOB 25 Aug I Nerve Assist
HCOB 25 Aug II Touch Assists, More About

The Game Called Man

by L. Ron Hubbard

Transcribed from a recorded lecture. International Association of Scientologists special gift edition. Published by Bridge Publications, Los Angeles, California.

Issues

HCOB 28 Oct The Auditor Admin Series for Use by All Auditors *Auditor Admin Series 1RA*
HCOB 29 Oct The Folder *Auditor Admin Series 4R*
HCOB 30 Oct The Yellow Sheet *Auditor Admin Series 6RA*
HCOB 31 Oct The Folder Summary *Auditor Admin Series 7RA*
HCOB 1 Nov OCA Graphs *Auditor Admin Series 8R*
HCOB 2 Nov The Program Sheet *Auditor Admin Series 9RA*
HCOB 5 Nov The Auditor's Report Form *Auditor Admin Series 13RA*
HCOB 6 Nov The Worksheets *Auditor Admin Series 14RA*
HCOB 9 Nov Dianetic Assessment Lists *Auditor Admin Series 19RA*
HCOB 10 Nov Miscellaneous Reports *Auditor Admin Series 20RA*
HCOB 11 Nov Folder Error Summary Format *Auditor Admin Series 22RB*
HCOB 12 Nov Invoice Form and Routing Forms *Auditor Admin Series 23RB*
HCOB 13 Nov The Pc Folder and Its Contents *Auditor Admin Series 3RA*
HCOB 14 Nov I Expanded ARC Straightwire Grade Process Checklist
HCOB 14 Nov II Expanded Grade 0 Process Checklist
HCOB 14 Nov III Expanded Grade I Process Checklist
HCOB 14 Nov IV Expanded Grade II Process Checklist
HCOB 14 Nov V Expanded Grade III Process Checklist
HCOB 14 Nov VI Expanded Grade IV Process Checklist
HCO PL 27 Nov Examiner's Form—Additional Data *Auditor Admin Series 11-1*
HCOB 28 Nov L&N Lists *Auditor Admin Series 18RA*
HCOB 29 Nov Correction Lists *Auditor Admin Series 16RA*

1988

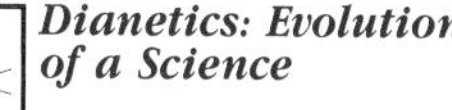

Dianetics: Evolution of a Science

Based on true incidents in the early history of Dianetics, the story of a promising young football player paralyzed from the waist down in an accident, and his road back through Dianetics. Produced in English, Danish, Dutch, French, German, Italian, Spanish and Swedish.

The History of the E-Meter

A technical film covering the development of the E-Meter, produced by Golden Era Productions in English, Danish, Dutch, French, German, Italian, Spanish and Swedish.

Issues

HCOB 8 Apr The "Bring Back to Life" Assist
HCOB 10 Apr R3RA Service Facsimile Handling Action Eleven *NED Series 30*
HCOB 4 May R Rev. 19 Jun 89 False Purpose Rundown Executive Posting Qualifications Form *FPRD Series 10-L*

Man, the Unfathomable

An hour-long film, narrated by L. Ron Hubbard, that takes the viewer through various times in the history of man in which he has been trying

INTERNATIONAL ASSOCIATION OF SCIENTOLOGISTS PINS

Earned by patrons who have contributed to the International Association of Scientologists: Patron with Honors Pin.

RELIGIOUS TECHNOLOGY CENTER RING

A gold ring with the Religious Technology Center symbol.

HUBBARD PROFESSIONAL MARK SUPER VII E-METER

On March 13, 1988, the Mark Super VII E-Meter, designed according to L. Ron Hubbard's specifications, was released. It is the most precise and accurate E-Meter ever built, especially suitable for the upper OT levels.

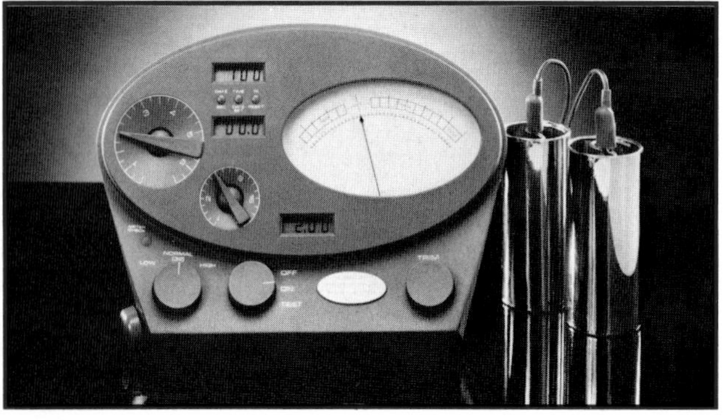

to cure his fellows of nonoptimum conditions. The film establishes man's need for Scientology and the E-Meter. Produced by Golden Era Productions in English, Danish, Dutch, French, German, Italian, Spanish and Swedish.

NEW OT VIII: TRUTH REVEALED MATERIALS

The materials of this Solo-audited OT level were released 7 June 1988 aboard the *Freewinds*.

ISSUES

HCOB	1 Jul	Questionable Auditing Repair List Word List
HCOB	2 Jul	Field Staff Member Repair and Revitalization List Word List *FSM Series 9-1*
HCOB Rev. 28 Mar 90	4 Jul R	Purification Rundown Correction List Word List *Purif RD Series 10-1R*
HCOB	5 Jul	The End of Endless Drug Rundowns Repair List Word List
HCOB	6 Jul	Crashing Mis-U Repair List—LC1R Word List *Product Debug Series 4R-1* *Word Clearing Series 62R-1*
HCOB	7 Jul	Product Debug Repair List Word List *Product Debug Series 10R-1*
HCOB	8 Jul	C/S Series 53RM (Short Form) Short Hi–Lo TA Assessment C/S Word List
HCOB	11 Jul	False Data Stripping Repair List *Product Debug Series 11*
HCOB	12 Jul	False Data Stripping Repair List Word List *Product Debug Series 11-1*
HCOB	20 Jul	Happiness Rundown Repair List Word List *HRD Series 5R-1*

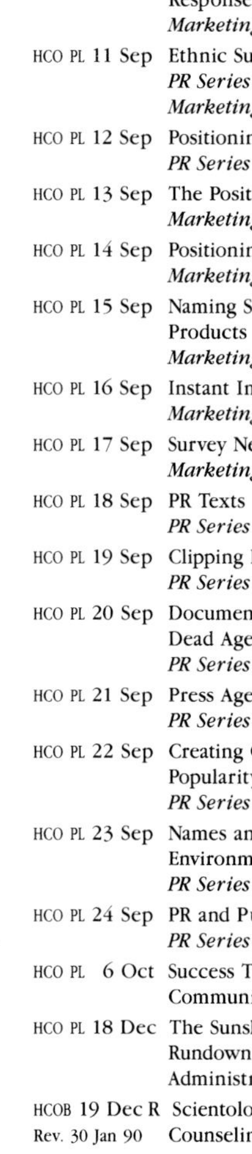

HCO PL	10 Sep	Tabulating Survey Responses *Marketing Series 22*
HCO PL	11 Sep	Ethnic Surveys *PR Series 15* *Marketing Series 23*
HCO PL	12 Sep	Positioning in PR *PR Series 29*
HCO PL	13 Sep	The Positioning Era *Marketing Series 24*
HCO PL	14 Sep	Positioning Surveys *Marketing Series 25*
HCO PL	15 Sep	Naming Services and Products *Marketing Series 26*
HCO PL	16 Sep	Instant Impression *Marketing Series 27*
HCO PL	17 Sep	Survey Network *Marketing Series 28*
HCO PL	18 Sep	PR Texts *PR Series 16*
HCO PL	19 Sep	Clipping Books *PR Series 24*
HCO PL	20 Sep	Documentation and the Dead Agent Caper *PR Series 32*
HCO PL	21 Sep	Press Agentry *PR Series 33*
HCO PL	22 Sep	Creating Overwhelming Popularity *PR Series 41*
HCO PL	23 Sep	Names and the Local Environment *PR Series 42*
HCO PL	24 Sep	PR and Purpose *PR Series 43*
HCO PL	6 Oct	Success Through Communication
HCO PL	18 Dec	The Sunshine Rundown: Administration
HCOB Rev. 30 Jan 90	19 Dec R	Scientology Marriage Counseling

E-METER ESSENTIALS

by L. Ron Hubbard

New edition. Published by Bridge Publications, Los Angeles, California. *TRANSLATIONS:* Dutch, German, French, Spanish and Italian.

INTRODUCING THE E-METER

by L. Ron Hubbard

New edition. Published by Bridge Publications, Los Angeles, California. *TRANSLATIONS:* Dutch, German, French, Spanish, Swedish, Danish and Italian.

THE BOOK OF E-METER DRILLS

by L. Ron Hubbard

New edition. Published by Bridge Publications, Los Angeles, California. *TRANSLATIONS:* Danish, Dutch, German, French, Spanish, Swedish and Italian.

UNDERSTANDING THE E-METER

by L. Ron Hubbard

New edition. Published by Bridge Publications, Los Angeles, California. *TRANSLATIONS:* German and Italian.

INDIVIDUAL TRACK MAP

by L. Ron Hubbard

New edition. Published by Bridge Publications, Los Angeles, California for use with New Era Dianetics.

BASIC DICTIONARY OF DIANETICS AND SCIENTOLOGY

by L. Ron Hubbard

New edition. Published by Bridge Publications, Los Angeles, California. *TRANSLATIONS:* Italian, Swedish, Dutch, German, Japanese and French.

The Married Couple

The story of a once-happy couple whose relationship deteriorates to the verge of divorce. They receive marriage counseling at a church of Scientology, find the source of their problems and begin to build an honest and lasting relationship. Produced by Golden Era Productions in Danish, Dutch, English, French, German, Italian, Swedish and Spanish.

"MAN, THE UNFATHOMABLE" MUSIC

The unique music composed by L. Ron Hubbard to accompany the film, "Man, the Unfathomable." Produced in Clearsound.

THE TROUBLESHOOTER

This package contains L. Ron Hubbard's bulletins for analysis and handling of difficulties which may be encountered in an auditing session.

PASSPORT UP THE BRIDGE TO FREEDOM

This unique document lists out the training and processing steps on the Bridge to Total Freedom, as well as every book, film and cassette by L. Ron Hubbard. Whenever a step is completed it is officially validated at a Scientology organization with a special passport stamp.

1989

ISSUES

HCOB	8 Mar	Word Clearing—Key Datum *Word Clearing Series 45*
HCO PL	21 Mar	PTS People and Leaves

Assists

This film supplements Dianetics and Scientology written materials and lectures about assists. It includes representation of some of the theory of why *they work and accurate demonstrations of* how *they are done. Produced by Golden Era Productions in English, Danish, Dutch, French, German, Italian, Portuguese, Spanish and Swedish.*

ISSUES

HCOB	2 Jun I	Auditing Repair List for People from Est
HCOB	2 Jun II	Est Confessional Form *Confessional Form 13*
HCOB	3 Jun	Auditing Repair List for People from Est Word List
HCOB	5 Jul	Coaching TRs 0–4
HCOB	24 Sep	Repair List for Treatment from Psychiatrists, Psychologists and Psychoanalysts
HCOB	25 Sep	Repair List for Treatment from Psychiatrists, Psychologists and Psychoanalysts Word List
HCOB	26 Oct	TRs Clay Table Processing: Instructions for the Student Auditor
HCOB	27 Oct	How to Do Clay Table Processing
HCOB	29 Oct	Clay Table Processing Repair List—LCTR
HCOB	30 Oct	Clay Table Processing Repair List Word List
HCOB	16 Nov	Art and Equipment *Art Series 17*
HCOB	23 Dec	TR Debug Assessment Word List

RESEARCH AND DISCOVERY SERIES, VOLUME 10

Compiled from the taped lectures of L. Ron Hubbard, January to February 1952. Published by Bridge Publications, Los Angeles, California.

CLAY TABLE PROCESSING PICTURE BOOK

by L. Ron Hubbard

For use by students on the Hubbard Professional TR Course only. Published by Bridge Publications, Los Angeles, California. TRANSLATIONS: Danish, Dutch, French, German, Hebrew, Italian, Japanese, Portuguese, Norwegian, Spanish and Swedish.

TRs in Life

Written and narrated by L. Ron Hubbard, this film shows how—without TRs—life is a struggle instead of a game. It depicts the common denominator of all failures to confront and handle life, why each TR exists and what each is designed to handle. Produced by Golden Era Productions. TRANSLATIONS: German, Spanish, Italian, French, Norwegian, Portuguese, Danish, Dutch, Swedish, Hebrew and Japanese.

1990

ISSUES

HCOB	27 Mar I	The Purification Rundown and Radiation *Purif Rundown Series 13*
HCOB	27 Mar II	The Purification Rundown: A Long-Range Detoxification Program *Purif Rundown Series 14*
HCOB	28 Mar	The Role of Oil on the Purification Rundown *Purif Rundown Series 15*
HCOB	1 Apr	CCHs 8–10
HCOB	2 Apr	Additional Objective Processes for TRs and Objectives Co-audit
HCOB	4 Apr	Model Session for Objectives Co-audits
HCO PL	4 Apr	Course Schedules
HCOB	9 Apr	Objectives Correction List
HCOB	10 Apr	Objectives Correction List Word List
HCOB	12 Apr	Clay Table, Definition of Terms

HUBBARD KEY TO LIFE COURSE BOOKS

by L. Ron Hubbard

The Hubbard Key to Life Course is the ultimate answer to the widespread illiteracy ravaging our society. The books used on the course are themselves a spectacular achievement. Designed and written by Mr. Hubbard and containing over 4,000 illustrations, these 13 books are not only powerful technical texts, they are true works of art.

Dianetics: The Dynamics of Life

A film showing the true story of how L. Ron Hubbard embarked on the most daring exploration in all human history—a journey to confront and answer the riddle of life itself. Produced by Golden Era Productions in English, Danish, Dutch, French, German, Hebrew, Italian, Japanese, Norwegian, Portuguese, Spanish and Swedish.

HUBBARD LIFE ORIENTATION COURSE BOOKS

by L. Ron Hubbard

The materials for the Hubbard Life Orientation Course consist of two books. The first is a large hardbound book, illustrated throughout with full-color artwork done by the same artist who illustrated the Key to Life Course books. The second book is illustrated with color photographs. The books form a complete package that can be continually referred to by the course graduate. TRANSLATIONS: French, German, Italian and Spanish.

ISSUES

HCOB	18 Jun	Pcs Who Refuse Auditing *C/S Series 124*
HCOB	30 Jul	Scientology Auditor Analysis Checklist *C/S Series 125*
HCOB	31 Jul	Confessional Auditor Analysis Checklist *C/S Series 126*
HCOB	1 Aug	The Test of a C/S *C/S Series 127*
HCO PL	2 Aug	Auditing Discounts
HCOB	3 Aug	Auditing and C/Sing Below One's Training Level

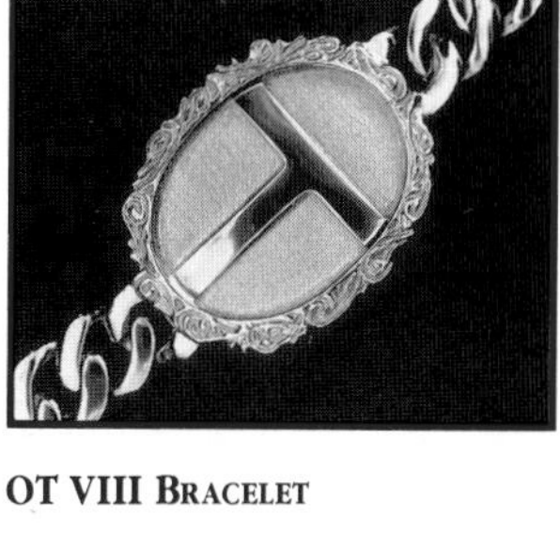

OT VIII BRACELET

A gold bracelet carrying the OT symbol in a wreath may be worn by a Scientologist who has attained the level of New OT VIII.

INTERNATIONAL ASSOCIATION OF SCIENTOLOGISTS PINS

Earned by patrons who have contributed to the International Association of Scientologists: Sponsor Pin, Senior Honor Roll Pin, Patron Meritorious Pin and Honor Roll Pin.

AUDITOR PINS

Class IV Auditor Pin, Class V Auditor Pin and Class V Graduate Auditor Pin.

FIELD STAFF MEMBER PINS

FSM Pin, Senior FSM Pin, Master FSM Pin and Power FSM Pin.

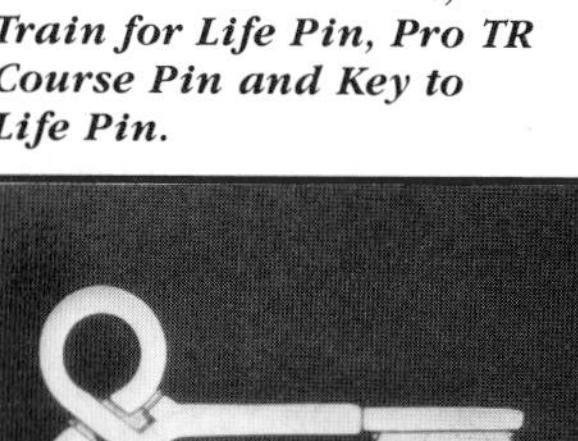

TRAINING PINS

Fast Flow Student Pin, Train for Life Pin, Pro TR Course Pin and Key to Life Pin.

HCO PL 29 Aug Using Orders or Policy to Create Problems
HCO PL 30 Aug Weekly Staff Meetings
HCO PL 10 Sep I The Quality of Division 6A, a Division 6A Checklist for Quality
HCO PL 10 Sep II The Quality of Division 6B, a Division 6B Checklist for Quality
HCO PL 10 Sep III The Quality of Division 6C, a Division 6C Checklist for Quality
HCO PL 5 Nov O/Ws and Evaluation *Data Series 51*

Upper Indoc TRs

This film, released by Golden Era Productions, shows exactly how Upper Indoc TRs are done and their results.

BASIC STUDY MANUAL

New edition compiled from the works of L. Ron Hubbard. Published by Applied Scholastics, Los Angeles, California. TRANSLATIONS: Italian, German and Spanish.

CLEAR BODY, CLEAR MIND: THE EFFECTIVE PURIFICATION PROGRAM

by L. Ron Hubbard

Makes the full technology of the Purification program available to anyone. Published by Bridge Publications, Los Angeles, California. TRANSLATIONS: French, German and Italian.

"DIANETICS: THE DYNAMICS OF LIFE" MUSIC

Motion picture soundtrack from the film *Dianetics: The Dynamics of Life.* In Clearsound.

THE SCIENTOLOGY CHARTS PACKAGE

A full package of sixteen Scientology charts and codes that help map the route to total freedom. These can be purchased separately or as a package in a special plastic envelope. The charts and codes in this package include:

Classification and Gradation Chart
The Bridge to Total Freedom
Hubbard Chart of Human Evaluation and Dianetic Processing
Hubbard Chart of Attitudes
The Tone Scale in Full and the Illustrated Tone Scale Chart
The Conditions Formulas
Evaluator's Know-How Chart
The Logics
The Factors
Code of a Scientologist
The Auditor's Code
The Code of Honor
The Creed of the Church of Scientology

1991

ISSUES

HCO PL 10 Jan Confusion Formula, Additional Data
HCO PL 11 Jan Telex Discipline
HCO PL 21 Jan Moonripping *Personnel Series 33*
HCO PL 22 Jan Consequences of Miscramming
HCO PL 23 Jan Senior Qual Network
HCO PL 28 Jan II The Tech Estimate Line
HCO PL 28 Jan III Marketing Posters *Marketing Series 31*
HCO PL 28 Jan IV Fliers, Definition and Use *Marketing Series 30*
HCO PL 29 Jan I Repetition of Message *Marketing Series 29*
HCO PL 29 Jan II Technical Specialist Courses
HCO PL 11 Feb Upper-Org Central Files and New Names to CF
HCO PL 21 Feb Religious Influence in Society
HCO PL 22 Feb Volunteer Ministers
HCO PL 23 Feb Body Routing and Its Use
HCO PL 25 Feb Delivering Public Division Courses
HCO PL 26 Feb The Organization of the Public Divisions

THE ORGANIZATION EXECUTIVE COURSE VOLUMES

by L. Ron Hubbard

Updated edition containing every issue on administrative technology written by L. Ron Hubbard. Volumes 0–7. Compiled by staff and published by Bridge Publications, Los Angeles, California.

Volume 0: Basic Staff Hat
Volume 1: HCO Division
Volume 2: Dissemination Division
Volume 3: Treasury Division
Volume 4: Technical Division
Volume 5: Qualifications Division
Volume 6: Public Division
Volume 7: Executive Division

THE MANAGEMENT SERIES POLICY VOLUMES 1–3

by L. Ron Hubbard

Updated edition of the Management Series *in three volumes, published by Bridge Publications, Los Angeles, California. Contains the Data Series, Public Relations Series, Marketing Series, Personnel Series, Organizing Series, Finance Series, Executive Series, Establishment Officer Series, Computer Series, Target Series, Admin Know-How Series.*

THE OEC AND MANAGEMENT SERIES POLICY INDEX

An index to the new Organization Executive Course *and* Management Series *volumes, published by Bridge Publications, Los Angeles, California.*

ISSUES

HCOB 19 Apr A Key Cramming Question *Cramming Series 18*
HCOB 20 Apr Cramming and Basics *Cramming Series 19*
HCOB 21 Apr Auditor Coordination Drills *Cramming Series 20*
HCOB 22 Apr What a Cramming Officer Has to Know *Cramming Series 21*
HCOB 23 Apr The Tools of a Cramming Officer *Cramming Series 22*
HCOB 24 Apr Modification of the Primary Rundown
HCOB 25 Apr Between Session Notes from Pcs
HCOB 26 Apr Handling Undeclared States of Release
HCOB 27 Apr I Discovery on PDH (Pain-Drug-Hypnosis)
HCOB 27 Apr II PDH Confessional *Confessional Form 14*
HCOB 27 Apr III Prepared List for Still Needles
HCOB 28 Apr Barley Formula for Babies
HCOB 29 Apr Data About Fragrances
HCOB 1 May I Study of Expanded Dianetics *Expanded Dianetics Series 0*

HCOB 1 May II Expanded Dianetics Repair List—L3 EXD *Expanded Dianetics Series 2*

HCOB 1 May III Expanded Dianetics Repair List—L3 EXD Word List *Expanded Dianetics Series 3*

HCOB 1 May IV Auditing Commands for Running Evil Intentions in Expanded Dianetics *Expanded Dianetics Series 26*

HCOB 1 May V Preassessment for Expanded Dianetics *Expanded Dianetics Series 27*

HCOB 1 May VI Preassessment List for Left-Side Rundowns *Expanded Dianetics Series 27-1*

HCOB 1 May VII Preassessment List for Right-Side Rundowns *Expanded Dianetics Series 27-2*

HCOB 1 May VIII Present Time Environment Rundown *Expanded Dianetics Series 28*

HCOB 1 May IX Handling Emotional Stresses *Expanded Dianetics Series 29*

HCOB 1 May X Past Auditing and Expanded Dianetics *Expanded Dianetics Series 30*

HCOB 1 May XI Handling Hidden Standards with Expanded Dianetics *Expanded Dianetics Series 31*

HCOB 1 May XII Wants Handled Rundown *Expanded Dianetics Series 32*

HCOB 1 May XIII Handling Stuck Points on the Track *Expanded Dianetics Series 33*

HCOB 1 May XIV Confessionals and Expanded Dianetics *Expanded Dianetics Series 34*

HCOB 1 May XV The Responsibility Rundown *Expanded Dianetics Series 35*

HCOB 1 May XVI Expanded Dianetics Service Facsimile Handling *Expanded Dianetics Series 36*

HCOB 1 May XVII Metalosis Rundown *Expanded Dianetics Series 37*

HCOB 1 May XVIII The OCA Rundown *Expanded Dianetics Series 38*

HCOB 1 May XIX C/Sing and Programing Expanded Dianetics *Expanded Dianetics Series 39*

UNDERSTANDING: THE UNIVERSAL SOLVENT

A volume of quotations from the works of L. Ron Hubbard. Published by Bridge Publications, Los Angeles, California.

NED FOR OTs AND SOLO NED FOR OTs NEW MATERIALS

On 6 May 1991, previously unreleased issues and rundowns for the New OT V, New OT VI and New OT VII were released at the Flag Land Base.

KNOWINGNESS

Second volume of quotations from the works of L. Ron Hubbard. Published by Bridge Publications, Los Angeles, California.

THE TECHNICAL BULLETINS OF DIANETICS AND SCIENTOLOGY
by L. Ron Hubbard

Updated edition containing all technical writings of L. Ron Hubbard on Dianetics and Scientology. Eighteen volumes, including thirteen chronological volumes, index and four subject volumes—the Case Supervisor Series, Technical Series, Auditing Rundowns and Grade Processes and Prepared Lists. Published by Bridge Publications, Los Angeles, California.

THE BOOK OF CASE REMEDIES
by L. Ron Hubbard

New edition including previously unpublished remedies and additional case remedy tools. Published by Bridge Publications, Los Angeles, California.

THE BASIC SCIENTOLOGY PICTURE BOOK
Taken from the works of L. Ron Hubbard

Published by Bridge Publications, Inc. New edition. TRANSLATIONS: Italian, Spanish, French, German, Danish, Dutch, Swedish, Norwegian, Hebrew, Japanese and Portuguese.

THE BASIC DIANETICS PICTURE BOOK
Taken from the works of L. Ron Hubbard

Published by Bridge Publications, Inc. New edition. TRANSLATIONS: Italian, Spanish, French, German, Danish, Dutch, Swedish, Norwegian, Hebrew, Japanese, Chinese, Greek, Portuguese and Russian.

L. RON HUBBARD: CALENDAR

Beautiful wall calendar featuring photographs by L. Ron Hubbard. First in a series to be released each year.

SCIENTOMETRIC TESTING

The manual on the technology of testing based on the works of L. Ron Hubbard. Packaged in a slipcase along with sample testing materials and grading tools. Published by Bridge Publications, Los Angeles, California.

1992

HOW TO USE DIANETICS: A VISUAL GUIDEBOOK TO THE HUMAN MIND

A video which explains exactly what Dianetics is and how to co-audit on Book One. Published by Bridge Publications, Los Angeles, California.

ART
by L. Ron Hubbard

L. Ron Hubbard's writings on art. Published by Bridge Publications, Los Angeles, California.

LIFE ORIENTATION PIN

Gold-plated "hat in life," symbol for the Hubbard Life Orientation Course.

SAINT HILL SPECIAL BRIEFING COURSE RING

Solid gold signet ring with crest.

AUDITOR PINS

Class VI Auditor Pin, Class VI C/S Pin, Class VIII Auditor Pin and Class VIII C/S Pin.

CHAPTER 43

LIST OF ORGANIZATIONS

Dianetics and Scientology organizations exist all over the world.

The address list that follows is as up to date as possible, but due to the expansion of the Church the number of organizations is rapidly increasing. Addresses are subject to change.

INTERNATIONAL ASSOCIATION OF SCIENTOLOGISTS

The International Association of Scientologists is a membership organization which unites individuals around the world in achieving the Aims of Scientology. Anyone in agreement with these aims may become a member.

For information concerning the activities of the IAS, to become a member or renew membership in the Association, you can write to:

INTERNATIONAL ASSOCIATION OF SCIENTOLOGISTS

C/O Saint Hill Manor
East Grinstead, Sussex
England RH19 4JY

INTERNATIONAL CHURCH ORGANIZATIONS

CHURCH OF SCIENTOLOGY INTERNATIONAL

Mother church of the Scientology religion

6331 Hollywood Boulevard, Suite 1200
Los Angeles, California 90028

RELIGIOUS TECHNOLOGY CENTER

Holder of the Dianetics and Scientology trademarks

1710 Ivar Avenue, Suite 1100
Los Angeles, California 90028

CHURCHES OF SCIENTOLOGY

CHURCH OF SCIENTOLOGY FLAG SHIP SERVICE ORGANIZATION

C/O *Freewinds* Relay Office
118 N. Fort Harrison Avenue
Clearwater, Florida 34615

CHURCH OF SCIENTOLOGY FLAG SERVICE ORGANIZATION

210 S. Fort Harrison Avenue
Clearwater, Florida 34616

WESTERN UNITED STATES

▲ **Continental Liaison Office
Western United States**
1307 N. New Hampshire
Los Angeles, California 90027

♦ **Church of Scientology
American Saint Hill Organization**
1413 N. Berendo Street
Los Angeles, California 90027

♦ **Church of Scientology
Advanced Organization of Los Angeles**
1306 N. Berendo Street
Los Angeles, California 90027

Church of Scientology of Arizona
4450 N. Central Avenue, Suite 102
Phoenix, Arizona 85012

Church of Scientology of the Valley
3619 West Magnolia Boulevard
Burbank, California 91506

Church of Scientology of Los Angeles
4810 Sunset Boulevard
Los Angeles, California 90027

Church of Scientology of Mountain View
2483 Old Middlefield Way
Mountain View, California 94043

Church of Scientology of Pasadena
263 E. Colorado Boulevard
Pasadena, California 91101

Church of Scientology of Stevens Creek
80 E. Rosemary
San Jose, California 95112

Church of Scientology of Sacramento
825 15th Street
Sacramento, California 95814

Church of Scientology of San Diego
635 "C" Street, Suite 200
San Diego, California 92101

Church of Scientology of San Francisco
83 McAllister Street
San Francisco, California 94102

Church of Scientology of Santa Barbara
524 State Street
Santa Barbara, California 93101

Church of Scientology of Orange County
1451 Irvine Boulevard
Tustin, California 92680

Church of Scientology of Colorado
375 S. Navajo Street
Denver, Colorado 80223

Church of Scientology of Hawaii
1148 Bethel Street
Honolulu, Hawaii 96817

Church of Scientology of Minnesota
Twin Cities
1011 Nicollet Mall
Minneapolis, Minnesota 55403

Church of Scientology of Kansas City
3619 Broadway
Kansas City, Missouri 64111

Church of Scientology of Missouri
9510 Page Boulevard
St. Louis, Missouri 63132

Church of Scientology of Nevada
846 E. Sahara Avenue
Las Vegas, Nevada 89104

Church of Scientology of New Mexico
8106 Menaul Boulevard N.E.
Albuquerque, New Mexico 87110

Church of Scientology of Portland
323 S.W. Washington
Portland, Oregon 97204

Church of Scientology of Texas
2200 Guadalupe
Austin, Texas 78705

Church of Scientology of Utah
1931 S. 100 East
Salt Lake City, Utah 84106

Church of Scientology of Washington State
2603 3rd Avenue
Seattle, Washington 98121

EASTERN UNITED STATES

▲ **Continental Liaison Office
Eastern United States**
349 W. 48th Street
New York, NY 10036

Church of Scientology of Connecticut
909 Whalley Avenue
New Haven, Connecticut 06515

Church of Scientology of Florida
120 Giralda Avenue
Coral Gables, Florida 33134

Church of Scientology of Orlando
1830 East Colonial Drive
Orlando, Florida 31802

Church of Scientology of Tampa
3617 Henderson Boulevard
Tampa, Florida 33609

Church of Scientology of Georgia
2632 Piedmont Road N.E.
Atlanta, Georgia 30324

Church of Scientology of Illinois
3011 N. Lincoln Avenue
Chicago, Illinois 60657

Church of Scientology of Boston
448 Beacon Street
Boston, Massachusetts 02115

Church of Scientology of Ann Arbor
122 S. Main, Suite 160
Ann Arbor, Michigan 48106

Church of Scientology of Michigan
321 Williams Street
Royal Oak, Michigan 48067

Church of Scientology of Buffalo
47 W. Huron Street
Buffalo, New York 14202

Church of Scientology of Long Island
99 Railroad Station Plaza
Hicksville, New York 11801

Church of Scientology of New York
227 W. 46th Street
New York, NY 10036

Church of Scientology of Cincinnati
215 W. 4th Street, 5th Floor
Cincinnati, Ohio 45202

Church of Scientology of Ohio
167 E. State Street
Columbus, Ohio 43215

Church of Scientology of Pennsylvania
1315 Race Street
Philadelphia, Pennsylvania 19107

Church of Scientology of Puerto Rico
272 Avenue Central
Hyde Park, Hato Rey
Puerto Rico 00918

Founding Church of Scientology of Washington, DC
2125 "S" Street N.W.
Washington, DC 20008

United Kingdom

▲ **Continental Liaison Office United Kingdom**
Saint Hill Manor
East Grinstead, West Sussex
England RH19 4JY

♦ **Advanced Organization Saint Hill**
Saint Hill Manor
East Grinstead, West Sussex
England RH19 4JY

Church of Scientology of Birmingham
60–62 Constitution Hill
Birmingham
England B19 3JT

Church of Scientology of Brighton
5 St. Georges Place
London Road
Brighton, Sussex
England BN1 4GA

Church of Scientology Saint Hill Foundation
Saint Hill Manor
East Grinstead, West Sussex
England RH19 4JY

Church of Scientology of London
68 Tottenham Court Road, London
England W1P 0BB

Church of Scientology of Manchester
258 Deansgate
Manchester
England M3 4BG

Church of Scientology of Plymouth
41 Ebrington Street
Plymouth, Devon
England PL4 9AA

Church of Scientology of Sunderland
51 Fawcett Street
Sunderland, Tyne and Wear
England SR1 1RS

Hubbard Academy of Personal Independence
20 Southbridge
Edinburgh
Scotland EH1 1LL

Europe

▲ **Continental Liaison Office Europe**
Sankt Nikolajvej 4–6
Frederiksberg C
1953 Copenhagen
Denmark

♦ **Church of Scientology Advanced Organization Saint Hill for Europe and Africa**
Jernbanegade 6
1608 Copenhagen V
Denmark

Austria

Church of Scientology of Austria
Schottenfeldgasse 13–15
1070 Vienna
Austria

Belgium

Church of Scientology of Belgium
61, rue du Prince Royal
1050 Brussels
Belgium

Denmark

Church of Scientology of Jylland
Guldsmedegade 17, 2
8000 Aarhus C
Denmark

Church of Scientology of Copenhagen
Store Kongensgade 55
1264 Copenhagen K
Denmark

Church of Scientology of Denmark
Vesterbrogade 66B
1620 Copenhagen V
Denmark

France

Church of Scientology of Angers
10–12, rue Max Richard
49100 Angers
France

Church of Scientology of Clermont-Ferrand
1, rue Ballainvilliers
63000 Clermont-Ferrand
France

Church of Scientology of Lyon
3, place des Capucins
69001 Lyon
France

Church of Scientology of Paris
65, rue de Dunkerque
75009 Paris
France

Church of Scientology of Saint-Etienne
24, rue Marengo
42000 Saint-Etienne
France

Germany

Church of Scientology of Berlin
Sponholzstrasse 51–52
1000 Berlin 41
Germany

Church of Scientology of Düsseldorf
Friedrichstrasse 28
4000 Düsseldorf
Germany

Church of Scientology of Frankfurt
Darmstädter Landstrasse 213
6000 Frankfurt 70
Germany

Church of Scientology of Hamburg
Steindamm 63
2000 Hamburg 1
Germany

Church of Scientology of Hanover
Hubertusstrasse 2
3000 Hanover 1
Germany

Church of Scientology of Munich
Beichstrasse 12
8000 Munich 40
Germany

Church of Scientology of Stuttgart
Urbanstrasse 70
7000 Stuttgart 1
Germany

Israel

Dianetics and Scientology College of Israel
42 Gorden Street, 2nd Floor
Tel Aviv 66023
Israel

Netherlands

Church of Scientology of Amsterdam
Nieuwe Zijds Voorburgwal 271
1012 RL Amsterdam
Netherlands

Norway

Church of Scientology of Norway
Storgata 9
0155 Oslo 1
Norway

Portugal

Church of Scientology of Portugal
Rua Actor Taborda 39–5°
1000 Lisbon
Portugal

Russia

Operation and Transport Liaison Office Moscow
48 Vavilova Street
Building 4, Suite 169
Moscow 117333
Russia

Spain

Operation and Transport Liaison Office Iberia
C/Montera 32 Piso 4°
28013 Madrid
Spain

Asociación Civil de Dianética de Barcelona
Calle Pau Clarís 85, Principal dcha.
08010 Barcelona
Spain

Asociación Civil de Dianética de Madrid
Montera 20 Piso 1° dcha.
28013 Madrid
Spain

Sweden

Church of Scientology of Göteborg
Odinsgatan 8, 2 tr.
411 03 Göteborg
Sweden

Church of Scientology of Malmö
Simrishamnsgatan 10
214 23 Malmö
Sweden

Church of Scientology of Stockholm
St. Eriksgatan 56
112 34 Stockholm
Sweden

Switzerland

Church of Scientology of Basel
Herrengrabenweg 56
4054 Basel
Switzerland

Church of Scientology of Bern
Dammweg 29
Postfach 352
3000 Bern 11
Switzerland

Church of Scientology of Geneva
Route de Saint-Julien 7–9
C.P. 823
1227 Carouge
Geneva
Switzerland

Church of Scientology of Lausanne
10, rue de la Madeleine
1003 Lausanne
Switzerland

Church of Scientology of Zurich
Badenerstrasse 141
8004 Zurich
Switzerland

ITALY

▲ **Continental Liaison Office Italy**
Via Torino, 51
20063 Cernusco sul Naviglio
Milan
Italy

Church of Scientology of Brescia
Via Fratelli Bronzetti, 20
25125 Brescia
Italy

Church of Scientology of Catania
Via Garibaldi, 9
95121 Catania
Italy

Church of Scientology of Milan
Via Abetone, 10
20137 Milan
Italy

Church of Scientology of Monza
Via Cavour, 5
20052 Monza
Italy

Church of Scientology of Novara
Corso Cavallotti, 7
28100 Novara
Italy

Church of Scientology of Nuoro
Via Lamarmora N. 115
08100 Nuoro
Italy

Church of Scientology of Padua
Via Mameli, 5
35131 Padua
Italy

Church of Scientology of Pordenone
Via Montereale, 10/C
33170 Pordenone
Italy

Church of Scientology of Rome
Via della Pineta Sacchetti, 201
00185 Rome
Italy

Church of Scientology of Turin
Via Guarini, 4
10121 Turin
Italy

Church of Scientology of Verona
Via Teatro Filarmonico, 3
37121 Verona
Italy

AFRICA

▲ **Continental Liaison Office Africa**
Security Building, 4th Floor
95 Commissioner Street
Johannesburg 2001
South Africa

Church of Scientology of Cape Town
St. Georges Centre, 2nd Floor
13 Hout Street
Cape Town 8001
South Africa

Church of Scientology of Durban
57 College Lane
Durban 4001
South Africa

Church of Scientology of Johannesburg
Security Building, 2nd Floor
95 Commissioner Street
Johannesburg 2001
South Africa

Church of Scientology of Johannesburg North
207 Bordeaux Centre
Corner Gordon and Jan Smuts Avenue
Blairgowrie
Randburg 2194
South Africa

Church of Scientology of Port Elizabeth
2 St. Christopher Place
27 Westbourne Road Central
Port Elizabeth 6001
South Africa

Church of Scientology of Pretoria
1st Level City Centre Arcade
272 Pretorius Street
Pretoria 0002
South Africa

Church of Scientology of Bulawayo
Southampton House, Suite 202
Main Street and 9th Avenue
Bulawayo
Zimbabwe

Church of Scientology of Harare
State Lottery Building, 1st Floor
PO Box 3524
Corner Speke Avenue and Julius Nyerere Way
Harare
Zimbabwe

Australia, New Zealand and Oceania

▲ **Continental Liaison Office ANZO**
201 Castlereagh Street, 3rd Floor
Sydney, New South Wales 2000
Australia

♦ **Church of Scientology Advanced Organization Saint Hill Australia, New Zealand and Oceania**
19–37 Greek Street
Glebe, New South Wales 2037
Australia

Australia

Church of Scientology of Adelaide
24–28 Waymouth Street
Adelaide, South Australia 5000
Australia

Church of Scientology of Brisbane
106 Edward Street
Brisbane, Queensland 4000
Australia

Church of Scientology of Australian Capital Territory
108 Bunda Street, Suite 16
Civic Canberra
A.C.T. 2601
Australia

Church of Scientology of Melbourne
42–44 Russell Street
Melbourne, Victoria 3000
Australia

Church of Scientology of Perth
39–41 King Street
Perth, Western Australia 6000
Australia

Church of Scientology of Sydney
201 Castlereagh Street
Sydney, New South Wales 2000
Australia

Japan

Scientology Tokyo
1-23-1 Higashi Gotanda
Shinagawa-ku
Tokyo
Japan 141

New Zealand

Church of Scientology New Zealand
32 Lorne Street
Auckland 1
New Zealand

Latin America

▲ **Continental Liaison Office Latin America**
Federación Mexicana de Dianética
Avenida Montevideo 486
Colonia Linda Vista
C.P. 07300
Mexico, D.F.

Colombia

Centro Cultural de Dianética
Calle 95 No. 19-A-28
Bogotá
Colombia

Mexico

Organización Cultural Dianética de Guadalajara, A.C.
Pedro Moreno No. 1078 Int 3
Sector Juárez
Guadalajara, Jalisco
Mexico

Asociación Cultural Dianética, A.C.
Avenida Revolución No. 1359
Colonia Campestre
C.P. 01040
Mexico, D.F.

Instituto de Filosofía Aplicada, A.C.
Durango No. 105
Colonia Roma
C.P. 06700
Mexico, D.F.

Instituto de Filosofía Aplicada, A.C.
Anaxágoras No. 231
Colonia Narvarte
C.P. 03020
Mexico, D.F.

Instituto Tecnológico de Dianética, A.C.
Avenida Nuevo León 238
Colonia Hipódromo Condesa
C.P. 06170
Mexico, D.F.

Organización Desarrollo y Dianética, A.C.
Sánchez Azcona No. 403 4° Piso
Colonia Narvarte
C.P. 03020
Mexico, D.F.

Organización Cultural Dianética, A.C.
Nicolás San Juan No. 1734
Colonia Del Valle
C.P. 03100
Mexico, D.F.

Venezuela

Asociación Cultural Dianética de Venezuela, A.C. Valencia
Avenida 101 No. 150-23
Urbanización La Alegría
Apartado Postal 833
Valencia
Venezuela

Asociación Cultural Dianética de Venezuela, A.C. Valencia
Avenida Principal de Las Palmas
Cruce Con Avenida Carupano
Quinta Suha, Las Palmas
Caracas
Venezuela

CANADA

▲ **Continental Liaison Office Canada**
696 Yonge Street
Toronto, Ontario
Canada M4Y 2A7

Church of Scientology of Edmonton
10187 112th Street
Edmonton, Alberta
Canada T5K 1M1

Church of Scientology of Kitchener
104 King Street W.
Kitchener, Ontario
Canada N2G 2K6

Church of Scientology of Montreal
4489 Papineau Street
Montreal, Quebec
Canada H2H 1T7

Church of Scientology of Ottawa
150 Rideau Street, 2nd Floor
Ottawa, Ontario
Canada K1N 5X6

Church of Scientology of Quebec
350 Bd Chareste Est
Quebec, Quebec
Canada G1K 3H5

Church of Scientology of Toronto
696 Yonge Street, 2nd Floor
Toronto, Ontario
Canada M4Y 2A7

Church of Scientology of Vancouver
401 West Hasting Street
Vancouver, British Columbia
Canada V6B 1L5

Church of Scientology of Winnipeg
Donald Street, Suite 125
Winnipeg, Manitoba
Canada R3B 2J4

CELEBRITY CENTRES

Church of Scientology Celebrity Centre International
5930 Franklin Avenue
Hollywood, California 90028

Church of Scientology Celebrity Centre Dallas
8501 Manderville Lane
Dallas, Texas 75231

Church of Scientology Celebrity Centre Las Vegas
1100 S. 10th Street
Las Vegas, Nevada 89104

Church of Scientology Celebrity Centre Portland
709 S.W. Salmon Street
Portland, Oregon 97205

Church of Scientology Celebrity Centre Nashville
38 Music Square West
Nashville, Tennessee 37203

Church of Scientology Celebrity Centre New York
65 E. 82nd Street
New York, NY 10036

Church of Scientology Celebrity Centre Washington, DC
4214 16th Street N.W.
Washington, DC 20011

Church of Scientology Celebrity Centre London
27 Westbourne Grove
London, W2
England

Church of Scientology Celebrity Centre Vienna
Senefeldergasse 11/5
1100 Vienna
Austria

Church of Scientology Celebrity Centre Paris
69, rue Legendre
75017 Paris
France

Church of Scientology Celebrity Centre Düsseldorf
Grupellostrasse 28
4000 Düsseldorf
Germany

Church of Scientology Celebrity Centre Hamburg
Sechlingspforte 2
2000 Hamburg 76
Germany

Church of Scientology Celebrity Centre Munich
Arnulfstrasse 197
8000 Munich 19
Germany

Scientology Missions

International Office

Scientology Missions International
6331 Hollywood Boulevard, Suite 802
Los Angeles, California 90028

Western United States

▲ **Scientology Missions International Western United States Office**
1307 N. New Hampshire
Los Angeles, California 90027

Missions and Dianetics Centers

Mission of Anchorage
440 W. 5th Avenue
Anchorage, Alaska 99501

Mission of Fairbanks
401 5th Avenue
Fairbanks, Alaska 99701

Mission of Phoenix
2213 East Campbell
Phoenix, Arizona 85014

Mission of Beverly Hills
109 N. La Cienega Boulevard
Beverly Hills, California 90211

Mission of Capitol
7637 Fair Oaks Boulevard, #2
Carmichael, California 95608

Mission of Sacramento
5738 Marconi Avenue, Suite 12
Carmichael, California 95608

Mission of Butte County
5 Williamsburg Lane
Chico, California 95926

Mission of Escondido
324 S. Kalmia Street
Escondido, California 92025

Mission of Brand Boulevard
144 S. Brand Boulevard
Glendale, California 91204

Mission of South Bay
3940 Marine Avenue No. B
Lawndale, California 90260

Mission of Long Beach
5951 Cherry Avenue
Long Beach, California 90805

Mission of Westwood
3200 Santa Monica Boulevard, Suite 200
Los Angeles, California 90404

Mission of Los Gatos
475 Alberto Way, Suite 110
Los Gatos, California 95032

Mission of Moreno Valley
22458 Barton Road
Grand Terrace, California 92324

Mission of Glendale
2254 Honolulu Avenue
Montrose, California 91020

Mission of Monterey
546-D Hartnell Street
Monterey, California 93940

Mission of North Hollywood
5213 Lankershim Boulevard
North Hollywood, California 91601

Mission of Berkeley
466 Santa Clara, Suite 310
Oakland, California 94610

Mission of Antelope Valley
712 W. R-8
Palmdale, California 93551

Mission of Palm Springs
44-855 Las Palmas Avenue, Suite F
Palm Desert, California 92260

Mission of Concord
3313 Vincent Road, Suite 207
Pleasant Hills, California 94523

Mission of Redwood City
617 Veterans Boulevard, #205
Redwood City, California 94063

Mission of River Park
1485 River Park Drive, Suite 100
Sacramento, California 95815

Mission of Salinas
908 Riker Street
Salinas, California 93901

Mission of San Diego Coast
3288 El Cajon Boulevard, #3
San Diego, California 92104

Mission of San Francisco
406 Sutter Street
San Francisco, California 94108

Mission of San Jose
826 N. Winchester
San Jose, California 95128

Mission of Marin
1930 4th Street
San Rafael, California 94901

Mission of Sonora
20100 Barnwood Court
Sonora, California 95370

Mission of Buenaventura
180 N. Ashwood Avenue
Ventura, California 93003

Mission of West Valley
20315 Ventura Boulevard, Suite A
Woodland Hills, California 91364

Mission of Alamosa
511 Main Street
Alamosa, Colorado 81101

Mission of Boulder
1320 Pearl Street, Suite B-50
Boulder, Colorado 80302

Mission of South Denver
6565 S. Dayton, Suite 1000
Englewood, Colorado 80111

Mission of Denver
6739 W. 44th Avenue
Wheat Ridge, Colorado 80033

Mission of Honolulu
941 Kam Highway, #207
Pearl City, Hawaii 96782

Mission of Golden Valley
5707 Highway 7, #140
St. Louis Park, Minnesota 55416

Mission of Espanola
401 N. Riverside Drive, Suite M
Espanola, New Mexico 87532

Mission of Casa Linda
10204 Garland Road
Dallas, Texas 75218

Mission of Houston
2727 Fondren, Suite 1-A
Houston, Texas 77063

Mission of the Woodlands
2727 Fondren, Suite 1-A
Houston, Texas 77063

Mission of San Antonio
10609 IH 10 W., Suite 208
San Antonio, Texas 78230

Mission of Bellevue
1545 134th Avenue N.E.
Bellevue, Washington 98005

Mission of Seattle
2124 3rd Avenue
Seattle, Washington 98121

Mission of University Way
15216 2nd Avenue S.W.
Seattle, Washington 98166

EASTERN UNITED STATES

▲ **Scientology Missions International Eastern United States Office**
349 W. 48th Street
New York, NY 10036

Missions and Dianetics Centers

Mission of Clearwater
100 N. Belcher Road
Clearwater, Florida 34625

Mission of Fort Lauderdale
371 E. Commercial Boulevard
Fort Lauderdale, Florida 33334

Mission of West Palm Beach
597 Caroline Avenue
West Palm Beach, Florida 33413

Mission of Champaign-Urbana
312 W. John Street
Champaign, Illinois 61820

Mission of Peoria
2020 N. Wisconsin
Peoria, Illinois 61603

Mission of Indianapolis
109 E. 9th
Anderson, Indiana 46012

Mission of Baton Rouge
7855 Jefferson Highway
Baton Rouge, Louisiana 70809

Mission of Albany
57 Wilshire Drive
Cheshire, Massachusetts 01225

Mission of Merrimack Valley
PO Box 6231
Haverhill, Massachusetts 01831

Cape Cod Dianetics Center
PO Box 2017
Orleans, Massachusetts 02653

Mission of Baltimore
410 Ingleside Avenue
Baltimore, Maryland 21228

Mission of Genesee County
PO Box 407
Davisburg, Michigan 48503

Mission of Burnsville
14750 W. Burnsville Parkway, #57
Burnsville, Minnesota 55337

Mission of Omaha
PO Box 670
Bellevue, Nebraska 68005

Mission of Greater Concord
228 London Road, Suite 5
Concord, New Hampshire 03301

Mission of Collingswood
Greentree Executive Campus
Lincoln Drive W. Route 73, 5001-G
Marlton, New Jersey 08053

Mission of New Jersey
810 Main Street
Hackensack, New Jersey 07601

Dianetics Center of Rochester
6 Bickford Street
Macedon, New York 14502

Mission of Rockland
7 Panoramic Drive
Valley Cottage, New York 10989

Dianetics Center of Charlotte
6201 Bevington Place
Charlotte, North Carolina 28277

Mission of Cleveland
18118 Harland Avenue
Cleveland, Ohio 44119

Mission of Northeast Ohio
PO Box 2002
Streetsboro, Ohio 44241

Mission of Lake Erie
C/O 460 E. 10th Street
Erie, Pennsylvania 16503

Mission of Harrisburg
150 Reno Street
New Cumberland, Pennsylvania 17070

Mission of Pittsburgh
RD #2 Box 379
Charleroi, Pennsylvania 15022

Mission of Charleston
1519-A Harbour View Road
Charleston, South Carolina 29412

Mission of St. Albans
103 6th Avenue
St. Albans, West Virginia 25177

Mission of Fairfax
7409-H Little River Turnpike
Annandale, Virginia 22003

Mission of Southwest Virginia
PO Box 205
Troutville, Virginia 24175

Mission of Milwaukee
710 E. Silver Spring Drive
Suite E
White Fish Bay, Wisconsin 53217

UNITED KINGDOM

▲ **Scientology Missions International United Kingdom Office**
Saint Hill Manor
East Grinstead, West Sussex
England RH19 4JY

Missions and Dianetics Centers

Mission of Wirral
Woodcroft Eleanor Road
Bidston Birkenhead Merseyside
England L43 7QW

Mission of Cambridge
21 Park Road
Cambridge
England CB5 8AR

Dianetics Information Center of Carlisle
37 Grey Street
Carlisle, Cumbria
England CA1 2HJ

Chichester Dianetics Center
76 Grove Road
Chichester
England PO20 6BR

Dianetics Information Center of East Grinstead
19 Portland Road
East Grinstead, West Sussex
England PO20 GRN

Dianetics Information Center of Leicester
29 Albert Street
Leicestershire
England

Dianetics Information Center of Hove
170 Sackville Road
Hove, East Sussex
England BN3 7AG

Mission of Kendal
Ashleigh Ashmount Road
Grange-Over-Sands
Cumbria
England LA11 6BX

Dianetics Information Center of Leighton Buzzards
Shenstone Acres
Stewkley Road, Soulbury
Leighton Buzzards
England

Dianetics Information Center of London
61 Lincoln Road
London
England N2 9DJ

Dianetics Center Camberwell
146 Frien Road
London SE 22
England

Dianetics Information Center of Norwich
11 Fir Tree Road
Norwich, Norfolk
England NR7 9LG

Dianetics Information Center of Bournemouth
East Wing Jolliffe House
32 West Street
Poole, Dorset
England BH15 1LA

Dianetics Information Center of Southampton
43 Butts Road
Sholing, Southampton
Soton 449077
England

Dianetics Information Center of Cornwall
9 Adela Road
Torpoint, Cornwall
England

Dianetics Information Center of Tottenham
98 Dowsett Road
Tottenham, London
England N17 9DH

Dianetics Information Center of York
9 Don Avenue
York, Yorkshire
England Y02 2PT

Cardiff Dianetics Center
12 Clare Road Grangetown
Cardiff, Wales

India

Dianetics Center of Patiala
Talwar House, 1st Floor
Opp. Bengali Garage
Phowara Chowk, The Mall
Patiala 147001
India

Mission of Ambala Cantt
6352 Punjabi Mohalla
Ambala Cantt 133001
India

School of Punjabi Studies
Punjab University
Chandigarh 160014
India

Ireland

Dianetics Information Center of Dublin
62/63 Middle Abbey Street
Dublin
Ireland

Pakistan

Dianetics Information Center of Hyderabad
306–307/ A Latifabad, Unit No. 11
Hyderabad (Sind)
Pakistan 71800

Nazimabad Dianetics Center
5 3, 23/13 Nazimabad
Karachi
Pakistan

Dianetics Center for Personal Excellence
7/213 Sirajuddaula Road
Dmmchs
Karachi
Pakistan

Ability Center of Rawalpindi
53-C Satellite Town
Opp. Wapda Office Chandni Chowk
Rawalpindi
Pakistan

Europe

▲ **Scientology Missions International European Office**
Sankt Nikolajvej 4–6
Frederiksberg C
1953 Copenhagen
Denmark

Missions and Dianetics Centers

Austria

Dianetik-Zentrum Salzburg
Rupertgasse 21
5020 Salzburg
Austria

Dianetik Wolfsberg
Wienerstrasse 8
9400 Wolfsberg
Austria

Belgium

Dianetics Center of Antwerpen
Lange Gasthuisstr. 13, Baite 9
2000 Antwerpen
Belgium

Mission of Brugge
Groene Poortdreef 15A
8200 Brugge
Belgium

Bulgaria

Dianetic Center Bulgaria
L. Karave Lov 67
1000 Sofia
Bulgaria

Dianetic Counselling Group Bulgaria
Akazia #2
1421 Sofia
Bulgaria

Czechoslovakia

Mission of Prague
Hastalka 4
11000 Praha 1
Czechoslovakia

Denmark

Dianetik Kursus Center of Aalborg
Boulevarden 39 KL
9000 Aalborg
Denmark

Mission of Copenhagen City
Bülowsvej 20
1870 Frederiksberg C
Denmark

Hubbard Kursus Center of Kolding
Ejlersvej 24 1 Sal
6000 Kolding
Denmark

Dianetik Lyngby
Sorgenfrivej 3
2800 Lyngby
Denmark

Mission of Fyn
Absalonsgade 42
5000 Odense C
Denmark

Hubbard Kursus Center of Silkeborg
Virklundvej 5
8600 Silkeborg
Denmark

Dianetik Sønderborg
Sankt Jorgensgade 14
6400 Sønderborg
Denmark

Finland

Scientology Mission of Helsinki
Alkukuja 2-6K
PL 8
00711 Helsinki
Finland

France

Centre de Dianétique de Bordeaux
4, cour de la Somme
33800 Bordeaux
France

Centre de Dianétique de Brunoy
2, rue Traversière
91800 Brunoy
France

Mission de Scientologie Gentilly
26, avenue Pasteur
94250 Gentilly
France

Centre de Dianétique de Lyon
3, rue du Dr. Augros
69005 Lyon
France

Centre de Dianétique de Marseille
6, cours Joseph Thierry
13001 Marseille
France

Centre de Dianétique de Missillac
Le Croissant
44780 Missillac
France

Centre de Dianétique de Montpellier
9, rue Fontaine St. Berthomieux
34000 Montpellier
France

Centre de Dianétique de Mulhouse
13, rue du Sauvage
68100 Mulhouse
France

Centre de Dianétique de Nice
1, rue Maurice Jaubert
06000 Nice
France

Centre de Dianétique de Paris
25, rue Levis
75017 Paris
France

Centre de Dianétique de Reims
36, rue Libergier
51100 Reims
France

Centre de Dianétique de Toulouse
31, rue Bernard Mule
31400 Toulouse
France

Centre de Dianétique de Vichy
1, passage de Venise
03200 Vichy
France

Germany

Scientology Mission Kiel
Dorfstrasse 12
2301 Achterwehr
Germany

Dianetik-Zentrum Bremen
Osterdeich 27
2800 Bremen 1
Germany

Mission Villingen
Schramberger Strasse 14
7211 Eschbronn 2
Germany

Dianetik-Zentrum Esslingen
Sulzgriesersteige 20
7300 Esslingen
Germany

Dianetik Dresden
Petersweg 29
8228 Freilassing
Germany

Dianetik Göppingen
Geislingerstrasse 21
7320 Göppingen
Germany

Dianetik und Scientology Heilbronn
Frankfurterstrasse 47
7100 Heilbronn
Germany

Dianetik-Zentrum Heiligenberg
Mühlenweg 34
7799 Heiligenberg-Steigen
Germany

Dianetik-Zentrum Karlsruhe
Kaiserstrasse 163
7500 Karlsruhe
Germany

Zentrum für angewandte Philosophie
Kaiserallee 36
7500 Karlsruhe
Germany

Dianetik Mannheim
Schwabenheimerstrasse 13
6800 Mannheim 10
Germany

Dianetik Husum
Husumerstrasse 27
2251 Mildstedt-Rosendahl
Germany

Dianetik-Zentrum Münster
Bernhard-Ernst-Strasse 7
4000 Münster
Germany

Scientology Mission Munich
Müllerstrasse 33 RGB 1. Stock
8000 Munich 70
Germany

Scientology Mission Nymphenburg
Nymphenburgerstrasse 186
8000 Munich 19
Germany

Scientology-Kirche Bayern
Nuremberg Mission
Farberstrasse 5, Postfach 4804
8500 Nuremberg 1
Germany

Dianetik Reutlingen
Heinestrasse 9
7410 Reutlingen
Germany

Scientology Mission Ulm
Eythstrasse 2
7900 Ulm
Germany

Dianetik Wiesbaden
Kaiser-Friedrich-Ring 70
6200 Wiesbaden
Germany

Greece

Applied Philosophy Center of Athens
Patision 200
11256 Athens
Greece

Applied Philosophy Center of Kolonos
Ioanninon 6
Kolonos
Greece

Hungary

Dianetika Egyesylet
Letet 215
1299 Budapest, PF: 701
Hungary

L. Ron Hubbard Misszio 2
1063 Budapest
Szekely Mihaly U 5 II 1
Hungary

Netherlands

Dianetics Centrum of Oostakapelle
Vronesteyn 27
4356 Ac Oostakapelle
Netherlands

Dianetics Studiecentrum of The Hague
Laan Van Meedervoort 542B
2563 BL 's Gravenhage
Netherlands

Romania

Dianetic Center Romania
NR 4, SC A
ET III, Apt 15
Iasi, Cod 6600
Romania

Russia

Mission of St. Petersburg
Bldg 17, Kor 1, Apt 14
195279 St. Petersburg
Russia

St. Petersburg Dianetics Group
Bldg 22, Apt 13
Kovalevskaya St
195043 St. Petersburg
Russia

Spain

Centro de Mejoramiento Personal
Cambrils 19
28034 Madrid
Spain

Centro de Mejoramiento Personal
Urbanización los Molinos Primera Fase 14
41007 Seville
Spain

Sweden

Mission of Hässleholm
Stobygatan 16
281 39 Hässleholm
Sweden

Mission of Norrköping
Vattengatan 13
602 20 Norrköping
Sweden

Dianetikhuset
Grev Turegatan 55, ö.g.
114 38 Stockholm
Sweden

Switzerland

Mission de Scientologie Chêne-Bourg
Rue de Genève 88
1225 Chêne-Bourg
Switzerland

Scientology Mission Luzern-Haldenstrasse
Haldenstrasse 37
6006 Luzern
Switzerland

Scientology Luzern
Sentimattstrasse 7
6003 Luzern
Switzerland

Dianétique et Scientologie Vevey
Rue d'Italie, 21
1800 Vevey
Switzerland

Dianétique Fribourg
Route de Moncor, 14
1752 Villars-sur-Glâne
Switzerland

Dianetik-Zentrum Zurich
Regensbergstrasse 89
8050 Zurich
Switzerland

Yugoslavia

Dianetic Center of Koper
Zupanciceva 39
Koper
Yugoslavia

ITALY

▲ **Scientology Missions International Italian Office**
Via Torino, 51
20063 Cernusco sul Naviglio
Milan
Italy

Missions and Dianetics Centers

Chiesa di Scientology
Mission di Aosta
Avenue du Conseil des Comis, 8
11100 Aosta
Italy

Chiesa di Scientology
Missione di Avellino
Via Derna, 3
83100 Avellino
Italy

Chiesa di Scientology
Missione di Barletta
Via N. Piccinini, 5
70051 Barletta
Italy

Chiesa di Scientology della Bergamasca
Missione di Bergamo
Via Camozzi, 77
24100 Bergamo
Italy

Dianetik und Scientology
Beda Weber Strasse 19
39031 Bruneck
Italy

Chiesa di Scientology
Missione di Cagliari
Via Einauidi, 12
09127 Cagliari
Italy

Chiesa di Scientology
Missione di Cantù
Via Magenta, 4
20038 Seregno (Milano)
Italy

Chiesa di Scientology
Missione di Castelfranco
Via Borgo Piave, 35
Castelfranco Veneto
Italy

Chiesa di Scientology
Missione di Clusone
(Valseriana)
Via Carpinoni, 11
Clusone
Italy

Chiesa di Scientology
Missione di Codigoro
Via Riviera Cavallotti, 15
44021, Codigoro (FE)
Italy

Chiesa di Scientology
Missione di Como
Via Borgovico, 155
Como
Italy

Chiesa di Scientology
Missione di Cosenza
Via Piave, 95 H
87100 Cosenza
Italy

Chiesa di Scientology
Missione di Enna
Via Franco Longo, 16
Enna
Italy

Chiesa di Scientology
Missione di Firenze
Via Borgo S. Lorenzo, 4
50100 Florence
Italy

Chiesa di Scientology
Missione di Lecco
Via Madonnina, 2
220404 Garbagnate Monastero
Lecco
Italy

Chiesa di Scientology
Missione di Livorno
Via della Madonna, 41
57123 Livorno
Italy

Chiesa di Scientology
Missione di Lucca
Via Tofanelli, 24
55100 Lucca
Italy

Chiesa di Scientology
Missione di Macerata
dell'Adriatico
Via Roma, 13
62100 Macerata
Italy

Chiesa di Scientology
Missione di Mantova
Via Bonomi, 6
46100 Mantova
Italy

Chiesa di Scientology
Missione di Milano
Viale Caldara, 27
20122, Milan
Italy

Chiesa di Scientology
Missione di Modena
Via Modonella, 21
41100 Modena
Italy

Chiesa di Scientology
Missione di Palermo
Via M. Toselli, 36/I
90100 Palermo
Italy

Chiesa di Scientology
Missione di Gaggino
V. Fornaci, 12
22027 Ronago (CO)
Italy

Chiesa di Scientology
Missione di Siracusa
Via Filisto Romeo II, 21
Syracuse
Italy

Chiesa di Scientology
Missione di Ragusa
Via Cascino, 36
97019 Vittoria (RG)
Italy

AFRICA

▲ **Scientology Missions International African Office**
Security Building, 2nd Floor
95 Commissioner Street
Johannesburg 2001
South Africa

Missions and Dianetics Centers

Ethiopia

Dianetics Information Center of Addis Ababa
PO Box 2852
Addis Ababa
Ethiopia

Mission of Ethiopia
PO Box 100505
Addis Ababa
Ethiopia

Ghana

Mission of Accra
PO Box 11584
Accra-North
Ghana 71800

Mission of Tema
PO Box 403
Tema
Ghana

Ivory Coast

Dianetics Center of Abidjan
01BP5003 Abidjan 01
Ivory Coast

Kenya

Dianetics Technology Center of Kenya
PO Box 1682
Thika
Kenya

Nigeria

Mission of Ibadan
PO Box 9943
University Post Office
Ibadan, Oyo State
Nigeria

Mission of Lagos
190/192 Ikorodu Road Palm Grove
PO Box 70745 Victoria Island
Lagos
Nigeria

Sierra Leone

Mission of Sierra Leone
PO Box 1396
Freetown
Sierra Leone

South Africa

Mission of East London
9 Salisbury Road
East London 53749
South Africa

Mission of Hillbrow
6 Palomar Heights
104 Claim Street
Hillbrow 2001
South Africa

Mission of Soweto
893 Moletsane
PO Box 496
Kwa Xuma-Soweto
South Africa

Mission of Norwood
18 Trilby Street
Oaklands, Johannesburg 2192
South Africa

Tanzania

Dar Es Salaam Dianetics Group
PO Box 9563
Dar Es Salaam
Tanzania

Zaire

Mission de Kinshasa
BP 1444 Fele No. 7
Kinshasa/Limete
Zaire
Africa

AUSTRALIA, NEW ZEALAND AND OCEANIA

▲ **Scientology Missions International Australian, New Zealand and Oceanian Office**
201 Castlereagh Street
Sydney, New South Wales 2000
Australia

Missions and Dianetics Centers

Australia

Mission of Camberwell
235 Camberwell Road
Camberwell, Victoria 3124
Australia

Mission of Perth
PO Box 1049
West Perth 6872
Australia

Japan

Mission of Tokyo
Park Heights Ikebukuro 1102
1-17-11 Higashi Ikebukuro
Toshima-ku 171
Tokyo
Japan

New Zealand

Mission of Christchurch
PO Box 1843
Christchurch
New Zealand

Philippines

Dianetics Center of Manila
PO Box 1182 MCC
Makati 1299
Metro Manila
Philippines

Taiwan

Mission of Taichung
51 Da Long Road
Taichung
Taiwan

Latin America

▲ **Scientology Missions International Latin American Office**
Federación Mexicana de Dianética
Avenida Montevideo 486
Colonia Linda Vista
C.P. 07300
Mexico, D.F.

Missions and Dianetics Centers

Argentina

Asociación Hubbard de Filosofía Aplicada
Neuquen 793-San Isidro
Buenos Aires
Argentina

Misión de Santa Fe
Prov de Santa Fe
La Rioja 3922
Argentina

Misión de Parana
Panama 911
Parana
Argentina

Brazil

Misión do Brasil
Rua Pedro Paulo Koerig 444
85670 Salto do Lontra
Estado do Parana
Brazil

Chile

Misión de Chile
Nuncio Laghi 6558
La Reina
Santiago
Chile

Colombia

Misión de Medellín
EL 32 No. 69B-33
Medellín
Colombia

Costa Rica

Misión de San Carlos
Hospital San Carlos
Alajuela
Costa Rica

Instituto Tecnológico de Dianética
Frente Oficinas Centrales Invu Calles
5-3 Avenida 9
Apdo 8099-1000
San José
Costa Rica

Cuba

Dianetic Counseling Group of Cuba
Calle 100 #3909
Apto. 1, Entre 39 y 41
Marianao 14, Havana
Cuba

Ecuador

Centro de Dianética y Cienciología
Elizalde 119 Y Pichincha
4 Piso, Oficina 2
Guayaquil
Ecuador

Guatemala

Misión de Escuintla
Ira Ave. 1-25
Zona 4
Colonia Los Naranjales
Escuintla
Guatemala

Dianética de Guatemala
Vía 1 4-51 Zona 4
01004 Guatemala Ca
Guatemala

Mexico

Dianetics Center of Aguascalientes
308 D-301
Triana
C.P. 20270 Aguascalientes

Mission of Ifa Bajio
Juárez No. 224
Leon GTO 37000
Mexico

Mission of Monterrey
Simón Bolívar No. 1335 NTE
Colonia Mitras Centro
Monterrey NL
Mexico

Mission of Mexicali
Av Nicaragua 807
Frac. Sonora
C.P. 21210 Mexicali
Baja California

Dominican Republic

Misión de Santo Domingo
Condominio Ambar Plaza II
Edificio II, Apto. 302
Avenida Saratosa Esq. Núñez de Cáceres
Bella Vista, Santo Domingo
Dominican Republic

Canada

▲ **Scientology Missions International Canadian Office**
696 Yonge Street
Toronto, Ontario
Canada M4Y 2A7

Missions and Dianetics Centers

Mission of Calgary
824 C Edmonton Train North East
Calgary, Alberta
Canada T2E 3J6

Mission of Halifax
1574 Argyle Street, Suite 11
Halifax, Nova Scotia
Canada B3J 2B3

Mission of St. Georges
130 125E rue St. Georges Est Beauce
Quebec
Canada G5Y 2X9

Mission of North York
227 Beverley Street
Toronto, Ontario
Canada M5T 1Z4

Mission of Vancouver
1892 Kings Way
Vancouver, British Columbia
Canada V5N 2S7

I HELP

(INTERNATIONAL HUBBARD ECCLESIASTIC LEAGUE OF PASTORS)

INTERNATIONAL HUBBARD ECCLESIASTIC LEAGUE OF PASTORS

1340 N. Berendo Street
Los Angeles, California 90027

FREEDOM MAGAZINE OFFICES

INTERNATIONAL OFFICE

Church of Scientology International
Freedom Magazine
6331 Hollywood Boulevard, Suite 1200
Los Angeles, California 90028

EUROPE

Church of Scientology of Belgium
Freedom Magazine
61, rue du Prince Royal
1050 Brussels
Belgium

Church of Scientology of Denmark
Freedom Magazine
Vesterbrogade 66B
1620 Copenhagen V
Denmark

Church of Scientology of Paris
Freedom Magazine
65, rue de Dunkerque
75009 Paris
France

Church of Scientology of Hamburg
Freedom Magazine
Steindamm 63
2000 Hamburg 1
Germany

Church of Scientology of Amsterdam
Freedom Magazine
Nieuwe Zijds Voorburgwal 271
1012 RL Amsterdam
Netherlands

Church of Scientology of Norway
Freedom Magazine
Storgata 9
0155 Oslo 1
Norway

Asociación Civil de Dianética de Madrid
Freedom Magazine
Montera 20, Piso 1° dcha.
28013 Madrid
Spain

Church of Scientology of Stockholm
Freedom Magazine
St. Eriksgatan 56
112 34 Stockholm
Sweden

Church of Scientology of Zurich
Freedom Magazine
Badenerstrasse 141
8004 Zurich
Switzerland

ITALY

Church of Scientology of Milan
Freedom Magazine
Via Abetone, 10
20137 Milan
Italy

AFRICA

Church of Scientology of Johannesburg
Freedom Magazine
Security Building, 2nd Floor
95 Commissioner Street
Johannesburg 2001
South Africa

UNITED KINGDOM

Church of Scientology United Kingdom
Freedom Magazine
Saint Hill Manor
East Grinstead, West Sussex
England RH19 4JY

CANADA

Church of Scientology Canada
Freedom Magazine
696 Yonge Street
Toronto, Ontario
Canada M4Y 2A7

LATIN AMERICA

Federación Mexicana de Dianética
Freedom Magazine
Avenida Montevideo 486
Colonia Linda Vista
C.P. 07300
Mexico, D.F.

AUSTRALIA, NEW ZEALAND AND OCEANIA

Church of Scientology of Sydney
Freedom Magazine
201 Castlereagh Street
Sydney, New South Wales 2000
Australia

Church of Scientology New Zealand
Freedom Magazine
32 Lorne Street
Auckland 1
New Zealand

Citizens Commission on Human Rights Groups

International Office

Citizens Commission on Human Rights International
6362 Hollywood Boulevard, Suite B
Los Angeles, California 90028

United States

Citizens Commission on Human Rights Phoenix
PO Box 16723
Phoenix, Arizona 85011

Citizens Commission on Human Rights Mountain View
483 Alicia Way
Los Altos, California 94022

Citizens Commission on Human Rights Los Angeles
6362 Hollywood Boulevard, Suite B
Los Angeles, California 90028

Citizens Commission on Human Rights Santa Barbara
1111 B Coast Village Road
Montecito, California 93108

Citizens Commission on Human Rights Riverside
17305 Santa Rosa Mine Road
Perris, California 92570

Citizens Commission on Human Rights San Francisco
83 McAllister Street
San Francisco, California 94102

Citizens Commission on Human Rights San Luis Obispo
PO Box 4134
San Luis Obispo, California 93403

Citizens Commission on Human Rights Orange County
23632 Via Halcon
Trabuco Canyon, California 92674

Citizens Commission on Human Rights Colorado
PO Box 21401
Denver, Colorado 80221

Citizens Commission on Human Rights New Haven
909 Whalley Avenue
New Haven, Connecticut 06515

Citizens Commission on Human Rights Clearwater
423 Cleveland Street, 3rd Floor
Clearwater, Florida 33515

Citizens Commission on Human Rights South Florida
1400 S. Dixie Highway #2W
Pompano Beach, Florida 33060

Citizens Commission on Human Rights Atlanta
2362 Piedmont Road N.E.
Atlanta, Georgia 30324

Citizens Commission on Human Rights Chicago
2370 W. Nichols Road, #E
Arlington Heights, Illinois 60004

Citizens Commission on Human Rights Boston
448 Beacon Street
Boston, Massachusetts 02115

Citizens Commission on Human Rights St. Louis
342 Tally Ho
St. Charles, Missouri 63301

Citizens Commission on Human Rights Buffalo
47 W. Huron Street
Buffalo, New York 14202

Citizens Commission on Human Rights Cincinnati
PO Box 1624
Westchester, Ohio 45071

Citizens Commission on Human Rights Portland
PO Box 1922
Portland, Oregon 97207

Citizens Commission on Human Rights Philadelphia
PO Box 171
Philadelphia, Pennsylvania 19105

Citizens Commission on Human Rights Austin
403 E. Ben White #A
Austin, Texas 78704

Citizens Commission on Human Rights Dallas
PO Box 742-826
Dallas, Texas 75374

Citizens Commission on Human Rights Houston
PO Box 22088
Houston, Texas 77277

Citizens Commission on Human Rights Seattle
300 Lenora Street #B-252
Seattle, Washington 98121

Citizens Commission on Human Rights Washington, DC
2125 "S" Street N.W.
Washington, DC 20008

Citizens Commission on Human Rights Governmental Affairs Office
301 4th Street N.E.
Washington, DC 20008

United Kingdom

Citizens Commission on Human Rights United Kingdom National Office
Saint Hill Manor
East Grinstead, West Sussex
England RH19 4JY

Citizens Commission on Human Rights Brighton
PO Box 529
Brighton
England BN2 2XX

Citizens Commission on Human Rights Bournemouth
PO Box 1546
Poole, Dorset
England BH15 1ZE

Citizens Commission on Human Rights London
28 Byron Court
Byron Road, Harrow
England HA1 1JT

Citizens Commission on Human Rights Northwest Office
3 Dorchester Avenue
Prestwich, Manchester
England M25 8LH

Europe

Citizens Commission on Human Rights Denmark
Lundegaardsvej 19
2900 Hellerup
Denmark

Finland

Citizens Commission on Human Rights Finland
PL 67
02771 Espoo
Finland

France

Citizens Commission on Human Rights France (CCDH France)
54, rue Custine
75018 Paris
France

Citizens Commission on Human Rights Angers (CCDH d'Angers)
42, rue Fulton
49000 Angers
France

Germany

Commission for Psychiatric Abuse Against Human Rights Germany
Postfach 620241
2000 Hamburg 62
Germany

Commission for Psychiatric Abuse Against Human Rights Düsseldorf
Beethovenstrasse 36
4000 Düsseldorf 1
Germany

Commission for Psychiatric Abuse Against Human Rights Frankfurt
Diersbachtal 13
6273 Waldems 3
Germany

Commission for Psychiatric Abuse Against Human Rights Göppingen
Geislinger Strasse 21
7320 Göppingen
Germany

Commission for Psychiatric Abuse Against Human Rights Karlsruhe
Am Wetterbach 100
7500 Karlsruhe 41
Germany

Commission for Psychiatric Abuse Against Human Rights Munich
Frankfurter Ring 105
8000 Munich 45
Germany

Commission for Psychiatric Abuse Against Human Rights Rodgau
Obere Markt Strasse 7
6054 Rodgau 3
Germany

Commission for Psychiatric Abuse Against Human Rights Stuttgart
Gaishämmer Strasse 12
7000 Stuttgart 1
Germany

Commission for Psychiatric Abuse Against Human Rights Wiesbaden
Mainzer Strasse 46
6200 Wiesbaden
Germany

Israel

Citizens Commission on Human Rights Israel
Suskin 9
Nahariya 22404
Israel

Netherlands

Citizens Commission on Human Rights Holland
Postbus 11354
1001 GJ Amsterdam
Netherlands

Norway

Citizens Commission on Human Rights Norway
Post Boks 237
1322 Hoevik
Norway

Spain

Citizens Commission on Human Rights Barcelona (CCDH Cataluña)
Apartado de Correos 30241
C.P. 08080 Barcelona
Spain

Citizens Commission on Human Rights Madrid (CCDH Spain)
Apartado de Correos 14.696
Madrid
Spain

Sweden

Citizens Commission on Human Rights Sweden
Hammarvägen 6
136 73 Haninge
Sweden

Citizens Commission on Human Rights Göteborg
Box 17100
402 61 Göteborg
Sweden

Switzerland

Citizens Commission on Human Rights Basel
Augsterheglistrasse 36
4133 Pratteln
Switzerland

Citizens Commission on Human Rights Bern
Postfach 338
3000 Bern 7
Switzerland

Citizens Commission on Human Rights Biel
Bei Baettig
Jurastrasse 53
2503 Biel
Switzerland

Citizens Commission on Human Rights Burgdorf
Hohengasse 3
3400 Burgdorf
Switzerland

Citizens Commission on Human Rights Geneva
Grand-Pré 2
1202 Geneva
Switzerland

Citizens Commission on Human Rights Lausanne
Boîte Postale 231
1000 Lausanne-7
Switzerland

Citizens Commission on Human Rights Thun
Bodmerstrasse 3
3645 Gwatt
Switzerland

Citizens Commission on Human Rights Zurich
Badenerstrasse 141
8004 Zurich
Switzerland

ITALY

Citizens Commission on Human Rights Italy National Office
Via Val di Porto, 19
20056 Trezzo sull'Adda (MI)
Italy

Citizens Commission on Human Rights Brescia
Viale Piave, 50/B
25125 Brescia
Italy

Citizens Commission on Human Rights Catania
Via San Camillo
95100 Catania
Sicily

Citizens Commission on Human Rights Monza
Via Nazario Sauro, 17
20049 Concorezzo (MI)
Italy

Citizens Commission on Human Rights Cantù
Via Fattori, 1
22063 Cucciago (CO)
Italy

Citizens Commission on Human Rights Como
Via Napoleone, 16
Como
Italy

Citizens Commission on Human Rights Milan
Fermo Posta Cordusio
20100 Milan
Italy

Citizens Commission on Human Rights Novara
Via della Riotta, 13
28100 Novara
Italy

Citizens Commission on Human Rights Padua
Via Buonarroti, 65
35100 Padua
Italy

Citizens Commission on Human Rights Pordenone
Casella Postale, 45
33170 Pordenone
Italy

Citizens Commission on Human Rights Turin
Via Luserna di Rora, 29
10100 Turin
Italy

Citizens Commission on Human Rights Vicenza
Casella Postale, 29
Montecchio Maggiore
36075 Vicenza
Italy

AFRICA

Citizens Commission on Human Rights South Africa National Office
PO Box 710
Johannesburg 2000
South Africa

Citizens Commission on Human Rights Cape Town
PO Box 374
Milnerton
7435 Cape Town
South Africa

Citizens Commission on Human Rights Durban
PO Box 24054
Hillary
4024 Durban
South Africa

Citizens Commission on Human Rights Pretoria
PO Box 11053
Brooklyn
Pretoria 0001
South Africa

AUSTRALIA, NEW ZEALAND AND OCEANIA

Citizens Commission on Human Rights Australia National Office
201 Castlereagh Street
Sydney 2000
Australia

Citizens Commission on Human Rights Adelaide
28 Waymouth Street
Adelaide 5000
Australia

Citizens Commission on Human Rights Brisbane
106 Edward Street
Brisbane 4000
Australia

Citizens Commission on Human Rights Canberra
15 Blythe Close
A.C.T. 2617
Australia

Citizens Commission on Human Rights Melbourne
44 Russell Street
Melbourne 3000
Australia

Citizens Commission on Human Rights Perth
39 King Street
Perth 7000
Australia

Citizens Commission on Human Rights New Zealand
32 Lorne Street, 4th Floor
Auckland 1
New Zealand

LATIN AMERICA

Citizens Commission on Human Rights Mexico
Tuxpan 68
Colonia Roma Sur
Mexico City
Mexico

CANADA

Citizens Commission on Human Rights Canada National Office
696 Yonge Street, Suite 802
Toronto, Ontario
Canada M4Y 2A7

Citizens Commission on Human Rights Edmonton
10187, 112 Street
Edmonton, Alberta
Canada T5K 1M1

Citizens Commission on Human Rights Montreal
4489 Papineau Street
Montreal, Quebec
Canada H2H 1T7

Citizens Commission on Human Rights Toronto
696 Yonge Street, Suite 601
Toronto, Ontario
Canada M4Y 2A7

Citizens Commission on Human Rights Vancouver
401 W. Hastings
Vancouver, British Columbia
Canada V6B 1L5

NATIONAL COMMISSION ON LAW ENFORCEMENT AND SOCIAL JUSTICE

National Commission on Law Enforcement and Social Justice
3917 Riverside Drive
Toluca Lake, California 91505

ASSOCIATION FOR BETTER LIVING AND EDUCATION

INTERNATIONAL OFFICE

Association for Better Living and Education
6331 Hollywood Boulevard, Suite 700
Los Angeles, California 90028

WESTERN UNITED STATES

Association for Better Living and Education Western United States Office
1307 N. New Hampshire
Los Angeles, California 90027

EASTERN UNITED STATES

Association for Better Living and Education Eastern United States Office
349 W. 48th Street
New York, NY 10036

UNITED KINGDOM

Association for Better Living and Education United Kingdom Office
Saint Hill Manor
East Grinstead, West Sussex
England RH19 4JY

EUROPE

Association for Better Living and Education European Office
Sankt Nikolajvej 4–6
Frederiksberg C
1953 Copenhagen
Denmark

Russia

Association for Better Living and Education Russian Office
48 Vavilova Street
Building 4, Suite 169
Moscow 117333
Russia

ITALY

Association for Better Living and Education Italian Office
Via Nerino, 8
20213 Milan
Italy

AFRICA

Association for Better Living and Education African Office
Security Building, 4th Floor
95 Commissioner Street
Johannesburg 2001
South Africa

AUSTRALIA, NEW ZEALAND AND OCEANIA

Association for Better Living and Education Australian, New Zealand and Oceanian Office
201 Castlereagh Street
Sydney, New South Wales 2000
Australia

LATIN AMERICA

Instituto de Tecnología Para La Educación, A.C.
Tetla #6 Colonia Ruiz Cortines
Delegación Coyoacán
C.P. 64630
Mexico D.F.

CANADA

Association for Better Living and Education Canadian Office
696 Yonge Street
Toronto, Ontario
Canada M4Y 2A7

APPLIED SCHOLASTICS

INTERNATIONAL OFFICE

Applied Scholastics International
7060 Hollywood Boulevard, Suite 200
Los Angeles, California 90028

WESTERN UNITED STATES

Applied Scholastics Los Angeles
503 Central Avenue
Glendale, California 91203

EUROPE

Applied Scholastics
F.F. Ulriksgade 13
2100 Copenhagen O
Denmark

AFRICA

Education Alive
CDH House, 3rd Floor
217 Jeppe Street
Johannesburg 2100
South Africa

AUSTRALIA, NEW ZEALAND AND OCEANIA

Applied Scholastics
319 Canterbury Road
Ringwood Victoria 3134
Australia

CANADA

Applied Scholastics
840 Pape Avenue, Suite 201
Toronto, Ontario
Canada M4K 3T6

CRIMINON

INTERNATIONAL OFFICE

Criminon International
6381 Hollywood Boulevard, Suite 420
Los Angeles, California 90028

WESTERN UNITED STATES

Criminon Western United States
PO Box 9091
Glendale, California 91226

Criminon Texas
805 South Jackson
Jacksonville, Texas 75766

Criminon Washington
4004 Island Crest Way
Mercer Island, Washington 98040

EASTERN UNITED STATES

Criminon Eastern United States
PO Box 6
Demarest, New Jersey 07627

Criminon Florida
639 Cleveland Street, Suite 210
Clearwater, Florida 34615

Criminon New Hampshire
282 Loudon Road
Concord, New Hampshire 03301

Criminon Minnesota
PO Box 82
Newport, Minnesota 55055

Children's Commission
Butler County Courthouse
700 Court Square
Greenville, Alabama 36037

EUROPE

Criminon Brussels
Rue Père Be Beken 6
1040 Brussels 4
Belgium

ITALY

Criminon Italy
Associazione Criminon
Via Nerino, 8
20123 Milan
Italy

AFRICA

Criminon Africa
82 St. Georges Road
Belleulle 2198
South Africa

NARCONON

INTERNATIONAL OFFICE

Narconon International
6381 Hollywood Boulevard, Suite 420
Los Angeles, California 90028

WESTERN UNITED STATES

Narconon Los Angeles
3429 W. Olympic Boulevard
Los Angeles, California 90019

Narconon Professional Center
4421 Lankershim Boulevard
North Hollywood, California 91602

Narconon Northern California
2718 Homestead Road
Santa Clara, California 95051

Narconon Chilocco
Route 2, Box 400
Newkirk, Oklahoma 74647

EASTERN UNITED STATES

Narconon Boston
1500 Main Street, Suite 4
Weymouth, Massachusetts 02190

UNITED KINGDOM

Narconon United Kingdom
Delivery Center Rannoch
Rannoch Road Crowborough
East Sussex
England TN6 1RF

EUROPE

Narconon Europe
Ny Carlsbergvej 37
1760 Copenhagen V
Denmark

Denmark

Narconon Denmark
Åmosevej 73
Skellingsted
4440 Mørkøv
Denmark

France

Narconon France
Rue de la Commande
Carrefour de la Croix de Dague
64290 Lasseube
France

Narconon Aquitaine
Rue de la Commande
Carrefour de la Croix de Dague
64290 Lasseube
France

Germany

Narconon Itzehoe
An der B 877
2210 Itzehoe
Germany

Narconon Schliersee
Neuhauserstrasse 1
8162 Schliersee 2
Germany

Netherlands

Narconon Holland (National)
C/O Gasthuissingel 16
2012 Dn Haarlem
Netherlands

Narconon Zutphen
Deventerweg 93
7203 Ad Zutphen
Netherlands

Spain

Asociación Narconon Los Molinos
C/San Nicolás S/N
Chalet Mari Solea
28460 Los Molinos de Guadarrama
Madrid
Spain

Asociación Española de Mejoras Sociales
Avenida de la Constitución No. 1 Primero B
41500 Alcalá de Guadaira
Seville
Spain

Asociación Narconon Retiro
Chalet Herrera
41500 Alcalá de Guadaira
Seville
Spain

Asociación Narconon Mediterraneo
Ctra. Alcalá—Dos Hermanas Km 2,5
Chalet San Luis
41500 Alcalá de Guadaira
Seville
Spain

Sweden

Narconon Sweden
Box 3081
143 00 Vårby
Sweden

Narconon Huddinge
Vårbackavägen 1
143 00 Vårby gård
Stockholm
Sweden

Narconon Knutby
Gränsta
740 12 Knutby
Sweden

Narconon Malmö/Eslöv
Södergård-Skarhult
241 00 Eslöv
Sweden

Switzerland

Narconon Romandie
Les Plans-sur-Bex 1888
Switzerland

Italy

Associazione Narconon Airone
C/O Villaggio Ionio
Via S. Francesco da Rena Fondo, 5
95100 Catania
Italy

Associazione Narconon Il Falco
Contrada Monti
Altilia
87040 Cosenza
Italy

Narconon Il Gabbiano
C/O Hotel Punta Dell'est
Strada Statale per Tarano
Zona 172/C
Taranto
Italy

Life Revitalization Center
C/O Albergo Colombo
Via Firenze, 29
Massa
Italy

Associazione Narconon per un Futuro Migliore
Via Cadamosto, 8
20129 Milan
Italy

Comunità Narconon Albatros
Strada Statale
18 Campora San Giovanni
87032 Amantea
Cosenza
Italy

Narconon La Fenice
C/O Hotel Holiday
Via Amalfi, 35
Villarosa di Martinsicuro
Teramo
Italy

Narconon Tucano
C/O Hotel Concorde — Val Canale
24020 Ardesio
Bergamo
Italy

Narconon Condor
Via E. Giusti, 68 BIS
21019 Somma Lombardo
Varese
Italy

Narconon Grifone
C/O Villaggio Ippocampo di Mare
Via S. Francesco la Rena
95125 Catania
Italy

Narconon Life
C/O Hotel Maya
66010 Palombaro
Chieti
Italy

CANADA

Narconon Vancouver
3240-4609 Kingsway
Burnaby, British Columbia
Canada V5H 4L3

Narconon Toronto
840 Pape Avenue, Suite 201
Toronto, Ontario
Canada M4K 3T6

THE WAY TO HAPPINESS

INTERNATIONAL OFFICE

The Way to Happiness Foundation International
6324 Sunset Boulevard
PO Box 2930
Hollywood, California 90028

UNITED STATES

The Way to Happiness Foundation New York
49 Saint Mark Place
New York, NY 10008

AFRICA

The Way to Happiness Foundation Africa
CDH House, 3rd Floor
217 Jeppe Street
Johannesburg 2001
South Africa

AUSTRALIA, NEW ZEALAND AND OCEANIA

The Way to Happiness Foundation Australia, New Zealand, Oceania
PO Box A1044
Sydney South, New South Wales 2001
Australia

LATIN AMERICA

The Way to Happiness Foundation Latin America
Tetla #6 Colonia Ruiz Cortines
Delegación Coyoacán
Mexico 04630 D.F.

Colombia

The Way to Happiness Foundation Colombia
Carrera 10 A, No. 27-71
Res Tequendama (Sur)
Bogotá
Colombia

EUROPE

The Way to Happiness Foundation Russia
Stoliarny Per 7-2
Moscow
Russia

WORLD INSTITUTE OF SCIENTOLOGY ENTERPRISES

INTERNATIONAL OFFICE

World Institute of Scientology Enterprises International
6331 Hollywood Boulevard, Suite 701
Los Angeles, California 90028

WESTERN UNITED STATES

World Institute of Scientology Enterprises Western United States Office
1308 N. Berendo Street
Los Angeles, California 90027

WISE Charter Committee Los Angeles
100 N. Brand Boulevard, Suite 501
Glendale, California 91203

WISE Charter Committee Orange County
29379 Rancho California Road, Suite 105
Temecula, California 92592

Hubbard College of Administration International
3540 Wilshire Boulevard, Suite 811
Los Angeles, California 90010

Hubbard College of Administration
Santa Clara Valley
2718 Homestead Road
Santa Clara, California 95051

EASTERN UNITED STATES

World Institute of Scientology Enterprises Eastern United States Office
349 W. 48th Street
New York, NY 10036

WISE Charter Committee Clearwater
628 Cleveland, Suite 300
Clearwater, Florida 34615

WISE Charter Committee Atlanta
33 Ponce de Leon, Suite 214
Atlanta, Georgia 30308

WISE Charter Committee Chicago
1 O'Hare Centre
Rosemont, Illinois 60018

WISE Charter Committee New England
246B N. Broadway, Suite 206
Salem, New Hampshire 03079

WISE Charter Committee New York
20 W. 20th Street, Suite 801
New York, NY 10011

Hubbard College of Administration Clearwater
1220 Turner Street
Clearwater, Florida 34616

Hubbard College of Administration Atlanta
1090 N. Chase Parkway, Suite 390
Marietta, Georgia 30067

UNITED KINGDOM

World Institute of Scientology Enterprises United Kingdom Office
Saint Hill Manor
East Grinstead, West Sussex
England RH19 4JY

EUROPE

World Institute of Scientology Enterprises European Office
Sankt Nikolajvej 4–6
1953 Frederiksberg C
Copenhagen
Denmark

Denmark

WISE Charter Committee Denmark
Svanemollevej 77
2900 Hellerup
Denmark

Germany

WISE Charter Committee Düsseldorf
Am Rottchen 32
4000 Düsseldorf 30
Germany

WISE Charter Committee Hamburg
Mittelweg 118
2000 Hamburg 13
Germany

WISE Charter Committee Stuttgart
Im Mahdental 24
7250 Leonberg
Germany

Netherlands

WISE Charter Committee Holland
Stadhouderskade 159
1074 BC Amsterdam
Netherlands

Russia

World Institute of Scientology Enterprises Russian Office
48 Vavilova Street
Building 4, Suite 169
Moscow 117333
Russia

Hubbard College of Administration Moscow
B. Pereyaslavskaya, 52
Moscow 129041
Russia

Spain

WISE Charter Committee Madrid
Calle Lanuza 9-1C
28028 Madrid
Spain

Sweden

Hubbard College of Administration Stockholm
Stockholmsvägen 70
181 42 Lidingö
Sweden

Switzerland

WISE Charter Committee Lausanne
Avenue de l'Université 18
1005 Lausanne
Switzerland

WISE Charter Committee Zurich
Bachstrasse 39
8912 Obfelden
Switzerland

Hubbard College of Administration Rolle
Rue de la Gare, 2
1180 Rolle
Switzerland

ITALY

World Institute of Scientology Enterprises Italian Office
Via Torino, 51
20063 Cernusco sul Naviglio
Milan
Italy

WISE Charter Committee Milan
Via Paracelso, 12
Palazzo Perseo
20411 Agrate Brianza
Milan
Italy

AFRICA

World Institute of Scientology Enterprises African Office
Security Building, 4th Floor
95 Commissioner Street
Johannesburg 2001
South Africa

WISE Charter Committee South Africa
PO Box 67675
Bryanstown 2021
South Africa

AUSTRALIA, NEW ZEALAND AND OCEANIA

Continental Office

World Institute of Scientology Enterprises Office Australian, New Zealand and Oceanian Office
201 Castlereagh Street
Sydney, New South Wales 2000
Australia

WISE Charter Committee Melbourne
1 Cuthbert Street
Footscray, Victoria 3001
Australia

Hubbard College of Administration Brisbane
119 Leichhardt Street, 2nd Floor, Suite 2
Spring Hill, Queensland 4000
Australia

LATIN AMERICA

World Institute of Scientology Enterprises Latin American Office Federación Mexicana de Dianética
Avenida Montevideo No. 488
Colonia Linda Vista
C.P. 07300
Mexico, D.F.

CANADA

World Institute of Scientology Enterprises Canadian Office
696 Yonge Street
Toronto, Ontario
Canada M4Y 2A7

WISE Charter Committee Toronto
873 Broadview Avenue, Lower Level
Toronto, Ontario
Canada M4K 2P9

PUBLICATIONS ORGANIZATIONS

BRIDGE PUBLICATIONS, INC.

4751 Fountain Avenue
Los Angeles, California 90029

NEW ERA PUBLICATIONS INTERNATIONAL ApS

Store Kongensgade 55
1264 Copenhagen K
Denmark

United Kingdom

New Era Publications, Ltd.
78 Holmethorpe Avenue
Redhill, Surrey
England RH1 2NL

France

NEW ERA Publications France
111, boulevard de Magenta
75010 Paris
France

Germany

NEW ERA Publications Germany GmbH
Bahnhofstrasse 40
2153 Neu Wulmstorf
Germany

Russia

New Era Publications Russia
B. Pereyaslavskaya 50, Suite 511
Moscow 129041
Russia

Spain

New Era Publications España, SA
C/de la Paz, 4, entpta dcha.
28012 Madrid
Spain

Italy

NEW ERA Publications Italia Srl
Via L.G. Columella, 12
20128 Milan
Italy

Africa

Continental Publications Pty Ltd.
6th Floor
Security Building
95 Commissioner Street
Johannesburg
South Africa

Australia

N.E. Publications Australia Pty Ltd.
68–72 Wentworth Avenue
Sydney 2000
Australia

Japan

NEW ERA Publications Japan, Inc.
5-4-5-803 Nishi-Gotanda
Shinagawa-ku
Tokyo
Japan 141

Latin America

ERA DINÁMICA EDITORES, S.A. de C.V.
Nicolás San Juan No. 208
Colonia Narvarte
C.P. 03020
Mexico, D.F.

Canada

Continental Publications Liaison Office
696 Yonge Street
Toronto, Ontario
Canada M4Y 2A7

All books on Dianetics and Scientology may be obtained directly from the organizations listed above.

GLOSSARY OF TERMS

Philosophy has always had the liability of gathering to itself a great many new words and labels. The reason for this is that the philosopher finds phenomena in the physical universe or in the mind or humanities which have not hitherto been observed or properly identified. Each one of these tends to require a new word for its description. In actual fact this cycle of new observations requiring new labels is probably the growth of language itself. Language is obviously the product of unsung observers who then popularized a word to describe what had been observed.

The system which has been followed in Dianetics and Scientology in labeling phenomena or observed things was originally to make verbs into nouns or vice versa. The practice of developing new nomenclature was actually held to a minimum. However, it was found that many old words in the field of philosophy, when used, conveyed to people an entirely new idea. The exactness of Dianetics and Scientology required a more precise approach. This approach was achieved by special naming with an eye to minimal confusion with already supposed or known phenomena. The Dianetics and Scientology vocabulary is nevertheless not large.

In the search which brought about Dianetics and Scientology many new phenomena were encountered which resulted, for the first time, in a workable, predictable technology of the spirit. The introduction of a few words of new meaning to make this possible seems to be a small price to pay.

This glossary contains the Dianetics and Scientology terms appearing in *What Is Scientology?*

aberration: a departure from rational thought or behavior. It means basically to err, to make mistakes, or more specifically to have fixed ideas which are not true. The word is also used in its scientific sense. It means departure from a straight line. If a line should go from A to B, then if it is *aberrated* it would go from A to some other point, to some other point, to some other point, to some other point, to some other point, and finally arrive at B. Taken in this sense, it would also mean the lack of straightness or to see crookedly as, for example, a man sees a horse but thinks he sees an elephant. Aberrated conduct would be wrong conduct, or conduct not supported by reason. When a person has engrams, these tend to deflect what would be his normal ability to perceive truth and bring about an aberrated view of situations which then would cause an aberrated reaction to them. *Aberration* is opposed to sanity, which would be its opposite. From the Latin, *aberrare,* to wander from; Latin, *ab,* away, *errare,* to wander.

ABLE: an acronym for *A*ssociation for *B*etter *L*iving and *E*ducation International. See Chapter 25.

action phrases: word phrases contained as part of the content of engrams which dictate some type of "action" in the mind.

affinity: the degree of liking or affection or lack of it. It is the feeling of love or liking for something or someone.

affinity-reality-communication (ARC) triangle: a triangle which is a symbol of the fact that *a*ffinity, *r*eality and *c*ommunication act together to bring about understanding. No point of the triangle can be raised without also raising the other two points, and no point of it can be lowered without also lowering the other two points. See Chapter 4.

analytical mind: that part of the mind which one consciously uses and is aware of. It is the portion of the mind which thinks, observes data, remembers it and resolves problems. See Chapter 4.

antisocial personality: a person who possesses a distinct set of characteristics and mental attitudes that cause him to suppress other people in his vicinity. This is the person whose behavior is calculated to be disastrous. Also called *suppressive person.* See Chapter 16.

AO: abbreviation for *A*dvanced *O*rganization. See Chapter 21.

apparency: something that seems to be, that appears to be a certain way; something that *appears* to be but is different from the way it looks. In Dianetics and Scientology *apparency* is used to mean something that looks one way but is, in actual fact, something else. For example, a person "gives an *apparency* of health," whereas he is actually sick. From the Latin, *apparere,* to appear.

ARC: a word coined from the initial letters of *a*ffinity, *r*eality and *c*ommunication. See Chapter 4.

ARC break: a sudden drop or cutting of *a*ffinity, *r*eality or *c*ommunication with someone or something. Upsets with people or things (ARC breaks) come about because of a lessening or sundering of affinity, reality or communication or understanding. Scientologists usually use the term *ARC break* instead of *upset,* because if one discovers which of the three points of understanding have been cut, one can bring about a rapid recovery in the person's state of mind.

assessment: an auditing technique which helps to isolate specific areas or subjects on which a preclear has charge so that they can be addressed in auditing.

auditing: Scientology counseling, taken from the Latin word *audire* which means "to hear or listen." Auditing is a very unique form of personal counseling which helps an individual look at his own existence and improves his ability to confront what he is and where he is. See Chapter 5.

Auditing by List: a technique used in certain auditing procedures.

auditor: a minister or minister-in-training of the Church of Scientology. *Auditor* means one who listens, from the Latin *audire* meaning "to hear or listen." An auditor is a person trained and qualified in applying auditing to individuals for their betterment. An auditor does not do anything *to* a preclear, he works together with the preclear to help the preclear defeat his reactive mind. See Chapter 5.

beingness: the assumption or choosing of a category of identity. Beingness can be assumed by oneself or given to oneself or attained. Examples of beingness would be one's own name, one's profession, one's physical characteristics, one's role in a game—each or all of these could be called one's beingness.

Book One: a colloquial term for the first book published on the subject of Dianetics, *Dianetics: The Modern Science of Mental Health*. A *Book One Auditor* is someone who knows the data in this book and uses it to audit others.

case: a general term for a person being treated or helped. It is also used to mean the entire accumulation of upsets, pain, failures, etc., residing in a preclear's reactive mind.

case gains: the improvements and resurgences a person experiences from auditing; any case betterment according to the preclear.

Case Supervisor: a highly trained auditor who is also trained in the technology of supervising auditing. The Case Supervisor reviews all auditing sessions done by auditors under his charge. His purpose is to see that the technology is standardly applied for the greatest possible benefit for the preclear. See Chapter 14.

CCHR: abbreviation for *C*itizens *C*ommission on *H*uman *R*ights. See Chapter 24.

charge: harmful energy or force contained in mental image pictures of experiences painful or upsetting to the person, which is handled in auditing. See Chapter 5.

Claims Verification Board: an official group within the Church of Scientology which facilitates refund requests.

Clay Table Processing: a particular process used in certain types of auditing.

Clear: a highly desirable state for the individual, achieved through auditing, which was never attainable before Dianetics. A Clear is a person who no longer has his own reactive mind and therefore suffers none of the ill effects that the reactive mind can cause. The Clear has no engrams which, when restimulated, throw out the correctness of his computations by entering hidden and false data. See Chapter 13.

control: the ability to start, change and stop something. One is successful in his life to the degree that he can start or change or stop the things and people within his environment. For example, a driver who cannot exert control over a car by making it start, move about and stop when he wants it to is quite likely to have accidents. A person who *can* control a car, on the other hand, will be able to arrive where he intends to.

counter-effort: an effort of something or someone in a person's environment against that person.

C/S: abbreviation for *C*ase *S*upervisor. Also used to designate a Case Supervisor direction of what to audit on a preclear (as in "he was given a new C/S"), or the giving of such a direction by the Case Supervisor (as in "the preclear was C/Sed for his next action"). *See also* **Case Supervisor** in this glossary.

CSI: abbreviation for *C*hurch of *S*cientology *I*nternational. See Chapter 21.

Data Series: a series of policy letters written by L. Ron Hubbard which deal with logic, illogic, proper evaluation of data and how to detect and handle the causes of good and bad situations within groups and organizations.

determinism: power of choice; power of decision; ability to decide or determine the course of one's own or others' actions.

Dianetics: comes from the Greek words *dia,* meaning "through" and *nous,* meaning "soul." Dianetics is a methodology developed by L. Ron Hubbard which can help alleviate such ailments as unwanted sensations and emotions, irrational fears and psychosomatic illnesses. It is most accurately described as *what the soul is doing to the body through the mind.* See Chapter 4.

dramatization: the acting out of an engram in its entirety or in part by an aberrated person in his current environment. Aberrated conduct is entirely dramatization. For example, a woman receives an engram in which she is kicked in the side and told that she is no good, that she is always changing her mind. At some time in the future, this engram could be reactivated and the woman might experience a pain in her side, feel that she is no good or get the idea that she is always changing her mind. This would be a dramatization of the engram.

dwindling spiral: a condition characterized by continuous worsening, decreasing or shrinking.

dynamics: the eight urges, drives or impulses of life. See Chapter 4.

E-Meter: short for *Electropsychometer,* a specially designed instrument which helps the auditor and preclear locate areas of spiritual distress or travail. The E-Meter is a religious artifact and can only be used by Scientology ministers or ministers-in-training. It does not diagnose or cure anything. It measures the mental state or change of state of a person and thus is of benefit to the auditor in helping the preclear locate areas to be handled. See Chapter 5.

engram: a recording made by the reactive mind when a person is "unconscious." An engram is not a memory—it is a particular type of mental image picture which is a complete recording, down to the last accurate detail, of every perception present in a moment of partial or full "unconsciousness." See Chapter 4.

enturbulence: turbulence or agitation and disturbance.

Est Repair Rundown: an auditing action designed to repair the damage done to a person mentally and spiritually by the practice of est (Erhard Seminars Training). Est was an offbeat group which used destructive techniques, and some people new to Scientology are found to have been previously involved with est. It is necessary to undo the harmful effects of est before such persons can make adequate progress in Scientology auditing.

exteriorization: the state of the thetan being outside his body with or without full perception, but still able to control and handle the body. When a person goes exterior, he achieves a certainty that he is himself and not his body. See Chapter 4.

floating needle: a rhythmic sweep of the needle on an E-Meter dial at a slow, even pace, back and forth, back and forth. A floating needle means that the charge on a subject being audited has dissipated, and is one of the indications of a process being complete.

FSO: abbreviation for *F*lag *S*ervice *O*rganization. See Chapter 21.

FSSO: abbreviation for *F*lag *S*hip *S*ervice *O*rganization. See Chapter 21.

genetic entity: a term coined in early Dianetics research to denote that part of a human being which takes care of the automatic mechanisms of the body, such as heartbeat, respiration, etc.

gradient: a gradual approach to something, taken step by step, so that, finally, quite complicated and difficult activities or concepts can be achieved with relative ease.

grant beingness: to let someone else be what he is. Listening to what someone has to say and taking care to understand them, being courteous, refraining from needless criticism, expressing admiration or affinity are examples of the actions of someone who can grant others beingness.

HASI: an acronym for *H*ubbard *A*ssociation of *S*cientologists *I*nternational. See Chapter 29.

hat: a Scientology slang term for a particular job, taken from the fact that in many professions, such as railroading, the type of hat worn is the badge of the job. The term *hat* is also used to describe the write-ups, checksheets and packs that outline the purposes, know-how and duties of a job in a Scientology organization.

hatting: the training given to a person so that he or she can successfully perform the functions and produce the products of a specific job, duty or activity. *See also* **hat** in this glossary.

havingness: the concept of being able to reach. By *havingness* we mean owning, possessing, being capable of commanding, taking charge of objects, energies and spaces. Specific processes exist in Scientology to help a preclear increase his havingness, and these are appropriately called Havingness Processes.

HCO: abbreviation for *H*ubbard *C*ommunications *O*ffice. See Chapter 20.

HGC: abbreviation for *H*ubbard *G*uidance *C*enter. See Chapter 20.

Hubbard Consultant Outpoint-Pluspoint List: a list of illogics (outpoints) and logics (pluspoints) used in an auditing process to help the preclear locate and handle illogical thinking in the area being addressed.

IAS: abbreviation for *I*nternational *A*ssociation of *S*cientologists. See Chapter 22.

I HELP: an acronym for *I*nternational *H*ubbard *E*cclesiastical *L*eague of *P*astors. See Chapter 21.

INCOMM: an acronym for *I*nternational *N*etwork of *C*omputer *O*rganized *M*anage*m*ent. See Chapter 29.

int: short for *interiorization,* the action of going into something too fixedly and becoming part of it too fixedly. *Int* is also used to refer to the auditing procedure which handles the adverse mental and spiritual effects of interiorization.

invalidate: refute, degrade, discredit or deny something someone else considers to be fact.

knowledge-responsibility-control (KRC) triangle: a triangle which is a symbol of the fact that *k*nowledge, *r*esponsibility and *c*ontrol act together as a whole entity. In order to handle any area of one's life, it is necessary to *know* something about it, take some *responsibility* for it and *control* it to the degree necessary to achieve the desired result. This triangle interacts best when used with high ARC, thus it interlocks with the ARC triangle. *See also* **affinity-reality-communication (ARC) triangle** and **control** in this glossary.

Listing and Nulling: a specialized technique used in certain auditing processes.

lock: a mental image picture of an experience where one was knowingly or unknowingly reminded of an engram. It does not itself contain a blow or a burn or impact and is not any major cause of upset. It does not contain unconsciousness. It may contain a feeling of pain or illness, etc., but is not itself the source of it. For example, a person sees a cake and feels sick. This is a lock on an engram of being made sick by eating cake. The picture of seeing a cake and feeling sick is a lock on (is locked to) the incident (unseen at the moment) of getting sick eating cake.

mental image pictures: three-dimensional pictures which are continuously made by the mind, moment by moment, containing color, sound and smell, as well as other perceptions. They also include the conclusions or speculations of the individual. Mental image pictures are composed of energy, have mass, exist in space and follow definite routines of behavior, the most interesting of which is the fact that they appear when somebody thinks of something. See Chapter 4.

MEST: a word coined from the initial letters of *m*atter, *e*nergy, *s*pace and *t*ime, which are the component parts (elements) of the physical universe.

meter: short for *E-Meter. See* **E-Meter** in this glossary.

missed withhold: a withhold which has *almost* been found out by another, that leaves the person who has the withhold in a state of wondering whether or not his hidden deed is known. *See also* **withhold** in this glossary.

NCLE: abbreviation for *N*ational *C*ommission on *L*aw *E*nforcement and Social Justice. See Chapter 24.

NED: an acronym for *N*ew *E*ra *D*ianetics. See Chapter 13.

New Era Dianetics for OTs (NOTs): a series of auditing actions, delivered as part of the OT levels, developed by L. Ron Hubbard during his research into New Era Dianetics in the late 1970s.

NOTs: an acronym for *N*ew Era Dianetics for *OTs. See* **New Era Dianetics for OTs** in this glossary.

Objectives: short for *Objective Processing,* an auditing action which helps a person to look or place his attention outward from himself.

OCA: abbreviation for *O*xford *C*apacity *A*nalysis. See Chapter 5.

Operating Thetan: a state of being above Clear, in which the Clear has become refamiliarized with his native capabilities. An Operating Thetan is knowing and willing cause over life, thought, matter, energy, space and time. See Chapter 13.

organizing board: a system of organizing that contains all functions a Scientology organization must perform in order to efficiently provide for its parishioners. See Chapter 20.

OSA: an acronym for *O*ffice of *S*pecial *A*ffairs. See Chapter 32.

OT: abbreviation for *O*perating *T*hetan. *See* **Operating Thetan** in this glossary.

overrun: continue an auditing process or a series of processes past the point of completion.

overt: a harmful act or a transgression against the moral code of a group. When a person does something that is contrary to the moral code he has agreed to, or when he omits to do something that he should have done per that moral code, he has committed an overt. An overt violates what was agreed upon. An overt can be intentional or unintentional.

pan-determined: able to view both sides. Pan-determinism is *across* determinism or determinism of two sides. If a person were playing both sides of a chess game, he would be exercising pan-determinism. *See also* **determinism** in this glossary.

PDH: abbreviation for *p*ain *d*rug *h*ypnosis, a behavioral modification technique used by military and intelligence services in which pain, drugs or hypnosis, or any combination of these, are administered to drive an individual into a state whereby he can be given suggestions or commands subconsciously. Dianetics auditing can undo the effects of PDH. For more information, see Chapter 31.

perceptic: any sense message such as sight, sound, smell, etc.

postulate: a conclusion, decision or resolution made by the individual himself to resolve a problem or to set a pattern for the future or to nullify a pattern of the past. For example, a person says, "I like Model-T Fords. I am never going to drive another car." Years later, no longer consciously aware of this postulate, he will wonder why he is having so much trouble with his Buick; it's because he has made an earlier promise to himself. In order to change he has to change that postulate.

potential trouble source: a person who is in some way connected to and being adversely affected by a suppressive person. Such a person is called a *potential* trouble source because he can be a lot of trouble to himself and to others. *See also* **suppressive person** in this glossary.

preclear: a person who is receiving Scientology or Dianetics auditing on his way to becoming Clear, hence pre-Clear. Through auditing he is finding out more about himself and life. See Chapter 5.

process: an exact set of questions asked or directions given by an auditor to help a person find out things about himself and improve his condition. See Chapter 5.

processing: another word for *auditing. See* **auditing** in this glossary.

PTS: abbreviation for *p*otential *t*rouble *s*ource. *See* **potential trouble source** in this glossary.

Qual: short for *Qualifications Division*. See Chapter 20.

RD: abbreviation for *r*un*d*own. *See* **rundown** in this glossary.

reactive mind: that part of the mind which works on a totally stimulus-response basis, which is not under a person's volitional control, and which exerts force and the power of command over his awareness, purposes, thoughts, body and actions. See Chapter 4.

reality: that which appears to be. Reality is fundamentally agreement—what we agree to be real is real.

rehab: short for *rehabilitation,* an auditing action which is used to help a person regain a former ability, state of being or more optimum condition which has been discredited, denied or suppressed.

restimulation: the "awakening" of an old engram, which occurs when a person's present environment contains enough similarities to the elements found in the engram to cause a reactivation of it. When an engram is restimulated, a person can experience similar pains and emotions to those contained in the original incident.

R6EW: the designation for the auditing process used on Grade VI. See Chapter 40.

RTC: abbreviation for *R*eligious *T*echnology *C*enter. See Chapter 21.

rundown: a series of related actions in Scientology which culminate in a specific end result. For example, the Drug Rundown consists of several different auditing processes and actions which, done fully and in sequence, result in the freeing of a person from the mental and spiritual effects of drugs.

Scientology: comes from the Latin *scio,* which means "know" and the Greek word *logos,* meaning "the word or outward form by which the inward thought is expressed and made known." Thus, Scientology means knowing about knowing. Scientology is an applied religious philosophy developed by L. Ron Hubbard. It is the study and handling of the spirit in relationship to itself, universes and other life. See Chapter 4.

Sea Org: short for *Sea Organization.* See Chapter 21.

self-determinism: the condition of determining the actions of self; the ability to direct oneself. *See also* **determinism** in this glossary.

service facsimile: a consideration that one must be consistently in a certain state in order to survive. This consideration will cause the individual to deliberately hold in restimulation selected parts of his reactive mind to explain his failures in life. For example, a person may keep an old injury in restimulation so that his family has to look after him.

SHSBC: abbreviation for *S*aint *H*ill *S*pecial *B*riefing *C*ourse. See Chapter 14.

SMI: an acronym for *S*cientology *M*issions *I*nternational. See Chapter 21.

SP: abbreviation for *s*uppressive *p*erson. *See* **suppressive person** in this glossary.

stable terminal: someone who is reliable, responsible and who can be depended upon to competently perform the duties of his job.

standard memory banks: recordings in the analytical mind of everything perceived throughout the lifetime up to the present by the individual except physical pain, which is recorded in the reactive mind. See Chapter 4.

suppressive person: a person who possesses a distinct set of characteristics and mental attitudes that cause him to suppress other people in his vicinity. This is the person whose behavior is calculated to be disastrous. Also called *antisocial personality.* See Chapter 16.

theta: energy peculiar to life which acts upon material in the physical universe and animates it, mobilizes it and changes it; natural creative energy of a being which he is free to direct toward survival goals. The term comes from the Greek letter *theta* (θ), which the Greeks used to represent *thought.*

thetan: an immortal spiritual being; the human soul. The term *soul* is not used because it has developed so many other meanings from use in other religions and practices that it doesn't describe precisely what was discovered in Scientology. We use the term *thetan* instead, from the Greek letter *theta,* θ, the traditional symbol for thought or life. One does not *have* a thetan, something one keeps somewhere apart from oneself; one *is* a thetan. The thetan is the person himself, not his body or his name or the physical universe, his mind or anything else. It is that which is aware of being aware; the identity which IS the individual. See Chapter 4.

time track: the consecutive record of mental image pictures which accumulates through a person's life. It is a very accurate record of a person's past. As a rough analogy, the time track could be likened to a motion-picture film—if that film were three-dimensional, had fifty-two perceptions and could fully react upon the observer. See Chapter 4.

TRs: abbreviation for *t*raining *r*outines, practical drills which can greatly increase a student's ability in essential auditing skills, such as communication. See Chapter 14.

unmock: become nothing, disappear, cease to exist.

whole track: the whole span of the time track. *See also* **time track** in this glossary.

WISE: an acronym for *W*orld *I*nstitute of *S*cientology *E*nterprises International. See Chapter 26.

withhold: an overt a person has committed but is not talking about; an unspoken, unannounced transgression against a moral code by which a person was bound. Any withhold comes *after* an overt. *See also* **overt** in this glossary.

WW: abbreviation for *W*orld*w*ide—the worldwide headquarters of the Church of Scientology at Saint Hill, where management was located until the early 1970s.

INDEX

A

D

E

F

G

H

I

J

K

L

M

N

Q

R

S

T

U

V

W–Z

EPILOGUE

The aim of this book was to answer the question, What is Scientology? The objective has been to provide you with information on how Scientology can change your life, and how it is changing the world. With all you have read, you now possess enough information to objectively evaluate the subject.

On a more personal level, however, the time has come to make a decision: You can close this book and walk away, or you can take, not your first step on the road to truth, but your next.